1862 - Tremaine Survey
Map of Adelaide Township

copied from linen map
University of Western Ontario

Adelaide Township...
A History

Township of Adelaide 1832

COMPILED BY ADELAIDE TOWNSHIP HERITAGE GROUP

DISCLAIMER

The descriptions, stories and anecdotes contained in this book are based upon interviews with surviving family members, family records, newspaper accounts of the day, church and cemetery records, and other historical sources where available. Although all reasonable attempts have been made to ensure the accuracy of the contents of this book, the authors, the editor and the publisher cannot guarantee such accuracy, and the authors, the editor and the publisher take no responsibility for any such inaccuracies, regardless of the source.

PERMANENT ACKNOWLEDGMENT

The Adelaide Township Heritage Group hereby acknowledges the financial support of the Government of Canada. The opinions expressed in this book are those of the Adelaide Township Heritage Group, and do not necessarily reflect the official views of the Government of Canada.

Published by
Adelaide Township Heritage Group, Strathroy, Ontario N7G 1R1
No part of this book may be reproduced for sale without permission of the Adelaide Township Heritage Group.

National Library of Canada Cataloguing in Publication Data

Main entry under title:

    Adelaide Township... a history

Includes index.
ISBN 0-919939-60-0

    1. Adelaide (Ont. : Township) – History. I. Adelaide Township History Book Committee.

FC3095.A32A44 2001   971.3'25   C2001-901333-7
F1059.A24A34 2001

Editorial Services By:

ON the MARK

144 High Street West
Strathroy, ON N7G 1G9
(519) 245-9239
onthemarkgb@execulink.com

Printed By: The Aylmer Express Ltd.

Limited Edition of 750 copies
Published August, 2001

For more information and orders contact:
Adelaide Township Heritage Group
14-307 Metcalfe Street East
Strathroy, ON N7G 1R1

Foreword

The Adelaide Township Heritage Group was formed when some Adelaide residents (and others with Adelaide roots) met to discuss collecting and preserving historical materials of the township and its families. Officers were elected at the first meeting on March 23, 1994. Vouchers were sold to provide working capital to publish a history book. Harold Eastman was named honorary president, and a tree-planting ceremony was held in his honour on July 1, 1994.

Research began in earnest—in family groups; at the Ontario Archives, Toronto; Middlesex County Land Registry Office; Reference Library, Toronto; University of Western Ontario; London Library; Strathroy Library; Strathroy Middlesex Museum; and from many other sources. Families with Adelaide connections were contacted through letters to newspapers and by means of a township canvass.

Funds were raised by diligent workers, who sold dozens of Adelaide shirts and caps, and tickets for draws on various items. They assisted at Irish Cabarets, yard sales, Canada Day barbecues, and special dinners.

Because of time constrictions and the complexities of publishing, some historical and family data is not complete. The original research materials and photographs are now located in the "Adelaide Collection" at the Strathroy Middlesex Museum. Individuals have access to these records to make additions to their family story.

Dedication

Westward they sailed—a six-week journey—across the dreaded Atlantic, the only route to the land of *Promise, Equality, and Opportunity*.

Dreams of a golden future made the known dangers ahead—privation, cholera, shipwreck—almost inconsequential, and fanned their fiery desires to flee to hope and freedom. No more hunger, religious restrictions, or landlords' greed! An escape from their assumed role in the class structure! Education for all children! Onward, to a place where one's destiny might be fulfilled and each family could own land! *Land!!!*

Presently, a poor servant to the wealthy would own many properties, marry across religious boundaries, and become the first Reeve of Adelaide Township!

Those who were educated and privileged brought money and furnishings to support a fresh beginning, where their level in society could be maintained and enhanced. Life as they knew it would continue—their wealth would hire labour to clear the trees and till the soil. Here in this untamed Adelaide, they might add to their fortunes and bring more honour and prestige to the family name. But pioneer life was a very humbling and leveling experience, and those whose fortitude was extended to the breaking point gave up the struggle against the trees, and moved to the new towns where they immediately gained recognition and power in the governing bodies.

Many were battle-weary soldiers, some leaders and others from Regiments of Foot, who for years had opposed Napoleon's threats in Europe. Later, they were sent to the West to continue the political fray in the War of 1812. Their service was to be rewarded with land in the recently surveyed forests of Adelaide Township, named for their Monarch's Queen.

Concerned with the limited future of the people on his estates, English landowner Lord Egremont devised and financed an emigration plan to open the doors of poverty and to provide magnanimous assistance for the emigrants. These settlers proved their abilities to overcome the challenges of this different world. Their descendants can be justly proud of their ancestry.

For their Loyalty to the British Crown, a small group of United Empire Loyalists made their way to Adelaide Township, to collect their property rewards according to the agreement. Their familiarity with the English system enabled them to make profitable leaps into entrepreneurial ventures, developing the village of Strathroy. Now, the mosaic of settlement was nearly complete.

Some English, who had put down roots in Quebec, felt the time was right to come to Adelaide, where they would be among neighbours of the culture of their homeland.

In later years, courageous men and women from the township made the name of Adelaide known, and well respected, through their heroic service in the two Great Wars. Then came waves of settlers from war-weary Europe, eager to start over in a fresh land. The resting Adelaide farms were ready for new ideas and manpower, to replace the Adelaide children who had left the land to hone urban careers.

To those who came before to clear the way and lay the foundations, we dedicate this book of the History of Adelaide Township. We are grateful for your struggles.

Residents of Adelaide Township, 2001 A.D.

A Reader's Guide

EDITORIAL STANDARDS

Editorial guidelines used in this book are from *The Canadian Press Stylebook* and Strunk & White's *The Elements of Style*. Other specifications were developed for consistency within the text. The following notations are included to aid the reader in understanding terminology that is used within the material.

DETAILS

When no township is listed after a named lot, the reader can presume the property is located in Adelaide Township. Other townships, where known, have been described by name.

When complete information was known, property has been described by lot and concession number.

Reference to "SER" and "NER" after the name of a concession indicates property located south of Egremont Road and north of Egremont Road.

The designation "townline" refers to a road between Adelaide Township and an adjoining township.

Within the many family stories, several items deserve explanation. For instance, in parentheses following names, a single date refers to the year of birth; a "d." preceding a year refers to the year of death; and hyphenation between years refers to both.

When "ca." precedes a date, this indicates "circa" or "about."

Occasionally, when a child died young, parents bestowed a desirable given name upon a child born later. This practise may be attributed to preference for a family name. In such cases, the given names are followed by "#1" and "#2" for clarity.

The term "issue" is used with some frequency. This refers to the placement of a child within a family, i.e., "fourth issue of John and Mary Smith."

The words "plough" and "plow" are both found in this book. The former is used when horses or oxen pulled the tool, and the latter when tractors were used.

The word "immigrate" is used when a person came to Canada to take up residence, and the word "emigrate" is seen when a person leaves one's place of residence to live elsewhere. Both usages are found in this book, although we have taken steps to be consistent within chapters.

NOTE FROM THE EDITOR

This book pays tribute to the pioneers of Adelaide Township and those who came after them. Determined individuals arrived in this area, firm in their resolve for a better future on Canadian soil. The volunteers and contributors who worked untold hours on this book personify their ancestors' enthusiasm and optimism. Without them and their spirit of co-operation, there would be no book detailing the history of Adelaide Township. I know that you will join me in applauding their concerted efforts.

Thank you, Adelaide Township Heritage Group, for the opportunity to work with you on this important enterprise. Your fascination with the past and your diligence led us through a mountain of paperwork and an ocean of historical data. It is my distinct pleasure to be part of this venture: a compilation of ancestral details, memoirs, places of the past and times gone by. Yours is an invitation to remember.

In the year 2000, we live in a world of burgeoning technology where the Internet, the PDA (Personal Digital Assistant), the GPS (Global Positioning System), genetically engineered food, and cloning are becoming commonplace. It is perhaps more important than ever to remember where we came from, and be mindful of the things that matter most.

Gena Brumitt
ON *the* MARK
Editor
CEO, Adelaide Township Heritage Group

WE REMEMBER

These volunteers shared their memories and knowledge of past days in Adelaide Township. Their research and written stories are appreciated. We regret sincerely that this book was not completed in the lifetime of many people who contributed.

We recognize the commitment of:

Harold Eastman
Mary (O'Donnell) Kelly
Alice (McKeen) Lumsden
Wilbert McKeen B.Sc., M.Sc., Ph.D.
Edward McLeish M.C., A.D., B.A., M.Ed.
Muriel (Petch) Sisson
Dorothy (Morgan) Winter
Hansford Wood

Table of Contents

Chapter One:
    Beginnings 1

Chapter Two:
    Family Stories 31

Chapter Three:
    Churches and Cemeteries 439

Chapter Four:
    Schools 467

Chapter Five:
    Communities 505

Chapter Six:
    Municipal Government 519

Chapter Seven:
    Communications 531

Chapter Eight:
    Architecture 543

Chapter Nine:
    Armed Forces 549

Chapter Ten:
    Agriculture 595

Chapter Eleven:
    Businesses 629

Chapter Twelve:
    Leisure Time 647

Chapter Thirteen:
    Profiles 653

Chapter Fourteen:
    Memories 667

    Group Vouchers 710
    Donors 711
    Sources 712
    Index 713
    Acknowledgement 715

THE FARMER

The king may rule o'er land and sea,
The lord may live right royally,
The soldier ride in pomp and pride,
The sailor roam o'er ocean wide,
But this or that, what'er befall,
The farmer, he must feed them all.

The writer thinks, the poet sings,
The craftsman follows wondrous things,
The doctor heals, the lawyer pleads,
But this or that, what'er befall,
The farmer, he must feed them all.

The merchant, he may buy or sell,
The teacher do his duty well,
The men may toil through busy days,
Or men may stroll through pleasant ways,
From king to beggar, what'er befall,
The farmer, he must feed them all.

The farmer's trade is one of worth,
His pasture with the sky and earth,
His pasture with the sun and rain,
And no man loses for his gain,
And men may rise and men may fall,
But the farmer, he must feed them all.

God bless the man who sows the wheat,
Who finds us milk and fruit and meat,
May his purse be heavy, his heart be light,
His cattle and corn and all go right,
God bless the seed his hands let fall,
For the farmer, he must feed us all.

-author unknown

CHAPTER ONE

Beginnings

Though the settlement of Adelaide Township followed the legal processes common to other townships in Southern Ontario, many aspects of its evolution varied distinctively with those of its neighbouring townships in Middlesex County. In order to understand the evolution of local government in what is now Ontario, it is necessary to provide an overview of the significant events of the previous 235 years.

"The British had just defeated the French in a global war that lasted seven years. Under the Treaty of Paris of 1763 that ended the war, the British took possession of the vast French territories in the new world. At the time 65,000 French settlers lived along the shores of the St. Lawrence River, but the land further west, including present-day Ontario, was unsettled bush. The British government, by the Royal Proclamation of 1763, split this western interior land tract off from Quebec and set it aside as Indian Territory that could not be settled. However political unrest in Britain's Thirteen Colonies made the British revise the boundaries of Quebec. Fearing that the rebellious spirit of the Thirteen Colonies along the Atlantic seaboard would spread north to Quebec, the British government passed the Quebec Act of 1774. This Act incorporated back into the province of Quebec the western portion of the region, including southwestern Ontario. It also guaranteed to the French settlers religious freedom and the continuation of a French system of civil law and landholding. These guarantees were successful in dissuading the French settlers in Quebec from becoming a fourteenth colony in the American Revolution of 1776.

Soon after the American Revolution, the situation changed again. In the mid-1780s, 6,000 to 10,000 United Empire Loyalists arrived in what is now Ontario. These refugees from the newly formed republic of the United States brought with them their loyalty to the British monarchy and to the British customs, forms of government, and social institutions, ideas very important in the later development of the province. The British government responded quickly to the desire of the Loyalist settlers to be governed by a British system of colonial government. As early as 1783, justices of the peace were appointed to administer local government, and English style townships were soon created in the settlement area. In 1788, four new districts were created. Ontario, previously under the jurisdiction of the District of Montreal, was divided into the Districts of Lunenburg, Mecklenburg, Nassau, and Hesse. These Districts were renamed in 1792, becoming Eastern, Midland, Home, and Western, respectively. (Present-day Middlesex County covers an area that was partly in the Home District and partly in the Western District.). However, these efforts to appease the Loyalists were only interim steps. The Loyalists were still under the remote administration of Quebec City for overall government and of Montreal for judicial purposes. As a way of giving the Loyalists their own district with their own local government, the British government passed the Constitutional Act of 1791, which divided the vast province of Quebec into two provinces— Lower Canada (modern southern Quebec) and Upper Canada (modern southern Ontario)." (Edward Phelps, Librarian. Regional History Collection, U.W.O., 1988)

In general, the settlement patterns of southern Ontario were naturally from east to west, with land being taken up along the Upper St. Lawrence River and Lakes Ontario and Erie; and, where feasible, along principle waterways. Access to the heavily forested interior of southwestern Ontario was contingent upon the building of roads. Eleanor Nielsen, who wrote *The Egremont Road*, has kindly permitted use of her extensive research.

In 1793, John Graves Simcoe explored the country between York, Lake Simcoe and Lake Huron. He began at once to construct a road between York and Lake Simcoe to be named Yonge Street in honour of Sir George Yonge, then Secretary of War. According to Gilbert Patterson, *"It was intended as a military convenience rather than an aid to settlement, being part of an overland route to Lake Huron by way of Lake Simcoe and Georgian Bay by which troops could be rushed to the upper posts on Lake Huron and Superior in case of war with the United States."* (Gilbert C. Patterson, *Land Settlement in Upper Canada, 1783-1840*, Toronto: Ontario Bureau of Archives 16th Report, 1920)

Yonge Street was completed in 1794, the actual construction carried out by the Queen's Rangers, a militia corps Simcoe had created to ensure the defense of the province, and to perform construction of roads and other public works.

The Queen's Rangers soon began construction of another great military highway paralleling Lake Ontario to be named Dundas Street, but the project was abandoned before completion and it remained for others to complete this major road, which eventually extended to the western frontier at Sandwich. That part known as Dundas Street ran from York, through the village of Dundas, as far as London. From London, or the Forks of the Thames as it was first called, there was good water transportation available along the River Thames to Lake St. Clair, and this method was generally used (Edwin C. Guillet, Pioneer Travel in Upper Canada, Toronto; University of Toronto Press, 1851). Later still, the Longwoods Road provided a further link in the chain of roads stretching toward the western border.

In 1809, a road was proposed through part of the London and Western districts close to the Lake Erie shoreline. Thomas Talbot, who had taken up the land at Port Talbot as early as 1803, was placed in charge of the lands adjacent to the road. In 1824, he supervised settlement along part of the same road running through the London District. This early road came to be known as the Talbot Road (G.C. Patterson, Land Settlement). Progress in road building was so slow that Thomas Smith wrote in 1825, with some exaggeration, that there were no roads or paths in the whole Western District, except along the creeks and rivers (Fred C. Hamil, *The Valley of the Lower Thames 1640-1850,* Toronto; University of Toronto Press, 1951).

According to Edwin Guillet:

"The most important addition to the highways of the province in the late 1820s was the Huron Road, which made available a means of communication by land between Lake Ontario and Lake Huron. This roadway was blazed largely through the lands of the Canada Company in 1827, and was an exception among early roads in that it was opened prior to the arrival of settlers. In the '30s, this road was still largely corduroy, with stumps two to three feet in height left standing, and it remained chiefly mud or corduroy until long after the middle of the century." (Guillet*, Pioneer Travel*)

When Sir John Colborne became Lieutenant Governor of Upper Canada in 1828, he realized that the existing road system in the southwestern part of the province, namely the Talbot Road and Dundas

Sir John Colborne
Lieutenant-Governor of Upper Canada

Map of Main Roads in Upper Canada, 1831

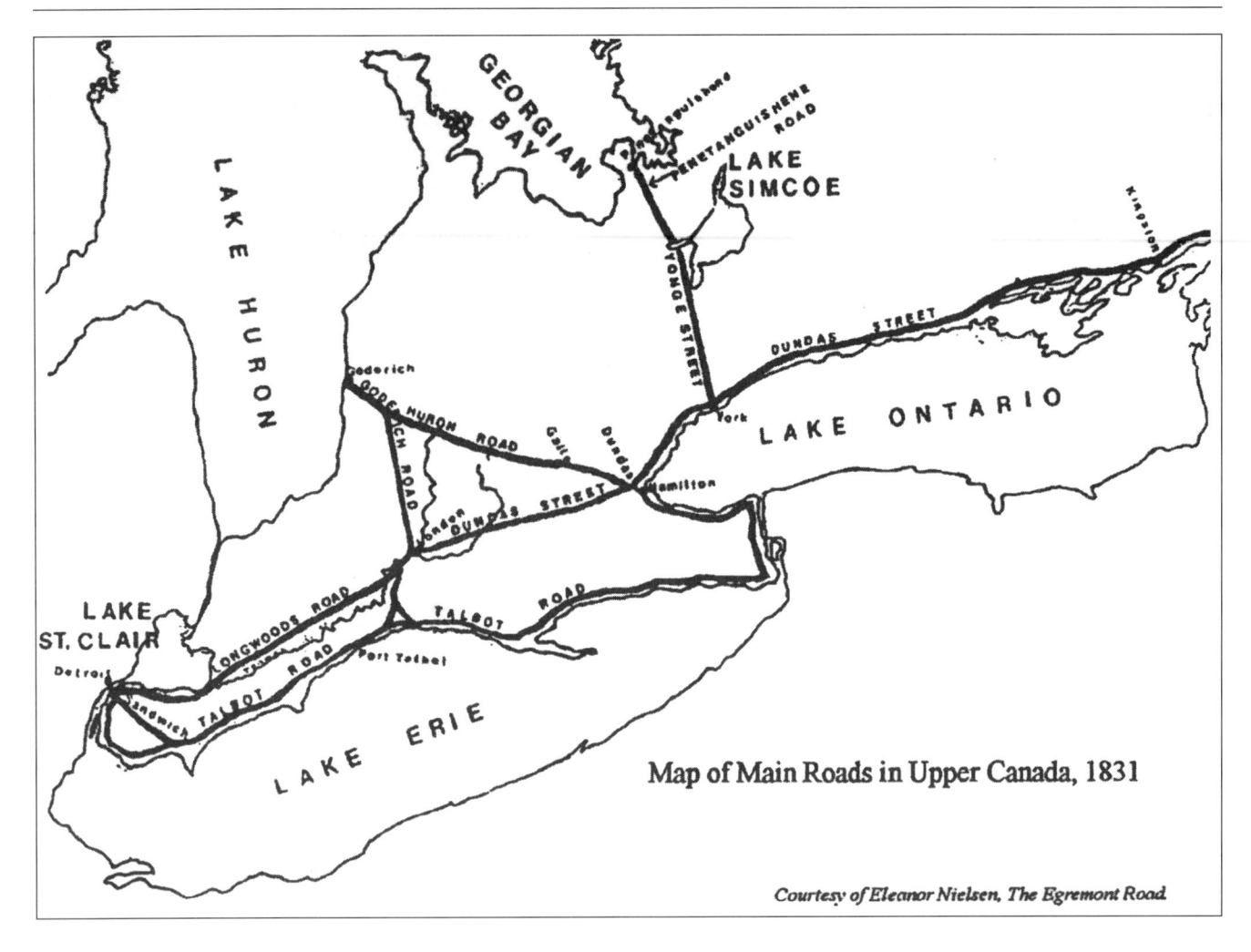

Courtesy of Eleanor Nielsen, The Egremont Road

Street, with the Huron Road and Yonge Street to the north, was entirely inadequate in case of a military emergency along the St. Clair River or the lower part of Lake Huron. At the same time, authorities in Great Britain had decided that the only way to lessen the pressures of over-population and unemployment at home was to step up emigration to North America. Great numbers of immigrants were expected to begin arriving in Upper Canada in the near future, and government officials needed to make advance preparations (Colborne to Right Honourable Viscount Goderich, December 12, 1831, *Blue Book of Upper Canada,* John Colborne Papers, National Archives of Canada, Ottawa).

The road that would satisfy military requirements and open up an area for settlement would become the Egremont Road, running from east to west through the yet unsurveyed and unnamed townships of Adelaide and Warwick.

Colborne turned to Peter Robinson, Commissioner of Crown Lands and Surveyor General of Woods, for assistance in opening up the northern (and as yet untouched) part of the Western District. Robinson's duty was to administer the sale of Crown and clergy reserves to immigrant settlers. He brought to his position the expertise gained a few years earlier when, in 1823 and 1825, he was in charge of transporting and settling two groups of Irish immigrants on their lands in the Peterborough area. Robinson's agent for immigrants to the new area in the Western District was Roswell Mount of Delaware, near Caradoc Township in the London District.

There was perhaps one person who had more knowledge of that part of the Western District than any official at York—Colonel Thomas Talbot. On a number of occasions, the government had made use of his services regarding roads and information on the Western District. It was natural, then, for Peter Robinson to write to Talbot about his plans for a road through the unnamed townships of Adelaide and Warwick, and through Plympton, which had been named in 1829. Talbot was delighted to be approached on this matter and replied, in part, as follows:

Port Talbot, April 3, 1831
My Dear Sir:
I decidedly approve of your plan for laying out a road from the N.E. corner of Carradoc to the mouth of the river Aux Perche, and am quite delighted that such a measure occurred to you, as I know of no part of the Province possessing greater capability for forming a good settlement than that tract affords, situated as it is between two noble rivers, the Sable on the north and Big Bear Creek on the south, which can furnish the settlers with excellent fish to feed them the greater part of the year, besides the land is of a very superior description, and in fact, when the communication is established, the distance from that part of Lake Huron will not be more than from Sandwich. (James H. Coyne, *The Talbot Papers, from Transactions of the Royal Society of Canada,* 1909)

An Exploration Trip Through the Woods

In late April, Talbot wrote to Robinson that he had engaged James Nevilles, a Captain of Militia, *"an intelligent and active man who will, I have no doubt, be of much use..."* to accompany the surveyor in exploring the proposed ground for the new road. At the same time, he recommended Mr. Peter Carroll of Oxford as a competent surveyor, adding that it would be necessary to send along two axemen with the party to carry provisions. (Coyne, *Talbot Papers*)

Peter Carroll was a young man of 25. Born in Oxford County, the son of Isaac Carroll, he had studied land surveying under Mahlon Burwell. His grandfather, John Carroll, U.E., had arrived from New Jersey in 1789, and is believed to be the earliest settler at Beachville on Dundas Street in Oxford County. (Walter H. Carroll, *John Carroll, U.E. and Some of his Descendants,* Hamilton, 1940)

Orders to Peter Carroll

Upon receipt of his orders from the Surveyor General's Office, Carroll began his exploration trip on June 12, 1831, accompanied by James Nevilles of Yarmouth. The men stopped overnight at Marvel White's Tavern on the Lobo-Caradoc townline and then set off for Mr. Townsend's on the River Aux Sable where they expected to meet with John McDonald, an official of the Canada Company to discuss the Company's southern boundary. Mr. McDonald failed to appear and, after waiting a couple of days in vain, the two men returned to Marvel White's tavern where they began to assemble the provisions for the exploring expedition. (Peter Carroll, *Diary Taken in the Survey of a Road from the North East Corner of Carradoc to Lake Huron,* June 9, 1831 to October 3, 1831, Archives of Ontario, Toronto, RG 01, CB-1.)

By June 16, 1831, the party got under way and starting from the northeast corner of Caradoc, they set out in a westerly direction through uncharted territory, making eight miles the first day and ten miles the second. June 18 was wet and rainy, but the party proceeded to the east line of the Township of Plympton and

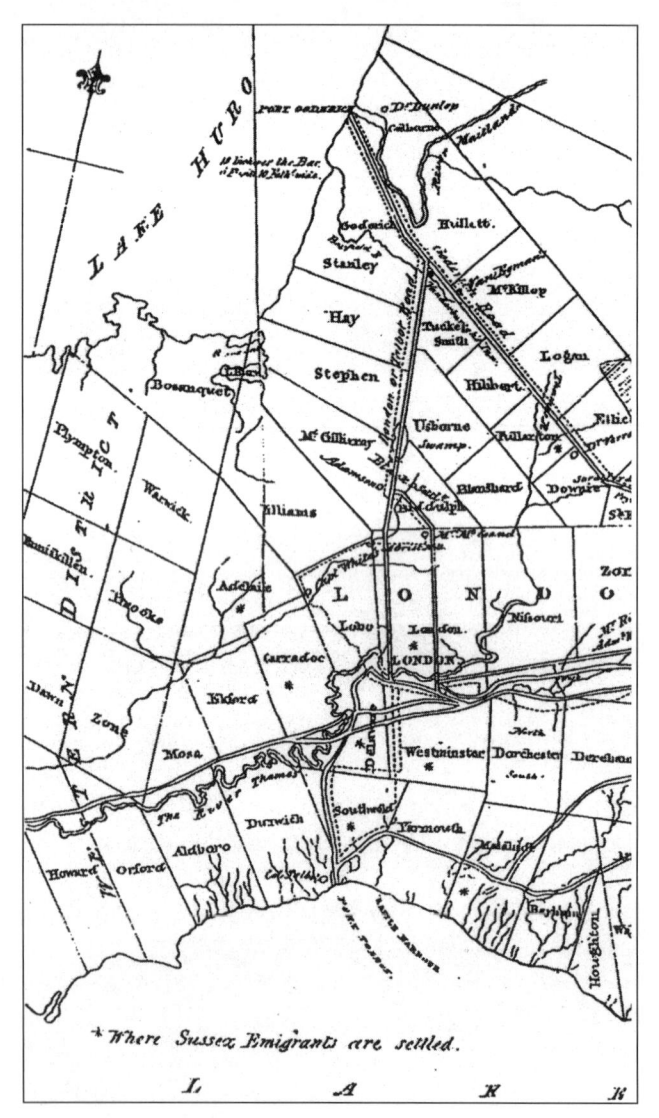

Section of "A Map of the Townships in the London and Gore Districts of Upper Canada Shewing Mr. Brydone's Route in 1834 by a dotted line"

encamped that night between the eighth and ninth concessions. Two days later, the four men arrived at Marvel White's. Carroll then spent several days making his plan of the proposed line of road and writing his report. On July 1, he and Nevilles presented the report to Colonel Talbot. (Carroll, *Diary*)

Talbot lost no time in writing Peter Robinson to acquaint him with the result of the exploration trip:

"I have now to inform you that our Surveyor and Explorer have returned from the New Tract of Country, and I am happy to add that they have been quite as successful as I could have wished, in finding an excellent line for the Road from the N.E. corner of Carradoc to Lake Huron... Surveyor Carrol said that he expected to be able to complete the Survey, in about six weeks, in which case you can commence work this autumn...

The best and cheapest route for settlers to get to the Road will be by vessels from Chippawa or Fort Erie to Port Stanley, the mouth of Kettle Creek, from thence there is a good road and plenty of wagons to be hired to Lobo or Carradoc...

I shall take constant interest in the Road and should like it to be called William the Fourth's Road." (Coyne, *Talbot Papers*)

Surveying the Main Road to Lake Huron

While Talbot was writing his letter, Peter Carroll was making the necessary preparations for the actual survey.

In his *History of Engineering in Lambton*, J.J. Klauke described conditions under which surveyors worked:

"Lambton's early surveyors worked in the bush utterly cut off from the rest of the world. They used chains, not tape measures, and marked out the concession lines by blazing (notching) the trees. They took a party of six to eight men with them and carried all their supplies, which were made up largely of flour and salt pork." (John J. Klauke, *History of Engineering in Lambton County,* London, Ontario, Lawson & Jones, 1972)

By July 6, the survey party was ready to begin. Carroll's orders from the Surveyor General were to survey *"...a Road from the North East corner of Carradoc to Lake Huron, with three tiers of lots on each side thereof."* (Carroll, *Diary,* July 6, 1831.)

Carroll soon established a routine in conducting the survey. He first produced the line for the main road across six to eight lots. The following day, he ran a proof line between two of the lots to the south of the main road and produced the road line between concessions two and three south of the main road, through the same number of lots. The group then returned to their camp on the main road and, the following day, repeated the procedure on the north side of the main road. In this manner, the survey party made their way west through Township AA (later Adelaide), completing, as they went along, the survey of the main road and three tiers of lots on either side.

By July 21, the survey party reached Township AB (later Warwick), where they planted large posts on the main road between the two unnamed townships.

When the survey party arrived at the tavern of

> Surv'y Gen'ls Office
> York 30th May, 1831
>
> Mr. Peter Carroll
> D.P. Surv'y
>
> Sir
>   In obedience to His Excellency the Lt Gov'r commands of the 28th Inst. Upon the application of the Hon. The Commissioner of Crown Lands to his Excellency of the 11th inst. On the Expediency of exploring a tract of Land between the North Angle of Carradoc and the River Aux Peches on Lake Huron with a view of ascertaining the best line for a Road to connect those two points ;—
>   "And if it should be found practicable to open a Road through Land fit for settlement that lots of 100 acres each may be laid out on each side of it" You will therefore proceed to the North angle of the township of Carradoc and run a line west by the needle until it intersects the Eastern boundary line of the Township of Plympton when it is supposed it will come in contact with the line between the 8th and 9th Concession of said Township, and which it apparently will or very nearly so: and if found upon examination by your associate James Nevelles Esq. It must be made use of as that shall save some later labor and expense by being already carried into effect (see Diagram herewith sent for your guidance), but should you and your associate be obliged to diverge from the direct line from the north angle of Carradoc to the River Aux Perches, either to the North or south thereof in order to obtain the desired situation for the intended Road then you will have to make a calculation of the breadth of the said lots accordingly as the rectangular lots are 30ch.00lk by 60ch.67lk. See also diagram.
>   The Honble the Commissioner of Crown Lands has suggested that should the land be found fit for Cultivation to the depth of two concessions of each side of the centre Road that the same may be laid out and as that will give three tiers of lots on each side thereof and by placing a small post in the centre of the front of each lot and marked thereon centre will divide the lots into 100 acres each as directed ~
>   As you have never been employed under pay and ration for yourself and party by the government the enclosed forms of the requisite vouchers which are to be made out after your survey is completed are sent for your guidance and must be sworn to.
>   You must keep a Diary of Time and Field notes of your operations in which you must note every thing of remark either for its utility or singularity which must also be sworn to, and you must make a general Report of your Survey all which must be returned completed with the Diagram and plan of operation.
>   I have the honor to be
>   (Signed) Wm. Chewett
>   Ass't Surv' Genl.
>
> P.S. you must wait upon the Honble Col. Talbot from whom you will receive any further instructions which he may be pleased to give relative to the aforesaid Survey

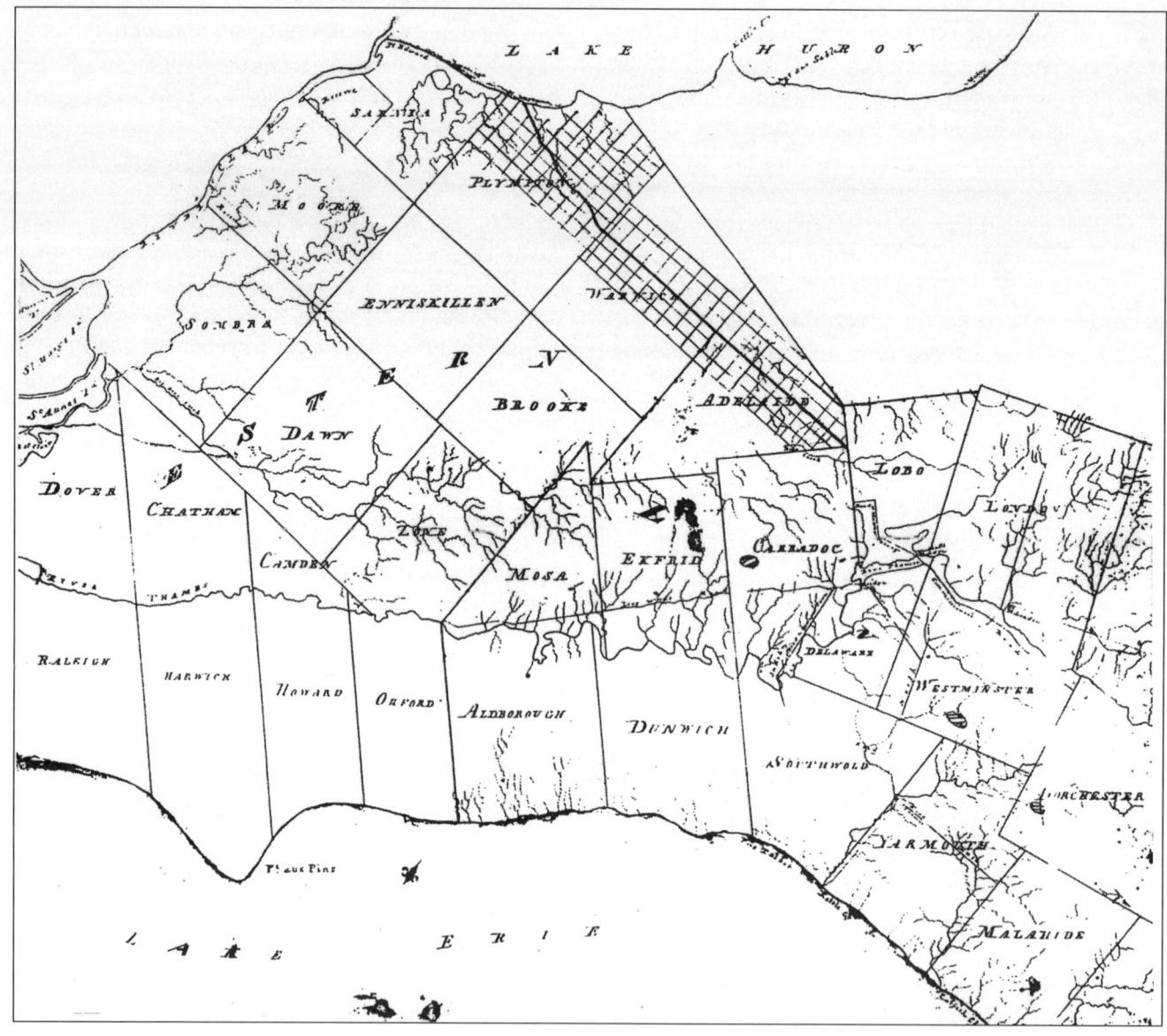

Map of the terrritory between Lake Erie and Lake Huron in 1831 showing Peter Carroll's survey of "a road from the N.E. corner of Caradoc to Lake Huron with three tiers of lots on each side" (A-17, (183-) (AO 234), Archives of Ontario, Toronto)

Marvel White in Lobo on August 30, the men received their wages and were dismissed. Carroll spent the next month preparing his financial accounts, survey plans, and field notes. On October 3, he presented them to the Commissioner of Crown Lands at York. The survey of the road from the northeast corner of Caradoc to Lake Huron was complete.

Survey of Adelaide, Warwick and Plympton Completed

In the spring of 1832, Peter Carroll was again called on by Peter Robinson, Surveyor General, to complete the surveys of the Townships of Adelaide, Warwick, and Plympton in preparation for the expected arrival of large numbers of immigrants.

On June 25, Carroll purchased provisions in London and hired eight men to assist him in the survey. The month of July was spent in surveying Adelaide Township, and on August 6, Carroll and his party proceeded to the south part of Warwick, marching along the town line to the main road.

The survey was completed October 18, 1832, and Peter Carroll and his party proceeded to the home of Asa Townsend on the River Aux Sable where they spent the night before returning home (Peter Carroll, *Diary 7, Completing Survey of Townships of Adelaide, Warwick and Plympton,* June

25, 1832 to January 8, 1833, D.B. Weldon Library, U.W.O.). With the townships of Adelaide, Warwick, and Plympton completely surveyed, all that was needed was settlers to populate them.

The First Settlers in Adelaide and Warwick

Even while Peter Carroll was completing the survey of the three townships of Adelaide, Warwick and Plympton in the summer and fall of 1832, settlers were converging on Adelaide Township. Most of the newcomers could be placed into one of four categories. The first to arrive that summer was a small group of well-to-do gentlemen from Ireland, who purchased several hundred acres of land in Adelaide.

Shortly after the Irish arrivals, Roswell Mount, agent for immigrants, faced the formidable task of assisting about 400 settlers from southern England sent out by the Petworth Emigration Society, who arrived at Kettle Creek the same day.

Discharged soldiers from Great Britain formed the third identifiable group. In 1832 and 1833, some 3,000 discharged soldiers, who had been allowed to commute their pensions for a sum in ready cash, were sent to Canada as settlers. The purpose of the pension commutation was to enable them to purchase land. On arrival at Toronto, the new settlers were sent to the best available districts for both settlement and employment. Many of these former soldiers were sent to Roswell Mount to be settled in the new townships.

The fourth group was composed of those sons and daughters of United Empire Loyalists who were entitled to free grants of land.

Irish Gentlemen in the Adelaide Bush

In the first group was a prosperous family from Ireland, William and Thomas Radcliff, sons of Rev. Thomas Radcliff of Clenmethen, County Dublin, Ireland. They arrived in Quebec with their families on July 16, and soon made their way to York, Upper Canada. They decided to settle in the newly opened Township of Adelaide. The first European women to come to this area were the Radcliff wives (Rev. Thomas Radcliff, *Authentic Letters from Upper Canada,* Dublin, 1833, Reprint Toronto: The MacMillan Company of Canada, 1952).

Because the services of a physician were always in great demand, their friend, Dr. Thomas Phillips, was granted a lot in the Town Plot along the recently surveyed Main Road. His house, the first house to be erected in Adelaide, was 24'x16' and consisted of one room downstairs, and an upstairs room reached by means of a ladder. He shared his house with the William Radcliff family until their own log dwelling could be completed. A good deal of the downstairs was taken up with a cooking stove belonging to the Radcliffs at one end, and Dr. Phillips' Franklin stove at the other.

William Radcliff's house, when completed, measured 46'x16' and was considered "the handsomest in the township." The Radcliffs each purchased 400 acres along the Main Road (Egremont) on the edge of the Town Plot of Adelaide. Thomas Radcliff, in a letter to his father, described his lot with enthusiasm:

"My lot is beautifully undulated. A creek or small river winding through its entire length, between rich flats, as they are here called, is bounded by each side, at some distance, by high banks, upon which I am leaving a belt of ornamental timber, which swells with the form of the hills, and is, in general, about one hundred yards in depth. Between those banks and the river, all trees are to be removed, except a few maples.

At a short distance from the site of the town, the right bank takes a bend, as it were, across the flats, and on that my house is placed, commanding from its windows a second smaller stream, with rising ground beyond, and a handsome point of land, embellished by a considerable clump of the best trees. The quality of the timber denotes the richness of the soil. Ours consists of maple, beech, butternut, elm, white ash, hornbeam, a sprinkling of oak, and some cherry and bass wood: all indicating a prime soil, and with great correctness, as I find it to be, in surface five inches of black vegetable mould, over a few inches of clay loam, with a substratum of strong clay—and almost all of my land, of this description, is an extended level of wheat soil, without the least unevenness. The knowing ones who have seen it, say it will give wheat forever and speak of fifty bushels to the statute acre." (Authentic Letters from Upper Canada)

Thomas also described his new log house:

"It consists of a cellar, three rooms and a small store room in the principal storey and two bedrooms in the roof, or RUFF, as the Canadians term it. The

edifice is thirty feet by twenty-five, from out to out. For the five rooms, we have three flues and two stoves, and mean to be very snug and warm." (Authentic Letters from Upper Canada)

Thomas was anxious for the freeze-up that fall so that the sleighs could be used to transport his furniture, which was still at Kettle Creek. Because of the extremely wet fall, he feared that the wagon and oxen would be swamped in the sloughs and mudholes. Indeed, that same year, Dr. William Dunlop of Goderich had advised intending settlers that there were *"...only two seasons when you can travel with any degree of comfort—midsummer and midwinter, the former by horseback or in a light wagon, the latter by sleigh."* (Authentic Letters from Upper Canada)

The Radcliffs and their friends were to form a distinct settlement in Adelaide because, unlike most of the settlers who arrived that year, they were gentlemen farmers able to hire help to clear their fields and build their houses. They planned to live the life of a gentleman squire as they had done in Ireland, with hunting, fishing, horseback riding, and social gatherings forming an important part of their lives.

There were, however, other, much larger groups of immigrants on their way to Roswell Mount's district who would pose a far greater challenge to the agent for immigrants.

Lord Egremont and the Petworth Settlers

Robert John Wilmot-Horton, the colonial under-secretary of the time, had investigated the costs involved in government-assisted immigration from the results experienced by the Peter Robinson Irish Immigration scheme to Almonte and Peterborough in 1823 and 1825, respectively; and had found them too high. Eventually, he concluded that if the financial burden of transporting the immigrants be excluded, the government could carry the costs incurred from the port of entry. He felt that a sum of £60 would see a pauper family of five (husband, wife and three children under the age of 13) safely established in the colonial backwoods. Even though the British government still considered this amount too high, they realized that something had to be done to relieve the mounting pressure of the superfluous poor in Britain.

In early 1832, the Petworth Emigration Society had been formed at the request of George Wyndham, the Third Earl of Egremont, to handle the details of sending out a number of people from Petworth Parish to Upper Canada. Many in England had reached the conclusion that the only way to improve conditions of unemployment and poverty caused by overpopulation, industrialization, and the flood of military men back in the country since the end of the Napoleonic War would be to encourage emigration from England on a large scale.

The Earl of Egremont was sympathetic to the plight of these victims of the times and, as a large landowner, he proposed to pay the travel expenses of any persons on his lands who wished to emigrate. His land included the entire parish of Petworth, Sussex, and property in varying amounts in nearby parishes. The scheme attracted large numbers of the poor and unemployed, as well as others eager to better their condition. At the same time, Sir John Colborne, Lieutenant-Governor of Upper Canada, always willing to assist the mother-country in its difficulties, was also anxious to increase the settlement of vacant land in Upper Canada by increasing the numbers of immigrants—more British—than that which existed from the influx of Loyalists and settlers from the newly founded republic south of the border. Because of this desire, the Crown Lands Department was prepared to assist newly arrived immigrants coming to Canada from the motherland.

Petworth, March 1st, 1832

Information to Persons Desirous of Emigrating from this Neighbourhood to Upper Canada

In the parish of Petworth, where the Earl of Egremont possesses nearly the whole of the land, his lordship has signified his intention of defraying the whole of the expense of persons of approved character wishing to proceed to Upper Canada; and, in any other parish in proportion to the property he owns in that parish.

Encouraged by this liberal support an engagement has been entered into for the ship Lord Melville, 425 tons register, A. 1, coppered and copper fastened, and sheathed with 7-foot height between decks and extra ventilating scuttles, which is to be comfortably fitted up at Portsmouth and to sail from thence for Montreal direct, on the 5th of April next. Passengers to be on board on the 4th at latest. A superintendent with his wife and family goes out with Lord Egremont's party and will conduct them direct to York, Upper Canada (in or near where he intends to settle), paying every attention to their comforts on the route.

A surgeon also sails in this ship, whose duty it will be to attend (gratis) to the health of the passen-

---

Adelaide, Upper Canada, July 28, 1832

Dear Mother, I take this opportunity to acquaint you that we arrived here safe and in good health on the 6th of July. Dear Mother, I was very fortunate in bringing my discharge with me, for I found in when I landed at York on the 23rd June that all who could show their discharge was entitled to 100 acres of land from the crown for their service, which I accordingly got; so if either of my nephews should like to come over here I will them some Land to work upon; tell them to bring some tools and all the money they can get with them, and some upland seeds of all descriptions, and garden seeds too, and barley in particular. Wm. Cooper's land joins mine, but have got to pay two dollars per acre for his, and 6 y'rs to do it in: here is a river runs through the corner of my lot, and plenty of fish in it, and here is wild deer and Turkeys, Pheasants, Partridges and Rabbits, and any body may kill them. Catherine is very well but she was very sea sick comin over for some time; she sends her kind love to Ruth and all her Brothers and Sisters and all friends. Copy this letter and send to my Sisters, and tell them I will build them a house if they come over here to live, so no more present from yours,

Edward & Catherine Boxall

Adelaide, Upper Canada, July 28th,, 1832

Dear Father and mother, brothers and Sisters, I hope this will finde you in good health as it leaves me preasant – I have been very well ever since I left England: we was seven weeks coming to Montreal, five weeks more coming up to Montreal, I have got 100 acres of Land at 2 dollars per acre and ¼ to be paid for at the end of three y'rs, and the rest in 3 y/rs more; in English money it comes to £41.13s.4d. in all; tell my brother James I saw Richard Carter and his wife at Little York, the are doing very well and said this would be a good opportunity for them to have come out this Country. I should for all my brothers to come here for here is plenty of work, and no dought but we shall do very well after next harvest. Edward Boxall and his wife and Wm. Philips from Merston and me have built us a shantee, and lives and works all together on our own land; we have got above two acres cleared and shall sow 6 or 7 acres of wheat this Autumn, and more in the spring. Dear Father I should like to have a malt mill and a few pounds of thread, and above all things a Newfoundland Dog for myself, and take this letter to Merston to Philips father and tell him to be sure to bring him a dog to catch the Dear and tell you what time of the year he means to come out so that you may all come together. Answer this as soon as you receive it; if you come in the spring or fall be sure you come by new York, and from thear to Buffaloe, and then cross the Niagara river at the ferry, and wait for the Chippeway Steem boat to bring you up to Kettle Creek. When you arrive at New York, send us a letter and we will meet you at Kettle Creek. I have to tell Wheat is now selling at 1 Dollar a bushel, beef at 2½d. Per lb. And mutton the same, and pork 4d. per pound in English money. Spirits is cheap here. Farmer's men gets from 8 to 12 dollars a month and board and lodgings and washing and mending. I have no more to say at present, so I must conclude with my kind love to you all. I remain Your dutiful son

Wm. Cooper

–direct to Wm. Cooper township of Adelaide to be left at Colonel Mount Delaware, North America

---

gers. The whole of the expence from Portsmouth to York, Upper Canada, is calculated for adults, £10, children under 14, £5, infants under 12 months free.

On these terms any person wishing to avail themselves of the peculiar advantages thus presented may join the Petworth party if they signify their intention to do so, on or before Saturday the 17th day of March instant, and make a deposit (at the printers) of £2 for every adult passenger and £1 for every person under 14 years; engaging to pay the remainder on going on board.

Persons particularly wishing to board themselves may be conveyed with the Petworth party, from Portsmouth to York, Upper Canada, medical attendance and every other expense included, for £5, or to Montreal only, should they wish to proceed any further, nor to avail themselves during the voyage of the assistance of the superintendent, for £3, 10s, but it is probable that they will find more comfort and on the whole less expence, by being board-

MORE ON THE PETWORTH EMIGRANTS

The Petworth Emigration Committee was established in 1832 in Sussex, England, to help poor people help themselves, and to relieve unemployment in the mother country. The amount of help varied from a minimum of a passage to North America, to a maximum of continued assistance in lands to enable the immigrant to North America to establish himself as a small farmer on a lot, which he would own outright at a future date. A passage was to be for one adult or for two children under 14 years of age.

At least three sponsoring authorities contributed:
(1) largely financed by Lord Egremont, by name George O'Brien Wyndham, 3rd Earl of Egremont (1751-1837), who was based on the Petworth Estate, one of the wealthiest landowners in Sussex, at Petworth, and in the surrounding or nearby parishes;
(2) the driving force was Thomas Sockett, the rector of Petworth. He planned and directed the emigrations; and
(3) the British Government, which backed the government-disbanded soldiers of the Perth and Richmond military settlements to areas. Major areas in Canada became known as Almonee and Peterborough.

The Petworth Committee chartered ships and hired a superintendent to take emigrants from Portsmouth to Upper Canada. In 1832, the Lord Melville and the Eveline sailed with 769 passages. A third ship, the England, sailed later but under similar conditions, so its 169 passages are often added to the Petworth Emigrants. For each of the following five years a ship was sent.

Thomas Sockett's choice of shipping agent was Carter and Bonus. Sockett wanted a ship certified A1, copper bottomed and copper fastened with steerage arranged and divided, so that single men would be separate from married men and the families. Also, water, fuel and cooking facilities were to be provided by the ship, and an allowance of 500-weight of baggage for each passage in addition to the weight of any provisions taken on board by the passengers themselves.

In Canada, the emigrants were kept on board to Montreal and encouraged to stay on board with the superintendent to York, where tradesmen often found work. A significant number took a steamer to Hamilton and formed clusters of emigrants at Ancaster, Dundas and Guelph. Many emigrants travelled through the Welland Canal to Lake Erie to the Township of London and to western districts being opened between Kettle Creek (now Port Stanley) and Sarnia. Those who came to Adelaide formed a large enough group to retain a community to commemorate their origin.

A preliminary list of emigrants from England contained the following names of people who came to Adelaide:

Boxall, Edward, Catherine - from Petworth, W. Sussex, 1832 Cooper, Wm.
Goatcher, Stephen (Wife still in England) from Pulborough, W. Sussex, 1832
Philips, W.J., from Marston, W. Sussex, 1832
Philips, Wm. Sr., Wife, 1 child - no date given

For passages not sponsored by Lord Egremont, various arrangements were used, sometimes by direct payments from leaders chosen to act by parties of emigrants, or by landlords and parishes sponsoring groups and individuals. For full assistance, the parish paid for travel from the home to Portsmouth, Lord Egremont paid £10 for passage to York, Upper Canada, and the government paid from York to a place to obtain land or find employment. Clothing and essential cooking utensils were sometimes provided by the parish. Sockett allowed £5 to outfit an adult and £3/5 for a child under 14. On April 11, 1832, the Lord Melville set sail. The Eveline reached Montreal on May 31, and the Lord Melville on June 8.

Letters From Emigrants
Describe the Landing Experience

A letter from Edward Boxall to his mother, dated July 28, 1832, indicated he had been a soldier in the 36th Regiment and later a resident of Colwaltham, Sussex. When he landed at York on June 23, he showed his discharge paper and was told that any soldier who showed his discharge paper was entitled to 100 acres from the Crown for his service. In the letter, Boxall offered some of the land to two of his nephews if they would come to Canada. William Cooper's land was adjoining his, for which he had to pay $2 per acre, payable in six years. A river ran through the corner of his property. Fish, deer, turkeys and pheasants, partridges and rabbits were abundant. His wife, Catherine, was very sick on the journey but was well now. He advised his nephews to bring seed, especially garden and barley, and all the money they could get.

On July 28, on the same sheet of paper and written across the above-mentioned letter, William Cooper wrote a letter addressed to his father, mother, brothers and sisters. It had taken seven weeks to get to Montreal, and five more to arrive in Kettle Creek. He got 100 acres of land at $2 per acre, one-quarter to be paid in three years, the balance in the next three years, the English equivalent of £41,13s,4d. He urged all of his brothers and sisters to come. He had built a shantee [sic] with Edward Boxall, his wife Catharine, and William Phillips. They lived and worked together on their land. They had cleared two acres and intended to sow six to seven acres of wheat in the fall and more in the spring. He requested that his letter be taken to Phillip's father, who should bring a dog to catch deer. Wheat was selling at $1 per bushel, beef at 2½d per pound, mutton the same, pork 4d per pound. Spirits were cheap. Labourers earned a good wage plus board, lodging, washing and mending. Mail was to be addressed to William Cooper, Township of Adelaide, to be left at Colonel Morants [sic], Delaware, North America.

A letter from Stephen Goatcher to his wife indicated that he was superintendent of the party in the Eveline. The date was July 6, 1832. He had not been sick on the trip, as many had been. It was very cold. At Newfoundland, there was snow on the mountains, but people were sowing wheat in Quebec. He saw Niagara Falls on June 2 at two miles off, and described it as "wonderful." Flies were abundant. He was on his way to Kettle Creek, where he was contemplating to settle. He had been inspected for cholera. He advised friends not to come to Canada. En route, he had 250 people to feed daily, a troublesome task. Mosquitoes were bad in the woods. He thought the land was very good—full of timber, no undergrowth, and could be cleared at £4 an acre. There were no stones in the area, and the soil was black loam. There was a road going through, and a coach was expected to operate soon. A mill was nearby and a sawmill was being built. The letter was addressed to Mrs. Goatcher, Pulborough, Essex.

In a letter from Adelaide, Upper Canada, dated July 28, 1832, William Phillips from Merston, Sussex, wrote to his father and mother that at York, three schooners took on passengers. Two schooners went to Hamilton, the third went through the Welland Canal with its 37 locks, to Chippewa two miles above the falls. He had gone under the falls to see it. From Chippewa, he had travelled in a party drawn by oxen, until they were opposite Buffalo. There, they were medically examined by American doctors but not allowed to cross the river. (Other letters had indicated that cholera was rampant; however, Phillips did not state any reason for isolation.)

The party landed at Kettle Creek on August 6. Phillips had gone by land to Delaware to Colonel Mount's headquarters. (Further reading indicated that Colonel Mount was Deputy Surveyor of the northwest corner of Carradoc [sic] to Lake Huron.) At Kettle Point, emigrants were placed under his management, care and attention. Many letters commended Colonel Mount. Phillips mentioned trees from which 6'-7' squares could be obtained, and said that, from root to branches was about 89'. He invited his father and uncle to come the following summer, and to bring seeds, and also cuttings of gooseberries, and apples (in a tub). He mentioned cohabiting with William Cooper, and Edward Boxall and his wife. He also stated that there were no game laws for hunting.

William Phillip's father arrived in 1833. He claimed that the principal road was almost impassable, and that he was advised to obtain a guide to get to a concession. Of mechanics and tradesmen who did well, the blacksmith, tailor, shoemaker and tanner were the best employed.

A letter from Mary and George Boxall, dated September 25, 1836, to George's father, mother, brothers and sisters at Farnhurst (near Haslemere) declared they had a good living in Canada. They had three children, and claimed they could keep three of them in Canada better than one in England. They urged the family to come to Canada, where they would find more friends in Canada in three months than they would in England in seven years. They were advised to bring all the goods and clothes they could, and named crockeryware in particular. They intended to rent 10 acres with an excellent house, and sell their own land. George's father-in-law, James Tilley, sent by the Petworth Committee in 1833, and his wife were well and established in keeping an inn at Bronti (now Bronte). Mail to James Tilley and wife was to be directed to them at Mr. George Chisholm's, Township of Nelson, County of Alton (Halton meant, no doubt) District of Gore, Upper Canada, North America.

No mention was made when Mary and George Boxall came to Canada and if they were part of the Petworth group. Nor could evidence be found in the 1842 census for Adelaide that they lived in the township—all this in spite of their letter being headed "Adelaide"!

From the 1842 census of Adelaide, the following information was extracted:

Lot, Concession	Head of Household	Occupation
E ½ 21 4	Boxwell, Edward	Farmer
E ½ 21 4	Cooper, William	"
W ½ 21 4	Cooper, James	"

From	Year	Males	Females
Eng.	1832	1	1
Eng.	1832	1	
Eng.	1833	3	2 (3 born in Canada)

Houses inhabited   246
Houses vacant   10
Houses building   12
Homes occupied: over 10 yrs, 21
                  10 yrs, 149
                  under 10 yrs, 80
Average residence in province, 9.6 yrs

Native to:

England	278	Canada Br.	404
Ireland	451	Europe	2
Scotland	59	United States	33

ed under his management. The sea stories contain brandy, porter and several other articles likely to contribute to the comfort of the passengers; to be given out under the direction of the surgeon, as circumstances may require.

Three ships were engaged, provisions for the voyage put aboard and transportation provided to move the travellers to dockside. The Lord Melville and the Eveline sailed from Portsmouth on April 11, 1832, while the England sailed almost a month later. Seven hundred and sixty-seven emigrants were aboard the three vessels. Upon their arrival in Canada in early June, a cholera epidemic was just beginning, and the emigrants were hurried on to York to be dispersed upcountry as quickly as possible.

Sometime in July of that year, 400 of these Petworth immigrants were met by Roswell Mount at Kettle Creek on Lake Erie and located on land in Adelaide Township. A number of these families settled on the shores of Bear Creek about six miles south of the Adelaide Township Plot. A few names of these Sussex emigrants have come down to us: Stephen Goatcher of Pulborough; James Parker; John Downer; James Napper; David Rapley; Edward Boxall from Coldwaltham; William Cooper from Burton; William Phillips from Merston; and Thomas Holden and Charles Rapley, both of Kirdford. It is also quite probable that the following families that settled in Adelaide may be added to the Petworth group: William Baker; George Carver; William Haslett; Frederick Hasted; Charles Hilton; John Hoare; John Humphries; James Joiner; James Knight; Charles Mann; William Pannell; William Pay; Richard Pullen; William Randall; Thomas Thomas; Francis Viney; and Edward White.

Army Pensioners

In August, several vessels bearing between 800 and 1,000 souls arrived on the same day at Port Stanley. Mount faced his most severe test to date in placing these settlers, many of them commuted army pensioners, with no experience at farming or clearing the land. In a report to Peter Robinson the following March, Mount told of some of his difficulties in dealing with this group:

"The Emigrants were no sooner landed than a fresh difficulty arose. At this time the cholera was raging with great virulence in the surrounding country and the inhabitants, apprehensive of infections from these destitute emigrants, could not be prevailed upon to receive them into their houses." (Roswell Mount to Peter Robinson, March 14, 1833, John Colborne Papers. National Archives of Canada)

"It therefore became necessary to remove them at the expense of Government to their destination. With much difficulty I succeeded in engaging waggons,(sic) for the inhabitants at first entertained such fears of contagion, that they were even unwilling that their waggons should be used in such a service." (Roswell Mount to Peter Robinson)

Mount finally moved the immigrants as far as the road would take them. When one case of Indian cholera occurred, he was obliged to set up a temporary hospital in a barn with one Dr. Starr in charge. Here, his charge were accommodated with temporary shelter and allowed some time to recover from the fatigue of their long journey before being located on their lands.

Mount's comments to Peter Robinson in his report of March 1833 clarify the tremendous challenges the agent for immigrants had overcome in the summer and fall of 1832. He wrote:

"In the month of July last, scarcely a tree had been felled in Adelaide. It is now densely settled— and numbers amongst its inhabitants many settlers of intelligence and property. In Adelaide and Warwick, I consider there are already between two and three thousand souls." (Roswell Mount to Peter Robinson)

Work Begins on the Roads

The policy in effect for dealing with new immigrants in 1832 was one of self-help, providing employment rather than direct aid. When immigrants began pouring into Adelaide in large numbers, Roswell Mount put them to work cutting out the roads, employing a few good choppers to instruct the newcomers in the use of the axe.

"When opening a road an 'explorer' went ahead, followed by two surveyors with compasses. Next, blazers notched trees intended to be the boundaries of the road, and woodmen chopped down those that were in the way. Gangs of men cleared away brush and trunks. Wagons with provisions brought up the rear. The resulting roadway was seldom straight as it wound around stumps, swamps and other obstacles." (J.J. Klauke, *History of Engineering*)

Military Land Grants in Adelaide Township

Name	Con	Lot
Joseph Abbott	4S	4
Henry Alguier?	13S	3
John Badger	7S	10
Jeremiah Baker	2S	2
Lewis Barnback?	3N	24
Robert Beattie	7S	6
Christopher Beer (Captain-R.N.)	10S	7+++
Edward Chicester Bolton	10S	11
Edward Boxall	4S	21
James Brown	2N	17
Edward Burke (Sergeant)	6S	10
William Butcher	7S	14
John Cahill	2N	18
Stephen Cain	7S	6
Patrick Callaghan	3N	15
Patrick Campbell (Sergeant)	2N	3
John Carruthers (Lieutenant)	1S	27
Samuel Chapel	7S	16
Joseph Clarke	7S	1
Hugh Corrigan	4S	1
John Crummer	2N	6
John Cully	5S	7
Dennis Cummins	2S	1
John P. Curran (Lieutenant)	1N	10
James Dillon	7S	1
George Dodd	14S	1
Patrick Donally (Surgeon)	1N	4
Henry Duggan	7S	7
Patrick Duggan	4N	9
Adam W. Emprey	7S	13
Peter Farrell	2N	20
Jonathan Fear	4S	14
Ryan Fitzpatrick	3N	1
John Gallagher	7S	7
Phillip Gallinger	5S	10
James Galloway	3N	2
Henry Gee	3N	5
James Gibson	2N	17
Alexander Glen (R.N.)	1S	3
Thomas Glynn	2N	16
Isaah Greason	2N	7
Michael Griffiths	5S	7
Robert Gripton	7S	13
William Groves	2S	10
George W. Hacke (Lieutenant)	9S	11
George Hamilton	2S	20
George W. Harris (Lieutenant)	7S	11
Thomas Harris (Captain)	1N	31
John Hays (Sergeant)	1S	24
James Healey	3N	5
George W. Henry (Lieutenant)	11S	9
Robert Henry	6S	1
John Hewitt	7S	14
John Hopper	14S	1
Paul Hughes	10S	10
Thomas Hussey	1N	23
John Jackson	3N	8
Thomas James	2S	11
Timothy James	5S	3
William James	3S	19
John Johnston	2N	4
Robert Johnston (Captain-R.N.)	8S	14
James Kelly	3N	17
Timothy Kennen	10S	2
Samuel Knight (R.N.)	2N	10
Matthew Lang?	6S	1
William Lawless	1S	6
William Lean	5S	9
James Lee	7S	9
Thomas Lee	7S	9
John Mahon (Lieutenant)	1N	22
Samuel Mather (Sergeant)	1N	2
William Maysent (Sergeant)	8S	9
Arthur McCollum	7S	10
Shepherd McCormick (Lieutenant)	2N	11
Thomas McHutcheon	2N	16
William McDonal?	9S	3
Alexander McDonald (Capain)	2N	26
Michael McDonough (McDonagh)	3N	4
James McFadden	1S	10
Mathew McGuinen	4S	2
Peter McHugh	5S	1
Baptist McIlwain	13S	1
Bernard McKenna (McKinna)	5S	1
Walter McKenzie (Lieutenant)	1S	28
David McPherson (Quarter-master)	4S	13
Donald McPherson	1N	23
Leslie McQuin	5S	9
William Middleton	4S	1
Robert Miller	2N	5
Simon Moak	3S	7
William Morgan	2N	19
Samuel Morrow	12S	1
Elijah Mudge	5N	2
Phillip Myers	5S	6
John Northwood (Sergeant)	8S	11
Thomas O'Connor	4N	6
Robert Pegley (Quarter-master)	1S	20
George Porterfield	3N	7
Charles Preston	10S	4
Robert Pullen	5S	10
Francis Quinn	8S	4
James Quinn	11S	1
John Radcliff (Lieutenant)	1S	13
Thomas Radcliff (Lieutenant)	1N	14
Patrick Redmond	4S	7
George Reid	9S	10
James Reiley	4N	12
James Renke	4N	13
James Riley	5S	6
Patrick Rones	2N	20
Arthur Ross	12S	2
Daniel Ross	12S	2
William Ryan	2N	19
John Smith	4S	1
Thomas Smith	10S	5
Frederick Somers	8S	13
John Sullivan	2S	4
Paul Sullivan	11S	3
Daniel Syne	4S	4
Thomas Thody	2S	10
Thomas Thompson (Officer)	1S	19
Charles Thrower	2S	11
William Tinkler	5N	2
Anthony Todd	3S	6
David Throwbridge	3S	3
Isaac Tuck	2S	10
John Tyneside	2S	1
William Vinery?	6S	14
Michael Walsh	6S	11
Joseph West?	6S	13
John Yonney	3N	4
Phillip Young	7S	16

ADELAIDE TOWNSHIP SETTLERS WHO WORKED ON THE EGREMONT ROAD IN 1832

Abbott, Joseph
Allen, Ira
Andrews, Christopher
Armstrong, Thomas
Armstrong, John
Ashbey, John
Baker, John
Baker, Jeremiah
Blake, William
Boddy, Michael
Boddy, Samuel
Boddy, Edward
Bradshaw, William
Brady, Joseph
Bray, William
Bray, Gregory
Brown, David
Brown, James
Brown, John
Brown, William
Bulger, James
Bulger, John
Bulger, Michael
Bulger, Edward
Burke, John
Burke, Edward
Butcher, William
Byrne, George
Callaghan, John
Callaghan, Patrick
Callaghan, William
Callaghan, Dennis
Callinan, Thomas
Campbell, Daniel
Campbell, James
Campbell, John
Campbell, Patrick
Caves, Henry
Clark, James
Collier, Thomas
Colton, Francis
Conaughton, John
Corrigan, Hugh
Corrigan, Michael
Corrigan, Thomas
Coulter, John
Coulton, Francis
Crone, William
Crummer, John
Crummer, James
Crummer, William
Cuddy, James
Cully, John
Curry, Duncan
Curry, Alexander
Donally, Patrick
Dougan, Michael
Dowding, Robert
Dowding, Thomas
Duggan, Henry
Duggan, Martin
Duggan, Patrick
Elliott, James
Fair, John
Farrell, Patrick
Farrell, Peter

Farrell, John
Feely, Patrick
Fitzpatrick, James
Fitzpatrick, Bryan
Foster, George
Freele, William
Gallagher, Michael
Gallagher, James
Galloway, Sholto
Galloway, James
Gately, Patrick
Gee, Henry
Glynn, Thomas
Glynn, William
Gosden, Edward
Gosden, John
Graham, Archibald
Greason, Isaiah
Green, George
Griffin, Michael
Groves, William
Groves, Charles
Hamilton, Jane
Harris, John
Harris, John J.
Harris, Samuel
Harris, Thomas
Harris, Joseph
Hart, Joseph
Hart, James
Harvey, Robert
Haslett, Matthew
Healy, James
Hopkins, William
Hughes, Richard
Hull, Cornelius
Hull, Jane
Hull, Robert Jr.
Hull, Blyth
Hull, Robert Sr.
Hume, Robert
Humphries, John
Inches, James
Ingram, Dennis
Iver, George
Jackson, John
James, Thomas
Jeminars, Thomas
Jeminars, Timothy
Johnson, Hugh
Johnson, Alexander
Johnston, John
Johnston, John Jones
Kelley, George
Kelly, Brien
Kelly, Arthur
Kelly, James
Kelly, William
Kenney, William
Kenny, Thomas
Kilbride, John
Kilbride, James
Knapton, Charles
Knight, Barnabas
Knight, James
Knight, Thomas

Lawless, Lawrence
Learey, William
Lee, James
Lee, Thomas
Lee, William
Lee, Frances Sr.
Lewis, Richard
Lewis, Charles
Livingston, William
Lyne, Daniel
Maguire, Thomas
Mangen, Matthew
Maysent, William
McCormick, Edward
McCutcheon, Richard
McCutcheon, Thomas
McDonagh, Michael
McDonald, William
McDonnell, William
McGinn, Thomas
McGinn, Leslie
McGugan, Neal
McGuire, Matthew
McGuire, William
McGuire, Charles
McIlwain, Babtist
McInnis, Thomas
McIntyre, Patrick
McIntyre, John
McKeawn, Hugh
McKelwain, James
McKenna, William
McKenna, Francis
McKenzie, John
McKenzie, Peter
McKenzie, Alexander
McMurrey, Owen
McMurrey, James
Middleton, Joseph
Middleton, William
Miller, Robert
Miller, William
Miller, John
Moore, William
Morgan, Joseph
Morgan, James
Morgan, William
Morris, John
Morrison, Archibald
Morrow, Samuel
Morrow, James
Murrell, John
Murrican, Michael
Nettleton, William
Newton, George
Nixon, Charles
Northwood, William
Northwood, John
O'Connor, James
O'Keefe, James
O'Neale, Terrence
Orr, Alexander
Payne, Joseph
Pegley, Anna
Pegley, George

Pegley, Henry
Pegley, Robert
Phillips, Peter
Phillips, Paul
Porterfield, John
Porterfield, George
Porterfield, William
Pullan, Richard
Quinn, Patrick
Quinn, Francis
Randal, William
Rapley, William
Reid, George
Reilly, Robert
Reilly, James
Rivers, Henry
Robertson, Andrew
Rones, Patrick
Rones, Thomas
Ross, Arthur
Rourke, John
Rowe, Robert
Salisbury, Daniel
Scanlan, Patrick
Shepherd, James
Sheppard, John
Sillington, William
Sissons, Thomas
Smith, John
Smith, William
Smith, Andrew
Smyth, Thomas
Stockdale, James
Stockdale, William
Sullivan, Paul
Taylor, Daniel
Taylor, Charles
Thody, William
Thody, Thomas
Thomas, John
Thomas, Enoch
Thompson, Alexander
Thompson, Peter
Thompson, William
Thorp, Sheldon
Thorp, Roxana
Travers, Jonathan
Walsh, Michael
Ward, Edward
Watson, George
Webb, Thomas
White, Edward
White, Richard
White, Daniel
Willey, James
Willey, John
Willey, Andrew
Willey, Joseph
Willey, Robert
Williams, Benjamin
Woods, John
Wynne, Samuel
Wynne, John
Young, John

Mount also realized, even if the newcomers did not, the absolute necessity of erecting houses to shelter them from the rigours of a Canadian winter. Accordingly, he contracted for the erection of a log house on each settler's lot where one had not yet been erected. *"These houses were built sixteen feet square, nine feet high, covered with shingles and rendered impervious to wet."* (Mount to Robinson) In all, Mount's expense account shows that 250 log houses were erected in the Townships of Adelaide and Warwick at a government expense of £947, 12s, 6p. The cost was to be repaid by each settler when established.

To deal with the roadwork, which was progressing in several locations simultaneously, Mount hired Ira Allen and Joel Westbrook as managers. Overseers were Cornelius Hull, Robert Hull Jr., and John Kilbride; Robert Pegley was designated as an issuer of rations. Four women were taken on as cooks: Roxana Thorp, Jane Hamilton, Jane Hull, and Anna Pegley. At the end of August, Patrick Rones was hired on as a butcher. He may have obtained cattle from as far away as Port Talbot on Lake Erie; in a letter to Peter Robinson in July, Thomas Talbot had written:

"By the way, when you write to Mount, pray have the goodness to say that should he be authorized to purchase Beef Cattle for the Emigrants that I have several head to dispose of." (J.H. Coyne, *The Talbot Papers*)

On October 20, Roswell Mount settled accounts with 386 persons who had been employed to open the roads, and wages to that day totaled £1,437, 15s, 6p. Anxious to reduce his expenses, he cut the rate of pay, hoping the settlers would be discouraged from further hired labour and go to their lands to set about the task of being self-sufficient. Even with a further wage reduction, however, he soon had 270 persons on the payroll, largely because of the continual arrival of poor immigrants and their totally destitute conditions. Many of the commuted army pensioners preferred working for wages (no matter how trifling), because their previous nomadic life style did not suit them for settling in the woods. Finally, late in January, Mount dismissed them all, but many were so destitute that he was forced to issue free rations to keep them from starving.

In attempting to explain his mounting expenses, Mount stated in his March 1833 report that the roads had been the heaviest expense and went on to describe his progress:

"The Main Road, nineteen miles in length, has been cut and made, through the townships of Adelaide and Warwick. The following roads have also been made. From Main Road in Carradoc to Bear Creek in Adelaide twelve miles—from thence to the Main Road in Adelaide near the Town Plot, six miles—from the encampment at Bear Creek on the line between the fourth and fifth concessions into Warwick, nine miles. The Roads on both sides of Bear Creek seven miles—making altogether fifty-three miles. Partial roads have also been cut in different directions to enable settlers to get to their locations... A way is now opened into the heart of a hitherto inaccessible tract of most valuable land." (Mount to Robinson)

The First Winter

Even Roswell Mount's optimism could not hide the grim reality that the winter of 1832-1833 had been a rough one for the new settlers. In January, Thomas Talbot wrote to Peter Robinson:

"The day before yesterday two gentlemen came on foot from Adelaide, a Mr. Alexander and a Mr. Wills. They gave a dreadful account of the roads, and the great want of provisions, and the consequent sufferings of the Emigrants."

C.O. Ermatinger recounts that *"In the winter of 1832-33, the Rev. Benjamin Cronyn, a clergyman near London, set out on foot with his friend Col. Curran, carrying a quarter of beef on a pole for the relief of starving settlers near Adelaide. Night came on and the raw beef attracted wolves, then common in the district. To add to their troubles the travellers lost their way in the dark, but finally came upon a chopper's shanty. Here they remained part of the night, making a fresh start with a lantern before daylight. When their light went out they lost the trail again, and the wolves were dangerously near when, fortunately, the two men were discovered by some of the settlers who had been on the lookout in expectation of their arrival with the anxiously awaited supply of food."* (C.O. Ermatinger, *The Talbot Regime*, St Thomas: Municipal World Ltd., 1904)

A Post Road to the Adelaide Town Plot

Early in 1833, the Village Plot of Adelaide was surveyed, ready for the land sale to be held March 25.

Sale of Public Lands in Adelaide Village made at Carradoc on the 25th day of March 1833 by Roswell Mount Esq. District Agent.

Description of Lot	No. of Lot	No. of Concession	No. of Township	Name of Purchaser	No. of Acres	Price/Acre	Total Amount	Amount of Installment	Whether Clergy Crown or Waste	Remarks
Village	1	Main Rd	Adelaide	Charles Willson	½	£6.14/-	£3/7/-	£-/16/9	C	Certificate given 26 Mar 1833
	2	"	"	Frederick Dillon	½	£6.10/-	£3/5/-	£-/16/3	C Pd for recently	1st Installment paid RM
	3	"	"	John Hoare	½	£6.10/-	£3/5/-	£-/16/3	C Paid for	1st Installment paid RM
	4	"	"	Mrs B. Westlake	½	£24.00	£12/-/-	£3/-/-	C Deeded	
	5	"	"	Charles Willson	½	£16/10/-	£8/5/-	£2/1/3	C #	Certificate given 26 March 1833
	6	"	13	Ferdinand Durand	½	£9.10/-	£4/18/-	£1/4/6	C Gone to US	1st Installment Paid RM
	7	"	"	Simeon Morrill	½	£8/-/-	£4/-/-	£1/-/-	C	
	10	"	"	Ross Robertson	½	£8.10/-	£4/5/-	£1/1/3	C	
	11	"	"	Joseph W. Neilson	½	£13/-/-	£6/10/-	£1/12/6	C these lots are built on and claimed by George B. Ivor	
	12	"	"	G. C. Clark	½	£1.2/-/-	£5/11/-	£1/17/9	C these lots are built on and claimed by George B. Ivor	
	13	"	"	William H. Dickinson	½	£14/-/-	£7/-/-	£1/15/-	C left country	Paid £1 on account to RM
	14	"	"	? Hart	½	£9/16/-	£4/18/-	£1/4/6	C	1st installment Paid RM
	4	Main Rol 2nd St	"	Mrs B. Westlake	½	£6.10/-	£3/5/-	£-/16/3	C	
	5	"	"	Charles Willson	½	£6.10/-	£3/5/-	£-/16/3	C #	
	6	"	"	William Wellwood	½	£6.10/-	£3/5/-	£-/16/3	C vacant	
	8	"	"	Lancaster Schofield	½	£6.10/-	£3/5/-	£-/16/3	C vacant	
	10	"	"	Frederick Dillon	½	£6.10/-	£3/5/-	£-/16/3	C	1st Installment Paid RM
Lot	15	1st Con South Rd	"	Dr. Thomas Phillips	200	£-/12/6	£125/-/-	£12/10/3	Clergy	Certificate given 22 June 1833
Lot	20	4th Con South Rd	"	James Inches	200	£-/12/6	£125/-/-	£12/10/10	Clergy	cancelled, resold 1st October, 1833
Lot	6	1st Con North Rd	"	John Boyce	200	£-/10/-	£100/-/-	£10/10/10	Clergy	Certificate given 16 May 1833
Lot	8	2nd Con North Rd	"	John Boyce	200	£-/10/-	£100/-/-	£10/10/10	Clergy	Certificate given 16 May 1833
Broken Lot	9	12th Con South Rd	"	Edward Boulton	104	....	....	....		Cancelled

these Lots were assigned for the Benefit of his Creditors.

[Source: Archives of Ontario: Facsimile copy prepared by D. F. Demaray]

The Main Road from Lobo to Adelaide Town Plot had been opened with the expectation that settlers would come into the township from that direction and would procure their supplies from farmers in Lobo. This expectation proved not to be the case on both counts. Settlers continued to arrive by boat at Kettle Creek on Lake Erie, or overland by Dundas Street as far as Delaware. It was soon realized that provisions could be procured from the southern parts of the Talbot Settlement cheaper and of better quality than from Lobo farmers. Mount said of this road, *"Without it, during the wet season, the Emigrants must have perished for want of food as it could not have been procured in any other direction."* (Mount to Robinson)

Yet another problem was emerging. In the confusion of settling new arrivals on their lands with some shelter and providing them with roadwork so they could feed their families, Roswell Mount had spent far more money than the Government had intended. When Colborne added up immigrant-related expenses for the whole country in 1832, he was appalled to find that more than twice the funds allocated for immigrant needs had been expended, with Mount being the worst offender (Peter Robinson, *Dictionary of Canadian Biography, Vol. 7*, Toronto: University of Toronto Press, 1988).

Settlement Expenses Curtailed

Early in 1832, Peter Robinson had personally directed Roswell Mount to look after the needs of the settlers and had authorized him to spend what was needed to see the newcomers established successfully on their land. Reluctantly, he was now forced to advise Mount that the government had cut off the flow of money for this purpose.

Unfortunately, the Main Road through Adelaide, Warwick and Plympton to Lake Huron was not yet completed. The 19 miles which had been opened carried the traveller only as far as Bear Creek, the future site of Warwick Village, and from this point to the shore of Lake Huron, the road was still only a surveyor's blaze, cut there in 1831 by Peter Carroll.

In May 1833, Henry John Jones, land agent for Plympton, was in York on business when he learned that, of nearly £13,000 slated for immigrant aid in 1832 for all of Upper Canada, 7,500 had been expended on the Adelaide settlers alone. There was talk that the Carroll Road (as they termed the Main Road), if finished at all, would be contracted. Later, Jones talked to Sir John Colborne and reported in his diary:

"Sir John wished to have a report made immediately on the probable expense likely to attend the completion of Mr. Mount's road. He cannot afford much and therefore wishes it at present to be as little as possible." (Henry J. Jones, *Diary, entry for May 17, 1833*, Lambton Room, Lambton County Library, Wyoming, Ontario)

Whether part of the remainder of the Main Road was built at Government expense is not known, but at that time, general practise in much of the country was for each settler to clear the road in front of his land as part of his settlement duties.

The Executive Council at York had issued a statement concerning settlement duties as follows:

"The Locatee shall clear thoroughly the half of the land width, opposite to the front of his lot... he shall cut down the stumps for a space of two feet from the centre of the Road, so low that a wagon wheel may easily pass over anything that stands within the space, and he shall sow with grass seed the Road so cleared.

Upon proof that this has been done, and that some person has been constantly resident upon the Lot for the space of two years, a Patent may issue without other conditions of Settlement Duty." (Minutes of Executive Council, Nov. 20, 1830, Land Orders)

In his report to Sir John Colborne in August 1833, Mount noted the population of Adelaide Township was 1,138 persons and that of Warwick was 852 persons, for a total of 1,990 souls. Eighty-eight families (452 persons) had temporarily left the two townships to secure paid employment in adjoining settlements but were expected to return to their lands. Therefore, 2,442 persons had been located in Warwick and Adelaide Townships between July 1832 and the date of the report. Included in this total were 176 commuted army pensioners who, with their families, comprised 666 persons. According to Mount, *"These pensioners were in a state of utter destitution when they arrived from Port Stanley... and I had no alternative but to give them assistance or allow them to perish."* (Mount to Robinson)

By August 1833, 1,630 acres of land were cleared in Adelaide and 1,166 in Warwick, of which 1,371 acres were actually in crop.

In his dealings with this first tide of immigration to the area, Mount displayed a remarkable degree of compassion and understanding not always present in government officials. He, of course, was in the midst of events as they unfolded and made decisions on the spot, knowing that many lives hung in the balance. Officials of the Home Government back in England, secure in the comfort of their government offices, and glad that the paupers were at last out of their jurisdictions, found it easier to be objective. Roswell Mount's considerable contribution to the settlement of this area was never fully acknowledged, nor indeed recognized by the Home Government. He died on January 19, 1834, at the age of 37 (The Canadian Emigrant and Western District Advertiser, Feb. 1, 1834, Obituary of Roswell Mount). No other settlement plans in future years ever received the degree of government assistance accorded to the Adelaide venture of 1832.

Obtaining Land

The process involved in acquiring title to land (right to ownership with or without possession) was most often complex and fraught with unimagined difficulties for the early settlers. It may have been an easier task to clear 100 acres of bush than to obtain the patent or title, but the acquisition of the patent was the ultimate goal for the settler, and it is the date of the patent that indicates the date of first ownership. Unfortunately, the events leading to the patent acquisition are not recorded in the Abstract Index to Deeds as held by the Provincial Land Registry Offices, and may only be discovered via a meticulous search of family records, court records, and other pertinent documents sometimes preserved at the Provincial Archives. In order to understand the nature of such documents, it is necessary to examine the process of land acquisition, which, although prescribed, did evolve and was sometimes circumvented by nefarious means.

The procedure that was in effect from 1796 to 1818 has been admirably described by R.W. Widdis in a paper, in which he describes three possible scenarios and entitles them as Land Grant 1, 2 and 3:

"The steps involved in obtaining title until 1818 are outlined below, as 'Land Grant 1':

1. a petition was submitted to the lieutenant-governor in council, and if it were received favourably, a grant was ordered by the council;
2. a copy of the order-in-council authorizing the grant was taken to the receiver general's office and the fees paid;
3. the receiver general's receipt was returned to the council office;
4. an order-in-council was issued to the grantee and taken to the attorney general's office;
5. the attorney general's fiat was then issued and taken by the grantee to the surveyor general's office;
6. in the surveyor general's office, the location was made, and a location and a description of the lot issue;
7. the description was forwarded to the provincial secretary, and it became his authority and guide for engrossing the patent.

In October 1818, an order was issued directing settlement duties to be performed. Evasion of these duties had long been an unsatisfactory element of the system. A certificate had to be filed with the surveyor general by each applicant to the effect that a habitable house had been erected and sufficient land cleared and fenced, i.e., a proportion of five acres in every 100. The procedure of 'Land Grant 2' involved:

1. submission of a petition;
2. a copy of the order-in-council authorizing the grant was taken to the receiver general's office;

Adelaide April 15/58

I hereby certify that I have surveyed the improvement made by Mr. James Abernathy in front of the East half of Lot No. 5. 2nd Con. South of the Egremont Road in the Township of Adelaide, County of Middlesex and that it contains 10 Acres or thereabouts.

I have also inspected and valued said half lot on which there are ten acres chopped and done in a workmanlike manner and preparing to log and burn it preparatory to a fall crop - said improvement has been done in the fall of 1857 and the early part of this year and that the sum of six dollars fee and is a fair and reasonable price therefor -

I further state that I am acquainted with the locality for the last fifteen years and that no improvement whatsoever has been made on it until the time specified within.

Geo. P. Liddy
P.L.S.

> I Certify that Mrs. Blanche Westlake has cleared that Lot alluded to in her Petition in the Village of Adelaide and built a Blacksmiths Shop thereon as stated and that the Petitioner is a Spirited and Improving settler, and deserves every encouragement.
>
> (Signed) Thos. Radcliffe
>
> Nov. 6 1837.

> In Council 26th April 1838
>
> Ordered that Frederick Hasted of the Township of Adelaide, Yeoman assignee of Charles Mann be allowed to purchase the West Half of Lot number nineteen in the Fourth Concession, South of Egremont Road in the said Township of Adelaide at the price and on the consideration to which Land, assigned to indigent Settlers are subject
>
> John ....
> Clerk Executive Council
>
> To: The Surveyor General

> Adelaide 9th June/51
>
> To The Honourable
> The Crown Lands Commissioner
> Toronto
>
> I arrived in this province from Scotland a short time ago but have not had the Good fortune to get settled on land to my wishes -
>
> I wish to purchase a lote of land from the Government and Lot No 25 First Concession South of the Egremont Road Township of Adelaide is still wild and not settled on. I sh'd like to purchase this lot - please let me know Pr return of Post if I can have this by paying the money for it as the summer will soon go past and I .... not answer one with a family to be in a Strange country long unsettled-
>
> Your reply by return of Post will oblige
> Your ob't Serv't
> Daniel McCubbin

3. location made and a ticket of location issued;
4. settlement duties performed within the time limit allowed and a certificate to this effect filed;
5. fees were paid;
6. the attorney general's fiat was issued and sent to the surveyor general's office;
7. the surveyor general prepared a description of the grant;
8. the provincial secretary prepared the patent.

The third procedure, which we will call 'Land Grant 3,' was followed when a person, after petitioning and receiving a location ticket, either died or ' legally assigned the land rights to someone else before receiving his patent.' For the historian, this can be confusing because the name on the petition and the name on the patent differ. In many cases, a relative or even a complete stranger eventually was issued the legal ownership of the lot.

If the original petitioner had died or assigned his rights to someone else, then the new claimant had to prove this claim before the Heir and Devisee Commission. The individual started this procedure by issuing a notice to the commissioner, claiming the lot in question. The notice was posted on the courthouse doors for three weeks so all could read it in case there were counterclaims. A bearing was established in which the counterclaimants could file proof (e.g., wills) backing up their claims. The committee would then study the various submissions and decide to allow or disallow the claim. If the verdict was to disallow the claim, then someone else might make claim to the lot. If the claim was allowed, the government then prepared a patent in the new name. Then the procedure outlined previously (Land Grant 2) was followed.

After the settlers secured a certificate sworn to by two witnesses that their settlement duties had been performed, they received confirmation of their grants. Many land owners, on receiving this confirmation, were content to put off patenting until a later date. Thus, in many cases, patents were not registered until quite some time after original settlement. In fact, property often was transferred several times before the patent was finally registered." (R.W. Widdis, *Tracing Property Ownership in Nineteenth-Century Ontario; A Guide to Archival Sources in Canadian Papers in Rural History, Volume II,* Gananoque: Langdale Press, 1980)

The period from 1818 to 1838 was one of almost chaos. Administrators of land policy changed frequently, often undoing the work and policies of their predecessors. Regulations set out by various governing bodies were often ignored and in some cases intentionally thwarted for personal gain. However, many of the same documents with only temporal alterations were used, and some examples relating to Adelaide have been included here.

LOYALIST LAND GRANTS IN ADELAIDE TOWNSHIP

NAME	DESIGNATION	LOT	CONC	ADDRESS OF LOCATEE	ORDER IN COUNCIL DATE
Peter Barkley	SUE	5 W 1/2	4 SER	Williamsburg Tp., Dundas Co.	18340201

Son of Peter Barkley, UEL of Williamsburgh Tp., Dundas County.

Andrew Willse Barnum	SUE	4 & 5	14 SER	Bayham Tp., Renfrew Co.	18321222

Son of Nathaniel Bunnell Barnum, UEL of Charlotteville, Norfolk County

Catherine Connor	UE	13 W	6 SER	Niagara Tp., Lincoln Co.	18370525
Catherine Connor	UE	14 E ½	8 SER	Niagara Tp., Lincoln Co.	18370525

Daughter of John & Sarah Connor, UEL of Kingston, Ontario. She married Peter Howe of Kingston son of William Howe, UEL of Kingston

Ann Cunningham	DUE	8	6 SER	Adelaide Tp., Middlesex Co.	18320723

Daughter of John Dingman, UEL of Westminster Tp. Corporal in Butler's Rangers. Ann (1795-) married Thomas Cunningham (1792-) and resided on Lot 8, Con 6 SER. Adelaide Tp.

Henry Dell Sr.	UE	22 & 23	3 SER	Wainfleet	18350821

Henry Dell Jr.	SUE	22 & 23	3 SER	Willoughby Tp., Welland Co.	18320417

Son of Henry Dell Sr.

Benjamin Green Jr.	SUE	21	1 NER	Townsend Tp., Norfolk Co.	18330906

Son of Benjamin Green, UEL of Sophiasburgh, Prince Edward County.

David Hicks	SUE	3	6 SER	Marysburgh Tp., Prince Edward Co.	18340605

Son of Benjamin Hicks, UEL of Sophiasburgh, Prince Edward County & grandson of Edward Hicks Sr., soldier with Butler's Rangers

Mary Hicks	DUE	14	9 SER	Marysburgh Tp., Prince Edward Co.	18380315

Daughter of Benjamin Hicks and sister of David (above)

Elizabeth Hill	DUE	26	1 NER	Edwardsburgh Tp., Grenville Co.	18320202

Daughter of Nazereth Hill, UEL of Marysburgh Tp., Prince Edward County. She married Samuel Hayes of Adolphustown Tp., Lennox County.

Elizabeth McLean	DUE	14 W ½	1 SER, NER	Yonge Tp., Leeds Co.	18360929

Daughter of David Hunter, UEL of Yonge Tp., Leeds County, and Leah McIlmoyle. She married Alexander McLean, (UEL?) of Yonge Tp., Leeds County. She resided at Ogdensburg, N.Y. on May 22, 1854.

John Brock Miller	SUE	3 W ½	13 SER	Hallowell Tp., Prince Edward Co.	18380329

Son of John Miller, UEL of Sophiasburgh & Hallowell, Prince Edward County

Mary Miller	UE	12	1 SER	Delaware Tp., Middlesex Co.	18321208

Daughter of John Miller & sister of John Brock Miller (above).

Edwardy Ryerson	UE/SUE	5	13 SER	Hamilton(T), Wentworth Co.	18360609

Son of Joseph Ryerson, UEL of Charlotteville, Norfolk County & grandson of Lukos Ryerson, UEL and Mehetable Stickney; and brother of Egerton Ryerson.

Rebecca Stover	UE	7	12 SER	Ernestown Tp., Addington Co.	18330103

May have been the wife of Martin Stover, UEL of Ernestown, Addington County.

Joseph Van Every	UE	3	4 NER	Stamford Tp., Welland Co.	18311201

Son of William Van Every, UEL of Niagara, soldier in Butler's Rangers and Elizabeth Stevens.

Catherine Willson	DUE	26	1 NER	Elizabethtown, Leeds Co.	18320202

Daughter of Joel Adams, UEL & Margaret Snyder of Edwardsburgh, Grenville County. She married Ebenezer Willson of Elizabethtown, Leeds County.

Richard Young	SUE	4	13 SER	Hallowell Tp., Prince Edward Co.	18370710

Son of Lieutenant Henry Young, Rodgers Rangers, NY of Sophiasburg & Hallowell Tp., Prince Edward County.

Perhaps no better summary can be provided than that prepared by Lillian F. Gates in her detailed study, *Land Policies of Upper Canada*.

"*Land of Upper Canada was initially regarded in Great Britain and in Canada as Crown land to be managed under the direction of the Colonial Office by the Lieutenant-Governor and Executive Council of the province, assisted later by an official who bore an English title, Commissioner of Crown Lands. The Imperial government was at first disposed to give the land away to reward loyalty and services; later it wanted to make the land pay the expenses of its administration; finally it became eager to develop a revenue from the Crown lands to further emigration from the mother country. Gradually, the land came to be thought of as public domain subject to the legislature of the province, and this foreign concept came to be accepted by the Colonial Office.*

Those who first devised and administered the land policies of Upper Canada were convinced that the American Revolution would not have occurred if there had been a loyal aristocracy and clergy of the established Church throughout the thirteen colonies, and if, in addition, the Crown had enjoyed a revenue independent of the legislature. They thought of Upper Canada as virgin soil on which political, social, and religious institutions of the right kind could be developed, and the specific land policies adopted reflected this belief. The Crown Reserves, the Clergy Reserves, the limited grants to 'common' settlers, the larger grants to officers and gentlemen- all were intended to establish the social structure that prevailed in the mother country.

The early land policies of the province were a failure because in 1791 Upper Canada was not virgin soil. Between 1784 and 1791, the province had acquired a body of settlers who had brought with them from the thirteen colonies, along with their loyalty, a preference for democratic institutions and a belief in religious equality. They were not likely to be weaned away from these sentiments on the Canadian frontier. Moreover, the physical and economic environment of the province was not suited to the development of an aristocracy of country gentlemen and to the maintenance of an endowed clergy but to the creation of a democratic society. The immigration of settlers from the United States and the very existence of the successful republic to the south strengthened this tendency. In addition, the devices from which Simcoe had hoped so much, the reserves, failed of their purpose because they proved to be obnoxious to the settlers.

The land policies in force before 1826 failed to attain their economic, as well as their political, objectives. One difficulty was that the policy was not a consistent whole, and parts of it, particularly the settlement duty requirements, were sabotaged. The free grant policy became in effect an inconvenient sales system, and, although it was the declared policy of the Crown to prevent speculation, the Crown and Clergy Reserves made the government

---

No. 3283

I hereby certify, that I have carefully examined the claims of Robert Hamilton of the Town of Queenston in the Niagara District Esquire and find him entitled to His Royal Highness the Prince Regent's bounty of a Grant of the waste Lands of the Crown, having served as a Captain of a Flank Company of the 2d Regt of Lincoln Militia on Service between the 1st July and the 31st December 1812

Certify, that at the Public Sale of Crown Lands held under the authority of the Commissioner of Crown Lands at *London* on the *Second* day of *July* 1833 *Walter McKenzie Junis* formerly of *Ireland* now of *The Town of York Upper Canada* became the purchaser of of Lot No. *28 & the West part 29* in the *1st Concession South of the Road* in the Township of *Adelaide* in the *London* District *Crown Lands* containing *Two hundred and thirty four* Acres, more or less at the rate of *twelve shillings & six pence* Currency, per Acre

And it is to be understood, that this Certificate shall be void, unless transmitted to the Commissioner for Crown Lands, at York, together with the amount of the first Instalment, being *thirty six eleven shillings & three pence* on or before the day of next, and the Land shall be liable to be re-sold at any future Sales.

On production of this Certificate, and payment of the first Instalment, the Commissioner for Crown Lands will give to the purchaser a written acknowledgment of the payment on account, and authority to take possession of the Lot. But the obtaining of a perfect title must of course depend on the punctual fulfilment of the conditions of the purchase.

the largest speculator of all. Finally, the Colonial Office, by yielding to the demands of special interests, such as the children of loyalists, contributed to the very speculation it wished to avoid.

In theory, a free grant policy was in force in Upper Canada prior to 1826 and a sales policy subsequently. In practice, there was neither. Paradoxically, the free grant policy became practically a sales policy, and, after a sales policy was officially adopted, free grants, free even of patent fees, continued to be made to such an extent that from 1826 to 1838 the Crown disposed of forty times as much land by grant as by sale, exclusive of the sale to the Canada Company.

Speculation might have been minimized... if an effective land tax had been imposed in the early days of the colony... Contemporary critics, however, advocated the adoption of the American system.

ARMY OFFICER LED THE WAY INTO ADELAIDE

The first "squatter" to locate in the Township of Adelaide was Malcolm McVicar, a veteran of the War of 1812. McVicar was prominent as a subaltern in the York Volunteers at Queenston Heights.

With his wife, an Irish woman, he settled in the township in 1829 between the second and third concession roads. They built themselves the typical back-woods cabin, cleared a space of land, and when others came a few years later, McVicar traded his "farm" for a job in the Huron Tract and departed.

(Excerpted from an article by Harold Eastman, Regional Collection, D.B. Weldon Library, University of Western Ontario)

This would have meant that no more scattered reserves would be created and that land would be offered for sale at what was practically a fixed price, for cash. It was recognized that this system played into the hands of speculators, but it was argued that this was an advantage. All, it was assumed, would be well if the simple, cheap, and quick American method of transferring the public domain into the hands of individuals was adopted.

In Upper Canada, however, it was not the system of free grants to immigrants that had failed, but the practice of using the land to reward U.E. loyalists, militia men, and officials already resident in the colony. Not one-sixth as much land was granted to later immigrants as to these classes of privileged persons. Yet, in 1826 it was made to appear that the free grant system had failed and it was abolished while the real evil was permitted to continue until 1837 and, in an altered form, until 1851, when scrip ceased to be issued.

No major questions of land policy had been set at rest by 1841. In Upper Canada, the Crown lands had been managed by the lieutenant-governor-in-council subject to such restrictions as the Colonial Office imposed; in United Canada, the Crown lands were managed by the governor-in-council subject to such restrictions as the colonial legislature

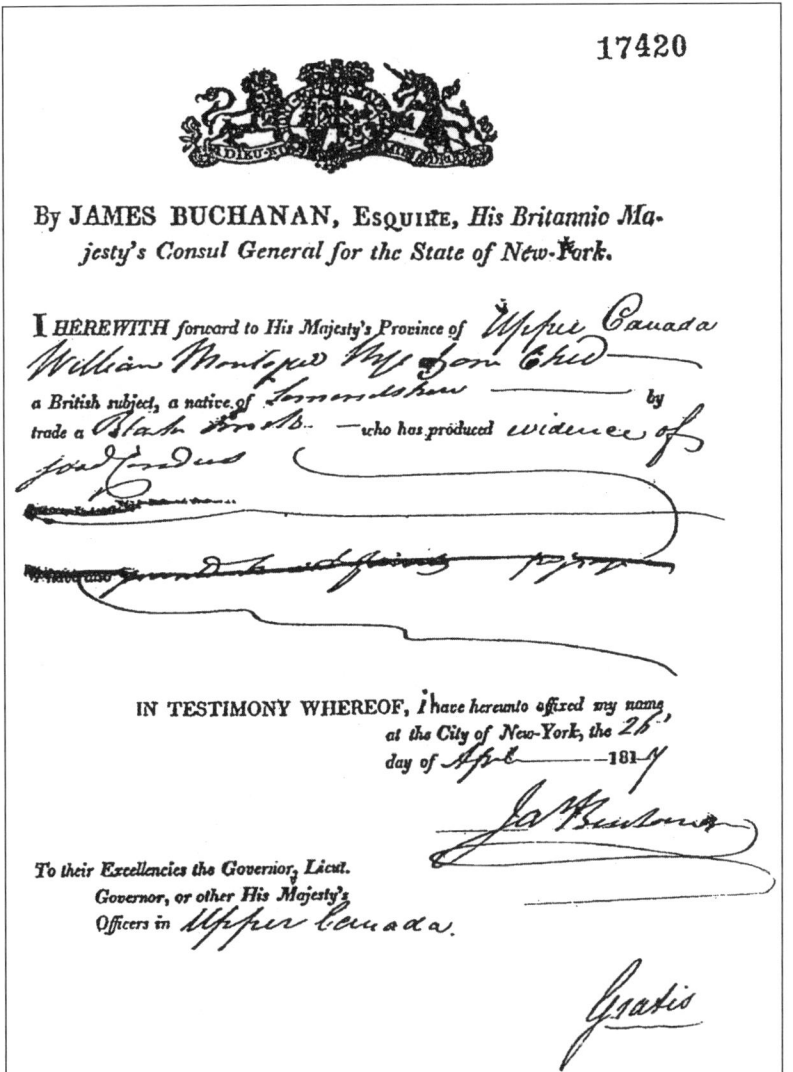

Location of Indigent Settlers in Adelaide Township

Name	Lot	Con
Michael ??	9 E½	11S
James Clark ?Souly	5 W½	2S
John Anderson	4 E½	4N
John. Armstrong Sr.	17 W½	3S
Thomas Armstrong	17 W½	3S
Michael Boddy	1 E½	3S
Samuel Boddy	1 W½	3S
John Bogue	6	12S
Edward Chicester Bolton	10	10S
Baryan Botately	17 W½	4S
Reys Bradley	14 E½	9S
William Bradshaw	13 E½	3S
Richard Brenan	13 W½	9S
John Brown	9 E½	3S
John Burke	11 W½	6S
John Butterfield	9 E½	2N
John Calison	1 W½	8S
Thomas Callaghan	4 E½	10S
William Callaghan	2 W½	8S
Colquhoun Campbell	25	3N
John Campbell	4 W½	4N
Robert Campbell	26	3N
James Carroll	17 W½	2S
George Carver	16 E½	5S
Henry Caves	1 E½	9S
Thomas Collier	8 W½	2S
John Connaughton	5 E½	6S
Joseph Cooper	7 W½	4N
Thomas Cooper	2 E½	2S
William Cooper	21 W½	4S
John Coulter	12 E½	7S
Thomas Coulter	3 E½	3S
William Crummer	6 E½	2N
James Cuddy	8 E½	3N
Robert Curry	1 W½	9S
Mathew Darvet	12 E½	2N
William Dodd	2 E½	6S
Patrick Donally	13 W½	3N
Robert Dowding	16 E½	3S
Thomas Dowding	9 W½	3S
Joseph Eastabrook	2 W½	6S
James Elliott	8 E½	2S
Silas Finch	18	3N
William Finkler	17 E½	5S
George Foster	7 W½	4S
Thomas Foster	4 W½	13S
William Freele	11 W½	3N
Samuel Gable?	11 E½	4S
James Gallagher	6 E½	4N
James Galt	1 E½	2N
Robert Gatley	5 W½	6S
Stephen Goatcher	20	5S
Thomas Goatcher	13 E½	5S
Edward Gosden	4 E½	6S
John Gosden	4 W½	6S
Thomas Hardy	1 W½	10S
Andrew Harkness	22 W½	3N
John Harkness	21 W½	3N
George Harris	14 W½	4N
Samuel Harris	12 E½	3S
Thomas Harris	17 E½	4S
William Heake	16 W½	5S
John Hoare	9 W½	1S
Thomas Holden	19 E½	4S
William Hopkin	7 W½	2S
Charles Hopkins	8	2N
James Hopkinson	4 E½	12S
Charles Houlton	14 E½	4S
Blyth Hull	8 W½	8S
Cornelius Hull	9 W½	9S
Robert Jr. Hull	9 E½	9S
Robert Jr. Hull	8 E½	8S
John Humphries	10 W½	3S
Thomas Hussey	23 W½	1N & S
Daniel Ingram	7 E½	2S
Hector Innis	2 W½	3N
George Ivor	11 E½	2N
John Johnston	4 E½	2N
James Joiner	12 E½	5S
James Jr. Kelly	17 E½	3N
Joseph Kelly	28	2S
Thomas Kenny	16	4N
Charles Knapton	15 W½	2S
James Knight	14 W½	2S
Thomas Knight	14 E½	6S
Laurence Lawless	5 W½	8S
William Little	14 W½	9S
Charles Mann	19 W½	4S
John McAlton?	21 E½	3N
Edward McCormick	14 E½	3N
William McDonald	3 E½	5S
Hugh McEwin	3 W½	9S
Thomas McGinn	4 E½	5S
Thomas McGuiver?	14 W½	3S
William McGuiver?	13 W½	3S
James McIlmurray	1 E½	8S
David McIlrea	11 E½	3N
Patrick McIntyre	3 W½	7S
John McKee(Ashkew)	20 E½	3S
Peter McKenzie	4 E½	2S
Owen McMurray	3 E½	7S
Duncan McVerrick	7 E½	2N
Patrick Mee	13 E½	3N
William Middleton	12 W½	7S
William Miller	5 E½	2N
John Miller	6 W½	13S
Andrew Minielly	1 E½	1N
James Mollineaux	4 E½	13S
William Moore	10 E½	4S
William Morgan	1 W½	2N
John Muirill	4 E½	7S
John Murray	26 W½	2N
Charles Napper	13 W½	4S
Robert Neilson	4	5N
George Newton	15 E½	2S
Samuel Nicholson	14 W½	3N
John Jr. Northwood	?	8S
Joseph Northwood	?	8S
William Orchard	4 W½	11S
Alexander Orr	17	4N
John Osburne	?	12S
William Paddy	14	2N
William Pannell	22 W½	3S
James Parker	15 E½	4S
William Parker	18 E½	5S
H. Pay	12	8S
Joseph Payne	18 E½	2S
Charles Peacock	12 W½	5S
William Philipps	15 W½	4S
Daniel Phipps	11 W½	4S
William Porterfield	7 E½	3N
Richard Pullen	17 W½	5S
Thomas Ragnan	22 W½	2N
Gilbert Ramsay	18,19	4N
William Randall	12 W½	3S
Charles Rapley	19 W½	5S
James Rapley	19 E½	5S
William Rapley	14 E½	5S
Richard Rees	1 W½	12S
William Robbins	4 E½	3S
George Robinson	13 W½	5S
John Robinson	1	3N
Thomas Rones	18 W½	2N
Robert Rowe	4 W½	9S
Edmond Russell	16 W½	3S
Daniel Salisbury	13 E½	2S
William Sangster	11 E½	2N
Richard Saul	4 W½	12S
Patrick Scanothing	3 W½	13S
Harry Setlington	7 E½	3S
William Setlington	7 E½	3S
Thomas Shain	9 W½	4N
Francis Shaughnessey	5	5N
David Shea	8,9,10	5N
James Sheppard	5 E½	4S
John Sifton	9 E½	1S
Francis Smith	9 W½	11S
William Smith	19 E½	2S
Philip Stacey	14 W½	5S
Thomas Steers	12 W½	9S
Thomas Steers	12	10S
William Steers	12 E½	9S
John Stillned	10,11	11S
Adharim Str_dut	13 W½	2S
Tunis Swartz	7	1S
Thomas Sykinic	14 E½	2S
Daniel Talbot	5 E½	10S
Daniel Taylor	4 E½	11S
James Thomas	18 W½	4S
Thomas Thomas	18 E½	4S
William Tinkler	22 E½	3N
James E. Tovier	13 E½	9S
Samuel Edison Turner	1 W½	1S
Benjamin Ward Bros.	24	2S
Thomas Webb	5 E½	2S
William Wells	18 W½	5S
Daniel White	4 W½	7S
Edward White	15 E½	3N
James Whiting	1 W½	11S
Daniel Whitley	19 W½	2S
John Willey	2 E½	14S
Robert Willey	2 W½	14S
Charles Wilson	3	5N
John Woods	4 W½	8S

Prepared by D.F. Demaray, Feb. 14, 2000.

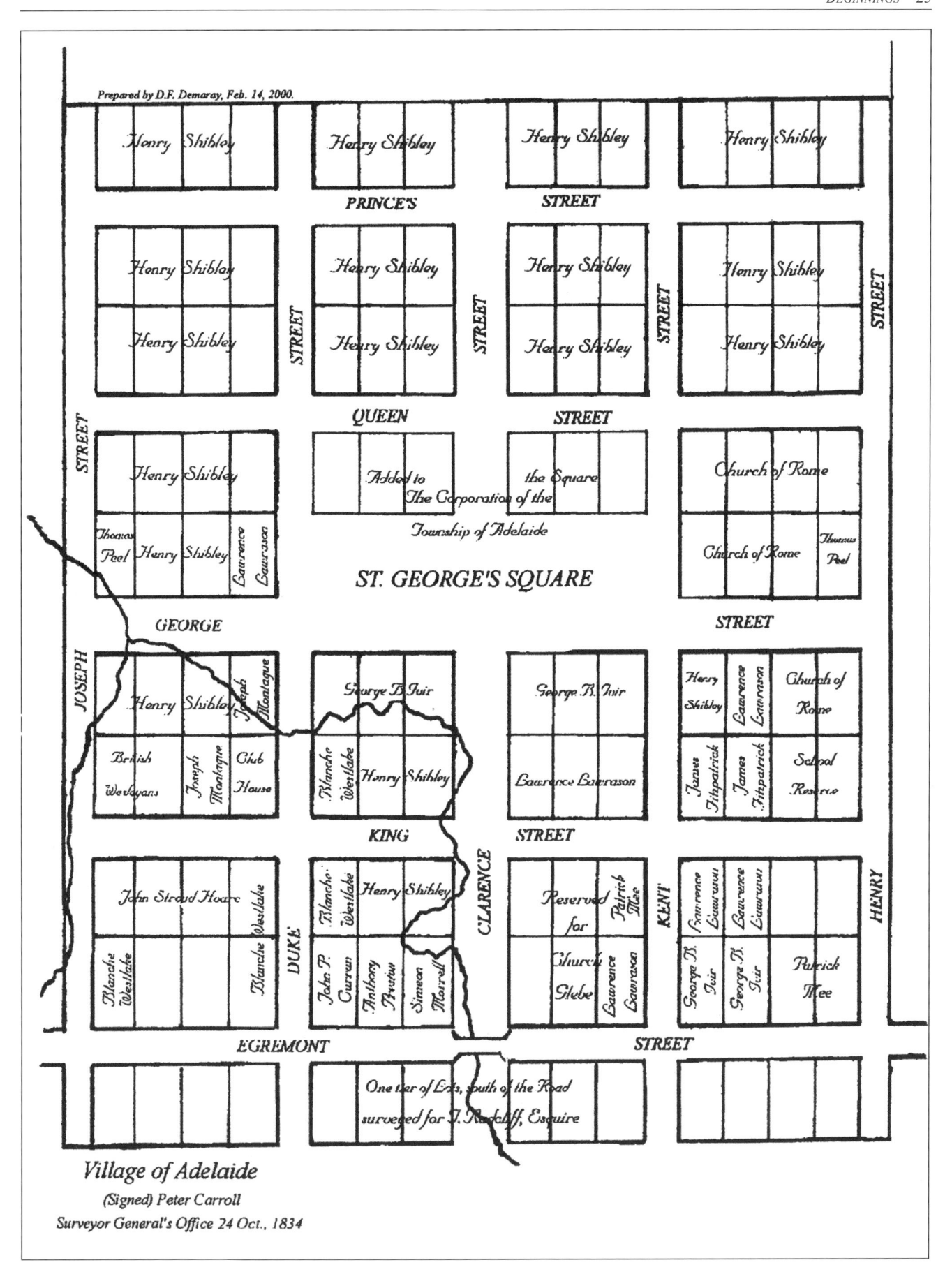

Village of Adelaide

Map showing lot assignments bounded by streets: Prince's Street, Queen Street, George Street, King Street, Egremont Street (running east-west), and Joseph Street, Duke Street, Clarence Street, Kent Street, Henry Street (running north-south).

St. George's Square is centrally located with the notation: "Added to the Square / The Corporation of the Township of Adelaide"

Lot holders shown on map:

North of Prince's Street: Henry Shibley (all lots)

Between Prince's Street and Queen Street: Henry Shibley (all lots)

Between Queen Street and George Street (flanking St. George's Square):
- West side: Henry Shibley, Thomas Peel, Henry Shibley, Lawrence Lawrason
- East side: Church of Rome, Church of Rome, Thomas Peel

Between George Street and King Street:
- Henry Shibley, Joseph Montague, George B. Fuir, George B. Fuir, Henry Shibley, Lawrence Lawrason, Church of Rome
- British Wesleyans, Joseph Montague, Club House, Blanche Westlake, Henry Shibley, Lawrence Lawrason, James Fitpatrick, James Fitpatrick, School Reserve

Between King Street and Egremont Street:
- John Stroud Hoare, Blanche Westlake, Henry Shibley, Reserved for Church Glebe, Patrick Mee, Lawrence Lawrason, Lawrence Lawrason
- Blanche Westlake, Blanche Westlake, John P. Curran, Anthony Freiva, Simeon Morrell, Lawrence Lawrason, George B. Fuir, George B. Fuir, Patrick Mee

South of Egremont Street: "One tier of Lots, south of the Road surveyed for T. Radcliff, Esquire"

Village of Adelaide
(Signed) Peter Carroll
Surveyor General's Office 24 Oct., 1834

imposed. The Reformers had contended for the regulation of the Crown lands by statute, but they did not achieve it. Administrative details relating to price, and to the terms and the conditions of sale, were left to the governor-in-council. This system remained in force until 1867. Between 1841 and 1867 the Executive Council resorted to many of the expedients which had been tried before and rejected: cash sale at fixed prices, local evaluations, graduated prices, credit policies, auction sales, settlement duty requirements, sales of townships or blocks of land to capitalists, and free grants in certain areas.

Legislative criticism of the way in which the Crown lands were managed was no less under responsible government than it had been prior to the Rebellion, both on questions of policy and details of administration. The malcontents continued to argue that population was wealth and that therefore the province would gain more by placing the land in the hands of settlers as quickly as possible than by administering it for the purposes of revenue. They pressed for lower prices, the credit system, free grants on colonization roads, and wound up advocating a homestead policy.

There was no more certainty, honesty, impartiality, and efficiency in the administration of the Crown lands after they came under provincial control than there had been before. The officials of the old Land Department of Upper Canada had been accused of feathering their own nests and of showing favouritism to insiders. The district agents appointed under the Union were accused of exactly the

Letter from the Enumerator, describing Adelaide Township
LONDON, C.W.
FEB 6TH, 1852

This Township of Adelaide was settled in the year 1832–principally by commuted pensioners and labourers who had not been accustomed to conduct farming operations. Consequently, the process of clearing proceeded slowly; till a new generation sprang up, who being used to bush labour, are now asking the forest recede rapidly, in a few years we hope to see the Township filled with enterprising, prosperous farmers. The greatest portion of the soil is capable of bearing any sort of crop. The soil of the western part bordering the Township of Warwick is of very superior quality, principally a sandy loam and gravel, worth 5 per acre. The southern part is partly sand and partly clay, the former worth 3.10 and the latter 4.10 per acre.

The corn, potato and oat crops have been greatly destroyed by squirrels and the other vermin this year, making the average produce much lower than in ordinary years.

More than half the farms in the Township have fruit trees planted on small patches of ground, but being cultivated as other crops and the trees not bearing, they are not marked as orchards on the Census sheets.

John A. Scoon
Enumerator
Township of Adelaide

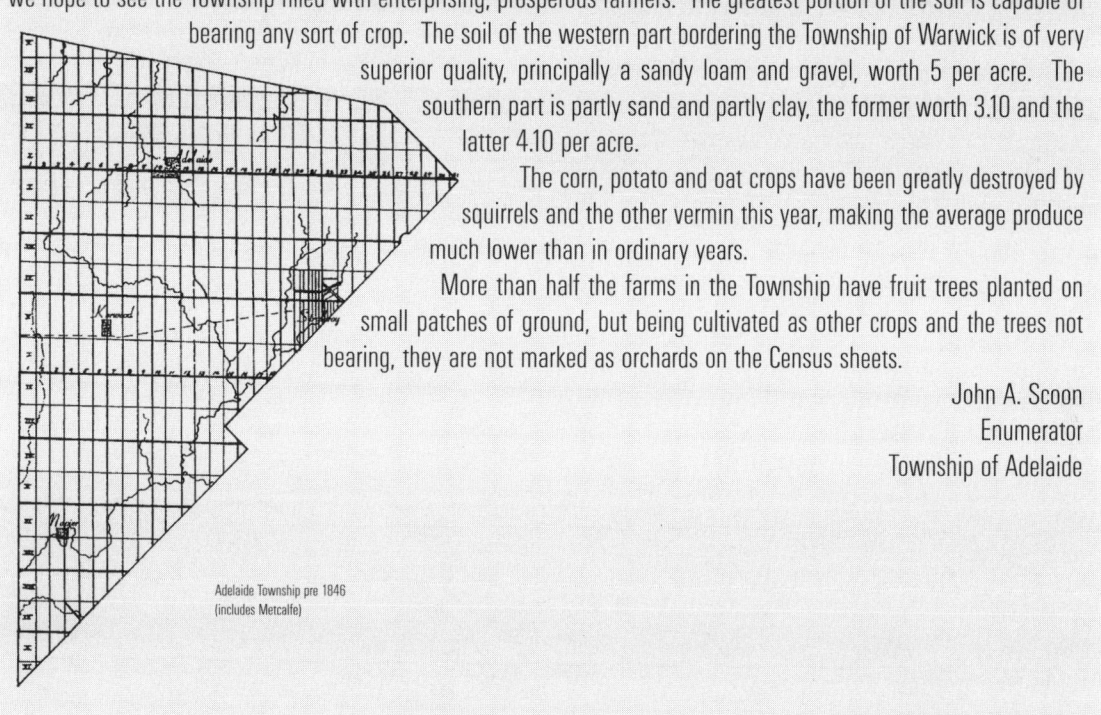

Adelaide Township pre 1846
(includes Metcalfe)

ADELAIDE TOWNSHIP
ABSTRACT OF THE CENSUS OF THE TOWNSHIP OF ADELAIDE, 1851
SUBMITTED AND SIGNED BY JOHN A. SCOON, ENUMERATOR, FEBRUARY 1852

Number of Males	1065		Church of Rome	212
Number of Females	914		Church of England	620
Total persons	1979		Presbyterians	93
			Free Church	76
Native of:			United Presbyterians	217
Canada	1032		Baptists	95
England	294		Wesleyan Methodists	497
Ireland	450		Episcopal	91
Scotland	119		New Connection	2
United States	61		Congregationalists	5
Wales	2		Universalists	32
Germany	9		Christian	1
West Indies	3		No Sect	27
Unknown	9		Unknown	70
Total	1979		Total	1979

ADELAIDE TOWNSHIP RESIDENTS

SOME RESIDENTS OF ADELAIDE TOWNSHIP
BORDERING THE FUTURE VILLAGE OF STRATHROY, 1851
(SOURCE – 1851 CENSUS OF ADELAIDE TOWNSHIP)

NAME	OCCUPATION	LOCATION
Frank, John,	Innkeeper	S4&5, NW 22 E
Celesta (2 children)		Church/School
Dell, Solomon	Millwright	Resident of Inn
Nevitt, John	Taylor	Resident of Inn
Cook, Timothy	Miller	S4, pt. 24 & 25
Harriett (5 children)	(grist mill)	
Slater, James	Miller	
Miles, David	Millwright	
Hemmingway, Moses	Sawyer	
Maria	Sawmill	
John (14)	Sawyer	
Vanvoltenburgh, Adam	Clothier	S4 - 23
Margaret	Carding & Fulling Mill	
Manson, Ralph	Merchant	S4 - 23
	store, distillery	
Page, John	Merchant	S4-23
Mary (2 children)		
Clark, Asahel	Cooper	S4-23
Mary (6 children)		
William John (16)	Cooper	
Andrew (15)	Cooper	
Robert (12)	Cooper	
Wilcox, Abel	Blacksmith	S4-23
Alice (5 children)		
Dell, Hiram	Merchant	S4-23
Ann (5 children)		
Thody, Thomas	Distiller	S4-23
Mary (3 children)		
Montague, William	Tanner	S4-23
Hartshorn, Skelvin	Tanner	Tannery and
Mary Ann		Methodist Church
McLaughlan, John	Farmer	S4-23
Catherine (5 children)		
Dell, Samuel	Labourer	S4-23
Louisa (2 children)		
Duncan, Thomas	Shoemaker	S4-23
Frances (3 children)		
Black, John	Carpenter	S4-23
Jessie (1 child)		
Archibald (27)	Carpenter	S4-23
Smith, William	Carpenter	S4-23
Mortimer, Thomas	Carpenter	S4-23
Mary (1 child)		
Segar, William	Carpanter	
Holden, Moses	Shoemaker	S4- 19&23

RESIDENTS OF ADELAIDE VILLAGE, 1851
(SOURCE - 1851 CENSUS OF ADELAIDE TOWNSHIP)

NAME	OCCUPATION	LOCATION
Mee, Patrick		
Mary (9 children)	Innkeeper	N1-12
Graham, Robert	Teacher	Resident at Inn
Mortimer, Arthur	Parson	S1-12
Mary (4 sons)		
Ivor, George (widower)	Grocer/Innkeeper	N1-11
(8 children)		
McAvoy, John	Innkeeper	N1-11
Emeline		
Franklin, Silas	Surgeon	Resident at Inn
Bray, William	Innkeeper	S1-W1/2 10
Armstrong, James	W.M. Minister	Resident at Inn
Smith, John	Shoemaker	S1-W10
Frances (6 children)		
Westlake, Blanche	Innkeeper	N & S1-9&11
Hoare, John Stroud	Storekeeper	N&S1-9&11
Ann (7 children)		
Preston, Anthony	Shoemaker	S&N1-11
Margaret (6 children)		
Freele, George	Shoemaker	
Tanner, Joseph	Shoemaker	
Preston, Charles	Shoemaker	S1-E1/2 10
Jane (3 children)		
Fitzpatrick, James	Tailor	S1-W11
Catherine (6 children)		
Maguire, Christopher	Wagon-Maker	S1-E1/2 9
Mary (4 children)		
Gare, William	Blacksmith	lives with Maguire
Hall, Charles	Iailor	
Mary (3 children)		
Charles (17)	Tailor	
Thomas (11)	Tailor	
Atkinson, Robert	Blacksmith	S1-Pt10
Jane (3 children)		
Upton, Edward	Farmer/Carpenter	S1-8
Fanny (7 children)		

OBITUARY

Died in Metcalfe on the 22nd inst, Christopher Beer Esq. Commander in the Royal Navy in his 82nd year.

A correspondent of the Free Press supplies the following particulars:

Deceased was the oldest settler in Metcalfe. Emigrating to this country in 1830, he secured a good location on the 10th and 11th Concessions of Adelaide, where he obtained a grant from the Crown of 800 acres of land for his services in the Royal Navy and, in 1832, returned to his forest home a second time, bringing with him his young family, where he continued to live up to the day of his decease. In his early days he saw a good deal of service, having served with distinction in almost every part of the world, and had the honor to hold a gold medal with two clasps to commemorate two of England's victories, fought and gained by English sailors, of whom he was one. Again he served on the Lakes of Canada during the rebellion of 1837 and 1838 and commanded a boat at the cutting out of the "Caroline" whose career was terminated by being launched over the Falls of Niagara. As an old settler he always had the heart to give and the hand to lend, and many of the early settlers have cause to look back with feelings of emotion at the rememberance of his many acts of kindness in bygone days of hardship and scarcity. He lived to see his family all comfortably settled around him and his last hours have been solaced by their kindness and attention and he has passed away without an enemy in the world, universally regretted by a large circle of relatives and friends.

(July 28, 1871 'Age')

same practices and, if Peter Robinson had failed to turn over his collections promptly to the Receiver General, so also did the district agents, and several of them became defaulters in the end.

After responsible government was achieved, order was gradually brought out of chaos... but not until United Canada had made many of the same errors that had been made by the lieutenant-governors-in-council and the Colonial Office. Nor was the task accomplished before all the land fit for permanent agricultural settlement had been disposed of. To the last, the debate continued among those who thought the government should be concerned primarily with getting revenue out of the land quickly and with as little trouble and expense as possible by disposing of the land in large blocks to capitalists, those who thought there should be no profit-taking intermediary between the government and the settler, and those who thought the government should be content to give the land away in small allotments to get it settled.

It must be admitted that those who opposed free grants or cheap land for immigrants and settlers with limited resources were often justified by the results. To entrust land to the uncoordinated efforts of such settlers was not to ensure the rapid development of prosperous agricultural communities or the most efficient use of the resources of the province. But these persons were not merely 'Instruments of production'—labour—they were human beings. The steam-boats and wagons that carried them to their destination were freighted not only with their pitiful possessions but with their high hopes as well. A paternalistic government might advise such settlers in all sincerity that it would be better for them to work as labourers for some years before going on the land; otherwise, debts insight deprive them of their hard-won equities in the end. On the other hand, a government indifferent to their wishes might prefer to risk entrusting the land to township promoters or land companies instead; this was a risk, as the experience of Upper Canada proved. But, given the values of the societies out of which most of the settlers came, what they wanted, what they had taken the risk of uprooting themselves for, was a chance at land and independence in the New World, or, in the case of native sons, on the newest frontier. Some of them made it—some didn't." (Lillian F. Gates, *Land Policies of Upper Canada*, Toronto: University of Toronto Press, 1968)

Switchboard in Telephone office of Meredith Morgan. L-R Cherry Dyer, Meredith Morgan and Mrs. John Morgan.

Waddell's Creamery Truck

Early 1900s Cadillac owned by James Richardson.

Kerwood CN Station, ca. 1908.

CHAPTER TWO

Family Stories

AARTS, Leonardus and Wilhelmina

On June 29, 1955, Leonardus and Wilhelmina Aarts immigrated to Canada on "The Maasdam." With them were their four children, Lena, Martha, Antoon and Theo. One son, John, was already in Canada with his wife, Dina, having immigrated in 1954.

Remaining in the Netherlands were a brother, Harrie (with his wife, Cisca), and two sisters, Jo (with her husband, Thijs) and Riek, who had entered a religious order.

The Maasdam arrived in Halifax, Nova Scotia, on July 6, 1955. The Aarts had lived in a small Catholic village and found Canada to be very different. In particular, they were amazed by the vastness of this country and the variety of religious practices. At first, the family moved in with John and his wife, in their rented house on Hwy. 22, just east of Hwy. 81 in Adelaide Township. Once settled, they joined All Saints Roman Catholic Church.

In the fall of 1955, the Aarts family bought a farm on Hwy. 22 at Lot 14, Con. 1 SER.

Lena Aarts married Peter Timmermans in 1958, and they moved to West Lorne, Ontario. Martha Aarts married John Van de Ven.

In 1960, Leonardus and Wilhelmina Aarts and their three sons, John, Theo and Antoon, sold the Adelaide farm and moved to Wainfleet in the Niagara Peninsula.

AARTS, Tony and Gerdie

Tony Aarts (1931) lived on a farm in Brabant, Holland, with his parents, Peter and Franciska (Vinken). Tony's mother passed away in 1937, when he was very young. He worked with his father on the farm until 1954, when he decided to immigrate to Canada. He first worked in Ilderton, for Tom Hughes, who operated a dairy farm. Two years later, Tony moved to Strathroy, where he lived with his sister and worked at the Strathroy Handle Factory. He met Gerdie Joris (1937) in 1955 and they married in May 1957. Gerdie had immigrated to Canada with her parents, Frank Joris and Nelly (Van Heugten), also natives of Holland. She moved to Strathroy in 1952 and worked at St. Mary's Hospital (now Marian Villa) in London before she met Tony. While still working at the handle factory, Tony and Gerdie bought a farm from Melvin Down and raised cows, but eventually changed to raising pigs. Later, Tony worked in construction but soon farmed full-time. As well, Tony and Gerdie drove a school bus. In 1979, the farm was sold to Don Ward. The Aarts bought a chicken farm from Frank Joris and they maintained that farm until 1996, then sold the farm to John Vervoordeldonk and built a home at 3225 Napperton Drive.

Tony and Gerdie have five children. Frances married Doug Lambert, and they have two daugh-

Tony Aarts Family

ters, Shelley and Krista. Frank lives in Calgary, Alberta, and has two children, Sheldon and Jessy. Nelly married Pete Smuckers and they live in Grand Bend with their four children, Nicole, Jeffrey, Stephanie and David.

ABERNETHY

This family is believed to have arrived in Upper Canada in 1842, settling in Adelaide about this time. Unlike many of their neighbours from County Down, they immigrated to Canada from Antrim County, Northern Ireland.

The first available record of the family was of the elder son, James, an auditor (meeting record of February 4, 1850), being appointed then by the Reeve of Adelaide.

James Abernethy (1822) was born in Antrim County, Northern Ireland, and has been described as a blacksmith. Other notations describe him as a shoemaker, so perhaps he was both. Early township records show that he resided on Lot 10, Con. 1 NER, with his mother, Ann, and a sister, Jamima "Jennie" (1824-1901).

The West Adelaide United Presbyterian Church records for 1853 show that James Abernethy was a supporter of the first chapel, erected on the corner of Lot 3, Con. 1 SER. Minutes in 1869 also state that he was an elected elder and a clerk of session for the early church. An 1878 map of Adelaide Township shows James residing on a 50-acre farm, which was part of Lot 5, Con. 2 SER. Little is known of the life of James Abernethy. It is unknown as to whether he married, and where he and his mother are interred, although the old cemetery at Wiley's Corners is a distinct possibility.

Jennie was born in Antrim County. She married James Shields about 1849. She is interred in the West Adelaide Cemetery with her husband. Jennie and James were the parents of six children (see SHIELDS, William and Lilly).

ABMA, Fred and Alice

Fred Abma and his wife, Alice, came to Canada in March 1953 from the Netherlands. They landed in the Owen Sound area but did not stay there very long. A month later, they moved to a farmhouse on the Plymouth/Warwick townline during the last week of April 1953. At 7:00 p.m. on the evening of May 21, the house was partly demolished by a tor-

Fred Abma's farm.

nado. Luckily, they were not in the house at the time but were having supper at a relative's home a mile down the road. It was an awful experience, especially since they had only been in Canada for a month! They moved that same night, with the help of neighbours who brought pickup trucks and helping hands, in just one hour.

In 1955, Fred and Alice moved to Watford and, in 1957, to Strathroy. In 1960, they lived in Ekfrid Township. In April 1961, they bought the "Parker Place" on the west half of Lot 16, Con. 5 SER, from John and Steve Kavinsky.

When they moved to the Adelaide property, they had five small children, Andrew, John, Janet, Richard and Christine. The Parker Place was a well-constructed house built in 1918 for the late Frank Parker. The maple and cherry lumber used to build the house came from one of the family's woodlots.

When Fred and Alice bought the property, it had a house, a double garage, and a barn on about eight acres of land. Fred was the sole breadwinner with a full-time job, and their initial farm livestock consisted of one cow. Soon, they bought some sows and started pig farming. Crops included wheat and corn, and for many years they had a big field of cucumbers. The children hated picking cucumbers, so the crop later changed to sweet corn.

In 1969, the Abmas had about 25 sows, many with a litter of piglets. The barn burned down one evening and only six sows and a boar made it to safety. The cause of the fire was never known and the money from the fire insurance was too low to cover the damage, but the neighbourhood and the church members held a collection. With that and a small bank loan, they were able to build a new pig barn the same year. With more livestock purchased later, Fred was able to make a living from the pigs and a part-time job driving a school bus for Langs Bus Line from 1976-1988.

Four more children were born on the Parker Place. Michael was born in 1962, George (the present owner) in 1963, Sylvia in 1968, and Francine in 1970.

The majority of Fred and Alice's married life was spent in Adelaide Township, from 1961-1993. George bought the property in 1993, and was married that summer to Amanda Anderson. Sylvia and Francine were also married that summer, only a week apart. It was a very busy and exciting time for the family.

During 32 years in Adelaide Township, the Abmas faced many challenges, but in general feel that they lived a good life there. Five children live in Western Canada, two in British Columbia, and three in Alberta. The remainder are in Ontario. All are married except the oldest son, Andrew, who lives in British Columbia.

ADAIR, James and Becky

William James Adair (ca.1825-1894) was born in Ireland and immigrated to Adelaide Township where he married Margaret "Becky" Conkey (1827-1895), also a recent immigrant from Northern Ireland, in 1850. They farmed at Lot 15, Con. 3 NER, and had 11 children.

Hugh (1851-1922) moved to Bounty, Saskatchewan, in 1902 and lived there as a bachelor until his death in 1922. His body was returned to Adelaide Township, where he is buried.

William John (1852-1918) married Elizabeth Baskier (1862-1909). They also migrated to Bounty, Saskatchewan, but little else is known about their lives.

James (1854-1940) married Mary Jane Clark (1863-1945) in 1887. They had five children in Adelaide, including a son who died in childhood (ca.1886-1889); Langford (1888-1988); Gertrude E. (1890-1981); Margaret (1892); and Mansell (1895). The family went west to Bounty in a covered wagon in 1904.

Robert (1856-1903) married Mary Jane Geary (1868-1968) and they had two sons, William (killed in WWI) and Franklin. Robert is buried in West Adelaide.

Arthur (1858-1931) and his wife, Emma Clarke Brown (1875-1941), who was most likely from Adelaide, moved to Bounty, Saskatchewan, in 1904 as homesteaders.

Sarah (1861-1887) never married. She died at the age of 26.

Henry "Harry" (1863-1895), who ran a brick- and tile-yard in East Williams Township, married Mary McLaughlin (1867-1967) about 1890.

David (1865-1947) married Annie Elizabeth Arrand (1867-1926) in 1892. They also moved to Saskatchewan, but to Saskatoon rather than Bounty. Their three children, Ada Manetta (1893-1993), Walter Stanley "Stan" (1898-1970), and Wilfred Charles (1902) were born in Adelaide prior to the move. In Saskatoon, the family adopted a daughter, Blanche Mark (1912).

Margaret Jane (1868-1943) married James Walker (1861-1924) and they lived on the Walker farm at Lot 19, Con. 1, where they had three children. William James Gordon (1893-1987) married Nettie Alveretta Brown (1898) and moved west. Margaret Ellen (1897-1977) married Roy Wilbur Smith (1894-1947) and lived in Lobo. Alexander Clayton (1898-1961) married Robena McKeen (1914-1944) and the couple lived on the Walker family farm. They had two sons, James Alexander (1937-1943) and Donald Gordon (1939). Donald took over the farm and married Catherine Anne Ford (1940). They had three daughters, Valerie Anne (1964), Elizabeth Margaret (1967), and Susan Jennifer Win (1973).

Thomas (1873) married three times. After his first wife, Christina McKenzie, died in 1897, he married her sister, Robina. The couple had two children before Robina died in 1902. The daughter, Christie, went west with her father while the son, Ernie, stayed in Ontario and was raised by his grandparents. Thomas met and married his third wife, Sarah Jane Glendenning, in Bounty, Saskatchewan. They had six children.

Samuel (1873-ca.1940) married Robina and Christina's sister, Minnie (1880-1980), about 1900. They left the area and went to Saskatchewan where one son, Alexander, was born.

ADAMS, Byron and Lois

William Henry Adams and his parents immigrated to Canada from Ireland. Unfortunately, both parents died en route, so William was raised by his brother. William married Mary Jane Hawes and they settled in Delaware Township. They had one son, Byron Alfred (d.1945), and three daughters, Ethel, Mary Anne and Alice. All are buried in Mt. Brydges (with the exception of Ethel, who moved west).

Byron was initially a labourer and he went west for two years when he was working for the Lowthians of Melbourne. When he returned, he married Lois Frances Miles of Caradoc and operated Adams' General Store in Mt. Brydges across from the Continuation School. Byron and Lois had three sons, Charles Wesley, John Byron, and Robert James, and three daughters, "Lois" Frances, Mina Louisa, and Mary Alice, who died when she was 10 months old.

As well as operating the Mt. Brydges store, Byron also operated a dray service, taking produce into London and returning with supplies. As his sons grew older, it became increasingly apparent that there was little for young men to do in Mt. Brydges, so Byron decided to sell the store in order to buy a farm which would provide work for his sons. Unfortunately, a fire at the store about this time left the family in somewhat strained circumstances. In October 1920, the Adams family purchased a farm in Adelaide, the west half of Lot 2, Con. 2 NER.

ALDERSON, Graham and Beverley

Graham Prosper Alderson (1931) worked at Carnation Milk in Kerwood from 1948-1982. He then worked at the local hospital for 14 years. Graham loved hunting, fishing and trapping, and spent a lot of time doing those things. He married Beverley Rose Morningstar in 1953, and they have five children, Michael, Belinda, Tracy, Elizabeth and Joel. Graham and Beverley are retired and live in Strathroy.

Michael Graham Alderson (1954) married Linda Lee Goulding in 1984. They have two children, Rhonda and Michael, and two grandchildren. Mike and Linda live in Strathroy.

Belinda Rose Alderson married Walter Michael Jakimczuk in 1975 and they have three daughters. April Rose (1975) married Jeffery Robert Graham (1973) and they have a daughter, Kaitlyn Rose (1998). The younger daughters are Michelle Belinda (1978) and Sarah Lorraine Elizabeth (1981). They live in Strathroy.

Tracy Lorraine Alderson (1959) also lives in Strathroy.

Elizabeth Ann Alderson married David Harold Sutherland in 1979. They have a son, Richard David (1983). They live in Strathroy.

Joel Vern Alderson married Mary Anderson in 1989. They have two sons, Cameron James (1990) and Ian Joseph (1992). They live at R.R. #1, Dashwood.

ALEXANDER, Joseph and Janet

Joseph and Janet Alexander were born in County Mayo, Ireland, in the late 1700s. Their four known children were William (1814-1885); John (ca.1821); Joseph W. (ca.1822-1884); and Thomas (ca.1824-1889), all born in Ireland.

William Alexander first married Jane (last name unknown) in Ireland. Jane died in Adelaide Township about 1854. Two children were born in Ireland, Margaret (ca.1845) and Joseph C. (ca.1849-1884), who married Isabella Campbell. They had two children, William D. (ca.1878) and Duncan L. (ca.1879), both born in Adelaide Township. They lived on the west half of Lot 19, Con. 3 SER.

After Jane's death, William married Rachael Harding (ca.1827-1912). William and Rachael were buried in Strathroy Cemetery. They had six children, all born in Adelaide Township. These were William H. (ca.1856); Jane (ca.1858-1925); Thomas (ca.1860); John A. (1863-1949), who married Alice M. Matthews (1874-1951); and Elizabeth A. (1865), who married William Carrothers (1858-1940), son of Thomas and Clarenda (Slack) Carrothers of Westminster Township. They had two children born in Adelaide, Alex Roy (1890-1917), and Irwin (1900-1970), who married Estelle Acton (1903). The youngest child of William and Rachael was Hannah (ca.1868-1935). Jane, John and Hannah were buried in Strathroy Cemetery.

No further information was available on John, second eldest of Joseph and Janet's children.

Joseph W. Alexander married Elizabeth Hodgins (1835-1906) in 1859. She was born in London Township, daughter of Henry and Mary (Stanley) Hodgins. They lived at Lot 19, Con. 3 SER, and in 1896, they moved to Strathroy. They are both buried in Strathroy Cemetery. Joseph and Elizabeth had six children, all born in Adelaide Township. Joseph H. (1861-1921) was a travelling organizer for the Canadian Order of Foresters He remained single and lived in Calgary. Mary Jane (1862-1931) married William Anderson Aitken in Adelaide Township in 1890. They had six children and lived in Metcalfe Township and later in Delia, Alberta. Margaret "Maggie" E. (1866-1926) married James Dunn. They had one daughter and lived in Calgary and Detroit. Martha A. (1868-1954) married William D. Radcliffe. They had two daughters and lived in Granton, Ontario. James S. (1870-1946) married Edythe A. (last name unknown) and lived in Calgary. Ida Hannah (1874-1944) married George B. Miller. Records show Ida lived at home in 1906, but she married and moved to Calgary in 1909, and later to California.

Thomas Alexander married Maria Hanna (ca.1825-1898) in 1851, daughter of John Hanna, born in County Mayo, Ireland. Maria came to Canada in 1843, settling in Adelaide Township in 1846. They lived at Lot 16, Con. 3 SER, and were buried in Strathroy Cemetery. They had eight children, all born in Adelaide Township. Joseph A. (1852-1892) married Sarah M. (last name unknown, d.1907) and migrated to Winnipeg. Robert (ca.1855) married Margaret J. (last name unknown, ca.1858) and they had two children born in Adelaide Township, George (ca.1887) and Gertrude (ca.1888), who moved to Toronto. John W. (ca.1857) moved to California. Thomas S. (ca.1859) became a doctor and also went to California. George (ca.1860) became a doctor and moved to Silver Creek, Michigan. Albert E. (1862-1945) became a doctor and married Sarah "Sadie" Andrews Maynard Luscombe (ca.1869-1904), born in Cornwall, daughter of Mr. and Mrs. Thomas Luscombe. They lived in Alvinston for three years and later moved to Williamston, Michigan. They had two children, Maynard (ca.1898) and Leola (ca.1900). Thomas and Maria's youngest children, George (ca.1864) and Richard H. (ca.1867), also a doctor, moved to Michigan.

ANDERSON, Alexander and Mary Jane

Alexander Anderson (1876-1958) was born in London Township. He married Mary Jane Scott (1870-1953), daughter of Robert Scott and Mary Cameron, who had moved to London Township ca.1882. Alex and Mary Jane moved to Belmont ca.1912 for four years, where Alex had a creamery. They came to Strathroy in 1917, where they were employed at Strathmere Lodge. Alex became the Superintendent and Mary Jane became the Matron. They bought the George Oliver house and lived on old Hwy. 22 near Strathmere Lodge. They both retired in 1944. Alex and Mary Jane Anderson were active members of Strathroy United Church and are buried in Strathroy Cemetery.

Alex and Mary Jane had two children, Arnold Clifton Anderson (1898-1966) and Velma Anderson (ca.1904-1927). Velma died during an operation for appendicitis. She was well known in musical circles in Strathroy, where she played leading roles in many successful theatrical productions. She owned and operated a successful millinery establishment in town. Velma is buried in Strathroy Cemetery.

In 1921, Arnold Clifton Anderson married Ivy Marie Plaxton (1893-1948), daughter of Edmund and Alice Ann (Wilkinson) Plaxton of Adelaide Township. They had two children. A daughter, Marie (1923), married Gordon Cuddy in 1941, son of Alfred and Harriett (McInroy) Cuddy of Adelaide Township (see CUDDY, John T. and Esther). An adopted son, William, now lives in London.

Marie and Gordon live in Strathroy, where Gordon has a furniture, appliance and repair business, in operation for 47 years. In his younger years, Gord worked for the Bank of Commerce, then went

Elizabeth (Hodgins) Alexander with children (ca.1900); back L-R, Margaret and Ida Hannah; front L-R, James, Martha, mother Elizabeth, Mary Jane and Joseph Jr.

Alex and Mary Jane (Scott) Anderson, ca.1942.

into military service during the war years, where he became very ill. He came home in 1945 and worked for the bank until 1952, then started Cuddy Furniture. Marie and Gordon have four children, Carol Elizabeth, Janice Louise, Judith Diane and Charles Edward. They are all married and live in Ancaster, London and Strathroy.

Arnold and Ivy Marie (Plaxton) Anderson were both chiropractors. Arnold was active in municipal affairs, first elected to Council in 1928 and re-elected in 1931. He was elected a Deputy-Reeve of Strathroy for 1932-1933. He served as Reeve for six years and was elected Mayor of Strathroy from 1940-1945. During this period, he began 23 years of service on the Public Utilities Commission. In addition to his activities on council and the P.U.C., Mr. Anderson was a charter member of the Lions Club, a member of Strathroy Parks and Fair Boards, and a Member of Session of Strathroy United Church. Keenly interested in horses and racing, he kept horses at his Caradoc farm.

Arnold Clifton and Ivy Marie (Plaxton) Anderson are buried in Strathroy Cemetery.

ANDERSON, Henry and Maggie

The west half of Lot 20, Con. 1 SER, was purchased November 29, 1881, by Henry Anderson of Westminster Township as a real estate investment. His son and daughter-in-law, Henry Arthur and Maggie (McDougall) Anderson, who were wed on April 18, 1888, moved to the farm as newlyweds.

A daily chronicle maintained by Henry and Maggie from 1888-1894 describes various details of their history. Lazarus Bates (perhaps a "home boy") is mentioned therein, having been hired to help clear stumps and plough the grassland. Henry and a neighbour, Ben Donaldson, bought a well-boring machine from Charlie Tanner in Strathroy. Together, they drilled many wells on neighbouring farms, and drilling replaced farming as a livelihood for Henry by 1896.

Social events recorded in the chronicle list many familiar Adelaide names: Robert, Jim and Alex Walker; Richard Brock; Miss Ingham; Ben Donaldson; George Brock; Kenning; Shipley; Dell; Thompson; Slater; Giffen; and Ireland.

Two sons, Henry McDougall and Arthur James, were born in 1891 and 1897 respectively. The family moved to Strathroy in 1903 but the farm remained in the family until 1956 when Alex Walker purchased it.

ARCHER, William and Della

William R. Archer bought the west half of Lot 17, Con. 5 SER, from the estate of Charles N. Parker.

William worked as a bridge foreman on the Pier Marquet Railroad until he developed rheumatism, then started farming. He married Della Mae Pike and they had two sons. In the 1920s, William and Della moved to Strathroy and leased out the farm and house. William had removed $600 from the insurance policy to save money and six weeks later, the house burned.

In 1980, part of the farm (92½ acres) was sold to Joseph and Emilie Van Damme. Five acres and the house and buildings were retained where Roelfina Archer, widow of Richard Gordon Archer, presently lives.

ARMSTRONG, John and Jane

John Armstrong (ca.1811-1854) and his wife, Jane Alwinter (ca.1819-1871), immigrated to Adelaide Township from Ireland about 1843. At least two of their children accompanied them, Ann (1834) and William (1839-1899). Four more children, Joseph (1844); Mary J. (1847); Jermina (1849-1923); and Franklin (1851) were born at their home on Lot 5, Con. 2. The family belonged to the Church of England until John's death, when they became Presbyterians.

After his father's death in 1854, William took over the family farm. The family had cattle, sheep, pigs and horses. In 1861, a census noted the following crops:

7 acres of wheat
5 acres of peas
5 acres of oats
1½ acres of potatoes
1½ acres of turnips and hay

William married Eliza Early in 1867 and moved to Michigan about 1878, leaving his youngest brother, Franklin, with wife, Martha Dowding, to live on the family farm. Franklin and Martha had at least three children, Harry Lorne (1898); Mary Jane Gertrude (1874); and William Herbert Wesley (1888).

Jermina married Thomas Kincade (1845-1915) and the couple moved to Michigan about the same time as William and Eliza. Joseph stayed in Adelaide, at Lot 7, Con. 2.

ARRAND, Clifford and Frances

Clifford Arrand and Frances Wilson married in 1944. Clifford was in the Armed Forces and went overseas in January 1945. After fighting in France, Belgium and Germany, he returned home in December 1945.

In 1946, Clifford and Frances bought a 50-acre farm, the south half of Lot 7, Con. 4 NER. In June 1946, they bought a house from Wilbert McLeish and moved to their property. Three years later, they purchased a barn from George Silver and moved it to the farm. The Arrands remember that putting the buildings on foundations took quite a bit of pioneering on their part. They worked at mixed farming for some years, then remodeled the barn for a three-floor hen operation, shipping hatching eggs.

Building of barn on C. Arrand property. Girls in front, L-R, are Della Jean McAdam and Mary Lee Arrand.

Family of Clifford and Frances Arrand, clockwise from top left, David, Brad, Frances, Clifford and Mary Lee, 1981.

Clifford also worked in cement with Gordon Plumb and later did contract work for the Department of Highways. In total, Clifford worked 25 years with the Department. During the months of July and August, the children and Frances traveled with Clifford, living in a trailer. The Arrands made the trailer their home, wherever Clifford parked his road machinery. This was a special time for the Arrand family. They still visit many of the friends they met during their travels.

Clifford and Frances have a daughter, Mary Lee (1947), who is married to Henry Pranger. They live in Belmont and have two sons, Brent (1974), and Christopher (1977). The Arrands have a son, David (1952), who lives in London with his one daughter, Heather (1981). The Arrand's youngest son, Bradley (1956), lives in Oshawa with his wife, Brenda. They have two sons, Mark (1984) and Thomas (1986).

In June 1993, Clifford and Frances sold the farm to Martin and Linda Peeters and moved to Strathroy.

ARRAND, George and Kathleen

George Thomas Arrand (1911-1988) and Kathleen Elizabeth Herrington (1921) were married in 1942 and lived on a rented farm owned by Laura Conkey of Strathroy. They lived there until 1947, when the farm was sold to Ray McPhail, the present owner.

Their possessions were few: a team of horses, a cow, and a turkey hen and gobbler. George worked with his father so he used his father's farm implements. The house did not have electricity or central heating. There was no water pressure system and therefore, no indoor plumbing. There were no built-in cupboards or closets, just bare walls. Kathleen decided that the living room needed paint and wallpaper. She asked the owner for permission to deduct some money from the rent and was granted a $5 reduction. The supplies cost $10. This was during the war and Kathleen worked at the Sommerville Factory in Strathroy, making ammunition cases for 18 cents an hour. The extra $5 was a lot of money, but she saved, and did the decorating work herself.

During the winter of 1944, a lot of snow accumulated. The snowplow only cleared one track on the Second Line, so the road was full of snow again soon after plowing. The sideroad wasn't plowed, so neighbours gathered to shovel snow and clear the road. Once a week, one of the men from the neighbourhood went to Arkona to the mill for chicken feed and returned with groceries for those in need. George and Kathleen had a few hens, and the income from an 11-quart basket of eggs bought groceries for a week. Life in the 1940s was very different from the 1990s.

George and Kathleen had two daughters, Ruby Jean (1943-1962) and Gloria Marlene (1946). Gloria married Ralph Marshall Dellow in 1963. They had four children, Robert John (1964); Elizabeth Anne #1 (1967, died a baby); Elizabeth Anne #2 (1969); and Allan George (1971). Gloria remarried in 1984, to Ken Russell Dennis.

Robert and Debbie McGillvery have a son, Johnathon Mark Andrew (1987).

Allan and Tammy Martin have a son, Justin Allan (1990). Allan married Lee Ann Elizabeth Highley in 1994, and adopted Kirsten Susan Elizabeth Williams. They also have a son, Cory Wyatt (1995).

Elizabeth married David Maycock in 1993, and they have a son, Joshua Darius (1996).

ARRAND, William and Della

William James Arrand (1880-1954) married Della Maud Gerry (1887-1947) in 1906. They had eight children. John Wesley (1907-1985) and James Bruce (1908-1984) remained bachelors. The third and fourth children were George Thomas (1911-1988) and Ida Pearl (1913, died an infant). Jean Lavine (1915) married Wesley McAdam (brother of Andrew McAdam) in 1936. They had two children, Della Jean (1947) and John Wesley (1950). They moved from Adelaide Township to Strathroy in 1959 and lived on the James Gerry farm, the east half of Lot 9, Con. 3 NER. Clifford Randolph (1917) and William Ralph (1919) were the sixth and seventh of William and Della's children. May Irene Arrand (1924), the youngest, married Andrew McAdam of West Williams in 1943. They had three children, William Harland (1950); Marilyn Dianne (1955); and Janice Irene (1959).

Irene and family moved to a farm at Lot 6, Con. 3 NER, in 1943, which they purchased in 1946 from LaVerne Topping of West Williams. They moved to London in 1963.

The William Arrand family owned 300 acres, parts of Lot 6 and 8, Con. 3 NER. They did custom-threshing, filled silos, trucked stock, serviced the community with farm supplies and a gravel truck, and collected milk for a cheese factory.

A clean, clear spring ran through the Arrand property. The James Rae farm was next door, and it made a good location for a swimming hole. A dam was built, making the water deep enough for a diving board. The swimming hole soon became a centre of attraction for the community, and people young and old came from miles around.

Reverend Stanlake from Kerwood decided it would be a good place to take a group of young boys from Kerwood and the surrounding area. He asked if they could sleep in the hayloft and store their food in the basement. He spent two weeks that summer with two different groups, using the Arrand's facilities. He taught the boys first aid, swimming, diving, cooking and good fellowship. They hiked and played games, and it was a happy time for all of them. The following year, Reverend Stanlake took the boys to Otterville and the younger Arrand boys were included.

The swimming hole had been used for many years when suddenly, tragedy struck. A Toronto boy, who was staying at the home of Richard Down, went for a swim one afternoon. He'd had surgery a few weeks before, and he suffered from cramps and drowned. He had called for help shortly before and, when the boys came to help, he said he was only fooling. Later, it happened again and no one responded. The swimming hole was not officially closed but after the tragedy, the community never used it again.

Silver Creek was enjoyed year-round for swimming, fishing, and skating. The hills on the Arrand property were also used for sleigh-riding. In the summer after a good dip in the creek, neighbours would often gather on the front lawn to visit. Those with musical talent, such as Reg Freer and the Murray brothers, brought their guitars and everyone sang along.

A mixed ball team formed called the Silver Creek Team. The ball diamond was on the Hodgson property where practices were held, and teams from surrounding communities came to play. When Silver Creek played against other teams, the players usually climbed into the back of the Arrand truck to be taken to the games.

There was never much money, but everyone was very rich with all the blessings that nature provided. Ralph Arrand and son, Donald, and his family remain on the old homestead, four generations of Arrands!

AULD, Robert and Joyce

Robert John Auld (1932) and Joyce Elaine Thomson (1932) were married in 1953. They had three children, Joan Marie (1955); John Robert (1959); and Ronald Allen (1962, died a baby).

Joan (Burden) lives in Sarnia. Her two daughters are Shannan Marie (1988) and Melissa Lynn (1989).

John married Joanne Marie Verboort (1956) in 1978. They live in Watford with their sons, Ronald John (1982) and David Albert (1984).

Robert and Joyce farmed 200 acres and milked cows in Warwick Township until they retired in 1981. They bought a three-year-old house and four acres in Adelaide Township from Jansen's in 1981, at Lot 1, Con. 3.

They have a gravel pit at their back door. They cleared trees and landscaped with stones from neighbouring fields. They built a dock so their grandchildren could fish, swim, and go boating.

They feed the fish, which have become like pets, so they are always thrown back into the water. The children have a trophy they pass around to the winner who catches the largest fish. The Auld farm is home to many Canada Geese. One pair nests on an island and raises goslings there year after year. The pit area became attractive to partying visitors for a time, but it is now fenced off and has become much cleaner and quieter as a result.

AUSTIN, Edward and Mary Ann

The 1864 directory of Adelaide Township shows Edward Austin and William Austin living on Lot 10, Con. 1 NER. Their occupations are listed as Joiner and Framer, so it seems they came here to earn their living as builders. Their father, Edmund Austin (1810-1864), was buried at St. Ann's Cemetery. Edmund and his wife, Sarah Goff (or Gouf), were born in England, and their children, William (1833) and John (1835), were born in the United States. Edward (1840), the youngest, was born in Westminster Township. He married Mary Ann Coates 1843) in England in 1861. She had immigrated to Canada with her family when she was eight years old, in 1851. During their residence in Adelaide Village, five children were born.

Mary Jane Austin (1862-1944) married William Miniely in Sarnia in 1885. She was buried in Edmonton, Alberta.

Sarah Ellen Austin (1866-1942) married David Kitchen in Petrolia in 1883 and was buried in Cass City, Michigan.

Emma Elizabeth Austin (1868-1961) married Alfons Stephen Kitchen of Petrolia in 1885. She died in Oil Springs.

Annie Laura Austin (1874) married John Hind of Petrolia and is buried in Austin Township, Sanilac County, Michigan.

George H. Austin (1877-1974) married Jessie McIwain and, later, Annie Chapman. He died in London, Ontario.

In the 1880 directory for Strathroy, William Austin was listed as miller for R. Pincombe, with a residence on English Street.

AYRE, Robert and Jane

Robert and William Ayre were the sons of William and Mary Ayre from Devonshire, England. Robert Veysey Ayre (1834-1892) came to Canada in

1855 from Lancashire, England. He resided in Adelaide Township on the Robotham Sideroad, on the south half of the east half of Lot 18, Con. 2 NER. He married Jane Robotham and they had three children, Bertha, Albert, and a daughter who died as a child.

Bertha married Bill Reid from London. They had four children, Robert Ayre Reid, who died on his 30th birthday in the armed forces during WWII; Jean (Allison); Marion (Bice); and Donald Reid, who also served overseas. Albert "Bud" was a bachelor who lived in Adelaide all his life. He and Cliff Branton were threshers.

AYRE, William and Mary Jane

William Ayre (1829-1897) came to Canada a few years after his brother, Robert, and resided in a house beside him. He married Mary Jane Sampson (1844-1918) and they had three children. Emma married Alfred Burrows and lived on the east half of Lot 14, Con. 2 NER. Mary Anne (1883-1969) married Silas Thompson (1875-1951), moved to Caradoc and had 10 children. The youngest, Grant "Stub," married Hazel Hill of Mt. Brydges and moved to the home of his uncle, Alf Burrows, in 1948 when Alf's wife, Emma, died of cancer. William "Billy" Ayre married Sarah "Sadie" Ellen Branton in 1918 and moved to a farm at Lot 30, Con. 3, in Warwick. They had a daughter, Mary Norma (1920). Norma attended school at S.S. #9. William loved music. He played the violin and was a square-dance caller. When Norma was about four or five years old, she went to the hall in Adelaide Village to a step-dance competition. Her Dad won first prize, which was $2. He said it was the easiest money he had ever earned. Norma played the piano for her father and the neighbours played the fiddle.

William Ayre, husband of Mary Jane Sampson.

Ayre family L-R, Mary Anne (Thompson), William James, Mary Jane (Sampson) Ayre, Emma Ayre (Burrows), ca.1895.

In 1944, Norma married Wilson McNab at West Adelaide Presbyterian Church. Wilson had graduated from the University of Guelph in 1941. They farmed on the McNab family farm on the east half of Lot 6, Con. 3 NER. Farming with horses was becoming obsolete, so they purchased a Willy's Jeep in 1948. It was used for transportation and working the land. In 1960-1961, Wilson attended O.C.E. Toronto and taught school for 15 years before retiring from Bruce Peninsula High School at Lion's Head where he taught for seven years. After retiring, he was an agent for East Williams Fire Insurance Company for 10 years. Wilson was the fourth generation of the McNabs to live on the McNab family farm. Wilson and Norma had three children, Karen Elizabeth (1948), Earl Douglas (1951) and Paul Martin (1955).

Karen married Bryce Cadman, who died in 1987. They had a son, Bryan (1987). Karen and Bryan live in London and she teaches at Lord Nelson Public School. In 1988, Earl and his wife, Ruth (Knip), purchased the McNab family farm and they represent the fifth generation to live there. They have three sons, Dwayne, Sheldon and Chad, and three daughters, Sarah, Julie and Penny. Earl also works at General Coach in Hensall. Paul and his wife, Laurie (Charlton), live in London and have two daughters, Krista Elizabeth and Lindsay Michelle. Paul is a registered nurse in the Intensive Care Unit at the London Health Sciences, University Campus.

Norma and Wilson retired and live in Strathroy.

BALL, Thomas and Emma

Thomas Ball Sr. (1829-1897) was born in Warwickshire, England. He married Emma Nichols Hancorne (1822-1869) near Swansea, Wales, and they immigrated to Canada in 1857. Their children were Thomas Jr., John Hancorne, Emma Nichols, and Robert Tudor (1865-1933). There is also a half-brother, William J., listed in the records.

Robert married Blanche Elizabeth Pincombe Brooks (1875-1964), the daughter of Hugh and Louisa (Pincombe) Brooks. Robert and Blanche had five sons, Thomas Herbert (1896-1953); Robert Hugh (1899-1983); George Edwin (1901-1986); John Russell (1905-1996); and Benjamin Walker (1912-1982). Both Hugh and Louisa are buried in the Poplar Hill Cemetery.

In 1907, Robert and Blanche and their family moved to the west half of Lot 7, Con. 1 SER, from their farm in Caradoc. The farmhouse, which had been built in the 1860s, needed a new roof and other repairs. The barn was also in poor condition; it was turned a quarter-turn, set on a new foundation, repaired, and is still in use at this writing. The 1½-storey farmhouse looks much the same as in the 1860s although an addition in 1984 added a double garage and laundry room. Prior to 1967, a large woodshed and a summer kitchen stood where the addition is now.

The Ball family attended West Adelaide Presbyterian Church until 1925. Robert Ball had voted for the Union between the Methodist and Presbyterian churches and, consequently, moved the family membership to Kerwood United Church. His sons, Hugh and George, attended this church as well as grandson, David, his wife, Beth, and their sons, Robert and Allan.

In the years following their move to Adelaide, Robert and Blanche enjoyed the friendship of the Callaghans, the McCarthys and the Walshes, their nearest neighbours. Games of euchre, group haircuts, and refreshments were enjoyed at these get-togethers. The youngsters would play card games such as "Flinch."

Adelaide Hall was the setting for concerts and community dances. Dances were also held in the homes and one story is told of the dining room floor of the Ball home falling through to the basement as a result of the enthusiastic dancing! This was long before the Ball family moved to Adelaide.

Herb was born with a clubfoot so his parents sought medical help. As a teen, he traveled to Toronto and the surgery received there was successful. He wore special shoes and walked with a slight limp for the remainder of his life. He attended Westervelt Business School and spent a long career with Lawson & Jones in London. During the war years, because of his disability, he was given an office job in the Veterinary Office at Carling Heights. He married Etta Staples in 1924 and they had one son, Robert.

Robert Hugh married Hazel Frieda Patterson (1903-1982), daughter of Robert Milton and Margaret Agnes (Meddie) Patterson of Adelaide, both of whom are buried in the Strathroy Cemetery. Hugh and Hazel adopted one daughter, June Helen. Hugh purchased a farm from Hazel's uncle, George Patterson, on the Fourth Line in Warwick, and the family owned and farmed 700 acres in Lambton and Middlesex Counties. The couple was very active in the Kerwood United Church. When June grew up, she married Finley Clyde Muirhead, and they had four children, John, Robert, Patricia and Linda. Hugh and Hazel lived on the farm for 45 years before moving to Strathroy, where Hugh sold real estate for a number of years before retiring.

George Edwin married Harriet "Hattie" Georgina Brown (1912), daughter of George and Anne (Graham) Brown, who was a schoolteacher at S.S. #6 Adelaide. Their three children are Ruth Harriet, David George and John Robert. George and Hattie farmed 550 acres at R.R. #3 Kerwood. Their son, David, studied agriculture at Guelph, and he and his wife presently own and operate the Robert T. Ball family farm at Lot 7, Con. 1 SER.

After Robert's death, Blanche lived with George and Hattie until her death at the age of 88.

John Russell was a teacher and, later, a principal. In Toronto, in 1933, he married Gertrude Stewart (1906), whose parents were the Rev. William A. and Jennie (McCoy) Stewart. They spent 1933-1934 in Britain on a teaching exchange. They had two sons, Roger John Tudor Ball, and Gordon David Stewart.

Ben attended the University of Toronto and graduated with a degree in Business Administration. He began his career with the Hudson's Bay Company. He married Rhoda Elizabeth "Betsy" Darnbrough (d.1959) in 1937. They had three children, Mary Elizabeth, John Michael, and Benjamin Walker Jr. Elizabeth died in a car accident in 1959 while returning to Toronto from the farm. In July 1961, Ben married Margot (Clark) Wilkinson and they had a son, Mark Andrew, and a daughter, Sarah Margaret. Ben died while on holiday with his wife in Mallorca, Spain. At the time of his death, he was President and C.E.O. of Federal Pioneer Electric, a company he had spent many years building.

BARKER, Paul and Brenda

Paul and Brenda (James) Barker and their three children, Jeremy, Tiffany and Kimberly, moved to Adelaide Township in 1986. Before moving to Adelaide, they had lived in Sudbury and in Papua, New Guinea. They were seeking a small farm with running water and a bush lot within commuting distance of London. They found these features at Lot 19, Con. 3 NER, where a house had been built for Earl Gartley and family.

BARRETT, Richard and Louisa

Richard Barrett (1832-1914) moved to the east half of Lot 10, Con. 1 SER, from Fingal in 1841 with his mother and stepfather, Daniel and Mary Ingram.

Home of Richard Barrett and daughter, Mary, ca.1911; now home of Tony Bycraft.

In 1859, Richard married Louisa Morse (1840-1891), daughter of William Dyer and Eliza Morse. Louisa was a talented spinner and seamstress. They had five children, George (1860-1952); Annie (1862); Frederick (1864); Mary (1867-1957); and Elizabeth (1870-1969). Richard and Louisa later bought the west half of Lot 10 and built a brick house there in 1874. The entire 200 acres of frontage had been divided into 1/2-acre lots.

Only Annie and Fred married. Annie married Albert Brock, youngest son of George and Isabella Brock. Fred married Annie Parker and they lived on the west half of Lot 10 with their three children, Winnifred, Myrtle and Lawrence. They moved to Saskatchewan in 1909.

George went to North Dakota to farm when he was 23. He later had a butcher shop in Idaho, and lived for some time in California. He returned to Adelaide in 1914 and farmed until he became blind in 1943.

Mary had attended Strathroy High School. She played piano, organ and violin. She played the organ at St. Ann's Church and gave music lessons. She became blind by 1930. Beth, Mary and George enjoyed the hockey and baseball games on the radio. They were keenly interested in politics and world news.

Elizabeth left Adelaide in 1911 and lived in Buffalo, then moved to California and lived there until 1933. She had trained as a milliner and she painted in oils.

Except for Fred, the Barretts are buried at St. Ann's Cemetery.

BAXTER, Reginald and Florence

On June 5, 1913, Mr. and Mrs. Samuel Baxter, with their two sons, Reginald and Edward, set sail for Canada. On June 16, they arrived at the farm of John Sercombe on the Fourth Line of Bosanquet. From there, the boys went to work at different locations.

Reginald had completed a course in gardening in England, so he sought employment in that field. In August, severe thunderstorms caused the collapse of many barns, and some burned to the ground. In October, the boys both worked on a 300-acre farm owned by E. Houlton, one mile east of Kerwood Road.

About November 9, the winds were exceptionally strong and many boats between Sarnia and Goderich sank. At this time, Reginald was 17 and Edward was 16 years of age.

Reginald got a job working for Robert Ball and for a few years, he farmed in the Kerwood area.

In 1916, Florence Thorne arrived in Canada from Tiverton, England, and became the wife of Reginald Baxter. They settled on a farm at Con. 5 NER in a small frame house on what is now Townsend Line. They had five children, Joyce, William, Fredrich, Nellie and Ronald.

Reginald became a fruit farmer and picked up berry pickers around Kerwood such as the Redmonds, Petches, etc.

Their daughter, Joyce (1919), went to school at the Keyser School. Two of her teachers were Mr. Fisher and Vivian McKenzie (who married Harry Conkey).

As a baby, Joyce won a high chair as first prize at the Adelaide School Fair and at the age of four, she was entered in a contest competing for "Most Beautiful Child." Joyce was one of the last to be entered, but received a beautiful portrait from the London Advertiser newspaper.

Because of a later move by the family, the other children did not go to the same school. One of Joyce's memories was of going down the road from the schoolhouse to William Parker's store to buy candy.

In 1927, Reginald's father, Samuel, went back to England. The family moved closer to Arkona where Reginald bought a farm from Mr. Gott.

Reginald rented the farmhouse in Adelaide for a few years and kept the land until William, his eldest son, married Reta Armstrong in 1946 and they moved into the old homestead.

Bill and Reta had two children, Ann and Allan. Reta died in 1981 and Bill in 1982. Their son, Allan, and his wife, Jackie Rutter, live with their family in a beautiful new house on this farm. Allan is employed with Strathroy Propane.

BELLAIRS, James Peel Stevenson and Maria

The Bellairs name can be traced to 1066, the time of King William the Conqueror, last successful invader of the British Isles. William Oscar Bellairs (1900-1978), who resided in Strathroy, had in his possession a large document tracing the history of the Bellairs family from King William in 1066, written in minute but clear Victorian script. In the 1960s, the London Free Press ran an interesting interview with William Oswald Bellairs, also of Strathroy, in which Bill recounted how Mrs. William Oswald McKenzie Bellairs brought this document from England. She had come to Canada in 1835 to join her husband, a British Army doctor, who had settled in East Williams. The Bellairs were a wealthy and influential family, both in England and early Upper Canada. Jean Goldrick Bellairs of Strathroy, wife of the late William Oswald Bellairs, donated this fascinating historical document to the Strathroy Museum in 1978.

Abel Walford Bellairs (1755-1839) was born in England in Penbridge, Derby County, England. He married Susanna Lowley, only daughter of Miles Lowley of Oakham. She died in 1823 and is buried in Bedworth, Warwick County, England.

They had five children, Emilia, James (1782), George (1787), Henry (1790), and William (1793), all born in Stockerston, Leicester County, England. Children of two sons, James and Henry, had connections with Adelaide Township.

James, second child of Abel and Susanna, married Elizabeth Ann Peel, born in Ardwick, Leicester County, England, eldest daughter of Laurence Peel and niece of Sir Robert Peel, Baronet. The famous painter, Paul Peel, had relatives in Adelaide Township, as he was recorded as coming to the township to visit family. James and Elizabeth were buried at Clifton, County Somerset, England. There is a curious clause in the Strathroy Museum document—in 1845 at about 63 years of age, James

Back L-R, Flossie on lap of father, Henry Oswald Bellairs, Carlotta Marie (Hunwick) Bellairs, Dorothy on lap of Carlotta's brother, Mr. Hunwick, and Henry Oswald's sister, Mary Foster Elliot, with Nona on her lap; front L-R, Norman, Sadie and William. Photo ca.1911.

was asked to sign a paper stating he would assume the name and arms of Stevenson instead of Bellairs, in compliance with the will of his cousin, William Stevenson.

The children of James and Elizabeth were James Peel (1808), Frederick (1810), and George (1817), all born in England.

James Peel Stevenson (Bellairs) was born in Uffingham, England. He was the first known Bellairs to come to the new country. In Adelaide Township in 1835, he married Maria MacKenzie, daughter of Col. Walter MacKenzie. Col. MacKenzie was a friend of the influential Col. James Fitzgibbon. They were together in the Battle of Beaverdam in 1812. It was to this (then Lt.) James Fitzgibbon, that Laura Secord gave her warning of the American intention to surprise him. Col. MacKenzie was given a large tract of land in Adelaide, shown on a ca.1840 map as Lot 28, 29, 30 and 31, on Con. 1 SER. Maria MacKenzie Stevenson Bellairs was given some of the land by her father. Records show that on February 2, 1835, James Peel Bellairs received the patent of the crown for the west part of Lot 30, Con. 1 NER, which he and wife sold to Thomas William on March 11, 1854. Curiously, he signs as James Stevenson or Bellairs, reverting to his birth name. James and Maria's three children, all baptised in Adelaide Township by Anglican clergy, were Elizabeth Anne MacKenzie Bellairs (1836), Walter George Bellairs (1838), and Mary Bellairs (1840).

James Peel Stevenson Bellairs was the first postmaster in Amiens in the early 1830s. The post office was situated in the tavern of Captain Marvel White in Amiens, another war buddy of Col. MacKenzie. In the History of the County of Middlesex (1889), James Peel is listed as having been commissioned in 1837 with a W. MacKenzie, Major, in the second Regiment of Middlesex Militia, which was raised in Adelaide Township. James Peel Stevenson Bellairs resigned from his Amiens postmaster position in August 1840. The family moved to Port Burwell, and James was listed as postmaster there in 1846. In 1853, James Peel and Maria sold the west half of Lot 7, Con. 1 SER, to Adolphus Mahon of Adelaide, for 137 pounds, 10 shillings.

Henry Bellairs, fourth child of Abel and Susanna, was born in Stockerston, Leicester County, England. He married Dorothy Parker. Henry was a Lieutenant in the 15th Hussars, and was wounded in the Battle of Trafalgar in 1805. He accepted Holy Orders and was ordained a priest in 1817 by the Bishop of Salisbury. Henry and Dorothy had 13 children. Some of their children were Henry Walford (1812), ordained by Bishop of Chester in 1835, who married Mary Hannah Albina; William Oswald McKenzie (1814-1897); Charles (1818); George Frederick (1825-1826); Arthur Heathcote (1826); and George Byng (1828), all born in England.

The only Bellairs to come to Middlesex County, according to our sources, was William Oswald McKenzie Bellairs, cousin of James Peel Stevenson Bellairs. William Oswald settled in East Williams and in 1852, he married Sarah Jane McKeichan (1825-1909), born in Benbecula, Isle of Uist, Inverness-shire, Scotland. On the family tree, Sarah Jane's name is spelled McEachern. Sarah's obituary mentions that Sarah came with her family to East Williams Township when she was about 20 years of age. Soon after her arrival, she met William Oswald, son of an English church clergyman, and they fell in love, although he spoke only English and she only Gaelic. They had a happy married life together. Her obituary also mentions her surviving sister, Mrs. Janet McCorkindale, who died at the age of 101 in Strathroy. William Oswald's obituary is slightly different, indicating he came to Middlesex County and worked as a schoolteacher for awhile, then moved to Detroit where he taught school and married Sarah Jane McKeichan of Detroit. It goes on to say they moved to East Williams and settled on Lot 14, Con. 8.

Sarah Jane McKeichan Bellairs had a baby who died in childbirth in 1860. In Adelaide Township, another family had a tragedy about the same time. Robert Bravener lost his wife, Sarah Ann, in childbirth when she gave birth to Oswald Henry. Robert already had four young children at the time of this baby's birth. Family legend has it that Sarah Jane Bellairs was very ill after the stillbirth and was not told her baby had died. Her husband, a doctor, brought the Bravener baby home with permission of Robert Bravener. When Sarah Jane Bellairs was well enough to be told about the death of her own baby she was so attached to this baby she would not give it up, although Robert Bravener wanted it back after his second marriage. Eventually, the Bellairs adopted Oswald Henry Bravener (1860-1935), son of Robert and Sarah Ann Bravener of Adelaide Township. Later, the Bellairs adopted a girl, Mary Jane Foster (1870).

In 1897 in Adelaide Township, Oswald Henry (Bravener) Bellairs married Carlotta Marie Hunwick (1875-1933) of London, England, living in Adelaide Township. They lived in East Williams Township. About 1913, they moved back to Adelaide Township. In 1921, Oswald sold his 100-acre farm (known as the Douglas Farm) on Second Line South to W.H. Edwards of Longwood, and bought 25 acres of land from R. Parker on the Fourth Line. Later, they retired to Strathroy.

An interesting article in a 1938 London Free Press newspaper relates the story of a family heirloom, a handsome writing desk. The desk was in the Bellairs family for generations in England and, later, in the forest home of his father by adoption, William Oswald Bellairs. Times were hard and Oswald sold the desk to a Mr. McDonald as payment for a couple of young pigs. Much later, children of this Mr. McDonald examined the desk closer and realized its value which, when closed and locked, measured only 24"x12". A London locksmith discovered 12 secret drawers, and in one of these, they found the family history now housed at Strathroy Museum. Eventually, this small desk came into the possession of Mrs. Russell Squire.

Oswald and Carlotta Bellairs had seven children, all born in East Williams. William Oswald (1900-1978) married Jean Lorena Goldrick (1910). Norman Henry (1901) married Pearl Dennison (1905). Sadie Jane (1903) married Thomas D. Gooden (1902). Flossie Isabelle Mary (1905) married Russell Squire (1905). Dorothy Edna (1908) married John Orval Barnes. Winona Etta (1910) married Louis Keck (1903). The youngest, Ada Violet (1912), married Philip Keay.

In 1886, Mary Jane (Foster) Bellairs (1870-1949), adopted daughter of William Oswald and Sarah Jane, married John Elliott of Adelaide Township (1862-1944), son of George Elliott and Margaret J. Spearman. They had nine children, all born in East Williams Township. Little is known about the eldest, James, or second eldest, Ella Marguerite (1888-1911). William Ernest (1890) married Lucy Jane Wardell of Adelaide Township, daughter of John Edward Wardell and Caroline Lindsay. The next four children were Earl Howard (1892-1893), Franklin Arnold (1893-1920), Earle Lloyd (1896-1897), and Thomas Arnold (1897-1898). Pearl May (1908) married Clarence Pearson, then Alfred Hall. The youngest child, George Stanley (1912-1985), married Marie Davidson.

BENEDICT, Ellwood and Alma

In the spring of 1936, Ellwood and Alma (Donaldson) Benedict moved from just north of Arkona to the east half of Lot 4, Con. 2 NER, the Duncan Robinson residence. They rented the farm from Mrs. Robinson, who had relocated to Strathroy. The Adelaide farm was close to the home of Loftus and Margaret (Donaldson) Wilson, Alma's sister. The Benedicts had a four-year-old son when they moved to the farm, Donald Lee. A second son was born in 1938, Loftus Rodger Benedict.

In the spring of 1942, Ellwood gave up farming and took a full time job at R.M. Rascombe & Sons Flour Mill in Strathroy. The Benedicts left the farm and moved to a house on Colbourne Street which was later torn down, and the Colbourne Street School was built there in 1945.

When the family moved to Strathroy, Rodger missed the farm so much his Uncle Loftus took him back to Adelaide. What began as a short visit became an extended one, which lasted from 1942 to the present.

BETT, Michael and Barbara

In April 1957, Michael Bett bought the farm at west Pt. Lot 26, Con. 2 SER, from Fred Rawlinson. The property is approximately 210 acres, with 50 acres on the south side of the concession road. The Rawlinsons vacated the house in September, and Mike and his new bride, Barbara, moved in after their October wedding.

Mike and Barb were the fourth owners of this farm. It was homesteaded by the Buttery family in the mid-1800s. Clarence and Pearl Pearson were the next owners, and they remained there for more than 30 years, until Clarence's death in the early 1950s. Fred and Nora Rawlinson became owners in 1953.

Mike and Barb did general farming during their 35 years on the farm, beginning with milk, hogs, eggs and cash crops, and ending with cattle and cash crops. With the switch from milk cows to beef, Mike became involved in local politics. In 1965, he was elected to township council with Reeve Clarence Stevenson, veteran Councillors Charles Nichols and Fred Hoffner Sr., and another rookie Councillor, David Ball, who was the youngest elected Councillor in the history of Adelaide Township. Following the unexpected death of then Treasurer, Clarence Fuller, in August 1966, Mike was appointed Treasurer. He began his duties on September 1, 1966, and remained a township employee until his retirement on August 31, 1996.

Mike worked with Clerk Wilfrid Wilson until his retirement at the end of 1967. Frank Gare took over as Clerk in 1968 and, upon his retirement at the end of 1981, Mike was appointed Clerk/Administrator, which incorporated the positions of Treasurer and Tax Collector. At the time of Mike's appointment in 1966, Alvin McChesney was both Assessor and Tax Collector. The Province took over the function of Assessment at the end of 1969, and Alvin retired as Tax Collector in 1972. Mike performed the Tax Collector's duties after Alvin's retirement. He was also Building Inspector, Dog Tax Collector, and Livestock Evaluator at different times while working for the township.

The Bett family included three children, Carol, Alan (deceased), and Sandy. The farm was sold in July 1992, and Mike and Barb moved to Strathroy.

BEYNEN, Hubert and Johanna

In 1953, Hubert and Johanna Beynen immigrated with their three children to Canada, moving from a small town near Sertogenbos in the Province of North Brabant. They arrived in Woodstock on a dairy farm with only $450 in their pockets. From there, they rented a farm from Sam Wiley in Kerwood. This farm was later owned by Peter De Jong, who was busy with a store he had built. The Beynens then bought a farm from Clayton King on Second Line North. Here they raised seven more children. Later, they bought a farm from Wes Demaray. Altogether, they purchased 350 acres, where they operated a Holstein dairy farm.

In 1976, the Beynens sold 200 acres to Gerry Devet and five years later, sold the remaining 150 acres to M. Malick. In 1981, they bought a house on Hull Street in Strathroy. When the 10 children grew up, they relocated to almost

Bett family home at Lot 26, Con. 2 SER, purchased by Mike and Barb Bett in 1957.

as many places: Sudbury, Timmins, Chesley, Toronto, Michigan, Cobourg, Poplar Hill, Kerwood and Strathroy.

Hubert and Johanna Beynen spend their winters in Florida.

BISHOPP, George and Mary Jane

George Bishopp (1813) was born in Dover, Kent County, England. He married Mary Jane Croucher and they immigrated to Canada in the summer of 1852. They settled on 100 acres of crown land, the east half of Lot 14, Con. 2 SER. With them were their three small children, George (5), Eliza (3), and Mary Ann (1). Mary Ann took gravely ill and they feared she would die at sea. She survived only until they reached Adelaide and was buried in St. Ann's Cemetery, Adelaide Village. A niece and nephew, George and Caroline Croucher, also accompanied the Bishopp family. A second son, Edward, was born in Adelaide in 1852.

Eliza married William Martin, son of Hiram Martin and Hannah Hollingshead, in 1869. They had 13 children. Of these, Emily married Elden Carrothers, Silas married Reta Mason, Calvin married Ella Wardell, and Ethel married Archie Muxlow. The rest of the family moved to Toronto, New York, and Saskatchewan.

BLOOMFIELD, Stanley and Betty

Betty Louise Richardson married Stanley James Bloomfield of Stratford on January 19, 1952. Since 1972, they have lived at 27748 Clyde Street, Kerwood, in a home that was her great-grandfather's. They have six children. James Fredrick married Marlene Ball, David Allan married Kim Whiteside, and Donna Louise married James Whiteside (they have since separated). William Robert married Jane Wilms, Douglas George married Julie Gallant, and Steven Edward married Mary Margaret Schutzbach. Betty and Stan have 12 grandchildren and two great-grandchildren.

Two of their sons, David and Douglas, work for CN Railway. When the tunnel was built under the St. Clair River to Michigan, David was the foreman who put in the golden clip (the last spike to complete the project).

BOERE, Jim and Susan

Jim Boere bought a farm at the west half of Lot 8, Con. 4 NER, in 1983. He moved to the area from Warwick Township. On August 11, 1984, he married Susan Soetemans of West Williams Township. They work together on the farm, raising pigs, crops, and children. Their family includes four of the latter, David, Jaclyn, Michelle and Bradley.

BOERSEMA, Marten and Elly

Marten and Elly Boersema were born in the Netherlands and immigrated to Canada in 1951 with seven children. Six more children were born in Canada. For the first nine months, the family lived at McKays Corners near Ridgetown, and after that, they moved to Keyser.

The Boersemas rented a farmhouse from the Herringtons, the former Glover place. The farm was sold to the Lentings, so the family had to move again. In 1954, Marten bought a house for $4,000 on Second Line South (Mullifarry Road) with 25 acres, Lot 19, Con. 3. That was a lot of money then, but by today's standard, it would be considered very inexpensive. The property was purchased from

George and Mary Ann (Croucher) Bishopp and back L-R, George, Elisa and Edward.

Marten and Elly Boersema family, 1968.

Teake Vander Wal, and the neighbours knew it as the Fletcher's place.

Marten and Elly were very happy in their new home. Marten made improvements to the house to accommodate the increase in family size. He was an architect and builder by trade in Holland and Canada, and built many houses in Strathroy and the surrounding area. He also built and repaired barns until 1969, when he was badly injured in a backhoe accident. He died a few days later in Strathroy Hospital and was buried in the West Adelaide Church cemetery.

In 1970, Elly began operating a health food store out of the house, modifying her husband's office to a small store and soon after, renovating the garage for additional space. She continued to operate the store there until 1998, when she built a new home and store on the property to replace the old family dwelling. Her daughter, Janice, joined her in the business in 1995 and has operated it since 1997. At the age of 83, Elly still likes to help customers from time to time. She has a burning desire to help people to recognize that God has given them bodies that can heal themselves, if they would only treat them with healthy respect and the necessary nutrients.

All of the Boersema children went to schools in Adelaide Township and all 13 attended Strathroy High School. Nine of the children went to university, and two went into the field of nursing.

Julie (1941) married Kees Lindhout, a lawyer in Toronto, and they have three children and eight grandchildren. Julie graduated as a teacher and taught for many years, then worked for various Boards of Education and finally for the Ministry of Education in Toronto. In 1999, she retired but does freelance work.

John (1942) married Jenny Mesu and presently lives in Ancaster. They have six children and five grandchildren. John began in the working world as a banker, then returned to school to earn his Doctorate in Business. He taught business at U.W.O. then worked with Imperial Oil in England. At present, he is a Professor at Redeemer College in Ancaster.

Doug (1944) graduated from Teachers' College in London and was one of the first teachers at Caradoc North in Caradoc Township. This was followed by various teaching positions in Ontario, Manitoba, Alberta and British Columbia. Today, he is working in his father's profession, in the building trade near Smithers, B.C.

Joe (1946) married Ena Pieterman and they have five children and six grandchildren. Joe worked with his father in the construction business in Strathroy, then obtained his realtor's license and now works for ReMax Realty in Burlington.

Rennie (1947) married Jack Pieterman and they have four children and four grandchildren. Rennie graduated as an R.N.A. and worked at Strathroy Middlesex General Hospital. She practiced nursing for many years while raising her family. Today, she helps her husband with their plumbing and renovation business in Hyde Park. They live in London.

Ralph (1949) married Lucille Jenkins and they have five children and four grandchildren. Ralph has a Masters of Divinity and after being a minister for a congregation in Calgary, Alberta, he became a missionary in Brazil, where he has remained for the last 20 years.

Attie (1950) married Henry Sandink and they live near Carlisle with their four children. She graduated from nursing in Brantford and practised her profession in London, Mt. Brydges and Burlington. Today, she works in Burlington as a lactation consultant.

Jack (1952) married Alana Meadowbrook and they have three children. He graduated from U.W.O. and then from the Royal Canadian Mounted Police College in Regina, Saskatchewan, and worked as a police officer in Alberta for five years. He then followed in his father's footsteps with his own construction business. He and the children presently live in Vernon, B.C.

Janice (1953) attended U.W.O. and returned to Strathroy to work in the office of the family construction business for a few years. She then moved to London and worked throughout southwestern Ontario in the sales profession. She joined her mother in the health food store and now operates the business.

Bob (1955) is married to Nancy Bouwsema. He joined his brother in the family construction business, then moved to Alberta and started his own construction business. He and Nancy live in Calgary with their three children.

Theresa (1957) married Talbot Bergsma and they have four children and live in Carman, Manitoba. Theresa attended U.W.O. and worked in business until her marriage. They lived near Bothwell and, after a few years, moved to Manitoba because of her husband's work. She presently works with the Corn Marketing Board in Manitoba.

Marcia (1959) is married to Ron Vandenbos and they have seven children and presently live near Carman, Manitoba. Marcia graduated from U.W.O. and taught in Orangeville and Hamilton, then moved to Carman, where she is a high school teacher.

Nick (1963) is married to Susan Bouwsema and they have four children. They reside just north of Guelph. He initially joined his brothers in the construction trade in Alberta, then attended university in Edmonton. After completing his degree, he returned to Ontario with his family and has worked in various sales positions. He presently works for Canadian Waste in environmental sales.

BOGUE, James and Ezelia

John Bogue (1800-1891) was born in Lanarkshire, Scotland. His parents died when he was still a child. He left his native land in his early youth to seek his fortune in England, where he was engaged in the occupation of landscape gardening. In 1826 in Sussexshire, he married Elizabeth Parrott (1800-1886), who was born in Somersetshire, England. In 1837, they immigrated to Canada. Elizabeth miscarried during the voyage. They settled in Westminster Township (now Brick St., London). It is possible that John had family there, as in 1836 a land transaction was recorded where Abraham Sloot (Baptist preacher, farmer, carpenter and handyman) purchased 200 acres for 550 pounds on Rymal's Corner from a Norman Bogue.

John and Elizabeth were members of the Baptist Church. They raised a family of six sons and two daughters, all born in Westminster Township. The eight children were John, Ann, Allan, Emma, James, Thomas, David and William Richard. John and Elizabeth were buried in Brick St. Cemetery. It is said that the Bogue men were big and handsome, prominent in their communities and genial, and that their word was as good as their bond. All of them were outstanding farmers and poultry men.

John Bogue (1828-1912) married Elizabeth Axford (ca.1840-1918), daughter of George Axford, a much-esteemed pioneer of Elgin County who was born in Devonshire, England, and farmed in Delaware. John and Elizabeth farmed on the east side of Talbot Road, 1½ miles north of Lambeth. Later, they moved into Lambeth. They were members of the Methodist Church and John was a Liberal in politics. John and Elizabeth had one son, Norman, who in 1906 married Annie Irving of Lambeth. Norman and Annie farmed on the homestead. John and Elizabeth were buried in Woodland Cemetery.

Ann Bogue (ca.1830-1916) married James Smart. James was a Sheriff of the united counties of Leeds and Grenville. They lived in Brockville.

Allan Bogue (ca.1832-1908) married Mary Jane Nixon (1874-1957). They farmed on the home farm on Brick St. Allan served on Westminster Township council. He was a noted poultry exhibitor at the fairs, and one of the best-known farmers and poultry men in Canada. He took a deep interest in the Western Fair since its inception. At the time of his death, he was Second Vice-President. He was also President of the East Middlesex Agricultural Society. Allan was recognized as a keen judge of poultry and officiated in that capacity at many of the largest exhibitions in Canada and the United States. Allan was also a member of the Masonic Lodge. Allan and Mary Jane had no surviving children; they were buried in Woodland Cemetery.

Emma Bogue (ca.1834-1913) married James Tunks. They lived in Westminster Township. In 1910, James was killed by a falling tree during a violent windstorm. In 1912, Emma lived in London. They were buried in Woodland Cemetery.

In Adelaide in 1867, James Bogue (1837-1921) married Ezelia Ann Buttery (1845-1931), born in England, daughter of George Buttery and Charlotte Rapley. In 1864, James settled on Lot 22, Con. 3 SER, and there he brought his new wife in 1867. Later, they also owned part of Lot 23. James was regarded as one of the most successful and progressive farmers in the district. He was one of the oldest members of Beaver Lodge, A.F. & A.M. They retired to Head St. North in Strathroy in 1908.

Ezelia Ann was influential in several organizations. She was the first President of the Strathroy branch of the Women's Institute, being a great believer in the importance of the contribution of rural women to the community. She was a member of the Hospital Auxiliary and was active in the work of the Baptist Church. In 1917, they celebrated their 50th Wedding Anniversary and in a delightful article in the Age, it noted that they were both remarkably active and in splendid health. Both were buried in Strathroy Cemetery.

James and Ezelia raised a family of three sons and three daughters, all born in Adelaide. Jessie (ca.1868) married Samuel R. Thompson in Adelaide in 1900. In 1921, she lived at home, and in 1931, she lived in Fort Frances. George A. Bogue (1870-1951) and John Bogue (1873-1945) never married, and they farmed on the Adelaide homestead. They also farmed on Lot 23, Con. 3. They were buried in Strathroy Cemetery. Edith (1875-1909) was a teacher and she never married. She taught in Poplar Hill, Springbank #4, Lobo and #11 Adelaide, and was regarded as one of the foremost teachers in this district. William (1877-1968) married Beatrice B. Robertson (1877-1940) in 1907 in Strathroy. They lived in Lambeth and later moved back to Strathroy. They had at least one son, James Robertson Bogue (1911). William and Beatrice are buried in Strathroy Cemetery. Charlotte Elizabeth "Bessie" (1887) married W.C. Scandrett and lived in Fort Frances.

In 1869 in Adelaide, Thomas Bogue (1840-1912) married Margaret Thompson (1848-1912) of Caradoc, daughter of John Thompson and Margaret Young, who lived on the townline of Adelaide and Caradoc. Thomas and Margaret farmed on the west part of Lot 25, Con. 2 SER. They had two daughters and two sons, all born in Adelaide. Ann and Elizabeth were both born in 1870 (Ann lived one month and Elizabeth 10 months). James Robertson (1875-1934) married Frances "Gertrude" Pincombe (1872-1940), daughter of Richard Pincombe and Amelia Martyn of Strathroy. They resided in Strathroy, where James was a prominent citizen. James was in the lumber business with his brother, Thomas Edgar Bogue. In Gertrude's obituary, daughter Margaret Bogue is mentioned as surviving her mother and residing in Strathroy. T. Edgar Bogue (1881-1948) married Grace McCracken (1877-1971). Until 1928, they farmed in Adelaide on Lot 25, Con. 2 SER, and then moved to London for a year before entering the lumber business in Strathroy. About 1909, Acme Lumber and Supply Ltd. bought the business and T. Edgar became general manager. He and his family were members of St. Andrew's Presbyterian Church. A daughter, Sarah, married C.M. Anderson and lived in Chatham. They had two sons. Donald Anderson is with Atomic Energy of Canada in Oakville, and James Anderson works for Reuters News Wire Service in Saigon, South Vietnam. T. Edgar died in a horrible car/train accident in 1948 as a result of a seizure. T. Edgar and Grace were buried in Strathroy Cemetery.

David Bogue (1843-1923) married Sarah Grace Axford (ca.1853-1922), daughter of George Axford and sister to Elizabeth Axford. They had two sons, George Allan and Chester Axford Bogue. They resided in Lambeth. As were his brothers, David was keenly interested in fairs and he won many prizes. In 1884, David was Worshipful Master of St. Paul's Lodge, No.107, Lambeth, A.F. A.M. In 1909, David was the auditor of the North St. Cheese Factory. In February 1912, Chester went out with his father and a hired man to cut firewood on their farm and was killed by a falling tree. His wife, Lillian Morton, who lived on Brick St. with their two small children, survived Chester. In 1919, David celebrated his 76th birthday at the Baker family's annual picnic in Westminster, and in 1921, David and Sarah lived in Lambeth. They were buried in Woodland Cemetery.

In 1916, William Richard Bogue (ca.1845)

farmed on Lot 24, Con. 2 and 3, and in 1917, he farmed on Lot 25, Con. 3 SER. Sometime after 1917, he moved to Moosejaw, Northwest Territories, where in 1919 he was Mayor. Records in 1920 list William Richard as a hardware merchant.

BOLTON, Richard and Frances

In 1852 in Adelaide Township, there were two families of Richard and Frances Bolton. Many of the children even had the same or similar names, and both families came from Ireland.

Richard and Frances came to Canada from County Wexford, Ireland, in 1840. They settled in Oxford County, where their fifth child was born. They came to Adelaide Township, the east half of Lot 11, Con. 4 SER, in 1852. Both Richard and Frances are buried in Strathroy Cemetery.

Elizabeth "Bessie" Bolton (1827) married David Jury. They had no children of their own, but they raised John Rinehardt, a neighbour boy. They gave him a good education and he went on to build a good business in Spokane, Washington.

Isabella Bolton (1829) married Rev. John Shaw. One of their sons went to New York City, where he was a professional singer in the large churches.

Richard William Bolton (1837) never married. He purchased the family farm in 1865.

Frances "Fannie" Bolton (1839) never married.

William Henry Bolton (1841-1930) married Elizabeth Hunter Harvey, in December 1865. Elizabeth Harvey was visiting her sister, Rebecca Jane (Harvey) Murdock, who lived on a farm at the southwest portion of Lot 12, Con. 4 SER. William and Elizabeth lived in Strathroy, where he worked as a carpenter. They had five children born in Strathroy. Their children were John Albert Ernest (1867-1952); Luella (1869-1960); Leander William (1870-1967); Andrew Harvey (1870-1947); Frances Elizabeth "Fanny" (1875-1959), who married James Henry Stephenson; Abigail Bertha Bolton (1881-1971); Eunice Myrtle Bolton (1883-1970); and Richard Franklin Bolton (1888-1954).

William and Elizabeth traveled by covered wagon when they moved to Greene, Iowa, in 1876.

Anna Maria Bolton married Edwin Wright. They had three sons and two daughters. Ada Wright married Alexander Forbes, and Lottie Wright married William Hall. John J. Bolton went to California.

BOLTON, William and Harriet

William and Harriet Bolton were married in 1826 in Denham, Suffolk County, England. They had four children before they immigrated to Canada in 1834. They initially lived in Bolton, a town that had been established by cousins. In 1837, after the William Lyons MacKenzie uprising against the government, the Boltons purchased land and settled on Lot 20, Second Line North. William never spoke of this time. The Bolton cousins fled to the U.S. with a price for their capture. It would not appear that William and Harriet were not involved in the uprising, as they were of strong religious beliefs. After coming to Canada, Harriet worked as a servant in Strathroy, and the Bolton family attended St. Anne's Anglican Church. They are buried in that cemetery, along with daughter Rachel, who died young, and four grandchildren.

Mary (1826-1887), the eldest child of William and Harriet, was born in England, and died in Strathroy. She married W.G. Watson, and had one child.

Pamily (1828) was also born in England. She married John Harkness of Adelaide Township in 1849. Pamily and John had three children, Harriet (1849); George (1850-1889), who owned a pharmacy in London; and Rachel (1854-1891), who married Thomas Wyatt after her Aunt Harriet died and left him a widower.

James (1831-1889), third child of William and Harriet, was born in England. James bought the farm from his father on January 19, 1858. He and Mary Anderson were married on July 19, 1859, by Rev. Bob Clarke of Methodist Church. James and Mary raised 11 children.

William James (1860-1890), eldest of James and Mary's children, married Ellen Wardell, and they had two daughters.

Charles Henry (1862-1933) married Margaret Graham and they settled in Caradoc Township. Their eight children were Mary, William James, Sarah Pricilla, Robert John, Lillian Amelia, Mabel Irene, Emerson Graham, and an infant son.

Sarah Jane (1864-1929) married John Graham, and they had six children, William, Annie Laura, Florence, Dougal, Nellie and Eva.

Elmia (1866) married William Pepper and they lived in Forest.

Joseph (1868), fifth of James and Mary's chil-

Charles G. and Barbara (Wyatt) Bolton family

dren, married Tena Smith and lived in Caradoc, then Metcalfe Township. They had two sons, Mac and Alex.

Elizabeth never married, dying at age 25.

Robert John lived in the Sarnia area.

Edmund (1872-1873) died a baby.

Hiram (1874) married Jessie Glen and they lived in Adelaide Township. They had two daughters who remained on the farm, Margaret, who married Dalton Walpole, and Mary.

Mary Emma (1876-1894) died in her teens.

Samuel Edwin never married. He worked on many construction sites in Adelaide, Caradoc, and Strathroy, doing cement work.

James was travelling to the gristmill the day he died. He had his loaded shotgun with him as he hoped to shoot some rabbits for supper. The gun dropped through the floor of the wagon and discharged, and the bullet struck him in the groin. He was taken to the Charles Demaray home, where he died before the doctor could arrive. He was well respected, as evidenced by the notice in the Age Dispatch: "The deceased was a native of Suffolk, England, and came to this country with his father's family in 1834, settling in Toronto. Some five years later, the family moved to Adelaide. The deceased therefore was a resident of the township for 50 years, where he was widely known as a man of great integrity and moral worth, and respected and esteemed by all classes… the funeral cortege was one of the longest that ever passed through Strathroy, there being in actual count 104 rigs in line."

Charles G. (1832-1906), fourth child of William and Harriet, was born in England. In 1859, he married Barbara Wyatt, daughter of Edward and Ann (Fraser) Wyatt, and they farmed on Second Line North. Charles and Barbara had 15 children.

William Samuel (1860-1931), the eldest of Charles and Barbara's children, was born in Adelaide Township. He married Sarah Gerry (1860-1945), and they had five children. They lived in a log house, which was papered every spring with clean newspaper. William eventually built a 2-storey brick house to replace the log home. They retired to 17 Duke Street in Strathroy after 28 years of farming.

William R. "Will" (1886-1915), the eldest of William and Sarah's children, never married. He served in the Army, and attended the Coronation of King George V.

Henry Franklin "Frank" (1890) farmed his father's land and retired to Strathroy. He is buried in Strathroy Cemetery.

Mabel Emma (d.1976), third issue of William and Sarah, was born in Adelaide Township. She married Fredrick H. Smith, and they had a dairy farm on Route 8 in London. They had two sons. Allan died at age three. Melvin Charles married Elizabeth Bray and they had two children. Robert resides in Hamilton and Catherine "Cathy" lives in London.

Evelyn Beatrice (1895-1971), fourth child of William and Sarah, married Clifford Branton (d.1943) in 1918 in Strathroy. They farmed on Lot 14, Con. 1 SER. Clifford was Road Superintendent until his sudden death, after which Evelyn moved to

Charles H. Bolton family, L-R, Charles, Mabel, Graham and James.

Strathroy, where she lived until her death. They had four children (see BRANTON, Thomas and Mary Ellen).

In 1950, Myrtle (1919) married Orland Akins of Wainfleet, Ontario. They had four children. Ruth married James Clark of Blenheim, and they had two children, Elizabeth and Mary Jane. Allan married Ann Ferguson. They live in London and have one son, Brent. Donald married Nancy Sprague. They live in Sauble Beach, and have two sons, Kyle and Brian. Joan married Terry Plant, and they live in Watford. They have two children, Jolene and Shannon.

Mabel Ellen (1920), second child of Evelyn and Clifford, married Walter Barkman. They live near Acton, Ontario, and have four children, Nicholas; Diane, who married Don Warren; Randolph; and Ellen, who married Steve Stanley.

Vera (1922-1996) married Lloyd Muxlow. They lived in Adelaide Township and had four children. Edwin, the eldest, lives in Edmonton. Peter lives in London. Douglas lives in Strathroy. Betty married Joseph Van Damme, and she lives in Adelaide.

Clifford (1934), youngest child of Evelyn and Clifford, was born in Adelaide Township. He married Andrea McAteer. They had one son, Clifford Darryl.

Edward James (1861-1908), second issue of Charles and Barbara, married Sarah Graham, then Eliza Graham. He had one daughter, Ethel. Edward farmed in Lobo Township.

Charles J. (1863-1940) married Sarah Annette Scott of Warwick. They moved to Chilliwack, B.C., and had three children.

Harriet Christena (1864-1941) married Thomas Nichols of Strathroy. She later married Sydney Loveless of London. Harriet is buried in Strathroy Cemetery.

Thomas Vinson (1866-1940), fifth child of Charles and Barbara, married Christena McDonald. They lived on Plank Road in Sarnia and had several children.

George Donaldson (1867-1929) married Isabel Scott. They lived at 6 Perry Street in London. George was the captain of the London Fire Department. They had two daughters.

Robert (1869-1882) was born in Adelaide Township and died young. He is buried in Strathroy Cemetery.

Sam and Sarah (Gerry) Bolton

Ann (1871-1960), eighth issue of Charles and Barbara, married Charles Nichols. They had two children. Their eldest, Edith, married William Mitchell and they had two sons, Clarence and Roy. Liza married Uri Pierce. They had three sons, Charles, Euart and Allan.

John (1873-1963) moved to Vancouver, B.C., in 1910. He was employed by U.B.C. in Engineering for 20 years. He was married twice, first to Louise Hall, then to Ella James. He had one son and one daughter.

Mary E. (1875-1876) died a baby.

Walter (1876-1955) married Emmaline Gerry (1877-1932). He was a farmer and an auctioneer. Walter and Emmaline moved to London, where he was a Liquor Control Inspector for 10 years. Walter later returned to Strathroy and married Mary James. Walter was the Mayor of Strathroy for two terms and a council member for eight years. He also served two years as a Councillor, and two years as Reeve of Adelaide Township. He later became the Inspector of Provincial Highway Construction. He had one son from his first marriage, Harold, who became a farmer and an auctioneer.

Adeline (1879-1957), twelfth child of Charles and Barbara, married Alex Wray. They farmed near Komoka. She later married John Gray and retired to Strathroy.

Hugh (1880-1957) married Florence Loveless. They moved to London, where he worked for the City of London. They had two daughters.

Pamily Levina (1882-1940) married James Graham. They lived in Watford before moving to Detroit.

Pte. David Bolton (1884-1956) was the youngest of Charles and Barbara's 15 children. He remained single, and served in WWI in the 124th Battalion C.E.F.

Rachel (1835), fifth issue of William and Harriet, was born in Canada. She died young and was buried in St. Anne's Anglican Cemetery in Adelaide Village.

William S. (1837-1902), sixth child of William and Harriet, was born in Canada. He married Sarah Jane Hansford, and William took over the home farm in Adelaide Township from his father. They had nine children, Harriet (1860); Philip A. (1861-1865); Mary G. (1864-1882); William Hansford (1868-1899), who married Mary Elizabeth Linton; Robert (1871); Ann Elizabeth (1872), who married Isaac Linton; Eveline (1873), who married David McIntyre; Alvina P. (1876-1882); and Affie (1878-1882).

Sarah (1838-1873) was born in Adelaide. She married Walter Hansford and they had four children.

Adeline (1842-1876) was born in Adelaide. She married Samuel Milliken and they had two children. Samuel remarried and had two more children.

Elizabeth Ruth (1843-1902), ninth issue of William and Harriet, married Philip George Hansford. They had 11 children.

Harriet (1846-1873) married Thomas Wyatt. She died after having four children. Thomas remarried after Harriet's death, to the housekeeper, Rachel Sarah Harkness, Harriet's niece. Thus, the children's new stepmother was their first cousin, Rachel, daughter of Pamily (Bolton) Harkness.

The youngest child of William and Harriet was Samuel (1848-1883), who married Ann Whyte (d.1935). They had four children, three daughters and a son, Samuel. None of the children lived beyond nine years. Ann never remarried after Samuel's death.

The Bolton clan, English and Irish, is very large with connections to many families. Barb Bolton (related by marriage to James Bolton) has a copy of William Bolton's will, made four days before his death in 1858. The time it took to be probated was 18 years!

BOS, Ralph and Jacoba

In 1953, Ralph Bos married Jacoba Plug in Sarnia, Ontario. They rented a farm in Adelaide Township from Fred Brent, who lived on the neighbouring property on the northeast corner of Egremont Road and Kerwood Road.

Two children were born to them at this location. David (1954) married Diana Graansma of Strathroy in 1976. They have three children. Peter John (1955) married Mary Sanders of Lobo in 1976. Their five children are Jason John (1976); Darryl Robert Martin (1978); Karen Annette (1981); Adam Peter (1983) and Steven Ralph (1986). The family resides at 3756 Egremont Drive in Adelaide Township, where they own and operate Ralph Bos Meats.

Ralph and Jacoba moved to Strathroy, and during the nine years there, four more children were born. Alice Irene (1957) married Mark Vandervennen of Chicago, Illinois, in 1984. They have three children. Irving Ralph (1958) married Margaret Zwart of Kitchener, Ontario, in 1981. They have three children. Annette Jacqueline (1960) married Edward Weesjes of St. Thomas,

Ralph and Jacoba Bos family; standing, L-R, Annette, Peter, David, Marvin, Alice and Irving; seated, L-R, Renee, Ralph, Randall and Jacoba, 1970.

Ontario, in 1978. They have four children. Renee Joyce (1962) married Paul Weavers of Woodville, Ontario, in 1986. They have three children.

Ralph and Jacoba bought a 100-acre farm at Lot 23, Con. 1 NER. They farmed cash crops and pastured beef cattle. The fertile clay soil produced bounteous vegetables for their growing family. Two more sons were born on the farm. Randall Keith (1965) married Margaret Veenstra of St. Thomas, Ontario, in 1987. They have three children. Marvin Timothy (1967) married Susan Cox of London, Ontario, in 1997.

In the spring of 1968, Ralph and Jacoba set up a butchering business, catering mostly to custom slaughtering for farmers in the area. In October 1968, an official open house was held. Peter and Mary now own and operate the butchering business, and live next door to the shop in a house they built in 1984. Their teenage children have become valuable helpers in the meat processing business.

BOSHART, Carl and Suzanne

Carl and Suzanne (Reeve) Boshart have lived in Adelaide Township since 1977, moving to the area from Wilmot Township in Haysville, Ontario. They moved into an older yellow brick home on the corner of the Old Pike Sideroad and Napperton Drive. The Bosharts have a family of three, Steven, Dawn and Dwayne. Carl and Suzanne presently live at Lot 25, Con. 1, and they have an antique business there called New Dawn Furniture. Steven and Jane live with Jane's daughter, Angil, in Embrum, Ontario (near Ottawa). Dawn and Dwayne both live in Strathroy. Dwayne and his wife, Tammy, have two children.

Carl and Suzanne established their business of "antiques and things" in 1982 when Carl was unemployed. Carl had built farm silos for many years, but the 1982 recession saw that business take a downhill turn. Their present business has developed into a place where the curious go to explore the past. More recently, they have added an auction component to their business, Suzanne being the auctioneer. Suzanne also works out of the home as a coordinator for a mental health service.

BOWLEY, Walter and Eva

In 1905, Eva Morgan married Walter W. Bowley in Napperton, Ontario. They lived on a farm on the Fourth Line, which is now owned by the Crandon family.

The Bowleys raised purebred Ayrshire cows and bulls and held a sale of the offspring annually. Potential buyers from everywhere were met at the railway station and brought to the farm for the auction. Eva prepared a cornucopia of food, ham and vegetables and a variety of pies, to feed them.

About 1910-1911, they entered an Ontario contest for "Best Farms" and were selected as one of the winners. Eva had kept properly detailed books, and Walter, of course, had the Ayrshires and had written articles on alfalfa for farm magazines. They received an engraved silver cup on an ebony base, which sat proudly on the living room table, quite an honour for the Bowley family.

BRADSHAW - LOUGHEED

Richard Bradshaw (1828-1879) was born in Ireland and, with his parents and siblings, settled in Middlesex about 1837, part of the large migration of middle-class, Protestant Irish who came to Canada before the famine. He married Matilda Lougheed (1837-1885) of Albion Township, daughter of Robert L. Lougheed and Jane Henry. In August 1871, Richard Bradshaw sold his London Township farm and moved his family to Adelaide Township, where they lived on 50 acres at the west half of Lot 6, Con. 2 SER. Five years after moving to Adelaide and in ill health, Richard relocated his family to a small five-acre farm on Con. 4, just west of Strathroy. They had eight children, the youngest of whom was born less than a year before Richard's death. The eldest daughter, Angelina "Lina" (1867-1954), who still lived at home, became a surrogate parent to her siblings. Her mother's older, unmarried sister, Anne Jane Lougheed (1832), who was confined to a wheelchair, assisted her in this responsibility.

The second and third eldest daughters of Richard and Matilda were Bertha P. (1861-1882), and Jane Louisa "Jenny" (1864-1944). Jenny married Isaac Henry Parker (1860-1933), a farmer at Lot 15, Con. 4 SER, in 1884. The four Parker children, all born in Adelaide Township, were Gordon; Velma; Frank P. (ca.1886-1954), who married Flossie McWhinney (1887-1936) and took over his father's farm; Bruce O. (1888-1948), who married Beryl Buttery Newton (1893-1971), daughter of

George and Alberta (Buttery) Newton. Bruce was a hardware merchant in Strathroy, in partnership with Parker & Sands Hardware.

In 1891, Lina married Colin Thompson, whose Con. 4 farm was very close to her family homestead. They had two daughters, Marjorie and Marie, both born in Adelaide Township. Colin died suddenly of acute appendicitis at age 39. Lina sold the farm and moved back to the family house, which burned down shortly afterwards. Undaunted, she had the house rebuilt and with "Aunt Jane," managed a household on their modest inheritances until Marjorie got a teaching position in Strathroy. In 1914, Marjorie married a Peterborough lawyer, Joseph Wearing (who later became the Senior County Court judge in London), whereupon Lina and Marie joined the newlyweds in Peterborough. Marie taught school in Peterborough until she married Alec Lamont, a farmer in Caradoc Township.

Richard and Matilda's two sons were Herbert S. (1869), listed as a bank clerk in Adelaide Township in 1891, and Ashley C. (1870), a teacher in Adelaide Township in 1891. Herbert and Ashley eventually moved to Manitoba. Lola Vanche (1873-1914) married a Michigan dentist, Edward Mayhew. Lola's obituary notes that a young family of four survived her. Margaret Ann (1873) married James Campbell, a doctor from Grand Rapids, Michigan. Lilian E. (1879-1909) married Wilmer Fitzgerald, the son of F.A. Fitzgerald, the first president of Imperial Oil. A year later, she died tragically during childbirth.

Richard Bradshaw's younger sister, Sarah, also lived in Adelaide Township. She was the widow of Ephraim Stoney and of Thomas Harrison. Toward the end of her life she lived with her daughter, Mary Adelaide Stoney and her son-in-law, Wesley Hollingshead Eastman (1855), son of Elijah and Abigail (Martin) Eastman. Wesley farmed on the east half of Lot 16, Con. 3 SER, and later in Glencoe. In their retirement, Wesley and Mary moved to Saskatchewan. The Eastman's four children were born in Adelaide Township. Berdella Frances "Birdie" married George Henry Petch of Adelaide, son of Joseph and Martha Jane (Parker) Petch. Edmund Wesley "Eddie" (1892) relocated to Regina and had a family there. Charles moved to British Columbia. William "Earle" (1897-1970) remained single and died in Regina. Another daughter of Sarah and Ephraim, Jennie, married Frank F. Downing of Strathroy.

Other Lougheeds lived in Adelaide Township, in addition to Matilda and Anne Jane. Their brother, Samuel, married Emeline Harrison, the daughter of Thomas Harrison, and farmed on Lot 6, Con. 3 SER. A nephew, Robert Henry Davis, married Mary Adelaide Pierce and was a grocer in Strathroy.

BRANAN, Richard and Anna Maria

Richard Wallace Branan Esq. (1796-1869) was born in Kings County, Ireland. Squire Branan owes his distinguished Scottish name to a family tradition that the Branans were related to Sir William Wallace, the famous Scottish patriot. Squire Branan was the Governor of the Bank of Dublin. He married Anna Maria Tobin (ca.1810-1892), daughter of William Tobin. William was a wealthy Irish Protestant, a widower, and Clerk of Court in Dublin. William's brother, James, had custody of William's three children. Anna Maria had been in a "Ladies' School" or convent and was talented in the art of needlework. James arranged a marriage between Anna Maria and Squire Branan, who was 14 years older. When one of Anna Maria's children later asked why she married a man who was so much older, and whom she did not know, she replied, "I knew no better than to do as I was bid." Squire Branan and Anna Maria had five children in Dublin.

In the spring of 1832, the Branans sailed for New York, along with James Tobin, his wife, and Anna Maria's sister and brother, Jane Charlotte and James. The Tobins, Jane Charlotte, and James stayed in New York. In 1833, Richard Wallace Branan and his family came to London, Ontario, and then moved to Katesville, where Richard obtained 400 acres at Con. 6 Adelaide (Con. 1 Metcalfe). Richard also owned part of Lot 17, Con. 5, South Adelaide, and from Thomas Bright in December 1843, he bought another 50 acres of that lot (which Thomas Bright had received as Crown land). In October 1848, he sold some of the lot to Thomas Rapley, and in November 1849, he sold 50 acres to Dudley Merrill and his wife.

Richard started a general store and hotel on the village Lot 17, Pt. Gore Con. 7, near the river. Here, he embarked on a career as general merchant and postmaster, and in 1839, he was elected magistrate. Richard and Anna Maria had three more children in Adelaide. In 1843, Squire Branan was elected

Ken and Mary (Branan) Foster, and Canada Post representative presenting watch.

Superintendent of Schools for Adelaide. When Metcalfe and Adelaide townships separated in 1845, Squire Branan was elected the first Reeve of Metcalfe, an office he held for eight years. Later, he bought a mill in Alvinston. When he died, John, the eldest boy, inherited the mill. His other children, Jane Charlotte Nugent, Emily Maria Smith, Cherry Charity Kellam, Naomi Ann Ireland, and William Wallace received 50 acres each in the Katesville area.

Anna Maria Tobin Branan never did any housework. Hired help was cheap and she always had women come in to clean until her daughters were old enough to help in the house. Anna Maria taught her daughters beautiful needlework and they sewed for many of the early settlers. Anna Maria died at the home of her daughter, Naomi Ireland.

John William Branan (1824-1895), eldest child of Richard and Anna Maria, married Arabella "Belle" Secord. They had four children, Anna Branan, who married a Mr. Ward; Jemie and Edward, who never married; and Kate, who married a Mr. George.

Jane Charlotte Branan (ca.1832) married Dr. Edwin Nugent, who had known the family in Dublin. Dr. Nugent practiced for a while, then they returned to Dublin and had six children there. Edmund died a young man with tuberculosis. Rhoda married Capt. Brabison. There is no further information on Louisa, Marian, or Florence. George was a surveyor; he died of yellow fever in Mexico. Jane and Edwin returned with their family to Strathroy for a brief time, then moved to California due to son Edmund's poor health.

Richard died young in 1841, and Elizabeth Catharine Frances died at the age of 16 in 1841. Both were buried behind the store.

Emily Maria (ca.1835-1879) married Edwin Smith, whose parents owned a mill in England. He had run away from home and come to Strathroy. His brother, Louie Smith, followed later. Edwin and Emily owned a drugstore and grocery store in partnership with Louie. At one time, they owned the Pincombe Block at the corner of Front St. and Caradoc St. in Strathroy. They had three children, Emily, Edwin and Dick, who never married.

Charity "Cherry" Judith Louise (ca.1834), born in Adelaide, married Thomas Kellam, her father's hired man. They moved to Dorchester. After Thomas' death, she married a Mr. Penwarden and moved to California.

Naomi Ann Tobin Branan (ca.1836-1910), born in Adelaide, married Joe Ireland. She died in Metcalfe Township.

William Wallace Tobin Branan (1838-1898), born in Adelaide, married Ellen Pike (1852-1928), born in England, daughter of William and Mary Jane (Bright) Pike, who were first cousins. The Bright family owned land along Lake Huron, and Bright's Grove got its name from this family. In 1856, William Wallace Branan, Gentleman, received from His Excellency Sir Edmund Walker Head, Baronet, Governor General of British North America, an appointment as Ensign in sixth Battalion of Middlesex Militia, granted for special confidence in his Loyalty, Courage and Good Conduct. Lucy (Branan) Van Belois, granddaughter, still has the official document of appointment.

William and Ellen had 13 children. Emily Ellen Branan (1870) married Ben Pierce in 1901. Little is known of Minnie Ann Branan (1875-1898). Lucy M. Branan (1877-1951) married a Mr. Trueman or Truman in 1906 and went to Hamilton. Ada May Branan (1878-1954) married Alex McDougall in 1906. William Wallace Branan (1879-1918) died in California. Bertha Sarah (1881-1960) married William Knight in 1904. There is no further information on Frederick R. (1882-1973). Dorothy "Dolly" Louise Branan (1884) married Alexander Smith. Ethel Almeda (1885-1979) married John A. Drake. Louis Tobin Branan (1888-1969) married

Mary Jane "Jennie" Stevenson in 1911. Oscar Tobin Branan (1890-1929) married Annie Cowan in 1923 and lived in Detroit. Little is known of Naomi Branan (1892-1983). John E. Branan (1895) lived in Winnipeg.

Of the children born to William and Ellen, only Louis Tobin Branan and his wife, Jennie, had descendants who lived in Adelaide. Helen Mae Branan (1912-1979) never lived in Adelaide. Mary Ethel Branan (1915) married Kenneth Foster, son of Charles and Bertha Sarah (Harris) Foster of Adelaide. (In addition to Ken, the Fosters had three other children, George Foster, who married Marjorie Westgate, and lives in Adelaide Township; Russell Foster, who married Viola Lythgoe, and lives in Kerwood; and Mary Foster, who married Leonard Johnson, and lives in Metcalfe Township.) Ken and Mary Ethel Foster had no children. They operated a gas station and garage for many years on the corner of County Rd. 39 (now Napperton Drive) and Kerwood Rd. Ken has retired, but the gas station and garage are still in operation. Ken also drew mail for Route 2 Kerwood from the Kerwood Post Office for many years, and he received a watch for this long service.

Richard Louis Branan (1918-1985), third eldest of William and Ellen's children, married Ada McArthur. George William Branan (1920-1977) married Evelyn Beck. Donald Alexander Branan (1927) married Madeline Grundy. These three couples resided in Strathroy. Lucy Jane Louise Branan (1931) married Cornelius Van Belois, and they lived in London, Caradoc Township, and Strathroy.

BRAND, David and Terry

The family of David and Terry Brand first moved to Adelaide in 1984, renting a home on the Second Line South. In 1987, the family moved to 29648 Kerwood Road, purchasing the 100-acre farm formerly owned by Jack and Bruce Arrand.

Production of prospect sale calves began with 35 commercial cows, and a spring auction for these calves was held in 1990. In 1991, David purchased a Full blood Limousin bull and later, in the spring of 1992, a Full blood Limousin heifer, which was shown as David Jr.'s first 4-H project. This commenced the building of a herd which today stands at approximately 40 head of Purebred and Full blood registered Limousin cattle.

David and Terry Brand, with children Lee-Ann and David.

David and Terry's children, David William Earl and Jaclyn Lee-Ann, attended Adelaide W.G. MacDonald Public School, graduating in 1995 and 1998 respectively. They are both attending North Middlesex District High School in Parkhill. David and Lee-Ann are current 4-H members and actively participate in many extra-curricular and community activities.

BRANTON, Thomas and Mary Ellen

Terence O'Reilly came to Canada in 1848. As the story goes, he dropped the "O" in the ocean and changed his name to Reilly. He immigrated with his sister, Eliza (Reilly) Brown, from Killishandra, County Cavan, Ireland, because of the potato famine. He married Mary Buxton of the Niagara area in 1853. They moved to Metcalfe Township at Lot 6, Con. 4, and had 10 children. Mary died three days after the birth of the tenth child. A daughter, Mary Ellen Reilly (1859-1899), married William Thomas Branton (1843-1929) and they had four children, Clifford Riley (1884-1943), Fredcrick Alfred (1887-1967), Sarah Ellen "Sadie" (1891-1967), and William Thomas (1893-1973). They lived in Caradoc Township.

In 1903, Thomas and Mary Ellen Branton moved their family to a farm in Adelaide Township on the south side of the Second Line North. Clifford R. married Evelyn Beatrice Bolton in 1918, daughter of William Samuel and Sarah

(Gerry) Bolton, who lived on the north side of the Second Line North (the farm is now owned by Wilbert McKeen).

Clifford and Evelyn moved to Lot 14, Con. 1 SER. Clifford farmed and threshed for many years with his partner, Albert "Bud" Ayre. To save money, he made culverts from old water heater tanks in his shop during the winter, and installed them throughout the township when needed. There is one still, in front of the McNab farm, just east of the lane. He was an Adelaide Township councillor for several years and Superintendent of Roads for the township at the time of his death, which occurred in a hunting accident. Evelyn sold the farm and moved to James St. in Strathroy. She died in 1971. Bill Nichols now resides on the farm.

The Brantons raised four children. Myrtle Agnes (1919) became an R.N. She married Orland Akins in 1950 and lives on Colborne St. in Strathroy. Myrtle and Orland have four children. Elizabeth Ruth Anne married James Clark, and they have two daughters, Elizabeth Ann and Mary Jane. They farm near Blenheim and train and raise Scottish Sheep dogs. Allen George married Ann Ferguson, and they have one son, Brent Allen. Donald William married Nancy Sprague and their children are Kyle and Brian. Marion Joan married Terry Plant and they live in Watford with two daughters, Jolene and Shannon.

Mabel Ellen (1920), the second eldest child of Clifford and Evelyn, left the farm in 1939 to go to the University of Western Ontario for four years and then to Teacher's College. She married Capt. Walter Barkman of the Lincoln and Welland Regiment in 1946. They lived in Brantford, Saint John, Toronto,

Clifford Branton's car.

Clifford Riley Branton (1884-1943)

and for the past 22 years, on 10 acres near Acton. Mabel and Walter's children were twins (died at birth), William Randolph, John Nicholas, and Diane Elizabeth.

Vera Evelyn (1922-1996) married Lloyd Muxlow (1917-1988) and lived on the Muxlow farm on Egremont Road at the east half of Lot 14, SER. Vera served in the army during WWII. She and Lloyd had four children, Edwin Lloyd of Edmonton; Peter George of Strathroy; and Betty Pearl (Van Damme) of Adelaide Township. Clifford William (1934) is a retired bank manager and lives in Belmont. He married Beverly Andrea McAtur and they have one son, Clifford Branton III, who lives in Windsor with his wife, Martha Anne.

Fred Branton married Lena MacDonald of East Williams and they lived on the farm at the east half of Lot 18, Con. 2 NER, until they retired to Strathroy. They had two daughters, Alma Evelyn (1916) and Freda Mary Ellen. Alma married Ken

Fred Branton with buggy.

Lightfoot in 1943. They lived on a farm in Metcalfe until they retired in Strathroy. Ken died in 1997. Their children are Kenneth Wayne Branton who teaches near Sarnia and farms with his nephew, Jamie Ireland, and family who live on the farm. Roslee Evelyn June Hamlin (Branton) lives near Hamilton.

Freda married Earle Lonsberry and lives in Woodstock. They have three children, Reginald, Janice and Elaine.

BRAVENER, Robert and Sarah

Robert Bravener was born in England (ca.1820-1883), and died in Adelaide Township. Robert married twice. His first wife was Sarah Ann (last name unknown). They had five children. These were John (ca.1847); Robert (ca.1848); William (ca.1853); Lucian (ca.1857); and Oswald Henry (1860-ca.1933). Robert's first wife died giving birth to Oswald Henry. Robert could not care for the baby, so Oswald Henry was adopted by William Oswald McKenzie and Sarah Jane (McKeichan) Bellairs from East Williams Township, and he became a Bellairs. The Bellairs family also adopted a girl, Mary Jane Foster (1870). William Bellairs came from a distinguished background; he could trace his ancestry to King William the Conqueror in 1066 (see BELLAIRS, James Peel Stevenson and Maria).

Robert's second wife was widow Sarah Ann Norton Frank of Westminster, daughter of Mr. and Mrs. Daniel Norton. Sarah had been married at age 16 to James Frank. The children from the Frank marriage, according to Sarah's obituary, were Cyrenous; Lucien, who lived in Ulby, Michigan; Mrs. Kelly of Carleton, Mississippi; and Nathan.

Upon the death of James Frank ca.1860, Sarah married Robert Bravener and they moved to Adelaide Township, where they settled on Lot 24, Con. 1 SER. Robert and Sarah had two children, both born in Adelaide Township, Lucinda (1861-1921) and George Henry (ca.1863-1937). Robert and Sarah were buried in the Fourth Line Cemetery in Adelaide Township. There was no further information about the children from Robert's first marriage.

Lucinda Bravener married Samuel Bird Plank (1853-1936), son of Henry and Ann (Holden) Plank, or Planck. Henry was a native of Pennsylvania and Ann a native of England. In Samuel's obituary, it stated that he was Strathroy's oldest native son, born in the town's early days. For 20 years, he worked in Herd's Sandstone Works, and then for many years at the Old Electrical Plant in Strathroy. Lucinda and Samuel Plank had five children. Alfred H. (1880) married Matilda A. Stacey. Frank (1880-1887) and Freddie (1886-1887) died young. Ruby P. married John Westley Nicholls. Lottie A. married George F. Stacey. In Samuel's obituary, Lottie A. Stacey and Alfred Plank were noted as the surviving children, both of Strathroy. The younger generations of Braveners live in the Owen Sound area.

George Henry Bravener, son of Robert and Sarah, married Emma Almus in December 1883 in Strathroy. George and Emma had three children, Henry, who married and lived in Owen Sound; Nora, who married Thomas Kelly in Strathroy in 1902; and Francis (1893).

BRENT, Fred

Fred Brent owned the east half of Lot 9, Con. 1 SER, which was used as a government demonstration sod pasture farm during 1951-1956. The 100-acre farm was divided into three equal parts. The back third was plowed up in the fall of 1951, and reseeded in the spring of 1952, with a mixture of Trefoil, Brome (waterways seeded with Reed Canary Grass). The middle third was the check portion; it received no treatment. The front third was fertilized. In 1956, the back and middle portions were plowed and reseeded with the same mixture used in 1952.

Fred Brent was also a cattle drover. He bought and sold cattle with Albert Brock and Howard

Mr. and Mrs. Fred Brent with daughter, Freda (Brent) Galsworthy, and son, Gordon Brent.

Brock. He rented farms in the surrounding community, and pastured cattle there in the summer. Some cattle were wintered in local barns every year. Fred fattened the cattle, and weigh scales (CNR scales from Mt. Brydges) were put in the shed at the front of the farm, installed by Waltham and Fuller. The cattle were weighed each month.

Fred drove cattle on foot to Kerwood, and trucked them in later years. The cattle were shipped by train to Toronto, Detroit, or Buffalo.

BROCK, George and Isabella

The Brock family has a long history in Adelaide Township beginning in 1853 when George Brock Sr. and his family arrived in five rigs from Quebec.

George Brock Sr. (1803-1884) was born in Fermanagh County, Ireland. He and his four brothers immigrated to Montreal in 1819. They farmed in Quebec until better land deals opened up farther west. George married his first wife, Mary McCourt, in 1830 and they had two children, Jane and Philip. It is told that Philip was kidnapped by natives and raised by a Catholic family. He was later located, but chose to stay with his adoptive parents.

After Mary's death, George married Isabella Moore (1817-1895) in 1836, daughter of Thomas and Elizabeth (Fowler) Moore. While in Quebec, nine children were born. These were William, Ellen, Elizabeth, Arthur, Isabella, Anne, Jemima, George Jr. and Richard. Two more, Maria and Albert, were born in Adelaide. Family stories are told that all the Brocks except baby Richard spoke French fluently.

In time, all but one of the Brock boys left Quebec. Philip (ca.1834) remained behind. William settled in London Township; Albert went to Enniskillen Township, near Petrolia in Lambton County; and Robert came to Adelaide near Napier (now Metcalfe). George Sr. and his family came to the Egremont Road area in Adelaide, where he bought 400 acres. The family's possessions were loaded onto five wagons pulled by three teams of oxen and two teams of horses. It is thought that they came all the way from Quebec by land as no stories are told in the family about passage on lake boats, and it would have been very costly for such a large entourage.

When the Brock caravan arrived in London, George Sr. was quite ill and he had to remain there until he was able to travel on. Because he was not expected to live, the rest of the family continued to the farm that day as the legal work on the property was completed. It was recorded on December 1, 1853, that George Brock purchased 200 acres of Lot 13, Con. 1 SER, from Laurence Lawrason, a well-known land speculator of London. It was late in the day when the family arrived at the home farm. They found a red brick house built close to the road in the centre of the acreage. This house was still there in 1943, at the time Ray and Donelda Brock's house burned. People kept stealing bricks from the old house until gradually nothing was left. It is thought that this large brick building with verandas on three sides was used as a barracks when soldiers were stationed in Adelaide Village at the time of the 1837-1838 Rebellion.

George Brock had also purchased 200 acres of Lot 17, Con. 1 NER. He was a successful farmer as his obituary states, "By industry and thrift, (he) made a good home for himself and his family." George Sr. and Isabella arranged a train trip back to Montreal to look at a stallion that he and his brother had bought together. They didn't trust the safety of railroads so, in their state of nervousness, they made their wills and left the lands to the boys. George Jr. inherited the west half of Lot 17, Con. 1 NER, William got the east half of Lot 17, Con.1 NER, and Arthur received the west half of Lot 14, Con. 1 SER (Bill Nichols' farm at the time of this writing). The railroad returned the Brock parents safely and the boys received their inheritances sooner than planned. Richard and Arthur were too young, so

George and Isabella (Moore) Brock

they didn't receive their share of the land at that time. Jane (ca.1832), daughter of George Sr. and Mary McCourt, had come to Upper Canada with her father. She married James Beacom and lived in Essex County.

William Brock (1838-1922), eldest child of George Sr. and Isabella, married Jane Moore (1845-1884). Their children were Margaret Jane (1868); William Albert (1870-1870); Anna Maria (1872); William Albert II (1874); George Arthur (1876-1877); Isabella Edith (1881-1882); and Arthur Norman (1883-1918). Arthur Norman married a neighbour, Lottie Nichol, and they farmed the west half of Lot 18, Con. 1 NER (see NICHOL, Edward and Maria). William Brock's second wife was Maria Moore (ca.1847-1922).

Ellen Brock (1840) married John Tyler of Sarnia, and Elizabeth Brock (1841-1867) died a young woman.

Arthur Brock (1844-1918), fourth issue of George Sr. and Isabella, and his wife, Esther Conkey (1844-1926), daughter of William and Mary Ann Conkey of Adelaide (see CONKEY, Arthur and Margaret) farmed the west half of Lot 14, Con. 1 SER. He built the brick house that still stands on the property today. Arthur was stunned by the same bolt of lightning that killed William Walker at McIntosh's gate near Adelaide Village in November 1885.

Arthur and Esther had a large family, including Arthur (1871-1877); Lavina Isabella Ellen (1873-1881); Margaret Anna (1875-1881, died of diphtheria or typhoid); and William Henry (1878-1922), who married Annie Howe (1881-1968). William and Annie's son, Edward (1907-1991), was born in Adelaide, and he married Katherine Bain, who now lives in Strathroy. Donna Brock married George Walker of Adelaide (see WALKER, Robert and Margaret). William and his wife moved to Port Arthur. Arthur Gourley (1880-1963) married Mary Freele (1881-1965), daughter of Thomas and Eliza Freele of Adelaide. Their three children were born in Adelaide, Clifford, Laila and Thomas Neil. Alice Jemima (1882, died an infant) was the fifth child of Arthur and Esther. Annie Marie (1883-ca.1963) married Frederick Ingham (1884-1916) and moved to Alberta, where Fred worked for the railroad. After his accidental death on the railroad, Annie returned to Strathroy where a daughter, Lillian Freddie Ingham (1917-1990) was born after the tragedy. Freddie married Fraser Galbraith (1912-1988) of Adelaide. They had two daughters. Ellen married Charles Feddema of Adelaide, and Jane Anne married Allen Delmage Dowding of Adelaide. Esther Brock (1885-1956) married William Brent (1880-1965). They farmed on the west half of Lot 8, Con. 1 NER.

Isabella Brock (1845), fifth child of George Sr. and Isabella, married neighbour O'Callaghan Charles Holmes and they farmed the east half of Lot 14, Con. 1 SER. Their children were Ellen Jane (1867); Emma Margaret (1873); Florence (1876), who married neighbour Frank Nichol (see NICHOL, Edward and Maria); Ida Almira (1879); Charles (1882); and Robert Lorne (1855). The Holmes family was hit hard by the diphtheria outbreak, which ravaged Adelaide in the late 1800s. The two oldest Holmes daughters died of the disease in February 1878.

Anne "Annie" Brock (1845-1887) married her first cousin, Robert Brock, and they lived in Enniskillen Township.

Jemima Brock (ca.1849) married Charles Sifton (see SIFTON).

George Brock Jr. (1851-1927) married Nancy "Annie" Mitchell (1857-1936) of Parkhill in 1881.

They had three children, Harold, Tyler Burton (died a baby), and Russell George. The little frame house on the west half of Lot 17, Con. 1 NER, was replaced by the huge brick house built about 1885, which cost $1,100 to build and still stands. George may have drawn up the plans, as he was very gifted in working with wood. He made a couch and a child's rocking chair, which are still in the family. The first American barn he built was raised on a foundation of stones brought from the McCabe farm on Lot 16, Con. 2 NER. The stonemason was Archie McNab. George Jr. was a busy man who combined farming with cattle buying, and he was also a Director of the East Williams Fire Insurance Company. The story is told that, since the company was owned by four Scottish men, "...they needed an Irishman for levity." As Russell grew old enough to take over the farming responsibilities, George Jr. retired to a house in Strathroy until his new house at 53 Caradoc St. was built. When Russell later retired, he lived in this home.

Harold (1882-1956), the eldest child of George Jr. and Annie, was born in the original frame house when the family arrived from Quebec. This house was made into a stable when the brick house was built. Harold started school at S.S. #10, which was then on the northwest corner of Lot 19, Con. 1 NER (Martin van Geffen's farm today). An old photograph shows it as a huge, brick, box-like building with chimneys at each end. The new school site was selected farther west as S.S. #12 in Adelaide Village was discontinued. The new site on Lot 17, Con. 1 SER was considered more convenient for children coming from the west. Harold told stories of the boys going into the woods in the spring during the noon-hour, picking leeks and bringing them back to share with their friends. One day, they reeked so strongly from the odour of leeks that their inexperienced teacher sent everyone home. We may wonder how many times they tried that trick to get a holiday!

When farm work slackened in the winter, Harold and other farmers worked at logging. With Rupert McNab, Wilbert Hodgson and Archie McNab (who later immigrated to western Canada), Harold logged the 200 acres bordering the Ausable River in West Williams Township, where the Nethercott farm is today. Another winter, he got work logging near Durham.

Harold married neighbour Maude Robotham in February 1906. They went to Enniskillen and bought a farm two miles south of Petrolia. Maude told that the roads were so muddy then, they would have to stop to dig the mud out of the buggy and wagon wheels. At times, Maude was so homesick for her large family (see ROBOTHAM, George and Margaret) that she would often go and sit in the milk house and cry where no one would see her. One day, she and son George were going to visit her parents and Uncle Russ Brock. Before they got to Wyoming, a car passed them. George said, "If we had a car like that, we'd be there in no time." A short time later, they came upon the stopped car and the driver was fixing a flat tire. They passed this car quite a few times on their way to Adelaide. The cord tires were narrow and the tube was pinched by the rim. When the Brocks arrived at Russell's on Egremont Road and had finished putting the horses in the stable, the once-envied car drove past the laneway.

George Brock Jr. (1855-1927) with Nancy (Annie) Mitchell (1857-1936), married January 1881.

Harold and Maude's children were George (1907); Ella (1909); Doug (1916); and Ray (1918). George died at age 12 after a tonsillectomy.

Doug left the farm and worked for the White Rose Oil Company, married Marie Wilson, and raised their family in Arkona (see WILSON, Samuel and Rebecca).

Ray came to Adelaide and took over the Charles Kerswell farm, the west half of Lot 5, Con. 1 SER, in the spring of 1938. He tried growing flax, which netted $25 an acre on 15 acres. He planted wheat and oats, and grazed cattle. Ray "batched" there in the summer for two years. In winter, he trucked the cattle to the Enniskillen farm and helped his father and brother with the farm work. Harold and Maude came to live on the property in 1940. Ray then had time to become active in community events and thus he met and married Donelda Jean Wilson (see Ray Brock).

Russell Brock (1887-1970) was a general insurance agent as well as a farmer. The story of how he met his future wife is interesting. Russell had injured his hand and was having trouble untying his horse from the hitching post in front of Butler's Department store. The Brown's daughter, Eva Marie, saw Russell struggling with the reins and she gave him a hand. He offered her a ride and the rest, as the saying goes, "is history." The Brown's dairy on Lot 20, Con. 5 SER, was home to Eva, daughter of Joseph and Rachel (Whiting) Brown. The Brocks enjoyed dancing and they were regulars at local dances.

Russell and Eva (1894-1974) had two daughters, Marjorie R. and Anna E. Marjorie became a teacher and taught at S.S. #10 Adelaide from 1935 to 1941. During that time, she was paid about $400 a year. She married Wilfred Sinclair and they live in Mississauga. Anna graduated from Strathroy General Hospital in 1942. She was a member of the second last class to receive Registered Nursing training from the hospital. Anna married Capt. Gordon Brent (1918-1987) whom she had met at school. Gordon was a career officer who served in WWII and the Korean War. They lived in Ottawa where they raised two children, Daniel and Paul. After Gordon retired from the service, the Brents relocated to the house Anna's grandfather had built on Caradoc St. in Strathroy. Dan Brent lives in Adelaide on his grandfather Brent's farm, the west half of Lot 7, Con. 1 NER, and he has two sons, Stacy and Tyler. Paul Brent is the Assignment Editor for CTV in Ottawa.

Richard "Dick" Brock (1853-1943) was a baby when the family made their exodus from Quebec. He was too young to have learned any French but it is remembered by the family that he had "the gift of gab." At an early age, he honed his ease of meeting people, and speaking, into a career as an auctioneer. A well-to-do neighbouring farmer was selling out, and he was concerned about the financial outcome of his sale because the usual auctioneer had "alcoholic tendencies." He went to young Dick and asked him to conduct his auction. George Jr. told his grandson, Ray Brock, about Dick practising his technique and lingo in the barn. His father would hold up a chicken and Dick would describe it and launch into his patter. This neighbour, who was well established, was able to procure auctioneer papers for Dick.

At age 18, Dick left the farm and began working in the oil business as a teamster, drawing oil from Bothwell to Petrolia. All the old Brocks were said to be good horsemen. Dick carried three barrels of oil on a stone boat and, when the mud was too deep for the load, he would roll the third barrel across to lessen the weight. He carried on with this work for a short time until he got the opportunity to go to South America to drill for oil. This was quite appealing, as the wages were high and many men came back after a few years with enough money to retire. Of course, there were the dangers of foreign drilling: malaria, disease and foul play. His father, George, didn't think much of this venture so he gave son Richard part of the home farm, the east half of Lot 13, Con. 1 SER, to encourage him to stay home and settle down. Richard married Harriet "Hattie" Ingham (see INGHAM, Samuel and Elizabeth), a sister of Maria Ingham who married Ed Nichol, a neighbour on the west half of Lot 15, Con. 1 SER.

Richard and Hattie had three children, Gertrude (ca.1883-1960); Melvyn Ingham (1885-1964); and Frank (1888). Stories are told of good times at Richard and Hattie's home on the Egremont Road. Hattie played the organ and Richard the violin. He was always on call to provide music at the local dances. The neighbours and relatives would drop in for euchre games. When the deck of cards couldn't be found, the blame usually fell on Hattie's visiting sister, Mary Jane "Jennie" Ingham (later married to

Ed McInroy), who was known to throw the "devil's toys" into the fire. Everyone laughed about it, then chipped in and sent somebody up to the village store to buy another deck! Richard was an active member of the Adelaide Village Orange Lodge.

Gertrude married David Moore and they farmed in Metcalfe and Enniskillen. Their son, Robert Moore, served in WWII. Melvyn and his wife, Olive Brooks, took over the farm. Two daughters were born, Merle and Muriel. Hattie and Richard moved to Watford, where he opened a farm machinery business. Melvyn later left the farm and went to London, where he became a successful insurance salesman. Frank had a banking career in Toronto.

In later years, Richard bought the west half of Lot 14, Con. 1 NER, and grazed cattle there. This was the former John Radcliffe property that was named "Oakdale Park" because of the stately oaks in front of the two-story, white frame house, which had an interesting roofline and a veranda across the front. After Hattie's death, Richard lived with his daughter in London and came out to spend the summer months in the Adelaide house. His "boys' parties" and "girls' parties" were fun and mentioned to this day. Myrtle (Branton) Akins tells that he would put up a swing in the front yard and serve ice cream to the boys and girls.

Maria Brock (1857-1949), the first Brock child born in Adelaide, married William Conkey (1848-1916). William's sister, Esther, married Maria's brother, Arthur Brock. All nine children born on the Adelaide farm moved with them in 1907 to Maymont, Saskatchewan.

Albert Brock (1859-1930) was the youngest Brock child. Albert was a man of many talents and he combined farming and cattle buying. He and his wife, Annie Barrett (1862-1944) lived on the home farm, the west half of Lot 13, Con. 1 SER (see BARRETT, Richard and Louisa). They later lived on the west half of Lot 10, Con. 1 SER, which Albert bought from his brother-in-law, Fred Barrett, who moved to British Columbia. Albert would drive his cattle by horseback to Kerwood, where they were loaded on railroad cars and shipped to the markets in Toronto, Detroit and Buffalo. Albert purchased five farms in Adelaide. He put an acetylene carbide lighting system in the house before installing hydro in 1930. They had two sons, Chauncey Howard (1882-1949) and Manfred Barrett (1887-1961).

Howard, the elder son of Albert and Annie Brock, and his brother farmed together for several years. In 1921, he married Sarah Lancaster (1885-1947), who clerked at the village store. She had come to Canada in 1911 from Appleby, England, with her two brothers. They lived in Saskatchewan and then Manitoba, and when war was declared in 1914, her brothers joined the Canadian Army and Sarah moved to Ontario.

Howard bought the store from John Muxlow. He delivered groceries and bought butter and eggs at local farms to sell in the store. Howard owned one of the first cars, including a Hupmobile, before permits were issued. A fire destroyed the store and house in 1924. He then went into the cattle business with his father. In 1927, Howard, Sarah, and their daughter, Dora, moved in with Howard's parents. After his father's death, Howard and Fred Brent bought cattle together for some years. Howard developed diabetes and was one of the first to benefit from the discovery of insulin. Both Sarah and Howard are buried in St. Ann's Cemetery.

Dora was born in the Strathroy Hospital in 1925. She attended S. S. #6 Adelaide, Strathroy Collegiate Institute, and H.B. Beal Technical School in London. In 1942, she married Andy Aitken (1917), son of John and Louisa (Waun) Aitken of Warwick. She worked in the office at National Grocers, a wholesale company in London, while Andy was overseas with the R.C.A.F. after July 1942. When Andy received his discharge in June, 1945, he and his brother, Jack, bought the Watford Grain Elevator and Mill from Andrew Hay. After three months, Andy bought Jack's share and he continued as owner and operator for seven years, with Dora keeping the books. They lived with Dora's parents. Their children are Barbara (1950) and Alan (1953). Andy built the barn and commenced farming in 1952 after selling the mill.

Barbara and Alan attended S.S. #10 Adelaide until the Adelaide Central School opened in January 1960. S.S. #10 was the same school where their grandfather, Howard Brock, had attended. Barbara and Alan both attended S.D.C.I. Barbara attended Teachers' College in London and began teaching at Hannah Memorial in Sarnia. She married Holger Peters, a Sarnia teacher, in 1972. They have three daughters, Sandra, Sara and Jennifer.

Alan attended the University of Guelph before commencing farming. In 1979, he married Catharin

Pety, a nurse from Tillsonburg, and bought the west half of Lot 10, Con. 1 SER, from his parents. They have two daughters, Heather and Kelly.

Andy and Dora built a new home at the east half of Lot 10 and moved into it on January 31, 1979. The next year Andy discovered golf, and joined Strathroy Golf Course.

Manfred, the younger son of Albert and Annie Brock, married Leda Fortner in 1909, and they had one son, Stanley James (1913). They left the Brock farm in 1925 and moved to Detroit until 1947, where they owned and operated a grocery store. They then lived at Silver Lake near Pontiac, Michigan, and finally retired to Florida.

Stanley married Lucille Thomas in 1941. They had two sons, Thomas (1943) and James (1945), who was killed in the Vietnam War. Tom married Ruth Darin in 1977 and they have two sons, David (1979) and Michael (1981). They live in Dearborn, where Tom is a police officer and Ruth is a teacher.

BROCK, Ray and Donelda

In 1942, Ray Brock married Donelda Jean Wilson (1923), the daughter of John David Wilson and Estelle Margaret Thomson.

Ray grew up in Enniskillen Township and attended a one-room red brick school before coming to Adelaide, where Donelda lived. Donelda's education concluded with Grade Eight. Her teachers were Margaret Bolton (Walpole) and Hattie Brown (Ball). Donelda's parents were both teachers.

Ray and Donelda bought a farm at the west half of Lot 5, Con. 1 SER, from Harold T. Brock, Ray's father, for a small sum. In March 1943, the house burned to the ground. Ray recalls it was probably the worst year of his life. At that time, in order to help with groceries, Ray and Donelda had been boarding the local schoolteacher, Beth Letherland, for $5 a week. When the fire broke out on that fateful day, she was resting in her bedroom. She jumped when the scream of "FIRE!" was sounded. She grabbed an armful of her things and ran to the front door. Donelda remembers that some underwear caught on the doorknob and, as she quickly detached them in her hurry to evacuate, paints fell from a school paint box and scattered.

Ray and Donelda received $1,000 insurance money, which Ray kept pinned inside his pocket, until the couple purchased a house from W.J. McChesney. The house was moved down the road and settled on a foundation that the neighbours helped dig with horses and scoop shovels. Donelda remembers the moving day well. With the help of Freda McChesney and Eileen Campbell, the women fed 100 men; it was like the parable of the loaves and fishes.

While the basement was being dug, Ray was deep in conversation with a dealer looking for a quick buck. In the meantime, the old horse, Jinny, ate a hole in the roof of their 1930 Pontiac, which had an upholstered top. The car was retired shortly after; roof or not, there was no money for gas.

However, once a roof was over their heads and the house was scrubbed clean, with a wood fire in the stove and a coal-oil lamp polished and lit, spreading its soft glow, the promise of a new home was heartening. This house still stands there.

Two children were born to Ray and Donelda. Richard Raymond lives in Kitchener, and Nancy Jean resides in Williams Lake, British Columbia. Ray and Donelda also have five granddaughters and one grandson.

BROOKS, Hugh and Elizabeth

Hugh Brooks (d.1871) and Elizabeth Jones were married in the chapel of Challacombe, south Moulton, in North Devon in December 1842. Hugh was in the employ of Lord Palmiter, and the Brooks family had lived in one of the buildings on Palmiter's Little Bray Estate. In April 1868 they left for Canada from Liverpool aboard the steamship "Belgium," which landed in Portland, Maine. Hugh and Elizabeth had with them 10 of their 11 children, John (1845-1845); Hugh Southwood (1848); Eliza (1850), whose husband William Paddison came with the family; Elizabeth (1852); William (1852); Thomas (1857); David (1859); Ellen Grace (1862); Harriet (1864); and Isaac (1866). Their eldest daughter, Mary Ann (1843), came to Canada the following year with her husband, George Sanders.

Before the Brooks family embarked, a salesman persuaded them to buy guns, telling them that Canadian law required all adult males to own firearms as protection against wild animals. He also induced them to buy leather leggings to protect them from biting snakes.

After landing in Portland, the family came to London, Ontario, by the Great Western Railway. They were dropped off on a Saturday afternoon at the corner of Burwell Street and Hamilton Road. Not knowing what else to do, they walked eastward along Hamilton Road for about a mile, carrying all their possessions. They stopped when they came to a vacant house on the north side of the road just west of Rectory Street. They decided that this was as good a place as any to spend the night, so they went inside while Hugh and some of the boys went off to find some furniture. They made some purchases on Dundas Street and settled in. On Monday, the owner of the building discovered the new occupants and agreed to take them on as tenants.

Hugh found work in the brickyards in South London and the family moved to a more suitable home on Brick Street. Later, they moved to Talbotville, where the men found work on farms. They lived in a house just north of the school, which the children attended when they were not working.

Once, while tending the fields, Hugh suffered sunstroke. That night he became worse, so Elizabeth walked about three miles to fetch Dr. Van Buskirk from St. Thomas. He rode on horseback to tend to the patient while Elizabeth walked first to the store to buy leeches and then home. The doctor placed the leeches on Hugh's neck and, after they were filled with blood, immersed them in salt water. This flushed out the blood so that they could be used again. Such was the practice of medicine in southern Ontario at the time. Hugh died on October 11, 1871, at the age of 50, and was buried in the cemetery at Talbotville.

Following her husband's death, Elizabeth moved to Con. 2 in Westminster Township in order to live close to her son, Tom. Several years later, she married John Pincombe. After his death, she made her home in Adelaide Village with her son, William, until she passed away in 1904. William was the first to move to Adelaide. He married Jane Ings and they had one son, Roy. Roy married Maud Ings and they had two daughters, Viola and Gertrude.

Most of William's brothers and sisters made their homes in other locales. John married M.A. Hutchen, and later died in a logging accident in Muskoka, in 1892. Ellen died in a farm accident at the age of 11 and was buried in Talbotville near her father. Mary Ann and her husband had no children, and she is buried in the Strathroy Cemetery. David Jones married Emily Head, Harriet married John Foster, and Isaac married Sarah Vanstone. Elizabeth married Edwin Campbell, Thomas married Jenny Foster, and Eliza and her husband, William Paddison, also moved away.

William's brother, Hugh, came to Adelaide. He married twice, first to Louise Pincombe and then to Jessie Ladell. Hugh and Louise had four sons, David Richard, Malcom, John and George, and one daughter, Blanche. David died young. Malcom married Ella Zavitz. John married twice, first to Emma Harten, with whom he had one child, and then to Nellie Schwartz, with whom he had four more. George married Bertha Campbell in 1912. They had four children who went to S.S. #6 Adelaide, and 11 grandchildren. Blanche (d.1964) married Robert Ball (d.1953) when she was 18 years old. They had five children. Two of them, George and R. Hugh, stayed in Adelaide.

BROOKS, Mike and Veryle

Milo (Mike) Edwin Brooks (1903-1977) was born in Thedford, Ontario. At the age of 15 he was working on the farm of his grandfather, Jim, in Keyser. He worked from 1920 to 1923 for James Wilson at the Forest Creamery, assisting in all departments. From May to October 1923, Mike worked for Ambrose Topping at Keyser, doing general farm work.

In 1924, Mike attended a dairy short course at the Ontario Agricultural College in Guelph. He was hired as head butter maker at the Kerwood Creamery on April 1, 1924. In 1927, he was promoted to plant superintendent in charge of plant employment and production. Carnation Milk Company bought the plant in 1941 and Mike was the plant manager until his retirement in 1968.

On April 18, 1928, Mike married Veryle Anna Gast (1909-1983), daughter of Elmer and Sarah Gast. Veryle came to Canada in 1917 from Elkhart, Indiana, with her parents and siblings.

Mike and Veryle resided in Kerwood, where they raised their family of four sons and two daughters, Edith, Robert, William, Marjorie, Richard and Joseph.

They were both very active in the village. Mike was the first Fire Chief of Adelaide Metcalfe Fire

Department in 1965. He also served as a village trustee for many years. They were members of Kerwood-Bethesda United Church. Veryle was a member of the choir, taught Sunday School, and was a member of various committees. She was also a member of the Rebeccah Lodge IOOF.

Mike's hobbies included repairing lawnmowers, especially powered ones, bicycles, and any small appliances. He was very handy as a plumber and carpenter, and at any other job that needed to be done. Mike always believed that no job was too big or too small and he was able to make things work most of the time, even if he had to make a part himself. He was seldom seen without his familiar pipe or cigar in his mouth.

Veryle was busy raising the family and running the household. She had many hobbies, including sewing, knitting, crocheting and other handiwork. Later, she enjoyed ceramics, oil painting, and listening to sports on the radio and television as well as attending hockey and baseball games with Mike.

Mike and Veryle especially enjoyed having their grandchildren visit. Mike always made sure there was a bike for them to ride and Veryle made sure the cookie jar was full.

BROTHERS

According to family tradition, the early Brothers families were Huguenots, who fled from France to England around the time of the Reformation. George Brothers (1803-1877) was born in Wiltshire County, England. In 1850, in Warminster, Wiltshire County, England, George married Mary Ann Harris (1816-1871), who was born in Westbury, Wiltshire County, England, daughter of Samuel Harris and Ann Nightingale.

They came to Canada in 1855. The 1861 census showed that George and his family were living in a one-story log house beside Mary Ann's father and brother, Samuel Harris and Thomas Harris, on Samuel's property, Lot 12, Con. 3 SER. Notes written by Leo Harris show that John Harris sold 50 acres, being the east half of Lot 7, Con. 2 SER to George Brothers. George sold this property in 1868 to James Dowding. The 1878 Middlesex County Atlas showed George and his family living on 35 acres, being the center third of Lot 12, Con 3 SER. They were members of the Church of England and were buried in St. Ann's Anglican Cemetery. They had four children, all except the last child born in England, Sarah (1851), Mary Ann (1853-ca.1928), George Edwin (1855-1928), and Mary (1860).

Sarah married George Adams.

Mary Ann married John Edmond Down (1852-1904) in 1876. John was born in Adelaide, son of George Down and Celia Weeks of Adelaide Township. They lived in Sarnia, where John was a foreman at Laughead's hub and spoke factory. John's clothes got caught in the revolving machinery while oiling the shaft. He was severely injured and died the next morning. In 1928, Mary Ann was living in Detroit, likely with one of her children. Mary Ann and John Edmond Down had three children, William H., George, and a daughter, whose name is unknown.

George Edwin, third issue of George and Mary Ann, married Mary Stacey (1860-1938), born near Toronto. The 1878 Middlesex Atlas shows that George Edwin resided on the family farm. Later, the family moved to Strathroy. George was an employee in the finishing department of the Strathroy Furniture Company. George and Mary were buried in Strathroy Cemetery. Their nine children, some of whom were born in Adelaide Township, were George M., Martin Edwin, Emily Laura, John, Stella May, Flossia, Frederick, Richard "Roy," and Vera Mae.

George M. (1877-1910) married Francis "Fanny" Roberts (1873-1958). They lived and were buried in Strathroy. George worked for the Strathroy Furniture Factory. They had a family of four children. Fanny later married George's brother, Martin.

Martin Edwin (1880-1958) was born in Adelaide Township. He first married Jeannette Haight (1882-1913), and secondly, his brother George's widow, Fanny Roberts. Martin had one son, James, by his first wife, and three stepchildren, Mrs. William Broomfield, Mrs. Albert E. Smith, and Wesley Brothers. Martin, Jeannette and Fanny lived in Strathroy and were buried in Strathroy Cemetery.

Emily Laura (1883-ca.1971) married Justin Jefferson Davis from Toledo. They lived in Detroit and Strathroy.

John (1885-1934) resided in Detroit.

Stella May (1887-1930) married William F.

Cooper (1881-1955). They lived in Strathroy, Mt. Brydges and London. Stella and William Cooper were buried in Strathroy Cemetery.

Flossia (1891-1967) married George E. Root (1869-1957) in 1916. They had a large family and lived in Strathroy and Mt. Brydges. Flossie and George were buried in Mt. Brydges.

Frederick (1894-1905) was killed in a hunting accident.

Richard "Roy" (1897-1971) married Helen "Ella" May Mills (1899-1971), daughter of William Daniel Mills and Ida Melissa Withers. Richard was in the Army and was badly wounded. Richard and Ella lived in Strathroy and had two sons. George William Brothers (1929) married Velma Irene Stewart (1923-1987) in 1956. They had one son. James "Jim" Richard Brothers (1958) married Elizabeth Ruth Shea (1958) in 1981. They have two daughters, Sarah Elizabeth (1982) and Nicole Ashleigh (1985). George and Jim own and operate Twin Elm Estates, a mobile home Park in Strathroy. Donald Roy Brothers (1933) married Edna Murray. Don was employed by Twin Elm Estates. Don and Edna live in Strathroy and have three children, Judy, Brian and Paul. Judy and family live in Prince Edward Island. Brian (1959) married Peggy Reason (1960) and they have two daughters, Amanda (1980) and Brianne (1983). Brian owns and operates Hy-Way Collision Ltd. on Highway 22 in Adelaide Township. Paul lives in Strathroy.

Vera Mae Brothers (1900-1963), youngest child of George Edwin and Mary, married Calvin Heard. They had a large family and lived in Detroit.

Mary, the last child of George and Mary Ann, was born in Adelaide Township, but died before the 1861 census.

BROWN, Allan and Mary Ellen

Allan James "A.J." Brown (d.1957) and Mary Ellen Noble (d.1976) from Lobo Township were married February 23, 1938, at the Ivan United Church manse. They took possession of the farm at Lot 16, Con. 4 SER, on March 1, 1938. The farm was located approximately two miles west of Strathroy on old Highway 22. Patricia (1940) was born at St. Joseph's Hospital in London. Carolyn (1942) was born two years later. James (1945) was born at Strathroy Hospital, rounding out their family of three.

Allan Brown family, August 1947.

Mixed farming was their forte with a large herd of dairy cows. In the spring of 1951, an additional 100 acres was purchased directly behind the home farm and facing the Second Line North.

Allan served for several years as an elected representative on the Adelaide Public School Board. He and Mary were also charter members of the first Farm Forum group in the area.

Mary was an active member of the Women's Institute. The family attended the United Church in Strathroy. All of the children attended S.S. #5 Adelaide Township Public School and later, Strathroy District Collegiate Institute.

In August 1957, a tragic farm accident claimed Allan's life. The farm was sold in October of that year and the family moved to Strathroy. Mary passed away in November 1976.

Pat moved to Windsor to become a nurse. There, she met her future husband, a high school teacher. They now live in Paris, Ontario, and have two daughters, two sons and grandchildren.

Carolyn attended Wells Business in London and has had a long and colourful career in varying businesses across Canada. She is married to a supervisor of a gold mine. Their home in Kimberly, British Columbia, is central to numerous stepchildren and stepgrandchildren.

Jim has operated his own truck service in Mt. Brydges since the fall of 1972. Racing a supermodified Indy-type car has been his obsession for many years, both in Canada and the United States. He is married to Joanne, a former Caradoc Township farmer's daughter. They reside in Landsdowne Park near Komoka. Together, they have three sons and one daughter.

BROWN, Gerald and Patricia

Gerald and Patricia Brown and family moved from London to their farm on the Second Line North in August 1971. The Con. 2 NER farm was formerly owned by Ken George. For Patricia, it was a return to familiar surroundings, having been raised in Adelaide Township, the daughter of Ed and Cecelia Healy, one of the pioneer families in the township.

Soon after buying the farm, a commercial cow herd was started and, in 1979, the Balador Farm purebred polled Simmental herd was established. Involvement with Simmentals resulted in Gerald becoming a life member of the Canadian Simmental Association, as well as the Ontario Association and the Southwestern Ontario Simmental Club. The herd was dispersed in 1993.

Gerald and Patricia have four children, Chris, David, Cathy and Paul. Chris is a graduate of Brock University with a BA in Business. He and his wife, Corinna, and son, Alex, live in Strathroy. David has his BA and MA in Communications from the University of Windsor and is now at Wayne State University for his PhD. Cathy is following her mother and grandmother Healy in the nursing profession. She lives in London and works at Marian Villa. Paul attended Huron College for his BA in History and the University of Western Ontario for an MA in History. He also graduated from the University of Windsor with a B. Ed degree.

Since moving to the farm, Patricia has worked as a nurse at the Strathroy Middlesex General Hospital. She also participated in the Palliative Care activities on the fourth floor at the hospital. She retired at the end of 1997. For many years, Patricia has been a member of the Catholic Women's League of All Saints Parish and has held numerous offices in the organization.

Gerald was briefly involved in local politics and for the years 1979-1982 was a member of the Adelaide Township Council.

Gerald and Patricia are both busy in retirement. Gerald raises and shows his Silver Laced Wyandotte bantams, and Patricia occupies herself working in her gardens, and doing volunteer work.

BROWN, James and Jane

The first of the Brown family to own land in Adelaide Township was James Brown (1834-1891), native of Cumberland County, England. The first Brown resident born in Adelaide Township was his eldest son, Thomas.

As a young man, James worked for several years in the gold fields of Australia. When he proceeded to Canada, his efforts in the gold fields provided the means for him to buy a farm with some improvements rather than rough bush land. In 1862, he purchased 100 acres located at Lot 6, Con. 7, West Williams Township. At the time, the property had 21 acres cleared for cultivation, with a log house and small barn.

By 1883, James had purchased the 50-acre farm adjoining his holdings. By 1886, James had cleared 90 acres of the 150.

In 1864, James built a new barn and a timber frame house to replace the original buildings. The census roll of 1891 shows the Brown family living in a 2-storey brick house of 13 rooms.

About one mile north of the Brown farm was the family of Donald and Ann (Lamont) McLeish, who came from Scotland in 1861. In 1863, James Brown took as his bride the second McLeish daughter, Jane (1839-1917).

Although the Brown and McLeish families lived in West Williams Township, they seem to have had "an Adelaide feeling." This was probably because their farms looked across the road to Adelaide, and many of their nearest neighbours lived in the township. They shopped in Adelaide Village or Strathroy and attended churches in Adelaide (St. Ann's Anglican in Adelaide Village and West Adelaide Presbyterian).

On March 22, 1888, James purchased the first Brown farm in Adelaide Township, situated at the

Tom and Melissa (O'Neil) Brown, wedding picture ca.1892.

west half of Lot 8, Con. 4 NER. James and Jane are both buried in Arkona Cemetery.

Upon his father's death, the oldest child, Thomas (1864-1938), inherited the Adelaide farm with the payment of $2,000 to the estate. About this time, Thomas married Melissa O'Neil (1870-1955), younger daughter of William O'Neil and Mary Fraser.

About 1900, Thomas built a new barn on the property. He built a new house about five years later. He must have built them well, for both buildings were still in use in 1994. The house has had no major changes to the interior in 90 years.

In April 1910, Thomas purchased Lot 15, Con. 8 in West Williams from his father-in-law, William O'Neil. This lot contained 85 acres. The estate of Thomas Brown sold this farm to Jack and Vivian Nethercott on January 5, 1955. Since Vivian Nethercott is a first cousin twice removed to Thomas, it may be said that this farm has remained in the O'Neil/Brown/McLeish family for 135 years as of 1994.

Sometime early in this century, Thomas Brown bought the east half of Lot 8, Con. 4 NER, Adelaide Township, which adjoined his farm to the east. This brought his holdings in the township to 200 acres.

Thomas and Melissa had two daughters, Mary Evelyn (1894-1972) and Margaret Winnifred (1899).

Mary married Munroe Fletcher (d.1966) of Adelaide Township on December 20, 1916. They lived all of their married life in Adelaide. Both are buried in the Arkona Cemetery. Mary and Munroe had one daughter, Evelyn Winnifred (d.1995, see FLETCHER, Donald and Annie).

Winnifred "Winnie" married Earl McInroy (d.1956) on October 20, 1920. During their married life, they lived in Adelaide Township. Earl is buried in Strathroy Cemetery. After his death, Winnie moved to London, where she resided at the time of her death. Earl and Winnie had one son, Keith (see McINROY, Alexander and Ann Jane).

Thomas Brown died in London at 74 years of age. Melissa O'Neil Brown died at 85 years at the home of her son-in-law, Munroe Fletcher. Thomas and Melissa are buried in the Arkona Cemetery.

The Brown farms in Adelaide Township have all been sold out of the family by the estate of Thomas Brown.

BROWN, John

John Brown (1805-1887) came from England in 1832 and settled in Adelaide Township, on the east half of Lot 9, Con. 3 SER. According to some records, he was married twice, since two wives are mentioned. He had five living children, Fanny (1835); John (1839); Joseph (1845-1932); Martha (1846); and Benjamin (1848).

Joseph married Sarah Gott (1849-1930) in 1871 in Sarnia and lived on the same farm as his father. Joseph and Sarah's five children were George Wesley (1872-1948); Wilbur Cecil (1876-1934); Olive Louise (1880-1965); Russell Louis Curtis (1884-1966); and Alma Augusta (1889-1961). Some stayed in the Adelaide area to farm.

Russell Louis Curtis Brown married Alma Ogilvie Knight (1884-1953) of Katesville in 1906. Russell and Alma had six children with four living, Raymond Arnold (1910-1991); Maurice Alexander (1914-1992); Everett Claire (1915-1970); and Kathleen Russell (1917-1996).

Russell remained in Adelaide Township throughout his life as a farmer. He and Alma lived for a short time on the Second Line of Adelaide but soon traded homes with his brother, George, and then resided with his parents on the home farm at Lot 9, Con. 3 SER. The house, which is still standing, was built by Joseph Brown in 1902, and the barn was built in 1906.

Raymond Brown married Ellen Gertrude Muma and they had three children, Vernon, Renita and Ronald. Raymond ran a garage on the Second Line until a fire destroyed it, and they moved to Highway 22 where his sons now run the garage.

Vernon Brown married Jill Crabbe in 1960 and they have two sons, Terry Andrew (1963) and Philip Wayne (1964). Both boys are married and have families.

Renita Brown married Charles S.T. Seed in 1958. They had four children, Christine Diane (1959-1960); Gwendolyn "Wendy" Lorraine (1960); Charles "Chuck" Frederick Raymond (1962); and Kimberly Michele (1963). Wendy lives in Toronto, and Chuck lives with his father. Kim is married to Ross Herrington and has a son, Donald.

Maurice Brown, second son of Russell and Alma, married Grace Emlin Freele (1917-1969) in 1939. Maurice and Grace had four sons, Cecil Frederick (1942); Jack Maurice (1947); Stuart Arnold (1948); and Glen Douglas (1951). Maurice and Grace farmed the home place, which has been in the family since 1832. Today, their second son, Jack, is farming the land.

Cecil married Winnifred M. Garrod (1941) in 1964 in Kerwood. They bought the Oliver Harris farm, the east half of Lot 8, Con. 3 SER. They have two daughters, Karen Grace (1970) and Deanna Lynn (1973). Karen married William Russel Clark (1968) from Petrolia in 1993. Bill and Karen have two sons, Todd William (1994) and Justin Robert (1997). They live in Petrolia. Deanna works and lives in Strathroy.

Jack married Diane I. Hall (1949) in 1971 in Brooke Township, Lambton County. Jack and Diane have three children, Michael Jack (1974); Paul Maurice (1976); and Sandra Diane (1979). All of their children live at home.

Stuart married Linda E. Daubs (1951) in 1973 in Strathroy. They have one chosen daughter, Caroline Dawn (1977). Stuart and Linda farm on the Second Line South of Adelaide.

Glen married Donna Richardson (1950) in 1971 at Kerwood. They have two sons, Glen Ryan (1976) and Randy Douglas (1978). They live on the Second Line South of Adelaide. Ryan married Sara Schyff (1973) in 1997 in Strathroy.

Everett Claire Brown, third issue of Russell and Alma, married Lillian Rozell and had two daughters, Elizabeth Louise (1938) and Patricia Ann (1940). Both girls are married and have families.

Kathleen married Robert Raymond Morgan (1916-1991) of Metcalfe Township on December 16, 1938, in Strathroy. Robert and Kathleen farmed in Metcalfe Township at Lot 10, Con. 2, growing crops, milking cows, and also tending to sheep, beef cattle, pigs and laying hens. Robert and Kathleen had three sons, Robert McIntyre (1942); Clayton Russell (1946); Evan Eugene (1947); and one daughter, Margaret Anne (1958).

The eldest son, Robert, married Dawna Aitchison of Lucknow in 1966, and owns a farm on the west half of Lot 9, Con. 2, in Metcalfe Township.

Clayton entered the banking trade for a time, married Janet Carroll of Strathroy, and then worked in automotive manufacturing and on the railroad before returning home to farm. They have five children.

Evan moved to Strathroy and married Myrna Kinsman. They have two children.

Margaret graduated from Fanshawe College as a Developmental Service Worker and worked in that field until she and her husband, Earl Salter, had their first of two children in Goderich, Ontario.

BROWNE, Matt and Lily

Son of James Brown (1834-1891) and Jane McLeish (1840-1917), James Matthews "Matt" (1875-1950) was born in West Williams Township and grew up in that area. He married Lillian "Lily" Elizabeth McChesney, daughter of David and Agnes Ann (Shields) McChesney on August 15, 1906. They were married at the family farm, on the east half of Lot 4, Con. 1 SER.

They farmed for approximately 10 years in West Williams Township before purchasing the McChesney home farm about 1915. Their family, Dorothy (Mrs. Clayton Beverly Morgan Carrothers); James David; Lillian Isobell; and Gordon were all born in West Williams Township.

The David McChesney farm was located at Lot 4, Con. 1 SER. Shortly after, James Brown purchased the Cleland farm at the west half of Lot 4, Con. 1 NER, and 38 acres that were part of the east and west half of Lot 4, creating a 100-acre parcel of land.

In 1919, he sold the Lot 4 home farm and moved to his mother-in-law's farm on the west side of Rapley Street in Strathroy. Agnes Ann McChesney purchased a house and lot almost directly opposite, on the east side of Rapley Street.

Matt and Lily resided on the Rapley Street property until Matt's death. Lily remained a few years, then sold the property and purchased a smaller house on Oxford St. in Strathroy.

The Adelaide property was sold out of the family by Matt's executors on April 21, 1954, to Mr. George Lothian, ending ties to the township for the family of James Matthew Browne.

BUCHANAN, John Stewart and Mabel

James Buchanan (1772-1851), the eldest of John Buchanan and Sarah Sproule's seven children, was born near Omagh, County Tyrone, Ireland, on the family estate, Strathroy. The word means "red valley." In 1798, he married Elizabeth Clark (1779) of Dublin. James became the British Consul in New York City in 1816 or 1819, a post he held until 1843. Following his retirement, he moved to Niagara Falls,

James Buchanan

where he continued to manage his numerous business interests.

James' eleventh child, John Stewart (1815-1875), was one of the founding settlers of Strathroy, Ontario. John Stewart was named for Sir John

John Buchanan family ca.1860-1863 (courtesy Strathroy and Middlesex Museum).

Stewart, a friend of his father. John was born the year before his parents and older siblings left Ireland for America. His paternal grandparents on the family estate raised him. His six younger siblings were born after his parents left Omagh.

In 1832, when John was 18 years old, he moved to Canada with his employee, Richard Avery, and Avery's wife and son. There he settled on 180 acres at Lot 25, Con. 3 SER, deeded to him by his father, James. In 1834, James received a patent from the Crown for 1,200 acres on Lots 22, 23, 24 and 35, Con. 4 SER, and Lot 22, Con. 5 SER, for services rendered to the Province. He also received the water rights on the Sydenham River, which John used to build a sawmill and, at the request of his neighbours, a gristmill. After the completion of the mills, James deeded or sold the 1,200 acres to John, who called them Strathroy after his family home. Many of the settlers in this area were Irish Protestants, like the Buchanans. In the 1840s, John Stewart donated land on Head St. to the Church of England for the building of a church.

In 1839, John married Mabel Ann Robinson in Toronto. By the 1850s, he had sold his land in Adelaide and the couple moved to Chicago. There, they had 10 children, Elizabeth Robinson (1840-died an infant); James R. (1841-1853); Samuel R. (1843-1904); Elizabeth R. (1845); John R. (1847-1883); Catherine Hume R. (1849-1880); William Hume R. (1849); Mabel R. (1851); James O.R. (1853); and Robert R. (1856-1905). John Buchanan died in Chicago.

BUNTING

Wesley Bunting bought Lot 24, Con. 3 NER from William Thompson on February 1, 1840. Wesley Bunting had immigrated to Canada from Ireland and bought this property. His sister, Lettisha (Bunting) Wardell was married to Joseph Wardell and they settled beside Wesley on Lot 25.

Joseph and Lettisha came from Ireland also. They celebrated their honeymoon traveling on the ship, a six-week voyage. They had nine children.

Wesley, second eldest son of Joseph and Lettisha, bought his Uncle Wesley Bunting's farm on Lot 24 in May 1899. On October 22, 1902, he married Mary Etta Zavitz and they both lived in Adelaide until their deaths. They had six children, four sons and two daughters. Two of their sons settled in East Williams Township and are now deceased. The other two resided in Adelaide Township.

In 1948, Idabelle, the younger of the two daughters, married Stanley Hemsted. She still resides on the family farm where she was born. Stanley (1916-1996) was born and raised near Regina, Saskatchewan.

The Hemsteds have two daughters. Leasa Sawyer lives in Toronto and Carol Pugh lives in Brooks, Alberta. Carol has three children, Brian, Stacy and Nicole. Both daughters attended Adelaide Central School.

BURDON, Benjamin and Wilhelmina

Benjamin Burdon (1827-1891) was a linen draper in Yorkshire, England, when he eloped with Wilhelmina Margaret Gelling (1830-1899) of the Isle of Man. Their immigration to Canada was probably in 1854 as their third child, Emma, was born at York, Upper Canada, and Ben Burdon was a tenant on Berkley Street at that time. In 1856, he was 35 years old and leased property in Owen Sound, possibly a store. Records in 1860 show the family leasing 100 acres in Lobo Township. In 1862, Benjamin Burdon was assessed for the west half of Lot 16, Con. 3 NER, in Adelaide Township. There were 18 acres cleared, and the lot was assessed at $600, and the personal property assessment was $448. He had more livestock in this area than any other farmer of the time. Very few had as many as 130 sheep, few had 12 cattle, and those farmers who owned horses had no more than two, whereas Ben Burdon had four. Total livestock in the township that year was: sheep 3,020; hogs 1,024; horses 120; cattle 2,978. The assessment shows 10 persons in the family, but his wife and the five children then born account for only seven. Perhaps his being a merchant and taking in livestock in trade could explain the large number of livestock, and the extra numbers in the family may have been clerks or servants. There may have been a store on this property at the time. In March 1867, Benjamin Burdon bought 200 acres, the whole of the lot from Andrew Heron, giving a mortgage for $1,200 with interest at 10%. He sold the east 100 acres in 1870 to John McClelland, a bachelor, and he sold the west half to James M. Henderson in 1872, taking back a mortgage for $1,700. In this mortgage, he is described as living in the town of Bothwell. Benjamin and Wilhelmina had eight children.

Wilhelmina Mary Jane (1850-1902) was born in England, and married John A. Cuddy (1846-1925) in 1869 (see CUDDY, James and Violet).

Annie Marie (1853-1907) was born in England, and married William Thomas Branston Lewies (1837-1922) or Lewis, a farmer in Adelaide, in 1872. Thomas W.B. Lewies bought the north half of Lot 24, Con. 1 NER, from Joseph Doyle for $2,000. He later sold it to his only son, William (1875-1945). Annie and William Lewies' oldest child, Lillian (1873-1930), a spinster, kept house for her father and ailing mother. After he left the farm, William moved to Kent Bridge and bought his wife's family farm (Langford) near there.

Emma Lavina (1855-1945) was born in Toronto, the first child of this family to be born in Canada. She married in 1871 at 16 years of age, to Joseph A. Pumaville, a schoolteacher at the old Mud Creek School in Adelaide. A family story is told that sisters Annie and Emma were out walking one summer day and they came upon a pool in the creek. As the day was warm and the pool inviting, they decided to have a swim. Joseph Pumaville came along and sat on the bank beside their clothes, thinking it a good joke. Emma's marriage was opposed by her parents as they thought Joseph was suffering from tuberculosis. He was never strong during their short three-year marriage. Emma frequently took his place at school. They had one son, Morley Franklin Pumaville (1872-1958), who became a teacher, a lawyer and later a magistrate in the new District of Temiskaming. After Joseph's death, Emma earned her living by dressmaking in Chatham. There she met John Trumpess, who became her second husband, and they had three daughters.

The (Pommaville) Pumaville family made an important contribution to the progress of Adelaide Township. The 1852 Adelaide census shows the family living on Pt. Lot 25, Con. 1 SER, where a store was on the property. Francis Pommaville, born in Lower Canada, is 41, a carpenter; his wife, Mary Ann, born in Ireland, is 39; Francis 15, born in Canada; the other children are born in Lower Canada, John 12; Eleanor 10; Elizabeth 8; Joseph 6 (the teacher); Mary Ann 4; Sarah 2. In the 1871 census of Adelaide, James Pumaville is recorded as a grocer on Lot 10, Con. 1 SER, where many businesses and the Royal Adelaide Inn were located at that time. Joseph Pumerville (sic) age 23, schoolteacher, a Methodist of Scotch origin, Mary Ann age 20, and Sarah age 18 are listed next in the census record.

Frederick Lionel (1856-1940), fourth child of Benjamin and Wilhelmina, was born in Owen Sound. He attended Toronto Normal School and taught school in Lambton County, then graduated from Ann Arbor Medical School and went to Edinburgh in 1892 and obtained degrees so that he could practice medicine anywhere in the British Empire. He married Mary Hooker in 1891, and had a very successful medical practice in London, Ontario, where they raised two children, Florence and Frederick.

Lucinda Priscilla (1861) was born in Adelaide. She moved to Kent County with the family in 1872. She married a farmer from the area, George Campbell Prangley, an ancestor of the Strathroy Prangleys.

Euphemia Alexanderina (1863) was born in Adelaide Township. She married Alfred James Pesha, son of a pioneer neighbour in Euphemia Township.

Benjamin Lincoln (1866-1951) may have been born in Adelaide before the family moved. He farmed in Euphemia Township and married neighbour Rachel Campbell.

Margaret Evelyn (1869-1924) attended high school in Wardsville. She married Manley Stafford Moorhouse, a neighbour.

BURROWS, Henry and Mary

Henry Burrows (1832-1916) was born in England to John and Grace Burrows. The child, later christened in the local Church of England, was destined to travel with his parents and a younger sister, over thousands of miles of land and water, before meeting and marrying the woman with whom he was to share his future. Current indications are that Henry's parents initially settled in what is now Darlington Township around 1837, about 20 miles northeast of Oshawa, Ontario, in the region of Durham. John and Grace had four more children together in Canada. Names of Henry's siblings were Sarah Ann (1835); Elizabeth (1839); Eliza (1840); Grace (1844); and John R. (1845).

John Sr. is believed to have died in Darlington Township between 1845 and 1848. His wife, Grace, appears to have then remarried, to a man named Robert Cauley, having a son, Robert, by him in 1849. In the meantime, Henry, then in his late teens, moved about 20 miles southwest of Oshawa, to Pickering Township. There he lived with, and worked as a farm labourer for, James B. Powell, a man who was to become a well-known Mason and civic leader in the town of Whitby. Henry later had his own farm on what is now the Greenwood Sideroad (near, or on, the present Greenwood Conservation Site). In 1851, Henry's mother, Grace, with her four daughters, two sons and new husband, Robert Cauley, were also found to have moved to Pickering Township. Grace appears to have died around 1854.

In England, Mary Elizabeth Rowe (1838-1922) was born to William and Elizabeth Ann Hick. Mary Elizabeth was baptized into the Church of England. About 1841, the Hick family, which is believed to have included three girls and three boys, immigrated to Canada. They initially settled in the Greenwood area of Pickering Township in what was to become Ontario County (later included in the Region of Durham). It was here that Henry Burrows married his new bride, Mary Elizabeth Hick, around the year 1856.

After the birth of their two eldest children in the Pickering area, Henry and his family joined William and Elizabeth Ann Hick in Brooke Township, Lambton County, taking up an offer of free government land. Present indications are that the two families lived side by side on adjoining parcels of land, each consisting of 100 acres.

Sometime between the census of 1871, and the drawing of a map for Adelaide Township in 1877, Henry Burrows and the family moved once again, this time about 15 miles northeast, with at least seven children. Their new residence in Adelaide Township was Lot 15, Con. 2 NER. Records indicate that the farm was settled in 1864, however the family was still shown to be residing on the Brooke Township farm as of the 1871 census. It may be that they chose to develop the new Adelaide property for a while before taking up full-time residence on it.

Records indicate Henry and Mary had 11 children, and were of the Wesleyan Methodist faith. Henry was buried at Strathroy Municipal Cemetery.

Mr. and Mrs. Alfred Burrows

Mary died in Chatham, Ontario, at the residence of her son, William George, and was also buried at Strathroy Municipal Cemetery.

William George (1858-1937), Henry and Mary's first child, married Mary Ann McKay at Mosa in Middlesex County in 1881. After the marriage, William and his bride moved to the Village of Glencoe, where William established a marble and monument business. He may also have been a building contractor and a mason in the Glencoe area, as some information indicates one or more of his younger brothers worked for him in those trades. Prior to 1900, William and his wife and three children moved to Chatham, where he again operated a marble and monument business, and later established a funeral home business with his son, William, known as Burrows and Son. William and Mary Ann appear to have had six children. William George is buried next to his wife in the old Mausoleum at the Maple Leaf Cemetery in Chatham.

Richard John (1859-1909), Henry and Mary's second eldest, was born in Whitby, Ontario, and may have lived his adult life in the area of London, Ontario. On December 24, 1890, he married Cynthia Murray (1864-1901). Cynthia was the daughter of Robert and Martha Murray. They are known to have had two sons, Manfred Walter Burrows (1895-died a baby) and Vernon Murray Burrows (1897-1958). Vernon is buried in Woodlawn Cemetery in London, Ontario. Cynthia was buried in the Municipal Cemetery at Strathroy with her parents.

Richard married a second time on November 8, 1904, to Ida Smith. A Middlesex County book on well-known people in the area indicates that Richard Burrows had a highly respected connection to the Masonic Order. Richard died at the age of 50 years, and was buried with his parents in the Strathroy Municipal Cemetery.

Norman (1862), third son of Henry and Mary, appears to have left the farm in his late teens to work as a bricklayer for his older brother, William, in Glencoe. Records show that he was living in Glencoe on December 26, 1888. In later years, he was known to have been a bricklayer and small contractor in Vancouver. He was approximately 50 years of age when he married the former Anna McIsaac.

Henry and Mary then had a daughter, Mary Grace (1864), who married George Alfred Brown of Strathroy (1863-1927). They appear to have left their farm prior to the 1891 census. When her sister-in-law, Mary Ann Burrows, died in 1935, Mary Grace stayed with and kept house in Chatham for her brother, William George, for a while. In 1940, Mary Grace was known to be living with her son, Walter H. Brown, and his family in Strathroy. Mary Grace (Burrows) Brown in buried in the Strathroy Municipal Cemetery.

Mary Grace had two children. Ethel Grace (1891), married an unrelated man by the name of Brown. It is believed that they had at least one child, probably a daughter. The family may have lived for a time in Detroit, Michigan, before moving to Florida. Walter (1893-1968) married Annie Olive Brent (1891). They had no children. Walter was in charge of the Roads Department for the Township of Adelaide. Both he and his wife are buried in the Strathroy Municipal Cemetery.

Henry (1866), fifth child of Henry and Mary, was gone from the farm before the 1891 census was taken. Very little is known of Henry. Records appear to indicate he moved to Detroit, Michigan, where he raised a family that included at least one granddaughter.

Annie Elizabeth (1868-ca.1917) was born the sixth child of Henry and Mary, probably on the farm in Brooke Township. She also left the farm before the 1891 census. On December 26, 1888, Annie married Steven Smith Waite (1861-1926), a baker. They had one daughter, Lina Maude Waite (1890). In 1901, the family lived in Strathroy, where Steven worked as a machine woodworker. Annie Elizabeth is buried with her husband in the Strathroy Municipal Cemetery. They were Methodists.

Walter T. (1871-1891) was the seventh issue of Henry and Mary. Records seem to indicate he was born on the farm in Brooke Township. He died from "La Grippe" at the age of 20, likely in Adelaide Township. He was buried in the Strathroy Municipal Cemetery.

Twins Allice Maud and Ella Maude (1872) were then born to Henry and Mary, possibly in Adelaide Township. They each lived approximately seven months, dying two days apart from congestion of the brain after a very short illness.

Emmiline (1873-1967) was born in Adelaide Township and was still on the farm at the time of the 1891 census. She married Peter A. Currie (1866-1951). In 1901, Peter was working as a carpenter in Strathroy. Emmiline had two children, both of whom died at birth. She may have lived in Sarnia around 1940. She died in London and is buried with her husband in the Strathroy Municipal Cemetery. They were Presbyterians.

Alfred E. (1876-1948), the youngest child of Henry and Mary, was born in Adelaide Township. He remained on the family farm his entire life. He died at the age of 74 when he fell off the roof of the barn while trying to repair it. His wife was the former Emma A. Ayre (1881-1948), who died one day before her 48th wedding anniversary. The couple had no children. Alfred is buried with his wife in the Strathroy Municipal Cemetery.

BUTLER, William and Mary

William Alfred Butler (1877-1955) was born in Warwick Township to Henry and Margaret James (Smith) Butler. In 1868, Henry Butler had come to Canada from Buckinghamshire, England, with his brother, Fred, and a cousin. William married Mary Timms (1888-1942). They purchased a fruit farm in Adelaide Township at Lot 1, Con. 5, possibly in the 1920s from Bron Bros. of Arkona.

William and Mary Butler had four children. Louella married James Wills, and they lived in Strathroy. Marian married Grant Ross, and they lived in Warwick Township. Evelyn married George Holmes of Arkona, and they lived in Forest. Robert Orval (1909-1951) married Pearl Marie Herrington, daughter of Charles and Clara (Muma) Herrington of West Williams Township. Robert

"Bob" and Pearl had two sons, Orval Fredrick (d.1976) and Raymond Arthur (1931-1998).

In the 1940s, Bob and Pearl Butler purchased the farm from his father, William. It became a thriving fruit farm with many kinds of fruit. They built a new house on the farm in 1948. Bob died from heart disease at age 42.

Orval married Evelyn Dibbly of Tilbury, where they resided. Orval and Evelyn had four children, Bonnie, Fred, Carl and John.

Raymond married Noreen June Zavitz of the Thedford area. Noreen was the daughter of Joe and Irene Zavitz. They lived in the old farmhouse and helped Pearl run the fruit farm after Bob's death. Raymond and Noreen had five children.

On May 21, 1953, a tornado struck the area near the Butler farm. Pearl, Raymond and Noreen had planted raspberries all day and had gone to Pearl's house for supper. At about 6:20 p.m., when they had just begun to eat, the wind became a terrible roar. They ran to the basement and got under the stairs. It was so dark they could not see each other. When it was over, most of the fruit orchards, the huge packinghouse, the barn, the drive shed, the older farmhouse and other buildings were all a pile of rubble. The new house was the only thing standing, but it was badly damaged. Many of the neighbouring farms were damaged, and this same tornado devastated the Sarnia area. Raymond and Noreen lost everything in their house, including Noreen's diamond engagement ring. Their daughter, Darlene, found it in the dirt 12 years later. It was in perfect condition, truly a miracle! Raymond and Noreen built a new home in 1972 beside the previous one.

Diane Marie (1953), Raymond and Noreen's eldest child, married Jack Bradley and they have

Butler family; L-R, Orval, Raymond, Pearl and Bob, ca.1943.

William Butler family, William standing, back L-R, Louella, Marian, Mary (Timms) Butler, front L-R, Evelyn and Robert, ca.1912.

since divorced. They had two children, Holly Rene (1971) and Nathan J. (1976). Diane, Holly and Nathan live in Toronto.

Robert "Bobby" Alan (1954-1968) was struck and killed while riding his bicycle in front of his home.

Darlene Marilyn (1957) married Christopher Rodgers of Timmins (1957). They have two children, Alex (1991) and Jacob (1997). They live in Timmins.

Rick M. (1960), fourth child of Raymond and Noreen, married Cathy McNeill (1962) of Sarnia. They have four children, Caleb J. (1987); Breanne A. (1989); Reagan V. (1992); and Isaac Raymond (1995). They live in Sarnia.

Debra Lynn (1962) married Nial Wilson of Arkona. They have two children, Rhea June (1984) and Eli Fredrick (1992). They live in Stirling, Ontario.

Diane started to school in the old Keyser's School but was moved to W.G. MacDonald School in her Grade One year. The other Butler children attended W.G. MacDonald and Strathroy Collegiate Institute. Raymond and Noreen did specialized fostering for 18 years, and many of those children attended the same schools.

After heart surgery in 1987, Raymond worked for Canada Post as mail delivery person for R.R. #1 Arkona. He retired in 1997.

The original farm has been severed for many years. Martin and Jo Thuss and family (Thuss Greenhouses) own the east part and live in the home that Bob and Pearl Butler built. Noreen lives on the two-acre lot in the center. Harry and Elsie Faulds of Arkona own the rest of the farm.

BUTTERY, John and Anna

It has always been stated that the Buttery family was the first to settle in Adelaide in 1832, and that the wife of John Buttery, Anna Wilkinson, was the first white woman in the township. While this statement is mostly true, John Buttery was not the first white man to live within the boundaries as surveyed in 1832.

John Buttery (1794-1853) was probably born near Marnham, Nottinghamshire, England. He married Anna Wilkinson (1897-1880), daughter of Joseph and Susannah Wilkinson of Weller, Nottinghamshire, in 1818. John and Anna came to Quebec City in 1820 after a tedious voyage of eight weeks, and then they traveled to Montreal. They located at Dunham, 60 miles east. The following is from The Age, February 11, 1880: "They had barely settled when both husband and wife were taken down with typhoid fever, and suffered for many weeks great distress, which, however, was greatly mitigated by the kindness of the neighbours. One family named Baker took their only son [George], less than two years old, and treated it as their own, until the parents were fully recovered."

They struggled hard to pay their bills and to simply survive. In the winter of 1828, they moved to French's Island on the Ottawa River, 40 miles northwest of Montreal. They remained there until 1831, when they moved west to Upper Canada. They visited York, Hamilton, Guelph and Galt, and for a time they resided at Ancaster, looking for a suitable location. Finally, encouraged by Peter Robinson while visiting with him at what is now Toronto Island, they decided to take up land in the "New Survey," in Adelaide Township.

John and Anna reached Lot 25, Con. 2 SER, on May 18, 1832, where they built their first log cabin, as described in The Age: "It had neither floor, window, nor door, bark being laid on the earth, and a blanket served for door and window for the entire summer." To this rude abode, they brought at least five children. George (1820-1909) was born in Nottinghamshire. Joseph (1822-1912); Susannah (1823-1906); Mary Ann (1825-1894); and William Isaac (1830-1903) were all born in Quebec. Caroline (ca.1835) was born in Adelaide. The names and birth dates of the other three children are unknown, but it is suspected that a son, Lance, was born about 1835. With all that is known of this family, it seems unusual that nothing is known of these three children.

John and Anna remained on Lot 25 until 1836, when they moved to Lot 27, Con. 3 SER. John and his sons, unlike many other settlers, cut and sawed their trees into lumber, which they sold to build Buchanan's mills and other structures in the hamlet that was to become Strathroy. As soon as there was a clearing, they planted fruit trees and prepared enough land for cereal crops to feed the livestock and family. The experience gained by having come to Canada in 1820, of having toured a fair expanse of the southern province while on their way to Adelaide, and of actually having learned what the new settlers would require, placed the Buttery family at a decided advantage over many of their neighbours. There was plenty of wild game in the forest, and Bear Creek teemed with fish. The son, George, was a hunter of some renown, and stated that he had "killed as many as 400 deer with one gun." [The Age, November 18, 1909.]

Mere survival had been replaced with decided agricultural advancement, and their prowess earned them the respect and admiration of their community. Education was deemed important in the Buttery family, and they played a significant role in the early development of the Methodist Church, of which they were lifelong members.

As a young man, George Buttery led a far from uneventful life. As his exploits are recounted in several other places in this work, they will not be repeated here. "George was a prominent Liberal in his political opinions, and for many years was one of the leading spirits of the Agricultural Association of West Middlesex. In 1853 he assessed the township, two years later was elected to the Township Council, and in 1856, he was elected Reeve, serving altogether nine years in the Township Council." [History of the County of Middlesex, 1889.]

George married Charlotte Rapley (1818-1895), daughter of James and Mary (Collins) Rapley, in 1846 (see Rapley). They raised seven children in Adelaide. Ezelia Ann (1846-1931) married James Bogue (1838-1922) of Adelaide (see Bogue). John W. (ca.1848-1890) married Margaret Heard of Elgin County. William George (1852-1942) married his first cousin, Lottie Buttery (1853-1887), and later Frances Barnes (1864-1940) of Strathroy. John T. (1854) married Mary Barnes (ca.1857) of Strathroy. Charlotte May (ca.1854-1910) married George Van Valkenburg in Adelaide in 1876 (they may have had a daughter, Winnifred, in Forest, who married H.B. Davis of Adelaide in 1906). David M. (1858-1896) died in St. Thomas, South Dakota. George A. (1860) was the youngest of George and Charlotte's children.

William George and Lottie lost their only child. After Lottie Buttery died, William George and Frances, his second wife, had three children, William "Bill" (ca.1924); George Howard (1926); and Frances (ca.1931). Bill was born in Adelaide, and he married Jennie VanBoven. George Howard Buttery (1926) was born in Brooke Township. He married Virginia Marie Gooden (1926), daughter of Thomas D. Gooden (1902) and Sadie Jane Bravener Bellairs (1903) (see Bellairs). George Howard and Virginia raised four children, Virginia Ann, Sharon Jane, Mark Howard, and Ann Marie. Frances married Earl Long and secondly, Ernie Carruthers.

John Thomas Buttery, brother of William George, and his wife, Mary, had three children, Howard R. (1886); Anne A. (1887); and Clara F. (1890).

Joseph Buttery, son of John and Anna, married Mary Rymall (1835) of Westminster Township on November 8, 1852, in Adelaide. He died in Smyra, Delaware, in the U.S. Joseph and Mary had three children, Joseph Thomas (1857-1946); Mary E. (1858), who married Andrew Thompson of Adelaide in January 1881 and is believed to have moved to Lambton County; and Desdemona (ca.1860).

Joseph Thomas Buttery married Lydia A. Barnes (1858-1936) and raised two children, Russell G. (1883-1953), who married Zada Blanche Taylor (1884-1943); and Ethlyn "Pauline" (1887-1975), who eloped with and married Charles R. Gundy of Wood-Gundy Investment House. Their son, Richard M. Gundy (1921-1971), carried on his father's business until his death.

Susannah Buttery (1823-1906), daughter of John and Ann, married James Thomson (1811-1889) of Caradoc Township. They raised three children, Samuel (1848-1866); William Alexander (1852-1936), who was a drover; and Carrie Thomson (1855-1929). Carrie is buried in Strathroy Cemetery.

Mary Ann Buttery (1825-1894), daughter of John and Anna, married Chester Miner (1821-1873). Chester was the son of Truman and Elizabeth (Morrison) Miner, formerly of Vermont (see Miner and Eastman).

William Isaac Buttery (1830-1903), son of John and Anna, married Nancy Eleanor Morden (1835-1891) of London, the daughter of a pioneer Methodist preacher. "Her father always stopped work at noon on Saturday to get ready for the Sunday service. He rode on horseback through the woods to the various places in which he preached" [The Age.]

William Isaac and Nancy raised nine children on Lot 26, Con. 2 SER. Margaret married Charles Davis and moved to Spokane, Washington. There is no further information on Amelia (d.1891) or John (1863-1866). Alberta Lucina (1865-1938) married George J. Newton (1863-1934). Charlotte "Lottie" (1867-1927) married George White (1867-1936). There is no further information on Effie Lora (1871-1892). William Ethelbert (1873-1935) married Charlotte Blanche Luscombe (1872-1934). Ralph Morden (1875-1935) married Margaret Jane McDonald (1878-1954). Mary Buttery (1881) married Andrew Thompson of Adelaide. "Mr. and Mrs. Buttery were very sincere in their religious life. In their home all food was prepared on Saturday, and no work done on the Sabbath except what was absolutely necessary. There was no Sunday reading of newspapers, and only sacred songs were allowed to be sung... When the family was at home they all attended church together, regularly, at both the morning and evening services, and usually stayed for Sunday School. The home was always open for social activities of the church. Mr. Buttery had a three-seated pleasure sleigh that was very well known. As well as being the family conveyance, it was always at the disposal of the Methodist to carry them to and from any of the activities in the country." [Diamond Jubilee of Strathroy United Church, 1939.]

William Isaac was a trustee and member of the Church Board for most of his adult life. After the death of Nancy Eleanor in 1891, William Isaac married Bessie Ellico (1854-1936). She died in Eugene, Oregon, in 1936.

Alberta Lucina Buttery, daughter of William Isaac and Nancy, and her husband, George Newton, had one daughter, Beryl Buttery Newton. Beryl married Bruce O. Parker (1888-1948) of Adelaide (see Parker), co-owner of Parker & Sands Hardware, Strathroy.

William Ethelbert and Charlotte had three children. Eleanor married Jack McDougal. George (1898) married Charlotte "Lottie" Frances Stevenson (1901-1982), and they had three children, Margaret "Maggie," Blanche, and George A. (1945), who died young. Vera (1902-1970) married a Mr. Morrison.

Ralph Morden Buttery and Margaret Jane had three children born on the home place in Adelaide. Marion Eleanor (1909-1998) married Stanley Coups, and then Berton Schultz. Ralph William McDonald (1909) married Helen Jamima Allum. Margaret Lucina (1914-1998) married Cyril Kendall and later, Robert Footwinkler. Ralph William McDonald Buttery and his sister, Marion, have been of great assistance in the preparation of this sketch of the Buttery Family. Ralph graduated as an engineer and spent much of his life in a supervisory capacity in the container manufacturing industry in plants across Canada. He and his wife, Helen, had two sons, Ronald Morden (d.1974) and Ralph James.

The reader is left with a long-held Buttery family mystery. At Longwoods Cemetery in Row 17, there exists a tombstone, inscribed as follows: "Mary Buttery 1806-1882/ Wife of William Wilkinson 1810-1874/ Infants Robert 1877/ Fanny 1879." Perhaps a reader will be able to shed some light on this curious inscription.

BYCRAFT, Craig and Patti

Craig Bycraft (1952) was born in Strathroy, the son of James and Thelma Bycraft. He grew up with five siblings on his parents' dairy farm in Lobo Township. Craig married Mary Patricia "Patti" Anne Regier (1952) on November 2, 1973. Patti is the daughter of Jerome and Catherine Regier, and also came from a farm background. She and her 12 siblings were raised near Chepstowe, Ontario. Patti had arrived in Lobo in the spring of 1970 to work as a mother's helper.

Craig purchased an Adelaide Township farm from his grandparents, Herbert and Violet Tomlinson, in 1979. This farm on Lot 30, Con. 1 NER, had been in the family since the 1850s.

Craig and Patti have three sons, Robert Jason (1975); Mark James Joseph (1981); and Daniel Craig (1982). They share the distinction of being the sixth generation of the Tomlinson family to live on this homestead. Property tax receipts dating back to the mid 1800s are displayed in the farm kitchen. In 1858, $11 was the total property tax on 110 acres.

Craig purchased the adjoining farm on Lot 29, Con. 1 NER, from Mel Laker in 1980, and a Lobo Township farm in 1981. Craig founded "Craig Bycraft Elevator" on his family's home farm in 1985.

Farming is not Craig's only interest. He is also a singer. Craig became a charter member of "Harmony Woods," a campground near Parkhill, and the Strathroy "Vocal Federation" barbershop chorus. Craig also sang with "Rural Roots," a quartet whose members all have farm origins.

BYLSMA, Rick and Jacqueline

Rick and Jacqueline Bylsma moved to their present address in 1985. Jacqueline was originally

Rick and Jacqueline Bylsma family, back, Jacqueline and Rick; front, Nicolis and Jason.

from Hickory Corners, and Rick was from the Ilderton area.

Rick is head of his department at Agra-Brands Purina in Strathroy, and has been working there since 1990. Jacqueline is an at-home Mom with two sons, Jason (1991) and Nicolis (1995).

The Bylsmas purchased the house where Stan and Bonnie Hodge lived for many years. They have done extensive renovations to their circa 1900 house.

Jason is attending Adelaide W.G. MacDonald School and is in Grade Two, while Nicolis will start Junior Kindergarten in 1999.

CALLCOTT, Bill and Joyce

Bill and Joyce Callcott have learned to say "The Old Galbraith House" when the locals ask where they live. They purchased the house from Roger and Aleta Cates, and moved to Kerwood in 1991.

Bill Callcott was born in 1950 in London and was raised in Lucan. Joyce Linker was born in Kalamazoo, Michigan. She came to Strathroy in 1962, where she lived until she married Bill in 1982.

Bill has worked for Canada Post since 1970, initially in London and then he transferred to Strathroy in 1985. He enjoys vegetable gardening, coin collecting, playing hockey, and car maintenance. He hopes to open a car wash business some day.

Joyce worked as a Registered Nursing Assistant at the Strathroy Hospital until 1991. She enjoys flower gardening, cross-stitching, and making jigsaw puzzles. She also enjoys volunteering in the library at the Strathroy Community Christian School. She plans, one day, to write a book about her experiences with cancer.

Bill and Joyce have two children, Darryl (1983) and Ashley (1986), both born in London.

Darryl is presently a student at S.D.C.I. He enjoys reading, composing music, and making amateur movies. When he is older, he hopes to be a police officer on a SWAT team.

Ashley is a student at Strathroy Community Christian School. Her hobbies are stamp collecting, jigsaw puzzling, and learning about and caring for animals. She hopes, one day, to be an animal biologist.

They are members of the Forest Christian Reformed Church and hope to be a part of Kerwood for years to come.

CAMPBELL, Archie J. and Annie

In 1919, Archie J. and Annie (Limon) Campbell came to the east half of Lot 25, Con. 3 SER, with their three sons. In 1927, they bought Lot 25, Con. 2, across from where they had been living and moved to this property. Their eldest son, Stewart, left home and moved to Welland where he worked for the C.N.R. as a telegraph operator. William and Murray, the younger sons, stayed in Adelaide and worked on the family farm.

William married Ella Chapman and died in 1970 at the age of 67.

Bill, Joyce, Darryl and Ashley Callcott.

Archie and Annie (Ireland) Campbell, ca.1934.

In 1931, Murray married Bessie Brown, whose parents, James and Maggie (Mahon) Brown, were from Adelaide. Her mother had gone to S.S. #3 in the late 1860s. Murray and Bessie moved onto the first farm which Archie and Annie had bought. They lived there together for 42 years.

Murray and Bessie's son, Donald A., was born on the farm on Con. 3, and in 1967, he brought his wife, Marilee O'Neil of London, to live there. Bessie and Murray built a new home for themselves on some land they owned on Lot 26, and lived there until Murray died at the age of 81 in 1983.

CAMPBELL, Ernest and Mary

Robert Earl Campbell (1929) was born in Toronto to Ernest Russell and Mary Christina (McLeish) Campbell, residents of that city. A second son, William Donald Campbell (1931-1956) was also born in Toronto.

In 1936, the family moved to a farm at R.R. #5 in Adelaide Township. On reaching school age, both boys attended S.S. #10 public school. On Sundays, they walked with other neighbourhood children to attend Sunday School in the Anglican Parish at Adelaide Village, approximately two miles from the farm.

On graduation from public school, Robert attended Strathroy Collegiate Institute in Strathroy. He rode his bicycle the five miles from the farm to school, but during inclement weather, he commuted via Jennings Bus Lines.

A daughter, Mildred Eileen Campbell (1937), was born in Strathroy. On September 5, 1959, she married Jerrold Lea Green of Sparta, Ontario. They now live in London, and have two sons and three grandchildren.

When Ernest died in 1944, Mary Christina sold the farm and moved with her three small children into Strathroy. She began employment as a secretary, first with E.G. Wright Utilities Ltd., and later with Middlesex Furniture.

Robert left school in early 1945 to sail on the Great Lakes. His first job as a stoker aboard the Canada Steamship Lines passenger vessel "S.S. Hamonic" was short-lived when the vessel burned at the dock in Point Edward early that summer. However, he continued sailing on other vessels of that line as a wheelman until the end of the 1949 shipping season. His brother, William, joined him in this vocation and for a couple of years they sailed together on the same ship, the "S.S. Huronic."

William left shipping in 1940 and took employment as a truck driver with Hawkins Lumber Company of Strathroy. He was killed in a logging accident while loading his truck. He had never married.

By this time, Mary had taken a position as office manager with the Municipal World Printing Company of St. Thomas and moved to that city with her daughter, Mildred Eileen. Mary died on January 8, 1990, at the age of 88 years.

Robert left the lakes in December 1949 and turned to a military career. He enlisted in the R.C.N., where he served in the seaman's branch on both the Atlantic and Pacific coasts of Canada for the next 14 months. He then transferred to the R.C.A.F., where he served for the next 20 years in the Security Services Branch. He was stationed at various bases in Manitoba, Ontario and Quebec, and in France. He attained the rank of Master Warrant Officer and, in 1971, retired from service as an instructor at the School of Military Intelligence and Security at Camp Borden, Ontario. He holds the Canadian Forces Long Service Medal.

Following Robert's military career and in view of his past marine experience, he attended marine college at Owen Sound and in due course obtained his "Home Trade" (Coastal and Inland Waters) Masters Certificate of Competency. He sailed as Captain of the pilot boat out of Sarnia for two years. With this vessel, during the night of January 5, 1972, he was successful in rescuing the Master and 30 crew members from the American steamer "Sydney E. Smith," which sank in the St. Clair River near the Bluewater Bridge, following a collision with the Canadian steamer "Parker Evans." For this action, he was awarded the Gold Lifesaving Medal by the United States Coast Guard in a ceremony held at Selfridge Air Force Base in Mount Clemens, Michigan.

In 1973, Robert joined C.N. Marine as a captain and sailed in that capacity until his second retirement 21 years later, in 1994. He presently lives in Sarnia with his wife, Ollie (Fichey) Campbell, an American citizen by birth, in their tenth floor condominium overlooking the St. Clair River. Robert and Ollie did not have children.

CAMPBELL, John and Nettie

John Alexander Campbell (1876-1954) and Nettie Ross (1881-1950), both of Lobo Township, were married on February 20, 1900. After a short stay in Lobo, they farmed for a few years at the east half of Lot 5, Con. 3 SER, then moved to the east half of Lot 2, Con. 1 NER, 1224 Egremont Drive. There they raised eight children.

John Ross Campbell (1901-1968) moved to Michigan, and married Inez Elliott. They lived in Plymouth, Michigan, and had four children, Peggy, Jack, Keith and Jerry. Ross worked in construction most of his life.

Sarah Jean (1903-1965) married Steve McLeish and lived near Sylvan. Jean was a member of the graduating 1925-1926 class from Strathroy School of Nursing, and was a nurse for many years at Strathroy Hospital. They had no children.

Mabel Catherine (1905-1934) married Orville Wardell. They lived in Adelaide Township and had one daughter, Eleanor, who married Ken Daniel of Lobo Township.

Lillie (1907-1996) married Howard Wardell and lived in Sarnia. They had four children, Jean "Marie," Donald, Marion and Catherine "Anne."

Annie Florence (1910-1924) died from diphtheria. She and Lillie were quarantined in the living room and food was passed to them through the door. Dr. Jones from Adelaide Village brought them comic books to read and then the books were burned.

Ellen Margaret (1912-1948), sixth child of John A. and Nettie, married Norman Wardell. They lived in Adelaide Township and had seven children, Alan, Ross, Roy, James, Helen, Lorne and Ila.

Gordon Peter (1923-1979) married Grace Gourlay (1925), formerly of Warspite, Alberta, on August 9, 1952. They resided at the family home, the east half of Lot 2, Con. 1 NER, where Grace still lives. They had two children. Lorne Gordon (1960) married Susan Hansen from Corunna. They live in West Williams Township and have three children, Katherine Marie, John Lorne and Karen Grace. Eileen Grace (1962) married David Hackett of Stratford and they live in Mississauga.

Gordon was born in the family home and worked in construction, including operating his own business in Adelaide Village for a time. During the latter years of his life, he worked for Moffatt and Powell in Watford. He spent a short time in the

Gordon P. Campbell family

army, stationed in Halifax during WWII. Grace was in the R.C.A.F. (Women's Division) during WWII, and spent most of her 2½ years of service in Edmonton and Calgary.

Annie Eileen (1925) married Arthur McKenzie of Parkhill and lives in Alliston, Ontario. They have two children, Marie and Donald.

The property was obtained from the Crown in 1836 by Emanuel Mathers. In 1837, the 100-acre farm was sold to David Wylie. John A. Campbell purchased the farm from Thomas Callaghan in 1911 for $4,700.

On August 1, 1918, John A. and John Ross Campbell had taken peas to the canning factory in Kerwood. Mrs. Earley met them on the way home and told them that their barn had been hit by lightning. They lost several loads of hay, pigs, and a colt. The pigs kept running back into the fire. There was a fence along the orchard then and the pigs had to be thrown over it in order to stop them from running back into the barn. Many implements were burned. The wheat was cut, but there was no place to store it. The threshers threshed the wheat in the field and sold it there for $2.50 per bushel (a good price then).

The cows had to be tied to the fence. By October 1, the new foundation and floor was in place for the new barn—then came the barn raising! John A. and Mr. Shanlow did the framing. Many men, and 30 women attended, and all the neighbours came. Nettie baked bread every other day.

John and Nettie used to have dances in their home. The kitchen table was moved to the corner and all the other furniture, including the stove, was moved out of the room. The floor was propped up in the basement so it wouldn't collapse. Mr. and Mrs. Billy McChesney sat on the table and provided the music. Mrs. McChesney played the autoharp and Mr. McChesney played the violin. Of course, their children were sent to bed before the dance began.

Many happy times were spent at Hillsboro Beach. The same group, mostly from West Adelaide Church, had a picnic there every year.

The Campbell girls attended the dances at Crathie Hall. Their father would drive them there and play cards while the girls danced.

Every year at Christmas, a goose-plucking bee was held. The first goose dressed was roasted for a dinner after all the work was done.

The tornado in 1953 took out all the trees in the laneway and some fruit trees east of the house. The car was moved from the east side of the house to the lawn on the south side and the outhouse was blown away from its place on the northwest side. The house itself could be felt swaying to the east but stood firm, although the front porch was taken off shortly afterward because of damage. All but three acres of the farm were sold to John Peters in 1966.

In the early years of their marriage, the neighbours visited each other frequently and often played cards. Lunch was served at the end of the evening. Gradually, this diminished as people became a little busier and more affluent, and went further afield for their entertainment.

CAMPBELL, John S. and Margaret

John S. Campbell moved to Adelaide Township in 1909 from Caradoc Township. His wife, Margaret (McKenzie) Campbell, moved to Adelaide Township in 1909 from East Williams. They lived on the Robotham Sideroad. The house was struck by lightning and burned down.

In 1928, they moved to the west half of Lot 11,

Campbell family, L-R, John, Rita, John Jr. and Keith Campbell, about 1982 (Colledge Studios).

Con. 2 NER. John S. and Margaret had four children, Dougal, Anna (Hendrick), Arthur and George.

Dougal's son, Jack, owned land and built a new house in September 1972, at the east half of Lot 5, County Road 12. Jack married Rita Edmondson, who was born in West Yorkshire, England. Their children are John A. (1971) and Keith S. (1974), who attended Adelaide W.G. MacDonald School.

CARROTHERS, John and Harriet

John Carrothers (1838-1917), first child of Nathaniel and Margaret Kirkpatrick, was born in the Village of London, Upper Canada (pop. 1,200). In 1860, he married Harriet Bratt (1842-1906) in Belmont, Westminster Township. In 1865, now a family of five, they moved to Adelaide Township, having purchased the east half of Lot 4, Con. 2 SER, from Peter McKenzie. McKenzie had received the patent from the Crown in 1848, and had cleared 20 acres.

John cleared and improved more land, erected large barns, and built a 2-story, 8-bedroom brick home with a "widow's walk." The family planted flowering shrubs and bushes, as well as a 4-acre orchard. They named their home "Mount Pleasant Farm" and it was said to be one of the finest homes in the township.

In 1878, they purchased the west quarter of Lot 4, Con. 3 SER from Mary Gregory. In 1889, John and Harriet rented both farms and moved to the Northwest Territories with 11 children. Harriet's brother, Jessie Bratt, who was married to John's sister, Rachael (1840-1916), and their family accompanied them. Together, they founded the settlement of Buck Lake on unoccupied, virgin prairie. It became part of the province of Saskatchewan when the government in 1905 created it.

In 1896, their eldest son, Austin (1863-1954), sold his ranch and a flock of several hundred short-wooled ranch sheep, and accompanied his parents back home to Mount Pleasant Farm. In 1896, Harriet purchased the west half of the west half of Lot 5, Con. 2 SER from William Thomas. She later sold this farm to James Wilson Thomas. In 1904, John and Harriet sold the Mount Pleasant Farm and moved to Regina.

Austin received title from his parents of the west quarter of Lot 4, Con. 3 SER. In 1897, Austin married Ida Thomas (1872-1899). She died a few days following the birth of their only child, Leonard (1899-1970). Austin's mother cared for Leonard until her death in 1906 in Regina. Shortly after, Leonard returned to Adelaide to be cared for by his father and stepmother.

Austin married Minnie Louise Morgan (1868-1938) in 1904. She was the daughter of Mr. and Mrs. William Morgan. They had two children, Clayton (1906-1996) and Evelyn (1909-1977).

As well as farming, Austin was skilled in carpentry and masonry. These skills were put to good use when on one occasion, Austin and his son, Clayton, were returning from Strathroy following a thunderstorm. They counted eight barns burning. The last barn was theirs. In 1911, Austin purchased the east half of Lot 3, Con. 2 SER, from Mr. and Mrs. William James Kincade. In 1944, he transferred the title to his son, Clayton, who sold the farm to Clayton Stevenson in 1949.

In 1916, Leonard lied about his age and joined the army. He spent his overseas duty skidding logs from the French Alps to sawmill camps, where they were made into thick planks to move the Allied guns through deep mud. Leonard was discharged from the army in 1919 and returned to his father's farm. He married Mete "Mae" Oliver (1903-1985). She was the daughter of William "Bill" Oliver and Minnie Arrand. Following their marriage, Austin transferred the title of the west half of Lot 5, Con. 2 SER, to Leonard and Mae. They had four children, Basil (1924-1978); Ivan (1925); Ilene (1929); and Vivian (1934). During the next 20 years, in addition to farming, Leonard was the township's assessor. One year, the township council instructed Leonard to do the unpopular task of reassessment. For a number of years, he was hired to grade and gravel the Second Line SER between the Lambton town line and the Currie Road (County Road 6).

Leonard and Mae moved to Sarnia in 1944. He was employed as a customs officer at the Bluewater Bridge in Point Edward until his retirement. Basil and Ivan continued to work on the farm until it was sold to William "Bill" and Bea Atchison in 1945.

Basil moved to Sarnia in 1944. He had three children, Jerry (1953); Betty (1955); and Rick (1957). After moving to Hamilton, Basil was employed by a Hamilton steel company as a transport driver until his death in 1978.

In 1945, Ivan married Mildred Murray. They had three children, Dennis (1946); Bradley (1950); and Gayle (1954). Ivan had a career in

Home of John and Harriett (Bratt), ca.1885, east half of Lot 4, Con. 2 SER. L-R, Eliza Jane Carrothers, mother Harriett, father John, Mary Ann "Minnie," William, Thornton, Austin; sitting are Fred, Ashton and Tirzah "Teasie" with Ina the rattail terrier. Property known as Mount Pleasant Farm.

sales and sales management. He and Mildred divorced, and he married Lily Atkinson.

Ilene married Robert Morgan in 1948. Their three children are Barbara (1949); Ronald (1951); and Wendy (1953).

Vivian married Bert Wellington in 1951. Their four children are Terry (1952); Rodney (1954); Robin (1957); and Darcey (1961).

Clayton Carrothers, son of Austin, married Dorothy Brown (1907-1998). They had two children, Donald (1930) and Joan (1938). Clayton helped Austin on the farm and at the same time was employed by the Howard McLean Grain and Feed in Kerwood and later by Pincombes Feed and Seed Store in Strathroy. Clayton and his family, including his father, Austin, moved to Milverton, Ontario, in 1944, where he managed a flour and grist mill. One Saturday, while oiling the mill machinery, Clayton was caught by a chain and sprocket. He was pulled in up to his shoulder and lost his right arm. Later, he owned a GMC dealership.

In 1930, Evelyn Carrothers married George Downer (1908-1991). George farmed for a short time before moving to Petrolia to work for a fuel company until his retirement. They had three children, Jean (1931); Marie (1934); and Ira (1942). Jean married Fred Ken in 1955. Marie married Donald Bustin in 1957. Evelyn was a devout member of the United Church and was an active community volunteer.

Leonard Carrothers (age four), ca.1903.

Carrothers (1935) celebration of 100 years of Carrothers family arrival in Canada. Standing L-R, Ninian (son of Samuel), Hugh Campbell (son-in-law of Michael), Eldon (son of Thomas), William (son of Joseph), Harry (son of Mark). Sitting L-R, Austin (son of John and grandson of Nathaniel), Amos (son of Micheal), Nathaniel (son of William), Mark (son of Michael) and William (son of Thomas).

CARSON, John and Eliza

John Carson (1815) was born in Ireland, and he married Eliza Gardner (1818) in Ireland. They immigrated to Adelaide Township about 1839 as the 1842 census states that John Carson had been a resident of Ontario for about two years, living on the east half of Lot 15, Con. 5 SER. He had not improved any of his 100 acres, and 70 bushels of potatoes were grown that year. John and Eliza had eight children, and information is provided for six of them.

Robert Carson (1838) was born in Ireland.

Jane Carson (1840) was born in Adelaide Township, and married Trustin Rowe (1859) of Metcalfe Township (he was born in Ireland).

Eliza Carson (1846) married James McGill, who was born in Michigan.

Hannah Carson (1850-1918), John and Eliza's fourth child, was born in Adelaide Township. She died in Solomon, Dickinson County, Kansas. In 1866, she married William S. Boyle of Metcalfe Township (1850-1914), who had been born in Scotland. To this union were born 13 children.

Jane Agnes Boyle (1867), Hannah and William's eldest child, was born in Metcalfe Township.

Martha Jane Boyle (1870); Margaret Ellen Boyle (1872); William Boyle (1874); John Harrison Boyle (1877); Charlotte Theresa Maud Boyle (1879); Ernest Walter Boyle (1881); and Hannah Carson Boyle (1883) were born in Brooke Township.

The later children were born in Solomon, Dickinson County, Kansas. These were Lillian, Thomas, and three sons who died shortly after birth.

Hannah Carson Boyle is buried in Solomon, Kansas, and her husband, William, is buried in Los Angeles, California.

John S. Carson (1852) and Thomas L. Carson (1854) were born to John and Eliza in Adelaide Township.

The 1852 Adelaide census showed that William Carson, 32, born in Ireland, and his wife, Lydia, were sharing Pt. Lot 15, Con. 5 SER, with William's brother. The children listed in the census are Jacob, age four, and Margaret A., age two. Rachel Marshall, age nine, born in Ireland, is living with the family.

Lydia died in 1871 in Adelaide Township at age 42. William Carson and his family are not shown in the 1861 Adelaide census.

CATCHPOLE, Alfred and Edna

Alfred and Edna Catchpole (deceased) moved from London to Adelaide on Concession 5 in 1953. They had two children, Elizabeth and Edward. Elizabeth married Jim Routley (see ROUTLEY, Jim and Elizabeth). Edward resided with his wife, Trudy, and their two boys, Tom and Bill, in Adelaide. They moved to West Williams. Tom now lives with his wife, Stephanie, and daughter Katelynn on Napperton Drive in Adelaide.

CAWRSE, Charles and Grace

Charles Cawrse (1801-1888), born in St. Neot, Cornwall, England, married Grace Rowe (1805-1883) in Cardynham, Cornwall, England, on April

Charles Cawrse Sr. at 85 years (1886).

16, 1827. In 1847 or 1848, they came to Metcalfe, then Adelaide Township, with nine children. In August 1848, Charles Cawrse Sr. bought the east half of Lot 9, Con. 3 SER, from Arthur Bowen and his wife. On the 1851 Metcalfe census they were living in a 1-storey log cabin with their nine children. They were members of the Anglican Church. Between 1854 and 1882, they bought parts of Lot 8, 9, 10 and 11, Con. 3.

In later life, the family turned strict Methodist and attended the Blackstock Methodist Church. At least one family member is buried in Blackstock Cemetery. Grace died at 82 years and is buried in St. Mary's Anglican Cemetery in Napier, beside two sons who died in their teens. The obituary said that her family was much scattered throughout Ontario. Charles died at 88 years and was buried in Strathroy Cemetery. His obituary refers to him as one of our most respectable citizens. Charles and Grace had nine children.

Elizabeth Ann (1828) first married Mr. Ross, a lawyer, then a Mr. Crane, then she married her third husband, William Dorgan, who also died young in 1868 and is buried in St. Mary's Cemetery, Napier.

Mary (1829-1921) married William Taylor from Metcalfe Township in 1852. They had two sons and five daughters. The daughters married into the Cowan, Smithrim, Dinning, Inch and Hawken families. The sons married Matilda Smithrim and Katherine McNeil.

Jane (1831) married Isaac Thompson from Metcalfe Township in 1862. They had five children and were living in Oregon in 1906.

Charles Jr. (1833) first married Jane Schusse from Westminster. They had one son, John William (1859-1927). Jane died in 1861 at the age of 20, and was buried in St. Mary's Cemetery, Napier. In 1863, Charles married Elizabeth Cleverdon from Adelaide Township. On the 1871 census, they lived in Strathroy and in 1875, Charles was listed in the Strathroy Business Directory as a grain buyer. He also dealt in cattle. They were back living on the Metcalfe farm by 1881 on Lot 10, Con. 3.

Their children were John William (first marriage), Mary, Charles, George, Maud, Ida, Frank, and a daughter who died young and is buried in Blackstock Cemetery.

John William went to London, Ontario, as a young man. He became a brick manufacturer. Later, he was prominent in building supplies, and he eventually became a member of the firm Morrison and Cawrse, real estate dealers. He was prominent in Masonic circles in London and district. He married widow Anna Skuse from London. Charles' and Elizabeth's daughter, Mary, died in 1887. She had caught a cold, which turned into consumption. The other children went to Portland, Oregon, with the family.

In 1888, Charles Cawrse Sr. died. Charles, who had mortgaged both farms to cover debts incurred by Lawrence Cleverdon in the Chicago stock market, lost the farms in 1889. Some time after his father died, Charles, Elizabeth and family left for Oregon.

George (1835-1852) was buried in St. Mary's Cemetery, Napier.

Grace (1837) married Charles Latour, a portrait painter, glazier and painter. They moved away from the area.

John (1842-1856) was buried in St. Mary's Cemetery, Napier.

Bedena (1844-1933) married Lawrence Cleverdon from Adelaide Township in October 1863. They had nine sons. They lived in Adelaide Township on Lot 2, Con. 2 SER, and then moved to Strathroy, where Lawrence was Mayor in 1877 and 1878. In 1888, the family left for the U.S. following failed business investments.

Ellen (1846-1891) married John Graham from Lobo. They lived in Lobo and moved to Adelaide to Lot 22, Con. 2 NER, in 1873. They had 10 children, including several who died in infancy. Ellen died in 1891 at 45 years. In 1896, John Graham married Sarah Jane Bolton of Second Line North, Adelaide Township. They had five children. Ellen was buried in Lobo Cemetery.

CHAMBERS, Thomas and Ann

James Chambers and Anne Ellis of County Cork, Ireland, had four sons and two daughters. Thomas (d.1883) married Ann Fuller. The second and third children were Charles and James. Marie married a Mr. Skuse from Byron or Komoka. Ursula married Robert Sadler, who was a tailor and Byron postmaster. They moved to Detroit, Michigan. Another son's name and whereabouts are unknown.

Thomas and Ann were married in County Cork, Ireland, in 1834. Thomas came to Canada in 1836

Grace (Rowe) Cawrse with children, Elizabeth Ann (or Mary), George and Bedena, ca.1850.

and made a home at the "Forks" or, as it is now called, London. Two years later, his wife and their two small children, Anne, aged three, and James, 18 months, joined him at the Forks. They lived there for about three years.

Deciding they lived too near a tavern to raise a family, they moved to Adelaide Township, settling on 50 acres at the west half of Lot 5, Con. 2 SER. While there, five more children were born, Mary, William "Willie," Thomas (1845), Charles "Charlie" and George. The farm was then sold to Mr. Kinney, a schoolteacher, for $800. They then bought 100 acres, the east half of Lot 1, Con. 2 SER, from Mr. Webb with his settlement rights for $100.

There was enough land cleared on this farm for a small garden, and the rest was solid bush with a small slashing. On the farm was a small log house and a stable. Mr. Wells and his family were to go to Sarnia that autumn but, due to soft roads, they had to return. Both families spent the winter together in a large oak log house, which was near the bridge on Con. 2 SER. In the spring, Thomas returned with his family to the east half of Lot 1, Con. 2 SER, and started to clear the land.

Thomas and Ann Chambers were members of St. Ann's Anglican Church in Adelaide Village, where both are laid to rest. This was the only church near them when they came from the Forks. St. Ann's was erected in 1833 and at the time of the Rebellion of 1836-1837, the church was used for a military camp. At this time, the floor was torn up, but it was repaired after the war. Later, a church was built at Wisbeach in 1856. The family then worshipped there, going on foot or in a farm wagon.

Five other children were born to Thomas and Ann, and of these, only two grew to adulthood, John and Rebecca.

When Thomas died, John and George Chambers, who had married sisters Eve and Elizabeth McQuillan, bought their father's farm, the east half of Lot 1, Con. 2 SER.

In the same year, John Chambers bought the east half of the west half of Lot 1, Con. 2 SER. It was purchased from James and Margaret Wakefield. This farm was adjacent to the farm purchased by John and George Chambers from their father's estate.

Subsequently, John and George split the farm that had been their father's. George retained 75 acres of this farm and John took 25 acres on the west side. This gave each of them a 75-acre parcel.

John moved a barn and an implement house as well as some fruit trees to his farm from the farm purchased by his father, Thomas.

John's farm is the one lived in and owned for many years by his son and daughter-in-law, Russell Chambers and Margaret "Nellie" Chambers.

Thomas and Ann Chambers had 12 children. Anne (1835) married James (or George) Clark. James married Hanna Bateman. Margaret married Robert Kerr, and then remarried, to John Reycraft. Mary married Henry Williams. William married Sara Clark. Thomas (1845-1930) married Margaret Bateman. Charlie married Fannie Moffatt. George married Elizabeth McQuillan. Beckie died in infancy. John (1854-1921) married Eve McQuillan, then Mary Brown. Twins unnamed, died in infancy. Rebecca married John Brown.

Anne and James (or George) Clark had nine children, Fannie, Annie, John, twins Mary and Jane, Beckie, George, Ida and Emma.

Fannie Clark married George Hodgson of Adelaide. Annie Clark married Nathaniel Seed. John Clark died in early manhood. Mary Clark married William Chapman of Saskatoon. Jane Clark married Jas Adair of Saskatoon. Beckie Clark married John Chapman of Moosejaw, then William Foller of Bounty, Saskatchewan. George Clark married Kate Tigner. Ida Clark married George Rogers of Victoria, B.C. Emma Clark married Walter Brown of Bounty, Saskatchewan, and then remarried, to A. Adair, also of Bounty.

John and first wife, Eva (McQuillan) Chambers, with daughter, Mary, and son, Russell, on horseback, in front of original house, ca.1895.

Living room of John Chambers home, Mary (Brown) Chambers (wife of John) and daughter, Mary.

James and Hanna Chambers, from May 8, 1863, to November 20, 1876, owned and resided on the east half of the west half of Lot 1, Con. 2 SER. At this time, the farm was sold to James Wakefield. Their children were Nancy, Thomas, John B. and Mary.

Nancy Chambers married Rev. Arthur (Grasset?) C. Smith, who went to the Yukon as a medical missionary and held funeral services for the native woman who first found gold in the Yukon. Their children were Noel, Gladys (Bates), and Harold. Thomas Chambers married Clara Dark of London, and their children were Adeline (Guest); Harold; Hannah (Clowes); Clara (Reynolds); Veronica; Dudley; and Maynard. John B. Chambers married Mary McCracken of St. Thomas, and they farmed near Muncey. Their children were Kathleen and Dorothy (Curtis). Mary Chambers married Myer McLaughlin and moved to Moosejaw, Saskatchewan. They had two children.

Margaret Chambers (1838-1917), third child of Thomas and Ann, had two children from her marriage to Robert Kerr (1837-ca.1870) of Warwick Township, Thomas (1864) and William (1868). Margaret and Robert farmed in Warwick Township. Thomas Kerr married Violet Bryce, and William Kerr married Liza Moffatt. From Margaret's second marriage, to John Reycraft (d.1914), three children were born, Rebecca, Swanton and Susie Reycraft. Margaret and John also farmed in Warwick Township. Rebecca Reycraft (1875) married Fred Westgate. Swanton B. Reycraft (1881) married Lizzie Moffatt. Susie Reycraft (1885) married Herman McNaughton. Margaret and John are buried at St. Paul's Anglican Church Cemetery in Wisbeach.

Mary Chambers married Henry Williams. They had seven children, Margaret Anne, Fred, Jennie, Thomas, twins Sara and Katie, and Charlie.

Margaret Anne married Jos. Richards. Fred married Sadie Utley. Jennie Thomas married John F. Jedds. Thomas married Emma Huxtable. Sara married George Gallanger. Kate married William Trescott. Charlie died a young man.

William "Willie" and Sara Chambers had six children, William "Willie" John, Frank, Fannie, James, Albert, and Walter. This family lived in Petrolia, Ontario.

William John Chambers married Lizzie Beach of Petrolia. Frank Chambers married Evelyn (last name unknown). There is no information on Fannie Chambers. James Chambers lived in Saskatoon, Saskatchewan. Albert Chambers married Lottie Astelle and they lived in Sarnia. Walter Chambers married Carrie (last name unknown) from Burford, Ontario.

Thomas Chambers, sixth child of Thomas and Ann, and his wife, Margaret, had seven children, Swanton, Essie, Hales (one of a set of triplets, two dying in infancy), Hilda, and James.

The family resided at the east half of the east half of Lot 1, Con. 3 SER. Thomas' brother, Charles Chambers, lived on the west half of the east half of Lot 1, Con. 3 SER, in the 1870s. Subsequently, Thomas bought out Charles and came into possession of the entire east half of Lot 1, Con. 3 SER. Upon Thomas' death, the farm was again split with Thomas' son, Swanton, who obtained the west half of the east half of Lot 1, Con. 3 SER.

Thomas Chambers' daughter, Hilda, who married Edgar Kerton, received the east half of the east half of Lot 1. Hilda lived for the rest of her life in the large cement block house on the property. On her death, the property became her daughter, Meryl's. Meryl married Earl Guest. The property burned while the occupant was Carlton Guest, Meryl and Earl's son.

Upon the death of his parents, the property was willed to Carlton Guest, who sold it in 1999 to Gary

Chambers, a great grandnephew of Thomas Chambers.

Swanton Chambers, Thomas and Margaret's firstborn, married Cassie Swanton, and they farmed near Watford. Essie Chambers married Richard Swanton. There is no further information on Hales Chambers. James Chambers died in infancy.

Charles Chambers, seventh child of Thomas and Ann, and his wife, Fannie, had two children, Maud and Charlie. Maud Chambers married Jas H. Bryce. Charlie Chambers never married.

George and Elizabeth Chambers had four children, Edward George, Annie, Mary, and John Thomas.

Edward George Chambers married Margaret Trotter. Annie Chambers married William Trotter. Mary Chambers married Jaret Trotter.

John Thomas Chambers, youngest child of George and Elizabeth, married Matilda Moore. They bought the west half of Lot 2, Con. 2 SER. A cheese factory was built on this farm at one time.

Russell and Nellie Chambers and firstborn daughter, Eva, 1917.

The cement top of the well that serviced the factory is still visible. John inherited his father's farm, the 75 acres at Lot 1, Con. 2 SER. John and Matilda had one son, John "Ross" Chambers. John and Matilda occupied the farm on which the cheese factory was built until John's death, when it was sold to the Verhoeven family.

Ross Chambers married Beryl Tedball. Ross and Beryl had one son, Gary Chambers. Ross and Beryl purchased and live on the farm at the west half of Lot 3, Con. 2 SER. This was purchased from Nelson Alderson, and was and is still known as the "Wonderland Farm." This was the site of the Wonderland Post Office. The tool shed, which is still on this farm, has the "pigeon holes" or letter slots from this building.

The original farm owned by Thomas and Ann Chambers was willed to Ross Chambers by his father. Upon Ross' death, Beryl deeded the east Pt. Lot 1, Con. 2 SER, to her son, Gary, who still owns the property. This farm has been in the Chambers name with direct line descendants for about 150 years, or five generations.

Rebecca, the youngest of Thomas and Ann's children, and her husband, John Brown, lived at Harbor Beach, Michigan. They had a very narrow escape with their lives when the great forest fire of Michigan in 1881 destroyed their possessions. Rebecca and her husband are buried in White Rock Cemetery near Harbor Beach, Michigan. They had two children, Margaret and William. Margaret Brown married William Bars. William Brown married Hazel Hill.

John Chambers (1854-1929) was married twice, and he had two children, Mary and Russell, from the first marriage to Eve McQuillan. Mary Chambers married Edward Hamer, and lived in Trail, B.C.

Russell Chambers (1890-1968) married Margaret "Nellie" Westgate (1894-1984) of Warwick Township. Nellie was the daughter of Thomas Westgate and Johnina Burgar. The couple took up residence in Sarnia, where Russell had a job at the Imperial Refinery. When his father, John, quit farming, Russell moved from his home at the west half of Lot 1, Con. 2 SER, to the large brick home his father had built in 1900 on the east half of the west half of Lot 1, Con. 2 SER. The summer kitchen on this house was the original farm home, and it is still standing at this writing. The couple purchased the west half of the west half of Lot 1, Con. 2 SER. Richard Routley had owned this farm. Upon the death of his stepmother, Mary, Russell moved to the family home next door to the property on Con. 2 SER. Russell and Nellie had six children.

Eva Marie Chambers, eldest child of Russell and Nellie, died in infancy from whooping cough. John Edward Chambers died March 4, 1944, still a young man. Thomas R. Chambers (1922-1982) married Wanda Ward, and they later divorced. There was one child from this marriage, Patricia Anne Chambers. Patricia married Neil Bolton. Thomas R. owned and farmed the north half of the west half of Lot 1, Con. 1 SER, from 1946 until his death in 1982, at which time it was purchased by Gary Chambers.

Evelyn J. Chambers (1926-1990), fourth child of Russell and Nellie, married Calvin Bryson and moved to New York State. After their divorce, she moved back to Canada, and purchased a home on Cockburn St. in Kerwood, where she resided until her death in 1990.

Cecil Laverne Chambers (1928-1984) married June Zink. Three children were born in Adelaide to this marriage, Brenda, William R., and Edward. Cecil farmed with his father, Russell, most of his adult life. He lived on the west half of the west half of Lot 1, Con. 2 SER. Upon his father's death in 1968, he farmed the land in partnership with his mother, Nellie.

Dorothy M. Chambers, the youngest of Russell and Nellie's children, married Lloyd Bryson of Warwick Township, Lambton County. Lloyd was an Inspector CID with the London Police Department at the time of his death in 1977. Dorothy lives in London.

Russell Chambers died at the home farm. His wife, Nellie, resided on the home farm until January 1981, when she moved to the Watford Nursing Home. She died January 19, 1984.

The family home on the east half of the west half of Lot 1, Con. 2 SER, is now owned by Barbara and Jason Caris. Barbara was a Chambers before she married, and is the great great-granddaughter of George Chambers.

CHOUFFOT, Jacques and Martha

The Chouffot family came to Adelaide in the spring of 1990. They were looking for a house in the country outside of London and were happy to find the Henderson farmhouse for sale. Martha's family is from the London area and Jacques came to Canada from France in 1985.

Pierre (1987) was two when he moved to Adelaide and Jean-Luc was born here (1992). History has come to meet the present in their house. Martha is a local teacher in Strathroy, as was one of the original Hendersons. Also, Jacques has a cabinet-making business on the property close to where Mr. Henderson had his shop. Here, all of the woodwork was prepared for the house.

CLELAND, Robert and Lillie

Robert (1805-1880) and Lillie (Wiley) Cleland (1804-1877) immigrated to Canada from County Down, Ireland, about 1837. With their six children, they came to Wiley's Corners in Adelaide Township, where other Wiley brothers and sisters had located in the new settlement of Adelaide (see WILEY, David and Ann; McCHESNEY, William and Jane; and SEED, John and Margaret).

The 1842 census lists the Cleland family living on the west half of Lot 3, Con. 2 NER, in a two-family household with Patrick Campbell. Campbell was a retired Army sergeant from Ireland, who had been in Canada about ten years (1832). Also in the household were Campbell's wife and one child, Ann. In 1836, Patrick Campbell received the patent for 200 acres, all of Lot 3, Con. 2 NER, for his military service. Campbell and his wife were Catholics, thought to be buried in St. Patrick's Cemetery. The Clelands supported the West Adelaide Chapel and later the Presbyterian Church, but they also had ties with St. Ann's Anglican Church where some family records are found. Louise Cleland (Maddeford) knows nothing of the Campbell family, so perhaps it was an arrangement of convenience between two Irishmen.

The 1842 Agricultural census shows that Robert Cleland occupied 401 acres of land with five acres improved. There are no records of the location of this acreage. In trying to provide farmland for his two sons, Robert Cleland divided his property, the north half of Lot 3, Con. 1 NER, and the west half of Lot 3, Con. 2 NER. This land was purchased in 1847 so that an extremely long laneway was necessary to access the farm buildings on the south half of Lot 3. The Campbell daughter, Ann, married to Thomas Ensign, sold the last of the property to Shalto Galloway in 1863.

In 1861, John Cleland purchased 35 acres, part of the west Pt. of Lot 4, Con. 1 NER, from Amasa Wood and wife, and five years later he purchased 73 acres of the same lot.

About 1870, the 2-storey frame house on the original north half of Lot 3, Con. 1 NER, was replaced by a magnificent red brick Georgian style home, a very ambitious project for the times! Family stories tell that the bricks were hauled from Arkona. In 1876, John Cleland deeded this property to his son, Robert Cleland Jr. The Cleland parents and their daughter, Isabella, lived in a white frame cottage on the southwest corner of Lot 4, Con. 1 NER, until their deaths. The Cleland family plot is in the West Adelaide Cemetery. In 1886, Hugh Wiley, brother of Lillie Cleland, bought the south part of the west half of Lot 3, Con. 2 NER, from the Cleland family. This property later became the Wilson family farm.

Robert and Lillie (Wiley) Cleland had nine children. Margaret Cleland (1827), born in Ireland, married John Riggs of West Williams in 1844. They raised nine children whose baptisms are in St. Ann's Adelaide church records.

David Wiley Cleland (1829-1896) was born in Ireland. He farmed in Adelaide and Warwick Townships, and never married.

Jane Cleland (1831) was born in Ireland. She married Robert Riggs of West Williams (no information on children).

Isabella Cleland (1833-1918), or Aunt Bella, as she was known in the neighbourhood, had a polio-like disease in Ireland when she was about three years old. She would talk about being carried on her father's shoulders around the farm in Ireland. She helped with the housework and cared for the babies in the new pioneer settlement, using a rocking chair as a wheelchair. That chair still exists and the rocker is worn flat. Many of the Wiley and Wilson children told stories of visiting Aunt Bella, who was a cheerful Christian lady. Dr. Oliver McGillicuddy, son of Elizabeth (Wiley) McGillicuddy, wrote in his autobiography about making a professional medical visit to Aunt Bella.

Allen "Allie" Cleland (1836-1903) married Margaret Campbell (1837-1919). They farmed on the Galloway farm and raised four children in the West Adelaide community.

Jack Cleland (1838-1933) was born in Canada. He married Catherine Wilkins of Adelaide and they moved to St. Clair, Michigan, and raised seven children.

Eliza "Lisa" Cleland (1842-1917) married veterinarian Dr. George Walker Fair (1831-1879) of Arkona. St. Ann's Anglican Church records show both Louisa Fair and Eliza Fair were baptized on July 13, 1875.

Ellen Cleland (1844) married businessman Robert Harper of Hamilton and raised three children there.

Robert James Cleland Jr. (1848-1926) married Mary Parcher (1852-1887). Robert raised his family in the West Adelaide community until he moved to the Adelaide/Warwick townline farm.

Robert and Mary (Parcher) Cleland had three children. Lillie Cleland (1880-1974) married William Cuddy of Adelaide Township (see CUDDY, James and Violet). Their children, Roma, Ruby, Eva, Clair and DeLos, attended S.S. #9 School.

George Cleland (1883-1954) married Bessie Watson (1880-1974) of Sarnia, whom he met when she was visiting her Watson relatives at Wisbeach. George and Bessie (Watson) Cleland had four children. Louden Parcher Cleland (1905-1991) lived on the Adelaide farm until he was 17, then moved to London. He married Hazel McLaughlin of Sylvan and they raised a daughter, Denise Cleland.

Mary Louise Cleland attended S.S. #6 Adelaide and the Wisbeach School in Warwick when her father was farming on the Adelaide/Warwick townline. Her schoolmates there were Freda Wiley, and Birdenia and Zelma Conkey. When the family moved back to the west half of Lot 4, Con. 1 NER, Louise's teachers at S.S. #6 Adelaide were Mr. Langan, Miss Tanner, Mr. Jones, (the doctor's father taught there during the war), Arthur Davidson and a "red-headed teacher" who boarded at Walsh's. She married Charles William Maddeford (1905-1989) and they lived in London, where he was involved in secondary school education. Their children are Dr. Bill Maddeford of Delaware; Ted Maddeford, a secondary school teacher in Ingersoll; and John Maddeford, a secondary school teacher in Parry Sound. Louise lives in Delaware at this writing.

Isabella Jean Cleland (1908-1989) married Lorne Graham (1911-1995) of Lobo Township, where they raised two sons, Gary and Dougal.

Lillian Cleland (1911-1997) married Maxwell McNee, with whom she had two children, Beverly and Donald. Then she married Ron Riddell, who was a mechanic in Strathroy. Their daughter, Linda, lives in Thorndale.

Bessie Hughena "Hughie" Cleland was named after the young Dr. Samuel Orville Hugh Jones of Adelaide Village. He asked that she be named after him, as she was his first delivery. She married Wesley Allen (1906-1980). Their son, Douglas Glen Allen, taught at a community college in Toronto.

Agnes Margery Cleland (1916-1994) married Donald Campbell (1907-1991) of Lobo Township.

George Watson "Wattie" Cleland (1916-1951) was killed in a gun accident in the bush.

Wesley Cleland (1886-1892), son of Robert and Mary (Parcher) Cleland, is buried in West Adelaide Cemetery.

John Cleland (1887-1962), youngest child of Robert and Mary, married Mildred Conkey (1887-1967) of Wisconsin, daughter of Alexander Conkey, originally of Adelaide.

CLELFORD, William and Ann

The Clelford family name first appears in the census in 1861. William Clelford (1810-1880), a carpenter/joiner, and his wife, Ann Neale (1820-1913), moved to Canada from England. Their two children, Phoebe (1844) and Charles (1847), were with them. Both William and Ann are buried in the cemetery of St. Ann's Anglican Church in Adelaide.

Their son, Charles Clelford, married a cousin, Priscilla Clelford, who had been born in Hamilton in 1871 but was raised by an uncle in Gananoque. She moved to Adelaide Township to "be with her own" but sometimes wished that the flat, landlocked township was a little more like her childhood home. When the cabin the couple had been living in behind St. Ann's Church burned down, they moved into a hotel that they operated for a good number of years. They had nine children, Annie (1873); George (1875); Mary Sophia (1875); Charles (1877); Rebecca (1878); Louisa (1879); Martha (1885); William (1885); and Emma (1890). William was the only one who did not survive his childhood years, and died in 1891. After many years of hard work at the hotel, and the farm they also ran, Charles and Priscilla retired and moved to Strathroy.

Their daughter, Rebecca, married a teacher, Charles George, son of James and Mary George, on December 23, 1897. They lived in Glencoe, where they raised eight children, Pearlie Jane (1900); Annie Edith (1906); Ethel (1908); Frederick James (1910); Charles (1911); Clara Mae (1912); Mary Eileen (1918); and Grace Isabel (1919). Because it was a busy time for the family, Clara spent the summers at her grandparents' hotel in the early 1920s.

CLEVERDON

Lawrence E. Cleverdon Sr. (1779-1845) was born in Pancrasweek, Devonshire, England. About 1835, he married Mary Watt (1805-1894), also born in England. Lawrence E. was 57 and Mary 30. They lived in Galshan, England, near Hartland, Devonshire. Their two children, both born in Hartland, Devonshire, England, were Elizabeth (1836) and Lawrence Ernest (1838-1911). In 1844, Lawrence, Mary, and their two children left England to come to Canada, landing in early 1845. Lawrence died soon after landing. His burial place is not known.

The 1861 Adelaide census shows that in 1848, Mary Cleverdon married Dennis Hodgson, freeholder, born in England ca.1805, of the Wesleyan Methodist faith. Mary, Elizabeth and Lawrence Jr. were Anglican. In November 1855, Dennis bought 100 acres of the west half of Lot 2, Con. 2 SER, from Jeremiah Baker. Dennis sold the property to Lawrence Jr. in 1860 for one dollar. The 1861 census showed that Dennis, Mary, Elizabeth and Lawrence Ernest lived in a log cabin. The farm was called "Garden Hill." They worked hard to clear the land, and Dennis and Lawrence sold greens from the farm.

In October 1863, Lawrence Jr. Cleverdon, now 25, married Bedena Cawrse (1844-1933) from Metcalfe Township at St. Ann's Anglican Church in Adelaide Village. It was a double wedding ceremony with Lawrence's sister, Elizabeth, 27, and Bedena's brother, Charles Jr. Cawrse (1833), from Metcalfe Township.

Lawrence Jr. was very active in politics and in 1865, Lawrence was elected a member of the Municipal Council of Adelaide and served as Councillor, Deputy-Reeve, and Reeve for years. In 1866, Lawrence bought 50 acres of the east half of Lot 2 from Blanche Westlake and 50 from Richard Randall. Less than 100 acres were cleared of the 200 acres. In 1871, Lawrence built the Victoria Cheese Factory, a large frame building on the south-

Bedena (Cawrse) Cleverdon and sons, 1887.

west side of Lot 2 with partner John Carrothers. The wood-lined well is still visible on the property. In 1871, Lawrence also formed a Pork Packing Company in Strathroy, a large brick building on Maitland Street with partners J.W. Squire and J. Lenfesty. In 1872, Lawrence severed the half-acre on which the cheese factory stood and in 1873, rented out the house and farm, now 120 acres cleared, to George Hodgson.

The Cleverdon family moved to Strathroy and became members of the Strathroy Methodist Church. Lawrence continued to run the Adelaide Victoria Cheese Company and he owned the Napier Cheese Factory in Napier. An article in the "Age" of February 20, 1874, reports, "The Napier Annual Meeting was most satisfactory. The stockholders received a dividend of 10% on the stock invested. Forty-one-and-a-half tons of cheese was made from the 20th day of May till the 31st day of October, which was sold for an average price of 11 1/4 cents per lb. Part of the cheese was sent directly to England." An article in the March 13, 1874, "Age" reports on "The Annual Meeting of the Victoria Cheese Company, owned and managed by Lawrence Cleverdon. There was a large attendance of the patrons, all of whom were thoroughly satisfied with the proceedings and also with the proceeds of the past year. There was 47 tons of cheese manufactured, which commanded the highest price in the market. August cheese was shipped direct to England and passed their close inspection, for First Class, as did also a carload from the Napier factory manufactured by the same company. Farmers are now alive to their best interest; they understand the advantage of pasturing their land instead of tilling it, and receiving $25 to $30 per season for each cow's milk, instead of less than half that amount for butter with more than three times the labor."

In 1875, Lawrence is listed in the Strathroy Business Directory as Lawrence Cleverdon, of Collett & Cleverdon, Pork Packers and General Provision Merchants, Cheese, Butter and Bacon, living on Albert Street with a Pork Packing Plant on Maitland Street, which Lawrence started with partners J.W. Squire and J. Lenfesty in 1871. In 1876, Lawrence dissolved his partnership in the Pork Packing Plant and became a heavy buyer of cheese for the English house of Collett and Company. In September 1876, the "Age" reports, "Lawrence Cleverdon holds 8,000 boxes of cheese, equal to about 480,000 lbs. or 21 carloads ready to be shipped to Liverpool, England."

In April 1877, Lawrence bought an elegant yellow brick house on 50 Oxford Street, with a large orchard. He sold produce from his garden and orchard. Bedena and Lawrence held many lawn parties for the young people of the church and the "Light Guard Band" played their first formal engagement on their lawn during a Lawn Social in 1879. Lawrence was elected Mayor of Strathroy in 1877 and 1878. Later, he became a Reeve. Through the years, Lawrence was a member of the Board of Trade, the Dairy Board in London, a member of the London Fair Board and President of the Railroad Board. In 1882, Lawrence sold the cheese factory and a half-acre to John Clark. In 1925, the frame building was sold to Russell Dowding, who lived across the road and used it as a drive shed. The

Dowdings had an aerial photograph made of their farm in the 1940s and it seems to be the only picture of the Victoria Cheese Factory. It blew down in the 1953 tornado. In 1883, Lawrence sold the Adelaide Lot 2 property to James Sullivan and 99½ acres to Charles Chambers. He bought two other cheese factories, one in Aughrim in Brooke Township near Napier and one in Shetland. The "Western Dispatch" reported, "Lawrence intends to give Mr. Richardson a close run this coming season."

Lawrence was a member of the Euclid Lodge. He was very active in church life, was a Methodist lay preacher and a Sunday School superintendent, and was on the building committee that built the present United Church in Strathroy. Lawrence chaired many temperance meetings, and was comfortable speaking to large audiences. Lawrence was an excellent and sought-after speaker, well liked and highly respected in the community. It was with much dismay and sadness in the family and in the community when it was discovered that Lawrence had left Strathroy for the U.S. one evening in May 1887, owing quite a bit of money. Often, he would play the Chicago commodities market. Winnings always went into the businesses, but in May 1887, after a stock market crash, he could not cover his losses and to raise money, Lawrence forged cheques for cheese not delivered in England. His wife, Bedena, and their seven sons, ranging from babyhood to 15 years, stayed in Strathroy to liquidate assets to pay their creditors. In an interview, she said she was owed gold. In June 1887, her sister's daughter, Mary, died at the age of 21, another blow. She sold their lovely home on Oxford Street in August 1887, along with other business holdings. Bedena's father, Charles Cawrse from Metcalfe Township, died in September 1888, and then Bedena and her sons joined Lawrence in Leavenworth, Kansas. Lawrence's mother, Mary Watt Cleverdon Hodgson, also went to Leavenworth. In 1889, Lawrence worked as a city circulator for the Leavenworth Kansas "Sun." In 1891, Lawrence was an insurance agent, and in 1893, he was listed as assistant superintendent for the Metropolitan Life Insurance Company. In 1894, the Cleverdon family had opened their own drugstore in Leavenworth, the "Cleverdon Bros. Drugstore," which was in the family for almost 50 years. They advertised their business as Druggists and Chemists, open day and night. Like all old-fashioned drugstores, they sold everything from drugs to paint.

It was also a sad year for the Cleverdons in 1894, as Lawrence lost his mother, who lived with them, and two of their boys. George died at the age of 10, and their oldest son, John Charles, died at the age of 27. The Cleverdons were devastated to have lost three of their family in one year. In 1898, they lost another boy, Albert Ernest, 27.

In the meantime, Lawrence Sr. was involved in developing the "Brighton Mine," also working later on a new invention, an iceless icebox (refrigerator). In 1911, while collecting insurance money from his clients, Lawrence was found robbed and murdered (a blow on the head left him bleeding to death) at 73 years old, a sad end for a man who endured great hardships and must have worked terribly hard to accomplish so much.

In 1917, Bedena, who was always helping in the family businesses, got caught in a tornado, which twirled her up in the air and left her with a broken hip. In 1933, Bedena died in Stillwater, Oklahoma, at the home of her doctor son, Lawrence.

All the Cleverdon boys were given an excellent education. Two became a medical doctor, several became pharmacists, one was a senior editor of a newspaper, one was the owner of a grocery store, and all became upstanding citizens who were much respected in their communities.

Lawrence Cleverdon and family.

Mary Watt (Cleverdon) Hodgson ca.1870s.

Lawrence and Bedena Cleverdon had eight children, the first three born in Adelaide. William H. (1864-1866) is buried in St. Paul's Cemetery in Wisbeach.

John Charles (1868-1894) became Chief Circulator of "The Times" in Leavenworth, Kansas. He died of typhoid fever. His obituary praised him as an industrious, faithful worker, a model man, a real gentleman and a true Christian.

Albert Ernest (1871-1898) received his doctor's degree, then two months after setting up practice, became ill with spinal meningitis and died. His fiancée, also studying to become a doctor, later married Albert's brother, Dr. Lawrence Cleverdon.

Lawrence Alexander (1873-1956) was the first of five children born in Strathroy to Lawrence and Bedena. Lawrence Jr. became a medical doctor in 1901 in the U.S.

Herbert Henry (1875-1934) operated a dairy, and later owned a grocery store. He died of cancer.

Alfred Russell (1879-1963) became a pharmacist and owned the Diamond Drugstore for many years. His father, mother, and brothers helped him in the store. He died at age 82 from complications of a broken leg.

George Watt (1884-1894) died at age 10 from a bowel obstruction caused by eating unripe fruit.

Frederick Norman (1887). Fred became a pharmacist and later operated the Cleverdon Bros. Drugstore in Leavenworth. He died sometime after 1934.

Looking back on the life of Lawrence and Bedena Cleverdon, and the parents on both sides, one has to admire the courage and fortitude of the early settlers. Middlesex County in the early- and mid-1800s was a harsh place, so full of hardships and set backs that many returned to England disillusioned. However, for all their trials and tribulations, the Cleverdons always made sure that their sons had a good education that led to productive and distinguished careers, which must have been a great source of pride for Lawrence and Bedena.

CONKEY, Arthur and Margaret

Arthur Conkey, who was already 57 years old, and his wife, Margaret (Ferguson) Conkey immigrated to Adelaide Township from Saintfield, County Down, Northern Ireland, in 1842. Six of their seven children were with them. Those who came to Canada with their parents were William (1817-1889) and his wife, Mary Ann Gourley; Robert (1821-1909); James (1825); Margaret "Becky" (1827-1895); Arthur (1829-1885); and John (1833-ca.1875). Mary (1813-1890), their eldest, stayed in Ireland with her husband, John Greer. However, after John and two of the couple's four children died during the potato famine, Mary's brothers, William and Robert, arranged to have her and the remaining two children brought to Adelaide. She married Stephen Jeffries of London and they raised four sons there.

Three of Mary's brothers left Adelaide. James married a woman from Lambton County and, according to family lore, became a lighthouse keeper in Port Stanley. Arthur married a woman from the Sarnia area and became a captain on a Great Lakes freighter. John married Elizabeth McChesney of Adelaide, and they and their children moved to Illinois.

The three Conkey children who remained in Adelaide were William, Robert and Becky. In total, they had 36 children.

William and his wife, Mary Ann, had 11 children. In 1875, William gave land to the West Adelaide Presbyterian Church, where a manse was built on the east half of Lot 3, Con. 2 NER.

Esther (1844) married Arthur Brock and they had seven children, three of whom died in childhood. The Brocks were farmers who lived on the Egremont Road about a mile east of Adelaide Village. Margaret (1846) first married Robert Seymour, who died at age 33, then his brother, Alexander. They had no children. William Jr. (1848) married Maria Brock (a relation of Arthur's) and they had nine children. They lived first on a farm on the Egremont Road, and then moved to Maymont, Saskatchewan, as homesteaders sometime between 1888 and 1891. Mary Ann (1850) married Stephen Kerswill in 1884 and had three children, one of whom died in childhood. The family left Adelaide in 1890 for Gladwin, Michigan. Thomas (1852) married Lillie Irvin around 1880. They were among the first Conkeys to leave Adelaide when they moved to Kansas City in the early 1880s. Their only child was born there. John Gourley (1856) joined his brother, Thomas, in the move to Kansas City. He married Alice Cox Reeder there in 1881 and sold dry goods, one of the first in his family to leave farming. Robert Deas (1857), the only sibling not to marry, also moved to Kansas City in the early 1880s. Henry Philip (1860) married Mary Agnes Douglas in 1887. They lived in Adelaide on Lot 3, Con. 2 NER, where they raised nine children. They are buried in Adelaide Township. Alice (1861) married her brother-in-law Stephen's brother, W. Giles Kerswell, in Richmond Hill. They raised four children on their farm near Elgin Mills. George Alexander (1865) died at birth. The youngest child, Walter Darius (1870), married his first cousin, Catherine Lillian Conkey in 1893. Darius had inherited the family farm upon his father's death in 1889. He and Lillian lived there with their three children until they sold the farm in 1907 and moved into Strathroy.

Harold Norman Conkey (1870-1962) married Ella Catherine Quick (1906-1998). After he returned from serving in WWI, he began a barbering business on the main street of Kerwood. This was expanded to a small grocery store and then a contract was ratified to operate the Kerwood post office on the premises. They raised six children who

George Conkey and his great-niece, Evelyn Pennington.

attended S.S. #7 Adelaide. Elva Conkey married Wilfred Jordan and they had four children. She later married Thomas Twiddy. They live on Lake Huron Shores. Norman Conkey married Barbara Jean Forton and they live near Arva with their two children. Leona Margaret Conkey (1931-1931) is buried in Strathroy Cemetery. Ronald Leland Conkey married Phyllis Anne Hunter and they live in British Columbia. They have two children. Glen Lawrence Conkey married Evelyn Parsons and they live near Woodstock with their two children. Glenna Loraine Conkey (Glen's twin) married Raymond Robinson and they live with their two children near Ilderton.

Clara Viola Conkey (1900-1956) married Lyle Knight (1896-1980) (see Knight). Winlow Robert Conkey (1909-1942) married Marguerite Frank (1908-1981) in 1941. Winlow and Marguerite both worked for the H.C. Downham Company. They lived in Strathroy beside Winlow's mother.

When Robert Conkey was 26 years old, he married 16-year old Jane Wiley, the daughter of John Wiley and Eleanor Davidson. Robert and Jane had 14 children, 12 of whom lived to maturity. They farmed a considerable amount of land and, in his obituary, Robert is referred to as "one of the grand old pioneers of Adelaide Township."

Their eldest son, David (1848) first married Elizabeth Miniely and settled near Wisbeach, where Elizabeth died giving birth to their second child. After this, David married Nancy Catherine Hall of Lobo, and they had three children at Wisbeach before the family moved to "the Dakotas" in 1884, where two more children were born. John (1849) married Mary Dale in Glendale, Ontario in 1876. They had one daughter, Laura, and farmed in Adelaide for many years before retiring and moving to Strathroy. Ellenor (1851) married Andrew Miniely, Elizabeth's brother, in 1870. They had two children before Andrew died. After the children were raised, Ellenor married William Rogers in 1903 and lived in Watford. She is buried in Adelaide with Andrew. Elizabeth (1853) married Joseph McChesney in 1881 and had three children. Robert (1855) married Jane Wallace in 1878. Margaret Jane (1857) died at age 10. Samuel (1859) also homesteaded in the Dakotas. He visited Lobo briefly, where he married Amanda Hall, a sister of brother David's wife. After a destructive fire in 1891, the family moved to Caseville, Michigan, and purchased a farm. They had five children there. William Nelson (1861) died at the age of two years. Alexander (1863) also went to the Dakotas with his brothers, Samuel and David. Like them, he married a girl in Lobo, Isabella Edwards, in 1888. They returned to the Dakotas and later moved to Wisconsin, where they had three children. Rebecca Ann (1866) married James Wallace, a neighbour boy, in 1890 (see Wallace). George Brown (1868) married Margaret J. Thompson in 1903. They farmed in the area until their deaths and are buried in West Adelaide Cemetery. They had no children. Catharine Lillian (1870), as noted above, married first cousin Walter Darius Conkey. Nathaniel Wesley (1872) married Ellen Seed in 1894. Nat and Ellen Conkey lived in various places in the local areas of Adelaide Township, the Wisbeach area of Warwick Township, and for a few years in Sarnia. They raised two daughters, Beatrice Birdenia "Birdie" Conkey (1898-1983) and Zelma Kathleen Conkey (1906-1959), who lived in Adelaide Township (see Pennington and Hodgson).

Frederick Goldwin Conkey (1874-1961), youngest of the 14 children, was born on his father's farm. He married (1896) Blanche Seed (1876-1946), daughter of William and Catherine (Brock) Seed. Her father had a blacksmith shop in Adelaide Village, where she was born. In 1901, Fred Conkey went with his father-in-law to B.C to work in Rossland Goldmines, doing blacksmith work fixing railroad tracks. He returned in 1905 to farm the west half of Lot 4, Con. 1 SER, one of the original Conkey farms. He did mixed farming, and raised cattle and prize sheep. He was a member of the Orange Lodge in Adelaide Village, a Past Master of the Masons in Strathroy, and a member of Adelaide council for many years. Fred and Blanche Conkey had five children. William George "Toots" Conkey (1896-1969) served overseas in WWI and, in Belgium, he married Maria Louisa Julia De Porte (1888-1977). They lived for 47 years in Strathroy where Toots was involved in local organizations and served on town council. Maria taught piano lessons. They raised a son, William Frederick Conkey, who began to play in military bands at age 10. In WWII, he was a musician with the R.C.A.F. He lives in Newfoundland. Toots also served in WWII as a Physical Training Instructor.

Fluddea Pearl Conkey (1902-1903) was born and died in Rossland, B.C. when her father was working in the gold mines.

Kathryn Jane Conkey (1905-1989) married Winfield "Pat" Waltham (1901-1967) of Adelaide Township in 1929. Pat helped his father, Richard Waltham, in the construction business and, during WWII, he and Kathryn lived in Windsor where Pat worked in a war plant. They returned to the Conkey family farm for a time, and then moved to Strathroy. Pat Waltham and Clarence Fuller owned a construction company and built bridges throughout Middlesex County and the neighbouring areas. Kathryn was a life member of the Eastern Star, and a member of the Rebecca Lodge in Kerwood for over 30 years. Pat was a member of the Imperial Order of Odd Fellows (IOOF) Lodge in Kerwood. Their son, Fred Richard Winfield Waltham, married Ruth Allison. They live in Clinton with their three children. Their daughter, Elva Marjorie Louise Waltham, married John Clark and they live in Etobicoke with their three children.

Florence Opal Conkey (1907-1909) died in a house fire at the Conkey farm. Gordon Nelson Conkey married Molly Kathleen Noble of London Township. Gordon served in the Canadian Army from 1943-1945 and returned home to the original Conkey farm to help his father. Before his retirement, he drove trucks for local firms. The farm was sold in 1981 to neighbour Bob Peters, and Gordon and Molly retained the lot and the house where they live. They raised four children. Cathleen Ann Conkey married Gerald Joseph Otremba and they live in London where she works at St. Joseph's Hospital as a medical records technician. James Gordon Conkey married Joyce Ann Lockwood and they live in Strathroy with their one child. John Frederick Conkey works in London. David Nelson Conkey married Kelly Ann Lawrence and they live in Sarnia with their two children.

Margaret married William Adair when she was 23 years old. They had nine sons and two daughters. Seven of their sons homesteaded in Saskatchewan, six of them in a town called Bounty.

Hugh (1851) moved to Saskatchewan in 1902 and lived there as a bachelor until his death in 1922. His body was returned to Adelaide Township, where he is buried. William John (1852) married Elizabeth Baskier. They also went to Saskatchewan, but little else is known about their lives. James (1854) married Mary Jane Clark in 1887, and they had five children in Adelaide before they moved to Saskatoon in 1904. Robert (1856) married Mary Jane Geary and they had two sons, William, who was killed in WWI, and Franklin. Robert is buried in West Adelaide. Arthur (1858) and his wife, Emma Clarke Brown, moved to Bounty, Saskatchewan, in 1904 as homesteaders. Sarah (1861) never married and she died at age 26. Henry (1863), who married Mary McLaughlin, died in 1895. David (1865) married Annie Elizabeth Arrand in 1892 (see Arrand). They had three children of their own and adopted a fourth. Margaret Jane (1868) married James Walker and they lived on the Walker farm on Hwy. 22, east of Adelaide, where they had two sons and a daughter. Both Margaret and James are buried in Strathroy. Thomas (1870) married three times. After his first wife, Christina McKenzie, died in 1897, he married her sister, Robina. The couple had two children before Robina died in 1902. Thomas' third wife, Sarah Jane Glendenning, whom he met and married in Bounty, Saskatchewan, had six children. Samuel (1873) married Robina and Christina's sister, Minnie, about 1900, before they headed out to Saskatchewan, where their only son was born.

COOPER

The Petworth Emigration Scheme recorded a succession of Coopers coming to Adelaide Township. In 1832, William Cooper from Burton, West Sussex, was the first. In 1833, William Cooper came from Tillington, West Sussex. In 1836, James Cooper arrived from Tillington, West Sussex, along with his wife, Harriet, and nine children. In 1844, John Cooper immigrated from Graffam, West Sussex, with second wife, Harriet Challen, and five children. Other Coopers came, but their information lacks details.

William Cooper (ca.1795), born in Petworth, Sussex, England, was the son of James and Sarah (King) Cooper. He was the first of the family to come to Adelaide Township. In 1832, he is listed on the Petworth Preliminary List of Emigrants. William came with a party of 150 sent by Lord Egremont in England who, upon arrival, camped at Captain White's property on the town line of Lobo and Caradoc until log shanties could be erected on their new farms.

William wrote in a July 1832 letter to his family that it took seven weeks coming to Montreal and five more weeks coming up to Kettle Creek. He had purchased 100 acres of land at two dollars per acre, one-fourth to be paid at the end of three years (without interest), and the remaining debt to be paid in another three years (with interest). William asked all his brothers to come, as he thought they would find an improved situation in Canada. He wrote that Edward and Catharine Boxall, who received a land grant, had no children, and that the Boxalls and William Phillips were his neighbours. Phillips, who was also single, wrote in a letter to his parents in 1832 that the three lived and worked together. In February 1833, William replied to a letter written by his brother, Christopher, "If father and mother will come over and keep house for me, I will keep them without work." William had built a 16'x22' log house, and he was planning to build a barn 20'x30', hoping that some of his brothers would come over to help him. He wrote that the government built houses for the married people, but the single men were expected to build one for themselves. He suggested his family bring all kinds of vegetable and fruit seeds and pips, bedding and woollen socks, needles, pins and thread, cooking utensils, knives, forks and metal plates, gunpowder, farthings and old halfpence, but no penny pieces. He also requested a dog for deer hunting, 12 pairs of leather gloves, tools, and many other items. William wrote about his beautiful lot at Lot 21, Con. 4 SER, where he had planted two acres of wheat and hoped to have four more acres ready by spring.

The 1842 Adelaide census showed William living on the east half (as did the Boxalls) and brother James and family, who came in 1836, on the west half, of Lot 21, Con. 4 SER. On the 1851 census of Adelaide, William, 56, was still single, and living with James and Harriet. No other information was found for William. Another possible family member, John Cooper (ca.1804), appeared on the 1851 Adelaide census, farming part of Lot 19, Con. 3 SER. John's daughter, Betsy, 22 years of age and single, was living with the James Cooper family at the time of this census.

James Cooper (1792-1883) was the eldest of six brothers and four sisters. In 1817, James married, first, Mary Lambert (ca.1792-1819). They had two daughters. In 1821, James married Harriet Carter (1802-1857), daughter of Henry Carter. They had five daughters and eight sons. Eight of these children were born in England and five in Adelaide Township. Four children died in childhood. In 1836, James and his family joined William under the Petworth Emigration Scheme. Harriet died in 1857 and was buried in the Fourth Line Cemetery. In 1858, James married a widow, Mahetable (Miner) Eastman (1806-1903) of Adelaide, daughter of Truman and Elizabeth (Morrison) Miner (see Eastman). They had no children.

James farmed next to his brother, William. He became a devoted member of the Wesleyan Methodist faith and held regular family worship three times a day for his household. He is credited with holding the first Methodist services in his log cabin and, in 1839, James became one of the first converts in this district into the Methodist Wesleyan religion, probably by a saddleback preacher. He helped build the first log Methodist church on what is now the Fourth Line Cemetery, just west of Strathroy. James was the first church class leader, a position he held for 45 years. In his 1883 obituary, his wife Mahetable, five sons and five daughters survived him.

Nine of his children were Harriet (ca.1823); Henry (ca.1827); Emma (ca.1827-1913); Caroline (ca.1829); Sarah (ca.1830-1896); William (ca.1832-1896); Catherine (ca.1834); Cornelius (ca.1835-1906); and Charles (ca.1841).

Harriet Cooper married George Pegley (ca.1808). They farmed on part of Lot 20, Con. 4 SER. They had at least four children, George M. (ca.1846); Mary Ann M. (ca.1849); Christian (ca.1851); and Christopher (ca.1851). In her father's obituary, Harriet lived in Minnesota (see PEGLEY, Robert and Mary Ann).

Henry Cooper married Elizabeth Martin (1825), daughter of Hiram and Hannah (Hollingshead) Martin. They had at least four children, David (ca.1854); Victor (ca.1857); Henry "Edward" (ca.1862), who went to the U.S.; and Hiram Cooper. Henry Sr. was a carpenter, and he had a wagon shop in Strathroy in 1851. He later moved to Detroit. In 1893, Edward Cooper married Alice Martin (1873-1952), daughter of William and Eliza (Bishopp) Martin of Adelaide. They lived in the U.S., where they had a daughter, Violet.

Emma Cooper married Thomas Rapley (1826-1906) in 1846, son of James and Mary Collins Rapley. They had the following known children, Caroline (ca.1847); Henry (ca.1849-1926); Thomas F. (ca.1849-1903); Mary Collins (ca.1853); Emaline (ca.1855); William J. (ca.1857); Sarah (ca.1859); Carrie; Sarah; Raida; Josephine; Jessie; Zorado; and Frank. Thomas had immigrated to Adelaide with his father and 11 siblings in 1832 under the Petworth Immigration Scheme. His mother had died shortly before leaving England, and his father died tragically, shortly after arriving in Adelaide. By 1851, Thomas was farming part of Lot 17, Con. 5 SER. It appears Thomas, Emma and family moved to the U.S. for a time as their four youngest children were born there.

Caroline Cooper married Thomas Holden (ca.1825-1877), son of Thomas and Margaret Holden. Thomas' father immigrated to Canada under the Petworth Immigration Scheme in 1832, a widower with seven children.

Thomas and Caroline farmed on part of Lot 19, Con. 4 SER. They had five children, John (ca.1848); James C. (ca.1849); Thomas (1853); Jeff (1856); and Cornelius (1858). Thomas was a bricklayer by trade. The family moved to Michigan in 1865, where Thomas died. He is buried in Strathroy Cemetery (see HOLDEN, Moses and Elizabeth).

Sarah Cooper married James Holden, brother to Thomas Holden. They also farmed on part of Lot 19, Con. 4 SER. They had at least seven children,

William J. (ca.1849); Henry H. (ca.1858); Hiram (1855); Harriet (1857); Mary A. (1860, died a baby); Caroline Enetta (ca.1866-1871); and Edith (1868-1949), all born on Lot 19 (see HOLDEN, Moses and Elizabeth).

William Cooper married Hanna Fraser in 1860. They had at least five children, William, Charles, Frank, Wesley and Gertie. In William's 1896 obituary, William, Charles and Frank lived in London, Ontario. His obituary tells us, "William Cooper was a prominent contractor and builder and consequently, the history of Strathroy is to a very large extent the history of himself, having worked upon the more projecting structures in our midst today."

No information was located on Catherine Cooper, seventh child of James and Mahetable.

Cornelius married and went to Yale, Michigan, about 1880. His obituary gives as survivors his wife, not named, sons James of Detroit and Emerson of Yale, and daughters Augusta (wife of John Hallock of Detroit); Mamie (wife of John Drennan of St. Ignace); and Lillian (wife of Herman Doelle of Croswell). Cornelius started his career as a blacksmith, and later was in the implement business and other businesses in Yale. He was a good singer in his day and took great delight in music.

Charles Cooper, the youngest child of James and Mahetable, married Katie O'Dwyer from Mt. Brydges. They lived in Strathroy.

John Cooper, who may have been brother to William and James, married Harriet Challen (ca.1827) in England. They farmed on part of Lot 19, Con. 3 SER. They immigrated with five children, Betsy (ca.1830); Sarah (ca.1833); Catherine (ca.1835); Charlotte (ca.1838); and Harriet (ca.1841). Known children of John and Harriet, born in Canada, were Caleb (ca.1846-1909); Emily Ann (ca1849); and Charles Christopher (ca.1850). In 1851, they lived in Adelaide Township, but by 1861 they lived in Strathroy.

Little information is found on the children born to John and Harriet, except Caleb, who married Hannah Wilmer. They lived in Adelaide for a while, then moved to Warwick Township and later to Strathroy. Caleb's obituary mentions that his wife survived him, with one daughter, Mrs. Thomas Stillwell of Warwick, and three sons, James, William and Elmer, all of Strathroy.

Other Cooper families lived in Adelaide Township, but they were not of English background and could not be connected to the original James Cooper family. The 1851 census shows:

A Thomas Cooper, 59, and wife Mary, 30, with daughter Ann, 9, and widow Ann Clark, 51, were living on part of Lot 5, Con. 4. Thomas is a labourer with English background, and a possible brother of William, James and John.

A widower, Joseph Cooper, 73, storekeeper, living with the Keyser family on Keyser Corners Lot 7, Con. 4, from the U.S.

A George and Phoebe Cooper with a large family, living with the Reid family on Lot 30 and 31, Con. 1 NER. George is listed as being a labourer from the U.S.

The Keyser book mentions a Samuel Cooper who ran the general store in 1871. Samuel is 32 in 1871, but he was born in Ireland and belonged to the Baptist Church.

The 1871 census shows three Cooper Head of Household names: John 67, Samuel 32, and William 19. There are no Cooper families on the 1901 census.

COWAN, Tyler and Kelley

In July 1994, Tyler and Kelley Cowan took up residence in Adelaide Township. Tyler, a Tillsonburg native, maintained his position as a Constable with the London Police Department. Kelley (Mason) Cowan, originally from Sarnia, works for the Lambton County Board of Education as a French Teacher at an elementary school in Forest.

Although they both endure a 30-minute commute to work, they feel the move to Adelaide from London has been positive. The beauty, space, and people of Adelaide Township have made the Cowans and their Labrador Retriever, Murphy, feel right at home.

CRANDON, Reginald and Frances

The Crandon family farm is at Lot 11, Con. 4 SER. Reginald, Edward, and Everett Crandon from St. Mary's purchased it in 1920 from Walter Watson Bowley, who had become ill, and died shortly after the transaction. Bowley had purchased the farm in January 1909 from his parents, James and Melinda Bowley, who bought the farm from its original owner, Paul Phipps, on April 24, 1882. Walter Bowley had built the present house after his pur-

Wilfred and Rose Crandon

chase. Phipps received the property from the Crown on August 22, 1851.

In March 1928, Reginald bought out his brothers' shares in the farm. Reginald and his wife, Frances (Ferguson), had two sons, Clare and Wilfred "Tiny." Frances died in 1953 and on June 29, 1956, Clare and his wife, Jennet (Teft), bought the property from Reginald. They raised a son, Larry, and a daughter, Lorraine. They had a herd of dairy cows.

In the spring of 1981, Clare and Jennet moved to Havelock Street in Kerwood and sold to son, Larry, and his fiancée, Fran Heuvel. They are raising three children, Tanya, Jennifer, and Jonathan on the home place. The farm is now a farrow-to-finish hog and cash crop operation.

CRUMMER, John and Margaret

John Crummer Sr. (1787) was born in County Cavan, Ireland. He was wounded while serving in the British Army under the Duke of Wellington in Babjaz, Spain, during the Napoleonic Wars. In Ireland, he married Margaret (1781-1881, last name unknown). Sometime between 1824 and 1832, he came to Canada. In 1836, he was granted land in Adelaide Township at Lot 5, Con. 2 NER, for his military service. For whatever reason, he was not found enumerated in the 1842 census of the township. In the 1851 census, Margaret, age 59, was enumerated as a widow. In censuses of 1861, 1871, and 1881, she was enumerated under her son, John. Her death is registered at age 100. Both John and Margaret are buried in St. Ann's Cemetery, Adelaide Village. They had five children. Mary (1817-1882) was born in Fermanagh, Ireland. A second child, a male whose name is unknown, died before 1851. The next three children were Mae Irene Queendrella (1822-1824); John Jr. (1824- 1897); and Margaret Ellen (1829-1850).

Mary married Patrick Mee of Adelaide Township in 1836 (see Mee).

John Jr. married Margaret Burns (1826-1855), who was born in Ireland. John was a farmer. He and Margaret had seven children, James Louis Henry (1854-1924); William Hubert Morrison (1855); Mary Ellen Anne "Minnie" (1856); John Percy Edward (1860); Helena Margaret Susan (1863); Florence Amy Sarah (1865); and Ernest Frederick Pelham (1867-1934).

Family lore relates the following story: an eighth child, Queendrella May, was born to John Jr. and Margaret, but died at about 1½ years. John and his wife had a "hired girl," a maid who was thought to have the "black hand." Strange events happened in the house. Eventually, the women were afraid to stay in the house alone while the men were doing chores in the barn. Windows and doors would fly open even though the windows were nailed shut and the doors locked. All these things stopped when the maid was dismissed. The baby died just before or after her dismissal. Alfred Cuddy, who lived across the road from the Crummers, related a similar story.

Margaret had a Dalmatian dog that ran under her carriage when she was driving. Her great-granddaughter, Mary O'Meara, believes Margaret may have been a United Empire Loyalist. As part of her children's education, she had them travel to Niagara Falls, a formidable trip at the time, even after the train came to Strathroy.

James Louis Henry married Elizabeth McCarthy (1856-1941) in St. Ann's Anglican Church, Adelaide Village. Both are buried in Strathroy Cemetery. She was the daughter of Martin and Anne (Moorehead) McCarthy.

Louis and Elizabeth lived on the Second Line North in Adelaide Township. The 100-acre farm was lost when Louis backed a $500 note for Herbert Mee, a first cousin, to buy a piano for his fiancée, Josephine Kearns. In the spring of 1890, he took his family west on a colonists' train. After two years there, they became homesick and returned to Adelaide to spend the winter with Cornelius McCarthy. The children had not seen apples in the west and they ate so many, they were all sick to their stomachs the first night home. They lived a few years in Adelaide, five years in Strathroy, and some time in Adelaide Village before moving to London in 1901. Louis and Elizabeth had nine children, May Irene Queendrella (1876-1949), born in Lambton; John Ernest (1878-1935); Annie Olive (1880-1969), born in Plympton Township; William Charles (1883-1952), born in Adelaide Township; James H. (1885-1951); Martin Howard (1887-1968); Louis Frank (1889-1969); a female infant (1894, died at birth); and Florine Elizabeth (1896-1963).

Of John Jr. and Margaret's children, limited information was revealed. William Hubert married Edith (1873, last name unknown). After her death in childbirth, he married a second time. In 1891, he was living in Vancouver.

There is no further information on Mary Ellen Crummer.

John Percy married Annie Jean Watson (1874) of Warwick, who died there in 1892, and was buried in West Adelaide Cemetery. John Percy moved to Vancouver.

Helena Margaret Susan married John McCubbin. She died in childbirth, the year unknown.

No further information was available on Florence Amy Sarah.

Ernest Frederick Pelham was born in Adelaide Township. He taught school before entering the Detroit College of Medicine. After graduation in 1896, he practiced in Essexville, Michigan. In 1903, he married Eva Grace Hall. They had three children. For several years, he was President of the town, as well as Postmaster for 16 years. He was also President of the Bay City Medical Society. After the sale of the east half of the east half of Lot 6, Con. 2 NER, to George Topping in 1895, and of the west half of Lot 6, Con. 2 NER, to William Charles Demaray in 1897, the Crummers moved to Strathroy.

CUDDY, James and Violet

James Cuddy (1806-1878) and his wife, Violet Smith (1813-1887), immigrated to Canada from County Tyrone, Ireland, in 1832. Goodspeed's "The History of Middlesex County" states that James Cuddy was one of the first settlers to arrive in Adelaide Township. His brother, John Thomas Cuddy, sister Margaret Cuddy, and her husband, Alexander Johnston, came later to this same area. James Cuddy's name is on the August 1, 1832-October 1832 payroll of those who worked clearing roads through the townships of Caradoc, Adelaide and Warwick, in the London and Western Districts. This was a government project to provide work and earnings for the early settlers. The lists of workers are compiled in "The Egremont Road," by Eleanor Nielsen.

The 1842 agricultural census gives statistics for the east half of Lot 8, Con. 3 NER: 16 acres of the 100 are cleared and produce consisted of 50 bushels of wheat, 20 of oats, 30 of peas, 100 of potatoes, 26 yards of flannel, and 15 yards of wool. There are 16 cattle, two hogs, 10 sheep and two horses. In 1845, James received the patent from the Crown for this property. By 1851, he had cleared 47 acres of this farm and the same year he received the patent for the east half of Lot 7, Con. 3 NER. The census of 1852 records that he, Violet, and family were living at this location, but no clearing had been done. By 1867, William and Archibald McNab were farming this lot.

The Adelaide Township Council minutes show that James Cuddy was appointed tax collector from 1853-1856. His name appears in 1853 as a subscriber to the first West Adelaide Presbyterian Chapel. He bought the east half of Lot 9, Con. 2 NER, from John Hamilton and sold it to his son, James Jr., in 1860. His sons, Walton H. and Edwin and their wives farmed this property until 1917, when it was sold to James Wilbert Hodgson. James and Violet had 10 children.

Esther (Truman) Cuddy (1826-1911), wife of John Thomas Cuddy.

James Cuddy Jr. (1834-1912) married Sarah Truman (1835-1893), the sister of Esther Truman who was wife of John Thomas Cuddy, and they raised their children on the Cuddy farms in Adelaide. James and Sarah had six children. The first two were Clara Cuddy (1862); and Emma Cuddy (1864-1938), who married Archibald Wiley (see WILEY, John and Eleanor).

Walton H. Cuddy (1865-1938) married Margaret McPherson (d.1917). They farmed on the east half of Lot 9, Con. 2 NER, until ca.1905. They moved to Strathroy, where Walton bought and sold timber, and then he started W.H. Cuddy Hardware, which became a very successful business.

Edwin "Ted" (1869), fourth child of James and Sarah, went to the U.S. after 1905. Augustus Truman (1871-1873) and John Arnold (1872) died as babies, and are buried in West Adelaide Cemetery in the family plot.

Elizabeth Cuddy (ca.1837), second child of James and Violet, married a Mr. Wodehouse (or Moorhouse) of Michigan. Her first cousin, Elizabeth Wiley, daughter of Mary Cuddy and D.D. Wiley, met her future husband, Dr. James McGillicuddy while visiting there.

Violet Cuddy (ca.1839) married a Mr. Donley. Sarah Ann "Annie" Cuddy (ca.1841) married a Mr. Martin. Esther "Essy" Cuddy (1843-1912) married Daniel Cruickshank of St. Catherines. Mary Cuddy (1846-1888) married David Duncan Wiley (see WILEY, John and Eleanor).

John A. Cuddy (1847-1925) married Wilhelmina "Minnie" Burdon (1850-1902). Her parents, Benjamin and Wilhelmina (Gelling) Burdon lived in many parts of Ontario until moving from Lobo Township to the north half of Lot 16, Con. 3 NER, in 1862. In 1876, John A. Cuddy purchased the east half of Lot 8, Con. 3 NER, from his parents. He stayed on this land until his death in 1925, when it was passed on to his son, William James Cuddy. The log cabin, built by James Sr., was sided and later used as a kitchen for the house he built. The Cuddys won many medals with their horses at country fairs.

John A. Cuddy objected to having an organ in the church sanctuary but the congregation decided otherwise. A Wilson nephew used to talk about the jars of dates that Minnie had that were a special sweet treat. John A. and Minnie are buried in West Adelaide Cemetery. John and Minnie had four children, William James (1870-1945); Walter Fred (1872-1893); Charles Arnold (1875-1932); and Pearl Elizabeth (1876-1959).

William James married Lillian Masselina "Lillie" Cleland (1880-1974) (see CLELAND, Robert and Lillie). William farmed until he moved to Strathroy in 1926 and worked for Downham's Nursery where the income was more stable. Later, the family moved to London. The children attended S.S. #9 Adelaide while they lived on the farm. William and Lillie's children were Roma Wilhemina (1904-1994); Ruby Isobel; Eva Cuddy; Clair Wellington Cuddy, who managed a Dominion Grocery Store in London; and De Los Cleland Cuddy, who served as a Lieutenant overseas in WWII and then worked in the federal civil service in Ottawa.

Walter Fred Cuddy is buried in West Adelaide. Charles Arnold Cuddy was a banker in Amherstburg. Pearl Elizabeth Cuddy, John and Minnie's youngest child, married Wesley Culbert of Biddulph Township.

Matilda Cuddy, eighth child of James and Violet, married James Barnes.

Thomas Alfred Cuddy (1850-1931) was a lumber merchant in Winnipeg. He took the Cruickshank nieces on trips and cruises. In 1929, he married his secretary, Frankie Chapman, and they moved to California. She took special care of her new husband and brought him much happiness in his last years. His burial service was from his home in

California and his obituary mentions his ornate copper casket.

Loftus Cuddy (1850), twin to Thomas Alfred, learned banking in Strathroy from his uncle, Alexander Johnston, who operated a private bank on Front Street. Loftus set up a private bank in Amherstburg. He then went to Cleveland and became involved in the coal business. The town of Cuddy, Pennsylvania, southwest of Pittsburgh, is named for him. While in Cleveland, Loftus built the first docks to move coal from hopper cars down funnels into the holds of ships. This revolutionized shipping on the Great Lakes. In 1946, these Cuddy docks were still standing. Loftus Cuddy also had interests in a fleet of lake carriers to haul coal and iron ore. He sold the coal business and entered the oil business, refining crude oil in Pennsylvania that was marketed in North America and Europe. The James Cuddy descendants wonder today who inherited his fortune!

CUDDY, John T. and Esther

Alfred Watson Cuddy and his wife Harriett (McInroy) Cuddy (1967).

In 1837 John Thomas Cuddy left his home in Tyrone County, Northern Ireland, and sailed to Canada to settle in Adelaide where his sister, brother, and their spouses were living.

After participating in the Rebellion of 1837 at Amhertsburg and being commissioned under Colonel McNab, he received a crown deed to the east half of Lot 5 and the west half of Lot 6, Con. 3 NER.

In 1840, he married Esther Truman, 14, at St. James Cathedral in Toronto. Her father was owner of Tavern Tyrone on Queen Street in Toronto, where Sheraton Centre is today. The two families had been friends in Ireland. She brought with her a wooden hope chest, which is now in the home of her great great granddaughter.

Their first home was a log cabin that was replaced in a few years by a 2-storey brick home heated by a fireplace. Their great-grandsons recall sliding with glee down the banister of the open stairway.

John Thomas carried wheat to Kilworth to be ground into flour, which Esther would use to bake bread. The nearest post office was in Adelaide Village, where they collected their mail. Squire John Thomas was involved in township government as a councillor, reeve, and justice of the peace. He was also a founding member of the West Middlesex Agricultural Society.

John Thomas and Esther raised nine children, Sarah (1842); John (1843-1906); Elizabeth (1845-1931); Thomas Alfred (1847-1933); Margaret (1849-1888); Arabella (1853-1874); Loftus (1857-1947); Mary (1861-1943); and Laura (1869-1952). They also raised a boy whose surname was Gordon, who enlisted in the 100 regiment and served in Gibraltar and later with the 93rd Regiment in Africa, earning the rank of Lieutenant.

In 1877 when their son, Thomas Alfred, married Sarah Matilda Stevenson of Croswell, Michigan, another brick home was built on Lot 6, Con. 3 NER, adjoining the first house. No interior doors opened into the other house! In 1915, a new barn was erected using brick from the Keyser brickyard for the foundation.

Thomas Alfred and Matilda had four children, Edna Stevenson (1884-1973); Allie Belle (1885-1961); Bessie Louise (1887-1972); and Alfred Watson (1888-1972). Thomas Alfred was left to raise the children after Matilda's death in 1892.

Edna became a seamstress who stayed with neighbourhood families for a week or so at a time, making clothes for them, as few ready-made clothes were available. She married Lawrence Marshall and moved to Warwick Township. Allie married Colin Duncan and lived in East Williams Township. Bessie, who was not married, worked for many years in Detroit for well-to-do families.

When Alfred Watson was nine years old, he quit school to help on the farm. His father had a small plough crafted so Alfred could help in the fields. In later years, he and Frank Pennington became champion ploughmen in area competitions.

Several generations of Cuddy men were interested in horses. Alfred loved to tell stories of racing along country roads in competition with his friends. A trip to the Dominion Day races in Strathroy was a real treat for him.

Mrs. Sarah Matilda Cuddy

Alfred married Harriett McInroy, who taught school at S.S. #9 Adelaide. The horse she drove from her home at Lot 12, Con. 3 NER, was stabled during the day in the Cuddy barn on "Bloomfield Farm." They had three sons, Alfred "Mac" McInroy (1919); Gordon Ingham (1921-2000); and George Beverly (1924-1990).

One day when gypsies came asking for food, Harriett left the lady holding baby George while she went to get maple syrup produced on the farm. What a risk Harriett had taken, but the gypsy lady proved trustworthy.

During the Depression of the 1930s, Alfred sold produce, eggs, poultry and homemade butter to customers in Sarnia each week. The butter was shaped in wooden molds or stored in small crocks and kept cool under rhubarb leaves for the trip. He enjoyed telling tales of escapades with unruly animals when he was trucking cattle.

It was fun hearing of the house parties he attended. The rugs would be rolled up, the furniture moved and dancing began to local musicians, often a pianist and a violinist. One of the men attending would call for the square dances. Sometimes these parties lasted until almost daylight. Alfred was known as a very good dancer, especially when a waltz was played.

Harriett was a long-time member and officer of the Ladies' Aid Society and Women's Missionary Society of West Adelaide Church and Keyser Women's Institute. She sang for many years in the church choir. She often had quilting bees at her home, and fundraisers for the Ladies' Aid.

Alfred "Mac" McInroy still lives in Adelaide, operating a turkey business. With his first wife, Dilys Scott (1924-1988) of England, he raised six children, Bruce, Barbara, Douglas, Robert, Brian and Peter. They all attended schools in Adelaide and Strathroy. He is now married to Patricia Van Oman of the U.S.

Over the years, Alfred M. had a stable of racing and riding horses. Several of his children rode horses in jumping competitions. He now has 17 grandchildren.

Thomas Alfred Cuddy

Gordon married Marie Anderson of Strathroy, where they now reside. He and his son, Edward, have a furniture and appliance store. They also have three daughters, Carol, Janice, and Diane, and 11 grandchildren. Gordon served as a member of the Strathroy School Board, Strathroy Council and the Strathroy Committee of Adjustment for a number of years.

George, who married Marguerite Willison, a teacher in Adelaide, remained on the homestead, which he operated as a dairy farm and later as a beef farm. He faithfully participated in the West Adelaide Church as an elder, a manager, and a choir member. As his father had done, he was a member of the Canadian Foresters in which they both served as treasurer and in other offices. For a number of years, he was secretary-treasurer of the Middlesex County Pork Producers. He was also secretary-treasurer of West Adelaide Cemetery Commission, a position that Marguerite assumed after his death.

Marguerite, a teacher in West Williams for 10 years, also participated in the life of the church as a Sunday School teacher, choir member, a leader of a Canadian Girls In Training group and as a member of the Board of Managers. She was also a 4-H leader and an officer in the Canadian Foresters. After the sale of the farm in 1996, Marguerite moved to Strathroy.

The farm now has new owners, Joseph and Johanna Minten, after belonging to four generations of Cuddys.

CUNNINGHAM, Carl and Margaret

Carl (1918-1995) and Margaret Cunningham lived at Lot 22, Con. 3 (69 Pannell Lane). They built their house and moved into it on November 1, 1965. This couple had previously lived at 170 Front Street East, Strathroy.

Carl worked at the Chevrolet-Olds Cunningham dealership in Strathroy from 1946-1966. He then attended Althouse College in London, after which he taught at Strathroy District Collegiate Institute for 10 years. Margaret worked for 13 years in the Sears Catalogue Order office in Strathroy. They are now retired.

Carl and Margaret had three children. Leslie married Jim Masterson and has three children, James, Kelly and Michael. They live in Toronto. Susan married Peter Parisi and has three children, Michael, Christopher and Jonathon. They live in Newmarket. John married Barbara Medwick and has two children, Stacy and Lucas. They live in St. George. Susan attended the Adelaide Township Central School, and the other children went to Strathroy schools. They all attended S.D.C.I.

The Cunningham's ancestors did not live in Adelaide. Carl's father and mother lived in London, and Margaret's family came from Moosejaw, Saskatchewan. Margaret's maiden name was Kelly. Her maternal grandfather, John Brown, had moved west in 1905 when land was being offered to farmers. He bought 640 acres of land, which Margaret believes is still in the family.

CURRIE/CURRY/CORRIGAN

The history of the Currie families begins in the village of Ballycastle, County Mayo, Ireland, when John Corrigan (1809-1893), a Roman Catholic, met Jane Garner (1804-1889), daughter of a coast guard petty officer and a member of the Anglican Church. Both were deeply religious. Courtship and love followed. In 1834, despite vigorous objections by both sets of parents, they married. John's parents insisted Jane become a Catholic. A battle of wills followed. For many months, this struggle continued. Jane refused to change her religion and her husband supported her. When it became evident that Jane would never become a Roman Catholic, arrangements were made to have John and Jane, their daughter, Ann (1833-1851), and son, Frederick George "Fred" (1836-1879), picked up by an emigration ship from an island off the west coast of County May. Mrs. Wardell writes, "Sailing time was eight weeks. They came to a sister-in-law's home near Kerwood, a Mrs. Munn. Two weeks later, John was born."

Upon their arrival, they changed their name from Corrigan to Curry and their religions to Methodism. These acts demonstrated their renunciation of their families because of the treatment they had received in their homeland. In 1838, John applied for and received title by government grant to the west half of Lot 14, Con. 5 SER. They would acquire 200 more acres over a number of years.

Jane Laughton, in a newspaper article about the Adelaide Township's Fourth Line Cemetery, gives the following information about the Curries (Currys): "Mr. Currie, who never used an axe, proceeded to clear the west half of Lot 15, Con. 5, and erected a log house. Hardship marked the early years. Mr. Currie crossed the St. Clair River at Sarnia to work at the mill. The first crop was planted in the fall, borrowing bushel-for-bushel of seed and sowing it, two bushels to be returned for each borrowed. At harvest time, Mr. Currie, like other settlers, flailed out the grain, carrying it in a sack on his back down the narrow, winding trail to the mill at Kilworth for grinding, returning before dark because wolves prowled." This is an indication of the pioneers' strength of body and will to succeed in besting the wildness of those times.

In 1856, John and Jane sold two acres of land for a railroad right-of-way. This provided them with a market for 4' lengths of cordwood, which the railroad bought for $1.25 per double cord.

The 1852 and 1871 census records show 10 children born to John and Jane Curry. The six sons were Fred, James John, William (died an infant), William Garner, Thomas Ornsby, and Isaac R.O., (ca.1850, died an infant). The four daughters were Ann, Eliza, Jane and Maria. Eliza, age six, died during a scarlet fever epidemic. Ann died at age 18 from inflammation of the bowel, or perhaps appendicitis.

In 1862, Fred, the eldest son, married Elizabeth "Eliza" Harris (1837-1871), daughter of Thomas Harris and Ann Phipps. The 1878 Middlesex Atlas shows Fred farming about 55 acres, the west corner of Lot 11, Con. 4 NER, in Metcalfe Township. NOTE: In 1843, a division line was set between Metcalfe and Adelaide. This line is still in place today.

Fred and Eliza had four children. Mary "Minnie" A. (1864-1962) married William "Will" John Donaldson. She died in Vancouver, B.C. Wilbert "Will" Case (1867-1945) never married. He died in Winnipeg, Manitoba. Louisa Jane (1869-1905) married George Herbert "Herb" Martin of Adelaide Township. He was born at Lot 10, Con. 3 SER. Thomas Frederick "Fred" (1870-1960) married Mary Wallace Bruce (1872-1955) in London, Ontario.

James John Curry (1838-1914) was the first Curry to be born in Adelaide Township. In 1864, he married Elizabeth "Liza" Morgan (1839-1883) in Adelaide Township. She was the daughter of John Morgan and Elizabeth "Eliza" Hughes. The 1878 Middlesex County Atlas shows James farming about 45 acres, being the east half of the west half of Lot 14, Con. 4, in Metcalfe Township. James and Elizabeth had seven children, Elizabeth, William "Filbert," Elmore, Della Jane, Lillian Maude, John and Cecil Pearl. Cecil was born in Bay City, Michigan, where James and Elizabeth had moved. At six months of age, following the death of her mother, she was sent to Con. 5 SER, to be raised by her grandmother. In 1909, Cecil married John Dufferin Brien of Kent County.

Following the death of his wife in Bay City, James returned to Adelaide Township. He died in 1914 and was buried in the Strathroy Cemetery.

Jane Curry (1843-1914), the sixth child of John and Jane, married Thomas Patterson (1819-1884) in November 1860. Thomas farmed the 100 acres located at the west half of Lot 15, Con. 4. They had nine children. They were Anna M., William A., Thomas, Louise E., Addie M. M., Alice A.G., Etta "Ettie" E.J., John A. and Richard E.

William Garner Curry (1845-1891) was the fourth son and eighth child of John and Jane. In 1868, he married Janet "Jane" Patterson (1848-1914). Jane was born in Ireland, the daughter of Thomas and Mary (Lighton) Patterson. William had taken over 48 acres of his father's farm, the west half of the west half of Lot 14, Con. 5 SER. Two acres

Crowds gather for the funeral of Sir Arthur Currie in Montreal, December 2, 1933.

had been sold previously for the railroad right-of-way. He also farmed the east half of the east half of Lot 13, Con. 4, in Metcalfe Township. William was active in municipal affairs. He was township counsellor and at the time of his death in 1891, was deputy reeve. He left behind his wife, Jane, and seven children.

The oldest, Almeda (1870-1907), became a teacher and followed her brother, Arthur, to Victoria, B.C., and taught in the same school as her brother. She later married the Rev. Leslie Reid, a widower with a daughter, Mildred. They had no children together.

The second child, John (1872-1942), along with his brother, Edward (1881-1916), remained on their parents' farm and continued to work it after their father's death. Neither brother married. John served a term as councillor of Adelaide Township and was Warden of Middlesex County from 1914-1918. He also managed the Middlesex Fruit Growers' Association for a number of years.

Arthur William Curry (1875-1933) was the second son and third child of William and Jane Curry. He suffered from stomach problems all his life. From early childhood, his main interest was playing soldiers. When he played with others, he was generally the leader. He attended public school at Napperton 1881-1888, then attended Strathroy Collegiate until Grade 12, when he quit because of a disagreement with a teacher. He went west to Victoria, B.C., and lived with a great-aunt, Mrs. Orlando Warner (nee Patterson). He attended Model School and obtained a third-class teaching certificate. He taught in a small village school at Sydney, 20 miles north of Victoria, during 1895-1896, then Boy's Central School 1896-1897. He became a teacher at Victoria High School in 1898-1900, then gave up teaching and became an insurance salesman. The following year, he became a broker and married Lucy Sophia Chadworth Muster. They had two children, Marjorie Victoria and Garner Ormsby.

His continued interest in the military resulted in his joining the B.C. Brigade, Canadian Garrison Artillery Reserves. He quickly rose in rank to Colonel, in command of the Fifth Regiment. Because his comrades in the regiment enjoyed making puns about his name, Arthur said, "I'll soon stop that!" and altered his signature from Curry to Currie. The rest of the Curry family later adopted this same spelling.

On August 4, 1914, WWI started and on August 26, Arthur left Victoria for Valcartier Mobilization Camp in Quebec. His rank was Brigade Commander in the Expeditionary Force. The people of British Columbia gave Arthur a horse. Arthur named his new charger "Brock" (perhaps in honour of Sir Isaac Brock). Brock was Arthur's companion throughout the war. He was at his master's side when King George V knighted Arthur in France in 1918. After the war, Sir Arthur and Brock returned to Canada and settled in Montreal where, in 1919, he accepted the position of principal of McGill University.

Upon Sir Arthur's death, pictures show Brock following the gun carriage that carried the flag-draped casket. Arthur's boots were reversed in the stirrups. Brock was retired to the family homestead at Napperton in Adelaide and could be seen at pasture from Highway 22. When he died, Brock was buried under a hickory tree close to the family home.

The three youngest second generation Curry children, Mary "May" (1878-1936); Ethel M. (1882); and Mabel Annie (1883-1936) never married and lived their lives with their brother, John, on the Curry homestead.

Thomas Ormsby "T.O." Curry (1847-1909) was the fifth son and ninth child of John and Jane Curry. He married Mary Ann Evans (1848-1924) of St. Mary's, Ontario. Thomas farmed the east half of the west half of Lot 14, Con. 5 SER, which was part of the Curry homestead.

T.O. and Mary Ann had three children, Elvira "Elvie" (1872-ca.1965); George E.R.O. (1874-1880); and Harold W.G. (1876-1955).

During his lifetime, T.O. had several careers. As a young man, he entered municipal life in Adelaide Township, and for eight years was an elected councillor. When the Patrons of Industry was organized, he took a prominent part, speaking through the province as grand trustee of the organization and afterward was elected vice-president. For some years, he was a very successful auctioneer, conducting numerous sales throughout the district. After the Patrons of Industry was dissolved, T.O. devoted a great deal of time in the interest of Liberal Government and spoke in many constituencies throughout the province. He was known as the "Silver-tongued Orator of Ontario." It was said of him that no reporter could quote him verbatim. He was a shareholder of the Farmers' Bindertwine Co. and was elected a member of the board of directors. T.O. was also bailiff of the Sixth Division Court for a number of years, but resigned in 1897, when Sir Wilfred Laurier appointed him to the position of Dominion Immigration Agent for the west, with trade quarters in Milwaukee, Wisconsin. He filled this position most successfully, almost up to the time of his death. He died at the homestead in Adelaide Township and was buried in the Strathroy Cemetery. There is no tombstone for T.O.

Harold, T.O. and Mary Ann's youngest child, married Estelle "Stella" Jury (1879-1960) in 1899. She was the daughter of Thomas and Mary Jane (McDowell) Jury of Napperton. Harold was past president of the Board of Directors of the United Farmers' Cooperative of Ontario. He served several terms as reeve of Adelaide Township, was warden of Middlesex County, secretary-treasurer of the local school board and served for 30 years as secretary of the Strathroy Dominion Day Committee. He was president of the Ontario Harness Horse Association and was widely known in the harness horse racing and breeding circles. Stella served as provincial vice-president of the United Farm Women of Ontario and was the organist for the Mount Zion Methodist Church at Napperton. Harold and Stella had three children, Lela (1903-1997); Verna M. (1907-1953); and Leonard (1910).

In 1929, Lela married Alton Oliver (1898-1975). Alton was the son of William Edward Roberts Oliver and Mary Ann "Minnie" Arrand. He worked for Mr. and Mrs. Meredith Morgan, who owned the Adelaide Telephone System, and went on to a 32-year career with Bell Telephone as a construction superintendent. At one time, Alton and Lela owned a standardbred horse named Corporal Lee who did all of his racing in the United States. He set two half-mile track records in the late 1930s, one as a two-year-old of 2:06½, and as a five-year-old, he set a record of 2:05. Alton and Lela had one child, a daughter named Marian (ca.1942). She married Roy Whitbread. They live in Brantford, Ontario.

Verna moved to Toronto to work and married George A. Philips (1907-1963). They had no children.

Leonard married Marjorie McEvoy. They moved to Vancouver following the birth of their son, Thomas, in 1944. Leonard was buried in the Strathroy Cemetery.

DALE

The Dale name is found in Adelaide Township records between 1880 and 1920. Oral family history suggests that the old Dales from Westminster Township bought 50 acres in Adelaide Township for each of their daughters and sent the sons to farm them. One was reportedly featured as a model farm in the Farmer's Advocate.

In 1881, Henry Dale (ca.1848) and William Dale (ca.1852) farmed in Adelaide. They were sons of Solomon Dale Sr. In 1872, Henry had married Anna Dale (1845), daughter of David and Elizabeth (Tunks) Dale of Westminster Township. Solomon Sr. and David were brothers. Henry and Anna had a chosen daughter, Clara, who married Robert Wilson in 1895. Another daughter of David Dale was Mary Dale (1850), who married John Conkey. They had a daughter, Laura, born in 1880.

In 1891, Richard Dale (1868) and James Dale (1870) farmed together in Adelaide. Their father, John "James" Dale of Westminster Township, was a brother of Anna and Mary. In 1892 in Arkona, Richard married Selinda Rosetta "Rosa" Edwards (1868), daughter of William and Mary (Patterson) Edwards of Lobo Township. Rosa had a sister, Isabella, who married Alexander Conkey, another Adelaide resident. In 1901, Richard was farming 50 acres at Lot 1, Con. 4 NER. James had moved to San Francisco, California, but another brother, Robert Dale (1872), was farming 100 acres on Lot 1, Con. 5 NER. Robert later moved to London, where he was a streetcar driver. Richard and Rosa's children, born in Adelaide Township, were John Edward (1893-1967); Mary Elizabeth (1895-1965); and Jeanette Isabell (1897-1990). According to his daughter, Mary, Richard always enjoyed a horse race and much to his wife's disapproval, challenged others to a buggy race with his new horse on the way home from the Baptist church. The Dale children attended Keyser School, S.S. #1 and #2 Adelaide, and West Williams. When it was time for Rosa's children to go to continuation school in 1909, the family moved to Strathroy. Richard continued to farm in Adelaide and in 1915, he bought a farm in Lobo

Township, where he and Rosa lived until her death in 1935 and his in 1959.

John Edward married Mary "Mae" Urzuhart. They farmed in Lobo on Lot 11, Con. 10, across the road from his parents. Their children were Margaret (London); Mary (Strathroy); Agnes Moore (1932-1996); Robert (Lobo Township); and Barry (Strathroy).

Mary Elizabeth married Hugh Jay, a Strathroy barber. Their children were Dr. H. John "Jack" D. (1913-1969) and F. William "Bill" (1915-1987).

Jeanette Isabell "Jean" was a teacher who married Martin Grieve. Their son, Richard Grieve, lives in Kitchener.

Most of the Dales who lived in Adelaide Township between 1880 and 1920 are buried in Strathroy Cemetery.

de BRUYN, Adrian and Joan

Adrian and Joan de Bruyn, Dutch immigrants, purchased the farm on Lot 12, Con. 5 SER, in 1964. They moved from the Komoka area with four children, John, Harry, Jim and Kathy. In 1971, their fifth child, Nancy, was born.

They raised hogs and worked their 97 1/2 acres of land while Adrian also worked in town for several years. The CNR tracks run through the farm.

There have been many improvements made to the land and buildings over the years. In 1989, Jim and his wife, Lisa (Meloche), purchased the farm. Lisa is from the Essex area. Adrian and Joan built a home near Adelaide Village. Jim, Lisa, and their son, Michael, moved to the farm in October 1989. In 1991, their second son, Bradley, was born.

Jim is a member of the Kerwood Fire Department. The children attend Adelaide W.G. MacDonald School.

DEKKER, Henry and Magdalena

When Henry Dekker migrated to Canada in 1951, he brought considerable energy to the venture, which is common to many of those who moved to this area from the Netherlands. This fifth generation florist built a thriving greenhouse business in Strathroy, Ontario.

After five years on the payroll of an Oakville landscape nursery, Henry Dekker and his wife Magdalena started on their own on January 1, 1957, with 10,000 square feet of greenhouses under glass. The greenhouses had been built about 40 years before and were purchased from Ernie Neilsen. There were two acres of land involved and the business was restricted to geranium propagation year-round and the production of flowers for the holiday markets of Easter, Mother's Day and Christmas. Everything was sold to retail florists in the Strathroy/London area.

In 1972, more land was purchased in Adelaide Township on County Road 39 west of Strathroy. The company expanded production facilities several times with the last expansion completed in 1987. At this time, there was a total of 455,000 square feet of greenhouse space with 25 acres of outdoor production facilities.

Henry Dekker Limited's production improvements and expansions were successful and this provided for increased volume and broader wholesale markets. Production included crops such as cut roses, cut chrysanthemums, tropicals and potted plants. There were 75 full-time employees with as many as 110 employees in the peak seasons. The markets included southwestern Ontario and Quebec, with holiday crops shipped to the U.S. Midwest, and southern and eastern seaboards.

Henry and Magdalena had six children. The two sons, Jim and

1994 wedding of Nancy de Bruyn and Dave Henderson.

George C., became actively involved as sixth generation florists. In 1987, Jim and George signed on as full partners, with Jim as Sales Manager and George as Production Manager. The daughters, Annette, Gwendolyn, Evelyn and Joyce, pursued other careers and moved out of the area.

Just prior to a 40th anniversary for Henry Dekker Limited in November 1996, Rose-A-Lea Gardens of Mt. Brydges purchased the company.

George has always lived in Adelaide Township. In 1968, he moved to a new home on Eastman Avenue. In 1985, George purchased the house at 124 Eastman Avenue, which was built by Frank Beute.

George married Florence Schenk of Sarnia in 1986. They have three children, Peter, Heather and Tina, and have been at the same address for 14 years.

DELL, Bassnett and Elizabeth

Bassnett Dell (1814-ca.1894) was born in Louth near St. Catherines, Ontario. His first wife was Hannah P. Jackson (d.1852). They married September 4, 1840. They had three children, twins Silvester and Silvia, and Melissa. Bassnett was the first shoemaker in Strathroy and he later took up residence at Lot 20 or 21 SER (Concession not mentioned; this was the first farm property on Highway 81 south of the 402 overpass, on the west side where the windmill and water tank once stood).

As quoted from a 1939 Age Dispatch article, Bassnett was the grandson of Empire Loyalists. "His first task in his new surroundings was to clear 10 acres and on this he built his log house and a barn." On settling in Adelaide Township, he married his second wife, Elizabeth MacNeil, on June 8, 1855. From the second marriage, there were six children, Nancy, Eli, Byron, Arthur, Hannah and William. Bassnett travelled on foot twice to visit his daughters from the first marriage, in Louth.

Each year, Bassnett made his children one pair of shoes, which had to last them the entire year regardless of tiny, growing feet.

When the children went to school for the first time after taking up residence in Adelaide Township, Bassnett went ahead of them to blaze a trail so the children wouldn't get lost coming and going to school. The school location was at the southwest corner or Lot 15, which later became S.S. #11 (Payne's School).

Silvester remained in Adelaide Township, where he married Emma Adelia Caldwell. Their children were Joseph, Emma Estelle, Mary Melissa, William Wallace and Matilda.

Nancy Dell married Paul Harris and they took up residence on the Second Line South. Eli moved to Port Huron, Michigan, and Byron remained in the area. Arthur settled in the Wallaceburg area. Hannah married her first cousin, Silas MacNeil. William remained in the area, living at the southeast corner of Highway 81 and the Second Line South. He was a good fiddler who regularly played for dances. William would often fall asleep and continue playing while he dozed! He died a young man, leaving a family of two sons, Angus and John, who were raised by their aunt and uncle, Paul and Nancy Harris.

DEMARAY/desMarets

The earliest records of the desMarets family are from the sixth century, and it is understood that these records were compiled by Louis XIV to authenticate the lines of nobility of France. David desMarets (1620-1697), with his parents, fled from France because of their Protestant religion. They, along with other Huguenots, went to Middleburg on the island of Walcheren, off the west coast of Holland. David married Maria Sohier in Middleburg on July 29, 1643. The first descendants of the desMarets family to come to America were David and Maria who arrived, with their four children, in the New Netherlands in April 1663 on the ship, "Bonte Koe," bound from Amsterdam.

David and his family first settled in a Huguenot village on Staten Island but because of the constant danger from Indian attacks and the threat of English invasion, moved to Harlem on Manhattan Island in 1665. After the Dutch fleet appeared in 1673 in New York Harbour and forced the withdrawal of the British forces, David became one of four magistrates of the City of New Orange. David was later selected for the high office of Constable in the restored English form of government. This honour and David's fidelity to the British Crown was to determine the future of this family in Canada.

David desMarets long had cherished an ambition to form a French colony. In 1677, he purchased about 2,000 acres of land, a tract approximately two miles wide and six miles long, lying between the

Hackensack and Hudson Rivers in New Jersey. Here, the family prospered and soon filled the entire tract. One of David's sons, Samuel desMarets (1656-1728), married twice and had 12 children. Baptismal records of these siblings are recorded in Pennsylvania, Virginia and New York. At the behest of Squire Boone, brother to Daniel, Samuel traveled to Pittsburgh, built boats, and traveled down the Ohio River to Louisville. Here the "Indian Wars" were intensely fought, with great losses on both sides. Sometimes the women were attacked and scalped, and children were carried off into captivity. One of the desMarets women who survived after being scalped refused to wear a wig, and showed her scars proudly until her death.

Samuel desMarets married Antie Losier (1661-1731) and they had two sons, David T. (ca.1729) and Niclaes (ca.1730). David T. remained in Orange County, N.Y., and Niclaes married Saurine Ackerman (ca.1733) and moved from Hackensack, N.J., to Schagticoke, Rensselaer County, N.Y. Niclaes and Saurine had nine children. The two eldest sons, Samuel and David, were soldiers with their father in the Revolution. David spelled his name Demoray, as did David T. and Niclaes. Samuel adopted the spelling as Demaray and founded the name in Canada.

Samuel (1754-1819) married Grietje Martin near Schagticoke. It is believed that they had 12 children, but not all have been identified. Among the known children are Nicholas (1776-1846); Richard (1778-1830); Gessie; John (1781-ca.1849); David (1782-1858); and Joseph S. (ca.1784-1855). All but John and Joseph were baptized at Schagticoke. Shortly after the Revolution, the Canadians were promoting the benefits of this country at northern U.S. border points, trying to attract prospective persons to settle in Quebec. About 1784, Samuel moved to Sutton, Quebec, and took up land at Sutton Junction, which is a rugged bit of country. Unless Gessie, of whom little is known, remained in Quebec, no other members of this family stayed in the vicinity.

In 1796, Governor Simcoe let the contract to build a road from Ancaster to Kingston. This road was used in 1813 to lead men safely to Kingston after the burning of Fort York (Toronto). It may be that the need for bridges on this stretch of road was the reason that Nicholas, David and John preceded their father to the area. David was definitely the "scout" for the family, as he has been found in 1814 in the area north of Whitby. Family stories indicate that David ventured as far west as North Dorchester Township and the "Forks of the Thames." Indians rescued him from exposure before 1810. Col. J.E. Farewell in 1907 stated, "The first three frame bridges in [Ontario] County were built by the Demarays of East Whitby."

Nicholas married Elizabeth Varnum (1777-1824) and they had eight children, Rebecca (ca.1811-1876); Richard (1810-1893); Benjamin (1812-1882); Nicholas (1820-1901); Eunice (1821-1873); Daniel Porter (1822); Abraham (1824); and Elizabeth (ca.1826).

Richard, second eldest known born to Samuel and Grietje, was born at Schagticoke. He moved with his parents to Quebec and finally to the Whitby-Cobourg area. He married Rebecca Varnum (1782-1823), daughter of Benjamin and Elizabeth (Porter) Varnum of Massachusetts. This union produced 10 children, Elizabeth; Margaret (d.1901); Sophronia; Samuel (1801), who married Rachel Demoray (1806); Cynthia (1802-1865); Eunice (1804); Asenath (1806); Electa (1808-1901), who married Edmund Newton Rogers; Benjamin Varnum "Big Ben" (1810-1891); and Richard (1812-1878), who married Jane Ann McNeill and farmed in LeMars, Iowa. Big Ben Demaray moved to Whitby, North Dorchester Township, and in 1862, became the first Demaray to settle in Adelaide Township.

John married Elizabeth Church (1792-1855) and they had 12 children. Most of them moved to the U.S.

David, son of Samuel and Grietje, came to Quebec with his parents and married Jane Marsh (1786-1885). Jane died in a nursing home in Arkona at the age of 98. David and Jane had 12 children, Ann (1804-1896); William (1806-1894), who married Margaret Marsh, then Rhoda Moore; Margaret (1808-1884); Eunice (1810-1871); Mary (1812-1894), who married Robsin Stevens, then Henry Groat; Sarah (1814-1862); Priscilla (1817-1901), who married William Molesworth; Samuel (1819-1907), who married Eunice Beacham (1820-1901); David Daniel (1820-1904), who married Margaret Molesworth, then Louise Snively, and thirdly Mrs. Eleanor Jane Spring; Jane (1823-1884), who married James Willer (killed in a train robbery while en route to Buffalo, N.Y.); Simeon (1825-1898), who married Annie Robson and moved to Sanilac County, Michigan; and Simon (1825-1885), who married Janet Willer and moved to Sanilac County. All of these children were born in Brome, Quebec, or Whitby Township, Ontario.

Joseph S., youngest issue of Samuel and Grietje, married Anne Stevens (ca.1803) and they had seven children who lived in the Durham-Muskoka District, Ontario.

The Demarays of Adelaide Township descend from two first cousins, Big Ben, ninth child of Richard and Rebecca, and Samuel, eighth child of David and Jane. Both of these men were born in Canada. Big Ben came with his family from Quebec to Whitby Township in 1816. He attended the district schools, where his teacher was the celebrated William F. Morse (a veteran of the War of 1812), and commenced farming on his own in 1834 in Whitby Township. He moved to North Dorchester Township in 1850, where he engaged in clearing land and farming. While there, he served as a member of township council for eight years and as Reeve from 1857-1859. He was a Reformer in politics, a member of the Methodist Episcopal Church, and one of the first persons to sign the Abolitionist petition in the township. Big Ben purchased 150 acres of Lot 28, Con. 1 SER, on August 17, 1861, from Norman Samis for $2,300.

Big Ben married twice. He first married Rebecca Varnum (1816-1855), daughter of Daniel and Nancy (Martin) Varnum, on November 23, 1833, at Whitby. It is interesting to note that Big Ben's mother was also named Rebecca Varnum. Big Ben and Rebecca had eight children, Stillman (1834-1892) who farmed at Winfred, South Dakota; Wellington (1836-1888), a farmer in Fillmore, Minnesota; Lorena (1838-1908), who married Alexander Newell and raised nine children (see Newell); Wesley (1840, died a baby); Abram (1842-1857), who died in South Dakota; Zemari (1847-1879), who died in an accident in South Dakota; Jannet Adelaide (1850-1868), who died in Adelaide Township; and Percival (1854-1946), who married Helen E. Johnson and farmed in South Dakota. After Rebecca's death, Big Ben married Martha Dicy (1832-1898) in North Dorchester Township and they had six children, Richard (1856-1918), who farmed in Adelaide; Cynthia Elizabeth (1859-1862); Mary Jane (1862-1921), who was born in Adelaide; Huldah Ann (1865-1899); Benjamin (1868-1941), who married Anne Shaver of Westminster Township and moved to California; and Wilbur William (1872), who married Bertha Frank Folkes of Strathroy and farmed in Lambton County.

Richard, eldest child of Big Ben and Martha, married Lucy Jane Johnston (1857-1936) and farmed on Lot 26, Con. 1 NER. He was a staunch Reformer and a consistent member of Bethel Methodist Church. When he died, the local newspaper stated that his funeral was one of the largest ever held in the township. Richard and Lucy had five children, all born in Adelaide, Joseph (1882, died a baby); Richard Ira (1884-1951); William Frank (1889-1914); Martha Mildred (1891-1893); and Lucy Lenore (1894-1919), who married Clifton L. Stoner. Lucy and Clifton farmed at Fernhill, Lobo Township.

Richard Ira married Martha Elizabeth Lewis (1874-1955) of Adelaide, and farmed on part Lot 21, Con. 1 SER. They had two daughters, Mildred Louise (1910-1993), who married Arthur A.O. Johnston and had two sons in Sarnia, then married Arthur Lewis (see Lewis); and Vera, who married William H. McDougall of Caradoc Township, Middlesex County.

Mary Jane, third child of Big Ben and Martha, married Brereton "Bert" Bunting (1857-1895) of Adelaide Township and had five children, all born in Adelaide. They were Benjamin Wesley (ca.1884); Herbert Edward (ca.1887); Melvin E. (ca.1889); and Minnie Pearl (1890). Melvin married and moved to Sault Ste. Marie, Ontario. Pearl married Hiram Dicy in Strathroy in November 1915. After Bert's death, Mary Jane married John E. Wardell in Strathroy in August 1915.

Huldah Ann, fourth issue of Big Ben and Martha, married Joseph Brown. They had five sons; the four known were William, Fred, Milton and Benjamin. After Joseph's death, Huldah Ann married John Wardell.

Samuel Demaray, first cousin to Big Ben, was born in Whitby, Ontario, and married Eunice Beacham (1820-1901) on December 6, 1838. Samuel and Eunice farmed in Whitby until about 1844, then moved to Dorchester Township, Middlesex County. They raised nine children, Araminta "Mint" (1839-1925); Aaron (1841-1914);

Charles Augustus (1842-1912); Rachel (1845-1913); William Alfred "Long William" (1847-1931); Simon (1849-1907); Dennis (1852-1926); Elizabeth "Betsy" (1854-1918); and Samuel (1861-1931). The first three children were born in the Scugog District near Whitby, and the remaining six were born in Dorchester Township.

Mint, the eldest child of Samuel and Eunice, married William Mahon (1831-1916) in North Dorchester Township, and they farmed there until they moved to Adelaide Township in the early 1860s, settling on the west half of Lot 25, Con. 1 NER (see Mahon). "Auntie Mint," as she was fondly called, was always considered the focal point of the Demaray family in Adelaide.

Aaron, second issue of Samuel and Eunice, married Amanda Catherine Johnstone (1843-1901) of Malahide Township, Elgin County. In 1864, Aaron and Amanda purchased a 125-acre farm on Lot 27, Con. 1 NER, from Robert Morehead. In December of that year, he sold half of the farm to his younger brother, Charles Augustus, who had followed him to Adelaide from North Dorchester. The land transactions between Charles A. and Aaron's son, William J. are too complex to be outlined here, but after Aaron's death, the properties on Lot 27 were sold to John and William Gunson for $5,500 on November 18, 1915.

Aaron was a farmer, lay preacher, Bible-School instructor, Steward, Elder, and member of the Methodist Church Board for both Bethel Methodist Church and the East Adelaide Methodist Church Council. He attended virtually all Methodist Church conferences across the province, and his advice was widely sought on church matters. For more than 20 years, Aaron was a director of the Lobo Mutual Fire Insurance Company. He was of a serious and devout nature, a strong abolitionist, but moderate in his Liberal political views. After Amanda died, Aaron married Margaret O'Neill (1849-1937) and they lived on Caradoc Street in Strathroy.

Aaron and Amanda had a family of seven in Adelaide, Martha Eunice (1863-1947), who married John W. Hansford of Adelaide and resided near Leamington, Ontario (see Hansford); Emily Jane (1864-1896), who married Robert Ramsay and lived in Lambton County; William Johnstone (1869-1933), who married Lucy Ann Thompson (1874-1912), daughter of Malcolm and Avis

Wedding photo of Sam and Susie (Giffen) Demaray.

(Downer) Thompson of Adelaide (see Downer); Amelia Minora (1877-1888); Samuel Aaron (1879-1925), who married Susan "Susie" Giffen (1879-1969), daughter of William and Isabelle (Harkness) Giffen of Adelaide (see GIFFEN, William and Mary Jane); Edgar Roy (1885-1925), who married Ethel Sissons and died in Vancouver, B.C.; and Bertha Amelia (1875, died a baby).

At 24 years of age, William J. received 75 acres of the east half of Lot 27, Con. 1 NER, from his father, Aaron. He married Lucy in 1895 and they had 10 children. The first seven children, born in Adelaide, were Elda Avis (1895-1988), who married Fred Abbot (1890-1952); Lucy Minora (1897-1986), who married James Davis (1897-1981); Robert Lawrence (1899-1986), who married Ruby Marie Evans (1896-1986) and retired as Director of the Board of Education at Guelph, Ontario; Leona May (1901), who married Harry Jackson (1903-1978); Beatrice Amanda (1902-1990), who married Vernon Harcourt (1896-1970); Norman Johnstone (1903-1986), who married Ila May Baker (1904-1983); and Joyce Emily (1905), who married Fred Finch (1906-1988). The next three children, born in North Dorchester, were Maxwell Downer (1906-1978), who married Vivian Mansfield (1910); Aaron Claire (1908-1997), who married Margaret I. Woods (1916-1993); and Dorothy (1911, died a baby). Aaron Claire and Margaret's second eldest son, Allen Roy, married Shari Ridley and moved to part of Lot 29, Con. 2 NER, where they built a fine house. The property is called "Demara Farm." Allen owns a plumbing business.

William J. and his family faithfully attended Bethel Methodist Church and six of his children were baptized there. They sold their 75 acres to John Robertson for $3,500 on September 12, 1906, and moved to Avon, North Dorchester Township, where William J. owned and operated a general store. Lucy died very suddenly one morning while preparing the family's breakfast. William J. married Edith Campbell (d.1928) in 1918, and after she died, he married Mary Tuffield (d.1943) in 1930.

Samuel Aaron purchased his father's 125-acre farm at Lot 25, Con. 1 NER, on April 6, 1909, for $4,232 and sold it six years later for $5,500. He and Susie moved to a smaller acreage just west of Strathroy on Con. 5. He then became the rural postman delivering mail to that part of Adelaide. Sam and Clarence Demaray spent many hours enjoying their common passion, fishing! Later in life, Clarence said that Sam Demaray had three loves—Susie, fishing, and the bottle, in that order! Sam's love of a "little nip now and then" made him the black sheep of the family in some members' eyes, but Sam was a little man with a giant heart. Before he was married, and still quite a young man, Sam moved to East Williams Township to care for a pair of orphaned boys after the tragic death of their parents. He continued to care for them until they were old enough to run the farm by themselves. After Sam died at age 45, Susie married Lewis "Lew" Marsh (1875-1960), a salesman in London, and even though she had lived with Lew longer than she did with Sam, Susie insisted on being buried with Sam. They had no children.

Charles Augustus, third child of Samuel and Eunice, married Isabella Ireland (1845-1919) and they resided on the 62½ acres of Lot 25, Con. 1 NER (see Ireland). Sometime before 1875, they moved to the south part of Lot 21, Con. 1 SER. Charles Augustus was a progressive farmer. He took a deep interest in all trends to improve agriculture and life on the farm. He was a prominent director of the old West Middlesex Union Agricultural Society and willingly lent his time and talent to increase its usefulness. Charles was a Methodist and a Liberal. He and Isabella raised four children in Adelaide, Jane (1866-1938), who married William Elliott (1860-1916), brother of Thomas (see Elliott); Lydia (1870), who married John Turner (1861-1928) and farmed in Lambton County; Effie (1872-1951), who married Thomas Elliott (1864-1986), brother of William (see Elliott); and Charles Allan (1875-1952), who married Margaret "Nettie" Ellen Hord (1875-1955) of East Williams Township.

Jane and William Elliott had five children, Ethel (1885-1959), who married Albert Dowding of Adelaide (see DOWDING, Thomas and Martha); Fred Harold (1886-1961), who married Ella Mahon; Edna Elliott (1889-1910), who married William Dowding of Adelaide; Lauretta Elliott (1895-1923), who married Claude Bishop (1886-1961) of Melrose, Lobo Township; and Bessie Blythe (1902-1990), who married Clarence Stevenson (1902).

Effie and Thomas Elliott had four children, all born in Adelaide, Allan Weston (1892-1978), who married Clara Adeline Smithrim (1893-1969); Norman Melvin (1893-1899); Ariel Acelia Elliott (1894-1993), who married Arthur Milton Morningstar (1902-1991); and Thomas Wilfred (1897-1993), who married Isabella Christine McLeish (1904-1987). Allan farmed for a short time in Adelaide, and worked at the refineries in Sarnia, but his greatest love was raising and driving racehorses, which he did for many years near Camlachie, Lambton County.

Charles Allen was born on Lot 21, Con. 1 SER, and lived his entire life on the farm. He continued in the enlightened traditions of farming as established by his father, Charles Augustus. He was a member of the Order of Foresters at Beechwood, East Williams Township. Allen and Nettie raised two daughters on Lot 21, Con. 1 SER, Elsie May (1897-1989), who married William Edgley (1892-1936) and farmed near Brockville, Ontario; and Margaret Ellen (1906), who married Cliff Wardell (1905) of Adelaide.

Shortly after their marriage, Margaret and Cliff moved to the Allen Demaray farm. For Margaret it was coming home; for Cliff it meant having a partner and friend on an established, well-cared-for farm. The two men built up a fine dairy operation with a registered herd of Holstein cattle. Soon, Cliff became known as an astute judge of cattle. By the mid-1940s, the war effort in Michigan and Ohio placed a huge strain on availability of dairy and beef cattle. Buyers came to Ontario from the Great Lakes states looking for fresh herds. With Cliff's acumen of cattle, he suddenly found he'd become a major drover in the district. Soon, he was shipping cattle to Michigan and Ohio. The re-industrialization of

Michigan, Ohio, and Pennsylvania during the war continued to attract a large influx of people to those areas and they had to be fed. The demand for Canadian cattle continued and Southwestern Ontario's reputation spread around the globe. It was not long before Cliff was hosting buyers from South Korea, Japan and Pakistan. Cliff continued working as a drover until he retired at age 75.

At the age of 15, Margaret (Demaray) Wardell had attended the Short Courses sponsored by the Ontario Department of Agriculture. As a young lady, she was involved in the work of the Strathroy Women's Institute, the Junior Farmers Organization, the United Farm Women of Ontario, Adelaide Branch, the Mullifarry Farm Women's Club, and numerous other agriculture-related programs. Throughout the years, she has held various positions of responsibility in these organizations, commencing with the Presidency of the Strathroy Junior Institute in 1933. She has held the position of President in each of these organizations and was elected President of the West Middlesex Women's Institute. Margaret was one of the prime forces in the restoration the Old Fourth Line Methodist Cemetery. Margaret also had her own turkey raising operation on the farm with often as many as 50 birds, and sold eggs to Bray's Hatchery at 50¢ apiece. She and Lyle Douglas of Lot 21, Con. 3 SER, employed experimental methods in their turkey raising operations in the early 1940s. Margaret is a devoted wife and homemaker, with a determined spirit, never afraid to espouse a worthwhile cause.

Rachel, fourth child of Samuel and Eunice, married John Johnston (1846) and they raised four children in the Strathroy area. Martha married Richard C. Archer (1852-1901), then Alfred Wall, and is believed to have moved to Rochester, N.Y. Edward A. (1874-1942) was a butcher in Adelaide and Strathroy. He married Ruth Butler (1876-1961) and they had a son, Edward (1904-1992), who married Norma Freele (1909). Ed and his brother-in-law, Bill Freele, owned and operated a hardware store in Strathroy (see Freele). John Henderson (d.1952), third child of Rachel and John, died in Pontiac, Michigan. An adopted son, Grant, became a dentist in St. Thomas.

Long William, fifth child of Samuel and Eunice, lived and farmed for a time in Warwick Township, Lambton County. He married Mary Sharp, who died young. He then married Mary Olive Woolley (1850-1929) of Springfield, Elgin County. Long William and his second wife had three children, Hiram Orlando (1871-1952), born near Arkona; George William (1876-1939), born near Lyons, Elgin County; and Olive Bertha (1881-1962), born in Springfield, Elgin County.

On September 7, 1875, Long William purchased 74½ acres of the west part of Lot 23, Con. 3 NER. Within 10 weeks, he sold 17 acres of that property to Andrew S. Heake. He retained ownership of the remaining property until his younger brother, Dennis, purchased it on November 20, 1878. It is possible that Long William and his family lived on this property for a short time and that Dennis may have helped him on the farm, but Long William and Mary Olive were residing near Springfield at the birth of their second child.

Simon, sixth child of Samuel and Eunice, married Ellen Elsie Venning (1853-1942) of North Dorchester Township on October 15, 1872, and purchased a 75-acre farm on Lot 23, Con. 2 NER, the following February. They raised three sons in Adelaide, Richard Venning (1873-1967); Andrew Frederick (1878-1952); and Oliver Roy (1883-1974). Roy was born on their new farm, which consisted of the west half of Lot 7 and the east half of Lot 8, Con. 4 SER, which Simon bought from Joseph Galbraith in October 1882. Simon and his family had attended Bethel Methodist Church before moving to the Fourth Line South. After the move, the family joined the Kerwood Methodist Church, where Simon served as Steward and Elder. In May 1891, he represented his church at conferences as Trustee of the Quarterly Kerwood Circuit. His middle son, Fred, was recording secretary of the Epworth League in July 1897, and his other son, Roy, was a member the same year. In 1898, Richard, the eldest son, married Carrie Sarah Inch (1878-1954), daughter of Francis and Mary (Taylor) Inch of Metcalfe Township.

Simon farmed on the Fourth Line South with his sons until he sold the property to Richard in 1904. At that time, Simon moved to Lot 6, Con. 2 SER. Fred was in medical school at the University of Toronto at the time. Simon did not enjoy his new property for long as he suffered severe sunstroke and was forced to leave farm work. They moved to

Carrie Street in Strathroy. He had always wanted to take his wife, Ellen, to Ireland, but it is believed they had to cancel the trip. After Simon died, Ellen continued to reside in the house on Carrie Street but later moved to live with her son, Roy, and his family in Adelaide.

Richard and Carrie had five children on the Fourth Line South, Winnifred Grace (1900); Oliver Earl (1901); Dena Elsie May (1903); Mabel Beatrice (1905); and Franklin Ross (1908-1975). In late March of 1920, Richard sold the property on the Fourth Line South, held an auction sale and packed their remaining possessions into a wagon, hitched up the horse, and "headed home away from this darn Adelaide clay." (The clay at the back of his property on the west half of Lot 8 had been used to produce brick and tile in the 1850s). They returned to North Dorchester. Clarence Demaray was 14 years old and went along for the ride. He well remembered how sore his backside was after bumping along for nine hours in that old wagon.

Winnifred Grace married Asahel Albert Bryson (1890) and raised a family on the Egremont Road in Warwick Township. Winnifred and Asahel were killed in a horrific automobile accident in Warwick Township. Earl married Myrtle Cole and they raised their family on a farm near Belmont. Elsie May married Lawrence A. Baker, then Frank Jackson. Beatrice married George Frederick Knowles (1926-1964) and they had two daughters. Ross married Dora Kathleen Copeman and farmed near Belmont.

Dr. "Fred" Demaray, second child of Simon and Ellen, married Mabel Armstrong (1882-1956) and they had three children in Toronto, Edna May (1907); Vera (1908); and Robert Frederick (1915), who was a Flight Lieutenant in the R.C.A.F. and a physician. After attending University of Toronto Medical School, Fred completed advanced medical training in Scotland before becoming a pioneering ophthalmologist in Toronto.

Roy, third son of Simon and Ellen, married Mary Elizabeth Smithrim (1883-1981), daughter of Richard and Elizabeth (Taylor) Smithrim of Metcalfe Township. Roy and Mary built a new house on Lot 6, Con. 2 SER. They had a family of five children, Richard Clarence (1905-1996), who was born on the Fourth Line South; Nellie Elizabeth (1908-1920); Elva Adeline (1910); Hazel Marie (1912-1973); and Stanley Roy (1918-1986). Because he found the land on Lot 6 difficult to drain, which made early planting difficult, Roy sold this farm in April 1922 and moved across the road to Lot 7, Con. 2 SER, where they enjoyed a larger house and what became possibly the best farmland in all of Adelaide. Roy and Mary always played an active role in the church. Roy served many terms as Steward and Elder of Bethesda United Church on the Second Line South. He was choir leader for more than 50 years, and he and Mary were always in demand as guest soloists for special services at all the district churches. Roy was a licensed auctioneer for several years in Adelaide. He served on the Adelaide Township Council as Township Adjuster, and was frequently called upon as arbitrator in local disputes. He raised purebred Clydesdale horses, and he and the Pedden family were well known for their breeding stock. He experimented with several sheep breeds, which included Suffolk, Lincoln, Border Leicester, and Corriedale, a particular favourite. He was proud to be called a "mixed-farmer" and was a husbandman in its truest sense. He was a beekeeper for many years, maintained an excellent fruit orchard, and developed several new strains of apples over the years. In the early years, they sold eggs and homemade butter on the Strathroy and London markets. Roy never applied artificial fertilizers to his land, and no pesticides or herbicides were ever used. Tractors on his land were forbidden, as he said all they did was "crush the life out of the soil." The family, while still at home, lived and worshipped in the Methodist tradition. There was no drinking, no swearing, no card playing, no dancing, no working on Sunday, and church and Sunday School attendance was mandatory. Moderation was the key word of the household. The family was never wealthy in monetary terms, but felt enriched in every other way.

On a Saturday in late spring in the early 1950s, right after the noon meal, Mary was tidying up some old papers, and put them in the cook stove to burn. The burning paper went straight up the chimney and landed on the dry shingle roof. Shortly after, she and Roy heard the general fire ring on the telephone, which was sent out to all houses on that particular party line. Mary answered the call to ask where the fire was and was told that her roof was on fire. Although friends and family members made every effort, the house burned to the ground in 45 minutes. The furniture and personal items they saved were moved into the barn/woodshed, and neighbours prepared food for the family and helpers. Within two months, a new house was built, all of the labour donated by friends and neighbours.

At the age of 83, Roy and Mary retired from farming. In June 1965, they sold their property at Lot 7, Con. 2 SER, and moved to a house on Drury Lane in Strathroy. With failing eyesight, Roy was unable to pass his driver's test, so Mary learned to drive at 83 years of age. They returned to Bethesda Church services whenever possible and were always revered guests of the congregation. They continued to maintain their little vegetable garden, and grew much of their own fresh produce. Mary continued to put down preserves, a skill that she had always performed with great success. They missed the farm and its way of life, but realized that there was a time for everything.

Clarence, eldest son of Roy and Mary, was born in Adelaide Township on the Fourth Line South. Before he was married, he worked on the farm, as an erector with a barn building company from Warwick, as a taxi driver in London, and as a barber. Much of this occurred during the "Dirty Thirties." Clarence often recalled that in relation to the costs of goods and services in those days, he had more money than he ever had in his entire lifetime. He often commented that there was lots of work to be had during the Depression if you really wanted to find it and didn't think the job beneath your dignity. From his experiences of the times, he believed that men simply found it easier to sit around, get drunk, feel sorry for themselves and blame their hard times on the government. Many enterprising men did become millionaires during the Great Depression and because of it.

Clarence married Alice Blanche Craig (1915-1989), whose family had come to Strathroy from the southern United States. Her father, Luther Vernon Craig, had been hired to re-tool and design the jigs and fixtures for the Turner Day Handle Factory (formerly Canadian Handle Manufacturing Company) of Strathroy. After his work was completed, Luther returned to the U.S. to re-tool the next plant. Blanche stayed on as housekeeper with the family of William Jackson, who owned the Handle Factory. In 1935, Clarence married Blanche in the Jackson home on Front Street, Strathroy.

When Blanche Craig arrived in Adelaide in 1935, it caused quite a stir in the community. She was felt to be an interloper and, with her southern drawl, locals felt she "talked funny." Nevertheless, one by one, neighbours welcomed her and she soon had many friends. She became president of the Mission Band Circle, the W.M.S. and several other women's organizations. Blanche used cornmeal muffins to prepare her stuffing, her use of spices was totally foreign to the women of Adelaide, and yet everyone wanted her recipes. She rarely used them, however, and many times she experimented on Clarence and her sons, only rarely with disastrous results. When it came to biscuit baking, she always bowed to Ella Harris.

Blanche prepared and organized the food for the Inaugural Banquet for Harold Eastman, when he was elected Warden of Middlesex County. To see and hear her talk and fret, it was as if she were planning an invasion of Europe. The day came and went with great success, as former Wardens and councillors stood one after the other and said that they had attended the finest banquet ever! For this former outsider, the ice in Adelaide had finally melted.

After their marriage, Clarence and Blanche rented a house and one acre of land on Lot 12, Con. 3 SER, from Clarence Fuller of Adelaide. They raised three sons on the property, Donald "Don" Frederick (1937); Robert "Bob" Irwin (1938); and Lee Roy (1939). The home was of brick construction, but it was quite possibly the worst built house in Adelaide. The foundation was built of mortar and 50% mud. The bricks in the lower walls had been reclaimed from the former house built in the 1850s. Every time it rained, or when the snow melted in the spring, the basement filled with water six feet deep and simply flowed into one side of the basement and out the other. The soffits had not been properly designed or constructed and subsequently the air passed through the house between the floors at will. When the wind blew, the linoleum on the floors in the bedrooms rose and fell with each gust, held down by only the furniture. There was no central heating in the house and to keep warm in very cold weather, the boys filled two-quart glass jars with hot water, encased them in knitted woolen socks, and put them in the bed near their feet. In the morning, the jars were often frozen and the broken glass was mixed with the ice in the socks. Blanche said that the boys never caught a cold until after a central furnace was installed.

The three boys walked two miles each way to S.S. #8, often accompanied by their dog, Mickey. As long as Mickey was present, other dogs stayed away from the boys, and he kept stray dogs from venturing near the schoolyard. The school children felt that it was an honour to share some of their lunch with Mickey and sometimes a fight broke out if denied that privilege. Audrey Atchison was their first teacher, followed by Rebecca Harris. When Anna Jean Wilson arrived as their next teacher, the prayers of the pupils had been answered. She was not much older than the boys in Grade Eight, she was fun, could really teach, and she could hit and catch a baseball better than any boy. Most of the boys had a crush on her and when she got engaged to Don Sullivan, many were disappointed.

Life at the school progressed smoothly and the pupils were happy there, until Payne's School on Second Line South became overcrowded and some of the pupils living just north of Strathroy were bused to S.S. #8. The Adelaide-East boys said that the "local home-grown" boys at the school were country hicks, the country boys called them "stupid city slickers," and Anna Jean did her best to keep the peace. Fistfights behind the school cleared the air and fortunately, the winners on both sides were about even. Understanding and mutual respect again prevailed.

Later, the Demaray boys rode the bus to Strathroy District Collegiate Institute and, with varying degree of success, graduated. While there, they excelled in sports activities and played on many championship teams. Strathroy Collegiate dominated in their league. In those days, outside the new gymnasium, there were plaques containing the names of former track and field champions. A few had their names listed more than once, and one name, that of George Downham of Adelaide, was especially prevalent. No name, however, had occurred more than three years consecutively and Don made it his goal to break that pattern. In the next four years, he achieved that goal and was proud to share his last senior track and field championship with his friend, Alexander McKenzie.

For many students, the Strathroy Cadet Corps was mandatory and merely something to be survived. This was not the case with the Demaray boys. Lee and Don soon became officers, and Lee rose to the rank of Regimental Sergeant Major. Strathroy won the Best Cadet Corps in Ontario that year. Because all three boys had learned to hunt at a very early age with their father, they dominated the Cadet Rifle competition for many years. One year, Lee won the most prestigious award for marksmanship in Canada, the Gold Star.

Clarence worked as a machinist and welder with Alton "Sonny" Wright in Strathroy and barbered part-time. In his spare time, he began to build his own drilling rig. Dug wells in the area were beginning to fail and small showings of crude oil had been discovered in Adelaide near Kerwood. Clarence could foresee a future as a driller of water, gas and oil wells. By working as a pipe fitter and welder at the Polymer Plant in Sarnia, he was able to provide the necessary cash with which to purchase tools and materials to augment his new drilling rig. The Canadian government informed him that he would not be eligible to enlist in the Canadian Army as his ability to drill and produce oil wells was important to the war effort. Very rapidly, he became a drilling contractor or in the jargon of the occupation, "tool-pusher." He required help in the form of "roughnecks," men who worked with him at the job. Many Adelaide boys filled this role. Ivan Carrothers, Bob and Roy Down, and Frank Baxter were just a few. Irwin Carrothers had assisted him in the early years and soon was qualified to become a tool-pusher himself. The old drilling rig was too slow, and could not hold enough steel cable to drill deep enough. Charlie Nichols and his brother, Bill, were already experienced well drillers and a partnership, Demaray & Nichols, was formed, thus providing sufficient capital to purchase the expensive rigs and tooling. The new partnership thrived and grew beyond their expectations. Soon, hundreds of thousands of dollars had been invested. Three drilling rigs were busy night and day, occasionally seven days a week. Clarence said that he would never ask a man to work on Sunday, nor would he do so himself. Shifts were twelve hours in length, excluding travel time. The work was dirty, hazardous, hot in summer and bitterly cold in winter, but the work just kept coming. Don, Bob and Lee worked on the rigs at various times, and it probably helped to decide that there had to be a better way to make a living. As careful as they were, both Clarence and Charles suffered very serious accidents. It was at times a very dangerous occupation. Clarence was the first to succumb and he required a very complex spine operation that nearly killed him. Charlie suffered a heart attack, but survived. Demaray & Nichols was no longer a viable enterprise, and was sold at great financial loss to both partners.

Clarence and Blanche moved from Lot 12, Con. 2 SER, to part of Lot 28, Con. 2 SER, in July 1965, which had been occupied by Hugh and Winnifred Dolphin since June 1952.

Don, eldest son of Clarence and Blanche, enrolled at the University of Western Ontario. After completing three years at U.W.O. in a science and mathematics program, he spent an additional two years in the study of history, economics and literature. During his last year, Don met and married Mary Gardner of South Porcupine, Ontario. They moved to Toronto, where Don accepted a job teaching secondary school science and mathematics. Mary and Don decided that Toronto was no place to raise a family, so they moved first to Prescott, and next to Fergus, Ontario. The family's last move was to London, where Don taught for the London Board of Education for many years. Don returned to Adelaide to care for his father in 1994, and purchased the property in 1996. He has numerous interests, including genealogy, and has owned his own design, fabrication and supply company for many years.

Don and Mary, now divorced, have two children, Craig Andrew Morgan and Kathryn Anne "Morgan." Craig married Nancy Patterson and they have two children, Grant Clarence Stanley and Nicole Katherine Louise. Morgan married Stephen Clark of Hamilton and they have a daughter, Mikaela Mary.

Bob, second son of Clarence and Blanche, attended Ridgetown Agricultural College and graduated with honours. He married Marie Morrow, great great great-granddaughter of John Morrow, who in ca.1841 hewed the giant white oak sills upon which St. Mary's Church was built. Bob pursued a career in Automotive Sales and Management in various places in Ontario. He opened a Chrysler dealership in Ridgetown, Ontario, and later sold it and went into house construction. He opened and operated a salmon fishing charter service for some time. He then invented, and started his own company to manufacture, industrial car and truck door removal equipment for the body shop industry. He saturated the Ontario market with his product, and retired. At present, he designs and builds custom cabinets for commercial and private customers.

Bob and Marie have two children, Joy Lynn and Robert "Bob" Allen. Joy married David Westelaken and they have two sons, Matthew David and Jason. Joy and Dave operate Empire Farms in Wallacetown, Ontario. Bob A. graduated from St. Clair College in Automotive Merchandising and presently works in new car sales in Chatham.

Lee, youngest son of Clarence and Blanche, graduated from Strathroy Collegiate and commenced a career in sales and management in the financial and building services industry. He married Anne Singer, a hairstylist in Strathroy. Lee and Ann have a son, Michael Andrew, who graduated from the University of Western Ontario and is presently teaching in Japan.

Elva Adeline, third child of Roy and Mary, was raised on Lots 6 and 7, Con. 2 SER, and as a young woman she moved to Strathroy to assist in the care of an aunt. The aunt resided on Victoria Street and at that time was a neighbour of Dr. Robert A. Willmott. Later, Elva became Dr. Willmott's assistant in his dental office. She met his son, George William "Bill" Willmott (1908-1993), also a dentist, and subsequently married him in 1935. Elva and Bill had two children, Sonya and Robert "Bob." Bill joined the Canadian Army in 1942 and served as Captain in the Canadian Dental Corps in England where he specialized in the treatment of servicemen whose faces were damaged as the result of war wounds. Upon returning in 1945, Bill set up his own practice in Strathroy. Sonya trained as an elementary school teacher and taught in Sarnia and London. She returned to Strathroy after her retirement in 1993. Bob joined the OPP and married Karen Kelleher. Karen and Bob have three sons. Jeffrey William works with handicapped children, Christopher John is a printer in London, and Joseph Robert Adam is a bush pilot in Northern Ontario.

Marie, fourth child of Roy and Mary, was born and raised on Lot 6, Con. 2 SER, and attended S.S. #8. She participated in several of the Short Courses with her cousin, Margaret. She attended hairdressing school and became a very accomplished hairdresser. She lived in London most of her life. At the age of 37, she met and married Russ Burchiel (1904), a widower, who was a Departmental Floor Manager at Simpsons. They had no children, and both died in London.

Stan (1918-1986), youngest child of Roy and Mary, was born on Lot 6, Con. 2 SER. He worked on the farm, but showed a real talent for radio electronics by dismantling every radio receiver he could get his hands on. He married Winnifred "Wynn" Darlow in Aylmer, and joined the R.C.A.F. in 1942. He became one of the most accomplished radar instructors in the R.C.A.F. He was stationed in many locations in Canada and only two of their children were born in the same place. The family spent many years at Zweibrucken, Germany, where he was Chief Radar Instructor for the Canadian Forces stationed in Germany and France. Stan, not wishing to be an officer, refused promotion after promotion and became one of the highest-ranking Chief Warrant officers in the Air Corps (he often said in jest that he'd only have to pay for his own uniform and that he'd rather be on the top of the bottom pile than on the bottom of the top pile). He retired in 1970 to live in St. Mary's, Ontario. Not being accustomed to sitting around all day, he joined the audiovisual staff at Fanshawe College in London, and became their top troubleshooter. Stan and Wynn had a family of one son and three daughters. Ronald "Ron" Stanley was born in Kirkland Lake, Ontario; Elizabeth "Lynn" was born in Strathroy; and Terry Ellen and Sandra Lee were born in Simcoe, Ontario.

Ron joined the R.C.A.F., trained as a pilot, and rose to the rank of Captain. Much of the time, he was stationed on Canada's east coast flying Argus surveillance and Albatross search and rescue aircraft. He spent the latter part of his career training pilots in the Canadian Forces. Ron married Leonice Yvonne Thibault and they have two children, Joanne Sylvia and Jeffrey Michael. Ron and Yvonne have two grandchildren.

After Ron retired, he became interested in researching the Demaray family. Frustrated by not being able to locate accurate cemetery records, he conceived of a giant database into which all burials would be recorded and indexed. He started with those cemeteries in which his ancestors were buried. Hundreds of records became thousands, and thousands became millions. Other volunteers joined his efforts and the Ontario Cemetery Finding Aid was born, a database that now contains an index of several million burials in Ontario. Because Ron resides in British Columbia, there is now a B.C. index, as well. The database grows daily, and it is very likely that it will eventually contain information on every known burial in Canada. This project has become one of the most significant contributions to genealogical research in Canada.

Terry, third child of Stan and Wynn, married Anthony William Eldon, and they have one son, Richard Anthony. Terry works as a set designer at the Niagara-on-the-Lake Theatre.

Sandra, youngest child of Stan and Wynn, never married. She works for the Federal government in Burlington.

Dennis, seventh child of Samuel and Eunice, married Angelique Plaxton (1856-1937) of North Dorchester on November 4, 1873 (see Plaxton). Their children were William Charles (1874-1946); Aaron Edgar (1877-1947); and Minnie May (1879-1962). The sons were born in North Dorchester, and Minnie May was born in their new home in Adelaide Township. The family continued to live there until Dennis sold out to William McKeen in 1885 and moved to the west half of Lot 12, Con. 2 NER, which he had purchased from Alexander Johnston. Dennis and his son, Edgar, added to their property in 1909, buying 80 acres of the east half of Lot 12, Con. 3 NER, from Arthur Brock. Dennis sold his 100-acre farm at Lot 12, Con. 2 NER, to Samuel E. McInroy in 1919.

Bill, eldest child of Dennis and Angelique, married Martha Elizabeth Hord (1876-1943) of East Williams Township, sister of Nettie Hord Demaray. In 1897, Bill purchased the west half of Lot 6, Con. 2 NER, from his father and the Synod of the Diocese of Huron. He also purchased the west half of Lot 7, Con. 2 NER, from the estate of Charlotte Arrand Simpson and Charles W. Arrand in 1927. Bill and Martha raised five children in Adelaide, Stella (1899-1962); Lloyd (1901-1991); Wesley "Wes" (1906-1985); Mary Elizabeth (1908); and Orval Hord (1912-1956).

Stella married Walter Haskett Jackson (ca.1895-1965) and they had a daughter, Abigail, who married John Thompson. Stella and Walter lived in West Williams Township.

Lloyd married Olive Inez Daley (1904-1994) and they raised five children near Parkhill, Ontario. At the time of his death, 24 grandchildren, 40 great-grandchildren and five great great-grandchildren survived Lloyd.

Mary Elizabeth married Russell Isaac and they had five children, Gerald Russell, William Raymond, Ronald Walter, Joyce Marie and Carol Ann. After Russell Isaac abandoned his family, Mary returned home to Adelaide to the home of her parents with the younger children. The older boys lived with their uncles. These children attended Adelaide elementary schools. Today, Mary Elizabeth lives with her son, Gerald, in Parkhill.

Wes and Orval never married but spent their entire lives farming in Adelaide. Their father, Bill, deeded 50 acres, the west half of the west half of Lot 6, Con. 2 NER, to Orval in 1938, and the remaining 50 acres of the west half to Orval in 1945. In 1927, Bill granted 50 acres of the west half of Lot 7, Con. 2 NER, to Wes. In 1944, Wes purchased the east half of Lot 4, Con. 2 NER. After Orval died of an accidental gunshot wound, Wes "inherited" Orval's property. Other than by the fact that these two men were bachelors, they led quite different lifestyles. Orval was a neat and tidy person, much like his mother. He was somewhat shy with strangers and possessed acceptable standards of hygiene. Wes was the antithesis of his brother. Although he was generous, kindly, a knowledgeable hog farmer, and a man who possessed a knowledge of the Bible that a minister would envy, his personal lifestyle and hygiene were beyond description. If it may be said that a farmer can best understand and appreciate his livestock by close observation of their behavior, then Wes understood such things better than most men. If a man may become a legend in his own lifetime, Wes Demaray did.

Aaron Edgar, second son of Dennis and Angelique, married Helena Harris (1876-1950) of Adelaide and resided on Lot 12, Con. 2 NER (see Harris). About 1923, they moved to Harrietsville, North Dorchester. They had one son, Clarence Laverne (1904-1963), who married Olive MacVicar. They raised their two children near Harrietsville.

Minnie May, daughter and youngest child of Dennis and Angelique, married George Henry Jarrett (1901-1963) and they raised two sons in Lambton County, Lyle Kenneth (1904-1993) and Oscar Keith (1912).

Betsy, eighth issue of Samuel and Eunice, married Isaac T. Spring (d.1877) and they had a son, Samuel Spring (1873-1916). After Isaac's death, Betsy married Benjamin Kirby (1852-1910) and moved to Detroit, Michigan, where a daughter was born, Theresa Pearl (1891-1912). Betsy was a large and powerful woman, and it was said that she was as strong as any man in the district.

Samuel, ninth and youngest child of Samuel and Eunice, remained in North Dorchester and married Ida May Sadler (1862-1947) on December 6, 1882. Sam and Ida had two children, Theresa May (1888-1958) and Howard E. (1905).

DEMARAY, Wesley and Orville

The Duncan Robinson farm was sold to Wesley E. Demaray in 1946. Wesley (d.1985) and his brother, Orville (d.1956), both settled in the area. Wes farmed the west half of Lot 4, Con. 2, and Orville the east half of Lot 5, Con. 2, both located on the present Cuddy Drive.

Orville suffered an untimely, unexpected death. He died from a gunshot wound while climbing a fence post in the field east of the house. Mr. Cuddy, a neighbour, found him. After Orville's death, Wes farmed both properties, as well as a 50-acre farm on Kerwood Road. One night, someone killed and skinned a cattle beast during the night (cattle rustlers were presumed to be the guilty parties).

Wesley was a well-known bachelor in his earlier years. He produced Shorthorn and Hereford cattle. In the latter years, he even hosted a cockfight in the wee hours of the night. Later, he was perhaps better known for his "housekeeping" to the local residents. A lot of stories have surfaced about Wesley's past, some true and some that can be left to the imagination.

Wesley had a variety of hired men. His nephews, Ron and Ken Isaac of Parkhill, worked for him. Other hired men included the Van Erp brothers, who helped him pick 50 acres of corn by hand one wet fall. How many farmers today would even let that cross their minds?

Wes had a great love of animals and they were well cared for. This included the rooster Wes kept as a pet in the house.

In the latter years, Wes' health deteriorated, along with his ability to care for himself. Dr. Wayne Johnson of Arkona visited Wes on many occasions, but one visit from any VON or health nurse was all they could handle. Wes was finally admitted to hospital with diabetes and a foot infection. Eventually, amputation of his feet and lower legs became necessary. Gangrene set in and death finally took its toll.

The stone house on this property is believed to be the only surviving stone building left in Adelaide Township. This building, sadly, has not been restored as a heritage site. The property was sold by the estate and is now a cash crop operation.

DEMPSTER, Robert and Elizabeth

Robert Dempster (1816) was born in Ireland and settled in Adelaide to farm before 1840. He married Elizabeth Shields (1821-ca.1901), daughter of William and Latetia Shields, in 1843. They had four children, Robert Jr. (1843-1884); James (1844-1845); Latetia (1846-1876), who married a Culbert before 1871 in Adelaide; and Elizabeth (1848), who also married a Culbert, some time before 1901.

Robert Jr. married Eliza Ann (1852-1890, last name unknown) in Adelaide about 1881. They farmed Lot 1, Con. 2 NER, according to the 1878 map, and they had two children, Robert Dempster III (1877-1887) and William Gilbert Dempster (1878-1884). All of the members of this family died within the span of six years. It could be assumed that a fatal disease was the cause. They are interred in West Adelaide Cemetery.

DERKS, Gerry and Mary

Gerry Derks (1930) was born in Schijndel, N.B., the Netherlands, and immigrated to Canada in August 1952. He first settled in London.

In August 1953, Mary Van Den Heuvel immigrated to Canada from Wijbosch, N.B., the Netherlands, and arrived in London.

The two were married in St. Martin Roman Catholic Church on August 29, 1953. In April 1955, they moved to Strathroy and started a garage specializing in general repairs. In November 1959, they moved to a new house on Pt. Lot 21, Con. 3, with their children, Anne Marie (1955); Albert (1956); and Frances (1958). They raised two more children in the new home, Gerald (1961) and Carolin (1964).

Anne Marie married Dale Satchell and moved to St. Thomas. They have three children, Christopher, Rebecca and Tracy.

Derks family, back L-R, Frances, Gerald, Carolin and Anne Marie, seated L-R, Gerry, Mary and Albert Derks, 1994.

Albert married Marietta VanDenBerg and moved to Ekfrid. Their three children are Jason, Cassandra and Amanda.

Frances married Rick Howe and moved to a farm in Melbourne. They have four children, Michelle, Gordon, James and Laura.

Gerald married Ruth Beimers and moved to Napier in Metcalfe. They have three children, Sarah, Rachel and Lucas.

Carolin married Charles McDonnell and lives in Strathroy. Their three children are Daniel, Nicole and Erica.

DEVET, Casey and Mary

Casey Martin (d.1979) and Mary Josephine (Hendrikx) Devet came to Canada from Baorle-Nassau in the Netherlands in April 1951. They bought the property at Lot 1, Con. 4 NER, from Jack Roland Sr., and moved there on March 13, 1953. They started a dairy farm with a few cattle and steadily increased the herd.

They had seven children. Lucy (1952) married Louis Hendrikx on April 27, 1973, and now lives in West Williams Township. Joanne (1953) married Harry Slaats on July 20, 1973, and now lives in West Lorne. John (1955-1973) died a young man. Frank (1956) married Elsie Soetemans on April 23, 1983, and lives in Warwick Township. Alda (1957) married Jerry Bongers on August 25, 1977, and lives in Warwick Township. Henry (1959) married Elizabeth "Betty" Vankessel on August 25, 1984, and lives on the home farm. Nancy (1961) married Martin Verberk (d.1997) on August 21, 1981, and she lives in West Williams Township.

Two years after Casey died, Henry purchased the farm from Mary. He changed the dairy operation to a hog operation in 1983. Henry and Betty had five children, triplet sons Brian, Casey and Jesse (1988; Jesse died in 1989); Victoria "Vicki" (1992); and Martina (1997).

Devet family, clockwise from left, John, Casey, Joanne, Lucy, Mary, Frank, Nancy on Mary's lap, Alda, Henry, ca.1963.

DOAN, Joseph and Edith

Joseph and Edith (Mellor) Doan moved to Kerwood where he was employed as a cheese maker. Frank (1913-1988) was born in Kerwood. The family moved several times, wherever a cheese maker was needed. These moves included Brigden, Belmont and Hickson, where Joseph Doan died in 1922.

Frank, his sister, Muriel, and his mother moved to Dorchester, where Mrs. Doan managed the telephone exchange. Frank obtained his high school diploma there and entered Normal School in London.

During the 1930s, they had a home built for their mother in Kerwood, which they retained until their deaths.

During WWII, Frank enlisted in the army but didn't go overseas as the war ended while he was still training in Calgary.

Frank obtained his BA, MA, and PhD while teaching in primary and secondary schools. He spent time in Houston, Texas, and was the first professor of Philosophy at Lakehead University in Thunder Bay, where he retired in 1978 at age 65. He died after a lengthy battle with heart disease.

DODGE, Henry and Elizabeth

Henry and Elizabeth (Smithrim) Dodge and their children, Rosella, Earl (d.1999), Velma (who now lives in Vancouver), and Calvin, all lived in Adelaide Township for eight years. Their farm in Metcalfe was small and a stream ran across from the front to the back, leaving only 50 acres of workable land. Earl remembers driving with his parents in the horse and buggy in 1919, looking for a bigger farm. They looked at Sam Demaray's property on the Second Line North and at the Andrew Douglas farm on Highway 81, north of Strathroy. Finally, the decision was made to buy 100 acres of the west half of Lot 18 from the estate of Norman Brock.

The family moved to Adelaide and settled there, between the farms of Russell Brock and Tom Walker. At this time, Earl's grandfather, William Dodge (who had married Martha Cook and after her death, to Maggie Chute from Caradoc), had a small acreage on North Head Street. He made a living growing vegetables and supplying the town. After Henry and his family moved to Adelaide, Grandfather William sold out and moved to California, to a small farm where he grew vegetables and grapes. When his wife Maggie died, he left the farm to his son, Norman, in Edmonton, and in 1926, he moved back to Ontario with his son, George Dodge, in Metcalfe, about a half-mile from the first farm. The Dodges moved to Adelaide on the Monday before Good Friday, 1919. The children were ready to attend S.S. #10 Adelaide after the Easter holiday.

Earl recalls his school days: "I entered Jr. III class [Grade 5] under the instruction of Greta Smith of Strathroy. I was always a bashful, shy kid, but the students at S.S. #10 made me feel at home. Hildegarde Web, a distant cousin of my Dad, from Byron, taught a year. Then we had Esther Bycraft, from Coldstream. I was then in Sr. IV and around Christmas time, the teacher decided that the four students in Jr. IV and Sr. IV, would take the work and try the High School Entrance Examinations. Graham Walker and I were the only two boys who passed. At that time, farm boys didn't go to high school, so

Esther Bycraft went to the high school and got books and teaching materials for Graham and me. The next June, Graham and I went into town and wrote the First Form Exams, which we passed. Then, we decided to go to High School in the Second Form. I got my Junior Matriculation and my parents asked me if I wanted to go to Guelph to Agricultural School. Because I was a quiet, shy boy, I decided to stay home and help Dad as he was working alone on the farm."

The Dodges returned to Metcalfe in October 1927, after buying the Smithrim family farm. They had never liked the Adelaide clay land. However, they kept the Adelaide farm and harvested hay each summer. Almost every summer, they had enough hay to fill their barn. In the spring, the farm was seeded to pasture. They would line the cattle on the road and drive them though a sideroad to pasture and later, drive them back in November.

When Henry died in 1946, Elizabeth sold the farm to George Elliott. He drained the farm and grew cash crops.

Calvin married Evelyn Howe and they built a small house across the lane from the old farmhouse. In 1936, when Earl was about 27, he and his father looked at a farm on the road south of them and they decided to rent it. In the meantime, an uncle's farm (William Hawkin), came for sale and Earl bought it. He had $1,000 saved in the bank from farming on the rental on Con. 4, Metcalfe.

Earl met his wife, Mae Watson (d.1995), through Thelma Payne. He had always chummed with her brother, Ormand Payne, in school. One Sunday, Ormand suggested they drive to Bright's Grove. They stopped at a cottage and Ormand went to the door. Thelma answered and when three other girls came out, Mae sat beside Earl, who soon realized this introduction had been arranged in advance. In 1946, after ten years of courtship, Earl and Mae were finally married, and they settled on his farm in Metcalfe on Con. 4. They had a son, Douglas, who lives with his wife, Diane, and their children, Megan and Ashley, on the farm. Mae taught at S.S. #9 Adelaide. After Mae died, Earl resided in Strathroy at Trillium Village, until his own death four years later.

DORTMANS, Harry and Nellie

Harry (1924-1996), and Nellie VandenBoom (1919-1996) were married in Canada in 1952 and resided in Rockwood, near Guelph. In 1954, they purchased Lot 14, Con. 5 SER, from the Currie family. They farmed dairy cows until 1972, when they began to include beef cattle and cash crops. They sold the farm in April 1979. The Dortmans then moved to another dairy farm on Lot 1, Con. 2 SER, of Kerwood. They sold this farm in May 1982 and retired to Forest, spending half of the year in Florida. Harry and Nellie raised eight children.

Hank (1953), the eldest sibling, has two daughters from his first marriage to Harriet Dorfmans (1953). Hank is now married to Linda Losh (1956), from West Chester, Pennsylvania. The couple lives in Carrizo Spring, Texas, raising two sons. Hank is a truck driver and Linda is a homemaker.

Trudy (1954) married Murray Bain (1954) of Strathroy in 1976. Trudy is a nurse and Murray is a sales representative. They currently reside at 317 Astoria Court in London with their three children.

Joan (1956) married John Aarts (1955) of Watford in 1976. They farm cash crops and live at Lot 23, Con. 5 SER, Warwick Township, with their three children.

Mary (1957), a nurse, married Roland Kroh (1954), a carpenter from Strathroy, in 1984. They reside in Strathroy at 23 Pannel Lane with their three children.

Frank (1958) married Sandy Veeke (1965) from Watford in 1984, and they reside in Watford at Lot 20, Con. 2 NER, where they farm cash crops. They have four children.

Rita (1959) married Rick VanGorp (1958) of Watford in 1979. They live in Watford at Lot 27, Con. 3 SER, where they raise hogs and farm cash crops and serve as the area Pioneer Seed Dealer. Rita and Rick have three children.

Ken (1962) resides in Strathroy and works as a labourer.

In 1992, Eileen (1966) married Kevin Peck (1964) of Dorchester, where they currently live. Eileen works for Canada Trust and Kevin is employed at Granger Fuels.

DORTMANS, Hein and Johanna

In 1923, Hein Dortmans (1896-1979) married Johanna Rooyackers (1892-1968) in Holland. Their eldest son, Harry (1924-1996), immigrated to Canada in 1948 and settled near Guelph. In 1949, Harry's brother, John (1927), immigrated to Canada and joined him.

In 1951, Hein and Johanna left their one son, Jan (1928), in Holland and immigrated to Canada with their remaining children, Gertrude (1925); Nolda (1929); Adrian (1934-1961); and William "Bill" (1936-1991). They farmed for one year near Guelph and then moved to Adelaide Township in the spring of 1952. Gertrude remained in Guelph and married Harry Schepters (1927-1998). The Dortmans purchased the east half of Lot 16, Con. 2 SER, from the VandenBoomens. In 1954, they purchased the west half of the same lot from Fred Rawlinson and moved to this property, where they continued to operate a dairy farm. In 1958, Hein, Johanna and Bill purchased 150 acres on Pt. Lots 16 and 12, Con. 2.

In 1960, Bill married Elizabeth Hendrickx of West Williams Township. Shortly after their marriage, Bill's brother Adrian died, and Bill and Liz took over the family farm from his parents. They ran a dairy operation until 1973, at which time they changed to beef cattle. Since that time, the farm has been a beef cattle and veal operation. In 1988, John H., Bill and Liz's son, and his wife, Rita, purchased the operation and continued the veal operation for a couple of years. The farm is presently rented by Nick Spruyt, and housing pigs.

Bill and Liz had a family of eight children. Adrian lives in Adelaide Village with his wife, Sue. John and Rita and their daughter, Abby, also live in Adelaide Village. Lia and Willy Toonen and their three daughters live in East Williams Township. Annie and John Rutten and their two daughters live in Forest. Rick and Julie Dortmans and their son, Riley, and Tony and Kelly Dortmans, live in

Dortacres Farm; Hein Dortmans with grandchildren, Annie and John, and Bill at driver's side.

Dortmans family, back L-R, John, Rick and Adrian, front L-R, Tony, Lia (holding Willy), Annie and Rob.

Adelaide Township. Rob Dortmans is presently living on the Dortmans home farm. Willy and Joanne Dortmans and their son, Billy, live in Warwick Township just over the townline.

DORTMANS, John and Nellie

In April 1956, John Dortmans (1927) and Nellie Peters (1933) of Kerwood married and purchased 100 acres from Clare and Muriel Sisson of Lot 15, Con. 3 SER. The Dortmans started with dairy farming and also raised turkeys. After four years, they remodeled their barn and began to raise pigs instead. The last change came eight years later, when they changed to heifers and concentrated on dairy farming.

The Dortmans raised eight children. All of them were very involved with farm work and participated in 4-H clubs and Junior Farmers.

In 1981, John and Nellie purchased Lot 16, Con. 4 SER, from Morris and Willy Hoefnagels (formerly owned by Clare Sinkey), and moved there in 1983 when John Jr. married. They resided there until 1989 when their son, Richard, married and took over the hog operation. The Dortmans then purchased and moved to Lot 18, Con. 2 SER, where they built their retirement home.

John and Nellie Dortmans and family, back L-R, Carol, Harriet, John Jr., Joanne, Maryanne, Richard, front L-R, Jenny, John Sr., Nellie, Lisa, 1976.

Joanne (1957), the eldest, married Tony Hogervorst in 1981. They grow vegetables in Warwick Township, Lambton County. They have five children.

In 1983, John P. (1958) married Shirley Mason, formerly from Coldwater (near Barrie). They took over the Dortman family dairy farm in September 1983 and are raising their three children.

Harriet (1960) married Leonard Duynisveld in 1983. They own a dairy farm in West Nissouri Township near Bryanston, and have four children.

In 1984, Marianne (1961) married Dale Donaldson. With their three children, Marianne and Dale raise geese and run a poultry processing plant in London Township, near Arva.

Also in 1984, Jenny (1963) married Ed Verbeek. In addition to raising six children, they are presently operating a hog farm in Warwick Township, near Arkona.

In 1989, Richard (1964) married Teresa Edgington, formerly of Ilderton, and they live at Lot 16, Con. 4 SER. They have a hog operation and are raising three children.

In 1992, Carol (1965) married Bill Geerts, and they are currently living at Lot 22, Con. 2 NER. They run hog and cash crop farms and have two children.

In 1992, Lisa (1966) married Brian Allen from Parkhill and they reside in Strathroy with their three children. Brian is a truck driver.

DOUGLAS, Thomas and Cicily

Thomas Douglas and his second wife, Cicily (Scott), moved from Lobo and purchased Lot 21, Con. 3 SER. He built the house now owned by A.M. Cuddy. His son, Andrew, lived there and later Liol, son of Thomas Waugh Douglas. Thomas and Cicily had seven children.

Isabella (1854-1948) remained unmarried, and worked as a housekeeper.

John "Jack" Scott (1856) later lived on Kittridge Avenue in Strathroy. He married Roseanne Murdock (see Murdock). They had two children. Hazel Douglas taught school at S.S. #11; her pupils included nephews Tom and Liol Douglas. Hazel married John MacDonald. Leila Douglas, the second daughter, married John Robbins.

Ann (1858) married a Turnbull and moved out west.

Andrew B. (1860) married Molly Pincombe. They had no children.

Thomas Waugh (1862-1938) married Florence Shipley, and he bought the "square" house at Lot 21, Con. 3 SER. He was a successful farmer raising purebred shorthorns, which he took by train to exhibit at the World Fair in Chicago in 1852. A family story of this event recalls that Thomas Waugh thought he wouldn't have to pay a tariff, but when he got to the border he wasn't allowed across so he telegraphed his father for more money. Eleven years later, he was reimbursed by U.S. Customs!

Thomas Waugh and Florence had three children, Thomas Anderson "Tom" (1905-1948); Lionel Scott "Liol" (1907-1948); and Florence Cicily (1908).

Tom was named after his maternal grandmother, who was an Anderson. He was engaged to be married and had started Veterinary School in Guelph, when he turned his new car in front of a Toronto streetcar and was killed. Tom is buried in Strathroy Cemetery.

Liol married Freda Oakes, daughter of William Oakes. Freda remarried after Liol's death, to a Patterson. She lives on a farm near Camlachie. They had two children. Mary (1957) married Terry McGregor. They had a son who lives in Ingersoll, and their daughter was killed in car accident. Margaret (1964) married Ted Gowan, but they separated. She lives in Dawson Creek, Alberta. They had two daughters, Susie and Beverley.

In her childhood, Florence C., third child of Thomas and Florence, was too "delicate" to attend school, so her mother taught her at home. She later attended S.S. #11 for two years and Strathroy town school for one year, then went to Strathroy Collegiate. She boarded with Rev George and Jessie Gilmore in London while attending Western University. She graduated with a BA, majoring in the classics as a Latin and Greek graduate. Her next level of education was at the College of Education in Toronto. There she received her teacher's training.

Florence taught school in Thedford and then in Wardsville. There were two teachers on staff, and Florence taught all subjects except French. She was proud of her boys' physical education classes, and one year she trained a WOSSA champion. Florence spent her last 15 years of teaching at the West Lorne Secondary School. She worked as a teacher for more than 40 years.

During her teaching days at Wardsville, Florence met her future husband, Bruce Dill, and they were married in 1945. They moved to Bruce's farm in Aldborough Township, Elgin County. A son, Thomas William (1952-1976), was killed in a car accident at a young age and is buried in Purcell Cemetery. Florence and Bruce Dill now reside at Beattie Haven, Wardsville, and Bruce continues to spend many days in his workshop at their Wardsville home.

George, sixth child of Thomas and Cicily, lived and was buried in Hamilton. He and his wife had two children, Helen and Jean, who remained single.

Jeanette Waugh "Nettie" (1873-1959), the youngest of Thomas and Cicily's children, remained unmarried. She trained as a nurse in London and nursed in Waterloo, Iowa. In later life, she and Isabella lived together in Strathroy. Nettie is buried in Strathroy Cemetery.

DOWDING, Thomas and Martha

About 1830, Thomas Dowding immigrated to Canada with his first wife and two children. They came from Westbury, England (near Bristol in the County of Wiltshire). Among their fellow passengers were the Randall, Brown and Harris families. The daughter died during the crossing and was buried at sea, and Thomas' first wife died shortly after landing. Thomas Sr. and his son, Thomas Jr., continued their journey accompanied by the Randalls, and settled in the Adelaide District.

Thomas (ca.1796-1870) asked Martha Randall (1816-1891), then 16 years of age, to keep house for him and look after his son. They later married and had ten children, Eliza (1834); Sarah (1837-1839); William (1840); James (1841-1914); George (1843-1927); Elizabeth (1845-1922); Harriet (1847), who married a Stover and resided in Chatham; Mary Ann (1849), who married a Toll; Samuel (1852-1854); and Martha (1854-1913). In 1851, for £25, Thomas purchased the property he had settled, being the east half of Lot 7, Con. 2 SER. Thomas Jr. is believed to have settled in the Arkona area.

Eliza Dowding (1834-1927) married Jason Holt (1829-1897), who farmed part of Lot 2, Con. 2 SER, and they had two children. Gilbert (1855-1885) married Minnie Roberts and they moved to Michigan. Estella (1873-1959) married William Langford in 1900.

William Dowding (1840-1912) married Ann Harris, daughter of Thomas and Ann (Phipps) Harris of Adelaide. They had three children, Ernest (1869-1956); W. Lawrence (1871-1936); and Mandana, who married John Sullivan (see Sullivan). William took over the homestead that, in turn, was later divided and passed down to Ernest and Lawrence.

Ernest married Anne Mildred Ferguson, daughter of Dougald Ferguson. In his early years, Ernest had a jewelry store in Watford. Later, he sold this business and moved to the Dowding crown deed farm, owned by his father. Ernest and Mildred had three children born in Watford, Dougald Ferguson "Ferg" (1908-1983); William Allen (1912-1990); and John Auld "Jack" (1913-1997). Ferg and Allen

Thomas W. and Florence (Shipley) Waugh, with Tom, Florence and Liol.

started an egg business in Petrolia and in about 1936, moved this business to Ridgetown; Jack stayed on the farm and worked with his father. Ferg joined the navy when WWII began, then returned to the egg business and finally started his own business in Aylmer. Allen continued the business in Ridgetown until 1948, when he sold it and moved to Lawrence's farm, which he had purchased from Irwin Carrothers in 1946. Originally, the Crown sold this farm to Thomas Collier on November 13, 1848. The old house was used by Jack Dowding as a granary. Jack and Allen remodeled the house, and the new plumbing included reversed hot and cold taps. This unique feature was always blamed on Jack, who was left-handed.

Ferg married Ruth Gosnell Taylor of Highgate and they remained in Aylmer. In 1938, Allen married Dorothy Delmege, daughter of Robert Delmege of Ridgetown. They had three children, Roberta Jane; William Ferguson "Bill"; and John Allen Delmege "Del." Jane married and lives in Strathroy. She worked as a receptionist for two local dentists. Bill graduated from Ridgetown Agricultural College in 1964 and continued to work on the family farm, which expanded to include a farrow-to-finish hog operation, laying hens, and broiler chickens. He served one term on township council and 15 years with the Adelaide/Metcalfe volunteer fire department. Del graduated from Fanshawe College as a licensed mechanic. Del is employed as foreman of the waterworks department of Strathroy P.U.C., where he has worked for 24 years.

Jack, youngest son of Ernest and Mildred, married Mary Anne Johnson, daughter of Walter and Irene Johnson. They had four children, John, James, Peggy and Debbie. Ernest passed his farm down to Jack, and Jack left the property to daughter Peggy, who is married to Brad Barclay. Peggy and Brad have two children, Katie Adene (1981) and William Ryan (1984). It seemed fitting that William receive the silver cup engraved "Bi-Centennial Baby 1984" for having been born closest to the anniversary date of the township, since he has such deep roots in Adelaide.

W. Lawrence, second child of William and Ann, married Elizabeth Westgate (1872-1957), daughter of George and Margaret (Lamont) Westgate of Warwick Township. They remained childless. In 1889, Lawrence acquired part of Lot 8, Con. 2 SER, and remained there for the rest of his life. They were members of Bethesda Methodist Church, where Lawrence was an elder. He was also a member of the Masonic Lodge, Napier.

In 1875, James Dowding married Margaret Arnot (1849-1907), daughter of David and Betsy Arnot of Walpole Township, near Simcoe, and formerly of Scotland. They farmed the west half of Lot 2, Con. 3 SER. They had six children, Millie (1873-1959), who married Alfred House of Port Dalhousie; Martha (1875-1972), who remained single; Albert Arnot (1877-1955); George (1880-1897), who died of typhoid; Russell (1883-1944); and William J. (1885-1976). All of James' children are buried in Strathroy Cemetery.

In 1908, Albert, third child of James and Margaret, married Ethel Elliott (1885-1959), daughter of William and Jane (Demaray) Elliott of East Williams. They had a son, Melvin, and a daughter, Irene (1913), who married Frank Gaunt (1911-1990) and resides in Corunna (Irene and Frank were the first couple married in Bethesda United Church, on July 23, 1908, with Rev. D.W. DeMille officiating). Albert farmed the west half of Lot 8, Con. 3 SER.

Children of Thomas Dowding and his second wife, Martha (Randall), back L-R, Martha Armstrong, George Dowding and Eliza Holt; front L-R, William Dowding, Hattie Stover, James Dowding, Mary Ann Toll and Elizabeth Thomas.

Four generations of Dowding family. Jane (Demaray) Elliott (grandmother), Ethel (Elliott) Dowding (mother), Isabella (Ireland) Demaray (great-grandmother) and Melvin Elliott Dowding (son), ca.1913.

This farm had been patented in 1854 by John Hanna and owned by the Kerswell family before being purchased by Albert. Albert and family were active members of Bethesda United Church (formerly Methodist).

Melvin, eldest child of Albert and Ethel, married Doris George in 1941. Melvin worked at construction in Brampton and Sarnia before returning, in 1945, to work the home farm. They built a new house and raised two children. Judy married Bill Morgan (see Morgan). Karen married Nelson Nichols and has a daughter, Emma. They reside in Strathroy where Karen works in the X-ray Department at Strathroy General Hospital.

In 1919, Russell Dowding, fifth child of James and Margaret, married Ada Bishopp (1895-1948), daughter of Ted and Emma (Downer) Bishopp. They had three children. Norman (1920) married Phyllis Hunt. Vera married Jack Kaler and they live in New Westminster, B.C., where they have two children, Ken and Karen Kaler. Ella married Isaac Van Belois and they live in London. Russell took over the family farm, the west half of Lot 2, Con. 3 SER, which was later taken over by Norman.

In 1910, William J. Dowding, James and Margaret's youngest child, married Edna Elliott (1889-1985), Ethel's sister. They had two children, Winnifred and Herbert (1914). William farmed the east half of Lot 4, Con. 2 SER, before moving to Strathroy in the early 1920s.

Winnifred married Arthur Pedden and they lived in the Crathie area of Adelaide before moving to Strathroy in 1972. They had three daughters, two of whom moved out of the area. Nancy married Larry Tomchick. They live in Strathroy and have a son and daughter.

Herbert married Norma White (1916-1986) of Poplar Hill. They lived in Lobo Township, where they raised four children, Vivian, Joyce, Carol and Ken.

In 1867, George Dowding, fifth issue of Thomas and Martha, married Mary Ann Shrier (1848-1917), daughter of Jacob and Mary (Mather) Shrier of Adelaide. George was a miller, who ran a large flour and feed store in Kerwood. They had five children, William H. (1869); Gilbert (1870-1925); Edith (1873-1955), who married Joseph Humphries (see Humphries); Mary (ca.1874); and Adella (1878-1907).

In 1898, William H. married Edna Freer (1874), daughter of Henry and Mary (Foster) Freer. They had at least one daughter, Dora. They lived in Kerwood, and like his father, William H. was a miller.

Gilbert Dowding married Elizabeth Ann Carrothers (1869-1946). They had five children, Orville (1894-1945), who married Lina Waite; Grace (1898-1968); Walter; Mattie, who married Harold Lucas; and Lloyd. Gilbert worked as a telegraph operator at the CNR station in Kerwood.

Adella, youngest of George and Mary Ann's children, married Albert Fuller (1876-1949), son of William and Mary (Valley) Fuller. They had two children, Clarence (1901-1966), who married Mildred Morgan; and Fred, who married Hazel Rummel.

In 1871, Elizabeth Dowding, sixth child of Thomas and Martha, married William Thomas (1837-1921), who had come from Scotland with his parents in 1840. They farmed the east half of Lot 5, Con. 2 SER, and had three children. James (1872-1938) married Mary Bishopp (1879), daughter of Ted and Emma (Downer) Bishopp. They had two

Syrup-making in the Albert Dowding bush, west half of Lot 8, Con. 3 SER.

sons, Bert and Floyd Thomas. Ida (1872-1899) married Austin Carrothers (see Carrothers). Lewis (1877-1946) married Jean Hedley (1889-1947) and they had two sons, Ronald and Kenneth Thomas.

Martha Dowding, youngest child of Thomas and Martha, married Frank Armstrong (1849-1821), son of John and Jane (Alwinter) Armstrong. They had at least five children, Mary Jane (1874); Delbert (ca.1876); Olive (ca.1878); Fred (ca.1883); and George (ca.1886). In the 1891 Adelaide census, Frank was listed as a carpenter and the family was living on the Second Line South. Martha, Frank, and family later moved to Saskatchewan.

DOWLING, Patrick and Mary

One of the lesser-known pioneer families in this area is the Dowling family. The family name varies from document to document as Doolin, Doolan, Doolen, Dooling, etc. The name has almost disappeared from the area, but there are still some descendants living in Adelaide.

Originally from Ireland, Patrick Dowling married Mary Flaherty in New York in 1837. As their family grew, they decided to move on to greener pastures and, in their search for a new home, they came to Adelaide Village. What attracted them to Adelaide, specifically, is not known. It is known, however, that on an 1859 excursion to this area, their eldest daughter, Catherine, met and married Terrance Callaghan in Port Huron. They moved to Adelaide Village and began to raise their family.

In January 1864, Anastasia Dowling married Edward Healy, son of James and Rosanna Healy. They resided in Adelaide and raised their family. In October 1868, Mary Dowling married John Johnson in Wyoming, Ontario. He was a farmer and resident of Plympton, in Lambton County. They remained in the area and raised a family of seven children. Margaret "Maggie" Dowling never married. She lived in Strathroy and worked as a seamstress. In October 1934, Maggie passed away, and she was the last person interred in St. Patrick's Cemetery. The resting place of Patrick Dowling is unknown. It is possibly in Wisconsin. Mary (Flaherty) Dowling died while living with Catherine and Terrance in Adelaide Village. She is buried in St. Patrick's Cemetery in Adelaide Village.

DOWN, George and Celia

George Down married Celia Weeks in Charing, Kent County, England, on February 2, 1841. They were married by Joshua Dix, Curate.

They took passage on the "Mediator" on May 16, 1841, from St. Katherine dock. The price was £10-10-5 or 10 pounds, 10 shillings and 5 pence.

They received 100 acres of crown land at the east half of Lot 15 SER (Concession not named) on August 23, 1844.

They had ten children, George, Eliza, James, Mary Ann, Charles, Elizabeth, John Edmond, Helen, Henry and William.

Charles married Hannah Edwards on February 11, 1879, in Warwick, Rev. J. Lince presiding. They had five children, Richard, Sarah, Amy, Rosetta and Wilfred.

Wilfred married Maude Stockton and they had three children. Melvin married Kay Shearer, Leola

Richard Down Family

married Russell Smith, and Roy married Betty Dennis. Roy and Betty had three children. Marlene married John Dorrestyn, Karen married Jim Mussell, and Gerald married Diane Watt.

Holstein cattle were bought in the 1920s and became a purebred herd in the 1930s. Dairy farming continued for more than 50 years. At present, the farm is in cash crops.

DOWNER - NAPPER

James Napper (1788-1875), son of Richard and Sarah (White) Napper, was christened in Pulborough, Sussex, England. James died in Petrolia, Ontario, probably at the home of his son, William. He married Avis Downer (1791) in 1820 in Wisborough Green, Sussex, England. Avis was christened in Wisborough Green, the daughter of John Downer and his second wife, Sarah (Miles), who was the widow of James Breeden. Avis died, probably before 1852, in Adelaide Township. James and Avis came to Canada in 1832, assisted by the Petworth Emigration Scheme. In 1822, James stated that he had not worked for a full year in the previous 10 years. He and Avis had six children, John (1816-1885); Charles (1821-1907); George (1823-ca.1832); William (ca.1826-1884); Mary Ann (1834-ca.1898); and a daughter, unnamed (ca.1836, died an infant). All of the children but John, who used his mother's surname, took the name Napper.

John Downer was born in Kirdford, Sussex, England, and was christened in Kirdford. The parish of Kirdford paid his passage to Canada in 1832, when his parents were sponsored by Pulborough. He died in Adelaide Township and was interred in the Fourth Line Cemetery. John was converted to Methodism in Adelaide and served as a lay preacher, exhorter and class leader. He married Lucy Rapley (ca.1823-1912) on November 30, 1843, in Adelaide Township. Lucy was christened in Wisborough Green, the daughter of James and Mary (Collins) Rapley. Lucy died in Adelaide and was interred in the Fourth Line Cemetery. John and Lucy had 12 children, Ann (1844-1935); Charles Henry (1845-1928); John Wesley (1847-1923); James Franklin "Jim" (1849-1923); Avis Lucy (1850-1898); George William (1852-1904); Emma Jane (1855-1928); Jesse (1857-1861); Mary Collins (1859-1861); Martha Sarah (1861-1864); Ira Edward (1863-1931); and Alexander David (1866-1874). Jesse, Mary Collins, Martha Sarah, and Alexander David were interred in the Fourth Line Cemetery in Adelaide Township.

Ann, the eldest of John and Lucy's children, was christened January 12, 1845, in Adelaide. All of her brothers and sisters passed away before her death. She married Elisha Saunders (1852-1894), the son of James and Ann (Johnston) Saunders, about 1881. Elisha died in Strathroy. They had three children. Johnston Rapley (1883, died an infant) was born and died in Adelaide Township, and his body was interred in the Fourth Line Cemetery. Annie Lucy (1884-1926) was born in Adelaide Township. She died after goiter surgery in Detroit. Her body was interred in Strathroy. Lucy was a high school teacher in Petrolia and Strathroy.

Roy Elisha (1886-1939), Ann and Elisha's third child, was born in Bothwell, Ontario. He died in Amherstburg, and his body was interred in Strathroy. He married Nellie Louisa Elliott (d.1927), daughter of Robert Elliott, on September 28, 1905, in Brantford. After her death, he married Bertha Riggle. Roy and Nellie had three children. Dwight Elliott Saunders (1906-1936) was born in Walnut, Iowa, and died in Detroit. He married Georgina Lafleur. Dwight's body was interred in Strathroy. Lucy June Saunders (1908-1987) was born in Ontario and died in Florida. She married Earl David Studer in 1927 and had two children, Roy and Lynne, who both have children. Dorothy Merle Saunders (1913-1995), third child of Roy and Nellie, was born in Flint, Michigan. She married Charles F. Pineau in 1939 in Dearborn, Michigan, and they had two children. Charles, the eldest, has children, and Michael Pineau (1950-1977) died young.

Charles Henry, second child of John and Lucy, was born in Adelaide Township and died in North Branch, Michigan. He married Sarah Moore Forsyth (1850-1922) in 1871 in Adelaide Township. He resided in Michigan. Witnesses of their wedding included Robert and Jane Forsyth. Also married that day by Rev. W.M. Roger were Annie D. Forsyth and Charles Wilson of Petrolia. Sarah was born in Londonderry, Ireland, the daughter of Alexander Forsyth and Annie Moore. Sarah died in North Branch and was interred in Pontiac, Michigan. Henry and Sarah had seven sons, John Alexander "Allie" (1873-1947); William Henry "Will" (1876-

1945); Ernest Robert (1880-1962); Fredrick Rapley (1882-1965); Franklin Forsyth (1886-1921); Charles Wesley (1888-1965); and Dr. Ira George Downer (1892-1977).

Allie was born in North Branch and died in Battle Creek, Michigan. In 1896, he married Gertrude E. Meade (1876), the daughter of Dr. C.H. Meade, in Olivet, Michigan. Allie was an electrical engineer. He and Gertrude had one daughter, Leita M. (1897-1963), who married Harold Gavin Ritchie Jr. in 1917 in Battle Creek.

Will was born in North Branch and died in Pontiac, Michigan. He married Margaret Brady in 1898, and they divorced about 1900. He married Clara Terry in 1904. Will and Margaret had one child, William (1899), but nothing further is known of him.

Ernest Robert, third son of Charles Henry and Sarah, was born and died in North Branch. He worked for General Motors. Ernest married Mary Georgina Rutledge in 1924, and they had four children, Henry Guerdon (1902); Ernestine Rutledge (1904); Roberta Eiliene (1905-1979); and Sarah Matilda (1907).

Henry Guerdon was born in North Branch. He married Viola Walker (1905-1928), the daughter of Joseph and Elizabeth (Kitely) Walker, in 1927. Viola was from Mayville, Michigan, and died in Pontiac. Henry then married Kathleen Alice Stevenson Andrews (1906) in 1935. Kathleen was born in Manchester, England. Henry and Viola had twin daughters, Mary Josephine and Viola Georgina, born in Pontiac. Henry and Kathleen had a daughter, Sharon Kay, born in Berea, Ohio.

Ernestine, Ernest and Mary's second child, was born in North Branch. She married Roy Harrison McKay (1894-1990) of Brown City, Michigan, in 1923. He died in Arizona. Ernestine and Roy had two children, Merle Marian, born in Oakland, California; and Max Millian, born in Mt. View, California.

Roberta Eiliene was born in North Branch. She married Harold Frederic Hobolth (1904-1993) in 1928. Eiliene and Harold Hobolth had five children, Marilou, Jean, Margarite, Billie Joan and Kirklin, all born in Pontiac, Michigan.

Sarah Matilda, the youngest of Ernest and Mary's children, was born in North Branch.

Fredrick Rapley "Fred," the fourth of Charles

Ira and Jennie Downer

Henry and Sarah's sons, was born in North Branch and died in Standish, Michigan. Fred was a druggist. He married Florence McGovern in 1911 in North Branch, and they had three children. "Junior" (1915-1917) died in Standish. Mary Jane married Harvey D Walker, lives in Saginaw, and has descendants. Bernice married into the Orr family and was divorced. She lives in Standish and has several children.

Charles Wesley, sixth of Charles Henry and Sarah's children, was born in North Branch. He married Winnifred Irene Hawkins in 1917. Charles and Winnifred had one child that was born and died about 1919. He married Maude Bentley in 1937. He then married Carrie Olvin in 1959 in Pontiac, Michigan.

Dr. Ira George Downer, youngest of Charles Henry and Sarah's children, was born in North Branch and died in Detroit. He married Jessie Maxwell Andrew (1894-1976), the daughter of Harry A. Andrew, in 1920 in Chatham, Ontario. Ira was a surgeon in Detroit and Jessie was a nurse. Jessie died in Detroit. They had four children. Jean Alice married Theodore R Hodges Jr. She resides in Grosse Pointe, Michigan, and has several children. Virginia Mary married James Howard, lives in Grosse Pointe, and has several children. Ira George Jr. died in WWII, and his body was interred in France. Harry Andrew (1927-1995) married, had two sons (one deceased) and one granddaughter.

John Wesley, third of John and Lucy's children, was born in Adelaide Township and died in Petrolia. He was interred in Hillsdale Cemetery. He married Esther Amelia Thrower (1851-1927) in 1870 in Adelaide Township, with Charles Mann and George Henry Parker serving as witnesses. Esther was born in Adelaide Township, the daughter of Isaac and Mary Jane (Humphries) Thrower. John had a farm implement agency, which grandson Wesley Thompson and his son, John, continued as a car dealership and chain of service stations. Esther died in Petrolia. John and Esther had two children, Minnie Esther (1871-1931) and Jesse (1873-ca.1874). Jesse was born and died in Petrolia. His body was interred in the Fourth Line Cemetery in Adelaide Township.

Minnie Esther was born and died in Petrolia. She was a music teacher. She married Richard Tate Thompson (1865-1894) in 1890 in Petrolia. Richard was born in Paris, Ontario, the son of Robert and Eleanor Harriett (Duesbury) Thomson, and brother of John J. Richard died in Enniskillen Township at age 29, killed by lightning. He was a bricklayer and Captain in the Salvation Army. Minnie and Richard had two children, Lucy Mary Ellen Esther Downer (1891-1984), who was born in Petrolia and died there at the age of 93; and Wesley Robert (1893-1948), who married Agnes McLachlan and had one son, John Wesley Downer, whose daughter, Jane, resides in Toronto.

James Franklin, fourth child of John and Lucy, was born in Adelaide Township and died in San Diego, California. Jim was a commander of the Macabees in Port Huron and Chicago. He married Ellen Ethel Boyd (ca.1842) on September 15, 1870, in Warwick Township, Lambton County. Ellen was born in Metcalfe Township, the daughter of Thomas and Charity (McLean) Boyd. James Franklin and Ellen had two children. Martha S. (1871) died in San Diego, sometime after 1948. She married Will J. Lange (1873) in Chicago, Illinois, where he was born. They had no children. Ida E. (1873-1948) was born in Strathroy. She married Robert R "Bob" McLean (1875-1941) in Chicago. They had no children. Bob was born in Oakland, California, the son of Rev. Thomas G. McLean. He was a County Agricultural Commissioner. Ida and Bob both died in San Diego.

Avis Lucy, fifth child of John and Lucy, was born in Adelaide Township and was christened on September 29, 1856. She married Malcolm M. "Mac" Thompson (ca.1843-1907) on May 19, 1869, in Adelaide Township, with John Buttery as witness. Mac was born in Adelaide Township, the son of James and Jannett Thompson. Both Avis and Mac died in Adelaide Township. Avis and Mac had seven children, including Arthur L. (ca.1871-1882); Janet May (1873-1963) and Lucy Annie (1875-1912). The fourth child, Charlotte (1876-1959), was born in Adelaide Township. She married (as his second wife) John Jameson Thomson (1868-1941) on September 22, 1924, in Adelaide Township. John was born in Paris, Brant County, Ontario, son of Robert and Eleanor Harriett (Duesbury) Thomson. John died while visiting Paris, and Charlotte died in London.

Lawrence Malcolm (1878-1882); Alida Kenressa (1880-1962); and Wallace Garfield (1883-1911) were the youngest three children of Avis and Mac.

Janet May "Nettie," second child of Avis and Mac, was born in Adelaide Township. She married Alexander "Alex" Smith (1863-1932) on December 7, 1898, in Adelaide Township. Alex was the son of Malcolm and Mary (McDonald) Smith. Nettie and Alex Smith had three children, Alexandria May (1901-1977): Donald Thompson (1904-1910); and Malcolm Elliott (1906).

Alexandria May was born in Fairview, Oklahoma, but her birth was registered in Ontario. May married Alfred Tennison "Fred" Sullivan (1898-1984), the son of John N. Sullivan. May and Fred Sullivan had five children, Donald; Margery, who married into the Bell family; Ruth, who married Ed Jarmain; Ila, who married Keith McInroy; and Lawrence. May died in Norwich, Ontario.

Donald, second child of Nettie and Alex, was born and died in Adelaide Township.

Malcolm Elliott, the youngest of Nettie and Alex's children, was born in Adelaide Township. He was a druggist in London.

Lucy Annie, third child of Avis and Mac, was born in Adelaide Township and died in Avon. She married William J. Demaray on March 20, 1895 (see DEMARAY).

Alida Kenressa, sixth child of Avis and Mac, was born in Adelaide Township. She married Richard William "Dick" Parsons (1876-1947) on December 24, 1902, in Adelaide Township. Dick was born in Lobo, the son of William and Mary

(Perry) Parsons. Kenressa's body was interred in Poplar Hill. Kenressa and Dick had five children. Avis (1907-1974) married Harold Tomlinson (d.1976). They had no children. Ross (1910-1984) was born in Adelaide Township and died in Strathroy. He married Lila Griffith (d.1992), and they had two children, Le Roy and Wallace. Ross's body was interred in Poplar Hill. Earl (1912-1978), the third child of Kenressa and Dick, married Freda Griffith, the sister of Lila Griffith. Earl and Freda had four children, Lawrence, Earlene, Janet and Richard. Earl died in London, Ontario. Joyce was born in Adelaide Township. She married Ellis Lachlin Stoner (d.1988), the son of Martin Stoner. Ellis died in London and was interred in Poplar Hill. In 1992, Joyce married Allan Pedden. They reside in Strathroy. Joyce and Ellis Stoner had four children, Glen, Wayne, Norma and Barbara. Phyllis, the youngest child of Kenressa and Dick, was born in Adelaide Township. She married Fraser Campbell (d.1985), with whom she had two children, Keith and Lynda Corinne. Fraser died in London.

Wallace Garfield, the youngest child of Avis and Mac, was born and died in Adelaide Township. He was a farmer. Wallace married Mary E. "May" McCubbin (1886) of Adelaide Township on November 4, 1908, in Strathroy. May was the daughter of Daniel and Jessie W. McCubbin. Wallace and May had a son, Alex McCallum (1909), who was born in Adelaide Township. Alex resides in Orangeville.

George William, sixth child of John and Lucy, was born and christened in Adelaide Township. He died of blood poisoning in North Branch, Michigan, where he was a miller with his brother, Henry. He married Hester A Sicklesteel (ca.1856) in North Branch. Hester was born in Chatham, Ontario. George and Hester had three children. Fannie (1877) married Otto J Briggs on May 23, 1900, in North Branch. They had two sons. Charles Herbert (1880-1965) married Jessie Ohwer and had two daughters, Dorothy and Janice. Jesse M. (ca.1890-1902) died in childhood.

Emma Jane, seventh of John and Lucy's children, was born and christened in Adelaide Township. She married Edward Bishopp (1852-1911) in 1872. Edward was born in Adelaide, the son of George and Mary Ann (Croucher) Bishopp. After Edward's death, Emma married Charles Gilbert Frank (d.1923) on January 3, 1912, in Adelaide. Charles was the son of Hiram Gilbert and Abigail Ann (Montegue) Frank. Emma and Edward Bishopp had five children, Alexander Edward (1874); George William (ca.1875-1879); Mary Elizabeth (ca.1879-1972); Jennie Lucy (1886), who married Rev. Nevilles; and Ada Irene (1895-1948).

Alexander Edward, the eldest child of Emma and Edward, was born in Adelaide Township. He married Musetta Mabel Evans (1879) on April 13, 1898, in Adelaide Township. Musetta was born in Lobo, daughter of John and Rachel Ann (Turner) Evans. Alexander and Musetta had at least six children. George (1901-1905) died in childhood. John Raymond (1902-1990) was born in Adelaide Township. He married Winnifred Eastman (1903-1978) on September 10, 1927, in Arkona. Winnifred was the daughter of Willard Martin and Anna (Love) Eastman. Ray and Winnie had two children. Robert "Bob," who married Emma Jean Swan, resides in Louisville, Kentucky. They have five children. Bette, Ray and Winnie's daughter, married Jim Derrick and has three children. She resides in Lakeland, Florida. Ray died in Lakeland, Florida. Other children of Alexander and Musetta include Grace; Mary; Dorothy, who married Horace Thompson and resides in Lakeland, Florida; and Ruth, who lives in Florida.

Mary E., third child of Emma and Edward, was born in Adelaide Township. She married James W. Thomas on October 11, 1899, in Adelaide Township. James (1872-1927) was born in Adelaide Township, the son of William and Elizabeth Thomas. After James died, Mary married George E. Oliver (1883-1972). Mary and James had two children, Floyd Thomas, who married Isabell (last name unknown); and Herbert Lancely (1901-1972), whose wife's name was Vera. Mary's body was interred in Strathroy.

Ada Irene, the youngest of Emma and Edward's children, was born in Adelaide Township. She married Lawrence Russell Dowding (1883-1944) on January 15, 1919, in Adelaide. Ada and Russell had three children. Norman Edward married Phyllis Hunt. Vera Emma Margaret was born in Adelaide. She married Jack Kaler (d.1973), and they had two children, Kenneth and Karen. After Jack's death, she married Winslow Hendrik. They reside in New Westminister, British Columbia. Ella Isabelle married Isaac Van Belois, and she resides in London, Ontario.

Ira Edward, John and Lucy's eleventh child, was born in Adelaide Township, where he was christened May 20, 1864. Ira continued farming on his parents' farm. He married Eliza Jane "Jennie" Houlton (1869-1908) on January 17, 1894, in Adelaide Township, with Rev. E.W. Hughes presiding; witnesses were Ernest H. Houlton and Louise Morse. Jennie was born in Adelaide Township and christened August 26, 1869, in Adelaide. She was the daughter of Henry and Eliza Jane (Morse) Houlton. After Jennie's death, Ira married Amy Mary Ellen Louisa Parker (1871-1944) on February 1, 1911. Louisa was born in Adelaide Township, the daughter of George and Rhoda (Thrower) Parker. Ira and Jennie had one son, George Houlton (1908-1991), born in Adelaide Township. Ira and Jennie both died in Adelaide

George Houlton married Evelyn Marjorie Carrothers (1909-1977) of Adelaide on September 10, 1930. Evelyn was the daughter of Austin Theodore and Minnie Louise (Morgan) Carrothers. George worked for Thompson's Service Stations. Evelyn died in Petrolia. George and Evelyn had three children. Evelyn Jean married Fred Kern, resides in Sarnia, and has three children and several grandchildren. Lucie Marie married Don Bustin, resides in Muskegon, Michigan and has three children. Ira George resides in Petrolia, where is he on town council. He has two sons, who are the only descendants with the Downer surname in Canada.

Charles, second son of James and Avis, was christened in Pulborough. He died at the home of his nephew, J.W. Downer, in Petrolia, and was interred in the Fourth Line Cemetery. Charles was a storekeeper at Napperton. He married Amy Parker (1820-1908) in 1845 in Adelaide; Ellen Mather and James Parker, the witnesses, were married at the same time. Amy was born in Sussex, the daughter of James and Amy (Steer) Parker. She died in Strathroy. Louisa Thomas (1850) lived with them and married Daniel McKinnon in 1868.

George, third issue of James and Avis, was christened in Pulborough. He died a young boy in Canada.

William, fourth child of James and Avis, was christened in Pulborough. He married Susannah Jury (ca.1833-1915), the daughter of William and Mary Jury. Both William and Susannah died in Petrolia.. William and Susannah had three children, Florence Augusta (1859-1939); Sarah Evelyn (ca.1862-1931); and Milton Melville (1864-1939).

Florence Augusta was a music teacher. In 1890, she married William R Thompson (1860-1923). They had a daughter, Evelyn Thompson (1894-1970), who owned a cosmetic company. She married William G. Davies, and after his death, she married into the Hyndman family. Evelyn and William had one child, Ruth (1916-1917).

Sarah Evelyn married Blake Lancey and moved to Toronto. They had a son who died at age 15, and a daughter, Florence (1890), who married Roy Stirrett of Swift Current, Saskatchewan.

Milton Melville, the youngest child of William and Susannah, was born in Adelaide Township and died in Talbotville, Ontario. His body was interred in Hillsdale Cemetery in Petrolia. Milton was a mechanic at Waterworks for Petrolia and Bakersfield, California. He married Mary Alvira Smith (1868-1886) on January 1, 1885, in Sarnia. Mary died in Petrolia at age 17. Milton then married Lydia Rowe (1863-1909) on November 6, 1889, in Kerwood, Ontario. Lydia was born in Bright, Ontario, the daughter of George and Martha (Gott) Rowe. She died in Bakersfield, California. Milton married a third time, to Lydia's sister, Cecilia Rowe (1865-1942), on October 9, 1912, in Woodstock, Ontario. Cecilia had first married William McRitchie on February 15, 1893, in Petrolia. Her children were Vivian, Clayton, and Rowe. Cecilia died in St. Thomas, Ontario.

Milton and Mary, his first wife, had one son, Lloyd (1885), who was born in Petrolia. He was residing in Detroit in 1939.

Milton and Lydia, his second wife, had three children. Vera (1890) was born in Petrolia. Muriel F. (1898-1953) was born in Bright's Grove, Lambton County, Ontario, married into the Langford family, and had two children, Florence, and Jeannie, who married into the Kennedy family. Inez (1900) was born in Petrolia.

Mary Ann, fifth issue of James and Avis, was christened on June 14, 1835, in Adelaide. Mary Ann is thought to have died in Michigan. She was living with James and Amy Parker in 1852. She married Mesach Mann (1830-ca.1898) about 1855. Mesach, son of Noah and Elizabeth Mann, was born in

Wisborough Green. Mary Ann and Mesach had at least three children, according to the 1861 census, Harriett E.A. (ca.1856); Mary S. (ca.1857); and Eanit F. (ca.1859).

DOWNHAM, Howard C.

In 1929, Howard C. Downham purchased 100 acres of land from the Buttery family, Lot 26, Con. 2 SER. He started the Downhamdale Dairy. On this farm, he had a prize herd of Holstein cows, which produced milk that was delivered by horse and wagon to customers in the Town of Strathroy.

Nursery stock was grown on this farm, and taken to H.C. Downham Nursery Ltd. in Strathroy to be distributed throughout the province. Howard's son, George F., purchased the Lot 26 farm from his father in the 1950s. George moved to the farm with his family in 1958.

In the 1970s, George married for a second time. His wife, Tina Nauta, came to Canada from the Netherlands in 1952 with her parents, Karst and Aley Nauta, and her six siblings. The Nauta family settled in Adelaide Township on the Egremont Road.

DUGGAN, Patrick and Annabella

In 1832, Patrick and Annabella (Kilroy) Duggan left Athlone, Ireland, and came to Canada. Patrick had been in the British Army and when he was discharged at Chelsea, he chose to go to Canada, hoping for a better future for his family. There is a record of a Patrick Duggan being baptized in 1789 at St. Peter's Church in Athlone, which would make him about 43 years old when he immigrated. Patrick and Annabella settled in Adelaide Township with their children, Martin (1820-1880), Lawrence, Mary Jane and Ellinor.

In the 1842 census, the Duggans are shown to be on Lot 5, Con. 5 NER, with six sons and two daughters. It is presumed that Martin and Lawrence are the elder sons, listed as being between 21 and 30 years of age. Four unidentified sons are under the age of 14, two still under the age of five. The records state that three of them were born after the family arrived in Canada. From this entry, it would suggest that Annabella was slightly younger than her husband.

There is an entry in the records at the Land Registry Office, which shows that Patrick Duggan bought 100 acres of land from George Goodhue and his wife in January 1854, also on Lot 5, Con. 5 NER.

The family was still at this location for the 1860 census. In the 1858 records, it states that Patrick sold 55 of the 100 acres to his son, Lawrence, who owned this land for 17 years before selling it in 1875 to Patrick Murray. There is also a mention of an Abigail Duggan, who may have been Lawrence's wife, in relation to this transaction.

Martin, Lawrence's brother, is the only other member of the family about whom we have information. He married Mary Bailey of Strathroy. She had come to Strathroy (probably from Athlone, like the Duggans) with her uncle, James Carley Jr., and her grandparents, Martha Carley (ca.1783) and James Carley Sr. (ca.1778-1851), who died of asthma. Martin, Mary, and their children left Adelaide for the Port Sanilac region of Michigan in 1853.

EARLEY, George and Jane

The original Earley ancestors came over from County Mayo, Ireland, about 1846. Some years ago, an Earley descendant (now living in Pennsylvania) visited the original stone home in Ireland and the dwelling was still occupied.

On October 15, 1860, George Earley and his wife, Jane (d.1885), bought the west half of Lot 3, Con. 5 SER. The Earleys were the first people to live on the land and farm it. Apparently, the Crown granted the land to a soldier in 1837, who then sold it to land speculators. They eventually sold it to George Earley.

George cleared enough land to build a log cabin, but was killed while cutting wood before they moved in. Jane and the children moved into the cabin before Christmas 1864. The youngest child, John, was then seven years old.

Jane died at 64 years of age. She and George were buried in the Fourth Line Cemetery near Strathroy. Unfortunately, the tombstones were destroyed and the church records were burned in a fire many years ago.

George and Jane Earley had eight children, Jane (1847-1923); Tilly; Ella; twins Maggie and Annie; Emily; Mary; and John James (1856-1924).

Jane married John Richardson (1837-1931) and lived next to her brother, John, on the Fourth Line, a mile west of Kerwood.

Tilly married William Henry Richardson and they lived in Brooke Township on Con. 10, halfway to Petrolia. Later, they moved out west.

Ella married Alex Bourne and lived in Enniskillen but eventually moved to Alberta.

Maggie married Henry Langford and lived in Port Huron, Michigan.

Annie married Sam Saunders and lived in Wyoming. Her husband was a blacksmith.

Emily married John Jackson and lived in Hesperia, Michigan.

Mary married Charles Richardson, and they also went to Hesperia, Michigan. The three Richardsons, William Henry, John, and Charles were brothers.

John James married Elizabeth Smithrim (1853-1941) on December 12, 1867, and lived on the homestead on the Fourth Line. They completed their new home in 1907, adjacent to the original log cabin. They bought part of the old church manse south of the railroad tracks in Kerwood when the Methodist Churches became the United Church. They moved this building to the homestead, where it was added to the portion of the new house that had already been constructed.

John and Elizabeth had five children, Minnie (d.1949); Mabel (1882-1917); Carrie; Howard (1889-1974); and Willard (1895-1956). They were very active in building the present United Church in Kerwood. John and Mabel sang in the choir, and Elizabeth was a lifelong member in the W.M.S. Organization.

Minnie, eldest child of John and Elizabeth, married Ernest Payne. Ernest was a policeman and they lived in Chicago. They had a son named Earl (1900-1980), who married Ellen Kordt and had one daughter, Jean. Jean married Harry Cook, a career Navy officer who was permanently stationed in Hawaii, where they still live. They have three children, Cathy, Carol and David.

Mabel married Elmer Langford (1874-1937). They farmed south of Kerwood on Kerwood Road and had five children. Basil married Lottie Lucas, a nurse. They lived in Columbus, Ohio, where Basil was an engineer for the school system. Basil and Lottie later retired to Strathroy. Neil (1905-1978), Mabel and Elmer's second child, married Ila Buchanon and they lived on a farm near Kerwood. They had five children, Elma, June, Mary Alice, Donald and Joe (1947-1962). Ena married Harold Irwin and they had a daughter, Yvonne. Some years after Harold's death, Ena married Bruce Evans. Joe (1913-1931) and George (1915-1919) died young.

Carrie, third eldest child of John and Elizabeth, married William Inch and they lived in the Kerwood area. They had three children, Jean, Donald and Leonard. After Carrie's death at the age of 37, the family moved to the U.S. The sons apparently moved to the northwest U.S., and Jean settled in Corpus Christi, Texas.

Howard married Lena Bourne (1893-1981) on July 11, 1914, in Alvinston. They had two sons, John Elwin (1916) and Raymond Howard (1923). Before her marriage, Lena taught school in Alvinston. When John Elwin was born, Howard was working out of Sarnia as an engineer on the railroad. Ray was born after their move to Columbus, Ohio, where Howard continued to work on the railroad. Later, he was employed by the Prudential Insurance Company, first as a salesman and later as a sales manager.

In 1937, Howard, Lena, and Ray returned to Kerwood to work the family farm, where Howard's mother had been living on her own. At first it was mixed farming, with mostly cash crops being grown. As Ray grew up and assumed an active partnership in the farm, they began to specialize in dairy farming.

In 1952, Howard and Lena retired to Watford to live. Howard still liked to "help out" on the farm. When he was 80, he still helped with the fall plowing.

John Elwin married Betty Tracy on November 14, 1936, in Columbus, Ohio. They had five children, Anne, John Allen, Vicki, Nancy and Steve.

John stayed in Ohio when his parents and brother moved back to Canada. He worked for Kenner Toys as their local plant engineer for many years. He and Betty are now retired and living in Middletown, Ohio.

Ray married Alice Mae Sutherland (1925) on August 14, 1944, and they had three children, Mary, Diane and Mike. Mary became a Registered Nurse, who now lives and works in Houston, Texas. Diane became a high school teacher and married Tom Patterson, another teacher. They have a son, Ryan, and a daughter, Heather, and live in St. Catharines. Mike, his wife, Christine, and their son, Christopher, also live in St. Catharines. His daughter, Sarah, lives with her mother, Joan, in nearby Virgil.

The first year of their marriage, Ray and Alice lived in Aylmer where Ray worked for the Stansell brothers, who had a large dairy farm business. The next year, they returned to the home farm to start developing their own dairy business. Ray gradually built up a quality purebred Ayrshire dairy herd. The original barn was renovated twice over the years, once to increase the size and later to accommodate the dairy herd and milk house.

In 1956 and 1966, Ray bought two more farms in the neighbourhood. These farms were systematically cleared of brush and tiled, bringing the combined acreage, including the home farm, to 300 acres.

In 1975, when Ray's son, Mike, became actively involved in the family dairy business, they gradually changed from Ayrshires to Holstein dairy cattle. A new 2-storey house was built for Mike on the site of the original log cabin. Ray and Alice stayed in the family home that had been completed in 1907, and they built an addition, including a family room with entryway and a carport and patio area.

On the evening of Thanksgiving Day 1982, the home farm dairy barn burned down. The cows that were not destroyed had to be sold, since there were no longer any milking facilities. Most of the younger cattle were in a barn on one of the other farms. The original cement silo west of the barn was destroyed by the fire, but the new, larger silo, which had been built east of the barn some years before, survived. The following spring the new dairy barn, which included a milk house and loose housing for the younger cattle, was finished and the dairy business resumed.

In 1982, Mike married Joan Murray, and three years later their daughter, Sarah, was born, the sixth generation of Earleys to live on the home farm.

By May 1987, Ray was no longer able to help with the milking due to advancing arthritis in both knees, and since reliable experienced help was increasingly hard to find, the farms were sold and the family moved to St. Catharines.

Ray has since had both knee joints replaced, and he and Alice are enjoying their retirement in St. Catharines.

Willard, the youngest child of John and Elizabeth, married Eva Humphries (1898-1977). They lived in Strathroy, where Willard built up a lumber business and Eva had the Gardinia Restaurant. They had seven children, Grant (1916-1978); Verne; Marguerite; Betty; June; Ruth; and Marilyn.

The home farm is now owned by a family who immigrated to Adelaide Township from Switzerland, and they have continued the dairy business. A large drive shed for machinery and storage has been added, but otherwise the farm appears much the same.

EARLEY

The first Earleys to immigrate to Canada were three brothers, James, George and Samuel. They came from Ireland in the 1840s, arriving in New York and then settling in Adelaide. The eldest brother, James, settled on Lot 7, Con. 3 SER, with his wife, Eleanor, and their new son, George Fawcett, who was born in New York.

George married Mary Jane E. Patterson and took over one of his father's farms on the west half of Lot 7, Con. 3 SER. This property is presently owned by Mike and Nancy (Beernink) Earley and their three children, representing the sixth and seventh generations of Earleys to live on the Kerwood Road.

George and Mary Jane had four children, Jim Wesley; Robert P.; Albert "Ted" O.; and Mary Lily, who married Milo Patterson. The eldest son, Jim Wes, married Della Edith Mae McKenzie in 1911.

Earley family presently residing in Earley homestead (Lot 7, Con. 3 SER), back L-R, Michael, Meaghan and Nancy; front L-R, Brooke and Kade.

James Earley with prize Angus.

Della was a dressmaker, and daughter of James and Elizabeth (Nichol) McKenzie of the east half of Lot 21, Con. 1 SER. Della's siblings were Cecil Edward (1887); James Alexander (1889); and Maude Isabel Jane, a teacher, who married Fred Poole of Lambeth. Her two brothers homesteaded in the Peace River area of Brownvale, Alberta.

In 1902, the front of the house at Lot 7, Con. 3 SER, was built and in 1911, because one or two teachers boarded there, Jim Wes added the back half. Della was humorous and well versed and, judging by the poems in her memoirs, well loved by everyone. Their home was very modern; the attic housed a holding tank for water, which enabled them to have a convenient flush-toilet that eliminated cold forays to the outhouse.

Jim Wes was a big man, and he was responsible for fixing the wet sloe holes at the butt line of his property on the Currie Road (now Kerwood Road). He placed stumps and logs in the bottomless sections, making travel to Kerwood a more pleasant trip.

Jim Wes and Della had four children, Eugene Wesley "Sparks" (1912-1979); James MacInroy Cecil "Jim Mac" (1914-1988); Calvin Clayton (1922-1923); and a stillborn daughter. They sold their livestock in 1924 (top milk cow sold for $90) and went west with their family to help Della's brothers, as they had expanded their grain farming to several sections of land and were running a large herd of beef cattle. Eugene and Jim attended school in Peace River while Jim Wes helped his brother-in-laws with the harvest. It was said that he could cut more grain in a day with horses and a binder than anyone else. Jim Wes considered homesteading there, but returned to Ontario the following year. There, he purchased cattle for less than half of what he had sold them for the year before. Della died in 1932 at a young age, a year after giving birth to their last child.

Jim Wes, Eugene, and Jim Mac managed on their own and purchased their first two Angus cows in March 1935. From this early start came the interest in fine cattle that both Eugene and Jim's family have shown. Six years after their mother's death, both boys married a Graham woman, but they were not related.

In 1938, Eugene married Margaret Jean O'Neil, daughter of Percy and Mary Graham of Springbank. Jim Mac married Jean Dorothy Graham, daughter of Edith and Dougal Graham, in 1938. The two couples and Jim Wes lived in the same house. Jim and Jean built a new home on the east half of Lot 6, Con. 3, across the road from bachelor uncles George and Sam, and their sister, Margaret Jean (children of Samuel Earley). This farm is presently owned by Cuddy Farms.

Earley Homestead

Eugene and Margaret had five children. Della Marilyn (1940) became a teacher. She married Hubert Freitag of Alameda, Saskatchewan. Beverly Eugene "Bev" (1941) became a high school teacher and married Janet Oakes of Strathroy. George Graham (1943) became a farmer and married Lynda Ann Stuart of Mt. Brydges. Robert Arthur (1947) became an accountant and worked for Deloitte & Touche. He married Susan Edwards of Watford. William Edward (1958-1959) died a baby.

Eugene was the local trucker and meat/chicken dealer in the area. He trucked chickens and pigs with a half-ton Dodge, the first flatbed 1947 Studebaker purchased from George Chittick, the Studebaker dealer in Kerwood. Weekly trips were made to Handleman's Poultry, Watford, Parkhill, and Detroit with deliveries. His first Aberdeen Angus cows came in 1935 from the Fraleigh Herd of Forest and Alloway Lodge Farm, owned by Col. McEwen of Byron, and are the foundation of the present herd of 175 cows, operated by Eugene's grandsons, Mike and Tim.

Eugene always loved politics, especially municipal politics; he would be upset to see what has happened in the last 10 years in Adelaide. He was a Councillor, Deputy Reeve and Reeve for many years. The County Road Committee was his favourite and he was responsible for chaining the county's cold-mix equipment to a tree and taking the committee and engineers on a road tour to view hot mix roads. They ended up in the Thedford Hotel and henceforth the county tendered and used hot-mix for the roads. His view was that the county-operated equipment was inefficient and unproductive. As chairman of the County Home farm (presently Strathmere Lodge), he made a number of improvements. A hen house was built for laying hens, a silo was built for the excellent Holstein herd, the residents did the chores, and the farm was financially in the black. The produce was used in the home, the morale of the residents was high, and the barns were the neatest and cleanest to be found.

Eugene added to his land base by purchasing part of Lot 8, Con. 1 NER, and the east half of Lot 7, Con. 3, and sold the low-grade gravel from this property to neighbouring farmers for laneways and barn foundations. (In 1992, George G. and Lynda tried to sever a marginal land lot off this property and, after being asked to plead hardship and dragged through an OMB hearing, the severance was finally granted and they built a completely accessible home in 1994.) Eugene enjoyed keeping everyone busy and organized and was notorious for his "to-do" lists (a genetic family trait).

In 1955, Eugene and George Morgan had an idea to build a pole barn, the first of its kind, 56'x96'. Red cedar posts were cut and trucked from Ottawa and elm logs were cut and sawed from the bush. The next challenge was to devise a method of digging postholes, as no one had invented the PTO posthole auger. They first tried boring a small hole and blowing it up with dynamite. This did not work. Charlie Robinson's tile ditching machine was brought in; the stakes were inserted and his machine dug the holes. This barn burned down in 1994.

Eugene's middle son, George, attended S.S. #8 with Anna Jean Sullivan (Wilson) as his teacher for all the grades. He graduated from Ridgetown Agricultural College in 1960. He and his brother, Bev, purchased Lot 12, Con. 3 SER, from Clarence Fuller in 1962 for $10,500. This was one of the first farms to be systematically tiled at four rods, and these tiles were split some 10 years later. George moved there after he married Lynda in 1965, and their youngest son, Tim, presently owns this property.

George and Lynda have four children. Michael Norman (1966) attended Michigan State University and Reich Auction School. He married Nancy Lee Beernink of Inwood in 1988, and they have three children, Meaghan Victoria (1990); Brooke Lee Ann (1992); and Kade Michael James (1998). Martha Lynne (1968) has an Ontario Agricultural Diploma. She married Rick DeBackere of Union in 1988. Timothy George (1969) went to Ridgetown Agricultural College of Technology. Sara Viola Jane (1975) is an O.A.C. graduate and works for Royal Bank. She married Peter Kendal from Port Credit in 1999.

George was a respected auctioneer (Reich Auction School, 1962) and judge of cattle across Canada and the United States. He imported Chianina cattle from Italy in 1974 and Belgian Blue's from England in 1986. He was President of the Canadian Angus Association (1979), the Ontario Angus Association (1974), Ontario Chianina Association and Western Fair Board Director, as well as an Optimist member and 4-H leader for 25 years. He was Adelaide Township Assessor, Dog

Tax Collector, Warblefly Inspector in the 1960s, and Councillor (1989-1994). He implemented tiling of township roads but failed to implement municipal piped water and a fully serviced industrial area for Adelaide Township.

George worked auction sales for Shore Holstein Limited (Glanworth), Walker Farms (Aylmer), Hays Farms (Oakville), Wilson Construction (Milton), Ontario Auto Auction (Toronto and Hamilton), Kitchener Auto Auction, Great Lakes Sales and Dow Downs Sales. He was Middlesex Farmer of the Year in 1984, and he received the 125-Year Centennial Medal in 1992. A round bale fell on him in a farming accident in 1990, and he is now an incomplete quadriplegic. He continues to judge and work with youth from his wheelchair and is farming 500 acres owned plus rented property in partnership with his sons, Mike and Tim.

The whole family has been involved in farming, 4-H, Brownies, Guides, fair boards, OFA and community activities. Mike has entered the auction business and is working as ringman at sales. They continue to show and sell cattle across Canada and in the U.S, and have proudly won many honours, including trips to Mexico and England. Achievements at The Queen's Guineas include George, Grand Champion (1959); Tim, Grand Champion (1984); Martha, Reserve (1985); Mike, Reserve (1987); Sara, Grand Champion (1993) and Reserve (1990 and 1991); and many Grand Champions and Reserves in both the carcass and live classes at the Royal Agricultural Winter Fair and shows across Canada.

In 1998, Hillcrest Farms (Mike and Tim) added the east half of Lot 11, Con. 5 SER, and continue to farm cash crops and breed quality cattle using embryo transplants, A.I. and selective genetic breeding to achieve cattle with hy-bred vigor with the consumer in mind. They continue to run an Annual Calf Sale at the farm, selling club calves and breeding stock to most Canadian provinces and in the U.S., and are leaders in the field in carcass excellence.

About 1940, Jim Mac became interested in fox ranching, so he decided to build a ranch. The Grahams, Jean's family, were in mink ranching. Jim purchased a few top breeders of silver foxes and, being a good cattle breeder, he soon became one of the top fox breeders in the trade. He was also one of the early breeders of arctic blue and/or white fox. Some of the shows where he won many champion ribbons were the Royal Winter Fair in Toronto and the Ontario Fox and Mink Show in Brampton. After many years of success, the styles changed to short fur such as mink, making fox ranching a losing game. Jim didn't care for mink, so he changed his focus to chicken and turkey broilers.

Jim and Jean had two children, Shirley Anne (1941) and Joan Marie. They raised purebred Angus cattle, exhibited many champions in the show ring under Hillcrest Farms, and later exhibited under Jim Earley.

In 1967, Shirley married Gerald "Gerry" Miller and moved to his home in Bowling Green, Ohio. In December 1968, they purchased the Atcheson property across from the home farm, Lot 6, Con. 2. Pioneer James Earley had owned the west half of this lot in January 1886, then granted it to Eva Tucker (Snell) in 1937, and Albert Jariott in 1948. Roy and Mary Demaray built on the east half of the property in 1918, and Leonard and Audrey Atcheson purchased the lot in 1953.

Shirley and Gerry have two sons, Rob James E. (1973) and Bradley G. (1977). In 1977, Shirley and Gerry purchased the south half of Lot 9, Con. 2, from Douglas and Marguerite Carrothers. This farm property had been in the Carrothers family for more than 100 years.

EASTMAN, Benjamin and Mahetable

The Eastman family traces their ancestry to Roger Eastman, who immigrated to Massachusetts from England in 1638. Roger prospered and raised a large family whose descendants scattered across the states of Connecticut, Vermont, New Hampshire, New Jersey and New York. A fourth generation descendant, Amherst Eastman (1768), entered Canada in 1785 and applied for a land grant in 1789, being a member of a Loyalist family. Amherst married Lucy Farmer. In 1803, Amherst received a grant of 200 acres in Augusta Township, Grenville County, Ontario. Later, the family moved to Nepean and then to North Gower, both in Carlton County. Both Amherst and Lucy died there after raising nine children.

In 1827, Amherst's fifth son, Benjamin Eastman (1804-1852), married Mahetable Miner (1806-1903), daughter of Truman and Elizabeth

(Morrison) Miner. They raised five children, Elizabeth (1830-1885), who married Moses Holden (see Holden); Elijah (1832-1891); Solomon (1834-1873); Silas (1837-1865); and Chester (1840-1889).

Benjamin engaged in general farming and pioneered in three townships, North Gower in Carlton County; Warwick in Lambton County, and finally, Caradoc in Middlesex County. The family, being Wesleyan Methodist, probably belonged to the Old Methodist Church that was located on the Fourth Line South in Adelaide. Benjamin's tombstone is one of the oldest still standing in the Fourth Line Cemetery.

There was a great deal of land speculation in the early years, from which the Benjamin Eastman family benefited. In 1842, Benjamin purchased 200 acres in Warwick Township for £10, and by 1845, he had sold this lot in two parcels for £102. In 1849, he purchased 100 acres in Caradoc Township, being Lot 10, Con. 9, for £75. Benjamin's eldest son and heir, Elijah, sold this property in 1854 for £500. The anticipated arrival of the Sarnia Branch of the Great Western Railroad had greatly inflated land prices. Speculators gambled that the railroad would pass just south of present-day Strathroy and they hoped to sell the land to the railroad or divide the property into town lots. This last land deal provided amply for the Eastman family. The family next moved to Adelaide Township where, in 1854, Elijah purchased 100 acres, being the east half of Lot 13, Con. 2 SER, from his uncle and aunt, Benjamin and Lucinda (Miner) Woodhull, for £225.

In 1853, Elijah married Abigail Martin (ca.1831-1910), daughter of Hiram and Hannah (Hollingshead) Martin. They raised seven children, Wesley (1855-1936); Willard (1857-1939); Annie (1859-1869); Minerva (1861-1945); Albert (1863-1943); Truman (1866-1950); and Effie (1868-1944).

Elijah engaged in general farming. He was active in the community, as a member of the board of trustees of the Strathroy Front Street Methodist Church, and a class leader in the Township of Adelaide. He was also a member of the Strathroy Council Royal Arcanum lodge (his estate receiving $3,000 from them after his death). In 1876, Elijah moved to the east half of Lot 9, Con. 4 SER. Two years later, he sold this farm and moved to Lot 24, Con. 3 NER, Warwick Township, near Arkona, where he spent his later years.

Chauncey and Isabell (Whiting) Eastman

In 1885, Wesley, the eldest of Elijah and Abigail's children, married Mary A. Stoney (1861-1936). They raised four children, Birdella (1885-1980), who married George Petch (see Petch); Edmund (1892-1972); Charles (1895-1969); and Earle (1897-1970). Wesley farmed on the Fourth Line SER and then near Glencoe, before moving to Western Canada with his three sons.

Elijah's other children left Adelaide. Willard moved to Arkona where he married Mary Charlotte Macklin, raising five children; he remarried, to Anne Love, and raised three more children. Annie died young. Minerva remained single and lived with her sister, Effie. Albert followed the tailoring trade and moved to Sturgis, Michigan, where he married and raised three children. Truman went to Arkona where he married Catherine Muma and raised six children. Effie, the youngest, married Tom Reycraft and moved to Orford Township in Kent County, raising 10 children.

In 1854, Solomon, third child of Benjamin and Mahetable, purchased 100 acres, being the west half of Lot 14, Con. 3 SER, from George Goodhue for £50. It was believed to be uncleared with no buildings. In 1860, he married Sarah Wiley (1843-1925), daughter of John and Mary (Martin) Wiley. They had two sons, Chauncey (1862-1947) and George (1868-1951). Solomon served as a trustee of the Ebenezer Methodist Church on the Second Line South. While building a wooden fence across the front of his farm in May 1873, he caught a cold. He was encouraged by his wife to rest, but he continued working. At only 38, he died of pneumonia, leaving a young widow and two small sons. Ordinarily, they would have lost the farm and Sarah would have had to remarry, but the farm was mortgage-free. Sarah also had the help of her still-single brothers, Joseph and Isaac Wiley. Joseph leased the farm for a few years.

When Chauncey was old enough, he took over the operation of the farm. Chauncey always said that he was doing a man's work by the time he was 14. In 1886, he built a large, 2-storey brick home that stood until 1998. In 1893, he married Isabell Whiting (1866-1942), daughter of David and Eliza (Balmer) Whiting. They had three children, Lela (1896-1988); Harold (1900-1995); and Bessie (1903). Chauncey purchased another 50 acres in 1915, being the east quarter of Lot 14, Con. 3 SER, increasing his farm to 150 acres.

Chauncey was a man of few words. It always took several days before his wife was able to pry out any news he heard when he went into town. Chauncey worked hard all his life, never going far from home. With his family, he would attend community gatherings but never became involved with the organizing committees, lodges or other societies. The work on the farm always took precedence. The only events that he never missed were the local agricultural fairs. His wife, Isabell, was well known as a good cook, and beloved by those who knew her. The late Margaret (Knight) Hammond lived directly across from the Eastman family when she was a child. In conversation, Margaret said that the Second Line South was a special place in which to grow up. She told of how Isabell would shout across to the children playing outside and ask if their oven was burning. Isabell would come over with a full cake pan or muffin tray and put it in the Knight's oven while she had tea with Margaret's mother. When the baking was done, she always insisted that everyone try the cake or muffins to see how they turned out. Nine times out of ten, Isabell went home with an empty pan.

In 1918, Lela, Chauncey and Isabell's eldest child, married Fred Cook. They farmed in Metcalfe Township. They had no children. After the death of her husband, Lela lived in Kerwood for several years, taking an active part in church work.

Harold, Chauncey and Isabell's middle child, was one of the few local farm boys who graduated from high school. Unlike some young graduates, Harold stayed on the farm, being much needed as an only son. He soon took over the family farm. He faithfully cared for his parents, his grandmother, and his great-uncle. In 1939, Harold married Gladys Johnson of Kerwood, daughter of William and Ada (O'Neil) Johnson. They had no children.

Harold loved his cheese. His mother never put the cheese on the table, so Harold would always get up after supper, go to the cupboard, and cut off a piece of cheese for dessert. When Harold, suddenly, at the age of 38, brought home a bride, the neighbours were curious. At one gathering of folks, Harold was asked how married life was going. Harold paused a moment and, with a twinkle in his eye, simply said, "Well, she puts the cheese on the table."

Soon after Harold's marriage, a few other changes took place as the farmer slowly transformed himself into a public servant. He became, if not the best known, certainly one of a few men known to all Adelaide residents of his generation. Harold would often say that, at one time, he knew the first name of every man in Adelaide, and then with a chuckle he would add, "... and some of the women, too." Starting in 1940, and for the next 34 years, Harold served the public. He was elected Councillor in Adelaide in 1940-1943 and Reeve from 1944-1949. He was chosen Warden of Middlesex in 1949, a year of celebration for municipal government, the 100-year anniversary of the Baldwin Act of 1849. Harold was the fifth and last Adelaide Reeve to become Warden. From 1950-1957, he was appointed County Treasurer, and from 1957 until his retirement in 1974, he was appointed County Clerk.

About 1950, Harold was also appointed a justice of the peace and served as the judge during jury selection when trials were held in London.

As his public service workload increased, Harold had less time for farming. He sold the "east 50" to Adrian Groot in 1950 and leased out the remaining 100 acres. Harold and Gladys spent their summers on the farm and their winters in London. Finally, in 1962, Harold sold the original homestead that had been in his family for 108 years. Adrian Groot purchased the property, and Harold and Gladys moved to London.

Harold will be remembered for his quiet sense of humour, his unique way with words, and his wonderful memory. Harold's memory was a treasure trove that went back to times most people had forgotten. He was always sought after to remember a few details about a person or an event. A few months before his passing, he gave another rendition of a poem he remembered from childhood, "There are strange things done in the midnight sun by the men who moil for gold. The Arctic trails have their secret tales that would make your blood run cold..." These, of course, are the opening lines of "The Cremation of Sam McGee," a favourite poem of Harold's, and he could recite all the verses.

Harold liked most people because he always saw something good in them. Sometimes he had a difficult time finding any redeeming qualities, but the worst thing he would say was, "Well, he wasn't good for much, but I liked him."

For his memory, wit, humour and friendship, Harold was the natural choice as honorary President of the Adelaide Township Heritage Group. He accepted and again served the people of Adelaide for the last 1½ years of his life.

Bessie, the youngest child of Chauncey and Isabell, attended high school in Strathroy and then trained as a nurse in Sarnia, graduating in 1924. She worked in nursing for several years but didn't find the job satisfying. When a wing was added to Sarnia Hospital with an X-ray machine donated by Imperial Oil, Bessie accepted the opportunity to study radiology in Detroit. She worked as an X-ray technician in Sarnia and then a year in Port Arthur (now Thunder Bay), before accepting a job at the new sanatorium in Cornwall. Bessie ran the X-ray department and laboratories there until she retired in 1968, when the sanatorium ceased to operate. She currently resides in Cornwall.

In 1893, George, Solomon and Sarah's second son, married Caroline Humphries, daughter of William and Caroline (Elliott) Humphries. They raised five children, Elva (1895-1979); Bill (1898-1990); Bertha (1900-1937); Annie (1903-1932); and Ken (1912-1996). In his early years, George worked in partnership with his brother on the family farm. In 1892, they purchased 50 acres, part of Lot 13, Con. 2 NER. In 1893, Chauncey and George ended their partnership, with Chauncey taking over the family homestead and George taking Lot 13, Con. 2 NER. In 1910, George purchased a neighbouring part of Lot 13 to make his farm 100 acres. George farmed for many years before retiring to Strathroy.

Elva married first, Ted Edgar, a barber in Strathroy, and second, Leslie Arnel. She had no children. Bill married Pearl White of Simcoe and had one daughter, Jane. Bill worked with an insurance agency in Aylmer, Ontario. Bertha married Jack Lee (see Lee). Ken married Margaret Sutherland and had one daughter, Lois.

Silas, the fourth child of Benjamin and Mahetable, worked as a clerk for Richard Dumbrill, a merchant in Strathroy. In 1859, with his share of the inheritance, at the age of 22, Silas formed a partnership with Richard Dumbrill and purchased the Montreal Store in Arkona. Silas managed the store and bought out Dumbrill's interest in 1863. In 1860, Silas married Ellen Rymal (1841). Still a young man, Silas contracted tuberculosis and went to Missouri hoping for a cure. He died there, but his body was brought back for burial at the Fourth Line Cemetery. Within a few months, a daughter, Ida (1865-1878), was born to Silas' widow, Ellen. The 1871 census shows Ellen and Ida Eastman living with Silas' mother, Mahetable, then the wife of James Cooper, in Adelaide. Ellen likely moved to Toronto, since her daughter is known to have died there at age 13.

In 1859, Chester, youngest child of Benjamin and Mahetable, attended Victoria University in London, Ontario, from which he withdrew because of poor health. He then went to work for his brother, Silas, and took over the Montreal Store after his brother's death. In 1865, he married Phoebe Wait (1838-1877) and raised five children, Jeremiah (1867-1889); Franklin (1868-1952); Herbert (1870-1952); Maggie (1872-1890); and Lillian (1875-1891). This family is an example of the devastation that disease caused in the 19th century. Within two years, Chester, Jeremiah, Maggie and Lillian died of tuberculosis. The remaining sons, Franklin and Herbert, moved to the U.S.

ELLIOTT, Allan and Clara

Allan and Clara (Smithrim) Elliott lived at R.R. #2, on what was then called the Second Line. The Elliotts had one daughter, Jean, who moved with her parents to Sarnia about 1929. Allan worked at Imperial Oil after leaving the farm, and he also

Allan and Clara Elliot with daughter, Jean, ca.1918.

owned racehorses. Allan and Clara moved to Strathroy when he retired.

Jean married Herbert Pyke and they raised two daughters, Dianne and Colleen. Dianne married Jim Colter and they have one son, Jason. Colleen married David Tyfe and they have two daughters, Tiffany and Caleigh. The Elliotts still reside in Sarnia and Point Edward.

ELLIOTT, Cliff and Kay

Cliff and Kay (Juba) Elliott moved to Southwestern Ontario following Cliff's service in the Air Force. Cliff found work in London as a stationary engineer. Later, he and Kay operated a restaurant and store in Blyth. By chance one day, the Elliotts saw an advertisement in the paper indicating Harry Joris was selling a country store in Adelaide Township for Peter de Jong. The Roosenaks, who previously managed the store, had returned to Holland and abandoned the store and its contents. Clifford and Kay arranged to look at the place, as it seemed the ideal situation for them. They started their business by first serving meals to local threshing gangs. However, this proved to be too strenuous a pace, so they changed to a combination lunch counter/grocery/variety store. In addition, they had a number of pumps installed and sold gas under the Texaco Company. The Elliotts and their business were warmly welcomed to the Main Road community of Highway 22.

After seven enjoyable years managing the store, tragedy struck in the early morning hours of August 28, 1970. At 6:00 a.m., the driver of an eastbound truck lost control and slammed into the southwest corner of the store. The driver, Martin Knudson of Don Mills, was hauling barbecue fuel to Toronto from Imperial Oil in Sarnia. The accident killed Knudson and left the Elliotts homeless with only the clothes on their backs and their pet budgie. The store, garage, and all living quarters were destroyed. Even items such as canned food spoiled and had to be buried in the dump. Following the accident, the community helped the Elliotts get back on their feet. At first, they stayed at the Bambi Motel down the road, and then they moved to Warwick Village while they began rebuilding their business. Within two years, construction was completed and they reopened.

The Elliotts operated their business for close to 20 years. Cliff's health deteriorated, and they sold to Herbert Joris and moved to Strathroy. Following Cliff's death in August 1983, Kay managed to keep very busy as an active community worker. She has donated untold time and energy promoting and fundraising for the Minor Soccer League, March of Dimes, Heart & Stroke Foundation, Cancer Research, Salvation Army, and Crippled Children Fund. One of Kay's greatest achievements came in April 1996 and again in January 1997, when she sent shipments of more than 700 teddy bears and clothes to needy children in Bosnia.

ELLIOTT, Thomas and Effie

Thomas Elliott (d.1896) married Effie Demaray and they farmed at Lot 24, Con. 2 NER. They had four children, Alan, Ariel, Melvin (died at age six), and Thomas Jr. (1897-1993). Thomas Sr. was killed at a barn raising when he was 32.

Thomas Jr. farmed for a time, then moved to Lot 21, Con. 1 NER, and remained there until retirement. He was on Adelaide Township Council and did road grading in Middlesex County, which later became the responsibility of the Department of Highways. He operated the grader in the early morning hours in the 1940s, before his farm work started.

In 1928, he married Christine McLeish (d.1987) of East Williams. They had five sons. Norman married Donna Wernham. They live in Strathroy and have two children, Sharon and Ray. Lorne married Elaine Park, and they live in London. John married Deanna Sutherland. They live at Lot 22, Con. 2 NER, and have a son, Richard. Ross (d.1985) mar-

Mrs. Effie Elliot and family, L-R, Tom, Ariel, Effie and Alan (Norman not in picture, died aged six in 1899).

ried Tina Nauta, and they divorced. He later married Lucy Ann Baird. They lived in Kitchener and had a son, Michael. Ross died at age 46. Grant married Lynda Patterson. They live in Strathroy and have two sons, Jamie and Jason.

All five boys attended grade school at S.S. #10 Adelaide, and high school at Strathroy District Collegiate Institute.

When they retired, the Elliotts moved to Caradoc Street in Strathroy. Christine died at age 83, and Tom at 96.

EMERICK, Francis and Susan

Francis Emerick (1791-1881) and his wife, Susan (1793-1877), were born in the U.S. Francis had a busy military career. He served as a Private in the Sixth Company, First Regiment of Lincoln Militia in 1819, and was at Niagara in June 1821 with the same regiment. He was in the Battle of Chrysler's Farm on November 11, 1813, and the Battle of Ogdensburg.

In February 1835, Francis Emerick wrote a petition to Lt. Gov. John Colbourne, asking that moneys he paid to James Stuart of Lot 19, Con. 3, Rainham Township, be repaid to him as this lot was "run off" in a survey of the Indian line, so that only 17 acres of the land remained of the 100 acres purchased. (A strip of land six miles wide on each side of the Grand River was granted to the Six Nations Indians at this time.) In his letter, Francis Emerick wrote that he was unable to support his wife and nine children, the eldest being 16 years of age, because of infirmities contracted while serving in the militia during the late war, for he had always served in flank companies. He was requesting other compensation for his loss, as he estimated the land was now worth $5 per acre because of improvements he had made. In 1836, after this and other correspondence sufficiently proved his case, Francis was given a free grant of Lot 3, Con. 10, Adelaide Township. He is thought to have come to Adelaide in 1832, but made no application for land at that time.

The 1851 census of Metcalfe Township lists Francis Emerick, 63, born U.S., farmer; Susan, 62, born U.S.; James, 23, born Ontario; Francis, 22; Peter, 21; Elizabeth, 20; Keziah, 26; and John, 13. Also listed are George, 32, born Ontario (Presbyterian); Elizabeth, 21, born U.S.; James, 3, born Ontario; and George, 1.

George Emerick is described as an innkeeper in the Village of Napier on Bear Creek in 1857.

Some of the Emerick children moved to Mosa Township, and some to Brook and Moore Townships in Lambton County. Elizabeth and her husband, Timothy Kenna Jr., moved to Sanilac County, Michigan.

EMMONS, George and Emma

In May 1914, George Roy Emmons (d.1957) and his family traveled on foot from their home at Con. 10, Lobo Township, to settle on the east half of Lot 2, Con. 3, in Adelaide.

With George came his wife, Emma Elizabeth (Skinner) Emmons (d.1955), and three sons, Lorne Roy "Bob" (d.1988); Gordon Douglas (d.1982); and George Henry (d.1982). Lorne, the eldest at 5½, rode in the wagon. A team of horses pulled the wagon, and the Emmons family also brought some cows, sheep, a flock of hens and some ducks. A daughter, Ada Elizabeth, was born a few years later.

The older Emmons boys were known for their strength and also their devilment. They were often in trouble at school. The boys could pick up a bag of wheat in each hand and walk the full length of the granary. They worked the gravel wagon from Gravel Hill (located at the north end of what is now known as Wilson Sideroad) at the Arkona townline, from daylight to dark. They slept on their way to work and also on the way home; the horses were either well trained or in a hurry to get home for supper.

Lorne began going to Goderich in his late teens, possibly following some of his Cline cousins. On a Saturday night, this took three or four hours (depending on the weather) in a Model-A, and he returned home in time to do chores Monday morning. On August 29, 1934, he married Clara Aileen Freeman (d.1979) from Point Farms, just north of Goderich. They lived in the Kerwood area for a time and then returned to the Goderich area, where Lorne trained to be a molder in the Goderich foundry during the war.

Gordon went to work on the railroad. He married Deborah May Rae and moved to Caradoc Township. They had two daughters, Mary (Wiwcharuk) and Jean (Van Erp). Deborah lives with her daughter, Jean. Deborah was 90 years old on January 18, 1998.

George married Joyce Borthwick, a relation of the Ross family, and moved into Warwick Township. They had two sons and two daughters, Violet Caley, Lee, Shirley Dolan and Ross. Joyce has lived in Strathroy since George's death.

Ada married Wilbert McLeish from West Williams Township, better known as "Cowboy McLeish." They had two sons and a daughter, Marjorie (Herygers); Donald (killed in a car accident); and Ivan.

In 1953, George and Emma sold the farm to their son, George. They moved to a little white cottage at the corner of Burns and Adelaide Streets in Strathroy. When Emma died, George sold their little house and lived with his daughter, Ada, until his death. Both are buried in Poplar Hill Cemetery.

Lorne worked in the Goderich foundry until the end of the war. After that, he farmed the Kilpatrick property and took up custom work in the winter, pressing hay from Goderich to Wingham.

In 1945, he bought a farm next to his father's property, on Con. 3. He and Aileen moved to the old Pete Reinhardt farm with their two daughters, Muriel Aileen and Donalda Jean.

The old house had been a granary for a number of years, so it took a lot of hard labour to get it into livable shape. Lorne worked nights at the Forest and Parkhill foundries and also worked on the farm, while Aileen kept the chores done and helped in the fields. He worked with Charlie Hill, better known by Donalda as the "Candy Man." Donalda would go with her father at night and play in the warm sand until she was tired, then curl up in his coat to sleep. In the morning, Charlie Hill would arrive for work with his pockets full of big white peppermints. Lorne finally gave up the foundry work and did farming and custom work for neighbours, threshing and filling silos, etc. When he was young, he was known as a daredevil. It was not uncommon to see him walking around the top of an empty cement silo while putting up the pipes. The pipes had just been set to fill Orval Demaray's silo on September 30, 1953. The next morning Lorne was "a shade out of sorts," as Orval put it; that's when he found out he had a third daughter, Georgina Elizabeth (1953).

In the late 1950s, Lorne discovered there was a need for hay in the southern counties. He had purchased the Freele place across the road and grew a good acreage of hay. He purchased a red 1950 Dodge cab-over-engine truck, and started trucking hay to Dresden, to Chatham, and to Tilbury, in small amounts at first and then later in larger loads. In the late 1960s, he bought a 1964 blue GMC cab-over-engine truck with a bed about 22' long. His load was eight tiers high.

He continued to buy hay from neighbours and deliver it south, which kept him busy all winter. He found a good supply in a northern county, at Goderich, and in the Lucknow area. Many Sunday nights he would leave home, drive to Lucknow and load 300 bales on Monday morning, then arrive home Monday night. Tuesday morning, he would leave for the southern counties, hoping to arrive home late Tuesday night. Sometimes he would bring back a load of fertilizer from the CIL plant in Chatham. The quality of the hay made it very easy to sell.

Not all of his trips were perfect. One time, he called home for his son-in-law, Rodger Benedict, to bring jacks and a tire. They found him near Oil City with a full load of 340 bales and a flat tire; he was perched up against a hydro pole, the closest high object. Another time, the load was too high to fit under a bridge. They took the bales from the first two rows onto the bridge and then drove ahead enough to unload the next ones and so on until the bales had been removed, reloaded on the other side of the bridge, and retied.

Rodger's son, Lorne, still sells hay. The difference now is that the trucks pick up the hay. Over the past years, they have loaded trucks for Windsor, Kalamazoo, Michigan, and as far away as Florida.

Both Lorne and Aileen are buried in West Adelaide Cemetery.

Muriel, Lorne and Aileen's eldest daughter, received her degree in Food Services in 1959 upon graduating from Guelph University. She was first employed at the Beck Sanatorium in Byron and then at Victoria Hospital in London, before being offered the job of setting up and opening a new facility at York Central Hospital in Richmond Hill. In September 1964, she married Ken Van Vugt from Maple, Ontario. She is now retired and resides in Midhurst near Barrie, Ontario. They have no family.

Donalda worked at Strathroy Hospital. In August 1964, she married Rodger Benedict, who lived with his aunt and uncle, Loftus and Margaret Wilson, on Lot 3, Con. 3 NER, just around the corner from her home. Rodger and Donalda lived at Lot 3, Con. 3, for 31 years, when they sold their farm to their son, Lorne. Rodger and Donalda then built a new home on her parents' home place at the east half of Lot 2, Con. 3 NER, where they still live. Rodger and Donalda have four children.

Lorne Allan (1969) lives with his wife, Tracy Lee (Miller), on Rodger's home farm on Wilson Sideroad. Lorne received his mechanic's license and farms full-time. Lorne and Tracy were married June 1, 1996. Tracy is a Registered Nurse, and works at a Rehabilitation Centre in London.

Barbara Lorraine (1974) is a Registered Nurse. In October 1997, she moved to Durham, North Carolina, where she is employed full-time at Duke Hospital and University.

Donna Marie Aileen (1978) is currently attending Bowling Green State University in Ohio, and intends to become a Registered Nurse.

Lorri Diane (1981) is presently attending Strathroy District Collegiate Institute and is planning a career in law enforcement.

Lorne and Aileen's youngest daughter, Georgina, married Earl Fleming, a butcher from Strathroy. They live on the front portion of the Freele place at the east half of Lot 2, Con. 2. Georgina is currently employed at S.A.D.C.C. in Strathroy. Earl and Georgina have three sons. Scott Kenneth (1976) is presently attending Fanshawe College in London and plans a career in computers. Mark Alexander (1977) attends school in London. Ryan Lorne (1984) attends Adelaide W.G. MacDonald School.

EVOY, Thomas, James and Elizabeth

Thomas Evoy, along with his eight brothers and sisters and a first cousin, James Evoy, set sail in June 1826 from Dublin, Ireland, and landed three months later in Montreal. From there, they traveled by oxen to Huntley, now Ottawa, in Carleton County.

James and his wife, Elizabeth (Wright) Evoy, and two small children, James and Mary, came with Thomas Evoy to settle in Adelaide. Thomas came alone as his brothers and sisters were not interested in starting a new settlement. He chose a location near the banks of a spring creek to ensure a good water supply. After some time, when an area was cleared and his home was built, he went back to Huntley to get his wife, Hanna (Jury), and their three small children, Susannah, Emily and Mary. They came by covered wagon to Lot 13, Con. 4 SER. Later Anne, George, Miriam, Naomi and Ephraim were born, and also a son who died in infancy. Since his siblings stayed in Huntley, Thomas lost track of them. Several houses were built on this farm as improvements throughout the years, and a portion of land was given for the Mt. Zion Methodist Church to be built. When it was torn down, the land was given back to the farm, then owned by Thomas' youngest son, Ephraim.

Thomas spent much time in the woods collecting herbs that he used as medicine. Neighbours called him "Dr. Tom" because he helped them with their ailments using these herbs. On one of his trips through the forest, he met a bear. With only a jackknife for a weapon, he started to run toward the bear. When the bear failed to run, Thomas halted beside a tree prepared to fight. Luckily, the bear walked off into the woods. Another time, he shot and killed a bear weighing almost 400 pounds, and the animal was used for food.

The closest mill was in Kilworth, about 25 miles away. The men would carry sacks of wheat on their backs through the woods. Often, there was a delay while the big water wheel turned and ground the grain into flour, and it took almost a week for them to return.

The farms where Thomas and James Evoy resided were close to each other and so the two families grew up together. Strathroy did not exist, and the nearest store was at Katesville. The older children would travel through the woods to get to the store.

Of Thomas' family, Susannah, the eldest daughter, did not marry until later in life, to a Mr. Joynes. She lived in a house on the old homestead, and they had no children. Emily married William Brandreith and had a son, Ozias, and four daughters, Louisa, Elizabeth, Vina and Emma. Mary married Bernard McMahon and had four sons and two daughters. Anne was a teacher, and she married George McNinch, an undertaker. He had a son, Asa, and a daughter, Jennie. They lived in Port Huron, Michigan. George Evoy, a butcher, married Sara Chard. They had two sons, Lovelace and Clarence. Lovelace died in young boyhood. Clarence married Annie McIntyre and had a dry goods store in Strathroy for many years. Miriam married Leslie Kimball. They had one son, Will, and one daughter, Priscilla (Armstrong). They lived near Petrolia. Naomi married Louis Harvey and had two sons, George and Will. Ephraim was the youngest son, and he and his wife, Emma (Rapley), also lived in a house on the homestead. They had one daughter, Isabel, who married Angus McLean. Ephraim farmed the land until retirement. He was very proud of the cream-coloured team of horses that he used for traveling to Strathroy and surrounding areas. In September 1947, after his death, Isabel and her husband moved into the old family home with three of their four children. Their youngest son, Grant, took over the farm in 1956 and lived there until 1995, when the property was sold.

FEASEY, Robert and Carolyn

Robert Angus Feasey (1939) and Carolyn Leone Giffen (1943) were both born in Strathroy Hospital and have resided in Adelaide Township since birth.

After their marriage on November 24, 1962, they lived in an apartment above Walter and Olive Feasey on Lot 11, Con. 1 SER. In the fall of 1964, they moved to a house at Lot 11, Con. 1 NER. This house served as the Adelaide Village Post Office around the turn of the century. When they were renovating the house, they found a letter dated 1905, edged in black bearing postmarks from Belfast, Ireland, and the Adelaide post office. It was addressed to Wilkins, a previous Adelaide postmaster.

Robert is the son of Walter and Olive (Macdonald) Feasey. Walter was born in London and his family lived in Metcalfe Township. Olive's family dates back to 1832 in Adelaide Township. One sister, Dorothy Vaughan, resides in London. Olive was born on the Macdonald farm east of Crathie at Lot 26, Con. 2 NER. Walter served as Reeve of Adelaide Township in 1950-1951, and was a renowned old-time fiddler and decorator in the area.

Carolyn is the daughter of James and Helene (McDonald) Giffen. They lived on Lot 22, Con. 3 NER, a designated century farm (1967). James was born on this property in 1881, and Helene was from Caradoc Township. Her father, John McDonald, was a half-brother to Walter Scott, the first Premier of Saskatchewan. Carolyn has a younger brother and sister, William and Dorothy.

Carolyn and Robert have three daughters. Deborah (1963) lives in Adelaide Village with her husband, Harry Bakker, and son, Richard. Cheryl (1964) lives in Port Stanley with her husband, Garret Warringer, and daughters, Jessica and Allison. Karen (1969) lives in Memphis, Tennessee, with her husband, Juan Carlos Altuzar, and daughter, Cassandra.

Robert was a member of Adelaide Township Council from 1967 to 1988, and served as Reeve for 14 years. He was a secondary school teacher and taught his entire career at Strathroy District Collegiate Institute, beginning in 1960 for a total of 34 years. He is a charter member of the Adelaide/Metcalfe Optimist Club, member of the Arkona Masonic Lodge, and Past President and longtime Area Director of the Ontario Federation of Snowmobile Clubs. Carolyn and Robert are members of St. Ann's Anglican Church in Adelaide.

In 1974, they decided to build a new house on the farm and did the work themselves. They moved into a small cabin on the farm that they had used for snowmobiling and other recreational activities. To give them more space, Robert built a platform next to the cabin for a sleeping tent for their daughters. Occasionally, the cattle would push down the rail fence surrounding the cabin and stick their heads through the tent flap, which scared the girls. The youngest, Karen, slept on a couch in the cabin with her parents. One year, they even canned some preserves on a small Coleman gas stove. They all have many happy memories of this family venture, but when fall arrived, they were glad to move into the new house.

In 1969, they bought an island (Loon Island) in the North Channel of Lake Huron, 4 km. off the east end of Manitoulin Island, and in 1991, bought a house on a canal in Punta Gorda, Florida. They are enjoying both properties in their retirement years.

FEATHERSTONE, John and Mary

John Featherstone (d.1861) and Mary Carley (1807-1907) were married in Ireland in 1829 when she was 22 years old, and the couple immigrated to Canada in 1834. They lived two years in Warwick Township, Lambton County, with an old country gentleman, Mr. Hill. In 1836, they purchased the west half of Lot 19, Con. 2 NER, from William Morgan. The 1842 Adelaide Township census records show that John Featherstone had lived in Ontario for seven years; there were 12 people in the household; two were absent at the time the census was taken; eight were natives of Ireland and four were natives of Canada; and the family religion was Church of Rome. Of the 50 acres occupied, five were improved. In that year, 25 bushels of wheat were produced, 10 of oats, 100 of potatoes, 80 units of maple sugar, and there were 12 cattle and seven hogs.

The 1852 census listed the family as follows: John, farmer, 50 years old; Mary 44; Patrick 20, born in Ireland, labourer (absent); James 16, born in Canada; Ann 13; John 11; Michael 9; Catherine 6; William 5; Robert 4; and Francis 2.

In 1859, John sold the north half of the lot to his son, James. In 1861, a corner of the lot on "Featherstone Sideroad" was sold for a school site to be S.S. #2, Mud Creek School (the forerunner of the next Crathie School). In 1865, Mary sold the 50-acre farm to Thomas Craig.

Mary Featherstone was a habitual pipe smoker and she was always seen puffing on her pipe when she went to town to do her shopping. For many years, she was thought to be "the oldest living woman in Ontario, if not the Dominion," but she was little more than 100 years of age. Old settlers in the area claimed that she was an old woman when they were boys, and estimated her age at about 110 years.

Her obituary states that Mrs. Featherstone was survived by six children, William of Carrolton; Francis of Grand Rapids; Michael of Merrill, Michigan; Robert and Henry on the homestead in Adelaide; and Mrs. P. Sheridan of Saginaw, Michigan. Mass was sung in St. Patrick's Church by Rev. Father Quinlan prior to interment beside her husband in the Roman Catholic Cemetery in Adelaide Village.

FEDDEMA, Gosse and Theodora

In 1947, Gosse Feddema (d.1968) and his wife, Theodora (1980), immigrated to Canada from the Netherlands with 10 children. In 1956, they purchased the Tom Redmond farm on Lot 5, Con. 3 SER, and became dairy farmers.

Their son, John, married Jenny Vanderhoek in 1969. They purchased the Redmond farm in 1970 from Theodora, who moved to Strathroy. John and Jenny raised six children. Barbara married Peter Robinson, has two daughters, Rachel and Emily, and lives in Cambridge. Jeff married Mary Creamer, has a son, Michael, and they live in Grand Rapids,

John and Jenny Feddema Family, 1998 (Colledge Studios).

Gosse and Theodora Feddema and their 15 children, 1964.

Michigan. Tracy married Dwayne Bulthuis and lives in British Columbia. Jennifer, Johnny, and Kevin still live at home.

In 1983, John bought the Redmond farm next door from Tony De Ruiter, who had purchased it from his father, John, three years earlier. Before that, Don Sullivan had owned the farm. Sullivan bought from John Shipley, who had purchased the property from Bob Redmond.

John, Jenny, and their children lived there from 1983-1993. In 1993, John bought Jim and Jean Earley's home on Lot 6, Con. 3 SER, then owned by Fernando and Julie Moniz who lived there for four years. The Feddemas have remained dairy farmers, milking cows on the original Tom Redmond farm.

FEDDEMA, Rienk and Pietje

Rienk and Pietje Feddema and their children immigrated to Canada from Holland in June 1949. After a short stay in Woodstock and later in Port Stanley, they bought a farm in Adelaide Township, being Lot 1, Con. 17 NER, known then as the Brooks farm. The family moved there on Valentine's Day, 1951. Rienk had been a potato farmer in Holland but when he came here, he decided to grow sugar beets, beans, peas and grain. A few years later, he started a dairy herd.

Rienk was also a busy man in the church and school. The first meetings of the Counsel of the Christian Reformed Church, the Christian School and the Christian Farmers Organization were held in their living room.

They had eight children, all born in Holland. Sjoukje became a Registered Nurse. John married Grace Hiemstra and moved to the U.S. Peter married Marg Everts and became a teacher. Grace married Ipe Vander Deen on April 15, 1954, and they rented a farm in Kerwood. After farming there for five years, they moved back to the home farm and worked as partners with Rienk. At that time, the first turkey barn was built. Jack married Ann Linker, and he became a salesman for Hollandia Bakeries. Ann became a teacher, taught for two years at S.S. #10, and a few years later, married Jelle Berg. Jane married Ed Ryken and moved to Edmonton. Rienk married Ann Schalk and is working in London as a Police Officer.

In 1961, Jack and Ann moved back to the home farm and soon a second turkey barn was built. After 11 years, Jack left the farm and became a salesman for Daco Laboratories.

Also in 1961, a bungalow was built, and in 1979, the farm was sold to Ipe and Grace Vander Deen.

Ipe and Grace have seven children. Patricia married Rudy Heidelberg in 1990, and they live with their three children in Edmonton. Ivan married Diana Schenk in 1978, and they live with their seven children in Langton, Ontario. Irene married Charlie Dyxkhoorn in 1982. They live with their four children in Springfield, Ontario. Richard married Barb Dekker from Chatham in 1982, and they have five children. Clarence married Irene Sikma in 1984, and they have five children. Sharon married Steve Talsma in 1987, and they have five children. John married Teresa Noorloos in 1992. They have three children.

Richard and Barb bought the dairy herd in 1986. In 1995, they sold it and bought a pig farm from John and Ann Van Erp at Lot 15, Con. 4 SER. The Vander Deens purchased the Robotham farm at Lot 18, Con. 2 NER, in 1983.

Presently, Clarence and Irene live on the homestead and Clarence is the turkey farmer. John and Teresa live in the bungalow and do the dairy farming. Ipe and Grace retired in 1994 and moved to Strathroy.

The Feddemas would like to express their thankfulness for the liberation of Holland in 1945 by the Canadians. When they go back to visit Holland, they often stop at the War Cemeteries. They see row after row of tombstones of young Canadians, and are reminded of the great sacrifice made by them and their families. They are very thankful to live in this great and beautiful land called Canada.

FINKBEINER, Samuel and Hazel

Samuel J. Finkbeiner (1895-1934) was born in Crediton, Ontario. He attended the Ross College of Chiropractics in Ft. Wayne, Indiana. There, he met Hazel L. Ramp (1891), who was born in Columbia City, Indiana. Hazel and Samuel were married April 25, 1923, in Michigan City, Indiana, where he opened his first chiropractic office. Eighteen months later, they moved to Milwaukee, Wisconsin, where he opened his second office and where their daughter, Shirley Jean (1925), was born.

In 1926, the family moved to Samuel's homestead in Crediton, where Maxine Lucille (1927) and Colleen Marilyn (1930) were born.

In late July 1930, they moved to Adelaide Village and purchased the general store from a relative, George Glenn. The three girls attended S.S. #6 and Strathroy Collegiate Institute.

After Samuel's death, Hazel and her daughters remained in Adelaide Village until November 1944, when the store was sold to Al Jervis. The family then moved to Hazel's former home in Indiana, where Shirley had taken residence earlier that year. The married names of the three daughters are Shirley Caldwell, Maxine Booth and Colleen Beck Fuller.

FLETCHER, Donald and Annie

Early one Monday morning in the spring of 1892, Donald Fletcher (d.1921) hitched up his horse and buggy and put a sharp spade in the back of the buggy. He told his wife he would return when he bought a new farm. He had been farming in Brooke Township, where the land was heavy. In his words, he was tired of farming land that was so heavy that, if you stepped in a puddle in the fall, the cast of your foot was still there in the spring. Thus, the purpose of the spade was to test the earth of any farm he considered buying (early soil analysis).

Three days later, Donald returned to tell his wife that they were moving to Adelaide Township. Shortly after, he, Annie, and their two small sons, Hugh Alexander (1884-1954) and Donald Munroe (1890-1966), moved to Lot 1, Con. 1 NER.

Donald was the son of Hugh Fletcher (1819-1880) and the former Elizabeth McCallum (1827-1892) of Nairn, Middlesex County. Donald's wife was the former Annie Fraser (1853-1945) of the Parkhill area, where Annie's mother had been a Munroe before her marriage.

Shortly after arriving in Adelaide Township, Donald Fletcher purchased 100 acres from John A. Miniely, the east half of Lot 1, Con. 1 NER, to the east of his original farm. Donald died at home at the age of 69 years. He is buried in London.

After Donald's death, his widow and son, Hugh, continued to live on the farm. On February 19, 1927, Hugh married Pearl Rowntree (d.1942) of London. At that time, Annie moved to Strathroy. She was buried from the home of her son, Munroe, with interment in London. In 1937, Hugh sold the original farm and he and Pearl moved to London. They had no family, and they were also buried in London.

In 1915, Munroe purchased the west half of Lot 2, Con. 1 NER, adjoining his father's property. On December 20, 1916, he married Mary Evelyn Brown (1894-1972), elder daughter of Thomas and Melissa (O'Neil) Brown of Adelaide Township. From his father's estate, Munroe inherited the 50-acre parcel of land adjoining his farm on the west.

Four generations of Fletchers, L-R, great-grandmother Mary O'Neil, grandmother Melissa Brown, daughter Evelyn Fletcher, mother Mary Fletcher.

Munroe continued to live on his farm until his death. He is buried in Arkona Cemetery. Mary continued to reside in the home she came to as a bride until her death. She is also buried in Arkona.

Munroe and Mary had one daughter, Evelyn Winnifred (1920). Evelyn trained as a teacher. On July 10, 1943, she married Ernest Lloyd Hockey Clifton at West Adelaide Presbyterian Church. After a career in the chemical industry, Lloyd entered training for the Presbyterian Ministry, and he was ordained in 1970. Evelyn and Lloyd have three children.

Evelyn and Lloyd's eldest child is Ernest Lloyd Munroe (1947), who entered the armed forces in 1979, serving as a major in the Canadian Military. He is presently stationed at military headquarters in St. Herbert, Quebec, and living in McMasterville, Quebec. He married Carol Ann Ford of Toronto in August 1974. They have two children, Carrie Evelyn Grace (1977) and Ernest Lloyd Ford (1980).

Evelyn and Lloyd's elder daughter, Evelyn Elizabeth Anne (1952), is a member of the Diaconal Ministry of the Presbyterian Church. She married Rev. George Yando in August 1980. They are presently living in King City. They have two children, Franklin Lloyd George "Geordie" (1982) and Evelyn Elizabeth Mae (1989).

Lloyd and Evelyn's younger daughter, Janet Isabelle Marie (1965), is presently working for Bell Canada in Toronto. She married Richard Meesters, a computer consultant in Toronto, in August 1989. They live in Brampton.

Lloyd had the privilege of conducting the marriage services for all three of his children. In the case of his daughters, he was assisted by his son, Rev. Lloyd M. Clifton. He also baptized his four grandchildren and, for Geordie Yando, was again assisted by his son. At their baptisms, Lloyd and Evelyn's daughters and grandchildren wore the long christening dress made for Evelyn's grandfather, Thomas Brown, in 1864.

When Lloyd and Evelyn retired in 1985, they returned to the Munroe Fletcher farm in Adelaide Township to live.

FLETCHER, James and Anne

James Fletcher (d.1929) and his wife, Anne, were residents of Strathroy but James, a farmer at heart, bought a 25-acre piece of land on the south side of the Second Line South, which may be part of Lot 15. One reason for the move was to be near his daughter, Mamie (Mrs. Harvey Harris).

He moved a frame house from Hyde Park to the small farm, which was no small feat. In the process, Mr. E. Frank received a broken arm. James intended to build a barn immediately but nature intervened, and he suffered the loss of his right leg. This delayed his work but after his leg healed, he worked on the barn and soon had a neat little building.

One of Anne's joys was her contact with children. Her big day was Halloween, which also happened to be her birthday. She always had cookies and a cool drink for any small callers who came.

After James died, Anne Fletcher continued to live in their home alone until ill health prompted her to move to her daughter's farm. The property now belongs to Elly Boersema.

FONGER, Ivan and Margaret

Ivan Fonger (1904-1991) married Margaret Hall (1911-1988) and in 1941, they moved from Metcalfe Township to Lot 9, Con. 4 SER. Their only child, Douglas, was born in 1942. At that time, Margaret left teaching but returned when Doug was older. She taught at the Napperton School and later at Adelaide Central, Grade 3 or 4.

In 1962, Doug married Carol Lythgoe of Strathroy. A year later, they bought Ivan's farm. They had three children, Darryl (1962), Steven (1967) and Lori (1969). Darryl married Jacqueline Kellestine in 1983 and moved to Melbourne, Ontario, where they have three sons, Derrick (1984), Craig (1986) and Devin (1991). Lori moved to Mississauga, Ontario.

Steve, Doug and Carol's middle child, purchased the Fonger farm in 1990. He married Barbara Lovell in 1992, and they tore down the original house in 1993. At that time, it was confirmed that the central portion of the original house had been an old granary, which was moved there about 1880, with regular barn beam construction. Ivan had previously told them, "There are braces and girths framing this [central] part of the house. It was built just like a barn was." The walls on this section of the house appear to be a foot (or more) thick. In the basement, the supports are old tree trunks with the bark still on them. When the granary was converted to use as a house, a brick veneer, one brick deep, was

Ivan and Margaret Fonger on their wedding day, September 24, 1938.

added, and the roof was raised to accommodate the second floor. The front of the house had six rooms downstairs, and five upstairs. The brick from the old house was reclaimed and used for the new house. During construction, a brick dated 1895 was found, signed by Pete Nicholes and Ed Clarke, Strathroy. While the renovations were ongoing, Steve and Barb lived in the driveshed for 4½ months. The new house is on the same location as the original house, and the interior has been completely modernized by the Fongers, who recently added insulation to the walls. Clay from this farm, west of the original house, was used to make the bricks for the Morgan house across the road. The date is said to be 1937.

Steve and Barb have two daughters, Sarah Elizabeth (1994) and Emily Louise (1996).

FOSTER, George and Laura

George William Foster (1898-1966), the youngest son of William Henry Foster, lived in Metcalfe Township in the little white cottage on the farm at Lot 7, Con. 1, now owned by Charles Foster. He helped farm with his father until August 31, 1926, when he married Annie Laura Pulling (1898-1954) and they moved to Lot 8, Con. 4, in Adelaide. Laura was the middle daughter of Charles and Charlotte (Bateman) Pulling of Strathroy. She was born in Mt. Brydges. Later, her family moved to Strathroy and she graduated from Normal School (London) in 1917. Laura taught in Metcalfe, Adelaide, and Caradoc Townships for nine years. She was a singer and sang in many of the area churches before being married.

Together, George and Laura farmed 50 (and later, 100) acres and Laura taught at S.S. #7 for two years. In 1934, George took over a Kerwood mail route (R.R. #3) from Mr. Smith and continued until his death 32 years later. Richard Morgan built their farmhouse in the early 1800s, at a cost of $100. The house had solid yellow brick walls made from a brickyard located on the farm.

George and Laura had a daughter, Gwendolyn Ann (1934), and a son, John James (1940-1996). In 1944, Laura suffered a severe heart attack and, following that, had very poor health until her death at age 55. Gwen and Jim attended R.R. #7 Adelaide and Strathroy Collegiate Institute. Gwen worked at London Life for one year and then returned home and worked at the Toronto Dominion Bank in Kerwood. Jim completed an apprenticeship for auto body mechanic with Ross Saunders in Watford and then worked for Percy Floyd in Strathroy, before opening his own business.

In 1956, George remarried, to Ruth (Brett) Brown of Strathroy, and they enjoyed a large combined family of 10 children. She was also a teacher, and she continued to teach for a few years after they were married. They sold the farm in 1964 to Douglas Fonger and moved to Kerwood to the house now owned by Randy Smith. George died suddenly of a heart attack at 68 years of age.

On May 21, 1955, Gwen married Norman Brooks of Metcalfe Township. He lived with Jack and Ruby Redmond, and was an agent assistant for the C.N.R. They lived in Burlington for one year, and then returned to the Kerwood area in 1956 and bought the John W. Redmond farm in Metcalfe. In 1963, after living in a house in Kerwood for a few years, they built a new house on their farm and moved into it. They farm cash crops, and raise beef cattle and Standardbred horses. Norman also worked for McLean Feed and Grain in Kerwood for 26 years. Gwen worked at the Toronto Dominion

Bank in Kerwood until she retired in 1995. They have also been mail carriers for many years (R.R. #2, Kerwood). Gwen and Norman have three sons, William Rodney (1956); James Bradley (1960); and Jeffrey Norman (1963).

Rod married Heather Elaine Wilson on August 17, 1991. Heather taught school at Colborne Street in Strathroy, and later at Adelaide-W.G. MacDonald. They have one son, Ian Wilson (1993), and they live at 37 Parkview Drive in Strathroy. Rod is the manager of ORTECH Corporation, Sarnia Operations. His company provides environmental services (air and water quality monitoring) to the petrochemical companies located in the Sarnia area. Bradley married Shirley Anne Morgan on September 28, 1991, and they live at Lot 5, Con. 5, the former C.D. Matthews farm. Brad is a mechanic and has worked at Wallis Motors in Watford since 1980. Shirley is the only daughter of Ernest and Joyce (Langford) Morgan of R.R. #3, Kerwood. She is a florist and works for Murray's Flowers with Flair in Forest.

Jeffrey married Linda Marie Watt on July 17, 1987. They have a son and daughter, Andrew Norman (1988) and Cassandra Lynn (1992). They live at Lot 7, Con. 2, Metcalfe Township, the former J.W. Redmond farm. They have a farrow-to-finish hog operation and cash crop farm.

John James "Jim" (d.1996), George and Laura's son, married Eva Doreen Gilbert (d.1993), third daughter of Frank and Betty Gilbert of Denfield, on June 3, 1961. They moved to an apartment on Victoria Street in Strathroy and later bought a house on Clarence Street. In 1968, they sold this house and moved to Lot 16, Con. 1, to a new home they built on a former old school house lot. On April 1, 1969, Jim, in partnership with Jack Harris, opened Hy-Way Collision in the renovated schoolhouse, where Jim's mother once taught.

Jim and Eva had two daughters, Laura Elizabeth (1968) and Brenda Anne (1971). In 1989, they built a larger home on a lot adjacent to their business. Their daughters both attended Adelaide-W.G. MacDonald Central School, Strathroy Collegiate Institute, and Westervelt Business School. After graduating, they worked as medical secretaries. On October 7, 1989, Laura married Larry Johnson, son of Gordon and Lenore Johnson of Strathroy. For a few years, they lived in the first house built by Laura's parents located in front of Hy-Way Collision. Larry is a horse farrier and Laura works as a medical secretary at Victoria Hospital, London (Children's Cancer Research). She also owns a women's clothing store (Perfect Plus) on Frank Street in Strathroy. Laura and Larry had a daughter, Kate Elizabeth (1994), then moved in 1995 to a farm at R.R. #2, Ailsa Craig, and had a second daughter, Michelle Eva (1997).

Brenda married Glenn William Arnold of London, on September 25, 1993. Brenda worked for a short time as a medical secretary at Victoria Hospital and then later opened a hair salon in her home. She purchased and operates a children's clothing store (Wearabouts) on Front Street, Strathroy, and continues her home business. She and Glenn have a son, John James (1994).

Together, Jim and Eva ran the body shop until 1993, when they sold the business to Brian (who worked for Jim) and Peggy Brothers. In October 1993, Eva became very ill and died of a brain tumor at 53 years of age.

Jim remarried, to Gayle (McKenzie) Griffiths of R.R. #2 Ilderton, on February 23, 1996. They sold his house in Adelaide and moved to Gayle's home. Jim then worked for an auto appraisal firm on York Street in London. During April 1996, he became ill and died shortly after of lung cancer, at age 56.

FOSTER, George and Marjorie

George Edward Foster (1918-1988) married Marjorie Westgate in 1941. George was enlisted in the army at the time. In 1944, George and Marjorie purchased a farm, the east part of Lot 7 and west part of Lot 8, Con. 5, near the Kerwood Road on the

Charles and George Foster cutting timber in 1943.

Farmers' milk in cans being trucked to Carnation Plant, Kerwood, January 1958.

Fourth Line. The farm had been owned by Mrs. Arthur Morgan. George and Marjorie had a mixed farm. They raised five children, Joyce, Louise, Erma, Glen and Charles.

Crops grown on the farm during the Foster ownership included corn, wheat, oats, soybeans and hay, which were mainly used for feeding the cattle. During the 1940s, the farm was worked with a team of horses, then a steel-wheeled tractor and later a rubber-tired tractor, followed by modern machinery. In the early days, haying was done by using a side rake, hay loader and a team of horses. Grain was cut and tied with a grain binder, and then the sheaves were stooked and hauled to a grain separator where the threshing was done.

George sold cream to Kerwood Creamery. Carnation bought Pollock's and George helped change the building over to accommodate cans of milk hauled by trucks from the dairy farmers. A few years later, George also hauled milk into Kerwood. His route took him out to Forest, Ravenswood and Ipperwash, before returning to the milk plant.

Helping neighbours in hard times is an attribute of Adelaide Township people. One day on the milk route, George wasn't feeling very well, and that night he had his appendix removed. The neighbours came with balers, tractors and wagons to take in the hay.

Since George's death, Marjorie continues to run the farm with the assistance of her sons.

FREELE

William Freele was born in Ireland (1807-1888). He married Catherine Seed (1807-1881) of County Down, Ireland. They immigrated in 1831 with their first two children, and travelled to Adelaide Township by ox cart. William farmed the west half of Lot 11, Con. 3 NER, and he and Catherine had 10 children. They both died in Adelaide Township.

Michael (1829-1862) was born in Ireland and is interred in St. Ann's Cemetery, Adelaide Township. He was a storeowner in Adelaide. He married Mary McKean and they did not have any children.

William (1830-1898) was born in Ireland. He married Rebecca Cummins in Adelaide Township in 1865, and they resided on Con. 3 NER. They had one daughter and three sons, Sarah, Michael, Charles and John. They were all interred in St. Ann's Cemetery.

Hugh (1833-1912) was the first child born in Adelaide Township. He became a farmer, and married Margaret Brians in Adelaide Township in 1858. They resided at Con. 3 NER, and had three sons and seven daughters. Their third son, Hugh (1834-1912), married Margaret Jane Briens (1868-1921), also from Ireland. They were the first couple married in 1858 at St. Ann's by the new rector, Rev. Alexander Sydney Falls, who came from Dublin. Hugh and Margaret also had 10 children, and farmed on the Second Line North. Some of their children farmed, some became storekeepers and shoemakers, and others moved to Detroit and South Dakota. Hugh died in Lambton County.

Hugh and Margaret's second son, James Spiers (1861-1937), married Alice Ham (1860-1941) from England. James and Alice farmed on Highway 22, just west of Hickory Corners. They had two children, Frederick George and Eva Pearle. Eva Pearle never married and is buried with her parents in Strathroy Cemetery. Frederick (1889-1958) married Bertha Davidson (1886-1971) from Caradoc Township. They farmed in the same area as his father, and had four children, George, Grace, Oscar and Alice.

George (1916-ca.1970), eldest child of Frederick and Grace, married Mary Yankovitch and had two children, Marion and Norman. Marion lives in the Glencoe area and Norman lives in Calgary. They are both married and have families.

Grace married Maurice A. Brown (1914-1992) in 1939. They farmed the east half of Lot 8, Con 3 SER. They had four sons, Cecil Frederick (1942); Jack Maurice (1947); Stuart Arnold (1948); and Glen Douglas (1951).

Freele family, back, William, Lavella, Eliza (Freele) Brent; front, father Thomas, Mary (Freele) Brock, Melissa (Freele) Wyatt, mother Eliza Ann (Neil).

Cecil Brown married Winnifred M. Garrod (1941) in 1964 in Kerwood. They bought the Oliver Harris farm at the east half of Lot 8, Con 3 SER. They have two daughters, Karen Grace (1970) and Deanna Lynn (1973). Karen married William Russel Clark (1968) from Petrolia in 1993, where they now reside. Karen and Bill have two sons, Todd William (1994) and Justin Robert (1997). Deanna works and lives in Strathroy.

Jack Brown married Diane I. Hall (1949) in 1971 in Brooke Township, Lambton County. Jack and Diane have three children, Michael Jack (1974); Paul Maurice (1976); and Sandra Diane (1979). All of their children live at home.

Stuart Brown married Linda E. Daubs (1951) in 1973 in Strathroy. They have one chosen daughter, Caroline Dawn 1977. Stuart and Linda farm on the Second Line South.

Glen Brown married Donna Richardson (1950) in 1971 at Kerwood. They have two sons, Glen Ryan (1976) and Randy Douglas (1978). They also live on the Second Line South. Ryan married Sara Schyff (1973) in 1997 in Strathroy. Randy lives at home with his parents.

Oscar (1918-1946), third child of Frederick and Grace, married Ethel Smith (d.1970s) of St. Mary's and they had one son, Gordon. Oscar died at the age of 27 in a garage explosion in London where he was employed. Ethel never remarried. Gordon married, has a son, Jeffrey, and lives in the London area.

Alice (1920), youngest issue of Frederick and Grace, married Donald K. Freer (1919-1996) in 1942.

They had three sons, Arthur, Kenneth and Bruce. Alice now lives in Strathroy. Arthur (d.1985) married Jean Emmons of Strathroy. Jean now lives in Strathroy. Kenneth married Margaret Van Dun from Petrolia. They have three children, Jason, Lisa and Charles. Bruce works in a hospital and lives in London.

George Freele (1836-1882), fourth child of William and Catherine, was born in Adelaide Township and was a shoemaker.

James (1837-1914) was born in Adelaide Township and died in Lambton County. He married Mary Whitlock in 1865. They had six daughters and nine sons, 10 of their children being born in Adelaide Township.

Matilda (1842-1921), sixth issue of William and Catherine, was born in Adelaide Township. She married William Whitlock and resided in Lambton County. They had four daughters and six sons.

Thomas Freele (1844-1922) was born in Adelaide Township and died in Forest, Ontario. He married Eliza Ann Neil (1856-1933) in Adelaide Township in 1876. She was the daughter of William and Mary (Flemming) Neil. He was the owner of the store in Adelaide Village. Thomas and Eliza had six children in Adelaide Township, Melissa L. (1887-1938); William E. (1879-1962); Mary Ethel (1881-1965); Lavella Catherine (1884-1966); Eliza Ann (1886-1969); and Leila Freele (1889-1891). Leila was interred in St. Ann's Anglican Cemetery.

Melissa married Lawrence Wyatt (1879-1956) in Adelaide at St. Ann's Anglican Church in 1910. He was the son of Edward Wyatt Jr. and Isabella Whyte. They lived in East Williams Township. Melissa and Lawrence had three children, Helen (1912); Lenore (1915); and Roberta (1917), all born in East Williams.

William married Margaret Galbraith in West Williams Township in 1911. He died in Forest, Ontario, and was interred in Strathroy Cemetery. They lived in Forest. William Freele and Margaret Galbraith had one daughter, Grace.

Mary Ethel married Arthur J. Brock in 1905. He was the son of Arthur and Esther (Conkey) Brock. They farmed at Lot 14, Con. 1 SER, and later moved to London. Mary and Arthur had two sons and a daughter, Clifford (1906); Laila (1908); and Neil (1912), all born in Adelaide Township.

Lavella lived at Lot 11, Con. 3 NER, and died in Strathroy. Her body was interred at the Strathroy Cemetery.

Eliza married Frederick Brent, the son of Joseph and Annie (Hodgson) Brent. They resided at Lot 7, Con. 1 NER. They had a daughter and a son, Freda (1916) and Gordon (1918-1987).

Catherine (1847-1913), eighth child of William and Catherine, married John A. Brown in 1880, and then Cornelius McCarthy in 1882. Catherine Freele and Cornelius McCarthy had three sons and three daughters.

Francis (1848-1907) married William Henry, a farmer and carpenter. He was a framing contractor when Charles Clelford's farm was erected. They had a family of two sons and two daughters. Francis was interred in St. Ann's Anglican Cemetery.

Robert (1849-1932), William and Catherine's youngest child, lived on Con. 3 NER. He married Maria Willoughby in 1874 in Adelaide Village. They had three daughters and two sons. Robert died in Strathroy.

FULLER, Obadiah and Charlotte

Obadiah H. Fuller (1841-1874), son of William and Isabella (King) Fuller of London Township, married Charlotte Maria Robbins (1840-1933), daughter of Walter L. and Sarah (Alway) Robbins of Adelaide Township, on October 30, 1863

They took up residence on the west half of Lot 29 SER (now 4397 Egremont Rd.). They had four sons, Hiram (ca.1864), who resided in Chicago and had no family; George (ca.1865), who married in Western Canada and had one son, Donald; Silas William (1866-1930); and Rodolphus "Rowe" (ca.1868), who died as a child. When Obadiah died, he left Charlotte with four young sons.

Up the road to the west lived John Smith (1829-1907), who had married Susannah Hunt (1832-1875) in 1853, and settled on Lot 26 NER (now 4074 Egremont Rd.). The Smiths had a family of seven children, Almina (1855-1943), Theopholis Courtland, Augusta Johanna, Nathan Arthur, Caleb William, Merci Ann and Amelia Jane (1865-1957). When Susannah died, she left her husband with seven children.

John Smith and Charlotte Fuller married in 1876 or early 1877, and lived in the spacious Smith home on Lot 26, with their combined family of 11 children. John and Charlotte had a daughter and son, Louette A. (1877-1967), who married Arthur B. Decker (1871-1960) of London Township in 1898, and had three children; and John A. (1880-1952), who married Laura E. Hodgins (d.1968) and lived in Adelaide Township.

The sons in the first Smith family all died young, and the daughters married and moved out of the township, except for two. Almina, the eldest, married William Gare (1852-1915) of Adelaide and had five children. John Charles, Ethel, Oliver Courtland, Annie J. and Manford were all born in Adelaide Township, but the family moved to Lambton County (see SMITH, John and Susannah). John Charles became a Reverend.

Amelia Jane, the youngest child of John and Susannah Smith, married Silas Fuller, third son of Obadiah and Charlotte Fuller. They settled on the Fuller farm and had seven children.

Oscar Murdick (1887-1972) married Katie Christena Campbell (1889-1970), daughter of Duncan A. and Flora (McIntyre) Campbell of East Williams, in 1911. They lived at 4074 Egremont Road and then moved to Lobo Township in 1927. They had three children. Alexander Campbell (1914-1936) died a young man. Hazel Aileen (1919) married C. Alex McGregor, son of Sam and Christina McGregor, in 1941. They live in East Williams Township, and have four children, Kenneth

Far left, Silas Fuller with dog; behind him, friend, Tom Whiting. L-R, beside Silas, Jack Fuller, Amelia Fuller, Dora (Fuller) Hardell, Charlotte Fuller; on porch is family heirloom bearskin.

Fuller homestead on Highway 22 (Egremont Road).

Alexander, Glen James, Hazel Christena and Bruce William. Duncan married Jean H. Parson, and they reside in Milton, Ontario.

Hiram Harold (1889-1984) married Lottie V. Cook (1888-1929) of Michigan in 1910, and lived in Michigan.

Joseph Arthur (1891-1985) married Ruby O. Gill (1899-1929) in 1914, and remarried in 1934, to Mary Wright (Watt) (1887-1984). They lived in Oakville, Ontario.

Dora Louetta (1893-1978) married George Wesley Wardell (1886-1943), son of John Edward and Caroline (Lindsay) Wardell. They lived in Adelaide Township and had four children, Earl Ray, Herbert Leslie, Leo Arthur, and Joseph George "Joe."

Vincent George "Dick" (1896-1990) married Mabel Kathleen Charlton (1902-1991), daughter of Robert and Hannah (Stonehouse) Charlton of Lobo Township. Dick served in the army in WWI, and they had three children. Cecil Vincent (1922) married Nona Jamieson of Salmon Arm, B.C., and resided in Thorndale, Ontario. They have a family of four children. Beatrice (1926) married Omie John Drysdale (d.1998), son of Jim and Florence (Waters) Drysdale of Lobo Township. They had three children, Karl, Glenda and Diane. Grant (1929) married Beulah Carter (d.1990) of London Township and resided in Strathroy. They had two children, Anne Marie and Lois.

Charlotte Beatrice (1898-1990), sixth child of Silas and Amelia, married Owen Eli Zavitz of Lobo Township. They had four sons, Ernie, Walter, Allan and Lyle. All of the children married and resided in Middlesex County.

John Obadiah (1904-1996) married Hilda Knight (1913-1977) of Oakville. They lived in Oakville and had three children, Gordon, Ronald and Shirley May.

The Fullers were a very musical family, and they all enjoyed playing musical instruments. They had many musical family get-togethers, and played for dances and socials in the area. Their musical tradition is being carried on through Oscar's grandson, Ken McGregor, whose band, "Beechwood," has been playing in the area for many years.

After John Smith died, Charlotte married a third time, to a Mr. Odlum or Audlum from Petrolia.

FULLER, William and Mary

William Fuller was born in Warwich Township. He married Mary LaValley and they moved to Adelaide. In the 1878 atlas, their property was the William Lagallce farm on Con 5. They had three children, Albert, Eda, and Mary Ann, who died at about age three.

Albert married Ardella Dowding and they had three children, Clarence, Ethel and Frederick. Clarence married Mildred Morgan. Ethel married Arthur Malleline and had one son, Raymond. Fred married Hazel Rummel and had one son, Ronald.

Ardella died and Albert remarried, to Ada Crawford. They had two sons, William and Harry. William married Daphne (last name unknown), a British war bride, and Harry married Jean Fydell. William and Harry both served overseas in WWII.

Clarence, Albert and Ardella's eldest child, was a bridge contractor in partnership with Winfield "Pat" Waltham. They built many bridges in Southwestern Ontario.

Fred was an electrician, who was responsible for wiring many Adelaide Township farms in the 1930s and 1940s, after electric power became available in the area.

Eda, middle child of William and Mary, married Frederich Richardson. They farmed Lot 3, Con. 4 SER. They had one son, Kenneth, who married Leila Muxlow, daughter of Archie and Ethel (Martin) Muxlow. Kenneth and Leila had a daughter and a son, Marilyn and Alan. Marilyn married Ivan Herrington. Their son, Alan, married Sandra

Harry and Jean Fuller

McAllister, and they have three children, Rebecca, Michael and Patrick.

The Fullers and Richardsons were active members of the Kerwood Methodist Church (later United Church).

FYDELL, Rev. Fred and Sarah

The Reverend Fred (d.1944) and Sarah (Wade) Fydell were moved from Camlachie United Church to the Kerwood charge in June 1939. Their son, Jim, was teaching in Northern Ontario, near Sudbury, at the time. He enlisted in the R.C.A.F. Ruth (whose husband, Gerald Galbraith, was also in the R.C.A.F.) lived with her parents when her husband was away. Jean attended Normal School in London and began her teaching career at S.S. #8 Adelaide. She then taught in the Essex area and married Harry Fuller in 1945. Jean moved to London, where she also taught.

Rev. Fydell died in Kerwood and Sarah moved to Smithville, where her sisters lived.

GALLOWAY, James and Anna

James Galloway (ca.1778-1864) was born in County Down, Ireland, on the estate of Lord Douglas. He worked on the estate as a gardener before he joined the Scots Greys as a trooper. After the Napoleonic Wars, he set up as a weaver in Glasgow. He married and he and his wife, Elizabeth, had six children, Robert (1814); Sholto (1819-1897); John (1824); two older daughters, and one infant daughter. Because of economic hardship, like many retired soldiers, John commuted his pension for a grant of land in Upper Canada. The eldest son, Robert, elected to remain in Scotland while the rest of the family prepared to immigrate to Canada in 1832. Unfortunately, Elizabeth died of cholera during the crossing, and the youngest child died shortly after. James remarried in Montreal on October 31, 1833. He and his second wife, Anna Haughlahan, with his remaining children, made their way to the east half of Lot 2, Con. 3 NER. James's land patent was for this 100-acre lot, granted June 17, 1826, 12 years earlier than the McChesney and Shields grant directly across the road.

In Adelaide, James and Anna had a daughter, Ann (ca.1833), and three sons, James (1835-1916); William (ca.1837); and David (ca.1841).

Census records of 1842 indicate James and his family had been in the province for 10 years, and that he was one of the earliest settlers in Adelaide. The same census states that James and his wife had three sons and daughters living away from home and two living at home. Four of the children are recorded as being natives of Ireland and one (Shalto) of Scotland; possibly at one time the family lived in Scotland.

The 1842 census states that James had cleared five acres of bush on his farm and by 1852 had cleared 35 acres. James was married and his wife died before 1851 in Adelaide Township, as James is listed as a widower in the 1852 census and was living with his son's family. An 1851 census records that James Galloway farmed in Adelaide Township and died after 1861 in Adelaide. His burial location is unknown.

The only one of James' children about whom we have significant information is Sholto, sometimes spelled "Shalto" in the records. A few sources state that he did not get along very well with his stepmother, and joined a cavalry regiment in 1837. He was stationed in Toronto and Fort Mulden. After his discharge, he took over the family farm. He married

Elizabeth Ann McGregor (1821-1891) about 1851 and they had seven children, Eliza Ann (1851); James Hy (1853-1916); William Thomas (1854); Frances Jane (1846-1884); Archibald (1858); Lucinda (1859-ca.1871); and Mary (1861). Shalto appears to have been an ambitious farmer as he accumulated 300 acres of land in his lifetime. He took over the family farm, then purchased 125 acres, the east and west parts of Lot 5, Con. 2 NER, and in 1836 bought the north part of the west half of Lot 3, Con. 2 NER.

Sholto makes an appearance as a coach driver in Anna Brownell Jameson's book, "Winter Studies and Summer Rambles in Canada." Jameson's class assumptions seem to colour her description of Sholto as a well-meaning but ignorant fellow with a "very demure and thoughtful though boyish face." When she holds forth on the principles of good health at some point in the story, she reports that he "listened with an intelligent look" and thanked her cordially. Sholto himself made some comment on this portrayal in the epitaph on his tombstone in cemetery of the West Adelaide Presbyterian Church. It reads, "In conclusion may I say that I think Mrs. Jameson was mistaken in the character of her man."

From Mrs. Jameson's report we also learn that Sholto's two older sisters had gone out to work as domestic servants and that his brother (probably John) had gone to work for a shoemaker in London.

Of Sholto and Elizabeth's daughters, we know little except that Frances Jane married Nathaniel Davidson. More is known about their sons.

Archibald married about 1887 and he and his wife, Barbara, had two children, Laura May (1889-1890), who is buried in the West Adelaide Cemetery, and Ethel M. (1891).

William Thomas married Mary (1854, last name unknown) in 1877. They farmed Lot 5, Con. 2 NER, and had five children, Catherine I.M. (Simpson) (1879); Mabel G. (Morgan) (1881); Chester (1883); Grace P. (King) (1887); and Roy D. (1889). James and Sarah are interred in West Adelaide Cemetery.

The eldest son, James Hy, married Sarah McChesney (1859-1909), the daughter of William and Jane (Wiley) McChesney, sometime after 1891. They owned the family farm originally settled in 1833, and in 1910, James was farming 200 acres at Lot 2, Con. 3. He and Sarah were active members in the West Adelaide Presbyterian Church, and had two sons, William Hy (1894-1947) and Albert James (1898-1981). William trained as a dentist and worked for many years in Blenheim where he lived with his wife, Mary Elizabeth Werden (1895-1992), and their daughter, Betty Jean (1926). Albert served in WWI and later became a freighter captain on the Great Lakes. He married Beatrice Zena Wilkinson (1898-1977) and had three children, Margaret Clarinda (1921); Zena Isabel (1927); and James Henry (1938).

GARE, George Sr. and Jane

George Sr. and Jane Gare immigrated to Adelaide Township about 1851 from Somerset, England. According to the 1851 census, George (1822-1909), farmer and wife Jane (1826-1907) and their family, George (9); Ann (5); John (3); and William (1) lived with Robert Pegley, a soldier farmer who was a widower with a family. In the same census, it lists a William Gare (the same age as George) as a blacksmith, living with a Maguire family. Unfortunately, no information could be found on this William. On the 1861 census, George and Jane had two more sons, Reuben and Moses.

George, Jane, and their family were members of the Bethel Methodist Church on Egremont Road. In an article from the "Age" paper on the Jubilee of Bethel United Church, John, son of George, one of the oldest residents, recalled very interesting scenes in the old school, before the church was built, when packed with people for special services. He said the very earnest powerful preachers of the early days hewed to the line and didn't worry where the chips fell. In the 1870s and 1880s, the Gare family lived in Lobo, on Con. 13. By 1890, they were back in Adelaide.

George Gare Jr. (1843-1928) married Elizabeth Grills (1851-1931) in 1872, and in the 1890s, George, Elizabeth, and their children, John (1874-1943), George, and Edith (d.1904) lived on Queen Street in Strathroy, on property purchased in 1896. The house is presently occupied by Jean (Gare) Miller and her husband, Elwood. George was a carpenter and well-known framer in the area. George, Elizabeth and their family were very active in the Salvation Army. Their daughter, Edith died at age 15 from diphtheria. She was well known for her "clear, soprano voice" as she worked industriously in open-air meetings of the Salvation Army.

John, first child of George Jr. and Elizabeth, married Sarah Amelia Werin (d.1900) of Thedford. In 1900, a daughter, Lena, died at three weeks of age, and her mother followed three weeks later. John married again, to Janet Annetta "Netty" Haldane (1872-1918) of Metcalfe. They lived on Queen Street in Strathroy next to John's parents. John and Netty were both active in the Salvation Army. It is said that John often walked all the way from Strathroy to Glen Oak to preach on a Sunday, and that Netty was an accomplished singer and records were made of her singing. John worked in the flourmills in Strathroy and later ran the Falconbridge General Store near Mt. Brydges. John and Netty had eight children, all born in Strathroy.

Manford Emile (1904-1989) married Freda Taylor (1910), who was born in England. Manford met Freda in Toronto while stationed there for the Salvation Army. In 1928, Manford and Freda opened a paint, wallpaper and flooring store on Front Street in Strathroy. They had two children. Kenneth (1931-1950) died in a motor vehicle accident at 18 years. Donald (1936) married Louise Thomas (1939). Don and Louise have three children. Brian (1958) married Winnie Linker and they have two children, Kelly and Bradley. Laurie Ferguson (1962) has two children, Kyle and Jasmyne. Steve (1964) is the youngest of Donald and Louise's children.

Estelle (1906-1968), second of John and Netty's children, married Lawrence George Noxell. They had no children, and lived on English Street, Strathroy.

Ewart Faye "Lefty" (1908-1982) married Florence Topping (1905-1982). Lefty ran the General Store at English and Caradoc Street in Strathroy for several years, and worked as a rural mail carrier on R.R. #6, Strathroy. Lefty and Florence had four children, Ewart (1932-1934); Betty F. (1930), unmarried; Robert D.(1936-1997) unmarried; and Jean, married to Elwood Miller from Strathroy. Jean and Elwood have two children.

Dwight (1908-1932), fourth of John and Netty's children, was single when he died in an accident.

John B. (1912-1992) married Reta Harding. John worked in the grocery business on Front Street in Strathroy, for Foodland and I.G.A., for several years. John and Reta had two children. Gregory

George Sr., John, George Jr., Manford: four generations of the Gare family.

(1947) married Sheila Kelly, and they have two children, Brian and Michael. Gwendolyn (1949) married Lorne Woods, and they have three children, Gary, Ronald and Darryl.

Orion (1912-1992), John and Netty's sixth child, married Charles Cooper. They had four children, Gordon (1932-1960); Marion (1943); Victor (1944); and Ruby (1945), who married Allan Truax. Ruby and Allan have a daughter, Ruth Anne (1965), who married Ronald Swain, and they have two children, Ronald and Brandon.

Wendall (d.1918) and Jean (d.1918), the two youngest of John and Netty's children, both died very young, the same year as their mother.

George (1875), second child of George Jr. and Elizabeth, married Jessie Jackson (1877). George was a butcher in Strathroy before moving to Toronto. They had two daughters. Emma married a Mr. Rowland, and Mabel died as an infant.

Edith (1888-1904) died of diphtheria at 15 years of age. She was well known for her clear soprano voice.

Ann (ca.1846), second child of George Sr. and Jane, died between the 1851 and 1861 census.

John (1851-1931) and Moses (1860-1932) never married and lived with their parents, George and Jane, on the farm in Adelaide Township. After their parents' death in 1907 and 1909, John and Moses moved to Strathroy, where they bought property on Front Street East, which later was occupied by Manford and Freda Gare and their paint and wallpaper business. In Moses' obituary, it records that he is the last of his family and one of the oldest members of Bethel Church on the main road.

Reuben Gare (ca. 1857) moved to the American Midwest in 1876 in search of prairie farmland.

William (1852-1915), fourth child of George Sr. and Jane, married Almina Smith (1854-1943) and lived in Lobo. In the late 1880s, William and Almina moved back to Adelaide. William and Almina had five children, all born in Adelaide Township. They lived in Adelaide for some time, then moved to Lambton County.

Rev. John Charles (1878), eldest of William and Almina's children, married twice, first to Sarah P. Vance, with whom he had 8 children, then to Margery (last name unknown), with whom he had two more children.

Ethel (1884-1958) married Henry Thompson, and they had two children, Irene (1915) and Melvin William (1913).

Oliver Courtland (1885-1968), third child of William and Almina, married Laura Ellen Vance. They had six children and two foster children.

Beatrice Ellen (1912) married Walter Heman Fox. They lived in London, and had four daughters.

Melvin William (1913) married Grace Evelyn Neely (1916). They had three children. Wayne Melvin (1940) married Inez Elizabeth Ferguson (1941). They have no children and live in Plympton Township. Ian Gordon (1945) married Agatha Maria Van den Broek (1946). They have a son and a daughter. Brian Franklin (1947) married Susan Jane Maw, and they have two daughters.

Lois Almina (1915), third child of Oliver and Laura, married Rowney Wiggleworth, and lived in Quebec.

Olive Gladys Mae (1918) married Burton Simpson (1938-1994).

Gordon (1921-1992) married Edna Annie Fradgley, and they lived in London.

Frank (1933), youngest child of Oliver and Laura, married Helen Riordan (1929). They lived in Keyser's Corners, Adelaide, and now Arkona. They had twins, Keith and a daughter who died, and Steven, who married Janet Milligan. They have two children, Jenna Lyn and Cyra.

Oliver and Laura's foster children were Tom MacLean (1946) and John MacLean (1947).

Annie J. (1887-1948), fourth child of William and Almina, married John Cable.

Manford (1890) was the youngest of William and Almina's children. He married Florence (1890-1969, last name unknown). They had two children. In 1937, Manford resided in West Kendall, New York.

Agatha Gare of Wyoming has information indicating the Gares were Huguenots in the Rebellion of France in the 1700s. The name at that time was Le Gare.

GAST, Elmer and Sarah

Elmer Wesley Gast (1880-1963) of Indiana and Sarah Hill Stone (1882-1974) of Michigan were married January 17, 1906. They had two daughters and a son, Vesta, Veryle and Loren.

The family immigrated to Kerwood in 1917. Their first night was spent at the O'Neill House in Kerwood.

Elmer and Sarah moved to Metcalfe Township, where Elmer worked for a cattle dealer, Charlie Murby. Eventually they bought a farm in Appin, but due to the Depression were forced to move to the Second Line of Adelaide Township, where they farmed for many years. Another daughter, Doris (1924), was born.

In 1953, Elmer and Sarah bought a house in Strathroy, where they enjoyed their retirement. They belonged to the Presbyterian Church and Sarah was very active in the W.M.S.

GEORGE, Edwin and Florence

The George family came to Canada from Twyford, England, about 1857. They came to the Arkona area and lived just north of the Ausable River. They stayed there for about 10 years and then moved near St. Thomas in Elgin County and then to the Shetland area of Lambton County.

George James George, was four years old when he came to Canada. He married Sarah Rickard in 1877. They had three sons and one daughter, all born at Shetland. The three sons went to

Saskatchewan. Edwin (d.1950) married Florence McPherson (d.1947) of Chatham, and they homesteaded near the town of Willow Bunch, Saskatchewan.

In 1937, Edwin and Florence returned to Ontario with their two sons, George and Lyle. They farmed in the Ingersoll area and in 1940, their eldest son, George came to Adelaide Township. He purchased a farm on the corner of Con. 4 NER and the Kerwood Road. In 1945, Edwin and family purchased the George Matthews farm in Kerwood. They moved to Kerwood in the spring of 1946.

When Florence died, Lyle purchased the farm from his father. He married Marion Muxlow, daughter of Archie and Ethel (Martin) Muxlow, on April 2, 1949. They have two children, Ronald Lyle (1950) and Sandra Marion (1956). In 1974, they moved to Strathroy and presently live at 306 Strathroyal Avenue.

Sandra married Rick Heinbuck in 1976 and they have two children, Derek and Janna. They live in Strathroy. Ron married Susan Hickey in 1991, and they live in London.

Edwin and Florence are buried in Strathroy Cemetery.

GEORGE, George and Doris

In September 1939, George and Doris George purchased the Ben Herrington farm at Lot 6, Con. 5 NER, moving in the following March.

The Georges had a couple of cows and four horses, and as time went on, they built up a milk herd by buying Holstein calves and waiting for them to become a paying proposition. Doris spent the summer and fall picking fruit. At only a few cents a box, it was a slow way to get rich, but each winter they had a supply of fruit, which was an extra bonus.

During the winter of 1941-1942, Fred Glover got George a job driving a truck for Clayton Edwards, picking up livestock for the Watford stock sale every Friday. The men were in Watford by 8:00 a.m., and after the sale was over, the truck was hired by the farmers to take their purchases home. If George had a good night, he returned at midnight and sometimes later. His pay was $1.00.

There were a few good crops and the calves became cows. Times were better, so the Georges started a family, and two daughters were born, Joanne (1949) and Lorraine (1951).

George had several attacks of sciatica and was laid up for short periods. He had a severe attack on January 1, 1954, and was a bed patient until well into June. Doris ran the farm with help from Dave Grogan, Bob Cathers, Earl Alderson, Morley Carson and Ross Herrington, who sent his two boys to stook, as well as many others. One day, George was lamenting about being no good at helping with chores, etc. Joanne said, "Never mind, Daddy, we'll keep you anyway, even you aren't any good."

In 1942, the Georges bought the south half of the north half of Lot 7 NER, for pasture, and then sold this property in 1974 to Martin Peeters.

Doris returned to her teaching career, and George returned to farming, but eventually rented the farm and went to work in the trailer plant in Strathroy.

From 1954 to 1974, George served on Adelaide Council. Because the hall was usually very cold, he carried a wool blanket to wrap himself in. He served under Reeves Angus McLean, Eugene Earley, and Charlie Nichols.

In 1974, Doris retired from teaching. Joanne had graduated with a Registered Nurse designation, but chose to work on a dude ranch in Bragg Creek, Alberta. Lorraine graduated as a Registered Nurse and was employed at a hospital in Kenora, Ontario.

The farm was sold to Joe Minten, and the Georges bought their present home in Strathroy.

GEORGE, James and Mary Ann

Samuel and Jane George lived in Twyford, Buckinghamshire, England, and had nine children, five of whom came to Canada, William (1813-1895); Richard, Jane, Benjamin and Samuel. Jane is buried in England. In 1879, William returned to England and brought his father, who was then 80 years of age, back to Canada. They were 11 weeks on the sailing vessel crossing the Atlantic Ocean. Samuel lived to be 92.

William, the eldest son, married three times, twice in England. By the first marriage (name of wife unknown), there were four children, Richard, Mary Ann, George and William Jr., who died crossing the ocean at age two. William, with his second wife, came to Canada in 1845 and lived near Arkona. In February 1853, he was ordained a Baptist minister in Lobo.

The Ken George family, L-R, Ron K. George, Margaret (George) Evoy, Doris (George) Kubecz, Evelyn (Pennington) George and Kenneth Brent George.

Mary Ann (1839-1899), the second child in the first family of William, married her first cousin, James George, son of her father's brother, Richard, and they lived in Adelaide Township, at the east half of Lot 11, Con. 2 NER. Mary Ann and James had eight children.

Albert (1867) married Maud Johnson. They had a son and moved out of the area. Lavina (1870-1898) married John Thompson. They had one son, and moved away. Charles (1872-1949) married Rebecca Clelford (1878-1957) of Adelaide Village in 1897. They had six daughters and two sons. They lived in Adelaide for a number of years, then in Glencoe where he taught school. James (1875-1921) married Mabel Brent (1885-1945) of Adelaide Township in September 1915. Mabel was an organist at St. Ann's Anglican Church for a number of years. They lived on the family farm, where he built a beautiful brick house. They had three children, Doris, Kenneth "Ken," and James.

Doris married Melvin Dowding in 1941, and they live at the west half of Lot 8, Con. 3 SER. They have two daughters. Judith "Judy" married William Morgan in 1970, and they have two daughters and a son, Jackie, Kim, and Andy. Karen married Nelson Nichols in 1979. They live in Strathroy and have one daughter, Emma.

Ken attended school at S.S. #4, and S.D.C.I. for two years. At the age of 16, he started farming the family farm at the east half of Lot 11, Con. 2. In 1956, he worked for Midrim Drilling, operating a diamond drill which was used to mine salt. In 1960, he drove a school bus at Adelaide Central School. In 1970, he worked at Murray's Feed Mill in Kerwood, but unfortunately, the mill burned. Ken was then hired at United Co-operatives in Glencoe as a feed truck driver. He worked there for 13 years, until he retired.

Ken married Margaret Evelyn Pennington, and they have three children, Margaret Elizabeth (1947); Ronald Kenneth (1949); and Doris Elaine (1960).

Margaret attended S.S. #9 and S.S. #4. On February 1, 1960, the new Adelaide Central School opened. Margaret attended S.D.C.I., and then in 1966 was accepted at St. Joseph's School of Nursing in Hamilton. She graduated as a registered nurse in 1969. She is now in charge of the Recovery Department at St. Joseph's Hospital, where she has been employed since graduation. Margaret married John Kenneth Evoy on September 27, 1969. They have three children, Carol Ann Margaret (1970); Sean Kenneth Douglas (1974); and Krista Susan Denise (1977). Carol Ann works in a retail fabric store, and Sean attends Brock University in St. Catharines. Krista is a hairdresser in Oakville.

Ron attended S.S. #9, S.S. #4, Adelaide Central, and S.D.C.I. After high school, he spent two years with Community Telephone Company and many years with Bell Canada. Ron married Femmy Winters on February 17, 1978. They live on a farm in McGillivray. Ron and Fem have two children, Susan Monica (1980) and Mark Ronald (1982).

George family ca.1900, back L-R, Tom, William James, Charles; front, L-R Albert, Mary, Rebecca, Nelson.

Susan is working as an esthetician in London, and Mark attends North Middlesex Collegiate. His interests include poetry, and he has been involved in school theatrical productions.

Doris, the youngest of Ken and Margaret's children, attended Adelaide Central until the family moved to Strathroy in 1971. After graduation from S.D.C.I., she worked at London Life for 14 years, and is currently employed with CIBC Mellon in London. Doris married Tibor Kubecz, and they have one son, Christopher Steven (1989).

James, third child of James and Mabel, married Catherine Aldridge of St. Marys. They lived in London for a number of years, and are now in Welland. Their son, Barry, has a son and daughter. Their daughter, Sheila, married Joe Petruzella, and they have a son and daughter.

Nelson, fifth child of Mary Ann and James, was a prominent London physician for 40 years. He was born in Adelaide Township, taught school in Warwick and S.S. #4 Adelaide, and was a business college teacher in London before entering University of Western Ontario Medical School, from which he graduated in 1909. At U.W.O., he distinguished himself in athletics, was president of the Athletic Society, and set a number of records in Track and Field events. Before commencing his practice, he interned at Victoria Hospital. During his career, he was a member of the Academy of Medicine and was on the staff of Victoria Hospital for several years. In 1912, he married Laura Diprose of London, formerly of Strathroy. They had no children.

Thomas (1881-1908) married Laura Conkey in 1907. They had two children and moved out west.

Mary (1883-1919) married Wellington Clendinning and lived at Banner near Thamesford. They had a son and daughter.

Sara (1875), the youngest child of Mary Ann and James, died at age 15.

GERRY, David and Jemima

Henry and Jane Gerry (1790) of Cornwall, England, and their two children, Sarah (1827) and Richard (1829), came by boat to Port Stanley and settled in Union, Ontario. Richard married Agnes Williamson Walker and they had seven children, Henry, James "Jim," Sarah, David, Richard, Mary and Emma.

Aggie Fletcher, Olive Gerry Payne, Gertrude McLean Fletcher, Myrtle Gerry Davis, and James Lesley Gerry.

David Franklin Gerry married Jemima "Mimie" Campbell in 1891. They moved into a log house in an orchard at Lot 18, Con. 3 NER. Their firstborn was a son, John Franklin "Frank" (1892).

One fine spring day, Dave and Mimie harnessed up the horse and wagon and went to town for supplies, leaving little four-year-old Frank with the hired man. He cooked eggs for breakfast and a spark from the chimney set the roof on fire. They came home to charred ruins. The granary was their home until the existing yellow brick house was built that summer.

David was a barn builder and his brother, Jim, was a house builder. His specialty was ornate cutout work on porches and stairways. Dave and his crew

Nola Bell Gerry with great-grandson, Alex James Dymond, one day old, 1995.

built the existing Gerry barn in 1905. The cost of a new barn in those days was $100, which included everything from cutting timber in the bush to a finished barn. They would take wagons, equipment, and a crew, and stay until the barn was completed. David and Jemima had another son, Archibald Campbell (1905), 13 years to the day from the birth date of their first child.

Frank married Erma Isobel James on October 6, 1971. They moved to London and had two sons, David James and Mansell Campbell.

Archibald married Nola Bell Desjardine on May 4, 1935. They stayed on the family farm and had two daughters. Mina Jean (1941) married Kenneth Johnston and they now live in Los Angeles, California. Mary Lou (1944) married James Allan Dymond and they live in Metcalfe Township. Mary Lou and James had two children, James Allen (1963) and Julie Elizabeth (1965).

James Gerry Sr., 1935.

James "Jamie" and Heather Wilton were married April 14, 1984, and built a house on Lot 18, Con. 3 NER (29863 Robotham Road). They started a dairy farm two years later. They have four children, Eric James (1988); Alannah Heather (1991); Alex James (1995); and Craig James (1997).

Nola Gerry still lives in the original Gerry house.

GERRYTS, Harry and Tina

Harry Gerryts (d.1994) and his wife, Tina (Bruinsma) Gerryts (d.1995), lived on the Second Line North, Lot 26, Con. 2. They had seven children, Lucy (Daniels), George, Angeline (Noordhof), Sidney, Tracy (Noordhof), Albert and Fay (Creasey).

The Gerryts moved to Canada in 1951 from the Netherlands and lived in different areas of Ontario until 1966, when they moved to Adelaide Township. They bought their farm from John and Catherine Noordhof, who ironically became the in-laws of both Angeline and Tracy (see NOORDHOF, John and Catherine). The girls often wonder if this arrangement was written into the purchase agreement when their parents bought the farm!

Although Harry was a truck driver, he and Tina enjoyed being hobby farmers. The family has many memories such as the snowstorms of the 1970s, the trials of using the four-party-line telephone, and euchre parties at Crathie Hall.

The original farmhouse burned down in 1977, and a new house was built. In 1989, Harry retired and they sold the farm and moved to Kettle Point.

GIFFEN, William and Mary

The Giffen property was the corner farm at Sideroad 24 and Highway 22. It was purchased in 1868 by William James Giffin (Giffen) from the Church Society of the Diocese of Huron. William was born and raised in Ekfrid Township and, for some years, resided in Plympton near Forest. He moved to Main Road, Adelaide Township, where he resided until he retired to Strathroy.

He and his wife, Mary (Janes), had seven children, William Charles (d.1967); Thomas; Frank, who became a dentist; Jenny, who married Herb Hall of Arkona; May, who married Ed Hull of Windsor; Annie; and Susie, who became an R.N.

William Charles married Annie Robotham (d.1967) of Adelaide Township on October 25, 1911.

They had two daughters, Helen Marie (deceased), who married Jack Colvin and lived in Lobo Township; and Evelyn Janes, who married James Charlton Sinker, and lives in Lobo Township.

Charles and Annie provided accommodations for tourists, including rooms and chicken dinners from 1927 to 1930. They also sold gas and operated a booth with soft drinks, ice cream, candy, etc. They met many interesting people from all over the U.S. and Canada. They lived on the farm until 1952, when they sold it to Mr. De Groot and Mr. Vanderbeeten. They built a new home in Poplar Hill, where they resided until their deaths.

GLENN, George and Margaret

In 1840, George Glynn (1809-1869) purchased 200 acres being Lot 16, Con. 1 NER, from Shepherd McCormick, a retired naval officer, for 10 shillings an acre or a total of £100. For the next 140 years, the east 100 acres of this lot became home to direct descendants of George Glynn.

George Glynn had been born near the town of Gort, County Gallaway, Ireland, and immigrated to Canada in 1832. The 1842 census reported that George Glynn was single and living on the property. Sometime in the mid-1840s George married Margaret Morrison (d.1853), who had been born in Scotland. George and Margaret had one son, James (1847-1913). By 1851, George had sold the west half of Lot 16.

George Glynn remarried, and he and his second wife, Mary (d.1879), had a son, George, (1855-1934), and a daughter, Catherine (1856). The 1861 census reported that the family lived in a single-story log house. In later life, the son, George, recalled that he and his sister had done their homework by firelight because candles and oil were scarce and expensive.

When George Glynn died, Mary and the two teenagers were left to run the farm. The elder son, James, had left Adelaide to study law. He set up a practice in St. Thomas, and in the late 1800s, many aspiring lawyers in the St. Thomas and Elgin County area trained in his law office under his tutelage. He was also one of the founding fathers of the St. Thomas Times Journal.

Mary Glynn and her son continued to farm the east half of Lot 16 until her death, when her son, George, took over the farm. The daughter, Catherine, became an elementary school teacher and taught in local schools. She married a Mr. Loud and moved to Romeo, Michigan.

Leota and Susan Giffen

The James and Mary Ann (Janes) Giffen family. Front L-R, James Franklin, Annie; middle L-R, James Giffen (father), William Charles, Thomas Allen, Mary Ann (mother); back L-R, Susan, Jennie, Mae.

In 1880, George Glynn married Margaret McKenzie (1861-1935), daughter of James and Margaret (Matthews) McKenzie. Margaret was raised on the east half of Lot 21, Con. 1 SER. After their marriage, the couple took up residence on George's farm. They continued clearing the land, removing stumps, and draining swampy areas. During their residency, the house that had replaced the old log building of 1851 was enlarged and bricked over. A large bank barn was built under the foremanship of Jack Drake, who resided on the east half of Lot 17, Con. 1 SER. In the late 1800s, the name Glynn was officially changed to Glenn. George and Margaret raised seven children.

The eldest daughter, Lulu (1881), married Leonard McKeen, and they farmed on the west half of Lot 15, Con. 2 NER.

Orville (1883) graduated in 1905 from the University of Western Ontario Medical School. He set up his medical practice at Wardsville, Ontario, where he practiced as a family doctor until his retirement.

Leonard (1888) graduated from the U.W.O. Medical School in 1912, and after additional training became a general surgeon in Chatham, Ontario.

Fred (1890-1919) purchased a farm on the concession north of Egremont Road. There is no indication that Fred actually lived on this property, but he did work with his brother, George. He never married and died during an influenza epidemic.

George B. (1893-1964) was the member of the family who made a lifelong contribution to Adelaide.

Laura (1895) attended London Normal School and became an elementary school teacher. In the 1920s, she moved to Windsor and taught there until her retirement in 1956.

Madeline (1897) graduated from St. Joseph's Hospital School of Nursing in Chatham in 1921. She pursued a career in nursing and eventually moved to California, where she was a nursing supervisor at Scrip's Memorial Hospital in La Jolla.

George Sr. bought two other properties on Egremont Road, a 100-acre farm at the east half of Lot 14, Con. 1 NER, and a 50-acre farm being part of Lot 14. He served as a trustee for S.S. #10 Adelaide for many years. Even though he had sold the home farm to his son, George, in 1928, he and Margaret continued to live on the property until his death, his wife dying a year later.

George B., the fifth child of George and Margaret, lived most of his life in Adelaide. In 1916, he purchased the west half of Lot 17 NER from Henry Tarrant and farmed there but continued to live in the family home. After the death of his brother, Fred, George took over Fred's farm on the Second Line North. He rebuilt the General Store in Adelaide Village, which had burned previously. He lived in the apartment above the store that he operated. He married Amanda Nichols (d.1981) in 1928 and the following year, they sold the store and moved to the family farm on the east half of Lot 16. George and Amanda raised six children there, Madelon, George, Margaret, Leonard, Marlene and James.

The family attended St. Anne's Anglican Church and took an active part in the activities of the church. From time to time, various members of the family sang in the choir, taught Sunday school, acted as interim Sunday School Superintendents, and as assistant organists. At this time, many of the social activities of the community, such as card parties and dances, concerts and garden parties, were sponsored by church organizations. Members of the family always took part in the planning and promotion of these events.

After the death of his father, George B. purchased the east half of Lot 14, Con. 1 NER.

For many years, George was a trustee of S.S. #10. He was a strong supporter of the concept of area school boards and worked tirelessly to establish the first Adelaide Township School Board. He served on that Board for several years. He also

Children in back row, L-R, Fred, Laura, Lulu, Orville and wife Florence, Madeline and George; front, George and Margaret, ca.1918.

served for some years on Township Municipal Council. In 1960, their children, with the exception of James, had moved from Adelaide.

Madelon taught for a few years in rural schools before moving to London. She graduated with a BA from U.W.O. and taught for the London Board of Education. She continued to reside in London after her marriage.

George farmed with his father for a short time. He trained as an accountant and worked at London Life. He married and resided in London.

Margaret completed a B.Sc. at U.W.O. and worked in the pathology laboratory at Parkwood Hospital. She married and resided in London.

Leonard farmed with his father and brother, James, for several years. He left the farm and moved to London, where he and his wife resided.

Marlene taught in Strathroy for a short time. After she married, she lived in London for a few years but she and her husband later moved to the Kitchener area.

James, the youngest son of George and Amanda, took over the family farm in 1960. He and his wife, Marilyn, purchased the west half of Lot 16, Con. 1 NER, thereby bringing the original land back under Glenn ownership. James served on the local school board. James, Marilyn, and their children, Robert and Lisa, were members of the church. In 1980, they severed a piece of land from the front of the farm, built a new home, and sold the remaining farm. They later sold this property and moved to Strathroy, ending the Glenn family's 140-year residency in Adelaide Township.

GLOVER, James and Eliza

James Glover (1833) was born in Lincolnshire, England. He came to Canada as a young man with his brother, William, and sister, Elizabeth (Glover) Colton. James settled in Adelaide Township on what is now Langdon Road, one mile west of Keyser's Corners. He married Eliza Anderson (1836), who was born in Adelaide Township. They built a new home, which still stands on Langdon Road. James and Eliza had five children, Sarah E. (1865, died an infant); John Thomas (1867-1895); James Henry (1868-1871); William Wilmore (1874, died an infant); Annie Louise (1879-1962).

John Thomas, the second child of James and Eliza, married Nellie Russell and lived on the home farm. They had two sons, Fred William (1892-1967) and Franklin Russell, who later moved to Detroit, where he died and was buried. Fred married Lena Oakes in 1921, and they had no children. He later moved to Arkona.

Annie Louise, youngest child of James and Eliza, attended Keyser's school when it was built on the hill. The students helped to carry the maps, books, etc., from the old school up the hill to the new school. She was just a young student but Annie remembered the move in the 1880s. She married Charles Wallace Gilbert (1871) of West Williams on April 19, 1905. They moved to West Williams and later moved back to the Fourth Line of Adelaide Township, on Langdon Road, east of Keyser's. Annie and Charles had 12 children, Wallace (d.1933); Erla Winnifred (1906-1984), who married a Fuller; Mary Gertrude (1908-1994), who married a Dove; Myrtle Louise (1909-1992), who married an Orr; Russell James (1910-1983); Thomas Grant (1912), who moved to Clarkston, Michigan; Lawrence Wallace (1913-1974); Irene Glover (1915), who married a McEachen and moved to Sarnia; Joe Verdun (1917-1977); Ernest Lloyd George (1918), who moved to London; Doris Laverne (1920), who married a Glenn and moved to Forest; and Donna Grace Gilbert (1923), who moved to Forest. Doris and Donna were born in Adelaide Township.

GOATCHER, Stephen

Stephen Goatcher of Pulborough, Sussex, was Superintendent of the Party who traveled in the ship "Eveline," one of the three ships carrying immigrants from Sussex to Upper Canada under the Petworth Immigration Scheme in 1832. His wife stayed behind in England. They traveled to Montreal in seven weeks, much longer than expected as the passage was rough, then in steamboats to York and to the Niagara River in schooners, through the Welland Canal on Niagara Falls, finally arriving in Kettle Creek. They completed the last 25 miles over land. In a letter written to his wife shortly after arrival in Adelaide, he said he had a great deal of trouble feeding 250 people every day. During the voyage, he lived with Captain Royal in his cabin and dined on fresh meat and fowl. Once settled, he found things were dear, and the flies and mosquitoes were numerous and troublesome. Stephen did not stay long in Adelaide, likely finding the pioneer life too harsh. Records appear to indicate he went to Melbourne, where he ran an inn. An article in the May 1933 "Age" relates how Adelaide Township was almost renamed "Goatcher" by a surveyor general, who considered changing the township's name in honour of Stephen Goatcher, one of the leading settlers for a short time.

GODDARD, Robert and Carolyn

Robert W. Goddard (1945) was born in Inverness, Scotland. He immigrated to Canada in November 1947 and lived in London. His hobbies are music and restoring old cars. His job is Occupational Health and Safety Officer for the Ministry of Labour. He is involved with several car clubs for the Sunshine Foundation.

Robert married Carolyn R. Bartlett (1947), who was born in St. John, New Brunswick. She moved to the London area in November 1948. Her hobbies are gardening, sewing and crafts. Carolyn is employed by Greendale Garden Products as a Southern Ontario Sales Representative. She belongs to the Strathroy Agricultural Society and the 4-H Horse and Home Making Clubs. In 1997, she was an Adelaide Councillor.

Robert and Carolyn have two children, Laura Leigh-Anne (1966) and Shelley Lyn (1968), both born in London. They attended school at Adelaide Public School and S.D.C.I.

Laura married Randy Wells of Strathroy and has two children, Amanda and Derick. They live in Ailsa Craig.

Shelley married Karl Cable of Arkona and has three children, Mark, Britteny and Bradley. They live in Strathroy.

GOLDRICK, Edward and Elizabeth

Squire Edward Goldrick (1815-1882), born in Dublin, Ireland, came to Canada about 1834. He taught school for a short time. In 1835, he began to purchase property with his savings and, after several property transactions, he settled on the north half of Lot 13, Con. 12 SER. He received the crown deed in 1847, and in 1869, he conveyed the west 50 acres to his son, Edward.

Edward married twice. First, about 1838, he married Elizabeth Jackson (1811-1851), daughter of John Flack Jackson (1784-1849) and his wife, Margaret. Elizabeth died of consumption at 40 years of age. Edward and Margaret had six children, Martha "Maria" (1839-1924); Gillman W. (1840-1909); Margaret J. (1843); Edward (1845-1911); Agnes "Nancy" (1849-1927); and Olive Elizabeth "Lizzie" (1852-1942).

In May 1852, Edward married the widow Sarah Penwarden (1831-1864) from Metcalfe Township, who had been born in England. The witnesses to this marriage were Thomas B. Winter and Maria L. Cook. The 1852 census showed a Caroline as his wife, so likely her name was Sarah Caroline Penwarden. Sarah's husband had frozen to death in 1851 according to the Metcalfe census. Sarah had four young children, but they were not living with them after she married Edward Goldrick. Perhaps they remained with family on the Penwarden side in Ekfrid or went to live with relatives in Elgin County. Edward and Sarah had three children, Albert "Bert" (ca.1860-1864); Edgar "Ted" (1861-1923); and Annie (1864, died a baby).

After the death of his first wife, Edward had purchased the store and hotel in Napier from Mr. Winter and the family lived there for some time. When Edward remarried, he returned to the farm. When Metcalfe set up their first Council in March 1851, Edward was appointed Clerk and was re-elected several times. The 1857 directory listed Edward as a

Robert and Carolyn Goddard family, clockwise, Robert, Carolyn, Shelley and Laura Goddard, 1981.

Edward Goldrick's log cabin.

merchant. He was a lay preacher and also the local magistrate. He was presented with a surveyor's chain to assess boundaries and such. The 1878 Atlas indicates that Edward Goldrick owned Lot 6, Con. 7; Lot 7, Con. 8; and Lot 13, Con. 12 Metcalfe (Lot 13 being his son, Edward's, by then). In 1851, they were members of the Wesleyan Methodist church, but when the Presbyterian Church was built in Napier, the family attended there. Edward and his two wives were buried in Brown's Cemetery, Metcalfe. Of the nine children, only two married and raised a family.

Maria, the eldest of Edward and Margaret's children, never married and lived with her sister, Lizzie, and brother, Ted, in the log cabin on the family farm. She was buried in Strathroy Cemetery.

Gillman W. married Elizabeth McIlwain (1847-1938), daughter of James and Clarissa (Martin) McIlwain, in 1868. Gillman farmed 50 acres, the west half of the north half of Lot 15, Con. 12, Metcalfe Township. Their children, all born in Metcalfe Township, were Clarissa, Trueman, Maria, Jerome, William and Frank.

Margaret J. married Jack Mann and farmed near Dutton, Ontario. They had four children, Ward, Wesley, Jack and Helen.

Edward married Mary Jane Robbins (ca.1841), daughter of Job and Christianna Robbins, in 1867. They farmed in Metcalfe Township. Edward and Mary Jane had 10 children, Gilman, John, Lawrence, James, Margaret, Edward, Herbert, Minnie, Maud and Mary "Ellie."

Nancy never married and lived for years in Dorchester with the Treharn family. She became an accomplished tailor and lived for many years in Chatham.

Lizzie never married. She is mentioned in the Napier History Books and gave an interview at 90 years of age, which is quoted herein. She lived with her sister and brother in the log cabin on the family farm. She could knit so fast that she could knit a sock in one evening. After her brother and sister died, she went to live with her nephew, James, and his family. She is buried in Strathroy Cemetery.

Bert, the eldest of Edward and Sarah's children, died in childhood and was buried in Brown's Cemetery, Metcalfe Township.

Ted never married. He lived with his unmarried sisters in the log cabin and farmed on the homestead. He is buried in Strathroy Cemetery.

Annie was buried in Brown's Cemetery, Metcalfe Township.

The following story is from an interview given by Miss Elizabeth Goldrick to Myrtle E. Home in June 1940.

"Miss Elizabeth Goldrick, who will celebrate her 91st birthday if she lives until August 24, declares that hard work never kills; in fact, she can account in no other way for her advanced age than by attributing it to the continuous struggle which pioneer days demanded of every woman as well as man.

Only two years of age when her mother died, she and her sisters, Maria, Nancy and Margaret, were early initiated into all kinds of household tasks. There were meals to be cooked every day for three brothers, Edgar, Edward and Gilman, and their father, and the equipment for such cooking was of the most primitive kind. Miss Goldrick recalls that at one time there was a period of six weeks in which they had no bread whatever, the mill in Alvinston, where their flour was usually ground, having broken down. She does not remember what they ate in place of bread, but they managed to exist. She also recalls a family living five miles distant who had absolutely nothing to eat for the same length of time excepting what the cows ate. To avoid using poisonous herbs, they followed the cows to the woods, and what they ate the family gathered too and cooked it, and on it subsisted until their crops were harvested.

In her early days, the Indians wandered through the forests surrounding her home, and it was no unusual sight to see 25 ponies with squaws mounted on them go by, the Indian braves on foot. Always the mother carried the papoose strapped onto a board, the board strapped to her back. One time when the family was alone in the house three Indians came in drunk, and one was so 'beastly' the children were terrified. These Indians wanted to stay all night, and they were told they might do so if they would sleep in the barn. In the morning, when the boys went out to do the chores, they found the cattle and stock all fed and the Indians gone. On another occasion they had a piece of meat in the kettle cooking over the fireplace, when an Indian named Black Hawk came in, took a fork and removed the meat from the kettle, and walked off with it without so much as 'by your leave.'

Miss Goldrick, who now lives with her nephew James Goldrick and his family on the old homestead, is the last surviving member of the family of Edward Goldrick, who as a young man of 19 came to this country from the neighborhood of Dublin, Ireland. For a time he taught school. Then, with the money he had saved, he bought a block of 85 acres in the heart of the forest, about a mile and a half from the present village of Napier. Presently came a chance to sell it for the sum of $20, after which he took up a farm adjoining it (the Goldricks still own this land, but now it is separated from the homestead by a road). The purchaser of Mr. Goldrick's farm cut down trees and put up the framework of a log house. The next year, meeting Mr. Goldrick one day, he said, 'If I had my $20 back again I'd make better use of it.' 'Well, here it is,' said Mr. Goldrick, handing him the money. And so the property became once more Mr. Goldrick's, and has ever since remained in the family. Miss Elizabeth's father then completed the log house, which, measuring 18 feet by 24 feet, boasted three rooms downstairs and two upstairs. The big logs (with much of the bark on) forming the outer walls of this pioneer home are still standing as a memorial to the energy and good craftsmanship of these early builders. As a matter of fact, this first house was lived in by the Goldrick family—one brother and two sisters always remaining here—until the present home was built by the nephew James, who has worked the farm since his uncle's death.

When Mr. Goldrick remarried they moved back to the farm again, and the children attended Yager's school (S.S. No.5). For several years after her father settled here there was no church and services were held once a month in the different homes by a visiting minister. Then for a time the Rev. Mr. Hutton preached in Yager's school. When the Presbyterian Church was built in Napier the family attended there

Miss Elizabeth recalls, her first teacher [at the Napier school] was Miss Toar, and another was Alex Leitch. In that early school there was a long desk down the middle of the room with benches on either side for the pupils, the boys occupying one side and the girls the other. There were large families in these days and Miss Goldrick remembers when Miss Campbell had 120 on the roll at one time. This teacher later married Mr. Dunlop, who owned and operated the sawmill in the village and made cheese boxes.

Miss Goldrick remembers well when the Napier road was chopped out. The first man to undertake this job gave up in despair and the work was completed by Jimmie Denshaw and his mother. The first man to drive over it was Thomas Winter, grandfather of George and Leo Winter, who own farms neighboring the Goldrick home.

There were many hardships in those early days, according to Miss Goldrick. She recalls that her father took a bag of maple sugar on his back and walked through the woods to Kilworth, a distance of 20 miles. There he sold it and with the proceeds bought his first logging chain. Settlers walked this distance too, carrying a bag of wheat to be ground at Woodhull's mill at Kilworth. Their grain was taken by team and wagon to market at St. Thomas. Before the Goldricks had horses and implements, however, haying and harvesting were laborious tasks. The hay was cut with a scythe and raked up by hand. Then Mr. Goldrick went into the woods and got four poles, two long ones and two short ones. He fastened the short ones across the long ones placed parallel; then he and his wife, each taking an end of this improvised rack, brought the hay into the barn. The grain was cut with a sickle and threshed with a flail. Then, Miss Goldrick further recalls, there came a time when her father and four other men went to London and bought the first threshing outfit in that section. It was the old 'spike' type and was replaced in a few years by a more modern outfit. With the early wood-burning engines that succeeded these, sparks often caused fires. As an emergency measure the engineer always kept a tub of water handy. On one occasion, when but a little girl watching the machine, Miss Elizabeth was held up by the engineer and told to pull a string, which she could just grasp. She did so, and was so astonished and frightened by the raucous whistle that she fell backwards and landed in the tub of water.

One other day, the roof of their barn caught fire in some manner and, the men being away, her mother undertook to save it. She climbed on the roof and pulled off three blazing boards, but in doing so fell back into the barn. She was not seriously hurt, but the barn was destroyed.

In this neighborhood in the early days dancing provided the merriest times, 'Old Dan Tucker' proving the most popular dance, although the settlers varied it with 'Two Sisters,' Scotch Reels and 'French Four.' Before fiddles came to the district Miss Goldrick's brother and another man would take turns in singing for the dancers. One can imagine that for these two at any rate a dance was not altogether a time of pleasurable relaxation.

Although almost 91 years old, Miss Goldrick has retained her faculties to a remarkable degree, her eyesight alone being impaired so that she can no longer enjoy reading and knitting, lifelong hobbies of hers."

GOSDEN

The names of brothers, John (1806-1886) and Edward Gosden (1811) have been found on the paylists of those persons who worked on the construction of the Egremont Road and the Currie Road (road running north and south between Lots 6 and 7) in 1832. On those same paylists, the names of Michael Griffin (Griffiths) and James McMurrey (McMurray) are included, and the families of these men play an important role in the Gosden family.

The search by descendants of this family, in an attempt to reconstruct its history, has been long and arduous, and much is still yet to be uncovered. At this time, this is their story in Adelaide.

Edward Gosden was born in England (possibly West Sussex) and there married Elizabeth McFarland (1774-1875), also of England. They had at least five children, all born in England, John D. (1806-1886); William (1810); Edward (1811); Harriet (ca.1813-1875); and Sarah (ca.1815). There may have been a fourth son, James, as his name appears as farmer and owner of the east half of Lot 4, Con. 7 SER, on the 1842 agricultural census of Adelaide.

Even though this family arrived in 1832, none of its members appear to have been granted a patent from the Crown.

The first census of Adelaide in 1842 was primarily an agricultural census, strong in agricultural data but including only the names of the heads of households. In this census of 1842 are found records for John Gosden (east half of Lot 11, Con. 6 SER); James Gosden (east half of Lot 4, Con. 7 SER); Edward Gosden (east half of Lot 4, Con. 6 SER); Michael Griffith(s) (west half of Lot 7, Con. 5 SER); and Edward McMurray (east half of Lot 3, Con. 7 SER). These men are all farmers and appear to have purchased their land.

John D., eldest son of Edward and Elizabeth, married Anne Burton in Adelaide on August 30, 1834, and the ceremony was probably performed by Dominic Edward Blake. John and Anne had a daughter, Elizabeth Anne (ca.1835). Nothing more is known of her. John's first wife died sometime before 1840, and he remarried, to widow Mary Laffey (ca.1815), on September 30, 1840, in Adelaide. Mary was born in Ireland and may have come to the marriage with two children, but virtually nothing is known about these children. John and Mary had six children, twins Jane (1843-1920) and Emily (1843); Sarah (ca.1844-1887); John D. (1845-1910); William (1847-1878), who was married (wife's identity unknown); and Harriet (1848), who married Edward Corcoran.

Jane married Henry Matthews (1827-1910) of Metcalfe Township. They had at least five children, John (ca.1858); Mary (ca.1859); Emily Jane (ca.1862); William (1866-1943), who married Stella Swayze (1867-1955); and Henry Jr. (1878-1920).

Emily, twin sister of Jane, married John McMurray (ca.1839), son of Michael and Clarissa (Whaley) McMurray, who lived on the east half of Lot 3, Con. 7 SER, in 1842. Michael McMurray (1810), who had worked on the Egremont and Currie Roads, was born in Ireland. John had six known siblings, James (ca.1835); Samuel (ca.1841); Elizabeth (ca.1843), born in Adelaide; Clarissa (ca.1844), born in Adelaide; Mary (ca.1846), born Adelaide; and Bernard (ca.1850), born in Metcalfe Township.

Sarah, third child of John and Mary, married James Griffin (Griffiths), eldest son of Michael Griffiths. Sarah and John had several children; the names known are Mary (d.1880) and James (d.1887). They are buried in Strathroy Cemetery.

Sarah's father-in-law had worked on the Egremont Road with her father. Griffiths was a discharged soldier when he arrived in Adelaide in 1831 or 1832. On May 26, 1836, he received his patent from the Crown for the west half of Lot 7, Con. 5 SER. This land, comprising the entire west part of Kerwood, was sold to William Shepherd on April 24, 1851. Had he retained this parcel for an additional four years, he would have profited from the sale to the railroad. The Gosden family would eventually purchase all of Blocks A and C, Plan 165 [Subdivision plan 165 as registered 23 April 1861].

The land holdings and dealings of the Gosden family are complex and are not fully described here. The following transactions, for the sake of clarity and continuity, are described in terms of the original Adelaide survey of 1832, and should suffice to give the reader an idea of the scope of the Gosden influence. This description does not include land owned by the sons-in-law of the Gosdens. By 1842, the Gosden family owned the east half of Lots 4 and 11, Con. 6 SER, and the east half of Lot 4, Con. 7 SER. On September 3, 1866, John Sr. purchased the southeast part of Lot 6, Con. 5 SER. This land was the location of the Canadian Hotel, the American Hotel, and future site in 1901 of the O'Neil House. John Sr.'s brother, William, purchased another parcel of the east half of Lot 6, Con. 5 SER, on September 14, 1867, from John I. McKenzie. Mary Gosden, probably wife of John Sr., purchased an almost five-acre parcel of the east half of Lot 6, Con. 5 SER, on August 12, 1873, which she held until its sale to William Newton in 1890. At the time of the 1871 census, the Gosden family owned Lot 7 on Con. 7 and 12 SER, and Lot 11, Con. 6. By the early- to mid-1880s, the Gosden family controlled all of Block A and C, Plan 165, in Kerwood. These parcels included the present lots from McKenzie Street, north to and including the Sports Complex, and the Morgan/Winter property at Grace and Cockburn Streets. An interesting and significant instrument appears in the land records dated 27 July 1901 with reference to Lots 1 and 2, Block C, Plan 165 of Kerwood, by which Sarah Griffiths, June Matthews, Harriet Corcoran, John Gosden and wife sold this parcel to Margaret Gosden.

In that there appears to be no evidence of leaseholds on the John D. Gosden Sr. property immediately southwest of the railway (location of O'Neil House), it may be assumed that John built or had built the wood-framed Dominion Hotel, later to be called the American Hotel. He and his son, John D. Jr., owned and operated this hotel until Mary Gosden sold the property to Frederick O'Neil on August 5, 1897. John D. Sr. is buried with other members of the Gosden family in Plot 204 of the Strathroy Cemetery. There is no headstone.

John D. Jr., fourth child of John and Mary, married Margaret Allen (ca.1849-1914), who had been born near Toronto. John and Margaret led an unusual lifestyle. Female descendants have stated that they would not have wanted to be married to John. John was born in Adelaide in that part which was shortly to become Metcalfe. Very shortly after their marriage, he and Margaret moved to Sanilac County, Michigan, where their two daughters were born. Mary Ellen (1873-1955) married Charles Stephen Marshall, son of Charles and Katherine (Cooper) Marshall of Adelaide, and Sarah E. "Sadie" (1876-1943) married Charles C. Driscoll. By 1881, this family had returned to Metcalfe and Kerwood. Details of John D. Jr. are still sketchy, but he could never stay in any one place more than a few years. John was a merchant in Kerwood; he also assisted his father in the hotel business. When John D. Sr. died, John D. Jr. took over the hotel and probably was responsible for its new name, "American Hotel." John was not a man of even, docile temperament. Family stories exist of him having defeated professional boxers from England, and of having received several knife wounds on a train trip that resulted in his partial paralysis. Perhaps a full account of this man will be discovered. John Jr. died in Detroit, Michigan. He and Margaret are buried in Plot 204 at Strathroy Cemetery.

William, brother to John D. Sr. and second son of Edward and Elizabeth, married Lucy Morgan (1814-1898), daughter of David and Lucy (Wellman) Morgan of Adelaide. William and Lucy had a daughter, Lucy Amelia (1847-1929), who died in Detroit, Michigan. William and Lucy moved to Worth Township, Sanilac County, Michigan, by 1860.

Edward, third son of Edward and Elizabeth, married Mary Welsh in 1851 in Metcalfe Township at St. Mary's Anglican Church. Edward and Mary moved to Sanilac County, Michigan, where their first two children were born, and then returned to Ontario, where their next four children were born. This family consisted of John (ca.1859), born in the U.S.; Edward (ca.1861), born in the U.S.; William (ca.1863), born in Ontario; James (ca.1866), born in Ontario; Richard (ca.1868), born in Ontario; and Thomas (ca.1870), born in Ontario.

Harriet, fourth child of Edward and Elizabeth, married George William Neaves (1809-1873) of Adelaide. In 1851, they resided on the east part of Lot 6, Con. 8, Metcalfe (east of Napier). They raised at least nine children, Phoebe (ca.1834); John (ca.1839); Frances M. (ca.1842); Harriet (ca.1840); Caroline (ca.1847); Thomas W. (ca.1850); Emily Jane (ca.1853), who married her first cousin, George Swaffer (ca.1846), at St. Mary's Anglican Church in 1870; George W. (ca.1859); and John M. (ca.1860).

Sarah, the youngest issue of Edward and Elizabeth, married James Swaffer (ca.1810), who had been born in England. James Swaffer/Swoffer/Swafford is still a mysterious figure. Mrs. Field, in her research, denotes James Swaffer as Commander Swaffer, but no other detail is given. Perhaps James commanded a gunboat or supply ship in the Rebellion of 1837. Sarah and Edward raised at least eight children, most born in Adelaide. These were Edward (ca.1834); William (ca.1838); John (ca.1840); James (ca.1842); Elizabeth (ca.1844); George (ca.1846), who married his first cousin, Emily Jane Neaves; Lucy (ca.1849); and Elizabeth (ca.1858-1910), who was born in Michigan and died in Buel Township, Sanilac County, Michigan. The Swaffer family lived on the east half of Lot 4, Con. 6 SER.

At the present time, it is not known if there are descendants of the Gosden family remaining in Ontario. There are many descendants in the U.S. It has been said that John Gosden Sr. was married a third time, to a widow by the name of Mary Welsh. This woman's identity is not known for certain, but the family suggests that it may well have been his brother's mother-in-law.

GOUGH, Steve and Betty

The last three or four generations of Goughs were born and raised in Caradoc Township, Metcalfe Township, the Glencoe area, and Western Canada. Steve was born and raised in Strathroy. His mother and stepfather, Shirley and Jim Merriam, and his brother live in Strathroy. Steve married Betty Joosten, daughter of Mathias and Elisabeth Joosten, who had moved from Holland to Watford in April 1952 with a son and two daughters. Two sons and two daughters were born in Canada. Mathias and Elisabeth live in Uxbridge, Ontario, and celebrated their 50th wedding anniversary in May 1998. The rest of their family live in Uxbridge, Markham, Brampton, North York, Lambeth, Forest and Kerwood. The family now has six sons and daughter-in-laws, 14 grandchildren, and one grandson-in-law.

Steve and Betty have a daughter and son, Kari and Tyler. The family moved to Kerwood in June 1986 from Strathroy.

Steve is a driver for Langs Bus Lines in Strathroy and operates Sky Top Kite, the kite store. Betty works with the administration at Carpet Care & Sales, Strathroy. Kari and Tyler are students at St. Thomas Aquinas High School in London. Kari's interests include Highland dancing and music. Tyler enjoys golfing, hockey, baseball and computer games. Their family includes four pets, Missy and Daisy (the dogs) and Melanie and Raine (the cats).

GRAHAM, Duncan and Mary

In the summer of 1837, John Graham, a weaver from Argyllshire, Scotland, arrived in Beauharnois, Quebec, with his wife, Nancy Livingston. John and Nancy soon moved on to Lobo, where they made their home

John Graham's eldest son, Duncan, lived northwest of Komoka in a white house with green shutters, justifying the name, "Green Shutter Grahams," to distinguish this family from the other Grahams in the area.

In 1861, Duncan and his wife, Mary (Ferguson), moved their family to Adelaide Township and settled on a farm, which they purchased from Adolphus Mahon. This was the east half of Lot 22, Con. 2 NER, which is the second farm east of Crathie Hall.

In 1869, the eldest of Duncan's 11 children, John F. Graham, took ownership of the farm. He and his first wife, Helen (Cawrse), produced nine children, Duncan, Mary, Grace, Charles, Neil, Alexander, Charles, John and Donald.

Graham family, ca.1948. L-R, Russell Oliver, Fred Braithwaite, Nellie Braithwaite, William, Pearl; sitting clockwise, Eva Gladwell, Christena, Arthur Gladwell, Donald, Robert.

After the death of his first wife, Helen, John F. married Sarah Jane Bolton. They had six children, Nellie, William, Annie, Dougald, Florence and Eva.

William married Pearl McAdam and continued operating the family farm. They produced three children, Christena (Gross); Norma (Lewis); and Donald.

Early in his life and in addition to farming, William worked with Harry Anderson drilling water wells and erecting windmills throughout the township. When electric pumps replaced windmills, he installed several farm and residential water systems in the area.

William and Pearl sold the farm to John and Deanna Elliott in 1971 and moved to Strathroy.

Christena and Jim Gross now reside in Port Perry and Norma Lewis lives in Scarborough. Roy Lewis passed away in 1997.

Donald and his wife, Shirley (McLeod), lived in Adelaide Township until 1998, when they moved to Strathroy. They have two sons. Gregory and his wife, Krista, live with their daughter, Makenna, in Toronto. Jeffrey and his wife, Susan, live with their daughter, Alexa, in Fenelon Falls, Ontario.

GREEN, Lee and Hazel

Lee and Hazel (Longstaff) Green moved to Adelaide Township on November 28, 1958, from Florenceville, New Brunswick. Lee had come to Strathroy hoping to see where seed potatoes he had sold in New Brunswick were grown, and he met the Woolley brothers, Earl and John. Earl Woolley mentioned that the Mitchell farm was for sale. Lee had wanted to move to Ontario for some time and finally, at age 50, he did. Lee was a farmer in New Brunswick and he continued to farm both locations for two years. He made many trips back and forth, bringing equipment and two herds of cattle, one Holstein and one purebred Herefords.

Lee and Hazel raised seven children, including Leslie, who lives in Strathroy; Oulton; Franklin; Leah, who lives in New Brunswick; Gideon; Thelma; and Wallace. Wallace was five years old when they moved to this area. He attended S.S. #5 and later Adelaide Central.

Lee has farmed all his life, growing potatoes for table and seed. It is likely that many Adelaide residents have purchased his potatoes over the years. The original barn was built in 1893, and still stands. Lee and Hazel built a new home on the original site in 1972, at Lot 17, Con. 4 SER.

Wallace married Darlene Pierce, and they live at Lot 17, Con. 5 SER, property previously owned by the Wright family. They moved from Strathroy in May 1984, and both work in the community. Darlene was raised in Metcalfe Township and born in Caradoc Township at Lucky Lodge on Highway 2, east of Melbourne. Wallace and Darlene have three sons, Nathan, Adam and Matthew.

GROGAN, Lawrence and May

In the early 1800s, Patrick Thomas Grogan and his wife, Clara, immigrated to Cornisteg, New York, from Monaghan County, Ireland. They had three children, John, Mary and Thomas (1854-1935).

Thomas married Adeline Allison (1845-1907) in 1874. After spending their early married years in Cornisteg, they moved to Toronto, where they resided for 10 years. Thomas and Adeline had one child, Lawrence (1876-1961).

In 1884, they moved to a farm near Arkona where they established a fruit farm. When Adeline died, Thomas sold the farm and purchased the Arkona Hotel, which he operated for many years. Thomas was very active and took a keen interest in baseball, especially watching his grandsons play the game.

Lawrence married May Alfretta Wiley (1878-1957) in 1897, and they made their home in Adelaide on Lot 4, Con. 5 NER. In the early years of their marriage, Lawrence and May grew many acres of apples and berry crops. This style of farming required numerous lengthy trips with horse and wagon from the farm to the London market to sell their produce. In later years, they operated a mixed crop farm. Lawrence and May raised a family of seven children, Marjorie Florene "Flossie" (1902-1987); Marion (1904-1983); Alfred (1907-1973); Ruby (1909-1989); David Thomas (1912-1993); Gordon (1913); and Walter (1916-1973).

Flossie became a public school teacher, and married Carman Hall on August 25, 1925. They resided in Warwick Township, and have one son, Lyle (1926). Flossie graduated from London Normal School in 1921 and taught at S.S. #6 Adelaide from September 1921 to June 1925. In 1941, she began teaching again due to wartime teacher shortages at S.S. #13 West Williams. She continued to teach at school sections in Adelaide (#9, #4, #9, #5, #1, and #2, which also included the Keyser school where she had received her elementary education). Flossie also taught S.S. #7 Kerwood, and retired from teaching in 1968 from Adelaide Township Central School, which is now the W.G. MacDonald School. Lyle married Roberta (last name unknown), and they have two sons, Ross and Andrew. Lyle worked at the post office in London, and lives in the London area.

Marion married Jack Fry, and they had no children. Marion attended Keyser Elementary School and later Strathroy Hospital Nursing School, where she graduated as a Registered Nurse. She practiced her profession for many years in the Strathroy area and resided with her husband, Jack, in Strathroy.

Alfred, third child of Lawrence and May, remained single. He attended Keyser Elementary School and spent most of his years working the home farm, except for a number of years when he worked at the A.C. Spark Plug plant in Flint, Michigan. Alfred was interested in sports and played baseball with many local teams.

Ruby married Reginald Scriven and had one son, Ronald. Ruby attended Keyser Elementary School and Strathroy Collegiate, and graduated from London Normal School in 1935. Ruby taught S.S. #4 Adelaide from 1936-1938; S.S. #12 London Township from 1953-1959; S.S. #25 Westminster Township from 1960-1965; Westminster Central from 1966-1968; and N.B. McEachren from 1969-1975. Ruby and her husband, Reginald, resided in London.

David married Hazel Merle Vernon (1910) on March 31, 1940. They bought a farm at Keyser's Corners and resided there for 37 years. In 1977, they moved to Strathroy, where Hazel still resides and is blessed with wonderful health. They had three children, James Barry (1943); David Glenn (1944-1985); and Carol Lynne (1949). In 1961, two foster children, brother and sister Dan and Linda Coward, joined the Grogan family.

David and Hazel operated a mixed farm, and raised and raced horses and competed at many local racing events. David was an avid sportsman, playing catcher for his brother, Gordon, as they played with the Arkona Giants baseball team. In competition with surrounding city teams, David also coached many boys' and girls' ball teams. He and his wife, Hazel, loved square dancing and he called the moves for square dancing at most of the local social functions.

David and Hazel were quite self-sufficient, milking the cows and using the milk, cream and butter for their daily needs. Chickens and a few pigs were also a common sight around the Grogan farm.

Barry married Sharron Elizabeth Burgess in 1964. They live in Strathroy and are both employed by the Thames Valley Board of Education. Barry and Sharron have two sons, Darren Gregory (1965) and Darryl Jason (1973). Darren married Kim MacDonald in 1988, and they have three children, Gregory James (1990); Shawn Michael (1993); and Bailey Jessica (1994). Darryl married Amanda Pitcher in 1997. Their two children are Karlyn Ivy (1997) and Gavyn David (1998).

David G. is buried in West Adelaide Cemetery with his father, grandparents, and other uncle.

Carol married Glen LeRoy McLean in 1970. Carol is an elementary school teacher for the Thames Valley Board of Education, and Glen manages a powder painting company in London. They reside in Strathroy, after living 23 years in Ekfrid Township. Carol and Glen had three children. David John married Tara Yamamoto in 1997, and they have a son, Brian Edward (1997). Brian Roy (1977-1996) died a young man and is buried in Strathroy Cemetery. Heather Lynne is in her first year of university at U.W.O. The three children attended the same high school as their parents, and even had some of the same teachers.

Lawrence Grogan

John Daniel Roy "Dan" Coward married Marilyn Galsworthy in 1976. They reside on the Galsworthy home farm. Dan is self-employed in the distribution of Abrasive Products and Marilyn works as a nurse at the St. Joseph's Health Center. Their three daughters are Jillian Nicole (1981); Rebecca Lynn (1983); and Jody Lee (1985). Jillian and Rebecca attend St. Thomas Aquinas in London, and Jody is a student at W.G. MacDonald.

Linda Coward now resides in London.

Gordon, sixth child of Lawrence and May, married Ruby Tuplin. They had no children. Gordon attended Keyser Elementary School and Strathroy Collegiate Institute, and graduated from London Normal School. He taught elementary school at North Caradoc School, and later taught for two years in Preston. While there, he was an outstanding pitcher with the Galt Terrier ball team in competition with other Ontario city teams. During this period, he was given an opportunity to try out with the Washington Senators of the American Baseball League; it was a wonderful experience, but he was going to be farmed out to a minor league so he returned to Ontario. Welland Ontario offered Gordon an opportunity to teach and play ball with a semi-pro league, so he began teaching there. While in Welland, he coached two minor league ball teams to Ontario Championships. Sal Maglie, who later was a star with Brooklyn, was one of Gordon's teammates on the Welland Semi-Pro team.

Gordon later moved to Allen Park, Michigan, where he took a teaching position in the Southgate Community. A new school was being built and Gordon was appointed Principal of the 22-room school. While there, he received his B Sc. and his Masters degree from Wayne State University. After 30 years as principal of the school, the community honoured Gordon by renaming the school in 1985 as the Gordon L. Grogan Elementary School. Gordon retired in 1987 and continued working in real estate and assisted his wife, Ruby, with her rose garden.

Walter, youngest child of Lawrence and May, married Elinore Holtz. They had no children. He attended Keyser Elementary School and Strathroy Collegiate, and graduated from London Normal School. He taught for several years at S.S. #16 Bosanquet Township. The school is now a private residence listed as 1880 Hickory Creek Line. He taught and later was Principal of the Amherstburg Central School. His last eight years were as Principal of Colchester School in the Harrow District. Walter also operated a store at Willow Beach near Amherstburg. Walter died during an Easter break while vacationing in Florida, and he was buried in Michigan. In 1998, the Grogan family arranged to have his body exhumed and transferred to the Arkona Cemetery.

GROOT, Adrian and Katrien

Adrian Groot (1922-1987) was born in Binnenwijzend, North Holland, the Netherlands, the son of John and Diewurtje (Lindeboom) Groot. He immigrated to Canada in June 1947 aboard the "Waterman," the first Dutch immigration boat bound for Canada after WWII. He spent his first summer in Manitoba working for relatives, and the first winter in a lumber camp in central Manitoba. For the next two years, he worked as a farm labourer and sharecropper in Blenheim and Tupperville, Ontario.

In early 1950, Adrian went to Holland to visit his family and to collect a small inheritance. He also met and courted his future bride, Catharina (Katrien) Keesom (1926), daughter of Wilhelmus and Johanna (Ruiter) Keesom. Katrien was born in Nieuwe Niedorp, North Holland. Adrian returned to Canada after arrangements were made for a marriage later in the year.

Back in Canada, Adrian looked for a farm in Kent County but found the land expensive. Through contacts, he heard that there were a number of affordable farms in Adelaide Township. These farms lacked buildings, the result of a tornado years earlier. In late summer, he purchased the east half of Lot 14, Con. 3 SER, 50 acres from Ralph Hendra and 50 acres from Harold and Gladys Eastman. It was always said that Adrian's was the third Dutch family to purchase a farm in Adelaide. The van den Boomen brothers were first and Jim Stokman, with his brother-in-law, Peter Verkley, were second. Adrian worked for and lived with the Eastmans until the end of that farm season.

Katrien Keesom arrived in Montreal at the end of October. Adrian met her and they proceeded to the home of her uncle, Johannes Ruiter, and his family. They had immigrated earlier that year to the village of Magog, Quebec. Katrien's father had agreed to the marriage only if she was married with relatives present. On Nov. 4, 1950, Adrian married Katrien Keesom in a little country church in East Bolton, Quebec. After a small celebration, they traveled by train to Strathroy.

They stayed with Harold and Gladys Eastman for a few weeks until the remainder of Katrien's belongings, which were packed in a large crate and shipped separately, arrived by train. Gladys taught Katrien her first English words. Katrien met all her neighbours at a small bridal shower held at the home of Orville and Sheila Down. She didn't know what they were saying, but she felt very welcome.

Much of the Groots' early furniture was purchased at local auction sales. They began to farm cash crops, and purchased a few milking cows. The early years were difficult. Adrian worked at several jobs off the farm. He harvested tobacco, and worked at the glass factory in Strathroy and the feed mill in Kerwood. One year, his sugar beet crop was totally washed out. An addition was built on the barn and Adrian raised pigs for a few years. Also, a small chicken coop was constructed for about 50-75 chickens.

Katrien, with baby Nicholas, went back to Holland to visit her family in 1960. In the 10 years she had been away, her 12 siblings had grown up and several were married. She enjoyed seeing her family again and getting caught up with their lives. Adrian stayed home, and the other children spent the month with family friends.

From 1962 until 1977, the farming operation slowly expanded. The neighbouring farm was purchased from Harold Eastman. This increased the Groots' farm holdings to 200 acres, including the remainder of Lot 14. The milking cows were moved to the larger Eastman barn. In 1962, construction was completed on a milk house with a cooler for milk cans; a bulk tank; a 14'x45' slab cement silo; a free stall barn; a 20'x70' cement silo; an outside auger feeder; more free stalls; a cemented and covered barnyard; a 20'x70' steel sealed silo for hay; a milk pipeline; and a 20'x27' steel sealed silo for high moisture corn. A milking parlor with a new bulk tank was constructed in 1977. The dairy herd grew to about 65 milking cows with 45 young and dry animals. A silo and free stalls were built in the first barn for the young cattle. Machinery was purchased and upgraded until the farm was self-sufficient. In 1980, Adrian and Katrien retired from farming and moved to Strathroy.

Adrian's most successful side business was the growing of cauliflower. Starting with a small acreage, he built his cauliflower business to the point where he supplied all the stores in Strathroy and one in London. His cauliflower developed the reputation as the finest and largest in the township. He also grew Brussels sprouts and various cabbages. Even after his retirement from farming, Adrian continued to grow cauliflower and potatoes on some

Adrian Groot Family

Jim and Mary Margaret Groot family, L-R, Joe, Brian, Mary Margaret, Jim, Laura and Sarah (1996).

rented land just outside Strathroy. He had a regular stall at the Strathroy Farmer's Market.

Eight children were raised on this farm, Divera (1951); Bill (1953); Jim (1955); John (1957); Nick (1959); Patricia (1960); Jeannette (1962); and Debbie (1970), all born in Strathroy. The Groots were members of All Saints Roman Catholic Church. All the children attended and graduated from Our Lady Immaculate School and Strathroy District Collegiate Institute, and they were active in the community. Most participated in 4-H, Junior Farmers, and the church youth group, as well as other church activities.

After getting a BA from Brock University, Divera graduated from Althouse College with a teaching degree. She lives in Mississauga, where she currently works as a teacher-librarian at Holy Name of Mary secondary school. She has traveled to several destinations and made numerous trips to the Netherlands, where she maintains close relationships with a large extended family.

Bill obtained a drafting technician diploma and worked five years at CPI Vampco in Strathroy. He returned to university for two years and then worked 16 years for NCR Canada Ltd., Waterloo, as a senior mechanical designer. He developed an interest in genealogy and local history, and served as a member of the Adelaide Township Heritage Group. In 1998, Bill married Rena Ali (1952) of Kitchener, Ontario. They now live in Waterloo.

In 1980, Jim married Mary Margaret O'Neil (1955), and they have four children, Sarah (1981); Joe (1982); Brian (1985); and Laura (1988). Some of Mary Margaret's ancestors from Adelaide were the Healys and the Carmodys. Jim and his brother, John, took over the family farm and worked together for 10 years. Then, Jim and Mary Margaret bought out John's interest and continued farming until June 1998, when the farm was sold. Jim currently lives on Egremont Drive in Adelaide, and Mary Margaret lives in Strathroy and teaches kindergarten in Watford.

In 1982, John married Elaine Royackers (1963), and they had four children, Jeff (1982); Michelle (1984); Jennifer (1986, died a baby); and Matthew (1988). They live on Centre Road, part of Lot 16, Con. 4 NER. John drives a truck for Ryder Integrated Logistics, who hauls car parts for General Motors. Elaine looks after a 450-sow pig barn for Lyle Hendrikx.

In 1986, Nick married Trudy McNab (1961). They had four children, Nicholas (1989); Wesley (1991); Emily (1993, died a baby); and Mary (1996). They live in Ingersoll, where they operate a Jersey dairy operation. Nick also works full-time for the Dairy Herd Improvement Association as a regional supervisor. Adelaide is part of his territory.

In 1987, Patricia married Terry Day (1960), and they have two daughters, Helene (1995) and Natalie (1998). They live in Dorchester. Patricia works part-time as a nurse at Victoria Hospital and Terry works as a property assessor, both in London.

In 1987, Jeannette married Scott Robinson (1962) and they have three children, David (1993); Renee (1995); and Stacey (1998). They live in Walton and run a swine breeding and finishing operation.

Debbie has a Developmental Services Worker diploma from St. Clair College, and an Early Childhood Education diploma from Fanshawe College. She lives in Strathroy and currently works as a teaching assistant at the separate school in Delaware.

Both Adrian and Katrien were involved in their community. Adrian was a committee member with the St. Willibrord Community Credit Union for 36 years. He served on the credit committee, supervisory committee and the board of directors. Katrien served on the executive, and is a lifelong member of the Catholic Women's League. She has volunteered as an assistant at Our Lady Immaculate School and taught crafts at the Strathroy SEARCH centre. She currently delivers Meals on Wheels, sings in the church choir, and helps at many church functions. Katrien lives in Strathroy and spends her winters in Lake Wales, Florida.

GUIKEMA, Martin and Jane

Martin and Jane Guikema live on part of Lot 19, Con. 5 SER. Their house is just west of Strathroy on County Road 39, across the road from Strathmere Lodge. They bought the house from Mrs. Agnes Hunter, who lived there for more than 20 years.

They moved on a snowy November day in 1989 with their four children. Monica has since graduated from university and lives in Waterloo. Rick, Sonya and Jody still live at home.

Over the years, the Guikemas have made many changes to the landscape. When they arrived, a broken fence and lots of trees and bushes surrounded the house. They cleared the land behind their home to enhance the view of the pond.

They enjoy living in this area with the open spaces and the sense of community among their neighbours.

HAAN, Al and Aafke

In the spring of 1949, Al and Aafke Haan immigrated to Ontario from the Netherlands with two sons. In 1962, they bought their present farm located on the east half of Lot 24, Con. 1 NER. This farm was previously owned by Stanley Newell, whose ancestors were the first settlers on this property.

When the Haan family moved to this location, they numbered 11, with six sons and three daughters. All are now married with families. Two sons, Ralph and Louis, stayed in Adelaide. The other sons live in Strathroy and the surrounding area, while the daughters moved to Sarnia, Watford and Dorchester. The children are Hank (1946), who married Ruth Kingma, and lives in Strathroy; Don (1947), who married Helen Lylstra, and lives at R.R. #2, Strathroy; Tina (1949), who married Dick Bouterse, and lives in Sarnia; Ralph (1951); Irene (1952), who married Don Van Gorkum and lives at R.R. #7, Strathroy; Willie (1954), who married Dorothy Bruinink, and lives in Strathroy; Yvonne (1955), who married Henry Beldman, and lives in Dorchester; Jack (1956), who married Nellie Rutten, and lives in Strathroy; and Louis (1961).

Off-farm income, such as construction, was

Al and Aafke Haan family, back L-R, Ralph, Don, Louis, Tina, Henk, Jack, Willie; front L-R, Irene, Aafke, Al and Yvonne, September 1995 (courtesy Luis Photography).

needed to support this family. At present, the farm is used as a cow/calf operation.

Ralph, the fourth child of Al and Aafke, grew up in Adelaide Township. He married Ineke Muis of Burlington in October 1975. They lived near Mt. Brydges, then Komoka, and finally moved to their present location on 3279 Mullifarry Drive in 1981, with their two children, Monique Michelle and Bryan Darrel.

Ralph has operated a backhoe business in and around Adelaide since April 1975. He has done most of the municipal drain repair for Adelaide Township for the last 10-12 years. His wife, Ineke, is the Director of Human Resources at Strathroy Foods. Monique is on a full track scholarship at Illinois State University in Normal, Illinois. Bryan is a Grade 12 student at London District Christian Secondary School in London.

Over the years, Ralph has met and worked for many fine residents of Adelaide, either on the drains running through their properties, or doing other backhoe work.

Louis moved to Alberta in 1979, where he built log homes for three years with his cousins, Jack and Bob Boersema. He framed townhouses for two years before he moved back to Ontario in 1984, with his wife, Carolyn (Holwerda). They were married on July 15, 1983. They moved around southern Ontario for 10 years before settling on the home farm. They built a new house on a 1-acre lot severed from the farm.

Louis owns and operates a small construction company called Haan Bros. Construction, founded in 1987.

Louis and Carolyn have four children, Stacey (1985); Dustin (1986); Maegan (1989); and Brittany (1991).

HANNA, John and Jane

The Hanna family immigrated to Canada from Ireland about 1843, and settled in Adelaide in 1846. John and Jane (ca.1785) Hanna had at least three children, Maria (ca.1825-1898), who married Thomas Alexander (see ALEXANDER, Joseph and Janet); John Jr. (1826); and George (1828). Another possible daughter is Ann (ca.1826-1851), who married William Morgan (see MORGAN, Richard Sr. and Jane). John Jr. and Maria were born in County Mayo. It is not known if John Sr. died in Ireland or Canada. The 1861 Adelaide census shows the family living on the west half of Lot 8, Con. 3 SER, on a farm named "Mount Pleasant Farm." Both sons are listed as being married. Robert Hanna (ca.1806), who could be a cousin or an uncle, is also living on the farm at the time of the 1861 census.

In 1859, John Hanna Jr. married Harriet Thrower (1840-1909), daughter of Isaac and Mary (Humphries) Thrower of Adelaide. They had at least six children. Mary L. (1860) married Jeremiah McKitrick and later, John Eagleson. She lived in North Dakota. Lavina (1861-1929) married her cousin, Christopher W. Hanna (1860-1938), in Sarnia. Esther (1863-1924) married Henry Carlton (1860-1913) and lived in Petrolia and Sarnia. The three youngest children were Adeline or Adlana (1866-1883); Wilbur (ca.1870) Hanna, M.D., of Michigan; and Dufferin (1877-1908). Dufferin had two sons, Frank (1902-1928); and Edward (1904-1986), who died in Salem, Oregon, leaving two sons and six grandchildren.

An 1881 Adelaide directory still mentioned John Hanna, but he isn't found in the 1881 Adelaide census. The 1861 Adelaide census also mentioned another John Hanna (ca.1839) from Ireland, working for Charles Rason.

Harriet (Thrower) Hanna joined a religious cult and moved to Benton Harbor, Michigan, where she died. Her death certificate was used to cover up the alleged murder of a young girl, and a subsequent court case was reported in the Toronto Telegram in 1911.

When Christopher Hanna died, his will was disputed in a major court case involving the Masonic Lodge, and at that time, Dr. Wilbur Hanna (named as an heir) could not be located.

In 1859, George Hanna married Jane Murdock (ca.1835), born in County Mayo, Ireland. They had two children, Rosanna (ca.1860) and W.J. (1862-1919). In 1861, George was listed as a farmer. He moved from Adelaide before 1871.

W.J. was born in Adelaide Township and died in Augusta, Georgia. He was MPP for West Lambton, Provincial Secretary, and President of Imperial Oil. He married Jean Neil (d.1895) in 1891. Their son, Lieut. Neil Hanna of the R.A.F., died in Italy just after the Armistice of 1918. W.J.'s second wife, Maud MacAdams, had two daughters. She left $10,000 to the city of Sarnia to purchase the land for Canatara Park.

HANSFORD, John and Mary

John Hansford (1795-1843) married Mary Noble (1802-1883), and they settled on Lot 28, Con. 1 NER, on April 13, 1836. They had four children. Walter (ca.1834-1868) married Sarah Bolton (1840-1873). Harriet (1836) married Thomas Woodward. Philip George (1838-1915) married Elizabeth Ruth Bolton (1843-1902), and they had nine children and moved to California. Sarah Jane (1840-1910) married William Sam Bolton (1837-1902).

Philip and Elizabeth's children were John William (1862-1924), who married Martha Demaray (1867); Philip George Jr. (1864-1947) of Brooke Township, who married Charlotte E. Bailey (1873-1943); Walter James (1867-1921) of Callander, Ontario, who married Jennie Johnson; Mary "Minnie" Vincent (1870-1935) of California, who married Alex McLachlan (1870); Harriet E. (1872-1948) of East Williams Township, who married Myron Linton (1870-1955) of Poplar Hill; Sarah Adelaine (1875-1954) of Strathroy, who married John W. Wood (1870-1934) of Adelaide, and had two children, Hansford and Mary Elizabeth; Thomas Wesley (1879-1930) of Saskatchewan, who married Jessie Robin Taylor; Charles (1882-1924) of Strathroy, who married Laura Giffen (d.1977) of London; and Isaac "Ike" (1887-1944) of Saskatchewan, who married Margaret Leona Murray (1892-1984).

The Hansford family attended the Anglican Church at Adelaide Village where they became members and the children were baptized. John was buried in the Anglican Cemetery in Adelaide Village. Walter took over the farm until he died. He was buried in the Anglican Church Cemetery. His son, Will, took over farming when he came of age. Will married Margaret "Maggie" Glen. He farmed until 1915, when he moved to Caledon East with his wife and family. He sold the farm to George Tomlinson, who sold it later to Fred Ramsay. When Fred retired, he sold the farm to Jan Pass, whose son, Charlie, is still on the farm.

John Hansford's widow, Mary, married Thomas Hindmarsh and they settled on Lot 28, Con. 2 SER, where she raised Harriet, Philip and Sarah until they were married. Philip took over the farm. Later, he sold it to Smith Mitchell and his son, Stewart. The property is now owned by the Department of Highways. Thomas and Mary were buried in the Hansford plot in Strathroy.

HARRIS, Samuel

Samuel Harris (1784-1864), a sheep shearer from Westbury, Wiltshire County, England, married Ann Nightingale (1785-1818) in 1803. They had nine children, Elizabeth (ca.1803); John (ca.1804), who died young; Jane (1809-1885), who married John Harris; Thomas (1810); Joseph (ca.1816); John #2 (ca.1816); Mary Ann (1816-1871), who married George Brothers (see BROTHERS); Samuel Jr. (ca.1818), who died young; and James (1818-1872). After Ann's death, Samuel married Sophia Orchard in 1819. They had two children, William (ca.1820) and Joshua (1822). Samuel remarried again, to Jesse (last name unknown), and they had one son, Samuel (ca.1823).

In 1832, Samuel Harris immigrated to Adelaide at the age of 54 with four sons, Thomas (1810-1885); John, James and Joshua. He left three daughters behind, although in 1855, Mary Ann came to Canada and later inherited 30 acres of land from her father. Samuel's remaining children and his third wife had all died. He settled on the east half of Lot 12, Con. 3 SER, a property on which he received a patent in 1849, after paying £25.

In 1834, Thomas married Ann Phipps (1810-1892), daughter of Paul and Frances (Francis) Phipps of Adelaide. The Phipps family had traveled from England with the Harris family and also came from Wiltshire County. Thomas and his father-in-law served in the 1837 Rebellion in the army.

Thomas and Ann had 11 children, Frances (1835-1922); Eliza (1837-1871); Ann (1839-1919), who married William Dowding (see DOWDING, Thomas and Martha); Thomas Paul (1841-1905); Joseph (1843-1927); David (1846-1909); Samuel (1848-1906); Mary Ann (1850-1853); William (1852-1853); Paul (1854-1914); and William #2 (1856-1914). Thomas farmed part of his father's farm as well as part of Lot 12, Con. 4 SER.

Frances, the eldest child of Thomas and Ann, married Thomas James (ca.1828), son of Thomas and Alice James of Adelaide. They had three children, Louisa (1858), who married George Miner (see MINER, Truman and Elizabeth); Lewis (ca.1860); and Alice (ca.1869), who married Ernest Houlton (see HOULTON, Henry and Eliza). In 1888, Lewis married Florence Houlton (ca.1868), Ernest's sister. They had two children, Harry (1890-1960), who never married and farmed at Anglia, Saskatchewan; and Gladys (1892-1982), who married Maurice Davis and lived in Dinsmore, Saskatchewan.

In 1862, Eliza, second child of Thomas and Ann, married Frederick Curry (1838-1879), son of John and Jane (Garner) Curry of Adelaide. They had four children, Minnie (1864-1962); Wilbert (1867-1945); Louisa (1869-1905), who married Herbert Martin (see MARTIN, Hiram and Hannah); and Fred (1870-1960). Frederick was born in County Mayo, Ireland, and came with his parents to Adelaide. He farmed in Metcalfe Township. After the early deaths of their parents, the children lived with relatives in Adelaide, then moved from the area.

In 1860, Thomas Paul, fourth issue of Thomas and Ann, married Harriett Martin (1836-1918), daughter of Hiram and Hannah (Hollingshead) Martin of Adelaide. They had five children, Ellen (ca.1860); Melvin (ca.1864); David (ca.1867); Alice "Allie" (ca.1873); and Hettie (ca.1877). Thomas and his family spent many years in Adelaide farming the east half of Lot 10, Con. 4 SER. The family moved from this area before the 1891 census. The eldest daughter, Ellen, married Fred Newland and had three children. Melvin married and had at least two children. David, a switchman on the railroad, married Hannah Kenniston and had two children. Allie married James Wade but had no children. Hettie married Robert Emerson, a minister, and had three children. Hettie and Robert spent many years in Japan as missionaries.

In 1865, Joseph, fifth of Thomas and Ann's children, married Caroline Croucher (1842-1913) of Adelaide. Caroline and her brother, George, were both born in England and came to Adelaide in 1852 with their aunt and uncle, Mary Ann and George Bishopp. Joseph and Caroline had six children, George (1866-1872); Annie (1867-1945), who married George Rivers; Caroline (1869-1871); Wes (1871-1943); Mary (1873), who married Robert Morgan (1865); and Fanny (1876-1977), who married Benjamin Pike and lived in Warwick Township. Joseph farmed and leased part of Lot 11, Con. 1 NER, and later, owned Lot 1, Con. 4 SER.

Wes, fourth child of Joseph and Caroline, married Justina Dell (1877-1932) of Adelaide, daughter of Alexander and Martha (Gill) Dell. Wes and Justina raised five children, Earl (1898-1975), who married Juliana van Damme; Elsie (1900-1977); Myrtle (1905-1992), who married Alfred Horne; Gordon (1909-1983); and Alex (1914-1992). Wes took over the family farm.

In 1940, Gordon, fourth child of Wes and Justina, married Lois Eakins (1913-1991), daughter of John and Laura (Owens) Eakins of Adelaide. They had two children, Garry and Donald (1946-1980).

Alex, the youngest of Wes and Justina's children, married Eva Humphries, daughter of Gordon and Ruby (Degroat) Humphries of Adelaide. They had one daughter, Nancy.

David, sixth child of Thomas and Ann, married Elizabeth Down (1851-1921) and they moved to Lot 5, Con. 3 SER. They had four daughters, Celia Rose (1870-1953), who married Robert Edwards of the Second Line of Watford and homesteaded in Michigan; Julia Florence (1875-1947), who married Asa Newell (see NEWELL, Alexander and Lorena); Helena (1879-1950), who married Aaron Edgar Demaray (see DEMARAY); and Annie, who married James Lotan and lived on a farm near Appin. David and Elizabeth also had two sons, Oliver George Lawrence (1887-1978) and Milton Cleveland (1893-1971), and raised George Jarrett, who married Minnie Demaray, sister of Bill and Edgar. David and Elizabeth, with three of their daughters, took part in the opening of the new school, S.S. #8, and the Bethesda Church.

David and Elizabeth moved their family Lot 23, Con. 2 NER, at Crathie. David did a large share of the threshing in Adelaide, working until nearly Christmas every year. In 1917, Elizabeth (by then a widow) moved with her sons to the present farm on Lot 9, Con. 3 SER. The Harris family was fortunate to move into a large, modern house, built by the previous owners, the Houltons.

In 1925, Oliver, the eldest son, married Ella Acton, who was teaching at S.S. #8 Adelaide and boarding with her aunt, Lizzie Dowding. Oliver and Ella built a new house on the west half of the 200-acre farm.

Oliver and Ella were very active members of Bethesda Church. Oliver sang in the choir and served as an elder, while Ella taught Sunday School and helped in the W.M.S. and W.A. Their son, Leroy, moved to Washington, D.C., where he worked as a senior research aerospace engineer. Phyllis worked for the Dept. of National Defence, C.O.D., in London. She was a talented musician who played for worship at Bethesda Church for many weddings and for wonderful singsongs at various social occasions. Oliver and Ella moved to Strathroy in 1965, after selling their farm to Cecil and Winnie Brown.

Oliver and his brother, Milton, had a threshing machine and did their own threshing, and contracted work for a number of neighbours. Although they had separate farms, they continued to share machinery and work together during planting and harvesting. They grew grain, corn and hay, milked Holstein cows, and raised some beef cattle on pasture.

In 1950, Oliver and Milton bought Lot 8, Con. 2 SER, which had been rented from the Houltons. The

Family of Thomas and Ann Harris, front, Joseph, Annie, Samuel; middle, Thomas, Thomas and Ann, Fanny; back, William, Henry Annett, David, Paul.

With stoneboat, from L-R, Byron Dell, Stanley and Harvey Harris, ca.1920.

property was used as a pasture farm. In 1963, Oliver traded his half to Irwin Carrothers for another pasture farm.

In 1917, Milton, the younger son of David and Elizabeth, married Rebecca Wilson, whom he had met while she was teaching at Crathie. Milton and Rebecca were members of Bethesda Church. Milton served on Adelaide Township Council and was a member of the Board of the Ontario Concentrated Milk Producers. He and Rebecca had four children. Arnold pursued a career as a mathematics teacher in Toronto, Kirkland Lake and London, with his last position as professor at Althouse College. David worked in Defence Industries Ltd. during the war and returned to work on the family farm, which he continues doing today. He gave up milk cows in favour of beef cattle. Marjorie married into the Heinbuch family and taught in Windsor. She has lived in Waterloo since her marriage. Marion married into the Oliver family. She has a degree in nursing and lives in Toronto.

In 1871, Samuel, seventh child of Thomas and Ann, married Mary Jane Crews (1851-1908), daughter of Joseph and Elizabeth (Burrows) Crews of Adelaide. They had five children, Elizabeth (1872-1922); Emma (1875-1923), who married Mayten Henderson (see HENDERSON, James M. and Bridget; William and Georgina); Annie (1875-1933), who married George Matthews (see MATTHEWS, William and Catherine); William Edgar (1878-1915); and Luther "Shoot" (1880-1935). Samuel first farmed part of Lot 10, Con. 2 SER, and later purchased his father-in-law's farm, being part of Lot 13, Con. 3 SER.

In 1900, Elizabeth, eldest child of Samuel and Mary Jane, married Herbert Greenfield (1869-1949). They had two sons, Frank and Arnold. The family homesteaded in Alberta. Herbert became involved in politics and served as Premier of Alberta from 1921 to 1925.

In 1908, William Edgar, fourth of Samuel and Mary Jane's children, married Mary Thomas (1878-1960), daughter of Henry and Mary (Shepherd) Thomas of Adelaide. They had two children, Evan and Edna. William farmed part of Lot 13, Con. 3 SER.

In 1942, Evan married Laura Whiting (1915-1990), daughter of William and Lavina (Patrick) Whiting of Caradoc. They had three children, Bill, Bruce and Mary. Evan took over the family farm in the 1920s. Bill became a veterinarian and is a professor at the University of Guelph. In 1970, he married Joanne Fraser and they have two children, Jennifer and Paul. In 1974, Bruce married a teacher, Donna MacVicar, and they built a second house on the farm. They have no children. Bruce changed the farm operation from dairy to beef production. In the summer of 1980, the barn was destroyed by fire. Shortly after, a large crowd gathered and witnessed the demolition of the partially filled 55' silo so that a new pit barn and silo could be safely constructed. In 1998, the farm was sold to Dan and Jen Parker. Bruce also had a tile drainage business for many years. In 1971, Evan and Laura's youngest child, Mary, a Registered Nurse, married Raymond Dodge (1947-1994). They had three children, Melissa (1974); Steven (1976); and Theresa. Melissa married Scott Berlemont, Steven married Jacoba Peters, and Theresa is presently studying at the University of British Columbia. Mary lives in Strathroy and has remarried, to Fred Butcher.

Luther, the youngest child of Samuel and Mary Jane, married Lydia Owens (1880-1914). They had a son, Samuel (1908-1984), who never married. After Lydia's death, Luther married Birdie Robotham (d.1948). They had no children. Luther farmed part of Lot 10, Con. 2 SER, before moving to Strathroy.

In 1878, Paul, tenth child of Thomas and Ann, married Nancy Dell (1856-1947), daughter of Basnett and Elizabeth (McNeil) Dell of Adelaide. They had five children, Franklin (1879-1880); Arthur (1882, died an infant); Ethel (1884, died an infant); Elmer (1887-1942); and Harvey (1895-1951). Paul farmed the west half of Lot 18, Con. 2 SER. His sons took over the farm. Elmer never married. In 1916, Harvey married Mary Fletcher (1891-1963), daughter of James and Mary (Ross) Fletcher. They had four children, a son; Lorein (1912); Elsie (1927-1995); and Paul Jr. Lorein married John Brown and lives in Mount Brydges. They have four children, James, Nancy, Kenneth and Delmar. Elsie married Ross Linton and had five children, Anne, Bruce, June, Ruth and Glen. Paul married Wandalee Bloomfield and lives in London. They have four children, Harvey, Anna, Mary and Evan.

In 1885, William, the youngest child of Thomas and Ann, married Melissa Dell (1863-1940), daughter of Sylvester and Emma (Caldwell) Dell of Plympton Township. They had eight children, a son (1886, died an infant); Thomas (1887-1888); Estella (1888-1981); Bertha (1890-1963); Ross (1893-1962); Jessie (1893-1980); Pauline (1899-1980); and Ferne (1904-1989). William lived his life on the farm where he died, taking over the farm from his father. He and Melissa are buried in Strathroy.

In 1911, Estella married Frank Inch (1888-1971). They had six children, Eileen, Audrey, Dorothy, Ross, Winnifred and Ruth. Frank farmed around Katesville in Metcalfe Township.

In 1913, Bertha, fourth child of William and Melissa, married Charles Foster (1888-1978), son of William Henry and Charity (Inch) Foster of Metcalfe Township. They had five children, Ken (1914-1992); George (1918-1988); Mary (1920); Russell (1922-1973); and Florence (1923, died an infant). In 1941, Ken married Mary Branan; they had no children. He operated a garage and service station at the southeast corner of the Currie Road and Fourth Line South in Adelaide. George married Marjorie Westgate in 1941, and they raised five children, Joyce, Louise, Erma, Glen and Charles (see FOSTER, George and Marjorie). Mary married Leonard Johnson of Metcalfe and they raised eight children, Nancy, Verna, George, Charles, Joanne, Gordon, Janet and John. Russell was a mechanic and truck driver. He owned and operated a trucking business in Kerwood. For many years, he picked up milk cans and delivered them to the Carnation Dairy in Kerwood. Russell married Viola Lythgoe and they had three children, Ruthanne, Wayne and Shelley.

In 1923, Ross, fifth issue of William and Melissa, married Kathleen Carrothers (1900-1968) of Thedford, Ontario. Ross farmed the home farm for a few years with his mother after his father's death, finally selling it in 1924. Ross moved to Centre Line, Michigan, where he had a barbershop and dry cleaning business. He and Kathleen had three children, Don, Ken and Bob.

In 1928, Jessie, sixth of William and Melissa's children, married Harry New. They had no children. He came from England and worked for many years as a farm labourer around Adelaide. He served in the Canadian army during WWI. After the Harris farm was sold, he moved to London and worked for the railroad. Jessie worked in Woolworth's in London. She looked after her mother, Melissa, and her grandmother, Emma Dell, during their final years. Both Harry and Jessie were members of the church choir, and Harry sang for the London Male Choir.

In 1921, Pauline, seventh child of William and Melissa, married Wellington Lucas (1898-1976), son of Hezakiah and Maria (Smith) Lucas of Adelaide. They farmed Lot 13, Con. 3 SER, and had three children, Bruce, Vern, and Betty. Wellington worked as a chiropractor in London, before moving to Detroit and working for the city gas company.

In 1930, Ferne, the youngest of William and Melissa's children, married Rex Arnold (1906-1992). They farmed in Sombra and raised two children, Bill and Keith. Ferne was a teacher for many years.

In 1840, John, sixth child of Samuel and Ann, married Sarah Ingram (ca.1821), daughter of Daniel and Mary Ingram of Adelaide. They raised nine

Family of William Harris, L-R, Bertha and Charlie Foster, Stella and Frank Inch, Kathleen and Ross Harris, Jessie and Harry New, Pauline and Wellington Lucas, Ferne and Rex Arnold.

children, Elizabeth (1841); Ruth (ca.1843); Sarah (ca.1845); Mary (ca.1849); Daniel (ca.1851); Absolum (ca.1853); Joseph (ca.1856); Angelina (ca.1858); and George (1861). John farmed part of the east half of Lot 7, Con. 2 SER. He sold this property in 1867 to his brother-in-law, George Brothers. The family moved away from Adelaide to an unknown destination. Nothing further is known about this branch of the Harris family.

In 1835, James, the youngest of Samuel and Ann's children, married Alice Stockdale (1818-1898). They had 11 children, Sofia (1843-1918); James (1845); Elizabeth (1846); Charlotte (1847); Bella (1848); Alice (1852-1881); William (1853); Margaret (1856); Isabella (1857); Mary (1860); and Anna (1862-1863). James helped his father and brothers clear the Adelaide farm. James owned part of Lot 12, Con. 4 SER, but farmed there for only a few years. Census records indicate he lived in Delaware Township and is buried in the Anglican cemetery there.

In 1845, Joshua, the youngest child of Samuel and Sophia, married Grace Elliott (1823-1900) of Adelaide. They raised 10 children, William (1846-1931); Jane (1847-1927), who married James Knight of Metcalfe Township and raised nine children there; James (1849-1894); Mary (1851), who married George Morris and resided in London; Robert (1854-1944), Albert (1856-1942); Sidney (1859-1901); Fred (1860), who died young; Thomas (1861) and Joseph (1864). All of the children were born in Adelaide, according to family stories.

Joshua was 10 years of age when he came to Adelaide, and would have helped his father and brothers in clearing the homestead. After marriage, Joshua did not stay in one place for any length of time. His eldest son was born in Sarnia, but the first four children were baptized in Adelaide. His name did not appear in the 1851 Adelaide census, but he may have resided in Katesville (Katesville is consistent with a family story about growing up on the banks of the Sydenham River near Strathroy). A 1939 newspaper article, featuring the reminiscences of George Shepherd, states that Joshua Harris had a liquor store in Katesville. The 1861 census finds Joshua as a labourer in Delaware Township, and the 1871 census has him in Adelaide, leasing part of Lot 9, Con. 1, with William, his son. In 1881, he was homesteading in Spence Township, Parry Sound County, with his sons, Albert, Joseph and William. Joshua and his wife both died at the home of their daughter, Mary Morris, in London.

In 1865, William, the eldest child of Joshua and Grace, married Mary Ann Baker (1849-1938), daughter of Thomas and Harriet (Channell) Baker. They raised five children, George (ca.1866); Sarah (ca.1868); James (1871); Frank; and Ruth. William worked closely with his father, and Mary Ann's parents were living with them at that time. The family accompanied Joshua to Spence Township, but later moved to Michigan, where William and Mary Ann passed away.

James, third child of Joshua and Grace, married Amelia Shepherd (1853-1906) of Adelaide, daughter of John and Elizabeth Shepherd. They appear to have lived for many years around Alvinston, Ontario, as they are buried there. They raised seven children, most of them homesteading in southern Manitoba.

Robert, fifth issue of Joshua and Grace, married Sara Ann Crawford (d.1944), who was born in Grand Rapids, Michigan. Robert met her while working in Michigan lumber camps. They married in 1878 and settled near Strathroy, where their two eldest children, Ernest and Laura, were born. Robert moved to Markdale, Grey County, before taking over his father's farm in Spence Township. His last move was to Durban, Manitoba.

Albert, sixth of Joshua and Grace's children, married Margaret Dickson in 1880. They raised six children. Albert farmed in Gravenhurst and Markdale, Ontario, before moving to Boissevain, Manitoba, in 1896.

Harris family, front, Oliver, Milton; middle, David, Helena, Elizabeth; rear, Annie, Rose, Florence.

Sidney, seventh issue of Joshua and Grace, married Harriet Lyons, and they raised seven children. He farmed in the Parry Sound area.

Thomas, ninth child of Joshua and Grace, married Minnie Pannell and moved to Bannerman, Manitoba.

The youngest son, Joseph, and his wife, Sarah, took over the Joshua Harris farm in Spence Township, near Burk's Falls, Ontario. They had no children.

HAWES, Alfred and Annie

Alfred John Hawes (1847) came from England and settled in Adelaide. In 1878, he was farming 50 acres, the east half of Lot 14, Con. 3 SER. The land registry indicates he purchased this property from James McNeice on May 2, 1876. Alfred died in Brown City, Michigan, and is buried in Carmen Cemetery in Lakeport, Michigan. His death record in the Sanilac County courthouse gives his parents as Thomas Hawes and mother unknown.

Alfred married Annie Sophie Paine, the daughter of John and Elizabeth (Rapley) Paine, on May 13, 1876, in the East Adelaide Presbyterian Church. Marriage records differ from Alfred's death record, and list his parents as Henry and Sarah Mitchell Hawes.

Alfred and Annie had seven children, among them Alfred John Montegue (1877), who married Alberta Dell Sheffer; Ernest Edward (1879), who married Maggie Mae Phipps; and Thomas Ethelbert, who married Mary Elizabeth Sly. The other children died young.

In 1879, Alfred sold the farm in Adelaide and moved to Section 25, Worth Township, Sanilac County, Michigan.

HEALY, James and Rosanna

The forefather of the Healys living in and around Adelaide Township was James Healy (1791-1861) of Port Arlington, Kings County, Ireland. He came to Canada in 1832 and settled on Egremont Road on 200 acres given to him as a pension settlement by the British Army.

James had joined the army, 37th Regiment of the Foot Hampshire Regiment, 2nd Battalion, on October 22, 1813, one of 40 new recruits who joined in September and October of that year, forming a compliment of 507 officers and men.

James Healy's regiment was sent to the Netherlands following Napoleon's escape from Elba, where they remained garrisoned at Antwerp until March 1817. In May 1817, James was transferred to the 1st Battalion, along with 270 other men. The 1st Battalion had been retired from the fray against Napoleon three years earlier and sent to Canada from Bordeaux on June 4, 1814, arriving in Quebec on August 3, 1814. The regiment was sent to join Sir James Kemp's brigade for service on Lake Ontario at Kingston to participate in an attack on the American naval base at Sackett's Harbour.

Historical accounts showed that the 37th of the 1st Battalion also spent time in Ireland, Bermuda, Jamaica and Ceylon. Following a transfer to Ireland, James fractured his leg from an accidental fall in May 1828 at Limerick while off-duty. He was discharged in Dublin soon thereafter, at the age of 39. James was described in discharge papers as being 5'6 ½", and having brown hair and gray eyes. Records stated that paymaster Richard Evans gave him 20 days' payment for 11 days marching time on August 24, 1830, to get him to Clonmill. Of his 200-acre pension, 100 acres was granted on July 31, 1832, by Sir John Colbourne, Lieutenant Governor of the Province of Upper Canada in the name of the Crown of England.

Some time after his return in Canada in 1832, he married Rosanna Callahan (d.1888) of County Caven. They had five children, Mary, Margaret, Edward, James Jr. (1838-1914) and John. James and Rosanna are buried together in St. Patrick's Cemetery, Adelaide Village. James was one of the earliest pioneers of the township of Adelaide.

James and Rosanna lived at Lot 5, Con. 3 NER, in a 1-storey log home. There were 50 acres of land on this property: eight with crops, four with pasture, and 38 acres of woods. They grew wheat, peas, oats, potatoes, beans and hay. Livestock on the farm included cattle, sheep and pigs. James was involved in the petition (May 27, 1844) for a Catholic church to be established in Adelaide, and is listed as having six family members that would attend. He and his family did attend after St. Patrick's Roman Catholic Church was built.

James Jr. married Joanna Walsh (1842-1918), daughter of Patrick (1800-1892) and Ellen (Quinn) Walsh (1818-1878) of Cashel, Tipperary, Ireland. They were married at the Walsh farm in Adelaide by the Reverend W.T. Lynch (Toronto) on April 5, 1864. They had nine children, John Edward "Ed" (1865-1936); Patrick James (Ed's twin, d.1866); Ellen (1866-1936); Rosanna (1869, died an infant); Teresa (1870-1927); Albert (1873-1944); Alice (1876-1952); Joseph (1879-1941); and Mary Elizabeth (1881-1959). James Jr. was a noted farmer and the director of the Strathroy Agricultural Society. He served the community as councillor for the Village of Strathroy, and as police magistrate. James Jr. was a banker in Strathroy when he bought "The Pines" in 1892. He lived there 22 years until his death. The Pines was sold in 1917.

Ed began the third generation of Healy's in Adelaide when he married Teresa Brady on January 16, 1895, at All Saints Church by the Reverend A. McKeon. Ed and Teresa had seven children, Wilfred (1896-1985); Helen (1898-1915), who died of lymphoma; Tom (1900-1921); Margaret (1901-1988); Alice (1903-1940); John Edward Jr. (1906-1995); and Mae (1913).

Ed inherited the family farm and lived there until his death. He died from a heart attack in the front yard 40' from where John Edward Jr. would eventually die of a heart attack in 1995. Renewing an old custom, John Edward Jr. was "waked" at home next to the room he was born in.

John Edward Jr. married Cecelia Euphemia and they had 12 children, Peter Joseph (1936); Teresa Josephine (1937), who married John Coupland; Patricia Margaret (1938), who married Gerald Brown); Donald Edward (1941); John James (1942); Mary Elizabeth (1943), who married Lyn Jones; Robert Marwood Gerard (1945); Timothy Francis (1947); Michael Patrick (1948-1977); Suzanne Cecelia (1950), who married Ron Hodgins); Monica Rose (1952); and Edward Robert (1954). The children attended Our Lady Immaculate School.

Robert Marwood Gerard, seventh child of John Edward Jr. and Cecelia, attended Napperton Public School, S.S. #5, for a short time, then O.L.I. He was named after Dr. Marwood Fletcher, who delivered all of Cecelia's children and patched them up over the years. Robert became a welder, and married Mary Lou McKim, the daughter of Elizabeth and Vern McKim of Essex, Ontario. They have three children, Mark Thomas (1980); Patricia Anne (1984); and Tara Leigh (1987). After Mark's birth, Robert and Mary Lou built a new house, and the little red house they had originally lived in was moved to a new location on the Second Line.

Michael Patrick, ninth child of John Edward Jr. and Cecelia, married Judith Diane Calcutt, and they bought a home at R.R. 7, Strathroy. The original owners of the property were Sam and Ethel Stevens (Sam worked as a gravedigger at Strathroy Cemetery). Michael and Judith had two children, Lisa Marie (1966) and Michael Edward (1969). They sold this property to Michael's brother, Robert Gerard, in 1974. In 1991, they bought ¾-acre of Ed's home farm, and built a new home. There, Daniel (1979) was born.

Wilfred, Ed and Teresa's eldest, married Malvina Dillon (1901-1977) and they had 10 children, Mary Teresa (1923); Ann (1925); Jack (1927-1975); Tom (1929); Eddie (1931); Jimmy (1933); Josephine "Joan" (1935); Rita (1938); Helen (1940); and Maurice (1943-1946), who died of diphtheria.

Tom, Ed and Teresa's third child, was called from western Canada to visit his mother before she died of diabetes, and on the way contracted scarlet

Cecelia and Edward Healy

fever and died a few weeks after his mother (due to medical neglect, according to family oral history).

Alice married Cecil Coughlin, and they had two children, Timothy and Jerry. When Alice died, Cecil married Alice's sister, Margaret. They had one child, James, who became a dentist.

Mae, youngest child of Ed and Teresa, married Jack McNamara.

Ellen, third child of James Jr. and Joanna, entered Sacred Heart Convent in London at the age of 20, and was subsequently transferred to Kenwood, Albany, New York (1893); then to Manhattan, New York; on to Grosse Pointe, Michigan; and finally to Montreal, where she died. She was an artist and painter. A large oil painting of hers of the Sacred Heart, which had been donated to All Saints Church in Strathroy, was removed from its frame by Father Moynahan and placed in the ceiling of the sanctuary during a renovation in the 1940s.

Teresa, fifth child of James Jr. and Joanna, was married to Lawrence Connelly by the Reverend T. Hogan in All Saints Church on July 22, 1902. They had two children, Helen (1903-1971) and Jim (1904-1948), who married Esther Hudnal, and had two daughters, Pattie and Suzie.

Albert married Grace Story (1881-1958) and they had three children, Marjorie (1907), who married Don Hansen; Jack (1909); and Helen (1911), who married Bill Lawrey. Albert eventually became a lawyer and Member of Parliament in Windsor. He was a major investor in the construction of the Ambassador Bridge in Windsor. Albert claimed the government engineers calling for larger cables than had been ordered (which forced the investors into bankruptcy) was due to the fact that the government was building the tunnel at the same time, and the bridge was in competition with the government project. Albert later moved to California.

Alice, seventh issue of James Jr. and Joanna, married Frank Vining in Zanzibar, Africa, in 1912. They had three children, Joseph (1914-1972), born in Aden, Arabia; Mary (1915); and John (1917). Alice died in Ogdensburg, New York.

No information was available on Joseph, eighth child of James Jr. and Joanna.

Mary Elizabeth, the youngest of James Jr. and Joanna's children, married Dr. Robert Ross MacDonald (1874-1949) at All Saints Church. Dr. MacDonald had a medical practice in Sarnia.

Descendants of this Irish pioneer family still live in the area.

HEMSTED, Donald and Anna

Donald John Hemsted (1913-1996) was born in Saskatoon, Saskatchewan. His parents immigrated to Canada from Iowa by train in 1910. This was at a time when Canada was encouraging settlers to populate the west.

After Donald was born, his parents purchased a half-section of land at Cupar, about 50 miles northeast of Regina. They carried on general farming, using four-, six-, and eight-horse teams, before the introduction of tractors.

The 1930s were difficult times, with the Depression and dust storms. During that time, the Hemsted family drove the horse-drawn school van, the forerunner of today's school bus.

Donald's mother died in 1935 of spinal meningitis, for which there was little known treatment. In 1937, the family left Saskatchewan to live in Ontario where they took up farming in West Williams.

In 1942, Donald and his brother, Stanley, enlisted in the R.C.A.F. They served as wireless technicians, stationed at Prince Rupert, British Columbia. The R.C.A.F. worked in conjunction with the American army, stationed on the Aleutian Islands to detect any Japanese activities within that area.

After their return, they purchased land in Adelaide Township. Donald purchased the "Pennington farm," the west half of Lot 15 and the east part of Lot 14, Con. 2 NER.

In 1947, Donald married Anna McDonald of West Williams. They have two children, Dianne and Lyle. Dianne works in Toronto as a Case Manager for the Ministry of Health. Lyle took over the farm after graduating from the University of Guelph. Donald and his wife retired and moved to Strathroy in 1979.

HENDERSON

Born in the township of Oxford, Upper Canada, James Michael Henderson (1837-ca.1934) was the third of eight sons of James and Dorothy Ann (Kenny) Henderson of County Down and County Cork, Ireland, who had immigrated to Canada in 1833. He grew up under pioneer conditions, helping with the arduous farm operations. He took a very active part in education, agriculture, politics, and the church. The Henderson name is on the June 7, 1903, petition to the Bishop for a new church.

In 1862, James married Bridget Burns (1833-1901) of Nissouri Township, originally from County Down, Ireland, in Ingersoll. They had five children, Theresa Jane (1862-1939); Sarah Ann (1865); Mayten James (1867-1948); Mary (1870, died a baby); and Frank (1871-ca.1961), all born in Ingersoll.

In 1873, James moved his family from Ingersoll by horse and wagon along Commissioner's Road to Adelaide Township, settling on the west half of Lot 16, Con. 3 NER, which he had purchased in 1872 from Benjamin Burdon. He was known as a progressive farmer, and he was director and, later, president of the West Middlesex Agricultural Society. He set up an apiary and named his farm "Honey-Hurst Farm." It is said that when he was working with the bees, he would come in for a meal and while at the table, bees would crawl out of his beard! For a short time, he was postmaster of the Crathie post office in his home. In 1886, he was appointed auditor for Adelaide Township. He took an active part in education (S.S. #4 Adelaide was next to his property) and he was interested in community affairs. He was a Roman Catholic in religion and an exceptionally well-informed Liberal in politics, holding "sound views on public questions."

James was a carpenter by trade, which was an asset for the Adelaide Second Line North neighbourhood. He was a fantastic storyteller, as his stories were based on actual experiences, whether recalling the arrival of the first train in Ingersoll (an event never to be forgotten), or hearing William Lyon McKenzie deliver a political speech after his return from banishment in 1849. Recounting his experiences with the Oxford Rifles along the Detroit River frontier, repelling the Fenian Raids, was always exciting for his Adelaide neighbours, who had not had such excitement in their lives since the 1837-1838 Rebellion! (Many years later, these volunteers for the Fenian Raids were formally recognized with a medal commemorating their service, and a land grant in newly-opened Northern Ontario).

Theresa Jane, eldest child of James and Bridget, married Edward Smithers (1866-1903) of Parkhill in 1884, and they moved to Michigan. They have descendants living in Michigan, New Jersey and Louisiana.

Sarah Ann married Cornelius Sullivan (1856-1917) of Metcalfe Township, and they had three children.

Mayten James was named for the date of his birth, May 10. He lived on the Adelaide home farm for 77 years and was considered a progressive farmer. He married Emma Jane Harris (1875-1923), daughter of Samuel and Mary Jane (Crews) Harris of Adelaide. They had 11 children, all born in Adelaide Township. Mayten is buried beside his wife in the Strathroy Roman Catholic Cemetery.

Angela Mary (1898-1928), eldest child of Mayten and Emma, married John Hubert McIntyre, and they had four children, Blanche, Velma, Norma and Emily.

Bridget (1900-1985) married a lawyer, Stanley Puffer, in Edmonton, and had four children. Bridget went to Alberta after the death of her aunt, Elizabeth Greenfield, in order to look after the household. She was made a princess of the tribe of Piegan Indians during the Ford McLeod stampede. She also had the distinction of being a guest of the Prince of Wales at a picnic at the royal ranch.

Madeline (1902) married Robert Henry McCarthy (1884-1969) of Adelaide. They lived in the Richard Brock house on the west half of Lot 14, Con. 1 NER. Robbie worked on the roads for Adelaide Township, running the road grader. Their three children were Constance, Aileen and James.

Wilfred (1904-1926) was the fourth child of Mayten and Emma.

Dorothy (1906) married John Scott.

Sarah (1908-1990), sixth issue of Mayten and Emma, was a telephone operator for the Adelaide Telephone Exchange, which was in the Henderson home. Many of the homes in the central part of the township had Springbank exchange numbers until they were changed to the Kerwood exchange. On a visit to the Henderson home today (Chouffort), telephone numbers can be seen inscribed in the brick. Sarah married Leo McIntosh (1908-1991) and they moved to Strathroy. Their son, Patrick, married Gisela Mantik, and they live with their son, Jason, in the Strathroy area.

Mary Stella (1910) married Wilfrid J. Gavan of Ottawa, and they had three children, Joan, Theresa and Jane.

James Patrick (1912-1978) stayed on the home farm for a few years. He married Ina Jean McNab (1922-1999) of Adelaide Township, and they had four children, Michael, Charles, Stanley and Janet.

Joseph Russell (1914-1988) served overseas in the R.C.A.F. during WWII. He married Barbara Dickson in England on November 19, 1944. Twin boys, Peter and Paul (1945, Paul died an infant), were born there before they returned to Canada. Five other children were born here, Mark, Michael, Christine, John and Tom. Russell worked as a bank manager for Toronto Dominion Bank and retired as Vice-President.

Mayten and Emma then had two children who died as infants, in 1916 and 1917.

Frank, the youngest child of James and Bridget, received local schooling in Adelaide Township and Strathroy and graduated from University of Toronto in 1903. He began his career with the Department of the Interior and was in charge of an Arctic Expedition in 1923 and 1924. He married Stella Lynott and they raised a son and five daughters in Ottawa.

James M. died at 97 years of age (his father had lived to the age of 103). James and Bridget are interred at All Saints Cemetery in Strathroy.

William Henderson, James M.'s brother and fourth son of James and Dorothy Ann (Kenny) Henderson, came to Adelaide Township and bought 50 acres, the west half of the east half of Lot 16, Con. 3 NER, beside his brother. William was 40 years old in the 1881 census list but had died by the time of the 1891 census, wherein wife Georgina (Fawcett) was then listed as a widow aged 44, with son Edward 20, and daughter Henrietta 18. In his 1884 will, the property was passed on to his wife. In an 1895 Quit Claim, Georgina and Hattie (Henrietta) Henderson transferred the farm to Edward, who sold the 50 acres to Walter Bolton in 1900.

Edward (1870) was born in Ingersoll and baptized there at Sacred Heart Church. His first communion and confirmation took place at All Saints Church in Strathroy, conducted by Archbishop Walsh. Edward was elected to the Adelaide Township Council in 1897-1898 and was Reeve of the Township in 1899-1900. He married Bridget Donough (or Donahue). After Edward Henderson left the farm, he took a business course in London and worked for Dominion Carriage Co. in Sarnia and Toronto. He also held important positions with the Toronto Separate School Board.

HENDRICK, John and Patience

John and Patience (Stevens) Hendrick homesteaded on the West Williams side of the townline beside the gore of Keyser with land holdings in 1861. Along with this property, they also had the east section of the gore and a farm across the road on the Fourth Line of Adelaide. John's parents were Michael (1790-1871) and Rebecca (1811-1887) Hendrick, Michael being from Monahan, Ireland, and Rebecca born in Ontario, both in the Keyser area at the time of the January 1852 census. Other records suggest the Hendrick family came from Pennsylvania's German settlement. The Stevens family was from Maryland's Irish settlement.

While in the gore area, John and Patience began raising a family of seven, George (1856-1930); Mary (1858); Emily (1860-1930); James (1864-1920); John (1865-1886); Manvil Lorenzo "Ren" (1868-1949); and Victor (1876-1929). In the early 1880s, they moved north of Keyser and south of the Ausable River in West Williams Township.

George left the area about 1900 to homestead in Foam Lake, Saskatchewan. He returned to Adelaide Township in 1930 in poor health, and died shortly after his arrival at the age of 74. Emma lived in the immediate area, spending time in Strathroy and Sylvan.

In 1902, Ren married Nettie Jane King (d.1952) of the Exeter area, and they had four children, Harry, Basil, Helen and Grant. Still living just north of Keyser in West Williams, they purchased Adelaide property at the east half of Lot 8, Con. 4 NER, in 1909. In November 1918, they purchased the Frank Langan farm at the west half of Lot 2, Con. 4 NER. This farm was originally settled by James Langan, deeded in 1861 and purchased from the Crown for $225. After this purchase, the Hendricks sold the Lot 8 farm. Ren and Nettie had a family of four children.

Harry (1903-1976), the eldest child of Ren and Nettie, worked on the home farm along with 50 acres, the west half of the east half of Lot 1, Con. 4 NER, just west of the home farm, which he purchased in 1924. He married Marjorie Blunt (1919-1988) of Warwick. They lived in Watford for five years and moved to Lot 2, Con. 4 NER, in 1953. They operated the farm as a general farm with hogs, chickens, milking cows and beef, while raising two children, Shirley and Bruce. Shirley became a Registered Nurse, currently residing in Strathroy and working in London. Bruce now operates the farm.

Basil (1907-1976) married Evelyn Hord of the Parkhill area. With the Hendrick family moving to the Langan farm, Basil and Evelyn moved to the original home farm in West Williams, north of Keyser. There they raised two daughters, Eva and Ruth. Basil died at the age of 69, and Evelyn still lives on the farm.

Helen, third child of Ren and Nettie, worked for several years on the farm and then moved to London.

Grant, the youngest issue of Ren and Nettie, married Anna Campbell. They live in London and have a daughter, Bonnie Ruth.

Victor, the youngest son of John and Patience, married Mildred Carrol in 1900. They took up residence at Lot 8, Con 1 SER, on the Sarnia Gravel. Victor was a well-known cattle dealer in the district. At age 52, after being sick for a short time, Victor died of quinsy.

Victor and Mildred had six children, John Wilfred (1902-1994); Laura Winnifred "Winnie," who moved to Detroit; Evan; Lewis Sherwood "Shady"; Eldred Edward; and Winslow Lorenzo.

John Wilfred left Adelaide when he was 17 for Western Canada. He married a woman there named Margaret Stevens, and they later moved to the U.S.

Anna and Grant Hendrick

Winnie married Howard MacNamee of Lucan and also moved to the U.S. Shady married Nellie Fletcher of Coldstream and their three children, Beverly, Ronald and Patricia, were born in Adelaide. The family moved away sometime in the 1930s. Eldred Edward went to Halifax and enlisted in the army. After the war, he moved to Windsor and then to Flint, Michigan. Winslow met his wife in Sydney, Nova Scotia, when he was sailing on the Great Lakes. The couple returned to the farm for a year, then moved to St. Thomas, London and Illinois. Winslow's second wife, Vera Dowding, grew up in the same area of Adelaide as the Hendricks and had gone to the same school, S.S. #6. Winslow was the youngest of the family and the only survivor when he spoke to us in May 1996.

HENDRIKX, Lyle and Mary Ann

Lyle Hendrikx (1951), son of John and Joanna (Jansen) Hendrikx, bought the Giffen place from Horst and Gertrud Buchardt in 1975 while living with his family in West Williams. Dry sows were kept in the barn. A line of trees in the middle of the east field was cleared. The house was rented out until early 1978. At that time, bride-to-be, Mary Ann Royackers, daughter of Albert and Joanne (Van Geffen) Royackers, also of West Williams, did some redecorating.

The newlyweds moved in after their March 31 wedding. That summer, a farrowing barn was built at the back of the bank barn, and the first litters of piglets arrived in the fall. So did Valerie, the eldest child.

In 1979, the decision was made to build a finishing barn for the weaners. Again, construction was completed in the fall. Shortly after the first pigs were born, Lyle and Mary Ann had a second child, Karl (1979). A third child, Daniel (1981), was born. Later that year, the couple purchased a 50-acre parcel from John Dortmans on Seed Road, close to Adelaide Village.

In 1982, Harold and Elizabeth Fish informed the Hendrikx family that they were interested in selling their house on the severed lot in the southwest corner of the farm. The growing Hendrikx family needed the space and moved in early March. Melissa, their fourth child, was born that May. In early July, Karl crawled under a fence and into the swimming pool. He was revived at the hospital, but died two months later after suffering severe brain damage, shortly before his third birthday.

Over the years, the family incorporated as Lymarikx Farms Limited and acquired more land at Springbank in East Williams and two parcels in West Williams.

The family was blessed with two more sons, Justin in 1983 and Nathan in 1985.

The Hendrikx family bought a parcel of 80 acres on Seed Road from Martin Timmermans in 1994. A 450-sow early weaning barn was built on the Adelaide 50 acres in 1996.

Of the early buildings, only the bank barn and driveshed remain, as well as a small shed that was a garage. The granny flat was burned since previous tenants had used it for a doghouse. The chicken shed with Mel Giffen's name etched in the beam was taken down to make room for manure storage. The farmhouse was in poor shape after a winter with only a raccoon for a tenant. The Adelaide-Metcalfe Fire Department used the house for some practice drills, then burned it completely in the final drill.

The children still live at home. Valerie works at the farm and the younger children are still in school.

HENRY, William and Francis

William Henry (1849-1930) was born in Chicago, Illinois, of English heritage. He came as a carpenter to Adelaide Village sometime before 1868, and worked with John W. Whitlock, and Edward and William Austin, framing barns and other buildings in the district. He married Francis Hannah A. Freele (1848-1907) on December 10, 1869, and commenced farming on Lot 12, Con. 1 NER. There, he and Hannah raised a family of four, Katherine Elizabeth "Lizzie" (1870-1918); Robert Thomas (1873-1930); Matilda "Tillie" Jane (1876); and Joseph William (1883). William combined farming with barn building and, by 1889, he was supervising barn raisings as head-framer, and built Charles Clelford's barn that year.

Lizzie married William John Brock (1861-1928), son of Thomas and Margaret Brock, storekeeper and postmaster (1886-1892) in Adelaide Village. William John described his occupation as "carpenter" at the time of his marriage to Lizzie. John and Lizzie had five children, Frederick "Fred"; Madeline Audrey (1895-1964); Ralph (1898-1980); William "Bill" Eldon (1901-1957); and Gordon Robert (1905-1980). William John attempted several enterprises but most of them failed. When Lizzie died, William John married Lottie Edna Nichol Brock (1888-1932), daughter of Edward Nichol and Esther Bella Seed, and widow of Norman A. Brock. She came to the new marriage with two children, Evelyn B. and Murray Brock. The new family arrangement proved to be incompatible; Lizzie's five children left Adelaide almost immediately to fend for themselves, and they did so most successfully. Before her mother's death, Madeline had married William Robert Kaye in Strathroy in June 1914, just before William Robert went overseas with the Canadian Expeditionary Forces. He was killed in action in 1916, leaving Madeline widowed, and with a baby, John Brock Kaye (1915). The exact chain of events is unknown, but eventually Madeline married I. John "Jack" Fox, who operated a jewelry store in Stratford, and Jack adopted John Brock Kaye. Madeline and Jack Fox lived separate lives, with Jack in Detroit and Madeline in British Columbia, where Madeline founded, owned and operated Debrett Candy Company, a very successful chain of retail candy and nut shops across the Canadian West and Ontario. Her older brother, Fred, operated one of these stores (called the "Nut House") on Christina Street in Sarnia. Fred Brock married and raised a family of four children in Sarnia. John Brock Kaye Fox married Clair Champer in Edmonton and raised a family in the west.

In the meantime, Ralph, Bill and Gordon Robert had moved to Kitchener and, probably with help from Madeline, they completed their education. Ralph and his wife, Olive May, had three children in Kitchener, June, Audrey and Jack. Bill trained as a professional engineer in Kitchener, married Betty Simon White, and had a son, William "Billie," who was ordained as a Roman Catholic priest. Gordon Robert became a corporate lawyer, Queen's Council, and senior partner in the law firm of "Brock, Trott, Artindale & West" in Kitchener. Gordon Robert married Antoinette Holle and they raised three children, Colleen Anne (1937); Gordon Robert Jr. (1938); and Thomas Louis (1952). Hardship and determination build character.

Robert Thomas, second child of William and Francis, was born in Adelaide and married Emma Louise Dickey (1877-1971) in Kerwood. They had three children, Edith Alma (1905-1906); Ernest A.

(1908-1924); and Ethel Lavinia (1910) who, in 1930, was living with her parents in Adelaide.

Tillie married James Bennett (ca.1868), son of James and Mary Anne (Hull) Bennett, in Kerwood on October 24, 1894.

Joseph William, youngest son of William and Francis, married Annie Elizabeth McCarthy, daughter of Cornelius and Sarah Ann (Moulton) McCarthy of Adelaide. They raised three children, Charles Edwin (1911); Edward Francis (1912); and Stanley Elden (1913). All of the children were baptized in Adelaide. The family later moved to Sarnia.

HERRINGTON, Roscoe and Mary

Roscoe Grant "Ross" and Mary Helen (Donaldson) Herrington had eight children, Kathleen; Donna; Grant; Lorne; Donald; Mac (1930); Helen; and George. They farmed in West Williams and operated a gravel pit from the farm. They sold the farm and pit to third child, Grant, and his wife, Eileen, and then moved to London. In 1957, they bought Lawrence Grogan's farm in Adelaide Township, where they lived for many years.

Mac was born in West Williams Township. He married Marion May Tackaberry (1939), who was born in London Township, the daughter of Benjamin Christopher and Emma May (Calcutt) Tackaberry. Benjamin and Emma had moved from Strathroy in 1945 to the Fourth Line of Adelaide. Marion has two brothers, George and Fred. Mac and Marion both attended S.S. #1 and 2, Keyser's School, and Strathroy High School.

Following their marriage, Mac and Marion lived in London. They bought five acres from Ross and Mary to build their home. They live on County Road 12, Townsend Line, and have two children, Kenneth James "Ken" and Jack. In 1991, Mac and Marion sold a corner of their lot, and the new owners built a house there.

Mac farmed with the family, and then changed his career to construction. He drove a gravel truck, and then operated machinery such as bulldozers and front-end loaders. He worked for Matthew's Group, Aztec-Ellis Don, Whimpey, and J-ARR Excavating Ltd., all from London. Mac was a foreman and superintendent for several years. This work, primarily with sewer and water mains, took him away from home to such towns and cities as Ottawa, Windsor, North Cobalt, Sudbury, London and Sarnia, as well as locals towns. Mac retired in 1994.

Marion worked for the Canadian Bank of Commerce in London, and then at home after moving to Adelaide. Later, she worked at Ausable Orchards and Rock Glen Fruit, packing and grading apples. She also worked at Dekker's Greenhouses in Strathroy.

Mac and Marion are now enjoying their retirement. They travel, play euchre, and enjoy music. They have lived in Adelaide Township for 40 years now, and have wonderful neighbours and memories. They are both Canadian Order of Forester members. Mac is a member of the Labourer's Union, and the International Operating Engineer's Union of North America.

Ken and Jack both work in construction. Jack is single. In 1981, Ken married Cyndy Butler of Oakdale, Ontario. They have two children, Toni Elizabeth (1984) and Bradley Kenneth (1986). They live at Lot 10, Con. 3 NER, which they purchased in 1976 from Mr. Martinus Vanderkant. There were many hills, gullies, and thorn trees on the farm, which Ken leveled and cleaned up to make it a straight 100 acres.

They built a new home on the farm in 1988 after selling the property they owned at Keyser's. An addition to the farm was Limousin cows in 1991. The name of the farm is "Adelaide Creek Limousins." As the cattle were growing to larger numbers and, with the addition of a hog-finishing business, the farm became a full-fledged, full-time farm.

In the spring of 1995, Ken and Cyndy purchased a 125-acre farm from Mrs. Ilene Dodge at Lot 11, Con. 3 NER. They count themselves very lucky to live in such a close-knit, caring community.

Family of Ken Herrington, Ken, Cyndy, Toni and Brad.

HERRINGTON, Trueman

In June 1850, Trueman Herrington purchased 84 acres of land at Lot 6, Con. 5 NER. The property went to Wesley Herrington, then Benjamin "Ben" Herrington (and possibly George).

Ben and his wife, Rose, lived on the farm and raised their son, Berton "Bert," who attended Keyser School. When Bert (d.1973) married Ethel Wilson (d.1973), Ben and Rose moved to Arkona, where Ben sold and repaired Massey-Harris implements.

While Bert and Ethel lived on the farm, they had six children. Marjorie Jean married Homer Carlym (deceased), and then James A. Dunn. Madge married William Vogel, and they had two children, Sondra and Harriet. Neva married Rex Davis, and they had six children, Donald, Richard, Rex Jr., Daniel, Bonnie and Michael (Bonnie and Michael died at five and six months of age, and are buried in Sunset Hills Cemetery in Flint, Michigan). Mary married Stewart Roloff, then Louis Schiller. She had three children, Linda Beth, Jon and Kathy.

After moving to Flint, Bert and Ethel had three more children. Betty married Lawrence (last name unknown) and they had seven children, Lawrence, Rebecca, David, Martha, Helen Mary, Sarah and Miriam. Robert married Regena Furtow and they had four children, Robert, Marianne, Michall and Jamie. James married Donalda Ivester and they had four children, Matthew, Timothy, Peter and Katie Ann.

After moving to Michigan, Bert worked for General Motors, Buick Motor Division, making crankshafts until his retirement. Bert and Ethel purchased 12 acres of land in Flushing, Michigan, and lived there during their retirement. They are buried in Grand Blanc, Michigan.

HICKS, Jack and Mary Lou

Jack (1936) and Mary Lou Hicks (1939) moved from Burlington to the east half of Lot 11, Con. 5 SER, in August 1975. With them were their three children, Nancy (1963); Steven (1964); and Sandra (1968), as well as their dog, Charlie. Jack, a civil engineer, had recently taken a position with Sifton Properties in London. He was born and raised on a farm near Goderich, and he wanted to return to the country.

The property was a very run-down, overworked nursery farm, which had been previously owned by Caradoc Nurseries of Strathroy, and Bill Earley.

The buildings were in poor repair, and the house was all but torn down (what was left was burned by the Adelaide/Metcalfe Fire Department). The drive shed and barn needed to be replaced.

The barn was originally an 'L' shape, but a training aircraft from Centralia (carrying live ammunition) ran out of fuel and crashed into one part of the barn, completely destroying it and killing some of the cattle in the yard. The pilot survived with only a broken ankle. Ammunition is still occasionally uncovered in the crash area.

With assistance from Roy Wardell, the barn and shed were raised and leveled, new foundations were

Cousins David Grogan and Jean Herrington in hammock, at home of David Wilson.

Jack & Mary Lou Hicks farm at east half of Lot 11, Con. 5 S.E.R.

made, and a steel covering was applied. Jack cleaned up the farm over the next few years and built a house while temporarily living in a mobile home.

Jack and Mary Lou's daughter, Nancy, is a nurse in Toronto. Steve married Rose Mary Aarts in 1992 and is now teaching school in Duncan, British Columbia. Sandra married Tom Taylor in 1994 and is now living in Maitland, Ontario.

Jack is employed by the Interprovincial Pipe Line in Sarnia, and is building up a cow/calf operation in his spare time.

HOARE, John and Anne

John Stroud Hoare (ca.1806-1881) was born in Cornwall, England. He married Anne Woolcock (ca.1806), who was born in England, on February 21, 1836. John was a storekeeper. He and Anne had seven children, Walter H. (ca.1836); Mary Jane (ca.1838); Elizabeth Anne (ca.1839-1857); George Stroud (ca.1842); William John (ca.1845); Philip Edward (1848); and John S. (ca.1851). John died in Adelaide Township. The Hoare family practised the Anglican faith.

Walter H. was baptized in Adelaide Township on March 5, 1837. He married Sarah (ca.1836, last name unknown), and they had four children, Edward; Frances Elizabeth (ca.1859); Charles Westlake (ca.1863), who was a physician; and Sarah Georgina (1867). These children were all born and baptized in Adelaide Township.

Elizabeth, third child of John and Anne, was baptized in Adelaide Township on January 10, 1841. She died in her teens, and her body was interred in St. Ann's Anglican Cemetery.

George was baptized in Adelaide Township on September 18, 1842. He married Sarah Naomi (d.1875, last name unknown).

Philip was baptized in Adelaide Township on June 4, 1848.

John was baptized in Adelaide Township on February 22, 1852.

HODGSON, Thomas and Elizabeth

In the early 1830s, three Hodgson brothers came to Canada from Yorkshire, England. One of these brothers was Thomas (d.1868). The names of the other two are not known, and a fourth brother stayed in England.

Thomas married Elizabeth Holmes (d.1876) in England. They came to Canada and settled in Westminster Township, where Thomas was a furniture maker. Thomas and Elizabeth had three children, John; Mary (1845-1855); and George Thomas (1851-1937). Thomas, Elizabeth and Mary are buried in the Brick Street Cemetery, near London (now in the London city limits).

George Thomas (1851-1937) lived in Adelaide Village. However, he spent some of his younger years in Stratford at a blacksmith shop, where he learned to make ploughs. For his first year's wages, he received $24 plus his board. During this first year, apprentice duties included cleaning the shop, so on Saturday nights, they worked until midnight. The second year, his wages were increased to $30 per year. Having gained his training and experience, he returned to Adelaide Village. According to Adelaide Council Minutes, Mrs. Westlake was the owner of the Royal Adelaide Hotel. She built a blacksmith shop in Adelaide Village and advertised for a blacksmith. John Hodgson applied for the job and was hired, and later became the owner of the shop. After a time, George bought the shop from his brother.

George married Fanny Clark (1857-1887) and they had two children, Wilbert (1881-1976) and Annie (1880-1971), who married Sam Wiley in 1903.

Wilbert lived in Adelaide Village until about 1896, when his father bought a farm at the west half of Lot 10, Con 2 NER. The house on this property had been the Presbyterian Manse, and had been moved to this location from the southwest corner, across from West Adelaide Church. Wilbert built a barn and, in 1904, he married Ida Marshall (1879-1954). They had two sons, John Thomas (1906-1959) and Wilbert Orville (1915).

In 1905, the Hodgsons bought the east half of Lot 10, Con. 2 NER, from John H. and Joseph W. Morse. In 1917, Wilbert bought the east half of Lot 9, Con. 2 NER, from W.H. Cuddy. Due to health problems, he rented out the farm. In October 1923, Wilbert and his family moved to Dorchester, where he operated a general/hardware store in partnership with Robert Henry. Two years later, in the fall of 1925, they returned to the Adelaide property and resumed farming. In 1933, they added Lot 9, Con. 3 NER, to their land holdings. Wilbert, Orville and John farmed all of this land, and had dairy cows, beef cattle, pigs and chickens.

John married Zelma Kathleen Conkey (d.1959) in 1931. At the time, Zelma was living in Sarnia with her parents, Nathaniel "Nat" Wesley and Mary Ellen Conkey. Nat was a Stationary Engineer at the hospital in Sarnia. After John and Zelma's marriage, the couple resided in Sarnia, where John was employed at Autolite. John and Zelma moved to the Hodgson farm in 1934, where John again farmed with Orville. Zelma's sister, Birdie Pennington, lived just around the corner.

In 1939, Wilbert and Ida moved to their home in Adelaide Village, where they resided until Ida's death.

The Hodgson farm was one of the first farms in the area to have electricity supplied by Delco Power. Zelma became a faithful member of West Adelaide Women's Missionary Society, West Adelaide Choir and the Women's Institute. She enjoyed playing the piano, singing, sewing, and many other handcrafts.

John and Zelma did not have children, but they enjoyed having family in for a singsong at the piano. On many Sunday evenings, they watched "The Ed Sullivan Show" on a post-card size (10") television, which they purchased in 1949.

For relaxation, the Hodgsons built a cottage at Rondeau in 1946. Here they enjoyed some leisure time and met new friends. Both John and Zelma died at about 52 years of age. After a year of illness, John died; Zelma, also fighting unknown health problems, died three weeks later. Shortly before their deaths, they had begun to build a new home. Unfortunately, neither John nor Zelma lived to enjoy it or see it completed. Their old home was moved once again and, at present, it is located on the corner of Highway 81 and the Second Line South. Orville continued to operate the farm for many years. Recently, it was purchased by the Strybosch family. Orville's keen memory has been the source of many stories throughout this book.

George and Fanny, Wilbert and Ida, and John and Zelma are all buried in the Hodgson plot in Strathroy Cemetery.

HOEFNAGELS, Marinus and Wilhelmina

The Hoefnagels family immigrated to Canada from the Netherlands in 1949. They lived in Mount Forest, and then moved to Adelaide. Marinus (Morris) Hoefnagels married Wilhelmina (Willy) Lamers in 1960. The Lamers family had immigrated to Aylmer. Morris and Willy settled in Adelaide on Lot 16, Con. 4 SER, and in 1969, they bought this farm from Clarence and Irma Sinkey. They sold the property in 1981 to John Dortmans Sr.

Morris and Willy have three daughters, Carolann (1961); Marianne (1964); and Patricia (1966). Marianne is married to Len Lewis and they live in Adelaide Township.

Morris and Willy now live on Lot 27, Con. 2 SER.

HOFFNER, Joseph and Theresa

In 1855, Joseph and Theresa Hoffner came to Canada from Wurttemberg, Germany (in the southwest region). They first settled at Baden in Waterloo County. Later, they moved to Rock Glen near Arkona, and finally resided in Adelaide at Lot 3, Con. 4 NER, where Gordon and Donna Hornblower now live.

From the diary of James Gerry, January 26, 1888: "Took job from Mr. Hoffner to build him a barn 36x52 feet—me to take out beams, plates, sleepers and overlays—him to furnish balance of timber—me to frame and finish outside and drive-floor according to the following plan—barn to be set on stone wall, agreeing to do the same for the sum of sixty dollars."

Joseph and Theresa had seven children. Two of them, Charles and John, died as children. The remaining children were William (d.1920); Joseph; Andrew; Mary; and Matilda.

William, a Roman Catholic, married a Presbyterian, Eliza Jane Shields (d.1942), in 1898. One presumes that the marriage created more than a passing discussion amongst neighbours.

In 1893, William purchased from Timothy Hay what is now the home farm of Frederick C. and Linda Hoffner, the east half of Lot 6, Con 4 NER. The farm cost $4,000. Today, over a hundred years later, the same land may be worth almost a hundred times that amount. Tim Hay had owned 550 acres when he died in 1907 at about 70 years of age. His obituary reads, "Timothy Hay, a conspicuous figure in the community at Keyser P.O., died rather suddenly... at the home of Joe Hoffner, a short distance west of the well-known corner. He suffered the misfortune of losing his residence by fire and he and his bosom friend and farm help, John Graves, rigged out quarters in his barn." Subsequently, Tim Hay caught pneumonia.

In addition to farming, William often attended cattle auctions. Becoming chilled at these events may have contributed to William becoming ill and dying at the premature age of 52, from pleurisy with effusion. William and Eliza had three children, Frederick William, Cecile, and John "Jack."

Frederick William became responsible for the farm management as a youth of about 16 or 17 years. He married Beatrice Oaks of Arkona. In addition to continuing with cattle farming and, later, mixed farming, Fred was quite interested in his community. He was involved on many boards, including the Strathroy Hospital Board, Ausable Bayfield Conservation Board, Municipal Council, the Milk Board, and others. He was pleased to support such projects as the first hydro line and the first telephone line, the Springbank Telephone System. The Hoffner telephone number was 51 R 4, which meant four long rings. The number for an emergency was one very long ring.

Beatrice enjoyed being a registered nurse, and was Supervisor of Nurses at Strathmere Lodge until her retirement at the age of about 67.

Fred and Beatrice have four children, Marjorie of Sarnia, William of Hamilton, Lola of London, and Fred, who lives with his wife and family on the home farm. As well as farming, they have an accounting practice in Strathroy. Their two children, James and Anne, represent the fourth generation of Hoffners living on the family farm. In 1993, the property became a century farm.

Cecile became a teacher, married Floyd Hillis, and moved to Sarnia. She currently lives with her daughter, Elaine, in Corunna.

Jack stayed on the home farm. He was buried in the same lot as his parents. Three tombstones created a problem for the Arkona Cemetery management. The initial two marble stones of Jack's parents were replaced with one granite stone bearing all three names. The question arose as to what the initial 'V' in William Hoffner's name referred to, and after having the initial put onto the stone, it was determined that in 1920, the letter 'V' was made for the letter 'U', which stands for Urias.

Joseph, son of Joseph and Theresa, married Mary Kearns, daughter of Sophrona and Thomas Kearns of Parkhill. Joseph and Mary left Keyser to live in Detroit, but they are buried in the Bornish Roman Catholic Cemetery. There are Hoffner descendants of Joseph in the U.S.

Mary married Bernard Reilly and lived in Elkton, Michigan. Times were hard and since the family was large, daughter Matilda "Tillie" was sent to Canada to live with her aunt and uncle, Matilda and Andrew, who had stayed on the home farm. Neither "Auntie" nor Andrew married.

Tillie married Blythe Rutter. They lived on the home farm, and Auntie lived with Tillie and Blythe until her death. In addition, Dan Cant lived with Tillie and Blythe during a period of time that included the 1950s.

HOFSTEEDE, John and Nellie

In June 1950, John and Nellie Hofsteede left the Netherlands and settled in Portage la Prairie, Manitoba. Nellie was the eldest of eight daughters born to Cornelius and Theodora Timmermans. John and Nellie lived for some time in Blenheim in Southern Ontario. They then rented a house from Donnie Wright on School Road, which was then called Sideroad 15. They later bought Donnie's 50-acre farm.

John and Nellie had eight children (the eldest daughter and her husband, Dave Cann, and their only child died in a car accident on Highway 81). The first two children were born in the Netherlands, while the remaining three sons and three daughters were born in Canada. John worked for the Strathroy Handle Factory and later went into the construction business. Most of the children settled in and around the Strathroy and Delaware area.

HOLDEN, Moses and Elizabeth

Moses Holden (1827-1904), son of Thomas and Margaret (Richardson) Holden, was born in Sussex County, England. In 1832, at the age of five, he came with his widowed father to Canada under the Petworth Emigration Scheme. After a stormy voyage of six weeks on the Atlantic, and a long, tedious journey along the lakes, they landed at Port Stanley. His father initially took up land in Warwick Township before settling in Adelaide on Lot 19, Con. 4 SER. Moses was one of the few men who saw the beginnings of Adelaide and Strathroy and the progress made into the 20th century. He learned the trade of shoemaking and followed it continuously throughout his life.

In 1852, he married Elizabeth Eastman (1830-

1885), daughter of Benjamin and Mahetable (Miner) Eastman. They raised seven children, Maria (1852-1935); George Richardson (1855-1933); Charles Wesley (1857-1947); Mahetta (1858-1926); Thomas B. (1861-1872); Harriet "Hatty" (1863-1926); and Edith.

Moses and his wife were very religious and they took an active part in the Methodist church. He served in several capacities, including choir member, class leader, trustee, and member of the board. He was one of the earliest members to tithe. All of the children were musically inclined and they were all members of the choir at some time.

Maria never married. She took care of her father after her mother's death. She was the organist for the Front Street Methodist Church for many years. After her father's death, she moved to Belfour, North Dakota.

George moved to Detroit and died in Seattle. It is not known if he married.

Charles was active in the local church and became a local preacher. He was later called into the active ministry and served in local churches before preaching in Michigan, South Dakota and Colorado. He retired in Michigan, after 50 years of service, at the age of 78. He married Emma (last name unknown) and they had three children, Herbert, Olive and Dwight. He married a second time, to Ella Mills, and they had a daughter, Florence Virginia.

Mahetta, fourth child of Moses and Elizabeth, married James Byron Vail of Strathroy. They had no children. James was a partner of Vail Bros. dry goods store in Strathroy. They moved to Belfour, North Dakota, and then retired to Redlands, California.

In 1890, Hatty married A. Judson Sayre, and they had one son, Harold Holden Sayre (d.1918). They lived in Harvey, North Dakota. Harold died in WWI.

Edith, the youngest child of Moses and Elizabeth, moved to Harvey, North Dakota, then retired to Redlands, California. She never married.

HOUBEN, John and Maria

In November 1950, John (d.1998) and Maria Houben married in the City Hall of Venray, Holland. In January 1951, they had a church wedding, after which the reception was held at Maria's house in Venray. The distance between John and Maria's homes was 26 kilometers. In that time, the trip was usually made by bicycle.

In March 1951, Maria and John left Rotterdam by boat. It was very difficult for the couple to leave their loved ones behind. There were more than 3,000 people on the ship and many were seasick. They were glad to arrive at their destination of Halifax, Nova Scotia, but walking was difficult after the long sea voyage. After two days and nights on a train, the Houbens arrived in London.

They bought their first farm, Lot 5, Con. 1 SER, from Clifford and Ilo Callaghan. There was much work to be done, and the little outhouse went first, special with little ones. In Canada, the soil was different than what one found in Holland, where John had a "mixed" farm. John built up a fine herd of purebred cows, which were milked in two milking parlours. They named their property "Asentray Farms." In the beginning, they grew sugar beets, cucumbers, grain and corn. They had never seen crops grow so fast in such a short time!

John and Maria raised 10 children, Mike, Pauline, Trudy, Mary, Gerry, Peter, Anny, Bernie, Joe and Teresa. The children all did their share on the farm. It was difficult for the older ones in school, but after learning English, they did well.

Houben family, Mike and Maria with Kristie, Julie and Kevin.

Mike, the eldest, went to school in Strathroy. He met Maria Vehaysen, the eldest daughter of Theodore and Anna Vehaysen, in 1970. Maria was born in Holland and came to Canada in 1952. She lived in Brooke Township for most of her life and went to school in Watford. Mike and Maria were married on May 6, 1972. The couple bought their farm in 1974 from Otto and Gladdis Zimmerman. They have three children, Kristie (1975); Julie (1977); and Kevin (1980). On the farm, Mike and Maria raised pigs and cash crops. They owned a service centre in Adelaide Village from 1975 to 1977. Mike was a member of Adelaide Council from 1982 to 1997 and reeve from 1995 to 1997. Mike and Maria lived in Adelaide Township until 1997, when they moved to Strathroy. They sold the farm to Bob and Willie Peters in 1995.

Pauline and John Bos moved to a farm near Parkhill.

Trudy and Hank Van Dyke, who farmed near Alvinston, are now living on a chicken farm at Lot 5, Con. 1 NER.

Mary lives on the original dairy farm and is very happy there.

Gerry and Peter went out west, to a beautiful part of the country.

Anny, who studied in London and at Georgian College, is now living in Orillia.

Bernie and Beth are building a new house on Lot 5, Con. 1 SER.

Joe and Fran live in Parkhill with their family. They are in the trucking business.

Teresa, who went to university at Western and Waterloo, has a double masters degree in gerontology. After working for planning boards in Essex and Toronto, she now works with the Fire Brigade.

After John and Maria retired in Strathroy, John returned many times to the farm. Maria moved to Trillium Village in July 1998, after John's death. The Houbens had 47 good years together in Canada: it was hard work, but they made it.

HOULTON, Henry and Eliza

Henry Houlton (1828-1901) immigrated to Canada from England as a bachelor and settled in Adelaide Village. He married Eliza Morse (1838-1906), daughter of William and Elizabeth Morse of Adelaide. They had four children, Amelia "Minnie" (ca.1865), who married Samuel Edwards in 1890; Florence (ca.1868), who married Lewis James (see HARRIS, Samuel); Jennie; and Ernest (1874). Henry farmed 200 acres, the east half of Lot 8, Con. 2 SER, and the west half of Lot 9, Con. 3 SER. Henry also ran a sawmill called Adelaide Mill.

In 1894, Jennie (1869-1908) married Ira Downer (1863-1931), son of John and Lucy (Rapley) Downer of Adelaide. They had at least three children, two infants buried in the Fourth Line Cemetery, Adelaide; and George (1908). Ira took over the family farm, part of Lot 13, Con. 4 SER. In 1930, George married Evelyn Carrothers (1909), daughter of Austin and Minnie (Morgan) Carrothers of Adelaide. George and Evelyn moved to Petrolia, where they had three children, Evelyn, Lucie and Ira.

In 1903, Ernest, the youngest child of Henry and Eliza, married Alice James (ca.1869), daughter of Thomas and Frances (Harris) James. They had four children, Clarence; Cuthbert (1906, died an infant); Frances (1911); and Lewis. Ernest took over the family farm, the west half of Lot 9 SER. Clarence remained single and worked for an airline in Los

Henry and Eliza Houlton

Florence Houlton

Jennie Houlton

Angeles. Frances remained single and worked as a nurse in Los Angeles.

HOWE, Russ and Jeannie

Russ and Jeannie Howe moved to part of Lot 19, Con. 5 SER, a property previously owned by Mary Butler. They rented the property for 1½ years before purchasing it. It is a unique property, consisting of a barn/house that was once a slaughterhouse. A lovely rock garden is located in the back yard beside a pond, where they were married on September 28, 1991.

The previous owner had resided in a small apartment in the slaughterhouse. After the Howes bought it, they renovated the whole building, making it an open concept home. The house is rustic in style with unique brickwork.

Russ and Jeannie have a daughter, Shannon Bailey (1993). They expect to continue renovations on the house for a long time to come.

HULL, Robert and Anne

Early in the 1800s, three Hull brothers left Londonderry, Ireland, for the New World. One settled in Nova Scotia, one in New England, and the third, Robert, settled in Metcalfe Township.

Robert and his wife, Anne (King), who was also from Ireland, had three sons, Cornelius (1804-1844); Robert Jr. (1811); and Blythe (1818). All three sons were born in Ireland.

In 1839, Robert Jr. married Anne Northwood (1824-1861), and their children were Anne (1839-1855); Jane (1840); Eliza; Robert (1842); John (1844); Mary Ann (1846); and Thomas (1849-ca.1851). By the 1861 census, Robert was listed as a widower and a labourer, living with Blythe's family. His children were not living with him.

In 1840, Blythe married Margaret Reed (1823), born in Scotland, and their children were Charlotte Jane (1841); Margaret Sophia (1843); Elizabeth (1844); Francis (1846); George E. (1848); James H. (1851); Agnes (1855); Thomas (1856); and Stephen (1857). In 1831, Blythe was living on Con. 8 in Adelaide, and by 1871, he and his family had left Adelaide.

Cornelius, the eldest son of Robert and Anne, married Mary Anne Summers (1817), born in Ireland, and their children were Robert (1842); Cornelius Jr. (1838); George Smythe (1840);

William and Charlotte Hull

William (1842); and Mary Anne (1844). Sadly, Cornelius died before Mary Anne's birth. Cornelius' widow, Mary Anne, later married Francis Smith and they had two known children, Jane and Francis.

On an 1831 land ticket map of Adelaide, Cornelius is shown on part of Lot 9, Con. 9 SER, which later became part of Metcalfe.

Robert, son of Cornelius and Mary Anne, married Orilia King (1840-ca.1870). They lived in Metcalfe.

George Smythe married Catherine Duffey (1834-1908), who was born in County Mayo, Ireland. Catherine had come to Canada in 1843 with her grandmother, Mary Columbine Wilson (Mrs. Matthew Wilson), and lived near Katesville. Catherine attended grammar school in Port Huron, Michigan, and taught school in Northern Michigan. She returned to Metcalfe to marry George and, for a few years, they lived on a rented farm on Con. 8 in Metcalfe. They later moved to the west half of Lot 6, Con. 5 SER, in Adelaide. This farm was "Pine Row Farm." Their children were William Columbine (1866-1941); Francis Smythe "Frank" (1868-1941); Cynthia Erma (1870-1879); and Annie Kate (1873-1951). George served for a number of years on the board of S.S. #7, Kerwood School.

In 1895, he purchased the south half of Lot 12, Con. 4 SER, from Uriah Stanley. Frank married Laura Gertrude Morgan and remained on the homestead. Annie became a teacher, and was married to George Linton Snyder. They had no family.

In 1897, William Columbine married Charlotte Elizabeth Wright (1872-1958). Their children were Hanson Wilfred (1898-1975); Leonard Franklin Bliss "Frank" (1900-1978); Ivan Alexander (1902); and adopted daughter, Dorothy Elizabeth (d.1983). William purchased the Lot 12 property from his father in 1908, and built the house that is there today.

Hanson, the eldest child of William and Charlotte, remained on the farm. He married Lillian Phillipa Lewis (1898-1965). They had three daughters, Phyllis Erma (1928); Elizabeth Ann Louise (1935-1994); and Norma Kathleen (1938). In 1962, Hanson sold the farm to Wietz and Sylvia Vanderhoek and moved to Strathroy.

In 1951, Phyllis Erma married Dr. William Butler (1929) and in 1974, they moved with their daughters, Joan Leslie (1955); Judith Ellen (1958); and Peggy Christine (1960), to Lot 25, Con. 2 SER. They lived there until 1983. The Town of Strathroy annexed this area in September 1980.

HUMPHREY, Mack and Eileen

Mack Humphrey (1919) was one of 14 children. He spent his youth in Caradoc Township, schooling, farming, trapping and hunting. During the Depression, Mack's father, Alfred, set up contracts for road building, ditch digging, well digging and tile drainage, which kept Mack and others occupied at a time when many needed work. Mack came to Adelaide Township in 1938 and worked for George and Jim Parker as a farmhand, then enlisted in 1941 in the Kent Regiment. He served his tour of duty in England and Europe. He was trained in the area of explosives, war gases, laying and removal of mines, jeep driving, etc.

On September 22, 1945, he married Eileen Winter (d.1995), and returned to Canada in November to await her arrival on July 1, 1946. Mack and Eileen moved to Strathroy, where they had two children, Danny Ernest (1947) and Linda Lee (1949). Danny married Janet Chepstone and they have four children, Angela, Melanie, Chad and Miranda. Linda married Ken Dowding and they have three children, Darren, Andrea and Ian. They all live in the Strathroy area.

The family moved to Adelaide Township in 1953, next to the Napperton School, S.S. #5, which Danny and Linda attended. When the new Central School was built, they attended school there.

Mack worked at Hawkings Lumber until 1960.

He then worked for E.J. Wright Central, where he remained until its closing in 1981. At this point, he began to rebuild homes and repair lawn mowers for a living. Eileen was janitor of S.S. #5 for several years, and worked as a lead hand at Craftmaster until it closed.

Mack still lives in Adelaide at the east half of Lot 14, Con. 4 SER. He has memories of loose livestock, dogs and cats, and raccoons in the attic, as well as fine neighbours, hard times, good times, and many summers of content in Adelaide Township.

HUMPHRIES, John and Maria

In England, about 1820, John Humphries (1797-1869) married Maria Ferris (1799-1885). They had three children before immigrating, in 1832, to part of Lot 10, Con. 3 SER. They had six children, Mary Jane (1822-1900), who married Isaac Thrower (see THROWER, Charles and Sarah); Rhoda (1824), who married Joseph Montague (see MONTAGUE, Joseph and Rhoda); William (1826-1912); Anne (ca.1834-1913); Henry (1838-1909); and Maria (1841).

In 1856, William married Caroline Elliott (1836-1892), daughter of James and Mary Ann Elliott of Adelaide. They had seven children, Emma (1857-1933); Mary (1859-1940), who became a music teacher and in 1913, married James Little; Louisa (1861); Annie (1863-1933), who married William Reilly in 1892; William E. (1865-1942); Harriet (1870-1920), who married into the Kincaid family; and Caroline (1872-1941), who married George Eastman (see EASTMAN, Benjamin and Mahetable) and resided on a farm near Strathroy.

William farmed the west quarter of Lot 10, on both Con. 2 and 3 SER. The Bethesda Methodist Church was built on a corner of his farm. He was a member of the Methodist Church, serving as class leader and school superintendent.

Emma married Harry Read, who owned London Dairy, in 1895. They lived in London, where they had three children, Edna, Eva and Harry. Edna married George McNaughton and they lived in Detroit. Eva married "Benny" Bennett and moved to British Columbia.

In 1889, Louisa Humphries (1861-1919) married William Beckton (ca.1859-1926), son of George and Mary (Stothard) Beckton of Kerwood. They had four children, Louella Merle (1889-1958), who married Harold Hyttenranch and had four children; Emma (1891); Evelyn Caroline (1894), who married Henry Tolson in 1923; and Anne (1896), who married William Simpson in 1924. Some records seem to indicate the second child was named Mae Hazel instead of Emma. William Beckton had immigrated to Canada from Scotland in 1869 with his parents. He worked as a cheese maker and farmed part of Lot 13, Con. 2 NER, before moving to Sarnia.

In 1893, William E., fifth child of William and Caroline, married Margaret Hunter (1863). They had two sons, James and John (1898), who both became medical doctors. James Humphries, M.D., married Margaret Maisey and lived in New Jersey. They had one son. After Margaret's death, Jim married a Nigle from Kingsville. John Humphries, M.D., married Olive Maisey, an older sister of Margaret. They had one daughter, Maisey, who lives in Windsor. William E. farmed on Lot 13, Con. 3 NER, for a few years and then moved to London.

Anne, fourth child of John and Maria, married a widower, Samuel Munn (ca.1794-1890) of Adelaide. They had three children, Josephine (ca.1855), who married James Brown, son of Joseph and Ann (Galbraith) Brown of Adelaide; Matilda (ca.1858); and John W. (ca.1865). Samuel farmed part of Lot 8, Con. 4 SER. His youngest son, John, took over the farm, but moved away in 1912.

In 1859, Henry, fifth child of John and Maria, married Bridget Galbraith (1842-1927), daughter of Ann Galbraith. They had seven children, Anna (1861-1933), who married Angus Knight (see

Henry and Bridget Humphries, west half of Lot 10, Con. 2 SER.

Willard Humphries, at 17 years of age.

KNIGHT, James and Jane); Harriet (1864-1934), who married Edwin Muxlow (see MUXLOW, Edwin and Harriet); Rebecca (1867-1870); Joseph (1869-1946); Willard (1872-1933); Adelaide (1878-1965), who married Joseph Petch (see PETCH, Francis and Mary); and Gordon (1887-1943). Henry farmed part of Lot 10, Con. 3 SER.

Joseph, fourth child of Henry and Bridget, married Edith Dowding (1873-1955), daughter of George and Mary Ann (Shrier) Dowding of Kerwood. They had a daughter, Eva Dowding (1898-1977), who married Willard "Bill" Earley, son of John James and Elizabeth (Smithrim) Earley. Eva and Bill had six children, Grant (1916-1978); Marguerite; Vern; Betty; June; and Ruth.

Willard, fifth issue of Henry and Bridget, married Annie Carroll (ca.1879-1910), daughter of John and Matilda (Carroll) Carroll of Adelaide. They had two children, Vila (1903), who became a nurse and married James Robinson, and Mable (1906-1960), who married Andrew Geddes (1901-1976) in 1925. Willard farmed with his father for a few years before renting farms in Adelaide for the next 12-14 years. By 1917, Willard had left Adelaide.

In 1915, Gordon, the youngest of Henry and Bridget's children, married Ruby DeGroat. They had three children, Earl, who married Florence Watcher; Eva; and Annie. Gordon took over his father's farm. He also had a sawmill in Kerwood, which he ran with his brother-in-law, Joseph Petch. Eva married Alex Harris, son of Wes and Justina (Dell) Harris. They had a daughter, Nancy, and retired to London.

Maria, the youngest child of John and Maria, married Robert Collier (ca.1830), son of Thomas and Sarah Collier of Adelaide. They had four known children in Adelaide, William (ca.1860); Thomas (ca.1863); John (ca.1868); and Albert (ca.1870). Robert farmed part of Lot 8, Con. 2 SER. By 1881, he had moved to Warwick Township.

INCH

William Inch bought the Keyser Cheese Factory in February 1916 from Mr. James Grieve and sold it in November 1918 to James A. Murray, giving Mr. Murray a total of 95 acres on that property. William and family do not show up in Adelaide or Metcalfe censuses for 1881, 1891 or 1901, and must have lived elsewhere, perhaps Strathroy, although most members of the Inch family lived in Metcalfe.

The Inch family is a very old family, traced back to the 1200s in Scotland, Ireland and England. There are many spellings of this name over the years. They were prominent families. Mr. Ron Cox from Quebec, in his Lightfoot book, relates many interesting legends about the early Inches:

"Many Inch legends exist which are only known to certain elders of the clan, and in the past, the Inch clan used to meet yearly at Inch (except the womenfolk who stayed home to do the work and those males who were in the stocks or otherwise employed in such institutions as Dartmoor or incarcerated in the dungeons of Exeter Castle) and at such meetings, all family matters were discussed, and certain monies or loot as it would be called today, were shared out."

During the Hundred Years War (1338-1453), the Inch clan received a terrible blow in battle through a misunderstanding. "With the 'English' force drawn up, the commander, one of the Arundells, was not too sure if the nearby woods contained any of the enemy, so, being cautious, he issued the order "Inch forward!" and to his amazement, all the Inch clan alone, leapt forward and charged the woods. Alas, the woods were alive with the French, and whilst they fought with all their skills and might, the Inch contingent was slaughtered almost to the last man before the rest of their comrades could make up the lost ground and reduce the French to a retreating rabble." Some drastic measures were taken at the next clan meeting concerning marriages, whereby the Inch males were asked to obtain a bride from the Hambly families by fair means or foul!

According to the Lightfoot book, a son, Frank H. Inch, married Hannah Josephine Wright. Three of five children were born in Adelaide Township, Alexander William (1885); Frank Bradford (1887); and Ruby Jemima Lilian (1889), but they are not on the 1881, 1891, or 1901 censuses of Adelaide and Metcalfe.

On the 1905 census, William, Frank and Richard Inch are recorded in the Foster's Middlesex County Directory, freeholders, all on Lot 6, Con. 5 SER, Adelaide Township, and in 1910, only Frank Inch is still living on the lot. By 1914, Frank has moved to Strathroy, according to information in the Age.

In a delightful story written by Jane Laughton about her Taylor connections, she recalls how her Uncle Frank, who operated a cheese factory in Kerwood (Frank must have taken over the factory), always bought the ham and cheese and sliced it up neatly, as her great-grandfather (Mr. Charles Cawrse Sr. of Metcalfe.) had arthritis. This Frank Inch (d.1917) was married to Grace Taylor, daughter of William and Mary (Cawrse) Taylor. Grace and Frank had one known son, Richard (1880-1941). It is unsure if there were two cheese factory owners named Frank Inch in Adelaide Township.

A Fred Inch lived in Adelaide Village on the north half of Lot 15, Con. 1, where he was a tenant, but he left the area by 1935.

INGHAM

Samuel Ingham (1821-1903) came to Canada from Yorkshire, England. He immigrated to the Rice Lake area of Ontario, where he taught school and farmed. During his marriage to Elizabeth Ellenor (1823-1875), they raised seven children. Three of these children spent their adult lives in Adelaide Township and died there, as did their father, Samuel.

The oldest Ingham, Maria Ann, married Edward Nichol and, by 1873, they were settled on the Egremont Road. While visiting her sister, Maria Ann's sister, Harriet, met Adelaide neighbour, Richard Brock. They married and lived on the west half of Lot 13, Con. 1 SER (see BROCK, George and Isabella), where they raised their family.

A year after Elizabeth's death, Samuel purchased the south half of Lot 18, Con. 1 SER, from Charles Oke. Ed Nichol, owned the north half of Lot 18, and in 1881, Ed bought Sam's half.

In the 1891 census of Adelaide, the youngest Ingham, Mary Jane, is recorded as a lodger with Richard and Harriet Brock; she is 26 years old and her occupation is "music teacher." At one time, she was the organist at Shiloh Methodist Church. Mary Jane met her future husband, Charles Edward McInroy, whose family had moved from the Belleville area to Lot 12, Con. 1 SER, next door. After their marriage in 1892 (see McINROY, Alexander and Ann), Samuel lived with the McInroys on Lot 12, Con. 2 NER. When the new brick house was erected in 1918, Samuel continued to live in the old log house in the yard. On his death, his body was taken by train to Cobourg and then to the Thackeray Cemetery on Rice Lake Road. His sons-in-law, Ed Nichol and Richard Brock, accompanied the cortege.

Alfred Ingham of Roseneath, son of William John Ingham, worked for the railway. He came to Adelaide Township to visit his aunts and grandfather and met the girl next door, Annie Mary Brock, daughter of Arthur and Esther (Conkey) Brock. They were married in Edmonton in 1913 and, three years later, he was killed in a railway accident. When daughter Freddie (Ingham) Galbraith (1917) was born, her mother brought her back to Strathroy to be among family. Alfred's sister, Mary Emily, boarded with her aunt, Harriet Brock, while she was teaching at S.S. #10 Adelaide. Mary Emily moved to Alberta in 1911.

IRELAND

William Ireland (1803-1856) was born near Girvan, Ayrshire, Scotland, and was the son of Bayne (1777-ca.1867), and grandson of William (1741), both born in Scotland.

The McCubbin family of Adelaide and East Williams Township came to the Ireland homestead when they first arrived from Scotland, and it was well known that the two families had been friends in Scotland. It has always been understood that William's fourth child was born at a place they called Springbank. Recent research indicates that there has not been a populated place with that name in the last hundred years, but this same research strongly suggests that the hamlet of Springbank lay near the present town of Campbeltown, Kintyre, Argyll District, Scotland. Campbeltown, Argyll, lies about 30 miles in a direct line across the Firth of Clyde and the trip by boat would involve sailing past the small island of Ailsa Craig and south of Arran Island. This entire region was a haven for whiskey smugglers. Campbeltown, Argyll is the location of one of Scotland's most renowned single-malt whiskey distilleries, called Springbank. Springbank was founded in 1828 by the local whiskey smugglers and this location was the source for the water for the distillery. Family tradition also confirms that old William did indeed like his whiskey. Margaret Demaray Wardell, granddaughter of William, recalls that Campbeltown was a place often mentioned by the Ireland family.

William married Jane Bishop (1813-1886) in Scotland, and they came to Lot 27, Con. 1 SER, with five of their 10 children, in 1843. Their children were Benjamin "Bayne" (1833-1895); Margaret Jean (1835-1916); Jennet "Jane" (1838); William (1839-1918); Jessie (1841-1927); James (1843); Isabella (1845-1919); Thomas (1849, died an infant); Allan (1852-1854); and John "Jack" (1855-1881). Thomas and Allan were born on the family farm and are buried in First Adelaide Presbyterian Chapel (Ireland) Cemetery. Margaret Jean married Robert Young in Scotland and they had a daughter, Ellen, who married Robert Black. This family stayed in Scotland.

Bayne never married. He lived his entire life in the original farmhouse on Lot 27 with his mother, Jane. This old house was located just to the west, across the lane, from the present Ireland house and Amiens Post Office.

Jane married John Wark of Caradoc Township, who was born at Jedborough, Scotland. From Caradoc, they moved to Speaker Township, Sanilac County, Michigan, in 1858. They raised six children, Jennie, Janet, William, John, Andrew and Thomas. The Irelands and Warks kept in close contact and held many family reunions with more than 50 descendants in attendance.

When William, fourth of William and Jane's children, was interviewed in 1889, the following events were recorded: "In making the voyage across the Atlantic, it took six weeks on the vessel California. They were among the first settlers of Adelaide Township, and erected their little home in the woods when wolves were numerous and troublesome. William and his family killed a bear about 100 rods from where the present residence stands, killing him with clubs and a dog. He was a student at the old log house of pioneer times, and was obliged to go two miles in order to get an education. He had followed agricultural pursuits all his life, and he now lives on the old Ireland homestead, which he owns, and which consists of 100 acres of well-improved land. Here he has resided for forty-five years. He was married October 26, 1863, to Miss Deborah Ann Donaldson (of Adelaide), who was born in Peterborough County, May 5, 1840, the daughter of George and Mary Ann Carroll, natives of Troy, N.Y., and Ontario respectively. The former was born in 1812, and was a soldier in the Rebellion of 1837. The latter was born in 1818. In politics, Mr. Ireland is a Reformer, and for twelve years has held the position of school trustee. He was an assessor of the township in 1873. In 1882 he was elected to the Township Council, and was defeated in 1883 by a majority of seven votes, but was elected to the same position one year later, heading the polls over twenty votes. He was elected to the same position in 1885 and 1886, and in 1887 was defeated by a majority of seven votes for the position of deputy-reeve. In 1888 he was elected to that position, which he now holds. He has been a life-long member of the Presbyterian Church, and takes an active interest in the affairs of the same. He was elected an elder of the Presbyterian Church in 1866, and appointed Justice of the Peace in 1874. His father was a member of the Presbyterian Church, and the first church (First Adelaide Presbyterian Chapel) of that denomination in Adelaide Township was built on the Ireland homestead in 1847, and Rev. William Howden was the first pastor. Mrs. Ireland is a member of the same Church." [History of the County of Middlesex, 1889]

On September 1, 1891, William was appointed Postmaster at Amiens Post Office, a position he was to hold for 22 years, the longest term of any that held this position, until the office was closed on April 30, 1913. This location at William's home on Lot 27 was a significant departure from the usual locations at or near Lot 31. The front room of the Ireland home was converted into a post office with one wall made into a postal unit with open boxes for each patron's mail. Mr. Ireland took his position and its responsibilities very seriously, as he never left his mailbag unattended, even among close relatives. Not only did he operate the office at his home, but travelled to Strathroy by horse-and-buggy or cutter five or six times per week, to pick up the mail 52 weeks per year. His daughter, Tootie, often assisted him with the mail. If he was seriously ill, his brother-in-law, Charles Demaray, made the run for him. He was also one of the first postmasters to experiment with semi-rural delivery before its inception in the period 1911-1914. William held many positions of trust within his community, but none was ever executed with such fidelity. He was truly the romantic figure of the old-time mailman!

William and Deborah raised five children at Laugh-Tree House (as the property came to be known), William Allan (1864-1892); George Mars (1866-1931); Anne "Annie" Mary (1869-1949); Margaret "Tootie" Jane (1871-1957); and John Donaldson (1876-1882).

William Allan never married.

George Mars married Betsy Ann Limon (1872-1946) of Caradoc, farmed in Adelaide on the home place, and raised four sons, Limon George (1901-1979); John Gordon (1905-1969); Donald Bruce (1908-1986); and William Duncan (1912-1992). These children attended S.S. #3 Adelaide.

Limon married Muriel Irene Luce (1903-1966) of Komoka and they farmed on the home place. Limon also worked for Harry Anderson for many years, and did roadwork for Middlesex County. Limon and Muriel had five children, Marion Jean (1931); Betty Marie (1932); Ronald George (1935); Dorothy Ann (1939); and William Keith (1944). Limon's first car was a Ford Model T Roadster, and on rainy afternoons you could find Limon at the blacksmith shop at Fernhill, getting Jimmy Drysdale to work on farm equipment. When Limon sold the Lot 27 home farm in August 1974, it ended more than 130 years of continuous ownership by the Ireland family.

Marion Jean, the eldest of Limon and Muriel's children, married Albert Cecil Ackland (1932) at Bethel United Church. Marion trained and worked as a nurse in London. They have three children, Jennifer Lee, Brenda Jean and Gregory Newton.

Betty Marie married Harold Lewis Caughlin of Lobo, and they have three children, David Lewis, Marilyn Joyce, and Susan Elizabeth.

Ronald George married Vivian McChesney of Adelaide, and they have three children, Sherry Lynn, James Dean and Lori Jean. They farm near Chatham.

Dorothy Ann married James Marwood Matthews of Adelaide. They have two children, Kimberly Irene and Katherine Anne. Dorothy Ann and James live in Brockville, Ontario.

William Keith married June Lightfoot and they had two children, Jeffrey and Jamie. Keith and June divorced in 1979. Keith married Linda Muylaert and they live in Katesville.

John Gordon, second son of George and Betsy, married Martha Emma Hiscox and raised three children in London, Margaret Ann (1931); Dorothy Jean (1934); and John Douglas (1938). John Gordon worked for Middlesex County Jail in London.

Donald Bruce, third of George and Betsy's sons, married Minnie Gertrude Malone (d.1989) and they had two children, Anne Elizabeth and Jean Isabel. Donald Bruce graduated from the University of Toronto as an engineer, joined Ontario Hydro as a lineman, and retired as an Assistant General Manager.

William Duncan, the youngest son of George and Betsy, married Sarah Ann Witherspoon. They had three children, Donna Ann, George Walter and Robert William. William spent many years as a barber in London, and served in the Canadian Army as Corporal from 1939 to 1945. After returning from overseas, he went to work for Ontario Hydro and lived near Forest, Ontario.

Annie, third child of William and Deborah, married Archie J. Campbell (1866-1937), formerly of Caradoc, and they had three sons, William "Bill," Murray and Stewart. Archie and Annie farmed on Lot 25, Con. 2 SER. Bill married Ella Chapman and lived near Fern Hill, Ontario (see CAMPBELL, Archie J. and Annie). Murray married Bessie Brown and farmed on Lot 25, Con. 3 SER. Stewart married Alberta Underhay, had a daughter, Victoria May, and lived near Welland, Ontario.

Tootie, fourth of William and Deborah's children, married Sandy Campbell (1869-1952) of Caradoc.

Jessie, fifth issue of William and Jane, married Robert Thompson (1840-1897), who was born in Scotland. They farmed in Caradoc and raised seven children, Bertha; Annie; Gordon (1869-1876); Margaret J. (ca.1870-1955), who married George Brown Conkey (1868-1955) of Adelaide; John W. (ca.1872-1918); and Silas (1875-1951), who married Mary Annie Ayre of Adelaide, and raised 11 children in Caradoc.

James, sixth child of William and Jane, married Angeline Lucinda Chute (ca.1846), daughter of Alfred and Olivia Chute of Caradoc Township. James and Angeline had four children, Effie, who married Emerson Steele; Edith, who married George Godden; Minnie; and Lily, who married John "J.C." McDonald of East Williams.

Isabella, seventh of William and Jane's children, married Charles Augustus Demaray (1842-1912) of Adelaide (see DEMARAY), and they raised four children in the township, Jane (1866-1938); Lydia (1870-1936); Effie (1872-1950); and Charles Allan (1875-1952).

Jack, the youngest child of William and Jane, married Amelia Johnson in North Dorchester Township and they had three children, Nina, who married Worthy Boyer; Blanche Alice, who married Harry McLean; and Melvin (d.1943), who married Ada Gilles and resided in Detroit, Michigan. Jack and Amelia lived in London, where Jack was a bank caretaker.

IRWIN, Joyce and Margaret

Joyce Irwin (1855-1935) was born in the County of Armagh, Ireland. He came to this country at the age of five and resided in Pine River (Huron County). On December 3, 1901, he married Margaret Dickson (1874-1947) at Pine River. Margaret was born at Amberley, in Huron County. They moved to Fernhill, where he had a blacksmith shop. While in Fernhill, they had a son, Harold (1902-1958), and a daughter, Elizabeth "Lizzie" (1904-1969). The Irwin family moved to the village of Kerwood in October 1904, having bought the house and blacksmith shop owned by John Armstrong (Lot 4 and the south part of Lot 5, Block "E" in the village of Kerwood). This location was on Cockburn Street, almost in the centre of the block between Grace and MacKenzie, on the west side. At some time previously, the Farmer's Bank was located in the house. Margaret's father, James Dickson (d.1920), lived with the family in Kerwood until his death.

After coming to Kerwood, three more daughters were born, Christena "Tena" (1906-1985); Trevah (1908-1984); and Muriel (1915-1998). The "h" was later dropped from Trevah's name.

Joyce was a faithful member of I.O.O.F. Lodge. The Lodge had oyster suppers at the Lodge hall, Margaret would cook the oysters in a copper boiler at the house, and the men came for them when needed. House dances (one or two each winter) were held at the house when the cook stove would be moved to the north end of the kitchen to make more room to dance. Margaret would make her delicious marble cake (the Irwin children didn't get to eat the cake then, because they would have gone to bed). Indians who lived in the village came and played the music for the dances. The dances were held until Joyce was afraid the floor would give way.

They looked after cleaning the bank (where the I.O.O.F. hall building is currently located), the I.O.O.F. hall, and the Anglican Church. Muriel recalled going along to the bank where she and Treva helped with the dusting, and cleaned the inkwells and refilled them. The floors were wood, there were teller "cages," and coal was used to heat the place. Muriel's daughter, Joyce (Langford) Morgan, remembers going to the bank with her Grandma when she went to clean, and being quite intrigued with the "cages" and the interesting smell, which may have come from a cleaning or preserving product used on the wood floors. Muriel also did housework for the W.R. Pollock household in Kerwood.

The eldest grandson remembers watching as Grandpa shoed horses in the blacksmith shop, and the young man pounded horseshoe nails into the bottom sill of the shop door. The sides of the doorframe were also full of nails, which the Irwin children had pounded there. Joyce Irwin was quite strict about his children not being in the blacksmith shop when he was working.

Before her death, some of Muriel's memories were recorded. She recalled that Saturday was the day to "set" tires, which was done in the back yard. Margaret and the children helped carry cold water from the pump to pour over the hot tires. The Irwin children would have gathered bark from along the railroad after school, which was used to heat the iron to "set" the tires. Muriel remembered pumping the bellows for her father when there were no customers in the shop.

On October 19, 1935, Joyce Irwin went to Wood's Store in the village in the evening, where he chatted and did some step dancing. When he was returning home at about 8:45 p.m., a car struck him as he crossed the street. He was taken to his home, where it was found he had a fractured skull, and he died shortly before midnight. Dr. Vine of Strathroy attended him. The funeral took place at the residence and Joyce was buried in Strathroy. Margaret remained at the residence on Cockburn Street in Kerwood for the remainder of her life, and the residence stayed in the family until Treva's death (she also died at the residence).

Harold, the eldest child of Joyce and Margaret, married Ena Langford of Metcalfe Township, daughter of George Elmer Langford, on April 15, 1933. They took up residence at Lots 7 and 8, Block "G" in the Village of Kerwood (Clyde Street). Harold was bookkeeper at the Creamery and Carnation Plant in Kerwood for many years.

Lizzie and Tena graduated as nurses in 1929 from Strathroy Hospital. Tena married Marvin Jones on June 23, 1930, and moved from the village. She died in Sarnia.

Lizzie married Bruce Evans (d.1992) on July 16, 1938, and they took up residence in the Irwin home on Cockburn Street. Lizzie nursed for several years and Bruce worked at the Kerwood Produce and at Muxlow's in Strathroy before taking over the Supertest gas station in Kerwood in the 1950s. In late 1946 or early 1947, Bruce started driving a school bus to Strathroy Collegiate. His first bus was a homemade plywood bus, cream-colour on the top, with a blue bottom. It carried 25-30 students and had car seats in it, one row on each side and one down the middle. The students called it "the shoebox." He bought a new yellow bus in the spring of 1948. Since Bruce was meticulous in the care of his vehicles, and back then, new vehicles had to be broken in, the first few days the bus was a little late arriving at school. While the bus went through Kerwood taking students home to the first road south of Kerwood, the students from the north would get off the bus and pick up snacks at Wood's Store, and then Bruce picked them up on his way back through the village.

After Lizzie quit nursing, she worked at the gas station. She pumped gas, worked at the counter and sold cigarettes, etc., and cleaned the windows of the cars Bruce serviced. Later on, in the late '50s, Bruce bought a second bus. Bruce began to drive the north route, and Ted Dennis drove the south route. Due to ill health, Bruce retired in February 1968, after driving bus for 21 years. A social evening organized by his former bus riders was held on June 29, 1968, at the high school. Many of the 300 students who had ridden on Bruce's bus attended, some from as far away as Downsview. He was referred to as the "best bus driver anywhere" and one of the most respected drivers the school ever had. Students could expect a little morning lecture, followed by an afternoon treat, at least twice a year.

Bruce and Elizabeth had one daughter, Margaret "Marnie" (1940), who married Jim Newman on October 7, 1961. Marnie and Jim had three daughters. Their youngest child, Michelle Elizabeth, married Steven Johnston of Ravenswood on October 8, 1994.

Joyce and Margaret at Harold and Ena's wedding, 1933.

A few years after Lizzie died, Bruce married Ena Irwin and took up residence at her home on Clyde Street in Kerwood. Bruce died suddenly of a heart attack in the pit of his garage, across the street from the house on Clyde Street. He had been heard to say on many occasions that the garage was where he would die. When Ena went to Strathmere Lodge in 1993, Michelle and Steve Johnston bought her house in Kerwood. They have done extensive renovations on the house and plan to do more.

Treva, the fourth child of Joyce and Margaret, was a bookkeeper for about 40 years for E.J. Wright Utilities and E.J. Wright Central in Strathroy.

Muriel, the youngest child of Joyce and Margaret, married Harry Langford in 1937. They had two children, Joyce (1938), who married Ernest Morgan; and a son, Paul (1946). The blacksmith shop was moved to Muriel and Harry's farm in Metcalfe Township on wagons pulled by tractor, and they used it as a garage for their car as long as they lived there. Muriel died at the Sprucedale Care Centre in Strathroy.

Elizabeth and Christena Irwin, graduation from Strathroy Hospital Nursing School, Feb. 8, 1929.

JACKSON, Jo and Vaike

Jo Jackson was born in the London area, near Fanshawe Dam. His parents were from Scotland and England. His wife, Vaike, was born in Geislingen, Germany, and her parents are from Estonia. They have three sons. Two reside in London and are married with children. The third son attends school in Rochester, New York, at the Rochester Institute of Technology, where his area of study is computer software design and repairs.

Jo and Vaike purchased their farm in May 1989 and have since built a driveshed to house the farm machinery, and also a lighted airstrip for their small airplane, which they use for enjoyment and travels from coast to coast. The property is called Mullifarry Landing after the Mullifarry post office, which was located less than a mile away.

Jo farmed in the West Lorne area for 20 years, where he grew cash crops and had cow/calf and sow/weaner operations. He worked in London for 30 years as a professional firefighter, where he advanced from hydrant man to district chief. When not farming his own land, Jo combines crops for neighbouring farmers.

JADISCHKE, Wilhelm and Frieda

The Wilhelm Jadischke family settled in Strathroy on September 24, 1950, after immigrating to Canada from Germany. The family was comprised of Willie, Frieda and their five sons, Gustav "Gus," Willie, Heinz, Arthur and Kurt.

Gus married Helen Louise Slater (d.1960), and they settled in Adelaide Township on the Second Line South. On November 9, 1972, Gus remarried, to Beverley (Wyborn) Tupholme, a widow from London. They have two children, Robert Andrew "Andy" and Deborah Louise "Deb." They grew up in Adelaide and attended W.G. MacDonald public school and S.D.C.I. Andy graduated in 1985 and Deb in 1995.

Andy finished his post-secondary education at Fanshawe College in London with a Motive Power Technology degree. He married Pamela Jane Drook in July 1993, and they reside in Kitchener, where he works for John Breuwer Car Parts Plus.

Deb graduated in May 1998 from Spring Arbor College in Michigan with a Bachelor of Arts degree in communication and an associate of piano pedagogy degree. She married Mark Raub Hirst on

January 10, 1998, and they reside in Spring Arbor, Michigan.

Gus is a self-employed heating contractor and Beverley is employed as an R.P.N. at Strathmere Lodge. They continue to reside at R.R. #7 Strathroy, Ontario.

JAMES, Thomas and Alice

Thomas James, a retired British soldier (ca.1788), received a Patent from the Crown in 1836 for 100 acres, the west half of Lot 11, Con. 2 SER. In 1841, Thomas and Alice sold 50 acres of their land (the east half of the west half) to their son, Henry. The 1852 Adelaide census shows Thomas James 64, a farmer of Wesleyan Methodist religion, born in England; and a son, Thomas Jr. 24, also born in England, whose occupation was blacksmith. Of the 50 acres occupied, 10 acres were cleared, crops grown were 15 bushels of wheat, 12½ bushels of Indian corn, and 50 bushels of potatoes. There were five cattle and three hogs.

Thomas and Alice had four children, Elizabeth "Betsy" (ca.1822), born in England; Ellen (1827), born in Nottingham; Thomas Power (ca.1828), born in England; and Thomas Johnston (1846).

Betsy married neighbour Charles S. Schweiger, a carpenter (ca.1809), who was born in Germany. The 1852 Adelaide census lists their children as Louisa 13; Henry 11; James 10; David 8; Thomas 6; Ellen 5; and Betsy 1.

In 1843, Ellen married William Miller (1814), who was born in Belfast, Ireland (see MILLER, Robert and Mary).

Thomas Power married Frances "Fanny" Harris (1835-1922) about 1855. Fanny was born in Ingersoll, the daughter of Thomas and Ann (Phipps) Harris. In 1861, Thomas Power owned the entire west half of Lot 11, Con. 2 SER. The east quarter of the west half was purchased from William Morse. He named his farm "Greenfield Farm" (1862 Tremaine Map). Thomas Power and Fanny had three children, Louisa Ann (1858); Lewis P. (ca.1860); and Alice Power (ca.1869).

Louisa married Chester Miner (1854), son of Chester and Mary Ann (Buttery) Miner, in 1882. They had two children, Lewis Chester (1884) and Florence Lillian (1887).

Lewis Chester farmed on part of his father's farm. He married Gertrude Margaret Eastman, daughter of Willard Martin and Mary (Macklin) Eastman of Arkona, in 1909. Later, they sold the farm and moved to Sarnia.

Florence married John Rosco McGrath (1887). Their eldest daughter, Beatrice May (1910), was born in Adelaide Township. It seems that the McGrath family moved to Saskatchewan as the other three children, Jack, Don and Florence Marie, were born in the Eatonia area of Saskatchewan.

Lewis P., second child of Thomas Power and Fanny, married Florence Ann Houlton (1868), daughter of Henry and Eliza Jane (Morse) Houlton of Adelaide Township, in 1888 on the James farm. Their son, Harry P. (1890), is thought to have later farmed in Saskatchewan. Their daughter, Gladys (1892), married and lived in Saskatchewan. Both children were born in Adelaide Township.

Alice, youngest of Thomas Power and Fanny's children, married Ernest Henry Houlton, son of Henry and Eliza Jane (Morse) Houlton, in 1903. Ernest was her sister-in-law's brother. Alice and Ernest had four children, Clarence, Frances, Lewis James and Cuthbert. In 1922, the E.H. Houltons were living in Strathroy.

In 1882, Thomas Power James sold the 100 acres of the original James farm to Isaac Thrower. At this time, records indicate that some of the James family moved to Saskatchewan.

JAMIESON, John

John Jamieson (ca.1798), one of the early settlers in Adelaide Township, kept a diary between April 1852 and June 1854. This document, a copy of which is in the library at the University of Western Ontario, has been invaluable to our understanding of life in Middlesex in the 1850s.

Jamieson had been a schoolteacher in the town of Largs in his native Scotland before he immigrated to Canada with his sister, Agnis (ca.1805), and his daughter, Jane (ca.1822). John's wife probably died before they immigrated; he is listed as a widower in the 1861 census. It seems that the Jamiesons had some fond memories of their old home. John notes in his diary that Agnis received annual flower seeds from Scotland, while he received the occasional newspaper with a letter.

Pioneer life was, in some ways, quite hard, and the Jamiesons were very much at the mercy of the Canadian weather, something which John carefully recorded in his diary. He noted late frosts, which destroyed everything he had planted, droughts that left the hay so short that it was impossible to cut, thunderstorms that brought down trees and, of course, snow. During one particularly dry period, a brush fire got out of control, burning a great deal of the Jamieson's fence line. Not only did they have to fight the fire, John also had to stay awake all night, guarding his crops from the neighbours' cattle. They came very close to losing their home to the fire, but were saved by a well-timed thunderstorm. The meticulous record Jamieson kept of the weather has been useful, recently, to scholars interested in climate change in the area. One interesting seasonal reference is to "The Canadian Band" starting each spring—it seems that this was the local name for the frog song on spring nights.

From reading the diary, one gets a fairly clear picture of the sort of person John Jamieson was. He was a religious man, a Presbyterian, who attended Sunday services whenever they were held and was concerned over their infrequency. One senses that he was pleased when the Reverend William Deas was appointed to minister to the community on a permanent basis. He almost always recorded at whose home the service was held, the subject of the sermon or the text that inspired it, and the attendance (which seems to have averaged about 30 people). In September 1853, the congregation held a meeting as to where and when they would build a church.

Just as there was no church building for the Presbyterian community, there was no schoolhouse for the children. In fact, there had not even been classes held for two years. Much to Jamieson's satisfaction, a resolution was passed to levy a tax to hire a teacher and provide the young people with an education. Although Jamieson had taught in Scotland, he had to go to London to write an examination in order to receive certification to teach in Canada. This took several days, because he walked there and back. He describes himself upon arriving home as being "quite crippled." This return to teaching meant that there was less time to work his land, only the mornings and evenings on school days.

Working the land meant clearing it, burning brush, dragging it, planting, hoeing, harvesting, and building fences to keep cattle and sheep out. One diary entry recorded how John and Agnis worked past midnight, in the moonlight, repairing their fences.

From the diaries, we know that the Jamiesons had an older cow named "Lilly" and a younger cow, "Plum." Cattle were not so much *fenced into pastures* as they were *fenced out of the crops,* and they often wandered quite a distance in the woods. One day, they spent most of the afternoon looking for Plum to see if she had given birth to her calf. They also kept some hogs, and a dog named "Dido." John Jamieson had to make the difficult decision to do away with Dido after he caught her worrying the neighbour's lamb, which died a few days later as a direct result.

In the entries about farming, it is most evident just how much neighbours depended on each other. People helped out when they were needed, not just when it was convenient for them. Agnis was called over to the McIntyre house to nurse a sick child, Mary, on New Year's Day 1853. Some of the people listed in the diaries as being part of this informal exchange of labour and expertise include Donald, Dugald and David McIntyre, D. Clelland, A. Clelland, W. Adair, James Murray Jr., David Wiley, John Wiley Jr., Pat Murray, Mrs. Livingstone, H. Shank Jr. and I.G. Shanks

These arrangements were by no means one-sided; while someone might have needed help one day, the next day he or she could be called on. One of the neighbours, David Livingstone, who was also from Scotland, suffered from rheumatism to a great extent and received help from the Jamiesons sometimes, but when he was better, he returned the favour. Work "bees" were held, where most of the community would come to raise a barn or harvest a crop.

At a house-raising bee in November 1853, John Jamieson was seriously injured. His leg was crushed beneath one of the logs for the house, and it was 11 weeks before he could get a shoe on the foot and much longer before he was really mobile. During the several months of recovery that followed, his neighbours chopped wood and made sure that he and his household got by.

As well as his constant interest in the weather, the church, the school and his farm, John's diaries also noted some social events, including weddings (one being his daughter, Jane, to David L.

McIntyre), funerals, school meetings and lectures. At one event, he noted that there was some sort of argument, which he blamed on "John Barleycorn," making his views on the temperance debate of the time quite clear. He also attended a lecture entitled "Liquor Laws in Maine."

Near the end of his diary, in May 1854, John Jamieson noted an important event, the arrival of his brother and his brother's family from Scotland. He says that they had travelled for eight weeks and were stuck in the ice for 17 days. Perhaps having his brother and nieces and nephews around occupied more of his time or resulted in his being less lonely but, for whatever reason, the diary trailed off after a few more cursory entries. He picked it up again briefly in May and August 1860, but used it only as a record of when he planted and harvested his peas and oats. The last entry in the diary reads "Aug. 17 cut oats" and, with that, the document ends.

John Jamieson continued to live in the community, and his name appeared as an elder in the session books of the West Adelaide Presbyterian Church in 1859.

JANSEN, Alfons and Lucia

Alfons Maria Peter Jansen and Lucia Catherine Teresa Van Gorp were married on April 14, 1948, in Alphen (North Brabant), located in the Netherlands.

At the beginning of their marriage, they rented a dairy farm from Alfons' brother-in-law, who had immigrated with his family to Canada. Within the next four years, Alfons and Lucia had three children, Louis, Jenny and John. Finally, they decided to pull up stakes and follow Alfons' dream of moving to Canada.

Alfons and Lucia saw the chance to own their own farm, fulfil hopes and dreams, and still have family close by to help with the adjustments of such a move. In March 1953, they and their three small children started the long journey towards the country that promised a better life. Alfons and Lucia had arrived with no money and no understanding of the language, and with a great sense of uncertainty.

Upon arriving in Canada, they stayed with Lucia's sister and brother-in-law, Sien and Chris Van Loon, who owned a farm on County Road 39 near Watford. Throughout their six-week stay, Alfons looked at different farms for sale. He decided on one owned by Fred and May Sullivan, Lot 4, Con. 2 SER, and they took possession on May 15, 1953. Along with the farm, there were 15 cows, 200 acres, and a small six-room house.

The way of life then was to grow and can fruits and vegetables, and help fellow neighbours during harvest time. The Kerwood Road was still gravel at that time and, when bad weather struck, farmers were responsible for transferring their own milk to the creamery in Kerwood.

During the next 36 years, the farm changed a great deal with new buildings, more cows, and 188 fattening hogs added to the livestock. Bigger and better machinery took the place of helping one's neighbours and made the labours of farming a little easier, thus making Alfons' decision to buy 100 acres from Clarence Matthews more realistic. In 1965, Alfons and Lucia saw a quota system introduced to the dairy industry, which produced a noticeable, profitable change in their lives. The house also saw many changes, considering there had been four more children born since their arrival in Canada.

On June 1, 1989, their youngest child, James Louis, bought the farm and two months later, married Tracey Robertson. Tracey is the eldest child of David Robertson, who farms the old Wilfrid and Mildred Wilson homestead on Lot 3, Con. 2 NER. She also has a brother, Jason, who still resides at home. An interesting fact is that the Robertsons are related to the Sullivans, who previously owned the Jansen farm.

Jim and Tracey changed the farm name to Janwood Farms, but still carry on the same farming traditions used by Jim's parents. They have two chil-

Alfons Jansen family, 1998.

dren, Ericca Leigh (1991) and Brett James Alfons (1992), representing the third generation of Jansens to live on the farm.

The following information was provided about other Jansens, but no details were given on the relationship, if any, to this Jansen family. Jenny Jansen, a hairdresser, married John Huybers, a civil engineer. They have three daughters, and reside in Courtright. John Jansen bought the old Donald Westgate farm in 1975 and also runs a 100 sow farrow-to-finish operation. He married Erna VanLoy and they have three children. Josie Jansen married John Bergsma, a teacher, and they have four children. They reside in Salt Spring, British Columbia. Margaret Jansen married Pete DeGroot, an insulator. They have three sons and live near Thedford. Pete and Jenny (Finkbeiner) Jansen and their three children have made the old Bill Edwards farm their residence since 1992. Pete is a cash crop farmer and seed dealer, and also works for Kenpal.

JANSEN, Lou and Mary

In 1971, Lou Jansen purchased Lot 2, Con. 2 SER, from Louis and Lena Langford, who retired to Strathroy. On July 3, 1973, Lou married Mary Scholten of Watford. They have three children, Michelle (1977); Brian (1979); and Heather (1982).

Lou was a hog producer from 1971 until 1998. They grow corn and soybeans on a ridgetill system. Lou also works in sales for the Forest Farm Equipment Case IH Dealership, and Mary is an educational assistant for the Catholic School Board. She works with young special needs children.

Michelle attends Ryerson University in Toronto, where she is in her second year of the photography program. Brian is in his first year at Ryerson, taking hotel management and tourism. Heather is in Grade 11 at S.D.C.I.

The family has many interests. Lou and Mary play baseball in Kerwood on mixed-league fun nights. Lou's love for reading brought about his participation at a London Trivial Pursuit Tournament and a Jeopardy Contestant Search. Mary's favourite hobby is photography. Michelle has enjoyed precision skating for many years and is presently skating for the Ryerson team. Brian's greatest pastime is downhill skiing and racing. He has coached a racing team, and is an instructor for the London Ski Club. Heather is an avid player on the senior high school basketball and volleyball teams. They all enjoy their homestead, and life in Adelaide Township.

JANSEN, Peter and June

Peter Jansen was born in Asten-Heusden, Noord Brabant, Holland, the son of Peter and Catharina (Vandenbroek) Jansen. He came with his family, including six sisters and two brothers, to the Watford area in 1956. They eventually settled on the line between Warwick and Adelaide Townships.

Peter married June Foot, the daughter of Albert and Flora (Moore) Foot, on November 12, 1971. June was born and raised in Galt, Cambridge, Ontario.

On April 1, 1974, the couple took up residence in Adelaide Township at Lot 8, Con. 1 NER, a farm they purchased from Ken and Nancy Galsworthy. The Jansens have four children, Jennifer (1974); Kristopher (1977); Ashley (1984); and Leanne (1984).

JOHNSTON, Alexander and Margaret

Alexander Johnston (1810-1880) of County Tyrone, Ireland, immigrated to Canada in 1834. His fiancée, Margaret Cuddy (1810-1857), followed him in 1835 and suffered the trials of travelling as a single woman on a ship crossing the Atlantic. She made her way inland, from the landing at Quebec to Adelaide Township, where her brother and sister-in-law, James and Violet, had settled on the east half of Lot 7, Con. 3 NER, in 1832. Alexander and Margaret were married and they made their home on the east half of Lot 6, Con. 3 NER. Margaret's brother, John Thomas Cuddy, would make his home on the west half of this lot.

Jansen family, L-R, Brian, Heather, Lou, Mary and Michelle, 1998.

The 1852 census shows Alexander Johnston 41; Margaret 42; William John 12; Alexander 10; James 8; and Thomas 6. The family is Presbyterian. Eighteen acres of the farm are improved. Crops grown include 60 bushels of wheat; eight bushels of oats; eight bushels of peas; 150 bushels of potatoes, and 40 units of maple sugar were produced. Johnston owns the home farm and the east half of Lot 11, Con. 2 NER, as well as 13 cattle, two horses, eight sheep and 14 hogs. Sixteen yards of flannel and 17 yards of wool were produced.

About 10 years later, the 1861 census shows that Margaret has died and Alexander has married a neighbour, Eliza Wilkins (d.1901), age 22, daughter of Matthew and Sarah Ritchie Wilkins of the west half of Lot 7, Con. 3 NER. Children listed are William John 21; Alexander 19; James 17; Thomas 15; and Margaret J. 2.

William John (1840-1911), the eldest child of Alexander and Margaret, moved to Strathroy and helped his brother, Alexander Jr., in his business enterprises. He and his wife, Agnes (1850-1960), had two children, Beatrice and Frederick. In November 1892, William wrote to Strathroy Council, asking it to purchase and plant five maple trees along the Centre Street wing of the new Post Office building.

Alexander Jr. (1842-1893), the second eldest child of Alexander and Margaret, was educated at London Grammar School. He opened a general store in Strathroy on Front Street east when he was only 18 years old. In spite of his lack of business experience, he was successful and continued in the business for eight years. He sold the store and opened the first private bank at the corner of Front and Colborne Streets, which was destroyed by fire in 1890. He relocated west of Frank Street on Front Street. His safe can be seen today in the store located on his business site. He became Mayor of Strathroy in 1889. In 1869, Alexander Jr. married Amelia Keefer, MD (1851-1914), daughter of James Keefer Esq., one of the founders of Strathroy. Alexander Jr. and Amelia raised two sons and three daughters. Alexander Jr.'s financial success is evident by the stately home he built at the corner of Kittredge Ave. and Caradoc Street on Quality Hill.

James (1844-1915), third issue of Alexander and Margaret, farmed the east half of Lot 11, Con. 2 NER. In 1865, he married Lydia Bryan (1844-1880) in County Antrim, Northern Ireland. Their children were Alexander (1868); John (1869); James (1871); Annie (1874); Margaret (1877); and Lydia (1880), who was born the year of her mother's death. James remarried, to Mary A. (1845-1933, last name unknown).

No further information is known about Alexander and Margaret's fourth child, Thomas (1846).

Alexander and his second wife, Eliza, had eight children. Margaret J. (ca.1859) became a teacher. Alfred (ca.1861) was a bank clerk, and probably worked for his half-brother, Alexander Jr., in Strathroy. There is no further information on Herbert (1865-1876); Martha (ca.1868); Ida (1870); Wellington (ca.1875); Maud (ca.1877); or Adeline (ca.1880).

In 1879, Alexander and Eliza sold the east half of Lot 6, Con. 2 NER, to Alexander Jr. By the time the census was taken in 1881, Eliza (Wilkins) Johnston, widow, is living on her son's farm and raising seven children; two are working and the five youngest are at home, ranging in age from Martha, age 12, to Adeline (1880), the baby. By 1901, this farm has been sold to Thomas Topping and wife.

James Johnston's farm, the west half of Lot 12, Con. 2 NER, was sold under a Power of Sale in 1885 by the Bank of Montreal to Alexander Jr. In 1885, it was sold to Dennis Demaray.

The pioneer of the family, Alexander, was buried in Strathroy Cemetery beside his first wife, Margaret.

The May 15, 1901, Age Dispatch reports the death of Mrs. Eliza Johnston, "Relict of the late A. Johnston, for many years a respected resident of Adelaide." She died at the home of her son-in-law, R.J. Coulton, in Detroit. Interment was at Woodmere Cemetery, Detroit. William John Johnston of Strathroy was in attendance.

JOHNSTON, John

John Johnston (misspelled on the 1878 Adelaide Township map) bought a farm on the Fourth Line, on the north side of the road, west of Kerwood Sideroad. There is little information about John or his wife, but they had at least nine children, five daughters and four sons, Ben, Alice Jane, David, Harry, Beattie, Eleanor, Maria, Sarah and Edith.

Ben, the eldest child of John Johnston, married Nellie Hume of Watford. They went west, where

Ben built railway grain elevators, and farmed on a quarter-section of land north of Provost, Alberta. He died in Saskatoon.

Alice Jane returned to the family farm from her home 20 miles north of Provost, Alberta, after the death of her husband, Rev. Alexander Rapson (d.1907). A son, Alexander, was born on the farm. Following his birth, Alice went back to Alberta to complete the "proving up" process on the two quarter-sections on which they had files. This done, she returned to Kerwood and stayed on the farm for a year or more. Alice's daughters, Philena and Emma Jean, attended the Kerwood school on the corner of the Fourth Line and Kerwood Sideroad. Alexander followed in the footsteps of his father, entering into the ministry of the United Church of Canada.

While living on the home farm, the barn (in which Alice had temporarily stored her things from the west) was struck by lightning and burned to the ground. In that period, too, David contracted tuberculosis, resulting finally in the sale of the homestead to Robert Galbraith Jr. David moved to Texas, where he died a few years later. He is buried in Kerville, Texas.

Harry married Della Currie. They lived on the Fourth Line, east of Kerwood Sideroad. They went to Winnipeg and Harry had a successful career as a travelling salesman for a Winnipeg wholesale company. They had three children, a daughter and two sons, all deceased.

Beattie lived on the Johnston farm for a time. He married the teacher who boarded at the Johnston home. Beattie bought a farm of his own and lived there the rest of his days. Once, when Alexander's regiment was on a training trip at Wainright, he borrowed a jeep and drove to see Beattie, which was a bit of a treat.

Eleanor married Charles Joynt of Camlachie. They lived in the Watford area. Some of their grandchildren reside in the Strathroy area, and the rest are scattered throughout Ontario.

Maria married Ed Symington of Camlachie. They moved just north of Provost, Alberta, where the Johnston family seemed to gravitate. Ed accumulated quite a few sections of land in his lifetime and, consequently, most of their family remains near Provost, Alberta. One son, Hugh, who is slightly younger than Alexander, still lives in Provost. Hugh and Alexander are the sole survivors of John Johnston's grandchildren, the number of which, by today's standards, is considerable.

Sarah married Thomas Somerville of Camlachie. How three Camlachie boys in the horse-and-buggy spent so much time in Kerwood remains a mystery. Thomas stayed on the Camlachie homestead. Of his grandchildren, Ann Marie lives on the homestead, Richard is a successful farmer, and Ian lives in Toronto.

Edith moved to Detroit and graduated as a nurse from Harper Hospital. Her classmates at Harper gave her the name "Johnny," which was soon adopted by most of the family. The children, however, were required to respectfully say "Aunt Johnny." She became a Detroit Public Health Nurse, working with children in a number of Detroit public schools. Late in life, she married John Parker, an old friend of the family, and came to live on his farm northeast of Watford, thus ending her days close to the place of her birth.

JOHNSTON, Steven and Michelle

Steven and Michelle Johnston were married on October 8, 1994. They moved to Kerwood that year, after purchasing Michelle's great-aunt's 66-year-old home at 148 Clyde Street. Although Michelle came from Wyoming and Steve from Ravenswood, Ontario, Michelle's roots are in the village, dating back to her great-grandparents (see IRWIN, Joyce and Margaret). She is the youngest child of Jim and Margaret (Evans) Newman, and is her grandmother's namesake. Michelle has two older sisters, Kim and Lisa.

JONES, Dr. Samuel O.H. and Agnes

Samuel Jones (1891-1932) was born in Adelaide Village on June 11, 1891, the son of William M. and Mary (Hughes) Jones. He graduated from the University of Western Ontario Medical School in 1913 and interned at Victoria Hospital in 1913-1914. He started his practice in Adelaide Village in 1914 and was there until 1925, when he moved to Sarnia. He practiced there until his death.

Dr. Jones married Agnes McLeish on April 17, 1918, and they had four daughters. May Louella was born in Adelaide and died at one year (buried in West Adelaide Cemetery). Lenore and Helen were born in Adelaide, and Mary was born after the couple moved to Sarnia.

Dr. Sam Jones' car (his first day in Adelaide Village).

Dr. Jones was a noted storyteller of "Mutt and Jeff" comic strip characters, and often drew the characters for his younger patients. His hobby was painting watercolour pictures.

JORIS, Harry and Maria

Harry and Maria Joris immigrated to Canada in 1951 with five sons, Hubert, Jack, Tom, John and Fred. They settled in Proton Township. In 1953, they bought a farm on Lot 4, Con. 1 SER, from Duncan and Emma Fletcher.

In 1963, Hubert married Rina Strik, and they have two sons, Rick and Dave. Hubert moved back to the farm in 1982 to look after his mother and take over the farming. Dave still lives on the home farm.

Rick, the eldest son of Hubert and Rina, lives on Lot 4, Con. 1 NER. He married Patricia Kristel in 1991, and they have two sons, Nick and Ben. In 1992, they moved into the former Elliott's Texaco Station.

Jack, Harry and Maria's second son, lives in Sarnia, and has remained single. The remaining family members are now deceased.

JOYNT, John and Edythe

In 1834, three Joynt brothers left County Mayo, Ireland, for Canada. These brothers, Christopher, Henry and Robert, initially settled in Lanark County between Ottawa and Peterborough. Robert came to Lambton County to a farm near Watford in 1847, with his wife, Maria, and their daughter, Alecia. On the farm, they had seven more children. Their son, Charles (1865-1915), married Eleanor Johnston (1866) in 1887. She was born between Kerwood and Watford. They lived on Lot 16, Con. 3 SER, Warwick Township, and their union produced John R. (1890-1981); Edith (1895-1959); and Clarence (1891-1977). Charles owned and operated a gas station in Watford and farmed the east half of Lot 17, Con. 2 SER, Warwick Township. Edith and Clarence are buried in Watford Cemetery.

John worked on the family farm until the mid-Depression years, and at a gas station in Watford. He married Edythe Styles (b. 1908) in 1935. They lived in Watford until 1940, and then bought a farm in Adelaide on part of Lot 20, Con. 4 SER. There was a large, impressive, red six-bedroom house, which John and Edythe filled with six children, John "Jack," Dan (Charles), Eleanor, Patricia, Marjorie and Carol. The farm possessed a soil that was highly productive for beans and corn. The beans were grown for the local canning factory in Strathroy and were picked by hand by the family, with the aid of several local families. Many stories abound about "picking beans and Joynts." John always took great pride in the corn crop on his 65-acre farm.

With the expansion of Strathroy, the Joynt's property fell within the new boundaries of the town and, in 1968, John and Edythe decided to build a new house in the front portion of the property. Edythe, who had worked at the Eatons' Catalogue order office for many years decided to retire about this time. Soon, a Sarnia construction company bought 44 acres of the farm for a new subdivision. The remaining 21 acres were sold to Cuddy Farms.

Jack was raised on the farm, attended Strathroy Collegiate, and after graduating, began his banking

Joris family at Hubert and Rina's wedding. Back L-R, Jack, Tom, Hubert and John. Front L-R, Harry, Maria and Fred, ca. 1963.

career. He married Sandra Wood of Belleville. Their son, David, and his wife, Cindy Janisse, live in Windsor. David and Cindy have one son, Dillon.

Dan married Bonnie Brown, formerly of London, and they still live on part of the home property. Dan worked for the Ministry of Transport until he retired in 1996. Bonnie worked at the Strathroy Hospital as an X-Ray technologist until she retired in 1997. Dan and Bonnie have two daughters, Anne and Janet. Anne graduated from the University of Waterloo with a degree in Science and later completed a degree in Occupational Therapy at Queen's University. Janet graduated from the University of Waterloo with a degree in Environmental studies and is presently working on her Masters Degree at Perdue University at Lafayette, Indiana.

Eleanor, John and Edythe's third child, is a resident of London and a graduate of U.W.O. She married Walter Huber from Germany, and is presently teaching at Parkhill High School. Walter is a personnel manager in London. Eleanor and Walter have two children, Peter and Heidi. Peter attended both Queen's University and the University of Toronto, and is presently a chartered accountant in London. Heidi graduated from Georgian College as a Cardiac Technologist, and married Christian Hamber, a lawyer. They have one son, Benjamin.

Patricia, fourth child of John and Edythe, married Lawrence Griffith of Poplar Hill. Larry was a Public School Principal for many years before his retirement. Patricia and Larry have five children, Brenda, Bradley, Annette, Jane and Michelle. Brenda, a graduate of Fanshawe College, is a Registered Nurse. She married Robert Sharpe, an optometrist, in London, and they have two sons, Ryan and Derek. Bradley is a graduate of Sir Wilfred Laurier University. He lives in London and works as a banker. Annette is a graduate Lab Technologist from Lambton College. She is married to Joe Yakobawski, a mortgage broker in London, and they have one daughter, Natalie. Jane is a graduate of U.W.O.. She is a teacher and is married to Rene Zwinkles, a Chartered Accountant in London, and they have one son, Patrick. Michelle, a graduate of Conestoga College, is a Registered Nurse. She plans to marry Jason Rapchan and reside in London.

Marjorie, fifth child of John and Edythe, married William Matthews of Kerwood, who operates a sand and gravel business on the Fourth Line South of Adelaide. They have two children, Jeffrey and Susan, both graduates of U.W.O. Jeff, an engineer, married Lynda Dymond, who is an Ultrasound technologist. Jeff and Lynda have two children, Jenna and Katie. Susan, a teacher, married Paul Findlay, who works for the Glencoe P.U.C. They have a son, Matthew, and reside in Glencoe.

Carol, John and Edythe's youngest child, married Daniel Smith of Port Huron. Dan manages a Wholesale Plumbing business in Port Huron, Michigan. Carol and Dan have three children, Tim, Stephen and Jennifer. Tim is an engineer in Virginia Beach, Virginia, and he married Bobbie Price. Stephen is also an engineer, and he lives in Toledo, Ohio. Jennifer attends the University of Kalamazoo in Michigan.

Edythe still lives in her home on the original farm, and is very proud of the family that she and John raised in Adelaide. John is buried in Watford Cemetery.

KAISER, Harold and Lynne

Harold Angelo Kaiser (1945) was born in London, Ontario, to Harold Wellington (1918) and Mary (Moschella) Kaiser (1913). Harold's heritage is German-Italian, and he is an only child. He resided in London for 33 years and was employed by the London Separate School Board as a plumber in the maintenance department.

On November 7, 1970, Harold married Lynne Beverley Clark (1953), who was born in London to Dick (1918) and Jean (Ferguson) Clark (1923). Lynne's parents had immigrated to Canada from Middlesborough, England, approximately 1 1/2 years before Lynne's birth, and Lynne resided in London for the next 25 years.

Harold and Lynne have one son, Anthony Harold (1971), and one daughter, Sherri-Lynne (1973). Both children were born in London. Harold and Lynne decided they would like to raise their children in the country, and in 1974, Harold purchased approximately 54 acres from Ken and Nancy Galsworthy. For the next three years, Harold and his father spent all of their evenings and weekends building a family homestead. In December 1978, the Kaisers moved into their new home.

Anthony started school at Aberdeen Public School in London and transferred to Adelaide W.G.

MacDonald Public School in 1978. He then went to Strathroy District Collegiate Institute. After graduation, he attended Lambton College, where he enrolled in the Law and Security course. He worked as a security guard. In 1995, he enrolled at U.W.O., where he completed his Bachelor of Arts in Psychology. Anthony married Lisa Duckworth on May 9, 1998. They live in London.

Sherri-Lynne also started school at Aberdeen. After Adelaide W.G. MacDonald Public School and S.D.C.I., she attended Westervelt Business School, where she was enrolled in the Restaurant Management course. She has two children, Jeffery Dugald Harold Stanley (1990) and Ashley Patricia Marie Frank (1993). Sherri-Lynne works as a manager at Taco Bell in London, where her family resides.

Over the last 20 years, the Kaisers kept a number of farm animals. They have raised standardbred horses for several years.

KELLY (CALLAGHAN), William and Mary

At the age of 12, William Callaghan came to America from Ireland in 1826. Eventually, he came to Ontario. He settled first near Warwick and later to the Sixth Line of Metcalfe Township, at Lot 10, Con. 1. He married Mary Burke (1851), who died of tuberculosis and left him with six children. William and his family attended St. Patrick's Roman Catholic Church in Adelaide Village.

William and Mary had six children, Luke (1837); Winnifred (1838), who worked on the Great Lakes and married in Chicago; Bridget (1841); Michael (1843); Sophia (1844), who married Henry Guilfoyle from the Sixth Line of Metcalfe in 1871, and had 10 children; and Edward (1847), who was a teacher in Katesville and other local schools.

Sophia and Henry's daughter, Margaret Theresa, married Jack "White Jack" O'Donnell of Plympton Township in Lambton County, Lot 24 at the Tenth Line and Uttoxeter Sideroad.

Edward and his family continued to live at Lot 10, Con. 1. He and most of the family are buried in All Saints Cemetery, Strathroy.

Pioneer Pat Walsh, who came to Canada in 1846, and his wife, Catherine (Quinn) were also early settlers. In 1858, they settled at the northwest corner of the Kerwood Road and Highway 22, and are buried in All Saints Cemetery, Strathroy.

Their son, Pat Jr. (1857), was born and died on the same farm, Lot 6, Con. 1 NER. He married Margaret Kearns in 1884, and they had three children. Annie (1885), the eldest, married James "Big Jim" O'Donnell (1914), who had been married once previously. They had five children, and lived out west. Theresa (1890) married Al Howe of Glencoe, and they had six children. Albert (1891) married Madeline Gearas and moved to Detroit, where some of their family still lives.

After Margaret died, Pat Jr. remarried in 1894, to Mary Ann O'Donnell (1865-1961), cousin of Margaret and daughter of James and Bridget (Kearns) O'Donnell. Pat and Mary Ann had seven children. Stella (1895), the eldest, married Durward Dewar of Plympton Township, and they had three daughters, Margaret, Mary Jane and Josephine (deceased). James (1897-1957) married Ruth Bradley. They had one daughter, Catherine, who married Gordon A. McKay, a lawyer in Kitchener. They have eight children. Joseph Leo (1899) died in his teens. Margaret (1900-1965) remained single and worked in Detroit. Wilfred (1902-1985) married Marie (last name unknown) and they had three sons, James, Joseph and Patrick. All are married and have families. Catherine (1904-1993) remained single; she was a beautician, and she died in London. Patricia (1905-1957) was a nurse.

Patrick, Wilfred's youngest son, lives at 12 Primrose Path in Kitchener, Ontario.

Nora and Jack Walsh farmed on the Egremont Road, and raised a nephew, Tom Ball. All are deceased now, and like many members of these families, they are buried in All Saints Cemetery in Strathroy.

KEYSER, Philip Henry and Maria

The early Keyser family belonged to the German Palatine group who came from Germany to the Schoharie area of New York in 1708. They suffered great hardships. Their story is well documented in the 1996 book, "Keyser Kith and Kin," by Lorraine E. Hodgins. There are numerous spellings for Keyser, such as Kayser, Kaiser, Kayser, Kiser, Keizer, Kaizer, Kizer, Kyser, Cyser and Kesser, but they all belong to the same family.

The first Keyser to come to Adelaide Township was Philip Henry Keyser (1778), son of Johannes (John) and Catharina (Braun) Keyser of Schoharie

County, New York. Philip married Maria Schaffer in the U.S. and six children were born in Schoharie, Catharina (1803); Maria (1806); John Philip (1808-1890); Anna Eliza (1812-1861); Jacob Henry (1814-1891); and Sophia Margaret (1816).

Philip came to Adelaide Township in the 1830s, without a wife and with four of his children, Maria, John Philip, Anna Eliza and Jacob Henry. "Keyser Corner" was a term that was coined in the early 1830s.

Maria married John Woodhull (1806-1866) in February 1830 in St. Paul's Anglican Church in London. They lived in Kilworth and had six children. They are buried in Woodhull Cemetery next to their house.

John P. married Elmira Dell (1814-1889) in Westminster Township in 1835. Since the 1830s, he had resided on Lot 7, Con. 4 NER. He bought this property in the 1850s from brother-in-law John Woodhull, who was granted the land from the Crown in September 1848. John P. and Elmira had nine children, all born in Adelaide Township, Philip Henry, John Woodhull (d.1917), Hiram Ransom, Joseph, Sarah Maria, Samuel, Eliza Jane, Royal Jacob and Elmira Ann. John and Elmira are buried in Arkona Cemetery, along with their youngest daughter, Elmira Ann (d.1877).

John and his sons farmed the land and made brick and tile from the clay pit near the creek. In 1871, they employed six people and worked five months of the year. Sons Royal Jacob and Joseph ran the business at various times.

In 1858, John leased land to the trustees of S.S. #1 Adelaide and S.S. #2 West Williams for a site for a school "there on partly erected by said trustees." If it was not used as a school, the property was to revert to the farm.

Philip Henry, the eldest son of John and Elmira, married Sarah Jane Jaynes, daughter of William and Rosetta Jaynes. They lived on the north half of the south half of Lot 7, Con. 4 NER. Philip was the first postmaster of Keyser, a job he held from August 1, 1864, until they moved to Michigan in 1867. Their first five children, William Henry, Sarah Caroline, John Washington, Charles Byron and Adeline M., were born in Adelaide. Philip and Sarah Jane moved to Bay County, Michigan, with their family. His lot was sold to James Gray and in 1869 to Samuel Cooper, who was postmaster until 1875 and ran a store until 1880. He sold to John McLeish. James A. Murray was the next owner. In 1936, it was purchased by Wilbert Murray, and is now owned by Bill and Doris Murray.

In 1860, John Woodhull Keyser, second eldest child of John and Elmira, married Louisa Mary York, the daughter of Daniel and Elmira (Norton) York of West Williams Township. John W. bought the south half of the south half of Lot 7, Con. 4 NER, from his father in 1859. Their first three children, Hosea Leonard, Elmira Jane and Mary Celesta, were born here. The family then moved to Parkhill and later joined Philip Henry in Michigan. They later returned to Ontario. After Louisa's death, John came to Adelaide where he died. The property was sold to James Langan. It went to William and Peter Langan in 1927 and was sold to Harold Westgate in 1943. In 1957, the International Pipeline Company located the Keyser Pumping Station on this property. The farm was sold to Clifford and Frances Arrand in 1965, and the present owner is Martin Peeters.

Hiram Ransom, third of John and Elmira's children, married Sarah Ann Stevens in 1863. She was the daughter of Benjamin W. and Jane (Harrison) Stevens, who also lived on Con. 4 NER. They lived in Strathroy until the mid-1870s. They moved to Adelaide Township, where they rented property on Con. 2 NER. Hiram was a thresher and farmer. They stayed until 1891, when they moved their family to Arkona, and later to Sanilac County, Michigan. Their children were Benjamin Charles, Nial Harrison, Eliza Jane, Emanuel, Margaret Emma, Hiram Leslie, Alva Morton, Milford Ellery, Mervyn Elmer, Vincent Edmond and Everalda May, all born in Adelaide Township.

Joseph, fourth issue of John and Elmira, married Mary J. Murray, the daughter of James and Catherine (Davidson) Murray of Keyser. Joseph and Mary bought Lot 7, Con. 4 NER, where their eight children were born. They were Ida M., Oliver James, Samuel J., Philip Arthur, George Alma, Iva Loretta, Elby Burton Everard "Bert," and an unnamed daughter. Joseph farmed and threshed for his neighbours. On this farm, they built a house and a barn foundation with Keyser brick. The house also has a brick floor. Joseph later bought the north half of the north half of Lot 7, Con. 4 NER, from his father, who retained a life lease. In 1904, Joseph sold the 50 acres to his son, Oliver, but was to have control of the brickyard for four years. In 1877, Joseph and Mary Keyser and Patrick and Elizabeth Murray sold one acre to the school trustees to build a school, which is still standing. In 1914, Joseph sold property to the Canadian Order of Foresters.

Joseph and Mary lived out their lives on the farm. Their eldest child, Ida M., married Hugh Davidson of West Williams, where they resided. Oliver James married Margery Maude Wilkie of West Williams. Ollie farmed and worked the brickyard with his father. Their children were Chester Murray, who died as a child; Arnold; James, who married Laura Sullivan; Ross; and Burton. They were all raised at Keyser and later moved to Toronto. Samuel J. married Lydia Ann Smith, the daughter of Henry and Mary Jane (Stevens) Smith, and they moved to Strathroy. Philip Arthur married Sarah J. McLean of East Williams. They lived for a short time on Con. 2 NER, and later moved to Strathroy. George Alma married Susan Cook and lived in Strathroy, but later moved to Ohio. Iva Loretta lived in Adelaide Township all her life. She cared for her father after her mother's death. In later years, she married Norman McLeish, the son of Malcolm and Catherine (Patterson) McLeish. They farmed in Adelaide on the West Williams townline. Bert married Marguriet Frances Thoman of Arkona. They moved to Toronto, where he was a barber at the Royal York Hotel.

Sarah Maria, the eldest daughter and fifth child of John P. and Elmira, married her neighbour, John Smith, the blacksmith of Keyser.

Samuel, John P. and Elmira's sixth child, lost his hearing because of being injured in a sledding accident. He was sent to a school for the deaf, where he met his wife, Isabel Alice Pirie from West Williams. Sam and Isabel leased the south half of the north half of Lot 7, Con. 4 NER, and purchased it in 1884. In 1912, Sam leased the farm to his nephew, Oliver. In 1919, the property was sold to father and son, Hugh and Arthur R. Davidson.

Samuel and Isabel's children were born in Adelaide Township. They were Robert A., Charles Royal Soloman, M. Lilly, I. Emma E., William T., Earl S., and Lloyd B. Robert and Charlie went to Strathclair, Manitoba, and Sam and the rest of the family followed in 1908. In 1942, George and Doris George bought the Lot 7 farm, and later sold it to Martin Peeters.

Eliza Jane, seventh child of John P. and Elmira, married William Henry Frank, the son of Hiram G. and Abigail A. (Montague) Frank of Adelaide Township. They were distant cousins. They lived in Adelaide Township, where William was a bricklayer. Their family consisted of Emma Jane, Royal Edward, Alice Clarinda, William Ernest and Edna Fern. Eliza and William moved to Sombra and continued west to Wisconsin and Minnesota, where Eliza died.

Royal Jacob, the youngest son of John P. and Elmira (Dell) Keyser, married Margaret Elizabeth Walker of Hyde Park. They lived at Keyser, where Royal Jacob ran the brickyard until about 1886, when they moved to Sombra Township (brother Joseph, and his sons, took over the business at this juncture). From there, they moved to Gladstone, Manitoba. Their first three children, Sarah E., David O. and John Frederick, were born at Keyser.

Of Philip Henry's other children, Anna Eliza, the third eldest child to come to Adelaide with her father, married Josiah Woodhull (d.1873) in Delaware in November 1829. Josiah was the brother of John Woodhull, Maria's husband. Anna and Josiah had 11 children. They farmed in Delaware Township. Both are probably buried in Woodhull Cemetery.

Jacob Henry married Margaret McStay (1816-1899) in Arva. They had six children and lived in Lobo Township. Before 1887, they moved to Birmingham, Michigan, where they are buried.

KINCADE, William and Eliza

William Kincade (1796-1885) immigrated to Adelaide Township from Derry or County Tyrone, Ireland, about 1840. He brought at least one family with him (he married two or three times), and fathered another family in Ontario with Eliza Graham (1814-1889), who was also born in Ireland. They may have married in Ontario.

William and his family moved to 100 acres on the east half of Lot 5, Con. 2 SER. In 1861, William farmed 20 acres, harvesting 10 acres of wheat, three acres of peas, two acres of potatoes, and hay. He raised three steers, five milk cows, 16 sheep and seven pigs, and he had four horses.

William Kincade immigrated with at least six children, Elizabeth (1821-1857); Jane (1822); Matilda (1828); Robert (1829-1909); Rachel (1834);

and William J. (1834-1925). Elizabeth married Angus McDougall and moved to the Wallaceburg area, Kent County, Ontario, probably about 1850.

William and Eliza had at least six children born to them in Adelaide Township. Thomas Herbert (1845-1915), the only one known to have had children of his own, married Jermina Geneva Armstrong of Adelaide (1849-1923) in 1877. They had a son, Anthony (1878), and in 1879, the family moved to Huron County, Michigan. Mary Elizabeth (1853-1926) married Edward Huggard Hastings (1840-1926) late in life, and died in Balgonie, Saskatchewan. She and four siblings, Letitia (1844); James (1847); Anthony (1849); and Angus (1854) moved to the Balgonie area about 1890 and stayed there until at least 1926, probably dying there. Another brother, George (1854), resided there in 1926, while James had moved to Kincaid, Saskatchewan.

In Michigan and Ontario, the surname was usually spelled Kincade, while in Saskatchewan, it was spelled Kincaid. Eliza died in Adelaide Township, as apparently did William.

Thomas and Mina (Armstrong) Kincade

Robert, one of the children William brought to Canada, worked on ships on the Great Lakes. He married Mary Mather (1833-1897) in 1851. Her father, Emmanuel (1798), opposed the match, saying he did not want his daughter to marry "that sailor," so Robert and Mary eloped in a lumber wagon to Delaware, where they were married by the Rev. R. Flood. The couple lived on William's farm in Adelaide, where their 10 children were born. Unfortunately, many of their children did not live very long. Rachel Isabella (1864-1868) and Susana Jane (1866-1868) died of "black diphtheria" in the same year. Later, between December 1876 and June 1878, four more children died, Sydney Jesse (1876, died an infant); Amanda Elizabeth (1856-1877); Robert John (1859-1878); and Lydia Matilda (1852-1878). Just a few years later, Rachel Susana (1869-1881) also died. Another daughter, Mary Ellen (1861-1889), married Rupert Robert Patterson before she died at the age of 27. Two remaining sons, William James (1854-1941) and Victor Albert Emmanuel (1872-1949), married and lived to ripe old ages. William married Mary Arrand, and Victor married Anna McFarlands.

The Kincades were active members of the West Adelaide Presbyterian Church. Robert held various offices and his half-sister, Letitia, was also a member of the church before she moved west. Robert and Mary were both buried in the West Adelaide Cemetery adjoining the church. There is a tombstone there, inscribed with the names of their eight children who predeceased them.

Like his father, Robert, William James was also a member of the West Adelaide Presbyterian Church. He and Mary Maria Arrand (1860-1898) were married there in 1880 by the minister at the time, Rev. Robert Scobie. Mary Maria was the daughter of Tom (1836) and Susan (Morden) Arrand. William James and Mary Maria farmed in Adelaide Township, where they had six children.

Their eldest child, Olive Mabel (1881-1950), married Robert Kelly and had one daughter, Valee. The second child, Hettie May (1883-1955), married first Charles Douglas and then Chris Jackson. She had two sons, Norman and Morris. Victor Roy Talmadge (1886-1921) married Hannah Morely, with whom he had four children, Orin, Berniece, Dorothy and Vera. Winnifred Victoria Pearl (1888-1975) never married but achieved many things in her lifetime, not the least of which was looking after her father in his old age. Myrtle Beatrice (1893-1968) married Allen Meredith (1894-1975). Her six children were James, Eldon, Edith, Madge, Ray and Don. Ivah Velma (1896-1988), the youngest, married Richard Hueston (1888-1961) in 1922 and had two children, Thomas William and Betty Yvonne.

Sadly, Mary Maria died at the age of 37. The two youngest children, Myrtle and Ivah, were only five years and 18 months of age at the time. They were sent to live with Mary's sister and brother-in-law, Lottie and Allen Simpson. Lottie was very kind to them, but Ivah remembers Allen as a cold, distant man.

Winnifred Victoria Pearl, known as "Win" to the family, was only 10 when her mother died. One of the more colourful figures in the Kincade family history, she got an education, and earned a BA and MA. She rode a motorcycle at a time when that was something ladies just *did not do,* and taught history at a number of Ontario schools. She also authored several books on Canada. Win used to say that her great-grandfather, William, married three times and had 23 children. If that is the case, there are still 10 Kincade ancestors unaccounted for, and, surely, many descendants in Ireland, Canada, and other locations.

KING, Fred and Elsie

In March 1925, George Frederick "Fred" and Elsie (Pressey) King moved from Parkhill to the east half of Lot 21, Con. 1 SER. Fred was born and raised in Brooke Township, Lambton County, and Elsie in Malahide Township, Elgin County. The couple brought their daughters, Inez Margaret and Gladys Muriel, who were seven and almost six at the time. Besides the family, Fred brought registered Jersey cattle, sheep, and Plymouth Rock hens for a poultry breeding station.

The first change Fred made upon moving to the farm was to reposition the barn to a handier location, and put a concrete foundation under it. (The big red barn on the corner of Highways 81 and 22, with G.F. KING R.O.P. JERSEYS painted on the side, was to become an important part of his daughters' memories.) Next, a windmill was built to pump water from the 125-foot deep well. Fred laid pipe to the house at a 4' depth, and forced water from the mill to a tank in the attic. He put an overflow pipe under the eaves, so the family would know when to shut the windmill off because the tank was full. The underground pipe was extended to the barn and a covered tank in the haymow. With this piping system, the cattle could drink from water bowls, and members of the household could use all the water they wanted, all by the use of gravity. Electricity became available by 1930, so the King family had lights and water in the house and barn—what a treat!

Fred sold Jersey milk to a Mr. Weedmark from Strathroy, who cooled it and bottled it for his customers. Later, the cooled cans were taken to the Strathroy Creamery, where the milk was pasteurized and sold.

The Jerseys were on R.O.P. (Record of Performance) with Ottawa. This meant that each cow's milk was weighed night and morning, and the amount written under her name. Every two months a government inspector came, took samples of each cow's milk, night and morning, and tested it for butterfat content. At the end of the year, Fred received a report as to the amount of milk and butterfat each cow produced, and over time, he had many high producing, prize-winning cows.

Meanwhile, Elsie was very busy each spring, hatching baby chickens in four incubators in the basement. The eggs were turned by hand each day. After a week, the trays were removed one at a time and candled (a light shone under them). Eggs that did not show a spot inside were discarded, for there was no chick inside. Coal oil burners heated the incubators, and water was kept in pans under the eggs at all times. When there were enough chickens for a flock, some were sold to other growers, and eggs were sold to other hatcheries.

Inez and Gladys attended S.S. #10 Adelaide. The teachers they remember were Misses Brett, Webb, West and Petch. The year Miss Velma Petch was their teacher, just five girls were in attendance. They were very well taught. Four of the girls were in Senior Fourth and ready for high school. The next year, three of the high school students stayed in Adelaide for Fifth Class, another family moved to the neighbourhood, and a new child began Grade One, so S.S. #10 was saved from closing.

After high school, Inez trained as a secretary. She spent the war years, 1941 to 1946, as a secretary in the British section of the Combined Chiefs of Staff in Washington, D.C. In 1946, Inez married

Richard Bettinson of Pelly, Saskatchewan, and they lived in Winnipeg, Edmonton, Regina, and finally Toronto. They have two sons. Richard lives in California and has two children, Kimberley and Bradley. Philip lives in Unionville and also has two children, Taylor and Jeremy.

Gladys married George Campbell (d.1991) from the Second Line North, Adelaide, in 1948. As Fred had died shortly before their marriage, Gladys and George moved in with Elsie and farmed the King family farm. Two children were born there. Margaret Anne married Allen Budden of West Nissouri Township, and they have three children, Stuart, Andrea and Stephen. Susan lives in Victoria, British Columbia.

The Kings sold the farm to Brian Butler of Strathroy in 1974, and Gladys and George lived happily in Strathroy for 17 years. After George's sudden death, Gladys moved to Admiral Drive in London. Fred, Elsie and George are buried in the Strathroy Cemetery.

KINGMA, Rimmer and Antje

In September 1951, Rimmer (d.1994) and Antje Kingma arrived from the Noord Oost Polder in the Netherlands, and settled in Brooke Township for four years. In September 1955, the Adelaide farm of Lewis Shepherd at Lot 19, Con. 3 SER (28332 Pike Road), was for sale and the Kingmas bought it for $10,500. They had six children, Patsy, Wilma, Jerry, Gretchen, Ruth and Corrie.

The barns and house at the Lot 19 property were in a serious state of disrepair, and everyone worked hard to make it possible to live comfortably. In 1956, electrical wiring and indoor plumbing were installed. Through a lot of hard work, such as growing green beans, sugar beets, cucumbers and turnips, they were able to establish themselves. Gradually, two dairy cows became a herd of 20. Several family members also spent many summers working out on tobacco farms.

In May 1961, Patsy, Rimmer and Antje's eldest daughter, married Hugh Pranger. They farm in East Williams Township. Two years later, Wilma married Wick Hamstra; they operate Carpet One in Strathroy.

In November 1966, Rimmer and Antje bought the farm across the road from Charles McCaffrey, when Jerry decided that he was ready to take over the farm. In June 1968, he married MaryAnn Van Arragon. Three months later, Gretchen married Gary Van Arragon, MaryAnn's brother.

In 1970, Ruth married Hank Haan, and in 1971, Corrie, the youngest daughter, married John Beintema from Watford.

Jerry and MaryAnn have five children, Raymond, Garett, Karen, Henry and Linda. At the time of this writing, Garett, Henry and Linda are attending university. Karen married Mark Howard and lives in Philadelphia, where she teaches Grade 5 students. When Garett finishes university, he plans to take over the farm. Raymond bought a house in Strathroy, and has worked in the greenhouse business for many years.

Rimmer Kingma died after enjoying many years of retirement in Strathroy. Antje Kingma moved to Trillium Village in Strathroy after her husband's death. She continues to enjoy gardening and crafts.

KLAVER - HOOGSTRA - SANDERS

Cornelius Klaver and Maria Van Lierope were married in Holland in 1950. They immigrated to Canada one month later. They lived in Watford for 15 years, where they had 10 children. In October 1966, they relocated to Lot 18, Con. 4 SER, because of Cornelius' new job at Cuddy's (now known as Cargill Grain on Con. 10, Caradoc Township). Their 10 children are Simon, John, Willy, Annie, Cathy, Alida, Mary, Peter, Tony and Bernadette "Bernie." The children attended Our Lady Immaculate School in Strathroy, and helped Lee Green pick potatoes for five cents a bushel.

Mary married Peter D. Hoogstra, son of John Hoogstra, in Adelaide. They purchased their home at Lot 18, Con. 4 SER, from Gordon Thomas on

The Klaver family, summer 1967.

October 8, 1983. They have three children, Bradley, Rebecca and Eric.

Bernie married Paul Sanders on June 14, 1986, and returned to Adelaide. They built a new home on Lot 18, Con. 4 SER (Napperton Drive), in July 1994. They have two children, Mark and Michael. Bernie works at Superior Propane. They love the area and hope to stay for a long time.

KLINKER, Bob and Jane

Bouwe (Bob) Wiebe Klinker (d.1962) married Jantje (Jane) Bos. Bob had worked as a hired hand since arriving in Canada from his native land, and relished the thought of farming for himself. In the fall of 1953, the Klinker family came from Oil Springs to take up residence in Adelaide Township. They rented a farm on the Egremont Road from Earl, Lester and Frances Wallace. Bob took great joy in working the fields and keeping a few head of cattle that he could call his own. However, farming was not Bob's real strength and, after facing the trials of farming for three years, he resorted to carpentry. As he was able to read a blueprint at a glance, he soon became Gord Campbell's right-hand man.

Bob and Jane had six children. Jane kept the home fires burning and cared for Jack, their youngest. Don and Effie attended school while Harry, Alice and Rennie worked at various jobs. When Alice became sick and died of kidney failure, the Adelaide community came forward to help the Klinkers. West Adelaide Cemetery holds three generations of their family.

In 1956, the family moved to Strathroy, where Jane still lives at Trillium Village. Harry and his wife, Riek, live in Sarnia. Don and his wife, Linda, live in Strathroy. Effie married Menno Eelkema, and they live in Listowel. Rennie married John Feddema, and they live in Metcalfe, and Jack resides in Surrey, British Columbia.

Klinker family, front L-R, Effie Eelkema, Jane (Tamminga) Klinker, Jack Klinker. Back L-R, Menno Eelkema, Linda and Don Klinker, Riek and Harry Klinker, Rennie and John Feddema.

KNIGHT, James and Jane

By 1831, Adelaide Township had been surveyed and opened up for settlement. A land patent was granted by the Crown in 1832 to James Knight (1792-1865) for the west half of Lot 14, Con. 2 SER. He may have been the original settler. He came with his wife, Jane, and a family of three children, James Jr. (1827); Henry (1829-1908); and Mary Ann (1831). A fourth child, likely born after their arrival, may have died early in life and is rumoured to be buried along with Jane under the front lawn of the house.

Initial hardship was the immigrant's lot. There were no roads, and necessary provisions had to be brought in either by horse or oxen and cart, or on one's back over barely passable bush tracks. The land was heavily forested with tall, old-growth trees. An initial clearing for a log house or shanty had to be made before land clearing could begin. These were usually crude structures to be replaced by more permanent quarters as time went by.

A pretty, yellow brick house was built in 1876, replacing the 1½-storey log house. Regrettably, James did not live long enough to see it. It was set back farther from the road, since they did not want to disturb the graves at the front of the property.

In due course, James sold the west half of his 100 acres to James Jr., who kept it for only a few years. This property changed hands several times thereafter and all trace of James Jr. is lost.

Henry, the younger son, inherited the farm. According to an 1878 Middlesex County map, he also owned or farmed another 50 acres, namely the west half of the east half of Lot 13 nearby. He married Elizabeth "Betsy" McNeil (1830-1902) of Scotland, who had immigrated to Ontario in 1849. They had four children, Angus (1856-1923); an unnamed daughter (1860-1863); Alonzo (1865-1939); and Elizabeth (1868-1896). Angus was nine years older than Alonzo, which may explain why he did not take over the family farm. Angus appears as the owner of other farm properties on the Second Line, judging from a township map reproduced on a

1918 calendar that showed the property owners at the time. He may have lived on the Groot's initial 50 acres; his father may have helped him get started.

Elizabeth, the youngest child of Henry and Betsy, married Jack Jefferson. She died at the age of 28, leaving two daughters, Gertrude "Gertie" or "Grace" (1891-1911) and Elizabeth (1896), initially in the care of their grandparents, Henry and Betsy Knight.

Alonzo married Marie "Minnie" Ann McInroy (1872-1936). Their children were Reginald Lyle (1894-1980); Henry "Bert" (1900-1982), who became a barber in Strathroy; Stewart (1905); Marguerite; and Helen Elizabeth (1910-1965).

In a will drawn up in 1905, Alonzo received the homestead in exchange for one dollar, and was to look after his aging father and pay $1,000 each to his two nieces upon attaining the age of 21. Should either one predecease the other, $2,000 was due to the remaining one.

Grace died at age 20, so at the age of 23, Elizabeth laid claim to the money. It was apparently settled by 1923, when Alonzo mortgaged the farm to James Patterson and received $4,600. He may have paid off his niece at this time and purchased the 50 acres to the west, thus making it a 100-acre farm once again.

When James Patterson died in 1929, his sons assigned the mortgage to Mary McKeigan of Strathroy. Alonzo had been making steadfast payments in the intervening years. It was near the stock market crash, however, and the beginning of the lean '30s. In 1932, he defaulted on the loan and the farm reverted to Mary McKeigan. It took until 1936 before the matter was settled.

For a full century, a Knight family member ran this farm; to some, it is still known as the "Knights' farm." Were it not for the Great Depression, a Knight might be working the farm now. Fifteen years later, in 1951, the Timmermans became the new owners, when they purchased the abandoned property from Mary McKeigan.

Reginald Lyle, the eldest child of Alonzo and Minnie, married Clara V. Conkey (d.1956), daughter of Darius and Lillian Conkey, on November 20, 1920. They had five children, Margaret (d.1998), who married Walter Hammond (d.1991); Evelyn, who married Carl Walden; Audrey, who married Frank Elliot; Grant, who married Ivey Smith; and Shirley Jean, who married Norman Giffen. The Knight family took up residence on the Second Line South in Adelaide Township, and lived there until after the cyclone of June 1944. They then moved to the Sarnia Gravel and Egremont Road, and purchased 100 acres, the east half of Lot 17, Con. 1, from Mary (McLeish) Campbell. Five years later, they purchased the west half of Lot 17, Con. 1 SER, from the McLeish family, and lived there until Clara's death.

Grant and his family continued to live on the farm until May 1963, when he moved to Port Huron, Michigan. Margaret and Walter moved to the farm in June 1963. After Walter died, Margaret continued to live on the farm. The property is still in the family, owned by Audrey's son, Russell, an Elliot who has farmed it for the past 27 years.

KOBES, Johannes and Gayle

Settlers do not arrive without a history of their own. Just before WWII, Johannes Kobes had been mobilized into the Dutch army, and in 1940, the country was invaded by Hitler's troops and had to capitulate after heavy fighting. Having come through unharmed, Johannes was released to tend his farm, to the great relief of his wife, Gayle, who had managed the farm and children on her own during his absence. The hometown, Zevenhuizen (Gron.), was liberated by the Canadian soldiers in April 1945.

The Kobes family immigrated to Adelaide from the Netherlands in June 1952. Johannes and Gayle first lived in what was known as the "Gerry house" on Lot 17, Con. 4 NER, on Highway 81, which was

Johannes Kobes family, furniture arriving from Holland in 1952.

then a gravel road. Their four children, Clarence (Klaas); Wiep; Evert; and Diane (1953) lived there with their parents. The yellow brick 2-storey house burned down after the Kobes family left, and a new house was built.

Except for Diane, the youngest, all worked at various jobs in and outside of the Adelaide community, to contribute to the family savings. In 1953, Johannes bought a farm at Lot 26, Con. 2 NER, from George and Mary Oliver, and the Kobes family lived there until 1965 (Ralph and Tina Boersma live there now).

The Kobes family participated in neighbourhood events held at nearby Crathie Community Hall. Euchre parties and dances were also held at Crathie Hall quite regularly in those days.

In 1959, Clarence bought 70 acres across the road from his parents' farm, from William James McDonald. This land, Lot 26, Con. 3 NER, was severed and 50 acres of it was sold to Albert Faber. Clarence became a secondary school teacher, and married Margaret Irwin from New Liskeard. Margaret worked at Strathroy Middlesex General Hospital from 1975 to 1992 as a Registered Nurse and Director of Education. In 1974, Clarence and his wife built a house in the woodlot on the remaining 20 acres, the south half of Lot 26, Con. 3 NER. This house and some acreage were severed in the early 1980s, and sold to John and Susan Kohler in 1991. Clarence built another house on the north end of the property, where he now resides. This is on the Adelaide-Lobo Townline. He had nine acres reforested, and he envisions this to be a new trend in Adelaide Township.

The earliest settler on this property was W. Linton, as recorded in the Historical Atlas of Middlesex County, by H.R. Page and Co., Toronto, 1878. This illustrates how properties continued to be severed into smaller parcels over the years.

Wiep Kobes and Bert Bandringa beside rail fence.

LAMBERT, Doug and Fran

Doug and Fran Lambert bought Lot 19, Con. 5 SER, and moved to this location in February 1982. Doug originally lived in Melbourne, but Fran, the daughter of Tony and Gertrude Aarts, has lived in Adelaide Township all her life. She lived on the Second Line South until she married Doug in September 1979.

Doug and Fran have two daughters, aged 11 and 14, Krista Lee and Shelly Lynn. They attend Adelaide W.G. MacDonald School.

LAMBIE, James and Edna

In 1944, James Lambie (1911-1981) purchased the James Murray farm, the east half of Lot 2, Con. 4 NER, through the VLA after his service at Dieppe. James Murray, the owner of this farm, had died from an accident on the upper barn floor. In 1927, his hired man, Frank Jones from England, died from a similar accident.

James Lambie married Edna Wilson (1917-1968) of the Arkona area, and they had two children, John and Marjorie. John resides in Owen Sound, and Marjorie married Ray Emery of the Glencoe area. James and Edna are buried in Arkona Cemetery.

Johannes Kobes family, L-R, Diane, Johannes, Clarence, Gayle, Evert and Wiep.

LANDON, Brian and Debbie

Brian and Debbie (Hudson) Landon and their two children, Eric (1981) and Jason (1985), live on part of Lots 30 and 31, Con. 1 SER. Brian was born in London and Debbie, whose family was originally from Scotland, was raised in London Township. They married in 1979, and bought the Adelaide property because it was affordable compared to land in the London area. Also, it was a short distance for Brian to travel to work in London. Debbie works at Strathmere Lodge.

LANGAN, James and Ellen

James Langan sailed from County Cork, Ireland, with his wife and infant, to change the life of a sailor's lot to that of a farmer. Soon after his arrival, his wife and baby died of a plague sweeping through the country, and he buried them beneath a large elm tree on his farm, adjacent to East Adelaide United Church, on Crown land.

He soon realized the poor qualities of his land and left it to seek better soil. He travelled westward and situated himself on a farm on the Fourth Line North, of Adelaide Township. His second bride, 20-year-old Ellen Cooper of Hungry Hollow, knew the rigors of raising a pioneer family. James was 40. He and Ellen had eight children, John; Mary; James; Thomas (1850-1939); Anne; William; Ellen; and Peter. Only two of the children married.

James was resourceful, sailing the Great Lakes for $40 per month. He hired men to clear his land for $5 per acre. James had once been shanghaied by British soldiers and had sailed in the Mediterranean Sea. He had a violin that was taken from an Italian boat as booty.

James built a log house on the south side of the road (west of Glovers). Later, he acquired a farm with a frame house on the north side of the road. In 1872, he built a large brick house. When the farm home was built, there was gold around the glass in the double front doors. The parlour, which was used just for funerals, was beautifully appointed. However, the Langan family lived only in the kitchen. They were thrifty people. They raised good cattle, sought after by the drovers every spring. In early days, Ellen and the three older children grew carrots and turnips to feed the pigs. When James took the pigs to market in London, Ontario, and spent the money on "Old John Barley Corn," Ellen would cry and then grow more pigs.

One time, Thomas went to the school at night to watch a lantern slide show, in spite of his mother telling him he could not go. Peter was born the following morning, and the promised whipping was forgotten.

As the Langan sons grew older, they took over, went to market, and prospered. Thomas married Mary Adeline (1870-1912, last name unknown), who was born at Napanee of the Bay of Quinto, of Pennsylvania Dutch stock. Her father was a well-educated man who could speak several languages, and her mother was Phoebe Henry. Adeline had three siblings, John, William and Elizabeth "Lizzie" (Moore). When Adeline's father left his wife and family, Phoebe married a Mr. Van Sickler and they had a son, Lorenzo. Adeline was put out as a nursemaid at seven years of age. John and William joined Mary Eddie Baker Christian Science and died as bachelors in an old soldiers' home in Michigan.

Adeline met Thomas Langan when he was in the East Nissouri area, packing apples. She was an attractive young woman. Adeline and Thomas were married in Nissouri Township, Middlesex County, and had at least seven children. Their son, James, was born in Vienna, East Nissouri, Middlesex County. Their second child, Ellen "Nellie," was a bright young girl who died on her seventh birthday, and was buried in the Roman Catholic Cemetery in Adelaide Village. Two more sons were born, Jonny and William, but both died from drinking impure milk. They were buried at Adelaide Village. Two of the surviving children, James and Viola, resembled Adeline. Two others, Harry and Gertrude, had bright blue eyes and light hair like the Langans.

The Langans were Liberals, but turned Conservative when the Liberal government built the railroad through Strathroy rather than Adelaide Village. The Langans were Roman Catholic and attended a church on land given to the Catholics by the Anglican Church. Later, they spearheaded a movement to build a brick church at the front of the Langan property. Rather than have it referred to as "The Langan Church," other Roman Catholics in the district contributed; however, the Langans gave the most. St. Patrick's Day was an occasion for celebration, as the Bishop arrived to name the building "St. Patrick's Church." Thomas took his 12-year-old daughter, Viola, and his son, Jim, for the ceremony.

Loftus Muxlow, then 16, went with Gordon Humphries and sat in the buggy, watching with curiosity. He did not know then that Viola would be his wife one day, and Thomas his father-in-law.

Thomas was tall, 140 pounds, with a big, square frame, sandy hair and a moustache. He carried himself with a jaunty air, a "man about town" staunch Conservative. He told stories of John A. MacDonald at political meetings. He joined the Salvation Army once to annoy the rest of the family. He died a Roman Catholic, but was indifferent about the church. He served as Reeve of Arkona twice. He was an apple packer and buyer for companies. He kept bees and, later in life, took pickle contracts for Libby's. He also grew raspberries and strawberries. Thomas made friends easily and enjoyed life, but he was not the best provider. In Arkona, he lived alone, with his old friend, Thomas Ridley, to keep him company. Mr. Ridley was an auctioneer. Very often, he took Thomas to auctions with him, and he would "knock articles down" to his friend, but, of course, the items were for Mr. Ridley himself!

When Thomas came to visit his daughter and son-in-law, Loftus would quit work and come into the house to hear Thomas regale the family with stories of people in Arkona. One time, when Loftus, Viola and family lived on the G. Petch farm, Thomas took a ride with Mr. E.I. Syerson. On their way to London, they stopped in to see Viola and family, then continued east. The family heard a crash, as Mr. Syerson hit the side of the bridge and they ended up in the creek. Loftus ran to help, but the men weren't injured, just shaken.

The only other child of James and Ellen who married was James. He married Maria Kearns and they had a family of two sons and two daughters, Frank, Leno, Zene and Celia. They lived on a farm in Warwick Township. When Celia was a teenager, she became very ill. Thomas, James' brother, went to spend the night with the family, but Celia died. Thomas later told his grandchildren that it was no wonder, because she was in an unheated room upstairs. James bought a family plot at Bornish and all of his family were buried there. The night Celia died, Adeline called for her daughter, Viola, "Shut the door from the dining room quickly, the little dog has gone mad. Go up to the sideroad to Mr. Smith's house and tell him to bring a gun and shoot the dog." Viola ran to Mr. Smith's place, and he came and shot the dog.

In later years, Thomas sold his little house to Walter Johnson for $500 dollars and went to live with Viola, Loftus and family. When they moved to the Nichol farm, he gave Loftus money to help build the barn. This money had been left to him in the will of his brother, Peter.

When Thomas died, there was a church service at All Saints Roman Catholic Church in Strathroy. In attendance was J.J. Johnson, an apple grower who had employed Thomas for many years. Matilda, the widow of Adeline's late brother, Harry, attended from Sarnia with their two daughters, Ellen and Muriel. John Armstead, a cousin from Michigan, also attended the funeral. The lane to the cemetery was muddy and the casket had to be carried. Reverend Buley, the minister, stopped in and helped.

The following story is told about the Langan brothers: They had a sugar maple bush, which proved to be an asset to the farm. One day, they had worked diligently gathering sap and boiling it down and, that evening, they were returning to the house with four wooden pails of thick, golden syrup. While climbing a fence on the way to the house, John tripped and dropped his pails. He was so frustrated that he kicked every pail over and all the syrup was lost. Even the pails themselves were demolished!

LANGFORD, Herbert and Margaret

Herbert J. Langford (1882-1986), son of George and Elizabeth (Foster) Langford, purchased the Adelaide farm at Lot 2, Con. 2 SER, in 1910. The previous owner, William Sullivan, moved to Strathroy.

On March 19, 1910, Herbert married Margaret Stella Mann (1881-1926) of Enniskillen Township. They had two sons and a daughter, Vance (1914); Annabelle (1915); and Louis "Lew" (1918). Unfortunately, Margaret died young and left her husband with the three young children. Herbert stayed on the farm and raised the children, and was a very good cook and homemaker. By signing up with the immediate neighbours, hydroelectricity was installed in 1928.

Vance moved to St. Thomas and Annabelle moved to Toronto, where they both still live.

In August 1943, Lew married Lena Atchison and they took up residence on the farm with Herbert,

Herbert Langford with children, Annabelle, Louis and Vance.

who left the farm in the 1950s and sold the farm to Lew about 1955. Lew and Lena moved to Strathroy in July 1971, when the farm was sold. Herbert was nearly 104 years of age when he died.

LARGE - BRAY - LANG

William Large, son of Robert, married Mary Ann Plummer, and they immigrated to Canada with their children from Purton, Wiltshire, England, in 1852. They settled in a part of Adelaide Township later designated Metcalfe Township, on a farm or place named Spring Bank. William, who was born in Christian Malford, married in Lydiard Tregoze (both in Wiltshire), and lived for a time in Lambourn, Berkshire, where James (1835-1912) was born. He had returned to his father's home parish, Purton, in order to make ends meet. His father's younger brother, another William, was a wealthy yeoman farmer who reached the rank of gentleman. His 1850 will, still in the family possession, along with various deeds and indentures dating back to the 1720s, forgave his nephew and namesake, William, of all his debts, and left him just enough money to immigrate with his family. The Larges had been settled in Purton since at least the time of the Great Fire of London, though register entries mention unconnected people of the name in Purton as early as 1558. In the Middle Ages, a "le Large," the French for generous (hence largesse), had represented one of the divisions of Wiltshire in Parliament. An extensive pedigree of the family has been constructed starting around the time of the English Civil War.

In Canada, the Larges intermarried with the Brays only once via the 1864 wedding of James and Blanche Louisa Bray (1835-1923) at St. Mary's, Napier. Blanche's godmother and namesake was Mrs. Blanche Westlake, a Cornish widow, proprietress of the local Royal Adelaide Inn, and probably a relation via her Cornish grandmother. The Brays felt that Blanche had married beneath her, because the Larges were not very successful then, and James was a failed barrister who was not much good at farming. His mother, though, came from a family of minor Purton gentry, the Plummers. Through the Plummers, James descended from the land owning families of Deane and more importantly, Sadler, for whom there is an early Visitation pedigree taking the family back to the time of Columbus.

James and Blanche had 11 children. The eldest of their children were born in Middlesex County, mostly in what is now Metcalfe Township. In the early 1880s, James, already nearing 50, decided to take up land in the Muskoka and Parry Sound district. The family settled in Perry Township, where Beatrice Florence Elizabeth (1885-1963) was born in the dispersed rural community of Swindon, presumably named after the Wiltshire railway hub that was close to the Larges' ancestral home. Beatrice married Herbert Chatterton Roberts, and was fifth of the six daughters born to James and Blanche. Beatrice also had five brothers.

A number of their Middlesex County neighbours accompanied them to Perry Township, including the Harrises and some of the Beers. By 1898, the family had moved west to Manitoba, where they lived at Orange Ridge, near Birnie, in the scenic but rocky Riding Mountain district. Walter Large's family of five sons remain there to this day, having struck it rich with oil found on their land.

Other sons of William and Mary Ann remained in Middlesex County, including the eldest, William, who married Elizabeth Collins from an Adelaide family, and settled in Strathroy, dying at the turn of the century. Henry went into brewing with his brother, Edward. Henry's widow, Alice (Mackintosh) Large, ended up in Neepawa, Manitoba. Edward married Elizabeth, daughter of Hamilton Dunlop, and after a stint in Thornhill, Ontario, went to Jamaica. His descendants, if any, remain untraced. Of James' sisters, Mary made a good marriage to Richard Becher Hungerford, an insurance agent in London, Ontario. Richard was the sometime Grand Master of the Masonic Grand Lodge of the Dominion. He came from an Anglo-Irish family, seated until recently at "The Island" near Clonakilty, County Cork. His elder son, had he wished to return to Ireland, would have been the head of the family, as this branch of the family eventually succeeded to the ancestral estates. Elizabeth married Walter Smith, leaving an only daughter who was a talented artist and nature lover, Mary Adelaide "Addie" Smith. The only other Large daughter, Mary Ann, died young in England before immigration. James' other brothers, Richard Plummer and Robert, both died in young manhood, unmarried.

Blanche's family, the Brays, came to Canada in 1838 in the person of William Bray, J.P., R.N. (1814-1882), a gunnery officer on one of the Royal Navy ships dispatched from Britain to help put down the Upper Canada Rebellion. Indeed, William is said to have fired the final salvo into the enemy's munitions dump, the windmill, at the Battle of the Windmill near Prescott, Ontario, in 1838, thus ending the battle and consequently the rebellion.

During his time on the Great Lakes Station, there arose a disagreement over William Bray's keeping of the naval stores at Kingston, which resulted in his arrest and imprisonment. With the young Kingston barrister, John Alexander Macdonald, as his counsel, he successfully sued his commanding officer, Capt. (later Admiral Sir) Williams Sandom, for false arrest, and was awarded £50 for damages. With this substantial capital, he elected to stay in Upper Canada, and married Eliza Jane Lang at Kingston in November 1839. They settled in Adelaide sometime between the birth of their eldest son in Kingston in 1841, and that of their next child in Adelaide in June 1843.

The most likely reason the Brays went to Adelaide was because William's father-in-law and mother-in-law, John (ca.1790-1864) and Ann (Treleaven) Lang (1781-1855), had settled there a few years after coming to Upper Canada in 1833. The Langs wanted to be near Ann's Cornish kinsmen following the tragic drowning/disappearance or murder of their only son, John, on New Year's Eve 1834, while crossing the ice from Bath Village to Amherst Island. The Moyles and Beers, and the interconnected Winlows, Westlakes, Morcoms, Hoares, Rundles, Harrises, Collinses, Brownes and Dunlops, had settled there, some since the township first opened up to large-scale settlement in 1829.

In relocating to Adelaide, John Lang also remained within the patronage of his noble employer, Lord Mount Cashell. According to the "History of the County of Middlesex," he had a house in the vicinity in an area now within Metcalfe Township. John Lang, many years a sawyer at H.M. Dockyard in Plymouth's Devonport district, had served as timber master on His Lordship's Amherst Island estates when he first came to Upper Canada. The family may even have been in Lord Mount Cashell's service in Ireland, as well (the elder Lang daughter, Maria Ann is listed in the census as having been born in Ireland in about 1819, though her parents waited until 1821 to have her baptized in Devonport, presumably upon their return to England.)

By a strange coincidence, William Bray's younger brother, Tom Cox Bray (1815-1881), also left their English birthplace, Portsea in Hampshire, for the colonies in the same year as William, choosing as his destination the free-settler colony at Adelaide, South Australia, to which he took his new bride, Sarah Pink.

In the Antipodean Adelaide, Tom set up shop as a shoemaker, as had his father before him. He grew wealthy, however, through owning stock in a shipping line. He obtained this stock, so the story goes, because, unlike his brother to the north, he was reconciled to his wealthy Bray grandfather, who had disowned their father for marrying "beneath himself" to Ann Cox, later Mrs. Winship, the daughter of a Southsea farmer. This money enabled Tom to return to England, where he lived as a gentleman in London and Harrogate, sending his eldest son to

Cambridge and into Holy Orders, marrying his daughters well, and leaving his younger son with sufficient funds to train for the bar. A political career followed that led to his election as the first native-born premier of South Australia, a knighthood, and participation as Sir John Cox Bray in the initial conferences leading to the establishment of the Commonwealth of Australia.

The Reverend Horace Edgar Bray (1859), an Anglican priest like his Australian cousin, and fifth of the six sons of William Bray, J.P., R.N., was born in Adelaide. He returned there many years later to preach at a centenary or some such celebration in the 1920s or 1930s. Horace's father gave up on Adelaide in the early 1860s, when he and his friend and connection, John Stroud Hoare, were unsuccessful in their bid to have the railway pass closer to Adelaide to ensure its prosperity. They met with the opposition of many of the retired British Army officers and Anglo-Irish gentry settled there, who wanted a quiet life and no risk to the local Jalna-esque squirearchy.

William, instead, removed to Petrolea (later Petrolia), where he set up shop as a chemist and druggist. It was here that his sons, John Lang and William Thomas, were trained as pharmacists, along with their sister Blanche. It was said by her daughter, a V.O.N. nurse, that Blanche was the first female pharmacist in Canada.

John Lang Bray, the eldest of William's brood, returned to his birthplace to study medicine at Queen's. He graduated just in time to volunteer for service in the Confederate Army Medical Corps, in which he served until the end of that war. He rose in his profession to become President of the Canadian Medical Association. So, like Sir Arthur Currie and the Hon. Edward Blake, Dr. Bray was an Adelaide boy who made good.

LEACOCK, William and Emma

William James "Billie" Leacock (1873-1961) was born in Alvinston, Ontario, to William John and Ellen (McLellan) Leacock. In 1904, he settled in Kerwood. Billie learned his blacksmithing trade from Mr. McNally in Alvinston.

On August 28, 1906, Billie married Emma Lydia Brandreth (d.1956) of Kerwood, in Strathroy. Rev. W. Conway, B.A., B.D., officiated, and the attendants were Emma's sister, Elizabeth Case, and her brother, Dr. Ozias Brandreth. Billie and Emma had a daughter, Anna (1907-1996), and many years later, a son, William George (1923-1997).

On January 15, 1909, Billie purchased a blacksmith shop on Grace Street in Kerwood, from Reuben Dowding. He bought a house from William Hull, on the Fourth Line of Adelaide Township, just west of Napperton. The house was built by William Murdock. Billie had the house moved during the winter, using horse-drawn sleighs to pull it to its present site at the corner of Grace and Clyde Streets. A little English lady rode in the house on the sleigh, and made meat pies and tea for the men transporting the house! It took three days to complete the trip. This house belonged to the Leacock family until 1995.

Group photo, L-R, Joe Brunt, Tom Brady, Jack Taylor, Henry Lambert, Will Leacock, Frank Mills and George Chittick.

Group photo, L-R, Art Such, Ern Tedball, Chuck Lougheed, Tiny Crandon, Harold Irwin, Mike Brooks; George Leacock and Ed Wilson in front.

William James and Emma (Brandreth) Leacock on their wedding day, August 28, 1906.

Cliff Winter and Billy Leacock.

Billie loved horses, and his work as a village smithy in Kerwood. He served as a county constable for a time. Emma was an active church member.

Billie and Emma are survived by their grandchildren, Stephen Leacock of Dorchester and Jane Graydon of London. Great-grandchildren of the couple include Stephen John Leacock of Tillsonburg; Jessica, Emily and James Houlachan of London; Allison and Gary Haldenby of Aylmer; and a great great-granddaughter, Haley Haldenby (1995).

LEE, John and Bertha

John "Jack" Mervin Lee (1902-1953) was born in England. He lived in England and Egypt, where his father, Frank Lee, was associated with the Suez Canal. Jack immigrated to Canada as a single man and first worked on the Adelaide farm of Lewis Miner. In 1927, Jack purchased a 100-acre farm from George Shepherd, the west half of Lot 15, Con. 4 SER. He married Bertha Eastman (1900-1937), daughter of George and Caroline (Humphries) Eastman, and they had two daughters, Carolyn and Bertha. After the early death of his first wife, Jack married Mildred Baxter and they had two children, John and Yvonne. Jack was killed in a car accident not far from home, and the farm was sold in 1955 to Harold and Helen Westgate.

Jack was said to be a marvelous piano player and, in his younger days, he formed a small orchestra that included Duncan Campbell as a fellow musician. They played at local community events.

Carolyn married Carlyle Wood and they have two children, Sharon and Bill. They farm in Lobo Township. Bertha married John Iles and they raised four sons, Bradley, Gary, Beverly and Mark. They farm in Essex County.

LENTING, Jacob and Jurjendina

Jacob (d.1975) and Jurjendina Lenting (d.1989) immigrated to Canada from Holland in October 1951. With them came four sons, Wes (d.1989); Rick; Harry (d.1993); and John. One married daughter, Grace Kok, was already here and another, their eldest child, Ann Smid, followed in 1953.

For about two years, Jacob and Jurjendina lived in West Williams Township behind the Ausable River. The house they lived in was demolished by the tornado of 1953, shortly after the Lenting family moved from this location. They relocated to Adelaide Township, where they rented rooms in the Laverne Topping house on the Fourth Line NER (this house is now owned by Dave and Linda Powell). The farm across the road, which was owned by Everett Herrington, was for sale. The Lentings bought it and farmed there for many years.

Rick, the second son of Jacob and Jurjendina, married Judy Overbeek. They sold the farm in 1981, and purchased Elmer Murray's farm across the Kerwood Road. This was sold in 1983 and, since then, Rick and Judy have lived on Lot 18, Con. 4 SER. John, the youngest son, lives in Strathroy. Ann Smid lives in Ailsa Craig, and Grace Kok lives in Strathroy.

The Lenting family never looked back after they came to Canada, and they adapted well to this country. One story the children still laugh about happened shortly after the family arrived in Canada. Irene Thomson and Ivy Herrington came to the door dressed in costume for Halloween. They stood, not saying a word, holding out their baskets. The Lentings, not being familiar with Halloween, thought they were being offered candy, so they all took something from the baskets. If Jacob and Jurjendina were alive today, they could probably write a book about those early years! They are both buried in West Adelaide Cemetery. Wes is buried in Exeter and Harry in Strathroy.

LEWIS, Frank and Isabell

In 1946, Frank (d.1953) and Isabell Lewis (d.1967) and their son, Richard, moved to Lot 3, Con. 3 SER, property purchased from Edwin Alfred Sullivan. Richard collected eggs and delivered them to Pollock's in Kerwood. In 1962, Richard and his mother sold the farm and moved to Strathroy. Ed Reitsma resides on the farm at this writing. Richard is now retired and living in Strathroy.

LEWIS, John Sr. and Elizabeth

John Lewis Sr. immigrated to Canada from Devonshire, England. He married Elizabeth Branton and lived at Lot 23, Con. 1 NER. He had two sons, William and John Jr.

John Jr. married Susan Daniels and they had 10 children, John Edgar, Albert, Martha "Hettie," Charlotte "Lotty," Charles, William, Morley, Frederick "Fred," Susan and Ivan Bertie (1893-1965).

Edgar married Isabelle McDonald and they had six children, Viola, who married Jim May; Cecil, who married Claire Woodings; Olive, who married William Burges; William; Calvin; and Donald. The three youngest sons never married.

Albert, second eldest child of John Jr. and Susan, married Anne Tomlinson. They had nine children, John, Jean, Irene, Ida, George, Verna, Alma, Lorne and Roy.

John, eldest child of Albert and Anne, married Elverta Orr. They lived at Lot 29, Con. 1 NER, then the west half of Lot 5, Con. 1 SER, and finally moved to Lobo Township in 1938. John and Elverta had three children. The only son, Grant, married Mary Guest. Doreen married Harley Black, and they lived in Strathroy. Doreen and Harley had two children, James and Steven. Laverne never married, and lived in London.

Jean married Gordon Wardell and they also had three children. Bruce married Jean McLean, Keith married Madeline Carroll, and Ken married Barbara Pedden.

Irene, third of Albert and Anne's children, married Cecil Pincombe. They have two daughters. Diane married Ken Veldhuis, and Carol married Mike Holt.

Ida married Harrison Meadows. They had two children, Arthur, who married Melinda Coyle; and Gary, who never married.

George, Albert and Anne's fifth child, married Pearl Skinner.

John Sr. and Elizabeth Lewis at daughter Hetti's wedding. The wedding took place at their home, Lot 23, Con. 1 NER (now Ralph Bos' home).

Verna married John Dennis and they raised three children. Betty married Roy Down; Dorothy married Walter Zavitz; and Frances married Gerald Bender.

Alma, seventh child of Albert and Anne, married Duncan Crawford, and they had two sons, Kenneth and Robert.

Lorne married Kaye Smith. They had two sons, Robert and William.

Roy, the youngest child of Albert and Anne, married Norma Graham.

Hettie, the third child of John Jr. and Susan, married Ira Demaray. Their daughter, Mildred, married Art Johnson. Second daughter, Vera, married Bill McDougall.

Lotty married Hiram Zavitz, and all three of their children married.

Charles, fifth issue of John Jr. and Susan, married Louise McGowan and they had one daughter, also named Louise.

William married Grace Millson, and they had three children. Raymond married Margaret Gray; Gordon married Marie Fletcher; and Grace remained single.

Fred, eighth of John Jr. and Susan's children, married Lorena Newell. They had four children. Florence married Joe Leslie; Carl married Dorothy McLean; Doris married Alan; and Ken married Lynda Sotterly.

Susan married Ross Woolley, and they had two sons. Earle married Margaret Innis, and Jack married Marguerite Earley.

Ivan, tenth and last child of John Sr. and Susan, married Violet Annie Dann (d.1984) on March 9, 1921. They had one daughter, Phyllis Jane (1926). Ivan continued to farm on the family farm as sole owner, later legally changing his name to Ivan Herbert Lewis.

The family attended Bethel United Church, where Ivan was the church treasurer. Violet was very active in the WMS, and was a Sunday School teacher. Phyllis played the piano for Sunday School.

Phyllis walked to attend S.S. #3 School in Adelaide and rode her bicycle to Strathroy District Collegiate Institute, where she graduated in June 1944. In February 1950, Phyllis had what the Age Dispatch referred to as "a disturbing experience." While working as a secretary at the Industrial Loan and Finance Corporation, she was forced at gunpoint to open the office for three thugs. They stole $600 in cash but were arrested a few hours later. Fortunately, no one was hurt in the incident.

Due to poor health, Ivan sold the farm and the family moved to Strathroy in 1952. Phyllis now lives in Strathroy.

LEWIS, Len and Marianne

Len Lewis (1962) was born in Belle Island, Newfoundland, the son of Harold and Jean Lewis. In 1988, he married Marianne Hoefnagels, the daughter of Morris and Willy Hoefnagels. Their children are Jamie Lee (1989); Bradley (1991); Nicole (1993); and David (1995).

The Lewis family lives in a home built by Marianne's father, on Lot 27, Con. 2 SER. Len works with the Canadian Pacific Railway, and Marianne works at Victoria Hospital in London and Strathroy Hospital.

LIGHTFOOT, Thomas and Jane

Thomas Lightfoot (1829-1908), son of Henry and Jane (Calvert) Lightfoot, was born in Yorkshire, England. He married Jane Mooring (1831-1901), also of Yorkshire, and they immigrated to Canada in 1851, shortly after their marriage.

Thomas had seven siblings, all born in England, John (ca.1826-1889), who married Sarah Bateman and, later, widow Margaret Copeland; William (1831-1903), who married Margaret Kirkpatrick; Joseph (1832-1916), who married Elizabeth Ann "Lizzie" Inch, and had a well known descendant, Gordon Lightfoot, the country music singer and composer; Mary (1836-1920), who married Henry Wright and, later, Capt. Elisha James Thomas; George (1838-1919), who married Jane Clarke and, later, Anna Maria Smith; Betsy (1840), who married John Finney and lived in the Dakotas; and Sarah (ca.1843).

Thomas and Jane were the first Lightfoots to come to Canada. They were followed by William, who was single when he immigrated. Joseph followed in 1854, and George and Mary came in 1856. Henry and Jane Lightfoot eventually immigrated, but the date is unknown. It is likely that they came with their youngest daughters, Betsy and Sarah. They all lived in Metcalfe and Brooke Townships.

LINKER, John and Helen

In 1974, John and Helen (McDonald) Linker purchased a three-acre lot from Dennis Molnar, across the road from Blanche Nethercott and formerly part of their farm. Helen came from East Williams Township. The couple built a new home at 436 Metcalfe Street West in Strathroy, and lived there for six years before moving to Adelaide Township. John and Helen have four sons, Andrew, Brian, Carl and Douglas. The country property was also home to a couple of ponies and many smaller animals and fowl. The Linkers decided to move again when plans for a subdivision became evident for the surrounding area.

The basement was begun at their present location on June 19, 1974. John constructed the new home in his spare time from his self-employed business. They moved into the partially finished home on August 14, 1974, and in September, the Adelaide school bus began to pick up three of their sons, as Carl was beginning kindergarten.

In May 1983, John and Helen purchased the 19 acres of river flats and bush adjacent to their lot, to add to their original "tiny acres." As hobby farmers through the years, they have kept sheep, goats, cattle and fowl, for pleasure only, not for profit. They now rent out the land for summer pasture, and keep a large vegetable and flower garden.

Carl lives at home and works at "The Pet Stop" in Strathroy. Andrew, Brian and Douglas are all married. They have acquired their father's building skills and constructed their own homes.

Andrew married Michelle Waun, and they live in Cairngorm.

John and Helen Linker property at part Lot 26 and 27, Con. 3 SER, ca.1990.

Brian married Corinne Speerstra in 1984, and they have four daughters, Melanie (1985); Julie (1988); Katie (1990); and Emily (1991). Brian and Corinne began residing in Adelaide Township in 1990, and the children attended grade school at Adelaide W.G. McDonald. Brian is a self-employed contractor and Corinne is a full-time mother.

Doug married Nancy Silva, and they also live in Adelaide Township.

John and Helen reside in a pleasant neighbourhood and appreciate their part of Adelaide Township, being part of Lots 26 and 27, Con. 3 SER.

LINTON, William and Elizabeth

William and Elizabeth Linton

William Linton (1840-1919) was born in Folkton, Yorkshire, England. On April 2, 1860, he married Elizabeth Ward (1839-1919), who was born in Reach Township, near Pickering, Ontario. Their children were Alice Jane, who married Samuel Edgar Wood; Isaac John, who married Annie Elizabeth Bolton; Mary Elizabeth, who married Hansford Bolton; Myron "Myde," who married Hattie Hansford; and George William, who married Edith Pearl Nichol.

In the 1871 census, William and Elizabeth were living in Reach Township on 50 acres at Lot 8, Con. 6. The family moved to a Con. 3 farm in Adelaide Township in 1871 or 1872. About 1908, William and Elizabeth relocated to a house on Victoria Street North in Strathroy. William and Elizabeth died in Strathroy.

LOCKE, George W. and Ruth

In 1950, George William "Bill" Locke (d.1990)

and his wife, Ruth, bought Lot 25, Con. 1 NER, from Fred and Lorena Lewis. The couple had four children, Dennis, Karen, Cheryl and Wendy. During the next few years, four more children were born, Bill, Bruce, Allan and Diane.

Dennis and Karen went to Crathie School. Their teacher was Miss Annie Courtis. They have many good memories of Miss Courtis playing ball, and of her powerful cars. Cheryl, Wendy and Bill attended Crathie and Adelaide Central School. Bruce, Allan and Diane attended Central School. There was a bad snowstorm in January 1971, and the children were unable to get home that night, so they were kept at the school. They were very tired and hungry when they finally arrived home! Another time, back in the 1950s, Tom Elliot and Bill went to get the children with a tractor and sleigh. The Crathie Christmas concerts were much enjoyed, and added to the excitement of the season. Bill was a school trustee for several years during the 1950s.

Oats, hay and corn were the main crops in the early years. Holstein cows were milked, and milk and cream were shipped to the Strathroy Creamery. As separating was necessary with surplus milk, a hog pen was built and skim milk was fed to the Landrace hogs.

In December 1959, the cattle were sold. In the spring of 1960, Bill, who had grown up on a farm with an apiary, bought about 1,000 colonies of bees from an apiary in Kent County. The crops varied over the years. The Lockes grew wheat, beans, corn and some hay, as there were usually a few horses

The Lockes, L-R, Dennis, Bruce, Bill holding Allan, Billie, 1960.

Robert Bruce Locke in bee yard.

around. On June 14, 1980, the barn and shed were torn down and replaced with a honey house. In 1999, after Bill's death, Bruce took over the farm.

MacDONALD, Angus and Sarah

Angus MacDonald (d.1925) was born in North Uist, Scotland, and immigrated to Canada in 1849. He settled in Adelaide Township and married Sarah Campbell (d.1916) of Adelaide in 1855, when they built a log house on Lot 26, Con 3 NER. There, they raised a large family. One son, Charles, eventually took over the Lot 26 farm. Another son, Duncan Lauchlin, married Edythe Isabelle Evans in 1899, and they lived with Angus and Sarah in a house across the road. This house was built by the MacDonalds, and all of Duncan and Edythe's children were born there. Angus lived to be 98 or 99. He and Sarah are buried in Nairn Cemetery.

Duncan and Edythe had five children, Gordon R.; Rheta; Dorothy (1907); Violet; and Robert (d.1980). The children attended Crathie School. Dorothy remembers that her last teacher was Fred James of Strathroy, who later became a famous doctor in London. Many of her schoolmates are still in the area, and two first cousins, Iva MacDonald and Olive Alderson (Feasey), live in Strathroy. Gordon R. is 91 years old and lives in London. He still drives his car, but plans to quit soon. Gordon was elected Warden of Middlesex County in 1955. He lived in Strathroy for several years and was Mayor of Strathroy in 1966, 1967 and 1968. Rheta and Violet are now deceased. Robert moved to Strathroy after he married, and lived there until his death.

Dorothy lived at home until her marriage to Howard Fisher of Caradoc Township in 1928. She visited her parents and friends in Adelaide and kept in touch with them throughout the years.

Dorothy writes, *"I have so many wonderful memories of my childhood and teenage years in Adelaide. We had so many friends in the community and all of us attended Crathie School; there always seemed to be concerts and get-togethers of some sort in the school at night. Later, when the community hall was built in the 1920s, so much took place there. What wonderful times we had at the many dances that were held at the hall!*

My family attended Bethel Church and lots of entertainment took place there, also. I can remember many of them from both school and church (and a lot of us, still on the go), namely the Wardells, Grahams, Olivers, Lintons, Woods, Tomilsons, Parsons, Boltons, and many more."

MacDONALD, Larry and Mary

Larry MacDonald grew up in Williamstown, Glengarry Township, which is in eastern Ontario. In 1967, he married Mary Pearson of Adelaide, the daughter of Len and Anne Pearson. In 1973, they moved into their new home on 1½ acres of the Len Pearson property.

Larry and Mary have three children, Tim (1969); Christie (1974); and Andrea (1979). Tim married Jennifer Grant in 1993, and they have a son, Jack (1999).

They have had a very happy life in Adelaide Township, where they also operate their business, Larry MacDonald Chevrolet Geo Olds Ltd.

L-R, Larry MacDonald and Alex Ferguson, in front of part Lot 22, Con. 3, in 1987.

MacDONALD, Morris and Vera

In 1934, Morris MacDonald (1908-1982) of Delaware, son of Bateman and Ethel (Lawson) MacDonald, married Vera Petch (1916), daughter of Morley and Harriet (Tout) Petch of Adelaide. They had three children, Gene (1935); Maryellen (1936); and Norma (1938).

Morris began to train horses. Training and then driving Adios Harry in 1954, Morris is one of the few Canadians to win the Little Brown Jug harness race in Delaware, Ohio. In 1958, he moved to the U.S., where he continued to train and drive horses. In the early 1960s, he was the leading driver at Yonkers Raceway in New York. In the mid-1960s, he began to purchase land in Adelaide Township. In 1968, he moved the family back to Adelaide, where they lived on Lot 24, Con. 3 SER. As well as his home farm, he acquired Lot 22 and part of Lot 23, Con. 1 SER. He also purchased part of Lot 22, Con. 2 SER, and about 90 acres across from the Strathroy Cemetery. In total, he owned about 700 acres, where he raised cash crops and pastured a quality herd of horses. He trained horses on his own track. He owned a well-known stallion named Newport Duke, which he bred to his own mares and to mares owned by others. Many of Newport Duke's offspring went on to make names for themselves.

Vera MacDonald pointing at her father's signature on the cornerstone of the former Downham Nursery (courtesy Age Dispatch).

Gene moved to the U.S., where he works in the horse business. He married Barbara Benoit in Rhode Island and they had three children, Sheila, Kenneth and Lisa, all born in North Carolina. Gene now resides in New Jersey.

Maryellen married Dow Wilson and they had two children, Joni and Steven. She remarried, to Graham Pincombe, and they have a son, Robert. She works as a secretary for Wright Photo Studios and Glendale Mobile Homes, both in Strathroy.

Norma married Daniel Talbot of Acton. They had two children, Michael and Margaret "Peggy." When Norma and Daniel divorced, she moved to the home farm to live with her mother. Michael is single. He lives in Strathroy and works in construction. Peggy married Robert Call. She works as a hairdresser in London.

MacKENZIE, John and Anne

John MacKenzie (1884-1961) was born in Scotland on the Isle of Lewis, as was his wife, Anne MacAuley (1884-1980). They were married there in 1914. Their two eldest children, Ian (1915-1942) and Jessie (1917), were born in the U.K., where John, a stonemason, served in the Royal Navy Reserve. In 1920, the family sailed from Glasgow aboard the S.S. Sicilian. They lived briefly in Toronto and Port Stanley, and then moved to London, Ontario, where the younger children, Donald Murdo (1921-1967) and William John (1923), were born.

During the Depression, the family moved to the east half of Lot 15, Con. 2 NER, at what was then known as Reynold's Corners. They lived there between 1929 and 1937. Ian attended high school in Strathroy, travelling there in Gordon Grogan's car each day. Bill, being younger, remembers going to school at S.S. #4.

After attending two years of university at McGill in Montreal, Ian enlisted in the R.C.A.F. While training in England, he met his death in a plane crash and is buried there near his birthplace. Donald also enlisted in the R.C.A.F. and served from 1940 until the end of the war. He was awarded the DFC. While he was overseas, he visited his father's parents, whom he had never met before.

Jessie left London in 1947 for Washington, D.C., where she held a number of international positions.

Bill enlisted in the army in 1942 in London. He

MacKenzie family, L-R, Donald Murdo, Ian, Anne (MacAuley), William John, Jessie, John.

completed Officer's training at Brockville the following year and was commissioned with the rank of Lieutenant. He completed his airborne training at Shilo, Manitoba, and was discharged at London, where he still lives. His parents are both buried there.

MAHON, William and Araminta

As a young man, William Mahon came from County Meath, Ireland, to London, Ontario; his father was a soldier. William had a team of horses and a wagon, which he used to convey newly arrived settlers from Hamilton to their destinations in southern Ontario.

William (1831-1916) married Araminta Demaray (1831-1925), and they settled on a farm in Dorchester, where she had immigrated as a child (see DEMARAY). They came to Adelaide in the early 1860s and settled on the west half of Lot 25, Con. 1 NER. They brought two children, John G. (1859-1940) and Ellen (ca.1859-1869). Two more children, Samuel (1861-1919) and Margaret "Maggie" (1870-1948), were born in Adelaide. They lived in Adelaide until William's death.

John G. married Mary Hansford (1863-1949) and they moved to Caradoc and then to Lobo (see HANSFORD, John and Mary). They had four children, William Emery (1888-1969); Annie A. (1891-1960); Fred (1899); and Ella (1903).

Samuel married Adeline E. Bolton (1868-1895) in 1894. Samuel then married Charlotte Noble (1866) and they had a daughter, Kathleen (1904). Samuel lived on the same farm as his father.

Araminta went to live with her daughter, Maggie.

Samuel sold the farm in 1918 and went to Calgary. He went to the Peace River with a survey party in 1919. He and another man were left to finish surveying while the rest of the party went on to make camp for the night. A blizzard came and all of the party's tracks had disappeared under the snow. When Samuel and the other man came to a fork in the road, they turned the wrong way. Their matches had gotten wet, so they couldn't make a fire. When the two men were found, Samuel had died from exposure. The other man's foot had to be amputated when they got him to Edmonton.

MANN

The Mann family came from West Sussex, England. Samuel C. Mann (1782-1836) and Ann Downer (1783-1845) were married in 1802 in Billingshurst, England. They had a large family of 12 children, 11 sons and one daughter (1815-1834). Ten sons eventually came to Canada. One son, Henry (1805), became a minister and stayed in England.

The first of the Manns to come to Canada was Charles (1811) in 1832, with his cousin, John Downer, who settled just north of Napperton. They came from Wisborough Green, West Sussex, on the Petworth Emigration Scheme sponsored by Lord Egremont. They were joined in 1835 by three other Mann brothers, Thomas (1813); John (1817-1891); and Samuel Jr. (1807-1841). In April 1836, Samuel C. and Ann left England for Canada with six of their sons, Noah (1803); George (1809); Mark (1819-1904); Eli (1821); Moses (1823); and Edwin (1825-1891). Samuel C. died during the voyage. One of Noah's daughters died in Brantford.

Samuel C.'s death left Ann alone to care for her young sons. She put some of them in "service" as she says in a letter to friends and relatives back in Sussex. Ann and her family stayed with Thomas Holden, a widower, who had immigrated with seven of his children in 1832. In 1838, Thomas Holden married Ann Downer Mann. Charles settled in Adelaide Township. Some of the Mann sons settled in Michigan.

Thomas Mann married Ruth Holden (d.1865), one of Thomas Holden's daughters. Thomas and Ruth lived in a log house on Pike Sideroad SER. It was on a little hill near a creek, and the property had an apple orchard. They lived in this log house for 28 years.

Thomas and Ruth had a large family of 12 children. Four of them died as babies and were buried in the Fourth Line Cemetery. Harriet, their eldest daughter, married Cyrus Hunter, and they lived in Strathroy for the rest of their lives. They had eight children. A number of Hunter descendants still live in Strathroy. William Hunter, a grandson, served on the Strathroy Council for a number of years in the 1930s.

Ruth Holden Mann and her adult daughter, Ruth, died less than a month apart and were buried in the Fourth Line Cemetery. Baby daughter Dorthea Annetta (1864) survived her mother. In 1867, Thomas Mann married a widow, Jane Patrick Clark. In 1877, when Dorthea Annetta was 13 years of age, Thomas Mann sold his farm and moved with his family to Cass City, Michigan. Some of the sons later returned to Canada. One settled in Sarnia and one in Strathroy. Some grandsons moved to London. When Dorthea was 16, she married George Kivel. They had one daughter and two sons.

Mark, son of Samuel C. and Ann, worked and lived in London for four or five years. In 1841, he married Sophia Rapley, one of Charles Rapley's two daughters. Charles (1800-1862) had immigrated to Adelaide Township in 1832 from Kirdford, West Sussex.

In 1844, Mark began to farm on Lot 14, Con. 4 SER, at Napperton. Mark and Sophia had 11 children, all born in a log house on this lot. The first house was close to the road but it was too damp, so

50th Wedding Anniversary of Mark and Sophia (Rapley) Mann, ca.1891.

Mann family, back L-R, George Mann, Eli Mann, Levi Mann. Middle L-R, Thomas Mann, Noah Mann, Thomas Jr. Mann, Harriet Mann Hunter. Front L-R, Dorthea Mann, Emma Hunter, Josephine Hunter.

they disassembled it and rebuilt farther back on a slight hill. Mark also owned a 100-acre farm near Petrolia.

Mark and Sophia's children all grew up on this farm. However, Alice Maude Maria died of scarlet fever at age four. She is buried in the Fourth Line Cemetery. Frances Elizabeth (d.1947) was the middle child.

Farming in those early years was hard work with primitive tools. Tree stumps took dynamite to remove and there was serious risk of injury. The older boys and Mark would take grain to the mill in sacks on their backs. They carried flour, shorts (bran) and other supplies home the same way.

Sophia's father, Charles Rapley, lived with Mark and Sophia until his death. Charles made some furniture for their house. Frances Elizabeth kept a red rocking chair, a cherry table, and a chest of drawers that he made. Charles Rapley and Mark Mann were members of the first Fair Board in Strathroy.

In later years, Mark and Sophia retired to a house on Albert Street West in Strathroy. A 50th wedding anniversary photograph was taken there in 1891.

Frances Elizabeth was born in the log house and lived all her life in Adelaide Township and Strathroy. She married William Cochrill (d.1929) in 1887, and they lived in the Mann log house where two children, Byron and Mae, were born. The log house and farm became part of the Currie farm to the east when the Cochrills moved onto a farm on Con. 10, in the south part of Strathroy. In 1915, they sold that farm and bought the Armstrong Homestead house on Victoria Street in Strathroy, where they lived for 32 years.

The Mann descendants have scattered far and wide, to the Canadian west and the west coast of the U.S., Tennessee and Michigan. One returned to Strathroy and then moved to London.

MANNING

David Manning (1819-1890) was the fourth child of William (1788-1860) and Phillipa (Parnell) Manning (1787). He married Mary Uglow Coulton and they had 13 children, David Jr.; Charles; Mary Ann; Alice; Grace Parnell (ca.1848); Nicholas (1848-1909); William Coulton (1852-1894); Sophia (1855-1898); Ellen (1856-1880); Coulton (1858-1871); and Sydney (1862-1938). Two children's names are unknown. About 1870, David and Mary, with 12 of their children, came to Canada. Mary Ann had married William Hoskings and they remained in England. At first, David, Mary and family settled in Middlesex County near Adelaide, but sometime after 1881, David bought a farm in Uttoxeter near Forest, where he raised heavy horses. The farm was later divided between two sons, Nicholas and Sydney. About 1905, Sydney sold out to Nicholas and bought a farm closer to Forest.

In the 1880/1881 Directory, a David lived on the same lot as Nicholas, the west half of Lot 1, Con. 4, Kerwood. They are listed as tenants.

David married Fern (last name unknown). John was a butcher. He and Fern lived in Sarnia and had three children.

Charles married Emily Rosa Pritchard in June 1879. The 1880/1881 Directory lists Charles as a grocer in Strathroy on Front Street, and their residence is at the corner of Centre and Caradoc St. Later, they moved to Collingwood, where Charles had a Flour and Feed Mill. They had five children.

Alice married George Stonehouse. George kept a store in McGillivray and was a postmaster for a time. They had one child.

Grace Parnell married Reuben Miner in December 1872. They had eight children.

Nicholas married Maria Langford, likely after 1881. The 1880/1881 Directory lists Nicholas as a grocer and a clerk. He boarded in the Commercial Hotel. Nicholas must have married after 1880. Later, he was a cheese maker. In 1906, he bought a cheese factory started by Louis Richardson in 1878. It stood on the southwest corner of Lot 28, Con. 9, about a mile east of the village and was called the Uttoxeter Cheese Factory when Louis Richardson owned it. When Nicholas bought it, the business was part of the Plympton Cheese Company, and he ran it until his death. His wife, Maria, sold the factory to John S. Clarke, who also owned the Warwick Village Cheese Factory. Nicholas and Maria had four children, Stanley, Gordon, Fred and Sophia.

William Coulton married Emma Crouse (1857-1943). In 1880, they lived in Kerwood on Lot 2, Con. 2 SER. He was listed as a tenant. Later, they resided in Forest, where William was a butcher. William and Emma had five children.

Sophia never married. She died at 33 years of age, and was buried in Beechwood Cemetery in Forest.

Ellen married Dr. William L. Crone (1856-1880) in 1878 in Adelaide. William was the son of William and Maria (Williams) Crone and was a graduate of the Ontario Veterinary College. They had one child, Frederick (1879-1939), who married Leona B. Henry in Vancouver. After Ellen's death, Dr. Crone married Caroline Craig (ca.1864-1907), daughter of John Craig of Adelaide, in 1887. They had two children, Leonard (1891) and Alverna Jane (1894). The family moved to Ovid, Michigan, but later returned to the area and lived in Watford.

Coulton died in Adelaide in his early teens. He was buried in St. Ann's Cemetery.

Sydney became a farmer. He married Elizabeth Shillington (1868-1944), and they had seven children.

The Age Dispatch lists a Thomas Manning, who married Jane Margaret Stewart in Strathroy on September 2, 1870. This could be one of the two children whose names are unknown.

MARSHALL, Robert and Vesta

Robert "Bob" and Vesta (Watson) Marshall bought their property in 1985, two years after Bob obtained employment at the newly formed Strathroy Foods. Bob travelled from Kirkton, their previous home, until they moved into their new residence in August 1986.

In 1987, their daughter, Lana, married John Seyler. They live in Innerkip and have two children, Rachel and Marshall. Their son, Brent, is a lawyer in St. Thomas. He has two children, Leah and Robert.

Vesta worked for 10 years at Expressions in the Kenwick Mall and retired in January 1998.

Bob was the plant manager at Strathroy Foods until January 1994, when he and Vesta purchased Strathroy Rent-All. This business has grown to include a fastening business called Marbolt. Vesta does the bookkeeping for the business.

They are both involved in Masonic organizations. Bob is a member of the Beaver Lodge and past president of Strathocha Shrine Club. They are

Jim and Eva Marshall on their 35th Wedding Anniversary in 1980.

both members of Veritas Chapter, Order of the Eastern Star. Vesta is past Queen of Omar Temple, Daughters of the Nile and a member of Strathocha Daughters of the Nile Club. Bob and Vesta are participating members of Strathroy United Church.

MARTIN, Hiram and Hannah

Hiram Martin (1794-1870) was born in New York into a family of United Empire Loyalists. According to oral tradition, he came to Upper Canada with his parents and several brothers about 1802, settling in Prince Edward County. By 1818, he was living in Mount Pleasant, near Brantford. In that year, Hiram married Hannah Hollingshead (1798-1877) in York, now Toronto. Hannah was the daughter of Isaac and Mary (Hill) Hollingshead. The Hollingshead family, also United Empire Loyalists, first settled in New Brunswick and then moved to a farm that is now part of Yonge Street, Toronto.

Hiram and Hannah had 10 children, Clarissa (1819-1888); Mary (1820-1884); Francis (1823-1895); Samuel (1825-1913); Elizabeth (ca.1828); Abigal (1830-1910), who married Elijah Eastman (see EASTMAN, Benjamin and Mahetable); Anne (1832-1919); Harriet (1836), who married Thomas Harris, son of Thomas and Ann (Phipps) Harris; Matilda (1839-1876); and William (1842-1924). Hiram farmed for several years in Mount Pleasant before moving to Oxford County, then to Caradoc Township, on a farm that is now part of the Strathroy Fair Grounds. The family finally moved to Adelaide during the 1850s. While in Mount Pleasant, Hiram is believed to have been one of the early teachers at the Mohawk Institute in Brantford. In Adelaide, Hiram settled on the west half of Lot 9, Con. 3 SER.

In 1842, Clarissa, the eldest child of Hiram and Hannah, married James McIlwain (1818-1879). They resided in Brooke Township, where they raised nine children.

In 1841, Mary married John Wiley (see WILEY, John and Mary). She remarried, to Stephen Cornwall of the Sombra area. They had a daughter, Harriet. After the death of her second husband, Mary came to live with her daughter, Sarah, in Adelaide. In the early 1880s, Mary made one trip to Western Canada. She is buried in Sombra.

In 1848, Francis married Harriet Waldron (1827-1901). They lived in Michigan, where they had two daughters.

In 1855, Samuel, fourth issue of Hiram and Hannah, married Beulah Miner (1831-1926), daughter of Truman and Elizabeth (Morrison) Miner. They had eight children, Frances (1856-1863); Electa (1858-1940), who married Hiram Kitchen; James (1860-1863); Martha (1863-1957), who married Samuel McCandless; Matilda (1866-1954), who married Robert Richards; Mary (1868-1932), who married Phillip Matthews; Hiram (1871-1875); and Silas (1874-1875). Samuel farmed part of Lot 15, Con. 2 SER, before moving to Strathroy.

Elizabeth, fifth of Hiram and Hannah's children, married Henry Cooper (ca.1827), son of James and Harriet Cooper of Adelaide. They had at least four children born in Adelaide, David (ca.1854); Victor (ca.1857); Edward (ca.1862); and Hiram (ca.1868). Henry later moved his family to Detroit.

In 1959, Anne married John Sydie (ca.1834) of Simcoe County. They resided there and raised six children.

In 1863, Matilda married Thomas Elliott (1840), son of Thomas and Mary Ann Elliott of Adelaide. They had three children, Thomas (1867-1872); Hannah (1870, died an infant); and Alice (1871-1872). Thomas worked in Strathroy as a carriage maker.

In 1869, William, the youngest child of Hiram and Hannah, married Eliza Bishopp (1849-1931), daughter of George and Mary

Martin family, back L-R, Francis, Carolyn, Gilbert, Alice, Louise, Silas. Second row, L-R, Emily, Calvin, Julia. Third row L-R, mother Eliza (Bishop) and father William. Front L-R, Maude, Ethel and Herbert. ca.1900.

Ann (Croucher) Bishopp. They had 13 children, Herbert (1869-1961); Gilbert (1871-1938); Alice (1873-1952); Emily (1875-1955); Silas (1877-1962); Francis (1878-1942); Lucretia (1881-1884), who died of scarlet fever; Caroline (1884-1950); Louisa (1886-1965); Calvin (1888-1925); Ethel (1890-1945), who married Archie Muxlow (see MUXLOW, Edwin and Harriett); Maude (1892-1970); and Leila (1894-1968). The first six children were born on the home farm.

Hannah, Hiram's widow, lived with William and Eliza after her husband's death. William continued to operate the family homestead until Hannah died, at which time the farm was sold to settle the estate. William moved his family to Port Huron and worked there for three years before returning to Adelaide in the early 1880s. William purchased the west half of the east half of Lot 14, Con. 3 SER, from Isaac Thrower. The farm was beside William's niece, Sarah Eastman, and across from his father-in-law. It produced a variety of fruits: apples, pears, plums and all kinds of berries, for which there was a ready market. This farm stayed in the Martin family until the late 1930s. William and Eliza are buried in Strathroy Cemetery.

The Martin family members were active in the Bethesda Methodist Church. Eliza was the first president of the Woman's Missionary Society of Bethesda. The children were members in the young people's groups and the choir. Ethel was the church organist for about 30 years.

Herbert, the eldest child of William and Eliza, married Louisa Currie (1869-1905), daughter of Fred and Eliza (Harris) Curry of Adelaide. They moved to Neepawa, Manitoba, where they had three children, Fred, Ethel and Susan. After Louisa died, Herbert married Margaret Stewart, and they had four children, Calvin Thelma, Jean and Elma.

In 1904, Gilbert married Mary Phillips. They lived in New York and had two children, Charlotte and Marion.

In 1893, Alice married her cousin, Edward Cooper (ca.1862). They lived in the U.S., where they had a daughter, Violet.

Emily married Eldon Carrothers (1872-1955), son of James and Helen (Thompson) Carrothers, of Adelaide. They farmed the south half of Lot 9, Con. 2 SER. They had a son, Douglas (1907-1977) and a daughter, Eldena (1913-1933), who died of diabetes. In 1937, Douglas married Marguerite Campbell, daughter of Archie and Isabel (McLean) Campbell of Adelaide. Douglas took over the farm and, with his cousin, Irwin Carrothers, purchased a trenching machine. They operated a tile drainage business for many years.

In 1912, Silas, the fifth child of William and Eliza, married Reta Mason (1892-1970). They farmed part of Lot 10, Con. 2 SER. They had three children, Aubrey (1913); Grant (1915-1968); and Flora (1917-1993). Aubrey married Anne Richardson and they had two children, Bob and Bradley. Grant married Margaret Lee and they had two children, Margaret and Kenneth. Flora married Ross Burthwick and had one son, Brian.

In 1908, Francis married Kate Cunningham (1878-1931). They lived near Hamilton, where they had three children, Margaret, Francis and Gwendolyn. Francis remarried, to Marion Waugh.

In 1909, Caroline married Bert Munson (ca.1882-1955). They lived in Ohio, where they had three children, Kenneth, Dorothy and Jean.

In 1913, Louisa married Archie Northmore (1888-1947). They lived in Toronto, where they had three children, Mary, Martin and Jack.

In 1917, Calvin married Ella Wardell (1888-1973), daughter of John and Carolyn (Lindsay) Wardell, of Adelaide. They had two children, Fred (1919) and Bill (1921). Calvin took over the family

William and Eliza (Bishop) Martin residence, Second Line South. Shown are Ethel, Leila and Maude.

farm, but died young. The family stayed together with the support of relatives and friends. The farm continued to provide fruits and berries for sale, and the cleared land was rented out to neighbours. The family moved to London in 1937.

Fred, the eldest child of Calvin and Ella, was educated at S.S. #11 Adelaide, Payne's School, Strathroy District Collegiate and, finally, Beck Collegiate in London. In 1929, he won a ribbon, which now hangs in the Adelaide Municipal office, for winning the most points at the Adelaide Fair. He started selling "Keith Seeds" in Adelaide by bicycle. After completing high school, Fred worked as meat-cutter. He continued in the meat business for 29 years, also serving in the R.C.A.F. for four years. A ruptured back forced a career change. Fred became a mutual funds salesperson for Regal Capital Planners, a job he thoroughly enjoys. His success parallels that of Regal, which grew to be the largest independent distributor of funds in Canada. Fred has won many top awards for sales, along with a diamond watch, a diamond ring, a gold cup, and trips around the world. He credits his success to the wonderful start he had in Adelaide and being raised by his mother, friends and neighbours. Fred is a great advocate of Adelaide and currently attends the S.S. #11 "Mullifarry Reunion" every year. In 1943, Fred married Mary Darby of Guelph, and they had three children, Bryan (1944); Heather (1955); and Jill (1963).

Bill, the younger son of Calvin and Ella, married Peggy Adams. They had two children, Lillian and Donald.

Both Maude and Leila, the youngest children of William and Eliza, remained single. They moved to Toronto and became successful dressmakers, although they returned to Adelaide often to visit family and friends.

MATTHEWS, Stephen and Hope

In 1937, Stephen (d.1956) and Hope Matthews (d.1947) and their teenage son, Andrew (1921), moved to a farm on the north side of the "Sarnia Gravel" (now Highway 22) between Hickory Corners and Highway 81. Stephen was born in England, and had served as a signalman in South Africa during the Boer War. He then moved with his father and brother to a farm in Saskatchewan between Battleford and Saskatoon. After a number of years, he left the farm to work in Calgary, Alberta, as a fireman on the railroad. He married Hope, and Andrew was born in Alberta. Less than two years later, Stephen moved his family to Detroit, Michigan, where he worked as a tool-and-die maker for the Packard Motor Car Company and, later, Ford Motor Company. Fourteen years later, he felt the urge to return to farming and they settled in Adelaide.

The farm supported a herd of 25 Jersey cattle. Cream and whole milk were shipped to a dairy in Strathroy. Andrew attended Strathroy Collegiate Institute and graduated in 1941. He went to the Ontario Agricultural College in Guelph for two years, and then enlisted in the R.C.A.F. in 1943. Hope died of cancer, and Stephen returned to England. There, he married Mary Seaton, a childhood friend and widow. He died of heart failure, and Mary died 15 years later at the great age of 105.

Andrew served overseas as a navigator in an R.A.F. Lancaster Squadron and, after the war, graduated from the University of Toronto in Engineering Science. He married Mary Elizabeth "Billie" Smith of Toronto in 1947. They had five children, Stephen; Nancy; Peter (d.1986); David; and Mary. After serving 15 years in the peacetime R.C.A.F., he joined RCA Victor (later Spar Aerospace) in Montreal. He retired in 1986.

Andrew and Billie's eldest children, Stephen, Nancy and Peter, settled in the Ottawa area. Nancy married Theophilus Reed, who works in the insurance business. Peter won an NSERC scholarship and took his Master's degree in computer science at Queens. He worked for BNR in Ottawa, and married Anne Booth (d.1986). He and Anne died in an automobile accident.

David, the fourth child of Andrew and Billie, moved to Edmonton. There he married Ann Rayment. He earned a BA and an MA at the University of Alberta, where he won a SSHRC scholarship. He went to the University of California at Berkeley, where he earned a second MA and completed his PhD in Linguistics and Slavic languages in 1997. He now lives near his parents in Ottawa.

Mary, Andrew and Billie's youngest child, married Peter Komarnitsky, a printer. They live in Guelph and have two children, Carolyn and Nicholas.

MATTHEWS

The earliest published article about the Matthews family appeared in the Strathroy Age on January 12, 1877, titled "A Few of The Old Folks." It states, *"Catherine, widow of William Matthews, remembers the Irish rebellion of 1798; came to America about 1850, lives with her son-in-law and daughter, William and Maria Sherman, not two miles west of toll gate, north of Strathroy; about 85."*

Another unpublished story was written by a great-granddaughter, Nellie (McIllmurray) Gotts Kreh of Michigan, in the 1980s. She states, *"William and Catherine Matthews, from Ireland, Ballina, County of Mayo, came to Niagara, Ontario, Canada in 1839. William died at Niagara and is buried there. Catherine (1783-1890) came with the family to Adelaide Township. The children were Margaret, Anne (my grandmother), Maria, Charles and George. They settled three miles north of Strathroy, Ontario. They were Church of Ireland, then became Episcopalian."*

An obituary of Catherine Matthews, which appeared in the Age on May 1, 1890, probably gives us the most accurate information. It states that Catherine Slush (1782) was born in Kilglass, County Sligo, Ireland, one of a family of five girls and two boys. She married William Matthews, who died before she immigrated with her family to the town of Niagara, Ontario, in 1847. They moved to Adelaide in 1850, where they purchased a farm on the main road. Catherine resided there until about four years before the date of the article, when she came to Strathroy with her daughter and son-in-law, Mr. and Mrs. William Sherman. Catherine died at the age of 107.

Merging the above three stories paints a fairly comprehensive picture. The year 1847 was at the tail end of the Irish Potato Famine. This might have caused the death of William and probably prompted the family to immigrate. In Canada, the family changed their religion from Catholic to Anglican, which agrees with another family story. Catherine's age of 107 seems incredulous, especially when you consider her eldest child would have been born when Catherine was 39, and the youngest, when she was 53. Census information and the "Old Folks" article suggests that Catherine was born about 1790 to 1792, which seems more probable.

The January 1852 census documents their residency in Adelaide, indicating they are living on part of Lot 21, Con. 1 SER. The Matthews children were Margaret (1822-1863); Charles W. (ca.1824-1915); Anne (ca.1826-1920); George (ca.1829); and Maria (ca.1836).

Margaret married James McKenzie (see McKENZIE, James and Margaret).

Charles, along with his brother-in-law, James McKenzie, purchased 200 acres of land from Andrew Heron on June 26, 1856. The sale was registered for this land, Lot 21, Con. 1 SER, in November 1856, along with conveyances that gave 1/3 (66 2/3 acres) to both Charles and George Matthews. James and George had been farming this property since at least 1852. A story that was passed down through the McKenzie line suggests that the lot was split as a favour to someone.

Charles was not recorded in the 1852 or 1861 Adelaide census. Despite the earlier purchase of land, Charles is not a confirmed resident of Adelaide until 1866, when he married Eleanor Earley (ca.1844-1928) of Adelaide, daughter of James and Eleanor (Fawcett) Earley. The marriage record indicates that Charles was born in Sligo, Ireland. In 1871, they are farming on Lot 21, but the 1878 Middlesex Atlas map shows Charles also on the east half of Lot 4, Con. 4 SER. The Lot 21 farm was sold in 1878 to Charles Demaray. Charles and Eleanor had seven children, James (ca.1867); William C. (1868-1933); George Henry (1872-1927); Anna M.

Matthews family, back L-R, George, Jim, Burton. Seated L-R, Clarence and Meryl Matthews, ca.1969.

George Matthews family, clockwise from back left, Brian, Larry, Wayne, George, Betty, Tyler, Sandra, and Jeannine.

(1874-1910); John W. (ca.1880); Lawrence Alexander (1883-1893); and Eveline (ca.1886).

James, the eldest child of Charles and Eleanor, became a doctor and moved to the U.S. A 1917 newspaper article notes that Dr. J.D. Matthews of Detroit, formerly of Adelaide, was going on active service with the U.S. Army Medical Corp in France.

William C. married Margaret Mitchell, (1855-1946) of Adelaide, daughter of John and Mary Ann Mitchell. They adopted a daughter, Ethel. In 1901, William was farming the west half of Lot 4, Con. 5 SER. Later, it is believed, he had a car dealership in Strathroy before moving to the London area. Ethel was very musical and played the organ. She married a Mr. Doherty, who made his living tuning pianos. They had no children.

In 1896, George Henry married Ida Isabel Westgate (1874-1961) of Warwick, daughter of George and Margaret (Lamont) Westgate. They had eight children, Clarence DeLloyd (1897-1974); Orville (1900, died a baby); Rheta Meryl (1902); Paul (1904, died a baby); Kenneth Earl "Ken" (1906-1973); Evelyn Dorothy (1910-1987); John "Jack" Ross (1913-1986); and Merlene Marie (1920). George took over the family farm, part of Lot 4, Con. 4 SER.

Clarence DeLloyd married Dora Meryl Freer (1901-1993) on November 28, 1924. Meryl was born in Metcalfe Township. They took up residence on Lot 4, Con. 5 SER, where they farmed and raised three sons, Burton "Burt" (1926); George (1929); and James "Jim" (1936).

In 1944, the family moved to Lot 5, Con. 5 SER, where they continued farming. Clarence also sold insurance for Mutual Life, Wawanesa and National Auto League. He and Meryl were both lifelong members of St. Paul's Anglican Church in Kerwood, Egremont Lodge 207, and Kerwood Rebecca Lodge.

Burt attended Agricultural College in Guelph and, after completing his education, became President of Waterloo and Guelph Universities. Burt married Lois Lewis of Ottawa on June 23, 1951, and they have two sons, David and Tom. Burt is now retired and living in Waterloo.

George farmed with his father on the home farm until his marriage to Margaret Elizabeth "Betty" Morgan of Adelaide on August 28, 1954. They bought a farm, Lot 5 Con. 4 SER, where George farmed. He also worked for Ken Matthews Ltd. George and Betty have three sons, Brian (1959); Wayne (1963); and Larry (1967).

Brian attended University of Waterloo and is employed with Toronto Dominion Bank in Toronto. He lives in Brampton with his wife, Jeannine.

Wayne attended University of Waterloo. He is a computer consultant with VERIZON Telecommunications Company in Texas. He married Reneé Couch in 1999, and they reside in Texas.

Larry attended Laurier University, and works for Percentage Plus Investment and Insurance Services Inc. in Brampton. He resides there with his wife, Sandra, and son, Tyler.

George and Betty severed a lot off the Matthews farm and built a new home on Lot 5, Con. 5 SER, in 1991. George is a member of the Kerwood Fire Department and also a member of Kerwood Egremont Lodge.

James, the third son of Clarence and Meryl, married Dorothy Ireland of Adelaide on May 21, 1960. They have two daughters, Kim and Kathy. After their marriage, Jim joined the O.P.P. He served in Brockville and Tillsonburg, where he now lives in retirement.

In 1940, Rheta, the third child of George and Ida, married William John Stuart Knox. They had no children. Rheta lives in Sarnia.

Ken, fifth issue of George and Ida, married Leila "Muriel" Waltham (1913), daughter of Richard and Elva May (Watson) Waltham. Ken operated the GMC dealership in Strathroy with Gord Galbraith in the late 1930s. Ken and Muriel also bought a farm and took up residence at Lot 4, Con. 5 SER, across the road from the Matthews home place. They started a trucking and bulldozing business in the late 1930s, which has been known as Ken Matthews Ltd. since 1964. Ken delivered gravel to the local farmers and area townships and he enjoyed visiting with his customers. Ken was a lifelong member of St. Paul's Anglican Church, Kerwood. Muriel still resides at Lot 4, Con. 5 SER, and is an active member in St. Paul's Anglican Church and continues to be active in the business. Ken and Muriel had two children, William "Bill" Earl (1940) and Judith "Judy" Ann (1943).

Bill attended S.S. #7 Adelaide and Strathroy District Collegiate. He belonged to the Kerwood Junior Farmers and Anglican Young People's Union. He went on to work in the family business and has been president of Ken Matthews Ltd. since Ken's death. Bill married Marjorie Joynt of Strathroy on September 29, 1962. They built a home on their farm at Lot 3, Con. 4 SER. They have two children, Jeffrey William "Jeff" (1965) and Susan Lynn (1970).

Jeff attended Adelaide Central School, Strathroy District Collegiate, and University of Western Ontario, where he received a degree in Civil Engineering. Jeff is a Professional Engineer, currently working for a consulting firm in London. Jeff married Lynda Elaine Dymond of Metcalfe Township on July 27, 1991. They have two children, Jenna Lynn (1993) and Katie Elaine (1995). Jeff and Lynda have purchased the family farm at Lot 4, Con. 5 SER, where they now reside. Jeff played guitar in the band "The Reflections" for many years.

Susan attended Adelaide Central School, Strathroy District Collegiate, and University of Western Ontario, where she received a Bachelor of Science degree and went on to earn her teaching degree at Althouse College. Susan is an elementary school teacher in Glencoe. Susan rode equestrian for several years and won many Ontario Championships. Susan married Paul Findlay of Glencoe on June 25, 1994. They reside in Glencoe and have a son, Matthew Paul (1998).

Ken Matthews family, L-R, Bill, Muriel, Kenneth and Judy, 1947.

Judy, Ken and Muriel's daughter, attended S.S. #7 Adelaide, Strathroy District Collegiate, and Teacher's College. She taught Grade Two at Adelaide Central School for several years. Judy married Robert "Bob" Dale of Lobo Township on July 10, 1965, and moved to Lobo Township, where they farmed. They raised three children, Karen Lynn (1967); Michael John Kenneth (1969); and Mary Ann (1972). Bob has been involved with Ken Matthews Ltd. for more than 35 years.

In 1941, Evelyn, sixth of George and Ida's children, married Ivan MacKenzie Parker (1908-1976). They had three children, Ivan "Mac," Isabel and Dorothy. Ivan was a successful breeder of Polled Shorthorn beef cattle in Wisbeach. With his wife, he established "Parker's Fireside Store" at the front of their farm. In 1954, he established "Order Groceries By Mail," a service that quickly gained many customers in Adelaide Township, especially among the growing Dutch population. Ivan's great-grandfather, Edwin Parker, immigrated to Canada from Ireland in 1855 and established a blacksmith shop in Adelaide Village. Ivan's grandfather, Benjamin Parker, was a bootmaker/shoemaker in Adelaide before purchasing a farm in Warwick Township.

In 1935, Jack, seventh issue of George and Ida, married Fay Geraldine Cockrane and had four children, Douglas, Arliss, Betty and Linda. Jack operated the family farm, part of Lot 4, Con. 4 SER. The farm was sold in 1945 to Edwin George, and Jack and his family moved to the Arkona area.

Merlene, the youngest of George and Ida's children, married Glen Moffat and had two children, Wayne and Sharon. The Moffats owned stores in Wanstead, Brigden, and Sarnia, where they retired.

It is believed that John W., fifth issue of Charles and Eleanor, went to the U.S. Nothing is known about Eveline, the youngest child.

About 1852, Anne, the third child of William and Catherine, married William Morgan (d.1855) as his third wife (see MORGAN, Richard Sr. and Jane). Anne was widowed with a six-month-old daughter, Mariah. With help, Anne operated the Morgan farm until her stepson, Robert, was old enough to take over. In 1863, Anne was called to the deathbed of her elder sister, Margaret McKenzie. Margaret asked Anne to marry her husband and look after her six children, aged two to 10 years. Anne accepted this responsibility and became the third wife of James McKenzie. By 1870, Anne was widowed again. She continued to operate the McKenzie farm with her stepchildren. Records show she is not residing on the farm in 1901. About 1913, Anne went to live with her daughter's family in Michigan.

George, the fourth of William and Catherine's children, married Mary Rychman (1841). They had eight children, Charlotte (ca.1859); Charles (ca.1860); Catherine (ca.1863); Mary Ann (ca.1865); William (ca.1869); George David (1870-1944); Emeline "Emma" (1873); and Caroline Jane "Carrie" (1874-1956). Mary Ann married a Mr. Gunyon (or Gunyu) and resided in Windsor.

In 1901, George David, the sixth child of George and Mary, married Anna Louisa Harris (1876-1933) of Adelaide, daughter of Samuel and Mary Jane (Crews) Harris. They had three children, William Samuel (1902-1986); Mary Georgina (1903-1989); and Ethel Irene (1904-1904). George took over the operation of the family farm, part of Lot 21, Con. 1 SER. The farm was sold in 1907, and George and his family moved to the Delaware area.

In 1892, Emma, George and Mary's seventh child, married William Blaine (ca.1862), son of John Blaine. They had at least four children, Cecil (1893); Alfreda (1895); Elizabeth (1897); and Ethel (1899). In 1901, William is living on the east half of Lot 5, Con. 5 SER. Adelaide township directories list William as a tenant in 1903 and 1905, and a freeholder in 1910. He left the township before 1914. Years later, Emma resided in Detroit, Michigan.

In 1901, Carrie, the youngest child of George and Mary, married William Patterson Carroll (1861-1932) of Adelaide, son of Thomas and Ann (Patterson) Carroll. They had three children, Rhena (d.1971); William Jr.; and Chester M. (1907-1960). William Carroll Sr. farmed part of Lot 2, Con. 4 SER. Rhena was married several times. Her first husband was a Hadden; other husbands were Forrest Hodge and Charles Towne. Rhena had a son, Francis Hadden, who stills owns property in Adelaide. Rhena died in Detroit, Michigan. William Jr. never married. Chester married Dorothy Westgate but had no children. Both William and Chester farmed on the Fourth Line South near Kerwood.

In 1858, Maria, the youngest child of William and Catherine, married James Williams (ca.1834) of Adelaide, son of John and Margaret Williams. James was born in Ireland. In 1866, Maria (Matthews) Williams married William Sherman (ca.1840) of Adelaide, son of Christopher and Margaret Sherman. William was born in Scotland. They farmed on part of Lot 17, Con. 1 SER. The 1871 and 1881 census shows that Maria's mother, Catherine, was living with them. Maria and James had no children, and they moved into Strathroy about 1886.

McADAM, Wesley and Jean

Wesley McAdam and Jean Arrand were married on October 24, 1936, at the parsonage in Ailsa Craig. They have two children, Della (1947) and John (1950). Della attended school at S.S. #9, where her teachers were Donald Heaman and Mrs. Hemstead. She recalls the square dances and card parties at Keyser's Hall, where her brother, John, usually fell fast asleep behind the musicians on a mattress of coats.

As well as mixed farming, Wes owned a tiling machine, which he used for additional income. In the 1950s, Wes went to work for Midrim Mining, a drilling company that came to the community to test for salt. Jean took in boarders who worked for the company. When the mining company left, Wes worked for the Middlesex County Roads Department. They moved to Strathroy in 1959.

Jean worked at the Middlesex Creamery in the snack bar and then for Bill Jervis at Jervis' I.G.A. In 1980, she retired from her last job as a cook at Strathmere Lodge.

McCABE, Ross and Mary

The original McCabes who settled in Adelaide Township came from Rockcorry, Ireland. Ross Miles (1785-1881) and his wife, Mary, settled on Lot 5, Con. 2, about 1849. Their son, Miles (1830-1915), and his wife, Mary (Elliott), raised a family of eight, including Sarah; Leo; Henry; John; William; James (1858-1936); and Angus Miles (1868-1944).

James taught school in Kerwood at S.S. #1. He became a doctor and started a practise in 1899. He also raised a family of eight, Frank, Victor, Allan, Joseph Ross, Leo, Theresa, Patricia, and Mary. Allan also became a doctor.

Angus Miles raised a family of three at Lot 16, Con. 2 NER. His children were Gladys, Miles and Evan. Evan stayed on the farm and married Elva Orr. They had one son, Joseph. The farm was sold in 1959 to Frank Feke.

Evan McCabe (in trunk) and Frank Bolton (on running board).

McCARTHY, Martin and Ann

Martin McCarthy (1816-1864) came from Roscommon County, Ireland. Through Colonel Talbot, he acquired a piece of land at the Forks of the Thames in London. Because of seasonal flooding, he moved to the east half of Lot 7, Con. 1 SER. He married Ann Morehead or Moorehead (1823-1897), who was born in Ireland. The 1842 census notes that Martin "Carty" has been in Ontario for seven years; he has improved 10 acres of his 100-acre farm, but there is no record of crops grown or any animals on the farm. This may indicate that he had recently moved to Adelaide from his London property. The land records show that Martin "Carty" bought 100 acres of the east half of Lot 7, Con. 1 SER, from John Peel Bellairs and his wife in 1840. In 1870, after Martin's death, his son, John, and the other children signed a quitclaim to Cornelius Carty. In the land records, it stated that "Cornelius Carty" was also known as "Cornelius McCarthy." At this time, Martin was 35 and Ann 28; the children listed were born in Canada, John 8; Cornelius 6; and Mary Jane 3.

Martin was buried in the Adelaide Village Roman Catholic Cemetery. His tombstone still stands, one of the few in this old cemetery. His wife, Ann, is buried beside him.

Martin and Ann had five children, John (1843-1900); Cornelius (1845-1939); Mary Jane (ca.1848-1925); William Martin (1853-1950); and Elizabeth McCarthy (1856-1916).

John married Elizabeth Wiley, daughter of David and Ann (Bradley) Wiley of Adelaide, in 1870 (see WILEY, David and Ann).

Cornelius married Sarah Ann Moulton, daughter of Israel and Serena Moulton of Forest, in 1880. On his golden wedding anniversary on June 20, 1930, Cornelius reminisced about driving the 20 miles by horse-and-buggy to claim her. Their honeymoon consisted of a return trip over the same route to his birthplace, the log house that was built by his parents. At the time when Cornelius and Sarah Ann began running the McCarthy homestead, there was an encampment of native Canadians on the farm. The braves trapped and hunted for their occupation. They also sold charcoal, which they made in pits in the woods. They burned limestone where they found it, and sold it for plaster and fertilizer, uses that were very familiar to the Irish settlers. The native women earned a little money selling their baskets. Cornelius McCarthy recalls that in his boyhood days, he played with these native children and could speak their language well. Deer, wolves and bear were common in the township and, as a boy, he had pet deer that drew him on a sleigh.

In an interview with the London Advertiser on June 20, 1930, Cornelius disclosed some little-known facts about life near Adelaide Village. He recalled that travelling Roman Catholic priests set up altars in the houses where those of the Catholic faith attended mass. Later, when a Methodist Church was built in the village, it served a large district. Many came from West Williams Township to the Adelaide Village church. The women came in their bare feet and brought knitting with them to work during the service. Later, Anglican and Catholic churches were built in the village. Cornelius attended school in the village, three miles away, at the time when the Egremont Road was only a trail through stumps. Cornelius admitted that he didn't attend school often—he was good at arithmetic but not so good at spelling.

Cornelius told of the days when Adelaide Village had a larger population than the Town of Strathroy. Until the chopping mill was set up in the village, the farmers had to take their grain to Kilworth, 20 miles distant, walking both ways. The mail coach stopped daily at Adelaide. As well as the mill, there were two harness shops, three general stores, three hotels, and two blacksmith forges.

Cornelius recalled that the 63rd Regiment was stationed at Adelaide Village and they were a fine lot of men. The government built the first hotel there. He remembered that, in those days, a bag of wheat was worth a barrel of whiskey in trade. Almost everyone "drank a drop," and whiskey was often kept in water pails in the house, but there were few drunks.

Cornelius said that oxen were only used for hauling, and he remembered six yokes of oxen hauling out the 14" sills for the barn—work that, later, one team of horses could do. There were no wagons used then, only sleighs in summer and winter, which were like huge stone boats. His father, Martin, had the second wagon in Adelaide Township, which was a "curiosity" made in Toronto.

In those days, there was plenty of timber and the farmers felled the trees, piled them in windrows and burned them, to clear the land for wheat. Mr. McCarthy speculated that [in 1930] *"The wood would be worth a great deal now."* He recalled going to funerals on horseback. The coffins were made of hewn or hollowed-out logs. The hearse was a sleigh. It seemed that there was more snow then in the winters. He referred to the doctor at Adelaide Village, who had a very large practise making his rounds on horseback.

In this interview, Cornelius concluded, *"I have read The London Advertiser for 60 years. At first it was published weekly, and it has come into our home ever since."*

A liberal in politics, the Adelaide octogenarian took an active interest in the affairs of his country. As a hobby, he favoured playing checkers and easily disposed of opponents half his age. In Sarah's opinion, a woman's hobby and life's work is wrapped in the development of her home and family. Both she and her husband weathered the years as pioneers well, and were happy to welcome their host of friends who feted them on their golden anniversary. They were presented with a pair of silver candlesticks and Cornelius received a gold-headed cane.

Cornelius and Sarah had six children, William Martin (1881-1930), who remained single and resided in Adelaide Township; Charles Wilfred (1884-1956), who married Loretta Jean Sullivan (1899-1973); Robert Henry (1887-1969), who married Madeline Henderson (see HENDERSON); Annie E. (1890-1956); Mary Jane (1893-1987); and Rena "Serena" Mary (1895-1984).

Annie E. married Joe Henry of Adelaide Village and Sarnia, and they had four children, Charles, Stanley, Edward and Marion. She later married Bill Yates.

Mary Jane married James Ignatius Sullivan (1894-1978) in 1926. They had two children, Larry, who lives in Sarnia; and Dorothy (1930-1986).

Serena married Miles McCabe. They had one son, James Malcolm McCabe. Serena is buried in the Roman Catholic Cemetery in Walkerton.

In his will, Cornelius made provision for his widow, Sarah, to have "home board and an annuity for life" in lieu of dower.

In 1940, the property was willed to Charles and his wife, Loretta Jean. Fred Brewer lived with this couple and rode the bus to Strathroy Collegiate with the other Main Road "kids." The Verkley family owns this farm today.

Mary Jane, Martin and Ann's third child, married (1869) David A. Wiley (see WILEY, David and Ann) in 1869.

William, fourth issue of Martin and Ann, remained single. As an adult, he lived with his first cousins, Bertha and Alice McCarthy, on the west half of Lot 15, Con. 1 NER.

Elizabeth, fifth of Martin and Ann's children, married Lewis Crummer (1854-1924) of Adelaide and Plympton Townships (see CRUMMER, John and Margaret) in 1875. They had seven children, Olive Anna Margaret (1880); William Charles (1883); James H. (1885-1951); Martin Howard (1887-1967); Louis Frank (1889-1969); an unnamed daughter (1894); and Florine Elizabeth (1896-1963).

Martin, the pioneer of the McCarthy family, had a sister, Nora (1800-1890), who was born in Dublin, Ireland. While there, she married Mike Regan (1790-1896). Their son, Michael Regan (1838-1928), married Margaret Herrington (1843-1919), who was born in Cork, Ireland. They purchased the east half of the east half of Lot 16, Con. 2 NER, and in 1927, Michael John Regan received the property in a quitclaim deed from Fergus Donahue. Nora, Mike, Michael, and Margaret are all buried in All Saints Roman Catholic Cemetery in Strathroy.

McCHESNEY, William and Jane

William McChesney (1810-1888) was born in County Down, Ireland. He and two brothers, Alexander and Joseph, immigrated to Adelaide in 1835. Alexander and Joseph settled on or about Lot 40, Con. 4, Warwick Township, and William settled in Adelaide.

On or about October 23, 1838, William signed purchase agreement #3395 for 100 acres of land, Lot 2, Con. 2 NER, from the Crown. This land had been set aside as a clergy reserve. In 1853, after he completed work requirements and yearly payments, a total cost of £50 sterling, the property was patented (Archives of Ontario RGI, C3, Vol. I, page 150).

The requirements of the land purchase included clearing 15 acres and erecting a house and/or barns in the first year. On November 4, 1838, William married Jane Wiley, also of County Down. They resided in Adelaide and settled on their farm. Their marriage is recorded with the Diocese of Huron in London, Ontario. They were married by license by D.E. Blake, St. Ann's Anglican Parish, Adelaide. According to an 1842 census, they had cleared the 15 acres and improved 11 more. The farm had produced 90 bushels of wheat, 20 of oats, 150 of potatoes, and 100 pounds of maple sugar. There were seven cattle beasts and three sheep. No horses are mentioned; one must assume the work was all done by hand or by oxen.

Nine children were born to William and Jane, and raised in the original log house, which consisted of one room and a loft. Eliza, the eldest, married John Conkey and settled in South Dakota. Mary married James Stalker and settled in Rockford, Illinois. Alexander died at age 13 and was buried in the West Adelaide Cemetery. Jane married Jack Grier and settled in Colfax, Washington. David (1848-1915) was born on the family farm. He was baptised by Rev. A. Mortimer; sponsors were Hugh Wiley, William McChesney and Jane Cleland. William James Jr. (1853-1929) farmed the homestead. Joseph (1854-1930) was born on the family farm. Henrey J. died at approximately 18 months, two days before his brother, Alexander. Sarah mar-

Agnes Anne (Shields) McChesney

Don and Lorna (Wilkins) McChesney on their wedding day, March 1946, in England.

ried James Hy Galloway, and both are interred in West Adelaide Cemetery. William Sr. and Jane are interred in West Adelaide Cemetery.

The office of the Registrar General records the marriage of David McChesney to Agnes Ann Shields (1851-1933), the daughter of James and Jennie "Jemina" Shields. They were married by Rev. Robert Scobie on October 1, 1873. Both are buried in Strathroy Cemetery. David and Agnes had six children, William James "W.J." (1875-1959); Elizabeth "Lilly" (1880-1963); Mary Jane (1883); Maude (1878-1948); Eliza "Lizzie" (1886); and Elva (1889, died an infant).

The Historical Atlas of Middlesex County, 1878 shows that David and Agnes owned a 100-acre farm, the east half of Lot 4, Con. 1 SER, and 38 acres, part of the west half of Lot 4, Con. 1 NER. David also purchased the west half of Lot 3, Con. 1 SER, from Charles Bolton and his wife on February 1, 1899. David assumed the two mortgages against the property and cash for a total of $3,150 and farmed there until selling the farm at Lot 3, Con. 1 SER, to his son, William, in 1905. He sold the rest of the farmland to his son-in-law, Matt Brown, and moved to Rapley Street in Strathroy to a farm that presently comprises most of Pannel Lane and area. In 1919, Agnes must have sold the property to Matt Brown and purchased the property across the street, a large, brick, 2-storey house on the east side of Rapley Street.

W.J., the eldest child of David and Agnes, was born at the family farm. He married Effie May Conkey (1880-1940) on December 25, 1900. They had one son, Robert Alvin (1902-1982).

W.J. served on the board of directors of West Adelaide Cemetery for most of his life, and was an elder of West Adelaide Church. He also taught the senior class in Sunday School. He and Effie May purchased Lot 3, Con. 1 SER, from his father in 1905, assuming the balance of the mortgage and one dollar. He put money aside in the Farmers Bank to build a new house and lost it all when the bank failed. Several years later, he finally built the house for his family at a cost of $750, key in the door, as the expression was at that time.

For a long time, W.J. rented the west half of the east half of Lot 2, Con. 1 SER, from his mother-in-law for the use of both cash crop and pasture. In later years, he also rented the front half of Lot 3, Con. 1 NER, from his father-in-law, Robert Conkey.

Sometime in the late 1890s, W.J. was kicked by a horse and the injury broke his leg. The leg was set at home and the cast was a wooden box fitted around

Alvin McChesney retirement party (tax collector and assessor for Adelaide). L-R, Charles Nichols, Frank Gare, Alvin McChesney and Frieda McChesney.

the leg and filled with gravel to hold the leg in position. It was not too successful, as the bones were out of place when the cast was removed. He walked with a limp for the rest of his life. Billy and Effie May are interred in West Adelaide Cemetery.

Robert Alvin was born at the family farm, Lot 3, Con. 1 SER. He married Anna Winnifred "Frieda" Wiley (1900-1984) on June 4, 1924, at West Adelaide Church. Witnesses were N.M. "Mac" Wiley and Flossie (Grogan) Hall. Frieda was born to William James "Jim" Wiley and Isabella (McKenzie) Wiley. They had four children, Donald, Vivian, Roy and Robert Alvin Jr.

Alvin farmed jointly with his father for a number of years and worked at a series of jobs at the GM Buick Division plant in Flint, Michigan. He worked as a lineman with the Springbank telephone system (with Ross Campbell). He was a trustee for the Adelaide School S.S. #6 for several terms. He was on the board of directors for West Adelaide Church, director on the West Adelaide Cemetery board (and custodian of the cemetery), a tradition that was carried on by Donald and now Roy McChesney.

Robert Alvin was the assessor for Adelaide Township during the war years and after, as well as the tax collector. A quote from Harold Eastman, July 1, 1995: *"Alvin and Frieda kept the neatest books I ever saw, and I have always considered them to be great friends."*

Roy, the third child of W.J. and Effie May, farms property that has been in the family since 1899. He remained single. Roy was injured in a snowmobile accident in the Muskokas several years ago and is now semi-retired.

Lilly, second child of David and Agnes, married James Matthew "Matt" Brown (1875-1950) on August 15, 1906. Both are buried in Strathroy Cemetery.

Mary Jane married Norman Burnet on December 21, 1913.

Maude, fourth of David and Agnes' children, married Daniel Parker on December 25, 1899. Both are interred in Watford Cemetery.

Lizzie married Fred Watson. She taught school for several years in Adelaide before moving to Butte, Montana. She died young, not long after the birth of her daughter. She is buried in Strathroy in her parents' family plot.

William James Jr. took over the family farm on July 26, 1886, due to William Sr.'s failing health. The 1891 census shows that William and his sister, Sarah, were then living on the family homestead. A marriage certificate indicates that on January 20, 1892, William J. McChesney and Ellen Jane Wilson (d.1925) were married in Adelaide Township by Rev. John H. Graham. The wedding was witnessed by David Wilson and Minnie A. Wiley. On September 18, 1909, William and Ellen sold the farm to William Gorman for cash and a mortgage of $4,500, and purchased a house on Metcalfe Street in Strathroy. William Jr. and Ellen remained childless. They are interred in West Adelaide Cemetery.

Joseph, seventh issue of William and Jane, married Elizabeth Conkey (d.1907) on November 23, 1885. They had four children, Eva Mabel, Nellie, David Henrey "Harry" and Herbert.

Eva married Walter Wilson. They farmed on the corner of Sideroad 27 and the Second Line North of Warwick Township. They had no children.

Nellie married Frank B. Summerfeld and moved to Dundurn, Saskatchewan.

Harry married Margaret Sargent. He became a doctor. Harry and Margaret lived in Seattle, Washington.

Herbert was killed in an automobile accident in his 20s, and is interred in West Adelaide Cemetery.

For a short period, Joseph and Elizabeth farmed the east half of Lot 3, Con. 3, but sold the property to James Sheilds on April 2, 1898. They farmed in Warwick Township until Elizabeth's death. Joseph spent the rest of his life with his son in Seattle, Washington, where he died. His remains were brought back and interred in West Adelaide Cemetery, with his wife, Elizabeth, and son, Herbert.

McDONALD, Hugh and Mary

In the late 1830s, Hugh and Mary McDonald came to Canada from Inverness-shire, Scotland. With them came their first four children, Mary (1821-1895); William (1824-1868); John (1827-1899); and David (1835-1855).

Mary married Alex Anderson and is the great-grandmother of Francis (Wilson) Arrand, and also Ruth, Eleanor and Jim Wilson.

William remained single.

John married Jessie McKenzie (1834-1926). John and Jessie are the great-grandparents of the

Pennington sisters, Evelyn, Kathleen "Kay" and Ann.

David (1835-1855) died suddenly while attending Queen's University, studying to be a minister.

After coming to Canada, Hugh and Mary had a fifth child, Hugh (1839-1907). He married Annie Cluness. They had six children, Hugh, Mary, Ann, David, Jim and Belle. Jim is the father of Nevie McDonald (now married to Arnold Watson).

Hugh and Mary settled on Lots 1 and 2, Con. 5, East Williams Township. This land was received from the Crown. Their first home was built on the property across the creek near the bush. It was the only clear land at that time. Hugh had been a blacksmith in Scotland and in order to continue his trade, he built a blacksmith shop near the road.

Most of these McDonalds are buried in the old Nairn Cemetery, except for John and Jessie and their family, who are buried in Strathroy Cemetery.

According to Adelaide land records, on January 15, 1857, Hugh and Mary McDonald became owners of Lot 16, Con. 4 NER, a farm consisting of 80.75 acres. This farm was probably bought for their son, John, who became owner in March 1863. It is supposed that about this time, John married Jessie, who had resided in East Williams Township. On this farm, they raised their five children, Margaret Sophia "Maggie" (1868-1907); Hugh (1871-1918); Mary Isabella (1872-1937); Jessie Henrietta "Ettie" (1874-1946); and John (1877-1952).

Maggie married Benjamin Pennington on January 1, 1894. They had two sons, John Leslie and Benjamin Francis "Frank."

Hugh remained single, and farmed with the family. He died at the age of 47.

Mary and Ettie remained single. They resided on the family farm.

John, the youngest child of John and Jessie, raised cattle on his pasture farms, and lived all of his life on Lot 16, Con. 4 NER, the original family farm. He remained single. Over the years, the McDonald family owned several properties on Con. 2 and 3 in Adelaide Township

During the last years of his life, John's great-niece and her husband, Kay (Pennington) and Wilfred Murray, lived with "Uncle John" and cared for him until his death. In 1956, Kay and Wilfred sold the farm to Cornelius and Louisa Verheyen.

McDOUGALL, Lloyd and Fieny

Lloyd and Fieny (Vanderheyden) McDougall moved to Adelaide Village from Strathroy in July 1979. Lloyd's parents had the BP Station on Highway 81 in Adelaide Township. Fieny had come to Adelaide from Caradoc Township, the lucky number 13 of 14 children.

McDougall family at the B.P. Service Station.

Margaret and Lorne McDougall

Lloyd and Fieny had a son, Gerald Jeffrey "Gerry." In 1994, Gerry married Erica Muyleart of Ekfrid Township. They reside in Strathroy.

The McDougalls lived in the Old General Store in the village, where they did some major renovations. Fieny had a hairdressing shop in their home, keeping business booming in Adelaide Village. She was on township council for one term from 1991 to 1994, and Lloyd was on council for the next term. Lloyd also worked in the construction industry.

McELMURRY

About 1835, the three sons of James (1809) and Fanny McElmurry immigrated to Canada from Six Mile Cross, County Tyrone, Northern Ireland. William (1804); Samuel (ca.1806-1887); and James (1809-1891) eventually settled in Warwick Township, near Arkona, where they split 200 acres. Before settling down, they may have spent time in Adelaide Township as they each married a young woman from Adelaide. James's marriage record in 1836 indicates he was a resident of Adelaide. Samuel's 1839 marriage record places him in Warwick working as a carpenter. William's marriage record has not been located.

The surname McElmurry has several variations. All three brothers were on the Warwick volunteers pay list in February 1838 with their names spelled McElmurry. However, the spelling varied on census and other records and each family line used a different spelling. William's line used McIllmurray; Samuel's line used McElmurray; and James' line used McIlmurray.

About 1838, William married Jane Morgan (1818-1893), daughter of Richard and Jane (Murdock) Morgan of Adelaide. They raised nine children, Marjory (1839-1902); Lucy Ann; John (1845-1913); Jane; Elizabeth; Fannie; William (1854-1931); Richard; and Angeline.

In 1871, Marjory married Robert Rowland (ca.1839-1900) of Warwick, son of Edward and Jane Rowland. Robert was born in Adelaide. They had four children, Clara, William J., Jane and Mary Lou.

In 1893, John married Priscilla Morgan (1847-1940), daughter of David and Ann Morgan of Adelaide, no relation to Jane Morgan's family. They remained childless.

In 1879, William, seventh child of William and Jane, married his cousin, Mariah Morgan (1855-1953), daughter of William and Anne (Matthews) Morgan of Adelaide. They had at least nine children, Pearl, Eva Pearl, an unnamed daughter, William, Maude Helena, Morgan Fred, Grover Cleveland, John Roy and Nellie May. The names of the first four children are uncertain as they all died young.

On October 22, 1839, Samuel, son of James and Fanny, married Ann Browne (1819-1911), daughter of James and Mary Browne of Adelaide. They raised 12 children, James, Mary, Fannie, David, Jane, Samuel A., William M., Ann, Lucinda, Elizabeth M., Alveretta and Albert A.. All of the children reached the age of 18, a notable achievement in those times.

On April 5, 1837, James, brother of William and Samuel, married Ann Johnston (1819-1899), daughter of Captain John and Mary Ann (Brock) Johnston of Adelaide. They had 11 children, Frances; Mary Ann; Catherine; Marjory; James; Jane (1852-1905); Isabella; Alexander; Kezia Ruth; William John Wesley; and Aramina Alice. In 1861, Isabella, Alexander and Kezia died of diphtheria, resulting in a funeral every Monday for three weeks.

Jane, sixth child of James and Ann, married Thomas Fydell, a Methodist Minister. Their son, Frederick (1880-1944), who also became a minister, served at the Kerwood United Church from 1939 until his death.

In 1911, Rev. Frederick Fydell married Sarah Alice Wade (1878-1957) and they had three children, James, Ruth and Jean. James married Jean Hindley and they had two children, Frederick and Catherine. Ruth married Gerald Galbraith and they had five children, Paul, Donald, James, Elizabeth and Judith. Jean married Harry Fuller, son of Albert and Adella (Dowding) Fuller of Adelaide. They had three children, David, Janet and Karen.

McGREGOR, Don and Karin

Don and Karin McGregor arrived in Adelaide Township in April 1994. They moved from Mississauga, where they had lived since their May 1992 marriage. They rent a farm owned by the Earley family. There are a variety of crops on the land around their house.

Don is a programmer analyst and Karin works as a claim adjudicator at Manulife Financial. Don and Karin enjoy recreational flying, gardening, camping, and hiking in their spare time.

McINROY, Alexander "Sandy" and Ann Jane

Alexander McInroy, his wife Grace, and their children immigrated to Huntingdon Township in Eastern Ontario, from Scotland, in the late 1830s. The third eldest, Alexander "Sandy" (1827-1909), married Ann Jane Reynolds (1837-1902) of Irish-born parents. They lived in the Madoc area, where nine children were born, Emily Jane (1856-1930); William Alexander "Alex" (1859-1934); Charles Edward "Ed" (1862-1928); Eliza "Lisa" (1865-1925); Isabella "Belle" (1866-1944); Alice Victoria (1869-1891); Mary Ann "Minnie" (1871-1936); Melissa Martha (1875-1951); and John Thomas (1879-1910).

This part of the province, with its stony terrain, was a marginal farming area, so, in 1883, the family moved with eight of the children to a more fertile farm in Adelaide Township. The 200-acre farm located at Lot 12, Con. 1 SER, at the eastern edge of Adelaide Village, was purchased from Francis and Mary Petch for $11,000. The farmhouse was located on a knoll on the western edge of the property near a clump of trees. The granddaughters told of visiting there and driving the horse-and-buggy across the wooden bridge over a stream to reach the house.

The 1896 assessment reported 160 acres cleared. The McInroy family attended West Adelaide Presbyterian Church. In 1890, Sandy was a school trustee of S.S. #12, the Adelaide Village School, and the same year his name appears with George Glenn as trustee for S.S. #10. (This is the year that S.S. #12 closed and S.S. #10 was built farther to the west, so that the students would not have to walk so far.)

In 1879, Emily Jane, the eldest child of Sandy and Ann Jane, married Mark Robinson (1846-1921), an Irish immigrant blacksmith of the Madoc area. James, Anna and Alexander were young when their father, Mark, went ahead to Michigan, where the lumber trade was boosting the economy, and built a house. His family joined him and three more children, Edward, Isabel and Emily, were born in Reno Township, Michigan.

Alex married neighbour Martha Miller (1862-1956) in 1888. Martha was the daughter of William and Ellen Miller, across the road in Adelaide Village. Alex and Martha had five children, Grace Mildred (1890-1978), who married Bruce Jones; Alice Helena (1892-1971), who married Alex Blair of Lobo Township; William "Kenneth" (1893-1976), who married Agnes Caverhill; Olive Alexandria (1894-1971), who married William Wilkie; and Henry "Murray" (1897-1957), who married Ethel Graham, and second, Ethel Hunt.

The 1896 assessment records show W.A. McInroy (Alex) living on the west half of Lot 18, Con. 2 NER. A ca.1904 school photograph of the students and teacher of S.S. #4 Adelaide includes Grace, Alice, Kenneth, and Olive. In 1904, the Alex McInroy family moved to a location near Saskatoon to homestead on the prairies. In 1912, part of the farm was sold for a location to build government grain elevators. The family returned to Ontario and purchased the Alex Stewart farm on the Nairn Road in Lobo Township. This farm, known as "Balmoral Farm" at Lot 12, Con. 9, became a very prosperous and modern operation as Alex built up his herd of purebred Highland cattle from stock he purchased in Scotland. He also owned a number of farms in Adelaide, Lobo, London and Biddulph Townships. Martha and Alex are buried in Ivan Cemetery, Lobo Township.

Ed, third child of Sandy and Ann Jane, married Mary Jane Ingham (1864-1958) in 1890. They met when she was visiting her sister, Harriet Brock, on the next farm (see INGHAM). In 1894, Mary Jane bought 100 acres, the west half of Lot 12, Con. 3 NER, in a Power of Sale from a loan company. This property was to become the McInroy homestead. The 1896 assessment shows 80 acres. In 1918, a

Family of Alexander and Martha (Miller) McInroy, ca.1904. Standing L-R, Kenneth, Grace and Olive. Seated L-R, Alice, Murray, Martha and Alexander.

modern brick home was built, which is a very comfortable residence today. This home was lighted by a Delco system, which was a luxury for the grandchildren in the 1930s and 1940s. Another marvel was the bathroom, with running hot and cold water and a flush toilet! In 1909, Ed purchased the east half of Lot 13 from William Humphries, and later the north half of Lot 14, which added more grazing land. Ed and Mary Jane had four children, Samuel Earl (1892-1956); Harriet Verne (1894-1981); Edna Bernice (1896-1975); and Mildred Elizabeth (1898-1990).

Samuel Earl attended Strathroy High School and London Normal School. He first taught at Poplar Hill and boarded with the McVicar family. Then, he was needed at home, so he helped on the farm and taught at S.S. #4 Adelaide. Some of his students, Ken George, George Robotham and Colin McKeen, have talked about being in his classes. Earl bought the farm across the road, Lot 12, Con. 2 NER, from Dennis Demaray in 1919. He married Winnifred Brown of Adelaide and they lived on this farm for many years. After his father's death in 1928, Winnifred and Earl shared the big house with his mother, Mary Jane. In 1949, the farm "across the road" was sold to Delmar Hayden, who lives there at this writing.

Earl had dairy cattle and beef cattle, and carried out mixed farming. Beginning in the late 1940s, he was secretary-treasurer of the Adelaide Township School Board for 10 years. He was a member of the Egremont Lodge and the I.O.O.F., and both Earl and Winnifred were members of the Rebekah Lodge in Kerwood. A son, Keith Earl, helped his father with the farm work. He took over his father's position as secretary-treasurer of the Adelaide Township School Board. Keith married Ila Doreen Sullivan of Adelaide. (see SULLIVAN, John and Letitia). They raised two sons. The eldest, Thomas Keith, married Barbara Grieve, and farms in McGillivray Township, where they live with daughters Kerrie, Linsay and Pamela. Donald Glen married Tina Bijelic of Strathroy. Keith and Ila changed the farm over to an egg-producing operation. Keith later worked for the Department of Agriculture until his retirement. In 1973, the McInroy farm was sold to Franciscus and Anna Vanden Ouweland, and Keith and Ila moved to Strathroy.

Harriet Verne, Ed and Mary Jane's second child, attended Strathroy High School and then London Normal School. She taught at S.S. #9 and met her future husband, Alfred Watson Cuddy, when stabling her horse in the Cuddy barn next to the school (see CUDDY, John T. and Esther).

As schoolgirls, Edna Bernice and Mildred, the two youngest children of Ed and Mary Jane, were given the responsibility of bringing the cows back and forth from the 75 acres, the east three-quarters of the east half of Lot 11, Con. 3 NER, purchased from the Thomas Raison estate. Edna was very skilled at needlework, a hobby that she enjoyed all her life. She married Lorne Stanley Murray of Adelaide Township in 1930 (see MURRAY, James and Catherine).

Mildred Elizabeth studied Toronto Conservatory piano and theory with Miss Meekison in Strathroy. She travelled by horse-and-buggy around the neighbourhood, giving piano lessons in pupils' homes. Kenneth Topping of Lot 4, Con. 5 NER, was one of her pupils. While playing the organ at West Adelaide Presbyterian Church, she met her future husband, Wilfrid Wilson (see WILSON, Samuel and Rebecca).

The Edward McInroy family attended West Adelaide Presbyterian Church as his parents did. Mary Jane, known as "Jennie" to some, was a member of the Women's Missionary Society. After the Union vote in 1925, the McInroys became members of the United Church in Strathroy. Ed drove a McLaughlin car, which was quite special at that time. The McInroy burial plot is in Strathroy Cemetery.

Lisa, the fourth child of Sandy and Ann Jane, remained single and lived in the family home. She was considered to be an accomplished dressmaker

Children of Alexander and Ann Jane (Reynolds) McInroy.

and was able to support herself. In his will, her father made provision for her by directing his son, John Thomas, to allow her the use of one furnished bedroom, her board and "lodging in the same manner, style and comfort as she enjoyed while residing with me." If she were to marry, the will stipulated that John Thomas was to pay her a legacy of $250.

Belle, fifth of Sandy and Ann Jane's children, told her grandchildren about helping with the farm work as a schoolgirl and milking six cows, morning and night. She graduated from London Normal School and, at age 19, she taught at S.S. #12 Adelaide Village School. A receipt dated March 3, 1885, shows her superannuation contribution as $37.28. An item in the Strathroy Age for January 3, 1886, shows M. McInroy in the 4th class, A. McInroy in Sr. 3rd and J. McInroy in Jr. 3rd. The teacher is Ellen Miller. Perhaps Isabella found it difficult to teach her siblings, so she found a position at the Nairn public school in East Williams. There, she met her future husband, Donald A. "Dan" Stewart. In the Age Dispatch December 21, 1892, East Williams news column, it is announced that Miss Isabella McInroy will teach in the Nairn school in January 1893. In 1895, she married Dan Stewart. They farmed in East Williams on the original Stewart family farm, where they raised their two children. John "Roy" married Margaret Howie, and Alice Maria married Erwin Scott.

Alice Victoria, sixth issue of Sandy and Ann Jane, died of typhoid fever after a three-week illness at age 22. According to her obituary, she had lived in Strathroy for about 18 months and was an active member of the Presbyterian Church. It is not known why she had moved there; perhaps she had employment.

Mary Ann "Minnie" married Alonzo Knight (1864-1939) of Adelaide Township (see KNIGHT, James and Jane).

Melissa Martha married a neighbour, William A. Brock. The Age Dispatch of June 28, 1900, reports a stylish wedding at the McInroy home on the evening of June 20, 1900, with 90 guests attending. The bride was assisted by Miss Annie Brock, and the groom by Albert Reynolds of Belleville. The ceremony took place on the lawn under evergreen arches decorated with flowers. Rev. Mr. Hannahson, pastor of West Adelaide Presbyterian Church, performed the ceremony, and Mrs. Hannahson played

Children of Charles Edward and Mary Jane (Ingham) McInroy. Taken on Mary Jane's 90th birthday, May 21, 1954.

the wedding music. After a "grand" wedding dinner in the dining room, a pleasant evening was spent on the lawn in "games, music and social chat." The couple left the township to live in "their far western home in Slate River Valley." Later, they lived in Fort William (1911) and California (1934). They raised five children. A grandniece remembers Aunt Melissa's visit to the family in the 1930s, and the enjoyable book that she brought as her gift.

John Thomas, the youngest of Sandy and Ann Jane's children, helped his father on the 200-acre family farm. He was a member of the L.O.L. (Loyal Order of the Orange Lodge) #310 Adelaide, and an active member of the Adelaide Band. He took an interest in horses, and stories were told of his joining others to race their horses on a track behind Adelaide Village on an 8-acre stretch of land now owned by David Campbell. In 1907, he married Macy Pearl MacDonald (1889-1979) of Caradoc. They had two children. Alexander Donald (1908-1947) married Wilma de Groat, and Gladys Jacqueline (1911-1992) married Bernard Barrowcliffe.

John Thomas inherited the home farm upon his father's death. A year later, John Thomas died of pneumonia after a week's illness. The Orange Order funeral service was conducted by Rev. Mr. Dehl of Adelaide and Rev. W.A. Hare of West Adelaide Presbyterian Church. Gladys Jacqueline was born just a few months after her father's death. The executors, Alonzo Knight and Donald Stewart, sold all of Lot 12 to Howard C. Brock in 1911. Macy remarried, to Hugh Byron McLeod (d.1942).

McINTYRE, David L. and Jean

David L. McIntyre (d.1890) probably came from Scotland and lived with his uncle, John McIntyre. This farm was likely left to David and he continued to farm this land until his death. David married Jean Jamieson (1823-1901), and they had six children, Rebecca "Bec" (d.1926); Janet (1855-1920); Margaret (d.1936); John (d.1926); Agnes (1853-1931); and Martha Jean "Matt" (1867).

Bec is thought to have been the eldest of the six siblings, and she chose not to marry. She worked as a gourmet chef in a hotel in Chicago. When she came home for visits she would stay with her sister, Janet, and brother-in-law, John Knight, first when they lived in Metcalfe Township and later at their home near the fairgrounds in Strathroy. One culinary delight that she bestowed on John and Janet upon returning from a shopping trip was a dish of sparrows, arranged neatly on a platter for supper. She is buried in the McIntyre plot in Strathroy Cemetery.

Janet married John Knight, son of Barnabas Knight of Metcalfe Township, on August 18, 1878, at Hillhead, Ontario. Their first child, Eugene, died at birth. The second, Alma Ogilive (1884-1953), was born on Con. 1, Metcalfe Township. Eva Kathleen Gordon, the third and last child, was also born in Metcalfe.

Alma married Louis Russell Curtis Brown on December 19, 1906, at an Anglican Church (probably St. Ann's in Adelaide Village). They had four children, Raymond, Maurice, Everett and Kathleen. Raymond married Ellen Muma and as a widower, married Irene Carruthers. Maurice married Grace Freele and as a widower, married Doris Gregory. Everett married Lillian Roselle. Kathleen married Robert Raymond Morgan of Metcalfe Township.

John and Matt, children of David and Jean, remained single. They farmed and lived at the family homestead until retiring to a home at the end of Dewan Street in Strathroy.

Margaret married George Marr, a photographer, and resided in Saskatoon, Saskatchewan. Margaret is buried in Strathroy Cemetery.

Agnes was a milliner in Strathroy. She married Theophile Smith about 1878. Little is known about the details of his death. Agnes then married John Anderson (1860-1942), who drove a hearse for Stewart's Funeral Home in Strathroy. They married about 1890 and then moved to Wyoming, Ontario. A daughter, Edith Winnifred (ca.1891), died a baby. Agnes and her family are all buried in Wyoming Cemetery.

McKEEN, William and Margaret

William McKeen, who was raised in East Williams Township, purchased 77 acres of property in Adelaide Township in 1875, being Lot 22, Con. 3 NER. He bought it from William Tinkler, who obtained the land from the crown in 1848. This farm extends from Crathie Drive to Wardell Drive. In 1885, he purchased 57½ acres on the east side of his original farm, from Dennis Demaray. In 1919, William and Margaret, his wife, moved to Metcalfe Township with their son, Oliver.

William married Margaret Vance on June 15, 1876, in the Township of Warwick. They had nine sons and three daughters, William (1877, died an infant); William Albert (1878-1919); Ezekiel Vance (1879-1956); James Herbert (1881-1941); Maggie Lovenia (1883-1901); Annie Edith (1885-1950); Arthur Frederick (1886-1963); Leonard (1887-1974); Olive Lulu May (1889-1977); Oliver Henry (1891-1970); Theodore Alfred (1893-1938); and Lawrence Wilfred (1897-1957).

Many of William and Margaret's sons became farmers in other townships. Herbert started working on the lake boats at the age of 17 and became an interior decorator in Detroit four years later.

McKeen/Campbell Family ca.1926. Back L-R, Dan, Ella, Agnes, Peter, Jessie and Archie Campbell. Front L-R, Cassie, Dan McKeen, Annie McKeen and Maggie.

Belle McKeen

Leonard bought a farm on Lot 15, Con. 3 NER, in 1912, and remained there until 1955. He retired in Strathroy.

In 1910, Ezekiel bought Dan McCubbin's farm at Lot 17, Con. 3 NER, and in 1919, he bought his father's 77 acres. He married Catherine "Cassie" Ann Campbell in 1910. Cassie and Ezekiel had four sons and two daughters, Alice Annie (1911); Margaret Robena (1913-1943); James Donald (1914-1993); Colin Douglas (1916); Lawrence William (1919-1994); and Wilbert Ezekial (1922).

Alice Annie married James Lumdsen in 1936. They lived in East Williams until they retired to Strathroy in 1971.

Margaret Robena married Alex Walker, and they lived on the Egremont Road in Adelaide Township.

James Donald farmed his parent's farm and helped his brothers.

Colin Douglas married Beatrice Green in 1942. He obtained his degree as Doctor of Philosophy in plant pathology, served in WWII, worked in the Federal Department of Agriculture in Harrow and Ottawa, and was an international scientist. He is retired in Orangeville.

Lawrence William married Doris Leitch in 1947. He lived on a farm in East Williams. In 1958, he bought a 60-acre farm at Lot 17, Con. 4 NER. In 1975, he built a house on this property. In 1995, Duncan, Lawrence's son, bought a 130-acre farm at Lot 11, Con. 4 NER. Duncan resides on his 200-acre farm in East Williams Township.

Wilbert Ezekiel married Joan Fall. He researched plant diseases and worked in the federal civil service for 10 years at Harrow, Saanichton and Vancouver. He was Professor of Botany at the University of Western Ontario for 34 years. His plant disease research was well known around the world.

In 1960, Wilbert bought a 100-acre farm at Lot 20, Con. 3 NER. He and Joan named the property "Bluegrass Farm," and frequently reside there during the summer. In 1995, they purchased his grandparent's farm at Lot 22, Con. 3 NER. This farm has been in the McKeen name since 1875.

McKENZIE, Duncan and Janet

In 1871, Duncan and Janet (McLeish) McKenzie bought 100 acres at Lot 9, Con. 4 NER, and moved into a log house on this property. The patent for this land originally went to Patrick Duggan in 1847. He sold the property to George Shanklin in 1848, and in 1854, it went to Benjamin Woodhull. Duncan and Janet had their first four children in the log house. Subsequently, Duncan built a large brick house and, in 1879, the family moved in shortly before the birth of their fifth child. Seven more children were born to the family. All of the children survived to adulthood except one son, Donald, who died at about age three. A second son, John, died in young adulthood, a victim of tuberculosis. The 11 members of the family who grew to adulthood settled in various parts of Canada, as far west as Victoria, B.C., and as far east as Marmora in eastern Ontario.

Both Duncan and Janet's ancestors came from Scotland. Janet's parents immigrated about 1862 and settled on the "island" farm in West Williams

Township. Duncan was the only member of his family to settle in Adelaide Township.

Angus, Duncan and Janet's son, inherited the home farm and it has remained in the possession of the McKenzies, except for some years during the 1920s to 1940s. During that period, Peter and Eva Campbell were the owners.

Angus married Annie J. McKellar, and four children were born on this property. Their son, Donald, is the present owner.

In the early part of the 20th century, a new foundation was laid using locally manufactured bricks. The original barn was placed on the new foundation. The barn has undergone several changes but is still in use. In 1968, a new modern brick home replaced the original brick home.

Duncan and Janet and their family were members of the West Adelaide Presbyterian Church and attended regularly. Their mode of travel was similar to that of their neighbours, a horse-drawn democrat or buggy.

Several community changes affected the McKenzie property and family, including the gradual shift of power source from horses to gas-powered motors (cars, tractors, etc.). Communication changed dramatically with the introduction of the Arkona telephone line about 1890. In the mid-1900s, hydroelectric power became available and, in 1996, a gas line passed the property, adding an additional source of power and heat.

When Adelaide roads were initially planned, the Fourth Line North met the county road by means of a gore about one mile east of Keyser's Corners. In the mid-1960s, the gore was eliminated and a curve substituted, changing the landscape. The curve is directly in front of the McKenzie property.

McKENZIE, James and Margaret

James McKenzie (ca.1812-1870) was born in Scotland. He immigrated to Canada before 1843, as his eldest child was born here the following year. A family story states that James, before coming to Adelaide, was a cabinetmaker in Niagara, Ontario. It was also said that he married three times. This story fits in well with the known facts. James's first wife is not known. James's eldest two children, William (ca.1844) and Jean (ca.1846), are offspring of his first marriage. James remarried, to Margaret Matthews (1822-1863), daughter of William and Catherine (Slush) Matthews. Catherine Matthews' obituary states that the Matthews family came from Ireland to the town of Niagara in 1847 and then to Adelaide in 1850. The 1852 Adelaide census confirms the residency of the Matthews and McKenzie families. They were farming parts of Lot 21, Con. 1 SER.

James and Margaret had seven children, an unnamed baby girl (1851, died an infant); Mary Ann (ca.1853); Elizabeth (ca.1854); James Jr. (1856-1891); John (ca.1858); Thomas (1859-1905); and Margaret "Maggie" (ca.1861-1965).

James' year of birth is unclear. His grave marker indicates that he was born in 1812. The Adelaide census for 1852, 1861, and 1871, as well as a newspaper death notice, indicate he was born ca.1819, ca.1820, ca.1804, or ca.1814. James was a wagonmaker in 1852 and a farmer by 1861. In 1856, he purchased 66 2/3 acres, being the north two-thirds of the east half of Lot 21, Con. 1 SER (see MATTHEWS). After Margaret's death, James married her sister, Anne (ca.1826-1920), who was the widow of William Morgan. James became stepfather to Anne's only child, Mariah Morgan. The 1871 census states that James died of "Gravel."

William, the eldest child of James and Margaret, lived in Port Huron and Rose City, both in Michigan.

Jean is not listed with her family in the 1861 census. Since her name does not appear as a survivor in subsequent family obituaries, it is assumed that she died young.

Mary Ann married a Mr. Gott. In 1881, Mary Ann Gott signed a deed to the McKenzie homestead in favour of James McKenzie Jr. In 1891, the Gotts were living in Brantford, and in 1905, Detroit.

Elizabeth married a Mr. Dreaver, and lived in Detroit, Michigan.

James Jr. married Elizabeth "Lizzie" Nichol (1850-1923), daughter of Edward and Margaret (Leitch) Nichol. They had four children, Isabella "Maude" Jane (1884-1979); Della Edith Mae (1885-1932); Cecil Edward (1887-1973); and James "Jim" Alexander (1889-1970). James Jr. took over farming the family homestead. He died a young man from inflammation of the lung and brain fever, leaving a young family. Seventy rigs attended the funeral procession despite inclement weather. Land registry records show no mortgage against the farm, so the family was able to keep the farm with hired help.

Maude, the eldest child of James Jr. and Lizzie, married Fred Poole (1877-1964), a widower, and they had two sons, Walter and Stan. They lived in Lambeth. Before marriage, Maude was a teacher for about 11 years.

Della married James Wesley Earley (see EARLEY).

In 1925, Cecil married Laura Gertrude Hawken (1890-1979) of Adelaide, daughter of George and Grace (Brent) Hawken. They had four children, June (1926); Gerald (1929); George (1930); and Donald (1934), all born in Brownvale, Alberta.

In 1967, Cecil wrote an interesting tale called, "On the Trail to the Lonesome Peace." The story tells of his experiences homesteading in the Peace River district of Alberta. He also records some of the McKenzie family history. At age 12, Cecil quit school because the family couldn't afford hired farm help. In 1908, he went west to work, returning in one year so his brother could work out west. Cecil worked in Wawanesa, Manitoba; Saskatoon, Saskatchewan; and Killam, Alberta. He had McKenzie relatives in Wawanesa, and Nichol relatives in Killam. In the summer of 1913, Cecil headed west to the Peace River district of Alberta and staked out a homestead. He returned to Adelaide that fall.

The Adelaide farm had poor soil and was difficult to work. It was sold on October 11, 1913. An auction was held on October 15. Della and Maude were both married and living nearby. Both Cecil and Jim went to Peace River to homestead. Their mother went to live with one of the sisters.

In 1929, Jim, the youngest child of James Jr. and Lizzie, married Mabel Mary Mitchell Irons (1896-1971) of Vancouver, B.C. They had two children, Isabel Joyce (1930) and Hazel Beatrice (1932), both born in Brownvale, Alberta.

John, fifth issue of James and Margaret, lived in Wawanesa, Manitoba, from the early 1890s to at least 1905. In the late 1920s, he was living in Vancouver. He had three children, Myrtle, Sherman and Fraser. In 1881, John signed a deed to the McKenzie homestead in favour of James Jr.

Thomas, sixth of James and Margaret's children, and his wife, Maria J., had five children, David A. (1888); Hazel M. (1890); John "Jack" T. (1891); Charles Stewart (1899-1900); and James "Jim." In the early 1890s, Thomas lived in Sombra Township, but by 1901, he was farming 100 acres in Adelaide, being part of Lot 15, Con. 1. Shortly afterward, he followed his brother to Wawanesa. Thomas was killed when a two-year-old colt dragged him for about a quarter-mile. Three of Thomas's children, Hazel, Jack and Jim were residing in Brandon, Manitoba, during a family visit in 1946.

Maggie, the youngest child of James and Margaret, married George Glenn of Adelaide. They had at least seven children, Mary "Lulu" (1881-1966); Orville (ca.1883); Leo (ca.1888); Fred (1890); George B. (1893-1964); Laura E. (1895-1983); and Madeline (1897-1979). In 1878, records indicate George Glenn was farming 100 acres, being the east half of Lot 16, Con. 1 NER. Lulu married Leonard McKeen. Orville was a doctor in Wardsville or Rondeau. Leo was a doctor in Chatham. George B. married Amanda V. Nichols. Laura lived in San Diego. Madeline married into the McCurry family. Maggie and her children, Lulu, George B., Laura, and Madeline are buried in the Strathroy Cemetery.

McLEAN

In 1903, William Howard McLean, the eldest in a family of seven, left home to seek fame and fortune. Howard went to London and joined the Volunteers at Wolsley Barracks. After a year, he took his discharge and joined the firm of British North America Life Insurance Company. He enjoyed the insurance business, but found it was a hard sell, as most people had never heard of life insurance.

In 1907, he learned that Saskatchewan was opening up for settlers. In 1908, he left for Saskatchewan with some farm implements and a team of horses. Howard was accompanied by Thomas Merrick from Metcalfe Township. The condition of the government was that, after three years, you were given the title to your homestead of one-quarter section (160 acres).

Howard had an excellent crop in 1910, but he was lonesome for home. He had a chance to sell everything, so he decided to return to his parents' home in Metcalfe Township. His father, at that time, lived on County Road Six on the farm (now owned by Jake Feenstra). He arrived in Kerwood by train and went to the Farmers Bank of Canada, which was located in the old Toronto Dominion Bank, and he

Lorna and Cameron McLean at Hamilton Lion's Club Convention, 1962.

deposited all the money he earned while in Saskatchewan. After depositing the money, he walked to his parent's farm. Early the next morning, his father woke him to take the team and wagon to Gravel Hill in Adelaide Township for a load of gravel. As he passed the bank, he noticed a small sheet of paper on the front door of the bank. He stopped and read the sign and learned that the bank had closed—it never reopened. So much for the three hard years of working in Saskatchewan. After the initial shock wore off, Howard borrowed $50 from his father and started over by buying 50 acres on the Brooke townline in Metcalfe. He was a very successful farmer and, by 1920, he had married Ada McGugen from Walnut. They had two children, Margaret (1917) and Cameron (1920), and purchased a 200-acre farm from James Cameron on Con. 10, Metcalfe Township, which was always known as "Cameron Farm."

In 1920, a group of area farmers formed a Co-op and named the group "The Kerwood Farmers Co-operative." The purpose of this group was to buy the grain elevator in Kerwood, which was owned and operated by Frank Mills, who wanted to retire. After purchasing the grain elevator, the group advertised for a manager. Howard was one of the applicants and was hired. Frank Mills owned the home next to Arthur Woods' store and it was sold to the group. When all arrangements of the sale were completed, Howard and his family moved into the house. This house was purchased by Eileen Freer (d.1999), and is now owned by her granddaughter, Lindsay Paine, and her husband, Steve Luis. While living in Kerwood, the family grew with the arrival of a third child, Marie (1925).

In 1924, the Co-op moved the feed warehouse from its location beside the bank, to the grain elevator property. In 1925, the Kerwood Farmers Co-op decided to disband. They offered the grain elevator, warehouse and office for sale by tender. Howard McLean and John Johnson were the successful bidders, and they purchased the assets of Kerwood Farmers Co-op. Howard continued as the Manager. In 1926, the partnership of Johnson and McLean purchased the elevator in Wyoming from the Mustard Brothers. Roy Stonehouse, a farmer in Enniskillen Township, was hired to manage the Wyoming operation. When Johnson and McLean decided to buy the Wyoming elevator, more capital was needed so Robert Galbraith was invited to join the firm. It was then decided to name the firm Johnson, McLean and Company. The company enjoyed prosperity. Unfortunately, the Wyoming elevator burned to the ground in 1929. Due to uncertain markets that year, the firm decided not to rebuild the Wyoming complex. Roy Stonehouse secured a position as grain buyer for Hiram Walker Distilling in Windsor.

In 1926, the Ralston Purina Company from St. Louis, Missouri, granted Johnson, McLean and Company a dealership. This dealership was one of three granted at that time outside of the U.S. In 1934, a gristmill was added to the Kerwood elevator allowing the company to manufacture poultry and animal feeds. In 1945, a new office and warehouse were built on the north side of the property.

In January 1946, Cameron was discharged from the Canadian army after serving four years. That summer, he was looking at an elevator in Clinton to purchase. Before this move was decided completely, Howard approached John Johnson and Robert Galbraith to ask if they were interested in selling their share in Johnson, McLean and Company to Cameron. Robert Galbraith declined but John Johnson agreed to sell his share. The new partnership became an incorporated company in the name of McLean Feed and Grains Ltd.

In 1955, a new grain elevator was built, consisting of four cement silos, a grain dryer and grain cleaner. This proved to be a turning point in the company as growth from then on was rapid. In 1958, the company started contracting out laying hens and raising their own replacements. At this time, the Galbraith family decided to sell their interest in the company. The growth in the laying hen department was rapid and required a lot of capital.

In 1963, Howard wanted to retire and since Cameron lacked capital, Cuddy Farms, their largest customer, were approached and A.M. "Mac" Cuddy purchased Howard's share. Mac Cuddy's business expertise was an invaluable asset to the company. In 1967, McLean Feed and Grain Ltd. purchased the grain elevator complex on Con. 10 of Caradoc, owned by Cuddy Farms.

In 1970, the company was approached by Maple Leaf Mills Ltd. to sell and this came about with Cameron remaining as Manager in Kerwood and Strathroy for a period of five years. At the end of that term in 1975, he was asked to remain and did until he retired in 1985. At the time of his retirement, Cameron was also managing the grain elevator complex in Greenway, Ontario.

McLEISH, William and Harriet

William McLeish (1866-1948) was the youngest child in the family of eight children born to John and Isabella (Currie) McLeish. William was born in East Williams Township. His father had settled there in 1855, after immigrating to Canada in 1842 from Kilfinan Parish, County Cowal, Argyllshire, Scotland.

On May 27, 1896, William married Harriet Wyatt (d.1947), the younger daughter of Thomas and Harriet (Bolton) Wyatt. The wedding took place at the home of the bride's parents in East Williams, at Lot 12, Con. 8, east of the Centre Road (ECR). Harriet Bolton was the youngest daughter of William Bolton, who lived at Lot 20, Con. 2 NER.

After their marriage, William and Harriet rented a farm in West Williams Township. Their two eldest children, Harriet Isabel and Ethel Ann, were born there. Their next home was in East Williams, where Mary Christine and William George were born.

In 1906 William purchased the east half of the west half of Lot 17, Con. 1 SER, where the family lived until 1948. On February 6, 1906, Thomas Gourie and his wife sold 50 acres, the east half of the west half of Lot 17, to William McLeish for $2,520. On April 12, 1912, Ida Pearl Parker and Harvey Parker Jr. sold the west half of the west half of Lot 17, Con. 1 SER, to William G. Robotham and David W. Robotham, contingent upon their assuming a mortgage to John and Moses Gare. This latter property of 50 acres was acquired by William on April 12, 1919, when he assumed the mortgage to John and Moses Gare. That mortgage was discharged in 1929. Thus, William held a clear title to the west half of Lot 17, Con. 1 SER, a farm of 100 acres.

On the east half of the west half of Lot 17 was a 2-storey white frame house, with no verandah, and a frame barn. In later years, a verandah was added to the north side of the house. Two orchards existed; one extended to the east from the house to the barn and the other was southeast of the barn. On the west half of Lot 17 was a frame barn, further south than the one on the east half, with a small orchard north of it. Brick remnants between this orchard and the barn, plus a well with a pump, gave evidence that a house had existed on the property at one time.

William McLeish engaged in mixed farming and raised cattle, horses, pigs and sheep. The poultry raising was done by Harriet, who was assisted by the children. From the livestock raised on the farm,

McLeish home ca.1910, Lot 17, Con. 1 SER. Children L-R, John, Harriett, Howard, Mary, Ethel and George.

William and Hattie McLeish with daughters, Harriet and Ethel.

most of the meat supply for the family was secured. The winter supply was either salted and stored in a barrel or preserved in glass sealers, which were stored in the fruit cellar. A root cellar below the kitchen served as a storage area for vegetables from the garden and for apples from the orchards. Oftentimes in winter, an apple-paring bee was held. Apples were placed on a forked spindle of an apple-peeling machine. By turning the crank, the apple turned against a sharp cutting edge that peeled the apple. Some peeling machines were capable of coring the apples as they were peeled. The peeled apples were cored and sliced and the slices placed on a wooden rack with a screened wire bottom. The rack was suspended by wires at the four corners from hooks in the ceiling above the wood-burning cook stove. Occasional stirring of the sliced apples allowed dried apples to be obtained for applesauce or for dried apple pies. Both were readily enjoyed by the family, especially when raisins were added flavouring.

While diligent in his farming, William maintained manual methods of farming well after more enterprising, progressive farmers were using modern farming equipment to lighten the heavy labour of farming. William's son, John, after finishing public school, remained at home to assist in the farming, and worked as hired help among neighbouring farmers.

As a boy, William and Harriet's youngest son, Ed, remembers driving the horse on a dump rake, tripped by hand, to rake the newly mown hay into windrows from which it could be piled into coils to dry. These coils were built by fork and after drying were pitched by forkfuls onto a wagon and hauled into the barn. When the hay was drawn into the barn, William pitched the hay into the mow by forkfuls, where John mowed it into the corners of the mow. Ed's task was to tramp the hay to help compact it. As he learned to balance on a moving wagon, Edward was taught the skill of building a load that would stand the rigour of a moving wagon on the field and into the barn. With use of a hay-loader (first borrowed from a neighbour and later a purchased one), the building of a load became more demanding—more volume at a faster rate.

Change came when a steel track was installed in the peak of the barn. By means of a hayfork and a system of pulleys, bundles of hay could be raised from the wagon. By sticking the hay fork to its maximum depth and locking it by a levering device, then attaching it to a pulley with a hayrope through it and assisted by a series of pulleys and ropes, the bundle of hay in the hayfork was pulled up by horses hitched, outside the barn, to the end of the rope. As the hayfork ascended, it locked into a car on the track and the car was pulled along the track over the mow. By means of a trip-rope, the bundle of hay was released from the hayfork over the mow. When the horses returned to the barn, the trip-rope could be used to pull the car back to its stop-block. Further pulling on the trip-rope caused the hayfork to descend for another bundle of hay.

Another task, when Edward was a boy, occurred when the grain was cut. At first, the binder did not have a sheaf carrier, so it was Ed's task to follow the binder around the field and throw the sheaves clear of the next round of the binder. It was necessary to learn how to twist stalks of grain into a band to tie the loose sheaves. When a binder with a sheaf carrier attached was obtained, the sheaves could be carried to rows. This facilitated the stooking. In stooking, two sheaves would be placed with their butts about 12" apart, so that the heads of grain in each sheaf supported the other. Long stooks, about 10 sheaves, would be built. Sometimes round stooks were built, especially when two people stooked using hayforks, and particularly when barley was stooked. Using hayforks for that job prevented the irritating itch caused by the barley ends. Most frequently, the grain was drawn into the barn and mowed until a threshing machine arrived in the neighbourhood. Fortunate indeed was the farmer who could thresh from the field! He had to be able to muster teams and wagons, as well as men, to assist in hauling the grain from the field to the machine.

It was a thrill to see the threshing machine arrive. Early machines were steam powered, so the farmer had to have ready a good supply of firewood for the machine. Clifford Branton used to do threshing for the McLeish family. It was a delight to the family to hear the distinct whistle of the machine, sounded by Clifford Branton, as the machine came in the lane, followed by a water tank drawn by horses. Harriet, sometimes assisted by a neighbour or two, would do the baking and serving of meals for threshers. Usually, several farmers on nearby farms would thresh in succession, so threshing became a community affair. The steam engine was eventually replaced by a large tractor.

William served as the Secretary for the three-member trustee board that operated S.S. #10 Adelaide, which was a yellow brick school situated on an acre of land of Lot 16, Con. 1 SER, adjacent to the McLeish property. He acquired this position about 1909, which he held about 20 years. As well, William helped his children do the janitorial duties at the school. In the winter, he went to the school early to start the fire, especially when it had not been banked the previous night. In the summer, a family effort was necessary to take down the stovepipes, which ran the length of the one-room school—from the wood-burning box stove at the rear, to the chimney above the blackboards at the opposite end of the room. After cleaning the soot from the pipes outdoors, the stovepipes had to be reconnected and hung near the ceiling. Then, the wooden floor would be scrubbed with hot water and homemade soap, which gave off a pleasant, clean odour. Initially, the desks were double, wooden, and fastened to the floor with screw nails through the iron legs. The first single desks to replace the double ones were small ones for the young children. Larger single desks were installed a few years later. Of course, all desks faced the blackboard. At first, the blackboards were of wallboard painted black or dark green. These were replaced by slate boards.

At S.S. #10 Adelaide, a pump just to the east of the school provided an ample supply of good drinking water. Children drank from a common metal cup, which hung on the side of the pump. As health measures improved and during winter weather, a pail of water was taken indoors and individual granite cups were used. These cups hung from hooks on a board attached to the wall near the coat hooks. Before the inclement weather of fall and winter, it was customary to carry blocks of wood from the woodpile outdoors to the lobby at the front of the school, so that dry wood was available for burning. Although there were separate entrances for the girls and boys—one on the east of the lobby and one on the west—Ed does not recall both being used. The east entrance was used for all children. Outdoor toilets were provided for each gender.

During winter, some of the teachers would prepare hot chocolate or soup on top of the wood-burning box stove.

William and his family attended Calvin Presbyterian Church, which was located at Lot 19 on the Adelaide side of the townline between Adelaide and East Williams Townships. William was an Elder there, and Harriet was a Sunday School teacher. After Church Union in 1925, the family attended St. Andrews Presbyterian Church in Strathroy. William served as an Elder there, too.

William and Harriet McLeish celebrated their golden wedding anniversary at their home in 1946. Edward decorated a three tier anniversary fruitcake that his wife, Laura Richardson McLeish, made for

Family of William and Harriet McLeish, ca.1962. Back L-R, Edward, Howard, John and George. Front L-R, Harriet, Ethel, Mary and Evaline.

the occasion. Harriet and William are buried in the Strathroy Cemetery.

William and Harriet had eight children, Harriet Isabel (1897-1973); Ethel Ann (1899-1988); Mary Christine (1901); William George (d.1973); John Thomas (d.1976); Howard Alexander (1908-1978); Eveline "Eva" Elizabeth; and Edward Archibald (1913-2000).

Harriet Isabel was born in West Williams Township. On July 17, 1926, she married Hugh Adair McKean (1898-1976), who was born in West Williams. Before taking residence in Strathroy, Harriet and Hugh lived in East Williams and Adelaide Townships. Before her marriage, Harriet attended the London Normal School and qualified as an elementary school teacher. She taught briefly at S.S. #9 Adelaide and boarded at the home of Mr. and Mrs. Alfred Cuddy. She taught also in schools in Nissouri and West Williams Townships. When Harriet and Hugh moved to Strathroy, Hugh worked for H.C. Downham Nursery and Harriet worked in some of the retail stores and later at Strathroy Collegiate Institute. Their son, Leroy, married Wilma Stirling, and their family lived in Strathroy where Leroy worked at the Canadian Tire Store, then later at Home Hardware. Harriet and Hugh are buried in Nairn Cemetery, East Williams Township.

Ethel Ann was born in West Williams Township. After completing high school, she remained at home and worked part-time for Mr. and Mrs. George Brooks, who farmed west of Adelaide Village. She became quite proficient in sewing, and assisted her mother in sewing clothes for the family. However, for a career, dressmaking was not adequately appealing. She qualified as an elementary school teacher and subsequently taught in schools in Lambton and Waterloo Counties. She married Anderson Marshall of Waterloo County and they farmed near Ayr about 10 kilometers west of Cambridge (Galt). Ethel and Anderson are buried in the Ayr Cemetery.

Mary Christine was born in East Williams Township. After her completion of public school at S.S. #10 Adelaide, Mary attended Westervelt Business School in London, and was employed as a stenographer for E.M. Flock, a prominent lawyer in London. On September 4, 1926, she married Ernest "Ernie" Russell Campbell (d.1944), who was an upholsterer for General Motors at a plant in Toronto. His uncle, George Campbell, had acquired the east half of Lot 17, Con. 1 SER and, on April 24, 1936, he granted that lot to Ernie Campbell. Along with his wife, Mary, and sons Robert Earl and William Donald (d.1946), Ernie took up mixed farming on Lot 17. Depression existed across the country and Ernie Campbell felt it acutely. As a cash crop, he contracted with the Strathroy Canning Factory to grow peas. When the peas were harvested and hauled to the canning factory, there were always loose pods on the field. Assisted by some of her siblings, Mary would glean those pods, shell them, and take the shelled peas in quart baskets to Strathroy. There, grocers were glad to purchase the fresh produce.

Born on the farm to Mary and Ernie was a daughter, Mildred Eileen. With her mother, Mildred went to Strathroy after Ernie's death in 1944. Robert Earl enlisted with the Armed Services. William Donald worked for T.M. Hawkins Company of Strathroy. He was killed by a log rolling off a platform truck that he was loading. Ernest, Mary and William Donald are buried in Strathroy Cemetery.

William George, the eldest son of William and Harriet, completed his high school education in Strathroy, where he was a star athlete. At home, he often rallied the neighbourhood children to start a game of softball in the pasture field on the farm of Russell Brock, at Lot 17, Con. 1 NER. The influence of Gladstone Mills of Strathroy convinced George that he ought to become a banker, so he

Grandma Currie McLeish

became an employee of the Canadian Bank of Commerce. He served in several communities in Southern Ontario, including Parkhill, Crediton and Delhi. He was manager in Durham and in Blenheim. He married Velma Gerhard (d.1994) of Delhi and retired there. George and Velma are buried in Delhi Cemetery.

John Thomas was born in Adelaide Township shortly after his parents moved to Lot 17, Con. 1 SER. After completion of public school, he remained at home to assist on the farm. He took over the orchards on the farm and, through a regimen of pruning and spraying, brought the neglected orchards to the point where they yielded an abundant supply of good fruit. He used his spraying equipment for whitewashing barns and stables, too. In later life, John became a weed inspector for Bosanquet Township, Lambton County. He retired in Forest. John is buried in Strathroy Cemetery.

When he was a young man, Howard Alexander worked for John Muxlow, who operated the General Store at Adelaide Village. Howard and John's son, Gordon, would pack the truck that John drove through the country to deliver groceries to farm homes. For those farmers who had telephones, grocery orders could be placed in advance. One summer, Howard went to Saskatchewan on a harvest excursion. He slept in a cabin with several other workers, who were provided meals at the owner's farmhouse. In Strathroy in 1937, Howard married Myrtle Catt, who was born in North Battleford, Saskatchewan. They took up mixed farming in Bosanquet Township, Lambton County, first near Thedford, then later near Forest. In later years, Howard operated an insurance agency from his second farm.

Two children, Joyce and Norman Howard (d.1949), were born to Howard and Myrtle. Joyce, a teacher, married Howard Pickard Jr., and lives near Lucknow. Norman Howard died at age five. After his death, Howard and Myrtle adopted Garry, who married and lives with his family in Forest. Myrtle remains on the farm, but rents most of the land to a neighbour. Howard and Norman Howard are buried in Pinehill Cemetery, Thedford.

Eva, the youngest daughter of William and Harriet, attended S.S. #10 Adelaide, and then went to Strathroy Collegiate Institute. She rode bicycles with her younger brother, Edward, over gravel roads

William and Harriett (Wyatt) McLeish, 50th wedding anniversary, ca.1946.

from their farm to Strathroy, a distance of five miles. In inclement weather, they used to drive a horse-and-buggy and, in winter, they travelled by cutter. Their horse would be left at the barn on the property of their Uncle William Wyatt in Strathroy. At the end of Second Form (so-called in lieu of Grade 10), Eva attended Westervelt School in London and then became employed as a stenographer for E.J. Wright and Son in Strathroy. She married Dwight Field (d.1986) and they lived in Forest, where Dwight was a successful manager of a Canadian Tire Store. Dwight is buried in the cemetery in Forest.

Edward Archibald, the youngest child in the family of William and Harriet McLeish, was very close to his sister, Eva. It seemed that anything Eva did, Edward had to do the same thing, knitting included (although he never did learn how to turn the heel of a sock!). Edward attended S.S. #10 Adelaide, and then went to Strathroy Collegiate Institute. Although alternating weeks for driving to school with Marjorie Brock, the task of feeding the buggy horse at noon fell to Edward. He would eat his lunch at school, then walk to his uncle's barn and feed the horse the bag of hay which had been packed in a burlap bag, at home, the previous night and tied on the back of the buggy. In cold wintry weather, bricks would be heated in the oven, then wrapped in several layers of newspaper and placed in the floor of the cutter to help keep the feet warm. A heavy blanket plus a buffalo robe over the knees was not always adequate protection from the elements. The bricks would be taken into the house at the Wyatt home. When it was time to return home from school, Aunt Maggie Wyatt would have the bricks heated for the trip.

Edward recalled that his father bought a driving horse from Tom Elliott. Normally this horse was a trotter, but if she heard the approach of another horse-and-buggy, she would start to pace. A slight slackening of the reins and an encouraging voice would be adequate to initiate a race. Margaret Holmes and Adeline Muxlow, who lived to the west on the Egremont Road, used to leave earlier than Edward but Edward used to be met frequently at the corner of the Egremont and Strathroy Roads (now the intersection of Highways 22 and 81) by buggies driven by Alice McKeen, coming from the north, and by Bill Ireland, coming from the east. At Con. 2 SER, buggies driven by Thelma and Ormond Payne and by Arnold Harris would be likely to join the cavalcade of horse-and-buggies into Strathroy on a school day. Between Con. 2 and Strathroy, the Patterson car, driven by Lawrence Patterson, would be likely to pass.

Edward graduated from Strathroy Collegiate Institute in 1932, and was the valedictorian for his class. Upon graduation, he was awarded a scholarship at the University of Western Ontario for highest marks in nine papers. He enrolled in Mathematics and Physics and graduated in 1935, with the degree of Bachelor of Arts in Honour Mathematics and Physics. After a year at the Ontario College of Education in Toronto, he started teaching at Melbourne Continuation School, a two teacher Secondary School that offered all courses to the end of Grade 12. (The designation of classes had changed from forms to classes.) Grades 9 and 10 were in one classroom, while Grades 11 and 12 were in another room. The Depression was a difficult time to obtain a teaching job, as school boards were economizing. After obtaining his permanent High School Teaching Certificate, at the end of two years of teaching, Edward became Principal of the school, a position he held until going into the army for WWII. After return to civilian life in November 1945, Edward was engaged at the Veterans' Rehabilitation School in London from November to August of the following year. A year teaching at Mount Forest High School was followed by 19 years in the Secondary Schools in Hamilton. One year at Henry Street High School in Whitby was followed by two years as Vice Principal at Courtice Secondary School just east of Oshawa. A move to become a member of the Faculty of Education, University of Western Ontario, London, ensued for a period of eight years. After 41 years of teaching, Edward retired in July 1977.

Edward married Laura Richardson of Fergus, Wellington County. They raised a family of four, two daughters and two sons. A move to Whitby with Laura and the two younger children lasted for three years. In 1969, the family moved to London. Edward was involved in local organizations and enjoyed gardening. He was active in bowling with the University Heights Bowling League and served it for many years as statistician and one year as President. He was a member of the Kirk Session of Elmwood Avenue Presbyterian Church, a member of the London Council for Adult Education, a member of the Senior Alumni of the University of Western Ontario, and a member of the Adelaide Township Heritage Group.

McNAB, John and Ellen

The McNab family farm, the east half of Lot 6, Con. 3 NER, was first owned by George Porterfield, a soldier, and his brother, William Porterfield.

John McNab (1805-1880) and his wife Ellen (1806-1888) were the first McNabs to come to the township. They had three sons and five daughters. One son, James, farmed in Inniskillen Township, Lambton County. William (1847-1906) and Sarah (Brooks) McNab (1847-1938) farmed the McNab farm. They had five daughters and four sons.

Mary Anna married Miles Currie, and they farmed the east half of Lot 6, Con. 2 NER. They had three children, Joy, Velda and Basil.

Ellen married George Young of Strathroy. They

William and Sarah McNab (ca.1865)

Earl and Ruth McNab

moved to Moose Jaw, Saskatchewan.

Elizabeth (1877-1948) married Duncan Laughlan McLean of the Strathroy area, and they moved to Cupar, Saskatchewan.

John married Agnes McLay (d.1923) of Warwick Township and they farmed the east half of Lot 5, Con. 3 NER. After Agnes' death, he married Elizabeth McLeish.

Archibald married Mary Jane Coulter of Strathroy, and they moved to Stoney Beach near Moose Jaw, Saskatchewan.

Frank married Nellie Hawkins of the Strathroy area, and they settled in Colonsay near Saskatoon, Saskatchewan.

Adeline married James E. Wilson of Forest, who owned a creamery. They had two sons and three daughters. The eldest son, Mac, was shipwrecked during WWII and, as a result of injuries he incurred at that time, lost both legs.

May (1885-1944), a twin sister of Adeline, never married.

Rupert Victor (1887-1973) married Ethel Wilson (1886-1951). He was the third owner of the McNab family farm. Rupert and Ethel had a son, William Wilson (1918), who married Mary Norma Ayre. They have three children. Karen Cadman has a son, Bryan. Earl Douglas married Ruth Knip, and they have six children, Dwayne, Sarah, Julie, Penny, Sheldon and Chad. Paul Martin married Laurie Charlton, and they have two daughters, Krista and Lindsay.

Rupert and Ethel had a daughter, Ina Jean (1922), who married James Henderson. They farmed the west half of Lot 18, Con. 3 NER. They had four children, Michael, Charles, Stanley and Janet (MacDowall).

Earl, the son of Wilson and Norma, and his wife, Ruth, moved to the farm from Hensall in 1989, and Wilson and Norma retired to Strathroy. Earl and Ruth represent the fifth generation of the McNab family.

McPHAIL, Ray and Ruby

Ray McPhail was born and raised in Brooke Township on the west side of the Middlesex-Lambton Townline, one mile west of Napier. In the fall of 1946, he purchased his first farm, 100 acres, on Lot 4, Con. 2 NER, from Laura Conkey. In the spring of 1947, he purchased 50 additional acres of that lot from Laura Conkey, directly across the road.

The back 50 acres of the home farm was completely covered with thorn trees and approximately 10 acres of scrub brush. There were many 25' thorn trees that grew so far out from the base, they were nearly as wide as they were tall. This acreage was used for pasture, and when one went into the field looking for cows, you could walk for half an hour and come out within one rod of where you went in, only to find the cows peacefully chewing their cuds behind some thorn trees. After much hard labour, this area was cleared and cleaned up.

In 1950, Ray married Ruby M. McCallum, R.N. (d.1981), who was also born and raised in Brooke Township, south of Alvinston. They had one daughter, Mary Catherine.

In the late 1950s, the McPhails installed plumbing and wiring. The Lenting Drain was dug, and all the land that needed tile was tiled. Ray said, "It was the best investment I ever made... the tiles sure paid for themselves."

In the early 1960s, a pole barn and two large fenced feedlots were built on the home farm. In

Ray and Ruby McPhail, 1980

1967, the McPhails added a cage layer henhouse on the north 50 acres, with automatic feeding and gathering systems. As years passed, the systems needed replacing, so the hens and quota were sold in 1992. On the home farm on March 11, 1994, fire destroyed the original barn adjoining one feedlot. It was replaced to continue fattening beef cattle. Presently, Ray and Mary Catherine farm beef and cash crops on their rich, slightly sandy, clay loam soil. Indeed, Adelaide Township soil has produced superior crops for many of its farmers.

MEE, Patrick and Mary

Squire Patrick Mee (ca.1809-1881) was born in Roscommon, Ireland. Patrick was among the earliest settlers in Adelaide. He had come to the township upon being hired by the Radcliff family to repair the old log house on their farm, when the Radcliffs were forced to return from Amhurst Island after a 10-year absence. In 1836, Patrick married Mary Crummer (1817-1882), born in Irwinstown Ct., Fermanagh, Ireland, daughter of the Battle of Waterloo veteran. In 1832, Mary came to Adelaide with her family. In 1837, she accompanied her volunteer husband to Amherstburg, where there was trouble, carrying her child in her arms. In those days, it was not unusual for a soldier's family to accompany his regiment. Mary found camp life disagreeable, so she returned to the Adelaide farm in the dead of winter, walking most of the way with her eldest child in her arms. After a time, she again joined her husband, in London, where they resided until after the birth of their second child. They returned to Adelaide and commenced hotel keeping, a business they followed for a number of years, and acquired a large property, to which they retired after Patrick's return from California. On this estate, they passed the remainder of their lives in peace and comfort.

Patrick petitioned for land on George Street in Adelaide Village for a Roman Catholic Church and glebe, and received four acres on March 31, 1849. The first church was a white frame building, and stood beside the Roman Catholic cemetery.

Patrick was an early councillor. In 1850, Patrick was the first reeve of Adelaide, re-elected in 1852. On the 1851 Adelaide census, Mary's brother, John 25, and her sister, Margaret 23, are both married and living with them. In a 1925 Age newspaper article, it notes that "In a township as Orange as Adelaide, Patrick had every man for his friend." He was well liked by everyone.

Patrick and Mary had eight sons and three daughters, William (ca.1829); Margaret (ca.1836); John (1839-1885); James (ca.1840); Anna (ca.1841-1886); Henry (1844); George W. (ca.1846-1867); Edward Walter (ca.1847-1894); Charles A. (ca.1850-1884); Ellen Marion (1851); Hattie E. (1855-1884); Thomas Herbert (ca.1858-1931); and William #2 (1862).

William was born in Ireland, and is perhaps a child from a former marriage. On the 1851 census, he is 22 years, single, living at home, and is listed as a shop man. He likely died before 1862, as Patrick and Mary's last son was also named William. In E. Walter Mee's obituary of 1894, Walter is referred to as the fourth son.

John was born in London. He married a "Miss Leonard" in 1874, and they had two sons, James (1874) and John Jr. (1883). John was engaged in many business dealings, and was a railroad superintendent for the Grand Valley Railroad in Eton Rapids. In 1867, he went to Manistee and was engaged in lumbering in partnership with his brother, James, and a Mr. Vincent, until 1872. He then bought James' interest in the hardware firm of Russell and Mee, buying out Mr. Russell to run the business by himself, of which he sold a part to Mr. Parry and engaged in lumbering with Mr. Leonard, whose daughter he married. Shortly before his death, he sold the business of Parry and Mee to their old foreman, George Billings, so he could have more time for lumbering. He was also a stockholder and director in the First National Bank. He was much loved and respected by all.

Anna married Thomas Seed (1847-1926) of Adelaide Township, where they resided after their marriage. They had six children, John T.W., who resided in Vancouver; Mary, who married Fred Farnsworth and lived in Illinois; Ethel and Queenie, who lived in Chicago; Annie, who married William F. Abbott and lived in Exeter; and Margaret, who married George A. O'Leary and lived in Windsor.

Edward Walter died in Duluth, Minnesota.

Thomas Herbert married Josephine Kearns (d.1953) in February 1887. He was the enumerator for the 1881 Adelaide Census, Division 3, and a well-known citizen of Strathroy. They had six children, Ellen (1887-1887); John Harry (1888-1891); Mary Marguerite (1890), who married Richard Stuart Wilson in 1916; Josephine (1892); Brian Patrick (1897-1926); and Herbert (1897). Thomas and Josephine are buried in Caradoc Township in All Saints Roman Catholic Cemetery.

MILLARD, Frank and Phyllis

When Frank and Phyllis Millard (d.1993) retired from farming in Shelburne, Ontario, they looked for a new home in Middlesex County. They wished to be closer to their daughter, Frances, who farms with her husband, Richard Kilbourne, south of Mt. Brydges.

Their search ended at the northwest corner of Kerwood Road and Highway 22. On September 6, 1967, they moved to the home on this lot, the site of the former school, S.S. #6 Adelaide. They purchased the property from Bill and Delores (Nichols) Carson.

The house is well built, with joists and hardwood floors from the school incorporated into its construction. The stone foundation from the school is buried on the lot in an area where the grass turns brown in dry summers. Former students recall taking classes in the shade of the large soft maple in the back yard. A large piece of cement discovered during the building of a fence was determined to be the floor of the school privy. Frank designed and built the attached garage and breezeway on the house.

For several years after the move to Adelaide, Frank was employed as a carpenter by Keith Hudson, who operated Strathroy Building Supplies on Highway 81. This business was relocated to London when the site became part of Highway 402. He then served for a period as Building Inspector for Adelaide Township.

Always keen gardeners, the Millards planted elm, ash, walnut, maple and pine trees on the lot. A balsam was brought back from a northern holiday trip, and an antique rose bush was rescued from a building site in Glencoe.

After his wife's death, Frank kept active playing the violin, doing woodworking, bird watching, and gardening. He now resides at Strathmere Lodge, and the property was sold to Jess and Jacqueline Robinson.

MILLER, Robert and Mary

Robert Miller (1786-1853) and his wife, Mary, immigrated with their children to Canada from Belfast, Ireland, in 1832. Land records show that in June 1836, Robert Miller, a British soldier, received his patent from the Crown for 100 acres, known as the west half of Lot 5, Con. 2 NER. The Adelaide census of 1851-1852 notes that Robert is a farmer, aged 66, and that he and his wife, Mary, aged 50, are affiliated with the Church of England. Three of their children were William (1814-1893) and Robert (1822-1906), who stayed in the area, and a daughter, who married a Dowling and lived in Minnesota. In 1851 or 1852, Robert and Mary sold 50 acres, the east half of the west half of Lot 5, Con. 2 NER, to their son, William.

The 1851-1852 census records that William, age 37, born in Ireland, and his wife, Ellen (James) of Adelaide Township (see JAMES, Thomas and Alice), age 25, born in England, lived on this property with four of their children. In 1854, the west half of the west half of Lot 5, Con. 2 NER, was sold to Shalto Galloway. William was educated in Belfast, and taught at the first school in the township, a log house at Lot 5, Con. 3 NER, on Squire Cuddy's land. It is said that William constructed most of the building with his own hands. William collected information for the 1861 census from residents on Con. 2 and Con. 3 NER, noting names of 585 individuals on pages 1-12. His obituary recounts William's active interest in municipal affairs, serving as assessor, councillor, reeve and clerk. He was assessor in 1838 or 1839 after his return from Windsor, where he served against the Patriots in the Rebellion. William was appointed township clerk in July 1878 after the sudden death of Anthony Preston, and he served in that capacity until 1891. William was also a local minister and he preached his first Methodist sermon in the log schoolhouse in 1841.

William and Ellen had nine children, Elizabeth (1844-1911); Robert (1847); Thomas (ca.1849); Henry J. (1850-1916); Mary (1853); Alice Power (1854-1933); Ellen Margaret "Nellie" (1857-1921); William (1859); and Martha (1862-1956).

Elizabeth remained single and was said to be "a woman of sterling qualities" and a "great cook." She stayed in the old home and later lived with her brother, Henry.

Robert married Margaret Cuddy, daughter of Thomas and Esther (Trueman) Cuddy. They lived in Sarnia and raised a family there.

Thomas is believed to have died at a very young age.

Henry lived on Con. 2 NER, until the family moved to Adelaide Village in 1878. He was "afflicted from childhood" and walked with a limp. A story written by his aunt, Ellen "Nellie" (Milliken) Wells, indicates that Henry fell and broke his hip and back when he was about nine years old. In 1891, Henry accepted the office of clerk of the township, following his father's term, and served until 1913, when failing health forced him to retire from active life. His sister, Alice, who did not marry, cared for him during his last illness. Henry was a member of the Methodist Church, but was always a faithful attendant and worker at St. Ann's Anglican Church in Adelaide, where his funeral service was held. Henry is buried in Strathroy Cemetery.

Mary married Ira Clark Burdick (buried in Arkona Cemetery), son of Caleb and Martha Burdick, in Adelaide in 1875. They had two sons, Herbert and William, who married sisters and lived in Winnipeg. Mary remarried in 1892, to Joseph Trott in Camlachie, Lambton County.

Alice became the second wife of Samuel Milliken in 1877. Samuel was first married in 1862 to Adeline Bolton, daughter of William and Harriet Bolton of Adelaide (see BOLTON, William and Harriet). Alice took on the responsibility of caring for the children from Samuel's first marriage, Mary (1865-1937); William Albert "Willie" (d.1923); Harriet "Hattie"; John Bolton "Johnny" or "J.B."; and Adeline "Ina." Samuel and Alice had three sons and three daughters, Alice (1879-1948); Thomas Chalmers; Samuel "Ernest" (1880-1947); Ellen Adelaide "Nellie" (1882-1967); Janet "Edith" (1884-1940); and Royden Stanley "Roy" (ca.1888-1951). For 56 years, Alice lived in East Williams on the townline, where all the children were raised.

Mary took care of the younger children when her mother died. She was a milliner who made straw hats, and a dressmaker. Mary did spinning and knitted socks and mitts from the yarn for the family. She took yarn to the woollen mill in Strathroy to be woven into blankets. Mary, who remained single, later trained as a Registered Nurse at the Ontario Hospital in London. She nursed many people in their homes. She stayed with her brother, Willie, in Adelaide Village before he died. Mary lived in Adelaide for 20 years and attended St. Ann's Anglican Church in Adelaide Village.

Willie, who remained a bachelor, knitted double mitts for himself and his brothers and sisters when he was young. Willie raised cattle on his 50-acre farm at Crathie, where his grandfather had lived. He lived with his older sister, Mary, on this property. Later, Willie owned a house between the Roman Catholic Church and the Anglican Church in Adelaide Village. He was township clerk for a time.

Hattie was a dressmaker. She married William Leckie and moved to Sarnia.

Johnny served in the Boer War. He obtained a B.A. in 1907, and a B.Sc. at Queens University in Kingston. For a time, he taught school near Toronto. Later, he worked in Ottawa as Dominion Land Surveyor in the Topographical Surveys Branch. He married Elvira Barker in 1913.

Ina, the youngest child from Samuel's first marriage, went to college in Chatham. She went to work for Tupper, Peters and Potts in Victoria, B.C. She married Archie M. Russell, and lived in Vancouver.

Alice (1879-1948) was the first child of Samuel and Alice. She remained single, and trained as a

Registered Nurse in Brockville "under the tutelage of her Aunt Ellen, superintendent there." Alice's nursing career took her to hospitals in Brockville, Lindsay (as assistant superintendent), and Renfrew (as superintendent). In later years, she looked after her ill mother, who was then living in Adelaide Village. Then she cared for her stepsister, Mary. Alice continued to live in the house in Adelaide Village after their deaths. When Alice died, the house, previously owned by her Uncle Henry, a bachelor, was sold out of the family.

Thomas became a teacher. He married Margaret Jemina McLeod. They lived in the Prince Albert area of Saskatchewan.

Ernest married Kate Kelsey Stewart in 1920. They lived in East Williams on the Milliken family farm.

Nellie trained as a Registered Nurse. She married John Wells and lived in Manitoba and Saskatchewan. Nellie wrote that "Mother was a wonderful woman, and a real mother and friend to my father's five children. In fact, I was nearly 20 before I knew that my father had been married before. We were just one big family…" and she was "a wonderful mother to us all."

Edith played the organ at East Adelaide Presbyterian Church. She married John McColl, and lived near Robsart, Saskatchewan.

Roy was employed first at the Royal Bank in Strathroy. Later, he was export sales manager for the Ford Motor Company, working in Australia, New Zealand, India, and other countries. He married Florine Schreiner.

After Samuel Milliken died, his wife, Alice, stayed on the East Williams family farm for a number of years until her son, Ernest, married in 1920 and took over the farm. She then went to Adelaide Village to live with her stepson, Willie, and continued to live there after he died, with Mary, her stepdaughter. About 1930 or 1931, her daughter, Alice, came to look after them both. The younger Alice continued to reside in the home after their deaths, except for a time when she worked as a nurse in Brantford.

Nellie, daughter of William and Ellen, taught at S.S. #12 in 1886. She trained as a Registered Nurse and was later superintendent in Brockville and Lindsay hospitals. Nellie remained single.

William, eighth of William and Ellen's children, became a minister. He married, and raised a family in the western United States after 1879, probably in Colorado.

Martha, the youngest child of William and Ellen, married William Alexander "Alex" McInroy in May 1888 (see McINROY, Alexander and Ann Jane).

Robert, son of Robert and Mary, was born in Belfast, Ireland, and came to Canada with his parents in 1832 at the age of nine. As a young man, he operated a sawmill and lumberyard in Middlemiss. He supplied materials for the government mail plank road between Port Stanley and Chatham, now known as the Longwoods Road. After his lumber business was destroyed by fire, he farmed for a time and then opened a meat market in Mt. Brydges. About 1877, he moved to Strathroy, where he was Chief of Police for 15 years. Later endeavours included working in the implement business, and working as caretaker of the Strathroy Collegiate Institute. Robert Miller married Mary Knott (d.1875) of Middlemiss, who died in Mt. Brydges. Two years after her death, he married Eliza Peters. Robert's obituary noted eight surviving children, John of Grand Rapids, Michigan; Frank of the Klondike; Mrs. D. Chisholm of Toronto; Stanley of Hamilton; and William, James, Wilbur and Emily of Strathroy.

MILLIGAN, John and Jean

John W. and Jean M. (Brennan) Milligan moved to Adelaide Township in November 1967, from London Township.

John is a plumber and farmer with a custom operation. He was a councillor for Adelaide Township from 1992 to 1997, and is serving as reeve at the present time. He is also a 4H leader.

Jean has been employed by the Middlesex Board of Education (now called the Thames Valley Board) for 17 years.

John and Jean have four children, Robert Glenn (1964); Kenneth John (1966); James Warren (1969); and Janet Ellen (1972).

Robert Glenn married Lisa Gregory on August 29, 1992. They reside in Strathroy.

Kenneth John married Alice Baird on October 9, 1993. They have one child, Nicole Elizabeth (1996). They live in Adelaide Township.

James Warren married Brenda Podolinsky on September 11, 1993. They live in Strathroy.

Janet Ellen married Steven F. Gare on June 18,

1994. They have one daughter, Jenna Lynne (1995). They live in Strathroy.

MILLIKEN, Earl and Ruth

Earl and Ruth Milliken were married in 1952 and had four sons, Doug, Paul, David and Tim. They have lived in Adelaide Township since their marriage. They built their first home on Highway 81, across the road from Jack Draper's store. They built their second home on Head Street. In 1961, they built a third home on Pannell Lane, and in 1965, a fourth house was built next door.

The old Levitt farm was purchased in 1968 and the Millikens developed Cedar Crescent off Pannell Lane. Over six years, they built three more houses and a duplex there. In 1971, they purchased the land and old house at the corner of Highway 81 and Pannell Lane. In the 1920s, Jim and Mary Thomas owned this house. They ran a boarding house for workers who came to town to work at Downham's Nursery. Frank Fidler boarded there in 1924.

The Millikens built a house on the side of the hill and tore the old house down in 1975. In 1987, they built the home on the corner, where they still reside. David and his family live in Adelaide on Charles Boulevard.

MINER, Truman and Elizabeth

In 1807, Truman Miner (1784-1866) married Elizabeth Morrison (ca.1787). There were eight known children, Mahetable (1806-1903; Arminda (ca.1810); Eliza Ann (1817-1893); Lucinda (1817-1881); Chester (1821-1873); Olivia (ca.1823-1877); Clarinda (ca.1829); and Beulah (1831-1926). The family originated in Vermont, where the first five children were born, with the remaining children born in Canada, probably Bytown (now Ottawa). The family next moved to Warwick Township and then to Con. 10, Caradoc Township, before moving to Adelaide in the 1850s. The 1861 Adelaide census shows Truman on the west half of Lot 16, Con. 2 SER. The census taker noted, "An old man, does not farm any." Truman's only son, Chester, is farming next to him, on the east half of Lot 16.

Mahetable married Benjamin Eastman (ca.1804-1852), son of Amherst and Lucy (Farmer) Eastman (see EASTMAN, Benjamin and Mahetable). It is believed that Benjamin worked quite closely with his father-in-law. Starting in Bytown, he followed, or preceded, every move by Truman with one of his own to a neighbouring farm. In 1858, after Benjamin's death, Mahetable married James Cooper (1792-1883) of Adelaide, becoming his third wife. James resided on part of Lot 21, Con. 4 SER. After the death of her second husband, Mahetable lived with her descendants, finally dying at the home of her grandson, Wesley Eastman, on the Fourth Line South.

Eliza Ann married John Crealy (1808-1844). They had three children, Truman (ca.1837); Hannah (ca.1840), who married James W. Smith in 1894; and Martha (ca.1842). They lived on part of Lot 20, Con. 4 SER. Truman married Ellen (ca.1845, last name unknown) and they had three children, John (ca.1872); Fred (ca.1876), who married Lulu Farthing in 1910 and then settled in Caradoc; and Ethel (ca.1882). Truman farmed the north half of Lot 18, Con. 3 SER, before becoming a photographer on Front St. in Strathroy.

In 1837, Lucinda, fourth child of Truman and Elizabeth, married Benjamin Woodhull (ca.1813-1878). They lived near Kilworth and Delaware. Another Benjamin Woodhull, who settled near Keyser's Corners, is believed to be a close relative.

In 1847, Chester married Mary Ann Buttery (ca.1825-1894), daughter of John and Ann (Wilkinson) Buttery of Adelaide. They raised four children, Reuben (1848); William (1850); George (1854-1918); and Ann (ca.1858). In 1881, all three sons were farming parts of the homestead, Lot 16, Con. 3 SER, but by 1901, only George remained.

In 1882, George, the third child of Chester and Mary Ann, married Louisa James (ca.1858), daughter of Thomas and Frances (Harris) James of Adelaide. They had two children, Lewis (1884) and Florence (1887). George and his wife sold part of the farm and moved to Kindersley, Saskatchewan, as did Florence and her husband, John McGrath. Lewis remained on the home farm and married Gertrude Eastman of Arkona. They had no children of their own but raised several foster children. They later moved to Sarnia.

In 1845, Olivia, sixth issue of Truman and Elizabeth, married Alfred Chute (ca.1822). Alfred was born in Nova Scotia. They had at least four children, Angelina (ca.1846); Martin (ca.1851); Harriet (ca.1854); and Andrew (1856). In the early 1860s, Alfred was farming part of Lot 26, Con. 3 NER, a farm he called Appleton Farms. Alfred was also a Baptist minister. The family later moved to London.

Clarinda married William Boville or Bovin, but had no family. After his death, she married Solomon Dell (ca.1823-1899), son of Samuel and Sarah (Wilkins) Dell. Clarinda was Solomon's second wife.

Beulah, the youngest of Truman and Elizabeth's children, married Samuel Martin (see MARTIN, Hiram and Hannah).

MINIELLY

The Minielly family is also known as McNeely, Manelly, Menealy, and Menely. The Minielly family originally came from the parish of Killahtee, Banagh, Donegal, Ireland. There were at least four children in Andrew and Sussanah's family born in Killahtee, William (1786-1829); Mary (1792); Andrew Jr. (1798); and Sarah (1807). They all came to Canada at different times.

William came under the Lord Bathurst scheme in 1815 and settled along the Scotch Line between Lanark County and Elmsley in 1816. He later lived in North Elmsley and, in 1846, moved to Plympton Township with his family. He married Elizabeth MacKay in 1831. There is a book written by Helen Minielly called, "The Minielly Family History 1815-1871," which deals almost exclusively with William's family. Andrew and Sussanah, Andrew Jr. and his wife, Isabella (Walker), and their daughter, Sarah, joined William in 1822.

Mary had married William Allingham of the parish of Inver in 1813. They raised a family in the town land of Fanaghan, parish of Inver (which is on the east side of Killahtee), and she stayed in Ireland until William died. Sometime in 1830 or 1831, Mary came to Bathurst Township, Lanark County, to join her parents with four of her five children. The eldest son, Edward, stayed in Inver. In 1832, Mary married William Fleck, a widower, in Perth. In 1836, they moved to Moore Township, Lambton County, with their own children and those from earlier marriages.

Sarah married Simpson Shepherd at the Perth Anglican Church on April 26, 1829, and they moved to Plympton Township, Lambton County (then Kent), in 1834.

Five children were born to Andrew Jr. and Isabella (Walker) in Bathurst Township, Lanark County, before they moved in 1833 to their land in Adelaide, Lot 1, Con. 1 NER. Their children were Sussanah (1822); Sarah (1824); John (1826-1902); William (ca.1828); and Anne (1831). Andrew Jr.'s parents must have moved at the same time—at least, there are two patents in the Andrew Minielly name dated 1836. Isabella must have died in the late 1830s, but no death record has been found. The Miniellys evidently had a private family graveyard on their farm; no death records were found for the parents. Andrew had died prior to the 1842 census, but Sussanah was still alive at that time and also in the 1852 census, when she was 91. The children were still living at the time of the 1842 census, but in 1852, only John and Anne were with the family.

In 1844, Sarah married William Shepherd of Plympton Township, brother of Simpson, but no marriage records were found for Sussanah, Anne, or William.

John, third child of Andrew Jr. and Isabella, married Margaret Ann Bowes, daughter of John and Jane (Dick) Bowes of Warwick Township, in 1861. John stayed on the homestead farm and when he died, his son, John Albert, resided there.

Andrew Jr. married for the second time on February 13, 1840, to Catherine Colter of Warwick (from Records of St. Ann's Anglican Church, Adelaide).

The Minielly family attended St. Ann's Anglican Church until 1844. After that, the children were baptised in the Wesleyan Methodist Church and are in the Central Baptismal Register. In the 1852 census and later, they are Wesleyan Methodist.

MINTEN, Peter and Jacqueline

Peter and Jacqueline (Aarts) Minten were married September 22, 1973, in Ingersoll. Their first home was in Watford.

In 1975, they bought a 100-acre farm from Raymond and Antje Kingma. It is located on Pike Road, R.R. #7, Strathroy. They soon started a hog operation, and Peter worked part-time doing construction. They farmed until 1986, when they sold 60 acres of farmland to their neighbour, Jerry Kingma. Peter then started a full-time woodworking business, and Jackie began working as a Registered Nurse at Craigholme Nursing Home in Ailsa Craig.

Their four children all attended Our Lady Immaculate School in Strathroy. Jeff, the eldest, 23,

Minten family, back, Peter and Jackie, seated, L-R, Mike, Becky, Jeff and Steve, 1998. (Courtesy Luis' Photography.)

went to Regina Mundi High School before attending U.W.O. in London. After graduation, he joined the Edmonton City Police Force. Steve, 21, attended S.D.C.I. and is now taking Construction Management Engineering at Fanshawe College. Mike, 18, is in Grade 12, and Rebecca "Becky," 14, is in Grade 9 at S.D.C.I.

MINTON, Joseph and Johanna

Joseph Peter Minton (1949) was born in Holland, and moved with his parents to Canada at the age of one. He lived on La Salle Line in Watford. Johanna Petronella (De Gouw, 1952) was born in Strathroy and lived on Bornish Road. They were married at St. Columban Church in Bornish on November 11, 1972. They moved to Watford on La Salle Line and lived there for seven months, then moved to Keyser's Corners.

Joseph, being a carpenter by trade, has been busy since then, building and rebuilding the house and farm buildings. The dairy barn was built in 1976, when they started the dairy operation. Their house was built between 1981 and 1985. A barn fire in the summer of 1987 leveled all the old barns to the south of the house, leaving only the two chicken barns to the east and the dairy barn to the west.

The Mintens have planted many trees and landscaped their property. Many of the old foundations north of the house and barns were removed. In 1992, they moved a caboose from County Road 39 to its present site for use as a playhouse for the children. In 1995, they purchased Lot 7, Con. 1, and Lots 6 and 7, Con. 2.

Joseph and Johanna have 12 children, Lucia (1974); Joseph Jr. (1976); Joni (1978); Ronald (1979); Kevin (1981); Matthew (1984); Krista (1986); Mary-Angela (1987); John-Paul (1989); Stephen (1991); James (1993); and Janessa (1995).

MITCHELL, John and Mary Ann

John (ca.1819-1890) and Mary Ann Mitchell (1822-1900) immigrated to Canada from County Armagh, Ireland, about 1850. They raised five children, Sarah (1851-1948), who married William Newton (see NEWTON, William and Christina); Robert (ca.1854-1935); Elizabeth "Margaret" (1855-1946), who married William Matthews (see MATTHEWS); Hannah (ca.1859-1954); and William (1864-1897). Sarah was born in Ohio, and William in Adelaide. When Sarah was a child, the family moved from Ohio to London Township and, from there, to Adelaide. John farmed 100 acres, being the west half of Lot 7, Con. 4 SER. An obituary of John's son states that John was a "well-to-do farmer."

Robert farmed part of Lot 7, Con. 5 SER, before retiring to London. He never married.

Hannah remained single and lived in London. She ran a boarding house.

William was described as being "…a young man blessed with a strong constitution and a vigorous mind." Endowed with these qualities, he went to London in 1880 and entered the Medical Department at Western University. He was a zealous student and in 1885, he graduated with honours, taking the gold medal in that year. He remained in London and was very successful in obtaining a practise. He was Professor of Anatomy at Western University for several years. He held a number of offices in the Irish Benevolent Society, and in 1895 was chosen President. Dr. Mitchell became Surgeon-Major of the Seventh Battalion and held that office up to the time of his death. He was also surgeon to the C.P.R. and for a number of benevolent societies. He was a member of St. John's Lodge, 209a, A.F. & A.M., and of the Foresters. He never married.

MITCHELL, John Sr. and Barbara

The elder John Mitchell (1737-1851) and his wife, Ann (1774-1851), were born in Ireland and came to Southwold Township in Elgin County some-

Smith Mitchell farm (ca.1923). L-R, Robert Stevenson (brother to Agnes), Eric Mitchell, Isabel Mitchell, Robert Mitchell, Stewart Mitchell, Agnes Mitchell, Smith Mitchell.

time after 1804. They received a location ticket for Lot D from Colonel Talbot. They came with at least three children, Margaret, who married a cooper, James Hepburn, and lived near Five Steaks Corners in Elgin County; John Sr. (1804-1886), who died in Adelaide Township; and Robert (1809-1867), who married Elizabeth Estlick and had at least nine children in Southwold.

John Sr. married Barbara McIntosh (1805-1885) from Scotland at Stirling (Hog's Hollow), Southwold Township, on November 24, 1829. After Barbara's death, John Sr. married Margaret Nicholson of Strathroy in 1864. John and Barbara had eight children, all of whom were baptised in the Old Anglican Church of St. Thomas, with the exception of the youngest daughter, Charlotte (1849). She was baptised in December 1857 in the old Methodist Church on North St. in Adelaide Township, an area that became part of the Village of Strathroy in 1860. John and Barbara's other children, who were all born in Elgin County, were Margaret (1830), who was living in Strathroy by 1857; John Jr. (1832); Alexander (1833), who married Rachel Marshall of Elgin County and had a son, George Edward (1867-1935), a cooper in Strathroy; Samuel S. (1836-1916), who married three times in Adelaide Township; William (1837), who married Elzina Stockton and farmed in Caradoc Township; James (1840); and Angus (1843-1943), who married Ann Jane Fitzpatrick (1848-1935) of Adelaide Township, and worked as a blacksmith in Watford. The aforementioned Charlotte married Robert Reed of Adelaide Township and settled near Picton in Prince Edward County, Ontario.

Angus and Ann Jane raised six sons in Watford.

T. Bert lived in Oshawa; Joseph H. farmed in Prince Albert, Saskatchewan; Harry was a farmer in Bousejour, Manitoba; Frederick J. (1874-1909) resided in Toronto; and Percy A. (1880-1916) was killed at Bologne, France, in WWI.

On May 13, 1863, John Sr. purchased 25 acres of the south part of the west half of Lot 18, Con. 5 SER, which he sold to Philip Jones on December 7, 1870. The following year, John and his family moved across the road to the farm that was to be known as "Maple Grove Farm" on the west half of Lot 17, Con. 4 SER.

The obituary of Samuel S., John and Barbara's fourth child, stated that he had come to Adelaide Township in the mid-1850s, and had resided in the hamlet of Strathroy for a short time before he married Robena Joanna Jones (1843-1861) of Adelaide Township. Joanna was born in Ontario, in Sidney Township, Hastings County, and had come to Adelaide with her parents in 1852. Sam and Joanna had one son, Edmund Samuel (1861-1924). Edmund married Louisa Smith in 1882 and they moved to Maple Valley, Sanilac County, Michigan. There, they raised six sons, Philip, Percy, Levi, Willard M., Witmar W. and Orville Edmund. By the mid-1860s, Samuel was farming on Lot 17, Con. 4 SER. After Joanna's death in Adelaide Township, Samuel married another Adelaide resident and close neighbour, Jessie "Isabel" Dubois (1844-1891), who had been born at Paris, Ontario, the daughter of Joseph and Mary Dubois of Con. 4 SER, Adelaide Township. From this marriage, seven more children were born in Adelaide Township, William George (1864-1915); Joseph H (1870); John "Cicero" (1872-1890); Frank J. (1875-1947); Smith Gordon (1877-1962); Maude E. (1880); and Royal Emmanuel (1883-1952). Two years after Isabel died, Samuel married Margaret Munroe. Samuel and Margaret had a daughter, Elizabeth "Lizzie" May (1894), who married Jay King of Strathroy. They resided in Oil Springs, Lambton County, and had a daughter, Helen.

Samuel and Isabel's eldest son, William George, married Sarah A. Luckins (1872-1952), daughter of Alexander and Phoebe Luckins of Adelaide Township. They farmed in Metcalfe Township, and raised two sons, Charles Samuel (1893-1978) and William Elgin (1894-1955). Joseph H. was born and raised on Lot 17, Con. 4 SER. and became a tai-

Eva and Jesiena Mitchell

lor in Mt. Brydges. John "Cicero" died of pneumonia in Adelaide at the age of 17. Maude E. was born on the home farm, and married Roy Nelson Theobald. They lived in Brantford, Ontario. Maude and Roy had five children, Elmor, Don, Marion, Margaret and Kingsley. Maude died in Brantford. Samuel and Isabel's youngest son, Royal, was raised in Adelaide. He became a Methodist minister and married Mary Coral Dale in Oil Springs, Lambton County in 1909. They moved to Phillips, Wisconsin, and later to Michigan, where they raised four sons and five daughters. Samuel's sons, Frank J. and Smith Gordon, farmed in Adelaide Township and, by 1914, these Mitchells owned and operated farms on Lot 17, 18 and 19, Con. 4 SER, as well as Lot 17, Con. 5 SER.

Frank remained at Maple Grove Farm, and married Isabel Giffen, daughter of William and Isabelle (Harkness) Giffen (1876-1953) of Adelaide Township. To Frank and Isabel were born two daughters, Jesiena (1910), who married Robert "Bob" McArthur, former owner of Pro Hardware on Front St. in Strathroy; and Eva (1912), who married James Marshall of Strathroy.

Smith Gordon purchased part of Lot 18, Con. 4 SER, and married Agnes Susan Stevenson (1880-1957) in September 1908. By 1914, he moved to Lot 19, Con. 4 SER, and purchased more land in 1921. The children remember that Agnes was not pleased about moving to a house that lacked hydro and was located far from town. Smith and Agnes had four children, Eric Samuel (1911); Robert (1913-1980); Isabel Susan (1915); and Stewart Gordon (1918-1992). The children attended S.S. #3 (Demaray's school) at the corner of Sideroad 27 and Egremont Road. Miss Anna Bycraft was their teacher. When the boys were old enough, they acted as custodians for S.S. #3—cleaning, fetching wood,

Samuel Mitchell with his third wife, Margaret (Munroe).

etc. Their most important job was to keep the fire burning in the winter, in order to heat the school and cook a big pot of potatoes for the children's noon meal. Eric believes the three boys received $50 each per year for performing custodial duties. Another one of their pastimes was to cut across the fields to listen to Mr. Wilson's radio, a rarity in the 1920s. When Isabel was just two years of age, she was thrown from the sleigh when her father took the curve too fast at the corner of Sideroad 27 and County Road 39. Smith simply stopped the horses, walked back to the snowy youngster, and plunked her back in the sleigh. Unlike much of Adelaide, Lots 27 and 28 offered much for its residents—many hills and valleys, a creek in which to fish and swim, Buttery's orchards, and later, Downhamdale Cemetery. Life was often hard for the "town-dweller" during the Depression, but for the mixed farmer, even without ready cash, no one starved.

Eric had always been fascinated with machinery, especially if it had an engine. His motorcycles were his pride and joy. It was not surprising that, after finishing high school, Eric joined Massey Harris in Brantford for a few years, worked for his brother in-law at Woods Transportation in London, spent some time with Universal Ignition, and finally worked as a mechanic for Muxlow brothers and A.C. Hall's in Strathroy. Eric married Violet Hymers from Perth County, and they had three children, Diane (1936); Beverly (1938); and Barry (1947).

Robert married Jean McGill of Lambton and operated a Fuel Distribution business in Watford. They had three children, Rick (1948); and twins, Jan and Joan (1951).

Isabel married Arthur "Harry" Woods (1908-1964) of Kerwood, founder of Woods Transportation of London. They raised two sons, John "Jack" (1938-1985) and Richard Stewart (1947).

Stewart was born on Lot 28, Con. 2 SER, and later purchased 65 acres on the southwest half of Lot 28 from Barney Campbell in 1948. Here he married Jean Truss of London and spent the remainder of his life. Stewart farmed with his father, and a second home was built on the farm for Smith and Agnes, where they lived the rest of their lives.

Jean and Stewart had no children. Stewart sold about one-third of an acre to Hugh and Winnifred Dolphin in 1952. In the 1970s, the Ministry of Highways started to accumulate land for the construction of Highway 402, taking about half of Stewart's property. Stewart severed several acres for a home, where he and Jean lived until his death. The land that remained was sold at public auction to Frank Kanters, who in turn sold it to Bob Marshall in 1985.

MONTAGUE, Joseph and Rhoda

In 1841, Joseph Isaac Montague (1818-1865), son of William and Maria (Sleigh) Montague, married Rhoda Humpries (1824-1905) of Adelaide Township. Rhoda, born in Trowbridge, Wiltshire, England, was the daughter of John and Maria (Ferris) Humphries of Adelaide Township (see HUMPHRIES, John and Maria). Joseph and Rhoda had six children, all born in Adelaide Township, Amelia (1842-1920); William Cyrenus (1844-1935); Thomas Edward (1847); Abraham Isaac (1849-1926); John W. (1850-1918); and William Humphries (1858-1915).

Joseph farmed Lot 17, Con. 1 NER, and worked as a blacksmith. The Montagues also owned other parcels of land. Rhoda continued farming with her sons after Joseph died visiting friends in the U.S. Rhoda was a woman of keen intelligence and sterling character. She was a devout Christian. Her tastes were cultivated and, even in old age, she devoted a considerable portion of time to painting and other artistic works.

The family left for Manitoba in 1879, and were some of the earliest settlers in that district. Rhoda died at the home of her daughter, Amelia, in Pilot Mound Glenora, Manitoba. Joseph and Rhoda are buried in Strathroy Cemetery.

Amelia married Edmund Crayston and had four sons. When her family moved to Manitoba, Amelia and her husband also moved, and settled on the shore of Rock Lake, 100 miles southwest of Winnipeg, where they had a beautiful home and a very large farm.

William Cyrenus married Mary Jane Petch (1845-1925) in Adelaide Township. Jane was born in Vaughan Township, the daughter of James (1816) and Millison (Keyworth) Petch, who were born in Lincolnshire, England. William and Jane farmed on the Montague farm until 1875, when they moved to Neepawa, Manitoba. William and Jane are buried in Riverside Cemetery in Neepawa. William's obituary stated that he took a keen interest in public affairs.

Two daughters and a son survived them in their obituaries, Mrs. Mildred Sproule (1884) of Killarney; Mrs. Alice Petch (ca.1875-1940) of Neepawa, who had married a Petch cousin; and Dr. Albert William Petch Montague of Minedosa, Manitoba, who practised as an eye, ear, nose and throat specialist in Minedosa and Victoria, B.C. Dr. Albert married Jessie Maria Sherrard in 1906 in Moncton, New Brunswick, and they had five children. William died in Victoria.

Thomas Edward was living in Galt at the time of his mother's death in 1905. He is buried at Trinity Anglican Church Cemetery in Galt.

Abraham Isaac lived in London at the time of his mother's death, but is buried in Zion Cemetery in West Nissouri Township. Abraham Isaac married Charlotte McDairmid (1847-1905). They had no children. In 1914, Abraham remarried, to Helena Augusta Saul (1879-1943). They had two children, Joseph (1916) and William (1917). They lived in West Nissouri, Thamesford and London. Helena was buried in Robins Hill Cemetery in West Nissouri.

John W. married Janet McKenzie. At the time of his mother's death in 1905, John was living in Winnipeg.

Walter Humphries married Barbara Ellen Angeline "Angie" Furry (1855-1945), daughter of Elias A. Furry, then reeve of South Cayuga, Ontario, and Henrietta Doan. They had two sons and two daughters. Walter and Angie are buried at Elmwood Cemetery, Winnipeg, Manitoba.

A large write-up is found in the encyclopedia of Canadian Biographies, penned when Walter was not yet 30 years of age. According to this biography, Walter was only five years when his father, an intelligent farmer and one of the most respected farmers in Middlesex, died on a visit to the U.S. while visiting friends. The article states: *"He has, like many who have risen to eminence, had to educate himself, and this he began while engaged as an errand boy in a country store. He qualified for a teacher's certificate in August 1874 and was employed at various points, one of them being in Adelaide in S.S. #6 in 1875 and 1876. An article in the Age Dispatch in 1875 mentioned that the school put on one of the most successful entertainment events ever held in Adelaide through the efforts of Walter. In 1882, he graduated in medicine in Ontario, then proceeded to Edinburgh, England, for further studies, coming back to Canada to practise in Dunnville, in the County of Monck. A few months after settling there, he very reluctantly accepted the nomination of the Liberal-Conservative Convention of Monck and became M.P. for Haldimand, Dunnville, Ontario, and though not yet 30, became one of the youngest members of the House of Commons in 1887. Walter was a supporter of Sir John A. MacDonald, but at the same time holding a liberal view upon public questions. In 1895, for a few months, he became the Secretary of State, then Minister of Agriculture until July 1896. He was one of the famous 'nest of traitors' that Prime Minister MacKenzie Bowell charged with conspiring against him. Walter dropped politics for a while and moved to Manitoba where, in 1913, he was elected to the Manitoba Legislature, serving as Minister of Public Works, a position he apparently held until his death."*

The article in Canadian Biographies finished with this statement: *"He is thoroughly Canadian in his aims and aspirations, and has an earnest and enthusiastic faith in the future of the country."*

Many relatives of Joseph Montague lived in the Byron area. Some of them came to the Adelaide area for a time. On the 1851 Adelaide census is listed a William Montague, 25, single, on Lot 23, Con. 4, who ran a tannery with a note beside tannery: M. church. Charles Montague and his wife in 1856 bought 50 acres of land, the northeast quarter of Lot 29, Con.1, which they sold to John Lamont in 1857.

According to the land records, in September of 1866, Catherine Montague of the City of Buffalo, wife of George Montague, purchased land in Adelaide from her brother-in-law, John Mitchell, whose wife, Margaret (Catherine's sister), was in ill health. The land included a Kerwood Village lot, and the north half of Lots 109 and 110 in the Village of Strathroy.

MOORE

The 1842 census for Adelaide Township lists a James More on Lot 15, Con. 1 NER. He is a non-proprietor, he and his wife are natives of Ireland, and they have been in Ontario for 10 years. One female child is listed, born in Ontario. James is a weaver.

On the same census is listed a John More on Lot 11, Con. 1 NER, also a non-proprietor. He and his wife are natives of England, and they have been in Ontario for 10 years. Three children were born to them in Canada, being two females 0-5 years, and one male 5-14 years. John is a carpenter.

Weavers and carpenters seem to move around a lot depending upon where the work is, so they are hard to trace.

A. James Moore married Anne Seeds on September 1840, according to the Anglican records for Adelaide.

One Moore daughter married William Brook of Adelaide, the mother being Margaret Moore, who died in Milton but is buried in St. Ann's.

There are no Moores recorded in Adelaide in 1851, but there are Moore families in Metcalfe, though not the same families. In 1861, there are Moore families in Strathroy, and there is a James Moore in Lobo, age 55, from Ireland, a widower with three teenage boys, and a Mrs. M. (likely a widow), with four young children, in the same household. Moores are also found in Lambton and East Williams Township at this time.

Although no ties have been confirmed between the Adelaide Moores and the Strathroy Moores, they all came from Madoc to Strathroy.

MORGAN, George W. and Elizabeth

George W. Morgan (1839-1892) was the son of Richard (1810-1882) and Catherine (Patterson) Morgan, natives of Ireland. Richard and Catherine married in 1834 and settled on Con. 4 in Adelaide Township.

George W. was born in Adelaide Township. He received a common school education and became a successful agriculturist. In 1867, he settled at Lot 7, Con. 4 SER, and in 1871, he married Elizabeth Cuddy (1845-1931) of Adelaide Township. George W. was given the title of Squire. He was conservative in politics, and he and Elizabeth were members of the Methodist Church of Canada. They had three sons, Alfred E. (ca.1877-1960); Ernest A. (d.1909); and George Elmer (1885-1968).

Alfred E. became a successful physician. He began his first practise in Adelaide Village in early 1900. He visited patients by horse-and-buggy. In 1904, he was largely instrumental in getting a telephone line established from Kerwood to Adelaide Village, and a telephone line was installed between his office and residence. In late 1906, Alfred relo-

George W. Morgan and Elizabeth Cuddy

cated to Toronto, where he practised medicine for many years. He married Elaine Russell (d.1913) of Wardsville, and they had three children, George (ca.1902); Russell (1906-1996); and Helen (1909-1912). After Elaine's death, Alfred remarried, to Ada Hughes from Western Canada. He died in Toronto.

Ernest A. died in Adelaide Township of a ruptured appendix. He was still a young man when he died at 33 years, three months and three days of age.

George Elmer was born in the residence at Lot 7, Con. 4 SER, and resided there until 1960. Elmer's mother, Elizabeth, died at the residence. Elmer was a successful farmer, and a noted breeder and importer of Cotswold sheep. His farm was known as "Maple Row Stock Farm," and he took many prizes exhibiting his sheep at fairs. He also sold insurance for Waterloo Mutual Insurance. He had a great

Mae and Elmer Morgan, 1967

interest in politics (conservative) and worked many elections. In his younger years, he played drums in the Kerwood Citizens Band. Elmer served on the Strathroy Fair Boards for many years. Elmer married Mae Fonger (d.1993), and they had three children, Elizabeth "Betty"; Alfreda (d.1993); and Ernest. Betty married George Matthews of Adelaide Township, and they had three sons. Alfreda married John Lambert (d.1994) of Watford, and they had three daughters and a son. Ernest married Joyce Langford of Metcalfe Township in 1960. The children of Elmer and Mae were all born in the residence at Lot 7, Con. 4.

When Ernest and Joyce were married, Elmer and Mae retired to a home in Strathroy. Elmer remained interested in the farm throughout his retirement, and visited at the farm frequently. He had a keen interest in sports, especially baseball, usually listening to one game on the radio while watching another on TV—and he knew exactly what was going on in both!

Ernest had already done the farming for several years because of his father's heart problems, and continued to for several years after marriage, until he began to work for Community Telephone (an independent company). Ernest worked out of the office in Kerwood until Bell Canada bought the system in 1980. He worked for Bell until his retirement in 1994.

Ernest and Joyce have two children, Shirley Anne (1963) and Allen Edward (1967). Shirley married Bradley Brooks and they reside in Adelaide Township. Allen was born on his grandfather Morgan's birthday, October 18, but unfortunately, before they could celebrate a birthday together, Elmer died. Mae died at the Victoria Manor Retirement Home in Watford in her 97th year. Their daughter, Alfreda, died later the same year after a battle with cancer.

The Lot 7 Morgan residence has seen many births, deaths and funerals over the years. Ernest doesn't remember his Aunt Jane Fonger (wife of Robert Murray), but he recalls that she died at the residence, and was carried out in a wicker basket.

Allen was christened in the home—probably just one of several children baptised there. The back half of the house was the original home, and the front part was moved to the lot from another location. These buildings were joined together, resulting in a double-width wall between the dining and living room areas. It is understood that the front part was moved during the winter on sleds pulled by horses. The stone used in the foundation of the barn came from St. Mary's to Kerwood by train, then was horse-drawn to the farm. The house has not changed much at all. The exterior of the house was clad in siding, and a sun porch has replaced the original open porch. Ernest and Joyce are proud and happy to be the third generation of Morgans to own and reside at Lot 7, Con. 4 SER, Adelaide Township.

MORGAN, Richard Sr. and Jane

The earliest story published about the Richard Morgan family appeared in the 1889 History of Middlesex County. It was recorded that, *"Richard Sr. and his three sons, John, Richard Jr. and William Morgan, emigrated from Ireland to Lambton County. They soon removed to Adelaide where Richard Sr. died at a ripe old age."* Another story, written by Mildred (Morgan) Fuller sometime in the late 1930s, states, *"About the year 1835, there left*

Joyce and Ernest Morgan, 1998

the County Mayo, Ireland, Richard Morgan and his wife, Isabella Murdock, and five children, Elizabeth, John, Richard, William and Jane. They landed at Quebec and settled on the Fourth Line of Adelaide." Both stories conflict with the obituaries of John and Richard Jr., which indicate John came in 1830, and Richard Jr., with his wife and daughter, came in 1835. According to the Adelaide 1841 census, William came in 1836.

A researcher in Ireland found Richard Sr. and Jane Morgan and the baptism of at least seven children, starting in 1805, in the Parish of Ballysakerry, County Mayo, naming them as Margaret, William, Richard, Susanna, Jane, William and Anne. The first William probably died as a child. It would first appear that this is not the right family, except further records show the marriage of William to Matilda Patterson, daughter of Samuel and Elizabeth. This couple came to Adelaide. The fact that Elizabeth and John are not listed only indicates that the family might have moved to Ballysakeery after Elizabeth and John were baptised or perhaps, earlier records didn't survive. This research also indicates Richard's wife is named Jane, which conflicts with the earlier mention of Isabella. Jane appears to be correct, because Richard's descendants use Jane as a family name while Isabella was never used.

There is a story by two independent sources that Richard Sr. was interred under a tree in Warwick Township, halfway between Kerwood and Watford. The tree, which is no longer standing, was pointed out to Dorothy (Morgan) Winter by her father.

Another short Morgan history was written by Jane Morgan's granddaughter, Nellie (McIllmurray) Gotts Kreh. Her story states that the Morgans had originally come from Wales and then, in the 16th century, came to Killala, County Mayo, Ireland. About 1970, Nellie visited a Murdock branch of the family who resided a few miles outside Killala.

Elizabeth (ca.1797), the eldest daughter of Richard and Jane, married James McAndrew. They had no children. It is not known where they settled. John, Richard Jr. and William all settled in Adelaide. While initially settling in Adelaide, Jane quickly married and moved to Warwick Township (see McELMURRY). There is no further information about the remaining Morgan children, Margaret, Susanna and Anne, except that Margaret married a Shannon.

The names John, Richard and William Morgan are still used today. A Richard and William Morgan both reside in Adelaide and a John Morgan resides in Ilderton.

John (ca.1802-1882), son of Richard and Jane, immigrated to Toronto from County Mayo, Ireland, in 1830. He obtained 200 acres of land in Enniskillen Township, Lambton County, but never settled there. In 1837, he married Elizabeth "Bessie" Hughes (ca.1822-1914) of London Township. They raised 10 children, Jennie (ca.1838-1911), who remained single and lived in Mt. Brydges; Elizabeth (ca.1839); Maria (ca.1841); Thomas (ca.1844-1851), who died of whooping cough; Sarah (ca.1845-1912), who remained single and lived in London; Margaret (ca.1849-1851), who died young of whooping cough; Margaret (ca.1853), who married Warner Brodrecht and lived in New Hamburg; John W. (ca.1856); Alice (ca.1858) and Richard "Dick" (1859). It is not known exactly when John settled in Adelaide. Land records show John purchased 100 acres in 1841, the east half of Lot 10, Con. 5 SER.

In 1864, John deeded an eighth of an acre, being the northwest corner of his lot, to the trustees of a New Connexion Methodist Church.

In 1864, Elizabeth, the second of John and Bessie's children, married John Curry (1838-1914) of Adelaide, son of John and Jane (Garner) Curry. They had at least seven children, Wilbert (ca.1867); Elmer; John (1876-1951); Della (ca.1872-1956); Lillian (1873-1917); Elizabeth "Lizzie" (ca.1881-1918); and Cecil (1883-1972). The 1878 Middlesex Atlas shows John Curry farming about 45 acres, being part of Lot 14, Con. 4, Metcalfe Township. The family moved to Bay City, Michigan, where Elizabeth died following the birth of Cecil. The 1891 census shows four of the children living in Adelaide. Wilbert and Della are living with their uncle, William Curry, and Lizzie and Cecil, with their grandmother, Jane Curry. It was said that Aunt Jennie and Uncle Dick Morgan raised Cecil from the age of six months. Wilbert moved to Toledo, Ohio. Della married Harry Johnston and moved to Winnipeg, Manitoba. Lizzie never married, and also moved to Winnipeg. In 1909, Cecil married John Brien in Adelaide. They resided in Ridgetown.

Maria, third child of John and Bessie, married James McCourt and raised at least six children,

Lizzie, Anna, Alice, John, Thomas and Richard. They resided in Petrolia.

About 1883, John W., eighth issue of John and Bessie, married Clara Cuddy (ca.1862), daughter of James and Sarah (Trueman) Cuddy of Adelaide, and raised one daughter, Gertrude (ca.1884). Starting in 1880, John acquired a total of 150 acres, being 50 acres from his father, Lot 10, Con. 5 SER, and two 50-acre parcels across the road, parts of Lot 10, Con. 4 SER. He was a well known and highly respected resident of Adelaide. He died at the age of 41, from inflammation of the lungs. In 1900, Gertrude married Dr. M.A. Giffen in Wisbeach. They had no children. Clara and Gertrude both moved to the U.S. The Adelaide family farms were sold in 1906.

In 1878, Alice, the ninth child of John and Bessie, married Herbert Stanfield of London. She later remarried, to James Austin. They lived in London.

Dick, the youngest of John and Bessie's children, took over operation of the family farm and acquired title after his father's death. He remained single, and farmed until his retirement.

Richard Jr. (1811-1882), son of Richard and Jane, married Catherine Patterson (1810-1892), daughter of Samuel and Eliza Patterson. In 1835, with a daughter, they left County Mayo, Ireland, and homesteaded in Warwick Township, Lambton County. In 1837, Richard Jr. moved to Adelaide when he found his land title was defective. They raised seven children, Eliza (1834), who married Henry Barr and moved to the U.S.; John (1837-1909); George (1839-1892); Matilda (1842-1897); Richard (1844-1918); Catherine (1849-1916); and Samuel (1855-1914).

Before their move to Adelaide, Richard Jr. worked off the farm for extra wages. On one occasion while he was away, wolves attacked the cabin. Catherine got the family dog inside and barricaded the door with benches, as there was only a quilt covering the opening. Richard killed 16 deer for venison in his first year; thus, they survived the early years. Richard prospered and, by 1852, he had 194 acres, being the east half of Lot 8 and the west half of Lot 9, Con. 5 SER, which he named "Cherry Grove Farms." He continued to acquire land until he had farms for each of his sons. He employed a private teacher for his children. Richard was also a Mason. The family attended the Methodist Church.

In his later years, Richard Sr., his wife, and son, Samuel, retired to a 50-acre farm, being part of Lot 9, Con. 4 SER.

In 1861, John, second eldest child of Richard Jr. and Catherine, married Rebecca Trueman (1844-1879), daughter of John and Sarah (Smith) Trueman of Metcalfe. They had eight children, Eveline (1862-1905); Loftus (1865-1956); John Harcourt (1867-1950); Norman (1869-1949); Wilber (1873-1943); Ettie (1875-1878); and twins, Thomas (1877-1877) and Alfred (1877-1881). After Rebecca's death, John married Dora Corneil (1844-1921), daughter of Christopher and Jane (Meadows) Corneil of Ekfrid. They had four children, Trueman (1882-1949); Emma (1884-1886); Walter (1887-1953); and Meredith (1889).

John lived the life of a pioneer farm boy, helping to clear and break up the land for crops. He was first elected as councillor for Adelaide at the age of 21 and also served a number of years as reeve. In 1880, he was the first Adelaide reeve to be chosen Warden of Middlesex County. This was an eventful year—the House of Refuge (now Strathmere Lodge) was built, and the Donnelly murders occurred in Lucan. John served many years on the church board of the Methodist Church, and was a member of the Masonic Lodge at Napier. He was also appointed a Justice of the Peace. He took over the family homestead, where he raised purebred shorthorn cattle, horses and sheep, and sold agricultural implements.

In 1878, two of John's children were involved in a tragic event. Wilber and Ettie were playing in their grandfather's barn (Lot 9, Con. 4 SER) when it caught fire. Joseph Galbraith, the next-door neighbour, saw the smoke and ran to help. With a coat over his head, he backed into the barn and saved Wilber, but couldn't locate Ettie before the heat and smoke made rescue impossible. Ettie died, and it was said that her death broke her mother's heart and led to her early demise.

In 1883, Eveline, eldest child of John and Rebecca, married James Cameron. They raised three children, Isabella (1884-1968), who married Watson Young; Evelyn (1885-1921), who married Winlow Bixel; and Alexander Cameron. The family lived in Strathroy.

Dr. Loftus Morgan married Lucia Aldrich. They raised four children, Elemore (1903-1966); Virginia (1906); Evelyn (1909-1995); and Lucia "Kitty"

(1910-1970). Loftus received a medical degree from the University of Toronto and served an internship in New York. In 1888, he moved to Baton Rouge, Louisiana, where he set up his medical practise. In 1912, he purchased a farm nearby and virtually retired from the practise of medicine. He took an interest in the formation of the 4-H movement and played a prominent part in the development and growth of that movement in Louisiana and throughout the South.

Dr. John Harcourt Morgan was born at Cherry Grove Farm. He attended S.S. #7 Adelaide and Strathroy High School. He was able to continue his education by preparing calves for the fairs and market, and he attended the Ontario Agricultural College at Guelph and received a B. Sc. in agriculture from the University of Toronto in 1889. He continued graduate work at Cornell University in the U.S. during the next 10 years, while working at the Louisiana State University at Baton Rouge. He aided in the fight to control the boll weevil, then first threatening the southern cotton empire, and worked on new methods of culture in orange groves and also on cattle tick controls. Dr. Morgan once said that he secured his first appointment in Louisiana because he was a Canadian and not a Yankee, and so could be accepted by southerners. He was President of the University of Tennessee from 1919 to 1933. In 1933, he became an original director of the Tennessee Valley Authority and then served as its chairman from 1938 to 1941. He also served on state and federal boards and committees, and received several distinguished awards, including an honourary degree from U.W.O. in 1939. Dr. Morgan was a quiet, unassuming man, humble in disposition. A memorial window was installed at Church Street Methodist Church in Knoxville, where he had taught Sunday School for 40 years. Morgan Hall at University of Tennessee was named after him.

He married Sarah Fay and they had four children, Dr. Harcourt A., John E., Fay, and Dr. Lucy Morgan. Harcourt subscribed to the Strathroy Age Dispatch, and often returned to Adelaide to visit his relatives and friends.

Dr. Norman Morgan, a veterinarian, moved to New Orleans, Louisiana, for his health and lived there the rest of his life. He remained single.

In 1899, Wilber, fifth child of John and Rebecca, married Carrie Jones (d.1944) of Guelph. They had two sons, an unnamed child who died in infancy, and George (1911-1970). Wilber was district superintendent of International Correspondence Schools for several years and was also on the staff of Shaw's Business College in Toronto.

Trueman, eldest child of John and Dora, married Ethel Reid of Aberfoyle, and raised five children, Gerald; Irene (1910-1992); Dorothy (d.1968); Muriel (1918-1997); and Norman (1920-1985). In 1910, Trueman moved to Castor, Alberta, where he raised his family. He worked as a mail carrier and freight agent for 35 years, and maintained a livery stable and implement agency. He served on the local school board and board of trade.

In 1911, Dr. Walter Morgan, third issue of John and Dora, married Flossie Steele in London. They had two children, Jack (1914-1993) and Marion (1885-1921). Walter received his medical degree from the University of Western Ontario and trained in New York. He practised in Arden, Ontario, before serving in France during WWI, as medical officer of the 42nd Battalion. He was wounded and awarded

Portrait of Dr. Alfred E. Morgan, ca.1925

the Military Cross for gallantry under fire. After the war, he practised in Ontario before serving in WWII., as chief of a hospital in St. John, New Brunswick, where he was awarded the efficiency decoration for long service. He retired and died in Belleville. On one occasion, during the first war, he was attending a wounded soldier named Stacey and found out that they were both born on the same farm. Stacey was born in a house at the back of the farm beside the railroad tracks. Stacey's father had rented land at the back and used the railroad bed as ingress and egress, because the Fourth Line road was not much more than a trail.

Meredith, the youngest child of John and Dora, married Ethel Patterson (1886-1967) of Cairngorm, daughter of Andrew and Agnes (Vincent) Patterson. They raised two children, Dorothy (d.2000) and Milo. Meredith was educated at S.S. #7 Adelaide and Strathroy High School. He attended Bliss Electrical School in Washington, D.C., with his friend, Bill Galbraith of Adelaide. After graduation, he worked for the London Power Co. As a hobby, he built and talked on telephones with his friends. He got the idea of building and installing telephones from his cousin, Dr. Alfred Morgan. Meredith got permission from township officials to string wire and poles along the township roads. All the holes were dug by hand. The first switchboard office was a small building on the main street of Kerwood beside the present Odd Fellows hall, on the property now owned by Mrs. Effie Wilson. It was installed by B.L. Balch, of Bell Telephone. The switchboard, which was later moved to a room in Meredith's Kerwood home, was still in use when dial service started in July 1965. Besides the telephone business, Meredith took over his Uncle Samuel's planing mill business. In 1928, Meredith sold the telephone business to William Wadsworth of Mount Brydges and returned to dairy farming. The Morgans were members of the Kerwood United Church and Meredith was a member of the Masonic Lodge, Napier.

Dorothy, daughter of Meredith and Ethel, married Clifford Winter (1909-1975) of Napier, and settled in Kerwood. They had no children. Dorothy was educated at S.S. #7 Adelaide, and Strathroy Collegiate. She worked as a telephone operator for a few years, before dial service, and then at Strathmere Lodge until her retirement. She also worked as a dispatcher for the Kerwood Fire Department. Cliff worked for several years at McLean's Feed Mill and then operated the Adelaide road grader. He also farmed on rented land in Metcalfe Township, and volunteered with the Kerwood Fire Department. Dorothy and Cliff were members of the Kerwood United Church where both served as elders for several terms. Dorothy was a member of the Irene Rebekah Lodge and an active member of the Kerwood Women's Institute, holding the positions of secretary and curator. Dorothy always had an interest in her family and local history, and collected roomfuls of material. She was much sought after to answer questions about the Morgan family and the history of the Kerwood area. She always said that she "will get it all organized one day" but it seems local community events, her little dog, and her cats take up too much time. She contributed a great deal to the Kerwood United Church history and to the history book for Adelaide Township.

Milo, son of Meredith and Ethel, married Mary Higman of Delaware. They raised two children, Susan and Richard. Milo was educated at S.S. #7 Adelaide and Strathroy Collegiate. He worked for Ontario Hydro, Delaware district (now Strathroy), and worked in Northern Ontario. He served for one

Morgan family homestead, Lot 10, Con. 4 SER, ca.1865.

term on the Adelaide council and was an original volunteer with the Kerwood Fire Department. Susan married Donald McLean and they have two children, Kenneth and Rebecca. They live in Strathroy, where Donald works for the Public Utilities Commission. Susan is the treasurer of the Strathroy Hospital Foundation. Richard married Sharon Fluney and they have two sons, Jamie and Shawn. They farm on the original Richard Morgan homestead, and are raising the seventh generation of Morgans in Adelaide. Sharon also works as an accountant at Gray's Egg Grading Business.

In 1871, George, son of Richard Jr. and Catherine, married Elizabeth Cuddy (1845-1931), daughter of Thomas and Esther (Trueman) Cuddy. They had three sons (see MORGAN, George W.).

Matilda, fourth child of Richard Jr. and Catherine, married George Foster (1837-1917), son of Charles and Selina (Parry) Foster. They raised two children, William and Lucy. They farmed in Metcalfe Township.

Richard, fifth issue of Richard Jr. and Catherine, married Elizabeth Orme (1847-1923). They raised four children, Edgar (ca.1874-1962); Sherman (ca.1883-1964); Mae; and Rena, who married a Smibert. Richard farmed on the west half of Lot 9, Con. 4 SER, before moving to London Township.

Catherine, sixth of Richard Jr. and Catherine's children, married John Trueman (1837-1929) of Metcalfe, son of John and Sarah (Smith) Trueman. They raised seven children, L.A., John, Richard, Ernest, Herbert, Lillian and Lena. They farmed in Metcalfe Township.

Samuel, the youngest child of Richard Jr. and Catherine, married Maud Rogers (ca.1856) of England. They raised six children, Richard (1878-1957); Nina (1880-1882); Lillian (1882-1968); Olive (1885); Lance (1888-1982); and Gladys (1893). A story is told that Samuel travelled to England on a cattle boat, perhaps to look after the cattle, and that he met his future bride during his travels. Samuel farmed the east half of the west half of Lot 9, Con. 4 SER, before moving into Kerwood to start a planing mill. The mill made wooden rolling pins, tongues, whiffle trees, etc., for horse-drawn implements. He also conducted a livery barn and coal yard business in Kerwood. Samuel died in Strathroy. His wife and children moved to Pincher Creek, Alberta, and Spokane, Washington.

Richard Morgan family

William (1814-1855), son of Richard Sr. and Jane, married Matilda Patterson (d.1845), daughter of Samuel and Elizabeth Patterson. About 1836, they immigrated to Adelaide from County Mayo, Ireland. They had two sons, Robert (ca.1843-1924) and William Patterson "W.P." (1845-1913). In 1848, after Matilda's death, William married Ann Hanna (ca.1826-1851) of Adelaide Township. The 1852 census records indicate that Ann died of "Erysiptus." They had no children. William's third marriage was to Anne Matthews, daughter of William and Catherine (Slush) Matthews, and they had two children, a son (ca.1853, died an infant) and Mariah (1855-1953).

Fortune didn't appear to favour William. With his first wife, Matilda, he settled on the west half of Lot 8, Con. 5 SER. Little is known about their lives. The first years must have been difficult. It appears that William might have settled in Adelaide before his brothers, Richard and John. Richard was still in Warwick until late 1837. John didn't purchase property until 1841, but might have rented nearby. Also, Matilda's family didn't arrive until about 1839. Several years went by before William and Matilda had two sons, only to have Matilda die shortly after the second birth. William was married to his second wife for three years, and then she died. Family records suggest he married his third wife, Anne Matthews, about 1850, but the 1852 census lists William as a widower. This census also shows that William's sons are living with their maternal grandmother, Eliza Patterson. His third marriage was more likely to have taken place about 1852. Six months after his daughter, Mariah, was born,

William died of appendicitis. The farm was left to William's widow, Anne, then upon her remarriage, was to go to William's son, Robert, and Anne equally. Anne (Matthews) Morgan married James McKenzie (See MATTHEWS).

In 1865, Robert, the eldest son of William and Matilda, married Anne Knight (1841-1906), daughter of Thomas and Susannah (Murdock) Knight. They raised nine children, William; Thomas (ca.1869), who became a doctor; Matilda (ca.1870); Murdock (ca.1873-1935); Granville (1874-1932), who never married; Milton Morgan (1875-1893), who drowned; Herbert (1877-1943); Arthur (1878-1941); and Mabel (ca.1883-1965). When he came of age, Robert received half of his father's farm, the west quarter of Lot 8, Con. 5 SER. He was a lifelong resident of Adelaide.

William, eldest son of Robert and Anne, married Margaret "Nellie" Foster of Kerwood, daughter of Samuel and Margaret (Carson) Foster. They had no children. William remarried, to Jennie Smith (ca.1870-1942), and they raised 10 children, Eva; Milton; Duncan; Georgina; Ralph; William; Marjorie; Edith (1908-1936); Francis; and Malcolm. They resided in Wawanesa, Manitoba.

Lewis and Margaret (Warren) Morgan

In 1898, Dr. Thomas Morgan, M.D., married Ada Whitehouse in London. They raised two children, Harry and Margaret. They lived in New York.

In 1892, Matilda married Thomas Hughes, and they raised three children, Clayton (1898-1905); Kathleen; and Nina. Kathleen married a Stevenson. Nina married into the Lewis family and has a son, Thomas Lewis.

Murdock married Emma Parker (1884-1972) and they raised 10 children, Mabel, Florence, Esther, Bertha, Mamie, Emma, George, Murdock, John and William. Robert went to Manitoba in 1901, where he taught school for about 15 years before engaging in farming.

In 1901, Herbert, seventh issue of Robert and Anne, married Margaret Richardson (1878-1956), daughter of James and Mary Jane (Smithrim) Richardson. They raised five children, Stanley (1902-1982); Dalton (1905-1971); Clayton (1907-1913); James (1908-1959); and Robert (1916-1989). Herb farmed on Lot 9, Con. 2, Metcalfe Township.

In 1938, Robert, the youngest child of Herbert and Margaret, married Kathleen "Kay" Brown (1917-1996), daughter of Russell and Alma (Knight) Brown of Adelaide. They had four children, Robert, Clayton, Evan and Margaret Morgan. Robert farmed in Metcalfe.

Arthur, the eighth of Robert and Anne's children, married Mabel Galloway (1881-1952). They raised one daughter, Gwendolyn. Arthur was a lifelong resident of Adelaide, and took over the operation of his father's farm, part of Lot 8, Con. 5 SER. Gwendolyn married James MacDonald and they raised three children, Suzanne, John and William.

Mabel, the youngest child of Robert and Anne, married James Galbraith. They had no children, and resided in Adelaide, in Crosswell, Michigan, and in Sarnia.

In 1865, W.P., second son of William and Matilda, married Mary Patterson (1846-1919) of Adelaide, daughter of Thomas and Mary (Lighton) Patterson. They raised seven children, William (1866-1950); Minnie (1868-1938); Annie (ca.1872-1934); Laura (1875-1963); Jean (1877-1960); Ira (1880-1953); and Eva (1883-1965), who married Walter Bowley in 1905 (see BOWLEY, Walter and Eva). Family records indicate that William was raised by his maternal grandmother, Eliza Patterson.

W.P. was an honourable gentleman. When he

and Mary Patterson were married, the minister stopped the ceremony to question, "Was William Patterson to be married to Mary Patterson?" The answer was clear, one of the names was spelled with one 'T'. Mary was born in Old Slego, County Connaught, Ireland. William lived his entire life on the same farm, Lot 11, Con. 4 SER, which was named "Meadow Vale Farms." He was treasurer of the township for 15 years. He took an active interest in church work, serving as Steward of the Mt. Zion Methodist Church for 31 years.

William, eldest child of W.P. and Mary, married Martha Bowley (1867-1964) and raised a daughter, Mildred Morgan (1904-1986). William was treasurer of Adelaide for many years. Mildred married Clarence Fuller, son of Albert and Adella (Dowding) Fuller. They had no children.

In 1904, Minnie, second of W.P. and Mary's children, married Austin Carrothers (1863-1954), son of John and Harriet (Bratt) Carrothers. They raised two children, Clayton (1906-1996) and Evelyn (1909).

In 1898, Annie married Frederick Shields in Napperton. They raised four children, Irene (1901); Clifford (1903-1935); Kenneth (1910); and Eva (1911-1989). They moved to Strathroy about 1909, where Annie was an active church worker for the Presbyterian church.

Laura married Frank Hull, son of George and Catherine (Duffy) Hull. They had no children.

In 1912, Jean, fifth issue of W.P. and Mary, married Andrew Kerr in Napperton. They resided in Embro. They had no children.

In 1910, Ira married Gwen Lewis (1885-1954), daughter of George and Phillippa (Inch) Lewis. They raised four children, George (1911-1987); Marjorie; Bev (d.2000); and Lewis (1922-1963).

One morning, while carrying two pails of grain to feed her chickens, Gwen was knocked down from behind by a ram that wanted the grain. Being Anglican and not Methodist, like her husband, she got up and proceeded to compliment the ram in quite colourful language. When she had finished, she heard chuckling noises coming from the silo chute. Apparently, Ira had seen the whole episode. On hearing this, Ira got the same number of compliments as the ram.

In 1940, George, eldest child of Ira and Gwen, married Velma Petch (1912-1990), daughter of Joseph and Adelaide (Humphries) Petch of Adelaide. They raised two children, Sylvia Bernice (1943) and William George "Bill" (1945). They farmed Lot 11, Con. 2 SER, and Lot 6, Con. 5 SER. Velma taught school in Adelaide and Metcalfe. George served as a Board of Education trustee when the Adelaide Central School was built. He also served as an Adelaide councillor.

George went to the Napperton School, which was across from the Currie farm. With some others, George used to wonder at the antics of Arthur Currie's horse, Brock, during a thunderstorm—was it the storm that caused his distress, or was it remembering the battles in Europe during WWI? On one occasion, Irwin Carrothers was visiting George while their wives went shopping. George was left home to baby-sit Sylvia, who was teething at the time, so she was quite irritable. George made frequent trips into another room to quiet the child. Finally, he said, "We'll just have to talk louder," to which Irwin replied, "She should have a full set in the morning."

In 1965, Sylvia married Jim McDougall of Caradoc. They had two children, Brian James (1966) and Kathryn Louise (1970). Sylvia and Jim farmed in Caradoc until they moved to Strathroy. Sylvia is a nurse. In 1992, Brian married Sandra Jones-Harris. They live in Caradoc, where Brian is Flood and Erosion Co-ordinator for the St. Clair Conservation Authority. In 1994, Kathryn married Martin Vander Velden and they live in Vancouver, B.C. Kathy manages a travel agency in Delta, B.C.

In 1970, Bill, son of George and Velma, married Judith Lynne Dowding (1949), daughter of Melvin and Doris (George) Dowding. They have three children, Jacqueline Joy "Jackie" (1972); Kimberly Lynne (1973); and Andrew William (1976). Bill farms the family properties as well as Lot 2, Con. 4 SER. In 1996, Jackie married John Buenen of Shedden, and they live in Chatham, where Jackie works in sales for a roof truss company. In 1995, Kim married Chris Helkaa of Strathroy. Kim and Chris live in Strathroy, where Kim is Parts Sales Representative for a Haggersville truck company. Andrew attends college and works on the home farm.

Marjorie, second child of Ira and Gwen, married Bernard Carstens. They have no children, and live in Ann Arbor, Michigan.

Bev, Ira and Gwen's third child, married Roberta Wyatt, daughter of Lawrence and Melissa (Freele) Wyatt. They raised two sons, James and John. James married Lynda Harris, and they have three sons, Chad, Christopher and Brock. They live in Leamington. John married Joan Bremner, and they have two daughters, Gillian and Kristin. They live in Ilderton.

Lewis, youngest child of Ira and Gwen, married Margaret Warren and raised seven children, Gail, who married a Schoeder; Joan, who married a Daniels; Warren; Brian; David; Ronald; and Donald. Lewis served in WWII. The family lived in Windsor, where Lewis worked for the Toronto-Dominion Bank.

Mariah, daughter of William and Anne, never knew her father, as he died shortly before her birth. When Anne married James McKenzie, Mariah went to live with them. James was a good and kind stepfather and she had six stepsiblings. The family went to Sunday School and church each Sunday. In 1870, Mariah learned over 200 bible verses in Sunday School, for which she received a prize book. She liked school and once even "spelled the school down." She took music lessons and went to London to learn dressmaking. In 1879, Mariah married William McIllmurray (see McELMURRY).

MULLAN, John and Ellen

According to the 1842 Adelaide census, John Mullin (also seen as Mullen or Mullan) had been in Ontario for 10 years. He was located on the west half of Lot 4, Con. 5 NER. In all, he occupied 168 acres with 13 acres improved. That year, 20 bushels of wheat were produced, 15 of oats, 18 of peas, 30 of Indian corn and 100 of potatoes. There are 11 cattle, nine sheep and seven hogs, and 28 yards of flannel and 12 yards of wool were produced.

Land records show that in 1848, James Langan and John Mullan received the Patent for Lot 4, Con. 5 NER, consisting of 126 acres. In 1849, John Mullan and his wife sold 60 acres of the east part to James Langan. In 1850, two acres of the southwest corner of the west part were sold to Daniel Root. A school was built on the west half of Lot 4 and, in the February 25, 1850, township council meeting Minutes, the election for St. Patrick's Ward was to be held in Mullan's School (the first Keyser School). John Dewan was to be returning officer. At the council meeting of January 21, 1850, John Mullan was appointed poundkeeper for Con. 4 and 5 NER.

The 1852 Adelaide census shows that there was a schoolhouse on the property. John Mullan, born in Ireland, a Roman Catholic, is 40, and his wife, Ellen, is also 40. Living in the same household are James Kelly, single, a labourer, born in Canada, 24; Mary Kelly 17, single, Canada; and John Kelly 14. Other residents of the home are Mullan children, born in Canada: Michael 14, Sarah 12, Francis 10, Hannah 9, Bernard 6, Henry 5 and Gregory 3.

In 1853, John Mullan and his wife sold the remaining 64 acres to Abraham Cleminhegg.

Several families who have recently lived on this property believe that a Catholic burial ground was located on the southwest part of the property, where large stones were piled on rough land.

MURDOCK, William and Ann

William Murdock and Anne Boyd married at Foxborough House, Ballybrooney near Ballina, County Mayo, Ireland. Anne was an orphan, raised by her father's brother, Thomas Boyd, in Foxborough. William Murdock was a laborer on the farm next door. About 1838, they came to Canada via Halifax, the voyage taking three months. They were not alone, as many friends from Ireland also came: the Morgan, Patterson and Curry families. They settled in Adelaide Township near Napperton, at Lot 12, Con. 4 SER. They lived on 200 acres, with the Curry and Patterson families living the closest. The families helped each other to clear the land.

William was an only son, but two sisters came to Canada with him and Anne. One was married to a Morgan, the other to a Rankin. Many of the Morgan family settled in Adelaide and Middlesex County, but many went to U.S. and were leaders in agricultural colleges. Some were prominent surgeons, and each one brought credit to their family.

William and Anne had 12 children in all, but we only know the names of nine. Henry married Diana Nelin, and they had 10 children. Isabel married Peter Cranston of Wyoming, and they had four sons. She remarried, to Charles Taylor of Sarnia, and they had four daughters. Mary (1819) was born at Foxborough. She married Thomas Hughes of Kerwood, and they had a daughter, Mary Jane. Sara married James Stanley of Biddulph Township, and they had 11 children. Anne married James Boyle, and they had six children. Jane married George Hanna of Brooke Township, and they had five children. Susanna married Thomas Knight in Ireland and remained there. Elizabeth married James Duncan in Ireland. Ellen, Sara, and William never married. Roseanne died very young. William Thomas (1835-1911) married Rebecca Jane Harvey (1844-1939).

Six of Susanna and Thomas' 10 children came to Canada, Jane, who married Thomas Irving of Watford; Mina, who married James Johnston of Brooke; Ann, who married Robert Morgan; Mabel; Florence; and Ester Irene.

William, the youngest child of William and Anne, met Rebecca Jane Harvey, daughter of Andrew and Abigail Harvey, through a cousin on the Boyd side of the family. Rebecca Jane was born in Windsor, Nova Scotia. When Rebecca Jane was six, the family moved to Vienna, Norfolk County, where her father served as an inspector of schools under the recently appointed Minister of Education, Egerton Ryerson.

William Thomas Murdock (1834-1911) holding Mac Gilmore.

Rebecca Jane had six siblings. Four of them, Eleanor, Sarah, Leander and Albert became medical doctors and practised in Watford and Wyoming. Elizabeth Hunter married William Henry Bolton of Kerwood (see BOLTON, Richard and Frances). Enoch moved to Michigan to farm.

William and Rebecca Jane were married in 1863 in Vienna. Rebecca Jane was asked to teach school the first year that she lived in Adelaide Township. They lived with William and Anne Murdock for about a year, while they built a house.

William and Rebecca Jane had seven children, Roseanne (1864); Mary Abigail (1867-1869); Helena Adelaide (1870-1874); William Harvey (1872-1874); Jessie Ann (1874-1948); Sara Alice (d.1928), who married Dr. Jack Armstrong of Alvinston; and Frederica (1881-1899). Helena and William died of scarlet fever, five days apart, and Rebecca Jane was hysterical with grief for weeks.

William was the reeve of Adelaide Township for nine consecutive years; at the end of his terms, he was given a gold watch and chain. William became tired of farming and sold his holdings. The family moved to Strathroy. There, William collaborated with G.W. Ross, and they built a block of stores called Ross-Murdock Block.

Eventually William moved his family to London, where he became the farm manager at London Psychiatric Hospital. He started having the residents help with the farming operations, a new idea for the hospitals of Ontario.

Roseanne, the eldest child of William and Rebecca Jane, became a teacher. She married John Douglas of Adelaide in 1891. John lived at Lot 22 Con. 2 SER, where Mac Cuddy later started Cuddy Farms. The Douglas family took in students from Adelaide to allow them to attend Strathroy District Collegiate.

Roseanne and John had two daughters, Hazel and Leila Isabel. Hazel also taught school in Adelaide Township.

Jessie Ann, the fifth child of William and Rebecca Jane, taught school in Adelaide for a year and then attended the University of Western Ontario, becoming one of the first two women graduates in 1900. The next year, she attended Toronto Normal School, and then taught school in Windsor for a year. She married Rev. George Gilmore. Jessie received an Honoree Doctor of Laws in 1948 from

The University of Western Ontario. Three of her children also graduated from U.W.O.

Many members of the Murdock family are buried in the Fourth Line Cemetery.

Some Murdock cousins remain in County Mayo, farming the same land in a beautiful farming area. Barb Bolton visited the area, and saw the house called Foxborough, soon to be torn down. They also saw the Ballybrooney Manor House, but did not get in. Someday, they hope to return for a longer visit.

The following account is an excerpt of a 55-page manuscript written in 1945 by Jessie Ann Murdock. Her granddaughter, Barb Bolton, questions some of the exact locations referred to in the story. Jessie was a good friend to Sir Arthur Currie, and a letter he wrote to her is in the Military Museum in St. Thomas. From *Through The Years,* by Jessie Murdock Gilmore:

"Adelaide Township was to be known as a unique settlement because of its type of settlers. A group from England joined the nucleus of Irish inhabitants, and among them all, town planning became a lively topic of conservation. They intended to build an opera house where the treasures of music would be available. Others felt that a club would provide cultural and social advantages. For the first few seasons, however, nothing mattered so much as to conquer the forest for the construction of homes, and to clear and till the unyielding earth. William Thomas Murdock was born in 1835, so everything was a real adventure to him. Anne loved music and would sing the old Erin songs. Tommy, as he was called, was soon joining her, and John Currie taught him to clog dance. He also loved to visit his grandmother Patterson who would tell him tales of Leprechauns that lived in the moors back home. "Tales or tunes are none better nowhere than in ould Ireland, my son, and don't you ever forget it."

Tremendous effort and adventures were reaping their rewards for our pioneers. Where once their cabin stood among dark and forbidding forest trees, now it was in sunlit clearing. There were fields of grain, a small orchard, a plot of green vegetables, and even flowerbeds. William was particularly interested in cattle, and had acquired a small herd of Shorthorns, three good horses and some pigs. Anne found time to care for the chickens and a few fat geese, so that the larder should have eggs and sometimes a bird for the table. Truly, as William said, the Lord had prospered all their undertakings, and they were happy.

Community life was not lacking in Adelaide, because the settlers made no pretense of living to themselves. The club and the opera house had never been realized, but a school and a church were in operation. Tommy Murdock attended the little log school for six months of the year, learning to read, spell, write and figure in a decidedly proficient manner. The school provided a meeting place for an occasional social and for worship on Sunday. Political meetings all took place at this sanctum of learning, upon which occasion all the eloquence and wit of these sons of Blarney came into play. Politics were keenly alive and hotly contested to the huge enjoyment of the settlers and the very definite benefit of the district.

Next door to the school property lived the Rapleys. David Rapley was a huge man with a remarkable tenor voice and two crippled legs, crushed by a falling tree in the first years in Canada. Anne told him, with evident wistfulness, of her love of music and lack of the instrument. Whereupon a plan took shape in David's mind that music should be a worthy part in this community, even without instruments. Accordingly, it was "given out" on Sunday that anyone desiring to join a choral society should come to the Rapleys' on Friday night. Nine people came. The next week the group numbers were twelve, and from that time David Rapley's Singing School played a wonderful part in the neighbourhood. It provided a choir for Sabbath day services; it was the background of all entertainments, and it meant pleasure and profit to every participant.

David Rapley died the second winter of his singing school. Illness came and became acute within hours, so his great voice was heard no more. The friends and neighbours gathered for David's funeral. He was to rest in a small plot of land owned and cleared by his son, William. When the service was over, William stood forth in the group and made an announcement.

"My friends," he said, "we are here today as a tribute of respect to your friend and my beloved father. You all know how his unfortunate accident crippled his activities. Yet he overcame his impediment to use his fine voice as a means of pleasure and

instruction in this settlement, still in its infancy. I know you wish to accord him an honoured place in your memories. Therefore I have decided to give this plot of land to the community as a resting-place for those who, like my father, have ceased from their labours. This land shall be the property of our church, and remain in our midst as a memorial to the pioneers in Adelaide Township."

There near the school and close to the Fourth Line road, was consecrated the first cemetery of the township. David Rapley's grave was almost a shrine in their midst for long years for those who had loved to hear his voice.

The Murdocks' youngest daughter was Roseanne. She was the delight of the family, but one day she fell ill with a high fever. Despite all efforts she died. Anne was stricken numb. So Roseanne Murdock, the darling of the house, went to a quiet spot in the graveyard where David Rapley lay.

Anne never recovered from the loss of her baby. She went about her duties as usual, but she never sang anymore. William watched her anxiously, and decided that a new interest must come quickly. A new house was to be built. Anne never showed great enthusiasm about the new home. William Thomas went to choir practice on Friday nights now, and William realized that he was growing up rapidly. William spoke to Anne that "We must have more young folks about now. Tommy must learn to be nice to the colleens."

So a Christmas dance was arranged.

With prodigal hand Anne sacrificed her finest fowls, and for days spicy odours of Christmas baking filled the house. Anne's cooking had long since become a fine art; her shortbreads, mincemeat and fruitcake were delicious to the last morsel. William Thomas and his father went back with the team to the woodlot for evergreens to trim the sunny rooms, and popped corn in great clusters to festoon a tree in the hall.

The party was a great success. William Thomas proved a capable host, dancing with the shy girls, joking with the saucy ones, and leading some carol singing in a strong clear baritone that reflected some credit upon Anne's training. Anne and William watched him with pride. What they saw pleased them and both wished that Uncle Boyd might have seen this boy, born in the Old World and reared in the new. Uncle Boyd was at rest with his fathers in a country churchyard back home, but name and memory were with the Murdocks almost daily."

MURRAY, James and Catherine

James Murray (1801) and Catherine Davidson (1807-1854) were born in Comber, County Down, near Belfast, Ireland, and were married in 1829.

In 1832, they immigrated to Canada with Catherine's parents, Nathaniel and Jane (Donaldson) Davidson, and Catherine's nine siblings. They had heard that Canada was a land of opportunity, where everyone who was willing to work could make a home and own a farm of his own.

They arrived in Quebec in the summer of 1832 in the midst of a cholera outbreak. After they received clearance to leave Quebec, they made their way by boat and wagon westward to Mount Royal,

Four generations picture. L-R, Eileen Trott holding Peter, Rebecca Murdock and Jessie Gilmore.

then to Kingston, and finally to the village of Cobourg. They resided close to a friend who had immigrated earlier and had written glowing reports of life in Canada.

Soon after their arrival, James and Catherine, with her sister, Eleanor, and John Wiley, worked a farm near Cobourg. They heard reports of good farmland in the newly surveyed Township of Adelaide, which would be better than the stony land they were farming.

In 1834, they left Cobourg, took the steamboat to Hamilton, and walked the rest of the way. They carried their most precious belongings and each couple had a small child. After weeks of travel, they reached London. When they arrived in Adelaide, they discovered there was a log shanty on one farm, but the other was completely wooded. They spent their first few nights in the shanty. With help, the young men erected a log cabin on each farm before winter settled in.

James and Catherine had seven children, Robert (1830), who was born in Ireland; James (1833); Elizabeth "Betsy" (1838-1919); Jane (1839-1887), who married William Brent; Ann (1841); Mary (1843-1868); and Eleanor (Ellen) "Nellie" (1849). The last six were born in Adelaide. Following Jane's death, William and his sons went to Stoughton, Saskatchewan, where he is buried. The exodus from Middlesex County to Saskatchewan was in the early 1900s, when travel was by covered wagon and train. Ann married James Lynn and lived in Glencoe. Mary married Joseph Keyser and lived at Keyser's Corners.

Catherine died from Black Diphtheria at 47 years of age. She is buried on the site of the log shanty in which they spent their first few nights in Adelaide.

James was a tax collector. He participated in the formation of the first chapel of West Adelaide United Presbyterian Church. Several church services were held in the home of James Murray before the completion of the church. Although there are no records available, it is believed that he is buried beside Catherine.

Betsy married Patrick Murray (1828) on April 20, 1852. He was born in Antrim County near Belfast, Ireland, immigrating at age 21 and settling in Adelaide. In the 1851 census, Patrick lived and worked with James Murray. Betsy and Patrick were married by Rev. Howden at the home of her parents.

According to the diary of a neighbour, John Jamieson, "The weather was cold and rainy from the east. They had a half-pleasant night of singing and joking. All the party seemed happy and merry."

They farmed at Lot 5, Con. 4 NER. He served for more than 20 years as a councillor, and for a number of terms he was Adelaide's representative at the county council. In 1882, Patrick and his brother-in-law, Joseph Keyser, sold the land for S.S. #1 and #2 Adelaide and West Williams. Patrick and Betsy gave the property adjacent to the school where the Salem Methodist Church was built. Patrick Murray, Nathaniel Davidson and Joseph Keyser were the school trustees.

Patrick and Betsy had eight children, Annie (1853-1856); Catherine (1854-1856); Mary Isabelle (1855-1856); Elizabeth (1858-1872); James Albert (1862-1939); George Washington (1865-1943); John Thomas (1867-1947); and Melissa Jane (1873-1942). Annie, Catherine and Mary Isabelle died of Black Diphtheria. These three and Elizabeth are buried beside their grandmother, Catherine, in the Pioneer Cemetery on Egremont Road. The last four children are buried in Arkona Cemetery.

When Melissa was two years old, the family moved from their log cabin to a new brick farmhouse that was built on the same farm. Family stories are told of putting Melissa in one of the dresser drawers to take her to their new house. Betsy and Patrick are buried in Arkona Cemetery.

John Thomas married Emma Isobel Chalcraft (1869) on April 3, 1895. They had six children, Earl, Ada, Norman, Irene, Geo, Stanley and Ivy Mable (1908-1992).

Ivy attended Keyser's School. She worked in London. She met William Everett "Ev" Herrington (d.1970) and they were married on August 4, 1941. They lived in Windsor after being married, and Ev was in the roofing business there.

Their first son, William John "Bill" (1945), was born in Windsor. On September 24, 1946, Ev and Ivy moved to the old Patrick Murray farm, which they had bought from Ivy's father. Ev and Ivy farmed this property, raising cattle and grain crops. Ev also did some roofing and ran a business selling farm fence, grain bins, etc.

The second son of Ev and Ivy, James Ivan (1948), was born at Strathroy Hospital. Even with all the hard work done during the day, the couple

L-R, Ada, Earl, Irene and Norman Murray (in front), eldest children of John T. Murray.

still enjoyed getting out to the local dances on weekends, where Ev did the calling for square dances. Ev and Ivy took their two young sons to the dances, as did many of the other parents. Thanks to their early introduction to country music, the boys learned to dance almost as soon as they did to walk.

As the boys grew and went on to school, first at Keyser's, Adelaide, and then to high school in Strathroy, they continued to help on the family farm. Ev began to custom farm, doing baling, swathing, combining, etc., for area farmers. The boys were kept busy most evenings and weekends with the custom work. Ivan says the smell of cut hay still brings back memories of blisters and sore muscles. Both boys were active in Junior Farmers at this time, and Ivan was pitching fastball. In 1965, Ev bought each of the boys a new Pontiac for helping out with the farming operation. For the next four years, both cars made a lot of trips south on the Kerwood Road. Ivan travelled to County Rd. 39 to the Richardson farm, while Bill went to Cairngorm to visit at the Smithrim home.

On August 9, 1969, Bill married Gayle Louise Smithrim, daughter of Mac and Margaret Smithrim, at Cairngorm United Church. On October 11 of the same year, Ivan married Marilyn Louise Richardson, daughter of Ken and Leila Richardson, at Kerwood United Church. Sadly, just a short time before the weddings, Ev was diagnosed with cancer. He endured many painful treatments, which proved unsuccessful. Ev died at the age of 63.

Bill went to work for the Bank of Nova Scotia, so he and Gayle moved with the bank to several homes for the next few years. While in Hamilton, their first daughter, Deborah Gayle "Debbie" (1973), was born at Henderson Hospital. Their second daughter, Diana Lynn (1975), was born at St. Mary's Hospital in Timmins. Debbie and Diana attended public and high school in Gravenhurst.

Ivan and Marilyn built a new home on the northeast corner of the farm, and they both worked for Brown Brothers in Arkona. Ivan worked the family farm and sold fencing, and drove a truck for Brown Brothers. After juggling three jobs for a time, he decided to quit the fence business and farming, and drive the truck full-time. Ivy rented the farm to Frank Verheyen, who raised cash crops on it for the next few years. He eventually purchased it in March 1989.

In 1987, Ivy decided to move to Orchard View Seniors' Apartments in Arkona. Ivan and Marilyn sold their home and moved into the old family home for the next two years. Ivy suffered a stroke while living in Arkona and, after being hospitalized, she moved into Strathmere Lodge. She resided there until her death.

Ivan and Marilyn built a new home, north of Grand Bend, in 1989. Marilyn continued to work in Arkona, and Ivan went to work for Hensall Co-op. In 1998, they sold this home and bought a new house in Grand Bend.

Bill became a bank manager in Gravenhurst, and worked there for a number of years while Debbie and Diana were in school. They decided they wanted to make Gravenhurst their permanent home so, rather than move again, Bill left the Bank of Nova Scotia and went to work for Gryvet Motors in Bracebridge, where he is still employed.

After completing high school, Debbie attended school at Wilfred Laurier, where she graduated with the Governor General's Academic Medal in Honours Bachelor of Science. She then completed her Masters degree in Waterloo. Debbie is now enrolled in Perdu University in Indiana, working on her PhD. Diana enrolled at Guelph University after high school, where she played basketball on the University Basketball Team. She graduated with the W.C. Winegard Medal in Honours Biological Science. Diana is now completing her studies at McMaster University and will receive her certification as a Physiotherapist in the fall of 1999.

James Albert Murray married Ann Eliza Stevens (1864-1936), daughter of John Stevens and Mary Jane (Sharpe) of Adelaide. Their marriage took place at the home of the bride's parents on September 30, 1885, by Rev. Dixon Sharpe, the bride's uncle. Annie was born in Lobo Township and came to Keyser with her parents in 1876. Albert and Annie spent all of their married life on the farm at Lot 5, Con. 5 NER. The house they lived in was built by Patrick Duggan, one of the Irish settlers on the Fourth Line North, who later moved to Michigan.

Albert and Annie had four children, Wilbert (1886-1963); Lorne Stanley (1888-1946); Minnie (1899-1956); and Hazel (1901-1930). Wilbert married Harriett Alberta Bennett (1891-1968) on December 14, 1910 at Parkhill Methodist Church. Harriett was the daughter of Luther Bennett, and her paternal grandparents were Rodney and Harriett (Hanna) Bennett of McGillivray. Wilbert and Harriett lived near Keyser's Corners, and had six children, Elmer Oral (1912-1990); Lawrence Arthur "Art" (1914-1974); Wilfred Austin (1916-1993); Marjorie Myrtle (1918); Harriet Mildred (1927); and William Albert "Bill" (1931).

Elmer, the eldest child of Wilbert and Harriett, was born in Adelaide Township, and lived near Keyser's Corner on County Road 6 with siblings Arthur, Wilfred, Marjorie, Mildred and Bill.

Elmer joined the Canadian Army in 1942 and was stationed in Newfoundland. In 1943, he left the army and joined the R.C.A.F. in Calgary until the war was over in 1945.

Elmer married Dorothy Donaldson in 1942. They had six children, Orla, who lives in Lucan; Lynn, who lives in Strathroy; Jean, who lives in Virgil; Ila, who lives in Bramalea; Jacqueline, who lives in Aylmer; and David, who lives in Sarnia.

In 1946, Elmer bought a farm, Lot 8, Con. 4 NER, now called Langon Drive. He lived there with Dorothy for 31 years and then sold the farm. Elmer bought four acres of land in 1977 on Lot 7, Con. 5 NER, and built a house on the property. This lot was sold and in 1987, they moved to Orchard View Apartments in Arkona.

Elmer is buried in Arkona Cemetery with his grandparents, parents, uncles, aunts, and brothers, Arthur and Wilfred.

Art, the second child of Wilbert and Harriet, married Alice Cochrane of Warwick Township. They moved from Watford to the home farm in 1946, when their son, Blair, was five years old and their daughter, Dianne, was three years old. A third daughter, Barbara (1948), was born in Adelaide Township.

Blair remembers the outhouse, oil lamps and the oil kitchen range. He was walking home from S.S. #1 and #2 Adelaide and West Williams in 1952, when the hydro poles were being installed. He recalls that Evan Stead wired the house and barn. Turning on the first switch was very exciting, as was getting the first milking machine.

Art built the first 2-storey chicken barn (30'x50') in 1957 with just a handsaw. At the same time, he started an egg pick-up service in a 1952 Chevrolet ½-ton. He delivered to Huctwith in Forest, and later to Tiffin's in London (King Street). During the summer holidays, Blair drove a 1955 Fargo two-ton truck. He and his sisters put together many of the 30-dozen cardboard egg boxes each week. They discontinued the egg business about 1960.

In 1963, Blair moved home to farm and bought the property in 1964. In 1965, he married Elizabeth Gardiner from Glencoe. When they moved to the farm, his parents and Barbara moved to Arkona. Dianne was married by this time.

Lorne and Edna (McInroy) Murray and daughter, Doris (Murray) Robotham, at Keyser's Corners, 1933.

In the early 1970s, Blair, Elizabeth, and their two sons, Kevin and Paul, moved to Arkona after selling the farm to Joe and Johanna Minten.

Wilfred Austin, Wilbert and Harriet's third child, married Mary Kathleen "Kay" Pennington, the daughter of John Leslie and Beatrice B. (Conkey) Pennington, on October 13, 1945. They moved to one of the Murray farms near Keyser and then to a farm owned by their uncle, John McDonald, on the Adelaide townline. They looked after John until his death. They farmed during the first 10 years of their marriage.

In 1955, the farm was sold and the family moved to a home on Adelaide Street in Strathroy. Wilfred and Kay had two children, John Alan (1950) and Janice Ann (1952).

They operated a City Service business and variety store, which they enlarged. It was a seven-day-per-week business, and they sold it several years later.

Wilfred was then employed by C.I.L. in public relations and sales in the Chatham district. They moved back to Strathroy in 1966, with Wilfred still employed by C.I.L. He purchased the Richardson Mill in Kerwood, which burned a few years later. A small, more efficient mill was built and opened in 1971 as C.I.L. Agromart-Murray's Farm Supply Ltd. After several years, this mill was purchased by another company.

Wilfred continued to work in Agra business with Brown Brothers in Arkona until his retirement. He had an adventurous spirit and each move was to his advantage. He enjoyed music very much and sang in West Adelaide's choir as well as in St. Andrew's in Strathroy, and at many social events. Another of his talents was carpentry, from houses to furniture.

Kay worked in ladies fashion stores, enjoyed sales and meeting the public, and made many good friends from this work.

John Alan married Nancy Elizabeth Herrington (1952) on February 25, 1972, at the West Adelaide Presbyterian Church. Nancy's parents are Grant McKenzie and Eileen Herrington. Alan and Nancy have a daughter, Melissa Kay Eileen (1977).

On November 1, 1978, Alan and Nancy established Murray House of Flowers in Arkona, a full-service retail flower shop in the two front rooms of their home. In 1984, they decorated the rest of the rooms in the house and invited customers to tour the home decorated for Christmas. In 1988, they purchased another retail flower shop in Forest, Flowers With Flair, and in 1996, they changed the name to Murray's Christmas House and closed the Arkona flower shop. They moved from the residence to have the Christmas store open for 300 days each year.

Janice Ann is a Registered Practical Nurse and a Music For Young Children teacher. The music program, which began in Ottawa in 1980, has grown worldwide and is endorsed by composers, conservatories, child specialists and music examiners.

Janice married Stuart Kettlewell, who works in a family business called Kettlewell Insurance and Real Estate. As a young person, he won awards in swimming and became a skilled pilot. They were divorced in 1996.

Janice and Stuart have three children, Laura Ann (1976); Murray Stuart (1979); and Carolyn Janice (1981). Laura earned the nickname "Blur" for her running abilities, which led her to become a great soccer and field hockey player. Her creative abilities and glowing personality took her to George Brown College in Toronto in the Fashion Design Program. Murray became a good boxer and an articulate sketcher, and has earned a private pilot's license. Carolyn did well in gymnastics and is creative in art. She enjoys being part of group planning for events such as the school prom. She works at Kenn's Printing and Cool Cucumber in Strathroy.

In August 2000, Janice remarried, to Mickey Prohaszka (1952). He played hockey and won many awards. He is now a licensed mechanic for Coldstream Concrete. His son, Chad Edward (1982), graduated from high school and now works with his father.

Marjorie Myrtle, fourth child of Wilbert and Harriett, attended Westervelt Business College in London. This led to positions with a grocery broker and a lawyer. While living in London, she met James Thomas Hill (1921) of Thorndale on a blind date. They were married one year and three months later, on June 26, 1943, in West Adelaide Church. Marjorie and James had five children, Murray Thomas (1945-1992); Glenna Yvonne (1948); Marjorie Patricia (1950); Debra Lynn (1956); and Douglas James (1961).

Murray married Linda Jean Chamings (1949) on August 9, 1969, and they divorced in 1989.

Marjorie Patricia married Glenn Edward Meadows (1947). They have three children, Andrew Glenn (1975); Erin Patricia (1977); and Lyndsay Ann (1985).

Debra married Dr. Frederick Neil MacKinnon (1960) on May 26, 1984. They have four children, Kara Lorraine (1987); Caileigh Rachelle (1989); James Edward Murray (1992); and Katherine Allena (1994).

Douglas married Karen Ann (1962, last name not mentioned) on November 21, 1982. Their three children are Tyler Douglas (1992); Jason Murray (1994); and Nicole Ann (1998).

Harriett Mildred, fifth child of Wilbert and Harriett, married Ivan Carrothers in 1945. They lived in Strathroy, Sarnia and London for 23 years. In 1977, she remarried, to Gordon Pond (d.1994) of London. Mildred received her Registered Nursing Certificate in 1969. She worked in London, for one year at St. Joseph's Hospital and 18 years at Victoria Hospital.

Mildred and Ivan had two children, Dennis Ivan (1946) and James Bradley (1950). Dennis became a Presbyterian Minister and lived in London. His children are David Ivan, who is studying architectural engineering; Jennifer Whitney, who is studying to be a customs officer at Niagara College; and Kathryn Elizabeth, who attends high school in St. Catherines. Bradley does landscaping in London and Port Stanley. His son, Jason Bradley, is a welder in St. Thomas. Jason has four sons, Jonathon, James, Justin and Jacob. Bradley's daughters are Kelly Ann and Julie.

Bill, the youngest child of Wilbert and Harriett, was born in Strathroy Hospital, when a total cost for a 10-day stay for mother and baby was $46 (when Mildred was born, the cost had been $42 for an 11-day stay).

Bill attended Keyser's Public School S.S. #1 and #2, and West Williams. His teacher in Grade 7 was Mary Ellen Paterson. The teacher told Bill and a classmate, Marjorie Hoffner, that if they tried hard, they might be able to take Grade 7 and 8 in one year. Bill feels that the credit is due to the teacher that he and Marjorie graduated the end of that year.

Bill attended Strathroy High School for a short time and then went to work with his brother-in-law, James Hill. Jim bought 50 acres of bush in what was known as the "Dorchester Swamp." They worked at cutting logs, wood, hydro poles and fence posts, etc.

Sometimes, he hauled logs to London to a sawmill to have them cut into lumber, and then he would haul the lumber to the London Airport. The truck he drove was a 1936 International with a stake body and hoist. He was just 15 and lacked a driver's license, but it didn't seem to matter in those days. The lumber was used to crate Anson bomber airplanes so that they could be put on flat rail cars and shipped by boat to England. When Bill turned 16 years of age, he borrowed James' car and drove to Ingersoll to get his driver's license. The examiner had him back out of a parking spot, drive around one town block, and then park in the same spot. He issued the license, and then Bill went across the street to the police station to have the Police Chief sign it. Shortly after this, Bill bought his first truck. It was a 1941 Ford short wheelbase, which reared up almost every time he spread a load of gravel.

Shortly before this, Wilbert had opened a gravel pit on the 50-acre farm he owned on the north half of the south half of Lot 7, Con. 4. The county used this gravel for roadwork. Bill hauled gravel from this pit to driveways, etc. At that time, he didn't have a loader, so he shoveled the loads onto the truck. After a year, he bought a new 1949 Ford dump truck. The price was $3,600, purchased from Carrothers Bros. Ford Dealership in Strathroy, which was situated where the liquor store is now. After two years, he bought a new Chevrolet truck, which he used for more than two years. He began hauling new cars to Alberta and Saskatchewan, driving a truck owned by Bob Bullock of Arkona. Bob had the trucks with Dominion Auto Carriers from Windsor. They were hauling Ford and Chrysler cars and International trucks, which were made in Chatham.

Bill met Doris Park from Parkhill, then working as a waitress in Frank's Grill in Parkhill. Later, she worked as a checkout clerk at Grant Pollock's I.G.A. store in Parkhill.

In 1954, when Bob Bullock quit the car hauling business, Bill went to work for Ken Pascoe of Parkhill. He hauled eggs from the grading station in Parkhill to various points in Quebec. Often, he had to deliver to private retailers in many parts of Montreal. He hauled seed grain from Stewart's in Ailsa Craig to points in Michigan and Indiana. At the end of September, he hauled to the southern U.S., taking turnips from Hensall to Georgia, Florida and Alabama. As a return load, he hauled grapefruit, oranges and vegetables to a chain of grocery stores and wholesale outlets in southern Ontario. If loads to the south were scarce, he hauled a load or two of baled hay to Florida for horse feed at the racetracks.

On September 29, 1956, Bill and Doris were married by Rev. John Barrett in the United Church in Parkhill. They moved a house onto the home farm. Bill and Doris have two daughters, Brenda Jean (1956) and Bonnie Lee (1961).

In the fall of 1959, Bill bought a truck from a man in Lambeth, which was connected with Leamington Transport. He was hauling freight from various points in Ontario to Winnipeg. A Leamington Transport rule was that two drivers were needed because a lot of miles were driven in a short time. Every trip had its own highlights. Bill's job kept him away from home for days and sometimes weeks at a time, so eventually Bill sold the transport and went back to the gravel and excavating business.

In 1975, Brenda married Joe McLeod and moved to Strathroy, where Joe works for Superior Propane (he has been employed there for 24 years). They have two children, Tammy Lee (1977) and Chad William Donald (1978).

In May 1978, Jeff and Mary Maes moved from Holland to Canada on their honeymoon trip. Jeff started working with Bill in June 1978. In 1979, they supplied all of the backfill for the sewer contract for the Town of Parkhill. More help was required. A neighbour, Morley Carson, operated the rubber-tired, four-wheel-drive loader, loading a fleet of as many as fourteen tractor-trailer dump trucks every day from 6:00 a.m. to 6:00 p.m. for about four months. That year was very busy. In 1983, Jeff bought the business and later, he bought the property. In 1982, Bill started working for Adelaide Township as Road Superintendent.

In 1984, Bonnie married Michael Vanos from Arkona. Michael owned and operated a service station with a lunchroom, until he sold it in 1988. Michael and Bonnie, along with his father, Tony, then built and operated an 18-hole golf course on their property, Arkona Fairways. Bonnie and Michael have three daughters, Katie Lee (1987); Shaina Lynn (1990); and Rebecca Jean (1993).

Bill retired from the township on August 31, 1996. In November 1998, Bill and Doris moved into Strathroy on Carroll Street.

Lorne Stanley, the second child of Albert and Annie, married Edna Bernice McInroy (1896-1975) on July 19, 1930. Edna was the daughter of Charles Edward McInroy and Mary Jane "Jennie" Ingham of Adelaide. They were married at the home of the bride's mother by Rev. George T. Watts of Strathroy United Church. They lived and farmed the same farm where Lorne was raised, Lot 5, Con. 5 NER. They had one daughter, Doris Alberta (1933).

Lorne grew wheat, corn, oats, barley and hay. Grain was taken to the mill to be ground into chop for the horses and cattle. He had an apple orchard and sold his fruit at the Sarnia Market, and to customers at the farm. The rich sandy loam of this farm produced sweet and sour cherries, black and red currants, rhubarb, horseradish roots, early and late strawberry crops, and a variety of vegetable crops. Edna preserved fruit and made pickles, jams and jellies. Root vegetables were stored in the cool basement as there was no furnace. The farm had chickens, laying hens, geese, ducks, turkeys, and even bantam roosters.

Threshing day was an exciting time. The big threshing machine, operated by John and Orville Hodgson, would come rolling in the lane. Edna was busy baking pies and cakes, and cooking big roasts with lots of potatoes and vegetables. The coal oil stove with its oven in the back kitchen was kept very

Doris and Bill Murray

busy and hot. It was a disaster if it rained, because there was no refrigeration, only the cool cellar to keep food chilled.

One very hot summer day in the early 1940s, the neighbour's hired man was using a tractor at the edge of the field, and a spark from the tractor landed in the dry grass. The hired man thought he had it stamped it out and drove away. The fire smoldered as it crept in the grass to Lorne's fence, into his dry grass, and then into the bone-dry, ready-to-harvest wheat field. The fire roared as it made a wide swath straight for Lorne's barn and all the buildings, including the house. One long ring on the telephone brought friends, neighbours and family, who could only stand helplessly by as the fire raged. A few hundred yards from the barn, the wind changed to the north and the fire sped to the roadway, where it burned itself out.

The fish peddler came to the farm from Port Franks with his fresh fish to sell, and the bread man from Birnam came in his truck filled with loaves of bread, fruit loaves and buns, with sweet, sticky icing. Traveling salesmen from Fuller Brush and Watkins usually came once a year peddling their wares. Their goods were excellent quality.

The house was heated by wood and coal. The coal man came regularly through the winter to dump coal into the coal bin in the basement and, later, in a corner in the back kitchen.

Hydro was installed in 1938. Three farms in a mile had to sign before the lines were installed down the road to provide electricity.

The farm also sold eggs, and when the hens were finished laying, they were sold to Ted Meadows from Arkona. The baby chicks needed lots of feed, water and heat to keep them alive and thriving in the colony house.

Even with their busy farm lives, Lorne and Edna found time to participate in community and church life. Lorne belonged to Arkona Masonic Lodge 307, was a member of Court Keyser No. 1295, and The Canadian Order of Foresters. He was a school trustee of S.S. #1 and #2 Adelaide and West Williams and, at the time of his death, was a councillor in Adelaide. He was a school trustee in 1945 when the school joined Adelaide Township School Area.

Edna belonged to Irene Rebekah Lodge #226 Kerwood, and was a member of Keyser Women's Institute, as well as the women's group at West Adelaide Presbyterian Church. With her busy schedule, Edna still always found time to crochet, do needlepoint and tat. Several pieces graced their home, but many were given to family and friends as gifts. She made aprons and housedresses for herself, and clothes for Doris. Embroidered articles were in abundance around their home.

Lorne enjoyed carpentry. He made twig chairs, fern stands and spool whatnots. He also kept busy repairing farm equipment.

With severe winter road conditions, the mode of transportation was horse and sleigh or cutter. Frisky horses raced over the snow, creating a challenge between driver and horse. Heated bricks wrapped in newspaper where their feet rested, and a buffalo robe over their knees, kept passengers warm. It was a thrilling experience with the horse kicking up snow in the passengers' faces. One severe winter, when Lorne was ill, Edna travelled by team and sleigh with Norman Murray across the fields as the roads were snow-clogged. They went to Arkona to get supplies for the house, and feed for the cattle and fowl, as no trucks could get through the roads for the entire winter.

Lorne and Edna are both buried in Arkona Cemetery.

Doris married George David Robotham (1919), son of David Whiting and Kate Elizabeth (Pulling) Robotham of Adelaide. They were married on July 16, 1977, by Rev. John B. Barrett in Strathroy United Church. They have no children, but George has a son, William George (1958), from a previous marriage, and two grandsons, David William Earl (1990) and Jamie John Charles (1993). Doris was raised on the home farm and attended S.S. #1 and #2 Adelaide and West Williams, and then S.D.C.I. She walked to the store in Keyser's to meet the Kerwood bus, driven by Bruce Evans. School days were long—she left home at 7:30 a.m. and returned after 5:00 p.m. In the winter, it was dark for both walks. She attended the London Normal School, the last of the Normalites.

Doris began a very rewarding teaching career in Colborne Street Public School in Strathroy in September 1953, and took early retirement in June 1984 after 31 years in the profession. She and Edna moved to Strathroy in October 1953.

Doris enjoyed childhood on the farm in

L-R, Lorne, Minnie and Wilbert Murray, the three eldest children of Albert and Annie Murray, ca.1900.

Adelaide. Feeding the calves, gathering eggs while trying to keep out of the way of a cross rooster, cleaning eggs (not a favourite task), picking fruit, grinding horseradish roots with lots of tears, making taffy on top of the snowbanks, walking behind the cattle being driven to the creek at Keyser's when the farm water table was low, and whirling the separator handle to separate cream from milk was lots of fun.

Doris was a member of several 4-H projects. She was involved in the life of West Adelaide Presbyterian church by singing in the choir, playing the piano in the Sunday School and attending the Young People's Group.

In 1966, Edna and Doris sold Lot 7, Con. 4 NER, their pasture farm at Keyser's Corners, where bricks were made at Keyser brickyard in the early 1900s. It was purchased by Blair Murray, a great-great-grandson of John Stevens, who had initially willed the property to his daughter, Annie Murray, then to her son, Lorne. Doris and George reside in Strathroy.

Minnie, third issue of Albert and Annie, married Thomas Valentine Ridley (1896-1974). They lived on a farm in Warwick Township, and had no children. Both are buried in Arkona Cemetery.

Hazel, Albert and Annie's youngest child, died at 29 years of age, which brought great sadness to her parents as it was just two months before Lorne and Edna's wedding. She is buried in Arkona Cemetery.

MUXLOW, Edwin and Harriett

Edwin Muxlow (1858) was born in Gosberton, Lincolnshire, England, one of 10 children of Thomas and Mary (Wilkinson) Muxlow. He immigrated to Canada in 1873 with his brothers, Isaac and William. He travelled to Petrolia with Mr. and Mrs. Benstead and spent some time there. Later, he worked for a farmer at Camlachie and also for William Parker in Warwick Township. While he worked for the Parkers, he attended a social evening at Zion Methodist Church, where he met his future wife, Harriett Serena Humphries, a daughter of Henry and Briget Galbraith (Humphries). They were married in 1884. Over the next few years, Edwin rented several properties in Adelaide Township on Con. 2 SER. He purchased his own 100-acre farm on Con. 3 SER, from Jacob Thrower in 1900.

Edwin engaged in mixed farming and also made maple syrup. He boiled the sap in a sugar shanty in the woods and carried the finished syrup to the house on a yoke over his shoulders. He was always

Four generations of Muxlow family. Bridget Humphries, Serena Muxlow, Loftus Muxlow and Adeline Muxlow.

interested in improved farming methods, a characteristic he passed on to his sons. Edwin suffered a serious heart attack in his early forties and was forced to leave the heavy work of farming. He was active in Bethesda Methodist Church. Edwin and Harriett had three children, Loftus, Archie and Pearl.

Loftus married Viola Langan, and they had three children, Adeline, Tina and Lloyd. He started farming on his own.

Archie married Ethel Martin in 1924, and they had two daughters, Leila and Marion. Archie farmed his own property and the home farm.

Pearl married Fred Petch and they had one daughter, Muriel (see PETCH, Francis and Mary).

MUXLOW, John Thomas and Ethel

John Thomas Muxlow was a son of John and Mary Ann Muxlow. His father came from England with four other brothers. Some of them settled in Lambton County, two of the brothers went to Michigan, and one brother settled in Adelaide Township. They came to this country about 1872.

John married Ethel Baird, and they had four children, Anna, Ralph, Gordon and Merritt. Anna married Dan McNeil, and they had two children. Ralph married Velma Parker, and they had one daughter and raised two foster daughters. Gordon married Jean Wright, and they had three children. Merritt married Norma Gallagher, and they had four children.

John had a butcher shop in Adelaide Village. He later moved to Strathroy, and operated a butcher shop on Front St.

At this writing, the descendants of John and Ethel are still alive, except for a daughter of Merritt and Norma, who was killed in a plane crash at Dryden, Ontario.

NAUS, Henry and Rosemary

Henry immigrated to Canada with his family at the age of 10, from the town of Neerkant in the Netherlands. Rosemary Nolan lived near Komoka. Henry and Rosemary were married on July 6, 1968, and they took up residence in the Town of Strathroy.

In February 1990, Henry and Rosemary purchased Lot 26, Con. 3, from Don Campbell, and Henry built their family home. The Naus family had always dreamed of living in the country, and their six children were very happy to move to this spacious 2½-acre lot.

The eldest daughter, Angela, moved to Ottawa to work for the Inuit Tapirisat of Canada after completing university. David

Edwin Muxlow family, L-R, Edwin, Loftus, Archie, Pearl and Serena (mother).

Edwin and Serena (Humphries) Muxlow in front of the Muxlow homestead ca.1905, with children Loftus, 20; Archie, 16; and Pearl, 14.

Henry Naus family, back L-R, Matthew, Jonathon, Maribeth, Angela and David. Front L-R, Kelly, Rosemary and Henry ca.1992.

is presently enrolled at the University of Waterloo, while Maribeth is a student at Queen's University in Kingston. Matthew journeys by bus each day to Regina Mundi High School in London, while Jonathon attends St. Thomas Aquinas High School, also in London. Kelly, the youngest daughter, is a student at Our Lady Immaculate School in Strathroy.

Rosemary is a kindergarten teacher at Our Lady Immaculate School, and Henry owns Naus Homes Limited with his brother, Herman. In 1992, Henry built a second structure on the lot, which he uses to store equipment for his business.

NAUTA, Karst and Aley

Karst and Aley Nauta and their seven children immigrated to Canada in 1952, and lived for four years in a house rented from George Freele on Lot 28, Con. 1 SER. The children attended school at S.S. #9, and were bused there by Bill and Alma Daniels. Some of their children and grandchildren now live in Adelaide, including Hilkie Hunter, Tina Downham (see DOWNHAM, Howard C.), and Laura VandenEynden.

NEELANDS, Rev. John and Anna

Rev. John Neelands (1836-1904) was the son of William and Sarah Neelands (1816-1908). William was a local Methodist preacher, as was his grandfather. John was born in Owen Sound, Grey Township. John had four brothers and two sisters who resided in Owen Sound, Manitoba, and the U.S. Sarah died in Owen Sound at 92 years of age. Early in life, John began to prepare himself for the Methodist ministry. His ordination took place in 1863, followed closely by his marriage to Anna "Annie" Williston (1838-1898), only daughter of the Rev. John Kellogg and Eleanor (Morden) Williston. Annie was born near Kingston. Even in childhood, Annie took great interest in the calling of her father and gladly did she enter into the work of her husband, John. She was universally beloved on every circuit on which they were placed. When John was away from home, Annie conducted regular family devotions.

The greater portion of their life was spent in Strathroy, Adelaide and Chatsworth. Also among John's charges were churches in Forest, Wyoming, Florence, Woodalee, Caradoc and Brooke. Rev. John was a member of the Court Sydenham, International Order of Foresters. While serving in Adelaide, Rev. John proposed the name "Bethel" for the new Methodist church dedicated on Dec. 25, 1870, on the Egremont Road. Their three children were Lavina "Vina," Mildred and Ella. Vina married Dr. Ozias Evoy Brandreth of Adelaide Township, son of William Brandreth and Emily Evoy. They lived in Cayuga. Mildred married Francis Ivor and they lived in Strathroy. Ella married into the Sullivan family.

NETHERCOTT, William and Blanche

William Henry "Bill" (d.1969) and Mary Blanche (Warren) Nethercott (d.1991) moved to Con. 2, Adelaide Township, with two daughters, Gwendolyn Blanche "Gwen" and Arlie Eileen, in the spring of 1935. They worked on the Stewart Scott farm on shares for one year. On April 1, 1936, the family moved to the 166-acre Buttery farm, owned by Vera C. and Eleanor L. Buttery.

Nethercott family, L-R, Blanche Nethercott, Bessie Campbell (neighbour), Bill Nethercott, Gwen Nethercott, Arlie Nethercott.

The farm was sharecropped for several years, and Bill purchased it about 1945. Fourteen types of apples grew in the orchards on this farm, including a variety of Pippens that required just one 20 oz. apple to make a pie! Eventually, there were so many apple orchards in this area that Bill bulldozed the trees and planted corn instead. The Nethercotts kept registered dual-purpose shorthorns for many years, and then raised Jerseys and sold the milk in Strathroy to Hunter's dairy. In the late 1930s, Bill, Blanche and Eleanor sold produce in the London Outdoor Market.

In 1965, Bill sold the land and buildings to George Downham, keeping only the house and one acre of land. In the 1960s, Blanche studied oil painting at Strathroy Collegiate at night school. Later, she taught as many as 24 students at a time in her home during winter months. Blanche continued to reside in the house after Bill's death until August 1981, when she suffered a stroke. In 1984, the house was sold to granddaughter Janet Smithrim and her husband, Doug Morton.

In 1946, Gwen married Peter Crawford. They reside in Lobo Township. In 1948, Arlie Nethercott married Evan Smithrim.

The Nethercott children remember the Second Line as being a wonderful place to live. There was a very strong community spirit as families worked together in good times and times of sorrow. The Nethercotts lived in Adelaide Township for 56 years.

NETTLETON, William and Jane

William Nettleton (1795) was born in Belfast, Ireland, and immigrated to Canada in 1836. He was granted Crown land at Lot 21, Con. 3 NER. After starting a business in London, he returned to the farm.

Henry Johnson immigrated to Canada from Antrim, Ireland, in 1848. For some time, he worked in Smithville, Canada West (Niagara District). In June 1849, Henry went to Quebec to meet his beloved wife, Jane (McConnell). Sadly, he was unable to meet them for he died of cholera on July 4, 1849, just a few days before their arrival. Jane, not knowing what had happened to her husband, made her way to London with their two small children, Alexander (d.1919) and Mary (d.1930). She stayed with her sister, Isabella, a milliner. Their sister, Sara, was married to William McKeen of Adelaide. Jane did not learn of her husband's death until October 12 of that year.

Early in 1850, Jane married William Nettleton and came to Adelaide to live in a log house. By 1890, they were living in 2½-storey brick house, "Orchard Lodge." Alexander Johnson had farms in East Williams and Adelaide, and remained single. Mary Johnson married Edwin Brock Van Camp (d.1926) of Merrickville and Petrolia in 1875. They moved to Nebraska in 1882. He died in Denver, Colorado, and she died in California, where four of their seven children lived.

William and Jane had seven children, Sarah Eleanor McConnell (1851-1948), who married John Thompson; Jane (1853-1940), who married

Nettleton family ca.1896, L-R, Mamie, Emma, Fred, Will Jr., Will Sr.

Sharman Swift; William Jr. (1854-1930), who remained on the farm and married Emma Marie Austin; Margaret Ann (1857-1940), who married Hugh McKeen; Susanna (1859-1960), who married Archibald McLeish; Arthur Henry (1862-1863); and Arthur Henry #2 (1865-1939), who married Alice McGill.

William Jr.'s in-laws, the Austins, were a United Empire Loyalist family. Emma Marie came from Simcoe to teach at Craithie School, which was on the Nettleton property. William Jr. and Emma had four children, Fred Austin (1887-1918); Mary Dibb (1891-1970); William Ryerson (1894-1981); and Alice Annie (1897-1918). Two children died during the flu epidemic in 1918. Alice Annie went to Oyen, Alberta, to teach school. While she was there, the school was closed because of the flu. She went to help at the hospital, where she contracted the disease. Her funeral was held from her parents' home, "Glenholme," on Kittridge Avenue in Strathroy.

William Ryerson, the third child of William Jr. and Emma, remained on the home farm. After Fred's death, William R. bought his brother's share of the farm from his widow. William R. married Elsie Jean Zavitz (1897-1997). They had one daughter, Donna Jean, who attended Craithie School, Strathroy High School, and U.W.O. She married into the Smith family and now lives in Kitchener.

NEWELL, Alexander and Lorena

Family tradition in the Newell family has always indicated that this family's roots lay in County Armagh, Ireland, and indeed the first Newell to come to Elgin County was born in Ireland. However, research done by Thomas David Foster Newell in 1998 indicates a Scottish origin going back to Archibald Newell (1520), born near Dumfries, Scotland.

Archibald Newell's son, Thomas (1545), was elected Burgess of Dumfries in 1601 and his grandson, Martin (ca.1570), held the same post in 1655. Martin Newell's son, John (1592-1658), was born at St. John, Town of Dairy, Scotland. Through the next three generations, Adam (ca.1638-1711), William (1686-1763) and Robert (ca.1734), were born near St John. However, Robert (ca.1734) left Scotland with his son, James Robert (ca.1754-1815) and daughter-in-law, Mary Manight (or McKnight), and their children, and settled in the Parish of Tynan, County Armagh, Ireland, about 1800.

James Robert and Mary had four children, John, Margaret, Mary and James (ca.1782-1859). Margaret married Robert Boyd, who had fought in the War of 1812 in Canada and returned to Ireland in 1814. Mary married an unknown Someral, perhaps the brother of Martha Someral (or Somerville), who married her younger brother, James.

James (ca.1782-1859) married Martha Someral in Ulster Province, County Armagh, and they resided in the town of Bryanlitte, County Monaghan, Ireland, where James was a weaver. James and Martha had a family of eight, six sons and two daughters. The eldest sons, Robert James (1805-1896) and John (1807-1894), with Robert's wife, immigrated to Canada in 1831 from Ireland, to an area 22 miles up the Gatineau River from Bytown (Ottawa). They worked in the lumber camps of Quebec. James and Martha and the remaining children, and the Lindsay family, followed in the summer of 1835. As bush camp life was unsuitable for families, this group moved west to Norfolk and Elgin Counties.

Robert James was born in County Armagh, and married Hannah Lindsay (1799-1869) in Ireland. Robert farmed in North Dorchester Township, where he and Hannah raised five children, Robert James (1829-1885), who was born in Ireland and died in North Dorchester; Alexander (1832-1904), who was born in Quebec and died in Strathroy; John (1838-1920), who died in San Diego, California; Margaret Jane (1835-1901); and George William (1841-1917), who lived near Ingersoll and is buried in Putnam Cemetery, Middlesex County.

Alexander, the second child of Robert and Hannah, married Lorena Demaray (1838-1908), daughter of Benjamin and Rebecca (Varnum) Demaray (see DEMARAY), in North Dorchester Township on August 31, 1865. They farmed there until the mid-1860s, when he moved to Lot 24, Con. 2 NER. Alexander and Lorena raised nine children. Henry Nassau (1855-1932) married Eliza Demaray, daughter of Richard and Ann Jane (McNeil) Demaray, and they farmed near Le Mars, Iowa. Henry became an Iowa State Senator. Wesley (1857-1910) married Mary Elizabeth Woodward of Lobo Township, and was a medical doctor in Lambton County. Robert Benjamin (1859-1937) married Priscilla Jamina Ramsay and farmed near West Bay City, Michigan. Ezra (1862-1940) married Margaret Ellen Slater (1868-1954) of Adelaide, and resided near Glen Rae, Metcalfe Township, and Saskatchewan (see SLATER, Thomas and Margaret). Naomi (1864-1906) married Warren Archibald Woolley (see WOOLLEY, Warren and Naomi). Cyrus (1867-1936) married Harriet Foster in Adelaide Village, and farmed near Fernhill in Lobo Township. Frank (1869-1943) married Jane White at Lambeth and they lived near London. Asa Roy (1874-1958) married Julia Florence "Flora" Harris (see HARRIS, Samuel) and farmed in Adelaide. Margaret "Jennie" (1880-1919) married Harry Patterson and lived in Strathroy.

Asa and Flora farmed on the home place in Adelaide and had three children, Lorena Elizabeth (1898-1955); David Alexander (1902-1946), who remained single; and Stanley Howard (1906-1992). Stanley married Martha Boyd (1902-1992) of Ekfrid Township, and they had a son, Larry Boyd (1943-1979), who married Hazel I. Mardlin and lived in London. Lorena married Fred W. Lewis (1890-1964) of Adelaide and farmed on Lot 25, Con. 1 NER. They had four children, Florence, Carl, Doris and Ken (see LEWIS, John Sr. and Elizabeth).

Of the eight children of James and Martha, three died in Lambton County, being John; Alexander (1817); and Mary (1822-1855). Four died in Elgin County, being James (1809-1871); Andrew (1819-1904); Martha (1824-1909); and Foster (1827-1867). Robert, the eldest, died in North Dorchester Township.

NEWTON, William and Christina

William Newton (ca.1810-1870) married Christina Burtwhistle (ca.1808-1868) in England. Both were born in England and died in Adelaide. They raised four children, Anne (ca.1843); William Jr. (1844); Richard (1846-1917); and Sarah (ca.1850-1884), all born in England. The family came to Adelaide sometime before 1861, and William farmed the east half of Lot 2, Con. 4 SER.

Anne may have married a Healey, of Irish origin, and had a daughter, Christina J. (ca.1872-1886). In 1881, Christina was residing with Richard Newton and in 1886, her funeral card states that she was a niece of William and Richard Newton.

William Jr. married Sarah Mitchell (1851-1948), daughter of John and Mary Ann Mitchell of Adelaide. They raised four children, Annie (1880-1964); William "Morley" (ca.1883-1960); Alfred "Gordon" (1887-1959); and John "Jack" Leonard (1891-1965). They farmed part of the east half of Lot 6, Con. 5 SER. They were both faithful members of the Kerwood United Church. Sarah was made a life member of the W.M.S. in 1928. She was known for her fig pies, scones and homemade bread, which she still baked when she was very old. She enjoyed quilting and made several quilts. She was pictured with one of her lovely quilts in the Age Dispatch, when she was in her nineties.

Annie, eldest child of William Jr. and Sarah, attended Watford High School and then took a six-month course at Model School in Strathroy. She taught at S.S. #7 for three years at a salary of $150 per year. In 1902, Annie married George Johnson (1868-1932), son of Hardy and Anne (Foster) Johnson. They raised nine children, Alice (1903-

Harriett Newton feeding turkeys, her daughter Gertrude in the doorway, ca.1937.

1966); Gordon Hardy (1904-1939); Harry (1906-1972); Florence (1908-1998); Evelyn (1910-1992); Mary (1914-1963); Kate (1916); George "Leonard" (1918-1989); and Annie "Laura" (1923-1973). The family farmed in Metcalfe Township. After her husband died, Annie operated a grocery store in London for 16 years.

Morley never married. He farmed the west part of Lot 7, Con. 5 SER, for some years and then sold his farm to his brother, Gordon. He moved to Winnipeg, Manitoba, where he made money on the grain market. He returned to the London area and lived with his Aunt Hannah Mitchell and Uncle Robert Mitchell. Morley retired to Victoria, B.C., where he died. He was once described as being an eccentric fellow.

In 1933, Gordon, third child of William Jr. and Sarah, married Eva Beatrice Foster (1902-1974), daughter of William and Mary "Charity" (Inch) Foster. Gordon farmed the west part of Lot 7, Con. 5 SER. They both sang in the Kerwood United Church Choir and contributed to quartets and duets. Gordon was a member of the Kerwood Citizen's Band. Beatrice sang a great many solos and was a loyal worker in the church and community. She was a longtime member of the Kerwood Women's Institute, and made a great effort to see that her nieces and many other young women became members. When anyone was sick in the family, Beatrice always brought a bowl of soup or a treat and lent a hand with the work. She was a wonderful hostess, and no one left her house without a cup of tea and some home baking. After her husband's death, she moved to Kerwood for several years. She married Hanson Hull and moved to Strathroy. Even though she never had children, she was very much a mother to her nieces and nephews and later, her step-daughters.

Jack, the youngest child of William Jr. and Sarah, remained single and became a farmer. He lived quietly with his mother. Jack took over his father's farm and also the west half of Lot 7, Con. 4 SER, from his grandparents. At one time, he delivered milk by horse and cart to the Kerwood Cheese Factory. It was his habit during the week (and also that of his brother, Gordon) to drop in at Woods' grocery store to exchange the news of the day around the stove. Jack was a member of the Kerwood Citizen's Band. He was rarely absent from the Sunday evening church service. He devoted his life to the care of his mother who lived to be 96. After her death, he could be seen visiting the pasture farm to care for his cattle, accompanied by his little dog, who was great company for him.

Richard, the third child of William and Christina, married Harriet Matilda Pennington (1863-1948), daughter of Thomas and Ann (Bridges) Pennington. They raised two children, Gertrude (1886-1943) and Leslie Richard (1892-1953). The children attended school at S.S. #7.

Richard first farmed his father's farm and then moved to the west part of Lot 1, Con. 5 SER, which was previously owned by William McKinney. He kept cattle, pigs, turkeys and chickens. Cows were milked by hand and then the milk was separated. The skim milk went to the calves and pigs, and the cream was sold in Kerwood. Eggs were also sold in Kerwood. The farm produced grain, corn and hay. The grain was cut with a binder and stooked in the field. At threshing time, neighbours came with teams and wagons and drew the stooked grain to the grain separator. The grain was stored in the granary for feed, and the straw was blown into a stack for bedding the livestock.

Gertrude married George Westgate, son of George and Margaret (Lamont) Westgate.

Leslie remained single, and farmed his father's farm all his life, keeping cows, chickens and turkeys.

Sarah, the youngest child of William and Christina, married Henry Rivers of Warwick Township in 1882. Sarah died just 20 months after her marriage.

NICHOL, Edward and Maria

The 1871 census of Alnwick Township by Rice Lake lists Maria Ingham (1846-1877), keeping house for her brother, William Ingham. A few farms away, Edward Nichol (1838-1926) is listed as a single farmer on his own land. Maria and Edward were married the next year, 1872, and they made the decision to come to Adelaide, where the land would not be as stony. Edward and Maria had two children, Frank (1874-1962) and George Albert (1876-1953).

Edward's sister, Elizabeth Nichol, also moved to Adelaide Township, where she married a neighbour, James McKenzie. The land records show that Edward purchased 100 acres of the north half of Lot

18, Con. 1 SER, from George Donaldson in 1873. In 1876, Maria's father, Samuel Ingham, purchased the south half of this lot from Charles Oke. In 1881, Samuel sold the land to Edward. By 1902, the 200 acres was divided again when Edward and Maria sold 100 acres of the east half of the lot to their son, George. After George's barn burned, he became involved with a fiberboard company. He got into financial difficulties, and the bank trustees of his property assigned the east half of Lot 18 to Loftus Muxlow in 1925.

Frank, Edward and Maria's first son, married neighbour Florence Holmes (1876-1962). They raised fruit on the light soil of their farm just east of Arkona, located on the townline of Adelaide and West Williams. They had a daughter, Alma.

George Albert married Annie Petch (1878-1917) and, after her death, Amanda Carriere (1888-1961). They lived in Elora, where they raised two children, Iona and Jack.

After Maria died, Edward married Esther Seed (1858-1935), daughter of Hugh and Jane Seed of Adelaide. Esther's sister, Lottie Seed, went to Roseneath to keep house for Edward's widower brother, Francis Nichol, and they later married. Edward and Esther had three children, Flossie (1882-1884); Edith Pearl (1884-1956); and Lottie E. (1887-1932).

Edith married George William Linton (1876-1948). They farmed at Lot 26, Con. 3 NER, and then retired to Strathroy. They raised four daughters, Edith; Leyta; Myrtle, who married T.H. McKinnie; and Ila, who married William Stuart.

Lottie married neighbour Norman Brock (1883-1918), and they farmed on Lot 18, Con. 1 NER. Their two children were Evelyn and Murray. Evelyn married Harold Prince. After Norman's death, Lottie married William John Brock of Adelaide Village. William was a carpenter, who is said to have worked on the construction of the S.S. #6 Adelaide schoolhouse.

NICHOLS, William and Mary

William James Nichols, the patriarch of the family, came to Canada from England with his wife in 1839. They first settled in York and then moved to Middlesex in 1851.

Their son, William James Jr., married Mary Ann McRann (1849-1873) in 1870 in Ailsa Craig. They lived in Lucan, where their son, William James III (1871-1946) was born. When Mary Ann died young, William James Jr. married Esther Amy Connor. They had a daughter, Loretta "Addie" (1876). Addie married Jerry Lintott. Jerry, Addie, and William James Jr. moved west to Brandon, Manitoba, where William died.

William James III married Wilhimina Lintott (1874-1902). After her death, he met Mary Ann Finkbeiner (1876-1954), who was born in Crediton, when he was working for a sawmill in Ailsa Craig. They married in 1903 (they were both Anglicans) and farmed near Brinsley. When they first moved to Adelaide, they rented a farm at Lot 3, Con. 2 NER, from William Conkey. They later bought a farm on Lot 11, Con. 1 SER, from the Baptist family.

William and Mary had 10 children, all born in West Adelaide. The children attended school at S.S. #9. Esther (1904-1912) died in childhood. Samuel Clarence (1905-1984) went to Strathroy to work as a mechanic, where he met and married Frances Snelgrove. Albert "Bert" (1906-1967) farmed Lot 13, Con. 1 SER, with his wife, Vivian (Berry).

Charles and Helen Irene (Robbins) Nichols, 45th Wedding Anniversary.

Orland Nichols and family, R.R. #5, Strathroy.

Amanda (1908-1981) married George Glenn (1892-1964), and is buried in the Strathroy Cemetery. Charles Walter Clifford (1909-1976) became involved in oil well drilling in Adelaide. Henry (1910, died at birth) is buried in West Adelaide. James "Jim" Edward (1912-1937) remained single, and died in his twenties of "quinsy throat." Orville (1915-1990) went to London as a young fellow and joined the R.C.A.F. He met Mary Tarbuck (1904-1981) in England and they were married. She came over as a war bride after he returned from overseas. Llewellyn "Bill" Nichols (1918), who was often referred to as "young Billy," was named after Doctor Jones' sister, Louella, who had looked after the Nichols children during an epidemic of the Spanish flu. Bill was a boxer in his youth before he went to war. He married Kathleen Fuller, who had moved to Canada from England with her mother after her father's death. Bill and Kathleen have two daughters, Carol Anne and Gloria Viola. The youngest Nichols child, Louise (1920-1983), married William Smith. They lived in London with their daughter and four sons.

Charles married Helen Irene Robbins (1913-1987) in 1934. They met at Huckley Valley. Helen worked at a restaurant/hotel there. Charles stayed in the hotel for two years while drilling oil wells. He was on township council from 1962 to 1966, and reeve of Adelaide Township from 1966 to 1976. Charles and Helen had four children, twins Orland James and Garfield Arthur (1938, Garfield died at birth); Dolores Irene (1940); and Charlotte Maxine (1941). Orland contracted polio at the age of nine. He spent nine months in hospital and, when he was released, he had a brace on his left leg. He wore the brace for about six months. One day, on the way out to the barn, he got disgusted with it, took it off, and threw it away. He never wore it again.

Orland retired from farming and now does contract fencing. He married Phyllis Gertrude Plumb (1941) in 1962. Phyllis farmed with Orland and was a bus driver for 19 years, but is now retired from both jobs. Orland and Phyllis have four children. Jo-Anne Elizabeth (1963) married Wayne Symington on April 18, 1998. Jo-Anne is a Minister of Religion in the Presbyterian Church in Canada. She was ordained June 26, 1990, at West Adelaide Presbyterian Church in Adelaide Township. Jo-Anne has very special memories of her grandparents—Charles sitting under a tree, doling out hugs and quarters, and Helen's wonderful home baked pies, buns and cookies. Wayne Charles (1965) married Tammy Payne on August 14, 1993. Wayne is an Executive Chef at the Delta Armouries in London. William Orland "Bill" (1967) married Tammy Richter on July 3, 1993. Bill works for the Adelaide Township Works Department. They have two children, Charles William (1994) and Laura Jeanette (1997). Timothy Duane (1972), the youngest child of Orland and Phyllis, married Corry Rombouts on October 17, 1998. Tim works at the office of Columbia Sportswear.

Dolores Irene, third of Charles and Helen's children, married Bill Carson in 1960. They were divorced and she married Bill MacDermid (d.1995) in 1981. Dolores taught school, worked at Sears, and presently works at Inkwell Printing. Dolores and Bill have two children from the marriage. Laura Jean (1962) married Raymond Tur in 1985 (they have since divorced). They have one child, Raymond Hubertus (1987). Laura works for an upholsterer and cleans houses. Teresa Charlene (1965) married Raymond Treve in 1987. She is the owner of Inkwell Printing.

Charlotte Maxine, the youngest child of Charles and Helen, married Peter Postma in 1962. She is retired from nursing at Strathroy Hospital. Peter is an owner-operator truck driver for Montgomery Tank Lines. Charlotte and Peter have two children, Charles Lyle Renault (1964) and Patricia Louise (1966). Charles married Kelly Wilkins in 1976, and they have a daughter, Carley Virginia (1995). Charles works as a Logistics Manager. Patricia is a manager for an affiliated brokerage company.

NOORDHOF, John and Catherine

John and Catherine Noordhof purchased Lot 26, Con. 2, in June 1956. They lived there until December 1966, then the family moved to Strathroy. John and Catherine are now retired and living at Trillium Village. Their six children are Arend, Henry, Tony, Ann, Emmy, and John.

Arend married Angeline Gerryts, daughter of Harry and Tina (Bruinsma) Gerryts. Harry and Tina had purchased John and Catherine's farm when they moved. Arend is a Kerwood volunteer firefighter, and Angeline is a former fire phone operator. Together, they operate Kerwood Auto Service. Arend and Angeline live at Lot 7, Con. 5, which they purchased in June 1979 from S. Algra. They have four daughters, Kathryn, Tracy, Amanda and Barbie. Kathryn married John Veltman in 1994, and they lived in Adelaide Township until 1998. They moved to Thorold, Ontario, but have since returned to this area and presently live in Strathroy. Tracy and Amanda live out of the area, and Barbie lives at home.

Tony married Tracy Gerryts in 1976 and they lived in Strathroy until 1986, when they purchased a home at Lot 22, Con. 3 SER. Tony and Tracy have two children, Michael and Lisa. Both children attend S.D.C.I. Tony is a partner with his brother, Henry, in Noordhof Bros. Contractors, and Tracy works for Zap Paintball.

Henry lives in Poplar Hill, Ann lives in Mt. Brydges, Emmy lives in Mitchell, and John lives in Oil Springs, Alberta.

Arend, Angeline, Mark and Amanda Greer, Barb, Tracy, Katherine and John Veltman and their children, Madison and Tyler, 1997.

O'CALLAGHAN, Terrance and Catherine

Terrance O'Callaghan (1883-1904) was born in County Cavan, Ireland. After the death of his mother and the remarriage of his father, he tried to leave home several times, but was unsuccessful due to his age. Finally, he left and sailed to the United States, where he spent some time in Philadelphia. He travelled to Port Huron and then journeyed to Adelaide Village, where he stayed with his aunt and uncle, James and Rosanna (Callaghan) Healy.

Catherine Dowling (1840-1929) was born in Massena, New York. In 1857, it is believed she moved with her family to Wisconsin. According to the story passed on by their children, during their travels to the new homestead, the Dowling family passed through Adelaide Village where Terrance and Catherine met. In 1859, Catherine travelled back with her sister, Margaret, to Port Huron, where Terrance met her. According to church records, Terrance and Catherine married at St. Stephen's R.C. Church in Port Huron. In 1860, they settled in the forests of Adelaide, where they lived for more than 47 years.

Terrance was always a staunch Liberal who took an active interest in municipal affairs, but he never aspired to any public office. He preferred to live a quiet, unostentatious life. In 1871, his farm at Lot 12, Con. 1 NER, had grown to 50 acres on which he produced wheat, oats, peas and potatoes. His livestock included horses, dairy cows, cattle, sheep and swine. For a brief period, he also delivered mail between Strathroy and Adelaide.

Catherine worked alongside her husband with the daily farm work and raised a family. She also aided materially in erecting St. Patrick's Church, where she was a devout member, active in church organizations.

Terrance and Catherine raised seven daughters and five sons. As in other families where the children had grown, some continued to live in the area and some moved to follow their dreams. Mary married Edward Sickles of Strathroy and moved to Flint, Michigan. Catherine "Kate" married Joseph Getty of Mt. Brydges and they made their home in Duluth, Minnesota. William married Annie Walsh of Warwick and they lived in the Petrolia area. Rosanna married John Walsh, brother of Annie, and they farmed around Reece's Corners. Lucy Margaret remained single and lived in Detroit, Michigan. Henrietta "Ettie" Maria married William Wilson of Strathroy. William was a marble cutter and they made their home in Petrolia. Thomas

"Tom" Joseph married Ann Jane Comiskey of Ingersoll and they farmed the family farm for some time and eventually moved to Watford where Tom was a cattle broker. Edward Frances "Frank" married Elizabeth (last name unknown) and after living in Duluth, Minnesota, they made their home in the Detroit area. James married Olivia Saunders of Watford and they lived in Watford where James was a stonecutter and Olivia was a milliner. Anastacia "Daisy" married Joseph Johnson and lived in Detroit, Michigan.

Terrance began to suffer from heart trouble, and this eventually took his life. Catherine moved to Petrolia to live with her daughter, Ettie. She remained there until her death. Terrance and Catherine were buried in St. Patrick's Cemetery in Adelaide Village.

OGG, Robert and Laila

In 1960, Robert Ogg (d.1988), a farmer in Caradoc Township, bought the Napperton School, S.S. #5, and the acre of land on which it was built. The school was razed, and a red brick, ranch-style home was built. Robert married Mrs. Laila Parker (McLean) on July 7, 1962. Along with her daughters, Barbara and June Parker, they moved into the new residence (see PARKER, James and Amey).

Robert and Laila Ogg, March 1988.

Robert incorporated a beam from the school into the basement of the new house, and fitted the school's front door into the entrance to the fruit cellar. He also moved the woodshed to the back of the property and covered it with aluminum sheeting (all of the carved initials are still on the inside of the woodshed).

Laila worked part-time for the licence bureau for 20 years. Robert worked for the Ontario Ministry of Transportation from the yard at Highways 22 and 81.

Following Robert's death, the property was sold, and Laila moved to Trillium Village in Strathroy. She enjoys playing piano in the community for Strathmere Lodge, Strathroy Hospital, for events at Trillium Village, and at Strathroy Baptist Church. She was an active member of the Caradoc Zion Ladies Aid group, and was one of the organists at Caradoc Zion Baptist Church until it closed.

OLIVER

George Oliver and his wife, Mary (Horswood), sailed from Lincolnshire, England, to New York in 1854. Sadly, Mary, two daughters, and George's sister died of cholera during the voyage and were buried at sea. A third daughter died just after landing in New York, and a son died shortly after the remaining family arrived in Ontario. The surviving children and their father settled in Delaware Township.

One of the children, Henry (1845-1940), married Ellen Augusta Hoskin (1848-1939) of St. Catharines. They moved from Bosanquet Township to Lot 26, Con. 2 NER, where they lived for 17 years. They retired to Con. 4 SER, west of Strathroy. Their property was later sold to Alex Anderson. Stories are told of Ellen Oliver leaving home at 4:00 a.m. in her horse and buggy to take butter, eggs and chickens to the market in London. Henry raised sheep and was well known as a good farmer and for his horses. When they retired, Henry and Ellen moved to the Fourth Line, where they celebrated 60 years of marriage in 1938. After Ellen's death, Henry lived with his daughter, Sarah Patterson, after her family returned from Alberta. His granddaughter, Marion Fuller, remembers being paid a penny to read the articles to him from the Strathroy Age Dispatch.

Henry and Ellen had six children. Charles Crawford (1879-1971) married Laura Belle Burdon

(1881-1958), and then Edith Jean Burdon Hull (1879-1962). They lived on the east half of Lot 25 or 26, Con. 2 NER. Nellie Frances (1881-1953) married William Henry Wardell (1873-1925) and they lived at Lot 25, Con. 3 NER, on the East Williams/Adelaide townline (see WARDELL, Joseph and Lettisha). George Emerson (1883-1972) married Lena Wood (1888-1933), and then Mary Bishop Thomas (1879-1972). He farmed the west half of Lot 26, Con. 2 NER, and retired to the north of Strathroy at the corner of Highway 81 and Pannell Lane (today Earl Milliken's property). Eli Elmer "Gibby" (1885-1980) married Ella Olstad in Alberta in 1914. He taught for four years in Adelaide schools and finished his teaching career in Alberta. Crawford Thomas (1887-1892) died young. Sarah "Sadie" Laura (1890-1974) went to Alberta in 1917 and married Merwin Coates Patterson (1888-1966). They raised seven children.

William Edwards Roberts Oliver (1867-1962), half-brother to Henry, married Mary Louise "Minnie" Arrand (1875-1958). They lived on several farms in Adelaide and the children attended S.S. #8 when they lived beside the school on the west half of Lot 7, Con. 2 NER (later Roy Demaray's farm). They moved to the Hodgson farm, Lot 10, Con. 2 NER, and the older children, Alton, Maye, Ruby, Hazel and Georgena attended S.S. #9 when Harriett McInroy was teacher.

William and Mary Oliver had 10 children. Joseph Henry "Alton" (1898-1975) married Lela Marie Currie (1903-1997, see CURRY-CURRIE-CORRIGAN). The next two children died young, Alma May (1900-1900) and Edward Lester (1902-1903). Mayetta "Maye" Pearl (1903-1985) married Leonard Carrothers (1899-1978, see CARROTHERS, John and Harriet). Annie Rubena "Ruby" (1904-1995) married Manville Bryce (1906-1983) of Watford. Mary Caroline "Hazel" (1906-1991) married Wilfred Manicom (1904-1970) of Warwick. Georgena Isabel (1908-2000) married Percy Manicom (1900-1964), then Clarence Randall (d.1987). Bertha Winnifred married John Bryce of Watford. Hilda Irene (1915-2000) married Gordon Gerry (d.1975) of Lobo Township, then Orville Williams (d.1983). Edith Louise married Winston Mahler of London. Bertha, Hilda and Edith attended S.S. #9 when Marie Reinhardt was the teacher. The Oliver family, like many others, was stricken with the 1918 flu and all but the mother were sick with it. Alton, a young man at the time, drove Dr. Jones of Adelaide Village on his rounds to see these flu patients. Alton would sleep while the doctor was tending the sick and then the doctor would sleep until they reached the next farm where there were more patients.

William Oliver continued to farm, except for a few years when he had a butcher shop in Arkona. He then bought a farm near Watford and left Adelaide Township in 1926.

OLIVER, Henry and Ellen

Henry Oliver (1845-1940) was born in Brothertoft, Lincolnshire, England. In the spring of 1854, he left England with his parents, George and Mary, and his brother and three sisters, along with an aunt and uncle. Cholera broke out on the ship and by the time they landed, his mother, aunt, and two sisters had died at sea, with his last sister dying soon after they arrived in New York. They made their way to Ontario, where Henry's brother died shortly thereafter.

On July 4, 1878, at the age of 33, Henry married Ellen Hoskin (d.1939), who was born in St. Catharines. Henry and Ellen farmed first in Delaware Township, then in Bosanquet Township, and finally, for about 17 years, in Adelaide Township on Lot 26, Con. 2 NER.

Henry and Ellen had a family of six children, four sons and two daughters. Their second youngest child, Thomas (d.1892), died at the age of five. Charles married Laura Burdon, Nellie married William Wardell, George married Lena Wood, Eli married Ella Olstead, and Sarah married Merwin Patterson.

The home of Henry Oliver, near Crathie. Sarah, daughter, and Ellen, wife of Henry, 1910.

Henry and Ellen retired to a home on the Fourth Line, near the present-day Strathmere Lodge. In 1938, they celebrated their 60th wedding anniversary there.

OOMEN, Chris and Nancy

Chris Oomen immigrated to Canada from Holland in June 1977. He bought a farm from Bouwe Zulstra at Lot 24, Con. 1 NER, in October 1978.

Chris married Nancy Van Kessel and they have four children, Lisa, Andy, Katy and Paul.

Chris worked for several area farmers before buying his own farm. The family enjoys participating in summer sports.

PAAS, Jan and Ebeltje

Jan and Ebeltje Paas and their three young children, Ina, Charlie and Steve, came to Ontario from Barrhead, Alberta. They were looking for a farm in this area because Ebeltje had a sister and brother-in-law farming near Watford.

In December 1951, they rented a house in Adelaide Township on Lot 19, Con. 3 SER. In the spring of 1952, Jan and Ebeltje bought the MacDonald farm located on Lot 27, Con. 3 NER. The farm consisted of 16½ acres of land in Adelaide and 50 acres across the road in Lobo, which is now Middlesex Centre. Some cows, pigs and chickens were purchased and the Paas family ran a mixed farming operation. It was hard to eke out a living on a farm in those early years, so Jan worked in construction to supplement the farm income.

During the 1950s, Jan and Ebeltje were blessed with three more sons, John, Dirk and Ralph. Later, when the price of milk increased, the farming future began to look brighter. In November 1965, they bought Fred and Mabel Ramsey's farm on Lot 28, Con. 1 NER. They moved to the new farm in April 1966. Mixed farming had become less popular and dairy farming provided the main source of income for the family.

In the 1970s, Charlie and Jan worked out an arrangement to begin farming with his father. Jan and Ebeltje decided to build a new house on Lot 28, Con. 1 NER, as Charlie planned to marry. In July 1974, Charlie married Grace Kloosterman, who had grown up near Brockville, Ontario. They have three children, Christie, Dale and Anita. In 1980, Charlie and Grace purchased the family farm and have continued in the dairy business since that time.

PAFF, Vern and Eileen

Vern and Eileen Paff moved to Kerwood from London in 1968. They have two children, Walter Verne (1962) and Barbara Ann (1970). The Paffs originated from Germany.

Walter married Kathy Wagstaff, who has a daughter, Giselle. Walter and Kathy have two children, Robbie and Ashley. They live on Havelock Street in Kerwood.

Barbara married Dave Westgate and has two children, Kaitlyn and Greg. They live on Confederation Line in Watford.

Vern worked for London Salvage and Trading Co. for 25 years. He retired in 1996. Vern and Eileen now spend spare time with their hobby, collecting antique cars. They own several that were restored by Vern, with help from Walter and Dave.

PAINE, Joseph and Elizabeth

Joseph Paine (1796) of Devonshire, England, married Elizabeth Ward (1797-1869) in 1818. Joseph and Elizabeth came to Canada and farmed 100 acres of land at the east half of Lot 18, Con. 2 SER. Their farm was named Peachtree Hill.

John Paine (d.1872), son of Joseph and Elizabeth, married Elizabeth Rapley (1823-1883), who was born in Sussex, England, the daughter of Charles and Frances (Adams) Rapley. Frances died in England and Charles brought his two daughters to Ontario. Charles is buried in the Fourth Line Cemetery.

John and Elizabeth had nine children, Elizabeth, Victoria, John Emanual, Wesley, Annie Sophia, James T. Arthur, Sarah Jane, Ernest and Sidney. Annie married Alfred Hawes, and they had seven children (see HAWES, Alfred and Annie). She died in Brown City, Michigan, and is buried in the Carmen Cemetery in Lakeport, Michigan.

The 1862 Tremaine map shows John Paine farming 100 acres at the west half of Lot 19, Con. 2 SER. The 1878 Middlesex County Atlas shows this farm labeled "Jno Paines Heirs." John died in Adelaide and was buried in the Fourth Line Cemetery.

The Paine schoolhouse was just west and across the road from the Paine homestead. It was hit by lightning and burned; only the foundation and water pump remain.

PARKER, James and Amey

In 1832, James Parker (1797-1864) and his wife, Amey (1797-1872), immigrated to Adelaide with their daughter, Amey (1819-1908), and sons George (1822-1897) and James Jr. (1824-1901). The children were then 13, 10 and 8. They came from Pulburough, West Sussex, England. His (Parke) ancestors had arrived in England with William of Orange from Switzerland.

Their first known homestead was a log house on 100 acres at the east half of Lot 15, Con. 4 SER. Later, this home was replaced by a large white brick farmhouse (this became the Clarence Sinkey farm).

Daughter Amey married Charles Napper (1821-1907), who became the first postmaster for Napperton. The post office was in a small house near the Mt. Zion Methodist Church on Con. 5. We believe that Napperton was named for Charles Napper. George married Sara Ann Hilton (1829-1898) and they had 10 children, George W., Harvey, Rhena, Martha Jane, Annie, Nellie, James, Charles W., Sadie and Ida.

James Jr. married Ellen Mather (1825-1895) of Adelaide Village in 1845 and they had seven children, James William, George Henry, Amanuel, Charles Napper, Robert, Amey Mary and Isaac (1860-1933).

In his will, James Sr. left the homestead property to James, and to George he left 100 acres at the west half of Lot 16, Con. 4 SER, which was across the sideroad.

In the area known as Napperton, there were many properties occupied by the children of George and James Jr. along Con. 4. Some of the Adelaide Township names which appear in the Parker family tree are Mather, Hilton, Rapley, Thrower, Humphries, Petch, Mann and Downer.

In 1878, George Jr. farmed Lot 14. About 1910, Lawrence David Parker (1881-1941), a descendant of James Jr., built a brick home on this lot, replacing a frame house which had been the home of his parents, George Henry (1848-1932) and Rebecca Roda Ann (Thrower) Parker (1849-1923). Lawrence's wife was Jenny Smith (1890-1965). Lawrence's sisters were Louisa (1871-1944), who married Ira Downer, and Gladys (1891-1944), who married Albert Levitt. George Henry and Roda were living in Strathroy on Albert Street, and operating greenhouses at this time. They were married in February 1870 in the Mt. Zion Wesleyan Methodist Church. Most of the Parkers are buried in the Fourth Line Cemetery near Strathroy.

Lawrence and Jenny had three sons, George Henry Smith (1912-1976); Charles Edward (1914-1968); and James "Jim" Dufferin (1917-1956). Along with farming, the family added gas pumps, log cabins, and a small store and curio shop, which were operated by the sons. One of the items in the curio shop, along with the arrowheads, etc., was a box on the wall with the sign "North American Monkey." When someone looked into the front of the box they saw their own reflection in a mirror. This was Lawrence's sense of humour. Jenny was known for her great cooking, homemade pies, and ice cream. During the war, gas rationing and the inability to obtain staples such as sugar and chocolate for the store caused its demise. Also, the completion of Highway 22 made direct travelling much easier from London to Sarnia, and travellers usually bypassed small towns and villages such as Napperton.

Charles married Doris Anthony (1914), and they moved to Timmins, where Charles worked in mining. Doris and their children, Pat, Larry and Linda, now live in the Toronto area.

In the 1940s and 1950s, Jim and his wife, Laila (McLean) Parker (1921), and their daughters, Barbara (1945) and June (1949), farmed the Lot 14 property. At the time, George and Evelyn (Ward) Parker (1919-1992), and their children, Bill (1941)

Bill, Bette, Julie, and Dan Parker in June 1997.

Dan and Bill Parker, cutting a 150-year-old log, March 1999.

and Jeanette (1949), farmed the west part of Lot 13, Con. 4 SER.

Barbara married Gerald Haumann (1944) and they have two children, Monica Lynn (1974) and Trevor James (1977). They live in East Williams Township in Nairn. June married Dieter Woerz (1944) and they have two sons, David Paul (1972) and James Michael (1975). June and Dieter live in London.

Jeanette married Doug Mahler (1949) and they have a daughter, Megan Ashleigh (1984). They live in Peterborough.

After Jim's death, George and Bill farmed both properties. Bill married Bette Vanderbeeten (1944), and they farm the properties with their children, Daniel William "Dan" (1970) and Julie Jeanette (1973). Bill and Bette continue making maple syrup each spring from their sugar bush. Dan and his wife, Jennifer (McDonald), are continuing a long tradition of farming in the Parker family. He is the seventh Parker generation to farm, and the fifth on the same property. The Parkers have been farming in Adelaide Township for over 165 years.

Isaac, the youngest child of James Jr. and Ellen, married Jennie Bradshaw (1864-1944) on November 27, 1884. They had four children, Frank (1885-1953); Bruce (1888-1949); Gordon (1895-1971); and Velma (1904-1964). Gordon was a veteran of WWI, and worked in Strathroy.

Frank bought a farm from his Uncle Charles, the west half of Lot 15, Con. 5 SER. He built a house there in 1918. The homestead was left to Velma and later sold to Dunc Campbell.

On March 19, 1919 Frank married Flossie McWhinney (1886-1936) and they had one child, Grant (1921). Frank was a farmer, and he served as a school board trustee for S.S. #5.

Grant is a veteran of WWII. While overseas in Europe, his grandmother, Lydia McWhinney, then 83 years of age, did a lot of knitting for the war effort and was described in the newspaper.

Grant met his future wife, Phyllis Coupland, in England. She was the daughter of a butler employed by a British movie star, Kenneth More. Grant and Phyllis were married in England on May 26, 1945.

After the war, they came to Adelaide and farmed, then moved to Kerwood. Grant and Phyllis have two children, Judy Ann (1950) and Michael Frank (1952).

Grant worked for Donald Pollock for several years and, in 1958, he and co-worker, Bill Jordan, bought Kerwood Poultry and Locker Service. They trucked milk, cream and eggs. Grant sold his share to Bill in 1963. He drove high school busses for several years and then trucks for Bluewater Milk Co-op, based in Wyoming, until his retirement in November, 1986.

Judy married Mike Olajos, a tobacco farmer from Mt. Brydges, on October 14, 1972. They have two children, Kimberly and Michael.

Michael, youngest child of Grant and Phyllis, married Sharon Hamilton of Strathroy on March 21, 1986. Sharon is a registered nurse working in London, and Mike has worked in Kerwood at the fertilizer plant (Cargill) for more than 25 years.

PATTERSON, Robert and Samuel

Robert Patterson (d.1866) was born in County Mayo, Ireland, near a little place called Killala. He came to Canada with his brother, Samuel, in 1836. They farmed for a few years near Cobourg, Ontario. In 1845, they came by horse and wagon to Adelaide Township, where Robert settled on Lot 10, Con. 5 SER. Samuel settled on Lot 11, Con. 5, the second farm to the east (now owned by Hillcrest Farms). Robert bought the 150-acre farm for £40, but the deal was not entirely closed until the railroad went through in 1856.

In 1852, another brother, William, came from Ireland with their widowed mother, Elizabeth, and they settled on Lot 11, Con. 4 SER (now owned by Bev Morgan). Two sisters, Matilda and Catherine, came a little later and were married to two brothers in the Morgan family. Matilda married William

From L-R, Clarence, Helen (Potter), Meddie, Hazel and Robert M. Patterson, 1934. (Note: This is second generation Robert M., son of Robert.)

Morgan, Bev Morgan's great-grandfather, and Catherine married Richard Morgan, Dorothy Winter's and Milo Morgan's great-grandfather.

In 1846, Robert married Margaret Carroll (d.1894). They lived in a log house (the front part of the present home; the kitchen was added later). Robert was a lay minister who preached in a little log church located on the northeast corner of his farm. At one time, the church needed repairs and each member pledged some money. Robert pledged $100, but died before he had it paid. They held Margaret responsible, so she borrowed the money from her brother, Thomas Carroll, who charged her 10% interest.

Family history indicates that when the church was dismantled, it was moved to Kerwood and used as a blacksmith shop. Robert and Margaret had five children. Mary Jane married George Fawcett Earley and lived at Reeces Corners. George married Maria Westgate and lived on a farm in Warwick Township (once owned by Hugh Ball). Thomas married Mary Jane Galbraith and lived across the road from his parents on the east half of Lot 10, Con. 4. Robert Milton (1862), the youngest, was only four years old when his father died. Apparently, there was no cemetery at the little log church on the farm, as Robert was buried in the Fourth Line cemetery just west of Strathroy. Robert Milton stayed on the home farm at Lot 10, Con. 5 SER, with his mother, Margaret.

In 1895, a year after his mother's death, Robert Milton married Meddie Patterson. They had three children. Bertha died at age four of diphtheria. Hazel Freida married Hugh Ball in 1924. Clarence Robert married Helen Potter in 1934, and they had two sons, Robert George and John Carmen. For several years, Clarence was secretary-treasurer of the Kerwood School situated on the Fourth Line SER.

Robert George married Donna Wernham in 1961. Robert and Donna live on the home farm and have four children, Kathy, Robin, Robert D. "Robbie" and Ryan.

Kathy married Jerry Hendrikx in 1987 and they live on a dairy farm near Parkhill. They have four children, Emily, Erin, Scott and Meaghan. Robin married John McLenan in 1992 and they live on the old Fourth Line, west of Kerwood. They have two children, Olivia and Daniel. Robbie and Ryan still live at home with their parents.

John Carmen married Judith Osborne in 1963 and they live in Strathroy. They have three children, Jackie, Leslie and Joseph Clarence "Joey."

Clarence and Hazel Patterson, 1911.

Jackie lives in Strathroy. Leslie lives with her parents. Joey married Lynda Brown in 1994 and they live in Strathroy. Joey and Lynda have two children.

The home farm at Lot 10, Con. 5 SER, is still in the Patterson family and has been home to five Robert Pattersons.

PATTERSON, Thomas

Thomas and Mary (Lighton) Patterson immigrated to Canada from County Mayo, Ireland. They came to Shedden near Port Stanley. Mary E. Patterson (1846) was born in Ireland, the first of two daughters. Janet "Jane" (1848-1914) was born on the ship or shortly after landing; Mary died in childbirth and was buried at Port Stanley Cemetery.

Shortly after coming to Canada, Thomas went to the gold rush, and later returned to Shedden. He and his two daughters moved to the Fourth Line, where his brothers lived.

Mary E. married Ivan P. Morgan in 1865, and lived where Bev Morgan now lives. They had seven children, William, Minnie, Laura, Annie, Jean, Ira and Eva. Eva married Walter W. Bowley and had four children, Mary, Anne, Jean and Walter.

Jane married William Curry and they had seven children, two of whom were Arthur and Ethel (see CURRIE/CURRY/CORRIGAN).

PATTERSON

Brothers Donald, Daniel and Hector Patterson came to Adelaide Township from Lobo Township. Land records show that on February 25, 1881, Daniel Patterson and his wife, Lizzie Nichols, deeded 100 acres of the west half of Lot 12, Con. 3 NER, to Hector Patterson. The 1891 census lists Hector Patterson, age 42, and his wife, Jennet Moore, age 35. Children listed are John Moore, 15; Jennet, 13; William H. 8; and Freddie, 4.

Hector had operated a blacksmith shop in Lobo, so his skills would have been most welcome in the Shiloh neighbourhood. In 1890, Hector served as deputy reeve of Adelaide Township. A young son, Leo John (d.1884), died a baby. Records indicate John Moore Patterson was killed in WW1 and is buried in France. The Patterson family had left the Adelaide area by 1901.

PEARSON, Len and Anne

Len and Anne Pearson moved to Adelaide in 1951. Anne had been raised in West Williams Township, and went to church at Bornish. The couple purchased 10 acres from Morley MacDonald and built a home. As Len had been overseas, they were able to buy through the Veteran's Land Act.

Len and Anne had three children. Mary married Larry MacDonald (Strathroy Chev-Olds dealer). John married Anne Pollock, and is a pilot with Canada 3000. Tom is a commercial fisherman. He lives in Comox on Vancouver Island, and fishes on the Pacific Ocean.

PEDDEN, Andrew and Margaret

Andrew Pedden (1805) was born in Scotland. He married Margaret (1815, last name unknown), also from Scotland, and they immigrated to Canada in the 1840s. Andrew and Margaret had 10 children, Joseph (1836); John (1837); David (1842); Jane (1844); James (1848); Agnes (1850); William (1853); Alex (1855); Mathew (1858); and Catherine (1863), who died at two days of age. Her body is interred in St. Ann's Cemetery, Adelaide Village. The first four children were born in Scotland, and the remaining six were born in Ontario.

John settled on Lot 16, Con. 7, East Williams Township. He moved to Adelaide Township in 1866 and settled on Lot 14, Con. 4 NER. On July 12, 1870, he married Nancy McLachlan (1847-1930). They had nine children, Margaret Ellen (1871-1941); John (1872-1940); Andrew (1874-1955);

Family of Archie and Dorothy Pedden (ca.1980), L-R, Shelly Meyers, Carole (Pedden) Meyers, Robert Meyers, Kimberly Meyers, Dorothy Pedden, Archie Pedden, Pamela Pedden, Brenda Pedden, Archie L. Pedden, and Archie L. Pedden Jr.

Catherine Jane (1876-1877); Joseph Alexander (1878-1892); Nancy (1880-1905); William James (1882-1971); David (1884-1942); and Archie (1889-1945). The family lived in a log house that was torn down in the mid-1930s, and a small frame house that is still standing. In 1902, the present home was built at a cost of $1,580, including the furnace.

William James married Elizabeth Watson (d.1907) in December 1906, and moved to a farm on Centre Road across from the Presbyterian Church. He remarried, to Margaret Ann Jenkins (1883-1968) on December 21, 1910. They had two sons, James Arthur "Art" (1913-1985) and Maurice Allan (1917). In 1917, they sold their farm in West Williams Township and moved to Lot 23, Con. 2 NER, in Adelaide Township, near Crathie.

Art married Winnie Gertrude "Winnie" Dowding (1912) on September 14, 1933, and they farmed the home farm and 150 acres of additional land. In 1958, they changed the farm operation from dairy/crop to cow/calf. Art also trucked cattle for many years. They moved to Strathroy after the 1972 sale of the farm to Ray and Joan Wardell. Art served on Adelaide Township council from 1957 to 1960. Art and Winnie had three daughters, Ruth Elaine (1935); Barbara Annie (1937); and Nancy Jane (1948).

Ruth married Lloyd Long of Poplar Hill in 1957. They reside in Oil Springs and have two children, Lorraine Ann "Lorrie" (1958) and Karen Elizabeth (1965). Lorraine married David Byers in 1982 and they have two children, Christopher Ryan (1984) and Marcia Leanne (1987). Karen married Christopher Strachen in 1997, and they live in Sarnia.

Barbara married Kenneth Wardell of Adelaide Township in 1958. They live in La Salle, Ontario, and have two children, Deborah Anne (1959) and Denise Deanna (1963). Deborah Anne (1959) married Robert Cassan in 1979, and they live in Windsor. They have two daughters, Sheri Anne (1983) and Carly Anne (1995). Denise married Scott Noble in 1986. They have a daughter, Shelley Marie (1985). Denise remarried in 1993, to Shawn McCann. They live in Essex, and they have a son, Bradley Ryan (1994).

Nancy, the youngest child of Art and Winnie, married Lawrence Tomchick of New Liskeard in 1968. They live in Strathroy and have two children, Darcy Ross (1968) and Terri Lyn (1971). Darcy married Maureen DeRuiter in 1995 and they have two children, Owen Lawrence (1997) and Olivia Marie (1999).

Maurice Allan, second son of William James and Margaret Ann, served as Provost Marshall in the army during WWII. He married Hannah McLeod (1907-1989) in 1935. They had two children, Joan Margaret (1938) and Donald Allan (1951-1991). After living in Strathroy for a number of years, Allan and Hannah bought the former Charlie Oliver farm on Con. 2 NER. John and Jean Milligan now own this home. In June 1993, Allan remarried, to Joyce Stoner.

Joan Margaret married Claire McLean in 1956. They have four children, Mark Edward, Martha, Mary Ellen and Marlene. Joan and Claire reside in Antigua, and their family lives in the London area.

Donald Allan, the youngest child of Allan and Hannah, was married to Jeanette McKenzie. They had four children, Sheryl, Catherine, Amy and David. The children now live in London.

Archie, the youngest child of John and Nancy, farmed the home farm in Adelaide all his adult life. He was very interested in horses and was the breeder of the famous racehorse "Grattan Bars." This horse held the record of 1:59 2/5 for many years. Archie sold Grattan Bars to Fred Thrower as a yearling colt for $300 and took calves and pigs as payment. As a three-year-old, Grattan Bars won three $25,000 stakes in 14 days.

Archie was also interested in politics and served on Adelaide Township Council for several years. In 1945, he ran for Member of Parliament for the Conservative Party against Robert McCubbin for the Liberal Party. He was defeated in the election and was killed by lightning two weeks later.

Archie married Melena May Marshall (1890) on May 4, 1915, and they had four children, Melena (d.1953), whose body is interred in Strathroy Cemetery; Margaret Nancy Ellen (1916); Eva Pearl (1919); and John Archibald (1925).

Margaret married Paul Bentley Butler on June 14, 1939, and they were divorced. Margaret then married Walter Charles Jowett on September 6, 1980. Margaret and Paul Butler had two children during the marriage, Kingsley Paul (1941) and Brian Duncan (1948).

Kingsley married Ruth Marjorie Allen (1944) on April 27, 1963, in Strathroy. They reside in

Wolfville, Nova Scotia. They have two children, Wendy Lynne (1963) and Stephanie Margaret (1970). Wendy married Timothy Arsenault on June 10, 1989, in Wolfville. They reside in Mahone Bay, Nova Scotia. They have one son, Jacob Kingsley John Arsenault (1995).

Brian married Sharon Anne Brooks on August 19, 1966, in Strathroy, and they were divorced. Brian married Marlene Armanda Chaput-Smith (1951) on September 4, 1992. Brian and Sharon had two children during the marriage, James Duncan (1967) and Tracey Lorraine (1969).

James married Jackie Alice Ysebert (1965) on December 20, 1989. They reside in Strathroy. They have two children, Jessica Mary (1994) and Nicole Sharon (1992). Tracey married Kelly Grant Dundas (1968) on March 11, 1995. They have two children, Ian James Butler (1993) and Rachel Anne Margaret (1997).

Eva Pearl, third child of Archie and Melena, married Robert William Elliott (1915-1994) on November 11, 1941. Robert's body is interred in Strathroy Cemetery. Pearl and Robert had two children, Diane Louise (1953) and Robert Darryl (1960).

Diane married William Quartel (1954-1996) on August 26, 1976. William's body is interred in Strathroy Cemetery. Diane now resides in London. Diane and William had two children, Sarah Katherine (1982) and Jessica Anne (1985).

Robert, Pearl and Robert's youngest child, married Susan Shilson (1960) on August 4, 1984. They reside in La Salle, Ontario. Their two children are Lauren Rebecca (1988) and Justin Robert (1992).

John Archibald, the youngest child of Archie and Melena, was born in Adelaide Township. He married Dorothy Harriet Topping (1927) on June 14, 1947. They have two children, Archie Lavern (1948-1993) and Carole Lynne (1951).

Archie Lavern married Brenda Lee Finkbeiner (1949) of Guelph on September 14, 1968. Archie Lavern died at 44 years of age, and his body is interred in Strathroy Cemetery. Archie Lavern and Brenda had two children, Pamela Dawn (1969) and Archie Lloyd (1970). The name "Archie" has been repeated through four generations of the Pedden family.

Pamela married Thomas Clare Breckles (1968) of Cambridge on September 14, 1996, and they live in Toronto. They have two children, Andi Elizabeth (1996) and Hannah Claire (1999).

Carole, youngest child of John Archibald and Dorothy, married Robert Burton Meyers (1949) of Galt on October 2, 1971. They reside in London, and have two children, Shelly Christine (1974) and Kimberly Dawn (1976).

PEGLEY, Robert and Mary Ann

Robert Pegley (ca.1781-1864), a native of County Down, Ireland, married Mary Ann (1796-1842, surname unknown) in 1802 in their home parish. The next year, at age 21, he enlisted in the British Army. After several promotions to Sergeant during his service in Europe, he was raised to the rank of Quartermaster for his participation in the Battle of Waterloo, where Napoleon Bonaparte was defeated. Robert Pegley retired with full pay in July 1821, from the Royal Veterans Battalion.

Robert came to Canada with his wife and 11 children and filed for free land in July 1832, based on his service in the British Army. By the birth dates of his children, it appears that he moved to Canada between 1829 and 1831. However, some records state that he had been a resident of the Province of Upper Canada since September 1825. From March 1827 until his petition of land, he was a resident of the Town of York while awaiting approval of his request. In 1832 and 1833, Robert Pegley was in Middlesex County working on the Egremont Road project from Lobo to Lake Huron. He was listed as "Issuer of Rations" for the workers.

In June 1836, Robert Pegley received the Patent from the Crown for Lot 20, Con. 1 SER, in Adelaide Township. He later lost this land and the records contain many letters that he wrote to regain the property. In one letter of July 1841, he stated that he had 14 children, some of whom had served in the Army. His wife died at Chatham, Kent County. Robert Pegley was able to reclaim his land as the 1851 census shows him living on the lot, a 71-year-old widower. In his household are daughter Anna Pegley Marsden 35, a widow born in England; son Henry Pegley 31, born in Scotland; Mary Ann Pegley 28, born in Ireland; Robert Pegley 26, born in Ireland, a surgeon who was absent on the day of the census-taking; Matilda Pegley 24, born in Ireland; Arabella 22, born in Ireland; John 20, born in Canada; Latitia 18, born in Canada; Charles 16, born in Canada; and Catherine A. 12, born in Canada.

The 1862 Tremaine Survey shows that Captain Pegley also owned 100 acres of Lot 20, Con. 1 NER.

As well as being an Adelaide Township farmer, Robert Pegley served as a Captain of Militia and as Justice of the Peace for Middlesex County and the London District. At the Feb. 17, 1851, Adelaide Township Council Meeting at Mrs. Westlake's Inn, Robert Pegley was appointed Treasurer for the year 1851. The Minutes of the Sept. 6, 1852, Council Meeting record that he was sworn in as Councillor for St. John's Ward to replace William Bray.

In his will, dated in December 1862, he named only a few of his children. A parcel of land was left to his son, John, and the remainder was set up in a trust for his unmarried daughters, who moved to Strathroy. In 1874, Matilda Pegley, acting as trustee, sold the 200 acres of Lot 20, Con. 1 SER, to William Niece.

There were 15 children born to Robert and Mary Ann, according to family research. Of the eldest, Christian (1805), there is no further information.

Second child, George (1809-1868), married Harriet Cooper (1822-1905), daughter of James and Harriet (Carter) Cooper, on Nov. 3, 1841, at St. Ann's Church in Adelaide. She died in South Dakota. George's name first appeared as a worker on the Egremont Road in 1833. He was a farmer living in a 1-storey log house on Lot 20, Con. 4 SER. George was a Lieutenant in the Second Light Infantry of Middlesex under Colonel T. Radcliff in 1837. Five children were born to George and Harriet Pegley while they were living in Adelaide Township, before they moved to Wisconsin in 1864.

Rowley James (1813), born in Ireland, came to Ontario with his father. He settled at Chatham, where he was a medical doctor as early as 1846, according to an advertisement placed in the Chatham Gleaner that located his office on King Street. He married Violet Woods of Sandwich, and they had three children.

Jane (1815), the fourth child, was born in Ireland. She married Dr. Thomas Cross of Chatham.

Anna Fry (1818), born in England, married Mr. Marsden of Strathroy. In 1865, she married Rev. Thomas Adams. Her third husband was Matthew Wilson.

Sixth issue of Robert and Mary Ann was Henry Porons (1820-ca.1863), born in Scotland.

William (1822), born in Ireland, was recorded in the 1851 census of Adelaide Township as living on the east half of Lot 17, Con. 1 NER. Also on the census were wife Cecilia 24, daughter of Captain and Mrs. Faunt; Henry 2; and Florence 1. Family records state that all of the children, except the first, were recorded at St. Mary's Church in Adelaide Township. The children were William (ca.1846); Robert Efan (1850); Florence (1851); Rosilie (1858); Thomas (1860); Ellen (1861); Cecilia Harriet (1863); and Sarah (1864).

Eighth child, Mary Ann (1823-1872), was born in Ireland. She lived in Strathroy, and remained unmarried.

Robert Cromwell (1825) was born in Ireland. He is listed as a surgeon in the 1851 census of Adelaide Township.

Matilda (1827-1899) was born in Ireland, never married, and lived in Strathroy.

Arabella (ca.1829-1904), born in Canada, married Charles Richard Atkinson.

John Kevin (1831-1878) was a merchant in Middlesex County in 1871.

Letitia Pegley (ca.1833-1873) never married, and lived in Strathroy.

Charles Edward (ca.1835-1897) married Martha Butler (ca.1845-1899) of Quebec in New York City in 1863. Charles was a lawyer in Kent County in 1871. They had six children.

The youngest child of Robert and Mary Ann was Catherine A.C. (ca.1839-1865), who remained unmarried, and lived in Strathroy.

After Robert Pegley's death, his children found property not covered by his will, which consisted of land in Strathroy. It included Lots 9 and 11 of Reid's Survey, south of the Railway Station, bounded by High Street on the South, Princess Street on the West, and the County Road on the East. This was formerly a portion of the N.W. Grant of Lot 12 on Con. 10 of the Township of Caradoc, according to the Survey and Plan of Samuel Peters, Surveyor of London.

The Robert Pegley family made important contributions to the development of the Township of Adelaide. The census records stated that they were Wesleyan Methodist in religion. Al Rhods of Madison, Alabama, a descendant of George and

Harriet (Cooper) Pegley, has been in Strathroy recently, looking for burial sites of his ancestors. He provided information on the Pegley family.

PENNINGTON, Thomas and William

Reverend and Mrs. William Pennington of the County of Yorkshire, England, had a family of six children. Two of their children, Thomas (1809-1895) and William, came to Canada in 1833. No further information is known about William Pennington.

Thomas married Ann Bridge (1818-1884). It is not known if they were married in England or Quebec, where they were living until 1856 when they purchased 100 acres from the Crown at the west half of Lot 15, Con. 2 NER. They arrived with 11 children. Two more children were born in Ontario.

Martha (1835-1920), the eldest child of Thomas and Ann, married John Ivor (1835-1907). They had three sons, David, Frank and Sidney. The 1861 census shows that John Ivor had a store and tavern in Adelaide Village.

John (1836-1884) married Esther Robotham (1842-1884). They moved to Frankfort, Kansas, where they were brutally murdered by their hired man. They had no children.

Hannah (1838-1900) married John J. Barber and moved to Birmingham, Alabama. They had two sons, one of whom was Donald.

Eliza (1841-1925) married James Sampson. They lived in Detroit and had a son, Herbert, and a daughter, Mabel.

Thomas (1843-1928), fifth child of Thomas and Ann, lived in Michigan. He was a farmer and carpenter. Thomas and his wife (name unknown) had two sons, Thomas Jr. and Roy.

Mary Ann (1845-1933) married William Pannell. They lived near Strathroy and their children were Fred, Blanche and Pearl.

William (1847-1920) moved to Oregon. He and his wife (name unknown) had a son, George, and four daughters.

Robert Clarke (1849-1935) lived in Kansas and farmed there. He and his wife (name unknown) had four children, Lawrence, Roy, Mabel and Nellie.

Benjamin "Ben" (1851-1914), ninth issue of Thomas and Ann, married Margaret "Maggie" Sophia McDonald (1868-1907), daughter of John and Jessie (McKenzie) McDonald of Adelaide, on January 1, 1894. Benjamin and Margaret had two sons, John Leslie (1895-1924) and Benjamin Francis "Frank" (1896-1967).

Ben bought the 100-acre farm at Lot 9, Con. 2 NER, which had been owned by David Wilkin (according to the 1878 Adelaide map). Life was not to be easy as Maggie developed tuberculosis and died at the age of 38 years. Ben had a great fear that his sons might contract the disease, so he built a new brick home on his farm in 1909. It is believed to have cost $1,800 to build. It had a complete basement, two storeys, and a large attic topped with a slate roof. A neighbour who was an excellent carpenter, James Gerry Sr., did the woodwork throughout the house, including a front staircase. The name of the builder is unknown.

Ben was unable to enjoy his home for long, as he caught a cold which turned into pneumonia, and he died at the age of 62. John and Frank were left alone at the ages of 17 and 18. Despite the big responsibility for the boys, they continued to farm with cattle, milking cows, pigs, chickens, and grain crops. They always had three horses to do the fieldwork. Frank also trapped animals and sold the pelts for fur. He had two large raccoon coats and hats made for himself and John. With extreme cold trips to the mill in Kerwood by team and sleigh, these coats made the trip bearable.

Frank was called up to the army during WWI. He trained with the First Depot Battalion, Western Ontario Reserve Regiment A Company, Fourth Battalion at Carling Heights. Frank had completed training and was ready to be shipped overseas the next day, when he contracted mumps. Frank never

Pennington Family Reunion, ca.1930.

fought a battle in WWI; his uniform was stored in a wicker hamper in the attic, complete with "putties" to wrap over pant legs and boot tops.

John's interests included photography, finishing his own photos, and playing the violin. On June 26, 1918, John married Beatrice Birdenia "Birdie" Conkey (1898-1983). Her parents were Nathaniel Wesley (d.1945) and Mary Ellen "Nell" (Seed) Conkey. The newlywed couple stayed on the home farm with Frank.

John and Birdie had two daughters, Margaret Evelyn (1920) and Mary Kathleen "Kay" (1923). The year after Kay was born, John contracted quinsy and died at the age of 29. Fortunately, Frank was still there to carry out the farm work. To supplement the farm income, Birdie churned butter and supplied a number of customers in the Sarnia area.

Many years of hard work passed for Frank and Birdie during the Depression. Margaret and Kay grew and attended S.S. #9, which was about 1½ miles from home. By this time, Frank owned the Currie farm, which was about halfway between home and school. Doing chores on two farms, both morning and night, left little time to relax. Margaret and Kay often stopped in at the Currie farm to put down hay and pump water for the cattle.

On September 3, 1932, Birdie and Frank were married. Frank had been a wonderful father to Margaret and Kay since John died. Soon, another daughter, Ann Berniece (1933), was born. Birdie said that Ann was named after her grandmother and a singer named Berniece that she had heard on the radio. Before hydro was available, the Penningtons were the first in the neighbourhood to have a battery-operated radio, and several families visited in the evenings to listen to the programs.

Frank was always very particular about his ploughing. He competed at ploughing matches and received at least six trophies for his championship work. He also received a trophy for Champion Bacon Hog. These winnings date from 1928-1930.

Evelyn's first teacher at S.S. #9 was Marie Reinhardt. When the weather was nice, Marie's sister, Marjorie, drove her to school in a very small cart, drawn by a very small pony. The students would all run outside to pet the pony. Other teachers Evelyn had included Viola Payne, Mildred Richards, Muriel Parker and Mae Watson. Every year, Evelyn entered her writing in the annual school fair. There was also a school parade, and each year, Ken Topping from Keyser won the soda-biscuit eating contest! One year, Evelyn and Kay decided to show their ducks in the fair. They wanted them to look nice and white, so they put bluing on them—that was the end of their plan to enter the ducks! Evelyn attended S.D.C.I. for two years, riding to school with Gordon Grogan, who charged just 25 cents a day.

Evelyn became a member of the West Adelaide Church and attended Young People's meetings. On September 4, 1943, at West Adelaide, she married Kenneth Brent George (1918), son of Mabel Euretta (Brent) and William James George (see GEORGE, James and Mary Ann). Evelyn and Ken have three children, Margaret Elizabeth (1947); Ronald Kenneth (1949); and Doris Elaine (1960). When the Helen Scott Society was formed, Evelyn became a member. Her hobbies included raising sheep and Dachshund dogs. She became a representative for Avon and has continued with Avon for 40 years. Ken and Evelyn moved to Strathroy in 1971 and now reside at 107 Princess Street.

When Evelyn married Ken George, their wedding was the first of dozens where Ann Dymond performed as a soloist. In early 1945, Birdie's father became ill, and her parents moved to the farm. Nat

John Pennington with mother, Margaret Sophia (McDonald) Pennington, and brother, Frank.

Conkey died that year, just one week after Kay married Wilfred Murray and they moved to their home near Keyser. Birdie's mother, Nell, continued to live with Birdie, Frank and Ann, sharing her time with her other daughter, Zelma Hodgson. During 1951, Frank and Birdie were less able to do all the farm work and began to think of retiring. In September 1952, they left the farm to be sharecropped by Mr. and Mrs. Gerrit Tamminga, and moved to Burns Street in Strathroy. Later, Frank sold the farm to the Strybosch family. They made a number of improvements, but the original home is still there. Frank Pennington died at the age of 71, and Birdie continued to live in Strathroy until her death at the age of 85.

In September 1951, Ann enrolled at London Normal School (Teachers' College) and graduated in June 1952. She began teaching Grade 2 at Colbourne School in Strathroy. In September 1953, Ann began teaching the Kindergarten class, where she remained until June 1958.

In July 1954, Ann married Robert "Bob" Dymond and moved to Metcalfe Township, where they still reside. Ann's teaching days ended in 1958, when she became a full-time mother to three children, John Robert (1958); Peter Francis (1962); and Mary Ann (1964). They began a mixed farming operation with Aberdeen Angus cattle, pigs, hens, and grain crops. Gradually, they discontinued farming livestock and grew only cash crops. Over the years, Bob has done custom planting and drying, has been field man for Green Giant, and for 23 years, Ann and Bob operated a cucumber grading station for Bick's Pickles. Bob still farms 213 acres, and Ann enjoys her hobbies, needlework and crafts, music, and even writes the occasional song or poem.

Ann and Bob's children attended Metcalfe Central School and graduated from S.D.C.I. John and Peter were involved in music through their teen years in local weekend bands, "The Chaparells" and "The Reflections."

At present, John is a musician, playing bass guitar. He lives in Toronto with his wife, Denise, and Denise's daughter, Bailey Brown. They were married September 27, 1998. Denise owns a hair salon, "Headstrong," located on Queen Street. John toured with many bands since beginning his career in March 1983. A few of these bands include k.d. lang, Bruce Cockburn, Randall and Tracy Prescott, Mercey Brothers, Lisa Brokop and Natalie

Frank and Birdie Pennington with grandson, John R. Dymond, 1959.

McMaster. He also does a great deal of studio work as a back-up musician on recordings. His music has taken him to many countries and continents and he has gained many friends and experiences, such as travelling to Bosnia to entertain the troops.

Peter learned the tool-and-die trade at Fanshawe College and Precision Tool in Cairngorm, following his graduation from S.D.C.I. He worked at this for a number of years before he got the urge to learn to fly. He has completed his flying examinations and at present he is flying for "Flightexec," a charter and air ambulance company operating out of the London airport. Last year gave him an unusual experience as he flew a "C46" out of Winnipeg into the northern areas.

Mary Ann, youngest child of Ann and Bob, graduated from Westervelt as an executive secretary and worked for 14 years at a Toronto Dominion Bank in London. In October 1986, she married Steven Martin. They reside in Strathroy with their two children, Allison Nicole (1991) and Brett James Robert (1997). At present, Steve is employed at Lang's Bus Lines and Mary Ann works at the Investment Centre in Strathroy.

Sarah (1853-1929), tenth child of Thomas and Ann, married William Earley (1851) and they lived near Kerwood. They had a daughter, Ida, and twin sons, Loftus and Earnest.

David (1856-1931) married Annie Jane Anderson (1866-1962). They lived on the home farm in Adelaide and had three children, Manfred, Clare and Eva.

Harriet Matilda (1860) died an infant.

Harriet #2 (1863-1948), the youngest child of Thomas and Ann, married Richard Newton (1847-1917). They lived near Kerwood and had two children, Gertrude and Leslie.

PERRIE, Rev. James and Marion

In May 1997, Rev. James "Jim" and Mrs. Marion (Heaslip) Perrie took possession of their 10-year-old retirement home, which had been owned by Allan and Kimberley Campbell. Adelaide Township was familiar to the Perries, as Jim had pastored from 1968-1975 at West Adelaide Presbyterian Church, which is part of the Beechwood Pastoral Charge. After marriage in 1974, Marion became fondly acquainted with the area as well.

Marion grew up in Princeton, Ontario, and graduated from Hamilton Teachers' College. After teaching for the Hamilton Board of Education for 16 years, she worked at Scripture Union in Scarborough until marriage and the move to Strathroy.

Jim also grew up with rural roots, on a farm near Brussels, Ontario, in Grey Township. After teaching elementary school for two years, Jim graduated from Waterloo Lutheran University and Knox College, Toronto. He was ordained to the Christian ministry within the Presbyterian Church in Canada in 1964 and served for 33 years in five pastorates, retiring to Kerwood from Geneva Presbyterian Church, Chesley, in Bruce County.

PERRY, Margaret

The 50-acre property on the south half of Lot 4, Con. 3 NER, was once owned by Mr. and Mrs. J.H. Richardson. They left it to their daughter, Mildred Richardson, who eventually sold it to her niece and nephew, Marian and Craig Cadman, of R.R. #3 Kerwood. Marian and Craig Cadman sold the farm to Margaret Perry on August 26, 1991. At the time of the sale, it was a wheat field with a 17-acre hardwood bush and a small creek.

Margaret moved into her house on the farm on June 8, 1992. At that time, she was finalizing her career as a school counselor at Montcalm Secondary School in London. The last 26 years of her teaching career were in London at Wheable, Beal, and Montcalm Secondary School.

Margaret was born on a farm on the Parkhouse Road, halfway between Appin and Glencoe in Ekfrid Township, and she lived there until she was 19 years old, when her family moved to Wardsville. She taught Grades 1 to 8 at S.S. #11 Aldborough for three years while living in Wardsville. Margaret lived in Lambeth for two years, when she taught Grade 2 at S.S. #17 Westminster, now the M.B. McEachren Public School. After living in Kingston for a year while she completed her B.A. at Queen's University, Margaret taught mathematics at Moira Secondary School in Belleville.

Country living always had a special appeal to Margaret, so farm life seemed the right direction in which to turn as she retired from teaching. She has not regretted the move.

Bonny Kish moved into the basement apartment at the farm on August 6, 1992. Bonny was born in London and lived there the first 22 years of her life. She also lived in Toronto, Woodstock and Thorndale. Bonny has always been employed in the health field. She is presently working for Dynacare Laboratories in London. She has been involved with horses since she was a child.

Bonny's daughter, Tracy, spent the first summer on the farm while she worked at a summer job. She completed her Bachelor of Nursing Sciences at McMaster University in June, 1994, and acquired her R.N. shortly afterwards. In August 1994, she went to Japan to teach English for two years.

The horses arrived at the farm in late August 1992, when the barn was finished. Margaret and Bonny each have horses, and they enjoy raising, riding, training and showing them.

PERRY, Robert and Thelma

Robert Perry was born and raised in Ekfrid Township, and educated at S.S. #13 and #5 Ekfrid, and Glencoe District High School.

Robert married Thelma Murray in a rural church called Riverside in Ekfrid (the church was later demolished). Thelma was born in Caradoc and raised in Ekfrid. She was educated at S.S. #1 Ekfrid and Glencoe District High School.

Robert and Thelma raised six children, Karen, who lives in Kitchener; Brian, who married Alexandra McEacheran and lives in London; Lorraine (deceased); Rob, who lives in Windsor; Bonnie, who lives in Toronto; and Greg, who lives in London. Several handicapped foster children were also a part of the family.

Robert and Thelma moved to the United Church manse in June 1988. Robert ministers to the United Church in Kerwood-Bethesda and Cairngorm.

Robert worked many years for Fennell Lumber in Glencoe, then operated a company known as Dun-Ald Construction from his home shop in Dutton, building new homes and doing repairs. He entered the ministry in 1979, with the intention of becoming ordained. The sudden death of daughter Lorraine at age 18 (in 1980) changed his plans, and he took Lay Pastoral Ministry training. He has served at Bluevale-Whitechurch, Cape Croker, and his present charge. Robert's hobbies are woodworking and heritage dancing.

Thelma taught school off and on. After Lorraine's death, she concentrated on being a foster mom until the death of a foster daughter while at Cape Croker. She worked at Cape Croker Junior School as a Tutor Escort, and after moving to Kerwood, Thelma worked for Bill Smith until his gift shop closed. She is now a Home Support Worker for Mardam Health Care Services, a Lay Supply Minister, and Facilitator of the Bereavement Program for the V.O.N. Her hobbies include gardening, oil painting, and heritage dancing.

PETCH, Francis and Mary

In 1842, Francis Petch (1814-1900) married Mary Moore (1815-1888). Francis and Mary were both of Yorkshire, England. They had one daughter before immigrating to Canada in 1844. They first settled in York County, Ontario, and some time before 1861, they moved to Adelaide Township to the west half of Lot 12, Con. 1 SER. According to family oral history, on the ship from England, Francis met (and kept in touch with) a Mr. Quantz, who settled in Adelaide. For reasons unknown, the two traded properties sight unseen.

Francis and Mary had seven children, Sarah (1843-1890); Thomas (1845-1920); Benjamin (1848-1863); James (1850-1918); Joseph (1853-1921); Mary (1856-1890); and Frances Jane (1860-1915). After Mary died, Francis married Ellen (1844-1915, last name unknown).

James Petch (1828-1894), brother of Francis, also farmed in Adelaide for a few years. With his wife, Sarah (1828-1893), he raised three children, Isaac (1861); James (ca.1862); and Sarah (ca.1869).

In 1869, Sarah, eldest child of Francis and Mary,

The morning after a garden party at the Fred Petch farm, Margaret Holmes, Muriel Petch and Stanley Brock, ca.1919.

married John Barron (1841-1916). They had no children. John had immigrated to Canada from England in 1855, probably with his parents. It is not known where he first settled. From the late 1870s until his death, he farmed in Adelaide on the west half of Lot 15, Con. 1 SER.

In 1870, Thomas married Sarah Thrower (1846-1913), daughter of Isaac and Mary (Humphries) Thrower. They had two children, Morley (1872-1944) and Whitford (1874-1929). Thomas farmed the west half of Lot 12, Con. 2 SER. About 1908, when Whitford married, Thomas, Sarah and Morley moved to a 13-acre farm, the southeast corner of Lot 21, Con. 3 SER, purchased from the estate of Sarah's father, Isaac. While walking home from a neighbour's house one day, Thomas was attacked and injured by a stray steer. He was found and taken to the hospital, but survived only a few days.

Both Morley and Whitford lost their hearing by the age of eight or nine as the result of a serious infection that accompanied a cold. Antibiotics, which can cure these infections today, were yet to be discovered. Before they became deaf, Morley and Whitford attended school and achieved a certain amount of fluency in speaking and an adequate vocabulary, so they were able to communicate later in life. However, this handicap prevented them from participating in many community events.

In 1914, Morley married Harriett Tout (1877-1945) of Toronto, and they had three children. Pauline (1915-1996) never married. Irene (1915-1963) married Peter Dodds of Watford in 1934, and had three children, Peter Jr., Robert and Barry. They lived in London where Peter worked at a grocery store, and then as an attendant at the London Psychiatric Hospital. Vera (1916), the third child of Morley and Harriett, married Morris MacDonald (see MacDONALD, Morris and Vera).

Morley initially worked on the home farm but did not care much for farming. He left the home farm to his brother and farmed his parents' 13-acre property, eventually acquiring it on their death. Morley had various other occupations. He was a builder and a good mechanic, often travelling from farm to farm, fixing machinery. He built a machine shop that made turned wooden parts for wagons and other farm equipment. He also designed and built his own cement mixer, which he used for building projects. He kept a pasture farm at Lot 16, Con. 1 SER.

In 1908, Whitford married Jessie Bell (1882-1950) and they had five children, Margaret (1911-1940); Jessie (1914-1997); Grace (1917-1921); Whitford "Whit" Thomas (1919-1996); and Edna (1923).

In 1938, Margaret married Verne Osborne. They had one daughter, Joyce.

In 1941, Jessie married Mandus Bice (1911-1987) of East Williams Township. They had two children, David and John. Mandus farmed in Adelaide at Pt. Lot 11, Con. 3 SER, then sold the property to his brother-in-law. He moved to Strathroy, where he owned the Canadian Tire store in the 1950s, and later, the Farmer's Outfitting Store.

In 1946, Whit married Helen Sutherland Begg (1924) of Scotland. They had three children, Whitford Jr., George "Wes" and Heather (1956-1959). Whit met Helen, who was working as a nurse, while serving overseas during WWII. Whit took over the family farm, and in 1946, he purchased the Bice farm. A fire in 1946 burned down the family home, along with Christmas presents and much family history. The family moved to the former Bice home across the road. Whitford Jr. became an architect and lives in Toronto with his wife, Eileen Lichti, and their two children, Matthew and Emily. Wes operates an import/export firm and lives in Grand Bend with his wife, Marie Campbell, and two children, Kathleen and Teresa.

In 1952, Edna, the youngest of Whitford and Jessie's children, married Ken Cornell and they had three children, Kirby, Kerry and Perry. Edna has a hairdressing shop in London, and Ken worked for the railroad.

James Petch, the fourth child of Francis and Mary, married Hannah Wiley (1845-1922), daughter of John and Mary (Martin) Wiley. They had four children, Frank (1873-1957); Joseph (1878-1963); Alton (1880-1955); and Sarah Jane (1884, died an infant). James farmed the east half of Lot 12, Con. 2 SER.

In 1918, Frank married Ida Galloway (1875-1959), daughter of Thomas and Jane Galloway. They had one daughter, Evelyn (1920). Frank started farming with his father and brothers on the home farm. He then farmed Lot 10, Con. 2 SER, with his brother, Joseph. About 1916, he purchased and farmed part of Lot 19, Con. 2 SER, for his remain-

Joseph and Martha (Parker) Petch in their wedding picture, 1876.

Fred Petch, Pearl Muxlow, and Muriel Petch in the early 1930s.

ing years. Evelyn worked for Revenue Canada in London, mostly as a secretary, for 35 years. In 1953, she married Robert Douglas Proctor (1918-1976). They had no children and lived in London, then moved to St. Thomas in 1962.

In 1900, Joseph married Adelaide Humphries (1878-1965), daughter of Henry and Bridget (Galbraith) Humphries. They had two children, Burton "Bert" (1908-1987) and Velma (1912-1990), who married George Morgan (see MORGAN, Richard Sr. and Jane).

Joseph worked with his father on the home farm and then with his brother, Frank, before farming part of Lot 10, Con. 2 SER, on his own. Joseph also worked part-time as a carpenter. His son, Bert, received a good education and wanted to pursue another career, but as an only son, remained to take over the family farm and faithfully looked after his parents. Bert was known for his sense of humour and had some skill with the written word. He was active in local community events, often composing skits and then writing up the events for the local newspaper. At the age of 62, he married a widow, Elva (Scott) Sparling.

Alton never married. He farmed with his father for a few years before farming on his own on Lot 17, Con. 2 SER. He was not listed in the 1925 Adelaide Directory. He died in Hespeler, Ontario.

In 1876, Joseph Petch, the fifth child of Francis and Mary, married Martha Jane Parker (1859-1928), daughter of George and Sarah Ann (Hilton) Parker.

They had four children, Anna (1879-1917); George (1882-1943); Lorne (1885-1948); and Fred (1891-1976). Joseph farmed the east half of Lot 15, Con. 1 SER. Joseph cleared five acres before building a cabin. He continued clearing land and in 1872, built a frame cottage with the harvested lumber. Candles were used to light the interior until 1877, when a load of lumber brought to London was enough to procure a lamp. The frame house was bricked over in 1897. The present Adelaide Central School is built on the original five acres that Joseph cleared.

In 1902, Anna, the eldest of Joseph and Martha's children, married George Nichol, son of Edward and Maria (Ingham) Nichol. They had no children. Prior to her death, Anna suffered from a long and trying illness. George farmed the Nichol homestead, Pt. Lot 18, Con. 1 SER.

George, Anna's brother, married Berdella Eastman (1889-1980), daughter of Wesley and Mary (Stoney) Eastman. They had three children, Edmund (1911-1916); Ruth (1914-ca.1991); and a son born in the west. George farmed across the road from Joseph and Martha. About 1916, he moved to Regina, Saskatchewan, where he worked as a firefighter.

Lorne, third child of Joseph and Mary, married Esther Seburn (1884-1917). They had one daughter, Jean, who resides in St. Thomas. After Esther died, he married Nettie McGeary, but they had no children. Thirdly, he married Dora Henry and they had two children, Lawrence and Lorraine. Lorne farmed Lot 13, Con. 3 NER, before he bought a store in Adelaide Village.

In 1912, Fred, the youngest of Joseph and Mary's children, married Eva Muxlow (1891-1971), daughter of Edwin and Harriett (Humphries) Muxlow. They had one daughter, Muriel (1916-1997), who married Claire Sisson (see SISSON, Herbert and Lottie). Fred took over the home farm. When he was young, Fred was a member of the Adelaide Band and played at many local functions. In 1914, he attended a six-week agricultural course sponsored by the Department of Agriculture. The graduating class voted to form one of the first four Junior Farmers' Improvement Associations in the province. This group was the predecessor of the Kerwood Junior Farmers. Fred and Eva held many garden parties on their farm. They retired to Strathroy in 1960.

Mary Petch, sixth child of Francis and Mary, married Harvey Parker, son of George and Sarah (Hilton) Parker (see PARKER, James and Amey).

Frances Jane Petch, the youngest of Francis and Mary's children, married her cousin, Isaac Petch (1859-1930). They had three children, Edna (1890-1950), who remained single; Gordon; and George (1892-1918).

PETERS, John B. and Hendrika

John B. Peters (1905) was born in Asten, North Brabant, Holland. He immigrated to Canada in March 1951 with his wife, Hendrika, and seven children.

They first settled on St. Ann's Island near Wallaceburg. Later that year, J.B. travelled to Adelaide Township to look for a farm to buy. In November 1951, they purchased 100 acres, the east half of Lot 3, Con. 1 SER, from Don and Anna Sullivan.

In the early 1950s, the eldest children attended school at S.S. #6 along Egremont Road, with Mrs. McNeil as their teacher. On many occasions, the Peters family received friendship and help from their neighbours, which made them feel welcome in the community.

The farm consisted of a dairy herd, pigs and chickens. Field crops they grew included sugar beets, cucumbers, picking beans, corn, oats and barley, with the children providing most of the labour. The eldest daughters worked as domestics in the winter.

J.B., a firm believer in good drainage, was one of the first farmers in the area to install tile drainage, which he did in 1959.

On the corner of the property along Sideroad #3 is the site of the former West Adelaide Presbyterian Church and Cemetery. In 1967, J.B. and the Junior Farmers cleaned up the cemetery as a centennial project. A monument was installed with existing gravestones dating back to the 1800s. The Peters family still maintains this property.

Several of John and Hendrika's children remain in Adelaide Township. Nellie married John Dortmans and moved to Lot 15, Con. 3 SER. Gertrude married John Timmermans and moved to Lot 11, Con. 2 SER. Ann married John Geerts and moved to Warwick Township. Carol married Louie Kennes and moved to Parkhill. John married Elsie Straatman and moved to Warwick Township, and

John Peters family in 1950, just before coming to Canada. Back L-R, Gertrude, Nellie; Front L-R, Carol, John Sr., Mary, John, Rita, Hendrika and Anne.

died the same year from injuries he suffered in a car accident. Mary died in 1955 after being struck by a car on Egremont Road. Rita married Frank Vander Kant and moved to Parkhill. Bob, the youngest and the only child born in Canada, married Willie Rombouts and lives on the home farm. They have five children, Ron, Michael, David, Robert and Melanie.

PHILLIPS, Ken and Phyllis

Ken and Phyllis (Down) Phillips reside in Adelaide Township at the corner of School Road and Mullifarry Drive. The history of this farm dates back to 1841, when Phyllis's ancestors, George and Celia (Weekes) Down, bought 100 acres of land. Later, George divided the farm and gave 50 acres to each of his two sons, Henry and Charles.

Henry married Mary Edwards and was given the 50 acres beside the sideroad, which became the east half of Lot 15, Con. 2 SER. Their six children were George, Arthur, Alma, Selinda, Laura and James Albert "Bert" (d.1952).

Bert took over the farm that was owned by his parents. He married Pearl Gill of Strathroy on January 7, 1920. They have four children. Ivan Russell married Marion Handley and they have three children, Stephen, Frances and David. Greta Winnifred married Ivan Linton. Lois Marion married James Watson and they have four children, Douglas, Margaret, Donald and Marion. Phyllis June married Kenneth Phillips in 1950 and they have two children, Marilyn and Robert "Robb."

Following Bert's death, Pearl sharecropped the farm with Phyllis and Ken, who had been living in

East Williams where Ken worked for his uncle, Bob McCubbin. In four years, when Pearl remarried and moved to Toronto, Ken and Phyllis purchased the farm. Marilyn married Burton Dolbear in 1970, and moved to Strathroy. Marilyn and Burton have three children, Laurie, Lincoln and Sarah. Robb lives at home.

PLAXTON, William and Susan

William Plaxton (1822-1909) was the fourth child of John and Elizabeth Plaxton, who came to Canada from Yorkshire, England, in 1827. About 1840, in Markham, Ontario, William married Susan Spring (1824-1905). They farmed in Dorchester, lived in Strathroy for seven years, and then bought property in Adelaide Township from Hugh Seed, the deed registered in 1889. They lived at the east half of Lot 12, Con. 2 NER. William and Susan had six sons and four daughters. Albert (1842-1912) was living in Strathroy in 1909, according to his father's obituary. Frances "Fanny" (1844) married W.J. Whyte. John (1846) resided in Markham in 1909. James Robert (1850-1914) married Ann Sinclair. They had seven children, none in Adelaide. In 1909, they lived in British Columbia. There is no further information about Dorothy (1852-1925). Peter (ca.1854) resided in Millington, Michigan, in 1909. Angelique "Angelina" (1856-1937) married Dennis Demaray (1852-1926), son of Samuel and Eunice (Beacham) Demaray, in 1873 in Adelaide Township. Angelina and Dennis farmed in Adelaide Township, and had three children (see DEMARAY). Thomas A. (ca.1858-1884) married Elspie Brown. They resided in Sandusky, Michigan, in 1909.

Edmund (1863), ninth child of William and Susan Plaxton, married Alice Ann Wilkinson (1864) in 1889. In 1899, Edmund purchased the home farm from his par-

Edmund and Alice Ann Plaxton on 50th wedding anniversary.

ents, and records show they were farming in Adelaide Township in 1901.

Edmund and Alice had two children in Adelaide Township. Oscar (1891) drowned in 1917 in Bindloss, Alberta, and Ivy Marie (1893-1948) married Arnold Clifton Anderson (1898-1966). Ivy Marie and Arnold had two children, Marie (1923), who married Gordon Cuddy; and William (see ANDERSON, Alexander and Mary Jane).

Alice (ca.1864), tenth child of William and Susan, married P.A. Sparling and lived in Blanchard Township, Perth County.

POLLOCK, William and Minnie

William Raymond Pollock and Minnie Ester MacPherson were married in Stephen Township in 1912 and lived in Corbett, Ontario, where William was employed by the Corbett Creamery. A short time later, they moved to Exeter, where he worked at the Exeter Creamery. Their first son, Mervyn Arthur (1913-1936), was born in Exeter, and while there, William attended the Ontario Agricultural College at Guelph, receiving his dairy qualification in 1915.

The following year, William was employed as a butter maker at the Kerwood Creamery, owned and operated by William Waddell, father of Mac Waddell, the owner of Strathroy Creamery for many years. During the time Raymond Pollock worked for Mr. Waddell, he also owned and operated a general store formerly run by the Armstrong family.

A second son, Donald MacPherson (1917), was born in the house known as the "Carmody House," located across the street from the Canadian Canner Pea Viner; it is now the residence of Margaret and William Jordan. The Pollocks then moved from this location to an apartment above the general store, which later became the residence of the Harold Conkey family. They operated the store and had the Kerwood Post Office in the front section.

William purchased the Kerwood Creamery in 1922 for $7,500 and sold the general store. One year later, he bought the former Waddell home, where he resided until his death in 1949. Two more sons were born there, Grant (1924) and Jack (1928). Mervyn, the eldest son, attended O.A.C. in 1935. He worked in the creamery until his death from streptococcus infection. Donald also worked in the creamery after leaving school.

Some of the other employees of the creamery were Russell Johnson, Reginald Willett, Harold Irwin, Milo Brooks, Ralph Brooks, Arthur Such, Charles Griffen, Ernest Tedball and Ed Wilson. Donald remembers that his father and his men cut ice from Cook's Pond, packed it in sawdust, and stored it in an icehouse. The ice was used to cool the cream after pasteurization.

Donald attended O.A.C. in 1940-1941 and worked in the creamery until it was sold in 1943 to the Carnation Milk Company for $35,000. Donald was employed by Carnation as a field man, and it was his job to convert 500 cream patrons to milk patrons and to set up milk routes and haulers.

In 1942, Donald married Margaret Isabelle Anderson, and they had three children, James Donald (1948); William Raymond (1950); and Anne Louise (1951), who married into the Pearson family.

After the creamery was sold, William started a new business, Kerwood Produce, which was an egg grading station and cold storage locker. He had a stroke in 1946, leaving him unable to operate his business. Donald left Carnation, bought Kerwood Produce, and started hauling milk to the Carnation plant. Some employees of Kerwood Produce were Anna Burdon, Bruce Evans, Bill Jordan, Grant Parker, Margaret (Taylor) Jordan, Ena Irwin, Douglas George, Earl Alderson, Cliff Winters, and John Raterink.

In 1953, Donald got involved in the truck leasing business with one tractor-trailer. He transported television cabinets from Middlesex Furniture Company to Toronto, where the components were then installed.

POSTHUMUS, Ypke and Gerda

Ypke Posthumus (1935), a dairy cattle farmer, was born in Jistrum F.R., Holland, the youngest of five children. Gooitske "Gerda" (1935) was born in Compagnie F.R., Holland, also youngest in a family of five. They married in 1959 and two children were born in Holland, Jacob (1961) and Eppie "Ed" (1962). After their immigration to Canada, three more children were born, Hein (1967); Pieter "Pete" (1973); and Grietje Aaltje "Greta" (1975).

Coming to Ontario represented a new beginning for the Posthumus family. In some ways, farming dairy cows is the same in Holland, but feeding, fieldwork and equipment are different here. Good neighbours taught Ypke and Gerda a great deal after their arrival. The primary focus of the farm is still dairy, with 200 acres of workable land.

In 1991, Ed married Gea (1964, last name unknown) of Barneveld Gld., Holland. They have three children, Trudy (1992); Ypke Jacob (1993); and Gonda Monique (1996).

In 1997, Greta married Andre Joosse from Strathroy.

POSTMA, Peter and Charlotte

Peter Postma immigrated to Canada from Holland in 1959 and settled in Ailsa Craig. He met and married Charlotte Nichols in 1960, and they settled in Adelaide Township. In 1964, they bought Charlotte's Uncle Bert Nichols' farm, which is located on Highway 22.

Peter worked as a truck driver. Charlotte was a nurse, but she also had an interest in politics (her father, Charles Nichols, was Reeve of Adelaide Township for more than 17 years). She ran for council and became the first woman on the Adelaide Township Council, a position she held for 15 years. Peter and Charlotte sold their farm and now reside in Sarnia.

A son, Charles, married Kelly Wilkins in March 1985, and they moved to the U.S. (Kelly is American). They have one daughter, Carley. A daughter, Patricia, is single, and lives and works in Sarnia.

POWELL, David and Linda

David Melvin and Linda Beth (Cerkan) Powell moved to Adelaide in the spring of 1972, after buying a farm at Lot 4, Con. 5 NER, from Ivan Small. They hadn't intended to move from their residence in Strathroy, but attended an auction sale at the farm in the company of an old university friend. He convinced them to make an offer on the property. They were very taken by the house and its unique architectural detail.

David and Linda have three children, David Scott (1972-1973); Jennifer Lynn (1974); and Nancy Ann (1978).

Linda's family roots go back to Poland although she was born in Wisconsin and spent most of her single life in Chicago, Illinois. David's family was from Brooke Township, where they had farmed since the mid-1800s. The Powells originated in Wales and came to Canada from Tipperary County in Ireland.

The house was built in the 1880s. It is probably the second house on the farm. The original frame structure was still standing (barely) when the farm was purchased. It was removed for aesthetic and safety reasons. The current house was built in front of the original homestead. The original residents, the Langans, held church services and funerals in the formal front rooms. There was a history of seafaring in the Langan family. It is understood that the original settler left his wife and family to clear the farm while he was engaged as a captain on a Great Lakes vessel. If you drive by, you will notice a wrought iron railing surrounding a "widow's walk" on the roof. This was a longstanding architectural tradition along seacoasts. You can see a long way from the rooftop, but not to any coastal shores!

PRESTON, Charles and Jean

Charles Preston (1791-1878) was born in Ballyclare in the County of Antrim, Ireland. He was a shoemaker by trade but served with the British Imperial Army. Charles fought with the Glengarry Highlanders on the Chrysler Farm, Ogdensburg, Ontario, in the War of 1812. As was the custom, Charles received a parcel of land in lieu of an army pension in 1831. The property was 100 acres in Napier, Metcalfe Township (now Adelaide Township). He married Jean Wilson (1792-1874). Charles and Jean had 10 children, Anthony (1814-1879), who married Margaret DeGraw and had nine children; Jane (1815), who married John Kearns; Thomas; Mary (1821), who married Joseph Hart; Charles (1832); Margaret (1832), who married George Perry; George (1836); Elizabeth (1839), who married John Old; Samuel (1840); and James.

When the Rebellion of 1837 broke out, Charles, then a Lieutenant, rejoined his regiment at Cornwall along with sons Anthony and Thomas. The Rebellion was short-lived, so they returned home to the farm in one year's time.

In the late 1830s, Charles donated four acres of his land for a church, cemetery, log schoolhouse, and rectory. The log schoolhouse was built in 1839, and it is believed the church, St. Mary's, was built in 1841.

As the children grew older, several of the Preston male children left the farm. Thomas moved to Wingham, Ontario, as a shoemaker. Charles moved to Ottawa, Illinois, as a farmer. George moved to Memphis, Tennessee, as a railway conductor, and James moved to Des Moines, Iowa, as a bridgemaster. Although no record exists of this, it is believed that one or two of the sons who moved to the U.S. fought as confederates in the American Civil War.

Anthony and his wife, Margaret, moved to Adelaide Village where he worked as a shoemaker. Nine children were born to them, Elizabeth (1839); Maria (1842), who married Sylvanus Gibson of Lucan in 1859; Charles Wilson (1844); Margaret (1846); Charlotte (1848); Sarah Anne (1850); Samuel (1853); Alice Alma (1855); and Antoinette (1858).

Anthony was appointed township librarian at the November 19, 1853, township Council meeting. The clerk was ordered to get "a desk for books to be of walnut or cherry." Since there was not a township public building at that time, one might assume that this Adelaide Township Public Library was in Anthony Preston's shoemaker shop. In 1855, Anthony was appointed Assessor for the Township. At the February 4, 1857, council meeting he was appointed Township Clerk, a position he held for 26 years. Anthony and Margaret are buried in Mount Pleasant Cemetery, London, in the Sylvanus Gibson plot.

Samuel, the youngest of the Preston children, became a hero in the U.S. Navy, but his life was cut short. In 1858, he was appointed Midshipman from the State of Illinois and entered the United States Academy in Annapolis, Maryland. He graduated at the top of the class. After the outbreak of the American Civil War, he was assigned senior duties of acting Midshipman. In 1863, Samuel was captured, and spent a year in Libby's Prison, South Carolina. He was exchanged in 1864 and had interviews with General Ulysses S. Grant and President Abraham Lincoln. He was killed in an attack on Fort Fisher, North Carolina, on January 13, 1865. His request was to be buried in the U.S. Naval Academy Cemetery if he was killed. He was the second person to be buried there and, after his death, six ships were named after him; four of these were destroyers that saw action in WWI and the Korean and Vietnam Wars.

It is believed that Charles and Jean later settled near Lucan to be close to their granddaughter, Maria Gibson.

St. Mary's remains in existence, and each June an annual service is conducted.

RANDALL, William and Ann

William Randall (d.1871), a weaver, was born in Wiltshire, England. His first wife died and he married Ann Ashley (d.1865), the woman who had been hired to look after his children. The family immigrated to Canada and settled in Adelaide between 1829 and 1832. It is possible that they came with the first group of Petworth Immigrants. The name "William Randall" appears twice on agent Roswell Mount's 1832 pay lists of people working on road construction in Adelaide and Warwick. It is likely that another Randall family who came in 1833 were related; this family came with the second group of Petworth Immigrants on the ship "England" to Lambton.

William settled on Lot 12, Con. 3 SER. In 1850, he is listed in the Adelaide Council minutes as a Pathmaster. At a later date, he moved his weaving business into Adelaide Village and remained there until the death of his wife. He moved to West Williams, where four of his children resided, and his body is interred at Sylvan Cemetery.

William's children were William Jr. (1818); Samuel (1823); James (1829); John (1838); Grace (1840); Mercy (1841); Mary (1843); Martha Ann (1836); and Marianne. The first three children were born in England, and the rest in Adelaide.

In 1842, William Jr. became a mail carrier, driving the stage between London and Sarnia. In 1843, he married Elizabeth Sitlington. They moved to West Williams in 1853, where he became one of the two founding settlers of the village of Sylvan.

Samuel married Harriet Sitlington and purchased Pt. Lot 9, Con. 3 SER, which he farmed until about 1857, when he joined his brother in Sylvan. The Lot 9 property then passed to his brother, James.

James married Elizabeth Mary Morse. James and Elizabeth's children were William Thomas (1855-1938); Eliza Ann (1857-1874); Arthur (1858-1882); Ellen (1860); George (1862-1925); and Lewis (1864-1937). Later, James and his family joined William Jr. and Samuel in Sylvan.

Of the remaining children, John married Sarah P. Smith in Strathroy in 1865. Nothing is known about Grace. Mercy married John T. Thompson of West Williams, and Mary married Charles Parker. Martha Randall married Thomas Dowding, and they lived on Pt. Lot 7, Con. 2 SER. Marianne (Mary Ann) married Stephen Thrower.

RAPLEY, Charles and Frances

Charles Rapley (ca.1800-1862), son of David and Ann (Stanford) Rapley (or William and Ann (Sanford) Rapley), was born in Sussex. Charles died in Adelaide Township and his body was interred in Fourth Line Cemetery. Charles was a brick maker in England. He wrote a letter in 1838 describing his activities with the militia in the Rebellion of 1837. He first settled on the west half of Lot 19, Con. 5 SER.

It seems quite possible that Charles is the child christened at Egdean, Sussex, on August 12, 1798. The parents of this child were William and Ann (Sandford) Rapley, married July 23, 1797, at Dorking, Surrey. There seems to have been considerable movement back and forth across the Sussex/Surrey border. If this William was the eldest child of William and Ruth (Court) Rapley, born about 1774 (no christening found), it would make James the uncle of Charles.

Charles married Frances Adams (d.1826) on November 11, 1822, in Stopham, Sussex. Frances was the daughter of Christopher and Sarah (Penfold) Adams, christened April 25, 1802, in Stopham. Frances died in Sussex.

Charles and Frances had three children, Sophia (1821-1903); Elisabeth (1824-1883); and Sarah (ca.1826). Sarah either died young or stayed in England.

Sophia was christened in Wisborough Green, Sussex, England, and died in Strathroy. She married Mark Mann (1819-1904) on March 8, 1841, in Adelaide Township. The following individuals are linked to this event: Charles Napper (witness) and John Downer (witness). Sophia and Mark celebrated their 55th Anniversary in 1896. Mark was born in Loxford and christened August 8, 1819, in Wisborough Green, Sussex, England. Mark was the son of Samuel and Ann (Downer) Mann. Ann was a half-sister of Avis Downer, wife of James Napper. Mark died in Strathroy.

Sophia and Mark had 11 children, John R. (ca.1842); Henry (1844-1912), who was a merchant in Petrolia and had two sons, John and Harley; Charles (1846); Malinda Jane (1849), who was christened May 6, 1849, in Adelaide and married William Luckham; Cynthia Ann (1851); Frances Elizabeth (1854-1947), who married William S. Cochrill (d.1929); Sarah Sophia (ca.1856), who married Zias B. Jury; Mark Wesley A. (1859); Jesse B. (1862); David Wallace (1864), who was christened April 1, 1864; and Alice Maude Maria (1867-1872).

Elisabeth, second child of Charles and Frances, was christened December 5, 1824, in Wisborough Green, Sussex, England. She married John Paine (d.1876) on November 29, 1842.

Elisabeth and John had nine children. Victoria A. (ca.1845-1925) married John James Douglas on July 12, 1864, in Adelaide Township. John (ca.1836-1893) was born in Ireland, the son of Melvin and Martha Douglas. Victoria A. and John had one child, Mable A. S. (d.1884). John E. (ca.1849), second child of Elisabeth and John, married Rachel M. Tuttle June 7, 1872, in Strathroy. Rachel (ca.1857) was born in the U.S., the daughter of Jacob and Eliza Tuttle. The remaining seven children of Elisabeth and John were Westley (1851); Anna (ca.1855); James (ca.1857); Arthur (ca.1859); Sarah Jane (ca.1862-1885); Alice (ca.1865); and Earnest (ca.1867).

RAPLEY, David and Harriet

David Rapley's father, James (1781-1832), was the son of William and Ruth (Court) Rapley, was born in Fittleworth, Sussex, England. He married Mary Collins (d.1831) in 1805 in Pulborough, Sussex. James immigrated to Canada in 1832 with his cousin, Charles Rapley, under the auspices of the Petworth Emigration Society. While staying in a camp in Delaware Township, James was visited several times by a doctor. He died soon after reaching his land in Adelaide. David (1817-1915), who had come to Canada with his father and several other siblings, petitioned to buy the land allotted to his father, the east half of Lot 19, Con. 5 SER.

David married Harriet Hilton (1821-1888) on March 23, 1840, in Adelaide Township. Harriet was born in Sutton, Sussex, the daughter of Charles and Mary Ann (Webb) Hilton. Both David and Harriet died in Adelaide Township. They had 10 children, Jesse (1841-1924); George (1842-1870); Mary (1846-1920); Charles (1848-1941); Esther Ann (1851-1924); David Alexander (1853-1864); Emma Harriet (1855-1943); Thomas James (1857-1921); William H. (1859-1935), who married Annie E. Jury (1868-1942); and Frederick (1862-1950), who remained unmarried, and stayed on the family farm.

Jesse, the eldest of David and Harriet's children, was born in Adelaide Township and died in Redwood City, California. Jesse was a rancher. He married Catherine Moore (1842-1916) in 1857. She was born in Kilkenny, Ireland. Jesse and Kate had three children, James David; Mary Ester "Minnie" (1870); and Maurice (ca.1878).

George, second child of David and Harriet, was a farmer in Adelaide Township. In 1866, he married Christina Lee (1845-1900), born in Scotland, the daughter of Andrew and Mary (McLaughlin) Lee. After George's death, Christina married George Thompson. George and Christina had three children, Mary Lee "Mame" (1868), who married Henry Thompson; Harriet Hilton (1869); and George (1870), who married Nell McPherson.

Harriet Hilton married Thomas Edward Pearce and they had four children, William; George; Charles (d.1917); and Harriet Lee, who married Alfred Bunting and had three children.

Mary, third issue of David and Harriet, married Alex Stevenson (1842-1927). Mary and Alex had two children, Jesse Rapley, who married Ethel Moore and had two children, Dorothy and Eileen; and Frederick David Stevenson, who married Edna (last name unknown).

Charles, fourth child of David and Harriet, married Amy May Parker (1856-1942) on February 22, 1883, the daughter of James and Ellen (Mather) Parker. They lived in London, Ontario, and had five children, Lena Myrtle (1885-1960); Georgina Edwina (1887-1958), who married J.O. Courtis and had one child, Eleanor Jean; Charles Ewart (1895-1916); and Blake Parker (1899-1993), who married Eirene Clara Jamieson in 1928. Eleanor Courtis married Donald Tuckey and has two children, Barbara and Ken.

Esther Ann, fifth of David and Harriet's children, was born in Adelaide Township and died in Edmonton, Alberta. She married James William Parker (1846-1916), son of James and Ellen (Mather) Parker. Esther and James had two children, Ethel Harriett, who married Earnest E. Sexsmith and had three children; and Harold Lancelot (d.1897).

Emma Harriet, seventh child of David and Harriet, married Ephraim James Evoy (1856-1943), son of Thomas and Hannah Evoy, and they had a daughter, Harriett Isabel Victoria (1897-1957), who married Angus N. McLean (1894-1956), the son of Aeneas H. and Dortha A. (Brigham) McLean. Harriett and Angus had four children.

The eighth child of David and Harriet was Thomas James, who died in Yale, Michigan. He married Rebecca J. Lowthian (1861-1945) and they had four children, Nina (1882), who married Bert Brown; Fred (1884-1966), who married Elizabeth Hodgins; Clare (1888-1930), who married Margaret Cavanaugh; and Hilton (1896-1987), who married Erma Reddicliff.

RAPLEY, William and Jane

William James Rapley (1814-1896) was born in Pulborough, Sussex, England, son of James and brother of David (see RAPLEY, David and Harriet).

William was a merchant, and Reeve and Mayor of Strathroy. He married twice. He married Jane Hilton (1820-1868) in 1838 in Adelaide Township. Jane was born in Sutton, Sussex, the daughter of Charles and Mary Ann (Webb) Hilton. After her death, William married his cousin, Jane "Jennie" Page (1847-1934) about 1874. Jennie was born in Sussex, England, daughter of John and Caroline (Rapley) Page (Caroline was the granddaughter of Charles Rapley and Jane Caern). Jennie died in Strathroy.

William and Jane had eight children, Mary Ann (1840-1906); Lucy (1841-1914); Charlotte (1843-1873); Ellen Maria (1845-1927); James W. (1848-1896); Sarah Jane (1850-1899); Manfred (1855-1935); and Herbert Sidney (1858-1936).

William and Jennie had two children, Dora (1877, died an infant) and Winfield Page (1883-1941).

Mary Ann, the eldest of William and Jane's children, was born and christened in Adelaide Township. She married James Manson (1836-1895) on November 1, 1860, in Strathroy. James was born in Wick, Caithness, Scotland, son of John and Isabella (Hoy) Manson. James was the founder of Manson's Bank. Their child, James W., died an infant. Mary Ann and James both died in Strathroy.

Lucy, the second child of William and Jane, was born in Adelaide Township. She married William Drynan (1835-1918), born in Girvan, Scotland. William was in dry goods. Lucy and William had six children, Mary Scott (1864-1958), who remained unmarried; William Rapley (ca.1870); Jennie (ca.1871-1891); James Herbert (1874-1960); Freddie (ca.1877-1884); and Thomas (ca.1881-1893).

William Rapley, second of Lucy and William's children, married Alice Innes. They had four children. Charles married S. Jean Moodie. James R. and his wife had two children, Scott and Christopher. Norman L. (d.1992) married Margaret Black and they had three children, John L., C. Douglas and Margaret. William Innes (1900-1981) was born in Buckingham, Quebec, and died in Hamilton, Ontario. William was president of Canadian Canners. He married Mary Kirk and they had three children, William Innes Kirk (d.1994); George; and Alice, who married John Lundon.

James Herbert, fourth child of Lucy and William, (1874-1960), married Jean Keith. They had a daughter, Mary, and a son, George Keith (1911), who married and had three children, Judith, James, and John. George is a lawyer.

Charlotte, third issue of William and Jane, was born in Adelaide Township. She married Rev. Joseph William Holmes (1834-1918), a Wesleyan Methodist minister. Joseph was born in Sligo, Ireland, and immigrated to Canada about 1862. Charlotte and Joseph Holmes had four children, Elliott, who married and was a dentist in New York; William Rapley (1867-1927), who was an actor in New York; Joseph H. (ca.1871-1873); and Charlotte Ann (1873-1962), who was born in Ayr, Ontario. Charlotte Ann married George Haldane in 1905 and they had a daughter, Josephine (1913), who married Dewitt Wilcox, M.D., in 1937. Josephine and Dewitt had three children, Christopher, Jennifer, and Mary Charlotte, who became an ordained Anglican priest in 1997. After Charlotte's death, Joseph married Amanda Lucretia Irwin about 1875, and they had three children.

Ellen Maria, fourth child of William and Jane, married John H. McIntosh (1844-1928), born in Paisley, Scotland, son of John and Julia McIntosh. Ellen and John had two children, William Ewing (d.1907); and John Rapley (1883-1959), who married May Patterson (d.1950) about 1920. After May's death, John married Susan Welles in 1953. He had no children.

James W., fifth child of William and Jane, lived in Kincardine. He married Charlotte M. Fawcett (1857-1946) and they had eight children who lived in various locations in Canada and the U.S. None appear to have resided in Adelaide Township, although some descendants live in Strathroy.

Winfield Page, son of William and Jennie, was a banker and broker in Montreal. He married Irene Burley (d.1958) in 1915. Irene was born in Portage La Prairie, Manitoba. They had two children and live in Dorval, Quebec.

RAWLINSON, Fred and Nora

Fred Herbert Rawlinson (1902) was born in Lincenshire, England, and came to southern Ontario six months later with his parents, George and Margaret Alice Rawlinson, and his sister, Beatrice. They lived in London. Fred married Nora Thrower, daughter of Jacob and Alice (Fortner) Thrower of Adelaide, in 1925.

Fred and Nora farmed 50 acres on Second Line South, across from Fred and Bill Martin. In 1933, Fred and Nora bought 100 acres to the east. They had three children, Eileen (1929); Ruth (1932); and George (1936).

The Rawlinsons remained at the farm until 1954, and then sold the property when they retired to Strathroy. Fred soon bought the Pearson farm, deciding to farm again, and later bought 12 acres on Con. 10 of Caradoc Township, where George and wife, Kathy, still reside.

REDMAN, Howard and Dora

In 1969, Howard and Dora Redman moved from Exeter to the Strathroy area. They lived on Front Street in Strathroy for one year, and then moved to Adelaide Township, where they rented a home at the corner of Highway 22 and County Road 6. They quickly became part of this friendly community.

Howard, Dora, and their family attended the West Adelaide Presbyterian Church on the Second Line North, where the minister at the time was Reverend Perrie. Dora belonged to the Helen Scott Society.

Howard and Dora have a son, Lyndsey, and a daughter, Laurie, who were seven and five when the family moved to Adelaide Township. The children attended Adelaide Central Public School.

The Redmans visited often with neighbours, especially Ray and Donelda Brock, who allowed the Redman children to ride the pony and help with gathering eggs.

Marguerite Cuddy often included the Redmans on trips to the sugarbush owned by Evan Stead, a real learning experience, where they sampled sap from the maple trees.

The soil where the Redmans lived was mostly clay, which made for harder digging, but they nevertheless planted a garden that yielded healthy, large vegetables.

Many summer days were spent at the park, where the children learned to swim. Howard made a backyard skating rink for fun times in the winter. He also included them on his weekly excursions to the township garbage dump, which was quite a different experience from setting garbage cans out in town.

In 1972, the Redmans purchased a home on High Street in Strathroy. Although their time in Adelaide Township only lasted for three years, it was an enjoyable part of life for their family, and many of their neighbours from that time remain close friends today.

REDMOND - JIGGINS

Thomas and Lillie (Ross) Redmond, formerly of Lobo Township, married in 1912 and took up farming on their 100-acre farm adjoining the Redmond homestead in Adelaide at the east half of Lot 5, Con. 3 SER. They had one daughter, Katharine Jean "Kay" Redmond.

In 1938, Kay married George Jiggins of Port Hope, a building contractor. They lived in several cities during the war, a few being Camp Borden, Barrie, North Bay, and Espanola (where P.O.W. camps were being built), and then went to Ajax to work for Defense Industries Ltd. George had a position as Building Superintendent and Kay worked in the Personnel Office.

In 1943, they returned to Adelaide Township and took over the Redmond farm from Kay's parents. Shortly after, the Redmonds retired to Strathroy. In 1956, Mr. and Mrs. Goose Feddema purchased the farm, and the property is now owned by John and Jenny Feddema.

George and Kay moved to Strathroy and George continued working in construction, specializing in custom-built homes.

REDMOND, William and Elizabeth

William Redmond (1831-1917) married

Elizabeth Venner of London, Ontario, and they had four children, Robert, Thomas, John and Teresa. William operated the Kerwood General Store. He and Elizabeth are both buried in the Strathroy Roman Catholic Cemetery.

Mathew Robert Redmond (1879–1956) married Margaret Inez Wilson (1890-1946), and they had six children, Matthew William (1912); Orville T. (1915); Inez Marion (1916); Eleanora Elizabeth (1919-1979), who married Fred Griffith of Strathroy; Gordon Arthur (1922), born in Watford; and James Pierce (1925), born in Forest.

Mathew and Margaret lived in Adelaide until 1929. They owned property at Con. 2 SER, beside the George Jiggins family. Gordon started school at S.S. #8 Adelaide and remembers his teacher was Marjorie Whiteoak. The family later moved to Warwick.

Gordon married Bertha May Tasker on June 8, 1946, and they had three children, Wayne David (1948); Gordon Bruce (1950); and Donna Marie (1954).

REINHARDT, John and Elizabeth

John Peter Reinhardt (1838-1913) was born in Germany. His parents sent John and his siblings to Canada because they were opposed to the strict military regime in Germany at the time. After they settled in Canada, John met and married Elizabeth McGugan (1839-1913) in 1862. Their children were Louisa Catherine (1863-1921); John Alexander (1864-1945); Hannibal Gary Adams (1866-1906); Fredrick William (1868-1932); Jennie (1870-1950); Mary Elizabeth (1872-1873); Isabella (1874-1949); Peter Mark (1877-1944); Elias (1878-1879); James Henry (1881-1959).

Louisa Catherine, the eldest child of John and Elizabeth, married James Henry Smith on December 19, 1888. They had five daughters and one son. Their eldest daughter, Jennie, married Lawrence Parker of Adelaide Township (see PARKER, James and Amey). They lived in Napperton at Lot 13, Con. 4 SER, where their grandson and great-grandson still farm.

John Alexander became a teacher and taught at S.S. #5, where one of his pupils was the young Arthur Currie. Also, because he was 13 years older than Peter Mark, he had been his brother's teacher. John Alexander and his family moved to the U.S., where he became the President of the Northwest Mutual Insurance Company in Washington.

Jennie, fifth issue of John and Elizabeth, married Norman McIntyre. One daughter, Mary Belle, did housekeeping for her Uncle Henry and never married. Another daughter, Elizabeth, taught at the Napperton School.

Peter Mark, eighth child of John and Elizabeth, married Rose Kenressa Thompson (1881-1939) of Caradoc. They had two daughters, Olive Marie (1904) and Marjorie Iola (1907-1984), and one son, John Murray, who was a twin to Marie and only lived a few months.

The family lived on Lou Shepard's property, which was east of the Napperton School, until they moved to Caradoc when Marie was five years old. Marie remembers that one of their neighbours in Napperton, David Jury, used to preach at Salem Church in Keyser. Her father would drive David to the church on Sundays so that he would not have to look after the horses.

About 1920, the family moved to Strathroy, where they lived for a year. Peter Mark bought a farm from James Galloway, the east half of Lot 2, Con. 3 NER. When the Con. 5 Reinhardt house burned down, the Reinhardts stayed in the Jury house for a time.

Marie attended Strathroy Collegiate. In 1923-1924, she went to the London Normal School to

Reinhardt family, back L-R, Isabella, Peter Mark, John Alexander, Hannibel G., James Henry. Front L-R, John Peter, Louisa Catherine, Frederick William, Jennet and Lizabeth, ca.1890.

become a teacher like her uncle, John Alexander. Her first placement was at S.S. #9, where she replaced Florence McPherson as teacher and taught for four years. She says that she was not only the teacher but, along with Margaret Conkey, also a janitor. They were responsible for building the fires and keeping the schoolhouse clean.

Marie (Reinhardt) Campbell, 95th birthday, 1999.

Marie married Murray Campbell in 1928. They lived in Adelaide Village, where they ran a store they purchased from George Glenn. Two daughters, Helen and Betty, were born there. In 1932, they sold the store to the Finkbeiners and moved to Prospect Hill, where they kept a garage. They had nine more children and Marie continued to teach for quite a number of years. Marie has 33 grandchildren and more than 40 great-grandchildren. Marie now lives in Nairn.

Mr. and Mrs. David Jury with John Reinhardt (child unknown).

James Henry, the youngest of John and Elizabeth's children, never married. He farmed at Lot 14, Con. 5 SER, despite requiring crutches from being stricken with infantile paralysis.

REITSMA, Edward and Elizabeth

Edward and Elizabeth Reitsma immigrated to Canada as newlyweds from the Netherlands in May 1956. The lived and worked in Sarnia for six years, and then on April 2, 1962, they bought the Frank Lewis farm at Lot 3, Con. 3 SER, to start a dairy farm and to grow crops to feed the herd. They were familiar with milking cows but had to learn about growing crops. With the help of good neighbours, they managed. Edward and Elizabeth had two daughters when they purchased the farm, Eleanor (then three) and Janet (then one). After they bought the property, two more daughters were born, Joanne (1964) and Dorothy (1970). The girls all attended Adelaide MacDonald public school and later went to S.D.C.I. One of the highlights, while the girls were growing up, was their participation in 4-H programs. The whole family was involved when they were showing their calves at the Strathroy and London fairs in the 1970s and 1980s.

Eleanor graduated and worked in offices, first in Strathroy and then in London, where she met her husband, Brian Campbell. They have two children, Elissa and Levi, and live in Wyevale, Ontario. Brian and his father operate a concrete business.

After graduation, Janet went to Calvin College in Grand Rapids, Michigan, to become a high school teacher. She married Steven Meyers and has two children, Hannah and Zachary. Steven is a social worker and they live in New Era, Michigan.

Joanne works at Glendale in Strathroy. She married Jack Huizinga from Petrolia and they have two children, Kyle and Lysa. Jack bought the milking herd from Edward and Elizabeth in August 1992, and is now doing the heavy work. They live a mile down the road in Lambton County.

Dorothy went to the London District Christian Secondary School in London and graduated from Brescia College. She worked with the school-age program for a few years and is now working at London Life/Great West Company. She married Larry Moraal of Leamington, and they live in London. Larry works in an auto parts factory in Chatham.

RICHARDSON, Clare and Jessie

Clare and Jessie (McCallum) Richardson, with daughter Marilyn (1936), moved to Lot 18, Con. 5 SER, in October 1938. Before this location, they lived and operated a dairy farm in Watford.

The couple established "Silvendell Farm" as a silver fox fur farm, and that same year a son, Bruce (1940), was born. Their small farm consisted of 10 acres with a house and barn, and a spring creek running through the back of the property. Clare always had a variety of animals, including a dairy cow, chickens, ducks, and a pig, to provide food and income for his family. They had apple, pear and apricot trees, and strawberry, raspberry and currant bushes, along with a large vegetable garden. Marilyn and Bruce attended public school at S.S. #5.

In the early 1950s, Clare and Jessie discontinued the fur business due to the loss of popularity of fox fur in ladies' fashion (which was replaced by a great demand for mink fur).

Marilyn married Larry Whiting and, since 1962, they have lived on Lot 22, Con. 2 SER, where Larry operates a two-way radio sales and service business.

Bruce married Rosalind Pane and moved to Milton. Bruce is employed in the petroleum industry, and he and Rosalind have two daughters, Darcy and Darlyn.

RICHARDSON, James and Mary Jane

John Richardson (1822), born in Leeds, England, married Margaret McDonald and they immigrated to Canada, to Metcalfe Township, in 1854. They brought their two sons with them, James (1846) and William.

James moved to Kerwood from Metcalfe in 1865. He boarded with a French family for a time and was manager of a brickyard in Strathroy. He purchased four acres of land and started a brick- and tile-manufacturing plant in Kerwood. Steam was used to power the machinery.

In 1872, James married Mary Jane Smithrim and they moved into a house made of Richardson brick. James bought 10 acres just north of the village, which he cleared and then traded for nine acres adjoining the four acres that came with the house.

In 1888, when the Grand Trunk Railway built the tunnel under the St. Clair River, James was contracted to supply the brick for the Canadian side. The business expanded to include a sawmill in Kerwood, a brick- and tile-works in Wyoming, and a sawmill at Walkers. James provided a lot of employment in the village in the late 1800s and early 1900s. In 1892, he had an agreement with the Grand Trunk Railway for a rail siding into the brick and tile yard.

James and Mary Jane had five children, Annie; John Henry; Frederick (d.1951); Margaret; and Dora.

John Henry married Sara M. Johnson of Metcalfe and they moved to Wyoming, where he managed that branch of the business until 1902. They had four children, Freeda M.; J. Frederick "Fred" (d.1971); Leslie (died at age six); and A. Mildred. In 1921, John bought the business from his father, then sold it to Fred at a later date.

Freeda married Rev. Alexander Sanderson and they lived in both Ontario and Alberta, where Alexander was a minister with the United Church. They had one daughter, Jeanne.

Fred married Nona Martha Wilson (d.1936) of Metcalfe and they had three daughters, Betty Louise, who married Stanley James Bloomfield; Ida Jean (died an infant); and Nona Marian, who married William Craig Cadman. After Nona Martha died, Fred married Irene Hillis in 1960.

Fred was very active in the community, the United Church, Mason and Shriners Lodge, and also in Ontario politics.

A. Mildred, the youngest child of John and Sara, was very active in the United Church Women's Institute and as a 4-H leader for years. She lived in Kerwood all her life and helped her brother, Fred, raise his daughters.

Frederick, third child of James and Mary Jane, bought 100 acres in Adelaide at Lot 3, Con. 4 SER, and married Eda Fuller in 1900. He built a home of sandstone brick. Frederick and Eda had one son, Kenneth, who married Leila Muxlow. They had two children, Marilyn Louise, who married Ivan Herrington; and Alan, who married Sandra McAllister. Alan and Sandra have three children, Rebecca "Becky," Michael and Patrick. Frederick continued to farm the Lot 3 property until his death.

Some items of note from the Age Dispatch regarding Kerwood Brick & Tile include the following:

Feb. 21, 1884: Mr. James Richardson has the contract of getting out timber for the new

Fourth Line bridge at Strathroy. The timber is to be first class swamp oak. One stick that he drew into his mill Saturday was 26 feet long and 4 feet at the butt.

Jan. 10, 1894: Mr. James Richardson of the Kerwood Brick and Tile Works is about to commence the manufacture of concrete tile.

May 8, 1895: Early Sunday morning the sawmill and brick and tile yard works and sheds of Mr. James Richardson were completely destroyed by fire. As there had not been any fire used about the premises for fully a week, it is supposed to be the work of an incendiary. The loss is somewhere in the neighbourhood of $2000 plus.

May 22, 1895: Mr. James Richardson, whose sawmill and drying sheds were destroyed by fire a couple of weeks ago, is now busy getting things in shape for business and expects to be running again this week. In the fall he intends putting up brick buildings making the sawmill as fireproof as possible.

Jan. 29, 1896: Mr. James Richardson had his face badly burned on Thursday last. He was engaged in running some bobbit metal into a circular saw boxing when dampness in the box caused it to explode, throwing the boiling metal into his face severely burning him. The new brick sawmill is completed and will be in operation by the end of the present week. The building is 60x70 of brick with iron roof, and is fitted with the latest and most improved machinery. It is certainly a credit to Mr. Richardson and the neighbourhood. A shingle machine had also been put in for the manufacture of soft elm and black ash shingles.

The Richardsons were very active in the Kerwood Methodist Church (later United) and they played a very significant role in the building of the church in 1923, as did many local families.

RIVERS

Major Rivers (ca.1770-1844) was born in England. He was an Officer in the British Army who saw active service in different parts of the empire. He served as Colonel Rivers under Sir John Moore at Corunna in 1808, where he received a rifle wound to the knee from which he never fully recovered. He also served with the 91st Regiment. Retiring from the army, he became a paymaster for the city of London, England, until 1832, when he came to Canada with his wife, Jane (last name unknown, ca.1790-1877), son Henry, and five daughters. They settled near London, Canada West. The Rivers family attended services at the Anglican Church. The aged officer died at his residence near London, C.W., from the effects of the wound he had received in the peninsular wars. The family came to Warwick Township and settled on a land grant received from the Crown. Jane Rivers died at the home of her daughter, Jane Crone.

Harriet Louise (d.1897), believed to be the eldest child of Major and Jane, married Lieutenant H.L. Deane. Harriet died at the home of J.H. English in Strathroy, where she had made her home for a number of years.

Elizabeth married Joseph Kennett. Both were recorded as being from Warwick Township, but they married in Adelaide Township on February 21, 1834.

Catherine Matilda (1814-1890) was born in Windsor, England. Her obituary said that in her earlier years she lived in England, France and Jamaica, receiving her education in England and France. Her obituary states the family lived in Adelaide Township for a while. She married Edward Bullock (d.1866), third son of Rev. John Bullock, Rector of Redwinter, Essex, England, in 1842, and resided near London. Later, she lived in Otterville, where Ed Bullock died. In 1870 and 1874, Catherine went back to England to visit family. In 1882, Catherine took up residence in Strathroy with her daughter, Mary Cecilia English (married to Jas. H.), where she died. She was buried in Otterville. Her obituary listed four surviving sons, J.E., H.E., and W.E., of Chicago, and F.G. of Otterville; daughter Mary of Strathroy; and her only surviving sister, Mrs. H.L. Deane.

Jane (1815-1895), born in Island of Wight, England, married William Crone (1809-1891), born in Cumberland, England, in 1832 in London, England. They farmed in Warwick Township at the east half of Lot 30, Con. 4 SER. William retired from the farm in 1862 and he and Jane moved to Strathroy, where William was a market clerk and commission merchant. Their children were William

(1834-1920); Sarah Anne (ca.1838); and Henry (ca.1845).

William, the eldest child of Jane and William, married Maria Williams (1832-1884), born in England and daughter of Dr. Roger S. Williams (1797-1880) and Maria Ann Dyke, in 1852. Dr. Williams had come to Adelaide in 1837 and lived on the Fourth Line SER. He practiced medicine for a season but later moved to Strathroy, where he died. William and Maria Williams Crone had a son, Dr. William L. Crone (1856-1908), who graduated from Ontario Veterinary College. In 1878, William L. married Ellen Manning (1856-1880) of Adelaide Township. Their son, Frederick (1879-1939), married Leona Blanche Henry in Vancouver, and they had a son, Wilbert Henry. In 1887, William L. married Caroline Craig (ca.1864-1907) of Adelaide Township, daughter of John Craig. William L. and Caroline had two children, Leonard (1891) and Alverna Jane (1894). The family lived in Ovid, Michigan, and later in Watford. They were members of the Episcopal Church in Watford.

Sarah Anne, second child of Jane and William, married Joseph Wilson (1835) of Welland County, son of William and Eliza Wilson, in 1861.

Nothing further is known of Henry, third child of Jane and William.

Henry G.R. Rivers (1825-1907), son of Major and Jane, was one of the earliest settlers in this district, when it was still a vast forest. He married Maria Westgate (1836), born in Ireland, in St. Paul's Cathedral, London, in 1854. He later married Sarah Newton (ca.1850-1884) of Adelaide in January 1882. Sarah was the daughter of William and Christiana Newton. Henry G.R. and Maria had seven children, Henry (1856); Mary Ann (1858-1950); George Russell (1860-1932); Maria (1862-1903); Samuel (1866); Eliza (ca.1868); and Jane (1870). Henry farmed the west half of Lot 30, Con. 4 SER, Warwick Township, by William and Jane Crone.

Henry, the eldest child of Henry and Maria, never married and lived with his bachelor brother, Sam.

Mary Ann married Isaac J. Kadey (1856-1923), and they lived in Warwick Township. They had two children, Lawrence R. (1893-1971) and Lottie (1895-1983), who married into the Perry family.

George Russell married Ann Elizabeth "Annie" Harris (1867-1945), born in Adelaide Township, daughter of Joseph Carpenter and Caroline E. "Carrie" (Croucher) Harris. In 1861, George farmed and operated a gravel pit in Adelaide Township on Lot 1, Con. 3 SER. George also owned basket factories in Niagara Falls, Leamington and Strathroy. George and Annie had five children, Robert (1887-1887); Gilbert "Russel" (1888-1950); Edward Henry (1891-1891); George "Norman" (1892); and William Henry (1897-1975).

Russel, second eldest of George and Annie's children, married Sarah "Delia" Thompson (1890-1961), daughter of Williamson R. and Sarah Lovica (Barnes) Thompson. Russ and Delia farmed near Watford and had a son.

Norman, fourth child of George and Annie, married Pearle Wilson (1898-1976) of Adelaide Township, daughter of Robert and Clara (Dale) Wilson. They had four children. The eldest, Wilson Bill (1920), married Betty Greenwood (1922) ca.1941, and Betty Jerome Leitch (1924) ca.1960. Bill and Betty (Greenwood) had two children, Winston Barry (1942) and Dianne (1943). The second eldest was Joseph (ca 1925). Raymond Keith (1928) married Marion Winterbottom (ca.1931). They had six children, Marilyn Jean, Bethel Louise, Raymond Douglas George, Donald John, Diane Marie and Deborah Elizabeth. The youngest child of Norman and Pearle was Clare (1933, died an infant).

William Henry, youngest child of George and Annie, married Ila Beatrice Huntley (1897-1987). "Henry" worked with his father in the Basket Works in Leamington and was a baker for a time. He established Rivers Shoe Store in Strathroy, which flourished for many years. Henry and Ila had three children. Lorna Mae (1920) married Cameron Howard McLean (1920), and they had one son, Cameron "John" (1944-1997). George Edgar (1922-1984) married Zeta Walsh (d.1993), and they had three children, George H., who married Sally Elstrom; R. Brian; and Catherine, who married Ian Preston. William John "Jack" (1926) married Reatha Elizabeth Watson, and they have three children, David George, Reatha Anne and William Steven.

Maria, fourth child of Henry G.R. and Maria, married Edwin Burlington in California, but they returned to Watford where Ed was employed. On a berry-picking trip, Maria died in a buggy accident.

Samuel, the youngest son of Henry G.R. and

Maria, never married and lived with his bachelor brother, Henry.

Eliza, sixth child of Henry G.R. and Maria, married R. Goodhand.

ROBINSON, Robert and Diana

Robert and Diana (Zaharchuk) Robinson live on part of Lot 28, Con. 2 SER, with their three children, Krista (1973); Robbie (1981); and Craig (1985). Robert, who was born in Strathroy, works at Ford of Canada in Talbotville, and moved to Adelaide about 10 years ago. Diana is a nurse at Strathroy Middlesex General Hospital. The Zaharchuks came from the Ukraine, and Diana's mother was from Norwich.

RUBOTHAM (ROBOTHAM), George and Margaret

In 1833, George (1792-1861) and Margaret (1812-1881) Rubotham immigrated to London, Ontario, from Wicklow County, Ireland, with sons William (1829-1887) and George Gideon (1833-1872). Two years later, they settled in Adelaide Township, purchasing 100 acres, the west half of Lot 18, Con. 3 NER, which they bought for £200. They built a log house, cleared land, and added four more children to their family, Jane (1839-1909); Esther (1841-1884); Elizabeth (1843-1932); and James (1845-1924). In 1848, they purchased an additional 100 acres, the east half of Lot 18, Con. 2 NER, for £62, 10s. At some point in time, the spelling of the family name changed to Robotham.

On the death of George, the Con. 3 farm was left to James, controlled by his mother until he reached age of majority, and with the requirement that he provide for her during her lifetime. The Con. 2 farm was divided, the south 70 acres to William and the north 30 acres (less Mud Creek School property) to George Gideon. William later purchased the north 30 acres.

In 1857, William married Ann Beaton (1830-1904), born of Scottish parents on Cape Breton Island. About 1849, she had moved to Adelaide Township, Lot 13, Con. 3 SER, with her mother and brother. William and Ann had four children, George Duncan (1858-1944); Annie Jane (1860-1959); Victoria Esther (1864-1963); and Willena (1868, died an infant).

While felling trees to create farmland in 1865, William was struck on the head by a tree limb. This nearly ended his life and made him subject to neuralgia; it also affected his hearing. This accident contributed to his death 22 years later, when he passed away two days after being afflicted with brain fever.

In 1883, George Duncan married Mary Whiting (1860-1923) of Lot 29, Con. 1 NER, and they set up farming in East Williams Township. Two daughters, Annie Eliza (1883) and Maude Belle (1886), were born there. When William died, George and his family moved to the Con. 2 property and resided with Ann. Three sons were born on this farm, William George (1888); David Whiting (1893-1964); and Manfred Beaton (1897). In 1918, George sold the Con. 2 farm to his son, David, and moved to Head Street in Strathroy. In the late 1920s, he married Maude Robertson of Strathroy, but they separated after a few years.

In 1918, David Whiting married Kate Elizabeth Pulling (1895-1966) of Strathroy. He was the only Robotham to spend his entire life on the Adelaide family farm. David and Kate raised seven children, George David (1919); Lloyd Charles (1920-1997); Wilfred Henry (1922-1974); William Walter (1924); Donald Ross (1928-1992); Betty Marie (1934); and Robert Gordon (1935).

Lloyd Charles attended S.S. #4 Adelaide. In spring and fall, he walked 1 1/2 miles to school, but in the winter, he travelled by horse, leaving the animal in the stable of Evan McCabe. He helped with farm chores before and after school, and did his share of custodial work at the school during his senior years. Lloyd was a bachelor. He stayed at home with his parents and helped to do the farm work with his father. From time to time, he helped the neighbours. Due to a health problem, he was not able to enlist, but spent one winter working at Sommerville's in Strathroy making war material.

In 1966, Lloyd Charles inherited his father's farm. He worked with Evan Stead, where he learned the electrical trade and went on to get his electrician's license. After the death of his mother, he sold the farm to Tom Muxlow and moved to Strathroy, where he worked as an electrician in Strathroy and the surrounding area. Many farmers from Adelaide as well as other townships called on his expertise.

The original Robotham farm on Con. 3 NER was sold in 1899 to William Nettleton for $2,500 following foreclosure. In 1949, David Robotham purchased the south 50 acres of this farm for $1,800. This was sold again in 1966.

Many Robotham family members moved away from the family farms.

George Gideon married Esther (last name unknown, ca.1843), who was born in Ireland, about 1862. They had three children, George Gideon (1863); John (1864); and Margaret A. (1867). Following the death of G. Gideon Sr., Esther married James Humphries and was living in Pestigo, Wisconsin, in 1889. Son George G., a bachelor, was also in Pestigo. In 1888, John was a bachelor and Margaret A. was unmarried; they were living in Adelaide Township. No further records of this family are presently known.

Jane, third child of George and Margaret, married Robert Ayre (1839-1898) of Lot 19, Con. 2, about 1870. Their children were William George (1873-1881); Mary A. Elizabeth (1870-1878); Albert R.J. "Bud" (1876-1949), who remained a bachelor; and Bertha A. (1880), who married into the Reid family and moved to London. Possibly Bertha had children, but no records have been found.

Esther married John Pennington (1836-1884) of Adelaide in 1871. They moved to a farm near Marysville, Kansas. In 1884, they were murdered by a hired man who robbed them of the proceeds from the sale of some pigs. The hired man was later captured by a group of neighbours and hanged from a tree. Esther and John had no known children.

Elizabeth, fifth issue of George and Margaret, married Archibald McKeen (1832) of East Williams about 1876. They had five children, Margaret E. (1877); Esther (1883); William (d.1930); Jane (1884); and Ida (1886). William is buried in Strathroy.

James, the youngest of George and Margaret's children, married Mary Ann (last name unknown, 1853-1905) in the early 1880s. They had three children, Pearl (1886-1974); Edwin James "Eddy" (1888-1970); and Mary E. (1890). Neither Pearl nor Eddy ever married. Eddy served in the army during WWI and later taught school, living in Adelaide and East Williams.

From William and Ann's family, Annie Jane, second eldest, married Duncan B. Campbell (1846-

Children of David Whiting and Katie Elizabeth (Pulling) Robotham, L-R, George David, Lloyd Charles, Wilfred Henry, Betty Marie, William Walter, Donald Ross and Robert Gordon Robotham, 1953.

1939) of Strathroy in 1882. They had seven children; four died in childhood. Their children were John G. (1888, died an infant); Duncan B. (1890-1892); Georgina "Geordie" (1892-1988); Ethel (1894-1984); Gladys R. (1897-1898); Gordon D. (1900, died an infant); and George Leo. Duncan Campbell was a contractor, building the CPR through the Selkirk Mountains. Annie was the first woman to cross the Kicking Horse Pass on steel when she went over on a handcar.

Ethel moved to Detroit where she worked until 1945, when she married R.A. McEachern and moved to Alvinston, Ontario.

George "Leo" trained as a dentist and practiced in Minnedosa, Manitoba. He married and had four daughters, Marjorie, Gladys, Donalda and Anna-May. Marjorie and Gladys are both deceased. They lived most of their lives in the United States. Donalda lives in Florida, and Anna-May is married and living in Winnipeg, Manitoba, as of 1996. Leo remarried.

Victoria Esther, third child of William and Ann, had a daughter, Birdie (1880-1948), who lived most of her life in Strathroy, having married Luther Harris (d.1935). Victoria remarried in the mid-1880s, to James Mitchell Roberts (1866-1948) of East Williams. They had three children, May Eileen (1888); Ann Eloise (1893-1914); and Eric Austin (1897-1951). They moved to Ottawa about 1900. May married Hugh A. Ross of Montreal in 1913, and they had three children, Garith (or Garth), Bobs (or Robs) and Eloise. Eric died a bachelor while serving in the Canadian army in Ottawa.

From George Duncan and Mary's family, Annie Eliza married Charles A. Giffen (1884) of Lot 25, Con. 1 SER, in 1911. They had two daughters, Helen Marie (1913) and Evelyn Jane (1917). Helen married John Roydon Colvin of Lobo in 1936. They had no children. Evelyn married James Charlton Sinker of Lobo in 1941. They had four children, William (1945-1945); Charles Edward (1947-1949); George Eric (1949); and Janice Ann Marie (1960). George is a lawyer in Strathroy at present, while Janice remains single and lives with her mother.

Maude Belle, second child of George Duncan and Mary, married Harold Tyler Brock (1883) in 1906. They settled on a farm in Lambton County near Petrolia and had four children, George Gordon (1907-1919); Mary Ellen Margaret (1909); Douglas Harold (1916); and Raymond Russell (1918). Mary Ellen Margaret "Ella" Brock married Carl Kavanaugh Sproule of Oil Springs in the mid-1930s. They had one daughter, Mary Nancy Colleen (1937, died an infant). Douglas Harold (1916) married Marie Wilson of Adelaide in 1942. They lived in Petrolia and Arkona and had four children, Pauline Marie (1943); Linda Louise (1947); Allen Douglas (1948); and Wilson George (1951). Pauline married Vernon A. Phibbs and currently lives in Fort McMurray, Alberta. Remaining family members include Raymond Russell Brock (1918), who married Donelda Wilson (sister of Marie above) in 1942. They settled on Lot 5, Con. 1 SER. They had two children, Richard Raymond (1944) and Nancy Jean (1950).

William George, the first of George Duncan and Mary's children to be born in Adelaide Township, married Leota Giffen of Adelaide in 1913. They farmed for a time in East Williams before moving to Flint, Michigan. They had one daughter, Marion Isabelle (1913). Marion married Floyd Thayer of Flint and they have two children, William Floyd (1943) and Sharon Lee (1946).

Manfred Beaton moved to Detroit, Michigan, and married Edna Elsie Reinholz of Detroit in 1921. They had one daughter, Donna Jean (1928), who married Carl Walter Schleicher in 1948. They had four children, Kathy Ann (1949); Ruth Lynne (1950); William Earl (1951); and Kenneth Robert (1953).

From David and Kate's family, George David (1919) married Loftena Muxlow (1915-1975) of Adelaide in 1954. They resided in Strathroy and had one son, William George (1958). In 1977, George married Doris Alberta Murray (1933) of Strathroy. William George married Mary Lee Thompson of Melbourne in 1989. They have two sons, David William Earl (1990) and Jamie John Charles (1993).

Wilfred Henry, David and Kate's third child, married Verna Chappell (d.1944) of Kensington, P.E.I., in Halifax in 1944. In 1947, Wilfred remarried, to Pat McGoun of London (d.1950). In 1952, Wilfred married Marjorie Chute of London (d.1995). They had one son, David Melvin (1953). David married Luanne Kerr of London in 1975. They have two children, Mark David (1979) and Erin Elizabeth (1981), and presently live in London.

William Walter, fourth issue of David and Kate, married Elaine A. McAndless (1926-1991) of

Toronto in 1951. They lived in Ottawa and raised three children, Katharine Helene (1957); James William David (1960); and Robert Elliott (1966). Helene married Randy Michael Zettle of Brampton in 1990. They live in Brampton and have three sons, Gaelen Alexander (1991); Zachary Clifford William (1993); and Logan Walter Charles (1996). James married Christine Marie Antaya of Petawawa in 1983. They have three children, Anna Christine (1986); Timothy James (1988); and Mary Elaine (1991). They live in Manotick, Ontario. Robert married Christina Marie Vadebobcoeur of Ottawa in 1995. They live in Ottawa.

Donald Ross, fifth child of David and Kate, married Ruby Davis and lives in Corruna, Ontario.

Betty Marie married William Wesley Brooks of Kerwood in 1953 and presently lives in Strathroy. They have two daughters, Karen Elizabeth (1957) and Kimberly Ann (1964). Karen married Michael Mace of Strathroy in 1979. They lived in Corruna and later divorced. Karen married Gary Mitchell of Lambton County in 1990. Karen is presently living in Strathroy. Kimberly married Ron Dymond of Metcalfe Township in 1985. They have three children, Wesley Ronald (1990); Amanda Marie (1993); and Daniel (1995).

Robert Gordon, youngest child of David and Kate, married Pearl (last name unknown) of Edmonton in 1959. They live in Calgary. They have three children, Norman (1962); Dale (1964); and Kathryn Elizabeth (1967). Norman married Debbie (last name unknown) in 1988. They have two daughters, Sierra Maria (1992) and Chantel Michele (1993). They live in Fox Creek, Alberta. Dale married Nancy Webb of Calgary in 1996, where they live. Kathryn lives in Colorado Springs, Colorado.

ROBOTHAM, George D.

George David Robotham (1919) is the eldest child of David Whiting and Kate Elizabeth (Pulling) Robotham. George was born and raised in the same house as his father, on Lot 18, Con. 2 NER. He attended S.S. #4 Adelaide, where Earl McInroy was his first teacher. When they were in the senior grades at S.S. #4, George and his brothers Lloyd, Wilfred and Bill were the school custodians.

Upon completion of Grade Eight, George attended Strathroy District Collegiate Institute for a short time. Money was scarce and with no means of transportation to school, he quit. In the spring of 1934, at the age of 15, George went to work for his Aunt Laura and Uncle George Foster. He worked six days a week and every other Sunday for $60 a year, plus his room and board. He remembers one summer without rain when they harvested only a couple of loads of hay and the crops were very sparse. Several sunny, frosty winter days found him with the horses and sleigh, cutting wood in the bush, which was then hauled to heat the farmhouse. Frozen food was a natural occurrence as the cold weather froze the sandwiches he took for his lunch.

George worked for, and lived with, Clarence and Helen Patterson for eight years. While at Pattersons he purchased his first car, a 1927 Chevrolet. He spent some time working for Fred and May Sullivan on their farm on the Second Line South of Adelaide Township. Later, he drove a gravel truck for Gordon and Dorothy Galbraith on Kerwood Road. Gravel was loaded from Gravel Hill at Sideroad #3 and the townline, now known as Townsend Road, as well as from Chambers Pit and several other surrounding area pits.

Later, George worked for Richardson Feed Mill in Kerwood. Some days he delivered feed to area farmers for their livestock and fowl. Some days he worked in the mill. At times, he was sent to Sarnia to get loads of lumber and steel roofing. He also delivered loads of coal to some of the area homes.

While working for Bob and Lottie McCubbin, George and Ken Phillips looked after the farming operation when Bob was this area's Member of Parliament in Ottawa.

George went to work for Bill and Alma Daniels of Daniel's Garage at Hickory Corners. While there, he helped to wire the garage for electricity. At this time, he began to drive a school bus, transporting students to Strathroy District Collegiate Institute. Sometimes he arrived with the tow truck at the scene of an accident.

At this time, George became a Mason, joining Masonic Doric Lodge 289 at Lobo Village. He married Loftena Pearl Muxlow (1915-1975), daughter of Loftus and Viola (Langan) Muxlow, formerly of Adelaide Township. George and Loftena had one son, William George (1958). For a short time, George worked for Jim Smith at Wards Water Supply London.

When Adelaide Township Central School opened in 1960 with Annie Courtis as principal, George became the full-time custodian and bus driver. He serviced the buses, which were kept in the bus barn at the school. He drove a regular route to Adelaide School until his retirement. Adelaide Township Central School became part of Middlesex Board of Education in 1969. In 1977, Adelaide Township Central School became Adelaide-W.G. MacDonald School, and special needs students became part of the student body. At this time, there were a number of upgrades to the building, including several new classrooms, a shop, a home economics room with kitchen facilities, and a much-needed gymnasium. Larry Smyth was principal.

In July 1977, George married Doris Alberta Murray, a teacher in Strathroy, who was the daughter of Lorne Stanley and Edna Bernice (McInroy) Murray of Adelaide Township. George retired in June 1984. He continued to drive bus for Langs Bus Lines until June 1996, when he retired for a second time, completing 45 years as a school bus driver. In 1990, George welcomed his first grandson, David William Earl, and in 1993 was delighted with a second grandson, Jamie John Charles. George and Doris reside in Strathroy.

ROMBOUTS, Adrian and Mary

Adrian Rombouts (1944) was born in Brecht, Belgian. He immigrated to Canada in the spring of 1951 with his family. Adrian's parents are Adrian Peter (1912), born in Rijsbergen Nederland, and Elizabeth Kustermans (1916), born in Achtmaal Nederland. His parents married in 1943 and moved to Westmalle Belgian. Adrian had two sisters and three brothers, Jacoba, Annie, Peter, Cornelius and Tony.

Adrian went to school in Warwick Township and worked on the farm with the family on Lot 26, Con. 2 NER, Warwick Township.

Adrian married Mary P. Hendrikx and moved to Lot 15, Con. 2 NER, a farm he bought from Harold Clapham, in October 1968. They have five children, Adrian (1969), who married Caroline Vanderheyden and moved to Forest; Anthony (1970); John (1972), who married Stacy Ormerod and farms Lot 15, Con. 2 NER; Joe (1974), who married Karen Redick and moved to Alvinston; and Mike (1975).

The Rombouts operate a 600-acre swine and crop farm and have been active in their parish council, Knights of Columbus, and Catholic Women's League. They have also been active in the farm community, MCFA, OFA, MCPPA and OPPMB.

ROUTLEY, Jim and Elizabeth

Jim and Elizabeth Routley moved from Strathroy to their Adelaide farm on Lot 3, Con. 4 NER, in June 1966. The farm was a fruit orchard for a few years, until Jim began raising pigs. He also worked off the farm, but is now retired. Elizabeth has worked at Strathroy Middlesex General Hospital since 1961. They have one son, Darren.

Elizabeth's parents, Alfred and Edna Catchpole (deceased) moved to Con. 5 NER in Adelaide from London in 1953. Elizabeth's only sibling is a brother, Edward (see CATCHPOLE, Alfred and Edna).

ROUTLEY, Ken and Marjorie

Ken and Marjorie Routley moved to Keysers at Lot 8, Con. 5 NER, in June 1968. They have two children, Roxanne (1975) and Jason (1980). Roxanne now lives in Strathroy and Jason lives at home.

ROWBOTHAM, Dan and Susaan

In June 1995, Dan and Susaan (Truppe) Rowbotham purchased the property located at 1290 Egremont Road, Pt. Lot 3, Con. 1 NER. This 2½-acre parcel was sold by Don and Lorna McChesney, and originally severed from the McChesney family farm.

Dan was born and raised in the Collingwood area, son of Donald and Carole (Eagles) Rowbotham. Susaan grew up in the Lambeth area, daughter of Walter and Donna (Lockridge) Truppe. Dan and Susaan both work for the O.P.P.

ROWLAND, Jack Sr. and Ethel

Jack Rowland Sr. (1889), who was born in England, came to Canada at the age of 16. He married Ethel Holmes (1891), who was born in West Williams Township, and they had six children. Evelyn, the eldest, was born in Strathroy. The next two, Nola and Pauline, were born in Adelaide Township just east of the property on Con. 4 NER, where Murray Thomson resides. Jack Jr. and Audrey were born in West Williams Township, near

Trucking raspberries, L-R, hired man, Jack Rowland Sr., nephew of J.R., and Carmen Jones.

Hungry Hollow. Bill was born on a farm rented from Wilbur Marsh, on Townsend Line.

In 1928, with an inheritance from England, Jack Sr. bought 100 acres on Lot 1, Con. 4 NER, where he moved his family. Jack Jr. remembers his excitement on moving day, when he drove a 1020 McCormick-Deering tractor from one farm to the other—at just eight years of age!

Jack Jr., Audrey, and Pauline immediately started to school at S.S. #1 and #2 at Keyser's Corners. They recall Vivian McKenzie being their teacher. Bill began school in 1932 and spent his entire public school years there.

As the family grew up, they gradually left home. Evelyn went to Sarnia to school and worked in a drug store.

Nola trained as a nurse and worked in a hospital in New York, where she dated and married the office boy who became Chief Administrator of the Hospital for Special Surgery.

After attending high school, Pauline worked in Arkona. She married Mike Fraser of Forest.

Jack Jr. worked winters in a box factory, and cut logs for Arnold Hodgins. During the summer, he worked on the Hamonic, a passenger boat on the Great Lakes. In 1943, he enlisted in the Canadian Army and went to Chatham for basic training. While there, he met Edna, who became his wife in 1948.

Audrey, like Evelyn, went to Sarnia and worked in a drug store. She married Thomas Romphf, a customs officer. They now live in Goderich.

Bill went to London to work at Coleman's Meat Packing plant. He married Patricia Quigley, and they lived in Dorchester. He worked there until the plant went into receivership. He was the last employee on the payroll.

After the war, Jack Jr. purchased a farm near his parents in Warwick Township, through the V.L.A., whose representative then was Mac Cuddy. He and Edna have a daughter, Jane (1949). Jack lived never more than three miles from his birthplace until he retired from Imperial Oil and moved to Sarnia.

Jack Jr. remembers his parents having a large raspberry patch. The berries were picked by many fine people in the neighbourhood: O'Hanleys, Niblocks, Dennises, Campbells, Conkeys, Elliotts, Grahams, Bices, McKenzies, Murrays and more. The berries were trucked to Strathroy, Sarnia and London to be sold.

Growing berries is very labour-intensive. Jack Jr. recalls that, if other farm jobs were completed, they automatically picked up a hoe and went to the berry patch. On his own farm, Jack Jr. did not plant one berry plant.

Jack Sr. and Ethel enjoyed their retirement in Arkona.

RUBY, Glenn and Lianne

In January 1991, Glenn and Lianne Ruby purchased Lot 8, Con. 2 SER, from Bill and Dorothy Dowding. They moved there with their baby son, Jacob. Two years later, Julia (1993) was born, and that same year the family left the farming business and moved to Hyde Park.

Greg and Karen Ruby and their son, Joshua, took over the farm. Jessica (1994) and Mark (1997) were born after they moved to the Lot 8 property.

The farm is operated as a broiler chicken operation, and Greg has a farm-related trucking business. He hauls chicken feed for their farm, as well as for

Dave Ruby (father), and John Ruby (uncle) of Strathroy. Karen works on the farm and does the accounting, and also works as a Registered Nurse at the London Health Sciences Centre.

RUPP, Christian and Linda

The Rupp family moved to the west half of Lot 16, Con. 1 NER, in June 1975. They bought the property from Gerrit and Charlene Weetering.

Christian Rupp grew up in Frauenfeld in Switzerland on a dairy farm. He served, as every male citizen must, in the Swiss Army. Linda Diver was born in London, Ontario.

Their children were born in Adelaide and went to Adelaide School and Strathroy District Collegiate Institute. Their children are Jennifer, Samuel, Heidi and Jonathan.

Jennifer is presently in the Canadian Air Force. She is attending University of Western Ontario to become a nurse in the Armed Forces, and works for the army the remainder of the year. She has been stationed in Chilliwack, B.C., for basic training, in St. John's, Quebec, and in Halifax, Nova Scotia.

SANDS, David and Margaret

In 1845, David Sands and his family, including wife Margaret (McPhedran) and four children, set sail from Glasgow, Scotland, on the Romulus (the ship sunk on the return trip). After a journey of seven weeks and three days, they landed at Montreal. In four more weeks, they reached Port Stanley by way of Bytown (Ottawa). From Port Stanley, they travelled by wagon to the Township of East Williams in Middlesex County.

The family settled in East Williams on Lot 12, Con. 7. A small log house, which had been built by other settlers, was their temporary home. Later, two more sons were born.

David Sands was a carpenter. When he immigrated, he brought a large box that contained saws and carpentry tools. He used the box to make a door for the first house he built.

In addition to his Bible, David brought an English prayer book from Scotland, and on many occasions he conducted funeral services. Sermons and prayer meetings were held in their log home. David played the concertina, and the neighbours sang hymns. This musical interlude was the community highlight of the week!

When David bought his farm in 1854, he paid £110 (approximately $530) for 100 acres. He was a lifelong member of the Presbyterian Church, and he chaired the committee that built East Adelaide Presbyterian Church in 1871. David was a prosperous farmer in the neighbourhood, and took an active part in municipal affairs. He was very interested in forming a union between S.S. #2 Adelaide and #14 East Williams. The first post office was located in a Sands home, named Crathie after a town in which they lived (near Aberdeen in Scotland).

Richmond Sands, David's eldest son, taught in Adelaide after 1852, then studied medicine and practiced in Nairn.

SAUL, John

John Saul (ca.1779-1855) was born in Lincolnshire, England. He married in England and had one child, Richard (1800-1877), also born in England. In 1832, John came to Adelaide with his son, who married a year earlier and became a Reverend, and his son's wife, Ann (1806-1893). John was a farmer. On the 1851 Adelaide census, John, a widower and by then 73 years of age, lived

Mrs. Richard Saul

with Richard and his family on the east half of Lot 20, Con 4 SER. He was buried in the Fourth Line Cemetery.

Richard and Ann originally settled in Metcalfe Township in what is now Napier. Five years later, they moved to the Adelaide property. Richard performed ministerial duties, but circumstances called upon him to attend to a large share of work that properly belonged to the professions of a doctor and lawyer. In the early days of Strathroy's incorporation, he was a member of the village council. For many years, Richard occupied a prominent position on the board of school trustees, and was township superintendent of public schools at one time. About 1862, he embraced the doctrines taught in the writings of Swedenborg, and united with the New Jerusalem Church. He was licensed to preach by the Canada Association of that church, but during the last few years of his life, his failing strength did not permit him to perform ministerial duties. When Richard died, Ann moved to the residence of her daughter, Mrs. Armstrong of Strathroy. Of the 12 children Richard and Ann had, only four were living at the time of Ann's death.

Elizabeth Saul (1835-1910) was born in Metcalfe Township. In 1855, she married William Henry Armstrong (1825-1889), born in Ireland, son of John and Margaret (Wallace) Armstrong. William H. came to Strathroy in 1854, where he conducted a general merchandising establishment for several years. In 1860, when the Village of Strathroy was first organized, he was appointed Treasurer, a position he held for over 30 years. He was also, for nearly 20 years, Collector of Indian Revenues. He was, for a time, inspector of weights and measures. In addition to his other duties, he was interested in agriculture, and specialized in raising stock. He owned 280 acres of land, 30 acres of it within Strathroy. Our present Strathroy Cemetery exists due to the 1861 purchase of nine acres of land from Mr. Armstrong. William and Elizabeth were strong Reformers and were highly respected and active members of the Methodist Church. William held many offices in the Strathroy Methodist Church and was recording steward and church treasurer for a great many years. They had 10 children. Only three lived to maturity, but they also died quite young. At their mother's death, only one child and four grandchildren survived her. The children of Elizabeth and William H. were John Wesley (ca.1855); Richard Wallace (1856-1915); William Alfred (1857-1907); Margaret (1864); Charles Ranby (1869-1871); George Albert (1872-1875); Alice E. (1874-1875); Sarah Maud (1876-1881); Susan Elizabeth (1879-1881); and Walter Henry Armstrong (1883-1890).

In 1862, Sarah Saul (ca.1838-1889) married Robert Nicholson (1828-1910), born in the North of England, son of Edward and Hannah (Mullcaster) Nicholson. Robert came to Canada in 1848 and to Strathroy in 1861, where he conducted a lumber and coal business and operated a planing mill. He also owned a farm just outside the town limits. Robert was prominent in the community and served as Reeve and Councillor. The Nicholsons took an active and prominent part in the life of Strathroy Methodist Church. Sarah and Robert had nine children. Six were alive at the time of their mother's death. The 1939 History Book of Strathroy United Church lists four surviving children, Annie (Mrs. G.L. Wagar of Bowmanville); Rev. R.R. Nicholson of Kemptville; Dr. J.H. Nicholson of Hart, Michigan; and Robert W. of Strathroy.

Richard R. Saul (ca.1838-1901) was born in Adelaide Township. He moved to Oelwein, Iowa, in 1877. He farmed with his brother, William, in 1893 near Mitchel, South Dakota, where he died. His wife died in 1879 in Oelwein, Iowa.

Amaziah H. Saul (ca.1840-1865) was born in Adelaide Township. He died young, and was buried in the Fourth Line Cemetery.

Rev. John S. Saul (ca.1844) was born in Adelaide Township. John died in the U.S. John was the owner of "The Age" in Strathroy. Later, he became the owner of the "Daily News" in Ashland, Wisconsin. In 1893, John was residing near Pontiac, Illinois. In 1910, he was living in Chicago.

William Harrison Saul (ca.1847-1917) was born in Adelaide Township. In 1877 in Strathroy, he married Phebe A. McLarty (1856-1901) of Strathroy, daughter of Robert McLarty. Phebe died in Mitchell, South Dakota. William remarried in 1906, to Phebe's sister, Mercy Jane McLarty (1859-1933). William and his wives are buried in Strathroy Cemetery. William's obituary listed two surviving daughters, Mrs. George Carlson of Mitchell, South Dakota, and Clarion Dewitt Hardy of Evanston, Illinois.

Ann "Alice" (ca.1850-1876) married Frank O. Buttolph and died in Greenville, Michigan.

SCOON, John A. and Helen

Squire John A. Scoon (ca.1800-1882), born in England, came to Canada in 1831 with his Scottish-born wife, Helen (ca.1801-1892), and their two children. They had a terrible voyage over; it took them more than two months to cross the Atlantic Ocean due to unfavorable winds. They settled a few miles northwest of Strathroy and farmed the east half of Lot 17, Con. 2 and 3 SER.

The Scoons owned 100 acres of farmland but had only cleared 20 acres for productive farming by 1842. As per the 1842 census, the family grew 90 bushels of wheat, seven bushels of barley, 100 bushels of oats, 80 bushels of peas, 12 bushels of Indian corn, 10 bushels of buckwheat, 130 bushels of potatoes, 630 units of maple syrup, and owned 10 cattle, 19 sheep and 15 hogs. Not only were the Scoons farmers, but they also ran a small store on their property and later owned a store in Sylvan.

In 1847, John A. Scoon, gentleman, was appointed Quartermaster of the Seventh Battalion, Middlesex. In 1851, John was appointed clerk of the newly elected Council, was an early councillor and served until 1856. John A. was a Conveyancer, a Justice of the Peace, and a Commissioner in the Court of Queen's Bench. He signed many of the early legal documents in Adelaide. John was the first steward of the Methodist Church and a Sunday School recording Steward. Squire Scoon gave a speech at the Annual West Middlesex pioneer banquet, held in January 1864, and attended by most of the early pioneers. In 1871, the Scoons lived in Strathroy, where John was president of the Woollen Factory, but in later life, they lived in the U.S., as John died there, tending his garden in Lapeer, Michigan. Helen returned to Adelaide and lived with her daughter, Jane, and her family living in Adelaide, where she died. John and Helen raised a family of five children, the first two in England, Jane (1829-1905); William A. (1831-1911); Joseph (ca.1832); John A. (ca.1835-1889); and Mary (ca.1839-1908).

In 1856 in Adelaide Township, Jane married John Waltham (1831-1897), born in Lincolnshire, England, son of John and Elizabeth Waltham of Adelaide. John and his parents had come to Canada in 1832. Jane and John had six children (see WALTHAM, John and Elizabeth).

William A. and his wife, Ann (ca.1831), settled on the homestead on the east half of Lot 17, Con. 3 SER. Ann died before the 1891 census. They raised a family of two boys and three girls, all born in Adelaide, W. John (1863); Mary (ca.1865); Helena "Nellie" (ca.1866); Thomas (ca.1868-1895); and Annie (ca.1871-1901).

W. John never married.

Mary married T.H. Price from Michigan at the homestead in December 1889, but it is believed she married a second time.

Nellie married Albert "Abe" Edward Thrower (1861-1935), born in Adelaide Township, son of Isaac and Mary Jane (Humphries) Thrower of Adelaide. Abe was one of the successful farmers in the district. He lived all his life on the home farm until he and Nellie moved to Strathroy in 1932. Abe had a son and daughter from his previous two marriages (see THROWER, Charles and Sarah).

Thomas never married and died a young man.

Annie never married, dying at 31 years of age.

Little is known about Joseph; perhaps he died young.

John A. married Mary Scales (1840-1890). As a young man, John lived for two years in California and other parts of the U.S. John and his wife lived in Strathroy where John, who was a druggist, had a store on Front St. In March 1868, the whole frame block burned down and John and his wife barely escaped with their lives. They settled in Parkhill, where John started again. His first business, "Scoon's Drug Store," a 1-storey building also used as a dwelling, was located on King St. and Westwood, but in 1869, he built the first brick building north of the tracks and had a prosperous business there. In 1887, this building was heavily damaged in a great block fire and the loss was $1,500, but John was fully insured. At death, his wife, son A. Scoon of Toronto, and daughter Jennie (living at home) survived him.

Mary, the youngest of John and Helen's children, married in 1861. Her husband was George Orchard (1833-1919), born in Somersetshire, England, son of James and Elizabeth (Court) Orchard. Mary and George settled in Strathroy. As a lad of 15, George had been sent to live with an uncle in New Brunswick, 60 miles from St. John's. After attending school there, he began life on a river schooner, working at intervals on farms. In 1851, he obeyed fortune's call to Western Canada. After adventurous trips to many places, he finally came to Strathroy in 1860 (interestingly, his obituary recalls the census having been taken in 1858) and at once entered into the drug business, which George pursued successfully for 12 years. In 1872, George sold his drug business to W.J. Dyas. From that time until 1900, his attention was occupied with several important trusts as executor and otherwise. In 1900, he resumed his former business. For many years, George was a member of the Public School Board, holding for a time the post of Chairman of the Board. He was also for some years a member of the Board of Health. Mary and George were members of the Methodist Church. Mary fell on a patch of ice coming home from church in 1907, and suffered a hip injury, from which she never recovered. They raised a family of five children, Dr. George Orchard of Windsor; Helen (married R.A. Willmott); Anna; Eva (married Gordon L. Cardiff); and Maud, who received her degree in pharmacy and eventually took over her father's business.

SCOTT, Robert and Martha

Robert Scott (1822-1912), the son of William and Anna Scott of Ireland, immigrated to Canada in 1842. He met and married a girl of German descent, Martha Matilda (1828-1874, last name unknown). He settled first in the Township of Hamilton, Northumberland County. By November 1855, he had purchased 100 acres in Adelaide from Michael Ring, the west half of Lot 18, Con. 2 NER. He also owned another 50 acres, the northwest corner of Lot 19, Con. 3 NER. Robert edited the Scott Bible, which is said to have been used by the Presbyterians. Robert and Martha had eight children, James Scott (1846-1906); Martha Lindsay (1848-1871); John (1851-1854); Sarah Eliza (1853-1924); William (1856-1943); Robert Walter (1860-1939); Henry Wallace (1863-1881); and Cornelius (1865-1934). The Scott children went to school at Craithie.

John Scott (1820-1897), younger brother of Robert, immigrated to Canada from Ireland in 1844. He married Eliza (1830, last name unknown), who had immigrated to Canada from Ireland. They had one son, William Joseph (1860). John lived at Lot 19, Con. 2 NER. He was a Methodist when he died. William J. was living in Manistee, Michigan, at that time.

Cornelius Scott (1865-1934) and Martha (Scott) Karr (1894-1954).

James Scott, eldest child of Robert and Martha, married Alexandra Anderson. Their children were Alexander Wallace (1891-1973); Martha Frances (1894-1910); Mary McDonald (1896-1969); and Robert James (1898-1909).

Alexander married Victoria Hodgins (1895-1985).

Mary McDonald (1896-1969) married Perry Albert Wilson. They had four children. Frances (1924) married Cliff Arrand. Ruth Alexandra (1926) married James Johnson. James Isaac (1931) married Ann Yorke. Eleanor Alberta (1933) married William Lambert.

Martha Lindsay, second child of Robert and Martha, married David Brown, son of James and Isobel Brown in May 1868. She died young and is buried in Strathroy Cemetery.

John Scott died in childhood and is buried in the Strathroy Cemetery.

Sarah Eliza, fourth of Robert and Martha's children, married William G. Duncan (d.1909) on June 25, 1873. They lived in Adelaide but moved to Winnipeg, Manitoba. Their stone in the cemetery reads: *W. Howard Duncan died August 13, 1910, age 20 years, 4 months; William G. Duncan died in Winnipeg January 31, 1909, age 60 years and Sarah E. beloved wife and mother died in Winnipeg December 25, 1924, 72 years; Lottie Mae died September 20, 1887, age 3 years; Wesley and Wilbert infant children of William G. and Sarah E. Duncan, no dates or ages.*

William Scott remained a bachelor and lived with James and his family.

Robert Walter, sixth issue of Robert and Martha, was born in Adelaide. When he was 21 years old, he received Crown land of a quarter section near Treesbank, which is southeast of Brandon Manitoba, for a home in 1881. He met and married Hannah Lamb (1867-1947), daughter of the teacher, William Lamb. She was born in Barrow in Furness, England. Their children were Arthur Wallace; Esther Maud (1890-1944); Edith May; Herbert; Louisa; Bessie; Robert James; Alice (married Art Barr); Betty (remained single); Kem; Richard; and John.

Esther Maud married Harvey Edward Rogers (1888-1960), who was born in Martinsville, Illinois. Their four children were Elmer Walter (1916-1994), who remained a bachelor; Robert (1918-1991); Edna Josephine (1922); and David Scott.

Robert, second child of Esther Maud and Harvey, married Diane (last name unknown) and they have three children, Lynn, Reggie and Barry. Lynn married Ed Mueller and has three children, Sherry, Guy and Donald. Reggie has one daughter, Michelle. Barry married Nora (last name unknown) and has one son. Barry died in his early 20s.

Edna Josephine, third child of Esther Maud and Harvey, married James Wilmot Parks (1916-1963). They had three children, Vera Olive (1941); James Blair (1945); and Terrance Alexander (1947).

Vera married Russell Clayton Woods (1930). They have two children, Sandra Anne (1968) and Gordon Russell (1970). Sandra married Mark Allen Thomson (1961). They have three children, Carling Allysa (1990); Jenna Oliva (1993); and Morgan Alexandra (1995). Gordon married Deborah Ann Strik (1970) and they have one child, Brittany (1997).

James Blair, second child of Edna and James, married Janice McPherson (1948). They have two children, Stephen (1970) and Michael (1972).

Terrance, youngest child of Edna and James, married Mary Lou Bruyere. They have three children, Troy; Terri-Lyn, who married Dan Davis and has three children, Dustin, Mary and Jamie; and James Ashley, who has one daughter, Jane.

David, youngest child of Esther Maud and Harvey, and his German wife, Juanita (1941), had four children, Stella, Christina, Rolf and Reiner.

Cornelius, youngest child of Robert and Martha, married Margaret McLean (1862-1936). They had a daughter, Martha A. (1894-1954), who married M.

William Scott (1856-1943)

Robert Walter Scott (1860-1939)

Alexandra (1860-1929) and James Scott (1846-1906)

Claude Karr (1885-1970). They had two sons, Edwin and Donald, and lived in Cass City, Michigan.

In 1877, Robert Scott remarried. His second wife was a widow, Margaret Harvey (Mitchell), who was born in St. Thomas, the daughter of John and Barbara Mitchell. She had a daughter, Addie. They lived in Adelaide. Robert is buried in Strathroy Cemetery.

SEED, John and Margaret

John Seed (1776-1878) immigrated to Canada about 1832 from County Down, Ireland, with his wife, Margaret (ca.1788-1860) and their family, including Catherine and her husband, William (Friel) Freele, and their two eldest children, Michael and William John; George; Hugh; Margaret; and Anne.

Catherine and William Freele had eight more children in Canada (see FREELE).

George (1810-1893), second child of John and Margaret, married Mary Wiley (1824-1881) in 1841 in Adelaide Township. Rev. Dominic Blake of St. Ann's performed the ceremony. Mary Wiley was a sister of John Wiley, Lillie (Wiley) Cleland, Jane (Wiley) McChesney, David Wiley, and Hugh Wiley of the West Adelaide community. It is not known if she had been acquainted with George Seed in County Down, nor is any information known about her immigration to Canada. The 1842 Adelaide Township census showed George Seed as a non-proprietor on the east half of Lot 12, Con. 2 NER. He had been in Ontario for 10 years and there were two people in the household (a reference to his bride, Mary). Fifty acres were occupied with 10 acres improved. That year, 80 bushels of wheat, 40 bushels of oats, and 100 bushels of potatoes were grown, and there were eight cattle.

George and Mary had 13 children. The 1852 census showed that George Seed was on the east Pt. Lot 12, Con. 2 NER. George was 38 and Mary 30, and children were John 10; David 8; Thomas 6; William 3; and George 2. By 1853, George Seed and his brother, Hugh, had purchased the east half of Lot 12 from George J. Goodhue, a wealthy entrepreneur and land speculator of London. Hugh located on the north half and George had 50 acres on the south half of the east half of Lot 12.

John (ca.1841-1872), eldest child of George and Mary, was a teacher who also did some preaching at Shiloh Methodist Church. He married Maria Ellen Willoughby (ca.1851-1927). They had one daughter, Mary Ellen "Nell" Seed (1871-1966). Shortly after her birth, her father died. The date and cause of death are unknown. There is a stone in St. Ann's Cemetery close to the other Seed monuments, engraved "In memory of John, son of…" and the rest is not visible. Nell lived with her Willoughby grandparents near Kerwood and in 1894, at age 22, she married Nathaniel "Nat" Wesley Conkey, also aged 22, son of Robert and Jane (Wiley) Conkey of Adelaide (see PENNINGTON, Thomas and William). After Nat's death, Nell married Robert F. E. Freele, and she was buried with him in Strathroy Cemetery (see FREELE).

David (1844) was listed in the 1880 Directory of Adelaide Township as owner of Pt. Lot 14, Con. 2 NER. His brother, George Seed Jr., was also listed as owner of this property. In June 1868, at age 24, David married Margaret Adair, 22 (ca.1845-1869), born in Niagara, daughter of James and Margaret Adair of Adelaide (east half of Lot 13, Con. 3 NER). After Margaret's death, David married Mary Adair (ca.1841), sister of his first wife. David and Mary had five children, Margaret "Maggie" J. (ca.1878); Harry (ca.1879); Mary (1880); Lottie M. (ca.1881); and Truman Eldon (1887), who was baptized at West Adelaide Presbyterian Church. David Seed's name was recorded on the West Adelaide congregational list. In November 1896, David Seed was a pallbearer at Wiley Cleland's burial. In the November 15, 1917, Age Dispatch obituary of William Seed, it was reported that Mrs. David Seed of Detroit sent a spray of flowers. No other records of this family have been located.

Thomas (1845-1926), third child of George and Mary, married Maria Mee (1843-1886) in 1871. The 1880 Directory of Adelaide Township showed Thomas Seed farming the north quarter of Lot 13, Con. 2 NER. Their children were all born in Adelaide Township and baptized at St. Ann's. Mary (ca.1872), the eldest, lived with her widowed grandfather, George, in 1891. She was a popular high school teacher in Illinois. She married Fred Farnsworth and was buried in Chicago. Margaret "Maggie" Ella (1874) was raised by the Mees after her mother's death. She was married in All Saints Church, Strathroy (1900), to George O'Leary and moved to Windsor. Quinnie "Queeny" Stevenson (1875) was unmarried and lived in Chicago. John Thomas Walton (1876-1949) lived in Vancouver. Annie Maria (1878) married W.F. Abbott of Exeter, and they had three children. Ethel Winnifred (1880-1952), sixth of Thomas and Maria's children, was unmarried and lived in Chicago.

Thomas moved to Strathroy, where he operated a harness shop. He married a second time, in 1893, to Sarah Hodgins (1848-1920) of London. His uncle, Hugh Wiley, died in 1906 at his McKellar street home in Strathroy. Thomas Seed died 1926 in Exeter at the home of his daughter Annie (Mrs. W. F. Abbott).

Hugh Seed family, back L-R, Elizabeth Jane Heake, William John, Margaret (O'Neil) (Demaray). Sitting L-R, Hugh (father), Esther B. (married Edward Nichol), Emily (Rutledge), Jane Hodgins (mother). Front L-R, Anna "Annie" Louise (Hughes) (Orme), Charlotte "Lottie" (married Francis Nichol Roseneath). Mary (deceased) and Matilda are not in photo.

William (1848-1917), fourth eldest of George and Mary's children, apprenticed in the blacksmith trade in Strathroy and operated a shop in Adelaide Village at the east half of Lot 10, Con. 1 NER. In 1869, he married Catherine Brock of West Williams Township, daughter of David and Margaret (Fair) Brock. William and Catherine had five children in Adelaide Township, Eliza A. "Ida" (ca.1871), who married George Sharen of Wallaceburg, and had four children; David Frank (ca.1872), who practiced veterinary medicine in Wallaceburg and continued his practice in North Dakota, where he married Mae Dasbinder; Birdie (1874-1877), who is buried in the William Seed plot in Arkona Cemetery; and Blanche Louise (1876-1946), who married Fred Conkey. Blanche and Fred raised their children on the west half of Lot 4, Con. 1 SER. The eldest, William G. "Toots," served in WWI and WWII. Pearl (1902-1903) died in Rossland, B.C., when the Fred Conkey family went out west for four years to work with father-in-law, William Seed. Kathryn married Winfield Waltham. The fourth and fifth children were Florence and Gordon (see CONKEY, Arthur and Margaret). Margaret (ca.1878), eldest child of William and Catherine, married Duncan Ferguson and lived in California. In the 1880s, the William Seed family moved to Wallaceburg.

The neighbours, organized by Thomas Seed, T.H. Mee, D. Adair and E.F. Henderson, along with about "one hundred-and-eighty others" met at the home of Mr. and Mrs. W.J. Seed at their residence on the Second Line North for "the purpose of testifying their regret at the Seed family departure." The entertainment consisted of a solo by Miss Kearns, speech by J. Bogue, violin solo by Wallace Brown, a "capital" speech by Jas. M. Henderson, and "sweetly captivating music on the violin" by Messrs. McLaughlin and Adair. E.F. Henderson read an address and two "handsome easy chairs" were presented to Mr. and Mrs. W.J. Seed, who replied in an "appropriate and feeling manner." Next came an instrumental solo by Miss Maggie Seed, followed by a speech by Mr. J.H. Alexander, then a duet by Miss A. Kearns and Mrs. Mee. The chairman announced that supper was ready and there were many delicious morsels, "chief among which was the palatable oyster." Afterward, conversation and dancing were enjoyed until an early hour.

A few years later, William and Catherine Seed went to British Columbia, where William found that blacksmiths were needed in the mining business. Many railroad tracks were built and maintained for the ore cars that were used to transport the minerals. They spent about 16 years there before returning to Wallaceburg. After William's death in 1917, Catherine married Joel Thorpe of Wallaceburg. According to her obituary, she was buried with her first husband in Arkona Cemetery. (The Arkona Cemetery records have not listed William and Catherine in Lot 11, the William Seed plot).

George (ca.1849), fifth eldest child of George and Mary, was a shoemaker. In the 1881 census, he was 30 years old and living with his parents, George and Mary (Wiley) Seed. It is thought that he died of tuberculosis at an early age.

Hugh (1852) is listed as the next child, and his tombstone states that he was the son of George and Mary Seed, but the rest of the stone is buried in concrete.

Robert Alexander (1854-1878) was a blacksmith. He was buried at St. Ann's. The broken tombstone is set in concrete beside that of Hugh.

Nelson (1857-1928), eighth child of George and Mary, married Annie Adair (ca.1860-1907) in 1881. He farmed in Adelaide with his parents for a few years, and three children were born, Herbert (ca.1882); Olive (ca.1888); and Birdena (1890). Nelson joined the Orange Order when he was 17 years old and was said to have held every office in it, including that of grand lecturer and grand censor. During his early days in Adelaide, he was a school trustee. Nelson was enumerator for the 1891 census of the village of Adelaide and Keyser's Corners. He started the enumeration on April 6, 1891, and completed it on April 27, 1891. He attended West Adelaide Presbyterian Church. Nelson left the farm in Adelaide and moved to Warwick Village where he entered the butchering business. After two years there, he moved to Wallaceburg, where he became involved in the painting and decorating business. At the time of his death, he was deputy grand master of the Grand Black Chapter, Royal Black Preceptory, Ontario West, and his interment was under the Chapter's auspices with service at the Knox Presbyterian Church and burial in Wallaceburg Cemetery. His survivors were listed as Herbert Seed of Wallaceburg and Miss Olive Seed of Detroit.

There is little information on James Henry (1860-1878). His tombstone, which shows his date of death, is partly buried in concrete beside those of his brothers, Hugh, Robert Alexander and John, whose tombstones are in the same condition of preservation.

Nathaniel (1862-1924) married Ann Clark (1860-1911), daughter of James Clark and Ann Chambers, in 1882. Nathaniel and Ann were recorded on various properties in the township. In 1888, his father, George, deeded Nathaniel part of the east half of Lot 14, Con. 2 NER, and also the south 25 acres of Lot 13, Con. 2 NER. In 1892, his father deeded him 50 acres at the south half of the east half of Lot 12, Con. 2 NER. Nathaniel and Ann's five children were born in Adelaide Township and baptized at St. Ann's. Henry Alexander (1883-1951) married Annie Moore (1883-1961) and they farmed in Adelaide Township on the east half of Lot 5, Con. 1 SER. They had no children. Maud May (1884) married Hezekiah Higgins of Brooke Township in 1917. Leo Wellington (1886-1957) married Gertrude Spalding (1890-1921) in 1915, and they had a daughter, Agnes Ann, who, from the age of nine months, was raised by her grandparents, the Clarks, when her mother died. Nathaniel Frederick (1889-1959) married Amelia Lazenby from England in 1923. They lived in Strathroy, where they raised four children. Mary Florence (d.1988) married Norman Cecil Keck (d.1992). Evelyn Irene married Mel Laker and they had three children, then she married a second time, to Thomas Edward Crossan (1932-1999). Charles Frederick, a United Church minister, married Renita Brown (1938-1992) in 1958 (see BROWN, John), then after Renita's death, married Joyce Gibson in 1993. Robert L. died young. John Sanford (1898-1961) married Elzina Lucille Moore in 1924. They farmed on the Seed homestead at the east half of Lot 12, Con. 2 NER, and raised four children in Adelaide, John Franklin "Frank," twins Freda Maude and Frederick Alexander, and Edward Douglas "Ted."

Samuel W. (1865-1884), eleventh issue of George and Mary, was buried at St Ann's Cemetery, having died of bronchitis.

Walter Joseph (1871) was living with his father, George, in 1891, and was mentioned as living in Wallaceburg in the 1928 obituary of his brother, Nelson.

The name of the thirteenth child of George and Mary, a son, is unknown.

Hugh (ca.1818-1890), third child of John and Margaret, married Jane Hodgins (1821-1905) of Ireland in 1846, in Adelaide Township. Hugh farmed on the north half of the east half of Lot 12, Con. 2 NER. John and Margaret Seed lived in his household. Hugh and Jane had 12 children.

Elizabeth (ca.1846-1909), eldest child of Hugh and Jane, married Andrew S. Heake (1843-1897), son of Andrew Heake and Amelia Samules, in Adelaide in 1865. The Heake family came to Canada in 1851 from Newfoundland and lived in London until 1855, then settled on Lot 23, Con. 3 NER. In 1881, Andrew S. Heake was appointed Justice of the Peace for Adelaide Township. Elizabeth and Andrew Heake raised their four children in Adelaide Township, William Andrew (1866); Eliza Jane (1870); Mary Clara (1872); and Malinda (1874).

Margaret (1849), second child of Hugh and Jane, married Dennis O'Neil in (1871), then after his death, married Aaron Demaray

Emily Hawkins (1852-1919) married John Thompson Rutledge (1844-1919). He immigrated to Adelaide Township from Enniskillen, County Fermanagh, Ireland, at age 18. In 1878, he and his wife moved to Portage la Prairie, where they raised four sons and a daughter.

Matilda Catharine (1854-1886) may have married William J. Polley of Wyoming (insufficient research to prove this).

There is no further information on Mary (1856-1875).

William John (1857-1930) worked for many years on the staff of the hardware store of Marshall and Mason in Strathroy. He was a member of the Masonic Order, belonging to the old Euclid Lodge, Strathroy, and later was Master of the Beaver Lodge. He went west in 1909 in the early boom days on the prairies and operated a hardware store at Vermillion, Alberta, where he was mayor of the town for five years. His interment was in Vancouver where he resided after his retirement. His wife, Annie (Welsh), survived him.

Esther Bella (1858-1935), seventh child of Hugh and Jane, married Edward Nichol, a widower, and lived on the Egremont Road in Adelaide Township (see NICHOL, Edward). They had two daughters, Flossie M.J. (1883-1884), and Lottie Edna (1887-1932), who married Norman Brock, then William J.

Brock, with whom she had two children, Murray and Evelyn.

Anna Louisa (1861) married Rev. Thomas Orme and they lived in Buffalo, N.Y.

Charlotte Lavinia "Lottie" (1861), ninth issue of Hugh and Jane, married Francis Nichol of Roseneath, Ontario, brother of her sister Esther's husband, Ed. Their youngest son, Sergeant Heber Nichol, was killed in action in France in 1915.

No records were found of the three youngest children, Andrew George Hugh (1866); Edwin (ca.1871); or Rupert (1878).

Margaret (1818), fourth child of John and Margaret, married James Kelly (1817) of Ireland. The Adelaide Township land records showed that in 1849, James Kelly received the patent for the east half of Lot 17, Con. 3 NER. In 1850, James Kelly and his wife sold their property to Daniel McCubbin Sr. (In 1910, Ezekiel McKeen purchased the farm from Daniel McCubbin Jr.). In 1850, James Kelly received the patent for the west half of Lot 17, and in 1854, the 100-acre lot was sold to Richard Gerry. The 1842 census listed James Kelly on the east half of Lot 17, Con. 3 NER, at which time he had been in Ontario for 10 years. Of the 100 acres, four acres were cleared, and 15 bushels of wheat and 50 bushels of potatoes were grown. Livestock consisted of one cattle and one hog. The 1852 census showed Margaret (Seed) Kelly, age 34; James Kelly

George and Mary Wiley Seed

35; James Jr. 11; Ellen 8; John 7; Jane 4; and Arthur 2. The Kellys left Adelaide after their farm was sold, and no other information was found.

Anne (1820), youngest child of John and Margaret, married James Moore of Adelaide Township in 1840. Rev. E. Blake of St. Ann's performed the marriage. Witnesses were George Seed and George Glynn. The family was not included in the 1852 census of Adelaide Township. Anne and James had three children (baptisms were recorded in the St. Ann's records), William John (1841); Margaret (1842); and Anne (1844).

SHAMBLAW, John and Lily

The Shamblaw family originally came from England. They lived first in Metcalfe Township and in 1948, when their youngest child was six months old, they moved to Kerwood. They moved into the house at what is now 27769 Havelock Street in 1953. John and Lily had four children, Robert William, Loreen Ann, Barbara Jean and Mary

William and Katherine Seed family, ca.1893, back L-R, Louis Conkey, Dr. Frank Seed, Ida Sharen (George). Front L-R, Katherine, Margaret Ferguson, William Seed, seated is Leota Carr.

Lynne. They attended Adelaide Central Public School. Robert married Bernice Smith from Glencoe. Loreen married D. Krause and Mary Lynne married Leroy Weber, both of Strathroy. Barbara married Ross Sutherland.

Lily says that John (d.1988) had many different interests, some relating to the history of the area. John had served in the army and was a motor mechanic by trade. He worked for George Chittick at first and then worked for Fred Griffith in Strathroy until he retired. He had an interest in antique equipment and owned a Bell steam engine and a John Deere tractor and water wagon, all of which he had restored himself, which he would show at fairs and steam shows. After his retirement, he taught himself to play the violin and played with the Old Tyme Heritage Group. Other members of that group included Reg Freer, Mabel Waltham, Gwen Waltham, Cora Brown, Ross Brown and Clarence Lewis. It was part of the group's mandate to preserve specialty dances from the past, like waltzes and square dances. John is buried in Strathroy Cemetery.

SHIELDS, William and Latetia

There were two Shields families living in close proximity in Adelaide Township. Often in those early days, when many families named their children after living relatives, it created problems in identifying individuals; nicknames such as "Red John," "Big John," "Long John," etc., were common. The Shields families were identified as "Irish Shields" or "Scotch Shields."

William Shields (1790-1870) and his wife, Latetia "Lilly" (1791-ca.1871) were both born in Northern Ireland, as were their three children, John (1816-1901); Elizabeth (1821-ca.1901); and James (1826-1886). John never married and is interred in West Adelaide Cemetery. Elizabeth married Robert Dempster (1816-1884) in Adelaide (see DEMPSTER, Robert and Elizabeth). James (1826-1886) married Jemima "Jenny" Abernethy (1824-1901) in Adelaide about 1849. She came from Antrim County, Northern Ireland, about 1834.

The family immigrated to Upper Canada, or as it was referred to then, Canada West, from Ireland in September 1837. They made an application for conditional purchase of the east half of Lot 2, Con. 2 NER (clergy reserve lands, which were set aside to

Jemima (Abernethy) Shields ca.1865.

retain clergy and sustain their needs) in October 1837.

William and his two sons set to work to clear the virgin forest and, by 1841, had constructed a log dwelling and barns, and cleared 11 acres of cultivated land with 90 acres of bush remaining. By 1851, they had cleared 50 acres and the family had moved into a 1-storey wood frame house, an improvement on the log home of 1841.

After his parents died, John continued to farm the Lot 2 property. As well as being a successful farmer, John was a partner in the private banking firm of E. Rowland and Company of Strathroy. His interest in the firm at the time of his death was $16,000. John left the farm on September 9, 1879, and purchased a two-acre plot on the western limits of Strathroy. This was on the south side of the Fourth Line (now Albert Street), where he resided with his sister, Elizabeth Dempster, and her son, James. The homestead was left to his nephew, Julius, who was a bachelor.

James, the youngest child of William and Latetia, was a farmer by trade. He purchased two

100-acre farms, first the west half of Lot 2, Con. 3 NER, and later he purchased the east half from Joseph McChesney. James and Jenny had six children, Agnes Ann (1851-1933); Julius (1853-1931); Lilly Elira (1859-1936); John J. (1863-ca.1934); Eliza Jane (1865-1942); and Frederick Charles (1866-1947).

Agnes Ann married David McChesney (McCHESNEY, William and Jane).

Julius farmed the homestead of his grandfather, receiving the property from John Shields on September 9, 1879, and selling it to Duncan Fisher for $3,900 on November 15, 1902. He followed his uncle into the banking business. Julius never married. He purchased a home in Strathroy, where he resided until his death. He is interred in Strathroy Cemetery.

Lilly Elira never married and is interred in Strathroy Cemetery.

John J. married Minnie Shields (of the Scotch Shields). He farmed in Warwick and they had one son, Laurier.

Eliza Jane married William Hoffner (1867-1920) in 1898. They had three children, Frederick William, Cecil, and John "Jack" (see HOFFNER, Joseph and Theresa).

Frederick Charles, youngest child of James and Jenny, married Annie E. Morgan (1875-1934). He farmed the west half of Lot 1, Con. 3 NER, as well as the east half of Lot 1, Con. 3 NER. He sold out to his brother-in-law, William Hoffner, on May 5, 1910. Frederick and Annie had four children. Clifford (1903-1935) never married and is interred in Strathroy Cemetery. Irene M. (ca.1905) married Robert O. Hillis in 1924 and they had a daughter, Maryn. After Robert's death, Irene married Fred Richardson about 1949. Kenneth (ca.1907-1960) resided in London, Ontario. Eva (1910) was a resident of London in July 1988.

SHRIER, Jacob and Mary

Jacob Shrier (1808-1888) was born in Alsace Lorraine of German parents. Jacob was orphaned, and raised by a Catholic priest. Jacob immigrated to Pennsylvania, where he met Mary Mather (1827-1897), daughter of John and Mary Mather of Alsace Lorraine. Mary had immigrated to Pennsylvania with her parents. Jacob and Mary were married in 1842. The couple heard that there was land to be had in Canada, and set out on a trip that brought them to Adelaide Township. This trek was made on foot.

Upon reaching Adelaide Township in late 1842 or early 1843, Jacob Shrier purchased 100 acres of crown land on #3 Sideroad, Lot 3, Con. 4, and Lot 4, Con. 3 NER.

The first home was made of sod, and the building of a log cabin followed. In due time, as the farm was cleared and the family grew, a large brick home was built. The brick for this house came from the Keyser Brick Yard. The family church affiliations included both Anglican and Presbyterian.

There were 13 children born to the Shriers, Mary (1848); William Henry (1849); Sophionia (1851); John Thomas (1854); Jacob (1856); Nelson (1858); Francis (1860); Ordelia (1862); Caroline (1864); Ann Elizabeth (1866); Simon (1869), who married Katie Vokes (see VOKES, James and Mary); James Gilbert (1871); and George (1874). Not all of these children survived to adulthood. Three children died before the age of five.

In the early years before flourmills were close at hand, Jacob Shrier and others would carry grain on their backs to be made into flour. These trips for flour and supplies would take the men as far as Kilworth or St. Marys. Mary was left on her own with the children while Jacob made these trips. Once when she was alone, four very hungry native Canadian men visited the homestead. Mary gave

Shrier family, L-R, Olive, Delman, Sarah, Henry and Cephas.

Shrier children, Simon, Gilbert, George, Annie and Carrie.

these men almost all the food she had, even though she was very nervous and had little food left for her children. Some weeks later upon arising, Jacob and Mary found half a fresh deer at their door, and they knew Mary's kindness had been remembered. Thus was born a tradition that no one was ever to be turned away hungry from the Shrier homestead.

SIFTON

John Sifton (1792-1848) and his brother, Charles (1797-1874), had set out for Cork on May 4, 1818, with the conception that they were to sail for Canada aboard the ship, Brunswick, almost immediately. They found that the Brunswick had not been outfitted, and they did not set sail until June 13. Many in the Talbot party, to which the Siftons belonged, were forced to spend much of their capital during the six-week delay at Cork, and were understandably concerned about the shortened growing season to prepare for their first Canadian winter. They did not anchor at Quebec City until July 29. Twenty-four children on board had died of measles, and an additional 11 died after reaching the Gulf of St. Lawrence. From Quebec City, the party travelled to Montreal by steamer at a cost of £3 for cabin passengers or 10s for steerage, provisions not included. The trip of 180 miles took about 36 hours. The Sifton brothers arrived in Montreal on July 5, 1818, only to find that no provision had been made for transportation to York and on to Port Stanley.

"Because of the rapids at Lachine, goods and passengers travelled overland by wagon from Montréal at this time. (The Lachine canal was opened to bypass the rapids in 1825.) Beyond Lachine towards York, flat-bottomed boats, about 40' x 6', a small mast, sails, an anchor and a cooking platform, with four men and a pilot, were able to carry about five tons. Once reaching the rapids around the Cascades, approximately 30 miles west of Montréal, it was necessary to "pole" using 9' metal-tipped poles. A small canal and locks had already been built between the Cascades and the Cedars. In many cases, towing was necessary—with the passengers assisting. It generally took 10 days to get to Prescott, Ontario, a distance of 120 miles. For the Talbot party enroute to York, it took 13 days from Lachine.

Beyond Prescott, ship navigation recommenced. The group heading for York/ Toronto travelled on the schooner Caledonia, taking six days to travel the 250 miles, arriving on September 9, 1818, 84 days after they left Cork. A few days later, they boarded a schooner to Queenston on the Niagara River, then overland to Fort Erie, and by schooner again to reach Kettle Creek/Port Stanley, but with a shipwreck enroute on Lake Erie—adverse winds forced the Phoenix aground about 40 miles southwest of Buffalo, New York. The ship broke up on the rocks, and one of the settlers died as a result of the cold and fatigue.

A small schooner, the Humming Bird, happened along, was engaged, and after three crossings of Lake Erie, they were all eventually in Kettle Creek. The last group to cross was forced ashore by winds in the Long Point area, and hence proceeded to Kettle Creek by wagon. By late October, some settlers were settling by the Thames River near London, Ontario—London Township." (This information taken from: *Richard Talbot, The Tipperary Irish, and the Formative Years of London Township, 1818-1826,* Daniel J. Brock, MA thesis, University of Western Ontario, 1969.)

John and Charles Sifton received land in London Township. The rest of the family, with the exception of Bamlet (1793-1876), came to London Township in 1819. Bamlet Sifton came to London Township in 1832. The father, Charles Sifton (1752-1842), son of Joseph (ca.1720) was born in Clonmel, Tipperary, Ireland, where he married Rebecca Wright in 1785. Charles and Rebecca raised eight children in Ireland, Eliza (1791-1819), who died on the voyage to Canada; John (1792-1848); Joseph (1792-1875); Bamlet (1793-1876); Charles (1797-

1874); Rebecca (1804-1879); Robert (1810-1877), ancestor of Mowbray Sifton of London; and Maria (1812-1898).

Joseph Sifton married Catherine Hogan in Ireland and they raised five children in London Township, Joseph Bradshaw (1815-1875); John (1822-1858); Rebecca (d.1882); Charles Wright (1824); and Bamlet Esdras (1828-1890). The son, John, was the first Sifton to commence several of their forays in Adelaide. At the age of 27, he received the patent to the east half of Lot 7, Con. 1 SER. From the land records, it seems obvious that he was having financial difficulties, because his younger brother, Charles Wright, loaned him money via a mortgage in April 1851. Two years later, this mortgage was assigned to Henry L. Thompson. However, John Sifton died in 1858 and John's older brother, Joseph Bradshaw, sold this land to William Conkey in June 1869 in order to discharge the mortgage still held by Henry Thompson. After 20 years of ownership, this property was lost to the Sifton family.

In the meantime, Joseph Bradshaw purchased the east half of Lot 9, Con. 2 NER, from George Ivor in October 1853 and sold it six months later to John Hamilton.

Joseph Bradshaw married Mary Goulding (1819-1905) and they had eight children, one of whom was Charles Goulding (1847-1884). Charles Goulding purchased the west half of Lot 17, Con. 1 NER, on November 9, 1877, and three months later he married the next-door neighbour's daughter, Jemima Brock (1850-1899), at St. Ann's Anglican Church in Adelaide (see BROCK, George and Isabella). Charles and Jemima had twin daughters, Mary Ida Christine (1880-1964) and Anne Augusta Jane (1880, died an infant). Mary Ida Christine married John H. Simmons (1875-1956). When Charles died, he left the land to his wife, Jemima; when she died a year later, she left the property to Mary Ida, who sold it to Henry Tarrant in 1903.

Throughout this chain of events, Bamlet Esdras Sifton, youngest brother of John Sifton, the original Sifton landholder, was buying and selling mortgages throughout Adelaide and other locations in Middlesex County. He became quite wealthy.

It was not until March 1937 that Clarence Sifton (1890-1951), great-grandson of John Sifton, one of the original two brothers who came to Canada, and grandson of Joseph Sifton (1828-1900), the cheese maker in Metcalfe, came to Adelaide. He and his wife, Gladys Dodge (1894-1978), came to Lot 11, Con. 5 SER, renting the farm from the owner, Henry Humphries. It is recalled by the family that this wood frame house was in deplorable condition and that the "insects merely stopped for lunch on their way through the walls." Clarence and Gladys had four children, Kenneth (1918-1991); Lawrence (1922-1997); Douglas (1928); and Victor (1930). While on Lot 11, Douglas and Victor attended Napperton School and the rest of the family was involved in operating the farm. Victor attended Napperton for the full four years, but Douglas started at Strathroy Collegiate Institute in 1940. Vic recalls that his classmates at Napperton included Phyllis Hull, Mildred and Bruce Dixon, Margaret and Dawn Muxlow, Mike and Harry Shepherd, Bruce and Don Wright, Edwin and Esther Grundy, and Clare Temple. Two of their teachers were Kathryn "Kate" Murphy and Norma Wright. *"The students at Napperton used to enhance their diet with apples liberated from Jack Lee's orchard to the east of the school, or the Currie orchard across the road. Apples recovered but not eaten immediately were stored in the school woodshed."* In March 1941, the Sifton family moved to farm in Brooke Township, Lambton County.

SISSON, Herbert and Charlotte

Herbert (1871-1938) and Charlotte "Lottie" (d.1960) purchased a 50-acre farm at Lot 15, Con. 3 SER, from John Watson and his sister. They took possession in February 1907.

French genealogy shows that the Sisson families lived in France. They traded with passing caravans for several centuries until the Massacre of Huguenots in 1572, when they had to flee to save their Protestant faith and their lives. Some reached England in the early 1700s, and in the early 1800s, some came to Canada. Herbert Sisson's family settled near Bethany in Durham County, where he was born. Charlotte's family (Atkinsons and Cairns) came from Ireland and settled nearby at Lifford.

When Herbert and Lottie were married, they left the hilly, stony fields of their youth and settled on a Warwick Township farm, where their first child, Gladys (d.1991), was born. In February 1907, they moved to an Adelaide farm at Lot 15, Con. 3 SER,

The Herbert Sisson family in 1933, L-R, Herb, Eileen, Lottie, Gladys and Claire.

formerly owned by John Watson and his sister. It was across from the Mullifarry Post Office. A few months later, a second daughter, Eileen, was born, followed three years later by a son, Claire (1910-1975).

Lottie was a charter member of the Mullifarry U.F.W.O., and Herb belonged to the United Farmers. He enjoyed working with wood and made many articles for the house, as well as things for his children's enjoyment, such as stilts, bow and arrows, and a bobsleigh and harness for the dog. He also mended the family's shoes. Lottie was kept busy with the everyday housework, sewing the family's clothing, tending her garden and poultry, preserving and pickling, churning, helping with the milking and farm work, and baking (some of our classmates offered a whole baker's bread sandwich for one of our crusts).

The children attended S.S. #11, Payne's School, which was destroyed in the tornado of 1943. When Gladys started high school in Strathroy, she had to pay tuition fees and board in town. In following years, two or more made the trip daily with a horse and buggy or cutter. The cutter rides were rather tipsy at times as the cutter runners were considerably narrower than the tracks the cars made in the snow.

The Sisson family attended St. Paul's Anglican Church in Kerwood the first year, but changed to St. Ann's in Adelaide Village, as it was closer. They took part in many church activities. The children were all married there and the parents are buried in the cemetery.

Gladys Sisson married Harvey Robertson (d.1992), a teacher. They retired to Havelock near Peterborough and are buried there. Their two daughters, Joan and Elaine, also became teachers.

Joan Robertson married John Klenavic and they have three children. They live in Ottawa, where Joan teaches music. Their daughter, Jennifer, married Chris Whiting. She lives in Nepean. John, the eldest son, lives in British Columbia, and Michael attends university in Prince Edward Island.

Elaine married Ron Scott, and they live on a farm at Norwood near Peterborough. Both are high school teachers. They have three children, Kerstin, Andrew and Lindsay.

Eileen, the second child of Herbert and Lottie, married Archie Cameron in St. Ann's on August 25, 1934, and they settled on Archie's farm near Watford. On August 25, 1984, they celebrated their 50th wedding anniversary at St. Ann's with a service followed by a dinner, which was the first event in the new addition. The dinner was arranged by sister-in-law Muriel (Petch) Sisson.

Eileen and Archie have three children, Alice, Allan and Howard. Alice became a teacher. She married Bob Wilson, and they lived in Katesville across the road from the schoolhouse (has since been removed). They have three children, Susan, Brian and Steve. Susan, a Health of Animals Technician in Watford, married Frank Sweeney and lives north of Arkona with their three children, Ryan, Sean and Allison. Brian and his wife Janet live and work in Sarnia. Steve is working as a mechanic, and farming with his parents.

Allan, Eileen and Archie's second child, has a body shop in Watford. He and his wife, Joan, have four children, Sherri, Julie, Sam and Pam. Sherri is an X-ray technician at Sarnia General Hospital. Julie is a teacher; she married Calvin Fowler, and they live on a farm near Oil Springs. Sam works in a microbiology lab in Guelph. Pam is in university in Social Services.

Howard, the youngest child of Eileen and Archie, lives on his farm near Watford and tends his crops, cattle and pigs. He is a very active member of the Lambton Cattlemen's Association. He also does quite a bit of his own construction and machinery repairs and remodeling.

Claire (1910-1975), the youngest child of Herbert and Lottie, completed one year of high school, and then he stayed home to farm with his father. In 1925, they bought a 50-acre farm south of the original property. In 1928, he went with friends on a harvest leave to Alberta. He was there for two months and enjoyed the friendship of the people. On September 27, 1941, he married Muriel Petch (1916-1997). On September 27, 1942, their daughter, Donna Marie, was born. In the fall of 1943, they moved the house on the back 50 acres over for a hen house. In June 1944, a tornado came down the Second Line and destroyed a lot of property. Claire and Muriel's farm was no exception: the roof blew off of the barn, as well as the shed; the hen house was upside down on a cherry tree; the garage collapsed on the car; the roof was off the colony house on Lottie's doorstep; and the ceiling and roof blew off the kitchen. During the storm, trees were felled, and chickens were killed and maimed. Windows in the house were smashed, and a steel shingle blew in onto the dining room table.

In 1956, the Adelaide farm was sold, and Claire and Muriel lived with her parents, Fred and Pearl Petch. In 1957, they purchased a farm 10 miles west of St. Mary's. After Claire's death, Muriel sold the farm and returned to live in Strathroy.

SLATER, Thomas and Margaret

Christopher Slater (1798-1889) married Christianne Carr (1806-1881) at Yorkshire, England, in 1829. They came to Canada in May 1830. One of their sons, Thomas, bought the property at Lot 24, Con. 1 SER. Thomas and his wife, Margaret, had five children, Emily, Louise, John, Margaret and Catherine.

Emily married William Walker, and Catherine Agnetta married Thomas Walker.

John and his wife, Margaret, bought a farm on the Second Line South of Adelaide and had a son, Frank, and a daughter, Marjorie.

Frank and his wife, Eva (Moore), farmed the homestead and had two daughters, Ethel and Helen.

Marjorie and her husband, Crosby Southern, farmed in the Fordwich area. They had two chosen daughters, Shirley and Rosemary.

SMITH, Charles and Marie

Charles and Marie Smith moved to Kerwood from Strathroy on September 5, 1971. They purchased their home from Wilma and Bill Rate, who had purchased it from the Diocese of Huron (it was the Anglican rectory). Their three children, Randall, Bill and Gayle, moved with them to the property.

Charles opened a shop, Smith Upholstery, in the old Post Office building. He then built a shop at their residence, which he used until September 1985. At that time, Bill took over the business and opened a store in Strathroy.

The home of Charles and Marie was built with Kerwood brick. It was constructed in 1927, partly from a cottage that had been on the lot south of its present location.

SMITH, Everett and Betty

Everett Smith and his family moved to Adelaide Township shortly after his return from overseas service in 1947. He was in the first division of the R.C.R.'s and served in the Italian campaign and the liberation of Europe, and he was part of the post-war troops in the Netherlands. The Smith family rented a farm in Adelaide Township for the first year, and then purchased the farm where the township office now stands.

Everett worked for Gord Campbell and, when the place in Adelaide Village became available, he sold the farm and bought it. He remodeled it into a home. At one time, he operated "Adelaide Construction" from the location. He was also the agent for Holiday Homes.

In the early 1980s, the front part of the property was sold to Dortmans. Several years later, the barns and acreage were sold to Doug Dolbear.

Through the years, Everett was tile and drain inspector, building inspector, and one year he collected dog taxes for the township. He was also a bus driver and a custodian at Adelaide W.G. MacDonald School. Everett lived in Adelaide Township from the late 1940s until 1992, when he and Betty retired to Manitoulin Island.

William Blair purchased the farm from the Walthams and it was used for pasturing cattle. In 1974, he gave the farm to Everett and Betty Smith. They built a new home on the farm.

Betty had moved to Adelaide Township in 1974. She taught at Adelaide W.G. MacDonald School from 1976 until retiring in 1992.

In 1983, the land was severed and sold to John Aarts.

In 1993, Everett and Betty sold the house and shop to their daughter and son-in-law, Elizabeth and Andrew Forman. In 1994, Elizabeth and Andrew opened a gift shop and handcrafted wood shop.

SMITH, John and Susannah

John Smith (1829-1907) married Susannah Hunt (1832-1875) in 1853, and they settled on Lot 26, Con. 1 NER (now 4074 Egremont Rd.). The Smiths had seven children, Almina (1855-1943); Theopholis Courtland, Augusta Johanna; Nathan Arthur; Caleb William; Merci Ann; and Amelia Jane (1865-1957). When Susannah died, she left her husband with seven children.

John Smith married his neighbour, Charlotte Maria (Robbins) Fuller (1840-1933), widow of Obadiah, in 1876 or early 1877, and they lived in the large Smith home on Lot 26, with 11 children from their first marriages. Charlotte had four sons (see FULLER, Obadiah and Charlotte). John and Charlotte had a daughter and son. Louette A. (1877-1967) married Arthur B. Decker (1871-1960) of London Township in 1898, and they had three children. John A. (1880-1952) married Laura E. Hodgins (d.1968) and they lived in Adelaide Township.

The sons from John's first marriage died young, and the daughters married and moved out of the township, except for two. Almina, the eldest, married William Gare (1852-1915) of Adelaide and they had five children, John Charles, Ethel, Oliver Courtland, Annie J. and Manford, all born in Adelaide Township. The family moved to Lambton County. John Charles became a Reverend.

Amelia Jane, the youngest child of John and Susannah Smith, married Silas Fuller, third son of Obadiah and Charlotte. They settled on the Fuller farm and had seven children, Oscar Murdick (1887-1972); Hiram Harold (1889-1984); Joseph Arthur (1891-1985); Dora Louetta (1893-1978); Vincent George "Dick" (1896-1990); Charlotte Beatrice (1898-1990); and John Obadiah (1904-1996).

After John Smith died, Charlotte married a third time, to a Mr. Odlum or Audlum from Petrolia.

SMITH, John Graham and Francis

In 1849, John Graham Smith and his wife, Francis (Clark), arrived in Canada from Sunderland, County Durham, England, with their family of five sons and one daughter. After spending a year in Toronto, they moved to Adelaide Village. From there, they went to Williams Township. In 1854, they bought the Gallagher farm in Adelaide Township, the east half of Lot 6, Con. 4 NER. Their family consisted of Edward G., Henry, Elizabeth "Betsy," John Jr., William, and Russell Blackbird. John G. Smith was a shoemaker who travelled the area making shoes for the local families. He lived on this farm until his retirement, when he moved to Strathroy. His son, Russell, took over the farm.

Edward, the eldest son, married Mary Shephard and moved to West Williams.

Henry married Mary Jane Stevens, a neighbour, and daughter of Samuel and Ruth (Grainger) Stevens. Henry was a shoemaker like his father. They lived in Keyser and later moved to Oak Avenue, Strathroy, where he continued his trade.

Betsy married Richard Bell in 1854. Richard had also come from Sunderland, County Durham, England, in 1852. He was a tailor who worked in London until he and Betsy were married. They settled in Keyser in 1857, when Betsy's father sold them ½-acre of his farm. The economy was bad in 1857, so Richard taught at Keyser School from May until August because the farmers didn't have money to buy tailored clothing. Their first five children were born in Keyser, John Christie, George, Richard Jr., Robert William and James Sparkes Bell. The family later moved to Strathroy.

The family had severed 4½ acres of the farm for John Jr., who was a blacksmith. He also bought Richard and Betsy Bell's ½-acre in June 1864. On this property, he built his first blacksmith shop of wood, but replaced it with a brick building in 1881. In 1883, he had the present brick house built by John Murray, a contractor from Strathroy. John Jr. married Sarah Maria Keyser in 1864. She lived across the road on Lot 5, Con. 4 NER, and was the daugh-

The Fuller homestead in Adelaide Township on Highway 22, ca.1900. Silas in the democrat, Amelia standing beside it, daughter Charlotte, son Vincent, and Oscar in the cart.

ter of John Philip and Elmira (Dell) Keyser. John Jr. and Sarah had eight children. Two daughters died as children. The other children were Joseph R., Matthew Foster, Urias Francis "Frank," Effie Lena, Clinton Roscoe and Orval. Joseph, Clinton, Frank and Orval moved to Strathroy. Matthew became the blacksmith at Kinnard, Bosanquet Township, and later moved to Detroit. Effie married Walter G. Gilbert and moved to West Williams. In 1909, John retired to Strathroy and sold the property to Donald Gray, who built a store to the east of the blacksmith shop facing Con. 4. Gray sold to William W. Parker in 1919, and he moved the building to its present location about 1922. Parker sold to Laverne Topping in 1943. In 1964, Frank and Helen Gare purchased the property. The store was closed and the property was eventually purchased by Joseph and Johanna Minten.

William, fifth child of John G. and Francis, was a carpenter. He married Sarah Ann Cadman, the daughter of James and Margaret Cadman. They lived at Keyser until after 1871, when they moved to Sarnia. Their children, all born at Keyser, were John Wesley, Frances Ellen, William Henry, Margaret Jane and Sarah Elizabeth.

Russell Blackbird, the youngest child of John G. and Francis, bought 95 acres of land, the east half of Lot 6, Con. 4 NER, from his father. Russell married Lucinda Victoria Stevens, a sister to Henry's wife. Their children were Ruth Lydia, Eliza Maria, George Lindsay and Mary Lucinda. Lydia married George Washington Murray of Keyser. She died during the birth of their daughter, Lydia May. George married her sister, Mary Lucinda. Russell ran the Keyser Cheese Factory in 1885 and had the post office in the front of the building with Benjamin W. Stephens as postmaster. In 1891, he sold one acre that included the cheese factory to Hugh Wilson, who sold the factory to James Thomas Grieve in 1911. Grieve ran the cheese factory until 1916, when he sold to William Inch. In 1901, Russell sold the farm to his son, George Lindsay Smith. In 1918, James A. Murray bought 94 acres from George L. Smith and one acre from William Inch, giving him 95 acres. The farm went to Wilbert Murray in 1931, to Lawrence Arthur Murray in 1952, and to W. Blair Murray in 1963. It was then purchased by Joseph and Johanna Minten.

SMITH, Leonard and Marta

Leonard Everett "Len" Smith (1947) was born in Adelaide Village, the son of Everett "Spike" and Helen Smith. He attended S.S. #10. His wife, Marta Rose (Whiteside) Smith, was raised in Strathroy, the daughter of Grant and Irene Whiteside. Len and Marta bought their home at Lot 19, Con. 5 SER, in December 1973.

Len and Marta have four children, Theresa "Terri" Dawn (1968); Ryan Leonard (1971); Lyndsey Rose (1980); and Meghan Jean (1982). Ryan and Lyndsey were both born on Christmas Day. Terri, Ryan and Lyndsey attended Adelaide W.G. MacDonald School, while Meghan went to a French Immersion program.

After graduating from the University of Western Ontario, Terri spent 15 months teaching in Japan and then was employed by the Financial Post in advertising in Toronto. Ryan was employed by C.N. after high school and then began work with Ryder Transport in London as a technician in 1996.

Although Len and Marta lived at R.R. #7 Strathroy, Len travelled extensively within Canada while he was employed as a high-pressure welder doing pipeline work. In 1996, he was contacted by Bechtel International of Houston, Texas, and accepted a temporary position in Algeria, where he spent four months in the Sahara Desert on a gas pipeline job. Marta obtained a B.A. majoring in Sociology from the University of Western Ontario, and worked as a counsellor for Middlesex Community Living.

SMITH

In the 1852 census of Adelaide Township, Malcolm Smith (1826-1901), born in Scotland, was 25 years old in the listing of the John Smith family living on Lot 27, Con. 2 NER. His father, John Smith, farmer from Scotland, was a widower, age 65. Also listed were a brother, John, born in Scotland, age 34; his wife, Flora, also born in Scotland, age 30; and their children, Donald, 4, and Mary, 2, who were born in Canada. Later, a son, John, was born ca.1853.

According to family information, the Smiths immigrated in 1843, five years earlier than their Scottish neighbours, the McDonalds, who lived on the east half of Lot 26, Con. 2 NER. The family consisted of Christina McDonald, a widow, aged 56; John, 30; Hector, 27; Mary, 21; Angus, 20; and

Laughlin, 14. A non-member, Catherine McLoed, 14, of Williams Township, was listed in the 1852 census as living with the McDonalds. Mary McDonald told her children of leaving her home in Scotland as a young girl and immigrating to Canada with her mother and her brothers. Crossing the Atlantic took the usual three months and they made their way to Hamilton. The rest of the journey to London was made in wagons, and they made a clearing in the forest for their home.

Malcolm Smith and the "girl next door," Mary McDonald (1824-1908), were married ca.1853, and they resided at Lot 27, Con. 2 NER. They had 10 children.

Charles A. (1854) lived in London.

Hector (1855-1930) spent his life on the home farm. He was a bachelor who assisted his parents in "hewing a farm out of the wilderness" a mile north of Hickory Corners.

Donald lived in Omaha, Nebraska.

Neil (1861-1895) married Maggie Paul and they lived in Lobo Township.

John J. remained a bachelor. He resided in Boissevain, Manitoba.

Alexander (1863-1932) lived on the home farm until his death. He married Janet May "Nettie" Thomson (1873-1963). Their children were Alexandria May (1901-1977); Donald Thomson (1904-1910); and Malcolm Elliott (1906). May was born in Oklahoma, delivered by Alexander's brother, Dr. Malcolm M. Smith, when the family was visiting there. May attended London Normal School and taught at Napperton, S.S. #5 Adelaide, until her marriage to Fred Sullivan of Adelaide (see SULLIVAN, John and Letitia). She boarded with the Parker family, and Velma Parker (Mrs. Ralph Muxlow) remained a friend for many years. Malcolm Elliott was co-owner of the Smith Graham Drug Stores in London.

Mary Ann (1864), seventh child of Malcolm and Mary, married Malcolm McGurgan of Caradoc Township in 1885.

Malcolm M. (1866) was a physician practicing in Fairview, Oklahoma.

Christina "Tina" (1869) married Joseph Hezekiah Bolton of Caradoc Township in 1899.

Betsey, the youngest of Malcolm and Mary's children, was born the same year as Queen Victoria. She married into the McFarlane family of East Williams.

Malcolm and Mary are buried in Strathroy Cemetery. The farm was sold to Robert McCubbin.

SNELL, William and Henrietta

In 1911, William "Bill" Snell (d.1969), a coal miner from Yorkshire, immigrated to Canada and came to Renfrew, Ontario. He had found a job on a farm through an employment agent. A year later, his wife, Henrietta (Suggitt) Snell (d.1948); their only child, a daughter, Eva (1900); and Bill's brother, Charles, made the crossing on the "Empress of Ireland." Eva remembers that it took a week and the seas were rough, making people seasick. There was a woman on the boat with a small child who was allowed to run all over the ship. One night, the child upset the mentholated spirit lamp and the partitions in the woman's room burned.

Eva had never really seen snow before she moved to Canada. When her father came to pick them up in Renfrew, he arrived in a sleigh. Eva's mother asked, "How's that thing supposed to work without wheels?"

In 1914, the family moved to Adelaide Township, where they settled on the west half of Lot 6, Con. 3 SER. Charlie Snell did not settle in the same area and ended up in Superior, Wisconsin, where he married, had a family and owned a grocery store.

When they arrived, Eva and her mother worked at the Con. 2 SER Houlton farm, and for the bache-

Family of Malcolm Smith, front L-R, mother Mary (McDonald) Smith, Malcolm, Alex, Christina, and father Malcolm Smith. Back L-R, Donald, Neil, Mary Ann, Hector, Charles and John.

lor Earley brothers, Jim, George and Sam. Their sister, Liza Earley, was married and lived in Michigan, and their other sister, Maggie, had died, so they needed hired help in the house. Eva remembers that Jim Earley was a boxer and boxed in Detroit for the Golden Gloves. There was a lot of interaction between the two families. At some point, Jim purchased land from the Snells with the stipulation that Eva remain in the house as family.

In those days, the Snells and Earleys collected sap from the maple trees, and then boiled it to make syrup. In order to clean up the syrup, they put an egg and a cup of milk in the sap. Any bits of bark or dirt rose to the top in the egg/milk scum, and was skimmed off. Not wanting to waste anything, though, Eva and Lily Redmond collected the scum and put it into a pan, then cleaned it up again to get sufficient maple sugar to make tarts. One time when Roy Demaray was helping with the sugaring, they decided to burn old rubber boots to heat the boiler. This worked fine until Roy decided to put all of the boots in at once—it made such a thick cloud of black smoke that they could not even see across the road! It did work, though. The sap was boiling away to beat the band!

Bill Snell had received some formal education in England, a Standard 4 from the Beetley Board School in 1890. Eva had only gone to school until she was 10. She received a Standard 5, and looked after children after that. William also took some courses when he was working in the mines. In England, he had worked in the mines for 15 years. He said that, when he first went down in the cage he knew it was dangerous, so he took courses in medical and rescue work to help him understand the situation better. This part of his education became useful later, when his neighbour, Eugene Earley, had purebred cattle with broken bones that needed setting.

The Snells, like many other farm families in the early 1900s, did not have hydro for a long time. They used coal oil lamps and lanterns, which had to be cleaned and tended often. Everyone got up early to take advantage of the daylight to do his or her chores. The stovepipes needed regular cleanings as well, a messy job! Eva remembers that Jim Mac Earley once helped her with this and she ended up entirely covered with soot. From then on, she did all the pipes by herself. She said that it always seemed like the minister would drop by for a visit on the day she decided to do the pipes!

Sometimes there were fires because of the stoves. When the Demaray house burned down, the family came to stay with the Snells. Bill was living there alone as Henrietta had passed away, and Eva was keeping house for the Longmeyers in Strathroy. One of the few things saved from the fire was the Demarays' organ. However, when they brought it to the Snells' home, one of its legs broke through the floor. When Eva saw her father and Roy Demaray in the unfinished basement, staring up at the leg hanging through the ceiling, she laughed until she cried!

"Gypsies" used to pass through Adelaide every so often and they would park their wagons by Payne's Schoolhouse on Second Line South and use the well. They sold pots and pans in exchange for chickens and eggs. There was some question as to exactly how honest some of them were in their transactions, such as the time Bill saw a gypsy distract a customer while another put his foot on the scale to make their goods seem heavier.

Farmers at that time still used horses, and Bill ploughed his land with a team. In the 1940s and 1950s, tornados were active in Adelaide, and two of the stories Eva remembers about them involve horses. Fred Sullivan saw a tornado coming and moved his horse into the stable in time, but the tornado caused a big beam to fall on the horse, and it was injured so severely it had to be put down. Another neighbour saw a tornado coming while he was out in the field with a team of horses. Just as he got them unhitched, something hit and killed one of them, leaving the other completely unharmed.

When one of the Thomas's bought the first car on Con. 2, everyone went to have a look at this wonderful thing, which Eva remembers had curtains on the side windows. Because it was more difficult to get around in those days, many things were delivered. Harold Conkey delivered groceries from Kerwood, and the cheese factory came around and picked up the cream.

During WWI, Eva's aunt wrote from England, telling them about how things were there and about the sirens and the blackouts. There was rationing in Adelaide Township, and one could only get a limited amount of butter and sugar, which was measured by the hundredweight. Sometimes a neighbour gave coupons they did not need to another family, which was always appreciated.

Eva married Bill Tucker at the Kerwood United Church in 1932, and they had three children, Marjorie, Esme and Raymond.

Eva says that she has seen many changes in her lifetime. Many things that were almost unthinkable when she was young, such as airplanes, are now completely commonplace. Mother Shipton, a popular prophet, had predicted there would be horses flying through the sky and, as Eva says, she was absolutely right. Eva flew to England in 1970 to see the places where she spent her childhood and remarks that, although she liked living there in her youth, she could not really see any changes.

At the time of this interview, Eva resided with Raymond's widow, Betty Tucker, in Cambridge.

SOETEMANS, David and Riekie

In May 1992, Dave and Riekie Soetemans purchased 50 acres of land at Lot 1, Con. 1 NER, from Martin VanKessel. Dave grew up in West Williams Township and Riekie in Warwick Township. Martin and Wilhelmina VanKessel had purchased the property in 1965 from John Blanchard, and they had built a house and shed on the southwest corner of the land in 1981. Deeds date back to June 16, 1836, when Andrew Menely received the land from the Crown.

Dave and Riekie developed this land into orchards, with 40 acres of apple trees and the remaining acreage in peach, plum, pear and cherry trees. They named the orchard Soetemans' Treesweet Orchards. Dave and Riekie have three children, Devan (1988); Marcie (1990); and Monique (1993).

SPRUYT, Nicholaas and Wanda

Nicholaas Johannes Spruyt (1957) immigrated to Canada in 1975. Before coming to Canada, Nick lived with his parents, two sisters, and two brothers in the Netherlands. The family lived in a large town, and Nick's father worked in the grass seed business until his retirement. When Nick came to Canada, he resided for several years with an aunt and uncle on a small dairy farm in the Oshawa area. Soon after, he met Wanda Bostelaar (1959), who had immigrated to Canada from the Netherlands in 1979, following her graduation from Agricultural College.

Wanda's family lived in the small town of Rotterdam, where her father worked in the paint industry. Wanda's father passed away in 1993, and her mother and brother, Rob, have remained in the Netherlands. Later in 1979, Nick and Wanda moved to Windsor to work for a large cash crop farmer. The two married in 1980 and moved to the Tillsonburg area, where they began hog farming two years later. They have two children, Celia (1982) and Randy (1983).

In 1985, the Spruyt family bought a hog farm in Strathroy from Jack and Rose Caris, and a second daughter, Joyce (1985), was born. Located on the Second Line South at Lot 16, Con. 2 SER (now known as 2890 Mullifarry Drive), the Spruyt 50-acre farm is set up for hogs and is currently running a 200-sow farrow-to-finish operation.

STEAD, Henry and Effie

Henry Stead (d.1928) married Effie Morse (d.1919), daughter of William (d.1900) and Susan (Raison) Morse (d.1929). Effie's father had purchased 70 acres of land, the east half of Lot 9, Con. 1 NER, in 1866. After he built the barn, William built the house in 1869. Effie's siblings were Joe; Louise (d.1958); Jack (d.1957); Bertha; and Charlie. Joe married Violet Sinclare. Louise and Jack

Soetemans family, L-R, Marcie, Riekie, Dave, Dean and Monique, 1996.

remained single. Bertha (d.1975) married Walter Baynham (d.1966), and Charlie was married. Effie was the only Morse sibling who had a family after marriage. The Morse farm was operated by Jack, Louise and Bertha.

Henry and Effie Stead had five sons, Harry, Jack, Verne, George and Evan. When Effie died, Evan was nine months old. He went to live with his mother's family on the Morse family farm.

Harry, the eldest child of Henry and Effie, married Jessie Ann Wooten, and Jack married Marion Fowler. Verne married Velma Purdy, and George married Rene Mossip. Evan married Evelyn Sumner.

After Jack and Louise died, Evan farmed on his own until Walter and Bertha Baynham moved to the homestead in 1964. Evan married Evelyn Sumner in 1979. Evelyn had two daughters, Marie and Nancy. Marie married Randy Smith and Nancy married Doug Hepburn. Marie and Randy have two children, Lisa and Steven.

STEELE, John and Janet

John and Janet Steele moved from London to Adelaide Village about 1985. They have three children, Carrie, Shannon and Shane. Carrie married Roger Snell and has three children.

John and Shane work at George's Auto Wreckers in Lobo. Shannon lives at home but attends school in London. Janet works at the Children's Psychiatric Hospital Institute in Byron, where she has been employed for 19 years.

John and Janet say they aren't farmers, but manage to harvest a lot of cars from the area as well as car parts, since Shane has an interest in car racing and demolition derbys. They had hoped he would outgrow this interest, but he keeps winning.

They enjoy Adelaide Village very much and hope to retire there.

STEVENS, Samuel and Ruth

Samuel Stevens (1786-1860), of Irish descent with origins in Maryland, married Ruth Granger (1799-1876), also of the U.S. The 1776 Revolution forces show several Stevens on their rosters. A migration from Maryland found Samuel, along with other Stevens family members, in Delaware and Westminster Townships in 1852. Ruth seems to have been related to the Woodhills of the same district, with the Granger name used as the second given name for family members.

Their home in 1852 was at Lot 4, Con. 3, Delaware Township, about two miles south of Kilworth, with farming as an occupation. There was a family of 12, which included twins. The seven youngest were still at home in 1852. The third eldest, Sarah, was born in Delaware, and the two elder brothers were also Ontario-born.

Benjamin William (1820-1888) married Jane Harrison (1817-1895), who was born in the United States. They were in Lobo Township in 1852 and in the West Williams side of Adelaide Store in 1861. A daughter, Sara (1844-1921), married Hiram Ransom Keyser of Keyser. A sister, Eliza Jane (1846-1911), married Nial Thorp of the district. Benjamin later lived at the east half of Lot 8, Con. 4 NER, where he was postmaster from 1875 to 1888. A son, Charles (1853-1894), who married Mary Graham (d.1942), continued as postmaster until 1891. Mary, carrying on her husband's name, is the only Stevens on the 1935 voter's list. The census of 1881 shows

Keyser's Postmaster, Benjamin Stevens Jr., and wife, Sarah Ann, ca.1870.

Elizabeth, age 20, with Benjamin and Jane. Other children could have been missed.

The next son, Samuel Jr. (1822-1881), married Jane (last name unknown, 1826-1903), who was born in England. In 1852, Samuel purchased Lot 8, Con. 7, West Williams, and in 1870 bought the west half of Lot 7, West Williams, and part of Lot 8, Con. 4 NER, in Adelaide. Sam and Jane were living on the West Williams side in 1871, with a family consisting of Robert (1847); Lillie (1845); Esther (1850); George (1850); and Addie (1861). Two small children died, in 1861 and 1865, and were buried in Arkona Cemetery, a testament to their early arrival in the district.

The first daughter, Sarah (1825-1889), born in Delaware Township, married David Sells in 1844. At age 15, Sarah was converted at a religious camp meeting in Dorchester. She lived with her husband in Adelaide for nearly 20 years. They purchased 50 acres at Lot 8, Con. 4 NER, alongside Benjamin Woodhull. Sarah's home was opened to preaching service before a Methodist Church was established at Keyser. The Sells family moved to Melrose in Lobo, where their descendants became part of that community.

Lydia (1827), fourth child of Samuel and Ruth, married George Burdick, who was born in the United States. They were in Delaware Township in 1852, with a son, Charles, aged three. George was listed as a blacksmith. In 1871, George was a blacksmith at Keyser. This occupation appears to have moved the family throughout the local area.

Hannah (1828) doesn't seem to have a connection to the Keyser area, and her whereabouts are unknown.

Ann Eliza (1830) married Truman Ward of Lobo. The family in 1871 consisted of three children. Her descendants lived in nearby Lobo.

Ambrosia "Ambrose" (1832-1896) was living with his parents in Delaware in 1852. His wife was Harriet, last name unknown. When their son, Benjamin Franklin Stevens (1855-1935), died, it listed his mother as Harriet Zavitz and his wife as Dorothy Zavitz. The tracing of a maiden name can be a challenge. A Harriet Hendrick (1837), who was a neighbour to brothers Benjamin and Samuel, appears a likely fit for Ambrose's wife, but this is not confirmed. Ambrose and Harriet were at part of Lot 10, Con. 4 NER, in 1871, with Ambrose listed as a farmer and thresher. Other children were Charles (1858); John Wesley (1861-1943), whose wife was Marjorie Munroe; Michael (1862); Samuel (1863); Harriet (1865); James (1867); and Richard (1870).

Ruth (1834-1911) had a twin named Patience (1834-1882). It appears that the mother, Ruth, used the short list when naming these two children. Patience married John Hendrick, a neighbour of her brothers. Ruth spent time with other family members, including Ann Wood and John Stevens, in 1871. She was with sister Lucinda in 1881 and 1891 in Adelaide. Helping with her siblings' growing families was Ruth's calling. She is buried alongside her sister, Lucinda, in Arkona Cemetery.

Mary Jane (1836), tenth child of Samuel and Ruth, married Henry Smith in 1856 in Arkona. Henry was the son of John and Francis (Clark) Smith of Lot 6, Con. 4 NER, at Keyser. A daughter, born in 1872, married Sam Keyser, son of Joe Keyser. Their son, John Smith, was helping his blacksmith uncle (also named John Smith) when an incident occurred, involving the death of local boy

Keyser's Postmaster, Charles Stevens, and wife, Mary.

Elmer Barten, age 13, in March 1876. The details were printed in the local paper at the time, describing how John's hot iron inflicted what was to become a fatal wound on Elmer. He was charged, but acquitted. He later became a blacksmith at Cairngorm.

John (1838-1904) married Mary Jane Sharpe (1838-1914). In 1871, they were in Lobo with two daughters, Alice Victoria (d.1875) and Annie Eliza. Annie and her parents were in Adelaide near Keyser in 1881. Annie (1864-1936) married James Albert Murray of the area (see MURRAY, James and Catherine)

Lucinda Victoria (1842-1893), youngest child of Samuel and Ruth, married Russel Blackbird Smith, Henry's brother. They took over the parent's farm at Lot 6, Con. 4 NER, at Keyser, and ran the cheese factory and post office for a period of time. Their family consisted of Ruth Lydia (1865); Eliza Maria (1866-1880); George, who took over the farm in 1901, and Mary Lucinda (1874).

Six family members (Benjamin, Samuel, John, Ruth, Patience, and Lucinda) are buried in Arkona Cemetery. Ten of the 12 children lived in the Keyser area at some point. This family certainly impacted on Keyser's early years, with the later years dispensing many of the descendants to points beyond.

STEVENSON, Clarence and Bessie

Clarence Stevenson (1902-1972) was born in Metcalfe Township. He worked on a farm in Adelaide Township during his teenage years. He married Bessie Elliott (1901-1990), born in East Williams Township. Bessie moved to Adelaide Village with her mother and father when she was a few years old.

Clarence and Bessie were married in Adelaide Village on March 15, 1922, and moved to the farm on Con. 3 SER. They had two children, Clayton and Marie. The first Stevensons to immigrate to Canada came from County Antrim in Ireland.

Clayton (1925) was born on the west half of Lot 2, Con. 3 SER, and moved at a few months of age to the west half of Lot 3, Con. 3 SER. He married Evelyn Watt (1924-1980) on November 12, 1955. Evelyn was born in Brooke Township.

They moved to Strathroy in 1975. They raised one son, Glen (1958), who now resides in Strathroy with his wife, Mary-Anne Ford (1958). They have

Clayton Stevenson (courtesy The Age Dispatch).

two children, Chelsey (1986) and Paul (1996).

Marie married John Robinson and lives in Strathroy. John and Marie have two children, David and Lisa.

STILL, Charles and Frances

On April 5, 1834, Charles Jasper Still (d.1889) married Frances Jane Armstrong (1808-1881) in Captain Curran's house in Adelaide. The officiating minister was Reverend Blake, and the bondsmen were John Philpot Curran and John Garnett Armstrong.

The groom was a Royal Engineer, born in Cobh, County Cork, in the first decade of the nineteenth century. His father was also named Charles Jasper Still (1769), and he had been an Overseer with the Ordnance Survey on Spike Island, a penal facility in Cork Harbour. C.J. Still Sr. had joined the Ordnance Survey in 1797, and as of 1815, he had five children and was residing on Bare Island in Cork Harbour.

Family history has it that C.J. Still Sr. left the responsibility of the family's inheritance to his daughter, Louisa, with strict instructions that it be divided in such a way that each one of his children would remain at the same level. Louisa followed his instructions to the letter by giving everything to the Roman Catholic Church. This came as quite a shock to the Protestant family! The family took the Church to court to try to regain their inheritance, but lost their case. Their challenge to the Church subjected them to increasing persecution and they decided to leave Ireland. Louisa, not surprisingly, became a nun with the Poor Clares and may have become an abbess in a convent in Spain. At least one sister married a Bremyer and lived in New York City. Charles Jasper Jr. immigrated to Adelaide, marrying Frances, another Irish expatriate, who had been born in Dublin, although her family may have come from County Longford.

Charles Jasper Jr. belonged to the Middlesex militia. On March 31, 1847, he became a Captain in the 7th Battalion. He was promoted to Major on February 15, 1856. He and Frances both died in Strathroy.

Charles Jasper and Frances Jane had eight children, all born in Adelaide Township. The two eldest sons, Charles (1835) and Henry (ca.1840), moved to St. Joseph Island. Both are buried in Sault Ste. Marie.

The eldest daughter, Louisa (1837-1876), married W.H. Ewer and lived in Strathroy. They had three sons and a daughter, and after Louisa died, the children were sent to England to one of their Ewer relatives to be educated.

The other five children moved west. Armstrong (1844-1920) and Jasper Nucerman (1848-1924) homesteaded in Riding Mountain, Manitoba, although it was still part of the Northwest Territories at that time. Armstrong had a fiancée, but she died before they were married and he remained a bachelor. He died in Neepawa, Manitoba. Jasper married Caroline Brett, the daughter of the ornithologist and naturalist Walter Brett, in 1885. They had four sons. Jasper died in Winnipeg.

Frances Maude (1846-1921) married Count De Dory in 1886. They had no children. She is buried in Neepawa.

Claude (1851-1921) married Louise Rowe in Strathroy in 1883. They moved west in 1884. They had a son and a daughter. The daughter died at a young age, and they buried her on their farm. Claude was killed in a farm accident.

Jane Eliza (d.1906) married William Drever Jr. in Winnipeg in 1868. They had two sons and a daughter.

STIRTON, Gordon and Margaret

Stirtons have lived in Southwestern Ontario for

Ian H. Stirton, 23, in an announcement of his assignment to Vietnam.

many years. In 1820, James Stirton came to Canada, eventually settling on a farm located between Watford and Alvinston in Brooke Township. He was born in the Stormont region of Scotland, but lived for many years in England before moving to Canada. His son, John, eventually took over the farm. In 1870, John married Mary McIntrye from Brooke Township. In 1889, he and Mary, along with their eight children, moved to a farm in Michigan.

Mary's maternal grandparents, surnamed Patterson, were Loyalists from North Carolina. John's maternal grandparents, surnamed Brown, were also Loyalists from North Carolina. The Brown and Patterson families came to Canada together following the American Revolution, first to Maine, then Nova Scotia, and finally settling in Ontario.

In 1951, John's grandson, Gordon, moved from Michigan to a farm near Kerwood with his wife, Margaret (Howell), and their three children. A fourth child was born later. Gordon continues to live on the farm. His eldest daughter, Mary, taught school in remote parts of Canada for many years, but now lives with her own family on a farm in Manitoba. Ian, Gordon and Margaret's eldest son, works as a press officer for the Federal Election Commission in Washington, D.C. The youngest son, William H., is an officer in the American Merchant Marines. Alison, the youngest daughter, lives in London where she teaches dance.

STOKMAN, Jim and Gertrude

Jim Stokman (d.1995) arrived in Nova Scotia in February 1948. He worked there for a Dutch firm, which took down hangars that were shipped to Holland. He then moved to Quebec and worked for a farmer. In the spring of 1949, he and his brother-in-law, Peter Verkley, rented a farm near Hull, Quebec. This was only for a short period. In the fall of 1949, Jim travelled to Southwestern Ontario. With the assistance of Lloyd Hunter, from the settlement service, he looked for a farm, eventually purchasing property owned by Archie Muxlow on the Second Line South. It had 100 acres, a house, barn, and driveshed. There was snow on the ground, so he had to shovel the snow away to see what type of soil he was buying. He was also able to rent another 100 acres without buildings, with the option of buying the land in the future.

During that first winter in this area, Jim worked for Hunter's dairy in Strathroy and boarded at Walter Hick's. In the winter of 1952-1953 he worked for George Jiggins on the farm. Jim also worked for McLean Feed and Grain in Kerwood for a short time.

Jim and Peter Verkley farmed together until 1956. Jim went on vacation to Holland in the winter of 1951-1952, when he met his future wife, Gertrude.

Jim married Gertrude Dykzeul on August 1, 1953, at the Roman Catholic Church in Strathroy.

They lived in the upstairs of the big house, with Peter and his wife, Gerina, who lived downstairs. They got along very well together and it helped Gertrude to become settled in her new country. By 1956, Jim and Gertrude had two children and Peter and Gerina had six; the house had become too small.

Jim and Gertrude bought property from Christina Paine, widow of Archie Paine, which held 25 acres, a house, garage, and small henhouse. The house needed repairs. George Jiggins put in new windows throughout, which greatly improved the house.

Jim worked as a salesman for Surge, selling and servicing milk machines. He enjoyed that job very much as he liked to interact with people. However, because of health problems, he changed jobs and started a chicken farm.

Jim and Gertrude had four children. Nick, the eldest, is farming on the home place. Trudy married Phil Farster; she is a nurse and he is a mechanic. They have one son, Matthew. John is a teacher. He is married to Janice Wardell and they have one daughter, Emily. Andrew is married to Marian Van den Boomen and they have two sons, Mark and Andrew.

Jim lived in Canada for 47 years, 45 in Adelaide Township. Gertrude still resides on the farm, with their son, Nick.

STRYBOSCH, Harry and Josephine

Born in the Netherlands, Harry and Josephine Strybosch married in 1950 and immediately immigrated to Canada. After living in Strathroy and Metcalfe, they settled in Adelaide in 1956. They purchased a home and five acres on Highway 81 SER, just outside Strathroy, for $7,000. Harry made an even trade for his home and property in Metcalfe for the new home. At that time, they had four children, JoAnn, Martin, Wilma and Tony. Four more children followed, Harry Jr., Joe, John and Elizabeth.

In 1985, Harry and Josephine subdivided the property behind their home into five lots. A new street, Charles Boulevard (named for Charlie Nichols who was once Reeve of the township), was developed as a result of the subdivision of the Strybosch property. Harry and Josephine built a home at the far end of the street and continue to live there today.

Their youngest son, John, built a home in 1987 on the last remaining lot on the north side of Charles Blvd., where he, his wife, Sandy, and son, Curtis,

Jim and Gertrude Stokman, wedding day August 1, 1953, All Saints Roman Catholic Church, Strathroy.

Harry and Josephine Strybosch on their wedding day in 1950.

presently live. The other seven Strybosch children live away from the Adelaide area.

SULLIVAN, John and Letitia

John Sullivan (1801-1835) was born in Kill Parish, County Kerry, Ireland. As a young man, John had enlisted in the 13th Regiment of the Light Dragoons at Maidstone, County Kent, England. After seven years of service, he was given an honourable discharge for a medical condition, "cephalagia (severe headaches) of long standing." At some point, he married Irish-born Letitia Cassell (1795-1877) and in 1832, the couple immigrated to Canada with their children, John Jr. (1829-1904), James and Harriet. They landed at Piston and made a successful petition for land at York; they moved to the west half of Lot 4, Con. 2 SER.

When John died just a few years later, Letitia was expecting another child, Lettica (1836-1911). Letitia abandoned the property and remarried, to a man named Whiting. They moved to Lobo, where the couple had a daughter, Catherine. After Mr. Whiting died, Letitia lived with her son, John Jr., and his family in Adelaide until her death. All that is known about Catherine Whiting is that she grew up to marry a Mr. Hall of Delaware. Her half-sister, Harriet, fades into similar obscurity. We only know that she married a man named Mayo.

Lettica married George Curtis (1833-1901). They moved to London and had two children, a daughter, Lettica (d.1873), who died at the age of six, and a son, Silas (d.1870), who died at the age of 18 months.

James, second child of John and Letitia, became a blacksmith and settled in Woodstock. He married and he and his first wife, Alice, had a daughter, Maude. When Alice died young, James remarried. He and his second wife had a son, Russell, and two daughters, Grace and Hazel.

John Jr. trained as a carpenter and joiner and worked in Kingston for 17 years, where he helped to build the Kingston Penitentiary. In 1853, he submitted a claim for his father's land in Adelaide, which had been abandoned when his father died. In London two years later, he married Agnes Nichol (1831-1887), one of the four daughters of William (1775-1855) and Janet (McIntyre) Nichol (1793-1873). The couple saved until 1860, when they were able to return to farm the property in Adelaide. They patented the lot, and built a brick house there around 1878, which stood until 1920. Living on the original Sullivan lot, John purchased three adjacent farms on the Second Line, the east halves of Lots 2 and 3 on Con. 2 and the east half of Lot 2, Con. 2, all SER. John served on the township council for a number of years as well as being connected with a local cheese factory.

John Jr. and Agnes were predeceased by their two eldest children, Catherine (1857-1879) and John

Agnes (Nichol) Sullivan, ca.1874.

John Sullivan with Edwin and Harriett.

(1859, died an infant). Their seven other children were Harriet "Hettie" (1860-1945); James (1862-1914); William (1864-1952); Mary Ellen "Ella" (1866-1888); John Charles (1868-1952); Martha Jane (1871-1943); and Edwin Alfred (1874-1960).

Hettie married Peter Anderson, who farmed in the Watford area. They retired to Strathroy. Their children were Ethel, Bert and Ella. Ethel (Armstrong, later Lougheed) lived in the west and then in Toronto. Bert married Bessie Clark and taught school in Saskatoon. Ella (Fulton, later Atkins) lived in the west mostly, but later in Strathroy.

James married Emma Martin and farmed in Warwick Township. Their oldest child, Edgar, remained single and went west as a teacher. Paul married Pearl McLean and was a farmer in Warwick Township. Bertha died as a young girl. Lena was a teacher who went west, where she married Elmer Hagerty of Saskatchewan. Carrie, also a teacher, went west and married Gordon Pearce of Saskatchewan.

William married Rachel Clark and farmed on the Second Line. They had six children. Vernon was a teacher who went west and was later killed in the Great War. Freida became a teacher, married Archie Smiley, and lived in Northern Ontario. Mabel married Basil McCandless, a grocer in Strathroy. Harold was a businessman in Strathroy. He married Beatrice Burdon. Margery was also a teacher. She married Herman Durocher and lived in the United States. Dorothy married a banker, Dick Davis, and lived in Port Credit. William's second wife was Margaret McColl. Their children were Annie, who married Art Fidler, a nurseryman in Strathroy, and Hugh, a technician who married Mary Forbes. Hugh and Mary live in Sarnia.

John Charles married Mandana Dowding and they raised four children on a Second Line farm. Laura married Jim Keyser, an automobile dealer in Toronto. Fred married May Smith and also farmed on the Second Line. Hazel, a teacher, married Charles Adderley and lived in Port Arthur. Jack became a teacher in Toronto and married Joyce Rutherford.

Martha Jane married George Cawthorpe who farmed near Melbourne. They had two daughters, Harriet and Evelyn. Harriet married a McKay. She became a doctor and practiced in Sudbury. Her sister, Evelyn, also lived in Sudbury.

The youngest son of John and Agnes was Edwin Alfred, who married Clara Carrothers. They farmed on the Second Line and their children were Norman, who died in infancy; Stewart (d.1937), who was a farmer; and Helen, who married Art Clarkson, a London businessman.

Descendents of John Sullivan living in Strathroy and Adelaide include Annie Fidler, daughter of William Sullivan; Ila McInroy, granddaughter of John Sullivan; Eleanor Collings, granddaughter of John Sullivan, her two sons, David and Brian Collings, and her two grandchildren, Chad and Sara Collings; and David Robertson, great-grandson of James Sullivan.

SUMNER, Don and Evelyn

Don (d.1973) and Evelyn Sumner and family moved to Adelaide Township and lived on the McCarthy farm, the west half of Lot 15, Con. 1 NER, in April 1954. They grew corn, oats and sugar beets. Theirs was one of the last farms to have horses to work the land, and an old threshing machine.

They had two daughters. Marie runs the Kerwood Post Office and is married to Randy Smith. Nancy lives in London. When Don died, the property was sold.

At first, Evelyn and the girls rented a house from Don Walker. In 1979, she married Evan Stead.

Evelyn's mother was Flossie (Bellairs) Squire, who lived on the Marg Hammond and Paine farms when she was young. Flossie was caretaker of S.S. #11.

SUTHERLAND, Clare and Helen

Clare Sutherland was born in Caradoc Township. On March 10, 1945, he married Helen Thompson, who was born in McGillivray Township. In November 1947, they purchased Lot 16, Con. 2 NER, a 50-acre farm in Adelaide Township, from Harold Bolton. They had mixed farming. In the spring of 1950, they purchased the adjoining 100 acres to the east from John Regan. They had a dairy herd for a number of years and later, farmed cash crops.

Clare and Helen had eight children, Deanna, Dolores, Elizabeth, Wayne, Linda and Lenor (twins), Sandra and Deborah.

Deanna married Jack Elliott and has one son, Richard, who drives the road grader in Adelaide Township. Deanna and Jack still farm in Adelaide.

Dolores married Jack Lamont and has two sons, Robert and Raymond.

Elizabeth married George Dougherty. They have two sons, Christopher and Michael.

Wayne married Dennise Antaya.

Sutherland family, back L-R, Deanna, Dolores, Elizabeth, Wayne, Linda and Lenor. Front L-R, Deborah, Helen, Clare and Sandra.

Linda married Wayne Giffen and has two sons, Brian and Allan.

Lenor married Bruce Elliott and has three children, Jennifer, Heather and David.

Sandra married Ronald O'Niel and has a daughter, Shawna. After they divorced, she married James Lockhart. They have a daughter and son, Jessica and Joshua.

Deborah married Rich Huismann.

In March 1980, Clare and Helen sold the 150 acres to Cuddy Farms (the property is now known as Hilltop Farms, on Cuddy Road). At that time, they moved to their present home in Strathroy.

TAMMINGA, Gerrit and Bouwchiene

Gerrit Tamminga (1924) and Bouwchiene Nyburg were born in Harkstede, Holland. They married on February 15, 1949, and immigrated to Canada on March 7, 1949. They arrived in Halifax on March 14.

When WWII ended, there were no homes for young people to begin their lives. Due to the war, nothing was constructed for three years, and bombing had destroyed a large number of buildings. When the Canadian Army liberated Holland, it was a very joyous time, being free again! Having met the Liberators in April 1945, there was a bond between Canadians and the people of Holland, so it was only natural that the Tammingas later immigrated to Canada. The couple stepped on shore with $80 and a lot of energy to start a new life in Canada. They settled in Oxford County near Bright, where they worked on a dairy farm. In 1950, they worked in Chatham in a paper factory, C.I.L. Fertilizer, and also did seasonal work such as planting and harvesting sugar beets and tomatoes.

In 1952, the Tammingas moved to Adelaide Township, knowing land was less expensive here than in Chatham. For three years, they sharecropped on the Pennington farm on the Second Line North. There, they experienced their first tornado in May 1953. They were preparing the land for corn when the weather turned windy and cloudy. Around 5:30 p.m., it began to storm and when they tried to send the milk cows home out of the bush, they wouldn't budge. Next, metal fencing and poles were whipping through the air. It was extremely frightening! Not until two days later did they understand what had happened. Then Hurricane Hazel of 1954

Mr. and Mrs. Gerritt Tamminga and family of 13 children, 11 in-laws, and 43 grandchildren, 1995.

turned the fields to lakes. The Tammingas lost 15 acres of sugar beets.

In 1962, the Tammingas bought a farm at Lot 11, Con. 5 SER, County Road 39, where they raised 13 children. They had to look for ways to increase income to feed the many mouths. They grew asparagus, strawberries, cucumbers, potatoes, and tomatoes for Campbell Soup. In the meantime, they built up a sow operation of 125 sows, created more barn space, and sold weaners to Quality Swine Co-op.

Talo, the eldest child, along with Junior Routley, built the garage and upstairs offices in Adelaide Village in 1979. Talo was a firefighter for Adelaide/Metcalfe for 21 years. His younger brothers, George, Fred, and Adrian followed suit. The first two volunteered for five years and Adrian so far has worked 10 years and continues to do so today. Talo married Dina Kok and they have four children, Annette, Gerrit, Richard and Ivan. They live in Parkhill.

Ann married John Jongbloed. They live in Chatham and have four children, Bryan, Kerri, Michelle and Emily.

Mary married Rick Lenting. They live in Watford and have three sons, Rick, Andrew and Jeffrey.

Janet married Rob Vanderveen. They have four children, Kristin, Michael, Lisa and Nicole, and live in Thamesville.

Grace married Jacob Lenting. They live in Watford and have seven children, Gerald, Robert, Carla, Rebecca, Stephen, Natasha and Lynette.

George married Rolean Hulzebox. They live in Ancaster and have seven children, Rachel, Bradley, Ashley, Lauren, Jodi, Taylor and Mariah.

William married Phyllis Baartse. They live in Wyoming and have five children, Joshua, Helena, Matthew, April and Connie.

Fred married Jeanette Koster. They have four children, Brianne, Scott, Sarah and Kevin. They live in Smithville.

Benita married Peter Boersema. They live in Beamsville and have five children, John, Bernice, Gerrit, Jennifer and Victoria.

Trudy lives in Strathroy.

Adrian married Michelle Bork. They live in Watford and have three children, Denise, Allison and Chad.

Geraldine married Burt VanLuik. They live in Beamsville and have four children, Nicholas, Gavin, Brett and Natalie.

Lucy married Frank Viveiros and they live in Iona Station.

In 1993, the Tammingas toured Normandy, where all the Allied Forces landed. What a tragedy, to see so many young lives buried. Today, the Tammingas still hold all the Canadians who enlisted in the Army, Air Force, Marines and Supply Ships in high esteem for giving and risking their lives and helping Europe to be free from German Occupation. The Tammingas sold the farm and moved into Strathroy in 1998. The family feels Adelaide Township was, and still is, a good place to live and raise a family.

TAYLOR, Daniel and Elizabeth

Daniel (ca.1784) and Elizabeth Taylor (ca.1793-1851) originated from Yorkshire. They were early pioneers who came to Adelaide around 1832 and settled in Katesville. They farmed on Con. 11, at the east half of Lot 4, SER. On the 1842 Agriculture Census, they had 100 acres, of which 35 were improved. They harvested 50 bushels of wheat, 16 of barley, 18 of oats, 20 of peas and 30 of potatoes. They made 50 units of maple syrup, owned 10 neat cattle, four sheep and one hog. They spun 14 yards of wool. Elizabeth died during census taking, as there is a notation about her death as "liver complaint." Daniel and Elizabeth had at least eight children.

Rhoda (ca.1821-1923) married John Calcutt (1812-1896) in St. Mary's Anglican Church) in 1840. After receiving a Crown grant, they took up farming at Lot 7, Con. 8, in Ekfrid Township, later returned to Metcalfe Township, and then settled in Strathroy. They had 11 children, all born in Ekfrid Township.

Mary Anne (ca.1822) married Samuel Hawes in 1841.

Charles (ca.1823) married Catherine Emerick in 1846.

Harriet married John Emmons in 1847.

Maria married Isaac Castel Jackson in 1849.

Sarah (d.1848) is mentioned in Anglican Church records.

William (1828-1910) married Mary Cawrse (1829-1921), daughter of Charles and Grace (Rowe) Cawrse of Metcalfe Township, in 1852. They lived in a large brick house on Lot 1, Con. 4, Metcalfe Township, which is now only pasture. There is a wonderful Christmas story written about this family by Jane Laughton, a granddaughter. They had eight children, all but one married into Metcalfe families.

Darina (ca.1835) married Peter Emerick in 1852.

Since this part of Adelaide became Metcalfe, the Daniel Taylor family was not researched any further.

TEDBALL, Milton and Eileen

Milton Rolland Tedball (1919-1976), the son of Ernest Rolland and Margaret E. (Richardson) Tedball, was born in Glencoe, Ontario. While he was growing up, the family lived at Kerwood.

On July 4, 1942, he married Eileen Warner (1922-1995) of Strathroy, the daughter of John and Constance (Davidson) Warner. Milton and Eileen were married at the Kerwood United Church. Milton and Eileen lived in London (during the war), Kerwood and Strathroy, and had three children. They divorced during the late 1960s.

During WWII, Milton was a mechanic and he continued the profession after the war. He served as President of the Royal Canadian Legion, Branch 116, in Strathroy in 1960. Milton is buried in Strathroy Cemetery.

Eileen was a housewife, and she also looked after children from Children's Aid. Later, she lived in Sarnia and worked as a waitress. She remarried on January 2, 1971, to Osmo Falden, and they lived in Tiverton, Ontario. She is buried in Strathroy Cemetery.

Milton Roger (1943-1995) was born in Strathroy. He served in the Armed Forces from 1962 to 1969 with the United Nations in Cypress. He was retired from the Waterloo Regional Police Force. Along with his wife, Joyce, and son, Michael, he lived in Elmira. He was a member of the Elmira Legion.

Margaret Jo-ann (1948) and her husband, Eric, live near Wyoming, Ontario. They have two daughters, four sons, and two granddaughters.

Ernest John (1951) and his wife, Debbie, live in Forest with their two sons, Rusty John and Kyle Milton. Debbie is an Early Childhood Educator and works in a day care centre in Forest. They were married in June 1989. John is an ambulance attendant and an associate member of the Royal Canadian Legion Branch 176 in Forest. John fondly remembers attending Grade 1 at Crathie School with Miss Annie Courtis as his teacher.

TEDBALL, Orville and Evelyn

Orville (d.1993) and Evelyn (Wilton) Tedball were married in 1947. Orville was the son of William and Dora Tedball, who farmed in Metcalfe Township until retirement, when they moved to Kerwood. Orville's parents lived in Adelaide for 35 years.

In 1948, Orville and Evelyn bought property from Bill Nettleton, Lot 22, Con. 1 NER, where they built their first gas station. Highway 22 was a gravel road at that time, but it was paved in 1949. They sold this business in 1955 and, a few years later, the gas station burned down.

Later, they bought property from William Goff, Lot 19, Con. 5 SER, and built a house and a car body shop (Adelaide Crash) on County Road 39.

Orville and Evelyn Tedball's gas station on the corner of Highways 81 and 22.

They lived at the same location for 40 years, and had two children, Dwight and Brenda (Scott), who is married and has two daughters, Amanda and Alainna.

For two years (until the new Adelaide Central School was built), Evelyn drove Dwight to the one-room schoolhouse in Napperton on County Road 39, in a 1933 Ford Coupe. Because children in those days usually walked the long distance to school, Evelyn often had extra passengers to Napperton.

THOMAS, Gordon and Helen

Gordon Henry Thomas (1909-1983) was born in Adelaide Township. His father, Edwin, owned land at Lot 18, Con. 4 SER, and Gordon represented the fifth generation of the Thomas family to live on this land. During Gordon's lifetime, he would sell sections of this land, but it was still where he built his home.

On June 22, 1935, Gordon Thomas married Helen Elizabeth Knight (d.1965) at Kerwood United Church. They had three daughters, Marilyn Jean (1938); Elizabeth Anne (1944); and Linda Joan (1949), all of whom moved away from the Adelaide area. Marilyn married Charles Spalding and they live in Calgary, Alberta. Elizabeth Anne married Errol McIntosh, and they live in Hays, Alberta. Linda Joan married Robert Strub, and they live in Redwood Meadows.

THOMAS, Lou

Lou Thomas of the Second Line South (his property was later owned by Fred Wright) had two sons, Ken and Ron. Ken joined the Air Force at a young age and was a crack shot at Strathroy High School. He was on the Bessel Rifle team and, later, the World team. Ron was also in the Air Force. He went on about 40 sorties, encountering many dangerous situations.

Later, The Lou Thomas family moved to Dominion Street at the corner of the Fourth Line South, where Lou Thomas had a small acreage for market gardens. After the war, Ken bought a lodge in the Muskokas. He continued to improve his sharp shooting skills with the use of a bow and arrow.

THOMPSON - FAUNT

There are certain echoes of Jane Austen in the backwoods gentility that the Thompsons and Faunts brought to Adelaide Township, where four generations of Thompsons lived between 1832 and 1932. They made extended visits to each other, especially to those relations who had the good fortune to live in town. They conducted their own private quarrels over legacies and inheritances, and they devoted special attention to ensuring that their attractive daughters made "advantageous marriages."

Thomas Thompson (d.1855) was baptized October 29, 1775, in Cullicudden, Ross-shire in Scotland. Upon joining one of the Scottish Fencible regiments as a 16-year-old, he was commissioned as an adjutant, a title with distinction that he continued to enjoy for the rest of his life, in spite of having spent just seven years in the army. Upon being placed on half-pay, he settled in Ireland and married Isabella Campbell, whose brother, Colin, was a prosperous businessman in Jamaica. For at least 25 years, Thomas farmed near Tanderagee in County Armagh and later near Fivemiletown in County Tyrone. On the promise of receiving 200 acres of uncleared land in Upper Canada in exchange for relinquishing his half-pay pension (which was only two shillings a day), Thompson and his family immigrated during the summer of 1832. Tragically, his wife died en route, one of the thousands who succumbed to the cholera epidemic of that year.

Thompson received his grant of land at Lot 19, Con. 1 SER, one of a group described by the 1878 Atlas of Middlesex County as "English and Irish gentlemen, mostly retired officers." The majority decided they were unsuited to the regimen of pioneering, but Adjutant Thompson continued to farm there for the rest of his life, along with several of his children. He was buried at St. Ann's Church in the village of Adelaide. Thompson's son, George, inherited the farm, which was subsequently passed on to George's niece, Bertha Thompson, an action that produced several lawsuits among various nephews and nieces.

Adjutant Thompson and his wife had 10 children. The eldest, Lewis Mackenzie, worked on a coffee plantation in Jamaica. James Campbell, who married Caroline "Fanny" was a classicist who had his own private school in London, Ontario. John Creery farmed with his father and possibly returned to Ireland. Catherine married George P. Liddy. Isabella (d.1889), a spinster, was buried in Strathroy Cemetery.

Another son, Thomas (d.1887), acquired his father-in-law's farm at Lot 18, Con. 5 SER, and later farmed at Lot 19, Con. 4 SER. He married Ellen Faunt, the daughter of another Adelaide settler. Upon his death, his obituarist remarked that, apart from having served as an officer during the 1837 rebellion, "a residence of 56 years in a Canadian township is rather monotonous and uneventful, and does not present much variety for a biographer to expatiate upon."

Ellen Faunt's father had brought his family of nine children to Canada in 1833. Like Adjutant Thompson, he was a retired army officer, having served under Wellington in the Peninsular Campaign against Napoleon from 1808 to 1814. His wife, Elinor Egan, was the daughter of a prominent Dublin physician. Before immigrating, they lived near Mullingar, County Westmeath, on land held by Faunt's family. Upon resigning his army pension, Faunt was granted several parcels of land in Adelaide Township, including the one that was eventually passed on to his son-in-law, Thomas Thompson. In decorous tones, his youngest daughter's marriage was announced, "At Belfield, the residence of the bride's sister, Mrs. Thompson, William, fourth son of Robert Pegley, and Cecilia, second daughter of Captain Faunt, late of H.M. 34th Regiment." A few years later, Faunt argued determinedly—though ultimately unsuccessfully—that Ellen and Cecilia should be the exclusive beneficiaries of a £1200 legacy left to them by an Irish Egan relation. He argued that their older sister, also a beneficiary, had disappeared and should be presumed dead, according to Faunt's correspondence with a Dublin Egan, who was the estate's executor.

Thomas and Ellen Thompson's four sons and four daughters were all born in Adelaide Township. According to one family historian, "In those days, attractive girls of good families often found it difficult to meet suitable husbands, so relatives who were in a position to do so would take the girls into their homes to provide them with opportunities they would not otherwise have." This course of action produced "very advantageous marriages" for two of the daughters, Isabella Campbell "Pidge," who married George Moncrieff, a Petrolia lawyer, mayor, member of parliament and a founder of Imperial Oil; and Charlotte Eleanor "Minnie," who married Jacob Englehart, also a founder of Imperial Oil and later chairman of the Temiskaming and Northern Ontario Railway. Jacob established the Charlotte Eleanor Englehart Hospital in Petrolia in his wife's honour. Louis Henry married Elizabeth Tanner and became a veterinary surgeon in Attica, Indiana. Eleanor Charlotte apparently died young. George Margrave "Joe" married his first cousin, Bertha Thompson, and took over her uncle's farm where they had a family of six children, Connie, Catherine, Adelaide, Margrave, Helen and Jacqueline. Colin Campbell married Lina Bradshaw and inherited his father's farm, where he and his wife had two daughters, Marjorie and Marie, before Colin died suddenly at the age of 39 of acute appendicitis. Albert Edward married Evaline MacPherson, and then remarried, to her sister, Setta MacPherson. He practised medicine in St. Clair, Michigan. Katherine Campbell "Kate" married her cousin, Jack Toothe.

Another son of Adjutant Thompson and Isabella Campbell, David Margrave (d.1896), was a lawyer in London. He married Anne Smith and they had two children, Bertha (d.1932), who married the previously mentioned George Margrave Thompson;

and Jack, who was a doctor. D.M. Thompson retired to a farm at Lot 16, Con. 1 SER. He was buried in Strathroy Cemetery.

Another daughter, Charlotte Margaret, married Robert Toothe, a graduate of Cambridge and a farmer. Their seven children were born in Adelaide Township. Harriet married Rev. A.S. Falls. Charlotte married Thomas Boyer. Helen married Harry Dillon Lee and, later, S.K. Davidson, an artist and London high school teacher. Edith and Frances both died young. Richard became a London lawyer, and Jack married the previously mentioned Kate Thompson. Charlotte (d.1873) was buried at St. Ann's Church in Adelaide.

The last-born son of Adjutant Thompson and his wife was George Frederick (d.1899), a bachelor who inherited his father's farm. He was buried in Strathroy Cemetery.

Bertha was the last of the Thompsons to live in Adelaide Township.

THOMPSON, George and Eliza

George Thompson (18451-1924) was born in Caradoc Township, the eldest of nine children. His parents, John and Margaret (Young) Thompson, had immigrated to Canada from Glasgow, Scotland, in 1840. At age 21, George was a veteran of the Fenian Raids.

In 1866, he bought Lot 21, Con. 3 SER, and paid for it from the sale of potash. The land was thickly forested. He gradually burned the brush off and in the late 1870s, burned 22 acres all at once. George was a wagon maker by trade and in partnership with a man named Wilkinson. They travelled around the district with their high-sided wagon, trading soft soap for hardwood. One year they kept their supply of potash, forcing the price to double.

In 1866 or 1867, George built the house, which remains on the property, with three rooms downstairs and three rooms upstairs, at a cost of approximately $1,000. He built an addition later, and made the walls three bricks deep. George also harvested grain by cutting with a cradle and threshing by flail. He kept livestock and had a large garden.

During the 1890s, gypsies used to camp on the road behind the farm. The road was 50 feet wide and called James Street, and ran west from what is now Highway 81 along the southerly limits of Part Lots 3 and 6, and terminated at the eastern limits of Part Lot 8 (Plan 295, Adelaide Township). The gypsies camped west of the creek. They became a nuisance by trespassing and stealing. George and Lewis James eliminated the gypsies through a mutual agreement with Adelaide Township Council. Each man built a fence along the middle of the road.

George also owned 25 acres in Caradoc Township, and six acres and a house across the road in the town of Strathroy. His children attended the school in Strathroy.

George was highly respected in the community and was an elder in the Presbyterian Church from 1873 to 1913. He lived in the house he built until his death.

George Thompson married three times. He had two children, John Albert and Minnie Delilah (d.1873), with his first wife, Eliza (d.1873). He and Christina Lee Rapley (1845-1900) had four children, Robert Scobie (1876-1960); James Oliver (1877-1895); Andrew Young (1879-1939), who became a doctor and lived in the United States; and Robertina Lee (1889-1966), who was a nurse during WWI. Thirdly, George married Tina Black, and they separated in 1913.

Robert Scobie married Ida Elizabeth Thomson (1880-1940). In 1913, they moved to the homestead from the property across the road. Their five children were Oliver George (1902-1954); James Alexander (1904-1973); Mary Lee (1913-1991); George Robert (1915); and Patricia (1920-1989). In 1919, the barn was raised onto a brick wall and a silo was built. The silo blew down and the orchard was destroyed in the hurricane of 1944. For a few years in the early 1920s, Scobie had a milk route. He lived on the property until his death.

The title of the property went to James Alexander in 1946. He married Jessie J. Parker (1912-1992), and their children were Alan, Joan, Colleen, Jessie, Mary Lee, David, Ida and Kathleen. Alex enlisted in the Royal Canadian Artillery in 1939 and served until 1946. He sold nursery stock for H.C. Downham Nursery Co. for 20 years. He cash cropped the home property, as well as other acreage, for a few years. In 1956, he was employed full-time by the Department of Highways as a Property Agent for the Provincial Government, a position from which he retired in 1969. After James' death, the land was rented to Cuddy Farms from 1956 to 1979, at which time Alex's wife, Jessie, sold the property to Cuddy Farms.

THOMPSON, Grant and Hazel

Grant Gordon "Stub" Thompson (d.1982), son of Silas and Annie (Ayre) Thompson, married Hazel Katherine Hill. They lived on the east half of Lot 15, Con. 2 NER, and raised 10 children. This farmland was originally owned by Henry Burrows, whose son and daughter-in-law, Alfred and Emma (Ayre) Burrows, farmed it. They had no children. Stub, nephew of Alf Burrows (d.1949), moved with his family to the property in June 1948. After Alf's death, Stub and Hazel purchased the farm.

Donald Gordon (1946) married Marjorie McCaw in 1970. They have two children, Tracy and Paul, and live in Strathroy.

Terry Lee (1947) married Sherrie Cook in 1986. They have one child, Cody Grant, and reside in Woodstock.

Judith Rose Ann (1949) married Leonard Westgate in 1969. They have two children, Darryl and Debbie, and reside in Strathroy.

Ross Erwin (1950) married Sonia Renshaw in 1973. They have two children, Amy and Adam, and live in Nairn.

Jean Katherine (1952) married Ken Watson in 1971. They have two sons, Kal and Galen. They live in Sarnia.

Mary Ellen (1953) lives in London and is Assistant Director in Human Resources at McKerlie-Millen.

Roy Karl (1956) married Karen McDowell in 1990. Now divorced, they have two children, Tyler and Raylene. They live in Alberta.

Susan Marie (1959) lives in London and is employed at Early Childhood Resource Centre.

Barbara Gail (1961) married Lewis Carter in 1994 and they reside in London.

Anne May (1964) is a secondary school teacher. She taught in Aylmer for three years, at the International School in Vienna for two years in Austria, and is presently teaching in Laipei, Taiwan, for three years at the International School.

After Stub's death, the farm was sold to Ed and Lucy Luyten in 1989. Hazel now resides in Strathroy.

THOMSON - SHOTWELL

James Thomson (1811-1889) came from County Antrim, Ireland, and settled in Caradoc Township. He married Susannah Buttery (1823-1906) from Nottinghamshire, England, daughter of John and Ann (Wilkinson) Buttery. They had four children, Annie (1846-1923); William Alexander (1859-1939); James Samuel (1848-1856); and Carrie (1855-1929).

Annie married John B. Shotwell (1845-1920) and they lived on Hull Road at the edge of Strathroy. He taught school at S.S #8 Adelaide, driving out by horse and buggy. His salary was only $400 a year, but "my father's profession gave us a distinct place in the community." (from the Autobiography of James T. Shotwell–1961). John Shotwell also taught at the Model School in Strathroy, where he trained young people for careers in teaching with principal, J.E. Wetherell. William Sullivan, one of his Adelaide students, was invited to board at the Shotwell home when attending high school. John and Annie had two sons, William John (1872-1901), who became a teacher and attended University of Toronto, rooming with his younger brother when he, too, was studying there; and James Thomson (1874-1965), who became a noted "son of Strathroy" for his outstanding work as a history professor at Columbia University for over 50 years. He also was

John B. and Annie (Thomson) Shotwell.

a member of the Peace Commission organized to construct the Treaty of Versailles and an advisor to President Woodrow Wilson, helping plan for a League of Nations. In 1901, James married Margaret Harvey (ca.1874-1965) of the distinguished Harvey family of Windsor, Nova Scotia. Her grandfather, Dr. Harvey, a professor at the Windsor University, Nova Scotia, was sent to Upper Canada to help Egerton Ryerson set up his public school system. Margaret and her cousin, Jessie Murdock (see MURDOCK, William and Ann), had attended Strathroy High School and frequently played tennis on John Shotwell's lawn. Margaret and James were engaged to be married, but it was many years before the marriage took place as each graduated from Toronto University, Margaret spent two years studying in Europe, and James studied to win a scholarship to Columbia University.

At the close of WWI, Dr. James Shotwell organized and edited the world's most massive history project to date—the 150-volume history of WWI, consisting of volumes from each of the participating nations on both sides. This was the "Economic and Social History of the World War," funded by the Carnegie Endowment for International Peace. From that point, Dr. Shotwell's name was connected with every serious effort to procure and maintain peace throughout the world. His career brought him into personal contact with many others who were making history in that era.

In his autobiography, he reflects on early days at Strathroy High School, where he first knew Arthur Currie. They were in a Literary Society debate, both upholding the Liberal position of "Reciprocity with the United States." Shotwell recalls that on the way home from school that afternoon, as the boys were held up at the railway crossing by a long freight train coming east from Chicago, Currie pointed out the loaded cars as a final argument for free trade. Shotwell writes, "That is my last distinct memory of Currie until we met again in the fields of France in March 1919 some 40 years later."

James and Margaret Shotwell raised two daughters, Marguerite and Helen. Dr. Shotwell held 12 honorary doctorates and decorations from five governments.

William, second child of James and Susannah, married Sarah Kitchen of Caradoc. They moved to Strathroy and lived in a fine home on Victoria Street.

There is no further information on James Samuel (1848-1856), who died in childhood, or Carrie (1855-1929), the youngest of James and Susannah's children.

THOMSON, George and Irene

In 1938, George Thomson (d.1983), who lived in Warwick with his parents, James (1868-1937) and Jane (Pullen) Thomson (1865-1939), married Florence Irene Murray (1903-1981). George's grandparents, James (1826-1891) and Margaret (Moyes) Thomson (1826-1915), had immigrated to Canada in 1859 from Fife, Scotland, and settled on Lot 12, Con. 3 NER, Warwick Township. James and Margaret are buried in the Bethel Cemetery near Warwick Village. James Jr., Jane, and their daughter, Margaret (d.1947), are buried in Arkona Cemetery. James Jr. and Jane had three other daughters, Mary Ethel (d.1960); Grace; and Annie. Mary Ethel married John Smith and had six children. She is buried at Warwick Village. Grace married Robert Conkey and they had one son, Ken, who still lives in Adelaide on the home farm. Grace and Bob are both buried in the West Adelaide Presbyterian Church Cemetery. Annie married Orville Weaver of Forest.

Florence Irene Murray was the fourth child of John Thomas "Jack" (1868-1947) and Emma (Chalcraft) Murray (1870-1936), Jack being the second youngest of eight children born to Patrick and Elizabeth "Betsy" (Murray, no relation) Murray (1838). Betsy was born in Adelaide, one of seven children. Her parents, James and Catherine (Davidson) Murray walked from Cobourg to Adelaide in 1834 to settle on Lot 3, Con. 1 SER, after immigrating to Canada from Ireland. Jack and Emma are both buried in Arkona. Irene was born when they were residing at Lot 5, Con. 5 NER, the homestead of Patrick Murray. Irene attended school at Keyser S.S. #1 and #2 Adelaide and West Williams. As a young girl, Irene moved to Arkona and, for many years, worked for Dr. Russell Woods in his dental office and as a nanny for the Woods' three young sons.

After George and Irene were married, they farmed on the townline east of Arkona. In 1965, this farm was sold to Andy Veeke of Arkona. All of the remaining buildings have been removed. The barn burned down and, in 1954, the family moved to Lot

5, Con. 5, a 55-acre farm purchased from Edna and Doris Murray, widow and daughter of Lorne S. Murray. George and Irene lived there until ill health made it difficult for them to continue farming. George and Irene had two children, Murray (1939) and Marilyn (1944). Murray attended all eight grades at the school in Keyser, and Marilyn started school there, but continued at Adelaide W.G. MacDonald. They both attended S.D.C.I.

After school, Murray worked at several jobs until March 1958, when he started full-time at the Feed Mill in Arkona. After this, he was transferred to Fred Brown Seeds, in a new building on the southern outskirts of town. This building is now the location of Village Feed and Heritage Acres Seed and Grain.

In the fall of 1964, Fred Brown and his sons, Mason, Mack and Martin, built a new mill and grain elevator at the corner of what is now Birnam Line and Arkona Road. Murray moved there to work when it opened in November 1965 and is still employed there, recently celebrating 40 years of service. In 1989, following the deaths of Fred and Mason, the mill was purchased by Cargill Ltd.-Nutrena Feed Division.

In 1963, Murray married Alice Stephenson of Arkona. During their first year, they lived in Forest, where Alice was employed by CIBC. They returned to Arkona and remained there until 1975, when they purchased his parents' farm at Lot 5, Con. 5 NER, where they still live.

Alice has been employed by Peter Thuss and Sons Ltd. of Arkona for the past twenty years. She and Murray have three children, all born in Arkona. The eldest, Connie (1964), is married to Brent Thomas (1964) and has two daughters, Tonya (1986) and Sharie (1989). She lives in Granton and is employed part-time at a flower shop.

Jackie (1967) lives in Strathroy with her husband, Manuel Bettencourt (1965) and their two sons, Jason (1986) and Adam (1984). She works as a Certified Health Care Giver at Sprucedale Care Centre in Strathroy.

Brian (1972), youngest child of Murray and Alice, lives in St. Albert, Alberta, a suburb of Edmonton, where he is an E.M.T. and Emergency Medical Dispatcher with a Wainright Alberta Ambulance Service. In 1997, he married Julie Harris (1972), formerly of London. She is an Industrial Hygiene Technologist and is employed by the University of Alberta in Edmonton.

All three children attended Adelaide W.G. MacDonald School and then S.D.C.I. Brian continued his education at Lambton College, Sarnia, and Conestoga College in Kitchener.

Marilyn, youngest child of George and Irene, lives north of Parkhill with her husband, Wayne Scott. They have four daughters, Bonnie (1963); Brenda (1965); Barbara (1967); and Betty (1970). Bonnie is married to Gary Romphf (1960) and they have two children, Cory (1989) and Kady (1990). Brenda has three children, Mary-Lynn (1985); Brandon (1986-1987) and Jarrett (1988). Barbara is married to Charles Hall (1966) and has two children, Thomas (1993) and Amy (1995). Betty is married to Ron Smith (1967) and they have two daughters, Emma (1996) and Erin (1997). Marilyn's family lives in the Parkhill area.

George and Irene are buried in Arkona Cemetery.

THORPE, Ransom and Hulda

Ransom Thorpe (1784-1849) married Hulda Ogden (1784-1845) and they moved from the eastern part of the United States to Adelaide Township. In 1841, Ransom purchased Lot 3, Con. 4 NER, from Charles and Joseph Van Every. In 1848, he sold two 25-acre lots to Jacob Shrier and John Mathers. The remaining 150 acres were sold to his son in 1848. Ransom died the following year and was interred in Arkona Cemetery, as were all the Thorpes and interrelated families. Ransom and Hulda had two children, Roxina (ca.1811), born in the U.S.; and William Rupert (1822), born in Vermont in the U.S.

In 1843, William married Anna Cordelia Eastman (1827-1907), who was born in New York State. They had seven children.

Ransom (1844), the eldest child of William and Anna, was born in Adelaide Township. In 1866, he married Mary Coome (1847-1925), who was born in England. In 1880 to 1881, Ransom was a cheese maker for the Keyser Cheese Factory. Their daughter, Rosella Roxanna (1867-1927), one of 14 children, married Benjamin Herrington (1859-1943) of Adelaide Township, son of Truman and Sarah Catherine (Woodhull) Herrington, in 1884. Rosella and Benjamin raised three children in Adelaide

Township on Con. 4 NER. Berton (1884-1973), the eldest, married Ethel Mae Wilson (1888-1973) in 1910. They had nine children. Berton and Ethel are buried in Flint, Michigan (see WILSON, Samuel and Rebecca). Frederick William (1887-1968) married Myrtle White and they moved to Strathroy. They had four children. Sara Reta Herrington (1889-1979) married William Alexander Louie (d.1976) of West Williams Township in 1915. They had three children.

There are no descendants of the Thorpe family living in Adelaide Township today. The Thorpes contributed greatly to the economy and the social life of the Keyser's community. The young Thorpes attended the first school across the corner from their farm, on the John Mullan property at the west half of Lot 4, Con. 4 NER, and the Thorpe name appears in the Minutes of the Salem Church at Keyser. Many of the family and connections moved to Michigan, where the economy was stronger. These family records were provided by Jean (Herrington) Dunn, whose Berton Herrington family represents the fifth generation and the last Thorpe/Herrington/Woodhull residents of the Adelaide/Keyser Community. A Thorpe descendant of West Williams, Rose (McLeish) Carson, also provided family data.

Rosella's siblings, all born in Adelaide, included Benjamin (1868); Friend William (1869); Edith Estella (1871), who married Albert E. Augustine; Joseph Orman (1872); Salena Jane (1874); Sheldon Eber (twin, 1875); Lillian Maud (twin, 1878); Mabel Adaline; Sherman Rupert (1882); Nelson Theodor (1885); Susan Beatrice (1886-1887), who died in Adelaide of measles complications; and Charles Roy (1888).

Nial Thorpe (1845-1921), second child of William and Anna, married Eliza Jane Stevens (1846-1911), daughter of Benjamin W. and Jane (Harrison) Stevens. One afternoon in March 1876, Nial was at Graham Smith's blacksmith shop at Keyser's Corners having his horse shod. Two schoolboys, Elmor Bartram and Walter Gurney, stopped in to get a ride home with Mr. Thorpe. He wasn't finished with the horse shoeing, so he told the boys to go on. The blacksmith told the boys to leave or he would be after them with a hot iron. This threat was not taken seriously as young Bartram didn't move and said he wasn't afraid of the iron. Events got out of hand and Smith stabbed Bartram in the lower part of his body with the iron. Still, no one present seemed to think the wound was serious, but the boy fainted from loss of blood and was carried home. Doctors Dawes, Brett, and Eccles of Arkona did all that was possible to save his life, but he died in a few days. A postmortem examination was made and a Coroner's Inquest was held. Ten witnesses, including Nial Thorpe, were examined and their testimony led the jury to render a verdict of not guilty. Nial and Eliza Jane moved to a farm west of Arkona and then to Brown City, Michigan. Of their 10 children, nine were born in Adelaide, and one was born in Bosanquet Township.

William Nelson (1846), third child of William and Anna, married Sophronia Shrier (1851-1874), daughter of Jacob and Mary (Mather) Shrier, in 1872. After Sophronia's death, William Nelson moved to Sanilac County, Michigan, where he remarried.

Emma Jane (1850), fourth issue of William and Anna, was born in Adelaide.

Huldah (1851-1918), fifth of William and Anna's children, married Isaac Newton Ogden (1848-1918) in 1869. They had 11 children born in Adelaide, two born in Warwick, and one born in Michigan. The family moved to Imlay City, Michigan, about 1888.

Orman Thorpe (1856, died an infant) was born in Adelaide Township.

Sheldon Rupert (1859) married Elizabeth Ann Goodchild, born in Westminster Township, in 1883. After her father's death, she was taken in by the Benjamin and Sarah Ann Stevens family and adopted the Stevens' surname.

THROWER, Charles and Sarah

Charles Thrower (ca.1789-1879), born in England, was a soldier in the Battle of Waterloo. He married Sarah Bird (ca.1788-1845). The couple and their two sons, Stephen (ca.1815-1901) and Isaac (1819-1902), both born in Suffolk, England, came to Adelaide in 1832. In 1846, after Sarah's death, Charles married Mary MacAuley (ca.1809), a widow born in New York. In 1861, Charles and Mary were living in Delaware Township.

In 1842, Stephen married Mary Ann Randall (ca.1822-1901). They had at least nine children. Charles (ca.1843-1904) married Sarah (last name unknown) and they had four children; Mary Jane (ca.1844); Sarah (ca.1846), who married Henry London in 1865; William (ca.1847-1891), who married Elsie Bessie Murch in 1871; Ann (ca.1848); James (ca.1851-1908), who married Annie Summers and had one son in Woodstock; Eliza (ca.1854-1916); Elizabeth (ca.1855); and Martha (ca.1858), who married William Down (1857-1930) in 1878, son of George and Celia (Weeks) Down of Adelaide. Martha and William had at least five children. In 1852, Stephen was farming part of Lot 11, Con. 2 SER, but by 1861, was working as a gardener in Delaware Township.

In 1839, Isaac Thrower married Mary Humphries (1822-1900), daughter of John and Maria (Ferris) Humphries of Adelaide. They had 14 children, Harriet (1840-1909), who married John Hanna (see HANNA, John and Jane); Louisa (1842-1919), who married John Bages (or Boges) and had three children; Abraham (1844-1857); Sarah Maria (1846-1913), who married Thomas Petch (see PETCH, Francis and Mary); Mary (1848-1924); Rhoda (1849-1923), who married George Henry Parker (see PARKER, James and Amey); Esther (1851-1927), who married J.W. Downer (see DOWNER-NAPPER); David (1852-1932) unmarried; Walter (1855-1919); Jacob (1857-1941); Emma (1859-1883); Albert (1861-1935); Ellen (1862), who married James or Joseph Grummett in 1888, and had three children; and Etta (1866-1943), who married Donald McLennan. Mary, Ellen and Etta resided in Sault Ste. Marie. Isaac farmed part of Lot 11 on both Con. 2 and 3 SER, having bought his father's and brother's land, and later retired to Strathroy.

In 1871, Mary, fifth child of Isaac and Mary, married Charles Mann (1846-1886), son of Mark and Sophia (Rapley) Mann of Adelaide. They had at least three children, Ira (ca.1871-1947), who married Mary Ellen "Ella" Hutchinson (1874-1965); Lena (1875-1965), who married Charles Tancock; and Victor (1883-1959), who married Lucy Cooper. The 1871 census shows Charles as a tenant on Lot 14, Con. 5 SER. He died in Petrolia.

In 1870, Esther, seventh of Isaac and Mary's children, married John Wesley Downer (1847-1923), son of John and Lucy (Rapley) Downer of Adelaide. They had at least two children in Petrolia, Minnie, who married Richard Thompson; and Jessie, who died young.

Walter, ninth issue of Isaac and Mary, married Hannah Gamble (1863-1913). They lived in Brooke Township, where they had at least six children, William, Robert, Herbert, Mary, Abraham, and Florence. Descendants live in Watford, Petrolia, Ridgetown, Wallaceburg and Seattle, Washington.

Jacob married Nellie Prince. They had four children, Ezlie Irvilene (1890-1909); Lyman (1892-1895); Leta (1893-1990), who married Edward Scott and had two children; and Esther. In 1899, after Nellie died, Jacob married Alice (Parkinson) Fortner (1862-1939). They had one daughter, Nora, (1901-1985), who married Fred Rawlinson (1902-1966) in 1925. They had five children, Eileen; Ruth; George; Margaret (1934-1935); and David (1938, died an infant).

In 1886, Albert, twelfth child of Isaac and Mary, married Emily Heake (1868), daughter of Andrew and Elizabeth (Seed) Heake. They had one son, Fred (1889-1972), who married Mabel Calder, but had no children. In 1903, after Emily's death, Albert married Euphemia McLean (1865-1912). They had a daughter, Mary (1905-1944), who married Duncan Munroe and resided in Glencoe. In 1913, Albert married a third time, to Nellie Scoon (ca.1866), daughter of William and Ann (Siggins) Scoon.

Albert lived his life on the farm where he was born, until three years before his death. Fred took over the farm, and achieved some fame as the owner of Grattan Bars, a horse that won three American derbies within 13 days in 1928, bringing the owner $75,000 in prizes.

TIMMERMANS, Cornelius and Theodora

The Timmermans family is of Dutch origin. Its ancestry has been traced to the early part of the 17th century. The name appears to have been derived from the carpentry trade and translates literally into "carpenters," although their history has mainly been rooted in agriculture. Members of the Timmermans family are widespread in the province of North Brabant, with more than 10,000 occurrences. The family has spread throughout the world, with over 400 members in the U.S. and 520 in Canada; the name is also commonplace in Australia, New Zealand, Great Britain, Ireland, Germany, France, South Africa, Spain, Italy, and many other countries.

Cornelius (1892) and Theodora Timmermans (1893) were born in the Netherlands, where they were successful farmers, having acquired some 17 hectares of Crown land during 1927. He turned the first furrows with a one-furrow plow, pulled by three horses. During WWII, farm life in Holland became bleak; the farmhouse was burned down, and crops and livestock were lost. Restarting proved hopeless and, influenced by son Lenard's earlier departure for Quebec and Hubert's desire to leave, and upon hearing farmers were needed in Canada, it was decided that the whole family would immigrate. With James Tulley of Portage la Prairie sponsoring them, they left in May 1950 for Canada, in pursuit of a better future.

The couple arrived in Canada with five of their eight children. John, the eldest of the five, was 22; Betsie 20; Hubert 19; Maria 17; and Bernadette 15. Of the remaining three, Nellie had married John Hofsteede (see HOFSTEEDE, John and Nellie), Lenard had immigrated to Quebec, and Peter remained in the Netherlands but came a year later with his wife, Tera.

Everything was an unknown for the Timmermans family: language, culture, customs, work ethics, choice and preparation of food, etc. They had no idea of their destination or the enormous size of the country. Seventy-two hours non-stop in a coal dust-filled train gave them some insight, yet they had only travelled slightly more than halfway. Their house was a renovated horse barn that was unfit to live in during winter, and at that time, there was very little work.

John hitchhiked to Ontario one August morning because the trains were on strike. He got to Kenora, Ontario, on the first day. He was accosted by two large men who did not understand his language and were interested in his suitcase. Somehow, he got away from them and, as he didn't have much money, he stayed at the Salvation Army. They fed him breakfast and everything was free. John had no trouble getting rides and he felt the reason for this is that he was wearing wooden shoes, making it obvious to the drivers that he was Dutch.

John had some trouble in Sudbury when another big man seemed to want him to go behind a vacant paper mill. John ran and jumped into a waiting train that was going to North Bay; apparently, the strike was over, but unfortunately, the same man was on the train! Eventually, a family gave him a ride to Hamilton and, from there, he went to Blenheim and then Tupperville, near a farmer's tomato field. This episode took six days, with 32 rides; he lost ten pounds and spent a total of $36.

He stayed in a small cottage, where Adrian Groot lived and worked for the same farmer. John's family arrived and they all picked tomatoes for the rest of the fall, and topped six acres of sugar beets.

Adrian left for Montreal to meet his future wife, got married and bought a farm on the Second Line in Adelaide. Cornelius and Theodora purchased the west half of Lot 14, Con. 2 SER, formerly known as Knight's farm, from Mrs. Mary McKeigan of Strathroy, and moved there with their family on February 17, 1951. This farm was across the road from Adrian Groot's farm. The land was fallow for several years prior to this, and the only building on the property was the house. A large, L-shaped barn had once stood nearby, but had been blown down by a cyclone, probably in 1947. Only the footings remained. Ruins of a former homestead were also found on the western half of the lot. According to local hearsay, that building had burned down. There was no electricity or running water, nor indoor plumbing. These became priorities of the first order when Peter came from the Netherlands, as he was an electrician by trade. It was often said that the first

Cornelius Timmermans immigrated to Canada at age 57 to Lot 14, Con. 2 SER, in 1951.

Timmermans family, L-R, Martin, Gerry, John, Gertrude, Ken, Rita and Ted (Jack died in 1995 in a snowmobile accident).

immigrating generation died, the second went broke, and the third succeeded. Cornelius made it in the first.

When Cornelius and Theodora reached retirement age, the farm was handed down to Lenard, the eldest son, and in 1973, he sold it to John.

Initially, John worked in London for Ellis-Don, building an extension to the Colborne Street School. He worked with his parents until 1957, when he married Gertrude Peters (1934) and bought the John Hoefnagels farm, previously owned by Fred Thrower. The sign on the barn roof could still be read—Grattan Bars 1:59 2/5. The horse stalls were removed and replaced with cow stanchions. John and Gertrude farmed there for 26 years. They raised five sons and one daughter.

In 1982, they bought the Bambi Motel and changed the name to Country Side Motel. After six years, John and Gertrude sold the business and bought property in Strathroy, where they continue to reside.

The eldest son of John and Gertrude, Ken (1958), was born at the Second Line of Kerwood. As he grew up, he helped John on the farm after school and sometimes stayed home to help with spring work. John taught Ken how to drive at an early age. He remembers plowing with a four-furrow plow at the age of 10, and thinks the training paid off because he has never had a car accident.

After finishing school, Ken became a full-time farmer. In September 1980, he married Antoinette Momersteeg (1960) from Grand Bend. They moved into Cornelius' house, which John had bought in 1973, and worked the land as a family farming enterprise. They also work off the farm, Antoinette as a full-time librarian for the Catholic School Board, and Ken for Peter Timmermans at Timmermans' Electric in Lucan, where he picked up enough of the trade to do his own wiring. Ken and his brother, Martin (1959), each bought a farm on Seed Road at the Second Line North. They bought all of the machinery and livestock, and rented land and buildings from their parents, and farmed together for 10 years. This ended when Ken and Antoinette purchased the Dortmans farm property, the east half of Lot 13, Con. 1 SER. They built a new house on this property and remodeled the barn to be a full-time farming enterprise. They have three children, Jason (1982); Lynn (1984); and Julie (1986). Ken's hobbies are snowmobiling, trapping, and skill shooting. Ken and Antoinette grow about 160 acres of soybeans, wheat and corn, a total of approximately 400 acres.

Martin was born in Strathroy. He had lived all his life on the home farm in Kerwood. He attended school at Our Lady Immaculate, followed by high school at S.D.C.I. in Strathroy. After graduating high school, he went to Ridgetown College. Two years later, Martin graduated with a diploma in agriculture. He worked at home on his parents' (then) hog farm.

On August 12, 1982, Martin married Joanne Verberk (1962) from Arkona, and they began married life together on the home farm. For the next 12 years, besides taking care of the pigs, they busied themselves with barn renovation and house remodeling. In 1995, they bought Timmermans Irrigation and started another business. They were so busy keeping up with two businesses, they had to hire extra employees. They have four children, Michael (1984); Ryan (1986); Kayla (1990); and Rachel (1991). Martin spends his spare time with his children, playing soccer and enjoying other activities, such as baseball, hockey and snowmobiling.

Maria, John's sister, lived in Adelaide Township from 1951 to 1956. She remembers that the space in Canada seemed endless after living in a small country. She was homesick, and hated hoeing sugar beets. When her parents bought the home farm, the house was furnished, which she found very interesting. There were large rugs and a beautiful staircase in the living room. The five bedrooms were big and airy, and there were even some clothes in the drawers. She finally felt at home, that she belonged somewhere! The beginning years were very hard. They had to clear land and make it productive, buy a tractor and cattle, pigs and chickens. They picked beans for the canning factory, along with cucumbers and the sugar beets Maria so despised, but overall, Maria loved her new home in Adelaide Township. Quite often, she biked to Adelaide Village to buy candy and cigarettes at the store, which is now the home and beauty salon of Lloyd and Fienny (Vanderheyden) McDougall.

Maria relates a funny incident from her youth: *"We used to cut down the brush (some were thorn bushes) to burn in our stove. I had to leave at 7:00 a.m. one Monday morning and I thought 'I'll just fill the stove and shut it down so Mother wouldn't get cold.' It was a stove with a warming shelf and reservoir for water. Dad was in the barn. Mother got an eerie feeling and, as she looked over, she saw that the stovepipe, which came halfway up through the bedroom, was red-hot. She went down and there was that old brute of a stove as red as anything—right to the back, with the water boiling in the reservoir and the coffee pot percolating on the warming shelf! It was scary for awhile, but we laughed about it later."*

Maria married Anthony "Tony" Vanderheyden (1930-1988) at All Saints Roman Catholic Church in Strathroy, on October 8, 1955. She now lives at Twin Elms in Strathroy, but her strong feelings for Adelaide Township remain.

TIMMERS, Johannus and Johanna

Johannus and Johanna (Sommers) Timmers bought a farm at Lot 4, Con. 1 NER, in December 1953. They had a mixed farm; they started farming in pigs with some chickens for the use of the family.

Six of their nine children moved with them, Adrian, Tony, Bill, John, Andrew and Antonia. Within six years, all the children were married.

In June 1960, the farm was sold to Adrian, the eldest son, and Catherine Vandenbroek, who moved in July 15, 1961, with six children, John (1955); Martin (1956); Wilma (1958); Mary and Marj (1960); and Paul (1961). Three children were born on the farm, Joanne (1962); Teresa (1964); and Frances (1966).

From 1960, the farm first started in dairy with 11 cows, and also pigs. After five years, they left the dairy to concentrate on sows and weaners. Three years later, they got out of farming pigs and raised veal calves. They also built a chicken barn. The veal calves operation was abandoned three years later to stay with the chicken (layers) operation, which is presently the mainstay of the farm. All through the years to the present, the land was also cropped.

Andy Timmers and his children in the cucumber field.

Timmers family, L-R, Mary, John and Kathy.

Martin and his wife, Mary (Aarts) from Watford, moved to the farm in September 1985 with two children, Rebecca (1982), who was named for her grandmother who died the same day, and Janet (1985-1990). Two more children were born on the farm, Kevin (1986), who was named after his father and grandfather; and Maggie (1988).

TOMLINSON, William and Ann

William Tomlinson (1820-1881), a native of Yorkshire, England, married Ann Parks (1821-1898). In 1862, they moved from Toronto Township, Peel County, to Adelaide. However, his name is on tax records as early as March 1856 and again in October 1860, for part of the west half of Lot 30, Con. 1 NER. William was a blacksmith and his shop was on his farm at the side of the road that is now Highway 22. It has been moved back to the house yard but is still standing. He wanted land so that his family could farm. William and Ann had nine children, Leonard (1848-1917); Thomas (1849-1928), who married Mary Jane Williams (1855-1929); William (1850-1927), who married Margaret Tuckey (1861-1892); John (1852-1927), who married Matilda Graham (1861-1953); Edward (1854-1860); Robert (1857, died an infant); Hannah (1858), who married Joseph Graham; Ann Jane "Jenny" (1860), who married Robert Lord; and Herbert William (1874-1954), who married Emily Frayne.

John and Matilda Tomlinson lived on the same property during their entire married lives, and farmed 100 acres. They were married May 24, 1881, in Lobo Township, home of the bride. Matilda was a daughter of John and Betsy (Rawlings) Graham, and a native of Cumberland, England. They moved to Markham about 1832, and then to Lobo Township. John and Matilda had nine children, Anne Elizabeth (1882-1963), who married Albert Lewis (1872-1949); Sarah Barbara (1884-1981), who married James D. McQueen (1881-1950); William John (1886-1965); George Leonard (1888-1976), who married Annie Crawford (1890-1973); Robert Edward (1892-1976), who married Gladys Bacheldor (d.1968); Herbert Park (1896-1986), who married Violet Rose Robson (1897-1989); Mabel Irene (1898), who married James McMahen; Olive Jean (1901, died of whooping cough); and Harold Graham (1901-1976), who married Avis Parsons (1907-1974). Three of John and Matilda's children farmed in Adelaide Township.

Anne and Albert farmed on the Sarnia Gravel. They had a family of nine children.

George and Annie farmed the corner of Hector Sideroad and Highway 22. They had two children. Margaret married Leonard Matheson and Ilene married Blake Gough.

Herbert and Violet farmed the Adelaide home farm, Lot 30, Con. 1 NER. They had one child, Thelma Louisa (1926), who married James Edward Bycraft.

Herbert and Violet's grandson and his wife purchased the farm in 1979. Craig Herbert Bycraft (1952) married Mary Patricia Regier (1952). They have three children, Robert Jason (1975); Mark James Joseph (1981); and Daniel Craig (1982). They also purchased the adjoining farm on the west side and, as of 1995, still reside there. The earliest tax receipt in their possession is for $11, dated November 12, 1858, for the west half of Lot 30. The tax collector was John N. Ashbee.

Herb and Violet had a mixed farming operation. There was a dairy herd of Holsteins, pigs, chickens, geese, turkeys, and an apple orchard. Herb had a weekly market route in London, where he sold eggs and chickens. At that time, the customer bought the whole chicken, head, feet and all (except the feathers), unless it was ordered "table ready."

Several generations lived together in harmony. Matilda was never in a hospital in her lifetime. She was a midwife and always had relatives to look after, or burials to prepare for, when she wasn't helping babies into the world.

TOPPING, John and Ann

John Topping (1809-1885) was born in England. He married Ann Bowman (1814-1892), also born in England. They farmed in East Williams Township. Both are buried in Carlisle Community Cemetery in East Williams Township. Their eight children were Thomas (ca.1837-1902); Jane (ca.1840); John (ca.1843); Henry (ca.1846); Georgina (ca.1846); George (ca.1848); Elizabeth (ca.1852); and Hugh (ca.1856). The last seven children were born in Ontario.

Thomas married Sarah Jane Calhoun (ca.1842-1903) in East Williams on June 26, 1860. Thomas and Sarah farmed on the east half of the north half of Lot 6, Con. 3 NER, on 50 acres. Thomas's brother, John, farmed the south half of the east half. Thomas and Sarah both died in Adelaide Township. They are interred in West Adelaide Presbyterian Church Cemetery in Adelaide. Thomas and Sarah had five children, George (ca.1868); Gilbert (ca.1870); William (ca.1874); Ambrose Arthur (ca.1876-1947); and Elizabeth Ann (ca.1880).

Ambrose was born in Carlisle, East Williams. He married Eliza Matilda Jane Morgan (1879-1953). They are interred in Arkona Cemetery.

In 1901, Ambrose bought Thomas's 50-acre farm and, in 1904, he bought John's 50 acres. Ambrose and Eliza farmed these 100 acres until about 1926. They then purchased the Langan farm on Lot 4, Con. 5 NER, where Ambrose died.

Ambrose was clerk of Adelaide Township for 31 years. He was a councillor for seven years and reeve for two years. In 1913, when the clerkship became available, he resigned the reeveship to accept that office, a position he adored and filled with great credit to himself and his township. He attended S.D.C.I. and graduated under principal J.E. Wetherell. Ambrose knew Adelaide and its people, and his word was his bond. He was a man of strong opinions, which were based on knowledge.

Ambrose and Eliza had three children, Thomas Robert Lavern (1900-1980); Ilo Jemima Jane (1903-1981); and Kenneth (1916-1932), who died as a result of a mastoid infection and is interred in Arkona Cemetery.

Ilo married Clifford Terrance Callaghan (d.1983). They resided in Adelaide Township, where they tended an apple orchard. In their retirement years, they moved to Watford, where Ilo died. She and Clifford are buried in Arkona Cemetery. They had one child, Kenneth, who died at birth.

Lavern married Alice Margaret Elizabeth Wilson (1905-2000) of Grand Bend on December 11, 1926. Laverne and Alice bought the farm from his father in 1926. They farmed the land until 1943, when they purchased the William Parker store at Keyser's Corners. Alice was a dedicated worker in the Keyser Ladies Institute and a talented seamstress. They kept the store until they sold it to Frank Gare in 1964. They then moved to the Langan Farm on Lot 4, Con. 5 NER, in 1964. They remained there until 1970, when they moved to North Street in Strathroy. Lavern died in Strathroy and is buried in Strathroy Cemetery. Alice resided in Strathmere Lodge after Lavern's death. Lavern and Alice had three children, Dorothy Harriet (1927); Doris Eliza (1930); and Ruby Alice (1934).

Dorothy Harriet married John Archibald Pedden (1925) of Adelaide Township on June 14, 1947, in West Adelaide Church. They farmed together on Lot 14, Con. 4 NER. They formed Walnut Ridge Poultry Farms, where they raised pullets and produced eggs. They had two children, Archie Lavern (1948-1993) and Carole Lynn (1951), both born in Strathroy.

Archie Lavern married Brenda Lee Finkbeiner (1949) of Guelph on September 14, 1968. They had two children, Pamela Dawn (1969) and Archie Lloyd (1970), both born in Strathroy. Archie's body is interred in Strathroy Cemetery.

Pamela married Thomas Clare Breckles (1968) of Cambridge on September 14, 1996. They reside in Toronto and have two children, Andi Elizabeth (1996) and Hannah Claire (1999).

Carole, second child of Dorothy and Archie, married Robert Burton Meyers (1949) of Galt on October 2, 1971. They reside in London and have two children, Shelly Christine (1974) and Kimberly Dawn (1976), both born in London.

Doris Eliza, second of Lavern and Alice's children, married John William Denning (1930) of Strathroy in Adelaide Township on May 26, 1951. They have three children, Richard Basil (1952); Randall William (1953); and Gayle Elizabeth (1962), all born in Strathroy. Doris and Bill reside in Strathroy.

Richard Basil married Lynn Marie Mills (1961) on June 7, 1987, in Strathroy. They reside in Caradoc Township. Their two children are Mary Lynn (1991) and Juli-Ann (1993), both born in London.

Randall William married Rebecca Ann Sage (1954) of Peterborough on March 25, 1977, in Thunder Bay, Ontario. They reside in Strathroy. Their four children are William Randall (1978); Joshua Basil (1979); Brett Anthony (1981); and Leslie Rebecca (1983), all born in London.

Gayle Elizabeth, youngest child of Doris and Bill, married Howard Allen Ramsay (1961) of Sarnia on May 26, 1984, in Strathroy. They reside in Exeter. Their two children are Brianna Sherry Elizabeth (1986) and Brooke Eliza Michelle (1988), born in London.

Ruby Alice, youngest child of Lavern and Alice, married George Edward Clark on September 25, 1954. They reside in Dartmouth, Nova Scotia. Their four children are Sally Lynn (1957); Jeffery George (1959); Gary Edward (1961); and Alison Ann (1964).

Sally Lynn married Hugh Ross MacIntosh (1954) in Nova Scotia on June 1, 1979. They reside in Stellarton, Nova Scotia. Their three children are Kaitlyn Elizabeth (1983); Jonathan Ross Clark (1985); and Lauren Alison (1986).

Jeffery George married Louise Fortin (1960) on May 27, 1989. They reside in Nova Scotia, and their three children are Jason Edward (1991); Adam Jeffery (1993); and Brandon Charles (1996).

Gary Edward married Donna Marie Benteau (1965) on September 14, 1996. They reside in Nova Scotia.

Alison Ann, youngest child of Ruby and George, married Walter Bryant Lenny (1951) on August 11, 1991, in St. Jacobs, Ontario. They reside in Lobo Township. Their two children are Alicia Kathleen (1993) and Elizabeth Ann (1995).

TOTH, Gary and Carol

Gary Toth was born in Melbourne and grew up in the Mount Brydges area, where he helped his father with their tobacco farm. Gary's parents, William (d.1976) and Gisella Toth, both immigrated from Dombrad, Hungary. Gary has two brothers and two sisters, all residing in Middlesex County, Ron, Roger, Linda and Betsy.

Carol Slottke was born in Toronto, but at age eight moved to the town of Strathroy with her parents, Heinz and Hanna Slottke, from Lithuania and East Germany respectively. An older brother died in 1974. Gary and Carol were married in 1986. Carol and Gary have one son, Stephen (1987), who attends Adelaide W.G. McDonald School. They resided in Strathroy for four years until they built their house in 1990, at Lot 28, Con. 2 SER, Adelaide Sideroad #27. Gary and Carol moved to this location because they liked the beauty of the land surrounding that short stretch of road. They had driven down that road many times over a span of about two years, wishing they could live there, until luck prevailed one day when they saw the "for sale" sign, and purchased the lot within 24 hours. Gary and Carol wish to stay in Adelaide Township and hope that, one day, they will be lucky enough to purchase more acreage a little further into the midst of Adelaide Township.

TRETHEWEY, Larry and Patricia

Larry Trethewey married Patricia Van Dinther, and they reside at Lot 3, Con. 5 SER (R.R. #3, Kerwood). This lot was previously owned by John and Joanne Van Dongen. Patricia, at one point, was a resident of Kerwood before she married Larry, who came to the community from Petrolia. Patricia, the daughter of Peter and Nellie Van Dinther, has many fond memories of her neighbours and is glad to be back in Kerwood.

Larry Tretheway and Patty Van Dinther, wedding day.

UNGER, Floyd and Shirley

Floyd Unger (1931) was born in the small prairie town of Laird, Saskatchewan. Prairie life in the 1930s was daylong hard work. With 12 brothers and sisters, there was no lack of laughter or quarrels. It was a hard life; three brothers died at a young age.

Floyd chose to join the army following the footsteps of three older brothers. He joined on December 10, 1952. Shortly after basic training, he was sent to Korea. Crossing the Pacific was rough, with endless days of seasickness and absolutely no appetite. To make matters worse, the movie of the week was "Titanic."

While in Korea, he became pen pals with a young woman by the name of Marilyn Scott. They had never met but, through letters, a friendship developed. When Floyd returned to Canada he visited Marilyn in Gananoque in eastern Ontario. He was introduced to her family, including her younger sister, Shirley (d.2000). It was Christmas 1954, and the family invited Floyd to join in the festivities.

On August 25, 1956, Floyd and Shirley were married. Their first home was the military base at Camp Aldershot, Nova Scotia. In 1959, they were sent to the Canadian Forces Base in Fort St. Louis, Germany. Shirley was to follow with all of their possessions packed in travel trunks. She crossed the ocean in the Italia. As it was hurricane season and the seas were high, everyone was instructed to remain below decks. Mealtime was interesting as the tables were bolted down, but the plates were not. The crew insisted on alternating the seating plan so that everyone could take turns eating on the low side of the table.

Floyd and Shirley returned to New Brunswick in early 1962, and shortly after, Floyd Jr. (1962) was born.

In 1965, Floyd transferred from the Black Watch to the Royal Canadian Regiment. The R.C.R. headquarters was located in London, so the family moved again, but soon returned to Germany. At the Canadian Forces Base in Fort York, Germany, Karen and Laure (1967) were born.

In 1968, they returned to Canada and settled in the Twin Elms trailer park in Strathroy. In 1970, they moved to the Garside house in Kerwood.

Floyd went to England shortly after the move. He was a member of the Canadian Rifle Team competing in the International Rifleman's Competition at Bisley. After the competition, he was sent to Cyprus as part of a United Nations peacekeeping mission, where he remained until the fall of 1970.

In 1973, Floyd retired from the Armed Forces and was finally able to enjoy his new home in Kerwood.

Floyd Jr. submits: *"I don't believe my sisters and I could possibly have grown up in a more magical place. We had the barn, where Dad would make us pick eggs from under the cranky old hens, pecking at our little hands. We had a puppy to play with and a bush to explore. Penny candy at Wood's [store] and sweet little old ladies with cookie jars full to the rim.*

Karen, the tomboy, would be two steps behind me, up the tallest tree, and Laure, the voice of reason, down below to watch us fall. Childhood memories that grow more precious each passing day!

After 28 years in Kerwood, I think we can truly call Kerwood home. The community has developed a certain character that has added a touch of charm to all our lives. If there is a perfect place to grow old, I would imagine Kerwood to be that place."

VAN AERT, Tony and Anne

Tony (1961) was born in Belgium to Joseph and Emma Van Aert. In 1967, the family immigrated to Canada, where they settled in Warwick Township on a dairy farm.

Tony married Anne Lambregts in 1981. Her parents had immigrated to Canada from Holland in 1958, and she was raised on a tobacco farm near Strathroy.

Tony bought a farm in 1980 from Cyril and Eunice (Irene) Reid, who were turnip growers. In 1953, a tornado had hit the farm, taking with it the chicken barn, house windows and a vehicle. The Van Aerts have recently built a new brick home. They demolished the previous home of James Wallace, which was damaged in that storm. The Van Aert dairy farm is at Lot 2, Con. 1 SER, where they reside with their seven children, Brigette 14; Brian 12; Sara and Laura 9; Catherine 8; Sheri 5; and Tracy 4.

VAN DAMME, Josephus and Emelie

Josephus C. Van Damme (1921) married Emelie Angela de Maat (1929) on April 9, 1953. The couple immigrated to Canada on April 14, 1953. When they arrived in Canada, they lived in Leamington and Bothwell, and then moved to Adelaide Township in 1961. They bought a tobacco farm on Lots 16 and 17, Con. 5 SER. This was the only tobacco farm in Adelaide Township at that time. They farmed until retiring to Strathroy in 1994. Joe Van Damme Jr. and his wife, Betty (Muxlow), and their three children, Andrea, Steven and Derek, have taken over working the farm. Josephus and Emelie had 12 children, Mary (1954); Margaret (1955); Matilda (1956); Marilyn (1957); Joseph (1958); Monica (1960); Marian (1962); Jeanette (1964); Michele (1965); Jacqueline (1967); James (1968); and Joanne (1970).

VAN de KEMP, Bert and Gloria

Gijs (Bert) Van de Kemp (1952) of Graveland, North Holland, Netherlands, was born to Jan (John, 1918-1990) and Sieboltje (Visser) Van de Kemp (Sylvia, 1915). The family of six immigrated to Canada from the Netherlands in 1954, settling on a farm in the Gorrie area.

Gloria Ann Ruttan (1958) was born in Wingham and District Hospital to Lloyd Ross (1929) and Margaret Beatrice Doreen (Latronico) Ruttan (1936). Gloria has one brother.

Bert and Gloria were married October 30, 1976, in Wroxeter, Ontario. They lived briefly in Listowel and Toronto and for 10 years in Gorrie. In September 1987, Bert and Gloria moved into their newly built home at 199 William Street in Wingham. They lived there for about seven years, until life began anew in Strathroy.

Bert is an electrician by trade. He worked for Western Foundry in Wingham as an electrician and maintenance supervisor for more than 17 years, until he accepted a transfer to their new machining plant in Strathroy, under their new name of Wescast. Wescast produces 45% of all exhaust manifolds manufactured in North America. They have four plants: two in Wingham, one in Brantford, and one in Strathroy. The Strathroy facility will machine about 60% of the manifolds that the Wescast foundries produce. Bert was instrumental in coordinating repairs to the plant, upgrading the electrical and plumbing systems, installation of the new equipment, and initial hiring of staff. He now holds the position of maintenance group leader, maintaining the entire facility and equipment.

Gloria's family history is very colourful and has deep roots in the settling of North America. Her great-great-great-grandfather, John Ruttan (1786), was born only two years after his parents settled in Canada. Later, John and his wife, Mary (Steel), lived at Ruttan's Point, a parcel of Crown land in Adolphustown, near present-day Kingston, which was granted to Captain Peter Ruttan (ca.1742-1829), who was Gloria's great-great-great-great-grandfather.

Peter fought in the American Revolution from December 1776 to its end in 1783. (He is said to have accompanied Chief Joseph Brant on a tour of observation from New York to "Western Canada" in 1778, and that they became faithful friends.) When the war ended, Peter left New York aboard the ship Hope, and eventually arrived in Adolphustown on March 20, 1784.

Peter's father, William Ruttan (ca.1710-1794) and Peter's grandfather, Paul Ruttan (ca.1685-1740), were both born in New York State. Abraham Ruttan (ca.1658-1713) was a Huguenot originally from the present-day France/Germany area. As a Huguenot, and after the Edict of Nantes (which had granted Protestants religious and political freedom) was revoked in 1685 by King Louis XIV, times became perilous, and thus began the Ruttan exodus to the "New World."

Bert and Gloria have four children, Jonathan Denver (1977); Anson William (1979); Elissa Ann (1981); and Hannah Sylvia (1984). All four were born in Listowel Memorial Hospital.

On November 28, 1994, Bert and Gloria Van de Kemp and their family of four children moved into their new home in Buttery Creek Estates. They had purchased the vacant lot, situated on Lot 27, Con. 2 SER, from George and Tina Downham, on July 28, 1994.

The Van de Kemp and Ruttan family histories are included in the book on the history of Howick Township.

VAN de VEN, John and Martha

On October 15, 1959, John (d.1984) and Martha (Aarts) Van de Ven settled on Lot 13, Con. 2 SER (now 2454 Mullifarry Drive). The farm was converted to a farrow-to-finish hog operation. Because of John's struggle with Parkinson's Disease, Martha learned to manage the farm and the family, for close to 20 years. Her motivation for such an enormous task was always her children. Martha hoped that one of her children would be able to keep the farm going after her. In addition, Martha found her dual role of being "half in the house and half in the barn," very satisfying, "because (in farming) you're running something yourself. It's your own business. I found it an accomplishment... being able to make a living for eight people." This quote is from an article in the Western Ontario Farmer (August 8, 1984), in which Martha's story of determination was told. During her years of running the farm, she managed to increase the number of pigs from 500 to 1,000.

John and Martha had six children. Anthony married Jane Van Oosten and settled in Strathroy. Wilma is married to Philip Andrews and resides in Oakville, Ontario. Trudy purchased a hairdressing business and lives in London. Leon took over the family farm. Eric lives in Strathroy and assists Leon with the farm. Christine is married to George Traubenberg and they live in London.

On January 14, 1994, Martha remarried, to Leo Gubbels from Delaware. They live on Pannel Lane in Strathroy.

VAN DINTHER, Peter and Nellie

Peter Van Dinther (1919-1990) was born in Erp, Gemert, Holland. Peter was on active military service as a private with the Royal Netherlands Army (draft 1939), 2nd Infantry Regiment, from October 24, 1938, until May 26, 1940.

On May 18, 1948, he married Nellie Migchels (1923) from Lieshout, Holland, and two weeks later, they came to Canada. It was a seemingly endless 11 days and nights on a boat named Kota Inten before they made it to their new homeland, Canada. They landed in Quebec and then travelled by train to Toronto and on to Chatham, where Mr. Nelson Doub from West Lorne sponsored Peter and Nellie. They worked together on a tobacco farm for Mr. Doub for one year, and then for Joe Bujack. The first years in Canada, they endured many hardships to save money and eventually have a place of their own.

On May 1, 1950, Peter and Nellie moved to Lot 1, Con. 5 SER, R.R. #3, Kerwood, where Nellie currently resides. Peter and Nellie raised six children, Martin, Mary, Peter, Ellen, Patrick (d.1962) and Patricia (twins).

Martin was married to Leola Hofsteede and they had four children, twins Michael and Steven, Mark, and Laura. They reside in Sarnia. Mary married Everett Thorne and they had four children, Jeffrey, Steven, Stacy and Brian, and reside in Watford. Peter married Elizabeth Koolen and they had two children, Lori and Scott, and reside in Kerwood. Ellen married L.H. James Gilroy and they had two children, John and Brian, and reside in Alvinston. Patricia married Larry Trethewey and they reside in Kerwood. The farm is still in the Van Dinther family.

VAN DONGEN, John and Joanne

John Van Dongen (1928) was born in the village of Zeelands, The Netherlands, and received his early education there; he was a plasterer by trade. He immigrated to Canada on February 28, 1953, and settled in London, Ontario.

Joanne Groot (1927) was born in Cromvoirt, The Netherlands, one of a family of 17 children. She received her schooling in Bluzemartel, North Brabant. She immigrated to Canada on August 19, 1953, and settled in London, where she was employed at St. Joseph's Hospital.

John and Joanne met through a mutual friend and were married December 28, 1954. They lived in Delaware for eight years and moved to Lot 3, Con. 5 SER, in June 1963. John continued his trade as a plasterer, and operated a mixed farming operation.

The Van Dongens have four children. Dorothy (1956), born in London, married Peter S. Van Riel of Thedford. They have four children, Paula, Brian, Kristy and Laurie, and are engaged in a hog farming operation. Murray (1957) was born in London. He is a house builder and lives in Delaware. Janey (1963) was born in Strathroy. She married Brad Scott of Exeter, and they have two children, Jordan and Sam. They own a grocery store in Delaware. Janey was a soloist with a musical group, The Reflections. Harriett (1966) was born in Strathroy. She married Dennis Szela of Strathroy, and they

Peter Van Dinther family, back L-R, Patty, Ellen and Mary. Front L-R, Peter Jr., Nellie, Peter Sr. and Martin.

John Van Dongen family, back L-R, Dorothy Van Riel, Janey Scott, Harriet Szela and Murray Van Dongen. Front L-R, parents Joanne (Groot) and John Van Dongen.

have one son, Kurtis. Dennis is a mechanic and Harriett is a hairdresser.

John and Joanne were members of the Brabanders dance group for several years and entertained at parades, fairs, Klompenfest, nursing homes, and retirement homes. They retired from the farm to Strathroy in 1989, where they built a new house on the western outskirts of town, still in Adelaide Township.

VAN ERP, Gerrit (Jerry) and Patricia

Gerrit (Jerry) Van Erp (1934-1996) was born in Oploo, Holland. He immigrated to Canada in 1952. Jerry married Patricia Armstrong (1935) of McGillivray Township on September 27, 1958. She was born in Arkona, Ontario.

Jerry and Patricia had three sons, Gary (1959); Michael (1960-1961); and Michael #2 (1962), who married Carrie Adams of Mississauga on August 18, 1984, and has four children, Jessica (1987); Victoria (1988); Stephanie (1990); and Joshua (1992). They then had a daughter, Linda (1965), who married Rod Hodgins of Ilderton on June 3, 1989.

In November of 1961, Jerry and Patricia moved to Seed Road and bought a house with 1½ acres of land. Later, they built a barn and a small building for their budgies and canaries, which they showed in different bird shows in Southern Ontario.

In 1962, Jerry began working for Bill Wright, managing a 500-acre farm that had cattle and Monadale sheep.

In 1971, they bought 50 acres next door on Lot 13, Con. 2 NER, where they had cows and calves on the pasture. In 1974, Jerry started farming for himself. They built a new house on the 50 acres, along with a pig and cattle barn. They also bought 94 acres on Lot 13, Con. 1 NER, in 1992. They raised cattle and pigs until 1981, but continued to cash crop.

Jerry was a volunteer for the Adelaide/Metcalfe Optimist Club in the 1980s. Since Jerry's death, Pat has continued farming with the help of her family.

VAN ERP, Theodore and Aleogonda

Theodore and Aleogonda Van Erp immigrated to Canada from Oploo, Holland, in 1952, with 12 children aged 18 months to 17 years. They bought a farm at Lot 15, Con. 4 SER.

Their son, John (1947), met Anne Verheyen (1945), also from Adelaide Township, and married in 1967. They have two daughters, Kim (1968) and Shelley (1973).

Both girls attended Adelaide W.G. McDonald School and S.D.C.I. After graduation, Kim went to work for six years as a groom for Cuddy's horse stables. She then went to work for Kaiser Aluminum in London, where she is still employed. She lives in Strathroy. Shelley went to Windsor University, Aylmer Police Academy, and Ontario Police College. She now resides in Kitchener and works as an O.P.P. Constable in Cambridge.

John and Anne sold the farm to Richard and Barb VanderDeen in 1995. They built a new home on Lot 17, Con. 5 SER, which they had purchased in 1985 from the late Bruce Wright. John and Anne had also bought a farm in Kerwood on Lot 7, Con. 4 SER, from Len Johnson in 1973, but later sold it to Rick and Anje Boer. John cash crops and works part-time as drain superintendent and building inspector for Adelaide Township.

VAN GEFFEN, Martin and Helen

Martin (d.1984) and Helen Van Geffen immigrated to Ontario from Vinkel, North Brabant, Holland, with nine children. They lived in Rockton for one year. They purchased Lot 19, Con. 1 NER, from Alfred and Myrtle Horne in August 1952. Helen now lives in Strathroy. Martin and Helen had 10 children.

Joanne, the eldest child, married Albert Royackers in December 1957 and moved to a pork farm in Parkhill. They have five children, Mary

Ann, Marty, Josie, Elaine and Susan. Mary Ann married Lyle Hendrikx and Elaine married John Groot. They now live in Adelaide.

Grada married Tom Vlemmix in May 1960 and moved to a vegetable farm in Grand Bend. They had four children, Raymond, Tim, Helen (deceased) and Helen #2.

Jane married Lambert Vanderkant in August 1970 and moved to a pork farm in Thedford. They have four children, Ken, Sandy, Ron and Karen.

Ann (d.1999) married George Lalich in October 1959 and lived in Strathroy. They had five children, Mary Ann, Kathy, Nancy, George Jr. and Robert.

Gertie married Perk Beaudoin in October 1964. They lived in Arkona, and are now in St. Thomas. They have four children, Portia Lynn (deceased), Marcia, Jacqueline and Wade.

Frank married Agnes Timmermans in December 1970 and moved to Lot 19, Con. 2 SER. This farm was purchased in 1968 from Ormand Paine. They have three children, Jennifer, Chris and Steve.

Norio married Ed Vanderheyden in February 1968 and moved to a pork farm in Forest. They had three children, Donna, David (deceased) and Rhonda.

John married Elsie Vandenheuvel in May 1971 and moved to Lot 19, Con. 2 NER. This farm was initially purchased by Martin, and sold to John in 1971. John and Elsie have four children, Jim, Laurie, Michael and David.

Martin Jr. married Rita Van Straaten in April 1974 and stayed on the home farm. He purchased the farm from his father in 1972. Martin Jr. and Rita have six children, Junior, Ricardo, Julie, Greg, Paulo and Ana.

Martin Van Geffen farm at Lot 19, Con. 1 NER.

Leo was the only child born to Martin and Helen in Ontario. He married Katie Van Gorp in April 1974 and moved to Lot 15, Con. 1 NER. He bought the farm, known as the Kaiser farm, in 1972 from Jim Canty. Leo and Katie have four children, Mark, Sara, Ryan and Lynn.

VAN GRINSVEN, John and Tina

In 1959, John Van Grinsven (d.1997) moved from Toronto to Strathroy to start up a deadstock business in Adelaide at Lot 27, Con. 1 NER. John rented the place from Charlie McCaffrey, a 5-acre farm property with a house and barn on it, which was more than 100 years old.

In 1960, he bought the property and renovated the barn into a slaughterhouse. In 1963, he started a mink farm, which he operated until 1967.

The deadstock business had grown so fast that John decided to get out of the mink operation. John bought the 100-acre farm next to his property and grazed cattle there. After that, the farm business was extended until it became a beef farm with acres of land.

In 1972, a new house was built near the feedlot. By that time, John and Tina had a family of four daughters and one son. At present, three of the children live on those properties.

A son, Murray, lives on the home farm, where he maintains the deadstock business and beef farm. Angela married Arno Janssen, and they have a pig farm. Teresa and her husband, Ron Fischner, operate an auto body shop.

John Van Grinsven died on what he still called "the home place."

VANDER VLOET, Tony and Mary

In October 1982 when they were married, Tony and Mary (van den Ouweland) Vander Vloet purchased the farm from Mary's parents, Frank and Anne van den Ouweland. Frank and Anne had immigrated to Canada from Holland in April 1973 and lived in a rented house near Arkona until June, then purchased the farm in Adelaide Township.

Tony was born and raised on a dairy farm in Parkhill.

On March 7, 1986, there was a snowstorm. Mary was due on that day to have a baby, and the baby couldn't wait for the storm to blow over. Mary's father made a path with the tractor for them

Tony Vander Vloet family, L-R, Paul, Mary, Tony, Brian, Laura and Karen, 1997 (courtesy Luis Photography).

to follow in their little car, a Bobcat, but the snow was too deep and the car became stuck. Next, they hooked a chain to the bumper, only to discover that it wasn't strong enough, and they pulled the bumper right off the car! Thank goodness for the Adelaide snowplow, and Lloyd McDougall and Richard Elliott, who were driving it. They came to lend a helping hand. It wasn't long before they met the ambulance, which took them to the hospital. They had just 15 minutes to spare when their daughter, Laura, was born! Laura has an older brother, Brian, and two younger siblings, Paul and Karen.

VANDERBEETEN, Anthony and Ardina

Anthony (d.1970) and Ardina Vanderbeeten (d.1976) came to Canada from North Brabant, Holland, between April 27 and May 6, 1948. The Vanderbeetens were one of the first families to immigrate to Canada from the small village of Erp, North Brabant. There were five children, and Ardina was expecting her sixth child in August, so it wasn't an easy journey for her. The new baby was born a Canadian.

Anthony was a hard working farmer who had fought in WWII. Times were hard and, to give their children a better life, they decided to leave their siblings, parents and friends, to start a new life in the "New World." Crossing the great Atlantic was a frightful journey that took 10 days.

The send-off in Rotterdam was tearful as the Vanderbeetens said goodbye to Gramma, uncles and aunts. Thinking they would never see them again, the family made their way toward the huge ship, the S.S. Tabinta, one of the old ships that had been used in the war. Anthony and Ardina told the children in later years, it was like going on board the Titanic. They thought they were doomed, but went full of hope and courage for a better life.

The ship was very large, so the children got into lots of mischief as they went exploring. On the fourth day at sea, a fierce storm arose. The ship rocked and waves crashed so hard, it sounded like cannon fire. There were many sick people. It was not a pleasant sight. The crew was busy with sick bags, trying to keep everyone calmed down. Finally, after many hours, the sun began to break through the storm clouds. The Vanderbeetens were excited to see the pretty rainbow, and were sure there was a pot of gold on the other side in the New World—what dreamers they were!

On day five, a baby was born in the ship's infirmary, so everyone seemed to be in high spirits. It was a new beginning and a good sign.

Once in a while, they sat on the deck late at night, looked up at the millions of stars, and made wishes. There was nothing but stillness and the lapping of water all around. They wondered if they would ever see dry land.

One day there was a party on board, to celebrate the birthday of a member of the Dutch royal family. Any excuse for a party! The children were given small cupcakes and, at night, there was dancing and lively music in the so-called ballroom.

The captain announced that they were halfway towards their destination. The ship had a speed of 30 km. per hour. No wonder it took so long to get to Canada!

The children found the kitchen and the cook always managed to have lots of fresh cookies for them to eat. They saw the occasional ship pass by— what a lovely sight! The adults played cards and sang Dutch songs to pass the time.

On the ninth day, there was a big party to celebrate Liberation Day. The ship was decorated in red, white and blue streamers.

The steward and crew gave a performance for the children and then they had to go to bed early. The adults dined and danced, and said farewell to their fellow passengers.

On the tenth day, the passengers arose early to see Canada. Everyone raced onto the deck to be the

This is a photo of the ship that was chartered for many immigrant families (Vanderbeeten family, 1948).

TABINTA - Built by Nederlandsche Scheepsbouw Mij, Amsterdam (engines by Werkspoor, Amsterdam) in 1930 for the Nederland Line, this was a 8,156 gross ton ship, length 469' x beam 62.2', one funnel, three masts, single screw and a speed of 15 knots. Launched on 21/3/1930, she was chartered to the Netherlands Government in 1948, who had established a line of ships to cope with the large scale level of emigration after the war. She made her first voyage from Rotterdam to Quebec in April 1948 and made a total of five roundtrip voyages to Quebec in 1948, plus four more in 1949. In July 1949, she made a single roundtrip voyage from Holland to New York. She was scrapped in Hong Kong in 1961 [North Atlantic Seaway by N.R.P. Bonsor, vol.4, p.1687, posted to The ShipsList by Ted Finch, July 11, 1998]

first to see the small white church and tiny houses in the distance. This was Canada! What a strange and wondrous feeling as the great ship got closer and closer to land. Daughter Bette still remembers the eerie feeling. They arrived in Quebec and no one was there to greet them or tell them what to do. Anthony produced a slip of paper with the name "Kingston, Ontario" on it. Little did he realize how far away it was. The children were too young to realize how difficult it must have been for Anthony and Ardina. They could not speak English so, as they told the children later, they used a lot of sign language.

The family first settled near the St. Lawrence River near Kingston. Anthony worked as a farm labourer. Later, the family moved to R.R. #5, Strathroy, on Highway 22, where the Vanderbeetens farmed for many years.

This was the beginning of life in Canada for Anthony and Ardina Vanderbeeten and their family. They had six children. Mary (1939) married John Does (1932-2001), and lives in London. Aubrey (1941-1991) was married to Ella Willing, and lived in London (Ella has remarried). John (1942-1997) was married to Joanne Lightfoot, and lived in Mt. Brydges (Joanne now lives in Strathroy). Elizabeth "Bette" married Bill Parker, and lives at Lot 14, Con. 4 SER. Paula married Gary Stevens, and lives in Thorndale. Rene married Gayle Muylaert, and lives on Pike Sideroad, R.R. #7, Strathroy.

Anthony and Ardina worked very hard to give their children a good future and a strong foundation to build on. The oral history of the family's immigration was repeated many times and eventually written down. Anthony always told his children, "You come from good people in Holland, so remember your roots."

VANDERHOEK, Wietze and Syke

Wietze Vanderhoek (1905) was born in the Netherlands. He immigrated to Canada in 1956 with his wife, Syke, and four sons, Gerry, Henry, Mike and Ray. They settled in Strathroy and bought a house with five acres, and started a dairy herd of Holstein cows, which had healthy heifer twins each year.

In the early 1960s, Wietze bought Lot 12, Con. 4 SER, from Hanson Hull. He brought 19 head of cattle to this farm.

In 1971, Ray married Hilda Hibma and they bought the farm from Wietze. Ray and Hilda have four children, Tracy, Shelley, Darcy and Timothy.

VEENSTRA, John and Jean

John Veenstra was born in the Netherlands on a dairy farm. After serving for 21 months in the Dutch navy, he immigrated to Canada in 1957, at the age of 22 years.

After working for a while in Ilderton on the dairy farm of Duncan and Mary Fletcher, John moved to Strathroy, where he worked for Statham Plumbing and Heating.

Veenstra home, formerly owned by Fred and Jean Wright, purchased in 1963 by the Veenstras.

In 1958, John met Jean Gerrits. She and her father, Herman, and mother, Margareth, and nine brothers and five sisters, had settled in the Clinton area. There, they bought a farm and started a broiler production.

In 1960, John and Jean married. They resided in Strathroy. In 1962, they purchased the east half of Lot 5, Con. 2 SER, from Fred and Jean Wright. In the spring of 1963, they moved to this property and began to operate it as a dairy farm.

John and Jean had three sons and one daughter, Susan, Gerald, David and Herman. They milked cows for 28 years and then changed the operation to a cow/calf farm in 1990.

In the fall of 1993, the barn burned to the ground. They replaced it with a small pole barn, suitable for a few beef cows and calves.

At the beginning of their marriage, Jean worked in the old hospital, and then worked the last five years in a retirement home in Watford. Now retired, she enjoys her many hobbies at home.

VERHEYEN, Brian and Lynn

Brian Verheyen grew up in Adelaide, the son of Frank and Mary Verheyen. The Verheyen family was involved in tractor pulls. Brian married Lynn Davis of London, and she moved to Adelaide after their marriage in August 1992.

Brian and Lynn have

Veenstra family, L-R, David, Gerald, and Susan, John with Herman on his knee, and mother, Jean.

Frank Cornelius Verheyen

two children, Calvin (1993) and Shelby Gail (1995).

Lynn is originally from Warwick Township, the daughter of Art and Grace Davis.

VERHOEVEN, Cornelis and Mary

On June 28, 1836, the Crown granted Jerimiah Baker 100 acres, the west half of Lot 2, Con. 2 SER. In 1923, John W. Langford (d.1949) sold the property to John T. and Mary Chambers. On December 8, 1954, widow Mary Chambers sold to Cornelis "Cor" and Mary Verhoeven from Watford. They had six children, Jim, Nellie, Anne, Bernard, Mia and Cory.

In 1965, Bernard married Elly Frensch from the Stratford area, and on November 6, 1967, Bernard and Elly took over the family farm from his parents. Cor and Mary then built a chicken barn and house on a 2-acre lot on the east side of the property.

Bernard and Elly raised four children. Lucia married Joe Kaak, a farmer from Shipka, Ontario, and they live in Strathroy. Ann Marie lives in Hamilton and is an Occupational Hygienist. Annette is married to Ken Hoeper, a farmer in Amberley. Bernie is a mechanic for Larry MacDonald in Strathroy.

A neighbour, Norman Dowding, told the Verhoevens some interesting facts about the farm. Apparently, there was a cheese factory located on the east side of the laneway, called The Victoria Cheese Factory. The well that provided water for it is still there. The building was later moved across the road to Norman's place and attached to his barn on the east side, but the wooden structure has since fallen down. The farm was also the site of one of the area's first gravel pits, located on the west hill side. Neighbours drew gravel out with horses and wagons, or sleighs. The property has an interesting history. It was often a gathering place for parties, with fiddle music and dancing in the kitchen.

Bernard Verhoeven home at the time Cornelius Verhoeven purchased it (the old John Chambers home, on Second Line South).

VERKLEY, Peter and Gezina

Peter Verkley (1918) married Gezina Stockman (1922) on March 1, 1949. They had 11 children.

John (1950), the eldest child, married Anne Marie Stock (1951) on June 17, 1972.

Their three children are Lisa Marie (1975); Brian James (1977); and Julie Lyn (1980).

There is no further information about Joseph (1951) or Paul (1952).

Frank (1953) married Carol Costello (1953) on June 16, 1976. They had three children, Amy Catherine (1977); Sarah Marie (1979); and Stephanie Danielle (1986). Frank remarried on June 23, 1990, to Dorothea Kelch (1954). Frank and Dorothea have two children, Greg Melanson (1975) and Chris Melanson (1977).

The fifth child of Peter and Gezina was Cecilia (1954).

Maria (1956) married Don Green (1961) on October 17, 1981. They have three children, Wesley Donald (1982); Tina Maria (1985); and Jesse William (1988).

There is no further information on Philip (1957).

Edward (1958) married Nora Vondijk (1960) on October 15, 1983. Their four children are Adam William (1985); Steven Peter (1986); Mark Nicholas (1991); and Benjamin (1994).

Thomas "Tom" (1960) married Catherine Hicks (1961), the daughter of Bruce and the late Betty Hicks from Sarnia, on November 1, 1986. Tom and Cathy have lived at 1817 Egremont Drive since their marriage. In 1996, Tom served as President of the Middlesex Soil and Crop Improvement Association and is a founding member of its Site Specific Management Club, which helps farmers use G.P.S. and yield monitors. Tom, Cathy, and their children, Patrick (1991) and Leahanne (1993), are members of All Saints Parish and folk choir in Strathroy, where Tom has played guitar in the folk choir since 1972.

After working with his two younger brothers for 21 years on the family dairy farm, Tom is now a broiler farmer at 1817 Egremont Drive.

There is no additional information on Philip David (1962).

Jeffery (1963) married Teresa Dekraker (1961) on April 11, 1987. Their three children are Scott Abraham (1989); Alexander Peter (1991); and Joshua Jeffery (1995).

VOKES, James and Mary

James Thompson Vokes (1825-1902) was born in Bridington, Yorkshire, England, the son of a Primitive Methodist Minister. This was the title given to a part of the early Methodist religion. James immigrated to Canada as a young man, and resided in the Province of Quebec for a time.

Mary Emerson (1829-1887) was a native of Fermanagh, Ireland, and immigrated to Quebec as a young girl. James and Mary met in Quebec and then married in 1852. They moved to Hamilton and then to Norval, Ontario. In 1870, they came to the Strathroy area.

James and Mary purchased property in Adelaide Township at Lot 21, Con. 3 SER, on the northern outskirts of Strathroy. This land later became part of the town. They spent the rest of their lives at this location. James was a master tailor and, if not the first tailor in Strathroy, he was certainly among the first shopkeepers to open a merchant-tailoring establishment. His store was located on Front Street, where he conducted a very rewarding and prosperous business. At one time, five of the Vokes daughters were working in this shop.

James and Mary had eight children, Francis Richard (1855-1872); Mary Ann (1857-1888), who married Gideon Adams; Sarah Jane (1858-1890), who married James Halpin; Margaret Elizabeth (1860-1916), who married David Smith and lived in Detroit; Susan (1862-1887); Ella (1865-1957), who married George Smith and lived in Minnesota; Robert Emerson (1867-1950); and Katie (1871-1968).

Emerson married Nellie Bavoss and they lived in Ontario, but after Nellie's death, Emerson moved to Duluth, Minnesota, where he was a building contractor.

Katie, the youngest child of James and Mary, became a teacher and taught at S.S. #8 Adelaide. She married Simon Shrier (d.1937) on December 26, 1894, and they lived in Michigan, where their first three children were born. Katie and Simon had four children, Emerson Nelson (1895); Olive Aileen (1901); Susan (1903, stillborn); and Gladdis (1909), who was born after Katie and Simon returned to Ontario (see SHRIER, Jacob and Mary).

Emerson Nelson married Katherine Clare of London, Ontario, on August 25, 1926. They had no children.

Olive Aileen married Harold Ogden in Gaylord, Michigan, on June 6, 1931. They had one daughter, June Marie (1933), and one son, William Harold (1937).

Gladdis married William A. McNaughton in Middlesex County on August 10, 1927. They have a daughter, Betty Marjorie (1930). Gladdis remarried, to Otto Zimmerman. They farmed at Lot 4, Con. 3 NER.

Katie and Simon are buried in Strathroy Cemetery.

James, Mary, and their family were members and strong supporters of the Strathroy Methodist Church. James served on the building committee for the church on Front Street, which is the present-day United Church. He was also a dedicated supporter and worker of the Liberal Party.

After Mary's death, James remarried on January 12, 1891, to Agnes Bowes (d.1925) of Wisbeach, Ontario.

WALKER, James and Margaret

James Walker (1829-1909) was born at Fernehurst, Roxburghshire, Scotland. Fernehurst is a castle in the border country near Jedburo, Scotland. (On February 14, 1861, he married Margaret Riddell (1834-1884) at Aberdeenshire, Scotland.) James and Margaret lived in the Belmont area after coming to Canada, then moved to Lot 19, Con. 1 NER, in 1866. James was a blacksmith. He had a shop on the corner of his farm at Lot 19 (Russell Smith has his anvil and Donald Walker has a set of scales that James made with his initials stamped on them).

James and Margaret had six children, James Jr. (1861-1924); Margaret (1863-1943); Helen Symington (1865), who was a nurse and moved to Western Canada; Sam (1867-1909); Alexander (1877), who was a dentist (when he moved to Oklahoma, he had to sleep with a rifle by his side because of Indians); and Andrew.

James Jr. married Margaret Adair (1868-1943) of Lot 19, Con. 3 SER, on October 28, 1891. They had three children, Gordon (1893-1987), who married Nettie Brown (1898) on January 28, 1918; Margaret (1897-1977), who married Roy Smith (1894-1947) on December 25, 1917; and Alexander Clayton (1898-1961), who married Robena McKeen (1914-1944) in 1936.

Gordon was a schoolteacher who taught at S.S. #4, then moved to Big River, Saskatchewan. Gordon and Nettie had two children.

Margaret and Roy lived in Lobo Township and had four children.

Alexander and Robena had two children, James and Donald. During an 11-month period, Alex lost his mother; his wife, Robena, through illness; and his son, James, who died as the result of a tractor accident. Alex later died of a tractor accident, at the scene of his son's death. In the 1940s, Alex was a Shur Gain fertilizer dealer.

Donald (1939) married Catherine Anne Ford (1940) of Bedford, England, on June 2, 1962. They had three children, Valerie Anne (1964), who lives in Toronto; Elizabeth Margaret (1967), who married Greg MacDiarmid (1962) on July 3, 1993, and lives in Chatham, New Brunswick; and Susan Jennifer Win (1973), who married Dave Noordermeer (1969) on August 9, 1997. Susan and Dave live in Mt. Brydges.

The original house at the east half of Lot 19, Con. 1 NER, was built in 1898, and the bank barn was built in 1900. The big silo and feedlot were built in 1972. The second house was built in 1967.

The original farm consisted of the east and west halves of Lot 19, Con 1 NER. The west half was sold in the early 1900s. The family continued to farm the east half of Lot 19, Con. 1 NER. In 1956, the west half of Lot 20 SER was purchased from Harry Anderson. In 1963, the west half of Lot 20 NER was purchased from Harry Carruthers. In April 1996, the farm was sold to Keith Nordemann, and Don and Anne Walker moved to Strathroy.

WALKER, Robert and Margaret

William Walker was born in Northern Scotland in the early 1800s. One of his sons, Robert, came to Canada and settled on Lot 18, Con. 1 NER. Robert and his wife, Margaret, had six children, William, James, George, Robert, Thomas and Elizabeth.

William married Emily Slater. He was later struck by lightning and killed while picking up milk

Robert and Margaret (George) Walker house, Lot 18, Con. 1 NER.

with horse-and-wagon on the Egremont Road.

Thomas married Catherine Agnetta Slater. They had four sons, William Thomas, John Russell, Graham Slater and George Arnold.

The Thomas Walker family had a family orchestra, which played at dances at Cairngorm and Crathie. Agnetta played the piano, Thomas played violin, and John and Graham played the saxophone and violin. George, at 10 years of age, played the drums. Later, George originated the Casa Royal Orchestra, playing every Saturday night in the Strathroy Town Hall. He arranged the music, and played in the orchestra until retiring in the later 1960s.

William Thomas purchased the old Slater homestead at Lot 23 and 24, Con. 1 SER, from his mother. He married Lillian Field and they had a son, George William, who married Donna M. Brock in 1955. George and Donna live on the Slater property and have one daughter, Marie Louise, who married Scott W. Baker. Marie and Scott have a son, Steven William (1993).

WALLACE

James Wallace (1826-1862) immigrated to Canada from Scotland, with his parents, John (d.1852) and Jane (Scott) Wallace. Also immigrating at that time were siblings Alexander Holcomb Wallace (1832); Elizabeth Wallace (1834); and Mary Wallace (1836). According to records of the time, they came to Ontario in 1846 and settled on the Egremont Road at Lot 27, Con. 1 NER, Warwick Township. The father, John Wallace, died from an ox cart accident and was buried in the Wallace

Cemetery on the corner of the Wallace farm (later the Watson farm). The old tombstones show that Jane and James are also buried there.

After his father's death, James applied to purchase the 200 acres of clergy land in Adelaide Township at Lot 2, Con. 1 SER. He received his patent from the Crown in 1852. The subscribers' list of 1853 for those contributing to the building of a Presbyterian Chapel at Wiley's Corners include James, brother Alexander, William Watson (now married to Elizabeth Wallace), and Richard Skillen (now married to Mary Wallace).

James married his neighbour across the road, Jane Wiley (see WILEY, David and Ann) and they had three children, Margery; Jean; and James Jr. (1862-1914). James was killed as a result of being kicked by a horse, and was buried beside his parents in the Wallace Cemetery.

In 1882, when James Jr. became of legal age, he received 100 acres, the west half of Lot 2, from his father's estate. His two sisters each received 50 acres. His mother, Jane, married James Marshall and the Wallace and Marshall children had made this their home until they married and set up their own households. Jane and James Marshall moved to the Marshall home on Con. 2 NER, Warwick Township.

James Jr. married Rebecca Ann "Annie" Conkey (1866-1954), daughter of Robert and Jane (Wiley) Conkey (see CONKEY, Arthur and Margaret). They moved into the old Wallace/Marshall house. James was an elder of the West Adelaide Presbyterian Church. He was a collector of taxes for Adelaide Township and a member of township council. He operated a mixed farming operation, and he and Annie raised four sons, Chester (1887-1941); James Earl (1893-1980); Stanley Clinton (1900-1980); and Frederick Lester (1910-2000).

Chester received training in Toronto and became a doctor and surgeon of veterinary medicine. For a short time, he had a veterinary practice in Arkona. He went to work in Toronto for the Dominion Department of Agriculture as an inspector of cattle at the abattoirs of the large packing plants. He married Pearl Irwin (1890-1976). Chester became interested in the Conkey family and he began the "Conkey Oak Tree" listing as many of the children and grandchildren as he knew. He continued his mother's album, which is a useful Conkey activity in every generation. Chester and Pearl are buried in West Adelaide Cemetery.

James Earl lived with his parents and helped on the home farm, then lived with brother, Lester, and sister-in-law, Frances, when they moved to a small farm in Caradoc Township.

Stanley Clinton went to Flint, Michigan, at the age of 21, to work for a plumbing company. There he married Mary McAlpine, and they raised two daughters, Marilyn and Darva. They retired to London, Ontario.

Frederick Lester remembers going to S.S. #6 Adelaide with all the Campbells, the Clelands, and the older Herringtons, who were living with grandparents Jim and Margery Wilson at the time. In 1942, Lester married Frances Iles (1913-1976). He carried on the farm work with Earl and they cared for Annie. Lester reminisces about the family's terrifying experience when the tornado of May 1953 hit their farm. Annie, who was recovering from a stroke, was lying on a blanket covering a hospital bed in the corner. The first sign of encroaching danger was a loud noise and the sound of breaking glass when the big east-facing window collapsed, and parts of the maple tree came in. Lester went under his mother's bed, and Earl wanted to go outside but Frances wouldn't let him leave. The next time they looked outside, they had no barn as it had collapsed. Lester said the duration of this was "one breath" as he remembers he couldn't get his breath once. His mother was lifted off the bed and the blanket on which she was lying was found on top of the windmill on the 50 acres east. On her bed were shingles, bits of board and chips from the barn, which was "ground up like hamburg." All the windows of the house were broken except those on the west side, and the panels were out of the inside doors. There were some pigs and an old bull in the barn—all were dead. Afterward, a sow was seen running around the yard with a board through its intestines! Four pups in the separator room survived and were running around on top of the barn debris. It wasn't long before the neighbours pulled in with their machinery and cleaned up the mess for about 60 rods around the barn. Eventually, they set fire to the remains.

After Annie's death, the farm was sold to Cyril and Eunice Reid, noted for their crops of turnips. In 1980, they sold to Tony VanAert who built a modern home on the property.

Lester, Frances, and Earl moved to the village of Mt. Brydges for five years, and then they moved to a 25-acre farm on Con. 8 in Caradoc Township, where Lester and Frances had two sons, James Lester and Frederick George.

James Lester married Barbara Hodgins. They live at R.R. #1 Hepworth, and have two children, Chadrick and Genna Rebecca.

Frederick George married Leslie Nichol, and are raising their daughter, Stephanie, in Strathroy.

After Frances' and Earl's deaths, Lester moved to an apartment in Strathroy. He remarried in 1987, to Edna Roulton, and they lived for a short time in Watford. They moved to an apartment at R.R. #3, Thorndale. Edna and Lester died several months apart.

WALSH, Patrick and Mary Ellen

In 1851, Patrick and Mary Ellen (Quinn) Walsh were living in Adelaide Township at Lot 6, Con. 1 NER, farming and raising their family of six children. Descendants of these Irish pioneers live in Middlesex County.

Mary (1841-1918), the eldest child, married Thomas Hickey and they farmed 100 acres, the west half of Lot 21, Con. 1 NER. It is thought that Mary was born on the high seas during the voyage to Canada.

Johanna (1842-1918) married the boy next door, James Healy Jr., and farmed and raised their family in Adelaide Township until moving to Strathroy later in life. Their family consisted of eight children. Some of the children stayed in the area—Sarnia, Windsor, Adelaide and London —while others left to find their fortunes as far away as Wyoming, Michigan and Arabia (see HEALY, James and Rosanna).

John (1843-1914) married Hanna Costello of London in St. Peter's Cathedral in London, and they returned to Strathroy where they farmed at Lot 21, Con. 1 NER.

Catherine (1847-1920) lived in the area.

Patrick followed in his father's footsteps and became a farmer. He lived and worked in Adelaide until his untimely death from appendicitis. He left behind a wife and 12 children.

Mrs. Mary Anne Walsh, 90th birthday celebration.

WALTHAM, John and Elizabeth

The first known Waltham to settle in Adelaide Township was John Waltham (ca.1808-1896), born in England. He and his wife, Elizabeth (ca.1810-1900), immigrated with their son, John (1831-1897), to Canada in 1832. The trip was smooth, taking only 30 days. John, being a labourer, settled with his family on Con. 2 SER. As were many English immigrants, John belonged to the Church of England. In 1851, the three Walthams lived on the east half of Lot 20, Con. 3 SER, residing with John N. Ashbee, who was 50 yrs. of age and single, owner of the farm. In later life, John and his wife moved to Caradoc Street in Strathroy, where John Sr. died. His obituary spoke in glowing terms of his sterling character and that "to know him was to respect him." John and Elizabeth were buried in Strathroy Cemetery.

Young John was born in Lincolnshire. He found his future wife, Jane Scoon (1829-1905), across the road from his parent's farm. Jane was born in Cumberland, England. They were married on December 9, 1856.

The Scoon family was one of the first to immigrate to the area in 1831. John A. Scoon and his wife, Helen, were Wesleyan Methodists, John being English and Helen being Scottish in ancestry. They owned 100 acres of farmland but had only cleared 20 acres for productive farming by 1842. As per the 1842 census, the family had grown that year: 90 bushels of wheat, seven bushels of barley, 100 bushels of oats, 80 bushels of peas, 12 bushels of Indian corn, 10 bushels of buckwheat, 130 bushels of potatoes, 630 units of maple syrup, and owned 10 cattle, 19 sheep and 15 hogs. Not only were the Scoons farmers, but they also ran a small store on their property and later owned a store in Sylvan.

John and Jane Waltham had six children, John A. (1857-1928); William (1860-1941); Scott Joseph (1862-1934); Helen Elizabeth "Ellie" (1866-1936);

Family of Richard Waltham, ca.1950. L-R, Marie, Winfield, Jack, Ross, Clare, Helen, Jean, Muriel, Irene, Dick and Elva (parents).

Henry Dale (1868-1943); and Richard Edward "Dick" (1874-1952).

William married Margaret Ann Richardson (1868-1949), daughter of John (1837-1931) and Jane (Earley) Richardson (1847-1923) of Adelaide Township, in 1888. They lived in Inniskillen and later went to New Westminster, B.C., where they were buried. They had eight children, John, Cecil Alexander, Basil, Eve Jane, Flossie Reta, Archibald, Adelbert and Vera, who was adopted. They all married except Basil and Eve Jane, who died as babies. All resided in Alberta and British Columbia.

Scott Joseph married Maudi Maher in Adelaide Township. They had a family of one son and four daughters, Arlie, Lydia, Lula, Corila and Vera.

Ellie married William Francis Pike (1861-1932), son of Benjamin and Margaret (Hanover) Pike, and they moved to Warwick. They had one adopted daughter, Maggie, who married a druggist in Wyoming.

Henry Dale (1868-1943) married Joanna Jones (1865-1953), daughter of Philip and Jane Ann (Fletcher) Jones, pioneers of Adelaide Township. Henry and Joanna lived in Cairngorm and had no children.

At the time of his death, John had been the assessor of Adelaide Township for nine years. He was a strong supporter of the Reform Political Party. John's grandchildren often heard stories of hardship. One such story related a buggy ride home from a party late at night. The buggy, drawn by two horses, was confronted by a pack of wolves. In order to save themselves, they released one of the horses, which the wolves chased. With the remaining horse still in the harness, they were able to arrive home safely.

Of the six children, only John A. and Richard Edward remained in Adelaide Township. Upon John's death, the homestead on the east half of Lot 1, at the Fourth Line SER, to which John received the deed in 1883, passed to his widow, Jane. Jane, in turn, passed the farm to Richard Edward. The farm was then inherited by his son, Kenneth Ross, in 1952. Upon his demise, his only son, Ken, inherited the farm.

John A. married Minnie Jones on March 28, 1888. They had four children, Winnifred Adeline (1889); Mary Jane (1891); William John (1893); and Helen Elizabeth (1896). The children were born in Adelaide, and all were baptized on April 25, 1897, and raised in the Anglican faith.

Dick married Elva May Watson (1881-1970) on March 29, 1900. They lived on Lot 1, Con. 4 SER. They also owned Lot 1, Con. 5 SER. Dick had a gravel pit on his property from which Basil Denning drew. Elva was active in Grace Anglican Church near Kerwood. Dick was in bridge construction, built bridges in the area, and had a business named Waltham and Kelly. Later, Dick was an Inspector of Highways. He was active in Lodge work and Grand Master of I.O.O.F about the 1930s. Dick's job often took him to Toronto, which was a full day's journey from home. When he and his wife were away, the raising of the children was left to eldest daughter, Jean, and the farming was the responsibility of the older sons, Pat, Clare and Ross. It was not uncommon for itinerants and hobos to come to the house and ask for food and/or lodging for the night. Both Richard and his wife are interred in Strathroy Cemetery.

Dick and Elva had nine children, Reginald Winfield "Pat" (1901-1967); Jean Alexandra (1903-1972); R. Clare (1908-1982); Kenneth Ross (1911-1997); Leila Muriel (1913); Helen (1915); Jack (1918); Lillian Irene (1920-1994); and Marie Evelyn (1922).

Pat married Kathryn J. Conkey (1905-1989) of Adelaide Township. They settled in Adelaide. Pat was also in bridge construction and owned Waltham and Fuller Construction. They raised two children. Fred lives in Seaforth and Marjorie resides in Toronto.

Jean married Fred Wright (1902-1962) of Adelaide Township. They settled on the Second Line. They had one daughter, Ruth Anne, who married Eric Hackle. They live in London and have a son, Fred. After Fred Wright Sr. died, Jean lived with her daughter, Ruth, and family in London, where she died.

R. Clare married Mabel Manicom (1902-1982) in Adelaide in 1934. Mabel was born in Cornwall, daughter of William Geake and Elizabeth (Hooper) Manicom. They settled on Lot 1, Con. 5 SER. The first oil well drilled in Adelaide Township was on Clare's property. Mabel sang in the church choir at the Anglican Church and sang duets with her sister, Gwen, on many occasions, as the Manicom girls were very musical. Clare was a member of I.O.O.F. Clare and Mabel had one son, Donald (1939), who married Norma Lightfoot (1938), daughter of Charles and Anne Lightfoot of Napier. Don worked for the Carnation Milk Plant in Kerwood, and for the Ford Motor Plant in Talbotville for many years, from which he retired in 1998. Don and Norma have two children. Brian (1958) married Denise Forgie from Brantford. They live in London and have two children, Matthew and Gregory. Kimberley (1961) lives in Strathroy.

Kenneth Ross married Gwen Manicom (1912-1992), born in Cornwall, England, sister of Mabel Manicom, and they settled on Lot 1, Con. 4 SER. Ross was well known for calling at square dancing events in the area, and Gwen played the piano. They were also part of the Heritage Group with Reg Freer and Walter Feasey, and were in much demand. Gwen was the church organist in the Anglican Church for many years. Ross was a member of I.O.O.F. Ross and Gwen had a son, Ken, who married Marilyn Smith. They live on the home farm and had two children. Clark (1962-1980) died young. Angela married Tom Lethbridge and lives in Sarnia. Angela and Tom have four children, Miranda, Scott, Nicole and Danielle.

Leila "Muriel" married Kenneth Earl Matthews (1906-1973), son of George Henry and Isabel (Westgate) Matthews of Adelaide Township, in 1937. Muriel and Ken resided in Adelaide at Lot 5, Con. 5 SER, where they operated Ken Matthews Trucking. Ken was a generous and warm-hearted man and always tried to help his fellow man. After Ken's death, Muriel stayed with the business. Muriel was also active in church. They had two children. Judith Ann married Robert Dale. They reside in Ilderton and have three children, Karen, Mary Ann and Michael. William Earl "Bill" (1940) married Marjorie Joynt, daughter of John R. and Edythe (Styles) Joynt. Bill and Marjorie live in Adelaide Township on Con. 4 SER, and have two children, Jeffery and Susan. Jeffery married Lynda Dymond, and they reside in Adelaide Township. Jeff is an engineer. He works for Dillon Consulting Limited in London, and also helps out at Matthews Trucking. They have two children, Jenna and Katie. Susan, the daughter of Bill and Marjorie, married Paul Findlay. They reside in Glencoe and have one son, Matthew.

Helen married Gordon Stinson (1905-1985). They reside in Rodney, Ontario. They raised two daughters, Anna Mae and Mary Margaret. Both are married and live elsewhere.

Jack married Beatrice Wickett of Caradoc. They lived in Adelaide for awhile, then moved to Stoney Creek, Ontario. They have two sons, Bob and Ray.

Lillian Irene married Chester Shortt (1918-1976). She was a nurse in Sarnia Hospital. They lived in Amherstburg and raised four children, Dick; Penny; Carol (d.1981); and David.

Marie married Lou Ballantyne (1920) of Caradoc Township. They reside in Strathroy. Marie enjoyed lawn bowling. Lou had the B.P. gas station on Caradoc Street beside Moore's blacksmith shop and behind the Derby Inn, now a parking lot. They moved to Ottawa and from there to the U.S., where they lived for 22 years before returning to Strathroy. They raised a daughter and son. Nancy (d.1999) was a nurse. She married Grant Oliver, and they lived in Caradoc. They had two children. Ross married Sandra Olafson Tyler, and they reside in Florida.

WARDELL, Joseph and Letitia

In 1853, Joseph (d.1925) and Letitia (Bunting) Wardell (d.1901) immigrated to Pickering Village from County Antrim, Ireland. Shortly after, they moved to Adelaide Township and settled on Lot 25, Con. 3 NER. In 1870, Letitia's brother and his wife, Elizabeth (Brady), moved from London to the farm next door.

Joseph and Letitia had eight children, Elizabeth (1857-1915), who married Charles Martin; John E. (1858-1926), who married Carol Lindsay; Elenore (1861-1940), who married James Bolton; Brereton

(1865-1939), who married Mary E. Orr; Mary (1866-1921), who married George Richardson; Isabella (1869-1940), who married Robert Graham; Wesley (1872-1947), who married Mary E. "Etta" Zavitz; and William (1873-1925), who married Nellie F. Oliver. Joseph and Letitia are the ancestors of many of the Wardells in this area. Their farm has passed down through four generations.

Wesley and Etta had a son, Borden, who married Evelyn Daniel. They lived on the townline between Adelaide and East Williams Townships, now known as Wardell Drive. Borden and Evelyn had a son, William W. "Bill," who lives at Lot 23, Con. 2 SER (now 28551 Centre Road).

Borden worked for Comstock for several years, converting electrical power from 50- to 60-cycle. He then worked for GM Diesel, from which he retired after several years. A few years after Evelyn's death, the farm was sold and Borden moved to London. The house on the farm later burned down. Borden remarried, to Ruth (Daniel) McNelles.

Bill grew up on the town line adjacent to the home where his father grew up. He has two sisters, Marion Heckman and Pat Richardson, both of Strathroy. As a teenager, Bill rode the road grader, which was tractor-drawn. After high school, he worked for Gord Campbell building drive sheds, rebuilding barns, and doing other odd jobs.

Bill married Lucille Wills (d.1993) and they had three children, William, Brian and Brenda Vianne, and five grandchildren. They resided in Strathroy for some time before purchasing their present lot from Bill's uncles, Fred and Walter Wardell, where they built a home in 1963.

Bill worked for several years for Wright Assemblies in Strathroy. In 1967, he started work at the Ford Motor Company while the plant was in the building stages, even before production began. He worked in Quality Control until he retired in 1994. Bill has been interested in cars all his life and continues to follow the automotive industry, both in production and sports.

William, the youngest son of Joseph and Letitia, had six children, Ethel, who married Melville Dennis; Olive, who married Russell Currie; Norman (1906-1987); Howard; Grace, who married Dwight Sexton; and Elsiem who married William A. Daniel.

In 1931, Norman married Margaret Campbell, daughter of John A. and Nettie (Ross) Campbell. Norman was raised on Lot 25, Con. 3 NER. When his father died, he took over the operation of the farm for his mother. Norman was also an electrician, and he and his cousin, Borden, wired many of the farms in the area. In 1948, he took on the job of Road Superintendent. He held the position until 1954, when ill health forced him to retire. In 1962, he moved to Strathmere Lodge, where he lived until his death. In 1962, son James and his wife and sons moved into the home farm and now James' son, Robert (1967), resides there.

Norman loved to play cards and dance, and call for square dances. When he saw a square next to his go ahead of the call, he would change the words to confuse them. He thoroughly enjoyed a good political discussion and didn't care what side he was on. Norman and Margaret had seven children, Alan; Ross; Roy; James; Lorne (d.1955); Helen; and Ila.

Alan married Joanne Parke, and they have three children, Michael, Lori and Faye. They live in Victoria, B.C.

Ross married Irene Baril. They have two children, Lori and Susan, and live in Edmonton, Alberta.

Roy married Kay Bennett. In 1960, he purchased S.S. #7 at Lot 6, Con. 5 SER, completed some major renovations, and made it into a home. They have a son, Mark (1965), who graduated from the University of Waterloo as a Computer Engineer. He works for Focus-Systems of Waterloo. In 1995, Mark married Margy Hartman of Zurich and they have two children, Hannah (1997) and Philip (1999).

Roy has been a carpenter, builder and general "fixer-upper" in the area since 1964. He has built homes, barns, additions and even the Fire Hall. He is on the Fire Department and was the Chief for 20 years. In 1995, he and Neil Bolton drove the new fire truck from Abbotsford, B.C., with a bent drive shaft—it was a bumpy ride!

James, fourth child of Norman and Margaret, married Joyce Merriam. They have two sons, Doug and Robert, and live in Strathroy.

Helen married Basil Martin (d.1984). They have four children, Basil, Samuel, Pamela and Leanna. Helen lives in Strathroy

Ila, the youngest child of Norman and Margaret, married George Herrington, and they have four children, Barbara, Donna, Clifford and Karen. They live in the Arkona area.

John E. and Caroline had six children, Lindsay; George (d.1943); Annabelle; Ella; Maud; and Lucy. George married Dora Louetta Fuller (1893-1978) of Adelaide Township on May 13, 1916. They lived in Lobo Township for two years when Earl was born. They bought a 100-acre farm in Adelaide Township in 1918 from Alex McCarthur, at Lot 20, Con. 2 NER. They attended East Adelaide Church. They had a general farm.

George and Dora had four sons, Earl Ray; Herbert Leslie (d.1991); Leo Arthur; and Joseph George. Earl married Beatrice Evelyn Augustine, and they had two daughters and one son, Fern, Joyce and Lorne. Leo, third son of George and Dora, married Dorothy Beck, and they have five daughters and a son, Donna, Carol, Marilyn, Dora, Connie and Pat. Joseph George married Ann May Hendra. They have three sons and one daughter, Charles, Douglas, Russell and Lorraine.

Herbert married Mearle Leone Watson in 1939. They had three sons, Lloyde, who has a son and daughter, Michael and Judy; Willis, who is unmarried; and Evan, who has a daughter, Josephine. Herbert took over the farm from his mother when his father died, and changed from general farming to beef cattle and a cow/calf operation until his mother died. He had worked with his father drawing gravel for the township roads from gravel hill with a team and sleigh or wagon. After Herbert was married, he worked for Norman Wardell, the Road Superintendent for the township, driving truck, grading, dragging, etc. Herbert also worked under Cliff Branton, Walter Brown, Wilfred Murray, Bill Baxter and Bill Murray. He worked with Cliff Winter and Reg Freer (grader drivers), as well as Orville Hodgson and Wes Smale (backhoe operators). Herbert worked on the road for 53 years. He farmed with his son, Willis, until his death.

WARDELL, Orville and Mabel

Orville (d.1930) and Mabel (Campbell) Wardell (d.1934) lived on a farm where Crathie Hall stands. They had a daughter, Eleanor (1930).

Orville was killed by lightning. Eleanor and her mother moved to Mabel's family home with her parents, John and Nettie Campbell. After Mabel's death, Eleanor lived with her grandparents until she married Kenneth Daniel in 1948 and moved to Lobo Township. They have five children, John, Catherine, Joan, Carol and Jim.

WARDELL, Raymond and Barbara Joan

Raymond Arthur Wardell, son of Walter and Mildred (McArthur) Wardell of East Williams Township, married Barbara Joan Westgate of Strathroy in 1968. They were married at St. John's Anglican Church in Strathroy. In June 1972, they moved to the west half of Lot 23, Con. 2 NER, which is now 3669 Crathie Drive. They have three sons, Bradley Joseph (1969); Wesley Raymond (1972); and Roger Walter (1976).

Ray attended Beechwood Public School in East Williams until Grade 5 and then went to East Williams Central. He attended North Middlesex District High School. As a farmer, he raises Charolais beef cattle and cash crops such as soybeans, corn, wheat, oats and hay. He is a volunteer in minor hockey in Strathroy.

Joan attended Colborne Public School in Strathroy and S.D.C.I. After graduation, she went into the Hamilton General Hospital School of Nursing Program and received her Registered Nurse's Diploma. She worked at Strathroy Middlesex General Hospital part-time for several years. Joan is a volunteer canvasser for Heart and Stroke and Cancer charities.

All three sons went to Adelaide W.G. MacDonald Public School and S.D.C.I., where they all earned O.A.C.'s.

Brad went to McMaster University in Hamilton to earn his Bachelor of Commerce Degree. He now works and resides in Mississauga. He married Lori Talefich of Mississauga on June 6, 1998.

Wes went to Wilfrid Laurier University in Waterloo to earn his Bachelor of Science Degree in Honours Computing and Computer Electronics with distinction. He works for IBM in Toronto. He married Heather Christine MacLeod of Richmond Hill on August 25, 1995. They live in Courtice, Ontario. He is a volunteer in Minor Hockey Olympics.

Roger went to Conestoga College in Kitchener and is now completing his third year in Radio and Television Broadcasting. He is a volunteer public announcer for all of the Strathroy Junior B Rocket home hockey games. He was known as "Rocket Roger."

WESTGATE, George and Gertrude

George Westgate (1868-1936), sixth child of George and Margaret Westgate, who immigrated to Canada from Ireland, was born in Warwick Township. He was known as "George on the Hill." George worked in the United States doing carpentry work for one winter and, while he was in the Cavalry, he earned honour standings. He played the violin at dances and travelled to Oklahoma and Texas to visit his sister and family on their cotton plantation, and made a trip overseas for cattle. George was a carpenter by trade and built cupboards for several neighbours. He was well known for his bee keeping skills. George married Laura May Edgar (d.1907), but she died young.

In 1915, George married Gertrude Newton of Adelaide. They resided in Warwick until 1924, when he moved the family to Lot 10, Con. 4 SER, Adelaide. The 10-acre parcel of land was purchased from Fred Shepherd. George made renovations to the home: he built a kitchen, entry, and veranda, as well as a garage and honey house. He also bored a well. Spruce trees were planted along the west side of the apiary. Honey was marketed in 60-, 10-, and 5-pound pails. The 10- and 5-pound pails were packed in boxes and stored upstairs in the house to keep the honey dry. George shipped the honey to Toronto, and sold honey to stores in Strathroy and the surrounding area. George kept two or three cows, a couple of pigs, and a few chickens. He bought hay from neighbours and stored it in the barn for the winter. The farm had a few apple trees and a small garden, and the remaining acreage was pasture.

Westgate family, L-R, Marjorie, Gertrude, Gloria, George and Harold.

Harold Westgate working in a bee yard.

George owned a 1914 Model T, one of the first in the area. There were three pedals on the floor, clutch, brake and reverse. On many occasions, the magnets had to be warmed on the back of the stove in the house before starting the engine. Raising the rear wheels also seemed to aid in starting the engine. The front window was two pieces of glass, but the other windows were made of mica and had curtains that buttoned to the side of the car.

George and Gertrude had three children, Marjorie (1920); Harold (1921); and Gloria (1922). After Gertrude's death, the farm was given to son, Harold, who later sold it.

Harold went to Napperton School when the road was gravel, and later went to the town school until his father died.

On November 17, 1943, Harold married Helen Eagleson from McGillivray. They lived on Lot 18, Con. 4 SER. Harold farmed and worked with Alton Wright on the snow plough in 1944. The roads were bad, so they had Jim Jordan follow with a truck to help out.

Harold and Helen also kept bees, which gave them honey all summer. They have three children, Leonard, Barbara and Denniss. Leonard married Judy Thompson; Barbara married Ross Prangley; and Denniss married Barbara Dodge.

In 1955, Harold and Helen bought and moved to the Lee farm in Napperton. Harold farmed and cut grain with the binder and threshed with Lew Shephard of Adelaide.

WHITING, David and Eliza

David Whiting (1838-1908), son of Henry and Rachel Whiting, married Eliza Balmer (1839-1906), daughter of John and Isabell Balmer. They raised six children, Rachel (1863-1898); Isabell (1866-1942), who married Chauncey Eastman (see EASTMAN, Benjamin and Mahetable); Thomas (1868-1949); Richard (1871-1950); Mary; and Annie. David farmed the west half of Lot 28, Con. 1 NER.

In 1884, Rachel married Joseph Brown (1859-1941) of Adelaide, son of James and Isabell (Wilkins) Brown. They had five children, David, Clifford, Eva Marie, Richard B., and Elsie Brown. Joseph farmed on the Fourth Line SER, just west of Strathroy, and sold milk to its residents. David married Robena McKellar and they had five children, Ellar, Jack, Joe, Mac and Ken. Clifford married Maude Wardell and they had three children, Norman, Mason and Marie. Eva married Russell Brock and they had two children, Marjorie and Anna. Richard married Ruth Jane Brett and they had eight children, Elsie, Betty, Robert, Dora, Myrtle, Richard, William and Ruth Ann. Elsie married Lorne Gibbs and they had two children, Leone and Douglas.

In 1899, Thomas married Mary Pilkey (1872-1953) and they had three children, Gladys (1905-1992); Ila; and Stella. Thomas farmed on Con. 1 SER, across from his father's farm. Gladys married Bert Knight, son of Alonzo and Minnie (McInroy) Knight of Adelaide. They had no children. Ila married Fred Eagleton and they had two children, Donald and Joyce.

Richard, fourth child of David and Eliza, married Mary Olive Dann (1892-1960). They had no children. Richard took over his father's farm and then retired to Strathroy.

In 1883, Mary, David and Eliza's fifth issue, married George Robotham of Adelaide, son of William and Ann (Beaton) Robotham. They had five children, Annie Eliza, Maud, William, David and Manfred (see ROBOTHAM, George and Margaret). Annie married Charles Giffen and had two children, Helen and Evelyn (see GIFFEN, William and Mary Jane).

In 1908, Annie, youngest of David and Eliza's children, married Gordon Johnston and had a son, Dwight. They lived in the Chatham area.

WILEY, David and Ann

David Wiley (1809-1888) of County Down, Ireland, married Ann Bradley (1808-1879) of County Dublin. They sailed to Canada in 1832 and located near Ingersoll. In 1836, they came to Adelaide, where brother John N. Wiley and sister Lillie Cleland were already settled. In 1837, David and Ann purchased 100 acres, the east half of Lot 2, Con. 1 NER, from Emanuel Mathers, who received his patent from the Crown in 1837. In 1874, this property was sold to William McCarthy and in 1903, upon his death, the land went to his executors, Margaret McCarthy and Samuel Wiley. By 1906, Margaret McCarthy had sold the property to James Comisky.

In 1837, David and Ann bought 100 acres, the east half of Lot 1, Con. 2 NER, from Alexander Glen, Royal Navy, who received this patent and also the patent for Lot 3, Con. 1 SER, and from whom David's brother, John N., and James Murray bought their farms. By 1842, the Wileys sold the land to Robert Dempster (see DEMPSTER, Robert and Elizabeth).

The 1842 census records David Wiley, a resident of Ontario for 10 years, lived on the east half of Lot 2, Con. 1 NER, with his wife and four children. Twenty acres of his farm were improved and he had produced 60 bushels of wheat, 70 of oats, 12 of peas, and 200 lbs. of potatoes. There were 14 hives of bees, 200 units of maple sugar, 14 yards of fulled cloth, 20 yards of wool, and 21 yards of flannel. As well, he owned 18 "neat" cattle, 11 hogs, 9 sheep and one horse. The 1851 census shows 45 acres of the farm cleared and the nine Wiley family members living in a 1-storey log house.

David Wiley was a founding subscriber to the West Adelaide Presbyterian Chapel in 1853. John Jamieson's diary records a church service held at David's new house in September 1853, with Rev. Howden as the minister. On June 2, 1854, John Jamieson wrote that he was at the raising of David Wiley's stable.

David and Ann had nine children, Jane (1837-1909); David A. "Daavy" (1837-1910); Elizabeth "Katie" (1840-1870); Susanna (ca.1843); Letitia (ca.1847); John (ca.1849), a joiner (carpenter); Hugh (ca.1851), a shoemaker; Sarah Ann "Sally" (ca.1855), who married William Ballagh of Teeswater; and William Deas (ca.1858).

Jane married James Wallace (1826-1862) of Lot 2, Con. 1 SER (see WALLACE). They had three children. Margery Ann "Maidie" (1858-1935) married James Wilson (1857-1938) (see WILSON, Samuel and Rebecca). Jean (1859-1941) married Robert Conkey (1855-1942) (see CONKEY, Arthur and Margaret). James (1862-1914) married Annie Conkey (1866-1954) (see CONKEY, Arthur and Margaret).

After her husband's untimely death, Jane married James Marshall (1833-1887) a widower of Warwick Township with two children, John and David. They lived on the Lot 2, Con. 1 SER property until Jane's children were old enough to inherit it and then the family moved to the Marshall farm on Con. 2 NER, Warwick Township. Their six children were born in Adelaide Township. George homesteaded in Manitoba and Saskatchewan. His nephew, Wallace Wilson (see WILSON, Samuel and Rebecca), worked for him for awhile. William (1868-1939), Jane's fifth child, married Ethel Muxlow and lived in Warwick Township. Mary Jane "Sis" (1870-1889) was shot by a deranged neighbour as she was returning with her friends from a Sunday evening church service near her home in Warwick. Susan "Toot" (1874-1944) married Walter Hall (1870-1951) of Warwick Township. They raised two children, Marjorie and Carman (see GROGAN, Lawrence and May). Lawrence (1877-1953) married Edna Cuddy (1884-1973). They raised five children in Warwick Township (see CUDDY, John T. and Esther). Ida (1879-1954), the youngest child of Jane and James, went out west when she was 19, and helped her brother, George, for several years. She married Wilbert Hodgson (1881-1976) of Adelaide (see HODGSON, Thomas and Elizabeth) and raised two children, John and Orville, in Adelaide Township.

Daavy, second child of David and Ann, married Mary McCarthy (1849-1925) (see McCARTHY, Martin and Ann). They farmed the east half of Lot 2, Con. 1 NER, the Wiley homestead. Their son, Samuel (1870-1958), married Annie Hodgson (1880-1971). They moved to the property at Lot 4, Con. 1 NER. Their son, George Christian (1907-1937), helped his father, and they had a reputation of being very "particular" farmers. One neighbour remarked that they never seemed to get any mud on their horses, the harness, or the implements, which mystified the other farmers as they coped with the Adelaide clay. George married Margaret Snelgrove (1908-1973) of Caradoc Township and they lived with George's parents. An unfortunate logging accident took George's life and his pregnant widow was left to care for their three-year-old son, Clarence (1934-1999). Margaret moved back to her parents' farm in Caradoc and daughter, Georgina, was born later that year. Clarence married Betty Lambert and raised two children in Mt. Brydges, Clarence Ronald and Barbara Ann. Georgina married Fred Payne of Caradoc and they raised four children, Brian Frederick, Elizabeth Ann "Beth," Blair Christian and Brenda Leah.

Land records of 1933 show that Samuel Wiley granted part of the east half of Lot 4, Con. 1 NER, to his wife, Annie, and in 1952, she sold 90 acres to Peter De Jong, who built a store on the front of the property. Samuel and Annie moved to Mt. Brydges to be closer to their grandchildren, and they celebrated their 60th wedding anniversary there.

Katie, the third child of David and Ann, married John McCarthy (1843-1870), brother of Daavy's wife, Mary Jane. They farmed the west half of Lot 15, Con. 1 NER, and raised three children, Alice Teresa (1871-1934); Bertha (1878); and John

Sam and Annie Wiley with Wilbert Hodgson, Nov. 1957.

(1880), who may have died an infant. Nephew Lawrence Marshall helped his Aunt Katie with the farm work after John McCarthy's death. When Alice and Bertha were left alone on the farm, William "Billy" McCarthy came to live with them and ran the farm.

After Ann's death, David and the family moved to Strathroy and resided in the Saulsbury Survey. The 1881 census lists: David 70; Sarah Ann 22; William D. 20; John H. 18; and Samuel 16. David, Ann, Daavy, and Mary Jane and an unnamed daughter, are buried in the family plot in Strathroy Cemetery.

WILEY, John and Eleanor

In 1832, John Nathaniel (1807-1892) and Eleanor (Davidson) Wiley (1805-1892), with baby daughter, Jane (1831), left their home in County Down, Ireland. They immigrated to Upper Canada with Eleanor's parents, and her six sisters and three brothers. The Davidson parents and the older boys took land in Hamilton Township by Port Cobourg. After helping the Davidson families settle into their new community and build log cabins, John and his brother-in-law, James Murray (married to Catherine Davidson), earned some wages around this bustling Lake Ontario by helping clear land on the concessions. They heard of better land deals in the newly surveyed township of Adelaide, so the Wiley and Murray families decided to take a risk and travel to this area. Each couple had a small child to consider on such a journey, Jane and Robert Murray (1830), who were also born in Ireland. There are differing stories of this trip west to Middlesex County, so the time and the route are not certain. Eleanor's obituary states that they set out in February 1834 and nearly all of the 220 miles was "accomplished on foot in the depth of winter through what was at the time a howling wilderness." Today, such a journey seems foolhardy, but perhaps their goal was to be ready to plant a spring crop.

The families arrived at a shelter at the south side of the Egremont Road. We know that this was on the 200 acres of Lot 3, Con. 1 SER, owned by Alexander Glen of the Royal Navy, who received his patent in December 1836. John bought 100 acres of the east half of the lot in January 1837, and his brother-in-law bought the west half (see MURRAY, James and Catherine).

The 1842 census shows that John N. Wiley had cleared 24 of the 100 acres. Crops grown that year included 50 bushels of wheat, 40 of oats, 14 of peas, eight of Indian corn, and 300 of potatoes. On the farm were three hives of bees, 200 units of maple sugar were produced, and there were 13 cattle, a horse, and nine hogs. The 1851 census records that there was a 2-storey frame house on the property that served as an inn, and lists the people staying there, one a doctor from Montreal.

In the Feb. 8, 1850, Adelaide Township Council Minutes, John N. Wiley is recommended to be licensed as an innkeeper. The Adelaide Township Council held their June 10, 1850, meeting at Wiley's Inn. No other record of a tavern license is found in later Adelaide Township Council Minutes, so perhaps spirits were no longer sold there. From family stories, early church records, and the 1852-1854 diary of John Jamieson, teacher at S.S. #6, it is noted that Wiley's Inn (West Station Inn) was a local point for neighbourhood activities. The stagecoach stopped at the inn delivering ministers, who would preach a Sunday service there. Rev. William Howden of Scotland, the first Presbyterian minister in Adelaide Township, served the Wiley's Corners Presbyterians, as well as those at the First Presbyterian Chapel and cemetery on the Ireland property, Lot 26, Con. 1 SER. In 1853, John N. and Eleanor gave ½-acre of land, the southeast corner of half of Lot 3, Con. 1 SER, for a West Adelaide Presbyterian Chapel and burying ground.

John and brothers-in-law, James Murray and Robert Cleland, were Charter Members of (Masonic) Beaver Lodge No. 83, organized on July 30, 1857, in Strathroy.

The land records show that Hugh Wiley, brother of John, has provided mortgage money in 1878 so that the west half of the east half of Lot 3, Con. 2 SER, was purchased by Rebecca Wiley Wilson, and then sold to her son, James Wilson. In 1886, Hugh assisted John to sell the east half of the east half of Lot 3, Con. 1 SER, to James Wilson, who lived with his elderly grandfather and took over the farm.

John and Eleanor had 12 children, Jane, mentioned earlier, who married Robert Conkey (see CONKEY, Arthur and Margaret); David (1831-1832), who was buried at Cobourg; John Nelson (1834-1916), the first Wiley child born in Adelaide at the West Station Inn; Rebecca (1836-1891);

Eleanor (1838-1878); Isabella Catherine "Cassie" (1841-1922); David Duncan "D.D." (1843-1912); Elizabeth (1846-1847); Mary Ann (1848-1917); Christina Howden (1849-1849); Nathaniel Davidson (1851-1935); and George (1871).

John Nelson married Margaret Jamieson (1836-1916) of Scotland in 1856. Her father, John Jamieson, was an active citizen of the West Station community (see JAMIESON, John). John and Margaret spent most of their life farming in Adelaide Township on the west half of Lot 3, Con. 1 NER, until their retirement to Watford. John Nelson served the new 1875 West Adelaide Church as treasurer for 36 years. He was a councillor for Adelaide Township and in the Council Minutes of January 21, 1867, he was paid $9.37 for his year's services. From 1869 to 1873, he was Deputy Reeve and during his service as reeve "he dealt fairly with all and made many friends."

John and Margaret had eight sons and one daughter. Two sons died in infancy, the three eldest became farmers, and the three youngest became medical doctors.

The nine children of John and Margaret were Nelson (1857-1906); Sanfield Archibald "Archie" (1858-1937); William Deas (1859-1963), named after the first United Presbyterian minister at West Adelaide; James M. (1860-1862); William James "Jim" (1864-1932); John Irvine (1866-1914); Walter Davidson (1870-1940); Frederick Charles (1872-1937); and Hattie May (1879-1971).

Nelson married Mary E. "Minnie" Crummer (1857-1925) and farmed in Warwick Township. They had no children.

Archie married Emma S. Cuddy (1860-1938) and farmed in Brooke Township. They had one child Mary Leila (died in infancy).

Jim married Isabella McKenzie (1865-1969) and farmed in Warwick Township. They had two children. Anna Winnifred "Freida" (1900-1984) married Robert Alvin McChesney of Adelaide Township (see McCHESNEY, William James and Jane). Nelson "Mac" McKenzie married Margaret Wade and lived most of his married life in Ailsa Craig. Mac and Margaret had two children. Barbara and John Wiley are married and raising their children in Mississauga.

Dr. John Irvine Wiley, sixth child of John and Margaret, attended S.S. #6 Adelaide, Strathroy Collegiate, and Trinity Medical School in Toronto (1888-1889). At one time, he had a practise in Arkona, then he moved to Dresden. He married Jeanette Douglas Whillans (1867-1940) and they were parents to six children. The eldest, Dr. Irvine Wiley, had a practise in Windsor.

Dr. Walter Davidson Wiley attended Strathroy Collegiate and Trinity Medical School in Toronto. He married Carrie Love (1871-ca.1915) in 1900, and moved to Brantford, where he was coroner and Chief of Staff for the Brantford Hospital and medical officer in the local schools. They were parents to two daughters, Mary Love (1902-1904) and Lois Wiley (1905-1978). Lois married Albert Mellish, and they lived in the western part of the U.S., in Washington. In 1918, Dr. Walter Wiley remarried, to Gertrude Best (1875-ca.1946).

Dr. Frederick Charles Wiley attended Strathroy Collegiate and the Detroit College of Medicine. In 1897, he opened a practise in Pinnebog, Michigan, and in 1907, moved his practise to Pigeon, Michigan, and was Chief of Staff at Bad Axe Hospital. He married Janet Louisa Southern (1873-1940) of Sarnia, and they were parents to six children, all born in the U.S. Dr. Fred Wiley is reported to be the first person to own an automobile in Pinnebog. He is still remembered as a caring doctor by some of the older residents of that area.

Hattie May, the only daughter and youngest child of John and Margaret, resided for most of her life in Watford. She married Fred Bayley (1875-1920) and they raised a daughter, Margaret, who married George Cherry. After Fred's death, Hattie married Joe Edwards (1877-ca.1950), who operated a butcher shop in Watford.

Rebecca, fourth child of John and Eleanor, married Samuel Wilson (see WILSON, Samuel and Rebecca). They raised their children on the east half of Lot 3, Con. 3 NER.

Eleanor, John and Eleanor's fifth child, married James Stewart (1820-1904). They lived at Keyser's Corners on the northeast corner of the townline and Currie Road in West Williams Township. All of their nine children are buried with their parents in West Adelaide Cemetery.

Isabella Catherine "Cassie" married John Irvine (1836-1923), the son of her father's eldest sister and her husband, William and Elizabeth (Wiley) Irvine of Belfast, Ireland. Elizabeth died when John was

10 years old, and William immigrated with John and another son, David, to Canada, where census records show they worked for the Wiley relatives. John and Cassie lived on Lot 4, Con. 1 NER. Daughters Louise and Florence were baptized at West Adelaide church. David Irvine and his family also attended West Adelaide church. In March 1866, John Irvine sold 38 acres of Lot 4, Con. 1 NER, to his father-in-law, John Wiley, and the east half of Lot 15, Con. 1 NER, to Terrance Callaghan. At this time, the Irvine families went to Oelwein, Iowa, where they became prosperous farmers and businessmen. Rebecca Wilson travelled by train to visit her sister and the nieces, Louise and Florence, who spent summer holidays with their cousins, Wilfrid and Loftus Wilson.

D.D., seventh child of John and Eleanor, married Mary Cuddy (1846-1888), daughter of James and Violet Cuddy (see CUDDY, James and Violet). D.D. and Mary farmed on the east half of Lot 3, Con. 3 NER. They were very active supporters of West Adelaide Presbyterian Church. Sunday School picnics were held in their woods. In January 1899, D.D. invited the women of the congregation to his home to plan the organization of a Women's Missionary Society at West Adelaide. D.D. and Mary had five children, Minnie Ann (1867-1927), who married David Wilson (see WILSON, Samuel and Rebecca); Violet Ellen (1870-1941), who married Samuel Wilson Jr., brother of David; Emma Elizabeth (1876-1955); Mary Alfaretta "May" (1878-1968), who married Lawrence Grogan of Adelaide Township (see GROGAN, Lawrence and May); and David Walter (1880, died an infant).

Emma Elizabeth, third child of D.D. and Mary, married Dr. James McGillicuddy of Warwick Township. James had a medical practise in Lansing, Michigan. Their sons, Oliver and Robert, also became doctors there. They spent many holidays with their Canadian cousins, Wilfrid and Loftus Wilson.

Mary Ann, ninth child of John and Eleanor, secretly married her cousin, Thomas Davidson, when she was visiting her relatives near Cobourg in August 1871. She returned home by train and finished her teaching contract at the old school S.S. #6, which she had attended as a girl. The next year, she returned as a bride to the Davidson farm at Camborne and she and Thomas raised eight children there.

Christina Howden was probably named after Rev. William Howden, who was Presbyterian minister in the community before the West Adelaide Chapel was built in 1853.

Nathaniel Davidson eventually changed the spelling of the family name to "Wylie." He was secretary of the first meeting called to build the second West Adelaide Church, and was interested in all community affairs. In 1873, he married Susan Elizabeth Riggs. They farmed in West Williams along the Ausable River on the Currie Road, north of Keyser's Corners. For awhile, Nathaniel ran an implement business in Arkona. The family moved to 447 Dundas Street, London, and lived there for six years, when son, Hugh, attended Central Collegiate. In 1904, they homesteaded in Saskatchewan, where they raised their seven children.

George, the youngest child of John and Eleanor, is listed in the 1881 census as being 12 years old and living with 73-year-old John N. and 70-year-old Eleanor Wiley, who adopted him. In 1897, he married Ada Minielly.

WILEY, John and Mary

In 1841, John Wiley (1808-ca.1853) married Mary Martin (1820-1884), daughter of Hiram and Hannah (Hollingshead) Martin. They had five children, Hiram (ca.1842-1870s); Sarah (1843-1925), who married Solomon Eastman (see EASTMAN, Benjamin and Mahetable); Hannah (1845-1922), who married James Petch (see PETCH, Francis and Mary); Joseph (1848-1927); and Isaac (1849-1925).

John immigrated to Canada from Ireland, possibly with two brothers. He may have first settled in the Metcalfe part of Adelaide. By 1841, he was farming on Con. 10 in Caradoc. Sometime in the early 1850s, John was killed while cutting down trees on his farm. John's death brought hard times to the family, and the children went to live with relatives in Adelaide.

Hiram, the eldest child, lived and worked with his grandfather, Hiram Martin, and uncle, William Martin. Hiram was said to be "not kept right in the head." He died as a young man sometime between the 1871 and 1881 census. No death notice or burial records have been found.

Joseph first worked for his uncle, Samuel Martin, and then his uncle, William Martin. After the death of his brother-in-law, Solomon Eastman, he leased the Eastman farm for a few years. In the late 1870s, he borrowed money and went to Burk's Falls, Ontario, to homestead with his brother, Isaac. In 1882, after the soil lost its fertility, he sold his homestead, and homesteaded near Regina, Saskatchewan. He married Mary McMahon (1842-1930) and they had a son, R. Charles Wylie (1886-1975). About 1905, the family moved to Vernon, B.C., where descendants still reside today.

Like his brothers, Isaac was raised by relatives and worked for his uncles and brother-in-law. He spent some time in Burk's Falls homesteading, but came back after a few years. He never married, and lived with his sister, Sarah, and worked with his nephew, Chauncey Eastman. He was described as a quiet man.

WILKINS, Matthew and Sarah

Matthew Wilkins (1790-1855) married Sarah Ritchie in Ireland. He was a blacksmith. Sarah and son, George (1823), who married an Irish wife (1836), were also natives of Ireland. Matthew Jr. (1831) was born in Ireland, and the next child, Violet (1833), was born in Ontario, thus establishing their date of immigration to Canada as 1832. David (1836) married Margaret Jane Wilson, daughter of Hugh and Jane Wilson, also Irish immigrants, in 1858. Catherine (ca.1838) married John Cleland (see CLELAND, Robert and Lillie) in 1860. The youngest daughter was Eliza (ca.1838). These statistics are determined from the 1861 Adelaide census. Matthew is buried at St. Ann's Cemetery in Adelaide Village.

WILKINSON, Joseph and Mary

Joseph Wilkinson (ca.1804-1857) was born in the parish of Marnham, Trent, Nottinghamshire, England, where he owned a small parcel of land and also carried on agricultural pursuits on rented land. He married Mary Chambers (ca.1804-1855) from Muskham, Nottinghamshire, England. They became parents of a large family, the eldest dying in infancy. In 1851, they immigrated to Canada with their eight children. Leaving Liverpool on a sailing vessel, after a five-week voyage, they arrived in New York, then made their way up to Ontario, sailing the Hudson River to Albany. They travelled to Buffalo by railroad, and then took a little steamer to Port Stanley. From there, they travelled to Strathroy by wagon. Joseph bought a small farm and rented 300 acres in Adelaide Township and there they made their home on Lot 25, Con. 2 and 3 SER, when the country was little more than forested wilderness. Joseph and Mary were buried in Fourth Line Cemetery. The children were left to fend for themselves, which they did admirably well.

Reuben (1831-1916), the eldest child, lived with his family upon arrival in Adelaide, but in 1856, Reuben purchased a farm of his own on the Fourth Line. In 1857, he married Margaret Campbell. The 1861 Adelaide census records them as living in a log cabin. Residing with them is George Wilkinson, widower (ca.1795-1875). George, who may have been Joseph's brother, died on Con. 2 SER. On the same lot in 1861, but in a frame 1½-storey house, lived a William (ca.1834), teacher, with Jane and William, his wife and 1½-year-old son. William is the son of John and Elizabeth Willkinson (unknown), so he is not a son of Joseph but must be related. Whether this William is the son of John and Elizabeth is not known for sure, as there were many Williams around. The William on Reuben's farm married Jane Thompson on August 8, 1859. Jane was born in Woodstock. Later records show they may have a married daughter, E.C. Edwards, and a son, John (d.1874), who died in an accident in Texas. On the 1872 census, only Reuben lives on this property.

In 1865, Reuben and family moved to Strathroy, where Reuben lived until his death. He was buried in Strathroy Cemetery. Their children were Mary Jane (ca.1860), who married Frederick Havers; Sarah Elizabeth (ca.1862-1911), who married George Emmons, lived in London and had seven sons; Emilina (1863); Adeline (ca.1863), who married John E. Matthews of Chicago in 1890, and lived in Chicago; Alberta (ca.1867); Amelia (ca.1869); William George (ca.1869-1884); and Alice Ann (ca.1872), who married Edmund Plaxton and lived on the Second Line North (see PLAXTON, William and Susan). Some of the married names of Reuben's daughters were Mrs. Bert Warwick of Port Huron, Mrs. William McCormick, Mrs. C. Worden (or Ward) of Detroit, and Mrs. W. Smith of Toledo.

Ann (ca.1834), the second child of Joseph and Mary, married Jacob Hull (ca.1834-1888). In the 1881 Directory, he lived on Victoria Street in

Strathroy. Jacob left no surviving children at his death. After he died, Ann married James Jarrett in Kerwood in 1898. In later years, she resided in Michigan.

Joseph (1836-1927), third issue of Joseph and Mary, married Harriet Dodd (1844-1920), daughter of George and Robena (Johnston) Dodd, in 1865. Robena's father was a Highland pioneer, Robert Johnston, a Captain in the Militia. They settled on Lot 21, Con. 1 SER, which they bought from John Frank. In the 1878 Middlesex Atlas, they resided on Lot 12 and 13, Con. 1, Metcalfe Township. Joseph and Mary's daughter, Anna Robena Wilkinson (1879-1921), married Arthur B. Woods (1874-1937) of Metcalfe Township, in 1903. Arthur was the son of William and Jane (Carter) Woods. Arthur was a merchant, operating a general store in Kerwood according to the 1910 Directory. They had four children. Robena Jane (1905-1975) married J.W. Redmond in 1938. Arthur "Harry" (1906-1964) married Isabel Susan Mitchell (1915), daughter of Smith Gordon and Agnes Susan (Stevenson) Mitchell, in Kerwood in 1933. They had two children, John "Jack" Arthur (1938-1985) and Richard Stewart. The third child of Anna and Arthur was Anna Beatrice (1908-1953), who married Harry Newton Johnson, son of George and Annie (Newton) Johnson, in Kerwood in 1930. They had two children, Mary Anne (1934), who married Donald Franks and resides in Kingsville; and Freida (1940), who married Allan Lamont and resides in Komoka. Fourth of Anna and Arthur's children was Frederick Paul (1914-1979), who married Eileen Brigham (1918) of Metcalfe Township in 1946 in Kerwood. Fred and Eileen ran a store in Kerwood. They had two children, Joseph William (1949), who is also a storekeeper, and Patricia (1952).

Robert (ca.1838), Joseph and Mary's fourth child, was educated in the parish schools of his native country and the district schools of his new home. He had been reared to a life of hard work. After the death of his father, Robert faced the problem of self-support promptly and cheerfully, though he was still in his teens. He started to learn the carpenter's trade for a year, and then took up farm labour, working in the summer months at $10 per month and board, and during the winter months just for his board. Saving from his scanty earnings and a little money left to him by his grandfather in England, he had accumulated enough money by 1860 to make a payment on 60 acres of bush land in Adelaide Township on Con. 4/5 NER. He settled down to the life of a pioneer, and clearing part of his land, erected a log cabin. Also in 1860, Robert married Eliza Lambert of Lobo Township, daughter of John and Mary (Smith) Lambert of Lobo, in London. Eliza's grandfather, William Smith, worked on the Egremont Road in 1832. With hard work and tireless energy, they succeeded in clearing the farm. They made many improvements and erected good buildings. He bought another 50-acre tract in Adelaide Township. They resided for 10 years on their first farm, then one year on their second farm. In 1872, they settled on Lot 7, Con. 1 SER., west of Warwick village, and sold the Adelaide property. Robert specialized in the raising of Shorthorn and Durham cattle, and Leicester sheep, and was a lover of fine horses. He won many prizes at county and township fairs. For years, Robert was a member of the Dominion of Canada Shorthorn Durham Breeders' Association. He served as president of the Warwick Township Agricultural Society. Robert was strictly temperate in his habits and in his life was never addicted to the use of tobacco or strong drink. They reared their sons to this belief and, like their father, they believed that strong drink was the bane of the country. Robert's wife, Eliza, was a model housewife and won many prizes as a butter maker. They were members of the Warwick Methodist Church. Robert made two trips to Europe, first with a cargo of cattle for Mr. James of Bosanquet. He also visited the place of his birth. In 1898, he took a cargo of cattle to London for Thomas Brandon and visited Edinburgh, Scotland. In 1900, Robert and Eliza retired to Watford and left the management of the farm to their sons. In 1903, they moved to Warwick to reside in closer proximity to their children.

Robert and Eliza Wilkinson had four children. Delilah May married Charles Hawkins of Warwick Township and had four children. William Henry farmed in Plympton Township, married Agnes Montgomery, and had four children. John Charles farmed on the homestead in Warwick Township. He married Anna J. McRorie and they had four children. Edith Butler, the adopted daughter of Robert and Eliza, married William Ladell of Wyoming and they had two sons.

George (ca.1841) and Charles (ca.1843), the fifth and sixth children of Joseph and Mary, lived in Chicago, according to brother Reuben's obituary.

Mary Jane (ca.1846-1850) died of measles at four years of age and is buried in Fourth Line Cemetery.

Henry (1848-1893), eighth child of Joseph and Mary, died in Michigan. His obituary read: *In Detroit, on July 6th 1893, Henry Wilkinson, formerly of Strathroy, in his 45th year, brother of Reuben.*

There are several other Wilkinson families around the area, in Strathroy, Caradoc and Lambton County. A good guess is that old Joseph had brothers John, George and Thomas, possibly also a Robert and William. A George and Thomas Wilkinson from Laughton, East Sussex, came without families to the Americas in 1832 as Petworth settlers.

WILLIAMS, Roger S. and Maria

Roger S. Williams (1797-1880) was born in England and died in Strathroy. He married Maria Ann Dyke (ca.1803-1878), who was born in England and died in Strathroy. Roger was a surgeon and farmer in Adelaide Township and Strathroy. He came to Adelaide in 1837 and settled on Springfield Farm at Lot 1, Con. 4 SER. He later moved to Strathroy, where he continued his medical practice. The Williams family attended the Church of England.

Roger and Maria had 10 children, Roger (ca.1826-1896); Mary (ca.1827); Sarah (ca.1829); John (ca.1832); Maria (1832-1884); Lawson D. (1836-1900); William W. (1837-1870); Deborah (ca.1840); Ann (ca.1842); and Jane (ca.1844).

Mary married Richard Browne, son of Captain Browne.

Sarah married George Howard in 1867. George was a wool merchant in England until he moved to Adelaide Township in 1858, where he farmed. They moved to Watford, and George became a bookkeeper there for Mr. Dodds. Sarah and George had two children, Roger S. Williams and Oswald Wilfred Howard.

Roger, the eldest, married Jennie Tweddy, daughter of Gilbert Tweddy. Roger became an Anglican preacher and they lived in Mitchell, Ontario.

Oswald married Georgiana Gillespie, daughter of John Gillespie. Oswald became a professor in the Montreal Diocesan Theological College.

John, the fourth child of Roger and Maria, retired in Strathroy.

Maria, fifth issue of Roger and Maria, married William Crone (1834-1920), son of William and Jane (Rivers) Crone, in 1852. They had three known children, William L. (d.1908); Maria Ann; and John T. They lived in Warwick Township.

William L. married Ellen Manning (d.1880) of Adelaide Township in 1878. Ellen died, leaving one son, Frederick (1879). William married Caroline Craig (d.1907), daughter of John Craig of Adelaide Township, in 1887. Dr. William L. Crone was a graduate of the Ontario Veterinary College and practiced his profession in Watford and at Ovid, Michigan, for the last 10 years of his life. William and Caroline had two children, Leonard and Alverna Jane. Both resided in Michigan.

Lawson D., sixth child of Roger and Maria, was a farmer. He died unmarried.

Deborah married Charles Sewell, and they resided in Toronto.

Ann and Jane, the youngest of Roger and Maria's children, died unmarried.

WILLISTON, John and Martha

Rev. John Kellogg Williston (1807-1891) was born in the Ottawa District and came to the vicinity of Dresden with his family when he was still a child. Early in life, he was converted to Methodism and fitted himself for the ministry. He was ordained in 1829. Rev. Williston was married three times. In 1829, he married a Miss Dolson of Kent County, who died a few years later. They had one son, David, who predeceased his parents. In 1839, he married Miss Eleanor Morden of London Township, who shared with him all the joys and sorrows of ministerial life.

Rev. Williston was the Wesleyan Methodist minister of Queen's Avenue (London) Methodist Church in 1832, and minister for the Westminster Township circuit in 1835. He shared the St. Thomas circuit with Rev. Vandusen in 1837. He was minister of the Methodist Church in Strathroy in 1853, Wesleyan minister of Napier (formerly the Mt. Brydges circuit) in 1864, and Methodist minister at Moody's Corner north of the tollgate in 1889. In 1885, his name is associated with Lawrence Cleverdon of the Strathroy Methodist Church. In the records of the New Connexion Church in Strathroy, John K.

Williston was recorded as "superannuate" (from *History of Middlesex County*).

Rev. Williston and Eleanor Morden had two children. Upon reaching manhood, John Wesley Williston (d.1870), born in Lambton County, settled in the Canadian West. He joined the California gold rush, contracted typhoid fever, and died. Anna Williston (1838-1898) married Rev. John Neelands (see NEELANDS, John and Anna). Sometime after 1873, Rev. Williston remarried, to Martha Davidson (ca.1818-1889). They lived on the Fourth Line in Adelaide Township. After Martha died, Rev. John went to live with his daughter and son-in-law, who lived in Watford. His funeral was from his late residence on the Fourth Line in Adelaide.

WILSON, Ed and Effie

Ed Wilson (d.1990) and his wife, Effie (d.2000), met when they were both working in the same barbershop in London, Ontario. When they first met, they had no thought of getting married. Effie's job was to wash the floor, and Ed's task was to wax and polish it. There were two little dogs in the shop, a black terrier and one other, and Ed tied towels to the dogs so that they would polish the floor as they ran around. Effie remembers the man who drove the Canada Bread wagon. Because his horse knew where to go, he would just go to sleep. She says that sometimes, while he was napping, they untied his shoelaces for a joke.

When the shop got a new permanent wave machine, Effie learned how to operate it. She then moved to Stratford where she earned a good living doing perms. She also taught other people how to do it and made a commission on every lesson. Ed came to see her while she was there and asked if she thought she might come back. She said that she did not think so because she was making good money. They went out to dinner and over dinner there was more talk like this, until Ed said, "I do love you and want you to marry me." They were engaged at Christmas, although they could not afford an engagement ring, and were married January 28, 1931, by Reverend Crowfoot in the Baptist Church on Adelaide Street in London.

Someone suggested Ed should move to a small town, so he and Effie moved to Kerwood and set up a barbershop in Dorothy Winter's house. The couple bought a little house from Stanley Johnson, located on Front Street. Ed served overseas during the war for a time. When he returned, the house was renovated and made larger, and a barbershop was put in the basement of the house, where Ed continued to cut hair. Ed worked at the Carnation plant for several years and took a night course in engineering at Beal Technical School during the time he was at the Carnation Plant. Later, he worked at Westminster Hospital as an engineer, looking after the boilers, etc., until he retired.

Effie was a nurse at the old Strathroy Hospital for several years. They had five children, Kenneth (1932); Raymond (1933); Frederick (1935); Olive (1937); and Sidney (1940).

Ed and Effie would have been married for 60 years in 1991, but he died short of their anniversary.

Olive, Ed and Effie's fourth child, married Don Smith in 1955. They have lived in the Village of Kerwood for most of their married life. They have five children, Kathie, Terry, Dawn Lee, Denise and Tracy. Olive has been very successful working at Aloette Cosmetics for several years, being a manager for part of that time.

WILSON, Francis and Jane

Francis Wilson (ca 1821-1889) was an early pioneer of Irish descent, who settled in Katesville in the early 1840s. His mother probably accompanied him, for in the 1851 census she is living with Francis and his wife, Catherine, and is a widow. Possibly, his father immigrated with them. Francis had three wives.

First, Francis married Jane (d.1847), who was buried in St. Catherine's Cemetery in Katesville. His second wife, Catherine (d.1852), also died young and is buried in the same cemetery. His third wife was Martha Ellen Cutler (1836-1902), daughter of Jacob Cutler of Westminster Township. Francis had several properties, among them Lots 10 and 11, Con. 3, Metcalfe. Martha Ellen's obituary stated they had lived first on the Eighth Line and then at Lot 15, Con. 2 (Sixth Line). Francis was a bailiff. In 1851, he had two servants.

Francis had nine children, born to the three wives. There is no further information on John (ca.1844). Mary, also born to Jane (d.1847), was buried in St. Catherine's Cemetery in Katesville. Nothing is known of Matthew (ca.1848), born to Catherine. The remainder of Francis' children were born to Martha Ellen. William (ca.1854) went to Enniskillen. Thomas (ca.1857) and Hiram (ca.1859) went to Detroit. Albert E. (ca.1861) married Laney (Helen) Case (d.1898), who died two years after their marriage. Albert married again in 1902, to Florence Munroe from Poplar Hill. Mary E. (ca.1864) married William Lewis. David (1867-1951) married Ida Louise Lambert (1871-1933) and they lived on the family farm at Lot 15, Con. 2, Metcalfe Township, and had four children. George (ca.1869) went to Fort Trumble in the U.S. There is no further information on Annie (ca.1873). Jane (ca.1875) married Luther Harris and lived in Detroit.

A descendant of Richard Wilson, George Wilson, lived at R.R. 2, Kerwood. As one of the potato kings in the area, George won several prizes. He was also a member of Middlesex County Council in the 1940s, and president of the Strathroy Hospital Board in the 1950s and 1960s. Like many others in the Wilson family, George was very involved in the communities in which he lived.

WILSON, Hugh and Jane

Hugh Wilson (1790) and Jane Cuddy (1796) were married in their native Ireland. They made their way to the part of Adelaide Township where Jane's sister, Margaret Cuddy, resided with her husband, Alexander Johnston. Jane and Margaret's brothers, John T. and James Cuddy, were also residing in this area. It is thought that the Wilsons may have lived previously in an earlier settled part of Middlesex County, but research is not complete to establish this. In 1861, Hugh and Jane lived in a building on three acres of Matthew Wilkins' property, the west half of Lot 7, Con. 3 NER. James Cuddy resided on the 100 acres next to them, the east half of Lot 7, Con. 3 NER.

Hugh and Jane's daughter, Margaret Jane, married David Wilkins, son of Matthew and Sarah (Ritchie) Wilkins, also Irish immigrants, in 1858. Perhaps the Wilkins and Cuddy families knew each other in County Tyrone, Ireland (see WILKINS, Matthew and Sarah). Records show that James Cuddy immigrated the same year as Matthew and Sarah Wilkins.

WILSON, Hugh and Mary Ann

Hugh Wilson, the father of Ethel McNab, was a cheese maker at Keyser's Corners. He showed cheese at the World's Fair in Chicago and won a prize. The certificate he received is displayed at the Dairy Museum in Ingersoll.

Hugh married Mary Ann Duffin, and they moved from West Nissouri. They had five children. James became a cheese and butter maker in Forest (Blue Water Creamery). Stanley moved to Detroit. Lawrence became a druggist in Windsor. Jean married Bev Baker, and they owned a newspaper in Palatka, Florida. Ethel married Rupert McNab, and they farmed in Adelaide at Lot 6, Con. 2 NER.

WILSON, Samuel and Rebecca

Samuel Wilson (1826-1866) immigrated to Canada from Northern Ireland with Patrick Murray and Robert Conkey, according to family stories. The three young men made their way to Wiley's Corners on the Egremont Road. The first record of Samuel is his signature beside that of James Murray as witnesses on the marriage certificate of Jane Wiley and Robert Conkey in 1847. The next record is of Samuel as a subscriber in 1853 to the first West

Wilson family, back L-R, David, Robert, David's wife Minnie (Wiley), Samuel's wife Violet (Wiley), Samuel, and Robert's wife Clara (Dale).

Adelaide Presbyterian Chapel. About this time, he married Rebecca Wiley (1836-1891), the daughter of John N. and Eleanor (Davidson) Wiley, on whose farm the church and cemetery were located. (Before the church was built, services had been conducted by itinerant preachers and held at the Wiley home, which was also the stagecoach station and the inn. Perhaps that is where Samuel first met his future wife.)

Samuel's name appeared in the 1854 assessment rolls on 100 acres of land on the south half of Lot 3, Con. 3 NER. He did not yet own this land and was recorded as having no taxable property; he owed three days of road labour. Samuel and Rebecca's first home was a log cabin on the northern part of the property, which older Wilsons remembered. Assessment rolls in 1856 and 1857 show the family fortunes steadily improving. There is now $25 of taxable property, including a cow, horse, wagon and some tools. The next year, Samuel, 30, purchased the farm from Daniel K. Servos, a United Empire Loyalist, who received his patent from the Crown in 1836 for his loyalty to the King at the time of the American Revolution.

Samuel and Rebecca had six children, William J. (1856-1876); James (1857-1938); Ellen Jane (1858-1924); Robert (1861-1927); David (1864-1944); and Samuel E. (1866-1937), who was born the year his father died. Samuel Sr. was buried in the pioneer cemetery at Wiley's Corners. When the new cemetery at the second West Adelaide Presbyterian Church opened in 1882, Rebecca bought 16 plots and, after having a Wilson tombstone erected, had Samuel's body moved there.

Despite her husband's early death, a young baby, and five other children to raise alone, Rebecca kept the family together. With the help of nearby relatives, the farm prospered, and was valued at $740 in 1869.

Ten years after his father's death, eldest son William J. died suddenly at age 20 from pneumonia contracted while drawing gravel for the new house on the southern part of the property. The original stone foundation is in perfect condition today, after more than 100 years. A letter of condolence dated February 16, 1876, was sent to Rebecca from the Orange Lodge, of which William was a member.

James, second eldest, had the nickname of "Reddy Fox" because of his red hair. He was nine at the time of his father's death and, when William died suddenly, he had the responsibility of helping his younger brother run the farm. When ill health overtook his grandfather, John N. Wiley, James moved to his farm at Lot 3, Con. 1 SER, on the Egremont Road (see WILEY, John and Eleanor).

James and Margery "Maidie" Wallace married, and looked after the Wiley grandparents. Grandmother Eleanor died in 1885 and, the next year, John N. deeded the 100 acres to grandson James, who carried on the farm work and cared for his grandfather until his death in 1892. James supported the new West Adelaide Presbyterian Church and held the office of treasurer for some years. He was a member of the Adelaide Township Council and patron of the 1878 Historical Atlas of Middlesex County, which he purchased for $12. Eventually, James and Maidie acquired more land. Maidie inherited 50 acres, the west half of Lot 2, Con. 1 SER, from the James Wallace estate. The couple bought the farm across the road, the east half of Lot 3, Con. 1 NER, from the D.D. Wiley estate. A garden was planted on the west 50 acres and a pony and cart were used to go back and forth. The uncertainty of the harvest was reported by their son, Samuel, who told of harvesting 55 bags of potatoes one year and two bags the next off the same land. James and Maidie had five children.

Samuel (1883-1963), the eldest child of James and Maidie, never married. He stayed with his parents and worked on the farm until their deaths. Like so many men of that era, he couldn't cook for himself or manage a house, so he worked as a hired hand for area farmers and rented the farm to his brother, Jack, until it was sold to Don Sullivan in 1950. Sam was quiet like many other Wilsons, except on matters of family trees (anyone's family), Presbyterians and Liberals. He was known as a "walker" and he would often walk to the Wisbeach store in the evening to visit with other farmers, or walk long distances to visit relatives.

John David "Jack" (1886-1955), the second of James and Maidie's children, had a scholastic bent. After primary school at S.S. #6, where he later became the teacher, he attended high school in Strathroy, then Model School for teacher training. He taught the Fourth class as a student teacher and met his future wife, Estelle Thomson of Strathroy, in his class. Later, he attended the University of

Toronto with the intention of becoming a mining engineer. During his second year, while on job training near Cobalt and Sudbury, he became ill with typhoid fever. This left him in a weakened condition and he was unable to finish his education, so he came home to recuperate. In 1914, he went to Northern Alberta and obtained a piece of land near Stettler, which he homesteaded. He cleared enough land to build a small house and worked at different jobs to earn a living. He worked for International Harvester for a time, qualified as a Justice of the Peace, and worked as a chef at a lumber camp and the railway, which paid a good wage of $3 a day.

He wrote letters home and to his girl friend, Estelle, who was beginning her teaching career, describing the cold of western winters. He writes of kicking the carcass of venison in the shed and how it "rang like a bell." Jack returned home and he and Estelle were married in April 1916. They settled on the east half of Lot 3, Con. 1 NER, where they remained for the rest of their lives. Their children remember tax notices coming in the mail from Alberta, but in those Depression years, there never seemed to be enough money left over, so the Alberta homestead was returned to the government.

Jack and Estelle had four children, Harold William, Marie, Donelda and Kenneth John.

Harold William remained on the home farm. He married Glenys Robertson and her three children, Ian, Dennis and David Robertson, were raised by

Mrs. James (Margery) Wilson and grandson, Harold Wilson.

them. David helped Harold with the farm work and a laying hen operation. In 1969, he bought the 90-acre north half of Lot 3, Con. 1 NER, and the south-west part of Lot 3, Con. 2 NER, from Wilfrid and Mildred Wilson, who retired to Strathroy. David married Janice Cox and they both raised her children. Tracey is married to James Jansen of Adelaide (see JANSEN, Alfons and Lucia). Jason and his wife, Paulina (Van Rensen), live in the house on the Harold Wilson farm. David raises cattle and grows cash crops, mostly grain, corn and beans. He and his wife, Leota (Giffen), are serious antique collectors. They have made many improvements to the old Cleland/Wilson property.

Marie, second child of Jack and Estelle, attended S.S. #6 Adelaide, S.D.C.I., and then trained at Strathroy Hospital. She completed courses for an Ontario Registered Nurse certificate. She married Douglas Brock, brother of Donelda's husband, and they lived in Arkona, where they raised four children, Pauline, Linda, Allan and Wilson.

Donelda married Ray Brock (see, BROCK, Ray and Donelda) and they farmed in Adelaide on the west half of Lot 5, Con. 1 SER. They have two children, Richard and Nancy.

Kenneth John attended S.S. #6, S.D.C.I., London Teachers' College, and the University of Western Ontario. He taught at Keyser School, S.S. #1 and #2, and in London. Then he graduated from Knox College and was ordained as a Presbyterian minister serving congregations in Kirkland Lake and Guelph. He is semi-retired in Hamilton and he and his wife, Donna (Truscott), a former Deaconess with the Presbyterian Church, continue to work in a church community in Hamilton. His eldest son, John, and his wife, Charlene, are Presbyterian ministers in Ottawa. They have three children. The younger son, David, works in finance in Toronto and his wife, Rowena, is a pharmacist.

Ethel May, third child of James and Maidie, attended S.S. #6. She was organist for awhile at West Adelaide Presbyterian Church. In 1910, she married Berton Herrington, and their first home was at Keyser's Corners, the east half of Lot 6, Con. 5 NER. There they raised Jean, Madge, Helen, Wilson, Neva and Mary. The older children attended S.S. # 1 and 2, Adelaide. In 1926, the family moved to Flint, Michigan, where Berton found employment in the automobile industry. Betty,

Robert and James were born in Michigan. Close ties remained with their Canadian relatives.

Rebecca Jane, fourth issue of James and Maidie, attended S.S. #6 and completed first form there. She started high school in Strathroy, but had to quit to help on the farm. She returned later and attended Normal School in Hamilton. She taught at Sylvan and Crathie, where she met her future husband, Milton Harris (see HARRIS, Samuel).

Wallace (d.1918), fifth of James and Maidie's children, went to Saskatchewan in 1916 to work with his half-uncle, George Marshall. Wallace and Neva Cone were married in March 1918 and lived in Biggar, Saskatchewan, where they were working to rent or buy a place of their own. He was called into the army but was still working in the harvest. He and his bride died within a day of each other from the dreadful epidemic of Spanish flu. James Wilson went west in the spring of 1919 and brought back the bodies to their final resting place in West Adelaide Cemetery.

Ellen Jane was the only daughter born to Samuel and Rebecca Wilson. She married William McChesney Jr. (1853-1929) and they farmed on the east half of Lot 2, Con. 2 NER, before their retirement to Strathroy. They were remembered as a favourite aunt and uncle. Ellen left her nieces money because she felt the boys always got the land.

Robert, fourth child of Samuel and Rebecca, farmed the north side of the home farm. He was a teacher, probably at S.S. #9, and in this way he supplemented the farm income. He married Florence Crummer (d.1890), who lived beside the school. She is buried in the Wilson plot in West Adelaide Cemetery. In 1893, he married neighbour Clara Dale, daughter of Henry and Anna Dale (see DALE). While on the farm they had two daughters, Ruby (1896-1954) and Pearle (1898-1976). Robert, Clara, and the girls moved to Strathroy in 1910, where they operated Wilson's Bookstore in half of the present Foodland on Front Street. A third daughter, Margaret (1913-1994), was born. She helped in the bookstore until it was sold. Then Clara bought the Dampier home on Metcalfe Street (now Hornyak's Dentistry) and operated it as Wilson's Tourist Home. Many times, the nieces and nephews attending high school in Strathroy were welcomed when they were stranded in town during snow storms. Ruby was a teacher in Strathroy and Windsor. Pearle was a banker. She married Norman Rivers and they raised five sons, Wilson, Clare, Joe, Raymond and Robert. Margaret married John "Jack" Oakes (1915-1970) and they made their home in Strathroy, raising five children, Roberta (Giffen); John William Samuel; Nancy (Larocque); Norma (Robertson); and Debbie (Pereira). Jack and Margaret operated a gift store in Strathroy after his retirement. They were active volunteers in the community and Margaret was involved in the work of the I.O.D.E.

David, fifth child of Samuel and Rebecca, was two years old when his father died and Samuel Jr. was born. His schooling was at S.S. #9. He was an avid newspaper reader and a final perusal at midnight was his ritual before bedtime. His mother, Rebecca, was fortunate to have financial assistance from her slightly eccentric but mysteriously wealthy bachelor uncle, Hugh Wiley. Records show that "Uncle Hugh" assisted her sons, James and David, to become established on farms of their own. In 1888, Rebecca purchased the Robert and Lillie (Wiley) Cleland farm on the north half of Lot 3, Con. 1 NER, and southwest part of Lot 3, Con. 2 NER, for $3,600 plus interest. David went to live on this farm and "bached" for himself until his marriage six years later to Minnie Ann Wiley (1867-1927). They had one child, Wilfrid Stanley (1896-1975). David raised Hereford cattle and Durham milk cows. A cooling house for the milk, cream and butter was built over the spring on the east creek running by the barn. Mixed crops were the standard hay, wheat, oats, barley and sorghum. In the 1899 "Watford-Guide Advocate," it was reported that David Wilson had purchased "orchard fruit trees." In 1902, the farming operation was expanded by the purchase from Bert Dempster of 100 acres, the east half of Lot 1, Con. 3 NER. David made several train trips to Winnipeg to buy cattle. One year, he and his sister-in-law, Violet Wilson, made a train journey west to Norquay, Saskatchewan, to visit first cousin Lillie Wylie Abray, daughter of Rebecca's youngest brother, Nathaniel Wylie, who homesteaded there from his farm in West Williams Township. Installation of the telephone in 1913 and the frugal purchase of a Ford Model-T in 1919 (standard black with canvas side curtains) were progressive steps to easier neighbourhood access from the isolated location of the farm. David was Clerk of Session of West Adelaide Presbyterian Church from 1928 to 1942.

Wilfrid Stanley was named after the Prime Minister, Sir Wilfrid Laurier. Wilfrid and his first cousin, Loftus Wiley Wilson, six months younger, were close companions. They shared many good times together. They attended S.S. #9 and went on to Arkona Continuation School, where they stayed together at Mrs. Riggs' boarding house, a Cleland cousin (see CLELAND, Robert and Lillie). Visits to the Rock Glen dam with their classmates were frequent after-school recreation, as Wilfrid's photo album shows. The schooling here lasted only until 1910, so his desire to become a doctor was thwarted as he had to run the farm during his father's illness. For a few years, he played first baseman on the Arkona Baseball Team, using his height to his advantage. In June 1918, the two cousins were conscripted to army training at London and Sylvan. Wilfrid always claimed that the celluloid lining in the top of his army hat irritated his head, causing early baldness. An eight-year courtship with Mildred McInroy (1898-1990) began from their meeting at West Adelaide Church, where she had played the organ since age 13 (see McINROY, Alexander "Sandy" and Ann Jane). They were married in a garden ceremony at the McInroy home and, as many couples did in 1923, they took a honeymoon train trip to Toronto, Niagara Falls, and Cobourg to visit the Wiley/Davidson cousins and the McInroy cousins at Belleville. They lived and worked on the family farm with Wilfrid's parents. Wilfrid continued the same type of farming operation as his father, but made some innovations. For a few years, he sold a special variety of strawberry on the London market. Additional farm income came from his apiary. Honey, butter, eggs, and Mildred's turkeys were also sold at the market. Because of the isolated position of the farm, electricity was not installed until 1946, as the Wilsons had to build their own hydro line from ½-mile in from the Second Line North, across the Conkey farm. A pressure system was installed the next year to supply water to the house and barn and, in the fall, a cement silo was built. When first married, Mildred taught piano lessons in their home as Norma (Ayre) McNab and Marie and Donelda (Wilson) Brock recall. She continued to play the organ and served as choir leader at West Adelaide until her retirement in 1986. Wilfrid and Mildred were dedicated members of the church and community. Mildred was a hard working member of the W.M.S. and Ladies Aid church groups, and was the treasurer for many years. In later years, she belonged to the Keyser Women's Institute. Wilfrid acted as Sunday School Superintendent for years, and he was ordained as elder in 1942 and appointed Clerk of Session in 1951, until he moved to Strathroy in 1969. He sang in the choir for many years, providing a needed bass voice. He began his term as Chairman of the Cemetery Board in 1944. Wilfrid was a popular member of the community debating teams in his youth, and in later years he was often the chairman for programs, concerts and garden parties, and he served as the main speaker on many occasions. When a veranda was built on the front of the house in the early 1930s, the Wilson home was a location for community garden parties and picnics. Wilfrid's interest in politics was maintained by his role in the Liberal Association and, for a time, he was Official Agent for his friend Robert McCubbin, a Member of Parliament from 1940 to 1959. Wilfrid was elected to the Adelaide Township Council in January 1940, reeve in 1942 and he was appointed to the clerkship in 1944, holding this position for 27 years. The last Adelaide Council minutes he signed were on February 16, 1967. All of the records he kept for the township can now be read in the Lawson Library at the University of Western Ontario. In the office at his home, he spent many pleasurable hours typing letters, compiling records, "figuring" the taxes on an adding machine, and producing the annual voters' lists on an obstinate Gestetner—all before the computer age, which he would have enjoyed!

Retirement from the farm became a necessary decision as arthritis in his legs was compounded by a broken leg incurred from a fall from a ladder while trimming the evergreen windbreak. With no sons to carry on the family farm, Wilfrid hoped that David Robertson, stepson of Harold Wilson, would buy it, and this became fact in July 1969. Wilfrid had spotted the property at 299 Carrie Street and "took a notion for it" as a retirement home. While he was recuperating in Strathroy Hospital, Mildred attended to business and organized the laborious move to town. During his new leisure time, Wilfrid began to research the beginnings of the first West Adelaide Presbyterian Church in preparation for the 1975 centennial. Illness hindered his work, but the family continued it. Wilfrid and Mildred won recognition and an award from the Presbyterian Church in Canada for their history research. The Wilsons enjoyed their Fiftieth Wedding celebration in June 1973 with family and friends at Strathmere Lodge, where Wilfrid was a resident. Mildred celebrated her ninetieth birthday in 1988 at an open house at West Adelaide church.

Wilfrid and Mildred had two daughters, Anna Jean and Marjorie Elizabeth.

Anna Jean (Sullivan) (McCoskery) received her education at S.S. #9 Adelaide from teacher May Watson Dodge. Anna attended the Strathroy Collegiate Institute, London Normal School, University of Western Ontario, University of the Americas, Mexico City, and the University of Toronto. She began her teaching career in the one-room school at S.S. #8 Adelaide and then at Colborne Street School in Strathroy. Later, she took a teaching position in Etobicoke and then with Peel Board of Education, where she was a resource librarian in a French Immersion School. One summer, she taught teaching methods to high school teachers in Nigeria through the auspices of the Canadian Teachers' Federation. Since her retirement and move to the family home in Strathroy, she spent a year in the Czech Republic teaching English in a high school. She is an active member of Soroptimist International and the Ontario Genealogical Society, and she is involved in Presbyterian Church in Canada committees. She attends the West Adelaide Presbyterian Church as she did as a child.

Marjorie Elizabeth (Whytock) attended S.S. #6, S.S. #9 and S.S. #4 at the time when the smaller schools were alternating their closings. She went to Strathroy Collegiate Institute and Beal Technical School. Marjorie took vocal lessons, studied music theory, and earned credits from the Toronto Conservatory of Music. While at Beal, she performed in some of their musicals, which gave her confidence to try out for a part in "Guys and Dolls" at the Grand Theatre. For many years, she was a member of the Earl Terry Singers, and she was a contract soloist for the Christian Science Church for some time. She worked at London Life until a son, Todd Rae, was born during her marriage to Rae Whytock. Todd married Jennifer McCallum in 1993 and they live in London raising two sons, Connor Michael and Tiernan Wilson. Marjorie lives in London and she has recently retired from 3M.

Samuel E., the sixth and youngest child of Samuel and Rebecca, married Violet E. Wiley (1870-1941) in 1892. His mother had died the year before and Samuel and his brother, Robert, divided the land. Samuel farmed the south part and Robert the north.

Loftus Wiley (1896-1988) was the only child born to Samuel E. and Violet. He attended S.S. #9 Adelaide and Arkona Continuation School with his cousin, Wilfrid. After his army discharge, Loftus returned home to continue farming with his father.

Loftus was quite an actor and orator at the local dances and garden parties in his early years, extending from Arkona to Crathie and the Strathroy area. He often said he was lucky to have a horse that knew its way home. In 1919, he married Margaret May Donaldson (d.1980), eldest daughter of George and Jean Donaldson. They were married in the Arkona Baptist Parsonage. The newlyweds made a honeymoon trip by train to Cobourg and Rice Lake to visit the Davidson relatives.

At this time, Loftus's parents moved to a new home on Carrie Street in Strathroy. His father died of a heart attack after a short illness at the age of 70, and his mother died several years later. They are buried in West Adelaide Cemetery.

For many years, Loftus served as an elder of West Adelaide Presbyterian Church. Margaret was active in the Women's Missionary Society. Loftus continued to farm the family property, raising Registered Shorthorn cattle. Les Cline, an Englishman, was the hired help for many years. Loftus and Wilfrid often worked together, especially during haying and grain harvest.

Loftus and Margaret raised a nephew, Loftus Rodger Benedict, who was the youngest son of Margaret's sister and her husband, Alma and Ellwood Benedict. When his parents left the Adelaide farm in 1944 and moved to Strathroy, Rodger stayed with his aunt and uncle, as he preferred to be on the farm with Loftus and the animals.

Rodger married Donalda Jean Emmons in 1964 (see EMMONS, George and Emma). They helped to operate the Wilson homestead, raising laying hens and a yard full of cattle. Some changes were made with the building of a hen house, pole barns, and machinery sheds. Rodger and Donalda raised four children here, the eldest being Lorne Allan Benedict (1969). He always told his parents that some day they would be moving, as he was always going to stay on the farm. Lorne completed a farm mechanics course and, in March 1994, he bought his parents' farm. They made plans to build a new home on the Lorne Emmons farm and partially retire.

In 1996, Lorne Benedict married Tracy Lee Miller in the Melbourne United Church. Tracy is employed full-time at a rehabilitation centre in London.

Changes continue to be made on the Wilson homestead. While replacing the barn foundation in the spring of 1997, Jeff Maes, a local contractor, was removing the barn bridge and found a brick with an imprint of the word "KEYSER" very crudely incised in it. It is believed that the brick was made at the Keyser brickyard at the turn of the century. There is a similarly incised brick in Earl McNab's barn foundation, presumably also produced at the Keyser brickyard. Rodger quickly put the brick into safekeeping.

Lorne and Tracy have a daughter, Monique Elizabeth (1999). She represents the sixth generation to enjoy living on the Wilson farm.

Sometime after Samuel's death, Rebecca (Wiley) Wilson informally adopted a young girl named Lillie Ann Mahetable Ireland, who was about 10 years younger than her youngest child. Lillie's sisters, Effie and Irene, lived in the neighbourhood with the Cummings family, who operated a blacksmith shop. Lillie married John C. MacDonald of East Williams in 1894, when she was 18 years old. Their first child, Christine Minnie, died in infancy, and Lillie died giving birth to their second child, Lillie Marjorie Elizabeth (1907). Lillie Marjorie became a teacher and taught at Keyser for a year. She lives in London.

WOOD, William and Mary

Sam Carr left Yorkshire, England, in 1849 and came to York County near Toronto, Ontario. In 1851, his family came to Canada. His eldest daughter, Mary (1829), married William Wood (1822) in England on May 12, 1851. Mary and William spent eight weeks coming across the Atlantic on a sailing vessel, accompanied by her mother, Jane (Parks) Carr, and her siblings. Mary's sister married William Jefferson of Dixie.

William and Mary settled on Lot 28, Con. 2 NER, which he purchased from Ed Park, who resided on the north part of Lot 29. William and Mary had eight children, Sarah May (1855-1866); Martha Jane (1858-1875); Samuel Edward (1860-1921); Betsy Ann (1862-1910); Thomas Park (1864-1928); Hannah (1867-1934); John William (1870-1934); and Mary Anne (1872, died at birth).

When Samuel, eldest son of William and Mary, married Alice Linton, Lot 28 was divided into two parcels. Samuel had the south 50 acres and John the north 50. Samuel sold his farm to Mr. Ward and moved to the corner of Con. 10, Lobo, and Highway 22. Samuel and Alice had four daughters and two sons, Gertie, Ella, Lena, Laura, Edgar and Cecil. Gertie married Hiram Cutler, Ella married Clifford Zavitz, Lena married George Oliver, and Laura never married. When Edgar and Cecil married, Edgar moved to the Parson farm in Adelaide Township, Lot 3 at Highway 22. He and his wife had one son, Donald, who is in Ottawa. Cecil bought a farm in Lobo Township on Komoka Road at the corner of Con. 7. He and his wife had two children, Carlyle and Marjory. Carlyle and his son, Allan, are still on the farm. Marjory married Doug May, had one daughter, and lives in Poplar Hill.

Betsy Ann, fourth child of William and Mary, married Arthur Bener and moved to Michigan. They had one son.

Thomas Park, William and Mary's fifth child, married Della Thorpe of Arkona, and they moved to Brown City, Michigan. Thomas and Della had four daughters and one son, Wilfred.

Hannah, sixth issue of William and Mary, married John Luchenbill of Vernon, Michigan. They had two sons, George and Francis.

John farmed on the north 50 acres of Lot 28, Con. 2 NER, and married Sarah Adelaine Hansford on March 26, 1903. They had two children, Mary Elizabeth (1904-1996) and William Hansford (1911). Mary married Mast Thomas on November 20, 1926, and they had two children, Vera and Dorothy. Vera married Neil McLean and Dorothy married Keith Wilton. William Hansford married Anna Belle Galbraith (1918-1999) on March 6, 1943. They have two sons and one daughter, John William, Donald Keith and Nancy Dianne. John William married Maureen Reeve on May 27, 1967, and lives in Peterborough. They have three sons and one daughter. Donald Keith married Linda Roulston on April 9, 1977, and they live in Brampton. They have one son and two daughters. Nancy Dianne married Graham Auger on December 19, 1970, and they live in Tailand, England. They have one son and one daughter.

WOODS

The Woods family can be traced back to John Woods of Roscrae, Ireland, born about the middle of the 18th century. He married Mary Robinson, who was born near Shinrone, Ireland. Both are believed to descend from English settlers who were brought by Cromwell to displace the native Irish settlers in the mid-1650s. John's grandson, William (1837-1907), came with his mother, Elizabeth Searson, brother Thomas and sister Floranna, to Toronto on May 28, 1850. While there, William, in addition to learning the trade of soap and candle making, was a fireman on the Grand Trunk Railway. In October 1858, the family moved to Brooke Township, Warwick County, where they purchased three farms from the Hon. George William Allan.

William was an Anglican, a Conservative, a farmer and a drover. He was a thrifty businessman, with an abundance of energy and a kindly nature. About 1860, William returned to Toronto and came back to Brooke Township with his new wife, Jane Carter (1837-1905), who also had been born near Roscrae in County Queens, Ireland. William and Jane had seven children, Gilbert (1865-1943); John Thomas (1868-1928); William Hy (1871-1937); Arthur B. (1873-1937); Elizabeth (ca.1897-1928); Thomas Alexander (1875-1971); and Hiram (1878-1893). John Thomas became a dentist and William Hy was a physician who died in Mt. Brydges.

Arthur married Anna Robena Wilkinson (d.1921), daughter of Joseph and Harriet (Dodd) Wilkinson of Metcalfe, in December 1903. In 1907, he became the eleventh proprietor of a general store, a business originally established in 1864 by John I. McKenzie. John had once owned all of the land upon which Kerwood was to be founded. The store was taken over by R. Galbraith in 1865 and he continued to operate it until 1875. There were a succession of owners of this store for the next 30 years as follows: 1875—J. Irving; 1876—H. Ford and J. Green; 1877—H. Nelles; 1879—W. Kellett; 1901—J. Brunt; 1902—J. Denning; 1904—C. Johnson; 1905—A. Woods; 1906—A. Killpatrick; 1907—A. Woods.

Arthur and Anna lived above the store for several years before purchasing a house on Havelock Street, where they raised their four children. After Arthur's death, the house was sold to Arthur's brother-in-law, Robert Wilkinson. The house was torn down in 1994 and replaced by a new one built by Richard and Joyce Copp. Arthur and Anna were active members of St. Paul's Anglican Church in Kerwood, and Anna was an avid supporter of the Women's Institute. In 1920, Anna and her mother were too ill to care for the family alone. Ella D. McMahon, Anna's niece, came to live with and assist the family. Anna's mother died in 1920, followed the year after by Anna. Ella stayed on to help the remaining family. She was a much-accomplished dressmaker and caregiver, and admired throughout the Kerwood community.

To Arthur and Anna were born four children, Robena "Ruby" Jane (1905-1975), who trained as a nurse in 1928, and married J.W. Redmond of Metcalfe; Arthur "Harry" Woods (1906-1964), who married Isabel Susan Mitchell (1915) of Adelaide, daughter of Smith Gordon and Agnes Susan (Stevenson) Mitchell and founded H. Woods Transport in London (see MITCHELL, John Sr. and Barbara); Anna Beatrice (1908-1953), who married Harry Newton Johnson of Metcalfe; and Fredrick "Fred" Paul (1914-1979). These children were all raised in the house on Havelock Street, Kerwood, and all graduated from Strathroy District Collegiate Institute.

Having learned to drive at an early age, Fred always had a carload of fellow students on the way to Strathroy for high school. Upon finishing high school, Fred became the proprietor of Woods General Store in 1937 at the age of 23 years, after his father's death. He married Eileen Brigham, daughter of William "Bill" and Annie (Kells) Brigham of Metcalfe, in 1946. In 1949, the original store, which was located immediately at the corner of Cockburn and Grace Streets, was replaced by the current red brick building. It was built with living quarters above. Fred and Eileen had two children, Joseph "Joe" William (1949) and Patricia Ann (1952). Fred was an active member of St. Paul's Church in Kerwood and the Strathroy Lions Club.

Joe became Manager of Woods' Store upon his father's death. Joe married Susanne Taylor Holden in 1986, and they took up residence in Strathroy. Eileen and Joe continued to work in the store.

Patricia and her husband, Brian Peters, have resided in Victoria, B.C., since their marriage in 1986.

WOOLLEY, Warren and Naomi

The ancestors of Warren Archibald Woolley (1863-1918), who farmed on about 60 acres at Lot 21, Con. 2 SER, have been traced back to Edward (1568-1628) and Margaret (Fritchley) Woolley, who lived in the village of Crich, Derby, England. Their son, Emmanuel (ca.1628), moved to Monmouth County, New Jersey, before 1667. He and his wife, Elizabeth, raised a family of nine children, one of whom was John Woolley (1659-1743).

John married Mercy Potter of Rhode Island and they resided near Poplar, New Jersey, where they had a family of 11 children. As well as being a successful farmer, John "ran a whaling fleet with an Indian crew and became well-to-do." Their son, Benjamin (1691-1773), married Esther Stout in New Jersey. Benjamin and Esther raised two sons and five daughters. Their eldest son, Daniel (1716-1822), who married Patience Throckmorton at Shrewsbury, New Jersey, died at Dunboyne, Malahide Township, Elgin County, after having ridden horseback all the way from Monmouth Township to visit his son, Joseph (1759-1830).

Joseph was born in New Jersey, and married twice there. Both wives were called Mary, but their surnames are unknown. Three children were born to the first Mary and six to the second. From the second marriage, a son, John Throckmorton (1784), was born in Monmouth County. With his parents and siblings, John moved to Malahide Township sometime before 1814, and settled on Lot 14 along Catfish Creek. Joseph died in Malahide Township.

John T. and his wife, Mary, had a family of 11 children, six sons and five daughters. The eldest son, Henry (1811-1876), married Elizabeth Ann Brooks in 1836 in Malahide Township, and they also had a family of six sons and five daughters, Almrya J. (1837-1877); Martha Emily (1838-1873); John "Wesley" (1840-1905); William H. (1843-1879); Hiram C. (1845-1900); Mary Olive (1850-1929); Lewis Benjamin (1852- 1911); Srena (1854); Srienda R. (1856-1941); Joseph Milton (1860-1919); and Warren Archibald (1863-1918).

Mary Olive married William Alfred Demaray (1847-1931) of North Dorchester Township, and they raised three children, Hiram Orlando (1871-1952); George William (1876-1939); and Olive Bertha (1881-1962). Mary Olive and William Alfred had a very large and successful dairy operation near Springfield, Elgin County (see DEMARAY).

Warren Archibald, the youngest child of Henry and Eliza, married Naomi Newell (1864-1907) of Adelaide Township on March 24, 1885, at Bethel Methodist Church (see NEWELL, Alexander and Lorena). They farmed on Lot 21, Con. 2 SER. To Warren and Naomi were born two children, Gertrude (1887-1938) and Ross Earl (1888-1952). For many years, Gertrude was the telephone operator at Springfield, Ontario, where she died. After his first wife's death, Warren married Naomi's cousin, Elizabeth Newell of Warwick Township. In 1913, Warren sold the family farm and moved to Strathroy.

Ross Earl married Susan Mildred Lewis (1892-1970) of Adelaide Township in 1917, and moved to Riverdale Farm, on Lot 19, Con. 1, Metcalfe Township (see LEWIS, John and Elizabeth). Ross and Mildred had two sons, Earl Wesley (1915-1981) and John "Jack" (1919). Earl married Margaret Lothian Innes. They had no children. Jack married Edith Marguerite Earley and they started farming on Lot 19, Con. 4 SER, and became major potato producers for about 50 years. Jack and Marguerite had three children, Ross Willard; John Wesley, who died at the age of four; and Nancy Diane, who married

John Woolley in front of family barn at Lot 19, Con. 4 SER.

Frank Lane and lives in Seaforth, Ontario. Ross married Barbara Long and they have two children, Michelle and John Ross. Ross lives on part of the original farm on the Fourth Line South. He owns and operates Woolley Trucking.

WRIGHT, Edwin and Anna Maria

James Wright (ca.1789) appears to be the first immigrant from Ireland to settle in the area of Upper Canada. An assessor in London Township, James and his wife, Feby, had six children, Abigail (ca.1821); Mary (ca.1836); Edwin (ca.1837); Joseph (ca.1838); Justus (ca.1840); and Milly (ca.1858).

Of their children, Edwin married Anna Maria Bolton (1844) and resided in Adelaide Township in 1876. Edwin belonged to the Anglican Church but appears to have joined the Methodist Church before 1910.

Edwin and Anna Maria had five children. Ada (1865) married Alexander Forbes and moved to Detroit. Frederick W. (1866) married Lena North in January of 1900. Lena was 31 years old at the time of the marriage, very unusual for the times! Frederick and Lena had two children, Alton Verne (1901) and Violet Cleva (1903). Francis Herbert "Frank" (1871-1934) was born in Biddulph Township. He married Martha Esther Lambert (1873-1954). Lottie (1872) married William C. Hall in 1897. Edwin (1877) was the only child born in Adelaide Township.

Frank was by occupation a farmer, but he also delivered mail to the rural area around Kerwood. This family belonged to the Methodist Church in Kerwood. Frank and Martha had eight children.

Alvin DeLoyd "Deed" (1899-1981), eldest child of Frank and Martha, married Greta Richardson and remained on the home farm on the Fourth Line SER. He took over his father's mail delivery. They had no children.

Erna Mae (1899-1981) never married and resided in London most of her life. She is interred in Watford Cemetery.

Cyril Leslie (1901-1958) married Bessie Berry and moved to London.

Frederick Morley (1902-1962) married Jean Waltham and resided on the east half of Lot 5, Con. 2 SER. They had two daughters, Martha Mae (1938, died at birth) and Ruth Ann (1946).

Eva Fae (1904-1992) married Russell Johnson and moved to Toronto.

Minnie Kathleen (1906-1972) married Dalton Morgan (d.1972). They died six months apart in Toronto.

John Edwin "Jack" (1907-1976) married Helen Glover and moved to London.

Ada Ilene (1915-1990) married David Smith and moved to Watford.

Of Frank and Martha's eight children, only two remained in Adelaide Township.

WRIGHTMAN, Harvey and Irene

Harvey and Irene (Bauman) Wrightman live at Lot 5, Con. 5 SER, known as "the old Wright homestead." They moved to this location in 1974, and had three children, Daniel, Maria and Esther.

Irene was born in Elmira, Ontario. Her ancestors immigrated to North America from Switzerland in the early 1700s. They settled for some time in Pennsylvania, and in 1850, they moved to Waterloo County.

Harvey was born in Alvinston, Ontario. His great-grandfather immigrated to Brooke Township from Scotland in 1850.

WYATT, Edward and Melissa

Edward Lawrence Wyatt (1871-1956) of East Williams Township married Melissa Freele (1871-1938) of Adelaide Village. Melissa kept store at Springbank with her brother, William Freele. Lawrence and Melissa took over the Wyatt home farm in East Williams Township at Lot 10, Con. 7. They had three children, Helen, who married Russell Payne; Lawrence "Lorne" Edward Freele, who married Beulah Agnes Whittle of Saskatoon in 1941; and Roberta (1917-1996), who married Beverley Morgan of Adelaide Township (see MORGAN, Richard Sr. and Jane).

Lorne and Beulah sold the home farm and, in 1973, retired to Adelaide Township, part of Lot 19, Con. 4 NER. They have three sons, Neil Douglas, Ronald "Ron" and Robert "Bob." Neil married Sheila Pope. They have two children, Glenn (1964), who married Heather Harris of Arkona and has two children, Taylor and Brooklyn; and Shawn (1969). Neil, Sheila and Ron live in Adelaide on the site of the former Crathie School. Bob lives in Long Sault, near Cornwall, with his wife, Judy (Walker), and their children, Amy and Mitchell.

STORIES NOT ALPHABETIZED

BRANDON, Alan and Michelle

Alan and Michelle (Vail) Brandon live on part of Lot 31, Con. 1 SER. Alan was born in Sarnia, and Michelle was raised in the Watford area. Michelle works in London and Alan works for Union Gas at Ivan, in Lobo Township. They moved to Adelaide Township in 1994, and enjoy living here.

CALLAGHAN – WALSH – O'DONNELL

At the age of 12, William Callaghan came to America from Ireland in 1826. Eventually, he came to Ontario. He settled first near Warwick, and then on the Sixth Line of Metcalfe Township, at Lot 10, Con. 1. He married Mary Burke (1851), who died of tuberculosis. William and his family attended St. Patrick's Roman Catholic Church in Adelaide Village.

William and Mary had six children, Luke (1837); Winnifred (1838), who worked on the Great Lakes and married in Chicago; Bridget (1841); Michael (1843); Sophia (1844), who married Henry Guilfoyle from the Sixth Line of Metcalfe in 1871, and had 10 children; and Edward (1847), who became a teacher, and taught in Katesville and other local schools.

Sophia and Henry's daughter, Margaret Theresa, married Jack "White Jack" O'Donnell of Plympton Township in Lambton County, Lot 24 at the Tenth Line and Uttoxeter Sideroad.

Edward and his family continued to live on the home farm. He and most of the family are buried in All Saints Cemetery, Strathroy.

Pioneer Pat Walsh, who came to Canada in 1846, and his wife, Catherine (Quinn), were also early settlers. In 1858, they settled at the northwest corner of the Kerwood Road and Highway 22, and are buried in All Saints Cemetery, Strathroy. Their son, Pat Jr. (1857), was born and died on the same farm, Lot 6, Con. 1 NER. He married Margaret Kearns in 1884, and they had three children. Annie (1885), the eldest, married James "Big Jim" O'Donnell (1914), who had been married once previously. They had five children, and lived out west. Theresa (1890) married A. Howe of Glencoe, and they had six children. Albert (1891) married Madeline Gearas and moved to Detroit, where some of their family still lives.

After Margaret died, Pat Jr. remarried in 1894, to Mary Ann O'Donnell (1865-1961), cousin of Margaret and daughter of James and Bridget (Kearns) O'Donnell. Pat and Mary Ann had seven children. Stella (1895), the eldest, married Durward Dewar of Plympton Township, and they had three daughters, Margaret, Mary Jane and Josephine (deceased). James (1897-1957) married Ruth Bradley. They had one daughter, Catherine, who married Gordon A. McKay, a lawyer in Kitchener. They have eight children. Joseph Leo (1899) died in his teens. Margaret (1900-1965) remained single and worked in Detroit. Wilfred (1902-1985) married Marie (last name unknown) and they had three sons, James, Joseph and Patrick. All are married and have families. Catherine (1904-1993) remained single and worked as a beautician. She died in London. Patricia (1905-1957) was a nurse.

Patrick, Wilfred's youngest son, lives at 12 Primrose Path in Kitchener, Ontario.

Nora and Jack Walsh farmed on the Egremont Road, and raised a nephew, Tom Ball. All are deceased now, and like many members of these families, they are buried in All Saints Cemetery in Strathroy.

GOVERS - YOUNG

Rick Govers and Sandy Young live on part of Lot 28, Con. 2 SER. Rick was born in the Netherlands. His parents, Adrian and Marie Govers, immigrated to Canada and settled in Lobo Township. Rick works for D&B Electricians in Strathroy. Sandy was born in Thamesford. Her family was originally from Scotland. Rick and Sandy have lived in Adelaide Township since 1994.

438 ADELAIDE TOWNSHIP... A HISTORY

Woods Store - 1938

Fred Woods - operaterd Woods Store in Kerwood from 1937-1979

Group at Kerwood United Church representing many Adelaide Township families – 1929

CHAPTER THREE

Churches and Cemeteries

CHURCHES IN ADELAIDE

The early churches played a significant role in the life of the early pioneers. It gave their life stability, a sense of belonging, and was, especially in the early years of settling, the only social outlet. Theirs was an isolated existence filled with the hardship of basic survival in the wilderness.

From the description given above, it might be assumed that these early settlers in Upper Canada had the legal right and opportunity to practise their faith as they so chose but such was not to be their circumstances. Just as the official church of the mother country was the Church of England, so it was in Upper Canada. Even before it was made official by the Canada Act of 1791 (the Act which brought the province into existence), the representatives of the British Crown recognized the authority of the Church of England. The Act spelled out the legal basis for the special privileges with which the Church of England in Canada was endowed. From the sections of the Act that relate to religion, there can be no doubt that it was the intention of the British government to establish the Church of England in Upper Canada. Under the Act, the legal onus fell upon the local legislatures to ensure that this establishment took place and, even though this legalization never was enacted in Upper Canada, the authorities in England and in the province acted as if the establishment were a part of the constitution.

To make matters worse for non-Anglican settlers, the British Parliament in 1791 ordained that one acre in every seven that were eligible as a Crown grant was to be set aside for the support of a Protestant clergy—meaning the Church of England. The Church of Scotland (Presbyterian), which had for some time been recognized as an official church in England, argued their right with no effect until, in the early 1840s, when the Clergy Reserves were finally sold, they shared equally with the Anglican church in monies received. Other denominations received nothing.

Anglican ministers were the only clergy that had the privilege of administering the Sacraments of Baptism and Holy Matrimony. In the 1820s, Archbishop Dr. John Strachan fought to keep this privilege only for the Anglican clergy. So it was that in sparsely inhabited areas, Canadians had to wait to have their children baptized or get married, and often people lived together without the benefit of the clergy. Other faiths, such as the Methodist, had strong missionary programs. Saddlebag preachers were very active in the early years of settling, and they made many converts.

When Adelaide Township was created, the first church services were held in the open, weather permitting. Otherwise, they were held in the log cabin homes of the early settlers or in early school buildings. As the population grew and regular church buildings were needed, people pitched in, donated land and lumber, and helped build church buildings, which were often no more than a log or frame building with split lumber for seats. Later, these were

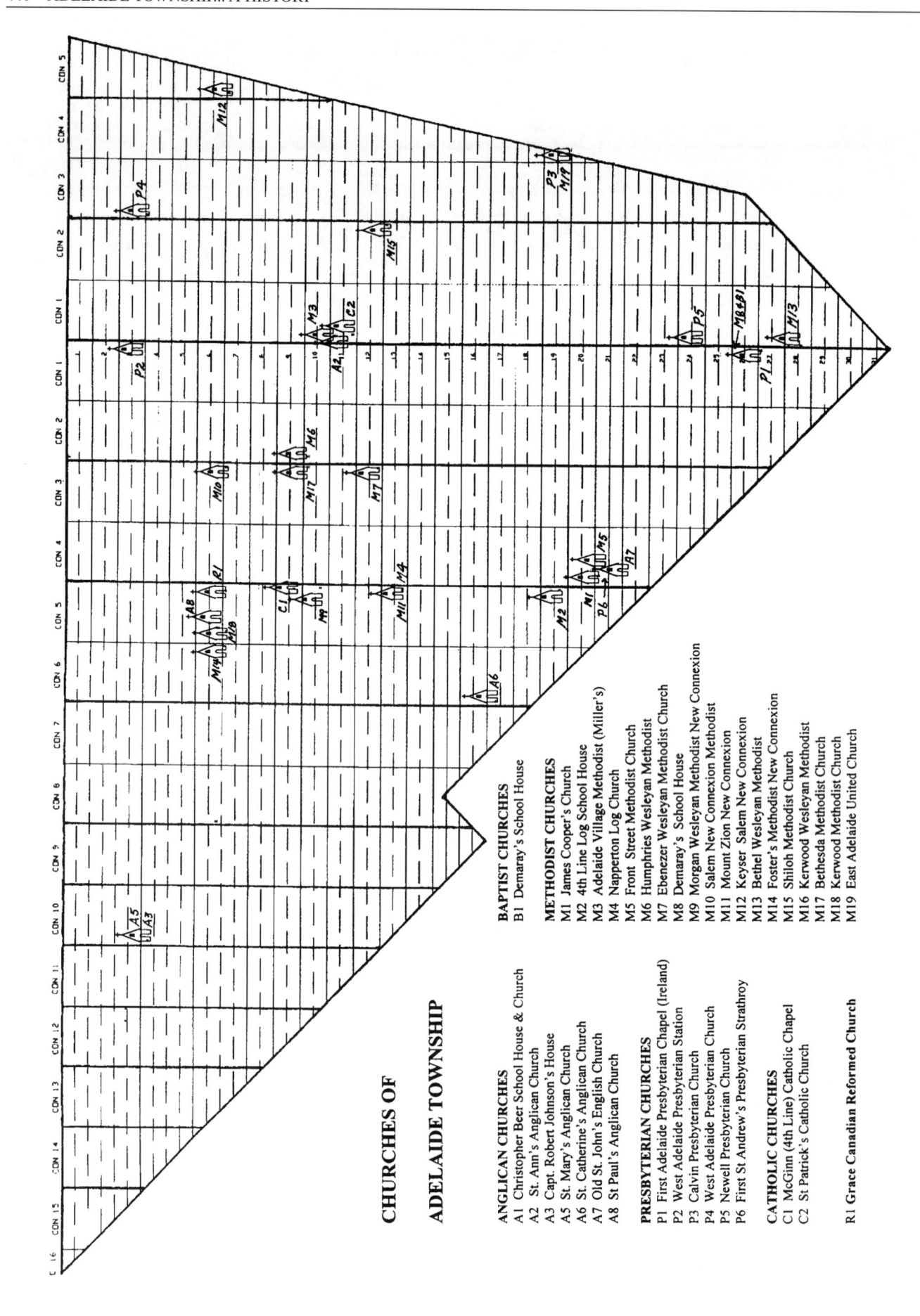

CHURCHES OF ADELAIDE TOWNSHIP

ANGLICAN CHURCHES
A1 Christopher Beer School House & Church
A2 St. Ann's Anglican Church
A3 Capt. Robert Johnson's House
A5 St. Mary's Anglican Church
A6 St. Catherine's Anglican Church
A7 Old St. John's English Church
A8 St Paul's Anglican Church

PRESBYTERIAN CHURCHES
P1 First Adelaide Presbyterian Chapel (Ireland)
P2 West Adelaide Presbyterian Station
P3 Calvin Presbyterian Church
P4 West Adelaide Presbyterian Church
P5 Newell Presbyterian Church
P6 First St Andrew's Presbyterian Strathroy

CATHOLIC CHURCHES
C1 McGinn (4th Line) Catholic Chapel
C2 St Patrick's Catholic Church

R1 Grace Canadian Reformed Church

BAPTIST CHURCHES
B1 Demaray's School House

METHODIST CHURCHES
M1 James Cooper's Church
M2 4th Line Log School House
M3 Adelaide Village Methodist (Miller's)
M4 Napperton Log Church
M5 Front Street Methodist Church
M6 Humphries Wesleyan Methodist
M7 Ebenezer Wesleyan Methodist Church
M8 Demaray's School House
M9 Morgan Wesleyan Methodist New Connexion
M10 Salem New Connexion Methodist
M11 Mount Zion New Connexion
M12 Keyser Salem New Connexion
M13 Bethel Wesleyan Methodist
M14 Foster's Methodist New Connexion
M15 Shiloh Methodist Church
M16 Kerwood Wesleyan Methodist
M17 Bethesda Methodist Church
M18 Kerwood Methodist Church
M19 East Adelaide United Church

CHURCHES AND CEMETERIES 441

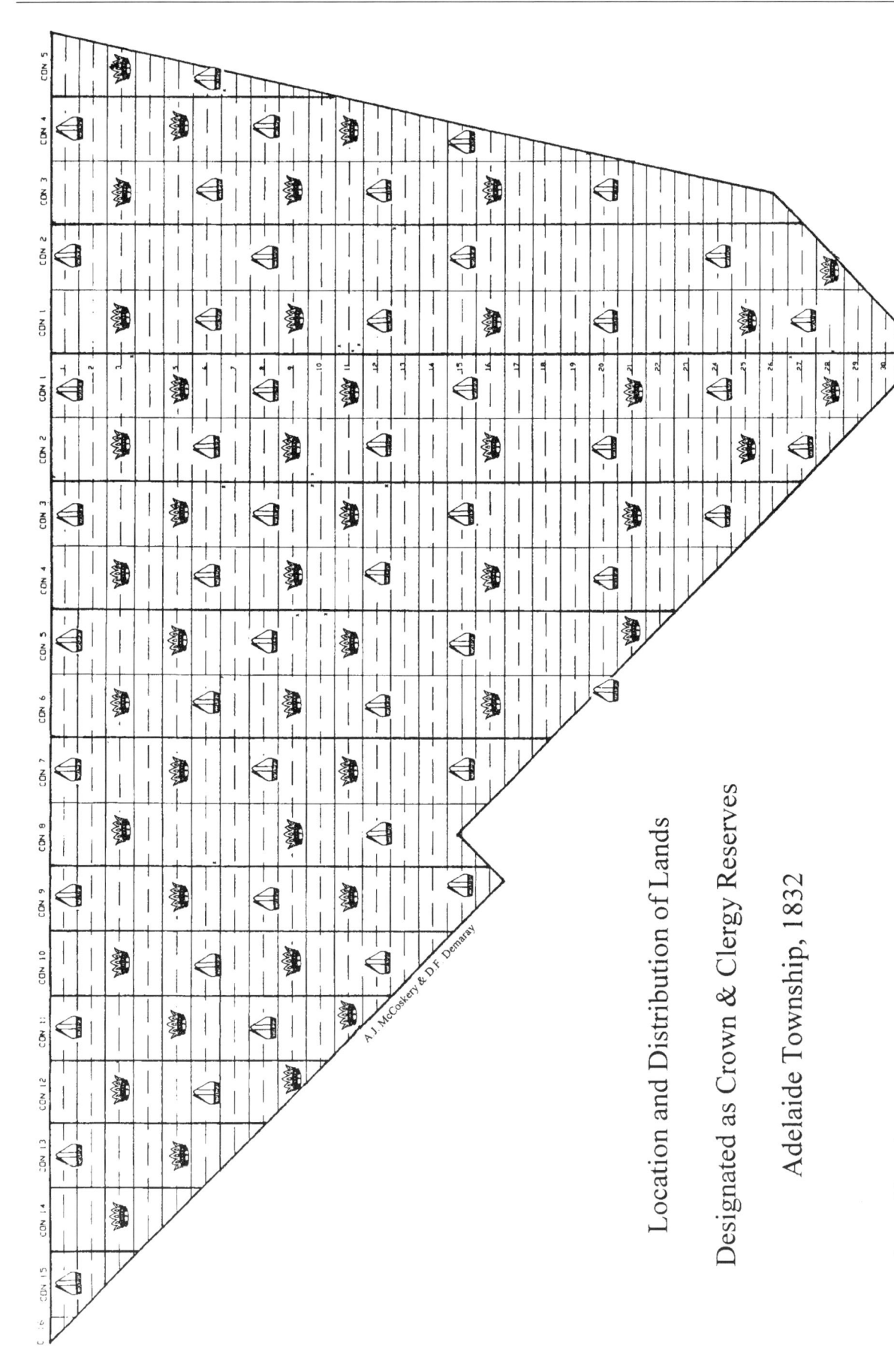

Location and Distribution of Lands
Designated as Crown & Clergy Reserves
Adelaide Township, 1832

Source: Archives of Ontario
Survey of Adelaide Township
by Peter Carroll (1831-32).

replaced by better frame buildings and, eventually, brick structures. Most churches had a colourful history of their progress and are documented in church history books already printed.

ANGLICAN CHURCHES
St. Ann's Anglican Church in Adelaide

In 1833, a log schoolhouse was used for church services until a frame church was built later that year with a rectory. We are told by Dora Aitkin in *A History of St. Ann's Church and Adelaide* that this little church stood on blocks, facing north, and that the pews and pulpit were not finished until seven years later.

The Rev. Benjamin Cronyn, who came from Ireland in 1832, was appointed the first rector of Adelaide in 1833. However, it appears that he was easily convinced by the people at the Forks of the Thames (London), where he had preached before coming to Adelaide, to stay and become rector there. In his place was appointed his successor and friend, the Rev. Dominic Blake who, with his brother, William Hume Blake, had come from Ireland in 1832. Rev. Blake ministered faithfully for nearly 14 years in this parish, which at that time included all of the Township of Adelaide.

Rev. Horace Bray, in a sermon he preached in St. Ann's in 1923 during the re-opening of St. Ann's Church, related a story about Rev. Cronyn. In the winter in 1833, Mr. Cronyn and his friend, Colonel Curran, were pursued by wolves while carrying a quarter of beef to the starving settlers in Adelaide. As darkness fell, the wolves came closer and, luckily, they found an uninhabited shanty, where they stayed until it was almost dawn. They lost the trail again when their lamp blew out. The wolves were finally closing in when they were found by the Adelaide settlers, who were anxiously looking out for them.

In 1836, Adelaide was created a Crown rectory and under Rev. Blake's leadership, St. Mary's Church near Napier and St. Catharine's Church in Katesville were built in 1841, while 1842 saw the construction of St. John's Church in Strathroy.

Rev. Dominic Blake was rector of all of Adelaide Township and more, and rode many miles on horseback through the bush, ministering to the people through the years. His brother, William Hume Blake, was later to become the first Chancellor of Upper Canada, while in 1857, the

Interior of St. Ann's Anglican Church in Adelaide Village.

St. Ann's Anglican Church, ca.1910.

St. Ann's Adelaide Church, 1908.

St. Ann's, last gathering of St. Ann's congregation in Adelaide Township Hall.

St. Ann's Women's Auxiliary, 1936 meeting at home of George Brooks, L-R, Mrs. Fred Ings, Mrs. Fred Petch, Mrs. George Glen, Mrs. A.J. Brock, Mrs. Russell Brock, Mrs. Robert Ball, Mrs. Lonzo Knight, Mrs. George Brooks, Mrs. Robert McCarthy, Mrs. Will Brent, Miss Mary Barrett, Mrs. Russell Dowding, Miss Lou Morse, Mrs. Fred Brent, Rev. Mrs. Harold Appleyard and Mrs. Howard Brock.

Ven. B. Cronyn became the first Bishop of the newly created Diocese of Huron.

In 1859, for a period of nine months between the departure of Rev. Arthur Mortimer and the arrival of the new rector, Rev. A.S. Falls, services were carried on by William Bray, a licensed lay reader. Rev. Falls lived in Strathroy rather than in the old rectory. In 1865, Katesville and Strathroy were removed from the Adelaide parish to form a new parish. In 1868, St. Ann's was destroyed in a windstorm, and the building of a brick church was begun that same year. Rev. Falls' wife, Anna Maria, died in 1869, and was buried in the cemetery. A white plaque was erected in her memory by the congregations of St. Ann's and St. Mary's.

Rev. John Kennedy, who followed Rev. A.S. Falls, bought the George Ivor hotel. He had it moved across the road, and then converted it into a rectory. The old rectory was demolished, and all of the land but two acres of the glebe land was sold for $7,700. This became the Adelaide Endowment, with the interest going towards the minister's stipend. In 1926, the rectory was sold to Walter Feasey, and a new rectory was built in Kerwood. In 1931, the church was wired for electricity, a gift from the A.Y.P.A., who earned the $105 needed by performing a play.

Many changes have taken place over the years, too numerous to mention, and St. Ann's continues to nurture her congregation.

St. Mary's Anglican Church, Near Napier

In the early 1830s, the first church services were held in Captain Beer's log cabin, likely the first Anglican service held in the area. When Captain Beer's cabin became too small, services were held in Captain Robert Johnston's large log cabin. Rev. Blake noted in his diary that the last service held in Captain Johnston's home was in 1839.

Rev. Benjamin Cronyn and later, Rev. Dominic Blake and his successors, preached at times. Saddlebag preachers occasionally conducted services.

Captain Johnston, Captain Beer, and later, Col. Arthur, could conduct baptisms and marriages, a privilege that came with being appointed a magistrate.

In 1839, a frame schoolhouse was erected during a "work bee" on property donated by Lieutenant Charles Preston, and services moved to the schoolhouse, which was situated, on what is now the yard of St. Mary's Church. This schoolhouse was also used by different denominations in turn, until several years later, when the Presbyterians, Baptists and

Methodists withdrew and built their own little white frame Union Church just north of the village.

In August 1841, the residents of the community sent a petition to Rev. John Strachan, Bishop of Toronto, requesting permission and financial assistance in building a church. Building began in the same year, likely taking only a few weeks. Captain Beer donated the lumber to build the church—lovely, dressed, black walnut lumber that he had saved for his own house. St. Mary's church is the oldest original standing church in Middlesex County.

St. Catharine's in Katesville

St. Catharine's Anglican Church was established in 1841 under the ministry of Rev. Dominic Blake, the minister of St. Ann's in Adelaide. It was situated east of the bridge over the Sydenham River, and northeast of the Sixth Line Road. Rev. Blake was their preacher until about 1846. Other ministers included Rev. Arthur Mortimer, who left in 1859, Rev. A.S. Falls and Rev. John Kennedy.

In 1865, Katesville was removed from the Adelaide parish and formed a new parish with Strathroy. Only a ghost of a picture of St. Catherine's has survived. It is known that it was constructed in the same design as St. Mary's and St. Ann's at Adelaide village. These churches were about 32' long, 27.2' wide, with walls 17.2' high at the eaves. The peak of the roof was 28.2' above the ground. A tower approximately 8' square and 32' high stood at the front, and provided an entrance to the church. St. Catherine's had three windows in each long wall unlike St. Mary's, which has only two.

Eventually, many people moved away from Katesville and what was once a thriving community, with hotels, businesses and a post office, became a ghost town. Membership in the church dwindled and, when the church closed in 1895, the contents and property reverted to St. John's, Strathroy. The church stood empty for some time and eventually gave in to the ravages of time. It was torn down sometime after 1895.

ANGLICAN RECTORS IN ADELAIDE TOWNSHIP

Rev. Dominic Edward Blake	1832-1844	Rev. Sutton	1897	Rev. Joseph A. Armstrong	1950-1954
Rev. Arthur Mortimer	1844-1859	Rev. F.C. O'Meara	1897	Rev. Erroll J. Shilliday	1954-1957
Rev. Alexander S. Falls	1859-1869	Rev. J. Connor	1897-1906	Rev. Sidney R. Lupton	1957-1959
Rev. R. Bentley	1860-1869	Rev. William E. Scott	1902	Rev. Leslie F. Harding	1959-1962
Rev. Weld	1865	Rev. Charles Mills	1906	Rev. Charles S. Ripley	1962-1967
Rev. G.L. Smith	1874	Rev. John William Jones	1906-1909	Rev. William Mercer	1967
Rev. F. McRae	1875-1881	Rev. Harry R. Diehl	1909-1926	Rev. George Hamilton	1967-1968
Rev. John Kennedy	1869-1883	Rev. J. McLeod	1912	Rev. Harold McKillopp	1968-1969
Rev. W.J. Taylor	1878	Rev. C.O. Pherill	1914	Rev. Morley Thomas	1968-1972
Rev. John Lees	1881	Rev. Newton Williams	1915	Rev. Claude Root	1970-1975
Rev. Babstone	1881	Rev. A.E. Duplan	1918	Rev. Denys Scorer	1973-1974
Rev. John Barry	uncertain	Rev. D.D. Douglas	1919	Rev. Coster Scovil	1974-1982
Rev. John P. Curran	1884-1886	Rev. T.J. Charlton	1919	Rev. Karl Hansen	1975-1979
Rev. William Hinde	1887-1889	Rev. John J. Fenton	1926-1928	Rev. John W. Hofland	1980-1985
Rev. Edward Softley	1881-1883	Rev. Stewart H. Brownlee	1928-1930	Rev. Robert Hayne	1982-1995
Rev. William Hinde	1889	Rev. Reginald T. Appleyard	1930-1932	Rev. Douglas Fuller	1985-1988
Rev. William Daunt	1881-1893	Rev. Harold F. Appleyard	1932-1938	Rev. Robert Towler	1988-1994
Rev. A. Fisher	1893	Rev. Bernard G. Buley	1938-1941	Rev. Peter Leonard	1995
Rev. E.W. Hughes	1889-1896	Rev. P.A. Rickard	1942	Rev. Leslie Peterson	1996
Rev. A.B. Bert	1894	Rev. W.J. Zimmerman	1942-1945	Rev. Virginia Lane	1996-1997
Rev. C.A. Anderson	1895	Rev. J.L. Ball	1946-1947	Rev. Frank Butt	1997-1998
Rev. Francis Ryan	1896-1897	Rev. J.E. Gordon Houghton	1947-1950	Rev. William Cliff	1998-

St. John the Evangelist Anglican Church, Strathroy

St. John's Anglican Church was established in 1842 under the ministry of Rev. Dominic E. Blake, rector of St. Mary's Church near Napier. The frame building was situated on four acres at Lot 23, Con. 4. The land was donated by John Stewart Buchanan, who had obtained the deed to 12,000 acres of pine forest along with the water rights to the Sydenham River (or Bear Creek, as it was then known) from his uncle James Buchanan, British Consul in New York. The church served for a time as the first school in the community. Rev. Benjamin Cronyn conducted the first Anglican service ever to be held in this area.

The small frame church soon became too small and, in 1860, under the ministry of Rev. A.S. Falls, a small brick church was built, which today still forms the nave of the church. The frame church was moved across the street, where it remains today as a private home.

In 1859, this area became the Village of Strathroy, separated from Adelaide Township. In 1865, Strathroy was removed from the Adelaide parish and formed a parish with Katesville under the ministry of Rev. R.S. Patterson. In 1870, a brick rectory was built beside the church. About 1874, under the leadership of Rev. James Smythe, a chancel was added to the church. In 1882, the first pipe organ in Strathroy was installed and, in 1883, an organ recital was given by Professor Charles Newman. When Rev. Hill was the minister from 1878-1885, there were plans to dispose of this church and buy the Frank Street Methodist Church. Many parishioners objected most strongly to the plan, being unwilling to sacrifice the beautiful grounds deeded to the church. The church continued to grow and many additions were added until it became the beautiful church that exists today.

St. Paul's Anglican Church at Kerwood

St. Paul's Anglican Church was established in 1857, Rev. A.S. Falls and Rev. J. Kennedy being the first rectors. In 1874, the hall in which services were held burned down, and there were no church services of this church until July 1880, when at a meeting it was decided to build a new church. On July 21, 1881, the cornerstone was placed by L.S. Richardson of the building committee, and on

St. Paul's Anglican Church

November 27, 1881, the new house of worship was opened.

St. Paul's has a faithful congregation who keep the church in good repair. Over the years, many memorial gifts have been donated, including several beautiful stained glass windows.

St. Paul's Anglican Church, Wisbeach

St. Paul's Church was established in 1856 through the efforts of Rev. P. Hyland. Although it is just over the Adelaide Township line, many of our Adelaide settlers attended this church. It is a beautiful little church with a well-kept cemetery. It is only open for services once a year in June.

PRESBYTERIAN CHURCHES
First Adelaide Presbyterian (Ireland) Chapel

The existence of the very first Presbyterian Church in Adelaide Township would have remained undiscovered were it not for a passage in Goodspeed's *History of Middlesex County,* in which it is stated that *"Mr. Ireland was a life-long member of the Presbyterian Church and took an active interest in the church affairs. He was elected the elder of the Presbyterian Church in 1866... His father was a member of the Presbyterian Church and the first church of that denomination was built on the Ireland Homestead in 1847, with Rev. William Howden as the first pastor."*

No record of this church is found in the land records for the west half of Lot 27, Con. 1 SER, the farm of William Ireland Sr., which he purchased in 1845 from William Bishop. A cemetery is known to have existed on this property as people living today recall its remnants. Two tombstones recovered from the old cemetery are that of Thomas Collier (d.1854)

Steel shed at West Adelaide Presbyterian Church, torn down during WWII.

and John Walker (d.1859). From past recollections of Ireland relations and neighbours, it is also known that there were at least 10 burials in this cemetery, which henceforth is to be known as First Adelaide Presbyterian (Ireland) Chapel Cemetery. In addition to the two former Amiens postmasters buried here, two Ireland children are interred at this location, Thomas (1849) and Allan (1852-1854). It is also strongly suggested that the chapel's first preacher, Rev. William Howden, is also buried at this site.

Rev. William Howden and his wife lived on one acre, part of the north part of the west half of Lot 23, Con. 1 SER, the farm of John McIntyre and his wife. The 1851 census listed Rev. Howden, United Presbyterian minister, 68 years of age, from Scotland, and his wife Elizabeth, 38, from England. The Irelands were from Scotland as were the McIntyres whose nephew, David, married Jane Jamieson, also from Scotland. Her father, John Jamieson, kept a daily diary from April 1852 to August 1860. From the Jamieson diary, some Presbyterian Church activities and the work of Rev. Howden can be constructed, as no official records are found before December 10, 1852.

In his diary entry of Sunday, April 11, 1852, John Jamieson writes *"Attended Divine service at James Murray's, the first sermon we have had in ten weeks. Mr. Howden's unhealthy state quite unqualified him for the regular discharge of his ministerial duties in such a locality."* It seems that Rev. Howden was serving both communities and the "West Adelaide Station," as well as the "Ireland Chapel," which is later called "East Adelaide" in the records.

On April 20, 1852, Rev. Howden performed the marriage of Pat Murray and Betsy Murray of the West Adelaide charge. Throughout 1852, John Jamieson noted each Sabbath by *"no sermon today"* or by stating the text that Rev. Howden used for his sermon. At the service on April 25, 1852, also at J. Murray's, Mr. Jamieson mentioned that 26 *"old and young"* attended. In May, Rev. Howden preached only twice to his western congregation. On June 20, he announced that he had handed in his demission to the presbytery at the last meeting.

On July 2, 1852, John Jamieson and William Shields called upon *"the members of our congregation who lived on the second line north and who had absented themselves from the meetings for some months past, to see what they had to say in the case of Mr. Howden's leaving. They would give no support to Mr. Howden unless he went to their houses to preach on Sabbath days."* On July 5, John Jamieson wrote a letter to the presbytery to send with Commissioner Shields from the west section of the congregation. On July 11, Mr. Frazier of Chatham preached, as appointed by the London Presbytery, to bring word that Rev. Howden's resignation was accepted and the congregation was declared vacant. On August 1, there was no sermon because of *"bad arrangements as the same hour was fixed at both ends of the township."* On August 11, Rev. Howden

Rev. Deas, West Adelaide Presbyterian Church, 1853.

performed the marriage ceremony of Jane Jamieson and David McIntyre at the Jamieson house. In August, one sermon was preached by Mr. Cavan; on September 5, the sermon was given by Mr. Greg; on September 19, the sermon was given by Mr. Sinclair.

The December 10, 1852, Minutes of the United Presbyterian Congregation, West Adelaide and Warwick are the first official record of the Adelaide Township Presbyterian Churches. It was agreed that each—Adelaide and Warwick—could raise £40 per year to pay presbytery for support of a minister. From the records, it is not known if the Adelaide West Station Presbyterians (those Presbyterians who resided in an area near or surrounding the stage-coach stop at Wiley's Inn on the Egremont Road, and who worshipped at services in local homes) worshipped with Warwick, or if this is a three-point charge with East Adelaide. According to the Jamieson diary, there were two visiting ministers in January 1853, and in February 1853, Rev. Deas preached twice. In March and April, there were no church services. There was one monthly service in May, July, and August.

The following is a list of the Presbyterian ministers who preached in Adelaide and Warwick township homes:

1852 – Rev. William Howden, Mr. Frazier of Chatham, Mr. Cavan, Mr. Greg, Mr. Sinclair

On September 30, 1853, a congregational meeting was held to discuss the location for a West Adelaide meetinghouse. A vote was held by those supporting the minister and the generous offer of John Wiley, tavern keeper on the northeast corner of Lot 3, Con. 1 SER, of ½-acre of land for the side of a chapel and burying ground was accepted over that of his brother, Hugh Wiley, a concession to the north on Lot 4, Con. 2 NER. A subscription committee was formed and $253 was subscribed. In the 1853 church records, these church members are listed as contributing toward the building of a chapel at the West Station:

David Wiley	James Marshall	Thomas Newgate	William Conkey
Daniel McIntyre	William Watson	Richard Skillin	Arthur Conkey
James Abernathy	Joseph Tanner (Warwick)	Alexander Johnston	Robert Campbell
John Bowes	John Evans	Robert Cleland	William Campbell
Harry Alison	James Cuddy	William McChesney	Arthur Ross (Warwick)
Dr. Bucke	James Shields	Robert Murray	Charles G. Tanner (Warwick)
Alexander H. Wallace	Joseph McChesney	William Macklin	Fred Rothwell
J.R. Robertson	James Billet	John Walker	James Wallace
John Shaw	Hugh Shanks Sr.	Michael McDonough (Warwick)	John Jamieson
Richard Wilson	Hugh Shanks, Jr.	Samuel Wilson	William Shields
James Cavers	Alexander Spalding	John Wiley, Jr.	John Wiley, Sr.
Alexander McChesney	George Watson	John Crummer	James Murray
John Foster	John Clark Sr.	Daniel Ingram	
Daniel Hayes	Thomas Edwards (Warwick)	William Adair	
Rev. William Deas	John Clark Jr.	Robert Conkey	

In addition to those persons listed above, the following neighbours, even though not of the same religious persuasion, made contributions to the building of the Presbyterian Church—a fine example of the munificence of the early settlers of Adelaide.

Thomas Chambers	John Miniely	John Black	Robert P. Tooth
Blanche Westlake	Frank Donelly (Warwick)	William Fuller	David Morgan
William Bray	William Thorpe	William Glen	R.L. Williams
Michael Freele	William Miller	George Fuller	James Galloway
John Fair (Warwick)	Mr. Hamilton	John Hoare	William Morgan
Joseph Morgan	Martin Carty	Robert Pegley	
William Freele	Andrew Black	Thomas Thompson	

1853 – Mr. Barr, Mr. Dunbar, Mr. Deas, Mr. Greg, Mr. Barr, Mr. Sinclair, Mr. Deas, Mr. Cavan, Rev. Skinner, Rev. William Deas

On September 7, 1853, Mr. Jamieson records *"Mr. William Deas, preacher of the gospel under the inspection of the United Presbyterian Synod of Canada, was ordained at the pastoral charge of the United Congregations of Adelaide and Warwick—the burning of my place prevented my attending."* The September 11, 1853, diary entry reads *"Sabbath—Mr. Deas preaching in David Wiley's new house—good meeting."*

West Adelaide Chapel

A building committee consisting of Rev. Deas, Robert Robertson, James Wallace, James Shields and James Murray agreed that a frame building 29'x36' with floor-to-ceiling height not less than 16' would be suitable. They ordered 28,000 red bricks from the Randall brick maker, and members of the congregation hauled them from the kilns to the site by July 1, 1854. Hugh Wiley offered to haul 1,000' of lumber from London for $2, the amount of his subscription. The church was built by the congregation and, by September 25, 1855, the first meeting of the congregation was held in the new chapel to discuss seating, and finishing the building. It was decided to borrow money and finish it immediately. John Jamieson was appointed caretaker for the sum of £3, 5s. per annum. In January 1856, managers were appointed: James Shields, James Wallace and Samuel Wilson. This was the main source of revenue as the quarterly offerings were small. Rev. Deas received a salary of $300 a year. In January 1860, subscriptions were taken to provide Rev. Deas with a cutter and a buggy, because his health was delicate. At the November 1857 meeting, it was decided to charge $1 per quarter for pew rents—a system retained until 1866. The church had a membership of 28 families in 1862.

Strathroy Presbyterians

Up to 1862, very few Presbyterians had settled in the Village of Strathroy. On rare occasions, Rev. Skinner of London Township or Rev. Deas of Adelaide came to the home of John Thompson on the townline of Caradoc east of the village until Mr. Thompson moved into Strathroy. At this time, the London Presbytery sent a regular supply of ministers to Strathroy meeting places in the homes. As a show of affection in March 1862, it was decided that a sum of $50 be collected by subscription, so that Rev. Deas could return to the "old country" where his native air might improve his health. In Rev. Deas' absence, the preachers were boarded at John Wiley's inn at the rate of $2 a week.

On May 24, 1863, the first Presbyterian communion in Strathroy was celebrated. As the congregations of East and West Adelaide were vacant, they asked the London Presbytery to conduct the services. The Session of East Adelaide, expecting a large attendance, felt that their chapel would be too small, so the service was held in the Episcopal Methodist Church in Strathroy, where the Presbyterians sometimes met. In all, 45 people were admitted to the church. Application was made to form a congregation and Strathroy was placed in connection with East and West Adelaide, forming one charge, Strathroy to have service every Sabbath afternoon, and East and West Adelaide every alternate Sabbath forenoon. The three charges shared the minister's salary: Strathroy $200, East Adelaide $100 and West Adelaide $150. At this time, the Strathroy Presbyterians began to build their church.

East Adelaide Presbyterian (Newell's) Church

During the summer of 1867, the Presbyterians built a frame church on the southwest corner of the Alexander Newell farm, Lot 24, Con. 1 NER. Many from the Second Line North and the townline attended. The last service was held on October 15, 1871, and the property was sold later that year. Nothing more is known of this church.

East Adelaide Church (Methodist)

At the annual meeting in 1867, there was discussion about repairing the west chapel. At a managers' meeting in May, 1868, a committee of David Livingston, John Cleland, William Forsyth, Robert Kincade and John Wiley Jr., were appointed to take charge of the burial grounds and to divide the church yard into regular spaces for grave plots. Graves were to be dug to an average depth of 5' for a charge of $2. There are no paper records of burials here—only the existing stones of the pioneer cemetery tell of the past.

In 1867, East and West Adelaide was disunited with Strathroy as it was felt that it was too difficult to procure a minister for three churches. Rev. James Donaldson ministered to the two congregations for four years. The elders from West chapel were: Robert Kincade, Alexander Rae, James Abernathy and David Livingston. Those of East Adelaide were: James Thompson, William Ireland and Mr. McChesney. Joint Session meetings alternated between the two churches. At a joint Session Meeting in February 1868, the elders rejected a grant of money by Synod to each congregation to assist with the purchase of a musical instrument as it was felt that it was "inexpedient to disturb the peace and harmony of the church." At the West Chapel, William Shields led the singing, and he was later replaced by Mr. W. Campbell.

The minister's house, situated at Johnston's Corners, Lot 7, Con. 2 NER, was in such a state of disrepair that, in October 1874, the congregation decided to build a new manse, one mile north of the existing church building, on the property of Mr. William Conkey, Lot 3, Con. 2 NER. Rev. James Laurence accepted a call to East and West Adelaide churches and lived in the manse until 1879. Because of the increasing number of members from the north side of the township, it was decided to build a new church, one mile north, at a more central location. The site on which it still stands was on the southwest corner of Lot 4, Con. 3 NER, on land donated by Robert and Jane Conkey. It is unusual that no records of the building plans for this church exist. Records of the new church, in the same book as the West Station Chapel records, begin February 19, 1877. The little red brick chapel was abandoned and, in 1880, the shed was sold. The proceeds were used toward the debt on the new building.

West Adelaide Presbyterian Church

The new West Adelaide Presbyterian Church was an impressive structure of white brick 34'x54' surmounted by an octagonal tower at the front. Interesting features were a fan-light window over the front door, a round coloured glass window in the rear wall behind the pulpit, and side windows of glass with coloured borders. Seating could accommodate 300 people. The church was lighted by kerosene lamps supported in attractive chandeliers. The new church was opened on Sunday, September 12, 1875. There were morning, afternoon and evening services with the minister, Rev. James Laurence, in the pulpit for the evening service. Hugh Wiley, chairman of the building committee, reported the cost of the new church was $4,400.

In 1877, the East and West Adelaide churches disunited, the Newell location was sold, and most of the East Adelaide congregation attended at Strathroy. Those not attending at Strathroy went to the Calvin Presbyterian Church, which had opened in 1871 on Lot 19, Con. 4 NER. The union of West Adelaide and Arkona came in 1878, with the minister residing in the Adelaide manse. For many years, the Psalms and Paraphrases were used. The words were printed on the bottom half of the page and the tunes for voice only were written as *"do, re, me, fa..."* on the top half. David Wiley and others led the singing. In 1880, the Hymnal of the Presbyterian Church was published and began to be

Mildred (McInroy) Wilson at the organ of West Adelaide Presbyterian Church, ca.1983.

used in Canada, and for the first time, hymns were included along with the psalms.

In 1882, ½-acre of land north of the church was purchased from Robert Conkey, to be used as a burying ground in connection with the church. The year 1885 marked the formation and opening of a Sunday School. A shed was built on the north side of the church in 1887. Miss Minnie Wiley was instructed to procure an organ for the Sunday School in 1893. The manse at West Adelaide was sold in 1894 and moved to the west half of Lot 10, Con. 2 NER, and used as a residence for many years. This building is still an attractive home on its new site at Lot 21, Con. 4 SER. In 1895, the Rev. A.E. Hannahson accepted a call to Arkona and West Adelaide. He was very musical and he persuaded the dissenting elders that an organ should be used in church services. After a new organ was installed, he formed and directed a choir and used hymn books.

In January 1899, a Women's Missionary Society was organized. A church library was established with Mr. John Robertson acting as librarian. The Envelope System for church offerings was introduced in 1913. Another ½-acre of land was purchased from John Conkey in 1915 for $150, as a site for a new shed and cemetery extension. Plans for the steel shed 100'x48' were prepared by James Gerry and built by G.O. Stevenson of Watford. A Young People's Society was formed in 1917 during the ministry of Rev. G.B. Ratcliffe.

In June 1925, the majority of the two congregations rejected "Church Union" and voted to remain Presbyterian. It was, by this time, 50 years since the church had been built, and plans were made to have a Golden Jubilee celebration on Sunday, September 6. Invitations were sent to former members and ministers. The following night, a fowl supper was held in the steel shed. Later that year, a call was extended to the Rev. A.E. Hannahson and, for the second time, he ministered to Arkona and West

1899 – 1999
West Adelaide Women's Missionary Society
In Memoriam

Mrs. Ben Arrand	Mrs. Annie Fletcher	Mrs. Ethel Marshall	Mrs. Edna Murray	Mrs. Clara Watson
Miss Emma Augustine	Mrs. Emma Fletcher	Mrs. Jane Marshall	Mrs. Hattie Murray	Miss Ella Watson
Mrs. Sadie Ayre	Mrs. Mary Fletcher	Miss Maggie Marshall	Miss Melissa Murray	Mrs. Hester Watson
Mrs. Robert Ball	Mrs. Pearl Fletcher	Miss Melinda Marshall	Miss M.J. Muxlow	Mrs. John Watson
Mrs. Beaman	Mrs. Marion Fry	Mrs. Effie McChesney	Miss Mary Muxlow	Miss Lizzie Watson
Mrs. Alma Benedict	Miss Mabel Galloway	Mrs. Freida McChesney	Mrs. R. Muxlow	Mrs. Belle Wiley
Mrs. T.J. Blakely	Miss Pearl Galloway	Mrs. Mary Jane McInroy	Mrs. E. Nethercott	Mrs. Emma Wiley
Mrs. Lily Brown	Mrs. James Geary	Mrs. Winnie McInroy	Mrs. Nichol	Mrs. Mary Wiley
Mrs. Melissa Brown	Mrs. Gilbert	Mrs. M. McIntosh	Mrs. Mary O'Neil	Mrs. George Wilkie
Mrs. Ila Callaghan	Mrs. Mae Grogan	Miss Annie McKenzie	Mrs. Chester Orr	Mrs. H.R. Williams
Mrs. Nettie Campbell	Mrs. Flossie Hall	Mrs. Annie McKenzie	Mrs. Mary Park	Mrs. Clara Wilson
Mrs. George Cleland	Miss Marjorie Hall	Miss Sarah McKenzie	Mrs. Sarah Parker	Mrs. James Wilson
Mrs. Kathaleen Clifton	Mrs. Susan Hall	Mrs. Duncan McLaughlin	Mrs. Birdie Pennington	Mrs. Margaret Wilson
Mrs. Grace Conkey	Mrs. A.W. Hare	Miss Annie McLeish	Mrs. Raine	Mrs. Mildred Wilson
Mrs. Lou Conkey	Mrs. Lorenzo Hendrick	Miss Millie McLeish	Mrs. Frank Reynolds	Mrs. Minnie Wilson
Miss Margaret Conkey	Mrs. R. Hendrick	Mrs. Reta McLeish	Miss Annie Robertson	Mrs. Estelle Wilson
Mrs. Margaret Conkey	Mrs. Ethel Herrington	Miss Addie McNab	Mrs. John Robertson	Mrs. Violet Wilson
Mrs. Marjorie Conkey	Mrs. Ivy Herrington	Mrs. Ethel McNab	Mrs. Belle (Shields) Samis	Mrs. Nelson Wylie
Mrs. Nel Conkey	Mrs. Zelma Hodgson	Mrs. Lizzie McNab	Mrs. Fred Shields	
Mrs. Phillip Conkey	Mrs. Aggie Jones	Mrs. Sarah McNab	Miss Mary Shields	
Mrs. Reta Crann	Mrs. I.B. Kaine	Miss McNair	Mrs. Kate Shrier	**Helen Scott Society**
Mrs. Harriett Cuddy	Mrs. Charles Kerswill	Mrs. Annie Mellish	Miss Pearl Shrier	**In Memoriam**
Mrs. Margaret Cuddy	Mrs. Phillip Keyser	Mrs. John A. Minnielly	Mrs. Irene Thompson	Mrs. Dilys Cuddy
Mrs. W.A. Cuddy	Miss Ollie Kincade	Miss A. Morgan	Mrs. D. Van Brenk	Mrs. Aileen Emmons
Mrs. Ida Davidson	Mrs. John Lewis	Mrs. Muma	Mrs. Annie Wallace	Mrs. Eileen McKenzie
Mrs. Dennis Demary	Mrs. Malcolm Lindsay	Miss Ada Murray	Mrs. Katherine Waltham	Mrs. Ruby McPhail
Miss Ada Emmons	Mrs. Edna Marshall	Mrs. Albert Murray	Mrs. Mabel Wardell	Mrs. Glenys Wilson

Adelaide. Two years later, Centre Road and West Adelaide were linked together, and Rev. Hannahson moved into the manse on Centre Road. In 1933, the church steeple was dismantled as it was considered unsafe. Rev. Hannahson retired because of ill health. He died several months later and was buried in West Adelaide Cemetery. His loss was greatly felt by all, as he and his family had been great assets to the church. By 1939, the Arkona church was closed and the manse was sold. While the West Adelaide church was being remodeled, starting in 1948, services and Sunday School were held in the S.S. #9 schoolhouse. During this period, the Helen Scott Society was formed under the leadership of Mrs. I.B. Kaine, wife of the minister.

The steel shed was sold in 1950 for $1,500. Many remember the good times and financial aid from strawberry socials, fowl suppers, skating parties and concerts, which were held in the shed for many years. West Adelaide and Centre Road joined with Beechwood in the fall of 1950. A house in Strathroy was purchased for a manse for the three congregations.

An electric Hammond Spinet organ was purchased in 1957. The first choir gowns were acquired in 1964. *The Presbyterian Record* was placed in every home of the congregation. The Strathroy manse was sold, and an apartment was rented for the minister's use. On September 7, the morning and evening Centennial Services were held in the church sanctuary, and the adjoining tent services were under the leadership of the minister, Rev. James Perrie. At the evening service, the guest minister was Rev. Lloyd Clifton, whose father was the minister at West Adelaide from 1936-1939. On Friday evening, September 12, communion was shared with friends and relatives from the congregations. Rev. Kenneth Wilson, a West Adelaide son, was the speaker. On Sunday, September 14, music was provided by members of the Hannahson family, children and grandchildren of the late Rev. A.E. Hannahson. The centennial project of the Church was the compilation of its history.

In August 1989, Rev. Lloyd and Evelyn (Fletcher) Clifton and family presented a memorial stained glass window illustrating *"He stands at the door and knocks"* in memory of their parents, Mr. and Mrs. Munroe Fletcher, and Rev. Ernest and Mrs. Clifton.

Ministers of West Adelaide Church

1853-1859	Rev. William Deas
1860-1864	Rev. William Fletcher
1867-1871	Rev. James Donaldson
1874-1879	Rev. James Laurence
1875-1881	Rev. F. McRae
1880-1883	Rev. James Carswell
1885-1891	Rev. Robert Hume
1893-1895	Rev. George Haigh
1895-1906	Rev. A.E. Hannahson
1906-1909	Rev. Malcolm Lindsay
1910-1916	Rev. A.W. Hare
1917-1921	Rev. G.B. Ratcliffe
1922-1925	Rev. James A. Gale
1925-1935	Rev. A.E. Hannahson
1936	Rev. James Hagen
1936-1939	Rev. Ernest Clifton
1939-1944	Rev. Robert Bruce
1945-1950	Rev. I.B. Kaine
1950-1960	Rev. H.R. Williams
1960-1962	Rev. T.J. Blakely
1963-1967	Rev. J.B. Robertson
1968-1975	Rev. James G. Perrie
1975-1983	Rev. Charles Falconer
1984-1991	Rev. Andrew Jensen
1992-2000	Rev. Douglas Miles

In 1999, the Helen Scott Society conducted a centennial and memorial service honouring the women of the West Adelaide Women's Missionary Society whose work for service continues today.

Calvin Presbyterian Church

In 1845, David Sands and his wife came from Glasgow, Scotland, and settled in East Williams Township near Nettleton's Corners. The Sands had many religious meetings in their home. It was decided to build a church, and a committee was formed of David Sands Jr., William McKeen, Charles Bolton, and Samuel and John Milliken. The church was located on Lot 19, Con. 4 NER. Archie McKeen cleared the land, and contractor Edward Austin of Coldstream built a frame church for $625. It was officially opened in 1871 with the Centre Road Church, where the manse was located as the other half of the charge. A Sunday School was established in 1872. In 1925, Calvin Church, also known as East Adelaide Presbyterian Church, became part of the United Church of Canada. Some members joined Centre Road Presbyterian Church.

The ministers of Calvin Presbyterian Church from 1871 to 1925 were: Rev. Lachlin McPherson (1871-1875), Rev. William Mildrum (1875-1877), Rev. John Lees (1878-1882), Rev. John McKinnon (1891-1904), Rev. John Moore (1904-1917), and Rev. George Aiken (1917-1925).

BAPTIST CHURCH

There is no evidence that the Baptists of Adelaide ever built their own church, but it is known that various Baptist congregations met in schoolhouses and Methodist and Anglican churches. Some of these schools and churches included those near Napier and Demaray's Schoolhouse at Lot 28, Con. 1 SER.

METHODIST CHURCHES OF ADELAIDE

In the pioneer days, once a district was even sparsely settled, the churches made a valiant effort to establish religious services. It was during this period that the Methodist saddlebag preachers and circuit riders were active, riding from settlement to settlement, holding services outside, or in homes if it could be arranged. Those saddlebag preachers and circuit riders endured great hardships, travelling the blazed trails through all kinds of weather, relying on shelter and food provided by the early settlers. T.W. Magrath, an Anglican adherent of Adelaide Township, wrote in his *Authentic Letters from Upper Canada... 1833*, that he appreciated the energy of the Methodist itinerants, *"Whenever a settlement is formed there, they are to be found... many of them are excellent men, and all of them are really or apparently zealous."* Magrath feared that the time had already passed when his own church (Anglican) could recover lost ground. *"The Methodist dissenters have obtained an ascendancy over our infant population. Their habits of domiciliary visitation, their acquaintance with the tastes and peculiarities of the Canadians, their readiness to take long and fatiguing rides, in the discharge of their self-imposed labours, render them formidable rivals to our more easygoing clergy."*

Methodist Church south of Kerwood, east side of County Road 6.

In 1834, shortly after the first settlers in this district arrived, a Methodist Circuit was formed which included Adelaide, Warwick and Strathroy, with the Rev. M. Ratcliffe in charge. These early Methodists were divided into five denominations: Wesleyan, New Connexion, Methodist Episcopal, Primitive and Bible Christians. Upon looking back now, the distinctions between the different groups may seem trivial, but they were considered significant at the time.

The first recorded Wesleyan Methodist services were held in 1836, in the home of James Cooper, who lived on the west half of Lot 21, Con. 4 SER (now Victoria Street, near the park). James Cooper had the distinction of being the first convert as a result of these home services.

Old Methodist Fourth Line Log Church and Schoolhouse

By 1840, more settlers had come to the area, and a log church was erected on the Fourth Line of Adelaide, on part of the east half of Lot 19, Con. 5 SER, on land donated by David and Harriet Rapley. James Cooper and John Buttery were two of the men who assisted at the erection of the log church. This building was also used for a school. In 1847, Adelaide became a separate mission, with Rev. Robert Corson appointed as pastor. He was succeeded by Rev. George Kennedy, John Webster, Rev. Ozias Barber, and Joseph Hill before 1850.

By 1851, the Methodist congregation numbered 178 souls. They had outgrown the little log building on the Fourth Line and, in that year, a quaint white frame church with a square tower was built on the east half of Lot 21, Con. 4 SER, on land donated by James Keefer, on the north side of present-day Front Street. Historically, this church has been called Front Street Wesleyan Methodist Church.

In 1855, the property where the log building stood was sold to the Wesleyan Methodist Church in Strathroy, to establish the Fourth Line Cemetery.

The Front Street frame church soon proved to be inadequate for the rapidly growing congregation and was sold for $500 to the Episcopal Methodist congregation, who moved it to Frank Street.

Adelaide Village Wesleyan Methodist Church (Miller's Church)

On November 5, 1845, the patent was received from the Crown for Village Lots 1 and 2 on the north side of King Street, on the west half of Lot 11, Con. 1 NER, in the Village of Adelaide. A Methodist church was built on this property and served the local community until the land was sold on June 6, 1893. Trustees at the time of sale were William Miller, William Chapman, James Carrothers, Aaron Demaray, Charles Demaray and William Thomas Galloway.

Rude Log Cabin Methodist Church at Napperton

After the Fourth Line Church/School was sold and the East Adelaide congregation held services on Front Street, the Methodist congregation built what has been described as a Rude Log Cabin Church near Napperton on the Fourth Line South in 1846. This building was used for both church and school. This rude log structure served until Mt Zion Church was built in 1868.

Humphries' Wesleyan Methodist Church

On September 28, 1855, a parcel of land 20 rods square was purchased from William Humphries on the west half of Lot 10, Con. 2 SER. A small log building was constructed, which served as both church and school. Church services and school classes were held here until about 1861. Twenty-six years later, another Methodist church would be built immediately across the road to the south.

Ebenezer Wesleyan Methodist Church

With the disappearance of Humphries Church about 1861, the Methodist congregation built a new wood frame church called "Ebenezer" on the northeast corner of Lot 12, Con. 3 SER, on land purchased from Samuel Harris. This church was going strong in December 1875. "A very gracious revival has just taken place at the Ebenezer Church… at which about 25 persons have decided to walk in 'wisdom's way'." This church burned during the winter of 1886.

Demaray's Schoolhouse and Church

The Methodists who lived in East Adelaide before 1862 had a great distance to travel to attend church in Strathroy, but after the arrival of Benjamin Varnum "Big Ben" Demaray, a schoolhouse was constructed on part of his property, the northeast corner of Lot 28, Con. 1 SER. Services at the schoolhouse eased the burden greatly. Big Ben had been an avid supporter of education while serving as reeve of North Dorchester Township and was a staunch Methodist. This historic little schoolhouse, S.S. #3, which was demolished in the fall of 1999 for the value of its old brick, served as a church for Methodists, Baptists and Presbyterians.

Morgan Wesleyan Methodist New Connexion Church

A wood frame Wesleyan Methodist New Connexion Church was built in the fall of 1865 on 1/8-acre on the east half of Lot 10, Con. 5 SER. Trustees were John Morgan Sr., Elizabeth Morgan,

Mt. Zion Methodist Church (Napperton)

Thomas Hughes, Henry Murdoch, John Truman, John Morgan Jr. and John Curry. It is not known when this church was demolished, but parts of it were used in the construction of Irwin's Blacksmith Shop at Kerwood.

Salem New Connexion Methodist Church

After the closure of Humphries Methodist Church and because of the long trip to Ebenezer Church, the Methodist congregation on the second line south in 1866 built a frame church on the west half of Lot 7, Con. 3 SER, on property purchased from James Earley. Trustees were John Sullivan, William Dowding, James Randall, John W. Brown, William Humphries and Robert Collier. This church was short-lived, as it was severely damaged in a great windstorm. Its remains were sold to the Salvation Army in October 1887, to be used as their new barracks.

Mount Zion New Connexion Methodist Church

In 1868, the old pioneer Rude Log Cabin Church disappeared to make way for the most distinctive church ever constructed in Adelaide. This beautiful brick structure was located on the northeast corner of the east half of Lot 13, Con. 5 SER. It served its followers faithfully for 44 years, and was the social centre for the neighbourhood until it closed in June 1912. Being located in the midst of a very talented group of musicians, Harold Eastman fondly recalled that, as a child, he attended Christmas concerts at Mt. Zion, and that Fred Shepherd had played the mouth organ. In the *Age of June 12, 1912, "Owing to a constantly dwindling congregation, the members of which have drifted away to other Methodist churches in the neighbourhood, it has been decided to permanently close the doors of this quaint little country edifice, within whose walls the gospel message has been proclaimed for many years."* Rev. C.F. Clarke was the pastor at the time of closing.

Salem New Connexion Methodist Church at Keyser's Corner

This church, which adopted its name from its predecessor on the Second Line South, opened in 1869, and was located on the east half of Lot 7, Con. 5 NER. The story of this church is included with that of Keyser's Corner.

Bethel Wesleyan Methodist Church (Stone Road Church)

Bethel Church was built in 1870 on the corner of the east half of Lot 28, Con. 1 NER, on property donated by David Whiting. During its construction, after the foundations were laid and the walls almost completed, a fierce wind storm in the middle of the night blew down the greater part of the work. With determination, it was rebuilt even stronger and was dedicated on Christmas Day in 1870. The first regular minister was Rev. John Neelands. Before the opening of Bethel, the congregation had held services at Demaray's Schoolhouse, which in those days was a red frame building. Members of the early Trustee's Board included the following family names: Hansford, Newell, Woodward, Smith, Gare, Demaray, Mahon, Lewis, Whiting, Grill, Copp, Wern, Matthews, Campbell, Robbins, Bishop, Thompson, Fuller, Barfet, Gunson, Tomlinson and Wark. As it was the custom for marriage ceremonies to be performed in homes or in the Manse, it was not until March 6, 1943, that the first marriage took place at Bethel Church. On this date, Anna Belle Galbraith was married to William Hansford Wood. The last marriage performed at the church was that of Mary Van Brenk in 1958. This church was closed on June 22, 1958, and the pulpit and two Bibles were given to the Poplar Hill Baptist Sunday School.

Kerwood Methodist New Connexion Church

At the south end of Kerwood, across the tracks, Mr. and Mrs. Charles Foster settled on Lot 7, Con. 6 SER, and in 1871, a piece of their land was deeded to the Trustees of the parsonage of the Canadian Methodist New Connexion Church. A parsonage was built in 1871, and the church was built in 1873. The church was dedicated on December 21, 1873, by the Rev. J. Medicraft, General Superintendent, whose sermon was highly appreciated. It was said that, "A greater discourse they never heard from any man." The following Monday morning, a tea-meeting was called, but the organizers "feared that it would be a failure, as the roads were fearfully bad, the worst they had been for years—mud knee-deep until Monday morning, when it froze a little. Notwithstanding these unfavourable conditions, the house was literally crowded and… it could be safely said that a more enthusiastic meeting had never been seen" by the observer.

In *Our One-Hundred Anniversary, 1873-1973*, an old-timer recalled her walk to church along the *"sidewalk of two or three inch planks, so constructed to make a walk about thirty inches wide; sometimes in wet weather the boards were so slippery, sometimes they were underwater in places... Growing by the wayside were orange lilies, daisies, buttercups, Sweet Mary, and a few weeds as well. Across the front of the church property was a picket fence and to the north and east of the church was the shed, to accommodate the horses that were driven to church... On either side of the long centre pews was an aisle from which shorter pews extended to the outside walls. Near the front of the north wall hung the clock. At the centre front behind the pulpit were two chairs and a settee. On the minister's right were the organ and the choir chairs. The carpet in front of the choir leader's chair was worn in a hole from the foot-tapping in time with the music. To the left of the minister were the desk and cupboard where the Sunday School secretary kept his papers and filled out the attendance book... The window panes were whitened, I suppose to subdue the light and also to keep people from looking in. At the sides of the windows were brackets for coal oil lamps, I do not remember the lamps being used, there was an acetylene plant at the east of the Church which provided the light for the building."*

The members of the Quarterly Board Kerwood Circuit on May 31, 1891, were: G. J. Kerr, David Jury, James Cook, John Jury, George Hull, G.W. Foster, Thomas Lightfoot, James Richardson, John Truman, William P. Morgan, Hardy Johnson, John Morgan, Simon Demaray, George H. Parker, William Fuller, and John J. Earley.

By 1886, the congregation had grown and it was necessary to enlarge the church. The parsonage was replaced by the present one in 1903 on the Gosden property, Lots 1 and 2, Block C. It is recorded that this decision probably created much discussion and maybe dissension; the reasons for this statement may never be known. By 1915, there was discussion about building a new Methodist Church at Kerwood, but it was not until March of 1920 that the stakes were driven for a new Methodist Church in Kerwood.

Shiloh Methodist Church

Unfortunately, almost nothing is known about this church or its congregation. It was built about 1873 on the corner of the east half of Lot 13, Con. 2 NER. This property was owned by Thomas Seed. Before 1910, Shiloh was part of the Adelaide Circuit, along with Bethesda and Bethel. From a financial statement of the Adelaide Circuit of May 31, 1903, as signified by Aaron Demaray, R.S. and Herbert J. Uren, Pastor, the following members made contributions to the Shiloh Church:

Thomas Arrand	David Adair
Henry Burrows	R.I. Coulton
Mrs. E.J. Coulton	Dennis Demaray
Edgar Demaray	William Elliott
John Elliott	Mrs. George Eastman
Mrs. James Geary	W.E. Humphries
David Harris	Samuel Ingham
E. McInroy	William Plaxton
Mrs. Edmund Plaxton	William Raison
Charles Tignor	Miss Lottie Arrand
Dan McCubbin	Mrs. Alfred Brown
Miss A. Robotham	John McLellan
Miss Rennel	Mr. Pennington
Mr. Adair	John Tignor
Thomas Raison	Alfred Burrows
John Arrand	Loretta Elliott
Milton Harris	Ivy Plaxton

Bethesda Methodist Church

After the loss of both churches (Ebenezer and Salem) on the Second Line South, the Methodist congregation, after much discussion, decided to build a new church on the northwest corner of Lot 10, Con. 3 SER. This church was immediately across the road from their first church, which had opened in 1855. Bethesda was dedicated in

Bethesda Methodist Church

September 1887. The new church cost $1,800 and had a seating capacity of 200. Rev. Mr. Pascoe, President of the Methodist Conference, preached the opening sermon to a densely crowded house, and the Rev. Mr. McDonagh spoke in the afternoon. The presence of this new Methodist church returned a social and religious cohesion to the Second Line South community such as had not been seen before. The church required almost all of its capacity most Sundays and, on special services such as Easter, Christmas and its Anniversary celebration, there was standing room only. Bethesda's choir, under the leadership of Roy Demaray, became renowned throughout the area, and was in great demand as a guest choir in other churches. Choir members over the years included: Leila and Marion Muxlow; Roy, Mary, Clarence and Don Demaray; Oliver and Phyllis Harris; Hilda Kerton; Doug Carrothers; Velma Petch; Russel Brown; Ruth, May and Helen Sullivan; Velma Petch; Blanche and Mary Down; Evelyn Carrothers; Marj and Marion Harris; and, at the piano, Mrs. Fred Thrower; Ada Dowding; Mrs. Ethel Muxlow; Harry Kerton; and Phyllis Harris.

The church was the centre of all community activities. At times, they met in one another's homes for social evenings and travelled by horse-and-sleigh to Zion in Warwick Township for oyster and ham suppers. There was a large shed behind the church and, every winter, weather permitting, the men flooded it and the water froze. There was ice for hockey, and they hosted a very popular carnival, which was attended by young people for miles around. The ladies of the church made coffee in a big copper boiler in the vestry, and also served hot dogs. One longtime member recalled that she had never tasted a better cup of coffee. There was always a Sunday School concert at Christmas, complete with tree, gifts, and Santa. The teachers spent many hours teaching the pupils recitations, dialogues and songs; there was a young men's chorus that sang several numbers, and a group of young ladies in costume who did drills.

Families attending Bethesda about 1920 were: Kerton, Dowding, Langford, Stevenson, Alderson, Sullivan, Carrothers, Shipley, Redmond, Snell, Earley, Demaray, Harris, Brown, Humphries, Muxlow, Petch, Eakins, Down, Eastman, Knight and Miner.

As the congregation grew older, sons did not always take over the family farms and, in the late 1940s, the immigrant Dutch families began to dominate the area. Many of these new neighbours belonged to the Catholic Church, and in 1968, after 80 years of fellowship, Bethesda Methodist Church was closed, with the remaining members attending at Kerwood United Church.

East Adelaide United Church
(Nettleton's Church)

This church, which was originally called Calvin Presbyterian or East Adelaide Presbyterian Church, became a United Church of Canada place of worship in 1925, after the Union with some of the Canadian Presbyterian churches. Its origin is included with the Presbyterian Churches of Adelaide. Some Presbyterian members continued with this congregation, and the church remained open until June of 1968.

In 1931, the church celebrated its Diamond Jubilee, with 12 original members present. Rev. Fred Milliken, who was born and raised in the community and a member, took part in the service.

After 97 years of worship, on the last Sunday of June in 1968, Rev. Griffiths preached the closing sermon of East Adelaide Church. On July 11, 1968, East Adelaide Church land, buildings and contents were sold by auction.

The proceeds from the sale of East Adelaide Church property was divided into five equal parts among the following: Strathroy Salvation Army, Canadian Institute for the Blind, Retarded Children's Fund, East Adelaide Friendship Circle and the Kerwood Cairngorm Charge.

The Kerwood Methodist Church
(Kerwood United Church)

The Trustee Board of the Kerwood Methodist Church met in January 1915 to discuss building a new church. There was no progress on the matter until Rev. A.I. Brown was minister. The subject of a new building was again discussed, and a committee was appointed to look for a suitable site. The committee decided to purchase the gristmill property. A subscription list was set up and, when subscriptions amounted to $12,530, the board decided the amount was sufficient to start plans for the building.

A church shed was built, and church services were held in this building until the new church opened in December 1923. The Rev. C.J. Moorehouse was the minister in 1923, when the church was built. There were special services and entertainment and, with subscriptions, concert offerings, unsolicited subscriptions, and further donations, the money kept coming in until the entire debt was pledged and no mortgage was necessary.

The Union of Methodist, Presbyterian and Congregational churches had been talked about for some time and, on June 10, 1925, the vote was taken. The name of the new church was changed to the United Church of Canada.

In 1967, the Bethesda congregation, which had been part of the Kerwood Cairngorm Charge, disbanded. The congregation joined with Kerwood, and the church was renamed Kerwood Bethesda United Church family.

Church groups played a very important role in the history of Kerwood Church: Sunday School, Epworth League, Young Peoples Society, Mission Circle (1920-1964), Baby Band (1924), Mission Band, Ladies Aid Society of Kerwood (1885), Junior Congregation, Young Women's Evening Missionary Auxiliary (1965), and since 1899, the Women's Missionary Society. Today, the organization of United Church Women carries on the proud tradition of these former groups.

The congregation of Kerwood United Church has always been a friendly group of people, somewhat cautious, sometimes conservative, but always community-spirited. No one in need was ever ignored. They especially warmed to their ministers,

Interior of Kerwood Methodist (United) Church, 1941 Anniversary, Minister F.J. Fydell.

who came with young families, and those ministers who were able to stay for any length of time were made to feel an integral part of the Kerwood family.

Early Methodist Ministers
Who Served in Adelaide Township

	Uncle Joe (Joseph Russell) Little
	Rev. John Saul
1832	Exhorter Creeley
1834	Rev. M. Ratcliffe
1835	Rev. Henry Johnson
1841	Rev. William Miller
1847	Rev. Robert Corson
1848	Rev. George Kennedy
1848	Rev. Joseph Webster
1849	Rev. Ozias Barber
1849	Rev. Joseph Hill
1850	Rev. John Hutchinson
1851	Rev. James Armstrong
1851/53	Rev. John Shaw
1853/55	Rev. John Kellogg Williston
1855	Rev. Thomas S. Howard
1856/57	Rev. Richard L. Tucker
1858/59	Rev. Nelson Brown
1859/61	Rev. John Baskerville
1860/61	Dr. Wild
1860/61	Rev. John H. Simpson
1860/61	Rev. James A. Ivison
1860/90s	Rev. John Neelands
1862	Rev. Joseph Follick
1863/64	Rev. W. Preston
1865/68	Rev. James Gundy
1868	Rev. Fancher

Kerwood Methodist (United) Church, ca.1940s.

1869/70	Rev. James Shaw		1912/14	Rev. Rufus I. Wilson
1870/72	Rev. John Walker		1914/17	Rev. John Ball
1870	Rev. B.T. White		1917/20	Rev. Asa I. Brown
1871	Rev. George Daniel		1917/25	Rev. George Aiken
1871/73	Rev. John Mahon		1920/23	Rev. C.J. Moorhouse
1871/75	Rev. Lachlin McPherson		1924/27	Rev. Reginald A. Brooke
1872	Rev. Henry E. Hill			Rev. Pentland
1872/75	Rev. Thomas Jackson		1925/28	Rev. A.E. Livingstone
1874	Rev. Ebenezer Teskey		1927/28	Rev. J.W. Johnson
1875/76	Rev. George C. Madden		1928-29	Rev. Poulter
1875/77	Rev. William Meldrum		1929/36	Rev. Colgrove
1875/78	Rev. John Russell		1936/38	Rev. Minielly
1877/79	Rev. William Shannon		1928/30	Rev. J.F. Sutcliffe
1878/80	Rev. Robert Smylie		1930/34	Rev. W.D. Stenlake
1878/81	Rev. Farquhar McRae		1934/36	Rev. Dr. Clendinnen
1880/82	Rev. W.W. Sparling		1936/39	Rev. D.W. De Mille
1880/82	Rev. William T. Turner		1938/47	Rev. G. Kilpatrick
1882/91	Rev. John Lees		1947	Rev. George Foster
1883/85	Rev. C. Barltrop		1947-48	Rev. W.A. Walden
1885/88	Rev. William H. Shaw		1939/45	Rev. F.J. Fydell
1887	Rev. J. Stonehouse		1939/45	Rev. Champion
	Rev. Kirkland		1945/56	Rev. R.C. Wright
	Rev. Harrison		1948/56	Rev. Dr. Treffry
1888/91	Rev. George J. Kerr		1956/68	Rev. W.S. Griffiths
1890s	Rev. Orme		1968/73	Rev. A.E. Wilfong
1891/93	Rev. R. Thomas		1973/79	Rev. Donald Glen Stewart
1891/1904	Rev. John McKinnon		1980-83	Rev. Robert Sinasac
1893/94	Rev. M. Griffin		1983/85	Rev. Eewart Madden
1894/97	Rev. J.B. Kennedy		1986/87	Rev. Michael Bohler
1896/1899	R. Fulton Irwin		1887	Rev. Kenneth Hick
1897/1900	Rev. A.H. Brown		1988-97	Mr. Robert Perry
1900/02	Rev. E. Kershaw		1997/99	Rev. Kristiane Charlton
1902/05	Rev. Leslie W. Reid			
1903	Rev. Herbert J. Uren			
1904/17/19	Rev. John Moore			
	Rev. Sawyer			
	Rev. Olivant			
	Rev. Kempster			
	Rev. Yelland			
	Rev. Mundy			
	Rev. Fortner			
	Rev. Walden			
	Rev. Hann			
	Rev. O'Kell			
	Rev. Armstrong			
	Rev. Thomson			
1905/08	Rev. W. Conway			
1905	Rev. T.J. Snowdon, Ph.D.			
1908/12	Rev. C.F. Clarke			

Grace Canadian Reformed Church, Kerwood

This congregation was formed in 1953 in Watford. In 1963, they moved to the former Grace Anglican Church, east of Watford. In September 1998, construction was begun for a new building, which was completed in 1999. The current minister is Rev. J. Van Woudenberg, the seventh Grace has had in its 46 years. Grace Canadian Reformed has a membership of 134 souls.

CATHOLIC CHURCHES

The first recorded Catholic chapel in Adelaide was located on part of the property of Thomas McGinn, the west half of Lot 9, Con. 5 SER, and the deed was formalized by the Rt. Rev. Alexander O'Donnell, Bishop of Upper Canada. Jesuit priests

PROVINCE OF CANADA

VICTORIA, *by the Grace of GOD, of the United Kingdom of Great Britain and Ireland, QUEEN, Defender of the Faith: - To all to whom these Presents shall come - GREETING.*
Know Ye, that we, of Our special Grace, certain Knowledge, and mere motion, have **GIVEN** and **GRANTED**, and by these Presents do give and grant unto.

The Roman Catholic Corporation of the Diocese of Kingston in trust for the site of a Church, burial grounds, and residence of a Clergyman or his Successors- heirs and assigns for ever, ALL that PARCEL or TRACT of LAND, situate *in the Town of Adelaide in the County of Middlesex in the London district*—in Our Province, containing a measurement of four acres be the same more or less, being composed of *lots number Thirteen and Fourteen on the South side of George Street and Lot Numbered Eleven, Twelve, Thirteen and Fourteen on the South side of Queen Street in the said Town of Adelaide. Also, Lot number Twelve and Thirteen on the North side of George Street in the said Town.*

Together with the all the Woods and Waters thereon lying and being, under the reservations. limitations and conditions, hereinafter expressed: To have and to hold the said Parcel or Tract of Land, hereby given and granted to the said *Roman Catholic Corporations and Successors* nevertheless, to heirs and assigns for ever: saving Us, Our Heirs and Successors, all Mines of Gold and Silver that shall or maybe hereafter found on any part of the said Parcel or Tract of Land, hereby given and granted as aforesaid; and saving and reserving to Us, Our Heirs and Successors, all White Pine Trees that shall or may now or hereafter grow, or be growing, on any part of the said Parcel or Tract of Land hereby granted as aforesaid.

Provided always, that no part of the Parcel or Tract of Land hereby given and granted to the said *Roman Catholic Corporation* and *their successors heirs*, be within any reservation and heretofore made and marked for Us, Our Heirs and Successors, or by Our Surveyor-General of Woods, or his lawful Deputy, in which case this Our Grant for such part of the Land hereby given and granted to the said *Roman Catholic Corporation* and *their Successors heirs* for ever, as foresaid, and which shall, upon a survey thereof being made, be found within any such reservation, shall be null and void, and of none effect; any thing herein contained to the contrary notwithstanding.

Given under the Great Seal of Our Province of Canada: **Witness**, Cousin Our Right Trusty and Right Well-Beloved Cousin JAMES EARL OF ELGIN AND KINCARDINE, Knight of the Most Ancient and Most Noble Order of the Thistle, Governor General of British North America, and Captain General and Governor in Chief, in and over Our Province of Canada, Nova Scotia, New Brunswick, and the Island of Prince Edward, and Vice-Admiral of the same: At *Montreal* this *Twenty sixth* day of *September* in the year of Our Lord, one thousand eight hundred and forty-*nine* and in the *Thirteenth* year of Our Reign.

By Command of His Excellency in Council
31 August 1839

from Sandwich and St Thomas ministered to the faithful occasionally. On Sunday, when there were no visiting priests, settlers rode horseback 30-40 miles to St. Thomas for Mass. This was the situation in 1844 and, with the increasing number of Catholics from Ireland and the Scottish Highlands, Reeve Patrick Mee wrote to Rt. Rev. Michael Power, Bishop of the Diocese of Kingston, requesting land for a rectory, cemetery and church. He included a list of 122 faithful, which was continuing to grow. The Kingston Diocese covered all of Ontario, as London, Hamilton, and others were not created until 1856. Immediately upon receiving approval from Bishop Power for four acres of land in 1849, the parishioners surveyed for the cemetery plot and began construction of the white frame church adjacent to the cemetery, which served as a Mission until 1904.

There are neither records nor pictures of this humble building, but it was apparently of sturdy construction. It served the parishioners well from 1849 until 1904. St. Patrick's was served as a Mission of Strathroy from 1869 until 1969.

In 1851, there were 50 Catholic families in Adelaide and 43 in Metcalfe. Not all attended St. Patrick's, as distances and the lack of regular instruction led to some drifting away from their faith. The first Catholic Church in Strathroy was called St Anne's until about 1869, when it was rededicated as All Saints. This resulted in a shorter trip to Mass for those living close to Strathroy.

The stalwart of St. Patrick's began planning a more substantial building, which materialized in 1904. With no resident pastor and no church organizations, most of the catechism lessons, prayers and devo-

St. Patrick's Catholic Church, Adelaide Village.

tions were taught at home. In the most steadfast Irish tradition, the Catholic faith was taught, practised, and passed on to the next generation. With the exodus of many people from Adelaide to Strathroy including parishioners of St. Patrick's, people despaired of ever having a resident priest. This factor contributed to quite a number of people joining others from Warwick and Plympton Townships in pulling up roots and moving to Michigan and other parts of the U.S.

By 1868, the Catholic population of Strathroy had increased significantly, and All Saints was upgraded from a Mission to a Parish, with Friar P.J. Brennan appointed pastor. St. Patrick's was now served as a Mission of Strathroy. In spite of setbacks, the little white frame building continued to provide for weekly Mass and Sacraments. Father John Scanlon, assistant pastor in Strathroy, took a special interest in the Adelaide Mission, endeavoring to care for the parishioners' every need.

A New Brick Church

After serving the parishioners for over 50 years, the frame chapel by the cemetery in Adelaide Village was torn down, and replaced in 1904 by a brick edifice on the north side of Egremont Road. The cornerstone was laid and blessed by Bishop Fergus McEvay of London on June 26, 1904, in the presence of 500 people.

This church, which stood as a centrepiece of Adelaide Village for 80 years, featured a small square tower at its southwest corner. It also had a choir loft, a compact pipe organ, and very artistic stained glass windows. Two of the stained glass windows on the west side of the church were donated by a well known pioneer, Miles McCabe, and his sons. On the east side, one window was the gift of Rt. Rev. Fergus McEvay, Bishop of London. Another read, *"In Memory of James and Ellen Langan—by the family,"* and still another was dedicated to the memory of Patrick Murphy.

The Finale of St. Patrick's

With no further need for the cemetery or church, St. Patrick's ceased to be a Mission of Strathroy in 1962. For the next 20 years, with no repairs or upkeep, part of the roof fell in and the building fell to the mercy of the elements and pigeons, both of which left their imprint. Eventually, the Diocese decided to raze the church in 1984. The demolition of this church was a melancholy experience for many of the elders, but their loss was somewhat appeased by the rescue of four of the beautiful stained glass windows. Those have been restored, and were erected in All Saints Roman Catholic Church in Strathroy, as a memorial to the devoted pioneers of St. Patrick's Parish in Adelaide.

The Legacy

The Catholic pioneers of Adelaide appear to have retained an affinity to their native Ireland in that their achievement and fame are often more recognized in a foreign land. The mass migration to the U.S. took the Catholic faith to Michigan and other parts of the U.S. One classic example is the grandson of Thomas Hickey, an Adelaide pioneer, who is now Cardinal James Hickey, Archbishop of Washington, D.C.

The only remaining evidence of St. Patrick's today is the cemetery with its 12 irregular tombstones paying a silent tribute to some 200 sons and daughters, and grandsons and granddaughters of Ireland who, through great adversity, firmly secured their faith in their new land.

Because the burial records as held by All Saints Church are incomplete, and the fact that no effort was made by the parishioners to maintain St Patrick's Cemetery at Adelaide Village, the following list of burials has been prepared from research completed by Mary Kelly before her death. Mary's research is invaluable to the history of Adelaide's Catholic community.

INTERMENTS AT ST. PATRICK'S CEMETERY

Marie Anderson	February 12, 1911
John Bulgar	1844
James Burns	1851
Catherine Burns	Aged 16 yrs.
Terrence Callaghan	December 27, 1904
Catherine D. Callaghan	January 29, 1929
Rosanna Callaghan	1812-1888
Terrence Callaghan Jr.	1913
Mary Elizabeth Callaghan	1924
Mrs. Callaghan	February 28, 1919
Patrick Campbell	
Derrick William Campbell	November 21, 1895
Sarah (Dubois) Campbell	April 4, 1872
Mrs. Thomas Carmoody	August 17, 1916
Mrs. J. Carty	January 20, 1916
Catherine Carty	1834
Thomas Cullinan	
John Cully	
Catherine Upton Cutler	September 3, 1903
Jacuit Cutler	August 30, 1903
Thomas Dewan	
James Dewan	
John Donnelly	January 5, 1882
Ellenor O'Neil Donnelly	November 27, 1914
Mrs. Mary Flaherty Dowling	1888
Margaret Dowling	October 11, 1934
Thomas Dunn	
Mrs. Featherstone	December 7, 1967
Michael Featherstone	June 8, 1932
Mary Carley Featherstone	December 5, 1907
Eugene Gallagher	
Mrs. Mary Gasden	July 18, 1900
Mrs. Edward Gasden	September 16, 1922
Patrick Gately	
Thomas Gately	
Michael Griffin	
Isabella Glen	September 6, 1892
George Glenn	June 21, 1869
Mrs. Mary Glenn	April 7, 1879
George Glenn	August 6, 1887
Margaret Glenn	1853
George Glynn	February 17, 1934
Thomas Glynn	
William Glynn	
Fred Glynn	
Mrs. Mary Gooden	July 1, 1900
Adeline Grogan	December 12, 1907
James Vincent Grogan	1873
John Hanley	September 6, 1878
James Healey	1792-1861
Edward Healey Sr.	December 22, 1895
Henry Healey	September 1874
James Healey	June 4, 1876
William Healey	October 18, 1878
John Healey	October 30, 1898
Mary Healey	August 7, 1890
Roseanne Healey	November 29, 1888
Annie Healey	June 9, 1892
Anastasia Dowling	1844
Cralty Henley (Koppelberger)	
Adeline Henry	1852-1917
John Henderson	1861
Dorothy Henderson	1900
Francis	1917
Henderson (two infant sons)	1917
Bartholomew Hickey	
Charles Bryan Hoffner	October 29, 1878
Mrs. Hoffner	January 22, 1909
Joe Hoffner	Feb 17, 1908
Jeff Hoffner	
Teresa Warner (Hoffner?)	
Henry Humphries	April 18, 1909
Oliver Ivirs	
Edward Ivirs	
Margaret Kelly	November 27, 1890
William Kelly	
Robert Kelly	
James Kelly	
Mary Kelly	
John Kelly	
James Kilbride	
John Kinna (O'Kinna)	September 20, 196?
Timothy Kinna	
James Langan	March 3, 1876
John Langan	March 31, 1909
Mrs. Ellen Langan	September 5, 1904
Anna Langan	January 13, 1919
Mary Langan	March 23, 1935
William Langan	July 2, 1928
Thomas Langan	October 9, 1911
Thomas Langan	1850-1939
Adeline Henry Langan	1852-1911
Ellen Langan	1873-1880
William Langan	1879-1879
John Langan	1881-1929
William Langan	1859-1928
Peter Langan	

462 ADELAIDE TOWNSHIP... A HISTORY

Annie Langan	January 3, 1919	William Morkin	November 10, 1892
James Langan	March 9, 1930	Samuel Morrow	
John Langan	1881-1881	Lizzie Woodward Morrow	October 17, 1889
William Mahon		Terry Mullen	
Patrick Malone	1861	Dan Murphy	
Rosie Murphy Malone	1957	Murrican	
Margaret Malone		Ethel Martin Muxlow	October 17, 1945
Martin Manion	June 5, 1912	Adeline Serene Muxlow	July 17, 1913
Martin Manion Sr.	January 10, 1864	Charles Muxlow	April 26, 1893
Patrick Manion		Lewis Francis Muxlow	November 4, 1897
Mrs. Mary Manion		Mrs. Edward O'Dwyer	March 28, 1879
Mile McCabe Sr.	June 5, 1881	Edward O'Dwyer	March 30, 1879
Miles McCabe Jr.	May 10, 1912	Patrick O'Keefe	January 3, 1903
Martin McCarthy	January 10, 1864	John O'Kinna	September 20, 1900
Mrs. Ann McCarthy	March 10, 1897	Ellenor Donnelly O'Neil	November 27, 1914
James B. McCarthy		Dennis O'Neil	July 8, 1897
Charles McCarthy		Palmer	
Elizabeth McCarthy	1916	William Redmond	
Nora McCarthy		Mrs. Michael Regan	March 11, 1919
Ann McCarthy	1997	Elim Salsbury	
Arthur McCohn	no date	Sarah Salsbury	
McDonagh		Jean Salsbury	
Leslie McGinn		John Salsbury	
Patrick McGuire	1887	John Salsbury	
Mrs. Ann McGuire	July 16, 1886	Alice Salsbury	
William McGuire		Bertha Salsbury	
Christopher McGuire		Dennis Shannigan	1833
Mary McGuire		Mrs. Dennis Shannigan	1879
Mary J. McGuire		Shannosy	
Catherine McGuire		John Small	
James McGuire		Robert Upton	February 5, 1907
Bernard McGuire	January 12, 1880	Margaret McKenna Upton	March 9, 1928
Ann McIntyre	January 26, 1878	Mrs. Robert Upton	February 5, 1910
David McIntyre	April 10, 1890	Mrs. Edward Upton Sr.	1895
John McIntyre	March 10, 1871	Richard Upton (murdered)	October 4, 1891
Patrick McGuire		Mrs. Robert Upton	March 12, 1925
Alex McInroy	February 25, 1869?	Patrick Upton	December 20, 1903
Anna Jane McInroy	March 6, 1902	Patrick Walsh Sr.	May 29, 1878
Mrs. William McKenna	1878	Patrick Walsh Jr.	1905
John McKenna	September 22, 1900	Margaret T. Kearns Walsh	April 17, 1893
Ellen McKenna	October 14, 1905	Ellen Walsh	June 1, 1878
Terrence McKenna	September 13, 1912	Patrick Walsh	February 18, 1892
Margaret McKenna	March 9, 1928	Agnes Welsh	January 21, 1897
Owen McMurray		John Woodlock	September 11, 1911
Mary McPhee	May 28, 1903	Mrs. Mary Woodlock	January 1920
Friar McKeon	1889	Duggan Woods	
Henry Mee	June 18, 1891	Ellen Wright	November 3, 1907
Patrick Monaghan	March 31, 1876	Mrs. Bridget Wright	December 27, 1899
Michel Monaghan	May 25, 1895	John Wright	April 14, 1918

CEMETERIES

Fourth Line Cemetery

In 1855, David and Harriet Rapley sold the east half of Lot 19, Con. 5 SER, to the Wesleyan Methodist Church in Strathroy. The Fourth Line Cemetery was established there for the token sum of five shillings. The signatures on this document, along with the Rapleys, included Rev. John Kellogg Williston, Charles Marshall, Richard Saul, George Pegley, Richard Kerr, Joseph Buttery, James Bond, Thomas and James Holden, trustees of the Strathroy Congregation of the Wesleyan-Methodist Church in Canada. Several early burials had already taken place there.

St. Ann's Anglican Church Cemetery

The cemetery is located in Adelaide Village and, together with the church, it covers an area of three acres. The cemetery was established in 1833, but there is one stone dated 1828.

The oldest recorded burial is that of James Lee, November 28, 1833. Despite the fact that many of the old tombstones have disappeared, there is still a wealth of history here. The tombstone of Blanche Westlake, who came from Davenport, England, and died in 1866, is in memory of one of the pioneers. She was the owner of the Royal Adelaide Inn. The tombstone of John Hoare, who died in 1844 and was postmaster of Adelaide Village for 40 years, is here. Donald Steward is commemorated in a stained glass window, and is buried here, as are the RadcLiff family. Here, also, are the ashes of William Radcliff, who died on a trip to Europe; he was cremated and his widow brought back his ashes for interment in St. Ann's Cemetery. The oldest stone that remains in good condition is that of Emmanuel Mather, who died in 1840.

An oak tree in the cemetery was brought from Windsor Castle. It was planted in 1938, to commemorate the coronation of King George VI and Queen Elizabeth. The tree died and was removed in 1996.

In 1928, a new cemetery committee was formed. The officers were Russell Brock, Fred Brent, Walter Brown and Robert Henry. At the same time, the Women's Auxiliary was established to assist the cemetery committee. The first officers were Mary Barrett as President, Mrs. Fred Brent as Treasurer, and Mrs. Howard Brock as Secretary. One of the auxiliary's goals was to collect $3,000 to be used to establish a fund to provide perpetual care. Donations were solicited from those whose family and friends were buried in the cemetery. In addition, fundraising events were held to restore as many tombstones as possible, and to build a fence. Shortly after the restoration, a new part was opened and the land was consecrated. Additional land was consecrated in 1933 and 1960. At the time of St. Ann's Centennial in 1933, the cemetery received favorable comments.

At the present time, the cemetery board is named by the Vestry. The current Chairman is Bob Feasey and the Secretary/Treasurer is Al Aitken. St. Ann's Anglican Church is responsible for the care and upkeep of the cemetery.

This cemetery is an integral part of St. Ann's Church and, as a result, many events have celebrated both church and cemetery. One such event was the pilgrimage led by Bishop G.M. Luxton that marked the Centennial of Huron Diocese in 1957. The London Free Press of June 30, 1957, reported that *"Four hundred Anglican pilgrims who came to mark the Centennial... found the pioneer churchyard unchanged... They inspected...the 122-year-old burial ground that occupied most of the churchyard... Former parishioners who had been away for years made the rounds of the grave markers, brushing at the eroded ones to distinguish dates and names... One small marker read 'John Seed, born March 31, 1766, died May 11, 1870, aged 104 years, 1 month, 11 days.'"*

This cemetery is thoughtfully and lovingly cared for by the descendants of those buried here, and by present members and adherents of St. Ann's Anglican Church.

St. Mary's Cemetery

St. Mary's Cemetery is in Napier in a part of Metcalfe Township that was formerly part of Adelaide Township. In 1845, the southern part of Adelaide and the northern part of Ekfrid were joined to form the township of Metcalfe.

One acre of land was donated by Charles Preston for a church and cemetery in the late 1830s or early 1840s. This land was also used for a log church school.

These first burials were very plain and simple. Kindly neighbours cut a tree of the proper width and length, an oak or cedar, hollowed it out for the body of the loved one, carefully dug a grave and reverently laid the body away, usually the next day; a prayer and psalm followed. People were literally buried in "the heart of an oak" like a King.

The first burial in what became St. Mary's cemetery was in 1832. The stone has been seen but it is now missing—either removed or beneath overgrown grass. A few years ago, a stranger took some stones from the cemetery, telling a neighbour that he was going to fix them. To date, they have not been returned. The cemetery has suffered one other major theft. At one time, there were white marble posts enclosing Captain Beer's family plot, draped with an iron fence in scallops. An anchor hung from each scallop. The chain was stolen during the iron shortage, in 1942 or 1943.

It is thought that Captain Beer officiated at some of the earliest burials. Captain Beer and his family were among the early settlers who immigrated about 1832. He was instrumental in developing the community, and was called the "shepherd of the infant community."

The first burial in St. Mary's Cemetery was that of Captain Caldwell, which took place on March 21, 1841. The last burial, that of James McKay, was in 1942. Some stones bear names not found in the parish records.

Joe Wrinkle, an escaped slave, came to the community around the 1840s. He was a well known and much loved man, who married after coming to Canada. Both he and his wife are buried in the cemetery. Their graves are marked by a marble stone that bears the name of Mrs. Wrinkle.

In 1860, the cemetery and church were consecrated by the Right Rev. Benjamin Cronyn, Bishop of Huron. In 1963, a plaque was unveiled, marking St. Mary's as the oldest-standing church in Middlesex County, and honouring the soldier's settlement of Adelaide.

This very old cemetery, nestled close to the church, is in a lovely setting. The grounds are cared for and beautiful wild flowers in season add beauty to the area. As in many older cemeteries, some of the tombstones need repair.

St. Patrick's Roman Catholic Cemetery

St. Patrick's Roman Catholic Cemetery is located in Adelaide Village, at Lot 11, Con. 1. It covers one acre of land, and is part of the original grant in 1848 of Crown land of four acres for a church, residence and cemetery.

Between 1849 and 1933, approximately 200 interments took place. The number of monuments was 65, with 16 on the ground. The oldest stone is dated 1864, that of Martin McCarthy, a native of Ireland.

The 1932 *Report of the Cemetery Board of the County of Middlesex* describes the condition of the cemetery *as "Very bad; found cemetery open for cattle to roam over and fences down...overgrown with poplars and weeds."*

By the 1960s, after some 30 years of deterioration, a local authority decided that some action must be taken, and the custodian and a group of volunteers began a massive clean-up. Trees and brush were cleared away. The ground was leveled and seeded, and fragments of tombstones were gathered and buried at the end of the lot. A new fence and gate were installed and the "consecrated pasture field" is described as being in "respectable condition." It was noted, "How much longer the 12 remaining monuments will survive is questionable since the quality of stone is not adequate to withstand the Canadian climate after so many years… even marble stones were over as the bases are of sandstone that, after a hundred years, begin to crumble."

The cemetery is owned and maintained by the All Saints Roman Catholic Church of Strathroy.

Strathroy Municipal Cemetery

Strathroy Municipal Cemetery is located at the southwest end of Metcalfe Street in Strathroy. The cemetery came into existence in 1862, when the town council purchased an acre of land for burial purposes and surveyed it into lots. However, it appears that a number of burials took place before 1862, as evidenced by one monument that carried the date of 1854 or 1856. When the cemetery was established, Strathroy had a small group of black residents, and the first person buried was one of their number.

A new part was added in 1868 and almost completely allotted by 1892. More land was purchased in 1892, 1924, 1953 and 1982. The cemetery currently covers approximately 40 acres of land. A columbarium was added in 1994.

Throughout the years as the cemetery was extended, changes were made to enhance the beauty of the area. Initially, plots in the old part were at random, and later, symmetry became part of the planning. In 1892, a drive was made through the centre and continued in a circle to the rear. In 1919, the older portion of the cemetery was improved. Graves were leveled, and old curbing was removed, thus making the cemetery more uniform. A new main entrance was built in 1955.

In 1872, the office burned and all of the records were lost. The office again burned in 1981, but records were not destroyed. The office is now computerized, and the caretaking and office staff is composed of two full-time employees and one part-time person.

The first sexton was William Hillyard, followed by William Richardson, Hiram Dell, William Wells, David Davis, Charles Davis, William Sullivan and Gordon Fletcher, who held the position for 31 years. The present incumbent, Mr. John Whiting, assumed the office in the fall of 1986.

A bylaw was passed in 1919 by the town council, placing the cemetery under the management of a committee. The first commissioners were J.C. Scott, S. Waite and J.R. Stevenson, with the mayor and reeve as members ex-officio. E.A. Baskerville was appointed to the position of Superintendent and Secretary-Treasurer in 1943. It is reported that he took a "faithful interest in the work and, under his supervision, the grounds were kept in excellent condition." He was still in charge in 1960.

Initially, the charge for the care of a lot was $1. The fee was increased in 1916 to ensure upkeep as needed. By 1960, 35% of the sale price was set aside for permanent care, as specified by the Cemetery Act. However, throughout the years, the return from investments has not been sufficient to meet all of the expenses, and the commission found it necessary to appeal to the town council for funds.

Strathroy Cemetery is a public cemetery that has been in existence and open for interments for many years. It is believed that several graves were moved from other areas in Adelaide Township to this cemetery during the 1930s and 1940s. Three graves are reported to have been moved from Katesville. One of Strathroy's best known public persons, Sir Arthur Currie, is buried in Strathroy Cemetery.

The grounds in this cemetery are particularly beautiful. In fact, it was described in the *"Strathroy Centennial 1860-1960"* as being *"one of the most beautifully kept in Western Ontario."* The entire area is carefully planned, with tree-lined paths and formal gardens. Norway spruce, flowering crab, and oak trees contribute to the beauty and the peace of this lovely cemetery.

West Adelaide Cemetery

In 1875, West Adelaide Presbyterian Church was built and a cemetery was established directly north of the church on Lot 4, Con. 3 NER. One acre of land was donated by Jane and Robert Conkey to the Board of Trustees, who were responsible for the management of the cemetery. The Conkeys had immigrated to Canada in the 1830s from County Down, Ireland, and settled near the site of the cemetery. The church and cemetery were very important to the Conkeys and other Irish and Scottish immigrants. This attachment in all probability motivated the gift of land. Although the cemetery was established adjacent to West Adelaide Church, its name "West Adelaide Cemetery" is for geographical reasons only, and it has no direct connection with the church.

In 1915, $1/2$-acre was purchased to extend the cemetery and build a shed. In 1925, the Cemetery Act Certificate defined the geographical area. Also in 1925, a cemetery commission was established with William McChesney as President and George Conkey as Treasurer. At that time, all records related to the cemetery were turned over to Wilfred Wilson and have remained the responsibility of the cemetery commission.

The symmetrically designed cemetery is in excellent condition and contains over 100 monuments dating from the late 1800s to the present. The tombstones carry a wealth of history, partly illustrated by the different styles that have evolved over the years. The monuments and the well-kept lawns and trees blend together to create a peaceful and tranquil setting.

The cemetery gates carry the inscription 1882-1927. However, the cemetery is still open for burial and has no restrictions of religion, race or colour.

West Adelaide Presbyterian Cairn

In 1853, part of the east half of Lot 3, Con. 1 SER, was purchased from John N. Wiley for a cemetery. The cemetery was free and open to all denominations of Presbyterians. In February 1854, a memorial deed was signed by James Wallace, John

Jamieson and David Wiley.

Information on the cairn indicates that the last burial was in 1881. Out of a total of 25 recorded interments, 11 died before age five, and four died as adults. We have no information on the remaining 10 burials. It is believed that some bodies were moved from this site to the new site of West Adelaide Cemetery. Those who were left were not exhumed and moved, for fear of transmitting the diphtheria germ that was prevalent at that time.

After 1881, the cemetery fell into disuse and, for a period of time, was badly neglected. In 1932, the condition of the cemetery was reported to the township. In the late 1950s, monuments were brought together in one place on the property and a plan for care was established. The Adelaide-Metcalfe Jr. Farmers took on this project and looked after the upkeep of the cemetery for a period of time. The Peters family took on the caretaking responsibility, and they continue to care for the cemetery.

PRIVATE BURIALS

There are several private cemeteries in Adelaide Township. Information on these sites is sketchy and largely dependent on memory. These sites include institutional burying grounds, as well as family grounds.

The House of Refuge Cemetery

This cemetery is on the grounds of the former House of Refuge. In 1985, Mona Aitken interviewed several persons who said they knew about a small cemetery for persons who died and had no one to take the responsibility for burial. In such cases, burial was a county expense. In addition, Strathroy municipal records indicate that there were 12 cremated burials. The grounds of the cemetery have since been plowed.

Mental Institution Cemetery

In the late 1930s during excavation, bones were discovered behind the bank on Front Street. The location was Lots 45, 46, 47 and 48. A longtime resident, Mr. Clark, said that there were persons buried on this property, the former site of the asylum.

Minielly Family Cemetery

This private cemetery, now non-existent, was established in 1880 on land owned by Andrew Minielly. The number of interments recorded in 1932 was 30 or more. There have been no burials since 1905.

Until 1960-1965, there were several stones and a small iron fence around the plot. It is thought that the stones were discarded to a nearby woodlot. Both stones and fence went missing around 1960.

Lot 22, Con. 2

This is now a radio-television business. The lot was previously owned by John Douglas. No tombstones exist, and no information regarding burials is available.

Lot 26, Con. 2

George Buttery is buried at this location under a big maple tree. No other information is available.

Lot 27, Con. 1

Two tombstones were on this property when it was owned by William Ireland. One tombstone was that of John Walker and the other one was Mr. Cooper. No burial data is available and the tombstones are no longer in existence, possibly buried under the road.

Con. 4/Wilson Sideroad

It is reported that some Roman Catholic family members were buried at this site. Among their number was Mary Climehegg, who lived on the property and was buried on November 2, 1879.

CHAPTER FOUR

Schools

Education in Adelaide Township

When the first settlers came to live in the forests of Adelaide, educating the children was an important consideration after basic needs were met for shelter, food, and clearing land for crops. If parents could read or write, such skills were passed on to their children in the evenings, around the fire or by candlelight. Many Adelaide pioneers were officers in the British military, and education or wealth had been the prerequisite for their position. It was very important for the officers' children to be literate, and to gain knowledge to improve their quality of life in the new world. In some wealthy households, a tutor or governess was hired to live with the family and teach the children, and perhaps the neighbours' children. Many less affluent citizens, who had been deprived of schooling in the "old country" for political or religious reasons, refused to tolerate such unfairness in Ontario. Thus, small log cabin schools, also used as a Sabbath meetinghouse, were built in the forest, and trees were notched to guide the way.

The first church services were held in Captain Beer's house, which was also used as a school. Captain Johnson provided similar facilities. A school was built in November 1839, and this was also used for Sunday School classes. Charles Preston donated land for a church school, church and cemetery. There was a school further west, across the road from Emerick's Hotel, which was built before 1836. It was close to the corner of Con. 10 and the Currie Road. St. Catherine's of Katesville opened in 1841 (perhaps the building was also used as a school at one time). A year later, John S. Buchanan gave land for a church and school, and the Church of England built an excellent schoolhouse where pupils were taught by William Hilyard. The old Methodist log church on the east half of Lot 19, Con. 5 SER, donated by David and Harriet Rapley, was also used as a school. The 1851 census shows another school on the Thomas Evoy farm, the east half of Lot 13, Con. 5 SER. In Adelaide Village, a school is listed, but we have no knowledge of who attended. Perhaps Robert Graham, a teacher staying at Patrick Mee's Inn, was the teacher of this Adelaide Village School. The 1851 census shows a schoolhouse on Thomas Cuddy's land, part of Lot 5, Con. 3 NER. This is said to be the first school in Adelaide Township, built in 1838, as the 1938 centennial was celebrated. In addition, a school is shown on John Mullan's farm, the west half of Lot 4, Con. 5 NER.

Before 1850, there were only a few private schools in Ontario. Some of the teachers were unqualified for their work, and teaching materials, as we know them today, were practically non-existent. Many children learned only what their parents could teach them. Most parents were proud to own a Bible, so this was the main textbook for all grades. A few free schools were started after 1850. In 1871, all schools in Ontario were available to students at no cost, thanks to the efforts of Rev. Egerton Ryerson, who is known as "The Father of our Public School System."

Teacher training did not take place, or the teacher-to-be attended the Model School in Strathroy, where a 2nd or 3rd Class Certificate was received. Those wishing a 1st Class Certificate earned this in Ottawa. Mr. Ross of S.S. #6 attended Ottawa Teachers' College. John Jamieson, a teacher from Largs, Scotland, writes in a diary entry of June 21, 1853, *"Appeared before the Education Board for examination, in order to obtain a certificate of qualification for teaching school. About 300 teachers present for examination. I passed and got my **TICKET**."*

It had taken him two days to walk each way and, unfortunately, Jamieson was caught in the rain on the way home, and the mud was unbearable as he was wearing "little shoes." He mentions a public examination of the school by Mr. Tooth, who had been appointed at the second Council Meeting of February 4, 1850, to be Superintendent of Common Schools in this township. Later, other Inspectors and Area Superintendents were Mr. Elliott, Mr. Carson, John Dearness (later Dr.), James Sexton, Gordon Young, Elwood Oakes, Graham McDonald, F. Stewart Toll, Don McIntosh, Don Dool, John T. Mackey, and (currently) Rene Trehan.

Adelaide Township showed some interest in providing books. On August 3, 1853, a committee was selected to buy books for the library with power to add to the stock. Anthony Preston, the Clerk, was appointed Township Librarian. He was ordered to get a walnut or cherry desk for the books. At the December 14, 1854, Council Meeting at the Royal Adelaide Hotel, Messrs. Scoon, Walker, and Preston were appointed to select books in the amount of $70 for the library. Mr. Preston was to cover them and prepare them for circulation. At the June 22, 1857, Council Meeting, £7, 10 shilling, was appropriated to the township library. Alex Forsyth was to assist the Clerk in choosing the books. On June 26, 1860, the Minutes record that... *"the Clerk of Adelaide, the Clerk of the Village of Strathroy and the Treasurer of Adelaide apportion to the Village of Strathroy, an equitable share in the Township Library. Aug. 5, 1861: $3.50 for dividing library books and apportioning books to Strathroy Library."*

On December 1, 1863, the Clerk was to receive $20 for serving as Librarian for 1863, $4 for repairing books for 1862-1863, and $1.50 for postage and stationery.

On May 5, 1873, at a Council Meeting at the Rychman Hotel, Edward Rowland, a School Teacher Representative for the School Teachers' Division of #1 of North and West Williams, sought a grant for establishing a School Teachers' Library. A grant of $12 was given.

THE SCHOOLS

S.S. #1 AND #2—ADELAIDE AND WEST WILLIAMS, KEYSER SCHOOL

S.S. #1 and #2 was situated in three different locations of Keyser throughout the years. The first school, a log building, was located west of Keyser Corner, on the farm of Lawrence Grogan (formerly the John Mullan farm), on the corner of Langan Drive and Wilson Road. Benches were placed along the sides of the room with desks in front. The girls and boys sat on opposite sides, with their backs to one another. The older children helped on the farms and therefore attended school only in the winter. The 20'x16' room was heated by wood, either in a fireplace or stove. In the Adelaide Township Council Minutes of February 25, 1850, it was stated that elections would be held in Mullan's School, Keyser.

The first teachers were Miss Lowes, Miss Currie and Miss Ann Dyer. Teachers usually boarded in the community. In 1857, Richard Bell was a tailor, but as times were hard, farmers had no money to buy tailored clothing. Richard Bell learned that Keyser needed a teacher. To augment his income, he applied for and received a certificate as teacher, which enabled him to teach from May to August.

S.S. #1 and 2 Keyser, ca.1905, teacher Mr. Courie; back, seventh from left, is Mary (Brown) Fletcher with sister Winnifred Brown (McInroy) on right holding date.

S.S. #1 and 2, June 1933, teacher Vivian McKenzie.

S.S. #1 and 2 Adelaide and West Williams, 1948.

The second school, probably a frame building, was situated across from the general store, a mile east at Lot 7, Con. 4 NER, on the farm of John Keyser Sr. On July 28, 1858, the land was leased to the trustees for .25¢ each year. The attendance was about 90, with desks large enough for six pupils to sit in. Once again, the girls sat on one side, and the boys on the other. The eldest pupils were seated at the back, the younger ones in front, and some were reported to have sat on the floor. Each family boarded the teacher for a period of time. Teachers of the school were John Winter, George Waters for four years (this Scotsman resigned to study medicine), Samuel Cooper, Adam Scott (an Irish gentlemen who could not manage the boys), and Richard Bell.

By 1877, the school was in need of much repair, as reported in the Strathroy Age of February 23, 1877, *"The schoolhouse is extremely bad, the pupils are literally huddled together. It is a great pity to see so many fine looking boys and girls forced to pass the day in such a wretched house. The trustees contemplate building very soon."*

In July 1877, the trustees purchased land from the Murrays and Keysers at Lot 7, Con. 5 NER, ¼-mile north of Keyser Corner, adjacent to Salem Methodist Church. The brick building had a bell tower (the bell had disappeared several times). In the Strathroy Age of October 6, 1881, it was reported, *"Trustees of Keyser School erected a $40 bell on the edifice last Saturday. May it swing longer than the last."*

The attendance was 110 students. The scholars marched from the old school to the new school in couples with guards alongside, under the direction of Mr. McTavish, who later became a lawyer in Parkhill. Later teachers were Mr. Anderson and Mr. Fovill. Mr. Rowland C. Wittett taught in 1871. Mr. O.C. Hodgins taught three years, from 1879-1881, for $275. He later became a Member of Parliament. Dr. McCabe taught from 1882-1885 for $252, which was considered to be high at that time, then left to study medicine. The average attendance was 66. Trustees were Patrick Murray, Nathaniel Davidson and Joseph Keyser.

Teachers were Mr. A.L. Leitch 1885, Miss Hannah Weir 1886-1888, Mr. Duncan Currie 1889, Mr. L.W. Cuddy 1890, and Mr. Ben Parker 1891. Ben Parker's salary was $480 his first year, with 72 pupils and an average attendance of 68. Mr. Parker's class carried off honours at Arkona Centre on entrance exams.

Mr. Johnson received the appointment of School Inspector following Mr. J.S. Carson. Trustees were Joseph Keyser, James Langan and Joseph Paterson.

Miss Jean Brown proved to be an outstanding teacher, and is associated with Red Cross work. Teachers were Mr. John Currie 1902-1908, Miss Belle Wyatt, Miss Kingsley, Miss Anderson, Miss Martha Milliken, Miss Pilkie and Miss Alberta J. Milliken. Mr. Murray McLeish taught 1914-1917, then went to St. Mary's and enlisted. Other teachers were Miss Jeanette I. Dale 1918, Miss Donna Tanner 1920, Miss Irene M. Shields 1921-1922, Mr.

S.S. #1 and 2

470 Adelaide Township... A History

HIGH SCHOOL ENTRANCE RESULTS

JULY, 1914 - ENTRANCE RESULTS FOR ADELAIDE STUDENTS

S.S. #11, Adelaide   Harold Eastman
  Charlotte Buttery
  Kenneth Thompson

S.S. #8, Adelaide   Hazel Sullivan

S.S. #5, Adelaide   Pauline Harris
  Franklin Hull
  Robert Paine

S.S. #10, Adelaide   Ethel McLeish
  George McLeish
  Jack Walker

S.S. #3, Adelaide   Annie Hansford

S.S. #7, Adelaide   W. Eddie Cooper
  Fred Richardson
  Cyril Wright
  Winnifred Waltham

S.S. #2, Adelaide   Mary Smith

JULY, 1915 - ENTRANCE RESULTS FOR ADELAIDE STUDENTS

S.S. #6, Adelaide   George Ball
  Ross Campbell
  Alvin McChesney

S.S. #2, Adelaide   Ethel Wardell

JULY, 1917 - ENTRANCE RESULTS FOR ADELAIDE STUDENTS

S.S. #7, Adelaide   Agnes Callaghan

S.S. #2, Adelaide   Olive MacDonald
  Gordon Wardell

S.S. #10, Adelaide   Elsie Campbell

JULY, 1918 - ENTRANCE RESULTS FOR ADELAIDE STUDENTS

S.S. #6, Adelaide   William Ball (Honours)
  R. McDonald (Honours)

(only Adelaide students to obtain honours)

Duncan C. Fisher 1923-1927, Miss Vivian McKenzie 1927-1929, Miss Lillian McKenzie 1930-1939, Mr. Ross Gregory 1940, Mrs. Jessie Bice 1941, Miss Mary Ellen Paterson 1942-48, Miss Mary Evelyn McLean and Mrs. Flossie Hall 1948-1949, Mr. Kenneth Wilson 1949-1951 (later became a Presbyterian Minister), Miss Gertrude Weishar 1951-1953, Mrs. Ruby Drake 1953-1955, Mrs. Hazel Gault 1955-1956, Miss Maxine Hunking 1956-1958, and Mrs. Bella McLellan 1959. Mrs. McLellan was the last teacher at S.S. #1 and #2 before the pupils moved to Adelaide Central School in January 1960.

For several years before 1945, Christmas concerts were held in the Canadian Order of Foresters' Hall, situated through the fields and across the creek on Langan Drive. There was a platform, curtains and chairs. Later, a movable platform was constructed by Gordon Plumb and used in the school.

The last trustees for S.S. #1 and #2 Adelaide and West Williams School at Keyser were Ivan McLeish, William Rowland and Lorne Murray. For 12 years, Wilbert Murray served as Secretary-Treasurer.

On January 16, 1945, the school section joined the Adelaide Township School Area. The five trustees were George Glenn, Harold Bolton, Howard Earley, Elmer Gast and Allan Brown. Earl McInroy was Secretary-Treasurer.

Mrs. Marguerite Johnson was itinerant music teacher. Mrs. Dorothy Hawkins was appointed Public Health Nurse. The electric lights were turned on December 17, 1945.

In 1943, a built-in cupboard was built at the back of the room, to store the storm windows. During June of this same year, the senior pupils painted the fence posts and outbuildings. Indoor toilets were built in 1950.

In 1960, the Canadian Order of Foresters bought S.S. #1 and #2 School, where Court Keyser and Court Bluebell held their meetings. In the early 1990s, after these two groups disbanded, the property was sold. It is now a private residence.

UNION SCHOOL, S.S. #2 ADELAIDE AND #14 EAST WILLIAMS
CRATHIE SCHOOL S.S. #2 AND HALL

About 1855, a log schoolhouse was built in

S.S. #2 Crathie, ca.1951

East Williams Township on Lot 16, Con. 7, on the property of E. Pedden. The first teacher was Tommy Robinett. Richmond Sands also taught at Pedden's School. By 1877, this Union School, S.S. #2 Adelaide and #14 East Williams, was in such poor condition that it had to be closed.

About 1876 or earlier, a movement was started to have a union school section formed including the eastern part of Con. 7, East Williams Township, and the eastern part of Con. 2 and 3, Adelaide Township. Considerable controversy arose, as some were in favour of a union, and others were not. If Pedden's School in East Williams was closed and a union school section was organized, the children attending there would have to go to Springbank School, which would be a long distance for some children.

Arrangements were finally completed and a union school was built on the Strathroy Road, Highway #81, on Lot 21, Con. 3 NER, Adelaide Township, and Crathie School, S.S. #2, was opened in 1879. When school opened, there were 50 pupils in attendance. The first trustees were James Jones, Andrew Heake and James Bolton. The first teacher was Miss Emma Austin, who later married William Nettleton, the owner of the property on which the school was built.

For many years, the school was painted white and will be remembered by the students of those days as "the white school on the hill." In 1930, the school was covered with red Insul-brick. The school was closed on December 31, 1959, and pupils attended the new school, Adelaide Central School, which was constructed on Lot 15, Con. 1 SER, and was opened on January 2, 1960.

LIST OF TEACHERS 1879-1959

1879	Miss Emma Austin
1887	Albert G. Bunting
1889	Osborne McPherson
1902	Dan Norris
1910	Maude McKenzie
	Mr. McPherson
	Miss Rebecca Wilson
1914	Miss Douglas
	Miss Iva Ingerville
1917-1918	Mr. Fred James
	Mrs. Taylor
1921-1922	Miss Jean McLeish
	Miss Ruth Amos
	Miss Allison Cameron
	Miss Irene Graham
1926-1933	Mr. Gordon McKean
1934	Miss Annie Sullivan (Fidler)
1938	Miss Marjorie Lyons
	Miss Aileen McKichan
1949-1959	Miss Annie Courtis

E.M. (Austin) Nettleton, teacher at Crathie School, 1881.

S.S. #2 Crathie, 1938. Back L-R, Marjorie Wardell, Christine Pedden, Marjorie McCullough, teacher Marjorie Lyons, Bill McDonald, Bruce Wardell. Front L-R, Betty Dennis, Donna Nettleton, Charlie Pedden, Allan Wardell, Murray Oliver, Douglas Pedden.

Some of the school trustees over the years were Wesley Bunting, William Graham, David Sands, James Bolton, Joseph Pedden and Albert Bunting.

Crathie Community Hall was built in 1921 by volunteer labour, and everyone was an active participant. Many events were held in the building, such as oyster suppers, box socials, card games, neighbourhood bridal showers, and debates by the Literary Society. Christmas concerts and competitive school musical concerts were held on a regular basis. Voting for the Federal and Provincial Elections were held in Crathie Hall. In the early days, a shed accommodated the horses and buggies. Many dances were held in the hall and, at one time, Guy Lombardo and his Orchestra played for a dance. Many people reading this will remember the good times at Crathie Hall!

Crathie School

S.S. #3 ADELAIDE

On December 6, 1861, Benjamin Varnum Demaray sold 1/5 acre of the west half of Lot 28, Con. 1 SER, to the trustees of S.S. #3 (B&S #2274 Middlesex County Land records). In the school log book of 1939, it is stated that the original building was used as a post office (Amiens) before it burned. The new school, possibly the brick building (demolished in 1999), had a dual purpose. It served as a school during the week and as a church on Sunday afternoons, with a Baptist Minister conducting the services (the accuracy of this early school history is uncertain). An organization called the "Patrons of Industry" used the building for meetings. Election speeches were also held here. When the itinerant "Magic Lantern" came to the area, it was given the use of the building. At the turn of the century, the school grounds were enlarged by the purchase of a piece of land to the east of the school, property owned by Thomas Whiting.

Trustees who served the section from 1885-1890 were Aaron Demaray, Malcolm Smith, M.M. Thompson, John Harten, Richard Demaray, William Demaray and James Giffen.

Some teachers listed include Mr. Pomeroy, Mr. Colin Johnston, Miss White, Miss Fitzgerald, Mr. Patterson, Mary Dibb, Lydia "Lizzie" Hyslop 1882-1885, Mary C. Cluness, Miss Fran Demaray 1885, Miss Sarah Ross 1886-1887, Malcolm Smith 1886-1889 (became a doctor in Oklahoma), Donald McLean 1889, Joan McDonald 1913-1918, Ethel M. Jury 1920-1923, Annie Bycraft 1923, Mary Edwards 1925, R.L. Walker 1927, Joyce Demaray 1927, Lena Pulling 1928, Rita Humphries 1929-1931, Margaret Bolton 1934-1936, Dorothy J. Bush 1937-1939, Edna Patterson 1940-1943, and Mrs. Mary A. Harris 1944.

S.S. #3 Adelaide

S.S. #3, back L-R, Jack Ramsay, Roy Lewis, Carl Lewis, Dorothy Bush (from Brigden), Phyllis Lewis, Thelma Tomlinson, Lyle Ramsay. Front L-R, Leslie Chisholm, Noreen Bell, Donald Wood, Marion Ireland, Doris Lewis, Betty Ireland; George Walker absent.

S.S. #3 Adelaide School Fair

Lena Pulling drove from Strathroy each day in her 1926 Model T coupe. If she had difficulty starting the car, student Bill Daniels would take out the floor boards and set the bands. Often, Bill and his brother, Alfred, rode their motorcycle to public school. Bill's dad had a similar car and Bill was interested in motor mechanics. After his school days, he operated the family garage at Hickory Corners.

New toilets were built in August 1934. Hot lunches commenced on January 1, 1936. The building was wired for electricity in March 1944.

The following students attended school during the period of September, 1925 to June, 1945: Stewart Mitchell, Almer Daniels, Olive Lewis, Alice Freele, Florence Lewis, Alfred Daniels, Ilene Tomlinson, Ruth Stiltz, Sadie Dewar, Roy Lewis, Carl Lewis, Phyllis Lewis, Jack Ramsay, Bruce Dixon, Mildred Dixon, Donald Wood, Thelma Tomlinson, Lyle Ramsay, Fred Tucker, George Walker, Marion Ireland, Howard McQuiggan, Betty Ireland, Lorene Bell, Leslie Chisholm, Doris Lewis, Anne Stanley, James Stanley, June Stanley, Bill Dennis, Isabell Chisholm, Ronald Ireland, Bernice Beatty, Douglas Finlay, Velma Chisholm, Doris Dennis, William Stanley, Priscilla Martin, Gordon Martin, Donald Martin.

The school closed in June 1945. It was sold to Mary Bolton to house her antique collection. The building was dismantled during the summer of 1999.

S.S. #4, ADELAIDE SCHOOL

S.S. #4 was located on the John Hanley property at Lot 15, Con. 3 NER, a brick building erected in 1879. Prior to this schoolhouse being built, the children of S.S. #4 attended classes at Mud Creek School, 1 1/4 miles east.

Some of the early names in the community were Henderson, Burrows, Pennington, McCabe, Brown, Hanley, McLellan, Gerry, Robotham, Seed, Ayre, Regan, McCubbin, Adair and Baskier.

The first teacher of S.S. #4 was Mr. T.M. Hamilton in the 1880-1881 school year. Subsequent teachers were Mr. Robert Coulton, Mr. Alexander James Anderson 1882-

S.S. #4, teacher Miss Laura Pulling.

1885, Mr. James C. Mitchell 1886, Mr. J. Mitchell Roberts 1886-1888, Mr. H.E. Manning 1889-1891, Miss Alice Dell, Miss Jessie Glenn, Mr. John Milliken, Miss Pauline Harris, Miss Minnie Milliken, Miss Annie Jane Anderson, Miss Blanche Pannell, Mr. Nelson George, Mr. Eli Oliver, Miss Marjorie McLeish 1913, Mr. Gordon Walker 1914, Miss Kate Pulling 1915, Miss Marjorie McLeish 1916-1917, Miss Pauline Lucas, Miss Marion Campbell 1920, Miss Martha McGeary, Mr. Samuel Earl McInroy 1921-1927, Mr. Wilbert McKean, Miss Alma Wardell, Miss Helen Alum 1930-1935, Miss Ruby Grogan 1936-1937, Mr. Aubrey Lyons 1938, Miss Irma Yake 1939, Miss Evelyn B. Campbell 1940-1941, and Miss Evelyn Windover 1942.

The school was closed in 1943. Mrs. Flossie Hall taught in 1944, until the school closed permanently in June 1945.

In 1943-1944, David Robotham drove Betty and Bob Robotham and Fred Bolton, who were the only S.S. #4 students still going to public school, to S.S. #9. The next school year, 1944-1945, Frank Pennington drove the few remaining #9 students to #4 school. These two years had #4 and #9 students alternating due to low enrolments in each area.

In 1946, David Robotham drove the three remaining S.S. #4 students, Betty and Bob Robotham and Ted Seed, to S.S. #10, where Mrs. Harris was the teacher. In September 1947, David Robotham drove Bob Robotham and Ted Seed to S.S. #10, then picked up Margaret Glenn and, along with Betty Robotham, drove them to the corner of Highway #81 and #22, where they met Bill Daniels, who drove them to Strathroy District Collegiate Institute. S.S. #4 remained empty for several years, and was then torn down. It is now a private residence.

The teachers boarded in homes in the school sec-

S.S. #4 Adelaide, ca.1905, back L-R, Kate Fraser, Mae McCubbin, Ethel Brown; 4th row, Eva (last name unknown, later Arthur), Matilda unknown, Oscar Plaxton, Earl McInroy, Walter Brown; 3rd row, Manford Pennington, Iva McCubbin, Elva McCabe, Laura George, Ivy Plaxton, Vernon Burrows, Manfred Robotham, teacher Blanche Pannell, Milo McCabe, unknown, Fred Seed (in front), Dave Robotham, Frank Gerry; 2nd row, Dorothy Henderson, Madeline Henderson, Edna McInroy, John Seed; front row, Bill Eastman, Fred Adair, Nelson McCubbin, Bertha Eastman, unknown, unknown, unknown, unknown, Eva Pennington; seated behind Eva are Harriet McInroy, Elva Eastman, Bridget Henderson and Mildred McInroy.

S.S. #4 Adelaide, teacher Nelson George.

S.S. #4 Adelaide, teacher Nelson George.

tion and walked to school. The school was heated by wood in a big stove near the back of the one-room building. In later years, an oil burner provided the heat. Senior pupils performed custodial duties. The building had a big bell in the bell tower, used to beckon the students to class.

Christmas concerts were held in Crathie Community Hall with S.S. #4 students joining Crathie students, performing songs, recitations, plays and drills. According to records: *"September 1, 1885, trustees John McDonald and James George with treasurer, J.M. Henderson, received a grant of $30.74, and March 4, 1890, trustees were John Pedden and William J. Adair, who received a grant of $31.24."*

S.S. #5 NAPPERTON

An article in the Strathroy Age, June 20, 1912, about the closing of Mt. Zion Methodist Church in Napperton states, *"A rude log church erected in 1846... was used for both church and school. This was the east half of Lot 10, Con 5 SER. It is possible that the school was moved to another structure before the log house was demolished and the new brick church was built in 1868."*

From the journal of the Municipal Council of the Township of Adelaide, February 25, 1850: *"Mr. Cook presented two petitions from Thomas Carrol and others praying for a new School Section, to be taken from School Section number five. Referred to School Committee. School Committee was moved by Mr. Hoar, seconded by Mr. Cuddy for two members. Carried."* The School Committee consisted of Mr. Hoar and Mr. Dell.

In 1881, a document (Instrument 6612) between David Rapley with his wife, Harriet, and the Trustees of S.S. #5, states $45 was to be paid for Lot 14, Con. 4 SER, 1/5 acre. The property was to revert to Rapley and his heirs *"in the event of the said lands not being used or required for public school purposes."* The trustees were to fence the lot at the expense of the school section, and maintain the fences. The trustees at that time were Jonas Jury, Thomas O. Currie and Andrew McCandless; the teacher, William James Smith, was the witness. Part of the school property was donated by Mr. Shepard, whose property was on the east side of the school (Mr. Rapley's land was on the west).

The frame schoolhouse on Lot 14, Con. 4 SER, was built about 1866. Early teachers were William James Smith and Mr. Botley. In the early years, the annual salary was from $240-300.

1885-1887	John A. Reinhardt
1888-1889	H.E. Manning
1890-1891	Miss Meada Curry
1893-1895	Miss Bishop
1896-1897	Laura Morgan
1898-1900	Addie Patterson
1901-1903	Miss M. McChesney
1913	Marjorie Thompson

1915-1917	Reta Collins
1920-1922	A. May Smith
1923-1925	Irene Shields
1926-1927	Elizabeth McIntyre
1928-1929	Alma Swift
1930	Mrs. Annie L. Foster
1931	Jean McGregor
1934	Nelson Johnson
1935-1938	Kathryn Murphy
1939-1941	Ilene Ada Wright
1946-1947	Mrs. Carman Hall
1948	Marguerite Willison
1949-1950	Mrs. Mary A. Harris
1951-1952	Mrs. Olive J. Burdon
1953	Mrs. Jean Colgan
1954-1959	Mrs. Margaret Fonger

Records indicate that Elizabeth (Dodge) Fisher was teaching in the 1940s. D. Jury was an early teacher. Before the school closed in 1959, Laila Parker offered the school board $500 to purchase the property. The school board then realized it did not own the land, which was to revert to heirs of the Rapley and Shepard families. Robert Ogg then purchased the property, paying Harold Westgate (the Shepard property) and Laila Parker (the Rapley property) and the School Board (the building). He razed the building and built a red brick ranch house in 1961, incorporating the school door and moving the woodshed to the back of the property.

S.S. #5, ca.1934, back L-R, Wilfred "Tiny" Crandon, Bob Topham, Grant Parker, Clare Crandon, Laverne Shepard, teacher Nelson Johnson; front L-R, Harry Shepard, Donald Jairts, Mervin Shepard, Bill Wilson and Dick Wilson.

S.S. #6 ADELAIDE

We know from the diarist, John Jamieson, that S.S. #6 was an established school section in 1853, as was S.S. #10. However, much to the distress of Mr. Jamieson, there was no schoolhouse and no classes had been conducted for two years. Previous to 1853, there is no indication as to where the classes were conducted—perhaps in someone's home or even Wiley's Inn.

On January 22, 1853, the ratepayers held a meeting and voted that a school should be opened as soon as a teacher could be obtained. Mr. Jamieson made an entry in his journal to the effect that school opened on February 15, 1853. There is no mention of where the classes were held or who the teacher was. On April 21, 1853, John Jamieson travelled to London to be certified to teach in Upper Canada along with 300 others. He was teaching in S.S. #6 shortly afterwards, and on April 30, 1853, he gave the scholars two weeks' holiday. His journal notes that school was opened again on May 23. Mr. Jamieson was engaged on September 21, 1853, to teach for six months.

S.S. #5 Adelaide, teacher John A. Reinhardt.

TINY ADELAIDE TOWNSHIP SCHOOL NOTED
FOR ITS MANY OUTSTANDING GRADUATES

Motorists leaving Strathroy and driving on Highway 22 in the direction of Kerwood soon pass the gray colored, tree-bordered school house of S.S. #5, Adelaide Township, through whose portals many a noted graduate has passed during the past three-quarters of a century, probably the most outstanding of them all being the late General Sir Arthur Currie, K.C.B. D.S.O. commander of the Canadian Army in WWI.

Although early records seem to have been lost with the passing of time, the fact is still known that two schoolhouses once were built within the environs of this school section. One had been erected on low ground and it was eventually decided to move to a better location. David Rapley, one of the old settlers, donated a site on a hill at the corner of his farm. The present frame edifice was built there in 1866 or about that time, and in the years following it became known locally as Rapley's School.

The other log school was in use for a time but was finally discarded and eighty years ago, in 1868, a brick church known as Mount Zion was built where it had stood. Henry Barr is recalled as one of the teachers in the school replaced by the church.

Early settlers in this part of Adelaide included the Morgans, Boltons, Murdocks, Jurys, Rapleys, Manns, Pattersons, Parkers, Carsons, Stills, Rowes, Tompsons, Campbells, Mitchells, Wards, Shepherds and the Jones and Thomas families.

The oldest resident of this school section at the present time is Fred Rapley, a son of David Rapley, now in his 86th year. Mr. Botley, who later retired and died at Watford, was the first teacher he remembers and is believed by local residents to have been the first teacher in the present building.

To Harold Currie, for 11 years reeve of Adelaide Township and warden of Middlesex in 1932, the writer extends thanks for many of these facts. His grandparents settled on land directly across the road from the present school in 1832, the property being later divided between their sons.

The late Thomas A. Currie, father of Harold Currie, was born there in 1848 and died in 1909. Mr. Currie himself was also born there as was his son Leonard and the latter's son, thus making five generations of the Currie family to occupy the same property.

We might add that Harold Currie served as trustee and secretary-treasurer of S.S. #5 for 30 years and regards it as the most important position that he ever held, owing to the excellent training he thereby received for the higher positions that were yet to be his.

Sir Arthur Currie was born December 5, 1875, and received all his public schooling at S.S. #5. Later accompanied by Harold Currie, who was his first cousin, he walked to Strathroy every day while he attended collegiate there.

John Currie, a brother of Sir Arthur, served as reeve of Adelaide for a term of five years and was warden of Middlesex in 1918.

The second oldest resident of this school section is W.A. Morgan, 81, who was treasurer of Adelaide Township for a period of 35 years.

Mrs. Carman Hall is the present teacher of S.S. #5.

The striking changes in the trend of rural population is demonstrated by some figures given to us by Harold Currie. Sixty years ago, the population of Adelaide was in the neighborhood of 4,000. Now it is less than 1,000. Six decades ago, Kerwood had a two-room school with 110 names on the roll. Last year, there were only 143 students enrolled in all of the 11 school sections of Adelaide.

(From The London Free Press, May 22, 1948)

Since the cost of paying a teacher's salary or building a schoolhouse seemed too high to consider, a proposal was brought forward to join with S.S. #10. This would have created a real hardship for many to attend because of the great distance, uncertain weather and poor roads. The matter was brought before Adelaide Township Council for a ruling. The Council decided that the boundaries of the school section should not be changed.

The time finally came when the ratepayers of S.S. #6 felt the need to build a schoolhouse. The site chosen was the northeast corner of Lot 5, Con. 1 SER, on the property of Alex Seed. The schoolhouse, probably erected in 1865, was built of logs. It was furnished as were many others, with benches. Since most of the writing was done on slates, desks were considered an unnecessary expense. Cash money was not plentiful, even in 1865. People were still taking butter and eggs to the store to barter for supplies. At this time, butter would give a credit of 7-14 cents a pound.

Since the number of scholars increased after 1865, it soon became evident that the little log schoolhouse was no longer adequate. Sometime before 1884, a new frame school was built almost across the road, on Lot 5, Con. 1 NER. There were

S.S. #6 Adelaide, teacher Arthur Davidson.

S.S. #6 Adelaide

originally four sections from Hickory Corners to the townline, with one school in Adelaide Village and one between Morse Sideroad and the townline of Adelaide-Warwick. Two families in Section Six applied to have their taxes paid to the village school. This caused a great deal of discussion and the result was a redivision of school sections into three sections instead of four. The village school was closed. School Section #6 extended from the townline to just east of the Township Hall. There were 4,200 acres in a school section.

One of the most successful entertainments ever held in Adelaide took place at S.S. #6 on the evening of November 12, 1875. The attendance was very large, many being unable to gain admission. Mr. N. Wiley occupied the Chair. The opening address, spoken by Master Charles Kerswill, was particularly well given and warmly applauded. The dialogues and the recitations were all first-class, reflecting the greatest credit on the pupils and on their teacher, Mr. W.H. Montague. Excellent addresses were given by Rev. Mr. Lawrence and Messrs. William Miller, J.W. Stewart, and the teacher.

Some of the teachers who taught at S.S. #6 before 1900 were Mr. John Jamieson 1853, Ms. Mary Ann Wylie 1865, Miss McKenzie pre-1884, Dr. Walter Montague 1885 (became a Member of Parliament, was elected as Minister of Agriculture in Manitoba), Mr. W.T. Miller 1878-1879 (son of W. Miller, the first teacher in Adelaide Township), Mr. A.B. Gilbert 1880 and 1882, Dr. Newell 1881, Dr. Kerswell 1883-1885, Mr. William Corpron 1885-1888, Mr. Walter Wiley 1889-1891, Mr. H.E. Manning 1892-1895, Mr. F.F. Saxton 1897-1898, and Mr. D.A. Ross 1898-1903.

The following is a list of some of the students who attended S.S. #6 with D.A. Ross as teacher:

GIRLS, 1897-1903

Winnie Barrett	Irene McCabe
Myrtle Barrett	Blanche McCarthy
Nellie Bennett	Annie McCarthy
Mabel Brent	Mary McCarthy
Olive Brent	Rena McCarthy
Madeline Brock	Lizzie McChesney
Martha Clelford	Millie McClinchey
Emma Clelford	Greta McGeary
Lottie Chapman	Pearl Minielly
Edna Chapman	Bertha Morse
Laura Conkey	Kate Upton
Eva Conkey	Anna Walsh
Hazel Conkey	Theresa Walsh
Laura Hawken	Stella Walsh
Eliza Freele	Ethel Wilson
Pearl Freele	Becky Wilson
Annie McCabe	

BOYS, 1897-1903

David Baptist	John Conkey
Willie Baptist	James Crummer
Lawrence Barrett	Howard Crummer
Frank Bennett	Frankie Crummer
Ernest Bishop	George Hawken
Russell Brent	Ross Ireland
Hubert Brent	Hugh Fletcher
John Cleland	Monroe Fletcher
Nat Conkey	Austin Kelly
Frank Conkey	Clarence Kerswell

SCHOOLS 479

S.S. #6, ca.1935. Back L-R, Gordon Conkey, Donald McChesney, Marguerite Brooks, Keith Highgate, Donelda Wilson, Doreen Hawken, Eileen Campbell, teacher Hattie (Brown) Ball, Shirley Finkbeiner. Front L-R, Grant Lewis, Colleen Finkbeiner, Evan Hendrick, Maxine Finkbeiner, Gordon Campbell.

S.S. #6, ca.1937, teacher Hattie (Brown) Ball. Back L-R, Evan Hendrick, Dora Brock, Ailene McCarthy, Gordon Campbell, Doreen Hawken, Eileen Campbell, Keith Highgate. Middle L-R, Laverne Lewis, Maxine Finkbeiner, Grant Lewis, Shirley Finkbeiner. Front L-R, Dorothy Feasey, Collen Finkbeiner, Eleanor Wardell.

Joe McCabe	Walter Rimmer
Leo McCabe	Harry Rimmer
Willie McCarthy	Wilfred Upton
Charlie McCarthy	Ruby Upton
Robbie McCarthy	Chester Wallace
Harry McChesney	Earle Wallace
Henry Miller	Albert Walsh
Joe Mills	Jimmie Walsh
Charlie Morse	John Wilson
Ruby Patterson	Sam Wilson
John Rimmer	Wallace Wilson

S.S. #6, ADELAIDE

June 29, 1888
On Saturday last the pupils of S.S. #6 assembled in Mr. D. McChesney's woods, the attraction being a "pic-nic." After the lengthy and animated program, besides many other amusements were concluded, the party sat down to supper, which was thought the best part of the entire "pic-nic" by those who were present.

July 13, 1888
Mr. William Corpron, teacher in S.S. #6, is spending his vacation in Strathroy.
Mr. A. Conkey and Miss Elizabeth Wiley, pupils of S.S. #6, attended the entrance examinations at Strathroy last week.

October 5, 1888
The usual monthly examinations for the month of September were held in S.S. #6, Adelaide, on Thursday and Friday, Sept. 28 and 29.

January 13, 1889
S.S. #6 has purchased a new supply of maps.

February 1, 1889
A meeting of the ratepayers of S.S. #6 will be held in the School House on Thursday evening, January 31, to discuss the proposed alteration of the School Sections.

(From the Watford-Guide Advocate, "Adelaide & Wisbeach" column)

In The Age, an article appeared on February 23, 1877 about the teacher at S.S. #6, Adelaide, *"Considerable improvement has taken place in the management of the school. Last fall, the pupils were nearly dead, now they are giving some evidence of mental power. Very much remains to be done before anything like excellence is obtained. Mr. Miller is working vigorously and promises to make his mark as a teacher. New maps have been furnished and a thorough and systematic drill commenced. Mr. Miller doesn't hold the geography in his hand while asking questions, thus avoiding the suspicion pupils might have that the teacher did not know the lesson. A celebrated clergyman once asked a servant girl for a pin to fasten the leaves of his sermon. "PIN IT IN YOUR HEAD" was the reply. This is the place teachers should pin the lessons they are to give every day."*

About 1889 or 1890, reference in the Minutes of the annual meeting of the ratepayers of S.S. #6 indicated that the building of a new school was to be undertaken. Considerable time (years) seems to have been taken up in debating whether to build a new school or repair the old one. Estimates were called for both solutions. In 1890, consideration was also given to moving the schoolhouse to a new site.

Two sites were proposed. The first was the southeast corner of John Woodlock's farm at the west half of Lot 6, Con. 1 NER. The second site was on the southeast corner of Patrick Walsh's farm at the east half of Lot 6, Con. 1 NER. The trustees supported the first site. When a vote was taken at a meeting held on January 29, 1890, the majority of the ratepayers voted for the second site. The trustees called for arbitration to settle the site. The trustees appointed Edward Rowland and the ratepayers appointed Duncan Robinson. At the same meeting, Patrick Walsh raised objection to the school site being on his property, as the site would be too close to his orchard and garden.

At the meeting of the ratepayers on February 18, 1890, there was a motion to accept the site on the Woodlock farm. There was a proposed amendment that the new school be built on William Conkey's farm. The amendment carried by a majority of three votes. At the meeting held on December 27, 1899, it was moved and carried that the trustees call for tenders for building a new school. It was also moved and carried that the trustees call for tenders for repairing the old schoolhouse. Apparently, the argument had changed from where to build a new school to whether one would be built at all.

On February 14, 1900, a ratepayers' meeting was held. It was found that the tender of Mr. W.J. Brock was the lowest. A large majority voted for building a new school. On April 19, 1900, the trustees were authorized to raise, by debenture, the sum of $1,300 for the building of the new school. The sum of $1,325 was received from William McChesney, for the debenture to be paid in five years. The building of the new school, a fine, large, brick structure on the Woodlock site, was completed in 1900, at a cost of $1,288.48. The old school was sold to John Woodlock for the sum of $74.40. It was moved to the Woodlock farm and sided with brick. It served the Woodlock family as their home for many years. New furnishings for the school must have been purchased as Minutes indicate that the old desks were sold for $2.30 each. Also, there are entries in the financial statements that indicate the purchase of a large desk, table, and several chairs. The trustees, being men of careful stewardship of public monies, made their purchases over several years.

School fairs were well supported by the trustees. This was a very exciting time for the students. It was an opportunity for all the schools in the township to come together in friendly competition. For the children, it was a highlight of the school year. In the early days, the school fair was held in Kerwood. After 1921, it was held in Adelaide Village. In the late 1930s, it was moved to Strathroy, to be held as part of the Strathroy Fair. The individuality of the school fair was lost in the hustle and bustle of the larger fair in Strathroy, so in 1945, the annual school fair was moved back to Adelaide Village.

The first mention of paying the Secretary-Treasurer was in 1915, when Sam Wiley was paid the sum of $10 after he had served in this capacity for several years. William McChesney served from 1916-1923, at the same salary. George Ball was the longest serving Secretary-Treasurer, holding the office from 1923-1941. In 1941, his salary was raised to the handsome amount of $15.

Prior to 1940, school libraries had very few books and most of them were old. In 1940, a circulating library for the township schools was intro-

SCHOOL FAIRS

At one time, the Middlesex Department of Agriculture representative came around to the schools and gave the interested students a dozen eggs. The student was to set the eggs under a hen (or hens) and raise the hatched chickens, the best of which would be shown in competition at the School Fair. The pupils were also given flower and vegetable seeds to be planted and cared for, without parental help; the resulting plants were also to be displayed at the School Fair.

> May 20, 1915
>
> **SCHOOLS GIVEN SEED POTATOES**
>
> H.A. Finn of the Middlesex Branch of the Department of Agriculture has been in the neighbourhood giving 1,100 pounds of seed potatoes to the schools of Adelaide, Lobo and North Metcalfe. There are about 21 schools engaged in School Fair work in the townships, and 11 of them centre around Kerwood, where the School Fair is held.

duced, and S.S. #6 subscribed to it. Each month, the school was supplied with a good number of books, which could be kept for the month and then passed on to another school.

In 1884, wood for the school cost $1.10 a cord—all beech and maple. Prices varied through the years but the highest price paid was in 1912, when the cost was $8 a cord. Wood always seemed to be bought within the school section.

The School Board consisted of three men (never women) who served a three-year term, with one member retiring each year. The list of trustees reads like a census list, as many men took on the responsibility. Between 1884 and 1940, approximately 45 persons were elected as trustees. The following is a list of trustees from 1885-1890:

July 28, 1885	Gavin Davison, John Galsworthy
February 26, 1886	John Galsworthy, James Wilson
August 26, 1886	John Galsworthy, Robert Upton
February 19, 1887	James Wilson, David McChesney
August 17, 1887	James Wilson, David McChesney
February 14, 1888	Robert Upton, D.D. Wiley, David McChesney
July 31, 1888	Robert Upton, D.D. Wiley, David McChesney
February 19, 1889	D.D. Wiley, David McChesney, G.S. Kerswell
August 1, 1889	David McChesney, Giles S. Kerswell, D.D. Wiley
March 8, 1890	James Wilson, Giles S. Kerswell, D.D. Wiley
March 18, 1890	James Wilson, Giles S. Kerswell, D.D. Wiley
August 18, 1890	James Wilson, Giles S. Kerswell, D.D. Wiley

On December 28, 1886, the school board received $60 from a clergy reserve fund. It is interesting to note how innovative the purchase of coloured chalk and plasticine was considered at one time.

From the record it was difficult to be sure who the teacher was. The entry would read *"hired a new teacher"* with no reference to name or salary. Prior to 1900, teachers were not always hired from September 1 to August 31 and Minutes were not always clear about the term. Prior to 1900, teachers seemed to be paid irregular amounts at irregular times. One entry reads *"Paid D. McDougall last half year salary $125."* In the Treasurer's Report, no reference was made to the first half year salary. On June 30, 1897, Mr. Saxton was paid $8 *"on salary."* In many cases, the teacher was also expected to do custodial work. Some samples of salaries paid are 1889 - $320; 1891 - $400; 1895 - $410; 1900 - $400; 1904 - $325; 1915 - $600; 1922 - $1,000; 1927 - $800.

Miss Marguerite Purdy was the first music teacher, engaged in 1939 at a salary of $60. She continued to teach after her marriage to Nelson Johnson. She was followed by Miss Gladys King (Mrs. George Campbell) and Mrs. Treffry.

The following is a list of teachers who taught in S.S. #6 after 1900:

1898-1903	D.A. Ross
1904-1904	Miss Crouse
1905-1906	Mr. John Wilson
1907-1911	Miss Maude McKenzie
1911-1912	Mr. Ryan
1912-1915	Mr. Leo Langon
1915	Mr. William Jones
1915-1918	Miss Donna Tanner (Mrs. William Illes)
1918	Miss Hazel Guest
1918-1920	Mr. Arthur Davidson
1920-1921	Miss Lenore Collins
1921-1925	Miss Flossie Grogan (Mrs. Carmen Hall)
1925-1927	Miss Vivian McKenzie

	(Mrs. Harry Conkey)
1927-1929	Miss Pearl Campbell
	(Mrs. George Hotham)
1929-1932	Miss Margaret Bolton
	(Mrs. Dalton Walpole)
1932-1936	Miss Harriet Brown
	(Mrs. George Ball)
1936-1942	Miss Adeline Muxlow
	(Mrs. Laverne Hawkins)
1942-1943	Miss A. Letherland
1944-1945	Miss Rebecca Harris
	(Mrs. Milton Harris)
1945-1951	Miss Mary E. Ross
1951-1957	Miss Kathleen E. McNeil
1958	Mrs. Hazel Beatty
1959	Miss Delores Nichols

The following is a report of the students who attended S.S. #6 in 1917, when the teacher was Miss Donna L. Tanner:

Jr. IV - Jack Ball, Clifford Callaghan, Jean Campbell
Sr. III - Mable Campbell, Winnie Hendrick, Louden Cleland, Kate Conkey
Sr. II - Louisa Cleland, Kate Walsh, Patricia Walsh, Sherwood Hendrick, Stanley Callaghan
Jr. II - George Wiley, Jean Cleland, Lillie Campbell, Sam Nichols, Dorothy Brown, Ernie Callaghan
Sr. I - Amanda Nichols, J.D. Brown, Stanfield Galsworthy, Bert Nichols
Jr. I - Arnold Galsworthy, Lillian Brown, Annie Campbell, Lester Wallace
Primer - Charlie Nichols, Lillie Cleland

During the summer of 1937, the school was rebricked and its foundation was replaced. During the summer of 1938, the school was redecorated by Mr. Feasey. New blinds were bought and storm windows were added. Musical contests were held every year after 1941.

In January 1946, the school was wired for electricity and, in August of the same year, Walter Feasey painted the interior and exterior of the school.

In 1945, S.S. #6 won First Place in the unison chorus and Beverly Hendrick won First Place in the solo class. In 1946, the school won First Place in the two-part chorus. In 1948, it again was the winner in the two-part chorus and Marjorie Wilson came in First in the Senior Girls' solo class.

In 1946, an old organ was replaced by a piano and, in April 1947, the School Board purchased a radio for use in the school. A Christmas concert was held every year.

The appearance of the school was improved by the addition of flower beds and a lawn. In 1947 and 1948, S.S. #6 was awarded the certificate from the Ontario Horticultural Association in recognition of the most outstanding work in the Township of Adelaide on Care and Improvement of Grounds.

From September 1946, the pupils of S.S. #9 were transported to S.S. #6 and in September 1950, the pupils from S.S. #11 also came by bus to this school. After 1959, S.S. #6 was closed, and the children attended the new township school, Adelaide Central School.

S.S. # 7 ADELAIDE

S.S. #7 Adelaide school was originally a small one-room building built on Lot 6, Con. 5 SER, sometime before 1872. Soon after 1872, two small frame buildings were erected. There were about 140 pupils. The Inspector was J.H. Carson, the Principal was Dr. McCabe, and the assistant was Miss Brophy.

The earliest records in the Minutes Book for S.S. #7 date from 1876, and show that the trustees hired a teacher named J.W. Torrence.

In 1877, there is an entry in the Minutes Book that concerns the building of a new addition. They planned to build it 4' to the north of the old building,

S.S. #7, teacher Mrs. Flossie Hall.

and shingle over the space in between to make a passageway. There was a stipulation that the windows would be let down from the top, and the walls would be given three coats of No. 1 lead paint—something that would never be done in a school now that lead is known to be toxic. The addition was to be completed by October 1, 1877; the builder was Mr. A. Wilton. The names of the trustees are written beneath the plan: Robert Morgan, George S. Hull, Henry Langford, Robert Galbraith and Thomas Harris. A decision was also made to rearrange the existing seats in the school, and install new ones. The trustees also intended to buy a half acre of land from Mrs. Reinhardt.

That same year, at a later meeting, it was moved and carried that the Secretary and the Treasurer each be given a salary of $5 per year. There was a motion made that they buy the land from Mrs. Reinhardt as soon as possible. In June 1877, they decided to advertise for a teacher. Mrs. Reinhardt was paid $2 for a portion of her expenses in the land sale. Interestingly, in the next motion, it was moved and carried that George S. Hull be paid $2.50 for his time and expenses in buying the land from her. The trustees also decided to insure the schoolhouse's contents with London Agricultural Mutual Insurance Company for the sum of $850.

In the Minutes for a meeting later in 1877, it was recorded that each of the men nominated for trustee would *"be allowed 30 minutes to explain their views, and 15 minutes to reply."* It was reported that *"Very eloquent addresses were delivered by the candidates for office—which were loudly applauded."* Nominees included Joseph Galbraith, R. Richardson, J. Richardson, C. Matthews and H.G. Ford.

Unlike other schools that required pupils' families to supply a certain amount of wood, the trustees at S.S. #7 put the contracts for wood delivery out to tender, and paid for the wood out of funds raised for the school. On Valentine's Day in 1878, just such a notice was drafted by Robert Morgan, Secretary-Treasurer, in the Minutes Book: *"Tenders will be received by the Trustees of School Section #7, up to 25th of February for the delivery of five cords of dry wood, two feet long, double, to be delivered to the*

S.S. #7 Adelaide, ca.1926. Back L-R, Ken Brooks, Muriel Irwin, Ilene Wright, Kay Bourne, Gwen Manicom, Muriel Waltham, Florence Edwards (teacher), Helen Glover, Dorothy Morgan, Joan Bourne, Anna Carroll, Helen Waltham. 2nd Row L-R, Howard Brooks, Fraser Galbraith, ? Winters, Alex Harris, Jack Matthews, Ken Richardson, Fred Woods, ? Winters, Mervyn Pollock, Grant Pollock, Don Pollock. 1st Row L-R, Ralph Brooks, Reg Carroll, George Carroll, Marjorie Bourne, Merlene Matthews, Irene Waltham, Milton Tedball, Mabel Carroll, Grace Glover, Milo Morgan.

S.S. #7 Kerwood, ca.1942; teacher is Edna Brown.

schoolhouse on or before the 10th of March, next."

In January 1878, Mr. Torrence was again hired as teacher at a salary of $400 a year.

S.S. #7 included Kerwood, up the Fourth Line to the Lambton townline, and east on the Fourth Line.

The dividing line ran between the Dick Morgan farm and Johnny Patterson farm on the south. On the north, the Ira Morgan farm had 50 acres in S.S. #7 and the remaining 100 acres in Napperton School, S.S. #5. George and Marjorie Morgan went to Napperton, but Bev and Lewis Morgan opted for Kerwood School.

The first school, with the addition, was a frame two-room school. There were two separate buildings (each with its own door) built in an L-shape. It was connected with a wooden platform or walkway that extended to the road. The second school ran north and south and the other east and west. The gate was in the shape of a western gate. These buildings were heated by wood and had coat racks on either side. Each building had its own teacher. Jack Correstine was the teacher in the Senior room and Ettie Patterson taught in the Junior room.

In 1899, one room was closed due to low enrolment, and Mr. J.V. MacDonald taught in the larger

S.S. #7 Kerwood School, ca.1895.

building. The smaller building was sold to Mr. J.H. Richardson of Kerwood, who used it in his brick- and tile-yard.

In the 1880 Minutes, it showed that money was borrowed from Richard Morgan, to build the schoolhouse and pay the teacher's salary. It also showed that they paid William and Mrs. Trotter $1 and $1.50 respectively, for splitting wood and cleaning the schoolhouse. There was a motion made by G.S. Hull, seconded by Mr. Jarvis, that the privies at the school were *"utterly useless and not fit for use as intended, and that we condemn them."* Plans were then made to draw up specifications for new ones. This project, like the stove wood, was put out to tender. Payments to the Age and the Dispatch for advertising space in relation to these contracts were recorded in the Minutes. From time to time, The Age also listed the Honour Roll at Adelaide Schools. On Valentine's Day 1889, the students listed were Mary Edwards, Flora Armstrong, Lena Richardson, Dora Richardson, Florence Maher, Annie Freele, Sarah Johnstone, Kate Robinson and Adella Dowding.

Another document of interest was the attendance record for several months in 1901. The children on the list ranged in age from 9 to 15 years older and were in classes V, IV, III, and Jr. III. Their names were Hattie Rodgers, Alice Morgan, John Smith, Elmer Morgan, Gertie Newton,. Ada Crawford, Frank Law, Walter Morgan, Gordon Newton, John Carroll, Wynnie Rogers, Millard Smith, Leonard Foster, Kate Dowding, Willie McIntyre, Lila Dowding, Eddie Galbraith, Willie Galbraith, Jennie Smith, Meredith Morgan, (first name unknown) Morgan, Annie Cook, Harry Rogers, Myrtle Richardson, Eva Dell, Ida McIntyre, Ross Madill and Howard Earley.

After a few years, a new school was needed. As the frame school was not in the centre of the school section, there was controversy over the location of the new school. Taken from Meredith Morgan's diary notation of February 13, 1912, *"There was voting at school for site of new school."* There was talk of the new school being built west of the farm that was later owned by George Morgan. In the early days, there had been a ruling that a school could not be built within a certain distance of an orchard. The owner of the farm immediately planted an orchard and, consequently, it was decided to build the new school just east of the old school.

S.S. #7, ca.1922

The new brick school was built in 1912, and the one remaining part of the old school was removed and became part of the Maher house around the corner. The Inspector at the time the new school was built was Mr. H.D. Johnson. Trustees were Richard Demaray, James Galbraith and Frank Hull.

The new school was a large, brick building with a good basement. It had a wood-burning furnace with two large registers at the back. The windows were in the north wall. The main entrance was on the west side, with double doors leading to a stairway up to the classroom. The boys' and girls' cloak rooms were on either side. A smaller door on the south side led to stairs going to the basement or upstairs to the cloak rooms and classroom. Lunches were put in pigeon holes along either side. There was a large attached library, also used as the teacher's room, along the south side. Blackboards were along the front and east end and down the south side. The seats were graduated in size—small for primers, mediums and larger for the higher grades. The younger children often started at Easter. Margaret McLean and Dorothy Winter started at Easter, taking turns sitting with Anna (Leacock) Burdon.

There were outside toilets, one for the girls and one for the boys, with a board fence in front to hide the doors. Water came from a well in the yard. In later years, indoor toilets (not the flushing type) were put in the west entryway, one on each side.

The school had a garden that the children worked in, and on Arbour Day, Mr. Pollock's horse-and-cart sometimes made a trip into James Galbraith's forest to get humus for the garden. In the summer, children played ball, had races, and played other outdoor games. In winter, they stayed inside by the registers and played "fruit-basket-upset," jacks, etc.

In the one-room school, the teacher taught all of the classes, one at a time. In 1918, one of the teachers at the school, Malcolm Fletcher, had enlisted and was going overseas. The community presented him with a silver watch as a memento.

S.S. #7 was made part of the Adelaide Township Area on January 1, 1945. The first trustee board included Elmer Gast, Harold Bolton, George Glenn, Howard Earley and Allan Brown. Earl McInroy was the first Secretary-Treasurer.

During the time Elizabeth Dodge was the teacher, 1945-1948, the children put on wonderful Christmas concerts at St. Paul's Anglican Hall in Kerwood.

Dr. Harcourt Morgan attended S.S. #7 while Mr. McCabe was the teacher.

S.S. #7 Adelaide postcard

Dr. Burton Matthews graduated from S.S. #7 and went on to be President of University of Waterloo, then Guelph University.

After the Adelaide Central School was built and opened in 1960, the S.S. #7 children were bussed there. Roy Wardell bought the school property and made the old school the attractive house it is today. Milo Morgan bought the school bell. The following is a listing of the teachers of S.S. #7 from 1877 to 1950:

S.S. #7, ca.1951, teacher Mrs. Flossie Hall. First row L-R, Bill Morgan, Larry Calcutt, Sidney Wilson, Joyce Foster, Sylvia Morgan, Louise Foster, Gary Maher, Ellen Galbraith, Chris Joris, Carmen Patterson, Leonard Hawkin, Dorothy Hawkins, Judy Matthews. Second row L-R, Douglas Fonger, Jim Foster, Marlene Calcutt, Bob Dennis, Betsy Vanderhyde, Marilyn Chittick, Jean Calcutt, Marnie Evans, Tom Scholte, Richard Brooks, Mildred Clothier, Ruth Ann Foster, Evelyn Clothier. Standing L-R, Donald Waltham, Catherine Wright, Peggy Brooks, Bill Matthews, Douglas Clothier, Albert Anderson, Ken Waltham, Fay Hawkins, Bill Wright.

1877	Mr. Torrence
1879	Emily A. Murray
1879	Jane W. Scatcherd
1880	Miss Grace Brophy
1880	Mr. J.R. McCabe
1881	Mr. Carson
1880-1881	Miss K. Church
1881	Mr. A.B. Gilbert
1882-1883	Miss Debb
1882-1883	Miss Austin
1883	Miss Mary Debb
1884	Alex McKenzie
1913-1914	Gladys E. Abbott
1914	Edna M. Moscrip
1914	Edward Callagham
1914	Miss Annie Newton
1916-1918	Mack Fletcher
1920	Mary M. Currie
1921	Merton Morely
1922	Nina Clark
1923	Melvin Lucas
1925	Annie L. Pulling
1927	Florence Edwards
1928-1930	Lenna Runnalls
1931	Dorothy Delmage
1934	Florence Edwards
1935-1936	Marjorie Parker
1937-1940	Esther Bateman
1941-1942	Edna Brown
1943	Dorothy Watson
1944	Aubrey Lyons
1945-1948	Elizabeth Dodge
1949	Harland Willison
1950-1959	Flossie Hall

S.S. #8

The Minutes of the annual meeting held January 9, 1861, are the first records we have of S.S. #8. We are very lucky to have Minutes for the meetings that were held between 1861 and 1877. James Galbraith was chairman of the meeting. Listed in attendance were John Sullivan, Anthony Douglas, William Fuller, John Alderson, Robert Collier, George Hannah, Richard Smith and William Dowding, although it is likely that other concerned individuals were also there. By law, meetings were held each year in January in the school building. At each meeting, a chairman, an auditor, and a secretary were appointed, and two trustees were elected. The first meeting was also attended by the teacher, John Hannah, who was 35 years old. A receipt of his salary is written into the Minutes: *"Received from the Trustees of School Section number 8, in the section of Adelaide, the sum of $186.66 in full for my salary as Teacher for the year 1861. Dated this 18th day of December, 1861, signed - John Hannah."*

1861-	John Hannah $186.66
1862 -	they were advertising for a teacher
1863 -	William Gleeson - $180.00
1864 -	William Gleeson - $220.41
1865 -	William Gleeson - $171.00
1867 -	John Bodaly - $200.00
1868 -	Sarah M. Barber - $192.00
1869 -	Sarah M. Barber
1869 -	Sept.-Dec. - Lizzie Barber - $64.00
1870 -	Lizzie Barber - $105.39
1871 -	Mary H. Bateman - $165.56
1872 -	Mary H. Bateman - $193.30
1873 -	Peter Anderson - $102.35 (ending July)
1873 -	Benjamin Donaldson $135.00 (ending December)
1874 -	John McIlwain - $60.90
1875 -	W. F. Mills - $88.22
1876 -	W. F. Mills $360.00 (full year)
1877 -	Robert H. Thompson - $314.00 (full year)

At the 1861 meeting, it was moved and carried almost unanimously that there should be a Free School System; that is, a general tax on all property in the section. There was some debate over this in later years because some people preferred the idea of a Rate Bill School. This question would be raised again in the Minutes over the years. It also agreed

S.S. #8 Adelaide, teacher Anna Jean Wilson, ca.1949-1950.

S.S. #8 Adelaide, teacher Eliza Payne, ca.1900.

that every student must provide ¼ cord of stove-length wood, to be delivered between January and April 1. This is a very important item, because the wood was necessary to heat the school. This subject is also discussed in the Minutes in later years.

The following is a list of some of the people who attended the meetings:

1864 - Lawrence Cleverdon, William Gleeson, Samuel Earley
1865 - John Harris, John Brown
1866 - D. Livingston, Thomas Fuller
1867 - James Thomas Sr., John Bodaly, John Carrothers, Mr. Martin, James Randall (trustee), Mr. Chambers, William Alexander (trustee), William Armstrong
1868 - William Humphries (gave the land for Bethesda Church)
1870 - James Dowden (Dowding?)
1871 - John Eakins (auditor), Mr. Tompkins
1872 - Thomas James
1873 - George Earley
1874 - John McIlwain, Thomas Collier, Samuel Lawhead
1876 - Mr. Bradshaw, Mr. Rogers, W.F. Mills, (Secretary)
1877 - J.C. Alexander, Mr. Sampson

YEAR	TRUSTEES	GRANTS
July 23, 1885	James Fortner Treasurer, William J. Kincade, James Carrothers	$54.20
Feb. 25, 1886	James Fortner, Amos Alderson, James Carrothers	$46.86
Aug. 5, 1886	James Fortner, James Carrothers, Amos Alderson	$45.39
Feb. 17, 1887	James Carrothers, William Dowding Treasurer, Amos Alderson	$39.78
Aug. 16, 1887	William Dowding Treasurer, James Carrothers	$36.28
Feb. 13, 1888	William Dowding, Amos Alderson	$31.45
Aug. 1, 1888	Joseph Brown, William Dowding	$42.12
Feb. 20, 1889	William Dowding, James Dowding	$31.43
Aug. 8, 1889	James Dowding, William Dowding	$28.62
Mar. 4, 1890	William Dowding, James Dowding	$21.33
Aug. 14, 1890	William Dowding, Joseph Brown, James Dowding	$24.35

(A year's grant to run the school—balance received from taxes levied on people of S.S. #8.)

A summary of expenses, dated at Adelaide, January 9, 1861, shows the funding for schools. The Sectional Funds were monies raised from S.S. #8 ratepayer taxes; the County Assessment was a grant from the County of Middlesex; and the Legislative Grant was from the Province of Upper Canada. When the Clergy Reserves were sold, this money also went to support the school system.

YEAR – 1861	TRUSTEES	AMOUNT
Jan. 9th	To Balance from 1860	$4.19
Mar. 4th	To County Assessment	$32.19
July 28th	To Legislative Grant	$38.24
Sept. 9th	To Clergy Reserve Mony [sic]	$56.64
Nov. 30th	To Cash from Sectional Funds	$30.00
Nov. 30th	To Cash from Appendages sold at schoolhouse	$8.55
Nov. 30th	Samuel Earley, Stovepipe	$.75
Dec. 18th	Cash from Sectional Funds	$26.29

From the records available, it seems that a school was built in 1861. The list of the bills for that year includes payments to James Eliott, for building the schoolhouse, as well as payments for the

S.S. #8 Adelaide, teacher Jeanette Taylor.

stovepipes and the stove from Thomas Crispin in Strathroy, fencing around the schoolhouse, and payment to John Black for moving stones, among other things. In the following years, the lists of expenses included brooms for .25¢ each, maps of Canada, a pound of chalk for .10¢, a pail for .25¢, and a tin dipper for .10¢.

In 1877, there was a section in the Age Dispatch entitled "Educational Notes." In a paragraph devoted to S.S. #8, the author writes that the trustees had been *"very much dissatisfied with the teacher who had charge of the school last year"* and that, as a result, they were only going to hire teachers on a six-month contract, which may be renewed, if the teacher proved satisfactory. The rest of the article is as follows: *"This is quite a stroke of policy; it is to be regretted the innocent may suffer and the guilty evade the penalty falling on the lost of his unfortunate successor. Of course, if the trustees are correct in their views of the late teacher, it is quite justifiable to be well guarded in the future. However, it is hoped that the lesson will be salutary and will learn teachers to be more cautious in their school duties. Mr. R. Thompson will, no doubt, be careful and redeem the opinion now prevalent in the section that inexperienced teachers are not reliable. The trustees must not be over critical and give him a fair chance."*

A new school was built in 1883, on the same grounds as the old one. This time it was a brick school rather than a wood frame building.

Taxation records show that many families whose members were school trustees in the 1860s were still living in the area in 1897, and paying taxes to support S.S. #8. These include the Dowding, Sullivan, Earley, Humphries, Eakin, Chambers, and Alderson families.

In the later years, there were a number of school reunions for people who had gone to S.S. #8. Sometimes these reunions were combined with church picnics at the Bethesda United Church, which was on the other side of the road. One of these combined reunions was held in 1937, in honour of the church's Golden Jubilee.

The following is a listing of the teachers who taught at S.S. #8 from 1880 to 1959, when the school was closed and the students were bussed to Adelaide Central School, which was built on Lot 15, Con. 1 SER.

S.S. #8 Adelaide, 1940, back L-R, Leroy Harris, Ila Sullivan, Eileen Carrothers, Ella Dowding, teacher Miss Jean Fydell. Middle L-R, Donald Carrothers, Graham Alderson, Evelyn Carrothers, Earl Alderson, Lawrence Sullivan, Marion Harris. Front L-R, Jack Alderson, Marie Stevenson, Phyllis Harris.

1880-1881 -	J.B. Shotwell
1882-1884 -	Philip Bartlett
1885 -	James Sutherland
1888-1889 -	Edward Hinde (e)
1890 -	W.J. Hanna
1912 -	Kathleen Dewey
1913-1915 -	Myrtle Crossley
1916-1917 -	Ethel Jury
1920 -	Jeanette E. Taylor
1921 -	Alice Wright
1922-1923 -	Ella Acton

490 ADELAIDE TOWNSHIP... A HISTORY

1925 -	Nellie Baker
1925 -	Annie L. Pulling
1927-1929 -	Marjorie Whiteoke
1927 -	Florence Edwards
1929 -	Melba Ward
1930-1931 -	Kathryn Murphy
1932-1934 -	Kathryn Murphy
1937-1939 -	Velma A. Petch
1940 -	Jean Fydell
1941-1942, 1944 -	Audrey Carrothers
1944 -	Felicia Reed
1945-1947 -	Mrs. Rebecca Harris
1948-1949 -	Anna J. Wilson
1950-1956 -	Mrs. Anna J. Sullivan
1957 -	Mrs. Ruth Foster
1958 -	Mrs. Marie Kearns
1959 -	Mrs. Margaret Redmond

Years unknown - Bessie Bogue, James Sutherland, Ida Terryberry, George Slaughter, Milton Campbell, Katie Vokes, Ena Iles, Eliza Payne, Laura Morgan and Ethel Currie.

Some of the former teachers changed their profession. Philip Bartlett became a lawyer and practised in London, Ontario. James Sutherland became a Medical Doctor in the U.S., in Oregon. George Slaughter became the Principal of a school. Wilbur Hanna was a surgeon. Milton Campbell became a doctor with a practise in the U.S.

In September 1960, Adelaide Central School was opened to replace the individual schools throughout the Township of Adelaide, thus marking the end of S.S. #8.

S.S. #8, back L-R, unknown, Ron Brown, Bill Dowding, unknown, Bruce Cuddy, John Laroque. Third row, L-R, Wesley Petch, Hugh Stirton, Del Dowding, Barbara Cuddy, unknown, Judy Dowding, Glen Brown, Jerry Levitt. Second row L-R, Whitford Petch, Ian Stirton, unknown, Joan Earley, Ruth Ann Wright, Bob Earley, Jack Brown. Front L-R, Doug Cuddy, Stuart Brown, Charlie Harnett, Jim Dowding.

S.S. #8, ca.1935. Back L-R, Basil Carrothers, Jim Tilley, Donald Sullivan, Ivan Carrothers, Clayton Stephenson, Reta Alderson, Bernice Baxter, Miss Kathryn Murphy. Middle L-R, Marjorie Harris, Marion Muxlow, Margery Sullivan, Ruth Sullivan. Front L-R, Marion Johnson, Ila Sullivan, Leroy Harris, Marion Harris.

In 1980, a reunion was held that was attended by former students from as far away as Washington, D.C., Toronto and Wyoming. Another reunion was held in 1983, at Adelaide-W.G. MacDonald School, at which time a collection was taken and the amount of $800 was given to the school to set up an S.S. #8 Reunion Fund. From this fund, an award is given annually to a Grade 8 student who has achieved both academically and socially. This award is still given each year.

S.S. #9

In 1838, Adelaide Township's first school, a private one, was a log cabin in the orchard of Squire Cuddy's farm, Lot 5, Con. 3 NER. The first teacher was William Miller.

From 1855 to 1890, pupils attended Crummer's School, at Lot 6, Con. 3 NER, built on property owned by the Crummer family. The location had been changed to be more accessible for pupils coming from the east. Because there was no schoolyard, the children often played on the road. When the enrolment increased, a number of families approached township council to ask that the township be divided into school sections. This resulted in the construction of three schools on the Second Line North. The old school building was moved down the road and became the home of Miles Currie.

The third log schoolhouse was built in 1890 in a more central location on Lot 5, Con. 3 NER, property owned by Mr. Gee, who donated ¾-acre for a schoolyard. Now, the students could play safely. In 1908, a woodshed was constructed. In 1909, this school burned down, the fire apparently caused by kindling that was left on top of the stove to dry. Another school was needed. For one year, classes were held in the home of John McNab.

On March 5, 1909, at a meeting of the trustees, John Cuddy moved and Ben Pennington seconded that a new school be built on the same site. It was decided that it should have a basement, a cement foundation, brick walls and a furnace. What a progressive group of people! Plans were drawn by James Gerry, a local architect and carpenter. So intricate were the plans that Mr. Gerry was called upon to assist with construction of the roof. A well in the yard supplied water to drink, and a tin cup hung from the pump. The toilets were wooden structures behind the school. Windows on each side of the building supplied the only light. Debentures were issued for $1,900, and the school was to be paid for in three years. In 1923, after consultation with the McClary Company over the furnace, a new pipeless one was installed for $265. This furnace was used until the school was torn down.

Trustees were men from the section who were elected at the annual meetings of the ratepayers. Meetings of trustees seemed to be held as business arose. Most often mentioned in the Minutes, available from 1905 to 1944, was the hiring of teachers, and the hiring of young men by tender to mow the grass, sweep the school, start the fire, clean closets, repair the building and fences. Often, there would be only a few cents difference among tenders. The Minutes also mentioned the ordering of supplies.

S.S. #9 Adelaide

Sometimes the trustees met to measure the wood (usually hardwood), which was purchased by tender from local farmers. The price of wood varied from $2 to $4.50 per cord as the economy dictated.

Teacher's annual salaries increased and decreased as the economy fluctuated. In 1914, Harriett McInroy was hired for $550 and was required to take a course in bookkeeping. In 1933, Mae Watson was chosen from 50 applicants, and paid $450 for the year. By 1943, only one teacher, Flossie Hall, applied for the position, and was paid $900.

In 1912, at the annual meeting, it was moved, seconded (names not mentioned), and carried, that a

S.S. #9 Adelaide, date unknown.

S.S. #9 Adelaide

The schoolhouse is more designed for preaching than teaching; the desks face the door; a niche in the front provides a suitable position for addressing and audience. The blackboards are at the sides, they might as well be in Keyser. There is considerable fair material in this section, but development must precede the higher standing anticipated under the guidance of Mr. Grigg. Vigorous teaching will bring about rapid results of the best kind; the trustees should second the teacher's efforts by getting the desks turned towards the west and also provide blackboard accommodation across the entire western end. Granting the use of the schoolhouse for meetings of various kinds is not a good policy. The generosity of the trustees should in many cases find an outlet in some other direction.

(From The Age, February 23, 1877)

library be established in the school. When the trustees met a few weeks later, the following was recorded in the Minutes: *"In regards to putting in a library, it was moved and seconded that we take no action at this time."* However, at the annual meeting in December 1914, $10 was allocated for the library. This began a pattern for ensuing years. In 1940, trustees voted to join the circulating library, headquartered in Coldstream.

In 1920, a consolidated school for the township was discussed but in 1924, Peter Reinhardt was appointed a delegate to the Trustees Convention in London, and instructed to vote against a "Township Board of Trustees." There was also mention of a Ratepayer Association.

Men of the community were appointed to judge the pupils' garden plots. In later years, women did the task. By 1934, there was no money for garden plots.

In 1937, the Board agreed, on the motion of Wilfrid Wilson, to purchase a sand table and Book of Knowledge. The Inspector also urged a higher salary for the teacher.

In 1938, a Centennial celebration was organized with invitations sent to former pupils and teachers and special guests, who included the Hon. J.C. Elliott, Postmaster General; C.M. McFie, M.L.A. Appin; Dr. G.I. Christie, President of O.A.C.; and Fred Laughton, former M.L.A. of Parkhill. The President of the Centennial Association was Ambrose Topping; Treasurer, John Hodgson; Secretary Loftus Wilson; and General Chairman Wilfrid Wilson. W.K. Riddell, Middlesex County Agricultural Representative acted a Chairman of the programme. Harold Currie, Reeve, unveiled a cairn, which is still standing, inscribed: *"In commemoration of the erection of the first school in Adelaide Township 1838-1938,"* a gift of the township council.

S.S. #9 Adelaide, 1935.

One special guest was 96-year-old Thomas Rowland of Michigan, who had attended school in 1848 in the original schoolhouse. He was presented with a gold-headed cane. Another special guest, James Langan, Postmaster at Balgonie, Saskatchewan (near Regina), came the farthest distance to the reunion. He was presented with a "luxurious upholstered ottoman."

To celebrate this day, activities such as ball games, sports for children, musical programs, speeches, visiting and meals were planned. What a gala event! It was long remembered and often mentioned in years after. It was reported in one newspaper that 1,000 people had attended the celebration.

During the 1940s, classes for schools #9 and #4 were amalgamated with each school used on alternate years, until the 1950s, when only S.S. #9 was used, because it was a better building. This necessitated transportation of pupils. During the wartime years of gas rationing, a special allowance of gas was given to the person who transported pupils by car. The first person to transport students was Laverne Topping, for $2.50 per day.

In 1960, the Central School System was adopted throughout the Province of Ontario, and Adelaide Central School was opened on January 25, 1960, for all students in the Township of Adelaide. S.S. #9 was eventually demolished, and James Doray built a new home on the site of the school.

S.S. #9 Adelaide

S.S. #9 Adelaide, Arbour Day 1924

S.S. #9 Adelaide, 1935. Front L-R, Anna Jean Wilson, Ellen Nielsen, Dorothy Topping. Middle L-R, Kathleen Pennington, Ina McNab, Mac Murray, Christian Nielsen, George Cuddy, Irene Arrand. Back L-R, Ralph Arrand, Jenny Nielsen, Edna Murray, teacher Mae Watson.

S.S. #9 Adelaide, 1952. Front L-R, Joe Swan, Barnard Nauta, Don Thompson, Paula Vanderbeeten, Dolores Sutherland, Deanna Sutherland, Martin De Groot, Clare Blanchard, William De Groot. Middle L-R, Donelda Emmons, Bette Vanderbeeten, Francis Vereyken, Tina Nauta, Dorothy De Groot, Loretta De Groot, Dorothy Nauta, Joan Giffen, John Vanderbeeten, Ron Blanchard, John Blanchard, Aubrey Vanderbeeten. Back L-R, Martina De Groot, Eileen De Groot, Mary Vanderbeeten, Muriel Emmons, Paula Vereyken, Hielkje Nauta, Rodger Benedict, teacher Don Heaman, Larry Blanchard.

S.S. #9 Adelaide, 1955, teacher Anna Hemstead.

S.S. #9 Adelaide

S.S. #9, 1951, by Don W. Heaman

My first year of teaching in 1952 was at S.S. #9 Adelaide Township, next to George and Marguerite Cuddy's farm, where I boarded. The school had been closed for several years prior to 1952. The influx of New Canadians after WWII necessitated the reopening. There were 29 students enrolled in Grades 1 to 8. Many of the students were of Dutch ancestry and were bused to the school from areas closer to Strathroy.

I enjoyed the neighbourhood and the students very much. It was at Orville Demaray's home where I saw my first television, 12" in black-and-white.

Mr. Earl McInroy was chairman of the Adelaide Township School Board. He not only hired me as teacher, but as school custodian as well. I split wood, stoked the old furnace and cleaned the school daily. Unfortunately, the old school was demolished.

After two years, I moved to Centralia Airforce School and then to London where I eventually served as Head of Geography in the high schools. I finished my 35 years of teaching in 1987.

S.S. #9 TEACHERS

1838-1855	William Miller
1855-1870	Ed Rowland
1870-1879	Ernie Crummer
1879-1880	Dr. McCabe
1880-1881	Benjamin Parker
1882-1884	William Mill
1887	Charles Anderson
1887-1889	J.D. Matthews
1890-1894	Sam Adair
1894-1895	Ema Iles
1896-1899	Truman Miller
1899-1902	Jennie Morgan
1902-1903	Laura Morgan
1903-1906	Miss Crealey
1906-1908	Mr. Dack
1908-1910	Edna Shawler
1910-1911	Miss Bragg
1911-1912	Florence Newton
1912-1914	Miss Holland
1914-1918	Harriett McInroy
1918-1919	Miss Hawkens
1921	Irene Morrison
1921-1922	Harriett McLeish
1922	Amie Monroe
1922-1923	Merle Dora Freer
1923-1924	Florence McPherson
1924-1927	Marie Reinhardt
1928	Miss Richards
1928-1930	Viola Payne
1930-1932	Muriel Parker
1932-1940	Mae Watson
1941	Marjorie Campbell
1942	School Closed
1943	Flossie Hall
1944	School Closed
1945	Flossie Hall
1946-1951	School Closed
1952-1953	Don Heaman
1954-1959	Anna Hemstead

S.S. #9 TRUSTEES (1905-1944)

Benjamin Arrand
Robert Wilson
F. McCabe
W.T. Galloway

John Robertson
D. Conkey
Samuel Wilson
Ambrose Topping
Miles W. Curry
William Demaray
John McNab
William Cuddy

Wilbert Hodgson
William Oliver
Gilbert Shrier
R.V. McNab
Alfred Cuddy
Loftus Wilson
George Emmons
Peter Reinhardt

Byron B. Adams
Frank Pennington
Philip Conkey
Earl Murray
Laverne Topping
Wilfrid Wilson
Bob Adams
Robert Conkey

S.S. #9 SCHOOL FAIR

S.S. #9 Adelaide held their school fair on Friday last, which was a profitable and enjoyable day for the people in the section generally. The children made splendid exhibits of farm and garden products, etc., and a good program of sports was also held. There was a good attendance of young and old and the fair was a decided success from every standpoint.

A school fair was held on the grounds of S.S. #9 Adelaide on Friday afternoon, September 27. The exhibits which were shown by the pupils were excellent, and it is evident everyone took an interest in it as shown by their attendance. A booth on the grounds managed by the pupils and the teacher, Miss H. McLeish, realized a profit of about $5 for the Red Cross.

The following is a list of the prizewinners:

EXHIBITS:

Corn Stalks - John Hodgson, Margaret Cooper, Marion Grogan;
Ear Corn - John Hodgson, James Gerry, Margaret Cooper;
Beets - James Gerry, Gladys Shrier, Marion Grogan;
Carrots - John Hodgson, Marion Grogan, Cameron Giffen;
Parsnips - John Hodgson, Cameron Giffen, James Gerry;
Onions - James Gerry, Mary Demaray, Marion Grogan;
Cabbage - Wesley Demaray, Cameron Giffen;
Potatoes - John Hodgson, Cameron Giffen, Wesley Demaray;
Pumpkin - George Arrand, Wesley Demaray, John Hodgson;
Tomatoes - John Hodgson, James Gerry;
Citron - Pearl Shrier;
Turnips - Wesley Demaray;
Mangels - Bruce Arrand, James Gerry, Wesley Demaray;
Apples - Marion Grogan, Pearl Shrier, John Hodgson;
Bouquet of flowers -
    James Gerry, Marion Grogan;
Plain hemmed handkerchief -
    Margaret Conkey, Mary Demaray;
Art - Marion Grogan, James Gerry, James Waite;
Writing Sr. - Marion Grogan, Robert Conkey, Wesley Demaray;
Writing Jr. - Cameron Giffen, Ruby Cuddy, Gladys Shrier;
Sports - Boys 8 and under -
    George Arrand, Willie Cooper, Gordon Emmons;
Sports - Girls 7 and under -
    Margaret Cooper, Isabel Giffen, Margaret Conkey;
Sports - Boys 9 to 12 -
    John Hodgson, John Arrand, Cameron Giffen;

Sports - Girls 8 to 12 -
    Mary Demaray, Ruby Cuddy, Pearl Shrier;
Sports - Boys 12 and over -
    James Gerry, Milo Brooks, Wesley Demaray;
Girls 3-legged race -
    Mary Demaray and Gladys Shrier, Ruby Cuddy and Margaret Conkey;
Boys 3-legged race -
    John Hodgson and James Gerry, John Arrand and Wesley Demaray;
Thread and Needle Race for girls -
    Margaret Conkey and Eva Cuddy, Margaret Cooper and Isabel Giffen, Pearl Shrier and Ruby Cuddy;
Sack Race for boys -
    John Hodgson, Cameron Giffen, Lorne Emmons;
Chariot Race for girls -
    Gladys Shrier and Mary Demaray, Isabel Giffen and Margaret Cooper, Pearl Shrier and Ruby Cuddy;
Chariot Race for boys -
    John Hodgson and James Gerry, Cameron Giffen and Bruce Arrand, John Arrand and Wesley Demaray;
Wheelbarrow Race for Boys -
    John Hodgson and James Gerry, Wesley Demaray and John Arrand, Cameron Giffen and Lorne Emmons.

(From The Age, October 3, 1918)

S.S. #10

The 1851 census shows that on George Ivor's property, Lot 11, (concession unknown) SER, there was an English school in the village. This was a church school, not a free public school. It was built after 1832. Due to the size of the section and for other reasons, dissension arose.

At a Council meeting on March 31, 1862, By-law 102 was passed, issuing debentures to raise $500 to be applied to building a brick schoolhouse in S.S. #10 Adelaide to be advertised in the "Home Guard." The section was divided ca.1869, and a school for the east half was built on the southwest corner of Egremont Road (Highway #22) and Robotham Road (at present, the Martin Van Geffen farm). This was a very large school, with chimneys on both ends for big fireplaces. From photographs, the structure appears to have been built of brick. This school was used until 1889, when the present school was built on Lot 17, Con. 1 SER. The contractor was Mr. James Gerry from the Second Line North. The first trustees were Charles Demaray, Alex McInroy and George Glenn, who also acted as Secretary. The school was first equipped with double seats and folding desks, a table for the teacher's desk, and frosted windows. The first teacher was Mr. Robert G. Walker, followed by Mr. Walter Campbell and Mr. John Cowie, all qualified with a 3rd Class Certificate. The subjects taught were reading, writing, arithmetic, grammar, history and geography. The enrolment was about 40 students. Mr. Walter Campbell, son of William and Jane Campbell of Main Road (Egremont Road) was the youngest of 12 children. In the 1880s and 1890s, he also taught at S.S. #7 in Caradoc, Longwood, Appin, and home

S.S. #10 Adelaide, teacher Velma Petch.

S.S. #10 Adelaide, June 1926. Back L-R, Tena Muxlow, Vera Demaray, Muriel Petch, teacher Miss Webb, Inez King, Frank Holmes. Front L-R, Lloyd Muxlow, Anna Brock, Myrtle Branton, Mabel Branton, Calvin Dodge, Jean Holmes.

school. He was a pupil of Strathroy Collegiate during the period when J.E. Wetherall was Principal. In the fall of 1892, he gave up teaching and moved west, locating in Washington and later in Oregon. He worked in the insurance business, real estate and ranching, and was elected to the Oregon State Legislature. At S.S. #10, the teachers were:

	Mr. Joseph Stewart
	Mr. S. Jones
1880	Dan Mitchell
1881	P.H. Bartlett
1882	John Baird
1883	Jane E. Pierce
1883	Jennie E. Price
1888	Robert Walker
1913	Beryl Chalmers
1914-1916	Florence Brown
1917	William Jones
1918-1919	Mary Ingham
1920	Greta Smith
1921	Esther Bycroft
1922-1925	Ruth J. Brett
1927	Hildegard Webb
1928	Ida Helena Eastman
1929-1930	Helen West
1931-1934	Velma Petch
1936-1940	Marjorie Brock
1941	Anne Humphries
1942-1943	Murray Squire
1944	Gladys M. King
1945-1947	Mrs. Mary Harris
1948	Doreen McBain

1949-1951	Marjorie Hamilton
1951	Harris Zavitz
1952-1953	Margaret McLean
1954-1955	Mrs. Ruby Drake
1956	Glenn Easterbrook
1957-1958	Ann Feddema
1959	Yvonne W. Thorpe

New seats, a false ceiling, and a woodshed were added in 1925, and enclosed toilets were added in 1929. The flagpole rotted off about 1920.

In June 1936, there was talk of closing this school, as there was an attendance of only four pupils. The trustees held a meeting at which the Inspector allowed them to keep the school open for another year. In the spring of 1937, the trustees took a petition to the people of the section and it was found that the majority wished the school to be kept open. The section later received word from the Minister of Education that the school would not be closed against the wishes of the section.

In August and September 1937, the school was redecorated inside and out in brown and cream. Walter Feasey of Adelaide Village was the painter. The bell, which had been broken, was repaired and again hung in the belfry. A new door was constructed and put on the west entrance. The frame on the back window, which had rotted away, was also repaired. In November 1938, a second-hand piano was purchased, and Frank Hendry of Strathroy began music lessons once a week. In December 1938, the steps on the east side fell apart, and new ones were built by George Glenn and William McCarthy. In 1942, a new cupboard was built for the windows. In the fall of 1940, the water in the old well was condemned, and a new well was drilled at the front of the school by Len Currie of Denfield. In February 1942, storm windows were put on the four west windows. The stove was moved to the middle of the room. In 1942, the pupils made a quilt and

S.S. #10 (new), part Lot 17, Con. 1 SER. Back L-R, Ethel McLeish, unknown, Harold Crawford, Beryl Buchanan, Carson Thompson, Jack Walker, Mary McLeish. Middle L-R, May Ball, John Browning, Mildred Thompson, Tom Ball, Verna Henry, Ena Pool, Gordon Crawford, George McLeish. Front L-R, Evelyn Brock, Cliff Brock, Margaret Demaray, Agnes Crawford, John McLeish, Leila Brock.

498 ADELAIDE TOWNSHIP... A HISTORY

S.S. #10 Adelaide, 1938. Back L-R, George Glenn, Earl Campbell, Leo Cushman, teacher Marjorie Brock, Madelon Glenn, Ray Jackson. Front L-R, Norman Elliot, Donald Campbell, Donna Carroll, Lenore Jackson.

sold tickets. They earned $11.70 and gave $5 to the Red Cross.

Some of the important people who attended this school include Dr. Orville Glenn, Wardsville; Dr. Leonard Glenn, Chatham; D. McKenzie, Hydro Commissioner; Laura Glenn, Teacher, Windsor; Graham Walker, Customs Official, Windsor; E.A. McLeish, B.A., Teacher at Melbourne, Sergeant in Middlesex Huron Regiment who won Military Cross, WWII in Europe, and was on the staff at Althouse College at U.W.O.

Some of the early treasurers and trustees were William Brock, Charles Demaray, Joseph Petch, B.J. Donaldson, James Walker, George Glenn, Alexander McInroy. Grants were an average of $25. During the 1920s and 1930s, teachers' salaries were about $150 per year. Mr. Joseph Stewart, who taught for two years, moved to Delaware, where he received an increased salary. He was considered a teacher of great merit who deserved his promotion.

Some of the treasurers from 1885 to 1900 were William Brock, James Walker, B.J. Donaldson, George Glenn and Alexander McInroy. Grants were about $55 per year from 1885 to 1900.

S.S. #11, PAINE'S SCHOOL

The first school to serve this area was a small log building located at the corner of the Second Line South and the Strathroy Road. Perhaps it was built about 1850. This school was used only a few years when a larger log school was built on ¼-acre of land on Lot 19, Con. 3 SER. This school was replaced by a brick school in 1876 on one acre of land on the corner of Lot 18, Con. 3 SER, at a cost of $1,300. It was destroyed by a cyclone on June 23, 1944. School was then held in Jack Hendra's house on the west half of Lot 16, Con. 2 SER, until the township school board was started in 1960.

In November 1875, this advertisement was placed in The Strathroy Age for a teacher, for January 1876:

> **Teacher Wanted**
> Wanted for S.S. #11, Adelaide, a male Teacher, holding 2nd or 3rd class certificate. Duties to commence on January 1st, 1876. Apply to either of the undersigned trustees.
> **JOHN WALTHAM**
> **JOSEPH ALEXANDER**
> **JAMES McNEICE**
> **TRUSTEES**
> **ADELAIDE, NOVEMBER 16, 1875**

The teacher who was hired from responding to this ad for the new school was Edward Rowland, who had been teaching at S.S. #9 Adelaide since 1855. The board trustees were John Waltham, Joseph Alexander and James McNeice. Edwin Morrow was treasurer. Mr. Roland eventually became a banker and moved to Strathroy. He later gave money for a scholarship to the graduating student at Strathroy Collegiate Institute who received the highest marks in mathematics.

S.S. #11 Adelaide

SCHOOLS 499

S.S. #11 Adelaide, 1941. Back L-R, Evelyn (Fletcher) Clifton, Ethel Slater, Eileen Rawlinson, Audrey Knight, Edith Down, Bill Gilbert, Rev. Fydelle. Front L-R, Ruth Rawlinson, Lois Down, Jean Knight, Paul Harris standing behind Donna Hendra, Phyllis Down, Grant Knight, unknown.

Other trustees for S.S. #11 before 1900 include John Douglas, Henry Robinson, Robert Frank, Wesley Paine, and D. Campbell. Secretaries at S.S. #11 include Edward Morrow, James Bogue, Peter Paine, J. S. Douglas, Archie Paine, Richard Down, Frank Petch and Fred Rawlinson.

Teachers following Mr. Rowland up to 1900 include D.A. Campbell, Bella Stanley, John A. McKane, Ellen M. Miller, and Albert McPherson. From 1900-1920, teachers were Mary A. Fletcher, Hazel Douglas, Mary Harris, and Edith Cummiford. From 1920-1944, teachers were Annie L. Pulling (Mrs. George Foster), Lillian Field

29th Annual Mullifarry Picnic for S.S. #11 Adelaide (Paine's School) at Poplar Hill picnic grounds, 1996. Photo taken and presented by oldest surviving male member of this era, late 1920s and early 1930s, Fred Martin. Back L-R, Evelyn (Brewer) Varley, Donelda (Ward) Lamont, Eileen (Sisson) Cameron, Evelyn (Petch) Proctor, Ruth (Rawlinson) Lamereaux. Front L-R, Phyllis (Down) Phillips, Blanche (Down) Gibson, Greta (Down) Linton, Ethel (Post) Mawson, Lois (Down) Watson, Leola (Down) Smith, Loreen (Harris) Brown, Margaret (Knight) Hammond.

(Mrs. William Walker), Mrs. E.A.C. Phillips, Eulalia Head, Ruby White, Thelma Payne, Shirley Langford, Evelyn Fletcher (Mrs. Lloyd Clifton, 1943), and Katherine Thornton.

DECEMBER 1914,
REPORT FOR S.S. #11, ADELAIDE
MISS M. FLETCHER, TEACHER

CLASS IV JR.	Vera Buttery
	Edith Thompson
	Bessie Eastman
	Lucille Moore
	Bert Knight
CLASS III SR.	Jessie Paine
	Orval Knight
	Norman Bellairs
CLASS II SR.	Eleanor Buttery
	Arthur Thompson
	Jack Buttery
	Willie Dell
	Sadie Bellairs
CLASS II JR.	Gladys Sisson
	Tom Douglas
	Liol Douglas
	Stewart Knight
	Joseph Roberts
	Flossie Bellairs (absent)
PART 11	Eileen Sisson
	Lottie Lucas
CLASS I (B)	Sara Bogue
	Marguerite Frank
	Marion Buttery
	Jim Thomson
	Rheta Knight (A)
	Dorothy Bellairs
	Nellie deGraw

A very successful entertainment was held at S.S. #11 on Thursday evening, December 23, 1915. The programme consisted of drills, dialogues, songs and recitations by the pupils. The pupils were assisted by Miss Nellie Watson, pianist; Miss Ruby Wilson, soloist; and Robert Latimer, cornetist, all of Strathroy. Dr. Jones of Adelaide Village delighted the audience with his comic cartoon sketches. The enjoyment of the evening was very much enhanced by music contributed by the Thomas Orchestra. Edgar Bogue acted as Chairman.

Teachers' salaries were never very high. In 1896, the teacher was paid $200 in two payments; in 1900, $250 was paid quarterly; in 1930, $975; in 1934, $450 (Depression); in 1936, $500; and in 1940, $600. Salaries also increased for experienced teachers.

School fairs were a popular day in the school year, early in September. There were classes in fruits, vegetables, pets, calves, baking, public speaking, spelling, singing and sports. Usually it was held at the township property in Adelaide Village. It always started with a parade and each school marched.

Their Royal Highnesses, King George VI and Queen Elizabeth, visited the area during the Royal Tour in 1939. The Board of S.S. #11 hired Alton Wright Transport to take the children to London to view the royal couple. The school was assigned a spot on the street to watch as they were driven by. After the King and Queen left, the group was taken to Springbank Park for a picnic. The Board paid Wright Transport $5 for the truck, and $2 was paid to reserve picnic grounds at the park. There is also a record that the teacher, Miss Shirley Langford, went to Ottawa on October 19, 1939, and met Lord and Lady Tweedsmuir and the Governor General.

Some of the students in 1942 were Audrey and Jean Knight; Edith, Phyllis, Roy and Lois Down; Eileen and Ruth Rawlinson; Ethel Slater; Paul Harris; and Donna Hendra.

As a Centennial Project in 1967, the former pupils of S.S. #11 started an annual picnic they called the Mullifarry Picnic, which has continued each Labour Day until the present time.

S.S. #11 Adelaide

S.S. #11 Adelaide

S.S. #11 Adelaide, ca.1920, teacher Miss Laura Pulling.

S.S. #12, ADELAIDE VILLAGE SCHOOL

This school in Adelaide Village was not opened as early as many other schools in the township. On May 5, 1849, the Council of the District of London gave Lots 13 and 14, one acre, on the north side of King Street in Adelaide Village for *"school purposes."* The Township Council Minutes of February 25, 1850, state that the Trustees of S.S. #10, John Stroud Hoare, Anthony Preston and William Bray, made application to council to have George Ivor take action immediately to open the streets so that the new school land could be accessed. From reading correspondence regarding Ivor, it seemed that he had fenced off this area and was using the land for farming.

In November 1875, this advertisement was placed in The Strathroy Age for a teacher for January 1876:

> **Teacher Wanted**
> Wanted for S.S. #12, Adelaide, a 3rd class teacher for the year 1876. Apply (if by letter) to Adelaide P.O., to the undersigned trustees,
> **JAMES LARGE,
> SECRETARY-TREASURER
> R. FORSYTHE
> H. HOULTON
> TRUSTEES
> ADELAIDE, NOVEMBER 30, 1885**

Few teacher records have been found. According to George Brock Sr., in an interview in The Age on January 28, 1929, the first teacher in Adelaide Village was Mr. Yeomans, whose salary was $300 per year. Other teachers were Annie Tweedle 1880-1881; Martha E.M. Rowe 1882; Maggie McKellar 1883-1884; Isabella McInroy 1885; Ellen Miller 1886; and Reta Clark 1887-1888 (she got an increase in salary the second year). In 1890, the school no longer existed.

Records of the school grants for S.S. #12 show that trustees on this school board from 1884-1890 were A. McJury, Richard Brock, George Baptist, William Gale, Albert Brock and Alexander McInroy. In 1890, Alexander McInroy's signature appeared as a trustee of S.S. #12, and also with George Glenn as a trustee of S.S. #10. This is the year that S.S. #12 closed and the new school, S.S. #10, was built farther to the west on Lot 17, Con. 1 SER, so that the students wouldn't have to walk as great a distance.

For the year 1886, the government grant was $70.09, and the remainder of the teacher's salary came from taxes levied on the landowners in school section #12. In 1889, the grant was increased to $84.67.

On January 11, 1889, a petition of the ratepayers of S.S. #12 was read at the Council meeting, asking for an increase of territory from the west end of S.S. #10, and the east end of S.S. #6. The clerk was instructed to notify the school sections interested. The petition of ratepayers from the west end of S.S. #10, asking to be attached to S.S. #12, was read. By the following year, the action was taken and S.S. #12 was closed.

MUD CREEK SCHOOL

In 1855, a school was erected on Lot 19, Con. 2 NER. The school was named for the creek that ran nearby. This school carried on its duties until 1879, at which time a new union school (Crathie) was completed about a mile east of this one, and another school, S.S. #4, was built a mile west.

Mud Creek School was a small frame building where 25 children of different ages sat in rows at long desks. One early teacher was a dignified woman who wore hoops under her long skirts. The children used slates and copybooks. They were taught reading, writing, arithmetic, spelling, history, geography and grammar, as well as deportment, and they learned their lessons well. The teachers in those days were very strict, and used a leather strap if there was a need for discipline.

Before they left for home, boys and girls lined up beside the door. Each girl would curtsy to the teacher and each boy would bow. The teacher would curtsy to every child in turn. The boys did not care for this dignified dismissal; they would try to get as close to the door as possible, duck their heads and run. The children set out happily for home, sliding and throwing snowballs in the winter, dressed in their woollen hand-made coats, caps, mufflers and mitts. In summer, they ran through the grass in their bare feet. What a change from today's school bus transportation to the door!

David Sands (later a doctor with a practise in Nairn) taught at Mud Creek School during the holidays.

The last teacher was Hugh McComb (or McKone), who married Margaret Nettleton. They moved to Parkhill and ran the stagecoach from Parkhill to Strathroy three days a week. They delivered the mail and often had one or two paying passengers on board.

Six of the last pupils to attend Mud Creek School met to hold a reunion in 1958, to celebrate the 100th birthday of Mrs. Sarah (Freele) Meek of Port Stanley. Other students of teacher Mr. McComb (or McKone) who attended this reunion were Mrs. Susan (Nettleton) McLeish, 99, of London; Mr. Roderick Campbell, 93, of Youngstown, Ohio and his sisters, Mrs. Isabelle (Campbell) Graham, 94, and Mrs. Emily (Campbell) Fay, 95, both of Colville, Washington; and Mrs. Annie (Robotham) Campbell, 98, of Alvinston.

ADELAIDE CENTRAL SCHOOL / ADELAIDE-W.G. MacDONALD SCHOOL

The education system in Adelaide Township changed in 1960 when all of the one-room schools were amalgamated into one school in the township. This school, named Adelaide Central School, is located on Lot 15, Con. 1 SER. The Principal appointed to this school was Miss Annie Courtis. During the 10 years she was Principal, she married and became Mrs. Annie Cannon. The custodian was George Robotham.

On January 1, 1969, the Middlesex County Board of Education was formed and all of the schools in the County of Middlesex were amalgamated under the new system. In June 1970, Mrs. Cannon retired, and the new Principal to start in September was Lawrence M. Smyth. At that time, the position of Secretary was added to the school, and Mrs. Donna Walker was employed on September 8, 1970. George Robotham continued as custodian. Attendance at this time was approximately 275 students, from Kindergarten to Grade 8.

In December 1976, trainable learning-disabled students from W.G. MacDonald School, who had been meeting in St. Andrew's Presbyterian Church, Strathroy, were moved to Adelaide Central School. The official opening of the new addition to the school was held in April 1977, and the name of the school was changed to "Adelaide-W.G. MacDonald School." Mr. W. Graham MacDonald was a Superintendent with the Middlesex County Board of Education for many years and was the organizer for the Special Education Program for the Mentally Retarded.

With the addition of the new students, the attendance increased to over 300. When this new wing was added to the school, it was said to have been the most modern structure for Special Education in Ontario.

In November 1990, a 30th Reunion was held. Reeve Frank Gare of Adelaide Township presented the school with a flag with the school logo on it.

There were many changes in staff and students over the years and, in January 1998, another change took place. The Thames Valley District School

Board was formed. This Board covers the counties of Middlesex, Elgin and Oxford, and the City of London, making it the third largest Board in the Province of Ontario, with 90,000 students.

During the 1997-1998 school year, a new school was being constructed on the north edge of Strathroy and, by doing so, many of the students from Adelaide-W.G. MacDonald School were moved to the new school, thus causing the population at the school to decline in September 1998 to about 215 students. The enrolment for the 1999-2000 school year is approximately 220.

The following is a listing of the staff members who were at Adelaide Central School and Adelaide-W.G. MacDonald School from September 1960 to June 2000:

STAFF MEMBERS	YEARS OF SERVICE
Lyons, Aubrey	1960-1962
Brooks, Norma	1960-1962
Redman, Margaret	1960-1963
Carson, Delores	1960-1965
Hall, Flossie	1960-1968
Cannon (Courtis), Annie, Principal	1960-1970
McLellan, Bella	1960-1971
Fonger, Margaret	1960-1975
Robotham, George, Custodian	1960-1984
Woodall, Joseph	1962-1963
Patterson, Raymond	1962-1964
Size, Mary Jean	1963-1965
Morgan, Velma	1963-1970
Pierce, Jean	1964-1965
Dale, Judith	1966-1967
Seed, Robert	1966-1968
Pierce, Margaret	1966-1970
James, Patricia	1966-1971
Ball, Harriet	1966-1972
Campbell, Gladys	1966-1972
Pucsek, Margaret	1969-1970
Duncan, Margaret	1969-1970
Dinnin, William	1969-1981
Alderson, Bonnie	1970-1971
Campbell, Janet	1970-1972
Hastings (Brown), Sandra	1970-1977
Smyth, Larry M., Principal	1970-1979
Walker, Donna, Secretary	1970-1998
Morgan, Peggy	1971-1973
Jeffs, Shirley	1971-1973

STAFF MEMBERS	YEARS OF SERVICE
Bergman, Paul	1971-1974
Cunningham, Laurel	1971-1975
Howard, Kitty	1972-1975
Walker, Marion	1972-1981
Osmond, Susan	1972-1981
Smith, Everett M., Custodian	1972-1982
Maycock, Marline	1972-1983
Hall (Hamilton), Marion	1973-1975
McDougall (LaCroix), Gloria	1973-1999
Smyth, Margaret, Vice Principal	1974-1984
Molineux, Margaret	1974-1991
McDonald, Connie	1975-1976
Williams (Thornicroft), Elizabeth	1975-1978
Walvius, Taisa	1975-1979
Bennett, Robert	1976-1977
Satchwell, Marion, Vice Principal	1976-1979
Zettler, John	1976-1981
Smibert, Marian	1976-1983
Hasan (Earnshaw), Barbara	1976-1985
Russell, Elaine, T.A.	1976-1988
Davis, Doris	1976-1988
Blair-Smith, Elizabeth	1976-1992
Goldrick, Dorothy, T.A.	1976-1999
Bishop, Jackie	1977-1978
Wagner, Barry	1977-1981
Higgins, Jean, T.A.	1977-1990
Jones, Christine	1978-1979
Thuss, Martin	1979-1980
Williams, Margaret, Principal	1979-1985
Patterson, Christine	1980-1984
Pedersen, Joyce	1981-1984
Ogg, John	1981-1984
LeFeuvre, John	1981-1987
Johnston, Lois	1981-1990
Unipan, Berta	1981-1994
Milligan, Jean, T.A.	1981-1994
Davidson, John	1981-1999
Zavitz, Ken, Custodian	1982-1988
Dinning, Ron	1982-1990
Lingard, Alice	1983-1992
Connor, Sandra	1983-1999
Lyon, Phyllis, Principal	1984-1987
Dargatz, Udo, Vice Pr./Principal	1984-1988
Hanson, Lynn	1984-1995
Brown, Marie	1984-1996
Ataide, Isaac, Custodian	1984-1996
Thody, Marie	1985-1988
May, Dianne	1985-1990

STAFF MEMBERS	YEARS OF SERVICE
Rowe, Donna, T.A.	1985-1996
Gear, Brenda	1986-1987
Campbell, Janet	1986-1987
VanderWoerd, Cindy, T.A.	1986-1990
Bennett, Donna	1987-1999
Brady, Wendy	1987-1990
Brown, Mary Anne, Vice Principal	1988-1988
Oldewening, Sadie, Vice Principal	1988-1989
Todd, Richard, Principal	1988-1993
Schofield, Nancy	1988-1994
Platts, John, Vice Principal	1989-1991
Kusters, Bert, Custodian	1989-1992
Wannamaker, Joan	1989-1994
Thomas, Judith	1989-1994
McLenon (Patterson), Robin, T.A.	1989-1994
Roby (O'Bright), Genyne	1989-1995
Woodford, Catherine	1990-1991
Houliston, Lisa, T.A.	1990-1992
Klein, Hannelore, T.A.	1990-1992
Smith, Janet, T.A.	1990-1994
Bailey, Marilyn	1990-1994
Dennis, Brenda, T.A.	1990-1997
VanKeulen, Edith	1990-1998
Graham, Elizabeth	1991-1992
Smith, Garnet, Vice Principal	1991-1994
Nicol-Wallace, Leslee	1991-1997
Pierce, Wendy	1991-1998
Platts, John	1992-1993
Hinton, Barbara	1992-1993
Howett, Clara	1992-1993
Campbell, Brenda, Custodian	1992-1997
Gee, Robert	1992-1998
Iszakovitz, Silvia	1993-1994
Oldewening, Sadie, Principal	1993-1998
Ataide, Carole	1993-2000

STAFF MEMBERS	YEARS OF SERVICE
Toll, Frances	1994-1995
Davidson, Tanya	1994-1996
Beaton, Marianne, T.A.	1994-1996
Van Daele, Dorothy	1994-1996
Smith-Gawne, Larissa	1994-1996
Henderson, Jane	1994-1999
Thompson, Judy, T.A.	1994-1998
Oliver, Charlene	1994-1998
Jackson, Ruth, Vice Principal	1995-1996
Fryer, Susan	1995-1996
Ridley, Judi	1995-1998
Brooks, Heather	1995-1998
Rae, Lisa	1996-1996
Wasko, Beth-Anne	1996-1990
McMillan, Betty	1996-1990
Fishleigh, Ruth, Custodian	1996-1998
Yamamoto, Ed	1996-1999
DeZorzi, Colleen	1997-1998
Pratt, Charlene	1998-1998
Bergman, Christine	1998-1999
Micks, Cathy, T.A.	1998-1999
Parker, Cathy	1998-1999
Varley, Sue	1998-1999
Black, Sharon, Secretary	1998-2000
Fex, Glen, Custodian	1998-2000
Hayter, Mary Louise, T.A.	1998-2000
Noble, Beverley, Principal	1998-2000
Piggott, Dianne, T.A.	1998-2000
Simmons, Tonya, T.A.	1998-2000
Assaf, Erica	1999-2000
Aylsworth, Jenny	1999-2000
Freeland, Frances	1999-2000
McLean, Pamela	1999-2000
Van DeWiele, Rose Anne	1999-2000

CHAPTER FIVE

Communities

ADELAIDE VILLAGE

Following are excerpts from "A History of St. Ann's Church and Adelaide" by Dora Aitken (this slim volume is still for sale, proceeds going to St. Ann's Cemetery):

"The first settlement at Adelaide village was chiefly composed of aristocratic army people, both English and Irish. In this it was similar to the Napier settlement. Some of these people remained and made a success of life in the wilderness, while others returned in a few years to their homeland. Early plans for the village included a Club House, an Opera House, agricultural grounds and a race track. The streets were laid out and named after thoroughfares in London, England. Duke St., Clarence St., St. George Square, Princess St., Queen St., King St....

In January, 1833, the Letters [Authentic Letters from Upper Canada] speak of a log school house being built and used for divine service until the church was built. In February of that year there were seven houses (two of them shops), and a hotel and a post-office were being built. A parsonage had begun, and the church was to be finished in the spring.

At the east of the village was the first Anglican rectory, built on the burying ground, just east of the present residence of Mrs. Vivien Nichols (part of lot 11, conc. 1N). This rectory was built in 1833. The old St. Patrick's Church (R.C.) was a white frame building by the R.C. cemetery. In front of St. Patrick's was a school, with two more houses to the west of it. The Township Hall was built in 1874.

...At that time, Mrs. Dempster lived west of the hall, and behind her house, the Murphys. Between Dempsters and St. Ann's Church was Miller's house. Across the creek were Brock's store, three houses (Fortner, Whittaker and Down), and the blacksmith's shop. Beyond it were a sawmill, a grist mill, and Freele's hotel. At the present site of Robert Feasey's house was the Post Office. Behind the present home of Edwin Brooks was a tile yard.

On the south side of the road, at the eastern end of the village, lived the Petch and Callaghan families—behind the present home of Walter Feasey. Along the bank of the creek were several houses belonging to army people. Next along the road were two houses (one owned by the Prestons), and then a wagon shop with the Orange Lodge above it. Then came the homes of George Hodgson and the Freele family. A family named Baptist lived in the old Nichols home (which is still in existence but not used as a residence). Next to it was the Doctor's house, and then the Methodist parsonage, the present residence of James Southern. Next was the Barrett residence (still in existence but unoccupied) and, west of it, a hotel...

Adelaide ceased to grow about 1856, when the Grand Trunk Railway Line from London to Sarnia was built through Strathroy rather than Adelaide. The railway had attempted three times to purchase a right-of-way through Adelaide, but unsuccessfully. Strathroy, which had a population of 14 in 1840, grew to 3,000 by 1870, when it was incorporated as a town.

The first postmaster at Adelaide was Col. Radcliff, followed by Richard Windsor, John Hoare, George Hoare, Thos. Brock and Mr. Wilkins.

Rural mail delivery commenced in 1912... The last site of the Post Office was the present residence of Robert Feasey...

In 1857, the population of Adelaide village was listed at 200. Township records include the following names and occupations: Wm.Bray, J.S. Hoare, Wm. Macklin, Robt. Atkinson, John Ivor, Robert Murray, John Stanley, all store or inn keepers; Wm. Cooper, steam grist mill; James Abernathy, Geo. Freele, Anthony Preston, John West, shoemakers; James Fitzpatrick and Chas. Hall, tailors; Wm. Clifford and James Brett, carpenters; Rev. Arthur Mortimer (Rector of St. Ann's); Robt. Pegley, magistrate; Thos. Sadler, harness maker; J.S. Hoare, postman.

From the time of Dr. Phillips' arrival in 1833, there appears to have been a doctor in Adelaide until 1932, when Dr. Roy McLeod moved away. Both Dr. Jones and Dr. McLeod lived in the house just west of the present Heaman's Service Station.

The London Free Press, February 15, 1947 edition has an article on the stagecoach which ran daily between London and Sarnia in the 1850's. The horses were changed at three stops, the first being Warwick Village, so probably Adelaide would be the second stop on the route.

The 11th Provisional Battalion in the 1837 war was commanded by Col. Radcliff and was stationed in London and in Adelaide Village. At this time St. Ann's was used as a barracks...

The last hotel in Adelaide was operated as a store for many years, and stood across the road from the present residence of Charles Nichols. The family of Frank Baxter were the last to occupy it before it burned down, about 1952. The last general store still stands, but has been closed since about 1955. The former storekeepers, Mr. and Mrs. Priestly, still live there. At present there is only one business in Adelaide Village—Heaman's Service Station...

The first telephone lines in Adelaide were installed by Meredith Morgan, and in 1911 and later there was a switchboard in the village, probably in the general store.

Hydro was installed through the village in the late 1930's. There were two petitions signed, one in June and another in August, before enough people could be persuaded to sign for the installation. Before this, several homes had a Delco plant, a 32 volt system which generated its own power."

Brutal Murder in Adelaide

**An Inoffensive Old Man the Victim
Particulars of the Tragedy and
Result of the Coroner's Inquest**

On Saturday afternoon last, one of the most brutal murders ever perpetrated in a civilized community was brought to light in Adelaide Township. The victim of the assassin was Jonathan Robinson, an old and highly esteemed resident of the township, who lived by himself in a house belonging to Samuel Harris, on the second concession south of the Egremont road, about four miles from Strathroy. The discovery of the body was made by Mr. Harris' two children and his hired man, James Clarke, about 3 o'clock, who at once notified the neighbours. Mr. Joseph Crews came to Strathroy to inform the Coroner and Chief of Police. The latter returned with Mr. Crews to the scene and inspected the premises, and then placed them in charge of two Special Constables.

The news of the murder soon spread and on Sunday morning, large numbers from town and country visited the scene, which presented one of the most sickening sights that one could conceive. Blood and grey hairs were noticed on stove and floor, while at the back of the stove lay the murdered man with his head smashed in, arms broken, and his head almost severed from his body. An examination of the premises showed that the house had been ransacked as drawers had been pulled out and valuable papers were lying about, while the money which the old man was supposed to have had was missing. In the shed at the rear of the house, an axe was found with grey hairs sticking to it, and just inside the back door, the old man's cap was picked up, which bore the marks of blows as would likely be made by the back of an axe, while one of the chairs had an indention in the seat as though struck by the same instrument. On a table near the front door was a lamp and paper, beside which lay a pair of spectacles. A chair stood near the table which gave the general impression that the old man had been reading on Friday evening, September 14th, the last night a light was noticed in his house, and had got up to answer a summons for admittance from the back door. On opening the door, he has been struck on the head with the back of the axe several times, and in his attempt to parry the blows his arms were broken. Stunned and bleeding, the poor old man appears to have fallen face forward on the stove, which stood nearby, as there were bloody hand marks and hair on the oven and lids, the latter being displaced. From here the assassin dragged his victim to the rear or back of the stove and cut his throat, as the blood was all underneath the body when found. Who the murderer is or when the deed was committed is shrouded in mystery, as the old man was last seen alive on Thursday, September 13th, on his way to Strathroy, but no one saw him return, and beyond the seeing of a light in the house by Mr. and Mrs. McDougal, on their way home from choir practice, the neighbours generally believed that Mr. Robinson was in Michigan as the blinds were down from Thursday, September 13th, up to the time the body was discovered on Saturday. From the advanced state of decomposition of the body, the murder must have committed on the night of the 14th or 15th.

Dr. Lindsay, coroner of Strathroy, acting under authority of the County Crown Attorney, proceeded Sunday morning to hold an inquest, and the following jury was empanelled with Mr. George Bishop, Sr. as Foreman: John Martin, Edwin Morrow, Paul Harris, George Miner, Charles Down, Henry Down, William Miner, James McNeice, John W. Watson, Henry Robinson, Angus H. Knight, Edward Bishop, William Martin, Henry Knight, Henry Bishop, William Ellis, John Eakins, Samuel Harris, William Humphries, Thomas Petch, Edwin Muxlow, James Petch and James Carrothers. The jury next viewed the body and made a careful examination of the premises, eliciting the facts above stated, and then adjourned to meet at the Firemen's Hall, Strathroy, at 10 o'clock a.m. on Monday to take evidence and receive the report of Drs. W.W. Hoare and A.S. Thompson, who made the post-mortem examination.

The unfortunate man has been a resident of Adelaide for years and was not supposed to have had an enemy in the world, which leads to the conclusion that robbery was the incentive to murder. Mr. Robinson was evidently a careful housekeeper, for the bedding and surroundings presented a very cleanly appearance. It was also learned that he had a deposit to his credit in the Bank of Commerce of $411, and was supposed to have had about $30 in the house, not one cent of which was found after the discovery of the tragedy. The remains were interred in the Strathroy Cemetery Sunday afternoon, a large number of neighbours and friends turning out to pay their last tribute of respect to the deceased. Rev. L. DesBrisay conducted the services.

Monday morning at 10 o'clock, the inquest was continued at the Firemen's Hall, before Coroner Lindsay. County Attorney Hutchinson, of London, appeared on behalf of residents of Adelaide and town. On the roll being called, all the jurors answered to their names. James Clarke was the first witness who deposed as follows: *"Worked for Mr. S. Harris in Adelaide; found the body of Jonathan Robinson on Saturday afternoon; had come down to do some work in the garden near Robinson's house, Emma and Edgar Harris accompanied me; I was putting the horses in the stable when Emma Harris, who had went and looked in the back door of Robinson's house, came and told me that there was a man in the house; Edgar was with me at the stable; I then went into the house and saw Mr. Robinson lying there dead* [Exhibit A, showing a plan of the situation of the house was here shown witness who said as far as he could remember it was a correct one]; *I entered by the back door; the key was in the outside of the door; did not notice cap or chair and did not see axe; I sent Emma to Mr. Ellis who lives opposite; and I roused other neighbours; Francis Smith was the first to the house; I went to the back door in the morning and saw the key in the back door; looked in, but did not go in as I thought I had no business there; knew deceased well and saw him last alive a week ago last Wednesday; I was cutting corn about 60 rods from the house and deceased came out to me and said 'Good day, James,' and I said 'Good-day, Mr. Robinson,' he gave me $2 to give Mrs. Harris for rent; he told me he was going to the states and then went into the house; the farm belonged to Mr. Harris, and I worked there; first started to work in the garden digging potatoes Friday afternoon; told Chief of Police I was not in the house until 3 o'clock, which was the truth."*

Edgar Harris, sworn: *"Am ten years old; know last witness; I and my sister were with him at Robinson's house last Saturday about 3 o'clock; don't think Clarke was in the house at that time, but he looked into the house over the partition towards the bed; did tell the chief that Clarke went into the house."*

William Pike of Warwick: *"Was not acquainted with deceased but knew he lived in a house on Samuel Harris' Farm; heard of his death about two weeks ago at a threshing at either Westgate's or Parker's; asked Joseph Harris a week ago last Friday if there was a man by that name dead; cannot remember who told me of the death; saw J. Harris at William Crone's; told the chief that I heard of the death at Westgate's on the 13th; heard that Robinson was found dead in bed and then that he was found outside near the fence; do not recollect who talked about the death; Jacob and William Cline, G. Routley, B. Pike, W. Widdis, Fred and George Westgate, W. Williamson, J. Harrower, G. Patterson, a man named Carr and myself were at Westgate's; William Williamson and J. Harrower were present near the engine when the person told that Mr. Robinson of the 2nd line was dead; I asked if it was Jonathan Robinson, but the party did not know; was filling an oil can and did not pay much attention to who told it; Westgate lives on the 4th line of Warwick; I told Joseph Harris it was Jonathan Robinson; Parker's threshing was two weeks ago Friday; Williamson, Harrower, Laverick, Widdis, myself and others were there; told Mrs. J. Craig, of Warwick, about Robinson's death, together with that of another man who had dropped dead on a straw...(?); I told Joseph Harris about the death at Crone's and Harris said it was the first he had heard; Crone's live between seven and eight miles from Robinson's; swear positively I cannot remember who told me of the death."* In reply to jurors, witness said he kept no book of dates of threshing and knew Robinson lived in Harris' house for a long time back.

Joseph Harris, of Adelaide: *"Knew deceased and live about eight miles from his house; knew last witness, and was talking to him at Routley's threshing a week ago last Saturday about Mr. McNeice's death; Pike next told me of Robinson's death; I asked if it was the one who lived in the log house or the one near the church; Pike said he thought it was the one near the church, and that he was found near the fence; I know it was Saturday because the engine went wrong; Pike told me of the death just as a mere rumour, and I thought it might be...(?); I knew the man had been sick."*

Joseph Crews, Adelaide: *"About 3 o'clock Saturday, James Clarke came running to where I was cutting corn and told me that Jonathan Robinson was lying dead in his house; Clarke appeared half scared to death; I went with him to the house and on going in I noticed blood and hair on the oven and lids of the stove and saw the body; I at once exclaimed, 'My God, this is foul play'; did not touch anything until the coroner came; think the blood might have been there a week; the house had been ransacked as drawers were out, table and papers scattered about; I afterwards learned that the papers were notes, (?) I hitched up and went to Strathroy for the coroner and police; I last saw Jonathan Robinson two weeks ago Sunday when I took him papers on my way to Church."*

Dr. Hoare then submitted the result on the post-mortem examination as follows:

"Post-mortem examination on body of Jonathan Robinson— External appearances—Body well nourished of a gangrenous colour, apparently 70 years of age, 5 feet 8 inches in height; hair grey; position of tongue normal; teeth, not good. Marks—1st over right frontal bone, above right eye, a deep bruise 2 1/4 inches long by 3/4 in. breadth; one of the upper part of the left parietal bone 1 3/4 in. long by 2 1/2 wide, and a second wound right in front about the size of an English sixpence; on the centre of the head, over the left parieto-occipital or back of head, a gaping wound 1 1/2 in. long and 3/4 wide; and a second 2 in. long by 3/4 in. wide; also a third over the right parietal-occipital region, through the soft parts and covering of bone, 1 1/2 in. long, by 3/4 wide, over the right occipital we find a severe contusion which, on cutting into, presents extravasated blood. Face—Advanced decomposition, and smeared with clotted blood. Neck—A deep gash extending from the trapexius muscle behind, on left side to the sterno mastoid on the right, severing the muscles of the neck and windpipe complete, also the blood vessels and extending into vertebrae. The left wrist smashed and both bones of the forearm broken; a wound about 1/4 inch behind third joint of little finger, fracturing metacarpal bone and on the posterior part, of right forearm a contused wound 4 in. long by 3/4 wide, which on opening presents a fracture of ulna. Thorax—On opening chest we find lungs soft and friable with considerable bloody serum in left cavity, and a good deal of hypostatic congestion of lungs. Heart—Soft and flabby, and completely emptied of blood about a tablespoonful of bloody serum in the pericardium or heart-sack. Skull—Find a fracture over right parietal bone extending from the temporal region 1 in. in front of ear upwards and backward towards the middle line of the parieta-occipital groove, and bloody clot immediately under the seat of fracture; membrane of brain apparently healthy; brain substance very soft and decomposed. Abdomen— Liver pale, not much decomposed, completely emptied of blood, otherwise healthy; kidneys pale and fatty; bladder empty; spleen soft, with decomposition. Stomach very much distended with fetid gas and containing about half a teaspoonful of partially digested pulpy food. From the foregoing we are of the opinion that the deceased came to his death from the above mentioned injuries."* W. W. Hoare, M. D. A. S. Thompson, M. B.

Dr. Hoare, examined: *"From the appearance of brain and lungs, deceased had been dead over five days, and might have been a week or more; no other cause were found than the injuries described to account for death; the injuries could not have been self-inflicted; the injuries could have been inflicted with the back of axe produced, grey and black hairs were found in wash dish, but might have been from the same head; the impression on peak of cap produced, corresponds exactly with the mark that might have been made by the axe, and a wound on the head fitted exactly with it; the throat wound was produced by some sharp instrument."*

Dr. A. S. Thompson corroborated the evidence of Dr. Hoare.

David A. Ellis, Adelaide: *"Am 13 years old and know the nature of an oath; knew Jonathan Robinson and saw him last a week ago Thursday, passing Paine's School house on his way to Strathroy; knew it was Thursday, the day before Mr. Smith was hurt in a well; saw a wagon overtake Mr. Robinson and he got in, but could not tell whose wagon it was."*

William Ellis, Adelaide: *"Am father of last witness, and live opposite deceased's house; recollect passing a remark asking where Jonathan Robinson was, when my little boy spoke up and said he saw him passing the school house on his way to town the day before; deceased was at my place Wednesday previous and complained of cramps, and I recommended some liniment; deceased was a pretty regular visitor to my house; from Thursday most, the day the body was found, the blinds were down, and I thought he was away from home; my daughter was over the day he went away and looked in; saw the bed with no one in it which satisfied us he was away from home; was talking with Joseph Harris, mail carrier who informed me that word had been left at S. Harris house that Mr. Robinson was going to Michigan; wasn't at home on the day of the well accident (?) o'clock, and saw no light on coming home, on the day the body was found the house had been ransacked; loose papers were lying around and Jonathan was a careful man in these matters; was informed that a light was seen in Robinson's house Friday night late by Mr. and Mrs. James McDougall; could not say whether Jonathan had any money in the house or not."*

Samuel Harris: *"James Clarke has worked for me about four years and has the run of the house the same as my own children; I told Joseph Harris that my family told me that Robinson had said he was going to Michigan; Clarke's statement about cutting corn and digging potatoes is correct; believe him to be honest but has a poor memory and is liable to contradict himself when bothered."*

Emma J. Harris: *"Was at Robinson's house Saturday afternoon at 3 o'clock; went to the door and found the key on the outside; opened it and went in and saw a man lying on the floor; ran out and told Clarke, who came in and saw it was Mr. Robinson, Clarke told me to go and tell Mr. Ellis."*

This finished the evidence. The coroner addressed the Jury, stating that there was little doubt in his mind that their way was clear to return a verdict of murder, but it was for them to say. Regarding the evidence as to when the murder was committed, it was more difficult to say.

The jury deliberated for a few moments and without leaving their seats returned the following verdict: *That Jonathan Robinson was, on some day to the jurors unknown subsequent to the 13th day of September, 1888, at the township of Adelaide in the County of Middlesex, feloniously and with malice aforethought, killed and murdered by some person or persons to the jurors aforesaid unknown.*

From what can be learned of the Robinson brothers, it seems they have been residents of Adelaide for upwards of 40 years. They owned a 50-acre farm west of where the murder was committed, which some years ago they deeded to William Alexander, on condition that he would keep Thomas and pay Jonathan a yearly annuity of $145. William Alexander died some years ago and his heirs will benefit by the old gentleman's death, one of them being Joseph C. Alexander of Michigan, whom Jonathan was supposed to have visited. Whether he did so or not has not yet come to light, and word from there is anxiously waited for.

Beyond the evidence of Pike, the murder is shrouded in mystery. And it does seem strange that this young man should have heard of Robinson's death at a threshing before the body was found and not be able to tell who his informant was. A great many present at the inquest think Pike should have told more than he did, and for his own sake it is to be hoped he will be able to explain the matter in a way that all can believe, for, as the inquest has left it, he occupies a position of doubt.

We understand that there is a movement in Adelaide to offer a reward of $500 for the apprehension and conviction of the murderer. If this is a fact, the Ontario Government should be asked to supplement it with an equal amount.

(From an unknown news source)

CRATHIE

The children sang the following song at the beginning of each meeting of the Literary Society. It was sung to the tune of a song about London, with the wording changed for Crathie. The song is copied from a London Free Press clipping dated March 17, 1925. The Society had excellent meeting programmes, and large crowds.

Crathie On The Hill
*Of all the places far and near
There's none that can compare
With dear old Crathie, Adelaide's boast
You're lucky if you're there*

*No place was ever known to be
So thrifty for its size
Let all the men take off their hats
And bow, in great surprise*

Chorus

*Crathie, Crathie that's the place for me
There's everything there from A to Z
Real good roads and shady trees
For work and comfort, the people all use skill
So let's offer a toast to Adelaide's boast
Dear old Crathie, on the hill.*

KATESVILLE

One of the earliest communities of Western Middlesex County was Katesville. Now a ghost town, it once existed and thrived on the Sixth Line of Adelaide, now known as Katesville Drive, Metcalfe Township. The community started on Lot 17, Con. 7 SER, Adelaide Township (now Lot 17, Con. 2, Metcalfe Township), during the mid-1830s. The community was established enough by 1837 to warrant a post office.

Previous to white settlement in this area, there was an aboriginal trail across the Caradoc Sand Plain that bridged Bear Creek at the future site of Katesville before carrying on to the Arkona area. This trail provided a link between various local rivers. It allowed local aboriginals to move between their seasonal camps, and gave them access to flint deposits in the Arkona area, as flint was not available on the Caradoc Sand Plain. The Tremaine Map of 1862 illustrates a meandering road from Mt. Brydges westward to Katesville and beyond to the Village of Adelaide. There is a good possibility that the construction of this road allowance followed the aboriginal trail through this area. There is evidence of an aboriginal presence at Katesville, as local residents have found numerous arrowheads in the vicinity. This trail and Bear Creek would have been natural avenues for the original settlers to enter the southern Adelaide Township area to homestead.

One of the original families to do so was the Blake family, devout Anglo-Irish gentry who immigrated to Upper Canada from Ireland in 1832. The Rev. Dominick Edward Blake had been appointed English rector for Adelaide Township and district. With him came his younger brother and sister-in-law, William Hume and Catherine Blake. The Blake family purchased Lot 15, Con. 7 SER, Adelaide Township, and then built a log cabin with the intent to homestead.

After a brief attempt at farming, William Hume Blake and his family moved away and settled in Toronto, where he continued his studies and rose quickly in legal, political, and social life. During their stay in Adelaide, William and Catherine had a son, Edward Hume Blake, on October 13, 1833, who later became the second Premier of Ontario (1871-1872).

The original purchaser of Lot 17, Con. 7 SER, the future site of Katesville, appears to have been Thomas Lyons. How it reverted to the Crown is unknown. However, on March 14, 1836, the patent for this 93-acre lot was transferred from the Crown to Thomas Radcliffe. Shortly thereafter, Thomas subdivided part of this land into village lots, some of which he retained for himself, and others that he sold. Some of the lots were sold to Richard Wallace Branan (November 3, 1836); Richard Brown (November 3, 1836); Charles Knapton (November 21, 1839); Henry Saul (April 14, 1845); William Fulton (May 13, 1845); Patrick Feenarghty (April 24, 1849); Alfred Sessions (April 7, 1854); and Edwin Burrows (June 1, 1854).

Richard Wallace Branan was an early settler and merchant in the area of Katesville. In addition to the village lot, he had purchased a parcel of land on Con. 6 SER, on June 30, 1836. Richard Branan and his family were probably the first to live in Katesville. To promote his new business venture, it is conceivable that Branan initiated the petition to acquire a post office. This would attract customers to his new general store, as they came to get their mail. By early 1837, the community name of Katesville was accepted enough by the locals to be mentioned on this petition that resulted in postal services being granted to begin on February 6, 1837, with Richard Wallace Branan being the first postmaster.

It is conceivable that, between January 1838, when Richard Wallace Branan received a license to keep a "house of entertainment" (saloon), and 1839, when he was appointed a magistrate, Richard Wallace Branan relinquished the position of postmaster to Richard Brown.

Under the direction of Rev. Dominick Edward Blake, the Anglican Church of St. Catherine's at Katesville, was erected at a cost of $50 in September 1841. However, it was not until March 19, 1846, according to the Metcalfe land records, that there was a transfer of 5 acres of Metcalfe land, part of the south half of Lot 17, Con. 1, from Matthew Kerr and his wife to the Church Society. Today, there remains no visual evidence of the church or its accompanying cemetery, but they were situated in the vicinity of the historical plaque, which is now located on Katesville Drive. It reads as follows:

KATESVILLE CEMETERY
ST. CATHERINE ANGLICAN CHURCH
ERECTED BY
THE PEOPLE OF METCALFE TOWNSHIP
IN MEMORY OF
THE PIONEER FAMILIES OF THE DISTRICT
BURIED HERE.
FIRST BURIAL 1840... LAST BURIAL 1874
FAMILY NAMES WHOM WE HAVE A RECORD OF:
BRANAN, BUCHANAN, BURGESS, GALE, KELLY,
KELLAM, MURPHY, O'REILLY,
THOMAS AND WILSON.
MAY THEY REST IN PEACE.

From the scarce records so far discovered, the following records of burials can be given:
William John Bennett (September 1, 1868, ae 15ms.)
Michael Boddy (December 22, 1852, ae 83)
? Buchanan
? Burgess
Richard Wallace Branan (February 26, 1869, ae 73)
Elizabeth Branan (d/o Richard W. child)
Richard Branan (s/o Richard W. child)
John Cook (h/o Annie Denning)
Dorothy Dinning (young sibling of Annie)
Mary Eleanor Fitzgerald (d/o Talbot)
Talbot Fitzgerald (1865?)
Jane Fuller (March 28, 1850, ae 1 yr)
? Gale
Robert Gripton (April 8, 1868, ae 96)
? Hull (August 26, 1866)
Mark? Kellam (March 30?, 1850)
James Kells (1857)
? Kelly
Eliza Knight (July 6, 1866, ae 49)
Harriet Matthews (August 12, 1873, ae2 2 yrs)
William McClatchey (March 10, 1869, ae 70)
Christopher Murphy (January 23?, 1865)
? O'Reilly
Albert Rhymes (September 29, 1874, ae 5 ms.)
? Thomas
Mary Wilson

During the mid-1840s, Katesville and its surrounding area transferred from the Township of Adelaide to the newly formed Township of Metcalfe. It was probably at its zenith during the 1850s, reaching a population of approximately 150. When the Great Western Railroad line was constructed through Strathroy rather than Katesville, the decline of the community was inevitable. The post office was subsequently closed in 1869, the church was demolished in the mid-1890s, and a cyclone destroyed the last of the original buildings in 1926.

KERRWOOD

In 1856, the Great Western Railroad went through from Toronto to Sarnia. Mr. William Kerr, a woodcutter by trade, came to the townline between Middlesex and Lambton Counties and began to cut timber to make ties for the railway trains to run on, but the further west they went, the more the land rose, making it impossible for the trains to stop and get started again. They came east two miles and named the place Kerrwood, (which eventually became Kerwood).

In 1862, Kerwood was a thriving village in the Township of Adelaide. Just four years prior, the site of the village was forest. Prominent merchant John J. McKenzie of Hamilton was the original landowner. He laid out the village into lots and streets. By 1862, there were plans for a railway station house to be built. The village at that time consisted of about a dozen houses, a post office, a general store, two hotels, a blacksmith shop, a shoemaker's shop, and a carpenter and joiner shop. The Rev. William Thorpe, Presbyterian, of Napier, preached fortnightly. Mails were received and dispatched three times daily, and the population was numbered at 50.

Alphabetical List of Professions, Trades etc.
Allen, James, blacksmith
Ball, Henry, hotelkeeper
Beaver Mutual Insurance Co.
Edwards, John, hotelkeeper
Edwards, James, hotelkeeper
Foster, Charles, Esq.
Harris, Isaac A., carpenter and joiner
Harvey, Michael, G.W.R.
Leonard, Michael, G.W.R.
McCartney, Hugh, shoemaker
Mathus, Susan
Revell, William, G.W.R.
Thomas, John H., general merchant

(Note: John H. Thomas was described as also being an express and land agent, postmaster, dealer in staple and fancy dry goods of the finest and newest styles, a large assortment of family groceries, drugs, medicine, wines, liquor, dye stuffs, hardware, Queensware, nails, woodenware, hats, caps, boots, shoes, ready-made clothing, parasols and umbrellas.)

In 1864, Mr. T. McKenzie built a store in the village (where Woods' store is now) that contained a butcher shop, as well as a general store. By 1871, Kerwood was sometimes called the Currie Road Station. The principal shipments were timber staves and cordwood. Mails arrived and were dispatched daily. The population was numbered at 80.

Some Additions to the List of Professions, Trades, etc.
Daly, M.F., innkeeper
Foster, George, farmer, J.P.
Foster, S., hotelkeeper

Irwin, James, postmaster, merchant and mill proprietor
Sommerville, H.D. general merchant
Walker, Rev. John, Methodist, N.C. Minister

A store was owned by Mr. Ford, where Chittick's garage now stands. He moved to the McKenzie store, which was later owned by Mr. Dowding. Mr. Shrier owned the gristmill, which was where the United Church now stands. John Gooden was a hotelkeeper, and Mr. Murdock owned the store we now know as Conkey's store.

The population of Kerwood in 1888 was estimated at 300. Charles Foster was the postmaster and he, with S. Foster and A. Rogers, were general merchants (during WWII, women carried on Red Cross work in A. Rogers' place); S. Jones had a boot and shoe store; T. Lynn operated the hotel; and J.J. Jury was proprietor of the meat market. James Richardson had come from England in 1853, and in 1876, he bought four acres of land in Kerwood and started a brick- and tile-yard. He made the bricks for the first Methodist Parsonage, which stood on the Charles Foster property. Other manufacturers were represented by George Downing's sawmill, Armstrong's carriage and wagon shop, and J. Perkin's cheese factory. In 1871, the cheese factory in Kerwood was opened with Mr. Richardson in charge; there was also one in Adelaide operated by Cleverdon and Caruthers.

G.W. Foster's field, now owned by Charles Foster, was the popular baseball ground. The Kerwood team was composed of James and Joseph Becton, Lewis Jones, Will Morgan, J. McMahon, Dr. Bruce Rogers, J. Richardson, J.J. Foster, Bob Wilson and James Pole.

The first and only resident doctor was Dr. Rogers. George Rowe and Sam Jones were shoemakers, as the shoes were made to order in those days. Sam Foster was a grain dealer and tavern keeper, who later kept a store where A. Rogers' store stood. Mr. William Redmond also kept a store there, and the women made butter and sold it for 8¢ a pound, that being the highest price of good dairy butter. The tailor shop was owned by Mr. Burdon. The brick-yard was then owned by James Dag; this lot is now the property of L. Cook. Mr. J.C. Jury was the first butcher.

St. Paul's English Church of Kerwood was contemporary with the village of 1857. Rev. A.S. Falls and Rev. J. Kennedy were the first rectors. In 1874,

DOCTORS WHO SERVED ADELAIDE TOWNSHIP RESIDENTS

The first physician in Adelaide Township was Dr. Thomas Phillips, an Irish friend of the Radcliff family (and fellow traveller). Reference is made to Dr. Phillips in Authentic Letters from Upper Canada, consisting of correspondence between the Thomas and William Radcliff families in Adelaide and their father, Rev. Thomas Radcliff, in Dublin, who published the book in 1833. Dr. Thomas Phillips settled on Lot 15, Con. 1 NER, beside Thomas Radcliff on Lot 14. We know from an August 1832 letter home by William Radcliff that Dr. Phillips was kept very busy, as a cholera epidemic had swept through the area. William Radcliff gives Dr. Phillips praise for his recovered health from the cholera, but unfortunately, Thomas Radcliff's young daughter died of the dreaded disease. Dr. Phillips' long house was the first to be completed in the township. He invited the Radcliffs to use the one room on the main floor, which had their cooking stove at one end and his Franklin stove on the other. Dr. Phillips climbed the ladder to his quarters on the second floor. Nothing more is known of his medical service in Adelaide.

The 1841 and 1851 censuses list George S. Williams, M.D., as a surgeon/farmer from England, in Canada for four years, aged 43. Eight of the ten children born to his wife, Maria, were born in England. The 1871 census placed him in Strathroy.

The 1851 census listed other doctors, but it is not clear how long they practised in the township: Robert Pegley Jr., a surgeon, aged 26, born in Ireland, son of Robert Pegley, an early military settler, on Lot 20, Con. 1 NER; Silas Franklin, 30, a U.S. surgeon, staying at McAvoy's Inn in Adelaide Village; Dr. Hennessey, a French-born surgeon of Montreal, staying at John Wiley's Inn, the east half of Lot 3, Con.1 SER.

It was reported in the Watford Guide-Advocate on September 7, 1888, that Dr. L.F. Cutten of Adelaide was spending a few weeks in the New York Hospital. Dr. Bateman of Caradoc took charge of his practise.

At this time (at the end of the century), some young Adelaide men were attending medical school at the University of Toronto. John Wiley of West Adelaide had three sons who graduated from medical school: Dr. John Irvine Wiley graduated in 1889; Dr. Walter Wiley graduated in 1892; and Dr. Fred Wiley graduated in 1894 from Detroit Medical School. Dr. J.R. McCabe graduated from the University of Toronto in 1899. In later years, Dr. Fredrick Demaray, son of Benjamin Demaray, received medical training to become an eye specialist.

Later, Dr. Bateman moved into the Barrett house on the

west edge of Adelaide Village. He had his office in a small building in front of the "Doctor's House" built by Mr. Raison. Dr. Bateman eventually bought the house and moved the small building to the west of the house where it remains today. Dr. Bateman moved his practise to Strathroy, and is listed there in the business directory of 1916.

Dr. A.E. Morgan was the village doctor at the time the telephone was installed, about 1905. Relatives tell of him installing a telephone between his house in Adelaide Village and his office. In 1906, he left Adelaide Village and established a practise in Toronto, which he had for many years. In 1916, Dr. Morgan joined the Royal Canadian Medical Corps and went overseas that summer.

Dr. Eckels is remembered as James Wallace's doctor in 1914.

Dr. Jones was a dedicated physician. His hobbies were drawing and oil painting. He entertained frequently at township socials, by drawing cartoons, which he called his "practisings."

Dr. McLeod was a well-loved doctor, as evidenced by the many stories about him. He hired drivers at night so he could rest between house calls. He left Adelaide Village to work among the native people on the Muncey and Oneida Reserves. When WWII began, he enlisted as a medical officer. Don McChesney tells of his surprise about having a medical examination by Dr. McLeod at Halifax, before his contingent boarded the ship. Dr. McLeod's wife died in a London Nursing Home in 1998.

The "Doctor's House" still stands in Adelaide Village and has been renovated again by the new owners.

**DEATH CERTIFICATES OF SOME ADELAIDE RESIDENTS
ARE THE SOURCE FOR THE FOLLOWING NAMES OF DOCTORS AND DATES OF DEATH
(DATES ARE NOT THE WHOLE TIME PERIOD OF THEIR SERVICE)**

Dr. Auld	1899	Dr. S. Jones	1914
Dr. F.J. Bateman	1920	Dr. Lindsay	1894
Dr. Berdan	1898 & 1926	Dr. H.C. McDougall	1928
Dr. Bettridge	1873 & 1888	Dr. McFadden	1920-1930
Dr. Billington	1872	Dr. J.R. McCabe	1889-1903
Dr. Boles	1921	Dr. McLeod	1930
Dr. Copeland	1909 & 1915	Dr. A. McTaggart	1872
Dr. Cutten	1887	Dr. James Newell	1898
Dr. Daws	1888	Dr. Newton	1945
Dr. C.B. Eckels	1910 & 1914	Dr. Ovens	1888
Dr. Marwood Fletcher	1929	Dr. Parker	1912
Dr. Robert Gibson	1902	Dr. Rogers	1892
Dr. Hanson	1878	Dr. Teasdale	1889
Dr. Harvey	1881-1887	Dr. A.S. Thompson	1872-1923
Dr. Walter Hoare	1873	Dr. G.D. Vine	1930
Dr. J.L. Huffman	1914		

the hall in which services were held was destroyed by fire. From this period until July 11, 1880, there were no services of this church at Kerwood. On the latter date, Rev. Edward Softley, of Brooke and Metcalfe Townships, held a meeting in the Canada Methodist Church. In October, he began the work of reorganizing the church. In December, a meeting was held at the Fourth Line schoolhouse, where Isaac Blain was elected clergymans' warden, and Reuben Parker was elected peoples' warden, and $150 per year was guaranteed to the clergyman. Church building followed and on November 27, 1891, a house of worship was opened. The cornerstone was placed on July 21, 1891. The contract was sold to W.F. Fawcett for $1,850, the site having been purchased from S. Earley for $140.

The New Connexion Methodist Church of Kerwood was dedicated some years ago, immediately after the organization of the church here. On the union of the churches, it merged into the Methodist Church of Canada.

The Methodist Church of Canada at Kerwood dates back to 1875, when John Russell was appointed minister. He was succeeded in 1878 by Robert

Smylie. Other ministers were W.W. Sparling in 1880-1881 and C. Barltrop in 1892-1894; Rev. George J. Kerr is the present minister.

At one point, the Methodists and Anglicans both held services over the hotel storeroom and stables of Sam Foster, which stood near the railway, on M.C. Morgan's garden lot. Hardy Johnson was the first Sunday School superintendent; he held the office for 30 years. Mr. Irwin was the first stationmaster. In those days, the trains ran so slow you only had to wave and they would stop and take on passengers!

After A. Rogers' house burned in 1942, the lot and store were sold to J.F. Richardson; there, he built a Supertest Service Station, which was operated by Bruce Evans. The blacksmith shop was owned by Ben Richardson, later by John and William Armstrong, and still later by Joyce Irwin. A creamery, which became famous for its Kerwood Butter, was owned by Mr. Waddell and later taken over by W.R. Pollock. This became the Carnation Milk Company receiving station.

KEYSER

Keyser is located on both sides of Langan Drive, west to Wilson Road and east to Townsend Line. It also includes the area on Kerwood Road north to the Townsend Line and south to Lot 7, Con. 4 NER, now occupied by Martin and Linda Peeters. Keyser was a hamlet, but never an incorporated village.

Keyser was named after the several Keyser families who moved to this area in the 1830s. John Philip Keyser came from Pennsylvania with his father, Philip, and his sisters and brothers. John Philip married Elmira Dell in Westminster Township. Elmira was a sister of Solomon, Hiram and John Dell, pioneer businessmen of Strathroy.

Keyser was locally known as Keyser's Corner, but the post office, located on the north half of the south half of Lot 7, Con. 4 NER, was called Keyser #57. The property is now owned by Jeff and Mary Maes. In 1869, mail was delivered three times weekly. In 1871, mail came twice weekly. Philip Henry Keyser was the first postmaster when the post office opened on August 1, 1864.

Samuel Cooper is listed as postmaster in 1869, a position he held until 1875. In 1871, Samuel Cooper is also listed as a storekeeper, so he must have had the two businesses together. The post office closed on October 30, 1913.

In 1871, the population of Keyser was 200; in 1880, the population was 60; in 1889, it was 65; and in 1891, the population was 45.

The story of the families who lived in and around Keyser's Corners is well documented in *"Keyser Kith and Kin,"* written by Lorraine E. Hodgins.

Early Keyser Settlers

The early settlers worked hard to clear the land and the farms became fertile and prosperous, with good grazing land. Some of the early settlers and their families up to 1888 were William Bartram, Josiah Bartram, David Brock, Joseph Colter, William Donaldson, Samuel Duggan, Lawrence Duggan, James Evans, Peter Fitzpatrick, James Glover, John Hendrick, Trueman Herrington, Timothy Hay, John Keyser, Hiram Keyser, John Langan, James Langan, Donald McLeish, John McLeish, Patrick Murray, Newton Ogden, William O'Neil, James Riggs, John Riggs, John Routledge, William Roy, Alberta Ryckman, J.S. Smith, Russell Smith, James Stewart, John Sharp, David Sells, Benjamin Stevens, Samuel Stevens, Ransom Thorpe, Henry Whiting and Robert Wilkinson.

Early Businesses

According to the 1868-1869 Local Directories and Gazetteers, the 1869 Province of Ontario Gazetteer and Directory, the 1871 Lovells Directory of Ontario, the 1888 and 1889 Farmers Business Directory, and the 1896 Morrey's Business Directory, the following businesses were operating in Keyser:

Brock, David	J.P.
Ogden, John	Harnessmaker
Burdick, George	Blacksmith
Richardson, Lewis	Owner of cheese factory
Cooper, Samuel	Postmaster, storekeeper
Smith, John	Blacksmith
Davidson, Nathaniel	Carpenter
Smith, William	Carpenter
Glover, James	Proprietor of cheese factory
Stevens, Ambrose	Music teacher
Hodgens, Charles	School teacher
Stevens, B.W.	Postmaster
Hendrick, John	Cheese manufacturer
Stevens, C.H.	Postmaster
Keyser, Jacob	Brick and tile maker

Thorpe, Ransom	Cheese maker
Keyser, John	Brickmaker
Wittett, Rowland C.	School teacher
Keyser, Joseph	Brickmaker

Brick- and Tile-yard

John Philip Keyser opened a brick- and tile-yard in Keyser behind his house, situated on Lot 7, Con. 4 NER, which he operated with the family. He supplied bricks for practically all of the buildings within the district. The yard steadily employed nine people. The business was later managed by his son, Joseph, and later by his grandson, Oliver Keyser. The last bricks made were used in S.S. #9 Adelaide (Cuddy's School), which was built in 1909.

Keyser Cheese Factory

In 1871, Louis R. Richardson of Kerwood established one of the first cheese factories in the area, and named it Adelaide Cheese Factory. In the first year, three tons of cheeses were made. In 1873, the name was changed to Adelaide Cheese Manufacturing Co., with John Murray as president. In 1874, it was called Keyser Cheese Factory. In an annual report of December 29, 1875, Thomas Beveridge was the secretary-treasurer of the Adelaide Cheese Factory. The Age Dispatch reports in 1880 and 1881 that Ransom Thorpe was the cheesemaker, and in 1885, Russel B. Smith was the proprietor. In 1886, Mr. Chalcraft was hired to make cheese and according to "The Age" was *"one of the best cheese makers of the West."* The 1887 Strathroy "Age" reports: *"Keyser Cheese Factory is receiving the largest amount of milk of any factory around, nearly 7,000 lbs. daily. In 1887, L.R. Richardson left the area and the cheese factory was now owned by R.B. Smith, who erected new buildings to enlarge capacity of milk received. In 1889, owing to the failure of the Mud Creek Cheese Factory, the milk route from there went to Keyser. In 1897, Hugh E. Wilson made improvements to the factory. In 1901, the post office moved to the cheese factory. In 1906 a new Success Churn was installed, which could make a ton of butter daily if enough milk could be supplied. In 1910, Hugh E. Wilson sold the factory which by now was a thriving business to James T. Grieve. In 1914, 64,838 lb. of butter and 110,006 lb. of cheese were recorded. In 1915, patrons received a record price for their milk of $1.63 per 100 lbs. In 1916, William Inch purchased the factory and was its cheesemaker. In 1917, a small fire did minimal damage, which was soon repaired. In 1918, William Inch sold the factory to James A. Murray."* The cheese and butter factory likely closed in the 1920s.

General Stores

In earlier years, there was a store on the Bill Murray property and Samuel Cooper was a storekeeper in 1871.

Keyser General Store was opened in 1909, built on the southwest corner of Langan Drive at Keyser, north around the curve by Donald (Daddy) Gray. In 1919, he sold it to W.W. "Bill" and Alice Parker, who moved the store around the corner, closer to his house, in 1922. They ran the store until 1943. Laverne and Alice Topping purchased it in 1943. They ran a grocery delivery service to neighbouring farms, where people could phone in their order and the Toppings delivered the order at the customer's door. They also delivered Master Feed products along with the groceries. The store was sold to Frank Gare in 1964. The store sold gasoline, meat, groceries, dairy products, cheese in bulk, hardware, dry goods and clothing, drugs, and produce in the summer. In 1979, Frank Gare closed the general store and opened an insurance office on the premises. This property is presently owned by Joseph and Joanne Minten.

Gravel Pits

Keyser had two gravel pits in later years. One was owned and operated by Bill and Doris Murray. The second was owned and operated by Cliff and Frances Arrand.

Blacksmith

Blacksmith John Smith did a flourishing business. He not only made shoes for horses, but also built carriages, wagons and farm implements. Uncle Joe Little, the pioneer minister who preached in the community, travelled on horseback, and it is said that he often left his horse at the Keyser blacksmith shop to be shod. With the advent of automobiles and tractors, the need for a blacksmith diminished and, in 1909, Smith sold his property to Donald Gray. He retired to Strathroy and sold the business to Lorne Davidson in March 1910. The blacksmith building burned down in 1913.

Salem Methodist Church

As in other early communities, the settlers of Keyser did not have a church. They held services in the neighbourhood homes, and a travelling minister preached. Marriages were often performed in the home of the bride's parents, or sometimes the parsonage in Arkona or Strathroy.

In December 1867, the appointed Trustees were given three acres of Lot 7, Con. 5 NER. Patrick and Elizabeth Murray charged them a dollar for the land, where a church was to be built adjacent to the school. On October 4, 1868, the dedication was held for the 32'x46' brick church, which cost about $1,200 to build. Hon. F. Smith of Florence preached at 10:30 a.m. and 5:00 p.m., and Rev. H. Kilty preached at 2:30 p.m. A dinner was held on Monday at 1:00 p.m., and a tea was hosted at 7:00 p.m. with an evening programme. A melodian was the instrument of choice. Rev. Fancher was the regular preacher when the church was erected. In 1895, the church underwent repairs, and Rev. Fancher (then of Bothwell) preached at the re-opening of Salem Methodist Church in December of that year.

The church served the community for many years. Social functions took place there, such as picnics, suppers and garden parties. In May 1905, the contributing members were: Joseph Keyser, Albert Murray, Benjamin Herrington, Bert Herrington, Mrs. Charles Stevens, Mrs. William Bartram and family, James Glover, Mrs. Bennett, Lorenzo Hendrick, Dan McLeish, Mrs. John Stevens, John Sharpe, Benjamin Arrand and Mrs. Hugh Davidson. Rev. T.J. Snowdon, Ph.D., was the pastor.

As the attendance dropped and expenses arose, it was decided to close the church. In January 1913, the Strathroy Age reported that the work of tearing down Keyser Methodist Church had begun, and that the material would be used to put a basement under Arkona Methodist Church.

School

Keyser had one school, but it was on three different locations over the years. The first school, a log structure, was located west of Keyser on the farm of Lawrence Grogan on the corner of Langan Drive and Wilson Road. It was about 20'x16' in dimension. The benches were placed along the sides of the room with the desks in front of them. The girls sat on one side and the boys on the other, with their backs to the girls.

The second school was likely a frame school and was situated across from the general store on Lot 7, Con. 4 NER. The third school was built on Lot 7, Con. 5 NER. The first teachers were Miss Lowes, Miss Currie and Miss Ann Dewar. In 1880, attendance was about 90 students. The wages were not very high, so teachers stayed at different homes in the section. Each family housed the teacher for a fixed period for their shares.

Armed Forces—WWII

A happy gathering was held in Keyser School when the neighbours met to welcome home their returned service men, Elmer Murray, Lorne Herrington, John McKenzie and Jack Rowland. An evening of cards and dancing preceded an address written by Mrs. Simon Shrier. A gift of a wallet with the owner's initials engraved in gold and each containing a sum of money was presented by Fred Hoffner Sr. and Otto Zimmerman, on behalf of the Keyser community. Keyser was fortunate to enjoy the safe return of its men who answered their country's call.

Village of Kerwood, 1957

HAMLETS AND VILLAGES
(From Business Directories of the Towns and Villages of Middlesex County)

1905

ADELAIDE - Population 150
Clelford, Charles	Hotel
Connor, Rev. W.J.	Anglican
Miller, H.J.	Township Clerk
Morgan, A.	Physician
Sawyer, Rev.	Methodist
Wilkins, F.	Blacksmith
Wiulkins, George	Postmaster

AMIENS - (20 miles west of London) - Population 40
Ache, Joseph	Apiarist
Cutler, J.O.	Builder and Contractor
Gowric, F.R.	Builder and Contractor
Harris, B.B.	Builder and Contractor
Ireland, William	Postmaster and General Agent
McGugan, Duncan	Auctioneer
Scott, Romph	Cattle Dealer

CRATHIE - (20 miles west of London) - Population 50
Brown, Margaret	Postmaster
Burdick, Gus	Blacksmith
Gerry, David	Carpenter and Builder
Henderson, James M.	Magistrate
McLean, James	Saw Mill and Lumber

KERWOOD - (on the G.T.R. 25 miles west of London) - Population 200
Armstrong, William and John	Blacksmiths
Beckton, George	Constable
Brock, John	Builder and Contractor
Brunt, J.M.	General Store
Cook, L.	Butcher
Denning, James	General Store
Dowding, George	Flour and Saw Mill
Dowding, Reuben	Blacksmith
Foster, Charles	Cooper
Kershaw, Rev. E.	Methodist
McMahon, John	Brick Manufacturer
Mills, John	Grain Dealer
Morgan, S.P.	Wood Turner
O'Neil, D.	Express and Railway Agent
O'Neil, Fred	Hotel
Richardson, Mrs. H.	Cheese Manufacturer
Richardson, James	Saw Mill and Brick Manufacturer
Rogers, Alfred	General Store and Post Office
Smith, William S.	Stonemason
Victoria Cheese Manufacturing Co.	
John Sullivan	Manager
Whiting, L.W.	Cheese Manufacturer

KEYSERS - (25 miles west of London) - Population 50
Keyser, Joseph	Brick Manufacturer
Smith, John	Blacksmith
Wilson, Hugh E.	Cheese Manufacturer

MULLIFARRY - (25 miles west of London) - Population 40
McNeice, James	Post Office

NAPPERTON - (24 miles southwest of London) - Population 50
Currie, Thomas	Justice and Government Agent
Jury, Thomas	Piano and Organ Dealer and Post Office
Morgan, W.P.	Insurance Agent and Township Treasurer
Rapley, C.	Grain Thresher

1910

ADELAIDE - Population 150
Clelford, Charles	Hotel
Eckels, Dr.	Physician
Miller, H.J.	Township Clerk
Wilkins, Eliza	Postmistress

AMIENS - Population 40
Ireland, William	Post Office and General Store

CRATHIE - Population 50
Brock, Richard	Magistrate
Campbell, J.S.	Butcher
Gerry, David	Carpenter
Gerry, James	Carpenter
Henderson, J.M.	Postmaster
McLean, James	Saw Mill

KERWOOD - on G.T.R. 25 miles west of London - Population 200
Armstrong, John	General Store
Beckton, George	Mail Carrier
Chittick, George	Hotel

Clarke, Rev. C.F.	Methodist
Cook, L.	Butcher
Dowding, J.G.	Railway Agent
Dunlot and McIntyre	Millers
Foster, Charles	Cooper
Foster, W.H.	Implements
Irwin, Joyce	Blacksmith
Leacock, W.J.	Blacksmith
McMahon, John	Brick Manufacturer
Mills, T.F.	Grain Dealer
Morgan, S.P.	Livery
Richardson, J. and Son	Sawmill
Rogers, Alfred	General Store and Post Office
Smith, William R.	Mason
Waddell, William	Creamery
Woods, Arthur	General Store

KEYSER - Population 50

Davidson, L.	Blacksmith
Grey, Donald	General Store
Keyser, O.J.	Brick Manufacturer
Wilson, Hugh E.	Cheese Manufacturer

MULLIFARRY - Population 40

McNeice, James	Post Office

NAPPERTON - Population 50

Currie, H.	Farmers' Agent
Currie, J.	Drover
Hull, W.C.	Postmaster
Jury, Thomas	Pianos
Morgan, W.A.	Health Officer
Morgan, W.P.	Insurance Agent and Township Treasurer

1914
ADELAIDE - Population 150

Clelford, Charles	Hotel
Eckel, Dr.	Physician
Petch, L.J.	General Merchant and Postmaster
Willoughby, W.	Blacksmith

1914
KERWOOD - Population 150

Armstrong, John	General Store
Beckton, George	Mail Carrier
Chittick, George	Hotel
Cook, L.	Butcher
Dowding, G.J.	Railway Agents
Foster, W.H.	Implements
Irwin, Joyce	Blacksmith
Leacock, W.J.	Blacksmith
Mills, T.F.	Grain Dealer
Morgan, S.P.	Livery
Richardson, J. and Son	Saw Mill
Rogers, Alfred	General Store and Post Office
Smith, William R.	Mason
Waddell, William	Creamery
Wilson, Rev. R.M.	Methodist
Woods, Arthur	General Store

NAPPERTON - Population 50

Currie, H.	Farmers' Agent
Currie, J.	Drover
Hull, W.C.	Postmaster
Jury, Thomas	Pianos
Morgan, W.A.	Health Officer
Morgan, W.P.	Insurance Agent and Township Treasurer

1916
KERWOOD - Population 200

Armstrong, John	General Store
Bank of Toronto	
Cook, L.	Butcher
Irwin, Joyce	Blacksmith
Lewis, Frank	Lumber
Mills, T.F.	Grain Dealer
Richardson, J. and Son	Saw Mill
Rogers, Alfred	General Store and Post Office
Waddell, William	Creamery
Wilkinson, R.C.	General Store
Willoughby, T.W.	Blacksmith
Woods, Arthur	General Store

1925
KERRWOOD (note change in spelling at this time) - Population 250

Bank of Toronto	
Chittick, George	Hotel
Conkey, Harold	General Store
Glover, Henry	Butcher
Humphreys and Petch	Lumber
Irwin, Joyce	Blacksmith
Kerrwood Creamery	
Leacock, William	Blacksmith
Richardson, John	Brick Manufacturer
Rogers, Alfred	Postmaster and General Store
Woods and Wilkinson	General Store

CHAPTER SIX

Municipal Government

Adelaide Township was settled in 1832 by John Buchanan on the north bank of the Sydenham River, near what is now Head Street in Strathroy. The township was named after Queen Adelaide, a German Princess from the House of Saxony, who became the consort of England's King George IV.

The township has boundaries with Warwick Township, Lambton County on the west, West Williams, East Williams and Lobo Townships on the north, Caradoc Township on the east, and Metcalfe Township on the south. The Town of Strathroy shares its north and west boundaries with Adelaide.

The township is physically made up of gently rolling clay-loam farmland, with some sandy sections, one example being a tobacco farm on Lot 16, Con 5 SER. It is located on the watershed of two rivers: the Sydenham, which outlets into Lake St. Clair at Wallaceburg, and the Ausable, which outlets into Lake Huron at Port Franks. Highway 22 (Egremont Road) is the approximate dividing line between the two watersheds. The intersection of Highway 402 and County Road 6 is the area of highest elevation in the township.

The original survey of the township used Egremont Road as Con. 1 (both north and south), north to Con. 5 NER, and south to Con. 10 SER. However, a dispute between the northern and southern parts of the township over a bridge to be built (over the Sydenham River in the southern section) led to a split. Those in the north felt they should not have to pay for the bridge, as their horse-and-buggies never travelled that way, and the subsequent formation of the Township of Metcalfe took place in 1846, with the addition of two concessions from Ekfrid Township. The new boundary between Adelaide and Metcalfe became the abutting line between Con. 5 and 6 SER. Ironically, because of current restructuring policies set down by the Provincial Government, the two townships will once again be united. The change will take place on January 1, 2001, following the November 13, 2000, election of a seven-person council to run the new Municipality of Adelaide and Metcalfe.

Living beside its growing urban neighbour to the southeast has not been without its problems for many Adelaide councils. One spring day in 1968, Reeve Charlie Nichols, members of his council, and the rest of the township residents, awoke to read a shocking story in the morning paper. The Town of Strathroy was proposing to annex 4,000 acres of township land, with the borders as Highway 81 on the west, Highway 22 on the north, and County Road 39 on the east. Further, the paper indicated that three members of the Town council, the Mayor, Reeve and a councillor, had optioned over 500 acres at Hickory Corners for an industrial park. This proposal was vigorously opposed by township council, and at a subsequent OMB hearing, the annexation proposal was turned down. This event led to the passing of the township's first Zoning by-law in 1969, followed by its first Official Plan in 1976, along with a revised Zoning

QUARTER SESSION OF LONDON DISTRICT

In the 1770s, the great influx of Loyalists to Canada from their homes in the United States increased the population of Canada rapidly, especially near Kingston, Toronto, and Niagara Falls. These settlers had remained faithful to the British Crown and Constitution. During the American Revolution (1775-1783), they believed that dispute between the colonists and the British Parliament over imperial taxation and trade controls did not justify rebellion against the lawful government. Also, they prized their civil and property rights, which were violated by the rebels. Loyalists remained true to their oath of allegiance to King George III, hence they opposed the radical protestors.

Loyalism was particularly strong in the middle colonies and in the deep south of the U.S. Most Loyalists were farmers and craftsmen. Only about one-quarter of them were British immigrants. As many of them spoke Gaelic, German and Dutch as spoke English. What these diverse people had in common were their political principles. Even before the 1783 peacetime, many persecuted Loyalists fled the territory of the southern states. It has been estimated that 50,000 of them preferred to leave rather than come to terms with the republic established by the rebels. Some 12,000 of them are reported to have come to Upper Canada. For many of the Loyalists, the houses they had occupied in the U.S. were destroyed after their contents were confiscated or burned.

The Loyalists desire for legality, compromise, representative government and constitutional monarchy laid the political background of modern Canada as a multicultural country. For their fidelity and sacrifices, the refugee Loyalists and their descendants were given the right to attach "U.E." to their names, and were awarded special land grants.

These Loyalist settlers to Canada were unhappy under French civil law and soon petitioned the government for some form of local courts and administration, for English civil law, and for separation from the area west of Montreal. In 1778, in recognition of the demands and requirements of the increasing British population in Canada, the British passed a decree that divided the Eastern settlements (which had been part of the District of Montreal) into four districts.

The districts were governed by a group of magistrates, usually supplemented by important merchants, wealthy landowners or leading political figures.

From this cross-section of society, 75 members were chosen, appointed by the Governor General. The members met to form the first Court of Quarter Sessions, which met quarterly. This Court assumed the judicial, legislative and administrative control of such matters as maintaining the peace, regulating domestic animals running at large, supervising the conduct of licensed taverns and houses of entertainment, appointing minor officials and superintending roads. Later, road superintendence went to County Councils, then ultimately to the Ontario Department of Highways.

In 1837, in the first session, an Act was passed that set forth the times and places of holding Quarter Sessions of the Peace in the several districts. In the District of London, Quarter Sessions

by-law to implement the policies of the OP. Planning has since become a major part of the township's everyday business. A peaceful annexation agreement was entered into between the township and the Town of Strathroy in 1980, where the township gave up 1,400 acres close to Strathroy, from the east half of Lot 22, Con. 2 and 3 SER, to the east half of Lot 25, Con. 2 and 3. The township kept the west half of Lot 22, Con. 2 and 3 along the east side of Highway 81, which has sometimes been dubbed Adelaide's Golden Mile, due to the high development of commercial and industrial properties along this stretch of the highway.

Before 1841, local concerns were dealt with at the Courts of Quarter Sessions. Magistrates, also known as Justices of the Peace, comprised these courts. These Courts were held in London.

In 1841, The District Councils Act was passed. People were now represented by a District Council. A warden, appointed by the Crown, would preside over the meeting. District Councillors were elected at an annual meeting of householders and freeholders and had a term of three years. Each township would have one District Councillor, or if there were more than 300 names on the assessment roll, two were elected. Adelaide Township was part of the London District.

In 1849, the Baldwin Act (or the Municipal Act) was passed. This was sponsored by Robert Baldwin, who was returned to power in the legislature in 1848. The Act became law on May 30, 1849, and came into operation on January 1, 1850. This Act gave to elected township councils the responsibility of handling their own local administration and removed the District Councils, which were replaced by County Councils.

were to be held "...in the District of London, at the Town of London, on the second Tuesday in January, April, July and October." By the same authority, "...no proceedings which have been had in any Court of General Quarter Sessions before the passing of this Act, shall be rendered illegal, or in any manner affected by the above recited Acts of any of them, or any part thereof, being hereby repealed." By the same Act, a subsequent paragraph stated "In time of war or other emergency, it shall be in the power of the Governor Lieutenant General or Person Administering the Government of the Province... to authorize the holding of the Court of General Quarter Sessions of the Peace in any District of this Province, at some place in the said District than is appointed by this Act."

Where the London District was first established in 1800, its oldest and most populated area was the Long Point Settlement at Lake Erie. It was argued that the administrative Quarter Sessions for the district should be conducted in that area. The courthouse for the District was promoted near Lake Erie on the town plat of Charlotteville, in spite of protests relative to the site's difficult access and to its lack of accommodations. In 1815, the provincial government realized Charlotteville would never amount to more than a hamlet. On March 14, 1815, an Act was passed, transferring the District town closer to the Long Point Settlement, and authorizing the construction of a new courthouse at Vittoria. By 1842, the work at Vittoria was complete. By this time, a large number of people had settled in the northern part of Middlesex County. These inhabitants of Middlesex County gave notice in September 1825 that they would petition the government to have their region declared a separate district at the next session of Legislature.

On the night of November 14 (or November 15), 1825, the courthouse at Vittoria burned, and was damaged so severely that it required rebuilding. This led to a prompt decision to transfer the district's administrative center to the Forks of the Thames River. It marked the beginning of the future of London. The official reason for the move was "to establish the district town of the London District in a more central location."

In 1829, work on the permanent courthouse in London began. During construction, the architect, John Ewart, had a frame structure built as a temporary location for the Sessions of the London District. Afterward, the building was used as the London District Grammar School.

With the older part of the district becoming more populated and with settlement pushing further north of the Thames River, many areas were dissatisfied with the centralized position of their district town. On March 4, 1837, provision was made for incorporating the County of Norfolk to become the District of Talbot and Simcoe, with Simcoe as the district town. Likewise, the District of Brock was established, with Woodstock as the administrative district town. On March 6, 1838, authorization was granted for the County of Huron to form a separate district, with Goderich as the district capital. With these changes, the judge of the elected General Assembly held power over a much smaller region.

The dates of the Courts of General Quarter Sessions of the Peace in Upper Canada were altered for London District. Quarter Sessions were scheduled for the first Tuesday of January, April and July, and the third Tuesday in the month of November.

When the Baldwin Act was passed, establishing the system of Municipal Government we know today, property owners in rural municipalities such as Adelaide were able to elect a Reeve and council to look after the day-to-day affairs of the township. Part of the Reeve's duties were to look after the general "good health and welfare" of the inhabitants of the municipality, "welfare" not having the same interpretive meaning 150 years ago as it does today.

One of council's duties was to appoint officials to deal with the administrative duties: a Clerk to keep records, take minutes, prepare by-laws, etc; and a Treasurer to receive and safely store funds, and pay debts owed by the township. These two primary administrative functions still exist today, though in some municipalities one person handles both positions. Early councils also appointed a Tax Collector; today, in many municipalities, tax collection has been included in the job description of Clerk or Treasurer. The Province is now responsible for property assessment, but early councils employed Assessors.

A Poundkeeper was also appointed by early Adelaide councils. Should livestock (cattle, horses) stray and be captured, and the owner not found, the animals were locked up in the Poundkeeper's barn until the owner turned up and paid all costs. Then, his animals were returned to him. If the owner was not located, the Poundkeeper advertised in the local paper in an attempt to find the owner; if this did not bring results after several weeks, the livestock were sold at a local auction sales-yard, and the proceeds (less expenses to the Poundkeeper) were added to the township coffers. With fewer and fewer pasture farms today, Poundkeepers are rarely used, the last time in Adelaide in the 1980s.

EXCERPTS FROM HISTORICAL COUNCIL OF ADELAIDE MINUTES

29 JUNE 1878
BY CALL OF REEVE FOR PAYING FOR WORK DONE IN THE SEVERAL E.D.'S AND FOR OTHER URGENT MATTERS.

- To D.D. Wiley $30 for grading on Side Road 3 and 4 N in E.D. and voluntary work having been done in proportion of $3 to $1 granted.
- To Wm. Ireland $4.49 for repairing 3 culberts and 4 cords of gravel in R.D. 8, E.D.
- Malcom Sinth applied for grant of $6 to cut a ditch on Side Road 27 and 28, 1 Con N, E.D. 3 - referred to Committee of E.D. 3.
- To James Thompson $77.75 to pay for gravelling in R.D. 3, E.D. 1.
- To Charles Cummins $62.20 being $54.20 for 542 loads of gravel at .10¢ per load, $5 for two apple trees, $5 for scraping surface on his land, to E.D. 2.
- To D. Brown $5 for 12 1/4 cords of gravel at 40 cents per cord charged to surplus a/c; also $4.70 for 11 3/4 cords of gravel both in E.E. 3, the latter amount Township funds.
- To William Henderson $16.12 for 43 cords of gravel at 37 1/2 cents per cord E.D. 2, Township funds.
- To D. D. Wiley $12.30 for grading on Side Road 3 and 4 in E.D. 2.
- To Mrs. Roberts a widow of Kerwood $10 to assist in supporting her large family.
- To John Bacton $12.25 for work on Curry Road, part of appropriation of $20 to said road.
- To James and Charles Bolton $54.20 for drawing gravel in E.D. 2.
- To Joseph Basker $16 for 40 cords of gravel for R.D. 4 and 5, E.D. 3.
- For work done in E.D. 2; G. Wilkin $13.80, D. Watkin $16.37, James Jones $48.25.
- For gravelling in D.D. 3; Nelson Wiley $27, R. Conkey $28, Giles Kerswell $17.50, D. Wiley $14; H & G Pagett $22.75, Wm. T. Gallaway $10.50 also $5 for [unclear], Wm. Glenn $5 for 4 days work, Carthy $3 for 1 days' work, John Wiley Jr. $3.12 for work D.E. 3 Balance of surplus account.

(Editor's Note: E.D. may mean Egremont District; R.D. may mean Road; D.D. and E.E. are mysteries!)

Livestock Evaluators were, and still are, appointed by local councils. The job of the Evaluator is to calculate the value of livestock, primarily sheep or baby calves, that the owner suspects were killed or injured by marauding dogs, generally when the livestock are on pasture. If the Evaluator agrees the livestock were killed or injured by dogs, he writes a report for council, who are obliged to reimburse the owner what the Evaluator feels is fair market value for the owner's losses. If the Evaluator feels the death or injury was not caused by a dog attack, he will also report this to council for their information, as the owner can appeal the Evaluator's decision. Rarely, the Evaluator is called upon to evaluate a poultry loss, where a dog has entered a hen house, causing great panic, and loss by smothering.

Another appointment Adelaide councils made is that of Fence Viewers. These gentlemen, three of them, visited the site of a fence dispute between two neighbours and dictated what repairs should be done, whether minor (such as a few strands of barbed wire and new fence posts) or major (where they decided a new page wire fence should be erected with new wood and steel posts). The Fence Viewers also decided who should pay what share of the repair, and stated a time limit for the work to be done. Should it not be done on time, the work could be done for the person designated to do it, and the cost added to his property tax bill. Should a property owner refuse to pay for his share of a repair, even though not designated to do the repair, it could also be added to his tax bill. Because of the emotions raised by fence disputes between neighbours, prudent councils had a stable of 10-12 Fence Viewers so they could, for example, appoint three viewers from the west end of the township to adjudicate a dispute in the east end. The two parties in a dispute always have a right to appeal the decision of the Viewers and, over the course of a century, the views of the Courts have changed dramatically on the need for a property owner to be responsible for a fence between his property and his neighbour's. The rule of thumb in the old days was that an owner would face his property lines; the right half becomes his to maintain, the left his neighbour's. An exception was that an owner maintained 100% of the road fence (except 400 series highways, a Provincial responsibility). As farming evolved over these many years, and pasture farms were plowed up to be used for cash crops, and many small lots were created by severance, the owners of cash crop land and small residential parcels of land increasingly appealed Viewers' decisions that they should be responsible for fencing their properties to keep their neighbour's livestock out.

A council-appointed position that has increased dramatically in visibility since the end of WWII as much as the Poundkeeper and Fence Viewer positions have decreased, is that of the Building Inspector. There has been steady growth in the township over the last 30 years, including increasingly bigger hog, poultry and dairy operations; new residential growth in Adelaide, Kerwood, the hamlet area north of Strathroy, and the Buttery Creek subdivision; and new and improved commercial and industrial facilities. Thus, issuing permits and inspecting new construction has today's Inspector working as many hours a week as the Inspector of 40-50 years ago worked in a month.

Another high profile, highly visible council-appointed position is that of the Drainage Superintendent. Municipal Drains have always been a fact of life in the township, and sometimes quite controversial. Many a story has been told about emotion-charged council meetings in the old Township Hall in the early years, where it was standing room only when a drainage petition was up for discussion. Friendships were lost, and neighbours sometimes became enemies. Council would divide the township into four parts, and the four councillors would each oversee the Municipal drains in a section. With the influx of settlers from Holland after WWII, Municipal drainage increased, and the supervision of Municipal drains became part of the Road Superintendent's job. After the 1968 Federal election that introduced the Trudeau years, the Federal Government decided to match the 1/3 grant paid by the Province toward construction of new Municipal drains. This was a development too good to pass up by astute drainage-conscious farmers, and Municipal drainage petitions blossomed. Municipal drains then became big business in the township; the township became better drained, and better for it with increased productivity.

With the increase in Municipal drains in the 1970s, it became impossible for the Road Department to keep up with requests for maintenance of these drains, and the inspection of the installation of new ones. Thus, in 1982, council hired a Drain Superintendent to look after all aspects of the drainage business, except for Tile Drainage Act loans. With these loans, the Province financed farmers who were privately tiling their farms, for up to 75% of the cost. The Province required an inspector to ensure the tiles were installed correctly, connections made, and outlets made properly into Municipal tile drains, Municipal open ditches or watercourses. Until recently, this position was a small part of the Building Inspector's job. Presently, the Building Inspector and Drain Superintendent positions are handled by one person.

As in all rural townships, dogs running at large and strays have been an ongoing problem for Adelaide councils. In an effort to discourage the multiple ownership of dogs in the township, councils past and present have levied a low tax on the ownership of a single dog, male or neutered female, but tripled or quadrupled the tax for multiple ownership, be it two or more of them. This tax offsets loss caused by dogs to sheep, livestock or poultry during the year.

Conservation Authorities have been a part of municipal government life since the end of WWII, created by the Province due to rising public concerns about the ecology. Their input is required by councils on new Municipal drain petitions, or the upgrading or improving of existing Municipal drains. The Authorities' input is also required in planning matters, be it the creation of a new lot by severance, approval of a subdivision, or amendments to zoning or the Official Plan.

The original Township Hall was built in the middle to late 1800s in Adelaide Village, with an outhouse at the back for those councillors who couldn't make it through some of the long drawn-out meetings of the day. The hall was heated by a wood-burning stove at the south end of the building. This stove, as the stories go, could roast councillors sitting at the table at the north end with their backs to the fire, but was not quite sufficient, when a bitter north wind was blowing, to take the chill out of those sitting with their backs to the north wall. In the early 1970s, an addition was built on the back of the old Hall, big enough for council meetings and perhaps a dozen spectators, and heated with electricity. If a large number of people were expected for a meeting, the old Hall was opened up and used again. In 1979, a new three-bay garage was built to house the township grader and truck. The back portion of the building contained an upper level, which doubled as a lunch room for the Road Department employees and a meeting place for council.

The old Hall was subsequently torn down, and old records were shipped off to the Regional Library at the University of Western Ontario in London for permanent storage. In 1982, the positions of Clerk and Treasurer were amalgamated, and the office was moved to the second level of the Township Garage. Because storage space was becoming almost nonexistent by 1989, the present Township Municipal building was built next door to the Garage, complete with a separate council meeting room, offices for the Clerk/Treasurer and Road Superintendent, a spacious concrete vault for record storage, a large outer office for a receptionist, and a small kitchen. The bottom level is laid out as a meeting room for organizations, or can be used for receptions and anniversaries. There is a large kitchen with a refrigerator and stove, complete with a separate ground-level entrance.

Prior to the building of the present Garage in 1979, a Quonset hut was used to house the grader and truck, located behind the old Hall since the end of WWII. Prior to that, graders and trucks were kept at the homes of the various Road Superintendents and their helpers.

One of the many stories that Harold Eastman delighted in telling about his days as an Adelaide politician took place when he was a councillor in the 1940s. In those days, winters were really winters; snowfalls generally accumulated higher than road fences, and drifts were twice as high. Most of the able-bodied men were fighting in the war, making it much more difficult for the older ones at home to keep the main roads plowed and passable, using the primitive equipment of the time. Uninhabited side roads were left to melt in the spring thaw. These conditions led one council to pass a resolution that "no woman shall become pregnant during the months of April, May or June." No mention was made about enforcement of the resolution.

**Reeves of Adelaide Township
—1900 to Present**

1900	E.F. Henderson
1901-1905	William Sullivan
1906	J. Wallace
1907	William Sullivan
1908-1911	D. Campbell
1912-1913	A. Topping
1913-1914	W. Bolton
1915-1919	J. Currie
1920-1926	J. Sullivan
1927-1928	J. McLeish
1929-1931	R. Waltham
1932-1942	H. Currie
1943	W. Wilson
1944-1949	H. Eastman
1950-1952	W. Feasey
1953-1954	A. McLean
1955-1964	E. Earley
1965-1966	C. Stevenson
1967-1976	C. Nichols
1976	E. Earley
1977-1980	R. Feasey
1981	D. Ball
1982-1988	R. Feasey
1989-1996	F. Gare
1996-1997	M. Houben
1998-2000	J. Milligan

**Reeves of Adelaide Township
Who Became Wardens of Middlesex County**

1880	John Morgan
1910	Dan Campbell
1919	John Currie
1942	Harold Currie
1949	Harold Eastman
1992	Frank Gare

Adelaide Township Office

MUNICIPAL GOVERNMENT 525

Council 1942: front L-R, A. Topping, Clerk; C. Branton, Road Superintendent; W.A. Morgan, Treasurer. Back L-R, F. Wright, Councillor; W. Feasey, Councillor; H. Currie, Reeve (Warden); H. Eastman, Councillor; W. Wilson, Councillor.

Centennial Council: front L-R, Bill Baxter, Road Superintendent; Mike Bett, Treasurer; Charles Nichols, Reeve; Frank Gare, Clerk. Back L-R, Robert Feasey, Councillor; George George, Councillor; Pete Smith, Councillor; David Ball, Councillor.

Council 1949: front L-R, W. Wilson, Clerk; H. Eastman, Reeve; C. Fuller, Treasurer. Back L-R, E. Carrothers, Collector; E. McCabe, Councillor; N. Wardell, Road Superintendent; W. Feasey, Councillor; A.M. McChesney, Assessor; T. Elliot, Councillor; J. Eakins, Councillor.

Council 1981-1982: front L-R, Frank Gare, Clerk; David Ball, Reeve; Bob Feasey, Deputy Reeve. Back L-R, Bill Baxter, Road Superintendent; Charlotte Postma, Councillor; Bob Sinasac, Minister; Fred Hoffner, Councillor; Jerry Brown, Councillor; Mike Bett, Treasurer.

Council 1955: front L-R, Wilfrid Wilson, Clerk; Eugene Earley, Reeve; Clarence Fuller, Treasurer. Back L-R, Milton Harris, Councillor; George George, Councillor; George Glenn, Councillor; Milo Morgan, Councillor.

Council 1983-1985: front L-R, Hansford Wood; Robert Feasey; Charlotte Postma. Back L-R, Frank Van Bree; Mike Bett; Frank Kanters; Mike Houben; Bill Murray, Road Superintendent; Rev. Jenssen.

Council 1991-1994: front L-R, Fieny McDougall; Frank Gare, Reeve; George Earley; Mike Houben. Back L-R, Mike Bett, Clerk/Administrator; Mr. Bob Perry; John Milligan; Bill Murray, Road Superintendent; Tom McChesney, Building Inspector; Frank Van Bree, Drainage Superintendent.

The first township council in the history of the new Township of Adelaide Metcalfe began its term in January 2001, as the amalgamation came info effect. Members of council are, front L-R, councillors Lyn Goddard, Rennie Feddema and Beth Ball. In back are councillors Adrian de Bruyn and Gerald Sanders, Reeve John Milligan and Deputy-Reeve David Clarke.

THE FIRE DEPARTMENT

In the late summer of 1964, a fire damaged the McMeekin house on Highway 81 in Adelaide Township, a few hundred feet north of the Pannell Lane boundary between the township and the Town of Strathroy. The Strathroy Fire Department answered the call to attend the fire, but refused to cross Pannell Lane into the township, preferring to watch neighbours and passers-by put out the fire. This was the latest in a series of refusals over the years by the town's fire department to attend fires in the township, in close proximity to the town's boundaries with Adelaide Township. The McMeekin fire was the catalyst that spurred the township council to think about setting up a fire department.

In February 1965, a 1,000-gallon 1959 Dodge gas truck was purchased, and retrofitted to carry a supply of water to a fire. At the same time, council was obtaining quotes from companies that built fire pumper trucks, and eventually chose a pumper built by the Thibeault Company, at a cost of $20,000. This truck carried 800 gallons of water. It was delivered to the township in May 1965, and housed in Chittick's Garage in Kerwood. The Dodge tanker was kept at the Carnation Milk Plant, also in Kerwood.

Now that it was obvious a fire department would be set up in the township, at a yet to be decided location, the council of neighbouring Metcalfe Township inquired about receiving coverage for the north part of their township, not covered by agreements with the Alvinston and Glencoe Fire Departments. Rather than Adelaide selling fire service to Metcalfe, the two councils agreed to operate the new fire department jointly, by adding the assessment of

Original Adelaide-Metcalfe Fire Department volunteers. Back L-R, Robert Dodge, Reg Freer, Ted Dennis, Neil Bolton, Dana Rutledge, Jim Bolton, Earl Bolton, Roy Wardell, Ed Reitsma and Paul Langford. Front L-R, Phil Giles, Cliff Winter, Milo Brooks, Bill Brooks and Ernest Morgan. Absent are Alick Ewen and Milo Morgan.

Adelaide-Metcalfe Fire Department trucks, late 1970s (after a third bay was added to the Fire Hall).

the area to be covered in Metcalfe to Adelaide's property assessment, and using one mill rate for this area to cover capital and operating expenses. And so, the Adelaide–Metcalfe Fire Department was formed (now Kerwood Fire Department).

Milo Brooks was chosen as the first Chief of the Fire Department. Along with Milo, the first volunteers to serve on the Department were: Robert Dodge, Reg Freer, Ted Denniss, Neil Bolton, Dana Rutledge, Jim Bolton, Earl Bolton, Roy Wardell, Ed Reitsma, Phil Giles, Cliff Winter, Bill Brooks, Ernest Morgan, Milo Morgan, Paul Langford and Alick Ewen. Four of the original members are still serving on the Department: Chief Neil Bolton, former chief Roy Wardell, Ernest Morgan and Robert Dodge.

The Department's first call was to Gordon McIntyre's home in Metcalfe Township on June 29, 1965. In the spring of that year, the Adelaide Council set up a committee of three members to search for a site to build a Fire Hall. The committee consisted of Reeve Clarence Stevenson, and councillors Dave Ball and Mike Bett. The committee visited stations in Middlesex and Lambton Counties during the spring and summer, gathering information on the design of various fire halls. It became obvious that the most suitable location for a Fire Hall was in Kerwood, because of its central location to service both Adelaide and Metcalfe. A site for a new hall was located on Grace Street East in Kerwood, on property owned by Norm Dowding. A house on the property had burned down the previous year, inhabited by Elaine Carroll, sister to the Jordan brothers, Bill, Wilf and Frank. A deal was made to buy the lot and, in late summer, Roy Wardell, a local contractor, was hired to build a two-bay fire station. The building was completed in late fall, and the official opening took place on December 13, 1965.

A system of three phones was set up in Kerwood to answer incoming fire calls. The phones rang simultaneously, and the three ladies answering the calls telephoned firefighting volunteers and informed them of the location of the fire. The first two volunteers at the Hall would then drive the pumper and tanker to the fire; the other volunteers would go to the scene directly in their vehicles. Dorothy Winter, Veryl Brooks and Norma Brooks were the first three volunteers to have fire phones installed in their homes. Following the resignation of Milo Brooks in 1966, Veryl Brooks' phone was moved to Eileen Freer's residence and Norma Brooks' phone went to the Carnation Plant, where husband Bill worked. Over the years, two more phones were added to the fire call system, so that the ladies who volunteered to answer fire calls

Receiving keys to the new fire truck. L-R, Frank Gare (Adelaide Reeve), truck supplier representative, Roy Wardell (Fire Chief) accepting keys, and Richard Bolton (Metcalfe Reeve), August 30, 1989.

would have time off for shopping and vacations; by agreement, there were always three people of the five at home to answer fire calls. When the fire phones were removed in 1990, Dorothy Winter had kept a fire phone in her residence for 25 years, and Eileen Freer for 24 years. Over the years, the following wives had fire phones in their homes: Marie Bolton, Mary Morgan, Kay Wardell, Pat Bolton, Joyce Morgan, Angie Noordhof, Dina Tamminga, Louise Bolton and Rolean Tamminga. Beginning in 1990, residents are required to phone the London Fire Department if they have a fire, quote their grid number (which located their lot, concession and township on a computer), and London alerts the pagers that each fireman carries and gives the location of the fire.

The Department has had five Chiefs in its 33-year history. Following Mike Brooks, who served from June 1965 to April 1966, Dana Rutledge served as Chief from April 1966 to April 1968, Bill Brooks from April 1968 to July 1969, Roy Wardell from July 1969 to January 1990, and Neil Bolton from 1990 to the present.

Shortly after the Department was up and running, a portable pump was purchased which could fill the tanker from a nearby pond or stream. Radios were installed in two trucks in 1975, and a base station in the Hall. In 1976, monitors were purchased for the firemen to wear; they can be paged when a fire call is received. The Fire Hall was expanded to a third bay which the firemen volunteered the labour to build in October 1978. This bay provides shelter for a new van, used to carry many of the necessities a modern Fire Department needs, such as Bunker gear, scott packs, tools, spare parts, etc. The tanker has been updated twice since 1965, the first time by a used milk truck and its stainless steel tank, and the second by replacing the chassis of the milk truck with a new one, while retaining the tank. The original pumper lasted 24 years, and was replaced in August 1989 with a new unit costing $113,000. When asked about their trip after driving the new truck home from the factory in British Columbia—through the beautiful Rockies, and lovely summer weather in the Prairies and Northern Ontario—Chief Roy Wardell and Deputy Chief Neil Bolton replied, "Somebody had to do it."

Van; tank truck delivered in June 2000, and pumper, in front of Kerwood Fire Hall.

530   ADELAIDE TOWNSHIP... A HISTORY

Ladies who maintained fire phones in their home before service went to central dispatch, March 1990. Back L-R, Louise Bolton and Joyce Morgan. Middle L-R, Angie Noordhof, Dorothy Winter and Eileen Freer. Front L-R, Pat Bolton, Kay Wardell and Dina Tamminga.

Fire Department 1971: front L-R, Ernest Morgan, Reg Freer, Roy Wardell, Robert Dodge, Earl Bolton. Back L-R, Bill Dowding, Alick Ewen, George Matthews, Cliff Winter, Ted Denniss, Talo Tamminga, Richard Bolton, Neil Bolton, John Tedball, Paul Langford, Milo Morgan.

CHAPTER SEVEN

Communications

The transmission of written communication has changed dramatically over the last 200 years and that communication through the mails was perhaps more important to the early settlers than it is even today. Not only was it an important vehicle by which to stay in touch with family and friends, it facilitated the opening up of new land, forced the improvement of transportation facilities by land and by water, and, indeed, the entire development of commerce in the new territories would not have been possible without mail service.

There were no postage stamps in North America before April 1851. The recipient of "letters" paid the cost of movement from place to place at often-exorbitant rates—often the equivalent of $10 to $15 for a three-page letter. Hence, many systems designed to cheat the mail service were rampant, including the placement of secret prechosen codes on the outside of the letters to signify that "Aunt Mary arrived safely at Napperton" or that "Uncle Archie got the money from his brother in Glasgow." These ruses were self-defeating, as they only denied the postal system of necessary revenue. Attempts were made as early as 1824 to improve the system, but with all revenues going to Britain, it was extremely difficult to make any progress.

In 1827, Thomas Allan Stayner was put in charge of a mail service in Canada and, even though he would be the last Deputy Postmaster to be responsible to the Postmaster General of Great Britain, he made several changes that expedited mail throughout Canada. Stayner introduced standardized postal markings at 105 post offices in Upper and Lower Canada. These marking devices recorded the place and date of origin, the dates and points through which a letter passed in transit and, finally, the date of receipt of the mail. With this system, local postmasters were made to be responsible for tardiness and other common abuses. In 1835, Stayner created the office of Surveyor (later to become Post Office Inspector) and these postal Surveyors were responsible for laying out mail routes, arranging for mail contracts, creating new post offices, and correcting "irregularities."

Letters to Adelaide, before the establishment of regular stagecoach service, were carried as "favour letters" by private individuals (neighbours, friends, relatives, store owners, etc.) or by persons who made a living collecting mail from Delaware, Hall's Mills, London, etc., and delivered to some pre-arranged location in Adelaide. It takes little imagination to comprehend the abuses available to unscrupulous individuals. These letters were nailed up on store notice boards and mill walls awaiting pickup. (When the Keyser Post office was located in the cheese factory, many letters were covered in mould and quite unsavoury!) Some were claimed by fraudulent claimants, and many were simply lost.

The advent of postage stamps in 1851 allowed for the pre-payment of mail and the improvements previously mentioned corrected many of the former abuses. Stagecoaches now carried the mails to post offices, however distant from the recipient. For the most part, postmasters were honest men, literate and highly regarded in their community, and of greatest importance, acceptable to the government of the times. With the "Family Compact" in power at York, former abuses were very often replaced with equally abhorrent practices resulting from government influence. Favouritism in the award of mail contracts, location of new offices, and other influence-related problems plagued the post offices well into the 20th century. Old-timers at Kerwood relate that the Post Office crossed the street after every election—an exaggeration but not entirely without merit.

Although there undoubtedly have been many petitions made to the Postmaster General on behalf of Adelaide residents, very few have survived. Among those that have survived is one put forward by several residents who resided in the Crathie area of Adelaide. It requests that a post office be established at the residence of Brereton Bunting. The petition was forwarded to the Postmaster General with implied recommendation for approval, but the petition was not granted and all records of the reason for refusal have been lost. It is interesting to note that even though the conditions as described in the following petition had not changed substantially, if at all, a petition which granted a newly opened Crathie Post Office was approved three years later for David Sands.

Post Office Inspectors Office
London
17 April 1884

Sir:

I have the honour to return herewith the petition of Messrs. James Bolton, Richard Gerry and others asking for the establishment of a Post office at Crathie.

In reference there to and beg to say that for some years previous to 1st October 1880 a Post office was in operation at Crathie, but owing to the resignation of the then Postmaster and the unwillingness of anyone to assume this position thus rendered vacant, the office was closed on this date stated. The residence of Mr. B. Bunting where the Office is desired to be established is located on Lot 21, Concession 2 of Township of Adelaide, County of Middlesex, West Riding 4½ miles South of Springbank, 5 miles north of Strathroy, 6 East of Adelaide, and 6 West of Amiens.

This locality is well settled and shows a tendency to improve although there is not any place of business in the immediate neighbourhood.

A Post office at Crathie would be of service to a community of about thirty families and could be served without any cost, daily (or rather tri-weekly) by courier if passing between Park Hill and Strathroy as this residence of Mr. Bunting is on the direct road travelled by the said Mail Courier-
I give sketch of locality herewith

I am Sir
Your Obdt. Servant
R.M. Barker
Post Office Inspector

With the arrival of the railway in Adelaide came the railway postal car, which was organized in the fashion of a complete post office and, in many instances, was far more elaborate than those existing in towns and hamlets. The mail was stamped with special markers to indicate the date, time, and sometimes route number of the train, and then resorted for its next destination. It is almost amusing to picture the rail postman looking out of the railroad postal car at the sign on the Kerwood railway station, which read "KERWOOD," and then stamping the mail from Kerwood with a hand stamp "KERRWOOD." It took the postal authorities almost 90 years to correct their error!

Post Office records available from the National Archives have been "cleansed" in recent years (as indicated by * in the following details) and are presented here in that form. However, research done over many years by a local postal historian has been included, in part, where considered applicable. All information in italics has been added for this book. The inauguration of rural mail delivery (RMD) occurred in Adelaide over the period from 1913 to 1915. Anna Bycraft Ward describes the system used after 1913 as being one, "…with post boxes located at railway stations and couriers contracted to deposit daily mail to boxes along numbered routes emanating from each office. These routes were planned to serve those roads most thickly populated which were concession roads and those living on sideroads were required to provide boxes at their nearest corner. As these latter householders also paid taxes with a right to the same service, the regulations were changed about 40 years later to accommodate them. Then, the mail couriers had to deviate from their course to place mail in boxes at their gates as well." Most persons in Adelaide received this "mail to door" service in the late 1930s and early 1940s.

Adelaide Post Office

Postmaster	Date of App't.	Date of Vacancy	Cause of Vacancy
Thomas Radcliff	PM in 1833	1839-07-06	Resignation

Lieut. Colonel Thomas Radcliff was one of the first settlers at Adelaide. He came with money and social position and rapidly was appointed Justice of the Peace. His home and post office, by the standards of the time, was nothing less than magnificent. If early land records are any indication, the first Post Office was located on Lot 11, C 1 SER.

Richard Winsor	1839-07-07	1842-09-06	Official Misconduct

Almost nothing is known of this man except that he was the son of Richard Winsor Sr. who was a bricklayer in 1842 and resided on the W ½ Lot 5, C 1 NER. Richard Jr. was listed as a farmer on Lot 11, C 1 NER, in the same census. It is not known why he was dismissed as Adelaide's second Postmaster.

John S. Hoare	PM in 1844	1869	Resignation

Store owner in the village of Adelaide on the W ½ Lot 11, C 1 NER.

George S. Hoare	1870-01-01	1870-12-31	Resignation

Store owner and son of John Stroud Hoare.

John S. Hoare	1871-01-10	1881-11-21	Death
George S. Hoare	1882-01-01	1886-06-21	Resignation
Thomas Brock	1886-08-01	1892-01-30	Resignation

Store owner in the village of Adelaide on the W ½ Lot 11 C 1 NER.

Thomas Freele	1892-04-01	1893-02-05	Resignation

Store and hotel owner in village of Adelaide, W ½ Lot 11, C 1NER.

George W. Wilkins	1893-05-01	1906-03-03	Death

Store owner on Lot 1 S. King Street on Lot W ½ Lot 11, C 1 NER

Mrs. Eliza Wilkins	1906-04-01	1911-09-13	Death

Assumed her husband's business and operation of Adelaide Post Office.

Thomas Freele	1911-11-22	1913-02-17	Resignation

Merchant in village of Adelaide.

Lorne Petch	1913-03-04	1914-06-30	Closed-RMD

Operated a General Store in village of Adelaide.

Amiens Post Office

Postmaster	Date of App't.	Date of Vacancy	Cause of Vacancy
James Peel Bellairs	Jan. 1837 or earlier	1840-08-06	Resignation

The first location of this Post Office was on Lot 1 C 8, Lobo Township at or near Captain White's Tavern in the hamlet of Amiens. This place consisted of merely half a dozen houses and one of the first grist mills in the district. All of the mail to Adelaide and Katesville was routed through Amiens from Delaware before the advent of the rail service at Strathroy. It is suspected that there existed some sort of mail service to Amiens by at least 1832 but this has yet to be proved.

James McKirdy	1840-08-07	No record 1840-1853	

James McKirdy lived in Caradoc Township, near Amiens, where he was a storekeeper and land dealer. No official records exist for the period 1840 to 1853. It is interesting to note that the 1851 Census of Lobo indicates that a Post Office existed at the location of Woodman's General Store but that Charles Woodman was not the Postmaster. It is, therefore, quite possible that Mr. McKirdy continued to operate the Post Office throughout this period. A contract was let to Robert Scoley on Jan 6, 1841, to provide mail service through Amiens twice per week from London to Port Sarnia for £160 per annum by horseback. A second contract was arranged in Nov. 1851 with Thomas Bath Winter to carry the mail from Amiens to Napier twice per week and he was to receive £29 per year. On July 1, 1853, Winter's contract was let to Henry Mouger. Strathroy Post Office opened in 1852 and received its mail via Amiens until the advent of rail service.

Thomas Collier	PM in 1853	1854-12	Death

Thomas resided on Lot 31, C 1, Adelaide Township (Hickory Corners); he died Dec. 24, 1854, and was buried in the Ireland Chapel Cemetery. The Post Office during this period was likely located on Lot 31, Adelaide, for when Timothy Cook (first Postmaster at Strathroy) inquired as to the reason why the Post Office had been moved from Woodman's, the reply from the Postal Inspector was that "the office was moved from Woodman's simply on account of Collier's place being considered a more eligible site" (Letter from M. Griffen to Mr. T. Cook, 18 Jan. 1854, on behalf of the Post Master General). Anna Bycraft Ward provides a most satisfactory explanation when she wrote, "As the tavern had been moved to the east end of Adelaide, the stagecoaches would be stopping there to change horses or to rest them, so it would certainly be more convenient to make one stop and also serve the Post Office. So Collier living nearby could easily be on hand to receive the mailbag from London and dispatch any mail to Sarnia." (Amiens: A Pioneer Settlement and Post Office Near Lobo Caradoc Townline in Middlesex County, 1985)

Chas. W. Woodman	1855-01-01	1856-07-25	Resignation

The Post Office moved again to Woodman's store on Lot 2, C 10, Lobo Township, east of Hickory Corners. By this time, any income from the Post Office was likely very meager, and not worth the inconvenience of having it located at the store.

H.P. Fuller	1856-11-01	1858-04-04	Resignation

Hugh Patterson Fuller, the brother of Obadiah Fuller of Adelaide, was a merchant all of his life and often moved from place to place in order to reap greater rewards. During Mr. Fuller's tenure as Postmaster at Amiens, he may have worked out of Woodman's General Store near Hickory Corners. As rail service to Strathroy replaced most of the stagecoach runs to Amiens and mail for Amiens began to be picked up at the railway station in Strathroy, he saw little potential for profit and moved on.

Amiens Post Office *continued*

Postmaster	Date of App't.	Date of Vacancy	Cause of Vacancy

John Walker   1858-04-20   1859-01   **Death**
John died in January 1859 and is buried at the Ireland Chapel Cemetery.

Ms. Martha Walker   1859-03-02   1859-03-31   **Resignation**
As the daughter of John Walker, Martha assumed the duties of her father.

John C. Collier   1859-04-01   1860-02-29   **Resignation**
Believed to be the son of Thomas Collier.

Duncan McArthur   1860-07-01   1864-10-14   **Resignation**
Duncan was a merchant at Amiens when the hamlet was located at the juncture of Lot 2, C 10, Lot 2, C 9, Lobo Township, and the Egremont Road. Duncan was probably the son of Charles McArthur.

Edward Stonehouse   1865-04-01   1866-03-31   **Resignation**
It is believed that Edward was born about 1832 in England, and that he tried to make a living as Postmaster at Amiens, but his attempt lasted only 11 months.

Charles McArthur   1867-08-01   1868   **Death**
Charles McArthur was born ca.1797 in Scotland and served as Postmaster for only a few months before his death in 1868.

John McArthur   1869-10-01   1875-12-22   **Resignation**
John resided on Lot 2, C 9, Lobo Township, at Amiens. John may have been related to Charles McArthur.

John Adams   1876-11-01   1886-06-15   **Resignation**
John was a shoemaker and appears to have had his shop in a small building that he apparently moved close to Hickory Corners on Lot 31, Adelaide Township, to better serve his Post Office, which he operated for almost 10 years. This building was purchased by Archie Campbell and became known as Campbell's "Hen House."

Joshua Lindsay   1886-10-01   1891-05-04   **Resignation**
Joshua lived at Hickory Corners, approximately at the site of "Daniel's Garage" (Lot 31). He closed in the veranda of his home, which served as the Post Office for almost five years.

William Ireland   1891-09-01   1913-04-30   **Closed-R.M.D.**
The removal of the Post Office to the home of William Ireland on the W 1/2 of Lot 27, C 1 SER, was a vast departure from the old hamlet of Amiens, which had long since ceased to exist. His story is recounted in that of the Ireland family. He was Postmaster for almost 22 years, during which many changes occurred in methods of transportation and Post Office service. For the majority of his tenure at Amiens, he picked up the mail at the railway station at Strathroy five or six times per week by horse-and-buggy or, in winter, by cutter. During his tenure, and because of the high esteem with which the Post Office Inspector held him, William was allowed to experiment with a variety of rural mail delivery schemes, such as special boxes at the end of side roads, drop-off points along his route, etc.

Katesville Post Office

Postmaster	Date of App't.	Date of Vacancy	Cause of Vacancy

R.W. Branan† 1837-02-06 1839 Resignation

Richard Wallace Branan was the first Postmaster at Katesville. The Post Office was located on Lot 17, C 7 SER, Adelaide Township, in Branan's store and tavern. It was in operation by February 6, 1837, and closed in May 1869. It would appear that the resignation of Richard Branan coincided with his appointment as Magistrate.

Richard Brown† 1839 1851-11 Resignation

Richard Brown was a merchant in Katesville. He assumed the position of Postmaster sometime in 1839 and continued in this position until he resigned in November 1851 in anger over the establishment of the Post Office at Strathroy. The inhabitants of the hamlet of Strathroy had attempted to send a petition to the Postmaster General requesting a Post office at Strathroy. The first was posted at Katesville, but never reached the Post Office Inspector. The petitioners tried again by posting their request at the Adelaide Post Office—mysteriously, this letter also disappeared. Finally, a local resident walked to Delaware carrying a third letter of request for a Post Office. This letter reached the proper authorities and it was not long before the petition was granted. It was said that this put an end to the tavern business in Katesville.

William Fulton† 1851-11 1853 Resignation

William Fulton operated a shoemakers' shop at Katesville, most likely located on Lot 17, C 7 SER, and assumed the duties of Postmaster in November 1851.

William McClatchey 1853 1869-05-11 Death

William McClatchey is the only Postmaster at Katesville to be acknowledged in the Archival Records in Ottawa, but research by Vaughan MacPherson has conclusively proved that Katesville had at least four other Postmasters (†). He ran several businesses from his residence on the W 1/2 Lot 18, C 7 SER. In addition to being the Postmaster, he was a chemist, land agent, and insurance agent.

Stephen Thomas† 1869 1869-05-30 Closed

Stephen operated the Post Office for only a few months but, with insufficient revenue, it was closed by the Postmaster General. Stephen then opened the Post Office at Mount Hope (Cairngorm). It is believed that Stephen later became a Member of Parliament.

Strathroy Post Office

Postmaster	Date of App't.	Date of Vacancy	Cause of Vacancy
Timothy Cook	1851-11-06	1865-10	**Death**

Timothy Cook and his partner, James Keefer, purchased Buchanan's grist mill, located on Lot 24, C 4 SER, in 1846. He opened a store on what is now Front Street East somewhere near the present location of All Saints Roman Catholic Church. In November 1851, after finally getting permission from the Postmaster General, Timothy opened the first Post Office in Strathroy. It has been recorded that his wife, Harriet, performed most of the Post Office duties. After a number of years, a few of the prominent citizens got together and raised enough money to build a new post office on Frank Street from which the Post Office continued to operate for an unknown length of time.

| **Mrs. H. Cook** | 1866-04-01 | 1867-09 | * |

Harriet "Hattie" Cook was appointed Postmaster after the death of her husband in the new Post Office on Frank Street.

Kerwood Post Office

Postmaster	Date of App't.	Date of Vacancy	Cause of Vacancy
J.H. Thomas	1861-12-01	1866-09-30	**Absconded**

Few details are known about Mr. Thomas or why he stole all of the money and stamps from the Post Office and left town, but land records indicate that he was also involved in some shady land dealings.

| **James Irving** | 1866-10-01 | 1875-03-31 | **Left the Place** |

James Irving, in addition to being the Postmaster, was a merchant, mill proprietor, and later, the Stationmaster for the Great Western Railway.

| **Charles Foster** | 1875-04-01 | 1888-05-19 | **Resignation** |

It is said that Charles Foster operated a Post Office on the east side of the main street in the proximity of Ella McMahon's house.

| **John C. Jury** | 1888-07-01 | 1895-10-21 | **Resignation** |

John Jury was a butcher. He owned a store on the main street of Kerwood.

| **James B. Denning** | 1896-02-01 | 1898-10-31 | **Resignation** |

James was a merchant in Kerwood.

| **Alfred Rogers** | 1898-11-23 | 1934-01-18 | **Resignation** |

Alfred Rodgers owned and operated a General Store on the west side of Kerwood from which he operated the Kerwood Post Office for almost 36 years.

| **Harold N. Conkey** | 1934-02-27 | 1943-01-18 | **Death** |

Harold Norman Conkey, for a number of years, ran a General Store on the west side of Kerwood. After the store was closed, the Post Office continued to be operated from their residence. Harold served in the Army for a couple of years.

538   ADELAIDE TOWNSHIP... A HISTORY

Kerwood Post Office *continued*

Postmaster	Date of App't.	Date of Vacancy	Cause of Vacancy
Mrs. Ella C. Conkey	1943-12-06		Acting

Ella, widow of Harold, carried on the duties of Postmistress for almost 16 years from her residence.

Mrs. Ella C. Conkey	1944-01-05	1959-10-19	Resignation

Reginald B. Freer	1960-01-17	1980-07-31	Resignation

"Reg" Freer operated the Post Office from his residence immediately north of Woods General Store. His wife actually performed the day-to-day duties, as Reg worked on the road crew for both Metcalfe and Adelaide Townships.

Linda D. Duval	1980-08-01	1985-12	*

Linda Duval operated the Post Office from the former telephone office, which had closed in 1965.

Marie Smith   1985

Marie Smith presently operates the Post Office on the west side of the main street.

Keyser Post Office

Postmaster	Date of App't.	Date of Vacancy	Cause of Vacancy
Philip H. Keyser	1864-08-01	1867	Removal from Country

Philip Keyser was a brickmaker. His property was located on N 1/2 of the S 1/2 Lot 7, C 4 NER. He operated the Post Office until he returned to the U.S. in 1867.

Samuel Cooper	1868-04-01	1875-01-02	Resignation

Samuel owned a General Store on the E 1/2 of Lot 8, C 4 NER, from which he ran the Post Office.

B. W. Stevens	1875-06-01	1888-02-24	Death

Benjamin W. Stevens resided on Lot 8, C 5 NER, and operated the Post Office from his residence.

Charles H. Stevens	1888-07-01	1891-05-23	Resignation-Closed

Following the death of his father, Benjamin, Charles continued to operate the Post Office at the same location. After his resignation, there was no postal service at Keyser for more than nine years.

Hugh E. Wilson	1901-07-01	1910-10-31	Resignation

Hugh Wilson opened a cheese factory at Keyser in 1901 on the E 1/2 Lot 6, C 4 NER, from which he also operated the Post Office.

James T. Grieve	1911-07-10	1913-10-30	Closed-R.M.D.

When James Thomas Grieve, a cheesemaker, purchased the business from Hugh Wilson, he inherited the Keyser Post Office. It is said that he took little interest or care in its operation and that the letters possessed the same flavour as the cheese.

Napperton Post Office

Postmaster	Date of App't.	Date of Vacancy	Cause of Vacancy
Thomas Jury	1870-09-01	1905-06-08	Resignation

Thomas Jury was crippled as the result of childhood disease. He lived on the property of his brother, David, on Lot 14, C 5 SER. Unable to perform heavy farm work, he ran a store from this house, selling binder twine and other farm supplies, as well as organs and pianos, and was the Napperton Postmaster for 35 years.

W. C. Hull (re-opened)	1906-02-14	1915-05-01	Resignation-Closed-R.M.D.

William Hull lived across the road from Thomas Jury on Lot 12, C 4 SER. The Post Office was in the north end of the house in a portion constituting the summer kitchen.

Crathie Post Office

Postmaster	Date of App't.	Date of Vacancy	Cause of Vacancy
James Anderson	1874-01-01	1880-06-10	Resignation-Closed

James lived on the E ½ Lot 21, C 2 NER, Adelaide Township. He was born in Ireland ca.1812 and was 62 years of age when he became Postmaster. He held that position until he resigned six years later. There was no Post Office in the district for the next seven years.

J. Sands (re-opened)	1887-04-01	1892-07-02	Resignation

John Sands lived in a log house on the south end of Lot 12, C 7, East Williams Township. The Post Office was in his house for five years.

Thomas V. Bolton	1892-03-01	1894-07-26	Resignation

Thomas Bolton lived on the S ½ Lot 19, C 3 NER, Adelaide Township.

Charles Post	1894-12-01	1895-02-19	Resignation
William Wilding	1895-08-01	1895-12-07	Resignation
Miss M. Brown	1897-03-01	1903-11-24	* (Dismissed)

Margaret Brown, daughter of David and Christina (Morrison) Brown, was born about 1855. She resided on Lot 18, C 3 NER, at the time she was Postmistress at Crathie.

A.R.J. Ayer	1904-01-01	1909-08-18	Resignation

Albert Robert James Ayer resided on the NE ¼ of the W ½ Lot 19, C 2 NER, Adelaide Township.

J.M. Henderson	1909-12-01	1913-11-29	Closed-R.M.D.

James Michael Henderson lived on the W ½ Lot 16, C 3 NER, Adelaide Township.

Mullifarry Post Office

Postmaster	Date of App't.	Date of Vacancy	Cause of Vacancy
James McNeice	1880-04-01	1900	Death

James lived on the NE corner of the S 1/2 of N 1/2 Lot 15, C 3 SER.

Ellen McNeice*	1900	1900-03-31	Resignation

Ellen, daughter of James McNeice, had assisted her father with the Post Office for several years and, after his death, she assumed his duties until the Post Office was moved across the Second Line South to the home of Charles Down. Ellen later married the Postmaster at Wanderland Post Office.

Charles Down	1900-04-01	1913-05-31	Closed-R.M.D.

Charles farmed on the W 1/2 of the E 1/2 of Lot 15, C 2 SER. The Post Office was located in the summer kitchen area of the house. Roy, Charles' grandson, still has the cupboard used to hold the mail in his grandfather's time.

Wanderland Post Office

Postmaster	Date of App't.	Date of Vacancy	Cause of Vacancy
Nelson Alderson	1908-06-01	1913-01-11	Closed-R.M.D.

Nelson lived on C 2 SER. He married Ellen McNeice, daughter of James, Postmaster at Mullifarry. At one time and for several years later, Nelson had a wrought-iron gate on the front of his property containing the word "Wanderland." It was stolen in the middle of the night in the early 1940's and was seen by an Adelaide resident at Jakie's scrap and junk yard in London—iron for another tank or gun!

The transportation of mail to the post offices before the advent of rural mail delivery is a subject far too complex to be described herein. Where post offices lay on major stagecoach routes, the process was relatively straightforward, with mail delivery contracts being arranged with individual carriers. After the arrival of rail transportation at Kerwood and Strathroy, the process became complex and subject to much change. For the greater part, records of contracts were kept in large ledgers by the Post Office Department on a regional basis commencing in 1877, and arranged alphabetically by post office name. Ledgers containing Adelaide records are included with those of all locations from Windsor to Georgian Bay. Of course, all records are handwritten and, in some cases, extremely difficult to decipher. Routes were subject to change as the Post Office attempted to increase the efficiency of the process. The "bidding" for contracts was at times intense, and the process hotly debated. Political interference in the process of awarding contracts, while always possible, was at times scandalous. It was, of course, easier and more efficient for the Post Office Department to deal with fewer individuals. Unscrupulous persons who were in a position to influence decision makers "bought up" smaller contracts, hired individuals to work at the lowest rates to make the actual delivery, and pocketed the profits. The entire process did, indeed, give meaning to the term "dirty politics."

The *"Voters' List of the Municipality of Adelaide"* for 1890 indicates that the township was served by 12 post office districts:

1. Strathroy
2. Napperton
3. Kerwood
4. Wisbeach
5. Adelaide
6. Amiens
7. Crathie
8. Springbank
9. Keysers
10. Mullifarry
11. Arkona
12. Forest

The northwest portion of Adelaide is still serviced by the Arkona Post Office.

The following persons have been involved in the delivery of mail both to the post offices in their respective area and to individual homes in the township. While this list is not exhaustive, it does represent the majority of those responsible for the delivery of the mails in Adelaide:

Joseph Harris
Terrence Callaghan
Cornelius McCarthy
J.S. Graham
M.O. Graham
Edmund Plaxton
William Ireland
Clifford Brown
A. Holland
Samuel A. Demaray
Allan Demaray
Richard Ira Demaray
Ernest Cawthorpe
Lloyd Stoodley
Merle Ruth Burdon
Shirley Gough
Lew Moses
Agnes Moses
Jim and Donna Case
John McMahon
William "Billy" Leacock
Frank Wright
Alvin Deloyd Wright
George F. Beckton
George W. Foster
William "Billy" J. McLachlan
Martha Esther Wright
Edward John Wilson
William Kenneth Foster
William R. Smith
Mrs. Martha Smith
Wilfred E. Rogers
Alfred Rogers
Harold N. Conkey
Mrs. Ella Conkey
Reginald B. Freer
Wilfred Harold Jordon
Mrs. Gwendolyn Ann Brooks
Charles Edward Calcutt
V.E. Kincade
Milton Hall
Helen Baxter
Raymond Butler
Shirley Brand

The covers shown below illustrate several interesting aspects of early postal service in Adelaide.

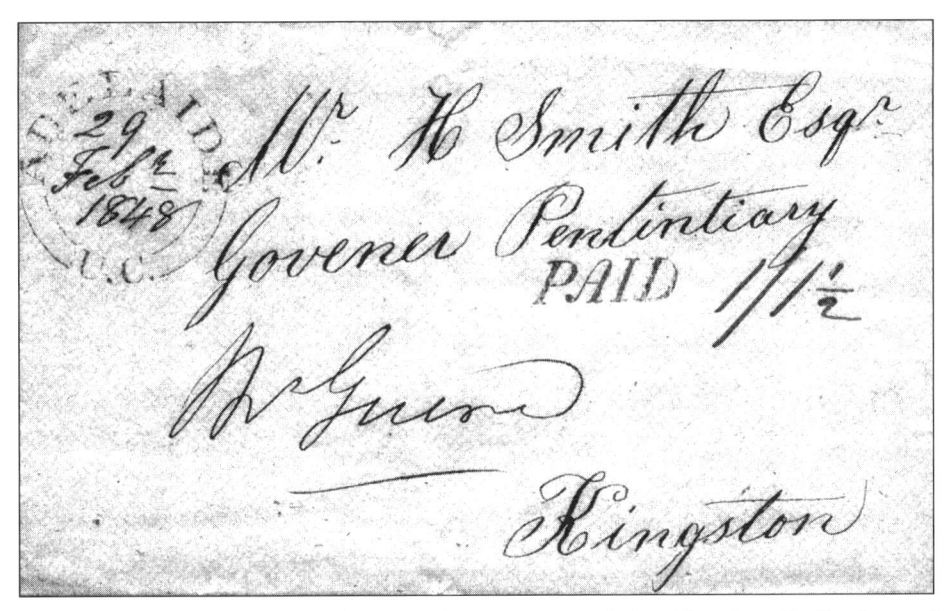

The cover from Adelaide village to the governor of the Kingston Penitentiary of 19 February 1848 shows that the cost of delivery from Adelaide to Kingston was 1 shilling 1 1/2 pence (a month's wages) and was paid by the sender. No postage stamp was affixed as adhesive postage stamps had not been introduced until 1851. It would be interesting to know the contents of this letter.

542 ADELAIDE TOWNSHIP... A HISTORY

By the 1850s postal rates had decreased substantially as shown by the cover from Katesville to William Street, Treasurer of Middlesex County, in London which incurred a fee of only 6 pence. It is interesting to note that this covers still bares no postage stamp. This occurrence was common in Adelaide township and might be explained by one or a number of reasons - the post master could not afford to purchase stamps from Ottawa, transportation to Adelaide was still too hazardous; or, as happened with the first post master at Kerwood who absconded with all the stamps and money, the Postmaster General did not have great confidence with Adelaide post masters.

The cover from Adelaide to the Commissioner of Crown Lands at Toronto shows the change from no postal fee, "FREE", (which was the custom to all government offices) to a charge of 3 pence from Adelaide to Toronto in 1858. The use of four-ring numbered cancels ("19" for Adelaide post office) was restricted to major post offices of the time. The use of this special cancel at Adelaide illustrates the confidence that the Postmaster General had that the village of Adelaide would become a major commercial centre.

CHAPTER EIGHT

Architecture

Many different styles of architecture are seen in Adelaide Township today, ranging from early frame Ontario Farm Houses and brick homes to recent modern, efficient, replacement homes.

There were many Ontario Cottages, which were basically frame 1-storey houses with a centre doorway and a window on either side. Frequently, there was space under the high roof for an extra room. These Ontario Cottages ranged from a very simple design to more elaborate, with features borrowed from other building styles.

The McCarthy frame home (east half of Lot 7, Con. 1 SER) replaced the first log cabin. The interesting feature of this Ontario Cottage is that everything is constructed of black walnut, even the eaves troughs! It is told that when the farm was sold out of the family, the new owners took the house apart and sold the valuable wood to discerning purchasers, then built a cheap frame house from their residence. The central doorway with small paned glass in the symmetrical windows shows a Georgian influence.

Ontario Cottage – McCarthy, east half of Lot 7, Con. 1 SER

Ontario Farm House – McNeice, south half of Lot 15, Con. 3 SER

Ontario Farm Houses dating from the 1860s had a mix of features copied from architectural styles of the day—a gable, Gothic window, and perhaps ornamental woodwork known as "gingerbread."

Often, the Ontario Farm House had the style of the local carpenter and was built of every conceivable sort of material within the budget of the homeowner. The James McNeice home (south half of Lot 15, Con. 3 SER) was the sight of the first Mullifarry Post Office. He was a finish carpenter, which accounts for the detailed work around the doorway and the trim around the windows.

Usually, the Ontario Farm House had a wing at the back for a kitchen, or sometimes at the side, giving the house a larger appearance. The wing may have been added after the main part was built, as a family increased and when money was available.

Some of the early brick homes had a Georgian influence—a symmetrical form, the centre doorway with windows on either side, and three windows on

Ontario. There were two brickyards in Adelaide, one at Kerwood and one at Keyser's Corners. Most of the bricks produced at this time were cream-coloured or yellow. The colour of the bricks was controlled by the composition of the clay. Before 1870, the bricks were sometimes pinkish (a deep pink or yellow), because the brick makers could not control the temperature of the kilns.

The home of Harold and Helen Westgate, of Lot 18, Con. 4 SER, has a Georgian entrance with gables on the ends, and nearly flat tops at the windows, but it is different in that it has a little gable sitting at the top. It is doubtful if this gable is original, but it may have been added about 15 years after the house was built, because centre gables were very popular and people "just had to have a gable." The same sort of thing happened in the 1920s—if homeowners lacked a front porch, they added one! Keeping up with the latest architectural styles seemed to be quite important!

There are many homes in Adelaide today, characteristic of Gothic Revival Architecture, which

Georgian Influence - Cleland/Robertson, Lot 3, Con. 1/2 NER

Georgian Influence – Westgate, Lot 15, Con. 4 SER

Gothic Revival – Conkey, Lot 3, Con. 2 NER

top balancing it, and a gable on both sides. Theoretically, this style ended when Queen Victoria came to the throne in 1837, but the influence of the Georgian style continued in Ontario home building into the 1850s and 1860s. This style is characteristic of the home of David and Leota Robertson, of the east half of Lot 3, Con. 1 and 2 NER. When renovating and removing the front veranda, built in the 1920s, they noticed a very large brick above the front door, which had an imprint of a child's foot. The Robertsons learned that a child's shoe was sometimes imbedded in a wall to represent good luck and to keep away "spirits." Their home, built in the mid-1860s by Robert Cleland Jr., has partitions from ceiling to basement of three layers of soft reddish brick, which is uncommon in this part of

ARCHITECTURE 545

Ontario Farm House - West Adelaide Presbyterian Manse, moved from Lot 3, Con. 2 NER, to west half of Lot 10, Con.2 NER, then to west part of Lot 22, Con. 3 SER

Gothic Revival - West Adelaide Presbyterian Church, Lot 4, Con 3 NER

Gothic Revival – Ball, west half of Lot 7, Con. 1 SER

became fashionable after the Georgian influence. The house at the east half of Lot 3, Con. 3 NER, built by widow Rebecca Wiley Wilson in 1875, is the home today of Lorne Benedict and family. The three important features of the Gothic Revival Architecture are seen: Gothic windows with flat-topped headings; finials—the carved wood at the peak of the gables; and bargeboards—ornamental woodwork around the edges of the gable. In most cases, there is a continuous board, which is very detailed. A news item of the day in the Strathroy Age refers to the 1875 building at the West Adelaide corner. James Galloway built a brick house of similar design on his farm at the east half of Lot 2, Con. 3 NER. That home has been recently demolished and replaced by a modern home, the residence of Roger and Donalda Benedict and family. The third house on the southwest corner of the east half of Lot 3, Con. 2 NER, built by William Conkey Sr., was a brick home of the same Gothic Revival style. It is standing today but is in disrepair.

On the corner by the sideroad, a frame manse was built—an Ontario Farm House that has stood the test of time well, having been moved to the west half of Lot 10, Con. 2 NER. The dwelling was used as a home by the Hodgson family and, after its second move, is a comfortable residence today on Highway 81, near Mullifarry Road.

The focal feature of the West Adelaide corner is the Presbyterian Church, built also in 1875. The church has pointed Gothic windows, rose windows front and back, ornamental brickwork, and buttresses on each side. This is a lovely Gothic country church, where weekly services are still held.

The Gothic Revival house that is the home of David and Beth Ball, at the west half of Lot 7, Con. 1 SER, was built in 1882, according to the date stamped on the doorbell. The bricks on the corners

Italianate – Carrothers, east half of Lot 4, Con. 2 SER

Italianate – Morgan, Lot 5, Con. 5 SER

are called "quoins," and there is interesting brickwork above the windows, which still have the original shutters.

An ornate Italianate home built by John and Harriet Carrothers about 1870, on the east half of Lot 4, Con. 2 SER, is now demolished. Italianate houses have brackets, frequently double brackets, all the way around under the roof. There is very heavy moulding at the top of the windows, and a keystone in the centre. A widow's walk on the top has turned pillars on the corners. Like the Gothic Revival style, there is a central gable.

This photo of the Hull/Morgan home, located at the west half of Lot 6, Con. 5 SER, was loaned by Bill and Judy Morgan. There is a very interesting double bay on the first floor, and a bay on the second floor above it. The partitions were filled with sand for insulation. No one lives in this house now. At one time, the windmill was fastened to the barn, the power used to grind grain on the lower level.

An Italianate home known as the Langan house, built in 1874, is now the residence of Dave and Linda Powell. Although the house is inland and far from water, Langan, a Great Lakes captain, built an elaborate widow's walk with beautiful metal work around the top, which is often called "Creston."

This home has everything found in an Italianate house—ornate double brackets, a picot detail underneath the eaves, and heavy headings at the windows, which are gently curved at the top. There is a beautiful slate roof. The porch has lost some of its detailed woodwork, but most of the essential features are still there. The beautiful fieldstones of the foundation are actually cut, and show a variety of colour.

The present manse in Kerwood, built in the early 1900s for the United Church, is Queen Anne Revival Style, which was very popular from 1885 until WWI. Features of this style include windows of different sizes and shapes, perhaps a "keyhole" window, side porches, and little bays, often described as having an "irregular footprint." On the front door, the glass window is etched "Methodist Parsonage." There are some stately Queen Anne Revival homes in Adelaide Township that were built just before or immediately after 1918. These homes replaced the second home, a frame Ontario Farm House, and some were modernized with Delco systems, and running water for bathrooms. Many Adelaide Queen Anne Revival homes retain features of Italianate architecture with double brackets supporting the roof.

The interiors of Victorian parlours displayed the current trends in decorating. This room in the

Italianate - Langan/Powell, Lot 4, Con. 5 NER

Queen Anne Revival - Methodist Manse, Kerwood

Meredith Morgan home in Kerwood has a picture rail, which made hanging pictures very convenient. There is a stained glass window that came into use about 1885. A decorated kerosene lamp waits for evening on the small table. Pianos were becoming popular in many homes. This photograph is of Dorothy Winter's childhood home in Kerwood. Dorothy's brother, Milo, still has the large painting of Windsor Castle. Family portraits, taken by a renowned photographer, were proudly displayed in the parlour, a very practical way to store them.

Interior - Morgan/Winter - Parlour interior, Kerwood

Ontario Cottage - Miller homestead in Adelaide Village, ca.1900

CHAPTER NINE

Armed Forces

A Military History of Adelaide Township

The following is excerpted from D. Colin McKeen's account of the influence of the military on the pioneer settlement of Adelaide Township and its subsequent development. It summarizes how the Militia was constituted, integrated with the Imperial Forces, and periodically changed to keep pace with the growing country's needs to defend its borders from invasion, and to ensure that the domestic rule of law be made secure.

The spirit of volunteerism shown by the early militiamen was maintained throughout the 1800s. This pattern served as a great incentive for the recruitment of personnel for military service both at home and overseas for both World Wars of the 20th century.

All documentary involves selection and inclusion, and is thereby subject to personal judgment, for history is particular in the events it chooses to retain. No pretense is made herein to act as a court of authority, only that this account carries a genuine degree of authenticity. For this reason, it is called "a" history rather than "the" history. The account terminates with the end of WWII.

The British Influence In North America

Soon after the landing of the Mayflower and the arrival of the Pilgrims on Plymouth Rock, Englishmen began swarming the American Continent. The English colonies formed were chartered bodies legally subordinate to the Crown. The reach of the colonies extended along the Atlantic Seaboard from Maine to the Carolinas, and west to the Allegheny Mountains.

The complacency of 18th century England was shattered by the revolt of the American colonies. In 1776, the 13 colonies declared their independence. Seven years later, they won their freedom from Britain. This revolution reverberated around the world, leading to the break-up of empires for more than two centuries.

Tensions and disharmony existed among the American Colonies as they set about their task of building a republic. After 1780 to the turn of the century, and even for a few later decades, hundreds of those remaining loyal to Britain came to British North America (later to become Canada) as United Empire Loyalists (UEL). In Upper Canada, they settled in pioneer communities near Lake Erie and Lake Ontario, and along the St. Lawrence River. Their loyalty to Britain never faltered. Nonetheless, for the UEL, there was no assurance of an easy life or a safe haven. The foundation of the Canadian Militia was laid in part by this gallant band of loyalists.

John Graves Simcoe, first Governor (1791-1794) of Upper Canada, always entertained the idea of a re-conquest of the United States. Accordingly, he visualized a central government at London on the Thames with operational arms extending from there. He divided the country into counties for Militia purposes, and enacted legislation for the role of the Militia. The aggression that he foresaw in the U.S. did not come, but about 20 years after he left office, the War of 1812-1814 broke out.

While fighting the Napoleonic War (1794-1814) against France, Britain found herself once again occupied with trouble involving the American colonies, primarily because of trading blockades with European countries. Due to failed negotiations, the War of 1812-1814 was the outcome. Canada was the objective of the U.S. "War Hawks," a group who wanted to see Britain thrown out of North America. Invasions of Upper Canada were attempted at Niagara and through Detroit. The invaders were eventually repulsed, with neither side making great gains.

In June 1814, the Duke of Wellington, with the help of the Prussians under General Blütcher, defeated Napoleon at Waterloo to end the Napoleonic War. On Christmas Eve of that year, peace between England and America was signed. In the peace negotiations, it was the shrewd Wellington (of Waterloo fame) who maintained that it was not in Britain's interests to demand territory from the Americans along the border that involved Upper Canada. Other boundary disputes, particularly regarding Maine, were settled soon thereafter.

The 1812-1814 war was a turning point in the history of Canada. Canadians took pride in the part they had played in defending their country, and this strengthened a growing national sentiment. After the war, anti-American sentiments ran high in Great Britain for several years. Because of this sensitivity, a simmering unease was engendered in Canada. To keep Canada secure, a reliable Militia had to be instituted and maintained.

The defeat of Napoleon in 1815 left Britain in unchallenged dominion over a large portion of the globe. For such victory, the cost was great, and she was exhausted. Furthermore, her pre-war industrial upsurge had been stalled by wartime trade blockades to her commerce. A succession of bad harvests made for increased food prices. The war debt had reached alarming proportions and Britain's economy was dangerously out of balance. Unemployment was high and, by 1826, a financial panic occurred. Authorities in Great Britain decided the sound way to lessen the pressures of unemployment at home (and to obtain some relief for the many thousands in distress) was to step up immigration to North America.

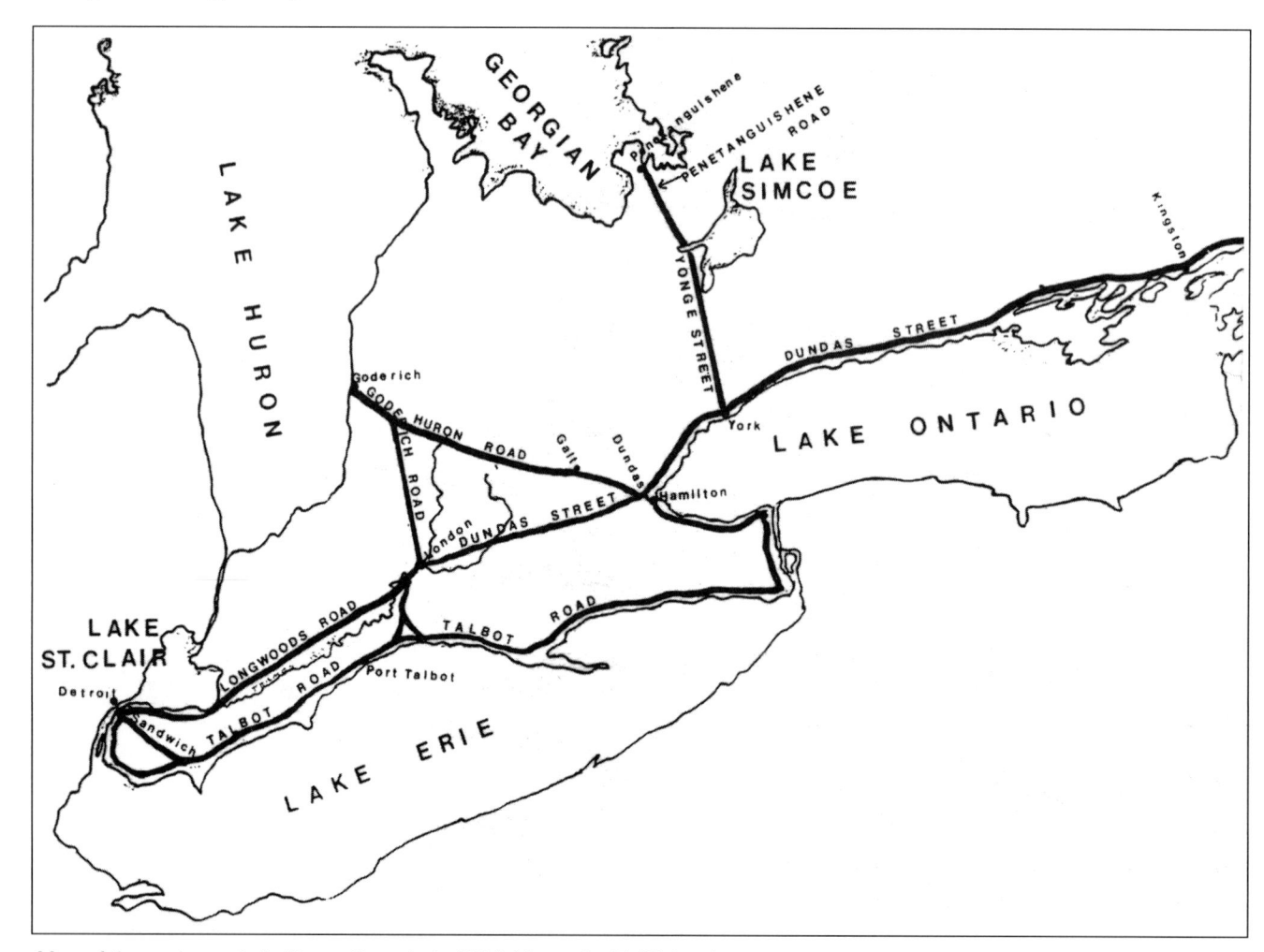

Map of the main roads in Upper Canada in 1831 (drawn by E. Nielsen).

With the expectation that a large number of immigrants would be arriving in the Maritime region of Canada and in Upper Canada, government officials were duty bound to make advance preparations. In Upper Canada, county surveys had to be initiated at once and roads constructed to permit an orderly settlement of the land. Because of the lingering threat of a military strike from the U.S., a good road system for the movement of troops was an obvious necessity (see Fig. 1).

In 1828, Sir John Colborne, Lieutenant-Governor of Upper Canada, realized the urgency of opening up the most westerly part of Canada West to colonization. Land surveys were organized. In 1831, a survey party began its task of laying out a road from the northwest corner of Caradoc Township westward through what was to become the Township of Adelaide in Middlesex County, Warwick and Plympton in Lambton County, to Lake Huron. This became the Egremont Road (see Fig. 2).

In the spring, summer and early autumn of 1832, the survey was completed, including three tiers of properties along the Egremont Road traversing the three aforementioned townships. When Adelaide Township was first surveyed, it included the southern part, which was separated off in 1845 to become the Township of Metcalfe.

Settlers were converging on Adelaide Township even before the official survey along the Egremont Road was completed. More of the original settlers

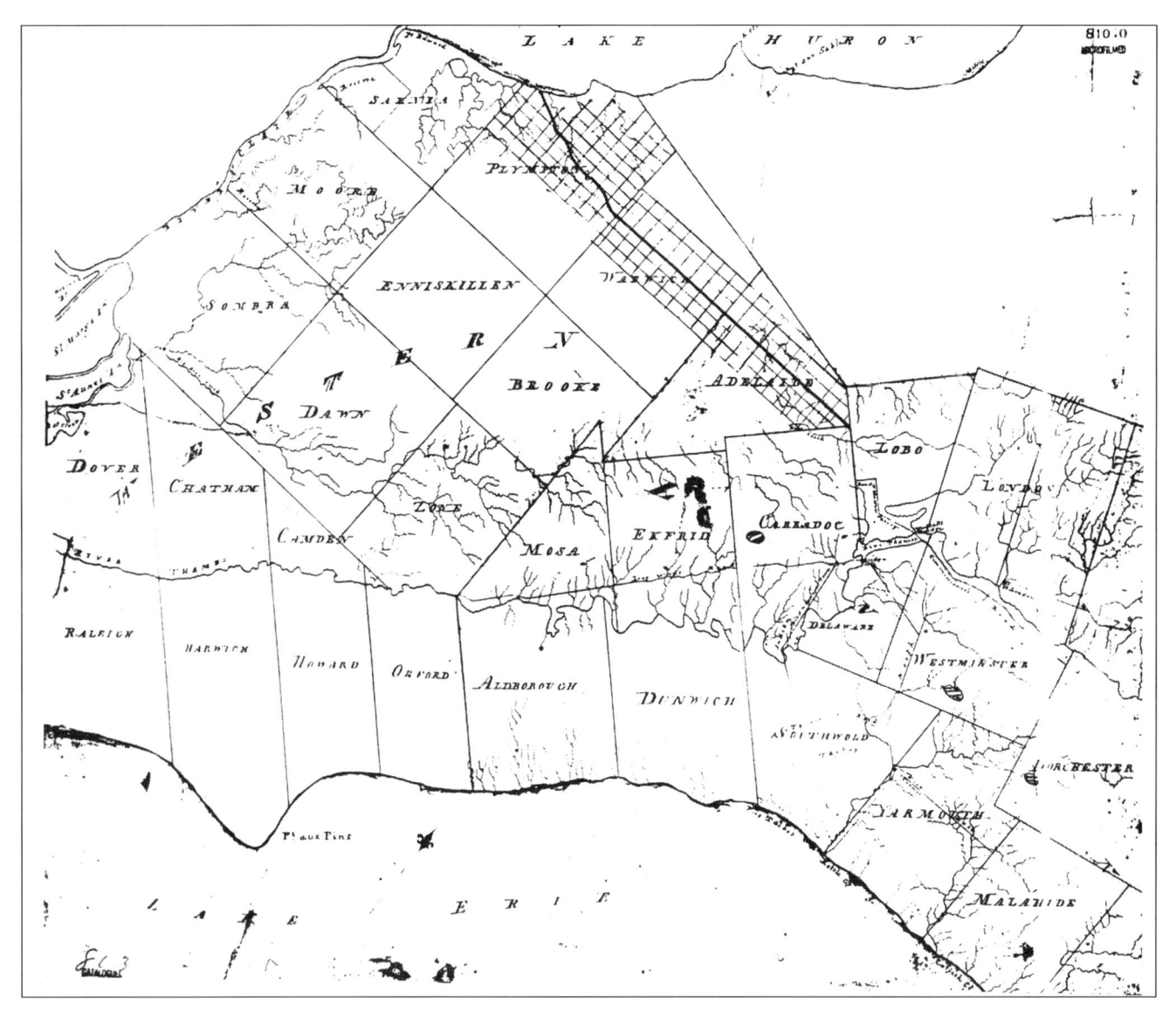

Map of the territory between Lake Erie and Lake Huron in 1831, showing Peter Carroll's survey of "a road from the N.E. corner of Caradoc to Lake Huron with three tiers of lots on each side." (A-17, (183-) (AO 234), Archives of Ontario, Toronto)

came in 1833, and subsequently for the rest of the decade. Most of the newcomers could be assigned to one of four categories: well-to-do gentlemen and their families from Ireland; Petworth settlers from the County of Sussex, England; discharged military men from Great Britain; and the United Empire Loyalists. The UEL were entitled to free grants of land—mainly 100-acre lots. Discharged British Army and Navy personnel were allowed to commute their pensions for a sum in ready cash to purchase land. In the 1834 Settlers' Map of Adelaide, there are 750 names. Out of a total of 497 in Adelaide, there were 85 discharged Army and seven discharged Navy personnel. Out of a total of 250 in Metcalfe, there were 49 discharged Army and one discharged Navy personnel. Eighteen UEL settled in Adelaide, and five in Metcalfe. Virtually all of the indigent settlers were sent out by the Petworth Emigration Society. (During WWII, the Toronto Scottish Regiment was stationed at and took training near Petworth, Sussex. When a lone German bomber was forced to hasten back to Germany, it dropped its load of bombs on Petworth and destroyed a school. The Toronto Scottish aided in the clean-up of the wreckage and so re-established Canada's link with Petworth.) The UEL and committed pensioners served in Upper Canada's earliest Militia, and indeed formed the backbone of the Adelaide Force.

Canada's Earliest Militia Formed

The Canadian Militia has a history of which it may well be proud. For more than a century, it had been the mainstay of Imperial interests in North America, and in the face of tremendous odds had greatly contributed to preserving half the continent for the British Empire.

In 1791, while Lord Simcoe was Governor-General, the provinces of Upper and Lower Canada were set up under Imperial Act 31 by King George III. In 1792, provincial and district boundaries and the representation of the provinces in Parliament were established. One year later, the first Militia Act was passed. Until then, the protection of the Province was entirely in the hands of the Imperial authorities. The Militia Act gave the young province the responsibility of organizing a Militia system that was to prevail in Canada for more than 100 years. Every able-bodied male inhabitant from 16 to 50 was considered a Militiaman. He was obliged to enlist on reaching the mandatory age of 16, under penalty of fine for failing to do so. The annual muster for all militiamen was June 4, George III's birthday. In the third Provincial Parliament (1801), regulations respecting "the better securing of the Province against the King's enemies" were passed for the further regulation of the Militia of the Province. In 1808, another act was passed, revising all previous acts for the raising and training of the Militia. The age for service was raised from 50 to 60 years in time of war or emergency.

The captains of Militia regiments were obliged to call out their companies not fewer than twice and not more than four times a year to inspect their arms and instruct them in their duties. Each man was compelled to outfit himself with a good musket, fusil, rifle or gun, with at least six rounds of powder and ball, and to come with these each time he was called out. No payment was made for Militia duty. Over time, appropriate amendments to the Militia Act were authorized. For example, sensing a threat of invasion from the U.S., a new Militia Act was passed in 1812 that extended the provision of the previous acts. It called for the formation of two Flank Companies by each county Battalion. Each Flank Company was composed of 100 men, volunteers from existing companies, who could be ordered by the Lieutenant Governor "to march to any part of the province upon any duty as he shall think necessary." Provision was made for the pensioning of soldiers who were permanently wounded in the War of 1812-1814, and for the maintenance of widows and orphans of those who lost their life.

The Fourth Regiment (Battalion) of Middlesex Militia was embodied under the act passed in 1793. In 1822, the Regiment was reorganized from the provisional basis under which it had existed. The citizen soldiers of the various regiments of Upper Canada served alongside British regular troops in defence of Canada. They took part in many of the important battles of the War of 1812-1814, including the capture of Detroit, the Battle of the Thames, the Battle of Lundy's Lane, Queenston Heights, Stoney Creek, Beaver Dams, etc. Other Militia fought at Chrysler Farm, Ogdensburg, etc., along the St. Lawrence River.

It is not the purpose of this account, written some 160 years after the original settlers came to

Adelaide, to detail the service of individuals. However, it would be remiss not to mention a few settlers who showed exemplary duty:

- Robert Johnson (1770-1868) settled in 1832 on Con. 8 SER (now Con. 3, Metcalfe). His blood relationship was to the Royal Stuarts. His grandfather was Lord Johnson of Annandale, Scotland. After the Battle of Culloden in 1746, the Johnson Estate was confiscated. Robert served under the Duke of Wellington in the Peninsular War (1808-1814) and was seriously wounded in the Battle of Waterloo (1814). He was 72 years of age when he came to Upper Canada. He brought considerable wealth with him. He received his commission as a Canadian Militia Captain under Sir Charles Metcalfe in 1843. Later, he was promoted to the rank of Major when Lord Elgin was Governor-General. He was popularly known as "Captain" Robert. He was a great benefactor to the community of Napier, building its first saw mill (1832), a grist mill (1838) and a carding mill. He signed his name "Robert Marquis" of Annandale. He lived to the age of 98.
- Corporal Charles Preston settled on Lot 4, Con.10 SER (Metcalfe) in 1831. He served in the War of 1812-1814 with the Glengarry Highlanders, and fought in the battles of 1813 at Chrysler Farm and Ogdensburg.
- Francis Emmerick came to Upper Canada from Holland via Pennsylvania and settled on Con. 10 SER (Metcalfe). In 1813, he fought in the battles at Chrysler Farm and at Ogdensburg. He also served in the First Regiment of the Lincoln Militia at Niagara (1819-1821).
- Rosewell Mount (1779-1834) was a Captain of the Second Company Middlesex Militia (1824-1830). When Peter Carroll, land surveyor, was commissioned in 1833 to survey the village plot of Adelaide in preparation for the public sale of lots, Captain Mount had already constructed a house on Lot 9, Con. 1 NER. He had high hopes for the village. In July 1832, when 400 Canadian immigrants from Petworth arrived at Kettle Creek on Lake Erie, Rosewell Mount was delegated to meet them and see to it that they reached Adelaide Township. In August, another 800-1,000 immigrants arrived at Port Stanley, and were shepherded by Rosewell Mount to Adelaide.

Those crossing the Atlantic in 1832-1834 faced a fearsome epidemic of cholera. The crowding of the immigrants in steerage with poor sanitation on the ships facilitated the spread of the disease, and resulted in the loss of many lives. The outbreak of cholera added to Rosewell Mount's burdensome chore of getting the Petworth settlers to their wooded Adelaide properties, where they had to construct shelters for the winter. Adding to the ill luck of the immigrants was an early August frost in 1832, which destroyed what they might have gleaned from nature's bounty. In the confusion of settling the new arrivals and providing them with road work so that they could feed themselves, Rosewell Mount had spent more than twice the government's budget. As would happen today, this overexpenditure created problems for Mount and the government.

In 1833, to facilitate the settling of Adelaide, Captain Mount was successful in getting a road opened from a point in Caradoc Township south of Longwoods Road to the town plot in Adelaide. This was of great benefit to the settlers in the southern part of the township, which became Metcalfe.

Dissatisfaction With
The Government Of Upper Canada

The decision to build the Egremont Road to provide military access to Lake Huron was soon justified. Although the perceived threat was from the U.S., as the War of 1812-1814 had reminded them, the problem came from agitators within Canada.

In the mid-1830s, the Government of Upper Canada, dominated by an influential group called the "Family Compact," faced a determined opposition championing reform. The "Reformers," led by William Lyon MacKenzie King, wanted a government modelled on the U.S. Declaration of Independence of 1776. After brief consideration of a long list of grievances tabled by the Reformers, the government refused to capitulate. The immediate option of the Reformers was to overthrow the government.

During 1837, many settlers were becoming more than a little interested in the political wrangling. The action of the Tories and the Orangemen in handling the parliamentary affairs of Upper Canada was disquieting. The leaders of the Reform movement were successful in convincing many settlers that rooting out a state of serfdom to which the secret society, the Family Compact, had subjected them was justifiable. In November, the Reformers of the London district were summoned to arms at Scotland Village, Grant County, by their leader, Dr. Charles Duncombe. The group disbanded when the Militia of Upper Canada was sent forward against them.

The Rebellion Of 1837-1838

The year 1837 brought serious crop failure, and the onset of a commercial crisis greatly aggravated the political unrest. Finally, the trouble came to a head in December, when an armed rebel group of Reformers led by MacKenzie was defeated at Montgomery's Tavern, just north of Toronto. When the uprising was quelled, MacKenzie and several leaders of the Reform movement escaped and fled across the border into the U.S. at Niagara. In the U.S., the Refugees banded together with American patriots, with the goal of liberating Canada from British persecution. Patriot forces assembled at Detroit, Niagara, and a few sites along the St. Lawrence River.

The Government of Upper Canada, firmly determined to maintain its constitutional monarchy, counted on the loyal support of farmers, new settlers, and most of the older residents. Yet, sympathy for government reform existed in the populace, so it was often difficult to ascertain whether one's neighbour was friend or foe. With imminent threats of invasion at Canada's borders, the Government ordered a full mobilization of the Militia. Sir John Colborn, Commander of the British Forces in both Upper and Lower Canada, held the British Regulars in readiness to counterattack where a border incident occurred. Consequently, the incorporated local Militia regiments were to be assigned front line duty at border posts.

During the initial settling of Adelaide Township (including what was later to become Metcalfe) in 1831-1832, 142 men had previous military experience. Several had fought under the Duke of Wellington at the Battle of Waterloo in 1815. Consequently, in the 1837 mobilization, Captain Thomas Radcliff of Adelaide Village had no difficulty in raising a regiment called the "Western Rangers." Radcliff (1794-1841) had obtained a commission in the Enniskillen Foot Regiment of the British Army at 18 years of age. He had fought in 19 battles under the Duke of Wellington in the Napoleonic War.

The official roster of command of the Adelaide Regiment at the time of recruitment under Thomas Radcliff, who received his rank of Colonel in 1837, was as follows: John P. Curran as Lieut. Colonel; Walter MacKenzie as Major; and William Radcliff, P. Hughes and Robert Pegley were old Captains. J.J. Buchanan, Thomas Groome, James Peel Bellairs, John Arthurs and E.G. Bowen were commissioned Captains in 1837. R.H. Allen obtained the rank of Captain in 1838. Of the Lieutenants, William Collins was commissioned in 1835; H.L. Thompson, T. White, G. Somers, R.L. Johnston, H.G. Bullock, E. Bullock and George Pegley were commissioned in 1837. Second Lieutenants J. Philips, D. McPherson, W. McKenzie, and C. White were commissioned in 1837. The Adjutant was Captain John Arthurs.

With some enthusiastic haste, Col. Thomas Radcliff raised the Western Rangers regiment. Soon thereafter, he was assigned command of the Western Frontier. He was then quartered at Amherstburg. After Col. Thomas Radcliff was assigned a higher command at London, his brother, Captain William Radcliff, was promoted to Major and given command of the Adelaide Company. Other companies of Militia were formed farther west on the Egremont Road in Warwick, Plympton and Sarnia.

During 1837, the Patriots and sympathizers increased in numbers and assembled support groups along the Detroit River. General Donald McLeod, a Canadian refugee and a veteran of the War of 1812, was appointed Commander-in-Chief of the Western Division of the Patriot Army. Patriots obtained arms and equipment by raiding local U.S. Government arsenals. Michigan officials sought, somewhat unsuccessfully, to discourage Patriot plans. On January 6, 1838, the Patriots seized the schooner "Ann" at Detroit, loaded it with stolen ordinance, and sailed it down river to Gibraltar, Michigan. There, with strengthened forces, General Sutherland assumed command of the Patriots. Since British Regulars had been ordered away from Windsor, Sandwich and Fort Malden for use in Lower Canada where a Rebellion was also raging, the Patriots were determined to make a landing on Canadian soil and set up a provisional government.

On January 8, the Patriot forces moved to Sugar Island and planned an assault on nearby Canadian Bois Blanc Island. They sailed "Ann" past

Amherstburg and fired several shots from her cannon into the town. When Bois Blanc was evacuated by the Canadians to strengthen onshore batteries, the Patriots took possession. Later in the day, the schooner cannonaded Amherstburg and the Patriots sought Fort Malden's surrender. Canadian Militia units returned fire on the vessel, damaging its steerings so that the vessel was soon grounded in Canadian waters. On January 10, Canadian Militia boarded the vessel, taking its commander and several others captive. This ended the fighting on the Detroit frontier for a month.

On February 24, the Patriots invaded Fighting Island in Canadian waters just off Sandwich. This was a fiasco for the Patriots; the Canadian Militia and British Regulars (now back on duty at Fort Malden) assaulted the island and drove the Patriots off. A much more serious invasion threat occurred on February 26 at Pelee Island from across Lake Erie. On March 2, an expedition of Regulars and Canadian Militia, dispatched from Fort Malden, drove the invaders back to the U.S. shore. In the Pelee Island skirmish, five were killed and more than 20 Canadians were wounded. The fleeing raiders lost 11 dead, and suffered total casualties of about 80 men. Other border skirmishes along the St. Clair River and on the St. Lawrence in Upper Canada were soon suppressed and the invaders thrown back.

The incident at Navy Island at Niagara, the headquarters of William Lyon MacKenzie, was an ill-planned adventure. To sever Mackenzie's supply lines and rout him from Navy Island, which was in Canadian waters, the Canadian Forces captured the Steamer "Caroline" in U.S. waters and set it ablaze. Its anchor was lifted and it was set free to float down over Niagara Falls. American feelings were inflamed by this incident, for this event reflected badly on the Government of Upper Canada.

Personal Involvements And Experiences Of Adelaide Militiamen In The Rebellion of 1837-1838

The active involvements of Adelaide militiamen in the Rebellion of 1837-1838 are, for the most part, sketchy. Major William Radcliff took the Adelaide Company of Militia to the Windsor Front. At the end of the Rebellion, in the winter of 1838-1839, he moved with his family back to London. A decade later, the Radcliff family returned to Adelaide Village.

A few military experiences are gleaned mainly from letters of veterans to parents, etc. George Buttery of Lot 26, Con. 2 SER, has given a few interesting reminiscences. The following are a few excerpts from his story—that of a 17-year-old warrior:

"The Militia gathered in the month of November near the old site of Underwoods Mill and thence marched to London. Early in January they started for Chatham, but roads were very bad and it took nine days to make the journey of 65 miles. There was a driving rain, then snow and frost, and sentries under blankets found themselves encased as in frozen shrouds, and boots so frozen that they had to be thawed before they could be put on or removed. Many of them slept in a hayloft and felt thankful for the privilege... The ration wagons that were to follow got stuck on the Longwoods Road and never came up so they had to do as best they could... A message from Fort Malden that they were threatening attack with the schooner "Ann" hurried them away from Chatham. They started from there on a steamer (Cynthia) and a schooner. When two miles from the mouth of the Thames River, the steamer was found to be on fire, and while stopping to put it out, the cold was so intense that she was frozen in. There was no way but to sit until the ice was strong enough so that the men might walk on it ashore... Going ashore Mr. Parker broke through and would have drowned if I had not gone to his rescue. They went on foot along the shore of Lake St. Clair to what is now called Windsor... On the way James Thompson complained of hunger and was supplied with the best they had, a chunk of frozen pork."

Mr. Buttery recorded that there was no battle while he was at the frontier. However, while on guard duty in front of an old storehouse, where the G.T.R. Station (Windsor) stood, cannonballs shot from across the Detroit River struck the building above his head. When he reported the incident to Sergeant Freele, he was ordered back to duty. When further shots struck the building, Sgt. Freele and Buttery left the site.

George Buttery related an altercation he experienced with Captain McCormick after the end of the Rebellion. The occasion arose over the responsibility of gate-closing at the time of trespass of the Buttery property, subsequent to a social ball that was given for the aristocracy of Adelaide by James Buchanan to celebrate the completion of his grist mill. Because he was not on military duty, Captain McCormick was forced to take orders from young Buttery—a form of retaliation to counteract McCormick's domineering spirit.

Charles Rapley, an Adelaide Militiaman, left an account of some of his experiences in a letter to his parents in Petworth, England, in October 1838. He was a drummer of the Adelaide Regiment. He mentioned that every man (between the ages of 16 and 60) was subject to call-up. He also mentioned that any who were thought to be disaffected were passed over. Fortunately, most, but not all, of the Adelaide settlers were loyal. In his account, he relates the frequency and seriousness of the Militia muster, especially the annual muster call. Rapley describes the weather and travel conditions that made moving to the frontier very difficult. The following is an excerpt from Rapley's letter via Nielsen:

"When we were out, our regiment searched homes, and disarmed several persons, but not a shot was fired by any of our regiment at any person, or at any of us by them; there was a schooner with some rebels, and cannons, arms, ammunition, etc., taken after considerable firing by the Chatham and Kent people at Amherstburg, about two days before we got there; we went from London to it, a distance of about 140 miles, and the travelling was very bad at the time; it had froze, then thawed, attended with heavy rain, then froze again. The marshes at the mouth of the River Thames were overflowed for about 14 miles, sometimes we waded through and sometimes we walked on ice."

Another soldier of the Militia was Patrick Mee of Lot 13, Con. 3 NER. Mee was an Irish immigrant who came to Adelaide with the Radcliffs. In 1836, he married a Miss Crummer, daughter of a Waterloo veteran who was also an early Adelaide settler (Lot 6, Con. 2 NER). In the winter of 1837-1838, Mrs. Mee, with a small child in her arms, accompanied her volunteer husband to Amherstburg. Later, Patrick Mee became the first reeve of Adelaide.

In addition to the Adelaide Militia Company commanded by Major Wm. Radcliff, an Adelaide Regiment of Express Cavalry was formed in 1838. This special regiment contained Privates from Warwick, Plympton, Sarnia and Moore townships, as well as Adelaide. This cavalry regiment was commanded by Colonel W.M. Johnston, with John Keyes as his Sergeant. A single record of this regiment survives, giving an account of allowances paid for billeting, stabling of horses, forage, rations, fuel and light.

Other military loyalties and anecdotes of Adelaide's early Militia may be contained in family accounts of the early settlers of Adelaide.

The Aftermath And Legacies Of The Rebellion

As 1839 continued, the drastic economic depression of 1837 was showing signs of clearing. Immigration to Canada from Britain, nearly halted by the bad times and political disorders, began to flow again. Trade was recovering and the pace of life started to quicken. From April 1939, knowledge of the recommendations in Lord Durham's report promised not only responsible government but also an end to the Compact rule.

The events leading up to and including the actual military involvement in the Rebellion imparted two chief legacies to the residents of Adelaide. First, an opposition to the Tory Government was firmly established. Adherents to this group were called "Reformers," and they preserved the reform movement in a political party known popularly as the "Grits." Second, the successful defence of Canada's borders put beyond doubt the principle of "volunteerism." This principle was fundamental in keeping a military presence in peacetime for the remainder of the century, and, more importantly, volunteerism was the backbone of Canada's outstanding military contribution in WWI and WWII.

It may be of interest in passing that, from 1832 through 1843, the price of a bushel of wheat at Toronto fetched from 3*s*. 9*d*. to a high of 8*s*. (about .90¢). The peak price was reached in 1837. By 1843, Adelaide farmers were reaping harvests ranging up to 25 bushels per acre.

Mid-Century Years For The Militia

It was customary in the Militia for the regimental officers to wear uniforms on duty. A wedding solemnized on March 18, 1848, between Jane Preston and John Kearns, a Sergeant of Her Majesty's 20th Regiment stationed in Adelaide

Village, was gay and colourful. Many of the attendees were dressed in the scarlet and gold uniform of the Kearns Regiment. The bride's father, Lieut. Charles Preston of Lot 4, Con.10 SER, was in a green uniform. This was the dress colour of a regiment stationed at Cornwall, in which Charles Preston served in the Rebellion of 1837-1838.

In the years after 1839 until the end of the century, the attraction for the military waxed and waned as significant world events came and went. Britain's involvements in the Crimean War (1854-1856), and the outbreak of the great mutiny in India among the native troops in the service of the East India Company in 1857, rekindled military enthusiasm in Canada. A visit to Canada in the summer of 1860 by the Prince of Wales, later King Edward VII, afforded an opportunity for Militia regiments to meet him. Although there is no authentic record, undoubtedly the Adelaide Militia would have appeared on parade before him.

The call for men in the American Civil War (1861-1865) touched the neighbouring people of Canada. The attractions of military life and the bounties offered induced several young Canadian men to enlist. In the early years of the war, Britain's ruling class sympathized with the Secessionist South. Canadians had divided sympathies; many favoured the South, while others sided with the Northern States. Although Canada was prepared to participate along with Great Britain in an invasion of the Northern States in 1861, actual involvement was averted by British diplomacy. Then, Britain announced a policy of neutrality with respect to the war in the U.S. Consequently, it was illegal for Canadians to enlist in the U.S. Forces. Nevertheless, a former Adelaide young man, Samuel Preston, enlisted and served with distinction. He was the son of Lieut. Charles Preston, Lot 4, Con. 10 SER. On graduating in 1861 from the U.S. Naval Academy in Annapolis, Maryland, he was commissioned and pressed into service in the Union Fleet. He was killed in the second naval attack on Fort Fisher, North Carolina, in 1865. His body was interred in the Annapolis Naval Academy Cemetery. In recognition of his meritorious service, four different U.S. destroyers were eventually named in his memory.

Spillover Effect Of The Crimean War (1854-1856) And The American Civil War (1860-1865) On Canada

During the Crimean War, the price of a bushel of wheat in Canada rose from .30¢ to $2.25. There was an unlimited demand in Great Britain because Russia had occupied the Danubian Principalities, cutting off wheat exports to Britain. In 1857, a Depression followed and the price of wheat fell to .69¢ a bushel, accompanying a low demand.

The American Civil War meant good economic times for Canadian agriculture. Beef, more than wheat, found ready markets in the U.S., and farmers increased their herds of cattle. There was also a brisk demand for horses for the U.S. Cavalry. These strong prices naturally reflected favourably on

---

Samuel William Preston

Samuel William Preston was born April 6, 1840, son of Charles and Jean Preston of Metcalfe Township. Charles was an army lieutenant. In exchange for a pension, he obtained land in Metcalfe in 1834, and in 1843, he donated four acres of land for a church and school house, resulting in today's St. Mary's Church. Samuel and his parents left the area and probably moved to Illinois.

He was appointed midshipman from the state, and enrolled in the U.S. Naval Academy in 1858. His class of 1862 graduated one year early due to the need of officers in the Civil War and he was top of his class. He went from Master, October 4, 1861, to Lieutenant August 1, 1862 and became Flag Lieutenant to Rear Admiral D.D. Porter. He was captured in September 1863, and taken to Libby Prison. Preston was exchanged for rebel prisoners in the fall of 1864. He had meetings with General Ulysses S. Grant and President Abraham Lincoln. He was killed in an attack on Fort Fisher on January 13, 1865. He was later buried at the U.S. Naval Academy Cemetery. Today, a Canadian flag decorates his grave site.

After his death, six ships were named after him, four being destroyers. Photographs of the four destroyers, U.S. Naval Academy Chapel, and the Commission Invisible Window were sent by the Naval Academy to be displayed in the vestibule of St. Mary's Church.

Due to the fact that St. Mary's Church only has one service each year, these pictures have been refurbished to be displayed in the Strathroy Museum, and are taken to the church for the annual service.

Anthony Preston, Samuel's brother, was Clerk of Adelaide Township for 36 years, from 1842 to 1878.

558 ADELAIDE TOWNSHIP... A HISTORY

Adelaide's economy, and caused a temporary boost in land-clearing of farmland.

The Fenian Threat

Since 1840, The U.S. had become home to many thousands of refugees from Ireland. The Fenian Brotherhood, a secret organization in support of independence for all of Ireland, took on a genuine significance in the 1860s. At the end of the U.S. Civil War, recruits from disbanded forces and jobless veterans joined the "Brotherhood." Britain and Canada learned of Fenian plans to invade and conquer Canada in order to use it as a means of driving the English out of Ireland. An alert for preparedness went out to all the military in March 1866. On June 1, a report was received and published by the *London Free Press* that a band of about 600 Fenians had crossed the Niagara border, were encamped near Fort Erie, and had plans to move farther inland. In March, a call had gone out to the Canadian Militia to recruit 10,000 volunteers. More than 14,000 presented themselves for duty. Volunteers from the Militia Forces at London, with additional troops from Oxford County, were dispatched to Niagara on June 2. A skirmish took place between the invaders and Canadian Militia near Ridgeway. The Fenians were routed.

Militias in the London District were also made ready to secure the U.S. border at Sarnia. This point was chosen because of its excellent connections with such nerve centres as London, Stratford and Toronto. Acting upon weighty rumours, on three separate occasions British troops and Canadian militiamen were ordered to Sarnia in 1866 to repel threatened attacks by Chicago-based Fenians. The threats proved to be groundless. Although the Adelaide Township Militia was in a state of preparedness, there is no official record of their involvement as a unit. James Henderson, who later resided on Lot 16, Con. 3 NER, served with the Oxford detachment that was dispatched to Niagara.

The Continuing Role Of The Militia And Its Changes

Prior to the mid-1850s, British North America had a "Sedentary Militia." The Militia Act of 1855 brought about an "Active Militia" of 5,000 men, armed and equipped, and 5s. a day for 10 days' training every year. At this time of prosperity, the London-Sarnia branch of the Grand Trunk Railway was constructed. Because of Adelaide's failure to negotiate satisfactorily with the railway, the village of Adelaide was bypassed, and by 1856, the town of Strathroy started to emerge as the new metropolis on the railway line (see Fig. 3). At that point, the Militia of Adelaide shifted from the village, apparently to Strathroy.

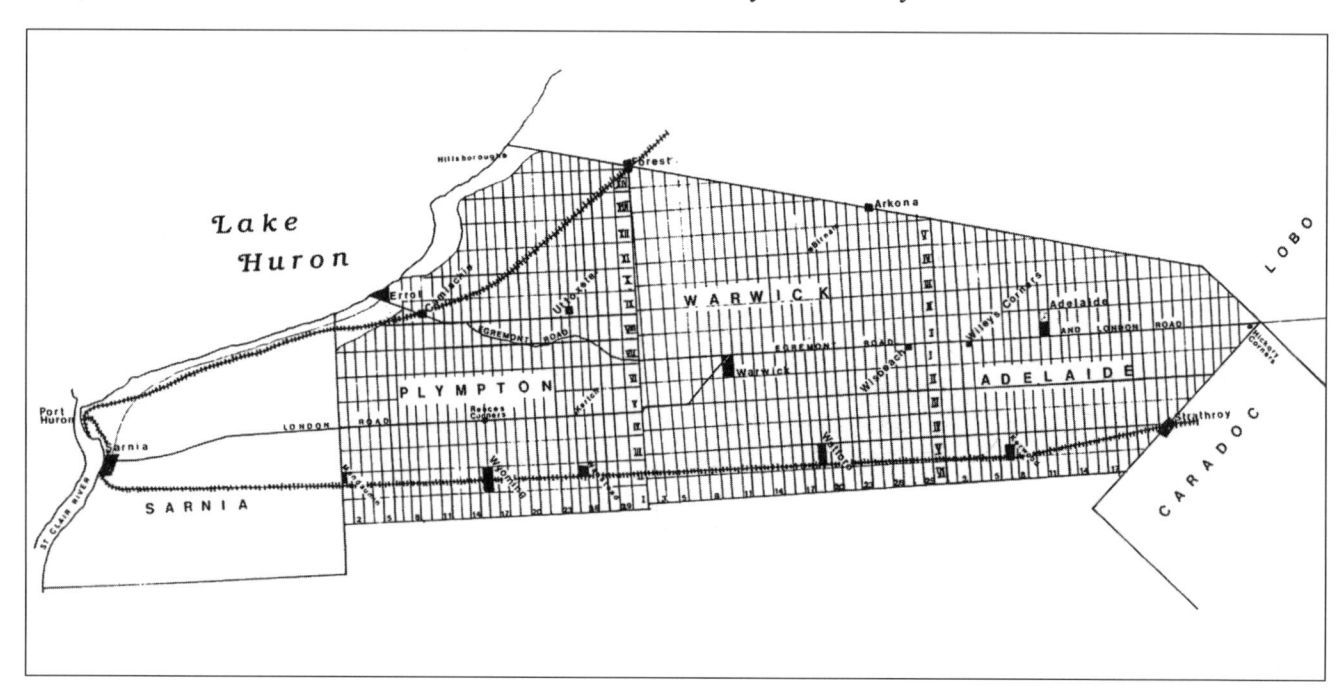

Map of Plympton, Warwick and Adelaide – 1866, showing the railways and new settlements (drawn by E. Nielsen).

Militia Reorganization Of District No. 1, 1870-1882

In 1870-1871, the First Brigade Division of Military District No. 1 comprised the regimental divisions of Essex, Kent, Bothwell, Lambton; West, North and East Ridings of Middlesex; West and East Ridings of Elgin; North and South Ridings of Oxford; and London City. The 26th Middlesex Regiment under the command of Lieut. Colonel William Graham had headquarters in London. It included seven companies, with No. 7 Company stationed at Strathroy under the command of Captain John English.

In 1873, the 26th Battalion assembled at Strathroy under the command of Lieut. Colonel Attwood and Major English. The entire Battalion numbered about 300, consisting of seven companies. Captain Irwin, Lieut. D.M. Cameron, and Ensign McKay commanded No. 7 Company from Strathroy.

Northwest Troubles Of 1885

The Northwest troubles of 1885 were due to grievances registered by "half-breeds" and native Canadians arising from railway construction across, and other concomitant changes to lands. They sought redress and failed to receive any. The complainants saw the Mounted Police force strengthened, while their situation was degenerating into one of ultimate servitude. At Duck Lake, the Northwest Mounted Police were defeated by the Metis.

To put down the Rebellion, Militia Forces were sent from many areas of Eastern Canada during the late winter and early spring of 1885. In April, the Seventh Fusiliers left London for the Northwest. The force consisted of 210 officers and other ranks. It is possible that one or more Adelaide volunteers were in this regiment. In all, the Canadian government had 8,000 men in the field. In mid-May, the Rebellion was quashed. The Metis leaders and Louis Riel were taken prisoner and sentenced. The Seventh Fusiliers returned to London in July.

The Northwest Rebellion demonstrated that the Militia of Canada, as reorganized after Confederation, was capable of carrying out its assigned duties. It is to be noted that the fighting forces were under the command of a British Army general. The Riel Rebellion did two other things: first, it helped change eastern attitudes about the Prairies, and second, because of rail transportation of Canada's eastern Militia forces to the west and back east, attitudes toward the C.P.R. were favourably changed. Both of these changes augured well for Canada.

Because Louis Riel was French, his hanging left a blot on the French-English relationship in Canada.

Canada's Military 1885-1913

In Canada in the 1880s, a Militia commission became a badge of respectability in a society acutely conscious of social status. In the 1890s, the Federal Government established permanent schools for the Militia. After the Liberal victory in 1896, Sir Wilfrid Laurier took the defence of Canada seriously and greatly expanded the Militia. The slogan "A National Army" for Canada was promoted.

As the crisis in South Africa deepened in 1899, Canada felt obliged to take a stand. Britain went to war. Laurier faced a much divided cabinet. Ontario's Members of Parliament clamoured to send a contingent, whereas French Canada thought that the Dominion had no business risking lives in England's colonial wars. Laurier agreed to support Canada's involvement. Between October 1899 and the end of the Boer War in 1902, Canada had sent a military force of 7,300 men to South Africa. It may be of interest to note that there is no record to show that any of Adelaide's men were involved in the Boer War.

For the Canadian soldiers participating in the Boer War, it made them confident about their capability of carrying their end effectively in the cut and thrust of battlefield experiences. Actually, service in South Africa set a precedent for Canada's role in WWI and WWII.

A new Militia Act was promulgated in 1904. Henceforth, command of the Militia would be open to Canadian officers. Nevertheless, British officers continued to hold the senior positions for another dozen years or thereabouts. The rate of military reform and military expansion between 1904 and 1914 was unbelievable. In retrospect, it is apparent that, by 1909, the Canadian Militia was being prepared for a role in the great European War, which seemed almost inevitable. Under the Liberal government, the budget for the Militia Department rose from $1.6 million in 1898 to $7 million in 1911. During the following three years, the Conservative government raised this Department's expenditures by another $3 million. The rise of military costs drew a strong and ready response from many Canadian citizens. Farm organizations deplored the waste of time and money on the Militia. By and large, Adelaide Township men looked with disfavour on military expenditures. Because the Militia was occasionally called in to break up strikes, a growing Workers' Union movement forbade members to join. Also, conscientious objectors could be found throughout Canada from several religious persuasions. It is also noteworthy that, beginning in 1909, many of the secondary schools in Canada offered cadet training. Several of the Adelaide men who found service in WWI and WWII took cadet training as part of their secondary school curriculum at Strathroy Collegiate Institute.

Preparation For WWI

The South African War had given Canada an opportunity to think about war. As well, a few keen officers had obtained experience under British instructors. One such officer was Col. Sam Hughes who, later, under the Conservative government elected in 1911, became its Minister of Militia and Defence. Canada had produced few characters to equal Sam Hughes, who was given the nickname, "Drill Hall Sam." In the words of one historian, he was "A man destined to live and die without a single doubt." He exuded self-confidence and was considered to be a blustering bully. Nonetheless, he was a staunch Imperialist, even though he had publicly criticized his British superiors for what he considered inept conduct in the South African conflict. Although his abrasive manner won him few friends in Ottawa, nothing diverted him from promoting military preparedness for Canada. Yet, when war broke out in August 1914, Hughes used his boundless energy and initiative to develop Canada's military machine. Although Prime Minister Robert Borden had some misgivings about Sam Hughes, he showed great tolerance toward his shortcomings. Borden wrote about him as follows: *"During about half of the time he was an able, reasonable, and useful colleague, working with excellent judgement and indefatigable energy; for a certain other portion of the time he was extremely excitable, impatient of control and impossible to work with; and during the remainder his conduct and speech were so eccentric as to justify the conclusion that his mind was unbalanced."*

By 1913, the world-wide Depression falling on the heels of the previous year's economic slowdown had taken the surge out of Canada's militarism. Unemployment soared everywhere. Crop failures hit the Prairies, and land and real estate prices fell disastrously.

Early in the summer of 1914, most Canadians were oblivious to the alarming events taking place in Europe. The newspapers from which Canadians obtained most of their news were not much better informed.

Canada Faces The Outbreak Of War

On August 4, 1914, at 8:55 p.m., news reached the Governor General's office in Ottawa that war between Great Britain and Germany had broken out. "When Britain is at war, Canada is at war," said Prime Minister Wilfrid Laurier in 1910. By the summer of 1914, it was still presumed to be true, although Laurier was no longer in power. Canada was a British nation and King George V was King of Canada. Patriotism could not be hidden. Canadians loyal to Great Britain called themselves Imperialists.

A government like Canada's, with little idea of what to do about the war—and fearful of doing too much—found volunteerism, a principle firmly established in the Rebellion of 1837-1838, a blessing. By August 7, Canada's offer to Great Britain, to bear the full cost of a contingent of 25,000 men, had been accepted. Soon thereafter, the War Measures Act was promulgated. Col. Hughes, now firmly established as the Minister of Militia and Defence, took immediate action and summoned volunteers for an Army, sending out hundreds of telegrams to Militia colonels. The response was overwhelming. The construction of a military camp at Valcartier, just outside Quebec City, was established as an assembly and training area for overseas volunteer recruits. A hastily trained contingent of men, with horses and equipment, was made ready for overseas departure on October 3.

Few in 1914, if any, in Canada and elsewhere, foresaw the terrible extent of the war. In December 1914, Prime Minister Robert Borden said, "There has not been and there will be no conscription." He announced later that the Canadian Expeditionary Force (CEF) would rise to 500,000 men. For a country of 8,000,000 people, it was a bold promise.

WWI
THE SALVATION ARMY SOLDIERS' TENT RECREATION AND READING ROOM FOR HIS MAJESTY'S TROOPS

From: Pvt. Conkey 7130   April 3, 1914
lst (Battalion) - 1st Brigade (Reg 4) D (Company)
Address to reply to:
W.G. Conkey
1st Batt. 1st Brg.
D Co., C.E.F.
France

Dear Mother,

I leave for the trenches for a second time at two this afternoon and as I have only an hour to scribble this and get ready to leave, I cannot tell you all I'd like to. I am at present in the county of Kent on the south coast 7 miles from Dover and in Shorncliff. It is said to be the finest country in England. It is only ten minutes to the sea or channel and on a clear day, the chalk cliffs of France are visible. I have lost all signs of the rheumatism now and it is nice and warm over here now. Well you don't need to write if you don't want to waste time and paper for it is ten to one I never get them.

Well, as the time is going, I will have to close. I will try to write oftener this time.

                 I remain,
                 "TOOTS"

P.S. I happened to meet Mr. Chesham or I would have been here for another month. We are the only ones from Strathroy in England. He is a transport officer.

Canada's First Contingent Overseas And Its Training For The Western Front

One Canadian who was somewhat reluctant to volunteer for Overseas Service was Arthur Currie, who was living in Victoria, B.C. He was a Lieut. Colonel, commanding the 50th Gordon Highlanders of Canada. Currie was experiencing serious financial problems; speculative holdings of real estate on Vancouver Island caused him to face bankruptcy when prices of real estate properties fell disastrously in 1913. To cover his real estate debt, Col. Currie had misappropriated $10,880 of Militia regimental funds designated for the purchase of new uniforms. He hoped that this misuse of funds would not surface until he could manage replacement. Rather than remain in Victoria in command of Military District 11, a post he had been offered by Defence Minister Hughes, he was persuaded by fellow regimental officers to look for something better. Minister Hughes then offered the 38-year-old Currie command of the Second Infantry Brigade. He accepted and left for Valcartier, Quebec. Neither the Prime Minister nor the Militia took any action on Currie's financial affairs, and Currie sailed overseas as commander of the Second Brigade.

Because Arthur Currie, who later became Canada's first general, was born and educated in Adelaide and at Strathroy Collegiate Institute, the residents of the township and town followed Currie's future and the progress of the war every step of the way.

Early on, Currie realized his lack of combat experience, showed constant devotion to study and duty, and his staunch dedication paid impressive dividends.

Minister Hughes was greatly displeased that he was adeptly manoeuvred from the position of Overseas Commander of the Canadian Forces. In October 1914, he managed a visit overseas in an unofficial capacity, and was awaiting the arrival of the troopship carrying the Canadian Contingent to Plymouth, England. He was given a grave warning by the Prime Minister to avoid friction with the authorities on the other side of the Atlantic. When he learned of the British plan to break up the Canadian Forces and assign them to British regiments, he "blew up" during a meeting with Lord Kitchener. He went further and demonstrated his unwillingness to take orders from the War Office in London, England. Lieut. General E. Alderson, a veteran of the British Army who had commanded the Canadians in the South African War, was appointed commander of the First Canadian Division Overseas.

The Canadian troops were destined to spend 16 memorable weeks on the Salisbury Plains. It was memorable for the appalling conditions of rain and mud, and housing in tents under cold, almost unbearable conditions. During January 1915, the weather improved somewhat, but not as the Canadian soldiers would have liked.

Col. Currie impressed British regulars attached to the Division. By his manner and physical stature, he created an atmosphere for himself. When General Alderson was asked by the Duke of Connaught to assess the Canadian Brigadiers, he replied, "Currie is out and out the best."

For his duties and responsibilities as the Minister of Defence, Col. Sam Hughes was given the rank of Major General by the Prime Minister.

Faults In Soldiers' Equipment

Although the Canadian troops endured their advanced training under harsh weather conditions, it was not their only complaint. Much of the equipment, including uniforms, boots, webbing, etc., that they took overseas did not stand up in service, and had to be replaced before the troops went to France. The only piece of equipment to survive was the Ross rifle, and its days were numbered. These shortcomings did not speak well for the manufacturers Defence Minister Hughes had selected.

Recruiting In Canada

Within a year of the declaration of war, 85 infantry regiments across Canada had been recruited or were recruiting. The Middlesex Regiment (135) was finally authorized to start recruiting on December 15, 1915. Meanwhile, volunteers from Adelaide joined up with other regiments.

Move To The Front And First Baptism Of War

On February 7, 1915, the First Canadian Division departed for France. Toward the end of the month, the Division was attached to General H. Smith-Dorien's Second Army. The water and mud that the soldiers knew on the Salisbury Plains was not a patch on that encountered in Flanders.

Col. Currie and the two other Brigade Commanders were made Brigadier-Generals to conform to the British ranks.

In mid-April, the Canadian Division was moved into front line trenches covering a sector 4,000 metres long in the Ypres salient. They relieved French troops. It was a bad defensive position, as the British had found out in the first battle of Ypres the previous autumn, because the Germans held most of the surrounding high ground.

In March, the Canadian Divisional Headquarters issued a document entitled "Principles of Defence," which declared that the cardinal principle of the defence scheme of the Division is a determination to hold the front line trenches at all costs! Where a trench was lost to the enemy, it was to be regained by a counterattack carried out promptly and with resolution. Canadians followed this dictum faithfully throughout the war. Acting aggressively and courageously became their motto.

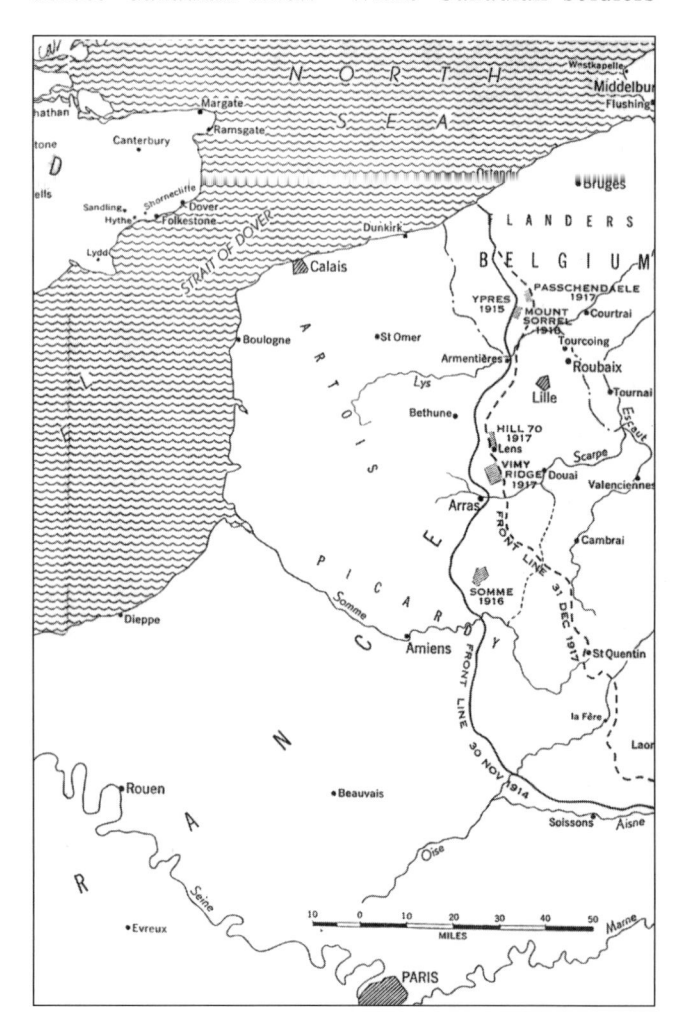

Rumours of the possible use of chemical gas by the Germans were heard, but discounted because of its disallowance by the International Declaration signed in 1899. At 5:00 p.m. on April 23, the Germans launched their offensive against the Ypres salient with a heavy artillery bombardment. The first use of gas in modern warfare was begun by the Germans a few minutes later. Chlorine gas exerted a ghastly effect on the exposed soldiers. In their part of the salient, the French troops fled and soon were in complete rout. Despite some breakthroughs by the enemy, the Canadian forces held on doggedly. The next day, the Germans continued their attack with more shelling, and more releases of gas drifted across Canadian lines. While Canadian soldiers were fighting with all the strength they could muster, their Ross rifles jammed under rapid fire. The flanks of the Second Brigade commanded by Currie were unprotected during a major part of this second battle of Ypres, but the Brigade fought well. The other two Canadian Brigades also performed admirably. At the end of the battle, telegrams were received by General Alderson, the Divisional Commander, from Field Marshall French, Commander-in-Chief of the British Expeditionary Forces (BEF) and from King George V, expressing admiration for the gallant conduct of the Canadian troops in repulsing the enemy. The battle of Ypres (see Fig. 4) cost the Canadians 6,000 casualties, nearly one-third of the Division's strength. It was a battle no Canadian wanted to remember, yet it marked a place in Flanders made famous by the courage and valour of the Canadian soldiers.

Trench Warfare

By the end of the second battle of Ypres, Canadian soldiers thoroughly understood that no-man's land was the space between their own and the enemy's trenches, pockmarked by shell holes and craters containing barbed wire entanglements, fragments of equipment and human bodies, etc. The idea of a trench war stalemate lasting for another 3½ years was inconceivable. Potent memories of the soldiers included persistent infestations of body lice and rats scavenging for food almost daily. Even worse were the frequent and sometimes continuous rain showers, resulting in waterlogged trenches. The Flanders soil was often churned into mud, which adhered to the boots, uniforms and equipment—an experience never to be forgotten.

Events Of 1915-1916

In the summer of 1915, Prime Minister Borden visited the Canadian Military Headquarters (CMHQ) in London, and also talked with the British High Command at the War Office. He had difficulty in convincing the British of the role that the Canadian government and their military leaders were capable of assuming in the execution of the war. He was frustrated with the level of consultation about a war in which Canada was playing so vital a part. After a determined stand, he won the right to have Canadian officers appointed up to the level of Divisional Commanders at the fighting front.

In the spring of 1915, the second Canadian Division reached England. It moved to France in September. Then the First and Second Canadian Divisions formed a Canadian Corps under the command of General Alderson. General Sam Hughes felt greatly slighted that he had not been given command of the newly formed Corps. However, in recompense for his other valuable services Hughes was knighted. Two Canadian Brigadiers, Arthur Currie and Richard Turner, were assigned command of the First and Second Divisions, respectively. They were promoted to the rank of Major-General to conform to British service. Hughes was shocked by the losses at Ypres and furious that General Alderson had replaced the Ross rifle with the Lee-Enfield. Hughes had despised British generalship in the South African War. Now, he raged that the generals were as hopeless against the Germans as they had been against the Boers. When General Alderson formed his new Headquarters, the Minister insisted that Canadians fill the staff jobs. His own son, Garnet Hughes, became a Brigade Commander.

The war in France did not go well for the Allies in 1915. In assaults on German Army entrenched positions, at Festubert on May 18 and at Givenchy on June 15-16, the Canadians did not fare well. Heavy casualties were sustained and the gains were minimal. France referred to the year 1915 as "l'annee sterile" (a year of no gains). In that year, General Sam Hughes insisted on spending much of the summer overseas with "his boys." The organization and training of the Canadian Forces in England was confusing and was not producing the fighting soldiers required as replacements for the casualties in France.

During the cold winter of 1915-1916, the Canadian Corps stood guard in front of the Messines Ridge. The Canadians were at a disadvantage because the Germans strategically held the surrounding higher ground. From the Canadian trenches, a series of underground tunnels was excavated across to, and under, the German trenches, enabling mines to be exploded in the spring offensive of March and April 1916. This offensive mounted against the Messines Ridge was soon blunted. It became known as the "battle of the craters." These assaults proved to be a costly experience in manpower and territory lost. As a result, General Alderson became the scapegoat and was relieved of the command of the Canadian Corps. He was replaced by General Sir Julian Byng. It took Byng upwards of a year to mould the Corps into a good professional organization.

In March 1916, the Third Canadian Division was formed from units already in France and England. Major General Mercer was given command. The Division saw its first front line action on June 1 at Mont Sorrel. In an opening deluge of enemy artillery fire General Mercer was killed. Major General Lipsett replaced him. Mont Sorrel was lost to the Canadians. A counterattack the next day by Currie's First Division failed. A second counterattack on June 13 by Currie's Division captured Mont Sorrel. Careful planning and preparation followed by a heavy artillery bombardment preceding the infantry advance was the key to success. Mont Sorrel had established Currie as one of the rising stars in the British Army. His pre-attack planning, ensuring that all officers and other ranks alike, knew their strategic objectives and the terrain over which they had to move—leaving nothing to chance—was his common sense way. The lesson that Currie and Byng learned should have been learned by other British generals before July 1, for on that day the long, costly, bloody Battle of the Somme was begun by the British Armies. By nightfall of the first day, 21,000 soldiers lay dead; these were the most terrible losses the British Army ever experienced in a single day.

The Canadian Corps was spared action on the Somme until September 15, when the British and Canadians attacked German front lines around Courcelette. Attacks and counterattacks characterized the bitter fighting around Courcelette before the Allies advanced to the Regina Trench. The fourth Canadian Division, which had arrived in France in August, joined the Canadian Corps. On October 10, this Division was assigned the task of capturing the Regina Trench—a low depression in the chalk down. After two unsuccessful assaults, the objective was taken on November 11. This was enough fighting for the year. Two months of fighting had cost the Canadians in excess of 24,000 in casualties—the equivalent of one complete infantry division. The Canadian Corps was exhausted. In November, the Somme offensive floundered in the mud with the Allies making no breakthroughs. British casualties exceeded 350,000 men.

The war on the Western Front in 1916 would not be complete without a brief mention of the horrific battles south of the Somme area around Verdun. On June 1, the Germans attacked Verdun and its two forward defence posts, Forts Vaux and Douaumont. To the French, Verdun was a sacred place. It was the best fortified area along the French border. To retain France's glory, Verdun could not be sacrificed. Continuous attacks and counterattacks carried on over more than four months did not result in a breakthrough for either France, or its inveterate enemy. In this long, horrendous battle, the French had suffered more than 360,000 casualties, while the Germans

Dr. Walter C. Morgan, received Military Cross in WWI (also served in WWII).

suffered in excess of 320,000. The year 1916 was a morale-destroying one for nearly all armies involved in this European War. For the Western Powers, the year closed in deep gloom.

Behind The Lines In 1916

A growing sense of dissatisfaction in the conduct of the war led to a cabinet revolt in the British government. This forced Britain's Prime Minister Herbert Asquith to resign on December 5. He was succeeded immediately by David Lloyd George.

In 1915, the Allies had pinned their hopes on Russia to defeat the Germans on the Eastern Front. Russia fell short on these expectations. Several of her armies had crumbled and, by the end of 1916, her capacity to muster adequate military strength had severely ebbed.

During the latter half of 1916, the sinking of Allied ships in the Atlantic, both naval and merchant, had increased four-fold. The indiscriminate German U-boat attacks would ultimately bring the U.S. into the war.

General Joffre, the French Army Commander-in-Chief, warned General Haig, Commander of the British Forces on the Western Front, that the British Army would have to assume more burden in 1917. Verdun had inflicted a very crippling blow on France's military strength.

The Canadian military administration in England was in a sad state of disorderliness. Borden knew of the trouble and had sent Minister Hughes overseas on two occasions to clear up the mess. He not only failed to improve the situation, but in the summer of 1915 created a Fifth Canadian Division in England for his son Garnet to command By September 1916, Borden had enough. Sir George Perley was appointed Minister of Overseas Military Forces of Canada based at London. Minister Hughes raged and protested back in Ottawa. On November 9, Borden dismissed his troublesome minister.

With the reorganization in the overseas ministry, the Canadian Expeditionary Force (CEF) in France came under Perley's authority. An understanding was reached that Canadian soldiers would still serve under British command as allies, but not as colonials. This change reflected a greater role played by Canada in the war.

Despite feelers for peace at the year's end and continuing into 1917 between the Western Allies and Germany, mediated by President Wilson of the U.S., nothing came of it.

History Of Middlesex 135 Infantry Battalion

By General Order 151 on December 22, 1915, the Middlesex 135 Infantry Battalion (Bn) obtained authority to mobilize with its headquarters at London, Ontario. The Battalion consisted of four Companies (Coys). "A" Coy recruited at Strathroy, "B" Coy at London, "C" Coy at Parkhill and "D" Coy at Glencoe. Many of the Adelaide boys were recruited to Bn 135 after November 1915. Under the command of Colonel B. Robson, the Battalion trained from November 20, 1915, to August 1916 at Carling Heights, London, and for six weeks at Camp Borden, before entraining for Halifax and departing for overseas on August 23, 1916. Advance training in England was at Witley Camp. On December 24, the battalion was broken up to reinforce other Infantry Battalions. "A" Coy was absorbed by 134th Infantry Bn (48th Highlanders of Canada); "B" Coy by 116th Ontario County Infantry Bn; "C" Coy and "D" Coy by 125 Infantry Bn (Brant County) and the Eighth Reserve Bn.

The History Of The Pride Of Middlesex

Just one short year has passed,
Since Middlesex gave birth,
To the 135 Battalion
The finest in all the earth.

It grew throughout the winter,
And when the spring came round
There was a strapping company
In each recruiting town.

"A" Company found its home
In the village of Strathroy;
And "B" Company contained
Full many a London boy.

Parkhill boasted "C" Company
As all of us do know,
And "D" was mustered up
'Round about old Glencoe.

And when the springtime came,
And the grass began to thrive,
Old London was prepared,
To welcome the 1-3-5.

They came from all the little towns,
And tented at the cove;
'Twas then we were real soldiers
In every act and move.

And when we finished shouting
To Carling Heights we moved,
And in the summer evenings
Through London streets we roved.

Then Sam Hughes took a notion
To profit on some land
So he made a summer training camp
At Borden in the sand.

He took us there with others,
To live in sand and dirt
And for weeks to never hear
The rustle of a skirt.

Six weary weeks had passed,
When we had to move once more
So they slipped us down to Halifax,
Upon the Atlantic shore.

We sailed the briny ocean,
In a trusty transport ship,
The sea was very calm,
And we all enjoyed the trip.

It was in the town of Liverpool,
We struck the land again,
And in the south of England
We went aboard a train.

We came into a camp
In the middle of the night,
We found that it was Witley,
When we saw it in daylight.

We lay around a week or so,
Then they gave us six day passes
Or eight days, if we wished to see
The Scotch or Irish lasses.

We started in to work again,
When we got back from our cruise,
And everything was going fine,
'Til along came old Sam Hughes.

Soon after his little visit
The orders came one day
That the 135th Battalion
Must shortly fade away.

The news came as a death blow,
To part us friend from friend,
For we'd meant to stick together,
Until the very end.

We left our heart-broken Colonel
On a misty October day,
And to join our future units,
We wearily wended our way.

"A" Company went to the kilties,
And "B" to the one sixteen,
"C" and "D" with the Brantford boys
Will show the Kaiser what they mean.

But friends when this war's over,
Those who are spared alive,
Will remember the Pride of Middlesex
And the good old 1-3-5.

Composed by Pte. Ferguson Maguire (1917)

Adelaide's Activities In Support Of WWI

In response to the Dominion Government's appeal for support for the Patriotic Fund, Adelaide Township Council took appropriate loyal action in November 1914. A grant of $2,000 requested by a newly organized Patriotic Committee was approved in December. To raise monies for the Patriotic Fund, local Patriotic Committees in many school sections sponsored picnics, garden parties and evening programs during the war years. On January 29, 1915, a Patriotic fundraising event was held at Payne's School House S.S.#11.

To meet the British Red Cross Society's urgent need for hospital bedding, equipment, medications, etc., Adelaide Council approved grants of $500 in both 1916 and 1917. Also, grants of up to $150 were approved for Red Cross Circles to help them finance their projects to supply knitted socks, scarves, balaclavas, etc., for soldiers overseas. In June 1915, the women of West Adelaide raised $90, and S.S.#4 raised $91.54, from a successful picnic on a Red Cross appeal. Township Council records list the following project leaders: Mrs. M. Brock, Adelaide; Mrs. A. Downer, Bethesda; Mrs. H. Dennis, Crathie; Mrs. J. Brunt and Mrs. Mills, Kerwood; Mrs. A. Cuddy, West Adelaide. Undoubtedly, there were several other leaders representing other areas of the township.

In the winter of 1914-1915, three pairs of woollen socks were knitted by Henry Miller of Adelaide Village, to be forwarded to the brave soldiers at the front. Henry, a retired township clerk, had been crippled for some years.

Reports Of Soldiers On Front Line Duty

Early volunteers from Adelaide saw front line action when the First Canadian Division was assigned duty in the Second Battle of Ypres in May 1915. Reports were received back home in June about the welfare of privates Jack Pcddcn, W.G. Conkey, and O'Dell. Lance Corporal R. Allan Bolton, Royal Canadian Engineers, had been injured in the battle of Langemarks.

Company Sergeant-Major Fred Piper Killed In Action

A few days before receiving word of his death at the front, Fred Piper's parents, Mr. and Mrs. Arthur Piper, received word from him about the horrible battles the Canadians were engaged in. Their son described acts of heroism and bravery. He concluded his letter as follows: *"It was simply hell—facing the shell, rifle and machine gunfire of the enemy. Some of the boys who were wounded may talk as they like about wanting to get back to the firing line, but not me, I never want to see the like again."*

Death Of Frederick Roy Adair

The funeral of Pte. Frederick Roy Adair, of "A" Company, Bn 135, who died in the military hospital, London on June 21, 1916, was held from the home of his uncle and aunt, Mr. and Mrs. Walter Bolton. Pte. Adair was born and grew up on Lot 15, Con. 3 NER. Six comrades served as pallbearers. Captain A.P. Malone and Lieut. D. Campbell dutifully represented "A" Coy.

Social Events

Communities of the township recognized the departure of soldiers and nurses for military duty at appropriate farewell parties. One such social evening was held on Good Friday evening, 1916, at Keyser's Forresters' Hall. Wrist watches were given to Lieut. Donald Campbell and Ptes. Beckett, Albert Galloway, William Tigner and Arthur Prittie (West Williams). Major O.L. Berdan of Strathroy, representing Bn 135, acted as chairman for the evening.

Clarence Kerswell, Popular Adelaide Boy, Enlists

A very enjoyable evening was spent at S.S.#6 on February 11, 1916, to honour Clarence Kerswell on his departure for overseas service with the artillery of the Middlesex Bn. He was presented with a silver wrist watch and a gold signet ring from his many friends.

Agriculture Is Put To The Test

By the end of 1915, Canadian agriculture was under heavy pressure to help keep the Western Allies supplied with food for humans and feed for animals. With French farms being stripped of manpower to meet military demands, and because Russian wheat shipments were blocked in the Black Sea, the Allies called for all the surplus food Canada could produce. The bumper cereal crops in the Prairies in 1915 saw much poorer harvests the following two years because of severe droughts and serious yield-reducing rust epidemics on "Marquis" wheat. In Adelaide, military recruitment and factory production needs were siphoning away farm help. Women had to go to the fields to assist men in gathering the harvests. Later, some food restrictions led to rationing. The Canadian slogan "Everyone must do his bit" struck a responsive chord in the hearts of all.

1917—The Western Front

During the cold, wet winter of 1916-1917, the Canadian Corps faced Vimy Ridge, a long slightly curved hill rising above the Douia Plain. It was capped by one small prominent elevation called the "Pimple." The Ridge remained securely in German hands since the autumn of 1914, although both French and British Armies had tried to capture it. It was a key fortress on the Hindenburg Line. Heavy gun emplacements supported with numerous machine gun pockets gave the Germans confidence that the Ridge was impregnable. General Byng gave the Canadian Corps the challenge of capturing the Ridge.

General Currie had visited Verdun the previous autumn to study the strategies that offered the most promise to the French Armies in that horrible and bloody stalemate. Over the winter, Currie decided how to implement some of these promising tactics at the Ridge. Generals Byng and Currie did extensive planning for the attack. Miles of tunnels, dug-outs and bunkers were excavated and stocked with ammunition and supplies. Every soldier was familiar with the terrain and knew his duty. Nothing was left to chance. Signallers laid miles of communication cable. The artillerymen knew how to pin-point objectives. They were thoroughly coached on how to advance their overhead firing to give the infantry the ultimate in protection.

In sleet and snow, the attack began on Easter Monday, April 9. All four Canadian Divisions were used. By noon on April 12, the capture of Vimy Ridge was complete. "It was a triumph of courage over terrible danger, but it was a victory of other qualities, too—discipline, foresight, ingenuity, hard work—virtues it had taken time for the Canadian Corps to develop." In the victory, nearly 3,600 Canadians lost their lives—that was the tragedy. The French said that at Vimy, the victory was "Canada's Easter gift to France." The American historian, William Manchester, said, "It was at Vimy Ridge that the Canadians won the reputation of being the finest soldiers on the Western Front."

In 1936, several hundred Canadian veterans went to Vimy Ridge to commemorate the unveiling of Canada's great memorial to her war dead.

After Vimy, General Byng was promoted to command the Third British Army. There was little doubt of who his successor should be. Sir Arthur Currie was given command of the Canadian Corps and promoted to the rank of Lieutenant-General. The gradual replacement of British officers in Canada's fighting forces was symbolic of a trend toward Canadianization. In the King's birthday honours list of June 1917, Currie was made a Knight Commander of the Order of St. Michael and St. George (KCMG).

In March 1917, Prime Minister Borden attended the first meeting of the Imperial War cabinet. In his spare time, he visited the Canadian troops in France, training camps in England, and every military hospital. Before returning to Canada, Borden had another problem on his mind. He was desirous of pacifying a still troublesome Sam Hughes. He asked Currie to accept Garnet Hughes as new commander of the First Division. Currie refused, replying that the ex-minister's son was incompetent. Borden dropped the issue; Sam Hughes did not. Knowing the urgent need for more reinforcements in France, Borden returned to Canada in May in a grim but determined mood.

In August, the Canadians were given a new objective—the mining town of Lens. Currie knew that the Germans held the hills flanking Lens and this would give the enemy a tactical advantage. Currie proposed taking one of the higher elevations, "Hill 70," knowing that the Germans would attempt to take it back. Currie was confident that with Hill 70 captured, the Canadian artillery under Colonel Andy McNaughton would be able to repulse counterattacks. Sir Douglas Haig, British Commander-in-Chief, approved the plan. On August 15, Hill 70 was captured following an exceptionally heavy artillery barrage. Then, as Currie had expected, the Germans mounted counterattacks, actually 21 in all, against the Hill. Canadian artillery with supporting machine-gun fire defeated every counterattack. The battle cost Canadians more than 9,000 casualties, while the enemy lost more than 20,000 men. It was a Canadian victory, but a costly one.

Jointly, the French and British armies had planned a summer offensive against the German lines. In the south, the French offensive failed. The British armies drove toward Passchendaele Ridge. The attack lay across reclaimed marshes. The very wet weather had clogged drainage and rendered the marshes almost impassable. British armies became hopelessly bogged down after suffering losses exceeding 68,000 men. In October, Passchendaele Ridge was still held by the Germans.

General Haig summoned the Canadian Corps. It was to be pulled away from General Byng's Army, holding fronts at Vimy and Lens. Remembering the horrible experiences suffered in 1915 at Ypres, Currie protested. Orders were orders. Currie obeyed and was granted some time to make plans. Wooden platforms to mount the artillery above the muddy bogs were improvised. Corduroy roads were constructed at critical sites. On October 26, the First and Second Canadian Divisions were committed. Little more than 100 yards were gained in four days. After a week's time elapsed to reconstruct roads and bring up supplies, the First and Second Divisions were replaced by the Third and Fourth Divisions. The final attack was begun on November 6. Ten days later, the Passchendaele Ridge was in Allied hands—but at a cost of more than 15,000 casualties, and memories of another horrendously muddy, bloody struggle. As was the loss of Vimy Ridge, so was the loss of Passchendaele Ridge to the Germans.

Farther south, Julian Byng's Third British Army showed what might have been accomplished had good foresight been used. British tanks had smashed through German lines on a six-mile front near Cambrai, but because of too few infantry, the advantage of the breakthrough was lost. A Canadian Cavalry group, along with a Newfoundland Regiment, fought valiantly around Cambrai, but in vain. Passchendaele and Cambrai had exhausted the British Army and discredited its generals.

Currie's Tactics And Strategy

Currie's blueprint for victory resulted from a visit to Verdun where the horrible four-month battle stalemate between the Germans and the French armies took place in 1916. Currie believed that the role of the artillery was vital. John Swettenham observed that, after Vimy Ridge, "It is significant that no later Corps attack, when planned by Currie, was ever unsuccessful."

Militia Fund Misappropriation Issue

In 1917, Arthur Currie made good the misappropriation of funds from the 50th Regiment, Gordon Highlanders of Canada, as of 1914. He acknowledged receipt of some financial help from fellow officers.

Canadian Political Events Of 1917

Politically in Canada, 1917 was a very difficult year. A grim Prime Minister Borden returning from London in May knew that reinforcements had to be found to maintain Canada's fighting forces overseas. On June 11, the Military Service Act was presented to Parliament and, on August 29, conscription became law. Sir Wilfrid Laurier, leader of the Liberals, had opposed the bill. Although conscription split both Conservative and Liberal parties, Borden could see no alternative. On October 6, Parliament was dissolved and a federal vote was called for December 17. On October 12, Borden

---

ALICE ANNIE NETTLETON (1897-1918)
V.A.D. (VOLUNTEER AID DETACHMENT)

Alice Nettleton, daughter of William and Emma (Austin) Nettleton, was born in Adelaide Township. She received her primary education at the rural school on the old homestead where her mother had taught. She attended East Adelaide Presbyterian Church and Sunday School. When she was 12 years old, the family moved to Kittredge Ave., Strathroy. After completing her studies at Strathroy Collegiate Institute, she took the V.A.D. course in London, and became a member of the St. John Ambulance Brigade. Then, Alice went to Oyen, Alberta, to teach school. When the school was closed because of the influenza epidemic in 1918, she turned to nursing in the emergency hospital at the nearby town of Cereal. After three days of illness from influenza, Alice died, and her body was brought back to Strathroy Cemetery, where she was buried on November 28, 1918.

This 20-year-old is the only woman named on the Strathroy Memorial Cenotaph.

---

announced his plan for the formation of a Union government. Laurier refused to become a part of the coalition.

Although conscription was a main concern of the election campaign, there were other issues. Despite General Currie's efforts to remain neutral in the election, his leadership became a political football. Charges were made that he had been reckless regarding the lives of Canadians. To him, the criticisms over casualties suffered, particularly at Passchendaele, were especially painful. False rumours had also been circulated that his health was failing. For military security reasons, a true historical account of the military events and battles involving the Canadian Corps in France at that time could not be made available to Canadians back home. Currie would give Borden a more complete account of Passchendaele later.

To maintain agricultural production, farmers' sons would automatically be exempted from conscription. Other exemptions stated that aging parents would not be left without a breadwinner.

In English Canada, newspapers were periodically leaking reports that Quebec was not giving loyal support to the national war effort. Recruitment of volunteers for military service in the province had become a dismal failure. French Canadians found reason to defend their stand with both politics and religion being involved. By mid-1916, French Canada's indifference to the war was hardening to anger.

The absence of uniform loyalty throughout Canada was hurting the cause of patriotism. Adelaide residents had strong prejudices, but openly expressed them with great reluctance. Assuredly, the residents of Adelaide would do their part.

Borden and the Unionists won a one-sided victory. The overseas vote was overwhelmingly in support of the government. The election pledge that all women would be entitled to vote was a big stride toward gender equalization. This and many other issues gave the Union government many challenges when Parliament opened on March 18, 1918.

War Weary: The Struggle Goes On

By the end of 1917, it was obvious that the war was not going well for the Allies. Menacing U-boat attacks continued to cripple British shipping. France had suffered severe humiliation because the strategies of its military leaders had not produced a single important victory. By November, the last of a series of provisional governments in Russia was swept away. The Tsarist monarchy had ended; civil war had broken out and, militarily, Russia was out of the war. The Austrians had almost destroyed Italy as a military threat. The bright spot was that the U.S. had entered the war on the Allied side.

Because of serious manpower shortages, the British High Command had decided to reorganize its armies with supposedly more effective fighting units—reduce the size of its divisions from four to three battalions and so on down. The War Office wanted the Dominions to follow suit. General Currie was insistent upon no change in the organization of the Canadian Corps. He was called to London to defend his views. He used Canadian battle records to justify his stand. A compromise was achieved when he recommended an increase in the size of the platoon (the functional, efficient fighting unit) from 30 to 40 men.

With Germany being relieved of fighting on the Eastern Front, the Allies anticipated new enemy offensives in France. During the winter of 1917-1918, the Canadian Corps was given the task of defending Vimy Ridge at all costs.

Leonard Carrothers, One Man's Story

Leonard Carrothers joined the 149th Battalion on January 11, 1916. The battalion soldiers received their training at Petrolia until May 1, moved to London for two months, then on to Camp Borden, which was occupied by 10,000 men in training. The 149th were perfecting hand-to-hand combat fighting with bayonets.

In the fall of 1916, the battalion returned to London at the Fair Grounds. Leonard was billeted under the grandstand. He transferred to the Signal Corps of the battalion and learned Semaphore and Morse Code signaling during the winter.

One day in the first week of March 1917, at 4:00 p.m., the 149th boarded a troop train at the C.N.R. station in London, heading for England via Halifax. At a stop in Moncton, New Brunswick, about 100 women met the train, carrying clothes baskets filled with food and pails of coffee. Leonard said it was a welcome change from bully beef and hardtack and greatly appreciated by the troops.

On arrival at Halifax, the battalion and three other battalions (4,000 men) were put aboard a White Star Liner, the "Lapland." The hold of the ship was filled with Red Cross ambulances.

When they steamed out of the harbour, the Halifax bands played "This is the End of a Perfect Day." Leonard stated that the first day out was calm but the rest of the trip was quite rough, with high seas created by March storms. He states he was one of a few soldiers who never got seasick during the crossing. On the ninth day, six English destroyers came out to escort the three troop ships in to Liverpool harbour. At 1:00 p.m., Leonard went on guard duty in the front steerage. His duty station was at the bottom of the stairs. His duty was to keep the troops that were bunked in this section from going down to secure blankets, etc., while the ship was in the danger zone.

"At 1:15 p.m., the ship hit a mine; the bow leaped up, then down. All I could see was water and kit bags rushing up from the two lower decks. I grabbed the stair railing and raced up. When I got to the top, water was about four feet behind me and 37 feet of ocean water was in the bow section below me. The mid and rear sections remained dry. As a result, the ship's propeller was just skimming the water. It took us almost four hours to reach Liverpool. Upon docking, we disembarked and went to Bramshot for a 10-day quarantine."

The army was looking for volunteers to go to France in the Canadian Forestry Corps—anyone who had experience working in the bush, a sawmill, or who could handle horses. Leonard applied as one of the teamsters, was accepted, and was sent to

Sunningdale (about six miles from Windsor) to select his team. He selected two matched heavy black Percherons. The Corps had 35 teams.

"We left Sunningdale around the first of May as '36 Company Canadian Forestry Corps' at 4:00 a.m. with each teamster astride one of his harnessed team, to travel nine miles to the station and be loaded on a train before sun-up in order not to draw attention from the air, etc. We went to Southampton, loaded our teams on a boat. They used a crane with a sling and swung the horses down into the ship's hold. We hit a storm crossing the channel to La Harve, and the breakers were so strong that the top deck was awash most of the way across. Many of the horses fell down and others would roll over them, so we had quite a time untangling and settling them down.

"At La Harve, we loaded eight horses with their food in each railroad car, along with two men. We were heading for the Jura Mountains; three days later, we arrived. All we could see around us were balsam trees. They picked a spot about half a mile from the station to build a sawmill. We slept under poles with brush on top. It rained most of the time; we dried out at night around brush fires. After we got the mill built, we got lumber to build a mess hall and kitchen, then huts to sleep in. We were put on French rations of black bread, horse meat, and rabbit once a week for about two months, then we got our own Canadian rations.

"The first six months I skidded logs with my team from 7:00 a.m. to 6:00 p.m., seven days a week. When winter arrived, I quit skidding logs in the bush to drawing logs by sleigh. The sleigh had 12' bunks with four corner binds, king pins on the front and back bunks. The bunks and sway bars would fold up when empty; when loaded the load would be approximately 14' wide on the bottom and decked to a peak of about 10'. We tried to keep the load to about 2,500 board-feet. We used a tandem team, my heavy team of Percherons on the pole with a light team on front. When the weather got cold, it was hard to keep your hands warm handling four reins. I was given a Russian prisoner to drive the front team. He was a good driver and could handle horses well. He couldn't speak English but could speak French, so we used French. Once I made a mistake of not locking the inside runner of the sleigh with a chain to act as a brake and to hold the sleigh straight to go down a steep grade for about half a mile. My team could normally hold the load but on this occasion the sun made the ice road slippery so the 2,500 board-feet of logs started to go sideways. We had to stop holding back on the load and let the teams at it to keep the load and teams from going over the embankment which was over 100 feet down. I was glad I had a good Russian driver with me; he didn't panic, he kept his team out front and didn't put any pressure on mine. When we got to the bottom of the grade, the teams were at a full gallop.

"I must say we got 500 Russian prisoners from the French to use for labour; they were fighting on the French front, had no money for two months and poor rations. They rebelled; the French turned machine guns on them. We got those who were left.

"In 1918, our mill and camp was moved up the mountain to within five miles of the Swiss border. We were now getting Sundays off. We would go to the top where the precipice was almost straight down into Switzerland. A great view; we could see Mt. Blanc to the left, Lake Geneva straight ahead, and ice peaks shining above the clouds. A beautiful sight to watch thunder storms crossing the country, lightning flashing above the clouds below your feet and the sun shining brightly overhead.

"After the Armistice was signed, our agreement with the French was to cut one-tenth of the forest and leave the roads in as good condition as we got them. We drew thousands of tons of crushed stone, which the Russian prisoners had made using 5-pound hammers.

"In February 1919, after the roads were repaired, we left France for England and were sent to a demobilation depot at Kimmel Park, a few miles from Ryle, Wales.

"Four days after a 3,000-man riot, the government quickly hired three White Star Liners from the U.S. I arrived back in London, Ontario, on March 21, and received my discharge from the Army."

The Closing Year Of The War

On March 21, 1918, three days after the 13th Canadian Parliament opened its session, the German armies struck. The British Fifth Army, which hadn't recovered fully from the Passchendaele mauling of the previous autumn, was routed within a week. The enemy penetration was deep. The First and Second Canadian Divisions were removed from the Canadian Corps to help plug the gap. Currie's appeal for their restoration went to the highest levels of the War Office. Keeping the Canadian Forces together was approved, but the First Division did not rejoin the Corps until June 1. The Canadians were responsible for covering a front of nearly 25 km., of necessity a thin line of defence.

In 16 days of fighting, each side lost 250,000 men. It was a frightful disaster for the British armies. Passchendaele Ridge, which was taken by the Canadians during the previous autumn, was retaken by the enemy after only token British resistance. The German spring offensive drove the British and French from some of the most blood-stained ground on the Western Front.

During the spring, General Currie used available non-combat time to improve the fighting efficiency of the Canadian Corps. In June, Marshall Foch, now supreme Commander of the Allies, visited Currie's Headquarters, and was impressed. The Corps, he said, was "an Army second to none, deriving its immense strength from the solid organization of each of its component parts, welded together in battle conditions."

In Borden's Union government cabinet, the Military Service Act was debated with acrimony. Exemptions to the Act were appearing farcical. One hundred thousand soldiers were needed overseas. On April 12, it was agreed that all exemptions from conscription would be cancelled. No longer were farmers exempt from military duty. Many rural populations of Canada seethed with rage—an election promise had been broken. By the end of the year, more than 99,000 Military Service Act men wore the uniform of the Canadian Expeditionary Force. In May, the Prime Minister had to leave Ottawa to attend meetings of the Imperial War cabinet. Borden called Currie to London to get the real story on Passchendaele. Currie told him of its horrors and that Canadian efforts were in vain. To boost morale in the French and British Forces was the political motivation for ordering the Canadian offensive against Passchendaele, Borden was told. Currie also related to the Prime Minister his own version of the March disasters. Later, Currie was told by Lord Milner, then Minister for War that, if the war went into 1919, he would be in command of the British Army.

Sir Arthur Currie and son, Garnet, at an official homecoming celebration in Strathroy, 1919.

Canada's Fifth Canadian Division in training in England was broken up to make available more than 20,000 reinforcements for the Corps in France. Toward the end of the Imperial War cabinet meeting, the Prime minister cabled Ottawa: "The Canadian Army is admittedly the most formidable striking force in the Allied Armies... To Currie's ability, I believe, he is the ablest Corps Commander in the British Forces."

Royal Visits

During the war, King George V paid several visits to front-line forces under British command. In 1918, a memorable inspection of a Canadian platoon of soldiers took place. His majesty stopped momentarily in front of Pte. William Tigner of Adelaide. It must have been obvious to the sharp regal eye that Tigner was considerably older than his comrades were. In speaking to Tigner, the King asked, "How old are you?" Putting regal dignity aside, he quipped, "How old do you take me to be?" The king smiled at him and then walked on.

The Last Hundred Days

In their March-April offensives, the German armies had been halted short of capturing the vital railway town of Amiens. Field Marshall Douglas Haig was given orders to push the enemy back in the Amiens sector. A consistently effective striking force had to be called upon. It was the Canadian and Australian units to which they turned. The Canadians and Australians had nine divisions in all. Enemy reconnaissance kept a careful watch on Canadian manoeuvres. Their position in the line was an omen of where an Allied offensive thrust might be made. A Canadian feint attack at Ypres was quickly followed by a carefully concealed march of the troops to the Amiens sector. Currie said, "We made the plan. We set the time and the place of battle." Artillery firing of 2,000 guns was integrated with a forward surge of 470 tanks. Communications were aided by aircraft spotters. The Australians, led by General Sir John Monash, were to advance simultaneously on the Canadians' left flank. French armies were on the right.

At 4:20 a.m. on August 8, the unsuspecting Germans were struck by the British First Army, spearheaded by the Canadian Corps. Surprise was total. The Canadians advanced 13 kilometres and the Australians almost as far. This was the greatest forward advance for any side in a single day of the war. The enemy front-line divisions almost ceased to exist. Many prisoners and guns were captured. The Canadian Corps lost 1,036 killed and 2,800 in other casualties. General Ludendorf, the German Chief of Staff, called Amiens "The black day of the German Army in the history of the war." It was the triumph the Allied generals had been waiting for.

On August 11, Haig allowed Currie to change fronts and start attacking the Hindenburg Line—a trench and fortification system that took two years to build. Once again, careful preparation took place with masses of critically aimed artillery fire. From August 20 to August 30, the Canadians battered a way

W.G. "Toots" Conkey, served in WWI and WWII.

Allan R. Bolton, Lance Corporal

Stanley Bolton

Pte. Archie Campbell

Lt. Art Anderson, Lt. Ashell Barry and Lt. Dan Campbell, 1919.

Charles Morse

through the Fresnes-Rouvroy section of the Hindenburg Line. Then, after a week's rest, the troops pushed through the more imposing Drocourt-Quéant Line. These offensives caused heavy loss of life. Some of the Military Service Act conscripts were now finding their way to the Canadian Corps as casualty replacements.

One major obstacle remained; the unfinished Canal du Nord. Once again, Currie insisted on time to prepare. The strategy devised, although risky, turned out well and again caught the Germans by surprise. The Canal du Nord battle started on September 26 and, within a week, the Canadians were on their way to Cambrai.

The use of the Canadians in almost continuous action as a spearhead for the British forces caused some soldiers to grumble that General Currie was a glory-seeker demanding the bloodiest tasks for his Corps. Australians made the same charges against their general, Sir John Monash. Without conscription to fill its ranks, the Australian Corps had to be pulled out of front line action on October 5. British divisions, partly as a result of organizational changes made the previous year, began to lack fighting endurance. However, on the whole, British armies were in far better shape than Marshall Petain's French forces.

The French town of Cambrai fell to the Allies on October 11. In retreat, the German soldiers fought a stubborn, well-disciplined rearguard action, relentlessly inflicting casualties on the advancing Allied forces. As Canadian soldiers trudged on, often soaked by the autumn rains, the First British Army directed the Canadian Corps on to Valenciennes. For four days, the Corps marched forward on paved roads, following the retreating German divisions. As they approached Valenciennes, it became obvious that the town was a key defensive point in the Hermann Defence Line. The approaches were dominated by a heavily defended hill, Mont Huoy. The Canadian artillery pulverized the hill with a massive use of shells. With comparatively low loss of lives, Valenciennes fell to the infantry on November 2. The triumphant Canadians swept on to the town of Mons. Elsewhere along the entire Western Front, German

Fred McKeen, enlisted 1917, served overseas in 1918 toward end of war.

resistance was collapsing. The border was crossed into Belgium. On November 10, Canadians entered Mons, where the war was begun for the British Expeditionary Force in August 1914. At 11:00 a.m. on November 11, the firing ceased. The war was over.

Pte. Robert James Foster

William Duncan Ireland

Dr. Alfred E. Morgan

Henry "Harry" New

Frank Pennington

Sgt. Emerson Shrier

Herbert Tomlinson

Clarence Ward

ADELAIDE RESIDENTS IN WORLD WAR I

Adair, William
Anderson, Arthur James
Anderson, W. H.
Armstrong, James Harvey
Bailey, John
Bailey, Maisie
Becket, W. P.
Bolton, Frank
Bolton, R. Allan
Bolton, Stanley
Bolton, William R.
Branton, Cliff
Buttery, Russell George
Campbell, Archie D.
Campbell, Donald McLean
Campbell, Ernest

Carrothers, Leonard
Chittendon, H. L.
Conkey, Harold Norman
Conkey, William George "Toots"
Currie, Sir Arthur
Fletcher, Malcolm C.
Foster, Robert James
Galloway, Albert James
Gilbert, Francis
Graham, Lorne Talmage
Graham, Herman
Haggar, William
Hansford, Isaac
Healey, Wilfred J.
Ireland, Clifford
Ireland, William Duncan

Kerswill, Clarence
Lewis, Fred
Lewis, George Samuel
McCabe, Leo James
McGeary, James Neil
McKeen, Fred
McKenzie, H. R.
Mee, Brian Herbert
Milliken, T. W.
Morgan, Dr. Alfred E.
Morgan, Dr. Walter Corneil
Morse, Charles
New, Henry "Harry"
Patten, George S.
Patterson, John Moore
Pedden, Jack

Pennington, Franklin
Ramsey, Wilfred "Fred"
Salsbury, J. R.
Shrier, Emerson Nelson
Sullivan, Harold Winston
Sullivan, Wilfred Vernon
Tarrant, Harry
Tigner, William Arnold
Tomlinson, Herbert
Ward, Clarence
Willoughby, Wesley
Wilson, Loftus
Wilson, Wallace
Wilson, Wilfrid
Wright, De Lloyd

Wilfrid and Loftus Wilson

**Armistice And Return Of Combatants
To Canada For Demobilization**

After the Armistice was signed, the First and Second Canadian Divisions marched to the Rhine and became part of the Army of Occupation. The Third and Fourth Divisions spent part of the winter of 1918-1919 in garrisons in Mons and Brussels. Demobilization plans moved forward as rapidly as possible, but not fast enough to satisfy homesick soldiers.

The endurance of more than four years of war had jaded the optimism of most adults on the home front. Tensions with deep political (and even religious) overtones had worn the spirit of Canadian unity thin. The sudden outbreak of the worldwide influenza epidemic saddened the grim outlook of the citizenry. The virus struck families with a vengeance, killing men and women in the prime of life even more quickly than the youngest and the elderly. By the end of December, nearly as many deaths resulted from the "flu" epidemic as from the war in Europe.

Fortunately, the war had some positive effects. As the Revolutionary War of 1776-1783 had won American Independence, WWI would move Canada a long way toward being a sovereign nation. Canada had a signature on the Peace Treaty of Versailles and became a member of the League of Nations.

Veterans streaming back to Canada from the holding camps in England and on the continent expected a hero's welcome. For the most part, the veterans with the longest service found, on returning home, that Canadians had learned to live without them. Currie was justifiably proud of the Canadian soldiers. He said, "Any success that has come to me has been won for me by the wonderful soldiers I have been privileged to command." He had hoped that each regiment would return to its home area as a unit. This was not possible. For the most part, veterans returned one by one to receive their welcome home. On July 1, 1919, Dominion Day celebrations at Strathroy featured a military parade of veterans.

In the immediate wake of the war, orthodox economics set in. With rising interest rates, there followed a downspin in the economy. The government insisted upon spending cuts. That was not what most Canadians expected of the peace—certainly not so for the war veterans who looked for rewards for their sacrifices. Government generosity was reserved for the disabled and for dependents of the war-dead. The able-bodied must fend for themselves. Consequently, war service gratuities were meagre and did little to help veterans adjust to a non-military society. General Currie fought hard for adequate war pensions. In the wake of WWI, several Veterans' Organizations sprang up across Canada. Pre-eminent among the groups was the Great War Veterans' Association (GWVA, 1917-1926). Through its monthly magazine, Veteran, it strongly espoused the causes of veterans, and it had the ear of government. At a National Conference in Winnipeg in November 1925, the GWVA surrendered its status in favour of forming the Canadian Legion of the British Empire Service League, as representative of all Veterans groups.

**Sir Arthur Currie Branch Of
The Royal Canadian Legion**

On January 19, 1928, a group of returned soldiers met at the Strathroy Armouries and formed a local Legion, Branch 116. The membership would be $3.50 per annum, Militia members would be allowed to join, and charter members would be those who enlisted from the Strathroy area with the longest service.

On September 6, 1961, the Legion members voted to name the branch after charter member Sir

Arthur Currie, a native of Adelaide Township. On December 12, 1964 the Ladies Auxiliary of the Sir Arthur Currie Ontario #116 was chartered.

Currie And The Aftermath Of The War

Sir Arthur Currie returned to Canada after receiving several honours overseas. He and his family came ashore in Halifax on August 7, 1919, to be greeted in a rather cool reception. A day later, he arrived in Ottawa by train where a formal, decorous ceremony was held for him on Parliament Hill. Because Prime Minister Borden was on royal duty, Sydney Mewburn, Minister of Militia and defence, honoured Currie at a banquet that evening where he was paid high tribute. Mewburn took the occasion to announce that Currie had been promoted to a full-ranking General. This was Canada's first soldier to achieve such a high honour. Mewburn also announced that Currie was being appointed to the position of Inspector-General of the Armed Forces.

Being unaccustomed to the deadening atmosphere of decision-making in federal politics, Currie was neither happy nor comfortable with the position of Inspector-General. However, during his brief tenure, he developed a plan for a Permanent Force and a Militia for Canada, which was introduced in the spring of 1920. But once again, public interest in the Militia, although newly organized, had begun to wane. In 1920, Currie resigned his position to become the Principal and Vice-Chancellor of McGill University—a post he held with great distinction until his death in November 1933.

Significant Domestic And World Events (1919-1939)

After the Armistice, Canadians were anxious to return to a normal life. Pacifism renewed its vigour. Agnes MacPhail, Canada's first woman M.P., was a devout pacifist, as was J.S. Woodsworth, who founded the Co-operative Commonwealth Federation.

In 1921, the federal Liberals formed a minority government under MacKenzie King. He had a marked aversion to the military life and the military mind. Keeping government costs down was of paramount importance. Defence needs were not seen to merit prime consideration.

In 1924, the Royal Canadian Air Force (RCAF) was legislated into existence. The Militia and Navy were envious of the RCAF's civil flying as a lever for public finds and fame.

Colonel Andy McNaughton, General Currie's chief artillery officer in WWI, was promoted to the rank of Major General and made Chief of the General Defence Staff. Under him there was close cooperation between the military and the National Research Council of Canada in fields of research that were a forerunner to radar.

During 1929-1938, all military budgets were chopped or reduced to find money for unemployed civilians. The budget for the Royal Canadian Navy (RCN) was reduced to almost nil. The Militia and RCAF fared slightly better.

In 1930, cadet training was still undertaken as a compulsory subject by male students attending Strathroy Collegiate Institute. Uniforms were changed from khaki to royal blue. Adelaide students well remember the drills during physical training class periods to promote military discipline. The annual inspection of the S.C.I. Cadet Corps in May was a significant event. The exercise ended in a parade through the downtown streets, marching to a drum and bugle band. For many years, this display of military training was under the command of R.L. Manning of the Collegiate Institute.

Wars And Stirrings Of War In The 1930s

In 1931, Japan marched into Manchuria and took possession. Other countries of the world found excuses not to intervene.

In 1933, Adolph Hitler came to power in Germany as leader (Führer) of the National Socialist Workers' Party, a right-wing party. It called for a rebirth of German pride and an end to the re-armament limitations of the Treaty of Versailles. His mesmerizing speeches were convincing to a following of ever-increasing numbers and strength. His party's domestic power soon began to overlook unseemly acts against the Jews. Hitler's strong following also led to the decline of political opposition showing any taints of Communism. He restored conscription and set out to build a powerful navy. The League of Nations was unable to demonstrate solidarity on any global issue.

In 1935, President Franklin Roosevelt signed the American Neutrality Act banning shipments of war material to nations at war. An amendment the following year prohibited financial loans to such nations.

Mussolini's Fascist Italy set out on a conquest of Ethiopia, and a year later, Hitler sent his troops to occupy the Rhineland without any outside opposition.

In the mid-1930s in the Far East, Japan was busy swallowing as much of coastal China as it could seize.

At the same time, the whole of Europe was seething with ideologies as workers' unions were clamouring for better deals. A nasty Civil War had broken out in Spain. Several political historians thought of it as the first real test of democracy against fascism. Representatives of all the ideologies of Europe became involved and sent combatants and weaponry.

In 1937, under communist Russia, dictator Stalin was carrying out a purge of the Army generals, politicians, intellectuals, and even ordinary citizens who dared to oppose the Communist Regime.

Later in the decade, it was Hitler's Germany that attracted most of the attention. In 1937, an Anschluss with Austria came about. The following year, Hitler annexed the Sudetenland of Czecho-Slovakia. The Munich Agreement signed in September 1938 gave Prime Minister Neville Chamberlain of Great Britain hope that a satisfied Germany would mean "peace in our time." By carefully crafted intrigue, Germany had rearmed its militant population with a powerful ideology and modern weapons, while the world watched and worried.

After 1935, the MacKenzie King government made tentative efforts to begin military preparations for a war many could see coming. These preparations were strongly opposed by the increasing number of pacifists. The Quebecois had memories of WWI and were determined not to be inveigled or conscripted into another British war. The political mechanisms for fostering war preparedness were all but choked off, even though the European storm clouds were threatening ominously. If war was inevitable, Prime Minister King was determined to bring Canada into it united, if at all possible.

Outbreak Of WWII

When the Panzer divisions of Germany crossed the border into Poland on September 1, 1939, Britain and France issued their ultimatum for a withdrawal. Germany ignored it. On September 3, war was declared.

The Parliament of Canada was called to a special session on September 7. After a three-day debate, Canada decided what its action would be. Prime Minister King made it clear that the decision reached should embrace an understanding "that our national effort might be marked by unity of purpose, of heart and of endeavour." The Prime Minister also repeated his pledge against conscription for overseas. On September 10, Parliament voted to enter the war on Britain's side, and Canada was then at war with Germany.

Despite Parliament's decision, many loyalties tugged at the minds of Canadians. The residents of Adelaide struggled with many of the same issues faced in 1914. Radios now carried news and messages into the homes that were carried only by newspapers in WWI. The time lag of news reporting was reduced, but it didn't alter people's concerns. As with 25 years earlier, loyalty to Canada's war effort would be the driving force.

Canada's unprepared fighting units were soon geared for a supreme war effort. At first, Members of Parliament were horrified to learn of the budgeted military costs for the first year of the war. Plans for the recruitment of three military divisions were reduced to two. Despite the Prime Minister's reluctance, the First Division would go overseas as soon as possible. Major-General A.G.L. McNaughton, a highly admired and successful artillery officer serving under General A.W. Currie in WWI, would be in command. The Division went to England in December and trained at Aldershot.

Patriotism invoked volunteerism. In September, 58,337 men and a few nursing sisters enlisted. In the first seven months of the war, nearly 85,000 Canadians had volunteered for active service. Recruiting for the Navy (RCN) and the Air Force (RCAF) was slower than for the Army at this time.

On December 17, a British Commonwealth Air Training Plan (BCATP) was created which was to deliver 20,000 pilots and 30,000 air crewmen per year. Most of the trainees were of Canadian, British, Australian and New Zealand origin. The construction of many air-training bases gave a boost to enlistment in the RCAF.

Germany Attacks On The West

In April 1940, Germany invaded Denmark and

Norway. Denmark fell at once and Norway held out only one week.

In Britain, Prime Minister Neville Chamberlain was toppled from power and was succeeded on May 10 by Winston Churchill. On the same day, Hitler released his Panzer divisions in a "Blitzkrieg" (lightning war) against the Low Countries and France. The German Air Force (Luftwaffe) added to the panic by dive-bombing attacks on enemy units. Holland was overrun in a few days and on May 20, the Germans were at Amiens, in France. Their fast-moving Panzer divisions swept up to the English Channel south of Calais trapping the British Expeditionary Force in a pocket along with the remains of the Belgian Army and a few thousand French soldiers. By a miracle, 338,000 British and Allied soldiers were evacuated from Dunkirk to England.

A hastily improvised scheme to construct and hold an Anglo-French fortress on the Breton Peninsula had to be aborted. France fell on June 12, and Hitler's puppet Vichy regime was installed. Canada now became Britain's biggest partner in the war.

Canada's Role Unfolds

By 1940, the seriousness of the war in Europe was touching the lives of all Canadians. Some provinces thought that Canada was weak and half-hearted in its war effort. The Royal Canadian Legion deluged Ottawa with telegrams calling for a complete mobilization of its manpower. On June 21, Parliament passed the National Resources Mobilization Act (NRMA) with registration taking place on August 19, 20 and 21. This gave the government powers to conscript for home defence. The first conscripts called up under NRMA reported to training camps across the country on October 9. At first, the call-up period of service was for 30 days. In February 1941, the period of service was extended to four months.

After France fell, MacKenzie King met with Franklin Roosevelt at Ogdensburg, New York, to establish a U.S./Canada Permanent Joint Board of Defence. To augment Britain's naval strength, Washington and London worked out a Lend-Lease Agreement. The Lend-Lease operated in favour of Britain's currency crisis by purchasing war orders through Canadian manufactured products. In the deal, many of Britain's colonial bases around the globe were leased to the U.S.

By late 1941, Canadians realized that their country was involved in a total war. To a degree unimagined in WWI, men and women were directed, advised and regulated. Major food items and gasoline were rationed. People purchased Victory Bonds and school children bought War Savings Stamps. Canadian manufacturing plants and workers were producing goods in a totally unparalleled manner.

The war created new opportunities for women—even if some were only for the duration. In 1941, women enlisted in the Army and Air Force; the next year, the Navy was opened to them. CWACS (Canadian Women's Army Corps), WRENS (Women's Royal Canadian Naval Service) and WDS (Women's Division, RCAF) enlisted in large numbers. Traditional male jobs opened up at home for females. Women drove buses and street cars, and worked in factories making weapons, munitions and a variety of goods to aid the war effort. On the farms, women drove tractors and helped harvest some of the most bountiful crops of the century. Also, by knitting woollen socks, scarves, sweaters, etc., women did their loyal duty for the military.

Children were also seen as a potential national resource. Those of public school age collected glass bottles, metal cans and milkweed floss. Those in high school tried to master arms drills in Cadet Corps.

For the only time in Canadian history, the whole nation was organized, involved and mobilized in a grand effort.

Germany Unleashes Its Terrors On Great Britain, Countries Of Central And Eastern Europe And North Africa

Two months after France surrendered, Hitler unleashed his powerful air squadrons against England. Fortunately, British Hurricanes and Spitfires outmatched the German Messerschmit fighter planes in the Battle of Britain. This thwarted Hitler's plan for the invasion of Britain.

At the same time, the Italians, who had joined the German cause in June, attacked British possessions in North Africa; control of the Suez Canal and the Mediterranean hung in the balance. The Italians invaded Greece. The Germans came to the aid of the Italians in the spring of 1941 to defeat Greece.

With an unbounded ambition, Hitler then moved his "Blitzkrieg" Forces to an Eastern Front and attacked Russia in June 1941. In six months, large areas of Russian territory had fallen to the German armies. They had overrun much of the Ukraine and were virtually knocking at the gates of Moscow. At this point, success for Germany and Italy in Europe was almost total.

Toward the end of 1941, the war became worldwide. On December 7, Japan bombed Pearl Harbour, Hawaii, catching the U.S. Pacific Fleet unaware, causing untold damage. The Japanese also struck at British Possessions of Hong Kong and Singapore. Two inadequately trained Canadian infantry regiments, sent in October to defend Hong Kong, were totally overwhelmed by Christmas Day by the invading Japanese Forces. Casualties were very heavy. Prisoners taken were often brutally treated, and many didn't survive to the end of the war.

The only bright spot for Britain and the Commonwealth at the end of 1941 was that the U.S. had declared war on Japan, and also on Germany and Italy.

Canada's War Problems

To safeguard the defence of Canada, the Federal government moved all Japanese Canadians inland away from coastal British Columbia, some as far east as Ontario.

The conscription issue raised its ugly head, as it had in WWI. The Right Honourable Arthur Meighen led the campaign for conscription. Meighen was the architect of the Military Service Act in 1917, and was brought back to lead the Conservative Party in November 1941. Volunteerism for overseas service was now failing conspicuously. The Conservatives pressed for conscription. Also, some serious disagreements within MacKenzie King's cabinet forced him to consider a plan to release the government from its pledge against compulsory overseas service. King gave the people of Canada the opportunity to vote in a non-binding plebiscite on the issue. The majority favoured conscription: 2.94 million voters were in favour and 1.64 million were opposed. The strong rejection in Quebec and in a few other smaller centres of Canada shook the confidence of the Prime Minister. He faced a seriously divided country and a split cabinet. It was at this time that the Prime Minister declared his stand with the ambiguous pronouncement, "Not necessarily conscription but conscription if necessary."

It was this vacillating stand by Canada's Prime Minister that tore at the hearts of Adelaide's residents, as it did all Canadians. Tensions developed among families and neighbours, as it had during WWI. Many were outraged at this Liberal dithering. Nonetheless, residents of Adelaide remained fully patriotic to their country.

The Dieppe Disaster

The Allies, particularly the Americans, wanted the earliest possible opening of a front in Western Europe. The Russians urged a diversion from the Nazi onslaught of their armies and people. A Canadian assault force was assembled and given the task of determining the feasibility of a cross-channel invasion. Dieppe, the little French town on the English channel about 80 km. south of Calais, was selected as a testing ground for amphibious warfare. The attack was made on August 19, 1942. The cost of the raid was very high in terms of military personnel killed and wounded and prisoners captured. Only a few of the objectives were attained. It was a costly learning fiasco for the Allied High Command. It was a crushing blow to Canadian morale that the media could not soften. Two more years of careful planning and preparation elapsed before the Allies felt ready to establish a Western Front on Fortress Europe.

Serious Losses In The Atlantic

With the fall of France, Germany took over the French ports and airfields. This increased the cruising range of German U-boats and the Luftwaffe. The Battle of the Atlantic intensified greatly. After 1940, the RCN had to assume responsibility for convoy escort, first south of Newfoundland, and a little later for the Western and North Atlantic. Convoys transported enormous tonnages of grains, foods, munitions and war equipment across the Atlantic. In 1942, the U-boat warfare reached into the Gulf of St. Lawrence and extended down the river as far as Quebec City. Consequently, in that year, shipping losses reached enormous proportions. It was in the Atlantic that the growing strength of the RCN was felt, where it acquitted itself well. Despite the price of naval inexperience, and though Canada was extremely unprepared, the growth and performance of the Royal Canadian Navy during the war was extraordinary by any standard.

The RCAF

The BCATP initially produced only pilots, air observers, and wireless operator/ air gunners. By the wrap-up of the plan, eight air crew categories were being produced. In all, 131,553 air crewmen graduated, of which 55% were Canadians. When the Canadian raid went in at Dieppe in 1942, 74 Allied squadrons, including eight from the RCAF, provided air support. Throughout the war, damage inflicted by aerial bombing, though terrifyingly dangerous, was severe, and civilian casualties were often staggering. Canadians had no chance to debate the strategy or morality of the bomber campaign. The claim had been established early in the war that air power would prove to be the decisive weapon of the war. Too much tribute cannot be paid to Canada's brave airmen.

A Turning Point Of The War

At the onset of winter 1942, the striking force of the German Army was stopped and trapped at Stalingrad in the Russian Caucasus. By January 1943, several German Divisions were demolished there. Subsequently, the Russians slowly but effectively started to push the German armies back along the Eastern Front.

By November 1942, General Montgomery's British Eighth Army had decisively defeated General Rommel's Africa Korps in the Battle of El Alamein inside the Libyan border in Egypt. At about that time, American and British Forces had landed in Morocco and Algeria, and would start their sweep across North Africa toward Tunis. By May 1943, the German and Italian Forces had been driven out of North Africa.

Italian Campaign

The next point of enemy engagement in the Mediterranean theatre was the invasion of Sicily with a start made on the plans of knocking Italy out of the war. Even before the invasion of Sicily, it was known that the Italian Armies were weak, poorly trained and badly equipped.

Ottawa and the Overseas Military Command decided that the time had come to split up Canada's Army. This decision was much to the disappointment of General A.G.L. McNaughton, who had led the Army since 1939. He was very adamant that the Canadian Army fight as a unit. However, that plan was scuttled, and the First Canadian Division with a Tank Brigade went to the Mediterranean to join the British Eighth Army for the invasion of Sicily on July 10, 1943.

After six weeks of fighting over very rough terrain, Sicily was in Allied hands. On September 3, the mainland of Italy was invaded, starting at the toe of the boot. While the Canadians worked their way northward with the British Eighth Army, the American Fifth Army made a successful amphibious landing near Salerno. After Naples fell to the Allies at the end of September, the Axis (German and Italian) resistance stiffened.

The original plan was that the Canadian First Division would return to England once Sicily was taken. Through a change of plans, this fighting unit remained in Italy and was joined by the Fifth Canadian Armoured Division to constitute the First Canadian Corps, with General Harry Crerar in command. Ottawa played a strong hand in the plan. Once again, the opinion of General McNaughton was overridden. It was felt that the time had come for more Canadian troops to see action and for its commanders to gain battlefront experience.

More Bitter Fighting In Italy

Hitler had ordered Rome to be defended at all costs. The enemy's Winter Line had been established south of Rome, cutting across the country from Ortona on the Adriatic through Cassino to the West Coast (see Fig. 5). Ortona was the anchor of the German Gustav-Hitler Lines and the capture of that sector fell to the Canadians. The attack began on December 6 and, after December 27, Ortona was in Canadian hands. During the three-week battle, all units of Canada's First Division suffered heavy casualties. The Germans finally withdrew from Ortona, knowing that every house and meeting place the Canadians might use was thoroughly mined and booby-trapped. Ortona will long be remembered by the surviving soldiers, their widows, and the grieving parents of the many Canadians killed.

During the winter lull, there were changes in the command of the Corps. The most senior and experienced commanders, Lieutenant-General Crerar and Major General Simmonds, returned to England to take leading roles in the First Canadian Army.

In May 1944, the fighting commenced again near Cassino. Before the end of May, the Hitler and Gustav enemy lines had been breached. By June 4, the American Fifth Army had liberated Rome. Two days later, the Allies established their Western Front in France. From then on, the Italian theatre became secondary in the minds of the people in England and Canada. This was due to the influence of the press, which gave its priority to the Western Front.

For the remainder of the summer and autumn, the Canadian Corps in Italy pushed northward, encountering stiff defensive rearguard action by the Germans. For all intents and purposes, the Italians were now out of the war.

The Apennine barrier was breached on September 22, with Ravenna being taken on December 16. At this point, the fighting in Italy ceased for the winter.

In February 1945, it was decided to have the Canadian First and Fifth Divisions transferred from the Italian theatre to join the First Canadian Army in Western Europe. This was accomplished in March.

In all, 92,757 Canadians served in Italy. Total casualties from all causes amounted to 26,254. As always, most of the losses were borne by the infantry.

The Western Front Opens

While theatres of WWII had been active in Eastern Europe, North Africa, Italy and the Pacific, the bulk of the Canadian Army remained in England—often bored with endless training exercises. The soldiers wanted field action. Although Canadians showed a warm affection for their leader, General A.G.L. McNaughton, it was not his fate to lead them into battle as a unit, as had been his firm resolve. The Allied Command always found reasons to oppose such a plan for the Canadian troops. In early March 1944, some two months after McNaughton was forced to relinquish his position and return to Canada, General Harry Crerar was assigned command of the Canadian Army.

By then, operation "Overlord," the secret code name for the invasion of Hitler's Fortress Europe, was well advanced in the final planning stages. Dependent on tides and weather, May and June were set as the two optional months for the invasion assault. At the final moment of decision, D-Day was June 6.

Mammoth preparations for "Overlord" involved the construction of two artificial harbours named "Mulberry," one for the British and one for the American Forces. They were floated across the English Channel and strategically sunk as embarkation points.

The German defence against invasion along the coast of France was in charge of General Rommel, who had built impregnable concrete blockhouses with fixed firing ranges commanding the beaches. This formed the "Atlantic Defence Wall."

Absolute air supremacy was the Allied Forces' chief asset. Canadian airmen and sailors were among the first into action. RCAF Lancasters of No. 6 Bomber Group dropped thousands of tons of explosives on enemy coastal defences. The Royal Canadian Navy provided 109 vessels and 10,000 sailors as its contribution to the massive invasion armada. Two Canadian destroyers, "HMCS Algonquin" and "Sioux," gave their utmost to silence enemy shore batteries. Armed merchant cruisers, "HMCS Prince Henry" and "Prince David," carried Canadian troops and the landing craft from which they made their run for the beaches.

In the pre-dawn morning darkness on June 6, 450 Canadian paratroopers landed behind German coastal defences. Canadian troops landed on the beaches a few hours later and waded ashore. Canada's Third Division, supported by the Second Armoured Brigade, went in on the assault. Although only one of the Canadian units reached its D-Day objective, the first line of German defences had been smashed. By the end of D-Day, successful bridgeheads had been established by the Allied Forces.

Almost immediately, all invaders met German counterattacks. The Normandy towns and countryside seemed a ready-made fortress for German troops, tanks, machine-guns, and formidable 88-mm anti-tank guns. German resistance stiffened when several Panzer divisions came to the aid of the defending forces. Canadian ground troops fought many bloody battles near Caen, which was an objective for the end of D-Day, but was only captured 33 days later.

General Montgomery, who had won fame by defeating General Rommel at El Alamein, was in charge of the British Forces. The Canadian Army, now led by General Crerar, came under Montgomery's command. By mid-July, Canada's Second Division joined the Canadian Corps and, two weeks later, the Fourth Armoured Division was in Normandy. Crerar's Army then included one British Corps and the First Polish Armoured Division, in addition to the three divisions of the Canadian Corps.

It was Montgomery's plan that the Canadian and British Forces would tie down the main German armour around Caen and serve as a hinge, while the two American Armies would sweep south in an encircling manner around on the Cherbourg Peninsula and cut off the German retreat. The plan did not turn out quite as conceived, because the Canadian and British Armies continued to encounter the cream of the enemy's troops. Several battles causing great losses of lives and equipment ensued. For the Canadians, the most bloody battles were fought around Caen, Verriere's Ridge and at the Falaise Gap.

By August 21, the Normandy campaign was ended. The Germans had suffered more than 300,000 casualties (killed, wounded and captured) in the defence of Normandy. More than 2,000 of their tanks and many of their deadly 88-mm guns had been destroyed. The enemy miscalculated by believing that Normandy would not be the major Allied invasion offensive. By the end of August, their forces were in retreat across the Seine. Canadian casualties in Normandy were 18,000; of these 5,000 were buried in France in war-grave cemeteries.

APCs Come To The Aid Of The Infantry

In the bloody Falaise battle, unusual Armoured Personnel Carriers (APCs) were designed and put into action by the Canadians. APCs were obsolete tanks (Canadian Ram and American M7), converted to serve as self-propelled vehicles carrying four or five soldiers. The gun turrets were removed and heavy metal plates welded over the vulnerable parts to give the driver and passengers protection from machine-gun, mortar and non-armour piercing fire. The vehicle came to be known as the "Kangaroo" and was used to attack enemy strongholds such as strategic road junctions, fortified road-blocks, etc. A Canadian Kangaroo regiment made up of two squadrons became an integral part of an armoured division. In addition to playing a valuable role at Malaise, they found effective use in clearing out towns, ports, etc., in other parts of the French coast and in Belgium, Holland, and even at the Rhine crossing in Germany. One four-man Kangaroo team consisted of two Adelaide soldiers, Alex Pedden and Russell Gerry, and two Strathroy men, Syd Welch and Gordon Downham. Three of the four combatants survived the war. Russell Gerry was killed in the Reichwald Forest encounter.

To Dieppe And On To Belgium And Holland

After the Seine was crossed, the Allied Forces

experienced the delaying effects of the ever-increasing lengthening supply lines. This slowed down the advance of the armies. By September 1, Dieppe was captured and the Canadians held a parade through the town to honour the dead of 1942.

On September 4, Hitler decreed that all fortressed towns with port facilities must be stubbornly defended to the very last soldier. Canadians would have to pay dearly for this decree for it was the assigned task of the Canadian Army to capture the coastal areas through to the Netherlands.

When the Canadians had scarcely reached the Belgian border, the Second British Army attempted a combined ground and air offensive (paratrooper landings) deep in the Netherlands on September 17. The plan was to secure crossings over the Maas River and the two main branches of the Rhine. Although paratroopers seized several bridges and established a bridgehead at Arnheim over the Rhine, they were unable to hold their gains. This failure was a serious loss, because the approaches to the valuable port of Antwerp, Belgium, were still in enemy hands. Antwerp lay on the Scheldt River about 50 miles from the sea. To the north of the Scheldt estuary was the peninsula of South Beveland and the strongly defended Walcheren Island. Much of this territory was low-lying, diked land. Many regiments of Canada's First Army fought bloody battles before Beveland was cleared of the enemy at the end of October. Walcheren Island was cleared about a week later. The capture of the Scheldt Estuary cost 6,367 Canadian casualties. At last, the port of Antwerp was open.

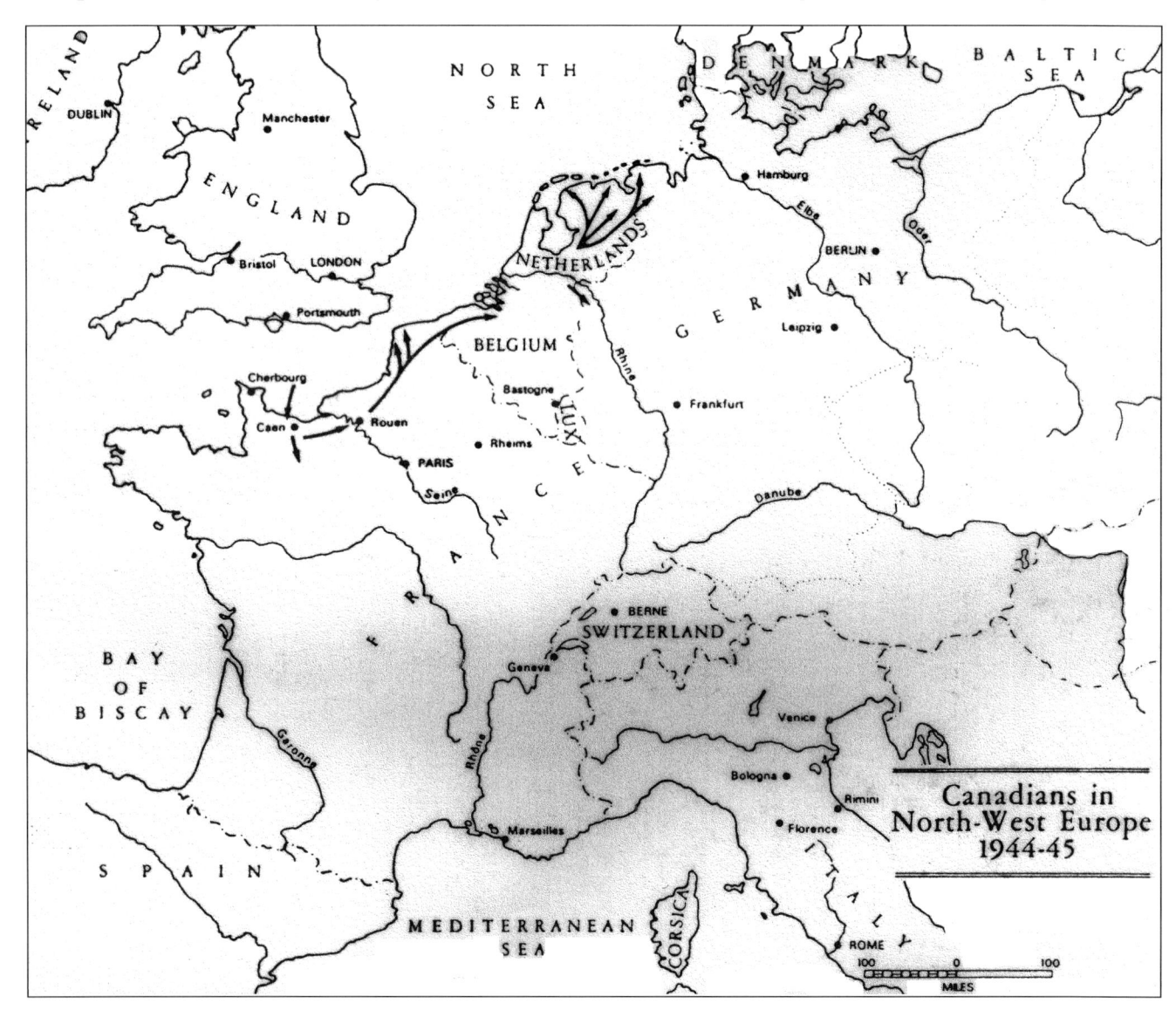

Canadians in North-West Europe 1944-45

After the Scheldt battle, the Canadian Army, now exhausted from five months of unrelenting warfare, entered a three-month rest period with only light action.

The Conscription Issue Rises Again

Casualties suffered on both the Western Front and in Italy were seriously crippling the Canadian Army's fighting efficiency. The critical issue was reinforcements. In September 1944, Colonel Ralston, the Defence Minister, had gone to Italy and Northwest Europe to study the manpower situation. The critical shortage of infantry reinforcements was much worse than he had anticipated. He returned to Ottawa, pointing out that a minimum of 15,000 reinforcements were required to bring infantry battalions up to strength (see Fig. 6).

MacKenzie King was of another mind and had decided that a push for conscription was part of a conspiracy of reactionaries. Because of his firm stand for conscription, Ralston was forced out of the Liberal cabinet on November 1. King's plan was to bring Canada's beloved old soldier, General McNaughton, into his cabinet as the new Defence Minister. Until a year earlier, McNaughton had led the Canadian Army through all of its war exercises and manoeuvres in Britain. He held a steadfast belief in volunteer recruitment.

The sacking of Ralston whipped up a public firestorm that blazed in newspaper headlines across Canada. It caused such a fury that McNaughton's appeals for overseas volunteers went unheard. The NRMA soldiers were not going to respond as he had hoped. The crunch was coming fast. On November 22, the Prime Minister informed cabinet that he had made a volte-face—conscription was now necessary to save democracy, he stated. The government then passed an order-in-council, sending 16,000 NRMA soldiers overseas. King survived a vote of confidence in Parliament.

Politically charged discussions tore at the hearts of Adelaide residents once again, as elsewhere in Canada. Despite political obfuscations, the Adelaide people could not turn away from the patriotic reality that Canada must stay the course until Hitler was brought down. Nevertheless, politics and patriotism were recurring themes in lively, often bitter, debates heard in living rooms and public meeting places throughout the township.

Victory In Europe

Except for Germany's final gasp on the Western Front, when its strong counteroffensive in the Ardennes led to the Battle of the Bulge from mid-December through mid-January 1945, it was downhill for the enemy since the Normandy invasion eight months earlier.

In February, the Canadians went back into action. The Reichwald was cleared and then it was on to the capture of the Hochwald. Many casualties were inflicted on the Canadian troops during the capture of both areas. In mid-March, the First Canadian Corps from Italy joined the Canadian Army, with General Crerar in command. The Rhine River was crossed on March 27. Beginning in April, the First Corps troops liberated the western Netherlands, while the Second Corps drove the Germans out of the northeastern Netherlands, and captured the German coast to the Elbe River.

The war in Europe was rapidly drawing to a close. On May 7, surrender negotiations were completed for northwest Europe. VE-Day was celebrated on May 8.

The Pacific War Continues

By May 1945, the Japanese Empire had been reduced to only a small part of its vast holding at the high tide of victory in 1942. The Japanese Navy had been all but destroyed. Now, in massive air raids, the American bomber squadrons were torching the wooden cities of Japan. The Japanese soldier still remained an obstinate foe who was expected to protect his homeland to the last.

Canada had committed itself in Parliament to participate in the invasion of Japan with Army, Navy and Air Force units. It was to be made up from volunteers who had served in the European war theatre. The Army division for the Pacific was to be the Sixth Canadian, and was to be organized on American lines to serve under them. The RCN would send "HMCS Cruiser Ontario." The RCAF would serve under U.S. command.

VJ-Day

The plans for the Canadian Pacific Force were almost completely in hand when the war against Japan came to its sudden end in mid-August. The atomic bombing of Hiroshima on August 6 and Nagasaki on August 9 forced Japan to sue for peace. The Pacific war ended on August 14.

Lt. Donald M. Campbell of the 48th Highlanders being decorated with the Military Cross at London, Ontario, by the Prince of Wales, September 1919.

Adelaide Soldiers Win High Military Honours

Men and women hailing from humble homes of Adelaide Township have left a rich legacy of service and duty in the military. Special honour fell to two infantry officers in WWI and WWII. Lieut. Donald M. Campbell, 48th Highlanders of Canada, won the Military Cross (MC) for his gallantry on the Western Front near Arras, France, in August 1918 (see Fig. 7 and 8).

In WWII, Lieut. Edward McLeish, an officer with the Highland Light Infantry of Canada, won the MC. His platoon was assigned the task of taking the enemy's last cross-channel firing-guns at Cap Gris Nez, France, out of action. Although wounded in action, he and his platoon successfully completed the task. Lieut. McLeish was

Award of The Military Cross to Lieutenant Edward Archibald McLeish Highland Light Infantry of Canada

Lieutenant McLeish, Platoon Commander of No. 11 Platoon, Highland Light Infantry of Canada at Cap Gris Nez on 29 September 1944, showed extraordinary courage and determination. On 29 September 1944, the Highland Light Infantry of Canada were ordered to capture the four large "Cross Channel" guns on Cap Gris Nez. No. 11 Platoon, under command of Lieutenant McLeish, was given the task of taking out No. 3 gun. This 16" gun had a 360-degree traverse, and was enclosed in a concrete emplacement constructed in tiers. An iron mail net was draped over the front of this massive cement structure. A heavy machine gun was mounted under the barrel. The emplacement was mutually supported by other gun positions. The determination, resourcefulness and example of Lieutenant McLeish, under concentrated shellfire, carried his platoon very rapidly through the initial deep minefields, then through thick wire entanglements that surrounded the gun position.

When the platoon reached the gun positions, the Germans threw grenades out of the slits. They filled the gun with cordite and fired at the platoon. While the gun was rotating, enemy machine gun fire sprayed the immediate area. Three men were wounded and one killed. Although the turret continued to revolve, Lieutenant McLeish seized the initiative, ordering his men to jump onto the gun platform. This Officer tried to force a surrender by throwing grenades into the apertures of the turret. Continuous fire was brought against him from mutually supporting gun positions. Eventually Lieutenant McLeish succeeded in placing a No. 75 grenade under the metal cover of the turret. When the grenade exploded, the gun was no longer able to rotate. This Officer continued to exhort his men, who closed in on the huge emplacement. They attempted to force a way into the encasement, firing at close range into the slits and throwing grenades through gaps between the concrete and the gun. The enemy, although in an apparently impregnable position, was forced to surrender by the determination and aggressive spirit of the men. The vigor, audacity and supreme courage of this Officer had an inspiring effect on his men at the critical moment, enabling the platoon to capture their objective, which greatly influenced the final capture of the Cap Gris Nez.

decorated by King George VI at a ceremony on May 1, 1945, at Buckingham Palace, London, England.

In The Aftermath Of WWII

The Canada to which the veterans returned in 1945 and 1946 was not the Canada they had left. The country had been changed. They, also, had changed. The past had to be put behind them now, as most were anxious to don "civies" and get on with their lives. Veterans had acquired the great discipline of service and these had imprinted indelible memories. Comrades who were left behind in cemeteries of the war's theatres would be remembered, and never forgotten.

Across Canada, the Royal Canadian Legion was strengthened by large numbers of returned veterans. Many communities erected new Legion halls. New programs were begun and were soon so entrenched that the Royal Canadian Legion became a community of weekly, monthly, and annual activities for returnees and their associates.

Canada's War Brides

One of the most popular characters of cartoonist Bing Coughlin was "Herbie," who appeared on a regular basis in the Canadian Army paper, "The Maple Leaf," depicting every stage and feeling of the Canadian service person overseas. One of these cartoons may best describe why there were so many war brides who came to Canada and, in fact, to our very own Adelaide. A quote: "They ain't got nothin' our girls ain't got, they just got it here."

Try to imagine being in another country across the ocean and not being certain of ever returning to our fair Dominion: the uncertainty of the future, never knowing what tomorrow may bring, for both civilian and military personnel. Boys being boys and girls being girls, romance was bound to flourish.

No doubt, there were heartbreaks for there were many Dear John letters, deaths, etc., in the course of events. Military leaders and military chaplains tried to discourage many marriages. They could see beyond the present and anticipate the difficulties that would arise. They failed miserably—at the end of 1946, there were 44,886 marriages recorded, and probably some that were not. In some cases, these were marriages between Canadian personnel, but the vast majority were between Canadian men and British women and these marriages were fruitful: the number of children reported by December 31, 1946, was 21,356.

The continental country to provide the most marriages was the Netherlands, where large numbers of Canadian service personnel were to spend the summer of 1945. By the end of 1946, there had been 1,886 Canadian marriages to Dutch women. There were also 649 Belgian brides, 100 French, six German, seven Danish, and 26 Italian marriages recorded.

Several clubs for war brides were organized, to educate them on Canadian ways and customs, and to dispel the many rumours about Canadian winters—they were reassured that they would not be living in igloos or having to apply for clothing coupons to buy fur-lined underwear. These first clubs were not very successful, and finally the bureaucrats realized these girls were Canadian citizens and were entitled to live in Canada. With that, the Canadian Wives Bureau was formed in London, England. It was established and run by the Canadian Army. The assistance of the Salvation Army and Red Cross was invaluable. Civilian Canadian girls worked with the Red Cross, crossing the ocean several times to escort the wives to Canada and assist some returning to England. One of these girls was Lillian McKenzie from Adelaide Township.

On arrival in Canada, there was more heartbreak and disappointment for some brides, such as going to live on a cattle ranch in Toronto, or language problems in Quebec, or the sudden change to life on a frontier farm on the Prairies. Some of these girls had never been out of the cities where they had been born, and they arrived in some homes to be snubbed and treated as servants. The homesickness of these girls was indescribable. They suffered from loss of family and friends with the ocean between them. Their plight is probably best described by one bride who wanted to go home in the worst way. Her husband told her, "I hope you swim well because I have no money to send you!" However, there is no doubt that the worst cases were often written about and that many more were welcomed and made part of their husband's family with no mention of homesickness. Many had no wish to go back to Europe or the U.K., other than for a visit.

Time and love can conquer all. Most of these brides have become loyal Canadian citizens who raised families, and are now grandmothers and great grandmothers.

Official List
Adelaide Veterans - WWII Overseas

Arrand, Cliff
Bice, Mandus
Brent, Gordon
Brown, H. "Bill"
Carroll, George
Crandon, Wilfred
Cuddy, A. Mac
Dewar, Arthur
Dowding, Ferguson
Down, David
Down, Ivan
Down, Jackson
Fry, Jack
Fuller, William
Gerry, Richard
Gerry, Russell
Harris, Arnold
Hawken, Gordon
Henderson, Russell
Lewis, Cecil
Lewis, Lorne
Matthews, Andy
McChesney, Donald
McDonald, Robert
McKeen, Colin
McLeish, Edward
Morgan, Lewis
Nichols, Orville
Parker, Grant
Payne, Chestle
Pedden, Alex
Petch, Whitford
Pollock, Grant
Prescott, Jim
Robotham, Wilfred
Robotham, William
Rowland, Jack
Tedball, Milton
Thompson, Alex
Thompson, George
Tilley, Jim
Wardell, Earl
Wilson, Ed

Headquarters, Fourth Army.

To Lieutenant D. McL. Campbell,
Canadian Machine Gun Corps.

5th October 1918

I congratulate you on the gallantry and devotion to duty for which you have been awarded

The Military Cross

Rawlinson Genl.

Commanding Fourth Army.

PRINTED IN FRANCE BY ARMY PRINTING AND STATIONERY SERVICES.

Adair, Robert

Aitken, W.A.

Arrand, Cliff

Brent, Gordon

Brown, William J.

Campbell, Grace

ARMED FORCES - WWII ADELAIDE RESIDENTS

ADAIR, ROBERT (killed in action - May 26, 1944, Italy)
AITKEN, W.A.
ARRAND, CLIFF
BRENT, GORDON
BROWN, WILLIAM J.
CAMPBELL, GRACE
CAMPBELL, ROBERT EARL
CRANDON, WILFRED H.
CRANDON, ROSE
CUDDY, A.M.
CUDDY, G.I.
DEMARAY, STANLEY
DOAN, FRANK
DOWDING, FERGUSON
DOWN, DAVID
DOWN, IVAN
DOWN, JACKSON
DOWNHAM, GEORGE (Military Cross)
ELLIOTT, CLIFFORD
FOSTER, GEORGE
FOSTER, RUSSELL
FREER, REG
FULLER, HENRY CRAWFORD
FULLER, WILBERT ALBERT
FYDELL, JAMES
GALSWORTHY, ARNOLD
GAMBLE, BEN
GEORGE, LYLE
GERRY, RUSSELL (killed in action - Feb. 9, 1945, Germany)

HARNETT, GLENN
HARRIS, ARNOLD
HAWKEN, GORDON
HAYDEN, DELMAR
HEMSTED, DONALD
HEMSTED, STANLEY
HENDERSON, RUSSELL
HENDRICK, ELDRED EDWARD
HUMPHREY, MACK
KINMAN, GEORGE
LAMBIE, JAMES
LEACOCK, GEORGE
LEWIS, LORNE
MARTIN, FRED
MARTIN, WILLIAM FRANK
MATTHEWS, ANDREW
MACKENZIE, DONALD
MACKENZIE, IAN (killed in action, Feb. 24, 1942, England)
MACKENZIE, WILLIAM JOHN
MCCHESNEY, LORNA
MCDOUGALL, LORNE
MCKEEN, COLIN
MCKENZIE, JOHN
MCKENZIE, LILLIAN (Red Cross Escort Officer)
MCLEAN, CAMERON
MCLEAN, MARGARET
MCLEISH, EDWARD (Military Cross)

MORGAN, LEWIS
MORGAN, DR. WALTER (also served WWI)
MURRAY, ELMER
MUXLOW, VERA (BRANTON)
NICHOLS, ORVILLE
PARKER, CHARLIE
PARKER, GRANT
PAYNE, CHESTLE
PEDDEN, ALEX
PETCH, WHITFORD
POLLOCK, GRANT
ROBOTHAM, WILFRED
ROBOTHAM, WILLIAM
ROWLAND, JACK
SEED, FRANK
SHAMBLAW, JOHN
SHETLER, ARTHUR
SMITH, EVERETT
TACK, HUBERT
TEDBALL, MILTON
THOMAS, KEN
THOMAS, RON
THOMPSON, GEORGE
THOMPSON, JAMES ALEXANDER
TILLEY, JIM
WARDELL, EARL
WARDELL, LEO
WILSON, ED

Campbell, Robert E.    *Crandon, Wilfred H.*    *Cuddy, A.M.*    *Cuddy, G.I.*

590 ADELAIDE TOWNSHIP... A HISTORY

Demaray, Stanley

Doan, Frank

Dowding, Ferguson

Down, David

Down, Ivan

Down, Jackson

Downham, George (M.C.)

Elliott, Clifford

Foster, George

Foster, Russell

Freer, Reg

Fry, Jack

Fuller, Henry C.

Fuller, William A.

Fydell, James

Galsworthy, Arnold

ARMED FORCES 591

Gamble, Ben

George, Lyle

Gerry, Russell

Harnett, Glenn

Harris, Arnold

Hawken, Gordon

Hemsted, Donald

Hemsted, Stanley

Henderson, Russell

Leacock, George

Lewis, Lorne

Matthews, Andrew

MacKenzie, Donald

MacKenzie, Ian

MacKenzie, William J.

McChesney, Donald

McDougall, Lorne | McKeen, Colin | McKenzie, John | McLean, Cameron

McLean, Margaret | McLeish, Edward (M.C.) | Morgan, Lewis | Murray, Elmer

Muxlow, Vera (Branton) | Nichols, Orville | Parker, Grant | Payne, Chestle

Pearson, Len | Pedden, Alex | Petch, Whitford | Pollock, Grant

Robotham, Wilfred

Robotham, William

Rowland, Jack

Seed, Frank

Shetler, Arthur

Smith, Everett

Tedball, Milton

Thompson, George

Thompson, James A.

Tilley, Jim

Wardell, Earl

Wardell, Leo

Wilson, Ed

Official List
Adelaide Armed Forces (in Canada)

Bates, Albert
Branton, Vera
Cuddy, Gordon
Demaray, Stanley
Doan, Frank
Fuller, Harry
Galsworthy, Arnold
Handley, William
Leacock, George
McKenzie, John
McLean, Cameron
Miller, Fred
Murray, Elmer
Parker, Charlie
Pedden, Alex
Seeds, Frank
Wardell, Leo

OTHER – ARMED FORCES ADELAIDE RESIDENTS

SERVED IN KOREAN WAR
UNGER, FLOYD

PRESENT DAY ARMED FORCES
RUPP, JENNIFER

Lt. Jennifer Rupp, Canadian Armed Forces, Air Force Division

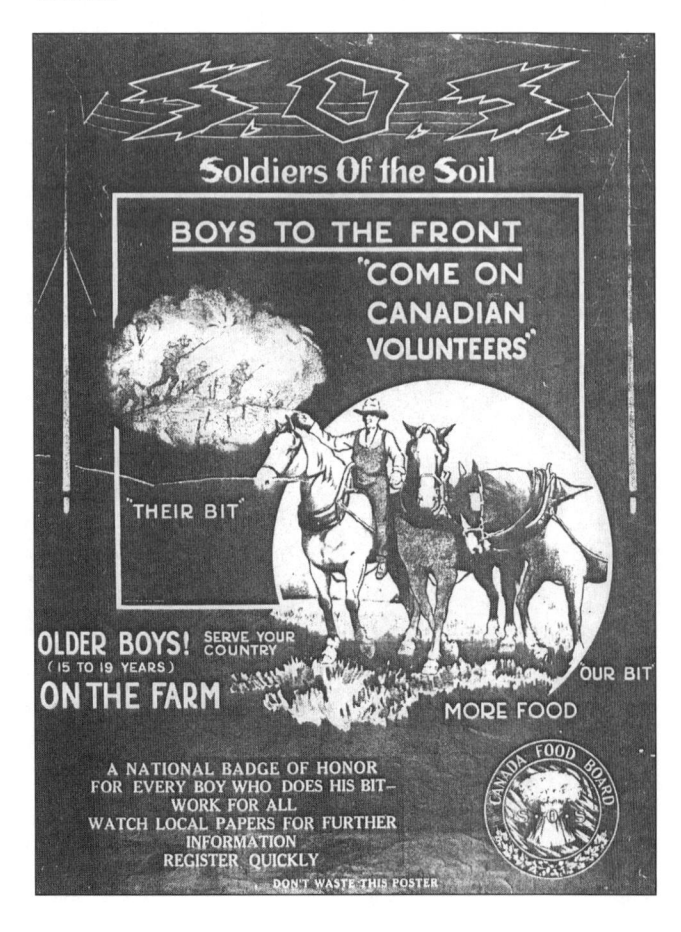

Floyd S. Unger in Black Watch uniform.

CHAPTER TEN

Agriculture

CATTLE

Until the 1940s, cattle had an enormous impact on all farm families. Much of the income and food was derived from cattle, and the farmer spent most of his time caring for them and obtaining food for them. The first and last job of the husband, wife and children, for 365 days a year, was milking and separating cream from milk.

On the barn floor, a local butcher usually slaughtered cattle, often fattened cows, for home consumption. Butcher Jack Campbell, who lived at Lot 18, Con. 3 NER, and later at Lot 28, Con. 2 NER, is one example. The beef was killed in December or January, quartered, and hung in the barn or work shed, where freezing resulted. Quarters were often sold to neighbours or relatives.

During the winter, cattle were chained to the side of the stall. They were released to the barnyard for a short while every day to obtain water from a large cement tank. During cold weather, ice (up to four inches in thickness) had to be removed from the tank each morning.

The older cattle were fed hay, corn sheaves or silage, and oat straw. The calves were often fed second-cut hay, and milking cows were given some chop and occasionally fed sliced mangels.

Downhamdale Farms

Pounds or enclosures were located throughout the township, and straying or trespassing animals were put in them until the owner paid a fine. In order to prevent straying, sometimes pokes were put on animals.

During the summer, the cattle were pastured in fields and even on the roadside. If a bull pastured with the cows, a good dog or a riding horse was used to bring the cows in for milking. The heifers were sold at one or two years of age unless they were used for breeding. The steers were frequently kept until they were four years of age and weighed as much as a ton. A hundred acres of pasture, and Adelaide had some of the best in Ontario, only supported about 20 big steers. Now, fertilized fields produce three to four times as much pasture. The main beef breeds were Hereford, Shorthorn, Aberdeen Angus, and dual-purpose Durham.

Dairy and beef cows and young cattle were sold at the Ontario Stockyards on Keele Street in Toronto. The cattle were walked to the closest railway station, Kerwood or Strathroy, and loaded on the train for shipping. Of course, fences lined both sides of the road, and so herding was possible. The large beef steers were frequently transported to a seaport and loaded on cattle boats that sailed to England, where the cattle were slaughtered. Sometimes, local young men got a free (or inexpensive) trip to England if they fed the cattle during their journey.

William Nettleton was a drover who lived in Adelaide on Lot 21, Con. 3 NER, and later in Strathroy. He owned 600 acres, which was mostly pasture land.

Cows sometimes became infected with Brucella abortus, which caused infectious abortion in cows.

Humans became infected with this bacterium if they drank contaminated milk, and then they suffered from undulant fever.

Mycobacterium tuberculosis was another bacterium that was transferred from cows to humans. During the 1940s and 1950s, the Ontario Department of Agriculture eradicated both bacterial species from cows.

Heel flies that laid their eggs during June and July unsettled the cattle on pasture. When the insect eggs were being deposited on their heels, the cattle became extremely irritated and scared, and ran long distances to escape this pest. During the next 10 months, the larvae developed in the cattle and then white round larvae (1"x1½") emerged from lumps on the cows' backs. In the 1970s, insecticides were used to eradicate this troublesome pest.

During the 1940s, farming became more specialized. This was due to more cash cropping, new machines, herbicides, electrification of the farm, use of commercial fertilizer, and better life in the city.

The cow/calf business diminished, and large beef feedlots appeared. These were easily recognized by their huge cement silos. Automatic mechanical unloaders became commonplace and, as a result, one farmer could take care of many (300-400) cattle. Ensilage, grain, corn, and protein supplement was fed to the cattle.

During the 1950s and 1960s, calves and yearlings were obtained relatively cheaply from the Western Provinces, first by train and more recently by truck.

Shipping fever, a very debilitating disease, frequently occurred and often killed numerous animals even when antibiotics were used. Calves were particularly susceptible due to great stress and a decreased immune system during the week-long train trip, when they were fed and watered just once or twice. More stress was added when the calves were not weaned before shipping. Now, all the calves and stockers are transported by truck, and travel stress only occurs for two days.

During the 1960s, beef consumers began to demand beef with less fat. Consequently, the European breeds, such as Charolais, Limousin, Simmental and other exotic breeds, began to replace the British breeds. These breeds do not fatten at an early age, nor do they gain as much on pasture. Now, the best restaurants in Toronto are obtaining their choicest beef from the U.S., where fatter cattle are available.

ADELAIDE PASTURES PRODUCED BEEF

In the late 1920s, the United States government imposed a restrictive tariff on Canadian cattle and cattle shipments to the U.S., as this is where most of the fat cattle produced in Adelaide were slaughtered up to this time. This action sent prices down, but the real slump came when the Depression came in 1929. With export markets practically non-existent, cattle sold at sacrifice prices. Cattlemen were encouraged to fatten and sell their cattle at lighter weights, and younger ages, as 3-4-year-olds that weighed 1,400 pounds were standard. By 1937, economic conditions began to improve. The U.S. tariff was lowered, and Canadian cattle were permitted to enter on more favourable terms. The outbreak of Foot and Mouth disease in Western Canada in 1952 and 1953 stopped all movement of beef export. Train cars were loaded from the C.N.R. Stockyards in Kerwood, where drovers assembled, weighed, and loaded these shipments of fat steers produced in Adelaide for shipment to Toronto, the U.S. (mainly Buffalo and Chicago), and Britain. Early township drovers included Howard and Albert Brock, Bill and Art Thompson, William and Fred Brent, Bill Nettleton, Ed and John Edward Healy, Jack Smithrim and John Johnson.

Some of the names of these beef producers pasturing cattle included William Brent, William Nettleton, Albert Brock, Doc Lambert, Jim Giffen, Andrew Pedden, Matt Brown, Bud Ayre, Art Conkey, Alf Cuddy, Fred Brent, Cliff McLean, Dan McIntyre, Hugh Ball, Tom Galbraith, Bob McCubbin, Clarence Patterson and Lorne Dodge.

Adelaide truckers included Jack Arrand, Jack Wooley, Howard McLean, Art Pedden and Ken Phillips.

ADELAIDE BEEF CATTLE AT THE ROYAL AGRICULTURAL WINTER FAIR

During the war, the Baby Beef Club program expanded at a remarkable rate in Ontario. Girls were admitted to membership and joined local clubs in large numbers. When the "Royal" resumed in 1946 after the war, provisions were made for the top calves in the local clubs to be shown a special class and sold by auction at the fair. This class was first

Ontario Junior Farm Clubs, 1936.

known as the King's Guineas, named after King Edward VII, who created a fund for use in developing agriculture in Upper Canada and placing it in trust with the Agriculture and Art Society, later entrusted to the Ontario Department of Agriculture to be kept in trust in perpetuity. Consequently, the King's Guineas became the Queen's Guineas when the present sovereign ascended the throne.

The Guineas now is a competition open to 4H youths in the Province of Ontario for showing market beef animals. Winners from Adelaide Township showing Grand Champions are George Earley in 1959, Shirley Earley in 1961, Tim Earley in 1984, Rob Miller in 1990, Sara Earley in 1993. Reserve Grand Champions have been exhibited by Martha Earley in 1985, Mike Earley in 1987, Sara Earley in 1990 and 1991, Lori Benedict in 1994, and Barb Benedict in 1996.

MARKET CATTLE

Ever since the "Royal" began in 1922, except during the war years, when the fair buildings on the grounds of the Canadian National Exhibition was used for barracks, the fair has been held annually in the fall. The Grand Champion Steer award has been one of the most coveted prizes at the show. Hillcrest Farm of Kerwood (George Earley and family) has won the Grand Champion Award five times, only surpassed by the University of Alberta, and the reserve Grand Champion Award eight times (also, the only farm to exhibit Grand and Reserve Grand Champion in the same year, in 1996). Gerald Miller won the championship in 1987 and 1994. Jim Earley showed the Reserve in 1962. Hillcrest Farms holds the record selling price of $37/pound for their Champion in 1991, for a steer purchased by Charles Coppa of Highland Farms of Toronto. In the carcass class, which is open to market steers and heifers, Hillcrest Farms genetics have dominated this class. They hold the record price of $60/pound for the Grand Champion, sold in 1990 to Steve Stavro's Knob Hill Store.

The Knob Hill Farms National Junior Heifer Show is a competition open to 4H members across Canada, exhibiting breeding beef heifers at the Royal Winter Fair. Local area winners include

Earley Brothers
Royal Champions 2000

David Brand of Kerwood winning the Knob Hill Jr. Heifer Show, Grand Champion Female in 1994. Other wins for his heifer include Ontario Provincial Jr. Grand Champion Female 1994, as well as winning Reserve Grand Champion Limousin Female at the 1995 Canadian Western Agribition in Regina. The Brand family showed their first Canadian Western Agribition Grand Champion Limousin Female in 1993.

Toni Herrington's 4H winnings at the Royal's Knob Hill National Jr. Heifer Show include Champion Angus in 1998. She also was awarded the honour of Ontario Limousin Queen 1998. At the 1998 Royal, Toni also won the National Junior Limousin Grand Champion Female.

Pure Bred Breeders past and present:

Aberdeen Angus: Eugene and Jim Earley, Fred Hoffner, Otto Zimmerman, Lew Shepard, Cliff Callahan, George Morgan, Lloyd Muxlow, Mac Cuddy, George Earley, Gerald Miller, Mike and Tim Earley, and Toni Herrington.

Hereford: Roy and Wes Demaray

Shorthorn: Joe Morgan, Gord Bolton, Loftus Wilson, Sam Wiley, Orville and Wes Demaray

Limousin: David Brand family, Earl McNab, Ken Herrington family

Simmental: Gerald Brown

THE DRAFT HORSE

In the early days of the township, many new settlers were from the British Isles. Many of these immigrants came from Scotland, so the Clydesdale horse was the draft horse of favour, to do the work in logging and working the land they had cleared.

The draft horse was the only source of power on the farm for many years. Most farms had a brood mare or two, and raised a colt or two every year to use or sell.

About 1923, Archie Pedden Sr. bought a Percheron stallion by the name of Syrus. The Percheron horse is believed to be native to France. Archie travelled Syrus from farm to farm to service the mares. The method of travel was by horse-and-buggy, leading the stallion along beside the buggy.

In the 1920s, Archie began to import registered Percheron and Belgian stallions from the U.S., because they were raising a better class of horse. At the beginning, these horses were brought in by railroad and unloaded in Strathroy. Several men were hired to lead these horses the nine miles from the station to Archie's barn. Later, trucks were used and the horses were delivered directly to the Pedden place.

These imported horses were sold across Ontario, with many going to Northern Ontario, where the draft horse was in demand for logging. The Mennonite community was another high demand area.

Through the 1930s, the draft horse was widely used for power, but by 1940, the tractor was replacing the horse. This spelled the end of the draft horse as a source of power, other than in the Mennonite community. The Peddens kept a Percheron stallion until 1945, but there was little demand for service.

OXEN AND HORSES

During early settlement, oxen were used for farming, but they could not be controlled as readily as horses and did not move as quickly. Their life span was half that of horses, but their hooves enabled them to move through swamps and mud more readily.

The oxen were soon replaced by draft horses, commonly used for drawing the wagon, sleigh, stone-boat and farm machinery. Most farmers used three heavy horses for drawing grain binders and two-furrowed plows. Because only one or two acres could be ploughed in a day, the farmer could only operate 100 acres.

The horses were "broken-in" or trained to work as a team when they were three or four years of age.

CANADIAN LIVESTOCK EXPORTS
1870 - 1941

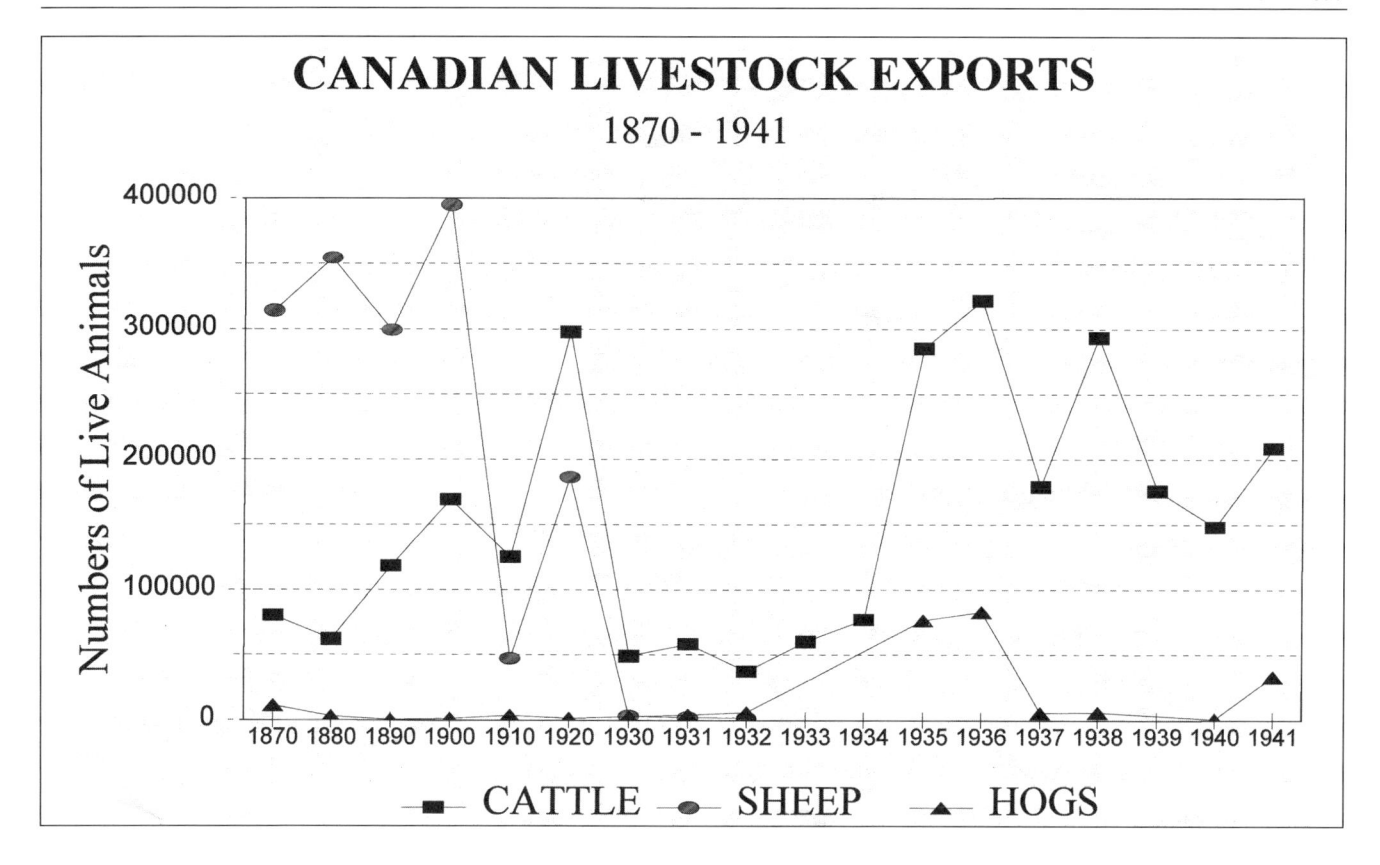

Chart showing Numbers of Live Animals (Cattle, Sheep, Hogs) exported from 1870 to 1941.

A neighbour often helped the first time a horse was hitched to a wagon, with an older, reliable gelding or mare. The horses soon learned "Gee," "Haw," "Get-up" and "Whoa," and could be left standing for long periods while hitched without being tied.

Horses idle during the winter sometimes developed sores on their shoulders if they were worked for long periods during hot weather. It usually took about a year for these sores to heal, even if shoulder pads were worn.

Most farmers had a blood horse, which was 400-500 pounds lighter than the draft breeds. It was faster, more temperamental, and used for driving and as a third horse. Good drivers could travel up to 50 miles a day while pulling a cutter or buggy, and were kept shod, or sharp shod on icy roads.

Often, farmers raised their own colts or fillies. A stallion was owned by a few farmers. During the spring and summer, the stallion was led beside a buggy as he weekly moved around the community. Sometimes, fences were ruined because horses trampled them and leaned their necks on them while they ate on the other side of the fence.

Cars and tractors replaced farm horses during the period between 1920 and 1940. Racehorses have increased in number during the last 50 years.

About 1930, Fred Thrower, who lived on the Second Line SER, owned Gratton Bars. This famous horse paced the mile in 1:59 2/5, an exceptional speed at that time. Mr. Thrower won $25,000 in each of three races on American tracks.

Arthur Currie trained and raced some good pacers and, a few years ago, Mac Cuddy sold a young standardbred stallion for $1,000,000.

Plowing ca.1800s, Bill Parker's grandfather, Lawrence, and great-grandpa, George.

EGG PRODUCTION 1940 TO 1995

In 1945, almost all farmers had a small flock of laying hens. By the mid-1950s, larger laying barns started to appear. One family, the Peddens, built their first egg barn in 1956. This barn was loose housing with chickens on the floor. With this type of barn, hens were kept in confinement all the time, and cannibalism and crowding were somewhat of a problem. In 1962, they built their first cage barn, and this was the beginning of a new type of housing in this area. Cage barns caught on very quickly and, through the 1960s, many barns were built. The 1960s were boom-or-bust times, with the large grocery chains dictating the price of eggs that week and the farmer paid for the special.

By the late 1960s, Adelaide Township farmers were beginning to see the result of overproduction and, by 1970, egg producers were not recovering the cost of production.

About 1965, the Ontario Egg Producers Marketing Board was formed. This board had little clout because they had no control over imports at the border. After two years of below-cost production, the Hon. William A. Stewart, Minister of Agriculture for Ontario, gave us the legislation to set quotas. Soon after that, the Hon. Eugene Whelan, Minister of Agriculture for Canada, made quota universal across the country.

The Canadian Egg Marketing Agency (C.E.M.A.) was formed and, with production under control in our country, the marketing board was better able to control imports at the border. This system of production control has worked well for the last 22 years, with the egg producers recovering the cost of production plus a moderate profit, with no subsidy from the government.

Allen Dowding farm at west half of Lot 8, Con. 2.

CHICKENS

At the turn of the century, most farmers kept about 100-150 hens, and three or four roosters who announced the break of day.

White Leghorn, Plymouth Rock, Black Minorca, Rhode Island Red, and crosses of these were usually housed in a hen house attached to a pig house. The hens, except during cold winter days, were allowed to roam in the barnyard and ingest grass, pebbles and bugs.

The hens were usually fed some wheat every morning and evening. A dish of oyster shell was usually left in the hen house. The hens laid few if any eggs in the winter because of short, dark days, coldness, and inadequate feeding. Consequently, the housewife sometimes stored eggs in water glass for winter consumption.

A row of nests about a cubic foot in size, with some straw in the bottom, served as laying nests. A nest egg was usually kept in each nest. Although hens might lay in any nest, they usually had their favourites in which most of the eggs were deposited. The eggs were usually gathered after the evening feeding and then wiped clean and stored in a basket or crate for a week.

If the road was rough when the farmer took his eggs to market in a basket in his buggy, especially if the basket was full, the eggs sometimes cracked—thus, the origin of the saying "Don't put all your eggs in one basket."

Frequently, the eggs were taken to an egg market (Charles Gill) immediately on arriving in Strathroy. The egg purchaser would give a deposit to the owner, who then would have money for shopping. By the time the owner was ready to return home, the eggs would have been graded and candled, and a final settlement was made.

In the spring, a few hens would be allowed to set on about a dozen eggs, which would hatch in 21 days. The resulting chickens would replenish the flock and serve for consumption during the year. Most of the roosters were eaten or sold.

The chicken in those days had a richer flavour, and the meat was not nearly as soft and tender as commercial chickens available today. The difference is caused by lack of exercise and forced feeding.

Now, one has to be a millionaire to get into the chicken and egg business. The rights-per-hen is expensive, and quota is controlled by the Chicken and Egg Marketing Board.

GEESE AND DUCKS

Most farmers had a pair of geese while others kept two geese and one gander. They often served as guard birds.

The goose began laying eggs every second day in the hay or straw in the barn in late March. The goose egg was always collected before nightfall and stored in a cool room in the house until the goose began to set and then the eggs were returned to the nest. The goose remained on her nest for 28 days, feeding for only about 10 minutes each day. After four weeks, about 10 beautiful, greenish-yellow, down-covered goslings broke out of the egg.

The goose and gander were very protective of their goslings. If one approached the goslings, he or she was likely to receive a terrific bang on their head from a wing. The goslings, when moving, always remained in a line behind the goose, which followed the gander.

Preparing the dozen-or-so geese for market before Christmas was always a challenge. A large copper kettle (now a prized antique) and one or two smaller black kettles were filled with water, which was brought to a boil. The recently killed goose was dipped in the boiling water the appropriate length of time, in order to loosen the feathers so that they could be readily pulled. The wing feathers always remained firmly in place, and the ones on the tips were sometimes left attached.

Usually, the birds were plucked in the kitchen, the only clean, warm place available in December. The down and small feathers were placed in a bag, except for several that floated around the room. This was a very busy day for everyone capable of plucking feathers. The bags of feathers were dried behind the kitchen stove for about a week and then were stored or used to fill pillows and ticks.

The geese were singed over a paper flame and placed in the cellar, and then transported to the butcher, who hung them in his store. If the geese were fed plenty of grain in the autumn, they were beautiful, fat, yellow birds. If one was eaten at Christmas, the fat was kept for cold remedies or applied to leather boots. Now, the raising of geese is the exception.

Only a few families produced ducks. They were nurtured in the same way as geese.

PIGS

On many farms, a building about 14'x30' was located close to the barn, as shelter for pigs and hens. The pig portion had two pens, with a cement trough in each. The sow and her litter occupied one pen, and the older pigs the other. During warm weather, the pigs were allowed to roam in the yard. A pig could be driven from one farm to another while controlling it with a long rope attached to its hind leg.

Pigs, mainly Yorkshire and other breeds such as Tamworth, were fed oat or barley chop, and refuse from the kitchen table. Sometimes, in the autumn, they were fed surplus apples.

Traditionally, farm families butchered pigs rather than cattle because pork was more readily preserved, it was cheaper meat, and pigs could be slaughtered more readily. Pork packed in salt in a barrel could be preserved in the summer, but beef could not.

However, butchering a pig required a little effort. A couple of butcher knives had to be sharpened and a large quantity of water had to be heated to boiling, either on the kitchen stove or in a large iron kettle. After the pig was bled, it had to be inserted and pulled from a barrel that was sloped against a low stand, upon which two men stood, raising and lowering one end of the pig into the boiling water. If the pig was properly scalded, the pig bristles could be quickly removed with sharp knives. The pig was then hung by the hind legs on a wooden fence rail sloped against a wall. A strong oak or maple stick, properly notched and about 18" long, was pushed under the hock tendons of the hind legs, and centered in a notch near the top of the rail. Thusly, the pig was hung so that it could be dressed.

Adrian deBruyn working land in September 1964.

Tamminga Farm

Bacon and ham was not cured; all the meat was left on the ribs. Often, a housewife made head cheese.

The price of pork, as well as beef, is determined by the American price. The price of red meat varies inversely to the price of corn, soybeans and barley. For the past 20 years, pigs have been sold in kilograms, while the cattlemen have retained the pound system.

For the past 20 years, marketing boards have controlled the marketing and sale of pigs in Ontario. Restructuring is occurring. Pig breeds are now thinner and longer and are butchered when they weigh about 85 kilograms.

Haying time

TURKEYS

Wild turkeys survived in Adelaide Township until the 20th century. Their numbers had fluctuated from year to year. They were greatly reduced when deep snow covered the ground for long periods. During the first half of this century, some farmers raised broad-breasted bronze or black turkeys, and kept a gobbler and as many as 10 hen turkeys. During the winter, they roosted in a shed or barn and were fed grain in the yard twice a day.

In the warm spring weather, the turkey-cock gobbled, strutted and mated. During late April and early May, the hens made nests in barns, sheds and protected spots. The brown speckled eggs were collected every day and stored in the house to prevent destruction and freezing.

When the hens began to set, 12-18 eggs were returned to the nest for hatching. The eggs were turned and kept warm for the next 21 days. For a short period each day, the hens would leave their nests to obtain food and water.

After hatching, the turkeys were moved to grassy areas. Every night, the hen turkeys were put in coops to prevent wandering. During the summer, the turkeys were allowed to roam in pastures and orchards. Those families who had adjacent pasture farms were very fortunate. The turkeys would sweep over fields and devour seeds, grasshoppers, crickets and other insects. Sometimes, the turkeys went into wheat and oat fields and trampled red clover seed fields. Grain and curd sometimes supplemented their diet.

Children assisted greatly in driving turkeys home and into coops, while one child tilted the coop up for the hen to be driven into it.

The black-head disease was sometimes common in turkey flocks, and there was no effective cure. Lice caused some debilitation as it does in wild birds.

Before Thanksgiving and Christmas, as many as 100 birds were prepared for market. If the birds were given the proper brainstick, the feathers could be removed in three or four minutes. The fuzz and tiny feathers were removed by singeing over a paper flame. The birds were sold undressed to the butcher, who hung them in his store window.

During the Great Depression, when live beef sold for 3-5¢/pound, turkeys were worth about 16-20¢/pound after plucking. Consequently, one can appreciate how fortunate an individual was if he or she could purchase a turkey for Christmas. Now, the relative price of turkey and beef has reversed.

The flavour, taste, and quality of the meat were more appealing than present turkey meat. Now, turkeys are grown only in large commercial farms, and exercise and food are different.

Mac Cuddy, an Adelaide Township farmer, started a commercial turkey farm about 40 years ago. He has been very capable and successful. He has a great international business, but most of his enterprise is in the U.S. He, like other large producers, grows white birds. In the wild, white birds would never survive, because they would be too obvious to their predators.

In 1990, wild turkeys from Michigan were introduced into the area north of Lake Erie. They are multiplying and may spread northward. However Adelaide Township is in the Snow Belt, and survival is difficult.

CORN

Corn was grown by North American Indians centuries before the white man grew it in Adelaide Township. The Native Americans developed the corn plant. It was their most important crop and, because they could dry and store corn seed, they were able to survive when other foods were scarce.

Now, corn is the most important crop in Adelaide Township and in North America, because it has several basic uses and demand is great. It is a

Ken Timmermans combining corn on his farm on Seed sideroad in 1998.

Alfons Jansen home farm at Lot 4, Con. 2 SER, ca.1940.

source of food for humans and animals, and a source of fructose, a very sweet sugar used in candy production. Corn is also used in the production of ethanol, a clean automotive fuel.

Only a small amount of corn was grown in Adelaide Township when corn was planted with a hand planter. After the introduction of the grain drill and the corn binder, each farmer, especially cow and beef farmers, produced a few acres of corn.

Throughout the 1920-1950 period, three to 10 acres of dent corn was grown on most farms. Most of this corn was cut into small pieces, using a cutting box, and blown through an 8" metal pipe into a silo.

The cement or wood silos were about 25-30' high and 14' in diameter, and were situated adjacent to a cattle barn. After the silo was filled in September or October, the silage fermented immediately into a preserved suitable cattle food, which provided feed during the winter.

Some farmers who lacked silos built corn shocks, containing 15-20 sheaves, in the corn field. The shocks were bound by twine and were drawn to the barn on a sleigh or stone boat as needed throughout the winter.

After the sheaves were placed in the manger, the cattle always devoured the cobs very quickly, but frequently left larger stalks in the manger. Each day, these stalks were collected and put in a pile outside the barn, and were burned when dry in the spring to destroy any corn borer larvae they may have contained.

Only a small amount of grain corn was grown before the 1940s, because an enormous amount of hard manual labour was required to remove the cobs and husk, and store it in corn cribs.

Load of men going to barn raising.

Taking in the hay harvest on the Albert Dowding farm ca. 1915, his wife Ethel and children Melvin and Irene in the foreground.

Beginning in the 1940s, corn production was revolutionized by the introduction of hybrid corn, herbicides, corn planters, combines and grain driers. This enabled Adelaide farmers to grow several hundred acres of corn.

Corn, like beans, had been a hoe crop. After the introduction of 2-4-D, the first herbicide, the hoe was no longer used in corn production. At the same time, the use of commercial fertilizer increased enormously and not only the corn, but also the weeds, were stimulated and became widespread throughout the fields. Before the 1940s, corn fields were generally pale green with yellow patches. With increased use of nitrogen fertilizer and better drainage, the corn leaves turned greener and greener and yields increased.

After 1940, very productive hybrid corn, which is a cross between two small inbred lines, replaced the open-pollinated corn or Indian corn.

The open-pollinated corn was heterogeneous, i.e., all characteristics varied. Some stalks were thick, some slender, some tall, some short, some had several cobs and some had none. The height of the cob on the stalk varied, and leaves varied in colour and size. Hybrid corn is genetically homogeneous and all plants in the same environment grow to the same size, ripen at the same time, and have the same susceptibility to pests. It is also more disease-resistant and cold-hardy. It does not grow below 50 degrees Fahrenheit, but may be planted as early as May 1, and every day earlier permits a higher yield. Open-pollinated corn was not planted until about May 24.

Between 1950 and 1975, due to the increase in the size and number of beef feedlots, very large silos up to 65' in height and 24' in diameter were built, and up to 50 acres of corn were required to fill these cylindrical chambers. Due to a lack of profitability in the beef feedlot industry in the 1980s, many of the large silos are in disuse, and have deteriorated due to acid and other chemicals.

Corn yields often reach over 150 bushels per acre. Some sweet corn is produced for home use and canning. Even raccoons, which are very numerous at the present time, prefer this variety—they eat and destroy sweet corn about two days before it is at the perfect ripeness for human tastes.

GRAIN HARVEST

Grain harvest has always been important in Adelaide Township, and has continued to increase in importance as the grain acreage expanded.

During the 1830s, the first years of settlement, small plots were cleared from the forest. Often, wheat and oats had to be planted around stumps and large stones, which oxen or horses could not pull. These stones were split later by dowsing them with cold water after they had been heated in a bonfire.

A cradle was used to harvest the grain. The cradle, an archaic implement, consisted of a wood frame with long bending teeth, fastened to a scythe for cutting and laying grain in a swath. Cradling was difficult work, but it has been claimed that some men could swath up to six acres a day.

Sheaves were bound by twisting heads of grain and dividing the attached stalks into two small bundles, and then wrapping them around a bundle. The lower end of the binding stems were twisted and pushed between the band and the bundle, and a sheaf resulted.

Cliff Branton operating steam machine.

The grain binder was invented in the latter part of the 19th century. It cut, bound sheaves with twine, and its sheaf-carrier deposited the sheaves in rows. Thus, less walking was necessary while stooking. The grain dried more rapidly in long stooks, but more bending and arm irritation occurred, especially if thistles were present. Round stooks were made with the aid of a 3-tanged pitchfork, with less energy. When the sheaves were dry, usually about a week after stooking, they were transported by a wagon to a mow in the barn. A pitchfork was used to lift the sheaves on the wagon and throw them into a mow, where the sheaves were layered over the mow. Later, sling ropes were used to remove one load in four bundles, using the barn track and a one inch hemp rope.

At first, a treadmill powered by horses was used to thresh the grain. At the turn of the century, the threshing machine was introduced. The owner of the separator threshed the grain of many of his neighbours, and charged either by the bushel or the hour. The size of the bushels varied greatly, which added to the gossip in the community.

At first, separators were powered by a belt from the steam engine, which usually burned wood to boil water and produce steam. It was necessary for the fireman to rise early to start the fire and boil the water. He often slept in the owner's spare bedroom. The steam engine whistle was always blown before and after work, and it could be heard for miles. Later, tractors replaced the steam engines, and sometimes the tractors had insufficient power to thresh damp or green grain.

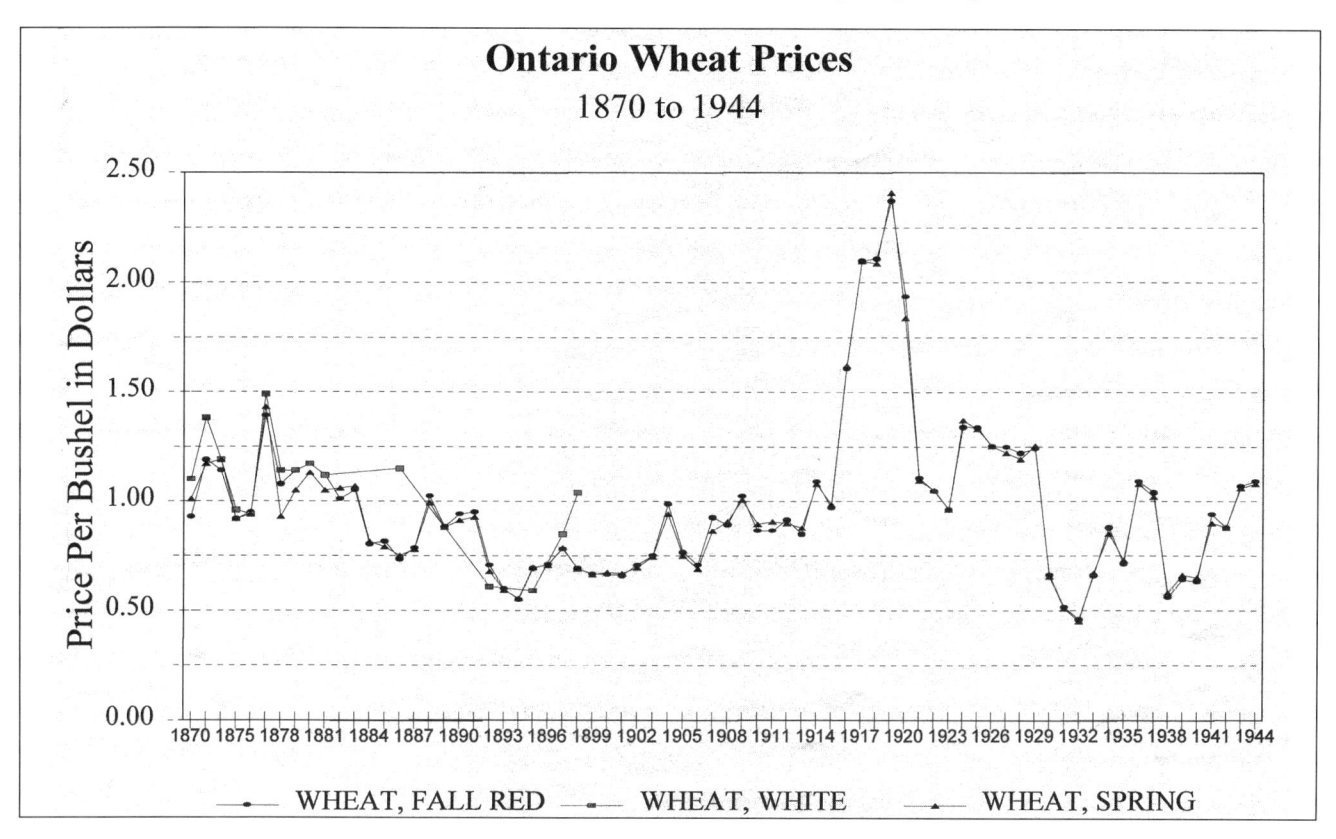

Ontario Wheat Prices
1870 to 1944

Model T converted into a tractor owned by Cliff Branton. Cliff and Myrtle (Branton) Akins on seat, Bud Ayre standing.

Threshing at Fred Petch farm, July 29, 1923.

The sheaves moved up the rotating feeder table and, as they entered the separator, rotating long, sharp, curved knives cut the stems and the binding twine. As the straw and grain passed over the shaking sieves, the grain dropped through and then was moved in an elevator to the top of the thresher, where it was released in bushel amounts down a spout into the granary.

The straw moved forward and was sometimes put through a cutting box before it was blown out a long, adjustable pipe (15" in diameter) to a stack or mow. If the mow being filled was in the same barn, the farmers were exposed to a great deal of dust, especially if the grain was smutty. Usually, the oat straw was blown into the barn, so it could be kept dry and then used for feed.

At the beginning of the threshing season, some stook threshing usually occurred, i.e., the sheaves were taken directly to the threshing machine. A spike-pitcher helped every load-builder to pitch off his load. It was a very strenuous job.

The wife of the farmer whose grain was being threshed always served an excellent meal, with plenty of meat and potatoes. Usually there was cake, fruit, and two or three pies for dessert, but pies were always the favourite, and men often consumed three large pieces, or half of a large pie.

During the late 1920s, when times were booming, the thresher offered the farmer the opportunity of having his threshing done with the "gang," a group of hired men. If this occurred, the farmer did not exchange help with his neighbours during threshing season.

In the middle of the century, combines began to be used. The grain was bagged on the combine, and the full bags were slipped down a metal chute to the ground while the combine was moving. A great deal of energy was required to lift the bags, especially wheat, onto the wagons and into the granary. The combines soon carried grain bins and elevators. Consequently, the farmer was obliged to obtain grain wagons whose walls sloped to a spout at the bottom of the wagon. Emptying was by gravity.

At first, there was difficulty in harvesting during a rainy season, because the damp grain could not be stored until the moisture content was sufficiently low (13% for wheat). However, commercial establishments obtained driers, and they could accept moist grain. Increased production caused a temporary shortage of storage space.

During the last 20 years, farmers have obtained large, round, metal storage bins with driers. Now, grain can be harvested with a fairly high moisture content, and one farmer can harvest up to 500-600 acres.

Clifford Branton's thresher.

OATS AND BARLEY

Until 45 years ago, banner oats were grown on 20 acres of most farms in Adelaide Township, and yielded about 50 bushels per acre. Oats were resistant to many diseases and were a reliable crop, even without fertilizer. They were the main spring grain.

Farmers liked growing a large acreage of oats, because oat straw contained considerable nutrient value, especially if cut slightly green. It was readily eaten by cattle after it went through the cutting box of the threshing machine. It supplemented hay. Oat grain was fed to pigs and cattle after being ground into chop. Considerable quantities of oats were always fed to race, carriage and draft horses, to make them frisky and lively.

On the other hand, malting and feed barley crops occasionally were good, but usually were poor, and so they were grown infrequently. In wet springs, barley would fail to emerge, and seedlings often did not tiller and were stunted. This was due to root destruction by the fungus Pythium. Nitrogen fertilizer greatly improved barley yields.

The barbs on barley awns caused great unpleasantness during stooking, loading, threshing, and working in the mow, especially if a barb got in one's eye. Thus, farmers liked to avoid planting and touching barley.

Recently, only a few acres of oats and barley have been grown, because more income is made from corn, soybeans and wheat.

WHEAT

Spring wheat has been grown to a limited extent, while fall wheat has always been an important crop in Adelaide Township. Farmers liked the golden sheaves and pretty stooks.

Wheat was an expensive commodity, about $2 per bushel, during the latter part of the 19th century and the early part of this century. Southern Ontario was the bread basket for Great Britain before the opening of the prairies. This valuable cash crop enabled farmers to build new houses and barns throughout the township from 1875 to 1910. Some wheat was required on all farms for chicken feed, livestock bedding, and even for filling ticks.

During the early part of this century, the Hessian fly caused a great deal of damage if wheat was planted during early September. The Hessian fly, a small, black two-winged midge, was introduced from

THE HARVEST OF 1835

An article in the July 12, 1889, Watford-Guide Advocate refers back 54 years to an exceedingly fine crop of wheat. As the harvest approached, the hopes of the settlers ran high. But just when the plump, golden heads of wheat began to bow, the weather broke and the rains descended. Although there were intervals of fine weather, showers followed so closely that the cut grain was drenched over and over and the uncut grain was laid flat. One farmer who remembers stated that all he managed to save in good condition was one stook of wheat, while bushel after bushel was fed to the cattle and pigs.

The bread made from the wheat of that year is reported to have been rather "waxy." But the wheat that wouldn't make flour would make whiskey, so the distillery at Kilworth did a booming business both that year and the following year.

The reporter commented that it is felt that the damage done to the Fall Wheat in 1835 is felt in the country today, as the stimulus given to the manufacture of whiskey has revived the "old country" habit of associating whiskey-drinking with almost every event that brought people together, such as work bees and house parties. The restrictions on the later Temperance Movements could be linked to the 1835 harvest!

Germany. This pest was eliminated with the use of resistant wheat and later planting.

In the 1940s, the combine began to replace the grain binder and threshing machine, and manual labour diminished. Now, moist wheat can be harvested because grain dryers are available at mills and on farms.

Also beginning in the 1940s, wheat yields began to steadily increase because of better soil drainage, new high-yielding varieties, and the application of fertilizer in the spring and autumn. Now yields are triple that of the early part of this century.

Even although inflation has increased a thousandfold, the price of wheat has only increased 50-100%. However, farmers now grow large fields of wheat. This is due to profitability, mid-summer harvesting, and planting after bean and corn harvest. The planting after bean and corn harvest is made possible because large machines are able to cultivate and sow large acreages in two or three days.

More recently, the no-till practice has been used to limited degrees, and this speeds the planting process.

BEE KEEPING AND BUCKWHEAT

In the 19th century and the early part of this century, some farmers kept a few bee hives. Large acreages of clover provided an ideal habitat for the bees. A considerable amount of excellent, tasty honey was produced. Pollination of flowers was assured.

A queen bee often escaped with part of the hive and made a bee-line to a preselected hollow tree. Farmers had to avoid their pathway but were forewarned by the approaching hum and buzz, and the thick cluster of bees.

A local understanding prevented farmers from planting buckwheat before July 1. By the time the buckwheat came into blossom, most of the good clover honey had been harvested, and a limited amount of undesirable, brown buckwheat honey was harvested during late summer.

In the 1930s, honey could be obtained from an apiary for 10¢/pound, and was usually sold in 5- and 10-pound tin pails, which could be refilled or used in other ways. For many years, Mr. Locke of Strathroy had bee hives in several spots in Adelaide Township.

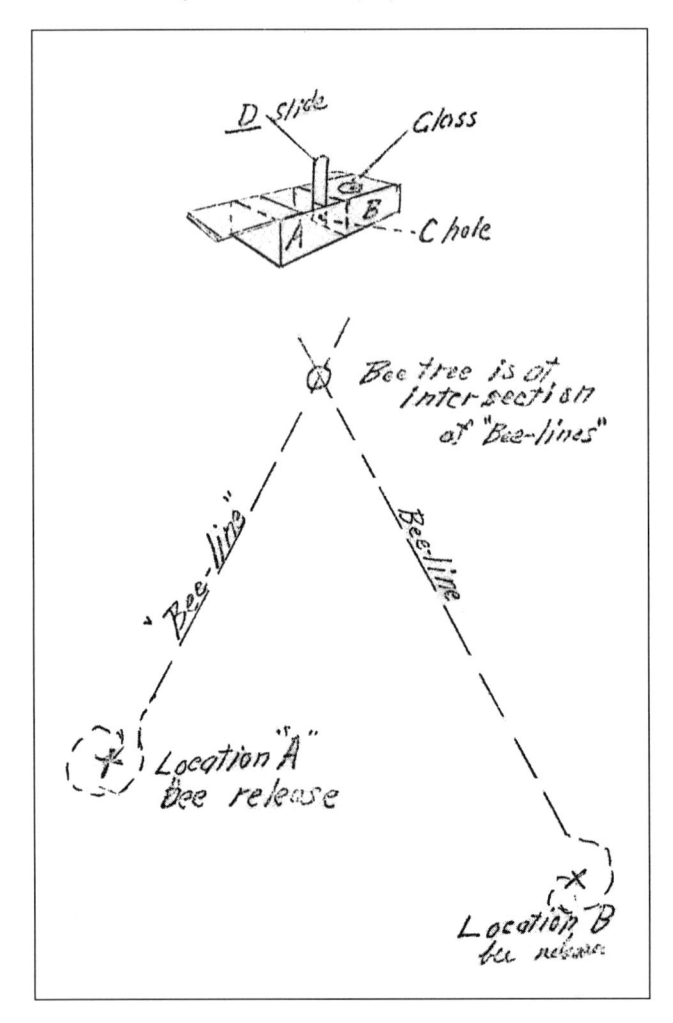

Recently, corn and soybeans have replaced much clover, and honey production has declined.

THE BEE BOX

At the Museum's Fair Exhibit an article was exhibited: "Used by the early settlers to get food when the country was largely woods." A prize was offered to the person or persons who correctly named the article and its use. The answer was "a bee box" and it was used to find wild bee trees and, thus, obtain honey.

The bee box is a wooden box approximately 3"x6"x12" with a partition across the center forming parts "A" and "B." The partition has a hole "D" closeable by slide "C." Each half of the box is covered with a sliding cover, that over part "B" has a glass window in the top.

To use the bee box, the operator or hunter should go into the bush in the flowering season and take a flower or two with wild bees on them. These are put into part "A." Close the lid and slide "C" closed. Put some honey on the floor of part "B" and almost close the lid. Open slide "C" and, when one bee comes through to the light, close slide "C." When the bee goes to work on the honey, keep the box still and remove the cover from "B" at location "A." When the bee is fully loaded, it will rise into the air, circle several times until it gets its bearing, and then make a "bee-line" to the tree. This direction should be noted carefully.

The hunter should move from location "A" at right angles to the bee-line, a distance of 75-100 yards to location "B," and repeat the procedure with another bee, by opening slide "C" and enticing it to the light and the honey. When the second bee is fully loaded, it will rise, circle, and make another bee-line to the hive. Where the two bee-lines cross is the location of the bee tree.

Teenagers and young men used to engage in this sport. When they located a bee tree, the usual procedure was to go to the owner of the tree and make a deal. The usual deal was for the youths to fell the tree, and cut it into saw logs. The owner would cut the limbs for wood and they shared the honey 50-50. It was not unusual in a big old hollow tree where bees had been working for years, to get two tubs (or even more) honey. If the owner was not co-operative and would not allow the tree to be cut, sometimes then, as now, "boys will be boys" and they would cut the tree at night and take the honey.

Mr. H. Anderson set up the exhibit at the fair. There were many interested and curious people, but they had no idea what the article was. Mrs. Marjorie Kellestine of Victoria Street was the only person to connect the article with bees, so she was declared the winner.

SOYBEANS

Soybeans were not grown in Adelaide Township until the middle of this century, and now are equal to wheat and corn in importance. Many fields, up to 100 acres in size, are grown. Weather conditions in North and South America have an immediate and direct impact on soybean prices. The increased demand for soybean oil and protein has advanced the grain price.

Short day varieties, cold hardiness, herbicides and combines have made increased plantings possible. Also, soybeans usually grow well in Adelaide heavy-clay soils.

Unfortunately, soybeans are susceptible to a water mould, Phytophthora, which develops extremely well in wet soil. Continuous planting of soybeans intensifies this disease, and aids in the development of new fungal strains. Good drainage helps prevent this disease.

New resistant varieties will help prevent the Phytophthora and white mould, another devastating disease.

Fortunately, the soybean is a legume, which adds nitrogen to the soil. Humus is also added, as only the soybean grain is removed from the field.

MAKING HAY

Adelaide Township farmers grew, sold, and fed a great amount of hay to their livestock until the 1960s. With the introduction of cash cropping and large beef feedlots, hay production was either eliminated or greatly reduced.

Also, the general use of commercial nitrogen fertilizer meant that clovers were no longer required to produce nitrogen in the soil. The nitrogen-fixing bacteria, Rhizobium species, in symbiosis with clover roots, produced nodules in which nitrogen was synthesized.

Until the 1960s, clover was rotated with oats, barley, wheat and corn, and the soil flora and pathogen population was greatly changed with each crop, to the benefit of the succeeding crop.

Timothy has always been a favoured feed for horses.

Alfalfa and red clover were the most common hay crop, while alsike and yellow and white clover were grown to a limited extent.

Alfalfa, a perennial, after a year or two, usually became less dense on the high ground and eliminated on the low ground, due to Phytophthora root rot. Consequently, farmers planted timothy with alfalfa in order to have hay throughout the field.

The first settlers used a scythe or sickle to cut the hay, and so its production was limited. Later, a mower, dump rake, tedder and hay loader were used. The mower had a 5' cutting bar. The cutting sections on the bar had to be sharpened after cutting about ten acres of hay, especially on stony fields. At the same time, knife sections broken by stones were replaced with new sections by riveting onto the cutting bar. Often, riveting was done on a large stone because the farmer did not have an anvil.

Big green horse flies were numerous in the hay fields, and these flies often caused a horse's stomach to become red with blood. The horses were greatly irritated.

After two or three days, the hay was put into windrows with a dump rake. The rake was operated by means of a foot pedal or a hand lever, which required a certain amount of strength. Driving was reduced to one hand. By means of the rake, the hay was gathered into windrows. If rain fell on windrows, a tedder (a machine with pitchfork-like tangs) was used to fluff the hay, enabling it to dry more quickly.

Sometimes, after raking, the hay was put in small piles or cocks to permit curing and prevent weathering, and put on the wagon with a pitchfork. If the hay was too green when it was put in the barn, spontaneous combustion might occur. Common salt added to the hay tended to prevent combustion. If the hay was not going to be thrown from the wagon with a pitchfork, the load was built in halves so that a hay-fork could be used to lift a large bundle of hay into a mow.

The hay-fork was u-shaped with two prongs about 2' long and 1½' apart. The metal fork prongs were pushed into the hay bundle, and by means of a handle and lever mechanism, 4" at the tip of each

Johnson Hay Loader; took two swaths from windrow, raking no longer required. James Fletcher, front; Paul Harris at loader; Harvey Harris driving the team, ca.1907.

prong was turned inwards and at right angles to the prong. Consequently, the fork was able to grasp the hay. The fork and hay bundle then could be raised by a rope, pulley and horse to a wood track below the peak of the barn. When the fork reached the car on the track, a lock was released and the car and hay bundle was pulled along the track until the hay-fork was tripped by a thin rope by the man on the wagon. Thus, the hay was dropped from the fork at the desired location.

During the early part of this century, a hay-loader was manufactured and it was pulled behind the wagon over the windrow. The hay was picked up by curved hooks that were attached to a rotating spindle between the loader wheels, which turned the spindle. The hay was moved up a rope and slat elevator, and dumped from the top of the loader onto the wagon.

The man on the wagon had to build the load as fast as the hay fell from the loader, or he became buried. The speed of the horses and the size of the windrow had a direct effect on the amount of hay arriving.

In the 1940s, movable balers came into use, and these produced rectangular bales. The bales were mechanically pushed onto the wagon. Sometimes, they were mechanically kicked into an enclosed wagon. Elevators were used to move bales into the barn.

More recently, large, round bales of various sizes, weighing hundreds of kilograms, are made. These bales are conveyed on wagons or tractor spears. The round bales have become popular because less labour is used. There is more deterioration of these bales, because they are too heavy to be put in the old frame barns and frequently are left outside. Often, they are wrapped in plastic or put in new steel sheds.

Sometimes, the clover and timothy is kept for seed. The first cutting of red clover is seldom used for seed. Timothy only produces one seed set a year. The price of seed varies greatly from year to year.

In the 19th century, farmers obtained timothy seed by having their young boys use scissors to cut ripe heads from the timothy stalks that grew along rail fences. The heads were placed in bags and flailed later.

CONTROL OF POTATO BEETLES

Although few potatoes were grown in Adelaide Township, farmers frequently grew enough for their own use and, if the family was large, they might produce one acre. Although Paris Green was the recommended pesticide, it was seldom used during the first 100 years of settlement because of its toxicity and its cost. In order to control pests, children were given a pail and asked to pick the beetles. The pail was held with one hand adjacent to the potato tops, and the other hand swatted the tops toward the pail opening in hopes that the beetles would drop into the pail. Sometimes, more than half of an 8-qt. pail was

Harvesting potatoes

collected, and taken to the house so that boiling water could be poured on the beetles. The procedure was repeated every day or every second day. This method of control was not completely effective, but it did reduce the population of beetles, saved the potato crop, and gave the children something to do. The devil has work for idle hands.

ORCHARDS

All farms had a wonderful orchard, which was composed mainly of apple trees, a few Bartlett pears, sometimes winter pears, two or three sweet and sour cherry trees, and a couple of plum trees. Occasionally, a few hardy peach trees, a concord grape vine, and a hope vine were present.

These orchards occupied about 5% of the farm and produced bushels and bushels of fruit. They were always adjacent to the farmhouse and added to the quality of farm life. The apples were used for eating, sauce, pies, apple crisp, and baking nine months of the year.

The orchards were good windbreaks for the home, and were excellent sanctuaries for many birds, especially bluebirds and flickers, which used hollow trunks for nests. Many songbirds made the orchard a cheerful place from sunrise to sunset, from early spring until late autumn. The orchards were beautiful during blossoming and harvest time. The grass under the trees served as pasture for calves. Larger cattle were not allowed to graze, because they browsed on the lower branches.

A large horizontal limb served as a support for a frequently used swing, made with a hemp rope that supported a wooden seat. The 1/2" rope was obtained from around a bag of binder-twine balls. Children used these swings two or three times a day, while they ate the most delicious apples at the ideal state of maturity. Children soon realized that, as the apple ripened, it became tastier and then gradually less desirable, at which time another variety was sought. Their choice changed from Harvest, Red Astrachan, Yellow Transparent, Tolman Sweet, Ben Davis, Winesap, Snow, Greening, King, Russet, Baldwin, and finally, Northern Spy. The taste of the later varieties was improved by frost.

All fruit trees, because they are heterogeneous and do not breed true, have scions grafted onto hardy root stalks, such as hawthorn. Some farmers also grafted onto main branches and, consequently, some trees supported three or four varieties.

During the later part of October and early November, large quantities of the choicest apples, mostly Northern Spy, Baldwin, and Greening, were picked and placed in large wood barrels, which were moved into the basement before frost became severe. Some apples were shipped to England, and windfalls were fed to pigs.

In October, the farmer would take sufficient apples from the cider apple tree to the local apple

ADELAIDE NEIGHBOURS HOLD A PLOWING BEE FOR JACK DOWDING

People passing the farm of Ernie Dowding in Adelaide Township last Tuesday would no doubt wonder what was going on. As they looked across the dull November fields, the thought of some belated plowing match being held would come to them. However, if they could see the way in which the soil was being rolled and uprooted, this thought would be quickly dismissed. It was just a plowing bee—uncommon these days—for Jack Dowding, an ambitious young chap, who intends to earn his bread by the sweat of his brow. He is going into the farming business when markets are bad, but if money can be made from this old occupation these days, John will make it.

Working through a dismal day that brought forth snow, rain and wind, 15 teams and a tractor plowed close to 20 acres. This land had not been broken for 30 years, and some of the participants in the bee had not then seen the light of day, and others were still dressed in Gandhi's garb. Most of the plowmen are neighbours, glad to give Jack a start, but there was also a minister, a produce dealer, an inspector, an ex-well-driller, and several philosophers present, each doing his share.

At a gathering such as this, there was no lack of comedy, and perhaps the biggest wisecrack was the one where the plowman, finishing up the ridge of another, said he had to stop his team, go ahead, and look around the corners to see that nothing was in his way. It is hoped that Jack's crops are better than some of the plowing he has to work on. Another feather on this unique day was the meals served. There was everything from soup to nuts, and the way some of the men ate, they must have been "nuts." This overeating, no doubt, made many of them drowsy, and accounted for the poor work they did. Nevertheless, it was a day that will long be remembered by the residents of the community.

(From the Age Dispatch, written by Bert Petch of Adelaide Township, Second Line South)

press, to obtain one or two barrels of apple juice. The children and parents would consume large quantities of this liquid during the next few days.

Mothers-of-vinegar, acetic acid-forming bacteria present in the old vinegar barrel, was usually abundant enough to provide inoculum for fermenting of the fresh apple juice. These bacteria gradually oxidized the juice into alcohol and then into acetic acid (vinegar). The vinegar was used by the housewife for the next year.

In pleasant weather, during February or March afternoons, the farmer spent considerable time pruning his trees and placing the discarded branches in a pile, which was burned.

The orchards were planted close to the house. Thus, the housewife could conveniently obtain apples, and the farm dog could prevent cottontail rabbits from girdling young trees. Pasturing the orchard also reduced girdling, by destroying the field mouse habitat.

The orchards were planted during the turn of the century and remained productive for about 75 years. It is surprising that apple maggot, codling moth and apple scab did not completely destroy the apples, because insecticides and fungicides were used only to a very limited extent. Blacknot often destroyed cherry and plum trees.

During long winter evenings, while the family sat around the cookstove, each member of the family would eat one or two delicious Spy apples and sometimes, for entertainment, the seeds were popped on the hot cookstove.

In most instances, the large orchards were never replaced, except for a few dwarf trees.

RASPBERRIES

Raspberries, both red and black, flourish where sunlight is somewhat reduced at the edge of woodlots and in areas where the woodlots have been completely logged. Although wild berry bushes are present on most farms in Adelaide Township, only occasionally do they occur in large, highly productive stands.

In the 1920s on the back 10 acres of the Glenn farm (Lot 10, Con. 3 NER), a solid stand of beautiful, wild, tasty red raspberries occurred for four or five years. Three or four teenagers could pick a 12-qt. pail of berries in two or three hours, every second morning during late June and early July. Picking

Eileen Sisson feeding chickens.

John Shamblaw cutting wood with steam power.

always occurred between hay and wheat harvest, when the temperature was high. A few other stands have developed throughout the township from time to time.

Upon arriving home, undesirable particles, leaves and insects were removed and the berries were placed in a large kettle. To each cup of berries, a cup of sugar and a cup of water were added. At the same time, 1- and 2-qt. jam jars were heated in boiling water. The jars were then filled, sealed, and stored in the cellar. Some housewives canned as much as 100 quarts.

Sometimes, the contents of the jars spoiled due to a poor seal and the entrance of micro-organisms. However, botulism caused by the extremely potent toxin, Clostridium botulinum, never occurred. Heat-resistant endospores of this bacterium were destroyed by boiling the acidic berries. The pH of a berry solution is below pH 3, and the spores are destroyed at a pH below 4. Also, the high sugar concentration produced a very high osmotic pressure and prevented the growth of micro-organisms, except for a few fungi such as Penicillium, which can grow even in maple syrup.

The berries made gourmet pies and desserts. Of course, the wild raspberries, like wild strawberries, are sweeter, tastier, and far superior to cultivated berries. Also, they are much smaller, and picking the same quantity requires more time. Only a few families, those with children capable of picking, were fortunate enough to obtain these delicious berries.

HAWTHORNS

Several cultivars of hawthorn grow in Adelaide Township on non-cultivated land, if it is not covered with forest. Originally, Adelaide Township was covered with hardwood trees and no hawthorns were present. After the forest was removed and pasture land and waste land appeared, hawthorn trees, an introduced species, began to spread.

The hawthorn seeds, which are produced in little red fruits, are spread by birds and cattle. The seeds are not destroyed in the cattle lumen or digestive system. Unlike other tree seedlings, hawthorns can readily withstand grazing because at the base of each leaf, a long sharp thorn is produced. In 25-50 years, these trees may completely cover a pasture field or farm.

If the hawthorn farms are left untouched, hardwood trees will grow through the thorn trees. Because the hawthorns are very sensitive to shade, all thorns will be killed in 50-75 years.

Frequently, half-hearted attempts are made to eradicate hawthorns by cutting them with an axe. This is a very difficult procedure because of injury by thorns, the hard work, and the fact that several new stems are produced where one existed before. Also, the hawthorn tree produces one main root, which develops horizontally about 6-24" below the surface of the soil, and it has the ability to send up several shoots.

The pasture farm on the east half of Lot 20, Con. 3 NER, was covered with small thorn trees in the 1920s. All of the thorns originated from one large thorn tree in the middle of the farm. Grass production was greatly reduced.

TREES AND WOODLOTS

Maple, oak, beech, elm, basswood, tamarack, hickory, poplar, ironwood, cherry, and willow, all deciduous, completely covered the Adelaide Township landscape until the white man began settlement. Pine and chestnut grew farther south, and hemlock grew farther north.

Environment influenced the density and prevalence of each species. Frequently, an oak, maple and ash mixture predominated. Tamarack prevailed in swamps (Lot 17, Con. 4 NER) until drainage occurred about 1900. The swamp was a good environment for red trilliums, jack-in-the-pulpits and ferns.

Hard maple was present on well drained soil, while soft maple grew in swampy areas. Willow also grew in swampy land and along creekbanks. Willow always spread along waterways because pieces of branches, after being washed downstream, would readily root, and grew if slightly buried in sediment.

Beech trees usually grew in clumps in lighter soil. Beech clumps resulted from the ability of beech to produce suckers from roots, which could grow into full-size trees. After a woodlot was cut down, oak and ash were usually the predominant trees in the second growth woods. Hard maple was often less prevalent.

Beautiful umbrella-shaped elms were quite common. They graced the fence lines and were more characteristic in Adelaide than hard maple, which had pretty red leaves in autumn. At the present time, with rare exceptions, only elms under 40 years of age grow, because the Dutch elm disease arrived in the 1950s and killed older trees. This disease is caused by a fungus and spread by two types of beetles. Elms begin to succumb to this disease after they are about 20 years of age.

In the past, elm served the farmer very well, as fuel, as timber in barns, and as structural frames in covered furniture. Elm wood was very strong, but had to be kept dry to persist. Rock elm was a favoured species. Hard maple and oak lumber made good hardwood floors. Oak lumber made beautiful flooring, paneling and furniture.

Intense shading in dense forests provided knot-free lumber because self-pruning resulted. The woodlots were distant from barns in order to conserve time to and from grain and hay fields, and to keep woodlot animals, such as squirrels, rabbits and raccoons distant from houses and gardens.

The size of the woodlots was continually reduced until they were eliminated or about 1/10 of

ASSISTANCE FOR ADELAIDE FARMERS

A special Adelaide Township Council Meeting was held on March 17, 1859, to discuss the existing economic situation, which would hamper many farmers from purchasing seed grain for the spring planting. Communication was made to Mr. A.P. McDonald, MPP, regarding passing an Act in Legislature granting aid for the purchase of seed for 1859. A petition was sent to Middlesex County Council to raise $3,000 for the township, to enable certain persons to sow their lands. There must have been results of these efforts, because the April 12, 1859, Minutes report a cost of $44.59 for distributing seed grain.

As may be expected, complaints of inequalities in charges for seed grain money were brought up at the February 1, 1864, meeting. Mr. Scoon was asked to investigate and report at the next Council Meeting. An item in the Minutes of October 3, 1964, records that Mr. Scoon was to receive $3.00 for investigating the seed grain account. The confusion in the seed grain account would be cleared as the August 7, 1865, Minutes state that the surplus of $69.34 was to be apportioned to each farmer who used this aid, and credit would be made on the collectors' roll. It would seem that government financial affairs often foment problems.

the farm acreage. The size varied widely, depending upon the amount of rough land and the philosophy of the farmer. Now, there is a provincial law that prohibits the reduction in woodlot size and some tax reduction is provided for woodlots.

In the mid-1800s, it was important to clear as much land as possible. The clearing of the land required an enormous amount of energy. Farmers and their children spent many hours cutting and burning trees and stumps during winter and springtime, in order to increase their arable land. Frequently, cultivation and cropping occurred around persistent stumps. This procedure took place from the 1830s until the present time.

Many straight, large, long, knot-free logs were harvested and used locally or shipped to England. Wood was the main fuel until the 1950s, and still is used to a limited extent. Indians made axe and hammer handles from hickory trees. Wiffle trees, double draw bars, and neck yokes were made from 5" tamarack trees cut longitudinally through the center. Round rungs were made in the same fashion as pins were made for beams in barns. The tamarack ladders were very straight, light and strong. Shellbark hickory nuts provided some tasty food.

Many trees and logs were cut by means of a cross-cut saw in about 12-14" lengths. These blocks were split into slabs, piled, and allowed to dry during the summer, before being placed in a woodshed. During the winter, the slabs were split into firewood suitable for burning in cookstoves. Tree limbs, except for the tiny ones, were placed in a pile and later sawed with a buzz saw after steam engines and tractors were available.

THE RAT PLAGUE

For a couple of years in the early 1930s, a rat plague occurred in Adelaide Township. The plague was caused by the Norway rat, the world's most destructive mammal, which reached North America by ship from Asia about 1775. It has been an economic and health problem since that time. It eats almost anything, plant or animal, dead or alive. It spreads disease and contaminates food. It has a high reproductive rate, an average of five litters a year with eight to 10 rats in a litter. Starting with a single pair, more than 1,500 rats could be produced in a year.

Suddenly, a large population of rats appeared in barns, hen houses and pig houses, and any other hiding place on the property. An army of rats invaded property after property. The rats made tunnels and nests through the straw and hay mows, and chewed holes in sacks, floors, doors and walls. They fed on grain, hen mash, and pig and cattle chop.

They could be heard at any time of the day or night. During the first hours of darkness, they left their hideouts and congregated in large numbers in the granary, hen and pig troughs. If one rushed into the hen house with a club at this time, there was the possibility of killing one or two rats as they scrambled up the 2"x4's.

No one would rush into the granary at night unless they banged the door before entering, and then only with a club. After entry, the rats scrambled and dashed in all directions, squealing and thundering about.

Three or four cats had no impact on the rat population. The cats avoided the rats, because several rats would stand their ground if a cat appeared.

Various techniques and traps were devised for catching the rats. Barrels partially filled with water and covered with a thin layer of chop were used for drowning the rats. All the methods failed to control the rat population.

In a couple of years, the rat population disappeared as quickly as it had arrived. The annihilation is thought to have been caused by a deadly virus or a bacterium.

FARM DOGS

It is believed that dogs, which may have developed from the wolf, originated in North America. Christopher Columbus reported their presence in 1492. The dogs have acted as the eyes, ears, police, playmates, and even confidants of Adelaide farmers. The presence of 160,000,000 dogs in the world attests to their widespread popularity.

Dogs contributed more to Adelaide farmers in the early settlement years when horses were used and general farming was practiced than they have since the introduction of the tractor and specialized farming, because fewer cattle and horses are pastured.

A good dog saved a farmer many steps when he drove the milk cows from the pasture to the barn and protected him from an attack by a bull. The dog kept cottontail rabbits far from the house, and protected the garden. Groundhogs, weasels and squirrels were also kept away from the yard.

A farm family always felt safe when they had a good watchdog. Boys and their dogs always enjoyed field trips, hunting rabbits, groundhogs, and even raccoons. The dogs were great companions.

The township was forced to have sheep and cattle evaluators because some dogs reverted to their ancestral habit of travelling in packs and capturing their prey. Sheep were very susceptible to injury and death.

Most dogs were cross-breeds or mongrels. Of the 400 distinct breeds in the world, the collie was the most common in Adelaide Township. The collie was developed in the Scottish Lowlands where they guarded the large flocks of sheep. In 1860, Queen Victoria brought some back to Windsor Castle, and the Britons and Americans fell madly in love with them. The collie was highstrung, sensitive, and anxious to please. They mistrusted strangers, but grew deeply attached to their owner and family. They were very effective watchdogs, intelligent, easily trained, and affectionate with children. The border collie was exceptionally intelligent and a superb sheep herder.

WELLS AND WINDMILLS

Water is our most valuable resource. The settlers at first relied on unpolluted and uncontaminated water from streams and ponds. For example, Mary Brown, who lived on the Featherson Sideroad, Lot 18, Con. 3 NER, obtained all of her water from Mud Creek until the beginning of this century.

For safety, convenience, and a reliable supply of water, wells were soon dug. Fortunately, an aquifer was present in Adelaide Township. The aquifer is a layer of sand saturated with water, of varying thickness and varying distances below the ground's surface. This stratum was the source of water for artesian and deep wells.

Some farmers relied on surface, shallow-dug wells, especially if creek water was available for livestock. Sometimes a tile drain emptied into their surface well in order to maintain a supply of water for a longer period of time. In dry periods, creek water was used to fill the shallow well.

Artesian wells were easy to construct and required little maintenance. They were made by boring a 2" hole into the ground, using 10' lengths of 1"-diameter steel rod, attached to a 2" auger about 1' in length. This apparatus was manually operated, and had to be extracted very often in order to remove the soil. After the aquifer was contacted, water moved up the hole due to pressure. If the water rose above the soil surface, an artesian well was constructed.

A pump log (a hollow log about 8"-9" in diameter and 7' in length) was inserted about 4' into the top of the hole, which was enlarged by an ordinary post-hole auger. A wooden spout was inserted into a hole in the log about 2'-3' above the ground.

EAST ADELAIDE

Our most up-to-date and enterprising farmer, Jonah Getty, Lot 25, Con. 2 NER, has improved the appearance of his farm by erecting a new windmill, of Toronto manufacture. It is Mr. Getty's intention to force the water to both house and barn and, no doubt, he will have arrangements made for pumping the water into the stables during the winter season. The neighbouring housekeepers are busy stirring up their sleepy husbands to "Go thou and do likewise."

(From The Age, August 16, 1900)

Water flowed continuously out of the spout into a wooden tank or trough.

Several of these wells at the north end of Con. 3 NER, between Lot 15 and Lot 18, produced satisfactorily until the 1940s. In this region, the aquifer was about 30' below the surface of the ground.

In most locations, dug wells had to be constructed. A well-witcher was often requested to find the most convenient location for the well.

A skillful well-digger with a strong back and a short-handled shovel (and without a hard helmet and hazardous duty pay) began to work with a couple of reliable helpers. The wells were about 3'-4' in diameter and up to 70' in depth, and required about a month for construction.

A wall or lining was installed as digging progressed in order to prevent cave-ins. Bricks usually formed the wall, but in the well at Lot 22, Con. 3 NER, the wall is composed of cone-shaped fieldstones, about 1' in diameter. This construction must have required great skill and careful selection from a large number of stones. In 100 years, no stones have fallen into this well.

Digging stopped prior to reaching the quicksand. A 2" hole was bored down to the quicksand and, if the water rose a few feet into the well, no further digging was required. A pump log was fitted into the top of the hole.

In order for the pump to be effective, the cylinder in the water pipe had to be 20' from the bottom of the well. Atmospheric pressure will not force water up more than 29'.

The leathers in the cylinder usually had to be replaced once or twice a year. Two strong men were involved in this procedure, because the pipe had to be pulled up until the cylinder was above the ground. A windmill above the well aided in this procedure. The leathers deteriorated most rapidly when the water contained sand. The well was protected by a cover. The cylinder had to be extracted if a mouse or frog was pumped into it, causing vacuum loss. Less energy was required for pumping if the cylinder was close to the surface.

Freezing of water in the pump and pipe never occurred, because a tap in the pipe about 4' below the lid of the well was left slightly open, and water drained through the tap, drop by drop. Consequently, water did not remain in the pump.

For the past 50 years, wells have been drilled. When the aquifer is reached, a point (a sieve apparatus about 6' long) is inserted into the quicksand and attached to the bottom of a 6" metal casing. If the sand is coarse, the point is very effective. An electric centrifugal pump, submerged in water at the bottom of the casing, forces water up a connecting plastic pipe.

Windmills were a great asset, but were only completely reliable if they were taller than the surrounding buildings and trees, and if the wind was blowing. The operation of the windmill could be completely automatic if a float mechanism in an adjacent water tank was attached to the break on the windmill.

CISTERNS AND RAIN BARRELS

The early settlers knew the value of soft water. Usually, deep-well water is very hard, while lake water is much softer. Surface and creek water is even softer, and rain water is soft. Water becomes harder as the concentration of salts increases.

At the present time, many water softeners and detergents are available for the removal of hardening compounds. In the past, fewer softeners existed, and they were too costly. Consequently, a technique for collecting and storing soft water was devised.

Except for the occasional time in August, most farmers had a good supply of soft water in their cisterns. The cistern was adjacent to the house, and was an underground cement structure about 9' deep and 6' in diameter. A manhole above the cistern projected up to one-third of a meter above the surface of the ground, and was covered by a lid, upon which a large heavy stone or weight sat. Overflow or excess water exited from the cistern by means of a tile drain, which emerged near the top of this storage reservoir. A pipe from an eavestrough from the house served to conduct water into the cistern. Sometimes, during dry August weather, the cistern went dry. This was an ideal time for the annual cleanout of this chamber.

A 2" galvanized pipe led from the bottom of the cistern to a cistern pump situated in the kitchen, summer kitchen, or wash area. The cylinder was in the pump because atmospheric pressure would force water up to the pump when a vacuum was created. During the cool weather, if the pump was not in a heated room, the pump-prime was released in order to drain and prevent freezing and breaking of the pipe.

If a cistern was lacking, a barrel was often placed below the eavestrough pipe, and soft water was available at least during the warm rainy season.

After electrification of the rural areas, hard water was pumped into farmhouses and cisterns, and rain barrels fell into disuse.

MUD CREEK

Mud Creek used to be a creek, not a drainage ditch. Many adjacent ponds and tiny lakes persisted throughout the summer. The water slowly seeped into the aquifer and downstream. Pretty water lilies were abundant in the creekbed, and cattails and swale grass occurred in inlets.

Children enjoyed catching chub and minnows by means of a handmade rod and line, and a hook with a worm. Then, a small tree branch with a side branch was made as a carrying device for the catch. The main branch was put through the gill and out the mouth of the fish, and the side branch prevented the fish from dropping.

If a goose and gander with their young goslings wandered to the creek, inevitably one or more goslings disappeared, because the turtles, up to a foot in diameter, would snatch and devour them. Now, the turtles are almost nonexistent due to the scarcity of water, and hunters who catch them and serve them as a delicacy.

Muskrats were numerous. Groundhogs always lived in tunnels on the banks and, every summer, a few migrated into farmers' clover fields to burrow and eat their favorite food. During the 1960s, a rabies virus annihilated them.

Obstructions such as old logs, water plants, and other constrictions in the creek have been removed, and the water from tiled fields goes downstream very rapidly.

FENCES

Fences have been used to mark the limits of properties and confine livestock within fields. If a fence has been in place for 10 years or more, even though it is not quite on the boundary line, it marks the property line—unless the fence is around a bend in a creek or river.

Bulls and poor fences have caused many quarrels between neighbours. Sometimes pokes, triangular wooden structures, were placed around the necks of animals, to prevent cows and pigs from passing through poor fences.

At the turn of the century, there were several fenced fields on a farm, but now few fences remain because pasturing of livestock is very limited. In the past, fences permitted the rotation of pasture fields with hay and grain fields.

Until recently, a provincial fence-line Act, which defined such things as type and standard of fence, was used. Three fence-viewers, appointed by the township, served as adjudicators to rule on fence disputes and, until about 1960, this procedure was generally accepted by farmers. Due to the change from general farming to cash cropping and the cost of fencing, two changes have occurred. First, a farmer can not force a cash cropper to build a fence on half of the property line, and second, judges now make the rulings.

Many materials have been used for fences. As farms were being cut out of the forest, sometimes stumps and stones were used. Also solid board fences were used occasionally. In the 1800s, rail fences were most commonly used. These fences were usually built in a zigzag fashion and were nine rails high. The ends of the rails were placed on top of each other, with a block under the bottom one. A pair of stakes were placed at the cross-over points and were wired together to prevent the rails from slipping sideways, and to give rigidity to the fence. The rails were 11' long and were split from straight oak or white ash logs. The oak rails lasted 50-60 years. These fences required about 6'-7' along the property line.

During the winter, huge snow drifts formed beside the fence, and these drifts were often indirectly responsible for the death of crops underneath them, such as Fall Wheat. Snow mould caused the death of the wheat.

In the early 1900s, straight wires were strung on posts and wooden pickets (1/2"x 2"x4') were placed in a vertical position and fastened to the straight wires by a hand picket instrument. Sometimes, commercial picket fences were used.

In the 1920s, page woven-wire fencing was introduced, and it was stapled to cedar posts or wired to steel posts, about a rod apart. Large anchor wooden posts, at the end of the fence or every 40 rods apart, were put deep in the ground after 3' cedar posts or planks were spiked at right angles to their bottom end. These cross-pieces prevented heaving if the cross-brace was parallel to the soil surface.

Fencing eight or nine wires in height and 20-40 rods in length were used. Until about 1970, post holes were manually dug with an auger, but since that time, power-driven augers have frequently been used. A fence stretcher was used to tighten the fence in order to prevent livestock from walking over it.

Sometimes five or six barbed wires were used to construct a fence. The wire fences were constructed much more rapidly than rail fences. Recently, fences three boards high have been built to confine horses. When the fence lines disappear, the limits of properties may be shifted unless surveyors' original starting points are made permanent.

FENCE-VIEWERS

The position of fence-viewer was created in 1793 by the first provincial parliament of Upper Canada. The first statute dealing with line fences was enacted in 1834. It was revised extensively in 1874 and 1913, and remained from that point as enacted until it was revised again in 1979, with further changes in 1986. The 1986 amendment made a significant change in that, where prior to this amendment, an appeal against a fence-viewers' award would go before a Judge of the Small Claims Court, a referee would now be appointed by the Provincial Cabinet to take the place of a Judge. The referee would have four deputies to go to various parts of the Province to hear disputes. The decision of the referee or deputy-referee is final, as was the decision of the Judge of the Small Claims Court.

Originally, the Act establishes the principle that, if a landowner wants a line fence to make the boundary between his/her land and the property of an adjoining owner, that landowner is entitled to construct a fence on the boundary line. If, however, neither owner wants a line fence, no fence is necessary. In the original versions of the Line Fence Act, both sides of the boundary were responsible for part of the line fence, either on a 50-50 basis or on a basis agreed upon between two property owners. The common law method of standing on one's property facing the fence and agreeing that the right hand portion would be his to maintain and fix has stood the test of time until recent years, probably to the early 1970s.

With the decline in the cattle population and the increase in cash cropping, farmers began to chal-

FARM MARKET PRICES IN 1888

September 7, 1888

Some very fast threshing was done in the vicinity of Adelaide by our popular threshers—the Adair Brothers, who are threshing 1,200 bushels of grain in one day.

Nov. 23, 1888

Mr. Robert Shepherd, who, for some time, has been purchasing geese, intends shipping a carload to New York presently.

January 6, 1888 - Watford Markets

Red Wheat 78 cents to 79 cents; White Wheat 78 cents; Spring Wheat 75 cents to 78 cents; Barley 55 cents to 60 cents; Oats 34 cents to 35 cents; Peas 55 cents; Eggs 16 cents; Lard 8 cents to 10 cents; Tallow 5 cents; Flour $2.00 to $2.25; Potatoes 75 cents; Butter 18 cents; Hay $8.00 to $10.00; Wood $2.25 to $2.50; Beef, fore quarter 5 cents; hind quarter 6 cents; Pork $6.00 to $6.30; Wool 20 cents.

(As reported in the Watford-Guide Advocate on June 29, 1888)

Pork in London is quoted at $6.50 to $6.75; eggs 14 cents a dozen; butter, rolls 15 to 16 cents; crock 18 cents to 20 cents.

Clover seed $4.30 to $4.50; Alsike $4.50 to $5.25; Timothy $3.00; Wool 18 cents to 20 cents.

lenge the notion that they had to put up a line fence just to protect their crops from the neighbour's cattle. Many court case appeals are recorded with the verdict in most cases going in favour of the cash crop farmer not being responsible for erecting a fence or maintaining a fence against his neighbour's cattle. In Adelaide Township, a judgment by the Honourable Sam Lerner, Small Claims Court, on October 1, 1985, further upheld this trend towards the livestock farmer being responsible for all portions of the fence enclosing his cattle. The Appellant, John Van Geffen, and the Respondent, Wilbert McKeen, had a difference of opinion regarding the properties on Con. 3 NER, being the south part of Lot 19 owned by McKeen, and part of Lot 20 owned by Van Geffen. In this case, McKeen had the cattle and Van Geffen had cash crops, and while Van Geffen acknowledged repairing an old fence to keep McKeen's cattle out, he refused to be part of building a new fence. McKeen then built a fence and appealed to the fence viewers for costs, which were awarded to McKeen. Van Geffen then appealed this award to Small Claims Court, resulting in the Honourable Lerner's verdict, allowing Van Geffen to be responsible for no part of the fence opposite his cash crop land, but to be responsible for part of the fence wherein he had a small orchard which could hold cattle of his own at some point. The decision boiled down to a 75% cost to McKeen, 25% cost to Van Geffen. This represented the percentage of fence, i.e., 75% opposite cash crop and 25% opposite old pasture/orchard. The township has on file awards dating back into the 1950s wherein, regardless of the type of farming operations on either property, awards are generally based on a 50-50 cost sharing basis.

LIVESTOCK EVALUATORS

Regarding livestock evaluators and fox bounties, the oldest form on file at the office indicates a dog tax and cattle, sheep and poultry protection Act in force in 1965, which would indicate the Act predates 1965 by a considerable number of years, perhaps going back into the 1920s and 1930s for a start-up point for the legislation.

Regarding fox bounties, they were in place by the Provincial Government in 1965. Chances are the bounty on foxes began sometime prior to 1965, and perhaps as far back as the end of WWII. At that time, sheep losses were running into the thousands of dollars per year, mainly due to a large sheep operation owned by Bill Wright on Seed Side Road north of Highway 22, and property to the west that was overgrown with thorns. This overgrown area proved an ideal spot for predators, such as stray dogs, foxes, and wolves, to hide in while preying on sheep. Councils in the period between 1965 and 1970 even hired trappers to trap the predators in the thorn trees in Adelaide Village. Farming practices changed in the 1970s and 1980s and, consequently, loss from predators has been drastically reduced. The evaluator may only be called out for one call a year, and in the late 1980s and early 1990s, there were no calls for the evaluator.

FARM SHAPE AND SIZE

Adelaide Township was originally laid out with a four rod road allowance between each concession, but only half of the east-west roads were built. In the instances where the roads were not built, half of the road allowances (two rods) was added to each farm. The 100-acre farms were surveyed to be 266 2/3 rods long and 60 rods wide, but without the east-west road, they were now 268 2/3 rods long and thus 2/3 of an acre larger.

This information was not known by all residents as evidenced by the fact that when farms were split in an east-west direction, the whole allowance, at least in some instances, went to one owner. Examples occur in Lots 19 and 21 NER. In Lot 19, the extra land joined the farm to the south, and in Lot 21, it was incorporated in the farm to the north. The farms on the gore roads vary in size and shape. In many other townships, however, the farms are not as long–120x133 1/3 rods or 80x200 rods.

In the past, when farms were divided into several fields, more fencing was required in Adelaide's long hundreds, and travel time to and from the barn to the fields was greater than in farms that were less elongated. Also the woodlot and wild animal habitat was further from the house.

Recently, however, since fields within the farm have been eliminated, the long hundreds are probably more convenient for tractor use. Also, individual farmers generally own more acreage.

FARM BARN

Typically, there were one or two barns on each hundred acres, and they were about 100'-200' from the farmhouse. If there were two barns, one was usually a cow-and horse-shed with a loft. The other one had a granary and large mows for the hay and grain on each side of the barn floor, which was wide enough to hold a team and wagon. A gangway always led to the barn floor. Sometimes, a room or roothouse was present under the gangway.

If there was only one barn, it was often raised on an 8'-10' concrete foundation, and cattle and horses were kept in the foundation part of the barn. If the barns were not raised, they were often supported on oak blocks that began to disintegrate after 40-50 years, and then sometimes were replaced with concrete.

A typical barn was 36' or 40' wide and 60'-70' in length. The main structure was built from hewn logs. The posts were 14'-16' in length, 12'-14' apart, and were embedded into the upper and lower plate. Tiebeams, across the barn, were embedded into the posts about 2' below the upper plate. All of these beams were about 1' square, sometimes the length of the barn, and often were made from rock elm logs. The logs were obtained from the farmer's woodlot.

The purlin, with its posts on the tiebeams, supported the rafters at their midpoint. The purlin and other tiebeams were about 8" square. The insert into plates, purlins, beams and posts were held securely by round wooden pins about 13" in length and 1" in diameter. Braces about 3'-4' in length were embedded into all timbers at all joints, to form a triangle with two 45-degree angles and one right angle. They gave rigidity to the barn. Each rafter, whether sawn or a pole, was spiked to the purlin and to the wall plate so that its upper tip met the tip of the rafter on the other side of the roof. The rafter projected about 2' out over the plate.

Sheathing and B.C. cedar shingles formed the roof. Hemlock boards 16' long and about 1' wide were fastened onto the sides of the barn with rock nails. Even though these boards were not painted in most instances, they lasted over 100 years, but became severely checked. All of the hemlock was obtained from Huron and Bruce County.

A 4" square wooden track was hung from the peak of the roof by metal rods attached to the rafters. This track was used to move bundles of sheaves and hay from the wagon to the mow. Dave and Jim Gerry framed many barns in Adelaide Township.

At one end of the barn, there were four horse stalls, and usually a box stall. In the remaining part of the barn, three or four rows of cattle stalls were present. Usually, two cattle were present in a stall, and they were held by a chain fastened to the side of the stall. The horses were always held by a halter and rope. When the barn was filled with livestock, its temperature was many degrees above the outside temperature.

Most of the frame barns were built at the end of the 19th century. They served very well. Many of these barns were burned so that they could be replaced with modern metal barns, which are used for livestock, machinery and hay storage.

FARMHOUSES

When our forefathers arrived during the middle of the 19th century, they had to hurry to build a log house before the winter. The original settlers were blessed with common sense and were very pragmatic. Their homes were always built on high ground and about 50'-200' from the road, unless the only suitable elevated spot was at another location. Thus, it was usually possible to have a nice lawn, and flowerbeds and lilac bushes near the road.

The original log houses were warm, well-insulated lodgings until sagging, rotting and cracks appeared. Usually, a ladder led to a loft, where the older children slept. Because of the paucity of rooms, privacy was at a premium. The log houses served as cozy homes until the latter part of the 19th century, and some were retained for storage and hen houses, etc.

The replacement houses were brick or wood, 1½- to 3-storey homes, which could accommodate a family of 12 to 15. The brick houses were solid brick (not brick veneer as is often built today) and always had at least two layers of brick. Most roofs were covered with B.C. cedar shingles, and sometimes metal and slate were used.

Wood lath and plaster was used throughout, except for the kitchen ceiling, which was usually wood. Occasionally, plaster was applied directly to the brick. A very cold house resulted, because an insulating layer of air was lacking. These houses never had the "new house" syndrome, which is common today.

Many houses had summer kitchens and some of these kitchens were added after the main structure was constructed. These additions tended to move slightly away from the main structure. The summer kitchens added greatly to the comfort of the home, especially from June to September, because all of the cooking was conducted in this summer room during hot weather.

In most instances, a good basement was built to store vegetables, apples, potatoes, preserves and salt pork.

Barn raising in Keyser's Corners, at the home of Albert and Ann Eliza Murray.

Newton barn raising

Heated rooms above the cellar prevented freezing in the basement. If no cellar was present, a log milk house adjacent to the house was often used for milk and preserve storage.

Typically, the front door of the house that faced the road was seldom used or opened, although they had fancy doorbells. Gingerbread was often present below the roof edge, especially on the verandah. Sometimes, very decorative structures were present at both ends of the roof peak. Tops of windows were often arched, and few storm windows were used. Frequently, a front and back ornate verandah was present. These structures gave valued protection from the elements and were an ideal place to sit and relax in the evening and during rainstorms.

During the 1930s, when ranch houses without verandahs appeared in the suburbs, many farm wives had the verandah closed in or removed.

Woodsheds were attached to the back of most houses, and stored several cords of dry wood. As the winter progressed, the wood slabs were split into firewood suitable for the kitchen stove. Kindling always had to be available for starting the morning fire. Cedar shingles from old roofs were treasured for starting fires. The fire in the kitchen stove was often the main source of heat in the house, and the housewife was responsible for its maintenance. If the fire was not properly maintained, a cake might fall during baking. In the ceiling, four large hooks around the stove supported wooden clothes dryers. Linoleum protected the kitchen floor.

One could always be warm in the kitchen on cold winter days if within 5'-6' of the stove. There was always enjoyment in rubbing one's hands above the hot stove, especially after coming in from a blizzard.

The husband was usually the first one to appear in the kitchen during winter mornings, and his first chore was to remove the ashes from the stove. They were put in a metal pail, which was dumped after the red coals cooled.

During cold winter evenings, the family often sat around the cookstove, put their feet on the damper, and watched the red coals in the open grate while they reminisced. The stove pipe did not go directly into the chimney, for it usually went up through a bedroom before entering the chimney near the ceiling. In homes without summer kitchens, the cookstove was moved across the kitchen for the winter so that more stovepipe was in the kitchen, to emit more heat. The same principle was used in the one-room schools.

If stovepipes were not cleaned two or three times a year, and more frequently if green damp wood was burned, creosote lining the inside of the pipe would ignite, and a roaring fire would occur within the pipe. If the stove vents were not closed immediately, and water was not poured on the metal collar surrounding the pipe in the ceiling, there was a possibility the pipes could collapse. Even the most easygoing individual became very agitated during this experience.

The parlor, seldom used except on Sunday, was kept immaculate and often had a pot-bellied stove, which radiated enormous quantities of heat. Both the parlor and the kitchen had lovely wainscoting that extended about 3' above the floor. The wain-

Line up of wagons of sugar beets to be unloaded.

AGRICULTURAL SOCIETIES

In the Regional Collection of the D.B. Weldon Library at the University of Western Ontario, London, an interesting old document written on blue parchment shows the concern of the early pioneers of the Adelaide area for becoming better farmers. This document, signed in 1859 by 80 members, states:

We, whose names are subscribed hereto, agree to form ourselves into a Society... for the encouragement of Agriculture, and also to provide for the promotion of Mechanical Science... to be called the "West Riding of Middlesex Agricultural Society."

Each subscriber agreed to pay the Treasurer five shillings (or $1.25) annually. The list of the 80 members followed the purpose stated, which was to hold a Fall Fair. As a result of the formation of this Agricultural Society, a Fall Fair was held in Strathroy the next year, 1860.

The following list of names are in the signer's script and may be transcribed inaccurately:

Christopher Beer	Hiram Carrol	Alexander Hilton	John Manning
Jacob C. Beer	Richard Coy	David Brown	Malcolm McArthur
Patrick Mee	Dr. Wm. R. Conarns	John Mortimer	Archibald Campbell
James Keefer	Jonas Jury	William Hawken	George Foster
James Gough	William Rapley	Frederick Harris	Jonas Jury
George Buttery	William Ewer	James Carrol	John A. Scoon
Joseph Buttery	G. Armstrong	John D. Harris	Joseph Scoon
William T. Buttery	Wm. Northcott	A.P. MacDonald	Horatio Sells
Frances Petch	Richard Saul (Rev.)	James Large	George Mortimer
William Brent	Philip Jones	William King	William Smith
James Cooper	John Pinkeren	A.H. Couse	George Parker
Amos Cutter	Samuel Hungerford	Walter Hoare	Robert Cleland
Hiram Dell	William Rundle	John Zavits, Jr.	Richard Garcy
Edwin Parker	Thomas Moyle	Timothy Cook	William Scoon
Richard Morgan	Robert T. Tooth	Richard Humphreys	David Wiley
David Rapley	Richard Moyle	John Carson	Alexander Levy
Anthony Preston	William Harris	John McGarvey	John Irvine
William Ireland	Robert Richards	Thomas Cuddy	Hiram Frank
Francis Frank	J.B. Winlow	William Robinson	John Frank
Mark Mann	W.M. Johnston	Stephen Boyd	Amos Culley

The document was written by Philip Jones, a farmer on the east half of Lot 17, Con. 4 SER, whose neat writing still stands out at the head of the list of signatures.

The Adelaide Township Land Records list a Crown grant of Lot 27, Con. 3 NER, on February 3, 1862, to be Middlesex West Agricultural Society of 55 acres. On 4 July, 1864, 16 acres of this property was sold by the West Middlesex Agriculture Society to Hector McDonald, a wagon maker.

In the Adelaide Township Council Minutes of June 26, 1869, it was recorded that the councillors decided to grant St. George's Square (in Adelaide Village) to the President and Directors of the Agricultural Society for "Annual Agricultural Shows or other matters connected with provision that the municipality could build a Town Hall and give free use of the same and of the land."

On October 7, 1870, The Age printed a full account by Anthony Preston, Esq., the Secretary of the Adelaide Agricultural Society of the Annual Show in Adelaide Village, "last Tuesday":

"Notwithstanding an unfavourably wet day and muddy roads, there was an excellent show of horses for general purposes, and draught horses, well able to turn over the soil in Adelaide of stiffer, if necessary. Of horned cattle, there was a good turnout, especially of Thoro-bred Durhams and Durham grades. A few sheep and pigs—owners not willing to bring them through the muddy roads. Of fruit and roots, a good

display, and also of mechanical work, plows, horse-shoes and a farmer's waggon, the whole manufactured by Parker and Hodgson of Adelaide Village, which for durability and substantial workmanship, could compete with any waggon shown at your last West Middlesex Agricultural Show. There were 182 entries. The following is the Prize List:

HORSES
Saddle Horse - 1st James Hamilton; 2nd G. Croucher, 3rd J. Wiley Sr.
Brood Mare - lst G. Brock, 2nd F. Petch
Three-year old Colt - lst G. Brock, 2nd G. Down
Two-year old Colt - lst H. Knight, 2nd P. Mee
One-year old Colt - lst G. Croucher, 2nd B. Burdon, 3rd G. Brock
Sucking Colt - lst F. Petch, 2nd G. Brock, 3rd G. Down
Horses, general purposes - lst Joseph Wilson, 2nd J. Carthy, 3rd P. Murray
Draught Horses - lst G. Brock, 2nd J. Carthy, 3rd J. Crummer

HORNED CATTLE
Thoro'-Bred Durham Bull (aged - lst D. M. Thompson, 2nd G. Brock
Two-year old grade bull - lst M. McCabe, 2nd F. Petch, 3rd J. Wiley Sr.
One-year old grade Bull - lst F. Petch, 2nd B. Burdon
Thoro'-bred two-year old Durham Heifer - lst S. Stephens
Milk Cow, grade - lst S. Stephens, 2nd G. Brock, 3rd B. Burdon
Two-year old grade Heifer - lst H. Knight, 2nd and 3rd S. Stephens
One-year old grade Heifer - lst, 2nd and 3rd S. Stephens
Heifer Calf, grade - lst S.Stephens, 2nd D. M. Thompson
Yoke of two-year old Steers - lst G. Brock, 2nd F. Petch, 3rd B. Burdon

SHEEP
Ram, aged - lst J. Healey, 2nd J/ Parker, 3rd F. Petch
One-year old Ram - lst J. Wiley, Jr.,
Ram Lamb - lst, 2nd and 3rd J. Healey
Ewe, aged - lst, 2nd and 3rd F. Petch
Ewe, Lamb - lst J. Healey, 2nd and 3rd F. Petch

PIGS
Boar, small breed - lst F. Petch
Sow, small breed - lst S. Stephens
Boar Pig - lst S. Stephens
Sow Pig - lst and 2nd S. Stephens

GRAIN
Fall Wheat - lst J. Parker, 2nd H. Knight
Spring Sheet - lst I. Carthy, 2nd G. Brock, 3rd, J. Parker
Barley - lst J. Parker, 2nd G. Croucher
Oats - lst and 2nd - G. Croucher, 3rd F. Petch
Peas - lst F. Petch, 2nd J. Healey, 3rd G. Brock
Flax Seed - lst F. Petch, 2nd J. Healey

FRUIT
Winter Apples - lst and 2nd G. Down, 3rd G. Brock
Fall Apples - lst G. Brock, 2nd and 3rd G. Down
Assortment of Apples, not less than 6 of each sort - lst G. Bishop, 2nd G. Brock
Potatoes - lst M. McCabe, 2nd G. Brock, 3rd F. Petch
Farmer's Waggon - lst Parker and Hodgson
Plow - lst and 2nd - Parker and Hodgson
Horse-shoes - 1st - Parker and Hodgson

On Sept. 30, 1870, The Age reported that The West Middlesex Fall Show in Strathroy, held the previous month, had a poultry class (turkeys, geese, ducks and hens), more classes of fruit, butter, honey, maple syrup and maple sugar, bread and homemade wine. There was a wide selection of ladies' craft work. Many Adelaide names appeared as winners—Armstrong, Buttery, Healey, Parker, Stephens, Campbell, Henderson, Saul, Douglas, Parker and Hodgson. The fall months of 1870 were busy times for Adelaide farm families!

In the March 20, 1874, council Minutes, it was proposed that $20 be paid to the Agricultural Society to assist in purchasing two acres from Mr. Mee. The site of the Town Hall was changed from St. George's Square to a lot on Front Street of Adelaide Village as the result of a petition by 66 ratepayers. The December 3, 1875, Minutes recorded that the Deed of the east half of Lot 12, Front Street, Adelaide Village, be made to the Agricultural Society. At the January 17, 1876, council meeting, a motion was passed that the reeve, John Morgan, Esq., forward $60 to John McDougal, MPP, to pay necessary expenses in getting a Bill passed by the Legislature of Ontario, authorizing the sale of St. George's Square in the Village of Adelaide.

scoting was childproof and a good insulator. Until the 1930s, a fancy couch, footstool, and a mouse-proof organ was often present in the parlor.

A fancy spare bedroom was present in every home and contained a nice bed, dresser, cane chair, and a lovely washstand with accompanying large, beautiful washbowl, magnificent large ewer, soap dish and comb holder.

Coal oil lamps were used throughout the house. Oil in the lamp was replenished every morning when the lamp chimneys were cleaned. Proper trimming of the wick was necessary if one side of the chimney was not to be blackened and illumination was to be at maximum for the next evening.

The dim lamp usually sat in the middle of the kitchen table and the children were frequently reminded not to jar the table while they ran around it during long winter evenings.

Magnificent hanging-lamps with large, decorative glass shades and hanging beads graced the parlor. Unfortunately, these beautiful lamps were rushed to the garbage dump when Premier Frost and Drew electrified rural Ontario about 1940.

Regular-sized wooden beds with 4'-5' tall headboards, and wooden slats to hold the tick, were used. Sometimes during the night, when the beds became older, a large bang or clatter would occur when a slat would come loose and fall to the floor. The slat would be put back in place the next morning.

Bright, freshly-threshed wheat straw was used to fill ticks. At first they were about 2' thick, but after a few days, they were compressed to about 6" in thickness, and became quite firm and comfortable. When the bed was made, the housemaid would move the straw to even out the tick.

Often, feather ticks made from down and small feathers from geese and ducks were used on top of straw ticks. Feather ticks were very warm and comfortable.

On cold winter nights, the housewife would heat an iron or brick and wrap it in newspaper or an old towel, and give it to the children to place at the foot of the bed.

A double-seat outhouse, 4'x5', built of hemlock barnboards, sat on wooden blocks or a cement foundation, and was situated 20'-50' from the back door of the house. This building did not have a window, but it gave protection from wind, rain and snow.

Newspapers and Eaton's catalogues gave a reliable supply of paper.

SOFT SOAP

Our ancestors liked to be clean and wear unsoiled clothes, and consequently, they required considerable amounts of soap. To meet this need, they produced a barrel of soap every spring from and with materials available on the farm. Although our progenitors did not know the chemical formula of soap or the chemical reactions involved in its production, they were skilled in its manufacture.

Part of the apparatus used in soap-making was a very large, hollow, basswood log about 6' in length and over 3' in diameter. It was placed on a low, sloping stand, covered with tin.

Every morning during the winter, ashes removed from the kitchen stove were placed in a pail, left to cool, and then dumped in the hollow log, which was always covered to prevent the entrance of snow and rain. All waste fat, especially fatty pork rinds, was stored during the cool season in the summer kitchen or wood shed.

In the spring, the large iron kettle (one was owned by every farmer) was placed under the lowest edge of the ash-stand. Some water was added to the ashes for several days and the lye, a brown liquid, drained from the ashes and dripped into the kettle until it was almost full.

The kettle was moved from the ash-stand, and the fat refuse was dumped into the lye. Wood below and around the kettle was ignited, and the mixture was heated for a couple of days. The result was viscous brown soap, which was carried to the soap barrel.

Watering the ashes flushed sodium and potassium hydroxide from the ashes into the kettle. When the mixture in the kettle was heated, the alkali metal (sodium and potassium) replaced the (OH) on the carboxyl radical on the end of the fatty acid chain, and soap resulted.

A SOFTBALL INCIDENT

During the summer in the 1930s and 1940s, boys and girls in their teens and early 20s formed softball teams, which played once a week in local pasture fields from 7:00 p.m. until dusk. Often, girls and boys played on the same team. Usually the girls wore skirts, not shorts, which were being slowly introduced. This more practical attire was opposed by mothers.

Frequently, the parents and neighbours would attend and enjoy watching and socializing while two area teams competed. Often, the season ended with an enjoyable corn roast.

One year in the 1930s, an Adelaide Village girls' team played a visiting Strathroy girls' team. During this game, a strong and vocal 14-year-old barefoot boy, wearing overalls, persisted in teasing and criticizing the Strathroy girls. He continued to annoy these spirited girls, even though they threatened to strip him if he continued his yapping. Finally, they decided to embarrass him. They grabbed him and pulled the trouser supports off his shoulders. After a short struggle, the girls yanked his trousers free.

Probably the bold town girls did not realize, or perhaps they did, that in the hungry 1930s, many of the farm boys did not wear underwear.

The town and local mothers began to talk about this unladylike act and the teams were immediately disbanded. The subdued victim never mentioned this embarrassing event.

SWIMMING HOLES

In the first of this century during the warm summer evenings in summer, the boys in the community used swimming holes in Mud and Gerry Creek. Very occasionally, in the muddy portions of the creek, they were bitten by bloodsuckers. Sometimes the boys ventured to the Ausable or Sydenham rivers, which were somewhat dangerous. In the month of June, some of the farm boys attending Strathroy District Collegiate would swim in a deep hole in the Sydenham on the golf club property. During a 1½-hour lunch break, there seemed to be plenty of time to swim and play. The boys were always in the buff, and girls never ventured near these locations.

Now this sort of recreation does not occur, partly because of more drainage, rapid water run off, and the presence of artificial swimming pools.

For a few years in the 1930s, the Arrand boys dammed Gerry creek on Lot 10, Con. 2 NER, about 200 yards from the Second Line North (Cuddy Drive). They used planks and mud, and raised the water level about 10', and backed it up about a mile. This was the best swimming hole in the area, and boys living within a three or four mile radius would often gather there in the evening to swim, dive and socialize.

One time, a young gentlemen from another community drowned in the murky water. The water was immediately released and the dam was never replaced. An inquest was not held.

FARM CHILDREN IN THE EARLY 1900s

In the first half of this century, farm children were raised in a very different environment to that of city children. It was sometimes believed that city children had more advantages than country children and thus were superior. The city folk had ice rinks, baseball diamonds, playgrounds and theaters, while farm children had ice on ponds or creeks, pasture fields for ball diamonds, and probably less spending money.

Farm children often went barefoot from May 24 until the first snowfall. Children raised on the farm had many more opportunities to work, make observations of nature and surroundings, experiment and investigate. They learned the meaning of work ethic.

The farm children always had something to do. They could do the following: bring the cows to the barn; milk the cows; feed the fowl; lock the hen house door in the evening; get a pail of water; split kindling; carry in wood; stook grain; pitch sheaves; plant, dig and pick potatoes; drive horses; pick berries; pick cucumbers; ride horses; jump in the hay mow; skinnydip in the creek; dig out groundhogs; chase rabbits; help butcher pigs; scuffle corn; pull mustard from oat fields; and help neighbours during harvest for a dollar a day plus dinner and supper.

BUTTER AND CHEESE

During the 19th and the first part of the 20th century, all farmers had income from either milk or cream. The cream was used for making butter, and the milk was used for making cheese.

During the 19th century, cream was obtained from fresh milk, which had sat for a few hours, so that the cream would rise to the surface. The cream was then skimmed from the surface.

At the beginning of the 20th century, the cream separator was introduced and used on every farm. After milking, the milk was poured through a milk strainer to remove debris, and into a large bowl on the top of the separator. The milk passed down

IN THE NEWS

August 9, 1913
SPECIAL TRAIN FOR APPLES

We understand that Peter McArthur, the well-known journalist and farmer of Ekfrid Township, is endeavouring to make arrangements with the C.P.R. for a special train of 25 cars to transport Middlesex County apples to Alberta this fall.

August 14, 1913
PEAS FOR CANNING CO. PAY BIG $

The farmers in this vicinity who grew peas for the Canning and Preserving Co. are well pleased. They received from $50 to $70 an acre. One farmer who grew eight acres received a cheque in the neighbourhood of $550.

March 12, 1914
RECORD YEAR FOR KEYSER CHEESE AND BUTTER FACTORY

Reports presented at the annual meeting of the Keyser Cheese and Butter Factory showed a splendid year's work. Over $31,000 worth of cheese and butter were made. The average price per pound for cheese was 13 cents and for butter 21.4 cents. If all the milk that the cream had been produced from had been made into cheese, it would have amounted to nearly 158 tons of cheese, an increase of nearly 10 tons over 1912.

August 28, 1913
AN ADELAIDE TOWNSHIP FARMER THRASHED [sic] 126 BUSHELS OFF TWENTY ACRES

Russell Parker of Adelaide has just thrashed 126 bushels of wheat off twenty acres and all through the district the yield is running from 35 to 40 bushels per acre.

Oats will break all records and in many places will yield 70 bushels an acre, the stacks standing over five feet in height. Cutting is now general. Potatoes will be a fine crop and barley is far above the average.

April 23, 1914
TWIN HEIFER CALVES - ADELAIDE

A cow belonging to Alex McArthur, Second Line North, Adelaide, recently gave birth to twin heifer calves, both of which are doing well.

July 2, 1914
LARGE RHUBARB LEAF

For luxuriant growth, John F. O'Neil, a Kerwood farmer, has a patch of pie plant, otherwise known as rhubarb, that is certainly worthy of note. The other day, one of the stalks was picked out for its unusual size and on examination, extraordinary measurements were taken. The big leaf was 27 inches in width and 16 feet and a half in circumference and the stalk and leaf four feet seven inches in length. Things certainly grow big at Kerwood. Who can beat it?

July 22, 1915
CROP REPORTS

The hay crop is short but the prospects for oats and wheat are immense. Some of the old timers never saw the like before, so heavy is going to be the yield. No starving on the land this year!

February 24, 1916
APPLES SHIPPED OVERSEAS TO CANADIAN SOLDIERS

Seven carloads of Ontario apples shipped to Canadian soldiers in British and French hospitals were badly frozen en route to the seaboard.

January 18, 1917
BOGUES WIN POULTRY PRIZES

Messrs. J. and O. Bogue of Adelaide have a large consignment of their fancy poultry, 117 birds, on exhibition at the Ottawa Winter Fair this week. John Bogue left Monday for the capital.

BASKET FACTORY

Mr. Rivers has a staff of twenty hands busy at the Strathroy basket factory, ten men and ten girls. He has sufficient orders now to keep the factory running continuously until mid-summer.

October 4, 1917
REAL ESTATE CHANGES IN ADELAIDE

Quite a number of farm properties in Adelaide Township are changing hands this fall. There is a strong demand for farms in this section of the county. Consequently, values are rising. Among the sales recently made were the following: Charles and George Oliver have purchased the 40 acres on the 2nd line N.E.R. owned by Harris Bros.; Ernest H. Houlton has disposed of his 200 acre farm on the 2nd line south, one of the most desirable and well improved properties in that part of the township, to Milton and Oliver Harris, consideration around $15,000. Mr. Houlton, we understand, intends to locate in Strathroy.

November 1, 1917
EFFECT OF DRAFT ON ADELAIDE FARMING

A letter published last week in a Toronto paper, states that farmers in the writer's section are hesitating about breaking up sod for the production of hoe or cereal crops next year until they learn what effect the draft is to have on next year's farm labour supply. The tendency to leave land in sod that should be broken up will be aggravated by the declaration by one responsible military authority that a man and a half are sufficient for the performance of the necessary work on 150 acres. If that ruling stands there will be little breaking up of meadows this fall and consequent reduction in more important crops, from a good standpoint, next year. A man and a half can handle 150 acres that are mainly in hay and pasture; it is wholly impossible for this force to take care of a similar area with three-fourths of it in grain and hoe crops. For years past farmers have been gradually changing their system of operation so as to meet the situation created by the steady drain of labour to the cities. This change has been accelerated of late years owing to the increased drain caused by the call to the trenches and the lure of high wages in munition factories. If, as a result of the draft, there is a further heavy drain this fall shortage of food in 1918 will not be confined to Europe; it will be experienced right here in Ontario.

August 22, 1918
CROP YIELDS

Some of the barley fields of the province this year will yield 65 bushels to the acre, according to the weekly report of the Ontario Department of Agriculture. The best average return for one county in Ontario last year was less than 40 bushels. The average for the whole province in the banner year of 1915 was only 36 bushels. Oats are also a bumper crop and will be considerably over the average in yield per acre. Essex and Kent report some fields running as high as 80 and 96 bushels to the acre, the official report says. The average for the province last year was 40.3 bushels. Spring wheat has done so well that it is likely to become a more established crop with some who have been neglecting it. Most of the barley and spring wheat and a considerable portion of the oats have been cut and stacked and some threshed.

February 6, 1919
SHIPPING BEEF TO EUROPE

There is an estimated decrease of 28,000,000 head of cattle in the principal countries of Europe. Years must elapse before European beef and dairy production is back to normal.

Shipments of beef to Europe under the conditions over there now pertaining are limited only by refrigerator space on the ships. As more tonnage becomes available, more beef will be shipped.

April 18, 1918
KEYSER CHEESE FACTORY BURNED

The Keyser cheese and butter factory was completely destroyed by fire Friday evening. The loss is covered by insurance. The fire is supposed to have been caused by some sparks from a stove pipe. No person was in the building when the fire broke out. The factory was owned and operated by Wm. Inch. There is a movement under way among the farmers of the district interested to have the factory rebuilt as soon as possible.

---

through a rapidly rotating disc-bowl that, by centrifugal force, separated the milk from the cream. Each emerged from a separate spout. The cream was stored in the cellar or milk house in large cream cans, and was sold at the creamery twice a week during summer and once a week during winter.

Butter was often made in the farm kitchen until the 1940s, especially during winter, when milk production was low. The cream was stored for about a week in the cellar, milk house or cool room. The Lactobacillus bacteria changed the milk lactose into lactic acid, which caused a natural souring. Consequently, fat globules clumped together.

The original and most primitive churn was a small barrel with a plunger (a flat, round piece of wood). A broom-like handle projected through a hole in the center of the barrel-lid. This handle was manually lifted upward and then plunged downward until the cream separated into butter and buttermilk. This tedious job sometimes took as much as an hour.

During the first half of this century, most families obtained a rotating churn with a capacity of up to eight gallons. Two short rods, 2" in length, were attached opposite each other to the center of the outside of the barrel (churn). The churn was suspended by the two rods, and supported in a U-shaped depression on the posts of a wooden stand. A handle could be readily attached to one of the barrel rods and then the churn could be rotated.

Churning was quickest when the barrel was

turned at a speed that allowed the cream and butter to drop from one end of the churn to the other. Sometimes during the winter, churning took a very long time, because the lactic acid-producing-bacteria multiplied very slowly in the cool environment. Churning was complete when all of the fat globules had adhered to each other to form butter masses.

The butter was removed from the churn and placed in a large wooden bowl. Sometimes, common salt and perhaps a little colouring were added and worked into the butter. If the butter was for sale, it was compacted into a rectangular wooden container, the butter-print, which held one pound of butter. The bottom of the print was movable, and could be pushed upward by a handle to eject the pound of butter onto butter paper used for wrapping. If the butter was kept for family use, it was often put in a roll.

In the spring, after the cows grazed on new grass, milk production increased and cottage cheese (curd), which resulted from precipitation of protein (casein), was frequently made from the surplus milk. Surplus cottage cheese was fed to chickens and turkeys after the family used as much as they desired. If too much was fed to turkeys, foundering resulted.

During winter, the butter became paler and paler, almost white. In May and June, butter was quite yellow naturally, due to the carotene from dandelions, which were plentiful in the pasture.

Farmers had to avoid feeding turnips to cows to prevent dairy products from having undesirable flavours and odours.

During the early part of this century, there were many cheese factories in Southern Ontario. The Shillingtons and then the Penningtons operated a cheese factory at Lot 13, Con. 3 NER, which burned down in the late 1920s. They obtained their milk locally and got ice from a pond at Lot 18, Con. 3 NER.

A TYPICAL DAY FOR A HOUSEWIFE IN THE EARLY 1900s

1. Ask her husband to arise and start fire in kitchen stove
2. Make children's school lunches
3. Help with milking
4. Get breakfast, eat, and wash dishes
5. Bathe baby
6. Wash milk pails and cream separator
7. Start yeast for bread (twice a week)
8. Make beds and empty chamberpots
9. Knead the dough
10. Clean lamp chimneys and fill lamps with coal oil, trim wicks
11. Put wood in the stove several times a day, in winter
12. Prime cistern pump and fill stove reservoir
13. Go outside to pump and bring in water three or four times a day
14. Sweep kitchen floor, dust with a goose-wing tip
15. Churn butter once a week
16. Change, and nurse baby several times a day
17. Wash clothes in hand washer or by scrub board, usually on Monday
18. Put clothes through wringer, or twist with hands to remove excess water
19. Hang clothes on outside line, even in winter
20. In late afternoon, bring clothes into kitchen, if frozen hang them above and around stove
21. Make lunch, eat, and wash dishes
22. Bake bread and buns, once or twice a week
23. Preserve raspberries and peaches, etc.
24. Preserve eggs in water glass for winter
25. Make applesauce and pies (have two or three pies for Sunday)
26. Make clothes, shirts, etc.
27. Attend women's Missionary Meeting (once a month)
28. Might go shopping Saturday afternoon
29. Feed hens and gather the eggs
30. Be home when children arrive from school
31. Get boys to split wood and fill woodbox
32. Prepare dinner, eat, and wash dishes
33. Light lamp
34. Milk cows and wash milk pails
35. Relax, knit and mend clothing, use at least one skein a week
36. Hang children's socks by stove to dry
37. Before sending children to bed, have them kneel at her knee and repeat a prayer
38. Heat and wrap a hot iron for children to put at foot of bed, in cold weather
39. Go to church on Sunday
40. Other duties included: preparing meals for as many as 10 men during threshing and wood bees, hire help, help shuck corn, put turkeys in coops, pluck feathers off geese, entertain friends
41. During her leisure time, she might listen on the telephone party line

CHAPTER ELEVEN

Businesses

22 AUTO BODY AND ACCOUNTING

22 Auto Body was established in 1989 by Ron Fischtner, and originally located in Lobo Township at Hickory Corners by Ron Fischtner. In September 1996, Ron and his wife, Teresa, built a new home and place of business on Lot 25, Con. 1 SER, 3801 Egremont Drive. The nature of this business is sandblasting, painting and repairing cars and trucks.

Teresa also has an accounting and bookkeeping business that she operates out of their home. She does the accounting for 22 Auto Body, as well as many businesses in the local area.

ADELAIDE CREEK LIMOUSINS

Adelaide Creek Limousins is located on a farm north of Kerwood on Cuddy Drive. The Herrington family owns 65 registered Limousin cattle. They started showing Limousins in 1994 with one bull.

In 1998, Toni opened some new doors with another breed. With the help of her 4-H leader, her boss at Cuddy Farms, John Squires (herd manager), and the Herrington family, Toni chose her first Angus heifer, "Early Sunset Queen."

Rewards in the show ring are not the only benefits to this business—Toni has developed many friendships over the past five years. She is very grateful for the respect she has from her peers, but most of all thankful for the support from her family, 4-H leaders and friends.

A.F.W. RESTORATION INC.

This business is owned by Harold Lewis and was established in 1991 on Lot 18, Con. 5 SER. With the use of high quality, modern, advanced equipment, repairs are completed on trucks and cars. Customers include insurance companies, dealers and the general public.

CARGILL LIMITED

In 1963, Scotch Fertilizer Company was built in Kerwood and later purchased by Cyanamid Fertilizers. This business was established as a farm supply outlet and service, and grain handling business.

Cargill Limited purchased Maple Leaf Mills Elevators in 1988, and in 1989, Cargill Limited purchased Cyanamid Fertilizers. Cargill Limited continued with the two establishments until 1994, when they demolished the Maple Leaf Mills Elevators.

Cargill Limited continues to do a thriving business with local farmers in handling their grain crops each year.

CATHY'S COUNTRY DINER

Cathy's Country Diner was owned by Cathy Holbrook. This was a restaurant and variety store business. This business closed in May 1999.

CITY SERVICE CENTRE

The McDougall family still hears from people who say that they miss City Service Centre, so easily accessible and on a well maintained lot. Here, you could fill up with gas, purchase oil or have mechanical problems corrected, then pop into a small variety store for your favourite treats or needed groceries from 7:00 a.m. to 11:00 p.m. for many years.

Lorne and Margaret McDougall developed a business where their children learned about all personalities—all of them helped with the store each day, even while attending Adelaide Central and Strathroy Collegiate.

Many fruit and vegetable crops were grown on the property to market through the store, and also later at the market in town.

City Service Centre on Highway #81

Lorne had many assistants from 1960 to 1966, when Margaret joined the business after being with the R.C.A.F., Downham Nursery, Vampco Aluminum Products and Middlesex Furniture. Her jobs took her from stenographer to computer operator, increasing her knowledge, which kept everything solvent in the McDougall enterprises.

Lorne filed saws and repaired many different things, with his mechanical knowledge and certificate from the Department of Labour, which he kept until his retirement.

For many years, this store was the information centre for lost travellers, at first trying to find Highway 22 and then Highway 402. The Americans turning off 402 onto 81 were mystified over the connection to Highway 2 and Highway 401. The store's "free" telephone greatly assisted salesmen, truck drivers and others to reach Strathroy addresses, helping them to keep appointments on time.

CORDEIRO'S AUTO EUROPEAN LTD.

Cordeiro's Auto European Ltd. was established on Lot 22, Con. 2 SER, on September 3, 1985. The owner is Michael Cordeiro.

This business consists of a service station, selling gas, oil and propane fuel. Mike also repairs foreign and domestic cars, and sells used cars. A towing service is also available through Cordeiro's. Mike's customers are local, although he often caters to customers off Highway 402, which is just north of the service station.

COUNTRYSIDE MOTEL AND RESTAURANT

In the early 1960s, Alex Clark bought a few acres on Highway 22 from Tom Elliott. By 1964, Alex had built a motel of units with a 2-bedroom apartment in the centre, along with a restaurant and a 2-bay garage. The business was named the "Bambi Motel," as Alex was a deer hunter. This was a family enterprise, and the whole family helped run the business. After 1½ years, they wanted to sell the business, which had become very time-consuming.

The motel was sold to Lou Chalmers of Sarnia, an Imperial gas and oil distributor. He sold the business to Reg and Jean Kemp in 1967. They ran the business as a 24-hour truck stop for nine years and then sold it to John Hagman of Toronto, in 1976. Unfortunately for the business, most travellers began to take Highway 402, which was being built at the time. The bank eventually took over the business, which remained vacant for some time. John Thyssen bought it from the bank in 1980. He built a 5,000 s.f. warehouse, and the restaurant was renovated into a 3-bedroom house, and the motel rooms were used for storage. He built trailers in the warehouse. A large supply of steel was needed for the trailer operation, and the bank refused a requested $100,000 loan to complete the venture. John Thyssen was forced to throw in the towel.

Again, the property was vacant, this time for almost a year. John and Gertrude Timmermans bought the motel from the bank in 1982. They moved into the house, which had a section partitioned off for use as a motel office. They spent $75,000 on repairs, and bought new bedding, carpeting and furniture. After 40 years of farming, they became motel keepers, changing the name of the business to "Countryside Motel and Coffee Shop." The 2-bay garage was rented to Bill Daniels, and cars were stored in the warehouse during the winter. In 1986, an addition of five kitchenettes and a storeroom were built. The

Countryside Motel & Coffee Shop
RR5, Strathroy, Ontario
¼ Mile West Of Highway 22 On Highway 22

Grand Opening 1983

Your hosts John and Gertrude Timmermans have for you:
* Newly Renovated Rooms   * Attractive Prices   * Waterbeds
* Family Atmosphere   * Picnic Tables   * Color TV
* Acres of Parking   * Located Away From Traffic Noise

OPEN HOUSE Saturday, July 2 10 a.m. - 5 p.m. & 7 p.m. - 9 p.m.

Drop in for coffee and donuts and meet the Timmermans

Located a short distance from Highway 402
For Reservation & Information
Phone (519) 245-0115

A Great Place To Stay Over On Turkey Festival Weekend

ALEX AND VI CLARK INVITE YOU TO THE
OFFICIAL OPENING
BAMBI ESSO SERVICE
Highway 22, 1 Mile West Highway 81, 3 Miles North Strathroy

ESSO SERVICE CENTRE
- ESSO GASOLINES AND LUBRICANTS
- 24-HOUR TOWING SERVICE
- ATLAS BATTERIES, TIRES
- MINOR REPAIRS

BAMBI MOTEL
- 10 MODERN UNITS
- WALL-TO-WALL CARPETING
- HOT WATER HEAT INDIVIDUALLY CONTROLLED
- 4-PIECE BATH
- TV IN EACH ROOM

BAMBI RESTAURANT
- MODERN, BRIGHT DINING ROOM FOR FULL COURSE MEALS
- LIGHT LUNCHES
- OPEN 6 A.M. TO 12 MIDNIGHT
- CATERING TO SMALL BANQUETS

Sunday, February 23/1964 2:00 P.M. TO 9:00 P.M.

COMPLETE Opening Special	COMPLETE Opening Special	COMPLETE Opening Special
ROAST BEEF DINNER $1.50	FRIED CHICKEN DINNER $1.25	FISH DINNER $1.35

Two Motel Units Open For Your Inspection — Come and see our New Motel and have Dinner in the Pleasant Surroundings of Bambi Restaurant.

Timmermans decided to sell the business in 1988. They sold to Walter and Ritva Kingo. Walter died in 1995, and Ritva and her son, Marcus, run the business now. This business has grown over the years, with the restaurant being licensed to seat 117 guests. Full-course meals are served in the restaurant to people in the local area, as well as those from London and Sarnia.

CUDDY FARMS

Cuddy Farms was established on June 15, 1950, by A.M. "Mac" Cuddy. This business started on the farm at Lot 21, Con. 3 SER. The operation consists of turkey eggs, day-old turkey poults, 3,000 acres of peas, corn, beans and carrots, as well as feed corn, wheat, hay and pasture.

Cuddy Farms is now known as Cuddy International Corporation, with farms in Ontario, Quebec, Nova Scotia, New Brunswick, Michigan, Ohio, Germany, Poland and Italy. The company has expanded into vegetable crops for Strathroy Foods, a division of Cuddy International, during the past 12 years.

The business first started with eggs and turkey poults and has since expanded to commercial turkey meat production. Cuddy Farms is known worldwide.

DAUGHARTY'S APPLIANCE CENTRE

Roy Daugharty is the owner of this repair business, located on part of Lot 22, Con. 2 SER, and was established on June 1, 1996. Local residents and those from the surrounding area come to Daugherty's Appliance Centre for good rebuilt appliances, and appliance repairs.

DORTMANS BROS./VILLAGE FEEDS LTD.

Dortmans Bros. is owned by John H. Dortmans, and was established in December 1980. This operation specializes in the selling of barn equipment, especially for swine and dairy.

Village Feeds Ltd. is owned by John H. Dortmans and Keri Evans, and was established in October 1990. Village Feeds sells a complete line of Nutrena Feeds for swine, dairy, poultry and pets.

Over the years, these businesses have grown from a 2-person operation to a staff of more than 10 employees. Customers for both businesses are from the surrounding farming district.

Keri Evans and John Dortmans held the grand opening for the county's newest feed outlet – Village Feeds – on January 9. Farmers from the area visited the business for feed specials, coffee, donuts and, if they arrived at noon, a light lunch.

ELLY BOERSEMA NATURAL HEALTH FOOD

This health food store is located on Lot 19, Con. 3 SER, and was established by Mrs. Elly Boersema in 1970. This business started in a small room in the Boersema residence, and is now run in a separate

Elly Boersema

store on the property. The business has grown over the years, with a much greater awareness of health food products for people who want to live a healthier life.

Elly's daughter, Janice, joined her in the business and has operated it since 1997, although Elly still assists customers in the store.

FIENY'S OF ADELAIDE

Fieny McDougall established a hair salon in her home in December 1985, on Lot 11, Con. 1 NER.

She has male and female clientele from the township, as well as from Strathroy. Many years ago, this house was a variety and grocery store (see THOMAS FREELE STORE).

G-P MOTORCYCLE AND SMALL ENGINES

Jerry Pawitch is the owner of G-P Motorcycle and Small Engines, established in 1988, which is located at Lot 22, Con. 2 SER. This business services rural and urban customers in the sales and repair of lawn and garden equipment.

GREEN SCHEELS PIDGEON PLANNING CONSULTANTS LTD.

Bill Green has been the township's planner since 1981. He was employed with the firm Proctor & Redfern, and had successfully represented a private client (Martin Strybosch) at an Ontario Municipal Board hearing against the township. Frank Gare was Township Clerk at that time, and suggested calling Bill when the township's former planner left the profession to pursue a career in the ministry. The early 1980s was a slow economic time for Ontario and the planning consulting business. The work performed for Adelaide was primarily commenting on consent applications and preparing site-specific zoning by-law amendments.

In 1989, Bill established William Green & Associates Planning Consultants, and Adelaide Township was one of his first clients. A new Official Plan for Adelaide Township was prepared by his firm and adopted by council in July 1991. A few years and a couple of partners later, a new Comprehensive Zoning By-law was prepared, and approved by Council in January 1997.

Bill has attended numerous council meetings, where he met and got to know many township residents.

Green Scheels Pidgeon Planning Consultants continues to provide planning advisory services to the township, and appreciates the opportunity to continue this longstanding relationship.

GRINSVEN ENTERPRISES

This business of dead stock removal was established by John Van Grinsven in the mid-1960s. It is located on Lot 26, Con. 1 NER, 7047 Egremont Drive. The present owner of this business is Murray Van Grinsven, son of John. This company services all of the local farming area, collecting and removing dead animals.

HICKORY CORNERS AUTOMOTIVE LTD.

Hickory Corners Automotive Ltd. was owned by Jim Zavitz and established October 14, 1980, on Lot 31, Con. 1 NER. This was an automotive repair and towing operation that serviced local residents and those from Strathroy. This business was closed in July 1999.

HY-WAY COLLISION LTD.

Hy-Way Collision Ltd. was established in 1969 by Jim Foster and Jack Harris on Lot 16, Con. 1 SER. The original building in which this business was established was at one time a schoolhouse. This business consists of an auto body repair service and paint shop.

During the 1980s, Hy-way Collision Ltd. was purchased by Brian and Peggy Brothers. The business now includes radiator repair services and a Krown Rust Control franchise. Many employees work here, mainly doing insurance work and restoring classic vehicles.

J.W.S. MACHINERY

J.W.S. Machinery was established in 1970 by John W. Stanley on Lot 22, Con. 2 SER, where hydraulic dump wagons, carts and trailers are built. The property also houses a small grain elevator for handling edible coloured beans. This business has diversified from an agriculture-based venture to a more urban operation. The property also includes a golf driving range, which is an attraction for many people of all ages.

KEN FOSTER GARAGE

In 1947, Ken Foster and his wife, Mary, bought the property at Lot 7, Con. 5 SER, from Peter Maher, who had operated a garage at this location that was destroyed by fire. Mary's father and brother, Louis and Richard Branan, and uncle, Clarence Stevenson, built another garage, a Texaco gas station. Don Branan worked as a mechanic for Ken Foster for 22 years, beginning in 1947. Ken Foster serviced and repaired automobiles, trucks and tractors.

Ken Foster Garage

Ken Foster Garage

Ken and Mary lived in the little house beside the garage where, in the front, was a spotless office. Here, Mary sold gum, candy, cigarettes, soda pop, etc, and customers paid their bills. Ken was a mail carrier for 35 years in the Kerwood area, and he kept his coat and hat for the job in a cabinet in the corner of this office.

The garage opened at 9:00 a.m., after Ken and Mary had finished the mail delivery. In October 1978, Ken sold the business to Spike Algra, and he and Mary retired to Strathroy after 31 years of faithful service to Kerwood and the surrounding communities. On November 8, 1978, an appreciation night was held in honour of Ken and Mary Foster, and nearly 200 people attended, a true testament to how well they were regarded. Spike sold the business to the Noordhofs, and it is now known as Kerwood Auto Service.

KEN MATTHEWS LTD.

In the late 1930s, Ken Matthews and Gordon Galbraith joined to form a trucking company, consisting of several 5-yard dump trucks. After two years, they divided their equipment and each started their own trucking business. Ken Matthews Company was formed about 1940, and more dump trucks were added to the fleet. The company supplied gravel, sand and stone for several local townships including Adelaide, Metcalfe, Mosa, East and West Williams, and many local farmers.

In the 1950s, dragline shovels and bulldozers were added to the expanding business. In the spring of 1964, the company incorporated and became Ken Matthews Ltd. The company consisted of Ken Matthews as President along with William Matthews and Gordon Aitken. With Ken's death in 1973, Bill Matthews became President.

Ken Matthews Ltd., ca.1948

Over the years, Ken Matthews Ltd. has employed numerous Kerwood area men, whose dedication to their work has helped the company to continue serving the area with pride.

KERWOOD AUTO SERVICE

Kerwood Auto Service is owned by Arend and Angeline Noordhof and is located on Lot 7, Con. 5 SER. This business, an automotive repair and gasoline service station, was established June 15, 1979.

This thriving venture services the areas of Kerwood, Watford, Strathroy and all of the surrounding farming communities.

KERWOOD CREAMERY

The Kerwood Creamery was purchased from Ray Pollock and started receiving milk from area farmers in 1943. Milk was received, graded and cooled before being stored in large storage tanks with a holding capacity of approximately 165,000 pounds, until tanker trucks from Aylmer Condensory could pick it up. The plant used a large volume of water, which at first was obtained from wells that were drilled by Clarence Demaray. However, the water had sulphur that blackened metal and caused it to rust. As a result, when a tanker came for a load of milk, it brought a load of water from the Aylmer plant. This plant operated from

Kerwood Creamery

Kerwood Creamery, 1923

1943 until the fall of 1981. Its closing was as a result of automation, when milk producers slowly changed to bulk tanks and producers changed to bottled milk under the direction of the Ontario Milk Marketing Board. The building was sold to the fertilizer plant.

The truck and pump in the photograph held 1,500 pounds. It had solid rubber tires and was the first to haul milk from Kerwood to Aylmer Condensory. Every few years, the size of the tanker got larger and when the plant closed, the largest truck held 54,000 pounds. Some of the people who

owned and operated trucks hauling milk to Kerwood:

Kerwood Produce, owned by Donald Pollock (and later by Bill Jordan and Grant Parker)
    Elton Freer
    Earl Rees (Ailsa Craig)
    Bill Baxter
    Donald Nevin (Parkhill)
    Grant Taylor
    Gordon and Merit Muxlow
    Russel Foster
    Alfred Hawkins
    Mr. Marsh (Arkona)
    Joe Van Bree
    George Foster
    Ben and Lawrence Glithero
    Grant Wilcox
    Bill Veich
    Ed Wilson
    George Brockie

People who worked at the plant were:
    Milo Brooks
    Harold Irwin
    Charlie Griffin
    Ernest Tedball
    Donald Pollock
    George Leacock
    Ed Wilson
    Dave Beveridge
    Fred Irish
    Bill McLaghlin
    Wilfred Crandon
    Graham Alderson
    Bill Brooks
    Donald Waltham
    Kenneth Waltham
    Adrian Vaane
    John Ratterink
    Richard Kelly
    George Johnson
    Robert Dodge
    Bob Shamblaw
    Frank Doan
    Dick Brooks
    Frank McCullough
    Doug Morningstar
    Steve Belinki
    Harold Nixon

L.A. POOL & SPA

Ron and Luise Thompson are the owners of L.A. Pool & Spa, which was opened in February 1992. The Thompsons are in the business of selling and installing swimming pools, and supplying pool chemicals and replacements parts. L.A. Pool & Spa also repairs existing swimming pools.

LARRY MACDONALD CHEVROLET OLDSMOBILE LTD.

In the 1930s, the Chevrolet Oldsmobile dealership was established in a new building at the corner of Caradoc and Metcalfe Streets in Strathroy. At the time, it was a modern new building and was operated by Clare Leitch. After WWII, the dealership was taken over by Carl Cunningham and John Robinson. They operated the dealership as a partnership until 1954, when Carl Cunningham took over the operation as sole proprietor. During this period, a showroom and shop were added to the original structure.

In 1959, Al Reddoch had a buy-out agreement with Carl Cunningham and, in 1965, Al was the operator. In November 1968, Larry MacDonald signed a buy-out agreement with Al Reddoch. During this period, the shop was enlarged again, and a parcel of land was purchased from Beaver Lumber. Larry took over as owner in January 1978 and, during the next few years, purchased the double house and the Markle house. The double house was demolished and the Markle house was moved to a new location. The vacant land was used as a display area and for a parking lot. The showroom was refurbished in 1979.

During the strong economic cycle in the mid 1980s, developers became interested in the Caradoc

Larry MacDonald, Opening Day, September 1988

Larry MacDonald turning the key to the new business, Larry MacDonald Chevrolet-Oldsmobile, Ltd.

Street corner, and a deal was made that enabled the Chev-Olds dealership to relocate on Highway 81, north of Strathroy. The new structure was built by Strybosch Construction with a showroom, parts area on two floors, 10 service bays, and four body shop bays. The operation relocated in September 1988, and an open house was held in March 1989. This is a thriving business where new and used vehicles are sold, and serviced.

LITTLE LAMBS CHRISTIAN DAY CARE

Little Lambs Christian Day Care, originally known as "Good Shepherd Day Care," is located on Lot 18, Con. 4 SER, 3114 Napperton Drive. The name of this non-profit, charitable organization was changed to Little Lambs Christian Day Care on February 15, 1994. It is administered by a Board of Directors. Children are cared for daily, on a full-time or part-time basis.

MIDDLESEX FARM SYSTEMS LTD.

Middlesex Farm Systems Ltd. is owned by Klaas Salomons and Son. This business was established on part of Lot 10, Con. 5 SER, in 1972. This business sells and services farm equipment that is used in the disposal of waste materials, in the industrial area and for farm use. Rental equipment is also available from this location.

NEW DAWN FURNITURE

New Dawn Furniture is owned by Carl and Suzanne Boshart and was established in 1983. Antiques and many other items are sold directly from this location, and sales are made by auctions held on the property. Carl and Suzanne also do refinishing of furniture at this location. Good used furniture and equipment are available at New Dawn Furniture, at reasonable prices.

ONTARIO HYDRO

The Ontario Hydro district office is located on Lot 21, Con. 1 SER, Centre Road. This building was constructed in the early 1990s to accommodate the offices and equipment of Ontario Hydro, which services the local rural area. Ontario Hydro was founded in 1906.

ONTARIO PROVINCIAL POLICE

For many years, the O.P.P. station was housed at Hickory Corners on Lot 31, Con. 1 SER. In the 1990s, a new building was constructed on Highway 81, north of Strathroy, and this became the new Ontario Provincial Police Strathroy Detachment. This Detachment became the administrative centre for Middlesex County in 2000, with Inspector John Stephens in charge as the Detachment Commander.

PARRISH & HIEMBECKER LTD.

James Richardson moved to Kerwood in 1865. It was at this time that Richardson's Brick & Tile Yard was founded. Bricks and tiles were the main business; pottery and crocks were also fired. Many of the houses in Adelaide Township were constructed from Richardson brick, as well as the Sarnia rail tunnel.

At the turn of the century, Kerwood was a bustling and thriving community. Business boomed and passed into the second generation with John Richardson. Lumber was increasingly in demand, and a sawmill was added to the operation. Early in the century, when the needs of the community changed and livestock and agriculture became the primary industry, a feed mill was started on the site. By the 1930s, brick and tile were no longer made, and Richardsons focused on feed and farm supplies.

Fred Richardson saw the opportunities in the feed business and capitalized on them. A rail siding was built, and boxcars of soy meal and grain were unloaded and processed into feed. Trucks were purchased, and a Shur-Gain dealership was started at Richardson's. A pellet mill was also purchased, at quite an expenditure for the time.

Many young men earned their living at the feed mill. Bill Morgan recalls unloading boxcars and, with a chuckle, remembers that it took much longer to do less work than it does today. Success rarely comes without setbacks. A fire in 1960 momentarily slowed progress, but the buildings were rebuilt and life moved on. A fire in 1968 destroyed a large portion of the mill. In 1969, because of poor health, Fred Richardson sold the business to Canadian Industries and a fertilizer sales representative, Wilfred Murray, to form a CIL Agromart, ending 100 years in the Richardson name. The business was renamed Murray's Farm Supply Limited. In 1970, a fire destroyed the original buildings, and only the office and silos were left standing.

In 1972, Don Waters of Waters Elevators in Parkhill purchased the facility. Murray Farm Supply became Waters Elevators. Almost immediately, money was spent to increase storage capacity and update the receiving facilities. Two years later, more storage was added and a white bean cleaning plant was constructed. Farm supplies, fertilizer and feed were still handled. Kerwood resident Dave McAllister managed the facility with his wife, Kit, as secretary. Many young men of the area filled the remaining positions, including Tony DeRuiter, Bill Dodge and George Tamminga. The coloured bean market proved lucrative for both producers and handlers. White navy beans, kidney beans, and black turtle beans were grown in the area.

Richardson's Feed & Supplies Ltd.

Richardson's Feed & Supplies Ltd., 1969

In 1982, the Falkland War broke out, sending Argentina to war with Great Britain. Argentina was no longer able to meet its contractual agreements with Canada. Waters Elevators was left with thousands of bushels of black turtle beans and no place to market them. The resulting financial hardships caused Waters Elevators to go into receivership.

Meanwhile, Parrish & Hiembecker, a strong player in the grain industry, was having success with their recent acquisition, Glencoe Grain & Seed Co. It was decided there was opportunity to expand by purchasing the now defunct Waters Elevators. In 1985, Parrish & Hiembecker Ltd. bought Waters Elevators, changing the name to Glencoe Grain & Seed Co., Kerwood Branch. Fertilizer and farm supplies were no longer handled; the business focused on grain and seed.

P&H's roots date back to 1909, when the Parrish family in the west joined forces with the Hiembecker family in Ontario. Strong family values paired with astute business fundamentals have secured a lasting station for P&H in the grain industry. Today, P&H divisions include New Life Mills, Butterball Turkeys, Martin Feeds, Cooks, Ellison Flour and Glencoe Grain & Seed Co.

Recently, the Kerwood area has shifted from a predominantly corn growing area to the more profitable soybean. With an ever increasingly global economy, the demand for specialty soybeans has increased. Nations such as Japan, China and Malaysia have started to import soybeans to meet the demand. Soybeans are processed, bagged and loaded into containers, which are transported by truck and then rail to be loaded onto ships bound for the Pacific Rim.

There have been many expansions in Kerwood since P&H took charge. Additional storage has been added, new warehouses built and cleaning equipment purchased. The success of the Kerwood branch has increased the workforce from two employees to six full-time positions. Following the retirement of the McAllisters, Roy Searson was hired as manager. Other employees are Lynn Beynen, Floyd Unger, Tony DeRuiter, Raymond Howe and Jim McCaw.

PARTS R US

In 1993, Doug Dolbear established Parts R Us. This is a very competitive business as larger parts companies have better buying power. At this location, they sell auto parts and body shop supplies to customers from the surrounding area and out of town.

PEDDEN'S COLLECTOR PLATES

Pedden's Collector Plates is owned by Dorothy Pedden and is located in her home on Lot 14, Con. 4 NER. This business was established on December 14, 1983.

At this location, there are many beautiful plates, dolls and collectables for customers to purchase. Over the years, the business has increased in size because of the interest in these lovely items, appealing to all age groups.

Dorothy Pedden in plate shop.

PETER MINTEN WOODWORKING

Peter Minten Woodworking started as a hobby and became a business in 1985. The shop is operated from the Minten home, where mainly custom-made furniture, cabinets and stairways are built, and renovations are done. Oak, walnut, pine, cherry and hickory are the main types of wood used.

The business involves the whole family in some capacity. As the kids grew up, they were always involved in helping assemble, sand, varnish and do whatever job needs to be done.

POLLOCK RENTALS LTD.

Pollock Rentals Ltd., located on Lot 22, Con. 3 SER, is owned by Donald M. Pollock. The business was moved to this location in 1973. Pollock Rentals is in the business of truck renting and leasing, truck body manufacturing, and dedicated contract carriage.

This company was founded in 1953 and originated in Kerwood. The original business was incorporated with one tractor-trailer under the name of D.M. Pollock Truck Leasing Company Ltd. In 1958, they moved to Strathroy, where the present fire hall is located. Originally, the business was a funeral coach rental operation that grew to include funeral coach and ambulance sales and leasing. The funeral coach and ambulance operations were sold in 1979. Truck body manufacturing started in 1968, and continues today.

The Transportation Division, called Partner Dedicated Services Inc., founded in 1995, was established to haul goods for certain dedicated customers.

Today, Pollock Rentals Ltd. services several hundred manufacturing, distribution and transportation companies in South Western Ontario.

PRIESTLEY'S ADELAIDE GENERAL STORE

The Priestleys lived on Highway 22 in the Adelaide Village General Store. Frank and Hilda and their two children, Donelda and John, arrived in the village in 1947. Frank was no longer able to farm so, after shopping around, he decided to purchase the store. They bought it from Charles Brandow and operated it until the store closed in 1957.

The General Store provided everything for the shopper's needs. Village residents and local farm families relied on this store for their regular staple food products. Here, you'd find block salt, cat chow, dog food, and calf meal. You could get kerosene or motor oil from the bulk tanks, or gasoline from the pumps. You could purchase buttons and thread, spices, lamps and parts, or just snacks. Ice cream, soda pop, candy, cigarettes and other tobacco products were regular items. Any household foods, including meats in the long counter, were located inside the one large room. Everything had to be packaged from the bulk containers.

The store was open from 7:00 a.m. until 9:00 p.m. The building also provided living quarters on the second floor. The 2-bedroom unit made for easy access to the store and to assist neighbours or travellers with late-night emergencies. Many bowls of soup were prepared and given to hungry and tired travellers. Sometimes they left money and sometimes they didn't. The building of Highway 22 required the removal of the front porch and the gravity-fed, glass globe, 10-gallon gas pumps out front. Most cars held eight gallons at that time. Gas was then .28¢ a gallon. Sometimes, regular customers put in their own fuel. The family members did all of the work, at any time it was needed.

The General Store was the main location for messages and local gossip. Members of the community met and traded stories and farm information. They sat on orange crates or hard wooden chairs. Until it was retired to propane, the pot-bellied stove provided a warm spot. On each side of the back door was a crank telephone—Kerwood was a long ring and a short 4-ring 1-1, and the other rang as 2-3, two longs and three short rings. Of course, each was a party line as well. Being on two rural telephone exchanges, the store often relayed messages from a person on one line to someone else on the other. This way, the families didn't have to go through the operator and get charged for the call. This created access to families on the Springbank telephone system and residents on the Kerwood system.

Sometimes the store was a central place for good old-fashioned fun. Ice-cream eating contests were held to see who could eat the most .10¢ hand-scooped cones. Lots of jawbreakers were also sold, at three for a penny, from the large, glass jar sitting on the counter.

RALPH BOS MEATS LTD.

Ralph Bos Meats Ltd. was established October 18, 1968, on Lot 23, Con. 1 NER, by Ralph Bos. It was a 1-man operation where cattle, pigs, sheep, etc., were butchered for the surrounding community.

Over the years, the business has increased in size and Ralph's son, Peter Bos, is now the owner of the business. Today, there are six full-time employees and four part-time employees. The business has also changed to be a wholesale as well a retail operation.

The customers come from as far away as Forest to the west and London in the east, as well as the local area.

RALPH HAAN BACKHOE SERVICE

Ralph Haan is the owner of Ralph Haan Backhoe Service. He digs trenches, basements and swimming pools. He is a licensed operator to install septic tank beds.

RANDEN TECHNOLOGIES INC.

John Randy Lee, owner of Randen Technologies Inc., operates this tool-and-die manufacturing business on Lot 31, Con. 1 SER, 4615 Egremont Drive. This business, which originated in September 1988, supplies parts for automotive manufacturers.

RANDY'S AUTO BODY

Randy's Auto Body is owned and operated by Randy Smith. This automotive repair and refinishing business was established in July 1985, and is located on Lot 7, Blk E PL165, in the Village of Kerwood. With the changes in the economy over the last few years, Randy has added radiator repair work and oil spraying to the work he does for his customers.

RAY TUFFIN PONTIAC BUICK LTD.

Ray Tuffin Pontiac Buick Ltd. is owned and operated by A. Ray Tuffin. It is situated on Lot 23, Con. 3 SER, 28478 Centre Road. This business was established in June 1970, and specializes in selling new and used vehicles. There is also a body shop on the premises where mechanical repairs are done. These cars and trucks are sold to the local residents of the town of Strathroy, as well as the surrounding rural community. Ray Tuffin also operates a leasing

Ray Tuffin Pontiac Buick Ltd.

business that supplies new and used vehicles to customers.

RICHARD COPP TRANSPORT

Richard and Joyce Copp are the owners of Richard Copp Transport, which was established in 1993 in the Village of Kerwood.

Steel is transported by this company for various manufacturing firms such as Magna Corporation, Samuel Steel, Stelco and numerous other automotive companies.

ST. WILLIBRORD COMMUNITY CREDIT UNION

In the early 1950s, a Dutch Priest, Rev. Jon Van Wesel, began to develop the idea for a cooperative banking system and credit union. He appointed the first executive committee, including Chris Van Bree and Martin Van de Boomen. A group of farmers met at the home of Martin Van de Boomen in 1951 to finalize the concept and start the business. There were initially 200 members, mostly Dutch Catholics. In 1999, the membership had grown to 30,000.

Other branches of St. Willibrord opened in the London area, and the region now covered includes Middlesex, Lambton, Perth, Elgin and Kent Counties, and the municipality of Waterloo. There are currently 10 branches.

St. Willibrord was an English monk who came to the Netherlands in the seventh century and became a missionary in the Province of Friesland. He became the Patron Saint of the Netherlands.

SKY TOP KITES

Sky Top Kites, established in June 1991, is owned and operated by Steve Gough and is located on Lot 7, Con. 2 SER, 28536 Kerwood Road. This business sells kites and air toys to customers in the surrounding area.

SOETEMANS TREESWEET ORCHARDS

Dave and Riekie Soetemans were married in 1996 and planted an orchard on Lot 1, Con. 1 NER. They planted approximately five acres to begin their operation, and continued each year until the 50 acres was filled with mainly apple trees of various varieties.

In 1998, they purchased another 50 acres and this is planted with peaches, plums, cherries, pears and apples.

The Soetemans have a retail store on the farm and sell fresh fruit throughout the year. The bulk of the fruit crop is sold to wholesale markets during the fall harvest.

STRATHMERE LODGE
(REPLACED HOUSE OF REFUGE)

During the early years in the district, public charity existed in a very crude form. Poor widows were sold by auction to the highest bidder, and proceeds of the sale were given to the public treasury. However, as civilization progressed, great advancements were made. In 1847, a suggestion for the building of a House of Industry in this area was presented to the authorities by a committee. The idea, however, was defeated in council.

After much discussion and thought, the institution west of Strathroy, known then as the House of Refuge, was erected in 1880 at a cost of $1,765. By 1881, there were 108 residents from Middlesex and Lambton Counties. The first Keeper and Matron were Mr. and Mrs. Archie Ballantyne, and the first physician was Dr. R.A. Stevenson. Other Superintendents and Matrons who have served at the House of Refuge have been Mr. and Mrs. James R. Hodgins, Mr. and Mrs. R.J. MacMillan, Mr. and Mrs. Alex Anderson, Mr. and Mrs. E. Miller, and Mr. and Mrs. R. Iles.

Between the Andersons and the Millers was Bob Clarke, a Superintendent who only worked at the facility for about 10 days. Pipes froze on the third floor, and he travelled up and down the stairs so many times, he had a heart attack and died.

When the Millers were hired as teamsters, they earned $400 per year and a free house; their hiring package also included lights (no heat), a garden, and a quart of milk a day. When they became Superintendents they put out tenders for new wiring for the whole building, and the contract was given to Clifford Hutton of Mt. Brydges. After the new wiring was installed, they painted the interior and exterior of the facility. After everything was completed, they held an open house.

Many improvements were made in both the building and the farm, which in 1880 consisted of 46½ acres of land. In 1928, 61 acres adjacent to the original farm were purchased for $3,500, and a new barn was built at a value of $6,000. These expenditures made the institution one of the finest in Canada.

Past, House of Refuge

Present, Strathmere Lodge

During 1953, the west wing of the House of Refuge was seriously damaged by a tornado. As a result, a new modern 1-storey wing was erected. This section included 26 rooms, which is now known as "A" wing.

In 1955, the name of the facility was changed to Strathmere Lodge, having been selected by the Board of Directors. Several meetings were held and, in 1961, work began on building a new structure on the same property as the House of Refuge.

Strathmere Lodge was opened in 1962 with a bed capacity of 168, which quickly filled, since it was a very modern building. In 1966, when Bernie Jordan was appointed as Superintendent, there was a long waiting list. The committee at the time took a proposal to County Council to add another 76 beds, and make changes in several areas. This was approved by County Council and the Homes for the Aged Branch of the Ministry.

Work started in 1967 and the project was finished in 1968. Again, there was a waiting list, and consideration was given to building another home in the eastern end of the county. Several sites were viewed and an option was taken on a piece of property in Dorchester. It was at about this time that Senior Housing started. Slowly, the waiting list got shorter, and it became obvious that another home was not necessary.

The year 1975 saw a major renovation to the kitchen, which cost in excess of $250,000, paid for completely by the County. In 1979, a new roof was installed at a cost of $45,000, split 50/50 between the Province and County.

Between 1880 and 1993, there have been many changes. This facility has improved from being a House of Refuge, where residents worked hard, to a Home for the Aged, where they are looked after. A 3-storey building became a 1-storey building, better for those with ambulatory difficulties. Residents originally numbered 108, to a high of 240, and finally, to the present 160 occupants.

The contractor for Strathmere Lodge was Ellis Don. Bill Galbraith was the first Warden to plant the "Warden's" tree. When Strathmere Lodge opened, the cows in the barn numbered 66. Phelps Symington was the first male resident to reach 100. House doctors following Dr. Stevenson include Dr. A. McCabe, Dr. Fletcher, Dr. Klahsen, Dr. Wolder and Dr. Fournier. Administrators at the Lodge were Samuel MacDonald, Bernard Jordan, and presently, Larry Hills.

STRATHROY HOME HARDWARE

Strathroy Home Hardware was located in Strathroy many years before moving to Lot 22, Con. 3 SER, in June 1994. This business is owned by Wayne and Susan Wilcox.

Before becoming Strathroy Home Hardware, it was known as Lamport Hardware and was located on Frank Street. This business was taken over by Wayne and Steve Wilcox and the name was changed to Strathroy Home Hardware. At this time, the business was moved to Front Street East.

After moving in June 1994 to Adelaide Township, a new building was constructed and the business expanded to include lumber materials. Customers from the town of Strathroy and the surrounding area are serviced from this new location.

STRATHROY MOTOR INN

Strathroy Motor Inn is located on Lot 22, Con. 2 SER, and is owned by Robert Hunter. This 22-room motel business was started in December 1987, by Wes Dixon and Bill Patten, and later sold to Robert Hunter in September 1989.

Strathroy Motor Inn

In August 1996, an 8-room addition was made to the motel, which serves customers in the commercial, industrial and tourist area, both locally and out of town.

STRATHROY RENT-ALL INC.

Strathroy Rent-All Inc. is owned and operated by Robert and Vesta Marshall. It is located on Lot 22, Con. 2 SER. This equipment rental business was established on February 1, 1994. Lawn and garden equipment and other items are rented to contractors, homeowners and farmers in the local Strathroy area.

STRATHROY ROOFING

Strathroy Roofing is owned and operated by Earl Pranger. He replaces and repairs roofs. Their motto is: "No job too small; no job too big; we do it all."

STRYBOSCH CONSTRUCTION

Strybosch Construction was established in 1967 and is owned by Martin John Strybosh. Commercial, institutional, industrial and residential construction is accomplished by Strybosch Construction.

SUPERIOR PROPANE

Superior Propane was established in 1974 at 29495 Centre Rd. The business supplies propane gas to residential, agricultural and commercial customers in Strathroy and the surrounding area.

SUPERIOR SALES

Superior Sales was established on September 9, 1987, by owner Doug Dolbear. This business sells automobiles, and also does auto body and mechanical repairs. Most of the customers come by referral.

THE CEDAR SHOP

The Cedar Shop is located at Lot 11, Con. 1 SER, 2235 Egremont Drive, and is owned by Peter Brander. This business was established in 1990. Peter does carpentry work in his shop, and products are sold to the general public.

THE FAMILY FLEA AND FARMERS' MARKET

Frank Vanderheide founded The Family Flea and Farmers' Market on September 2, 1992. It is located on Lot 22, Con. 2 SER, 28592 Centre Road.

This flea and farm market is open only on weekends. There are many vendors selling meat, eggs, produce, baked goods, crafts, clothing, etc., to the many local customers who look forward to a weekly shopping trip to the market.

THE GIFFEN HOME

Charles and Annie Giffen provided lodging for tourists in the late 1920s. They also sold gas, chicken dinners, soft drinks, ice cream and candy. The Giffen Home had guests from all parts of the U.S. and Canada.

THOMAS FREELE STORE OF ADELAIDE VILLAGE, ca.1910

Thomas Freele, the proprietor of this store, was born in Adelaide Township in 1844. Other proprietors of this store were:
Robert T. Lord (ca.1891)
Mr. Alexander
Thomas Freele

Thomas Freele Store, ca.1910

Jack Muxlow
Howard Brock
Murray Campbell
Samuel and Hazel Finkbeiner
Al Jervis
Mr. Gibbons
Charlie Brandow
Frank and Hilda Priestley
Mrs. Lou Moses (antiques store)
Sarnia couple (residence)
Fieny and Lloyd McDougall
(residence and hairdressing business)

In 1924, the store burned and the present building on the site at Lot 11, Con. 1 NER, was built by George Glenn.

THOREN'S NURSERY

Thoren's Nursery was established in 1970 by Henry and Barbara Thoren on Lot 18, Con. 5 SER. Since then their son, Frank, has taken over the business. The nursery has expanded in size and volume over the years. They grow nursery stock—trees, shrubs and evergreens—to supply landscapers and garden centres in the area.

THUSS GREENHOUSES AND GARDEN CENTRE

Martin and Jo Thuss established Thuss Greenhouses and Garden Centre on Lot 1, Con. 5 NER, in 1981. The original name of the business was Orchardview Greenhouses.

Over the years, the building has been enlarged from 1,500 s.f. to the present size of 22,000 s.f. In the beginning, the business of growing and selling bedding and potted plants was 50% wholesale and 50% retail. Today, the business is 100% retail sales.

They also sell plant-related products in their garden centre to their customers who come from the surrounding area.

Thuss Greenhouses and Garden Centre

TORONTO-DOMINION BANK

Toronto-Dominion Bank, formerly the Bank of Toronto, was established May 15, 1913, and is on the main street in the Village of Kerwood. This bank is very important to the local people, who appreciate doing their banking close to home.

Bank of Toronto, Kerwood, ca.1941

Bank of Toronto, Kerwood, ca.1920

VANDERCRAFT FURNITURE LTD.

Vandercraft Furniture Ltd. was established on Lot 22, Con. 2 SER, in September 1992. The present owner is John Vanderheide, who originally was in partnership with Frank and Rick Vanderheide. Excellent quality furniture is manufactured at this location by skilled craftsmen.

WALTER TADGELL & SONS LIMITED

Walter Tadgell & Sons Ltd. was founded in 1937, and originally was a gas station located in Strathroy on the corner of Front and Caradoc

Streets. When this business expanded to farm equipment, they had to find a new home. They located the business on the south side of Front Street, just east of the Age Dispatch. A few years later, another move was made, to a larger building across the street.

In the 1980s, another move was made, to Lot 22, Con. 3 SER, on Highway 81, north of Strathroy. This location gave the Tadgells more room for their farm machinery, lawn and garden equipment, and recreational vehicles, and also for sales and service areas. The Tadgells serve customers from Strathroy and the surrounding rural area. The present owners are Ron, Brian and Jamie Tadgell.

WEATHER-BOS CANADA LTD.

Weather-Bos Canada Ltd. is owned by Eric Bos and was established in 1991. Weather-Bos Canada makes natural stains that are environmentally safe. These stains are sold to retail paint stores, lumberyards and industrial businesses.

WESCAST INDUSTRIES INC.

Wescast Industries Inc. was established on Lot 22, Con. 2 SER, in July 1994. This building was previously occupied by Franklin Electric and Ontario Hydro.

This is an automotive manufacturing business making exhaust manifolds for cars. Their main customer is the General Motors Corporation.

WESTSIDE AUTO SALES - CANN BROS. HOLDINGS INC.

James L. Cann Jr. is the owner of Westside Auto Sales, established in February 1965, on part of Lot 19, Con. 5 SER.

Originally, this operation was known as Adelaide Auto-Craft and was an auto body repair business. With the change in name to Westside Auto Sales over the years, the company is no longer in the repair business, but reconditions and sells used automobiles. The majority of Westside's customers are from the London area and out of town.

WOODS GENERAL STORE

This business was established in 1907 by Arthur and Anna Woods. Following Arthur's death in 1937, his son, Fred, took over the store and it became known as Fred Woods' Store. Fred died in 1979 and his widow, Eileen, became the owner. The store has been managed by their son, Joe, since 1979, and mother and son still work in the store.

Woods General Store is located on the main street in Kerwood, and is a general store that sells food items, hardware, men's' work clothes and boots, as well as a variety of other items. Business has changed over the years, with bigger department stores being established in the cities of London and Sarnia, attracting people to shop away from the rural area.

WRIGHTMAN ALPINES

Wrightman Alpines is owned and operated by Harvey and Irene Wrightman. This nursery business was established in 1984, and is located on Lot 4, Con. 5 SER. Alpine plants are grown and sold to local gardeners and garden centres.

Woods General Store, Arthur Woods and family in front, ca.1912.

Keyser Store, William Parker and his dog, Laddie

BUSINESSES 645

O'Neil House

Kerwood Train Station

Keyser Cheese and Butter Factory

Green Pea Threshing Factory, which operated (where ballpark is now) until 1940s, then moved south of Kerwood.

Kerwood Farmer's Co-op, elevator and office (1921-1925)

646 ADELAIDE TOWNSHIP... A HISTORY

Rogers' General Store

Keyser Brickyard, ca.1920

Kerwood Produce & Locker Service, L-R, Cliff Winter, Doug George, Donald Pollock (owner), Bill Jordan and Grant Parker, 1948.

Original Keyser Store, ca.1909

Fertilizer Plant

Brooks farm, oil drilling equipment, ca.1900

CHAPTER TWELVE

Leisure Time

BOXING AT ADELAIDE VILLAGE HALL

About 1937 or 1938, during the winter season, boxing bouts were commonplace at the Adelaide Township Hall. There was no roped ring or mat on the floor. Except for boxing gloves, basic equipment was lacking.

This sport was initiated by Davey Long, and was very entertaining and well-attended every week. It became the topic of enthusiastic conversation, and young men in other townships came to show their prowess.

An attempt was made to match individuals of equal size and ability, but this was often less of a priority than simply having a fervent attitude toward the sport. Most young men in Adelaide participated in the weekly two-hour event. John R. Stewart of East Williams was in his late teens when he was matched with Herbert Wardell, who had never boxed. Stewart attacked like a wild man and, within a few seconds, Wardell was on the floor. He never boxed again. Among others, Stewart fought 19-year-old Lawrence McKeen, and Jim Earley, about 25 years of age. In each instance, Stewart attacked with all his might and connected some terrific blows, but was never a match for Earley or McKeen.

Jim Earley (who apparently had some practise at the Ontario Agricultural College in Guelph) was the champion at Adelaide Village Hall. A few individuals from other districts challenged Earley, but never succeeded in beating him.

SCHOOL FAIRS AND GARDEN PARTIES

The school fairs were under the care and guidance of the Department of Agriculture. Home Economics graduates acted as judges for the various classes, such as public speaking, home economics, and related subjects. Volunteer helpers took an active part in these events. The Adelaide Farm Women's Club of S.S. #10 Adelaide was active in these fairs. The school fairs were discontinued by March 1940.

Garden parties were a popular form of entertainment. A makeshift booth was set up where ice cream, candies, etc., were sold, and the profits were added to the admission fees. A professional chair-

Adelaide Orange Lodge Band

The Choral Group ca. 1941. L-R Tina Muxlow, Maxine Finkbeiner, Marguerite Walker, Joy Evans, Shirley Finkbeiner.

1920s Bethesda Girls' League

man, R.E. Roland, had an interesting variety of stories and jokes to entertain the audience.

THE "WHISKEY" PROBLEM

The liking for a "wee drop" was an aspect of the "old sod" culture that many immigrants brought (along with their Bibles) to Adelaide Township. Drink in moderation was an acceptable part of the Army and Church of England society, and "poteen" was a part of daily life of those oppressed by the old world class system. An Adelaide farmer of Irish background recalled that a pail of spirits was always kept in the kitchen. He commented that sometimes the women were so intoxicated at a barn raising "bee" that they had difficulty serving the supper. One Adelaide pioneer died when he set himself on fire lighting his pipe, on the long trek home from a Katesville saloon. The death of an Adelaide resident (the result of a drunken brawl in a Strathroy tavern) was documented in the 1891 Strathroy Age account of the court case, which found a Metcalfe man guilty of murder.

In a collection of family letters, reference to the problems of alcohol is made in a letter written May 17, 1902, by an Adelaide Township mother to her son in the Northwest Territories, later Saskatchewan. The mother tells of the sad death of a young doctor in Kerwood, whose death... *"should be a warning to all young men to refrain from intemperance for 'as ye sow, so shall ye reap.'"* Then she writes, *"Kerrwood has got to be one of the most drunken places that you would find in the universe."* She then mentions that *"the keeper of the O'Neil House was fined fifty dollars for 'selling on Sunday.'"*

TAVERN LICENCES ISSUED BY ADELAIDE TOWNSHIP COUNCIL IN 1850

Wiley's Inn
(East half of Lot 3, Con. 1 SER)
John N. Wiley

Ivor's Inn
(Lot 11, Con. 1 NER, Adelaide Village)
George Ivor

Bray's Hotel
(Lot 10, Con. 1 SER)
William Bray

Hickory Corner's Hotel
(Lot 31, Con. 1 SER)
Francis Frank

Royal Adelaide Inn
(Lot 11, Con. 1 NER, Adelaide Village)
Mrs. Blanche Westlake

Mee's Hotel
(Lot 11, Con. 1 NER, Adelaide Village)
Patrick Mee

McAvoy's Hotel
(Lot 11, Con. 1 NER, Adelaide Village)
John McAvoy

1859 - Licenses - $30.00 instead of the current $50.00

Royal Adelaide Hotel
Mrs. Blanche Westlake - 1869
James Donelly - 1861
Ambrose Wynne - 1863
Henry Gilldart - 1865
John Hamilton Sr. - 1866

Crown Inn - (name change)
John Hamilton Sr. - 1869-1876*

Canadian Hotel
(Lot 11, Con. 1 NER, Adelaide Village)
John Ivor — 1859
Robert Evans - 1863
Thomas Pennington - 1866-1869
Charles Clelford - 1874-1876*

Nahon's Hotel
(Lot 22, Con. 1 NER)
John Ryckman - 1859
Albert Ryckman - 1861-1873
James Anderson - 1876*

Hickory Corners Hotel
David Collier - 1862
Frederick M. Ladell - 1863
Robert Gilchrist - 1864
William Lea - 1872
Henry Carroll - 1874-1876*

Kerwood Hotel
Thomas Winter - 1864
John Gooden - 1866
William Connor - 1869
M.F. Daly - 1872
James Gough - 1873
John Hart - 1875
William Hart - 1876*

Dominion Hotel
(Kerwood)
Samuel Foster - 1867
Colin McKellar - 1874

*Records end 1876.
The Province issues licences in 1877.

Most Adelaide residents were disgusted by the drunkenness of some of their neighbours. Temperance Societies were formed, meetings held, and ministers repeatedly delivered remonstrances from the pulpit to try to change the behaviour of the imbibers.

The Adelaide Township Council tried to control the number (and quality) of taverns by issuing annual licenses at the rate of $20, plus $5 Provincial Tax, and appointing tavern inspectors to inspect the condition of each establishment. At the February 8, 1850, Council Meeting, a motion was passed that *"No tavern, ale house or house of entertainment, except as already licensed, shall be allowed in the township during the present year."* At the Council Meeting, Feb. 2, 1852, held at Mee's Inn, a tavern inspector was appointed for each of the five roads of the township (names of inspectors are not listed). Some Inspectors' names that appear in Minutes over the years: George Sloot was replaced (1852) by John Donaldson for Con. 4 and 5 NER. In January 1858, Johnston McNiece, Alexander Johnston, John Donaldson, John Brooks, and Charles Matthews are to be paid $2.50 for their services in 1857. Other inspectors appointed: John Paine (1867), George Brock (1869) and William Exander (1872).

At the January 1, 1853, Council Meeting, the Clerk was instructed to write the keeper of the Strathroy Hotel, asking that he enforce more "regularity." In August 1854, the Clerk was to write to Mr. Page in Strathroy to complain that he has been selling beer and wine in his tavern without a license. At the meeting of January 17, 1859, the Adelaide Council approved petitions from the Sons of Temperance and the Lodge of Good Templars *"to perfect a better system to suppress the evils of intemperance that now exist in the Township of Adelaide."* Captain Pegley was appointed to deal with this matter.

In 1876, Henry Carroll and William McKeown received a "Temperance and Victually House License" for their hotels from Adelaide Township Council. This was the township's response to the Canada Temperance Act (or Scott Act) introduced in 1876, which became law in 1878. The new legislation enabled the passing of a municipal by-law to prohibit the retail sale (but not the consumption) of liquor. The temperance supporters set out to gain cooperation to repeal the Scott Act. Now, the Provincial government took over control of issuing tavern licenses. The Adelaide Township Council members were probably pleased to be relieved of this responsibility!

ORGANIZATIONS

COURT KEYSER #1295
(THE CANADIAN ORDER OF FORESTERS)

In December 1914, Joseph Keyser sold a small piece of property to Court Keyser. A cement building was built on the 65'x54' lot located at the southeast corner of the Keyser farm. In 1960, Court Keyser #1295 sold this Hall to Elmer Murray, and then purchased the school and property of the former S.S. #1 and 2 Adelaide and West Williams.

For several years, the organization sponsored garden parties at the school grounds. Here, local talent and others from the surrounding area provided entertainment. The Paul Brothers and Shirley entertained on one occasion. Each December for several years, the organization held a turkey shoot, which was a major fundraiser. A ham supper was held for Court Keyser members and families during the spring break from school. Euchre was enjoyed following the meal.

The Canadian Order of Foresters for the ladies, Court Bluebell #1909, originated on September 29, 1961. They met in the Court Keyser Hall, but later, during the winter months, they met in members' homes. They held dessert/euchre parties. Court Bluebell provided financial help for the handicapped pre-schoolers who met daily in St. Andrew's Presbyterian Church in Strathroy. Members of Court Bluebell still meet socially once a month for lunch.

Court Keyser #1295 and Court Bluebell #1909 both disbanded in the early 1990s.

CRATHIE LITERARY SOCIETY

Crathie Hall was built in 1923 by neighbours of the community. Horses and buggies were kept in the nearby shed. Monthly Literary Society meetings, card games, bridal showers, Christmas school concerts (S.S. #2), birthday parties, picnics, stag parties, elections, debates, recitations, skits, euchre, fowl suppers and dances were held at the Hall. Fred Branton and Walter Brown played violin, piano, etc., and the Roy Kennings Orchestra played for dances.

West Adelaide Women's Missionary Society

The most famous musician to play in Crathie Hall was Guy Lombardo. He and his four or five-piece band (mostly his brothers) performed in Crathie in the early 1920s when he was a college student.

In 1930, during a well-attended goose supper, it snowed so hard that the entire crowd spent the night at the Hall, remaining there until the storm broke the next morning.

The box social probably caused the most excitement, tension and controversy. At this social, each girl packed a lunch for two people. She would then dine with the gentleman who bought her lunch at the auction. If there was a boyfriend, he was made aware of an identifying mark on his girlfriend's lunch. This was a great moneymaking scheme, as young men often had to pay dearly for the right to eat with their own girlfriends.

EGREMONT LODGE ODDFELLOWS

Egremont Lodge Oddfellows was instituted in Adelaide Village in 1877. One year, 23 members were initiated; the next year, 31. The first members were T.W. Evan (NG), John Coulter (VG), B. Rogers (RS), G. Hodgson (Secretary), Edward Austen (Treasurer), Andrew Weir (Warden), and J.S. Hoare (Conductor).

The Hall was rented for a while, but later was purchased. In 1883, the Lodge was moved to Kerwood where it remains today. In 1977, the organization celebrated its 100-Year Anniversary. The officers that year were Lorne Dodge (NG), Mac Smithrim (VG), Stanley Johnson (RS), Earl Dodge (FS), George Wilson (Treasurer), and George Matthews (Warden). The bottom storey has been rented from time to time but is now empty and used only for Federal and Provincial elections.

IRENE REBEKAH LODGE

Another branch of the Oddfellows was formed, encampment enterprise No. 38, which was instituted on May 6, 1925, with 30 members initiated. They met in the Oddfellows Hall until disbanding in 1990. The building was sold in 1999.

The Irene Rebekah No. 226 was instituted in May 1921, with 52 members initiated. Mrs. Richard Waltham was the first Noble Grand and became the first Deputy. Many of the members became District Deputies through the years. Many good times were had. Due to the lack of new members, the Lodge disbanded its charter in 1990 with those who wanted to join other lodges.

KERWOOD WOMEN'S INSTITUTE

The Kerwood Women's Institute was organized in August 1910 with 15 members joining that day growing to a membership of 44 by the end of the year.

Kerwood Women's Institute, gathering at Woods' house, 1913.

The branch has been active for over 90 years now- helping families in the community and donating to many charities over the years. In 1985 the W.I. erected a flag pole in the Kerwood Park and supply and maintain the flag that flies atop it. W.I. signs have also been put up at the entrances to the village of Kerwood.

The 90th anniversary was celebrated with an afternoon tea in August 2000-the highlight being the display and commentaries on 25 wedding dresses and accessories from 1880 to the bride, married only a few weeks before, who modeled her gown. There was one three-generation set of dresses.

Family members have given life memberships to Muriel Langford, Mary Johnson, Viola Foster, Joyce Morgan and Gwen Brooks.

KEYSER GRANGE

The Grange was a Lodge, but worked like a co-op. They purchased large quantities of goods and then sold them to members for a more reasonable price than retail. In February 1876, the Strathroy Age reports that Keyser Grange has received their first stock of goods.

KEYSER WOMEN'S INSTITUTE

In 1915, the women of Keyser's Corner, who were helping with Red Cross work in the surrounding towns, felt more could be accomplished by organizing a club of their own. On January 11, 1916, in Keyser School, Dr. McKenzie Smith addressed a group of ladies and organized the Keyser Women's Institute. At that time, Farmers' Institutes were held in many communities, where men met to talk about agriculture. The women convened at the school at the same time the men met at the Hall. During wartime, blankets and quilts, good clothing, socks, sweaters, and other goods were shipped to England. Boxes were sent regularly to the soldiers overseas. Through the years, the branch has been very active in community work. They remembered sick members, their families, and others with fruit, flowers and cards. They gave gifts of money to the Red Cross, Sick Children's Hospital, Strathroy Hospital, Cancer Fund, Institute for the Blind, Food Parcels to England, Mental Health Association, Food Relief, Fire disasters, 4-H Clubs, the Craft Room at Strathmere Lodge, and Strathroy Middlesex Museum. They gave two life memberships, the recipients being Mrs. Simon Shrier (on her 80th birthday) and Mrs. Lawrence Grogan. For several years, they held a garden party at Keyser School. Later, a euchre party, a bake sale and bazaar were held each fall instead of the garden party. Mrs. Simon Shrier and Mrs. Clifford Callaghan have served as District Presidents.

Keyser Women's Institute celebrated their 25th Anniversary at a regular meeting in Keyser Hall on March 26, 1941. On April 13, 1966, more than 125 women gathered in Keyser C.O.F. Hall to mark the 50th Anniversary of Keyser Women's Institute. President Mrs. Otto Zimmerman thanked the ladies for the privilege of being their president on such a memorable occasion. Her mother, Mrs. Simon Shrier, was the first President.

Mrs. Lawrence Grogan wrote in 1953: *"Keyser Women's Institute has done a great deal for the local Forester's Hall. We have had full use of it for many years. In return, we have equipped the Hall with hydro, new platform, stage curtains, piano, chairs, dishes, hot plates, and we have paid the Fire Insurance. At our last meeting, we improved the grounds by planting shrubs and perennials at the Hall."*

In 1976, members, former members, and friends of Keyser Women's Institute gathered in West Adelaide Presbyterian Church to mark the Branch's 60th Anniversary.

UNITED FARM WOMEN'S CLUB OF ONTARIO

Adelaide United Farm Women's Club of Ontario (U.F.W.O.) activities centred around S.S. #10. The club disbanded about 1928 or 1929. The group

Kerwood Citizen's Band

organized the United Farm Young People's Club (U.F.Y.P.O.), which disbanded about the same time. The Mullifarry United Farm Women's Club of Ontario was organized in 1921. Mrs. Danny Campbell visited the local women. She called a meeting at which the Mullifarry club was organized around S.S. #11, also known as Paine's School. In 1996, the former active club members were few in number but still gathered for luncheon meetings at their homes during the summer months.

Several of the club members were also active Women's Institute of Strathroy members. All were active in local programs to promote improvement in the communities.

UNITED FARMER'S ORGANIZATIONS

The Crathie United Farmer's Organization (U.F.O.) was located at the corner of the Second Line North and Highway 81. Local meetings took place in S.S. #2 in the early days. In 1923, a community hall was built on the corner. This was a very active centre for the community club, for public and social meetings, and dances.

The club ordered farm supplies for farmers from a central office near Toronto. A local farmer could order fencing, fence posts, salt and flour, and cattle feed through Crathie U.F.O. A rail car was parked on a C.N.R. siding in Strathroy, and farmers drove there to pick up their products with a horse-drawn wagon. When bulk feeds were shipped loose, these were used as livestock feed.

WOODMEN OF THE WORLD

The Canadian Order Woodmen of the World was incorporated in 1893. The head office was in London, Ontario. It was a fraternal association that issued insurance policies (from $250 to $3,000), sick and accident benefits (from $3 to $10 per week) and funeral benefits ($50 to $100). There are many tombstones in Strathroy Cemetery engraved with the W.O.W. crest.

In the April 13, 1899, Strathroy Age, it was reported that the Adelaide Camp 36, Canadian Order W.O.W., numbered 70 members, and five more were added to the camp. *"Refreshments were served of bread and butter, canned salmon, cheese, cream and sodas accompanied by copious draughts of hot lemonade followed by speeches and songs in which Messrs. Bennett, Dowding, Philips, Kerswell and several others took part."*

A notice in The Dispatch, May 23, 1901, stated that the Sovereigns of Adelaide Camp No. 36 C.O.W. are to attend service in Shilo Church on Sunday, June 2; Rev. H.J. Uren will preach. In February 1914, notice was made that the Adelaide Camp was disbanding and most of the "Choppers" were affiliating with the Strathroy Camp.

Woodmen of the World - Red badge worn at regular meetings.

Fishing on creek Adelaide Village, Lauretta Elliott and friends.

CHAPTER THIRTEEN

Profiles

EDWARD BLAKE, 1833-1912

Edward Blake was born October 13, 1833, on the family farm in Adelaide at the Bear Creek settlement later known as Katesville. His father, William Hume Blake, had studied medicine and surgery in Dublin, and then married his cousin, Catherine Hume Blake. When elder brother, Rev. Dominick E. Blake, was appointed rector by the Church of England for Adelaide Township and district, the three Blakes immigrated to Upper Canada. William and Catherine purchased a farm in the southern part of Adelaide Township, Lot 15, Con. 7 SER. The primitive conditions of Adelaide Township in this era were unimaginable to these educated upper-class immigrants who were suddenly faced with clearing land and operating a farm.

Shortly after the birth of their sons, Edward and Samuel, William and Catherine made the wise decision to leave this wilderness farm life for which they were unsuited; they moved to York (Toronto). William studied law and, in 1847, was elected to represent East York in the Legislature. He was appointed Solicitor General and, two years later, was appointed Chancellor of the University of Toronto.

Fortunately for Edward Blake, his father escaped the unforgiving backwoods, and Edward and Samuel had the opportunity to be educated in Toronto. Edward became a successful lawyer, followed by political associations at both provincial and federal levels. He married Margaret Cronyn, daughter of Bishop Cronyn of London. As a Reformer (Liberal) he served as Ontario's second Premier in 1871-1872. He held several federal appointments until 1892, when he was elected to the British House of Commons as an Irish Nationalist Member. He returned to his Toronto home in 1906. From a very humble childhood in Adelaide Township, Edward Blake took his place among the educated and influential politicians of the nation and Britain.

Hon. Ed. Blake Q.C.

WILLIAM BRAY, J.P.R.N., 1814-1882

Born in Portsmouth, England, William Bray went to sea at age 11 and made a voyage around the world on a 76-gun ship. From 1827, he was with the British Mediterranean fleet, engaged in freeing Greece from Turkish rule, and in manoeuvres against the Russian Navy. When Charles X of France was dethroned in 1830, William Bray was there during the three days' revolution. In 1835, his ship was ordered home and he was paid off after seven years of service in the Mediterranean. He rejoined the fleet to learn the art of gunnery, and as an instructor he was sent to the West Indies and Brazil. In 1837, he made two journeys across the Atlantic to Halifax and then to Quebec City, to aid in suppressing the rebellion. Here, he volunteered for Lake Service and was credited with firing the final shot into the munition dump at the Battle of the Windmill at Prescott, which consequently ended the battles. At the Kingston naval base, there was a disagreement over his keeping the stores, which resulted in his being fined and arrested. With the help of a young Kingston lawyer, John Alexander Macdonald, William Bray successfully sued his commanding officer and was awarded £50 in damages. With this capital, he decided to stay in Upper Canada.

In Kingston, he married Eliza Jane Lang, daughter of John and Ann (Treleaven) Lang. The Brays relocated to Adelaide Township sometime between the Kingston birth of their eldest son, John (1841), and that of the next child, Blanche Louise (1843). The 1852 census of Adelaide Township shows William Bray, age 39, enumerated as an innkeeper, with Eliza Jane, age 29; John Lang Bray, age 12; Blanche L. Bray, age 7; William T.M. Bray, age 5; Adeline E. Bray, age 3; and Caroline A.P. Bray, age 1.

William Bray turned his interests and energies to family, community and mercantilism in the developing settlement of Adelaide Village. He was a member of Adelaide Township Council, from which he resigned his position in 1852. His obituary and the family historian state that William Bray left Adelaide that year to visit his only brother, T.C. Bray, in Australia, and to inspect gold mines there. William returned to Adelaide and set up a joint stock company for milling purposes. In 1862, this mill burned down, a great financial loss for Bray.

During his residence in Adelaide Village, William Bray was involved in many enterprises: as a merchant selling dry goods, hardware, groceries and produce; township councillor and school trustee for many years; Captain, 7th Branch, Middlesex Militia; President of Adelaide Branch, Upper Canada Bible Society; first delegate from the parish of St. Ann's Adelaide to the first Anglican Synod in the Empire since the 1840s, held in Toronto; lay delegate to the synod of the diocese of Huron at London; in 1863, owner of a druggist's shop in Strathroy, which was burned out after only a few weeks; resettled in Petrolia, where he opened a chemist's shop in 1873.

When William Bray died, he left a wife and a large family, many of whom followed their father's example of perseverance, acceptance of change, and a willingness to help others. They too, accomplished great things!

JOHN STEWART BUCHANAN, d.1875

John Stewart Buchanan, eleventh child of James Buchanan and one of the first settlers of Adelaide Township, benefited greatly from his father's strong political and business dealings. James had studied law in Dublin, married "well," and become involved in profitable property transactions. He consistently sought advantages for himself and his 17 children. James was a religious man who published tracts about his ideas. In other publications, he discussed compassionate treatment of the native peoples of North America, a method of financing a railway into America's heartland, and the structure of an early pioneer settlement with mills, a school, meeting hall and bunkhouses for the settlers, a plan from which John may have culled some ideas.

In 1816, James left an appointed post in Paris to take the position of British Consul in New York City, which offered more opportunity for his eldest sons to find government positions and develop business enterprises. John was left on the family estate, where he was raised by his paternal grandfather. In 1831, James deeded John 181 acres, Lot 25, Con. 3 SER, in newly surveyed Adelaide Township, where John began farming in 1832. In 1834, Consul Buchanan received a patent from the Crown for 1,200 acres on Con. 4 SER, Lots 22 through 25, and Lot 22, Con. 5 SER. With the land, he also received the water rights on the Sydenham River. John built a small sawmill; neighbour George Buttery helped to haul the timber, assisted by William Benjamin. In 1836, the neighbours requested that John Buchanan also erect a grist mill, as the nearest one was at Kilworth. These mills were very important to the people of Adelaide Township. Many Irish, who were brought over to sharecrop on the "estates" near Adelaide Village, owned by military gentlemen, left and settled around Buchanan's Mills. By 1840, there were 14 inhabitants at Strathroy, so named by John Buchanan after his homeland.

John Buchanan was very active in the community. In 1837, he was a presiding magistrate; in 1842, he represented Adelaide in the Middlesex County Council; from 1845 to 1847, he was the Warden of Middlesex County. He deeded Lot 23, Con. 4 SER, to the Bishop of Toronto for an Anglican church and school.

In 1839, John Buchanan married Mabel Ann Robinson, daughter of an aristocratic Irish doctor, Samuel Robinson of Toronto. They returned to live in Strathroy, and some of their 10 children are registered in St. Ann's Adelaide records.

Sometime during the 1850s, John Buchanan sold all his land holdings. Most of the Adelaide land was sold to John Frank, who severed it into town lots for sale. Buchanan moved to Chicago with his wife and family. By 1870, John was a member of the firm of Buchanan, Carpenter and Company, dealers of Coach and Saddlery Hardware, in Chicago.

Without the land grant from his father at the time of the settlement of Adelaide, one could speculate as to how the future of Adelaide, Strathroy, and John Stewart Buchanan might have been different. Opportunity and timing were James Buchanan's legacy for development and economic gain in this corner of Adelaide Township.

GEORGE BUTTERY, b.1820

George Buttery was one of the most prominent, highly respected men in Adelaide Township. He was born at Marnham Nottinghamshire, England, and at two years of age, came with his parents, John and Ann (Wilkinson) Buttery, to Canada. By the spring of 1832, John and Ann had taken up land in Adelaide Township. In the same year, Lord Egremont sent out a number of immigrants, who took up land on the Fourth Line.

Charlotte Rapley became George's wife. George Buttery was one of the most active and successful of the Adelaide pioneers, both as a farmer and fruit grower. He also took an active part in public matters, and at different times filled nearly all of the township offices. He was assessor in 1853-1854, councillor in 1856, and subsequently reeve. He was appointed a Justice of the Peace and, after the rebellion, received a Lieutenant's commission. He was president and vice-president of the Adelaide Agricultural Society for many years, and director or president of the West Middlesex Agricultural Society for a long time. He took part in the revision of the Agricultural Act. At one time, George Buttery was sent on an important mission to Kingston in connection with agricultural matters, and he was frequently a judge at Hamilton and London on exhibits there.

A.M. "MAC" CUDDY, b.1919

A.M. "Mac" Cuddy was born on his maternal grandfather's farm near Kerwood. He attended S.S.#9 Adelaide, and graduated from Strathroy Collegiate Institute in 1938 with the Thomas E. Wilson Scholarship to Ontario Agricultural College. From O.A.C., he graduated in 1942 with a degree in Landscape Architecture, having earned Major "O" Athletic letter.

In June 1942, Mac Cuddy joined the Canadian Army and served overseas in the Royal Canadian Artillery until discharged in September 1946, with the rank of Captain.

On February 2, 1946, Mac married Dilys Diana Scott in Aldershot, England. After returning to

A.M. "Mac" Cuddy

Canada, Mac worked for the Veteran Land Act for four years. In June 1950, Mac bought a farm at Lot 21, Con. 3 SER, where he still lives. In 1953, Mac built his first turkey hatchery, where he pioneered the use of light to bring turkeys into off-season production, a technique now used globally. In 1955, he bought a part-ownership in Riverside Poultry and built another processing plant in 1967. In 1968, he entered the U.S. market with hatcheries in North Carolina, South Carolina, Virginia, Missouri and Minnesota. By 1970, Cuddy Turkey Farms had become the world's largest producer of turkey eggs and poults, and this status remains. Exports are made to more than 20 countries.

In 1983, Mac Cuddy was the first recipient of the Ontario Chamber of Commerce Businessman of the Year Award. From the University of Guelph in 1994, he was awarded an Honourary Doctorate. Also in 1994, Mac received the Master Entrepreneur of the Year Award. In 1995, he was inducted into the London Business Hall of Fame. In 1996, the "A.M. Cuddy Wing" was dedicated in his honour, housing the M.R.I. at John Robarts Research Institute in London, Ontario.

Mac Cuddy has also remained passionate over the years about the horses he bred, raised and raced. The following are the awards he won and the names of the horses:

- Governor General's Cup in 1963 with Reed's Russet
- Lieutenant Governor's Cup with Royal Commander in 1970
- Three-Year-Old Trotting Filly in 1972 with Speedy Carlene
- The Hambletonian with Bonefish in 1975
- Two-Year-Old Trotting Filly of 1978 with Imagery
- The Prix la Force in Paris in 1988 with the French thoroughbred Welkin
- Multiple Stakes races in Europe with Sea Cove in the 1990s including Elitlopp and the Prix d'Amerique
- Sovereign Award for Two-Year-Old filly with Larkwhistle in 1997

Mac Cuddy served as President and Chairman of the Lexington Trot Association, on the Board of Directors of John Robarts Research Institute, and on the Board of Ontario Jockey Club.

LIEUTENANT-GENERAL SIR ARTHUR CURRIE, 1875-1933

Sir Arthur Currie was born in Adelaide Township. He attended Napperton Public School, S.S.#5, from 1881-1888. Arthur Currie attended Strathroy Collegiate Institute from 1888-1892, and Strathroy Model School from 1892-1893. He received a 3rd class Teacher's Certificate, but received no teaching experience because of the economic downturn. He returned to S.C.I. in 1893-1894 but quit school in May 1894, before writing his exams. He took a train west to Victoria, British Columbia. While in British Columbia, he taught at Sidney, 1895-1896, at Victoria Boys' Central School from 1896-1897, and at Victoria High School from 1898-1900.

On June 5, 1897, Arthur enlisted in the Militia in the Canadian Garrison Artillery Regiment and was promoted to rank of Second Lieutenant on December 19, 1900. He was with the insurance firm of Matson & Coles in 1900-1904. On August 14, 1901, Arthur Currie married Lily Warner.

During his Militia service Arthur Currie was promoted to Captain in 1901 and Major in 1906. In 1908, he joined the real estate firm of Currie and Power. He was promoted in 1909 to Lieutenant Colonel of the Fifth Canadian Garrison Artillery Regiment and, on October 24, 1913, Currie was promoted to Colonel. He was given command of the newly formed 50th Gordon Highlanders of Canada. On August 12, 1914, Currie was promoted to the rank of Brigadier to proceed overseas as part of the British Expedition Forces.

Arthur Currie was part of the First Canadian Division and fought at the battles of Ypres and St. Julien. He made a strong case for keeping Canadian soldiers together in a true Canadian Division, and was successful in establishing this. He was the first Canadian promoted to the rank of General. He believed in fully preparing each member of his troops before a battle. Currie, nicknamed "Guts and Gaiters," was successful for the planning and execution of the battle of Vimy Ridge (the battle that many feel recognized Canada as a true nation). He visited his troops at the front and was involved in the controversial battle of Mons in 1918, when a number of troops were killed hours before the Armistice.

Arthur Currie received many honours. He was knighted by King George V in 1917 and received the following honours: Commander of the Bath, Legion of Honour, Knight Commander of the Order of St. Michael and St. George, Croix de Guerre, as well as Distinguished Service Medal (U.S.).

GEORGE GRAHAM EARLEY

For more than 40 years, George Graham Earley has dedicated his life to farming and the agricultural community. His induction into the Canadian Agricultural Hall of Fame on November 7, 1999, placed him alongside some of the country's most renowned agricultural pioneers. He has been recognized for his work not only in the breeding of cattle, but also for his efforts in promoting and protecting the beef industry. He is one of the youngest farmers ever inducted. George is recognized as one of the world's foremost breeders of purebred Angus cattle. Through the Earley family farm, Hillcrest Farms, he pioneered an aggressive import program for "exotic" beef breeding stock aimed at producing carcasses in response to changing market demand. George has clearly demonstrated that there is a place in the beef industry for crossbreeding alongside purebred breeding programs. He bred imported Chianina, Maine-Anjou and Belgian Blue cattle with his high-quality Angus stock to produce higher quality carcass animals. The goal was to use the Angus cow as a base and to improve on what she could offer. He has been called "one of the Great Stockmen of our time."

One of George Earley's greatest strengths has been to recognize market trends in the beef industry and to convince judges, exhibitors and market personnel to incorporate such change for the benefit of the industry. The results are improved breeding stock, additional show ring performance and financial success for those making the changes. His breeding programs result in an annual calf production sale that has become one of the most dynamic sources of show cattle in Canada. His influence also extends to the sheep industry.

In addition to establishing a judging reputation internationally in the show ring, George has been generous in sharing the knowledge he has gained through his years of experience. He carried his philosophy of innovation to his teaching of young people, which has earned him the respect and admiration of his peers. He has attracted many motivated youngsters to agriculture. As a 4-H leader for 25 years, George has served as a mentor to countless young farmers. He continues to encourage and counsel young people, and serves as judge for numerous competitions. His own children have been perhaps his best students. Sons Mike and Tim have taken over the operation of the family's Hillcrest Farms and daughters Martha and Sara both work in agriculture-related jobs. George and his wife, Lynda, took over the operation from his father, Eugene, who bought the family's first purebred Angus cow in 1936.

The family has enjoyed unparalleled success at the Royal Winter Fair. From 1959-1999, Hillcrest Farms has produced more Grand Champions, Reserve Grand Champions and Championships in live and carcass classes than any other sole exhibitor.

By focusing on specialized crop production in the mid-1960s, George demonstrated that a balanced interest in soils, crops and machinery could have a positive financial impact on his agricultural enterprises. He also has a passion for auctioneering and sales management, and his skills are recognized both nationally and internationally. He has established many contacts and friends around North America and many parts of the world.

George Graham Earley

JOHN FRANK, 1820-1886

When news reached Adelaide of the Great Western Railway coming from London to Port Sarnia, greedy schemes of instant riches were envisioned. Land values immediately skyrocketed, forcing the railway engineers to alter their planned routes. It was public knowledge that Richard Branan of Katesville increased the prices of his lots to such heights that the railway officials looked elsewhere. Thus, Katesville and Napier were left as hamlets. Adelaide Village was ignored for the same reason, in spite of the efforts of William Bray and John Stroud Hoare. Real estate sales boomed in the Caradoc-Adelaide corner of the township as speculators took advantage of the prospects of selling land to the railroad. Some investors held large quantities of land for years and were finally forced to sell it at a loss or lose it altogether. Farmers along the railroad anticipated selling firewood for the steam engines as this commodity was also increasing in value.

In 1846, John Frank of Westminster Township married Celestia Dell, whose brothers were prospering in this part of the township. In 1847, John Frank purchased a large amount of John Stewart Buchanan's lands. He hired a surveyor and had his new farm divided into lots. John Frank offered the Great Western Railway a free site for a station and right-of-way through his property. The first plans of the railway were to pass about a mile south of the settlement to avoid the flat, swampy land. After John Frank's generous offer and the intervention of some prominent businessmen, railway officials could not refuse. The railroad was built with station and yards on John Frank's farm at the south end of what became known as Frank Street. He profited from his generosity, and earned a reputation for having a liberal nature.

The centre of the village shifted to the western part of Front Street and businessmen bought lots on Frank Street, Centre Street and James Street, to be near the new railroad station. Even though the stumps were not yet removed from Frank Street and the mud was a foot thick after a rain, the business area expanded to this section.

In John Frank's obituary, his unselfishness and interest in the town are mentioned, as he "presented a market site" (actually, he sold it for $125 to the municipality in 1861). When plans were made in council on April 3, 1863, John Frank's offer was approved to loan the council $300 at 10% interest, payable in three years, to build a second Town Hall with a market house, costing $500 on the market square (Frank Street).

John was elected as councillor for several years and served as deputy-reeve. Today, John Frank's name is a reminder of his early altruistic interest in promoting growth and serving his community with unselfish public spirit.

DR. E. LEROY HARRIS, d.1978

Dr. E. Leroy Harris was a senior research aerospace engineer in the Research Department and employee of the U.S. Naval Surface Weapons Center White Oak Laboratory for 19 years. Dr. Harris was the son of the late Mr. and Mrs. Oliver Harris of Strathroy, and a native of Adelaide Township. He was educated at S.S. #8 Adelaide, and Strathroy Collegiate Institute. He graduated in Engineering Physics from Queen's University in 1951. After employment with the Defense Research Board, he did post-graduate studies at the University of Toronto Institute of Aerospace Studies. He received his Ph.D. degree in Rarefied Gas Flows in 1959, and did early research to determine the aerodynamic forces and heating of bodies flying at extremely high altitudes. This work had application to the Navy's major space and high-altitude missile programs.

Dr. Harris began his professional career at the U.S. Naval Ordnance Laboratory in 1959, continuing research in rarefied gas flows and viscous flows in the then Aerophysics Division. He later became chief of the division.

In 1961, Dr. Harris co-authored an important paper on "The Simulation of Re-Entry Conditions in the Wind Tunnel" for presentation at the Institute of Environmental Sciences. This paper heralded the directions his research would take over the next decade. In general, he researched the fluid and flight mechanics of reentry bodies released from long-range ballistic missiles. Specifically, he did the original aerodynamic design of a new class of wind tunnels, namely, hypervelocity tunnels. These tunnels simulate speeds of 7,500 to 15,000 mph (10 to 20 times sound speed) and are required for the development of advanced intercontinental ballistic missiles. Concurrently, he developed techniques for calculating the flight paths of lifting ballistic missiles reentering the earth's atmosphere as well as for calculating the interception of ballistic missiles by ground-launched interceptors. Details of the airflow over the surface of ballistic missile reentry bodies including magnetohydro-dynamic effects also claimed his attention. The significance of his research was recognized by his peers and acknowledged by the American Institute of Aeronautics and Astronautics through their publication of his work.

In the late 1960s and early 1970s, Dr. Harris turned his attention to lasers, and was an early pioneer in the fundamental research which led to major engineering programs for the gas-dynamic laser and the electric discharge laser. The significance of his research efforts was recognized long before the U.S. Navy became involved in developing large experimental lasers.

Dr. Harris was also actively engaged in research to determine the amount of rarefaction produced by a high-energy particle beam traversing a gas, in support of a major research program for the U.S. Navy. In this work, he pioneered in calculating the expansion and temperature of the gas column through which the beam is propagated.

Dr. Harris was a recognized expert in his field, gaining prominence nationally and internationally. He received the Meritorious Civilian Service Award in 1971 and a Superior Achievement Group Award in 1976.

JAMES HEALY, b.1838

James Healy was born in Adelaide Township, the son of James Sr. and Rosanna (Callahan) Healy. His mother was a native of Cavan County, Ireland, and his father came from Queen's County. James Healy Sr. served under Wellington throughout the Peninsular War, and on the great day of Waterloo performed garrison duty within sound of the battlefield. At the conclusion of the war, his garrison was sent to Canada, where he served 10 years, returning thereafter to Ireland. In 1832, he immigrated to Canada, where he had received a pensioner's land grant in the County of Middlesex. He was one of the earliest pioneers of the Township of Adelaide, where he lived until his death in 1861.

James Healy was educated in Adelaide. He attended the first school opened in that part of the country, a primitive log schoolhouse, and began his attendance on the very opening day of the school. His first teacher was William Miller, through whose efforts the school building was built (and whose hands did most of the building).

When James Healy grew to manhood, he engaged in farming and the raising of thoroughbred stock. In the latter business, he acquired a very wide reputation. In 1876, he was selected by the Dominion Government to represent Ontario at the World's Fair in Philadelphia, his specialty being thoroughbred sheep. On that occasion, he won three medals and three diplomas. In 1887, on account of ill health, he sold all of his thoroughbred stock and rented Grove Farm, and relocated to the Fourth Line of Adelaide, a mile from Strathroy. About this time, he formed a partnership in the banking business with Edward Rowland and Jack Shields, under the firm name of E. Rowland & Co. In 1878, James Healy was obliged to go abroad for his health. He spent several months in Old Ireland, visiting (among other places) the homes of his ancestors. In 1892, James Healy bought The Pines (the old Scratcherd homestead), and brought his family to Strathroy. In 1864, he married Joanna Walsh, who graciously presided over the domestic concerns of The Pines for many years. James and his family were members of the Roman Catholic Church. In politics, James Healy was a staunch Reformer.

James Healy was before the public eye for many years in many capacities. For more than 10 years, he was director of the Adelaide Agricultural Society. For 27 years, was director of the West Middlesex Agricultural Society. He served on Strathroy council, was elected deputy-reeve, and was made a magistrate in 1886.

JAMES HENDERSON, 1837-1935

Born in Ingersoll, the third of a family of eight sons whose parents came to what was then Upper Canada in the early 1930s, James Henderson grew up under pioneer conditions. Schools were scarce and teachers were boarded with families of the community. Farm operations were primitive. As a boy on his father's farm, it was James' job to take out a drink to the harvesters about the middle of the afternoon. This he did, using a tin pail and a tin cup or dipper—but the drink was whiskey, which in those days cost .50¢ cents a gallon, instead of water.

Being of a mechanical nature, James Henderson became a carpenter and builder, and erected a number of stores and dwellings in and around his native town that still stand today. At that time, when a man decided to build a home, he secured a pile of rough lumber and the carpenter did the rest. The carpenter dressed the lumber and made everything by hand, even doors, window sashes and mouldings.

In 1866, James Henderson enlisted with the Oxford Rifles to repel the Fenian Raids, and was out with his company along the Detroit River frontier. Many years afterward, the government recognized the services of these volunteers by a medal and land grant in New Ontario.

After an unsuccessful venture in commercial life, James moved in 1873 with his family to the homestead on the Second Line NER. He took an active part in education and the good of the community, and was known as a progressive farmer. He was exceptionally well informed, with sound views on public questions. He was particularly interested in the West Middlesex Agricultural Society, in which he served as director and later as president. He was Liberal in politics and a Roman Catholic in religion.

GEORGE BESTWICK IVOR, 1808-1897

The History of Middlesex County (Goodspeed) 1889, states that George B. Ivor and James Cuddy were the first settlers of Adelaide Township, arriving in 1832. This is a very curious statement and the basis for it is unknown. There were also other indigent settlers in Adelaide Township who were not part of the military group, with different arrangements for obtaining land.

Both Ivor and Cuddy were on the payroll of the construction of Egremont Road. George [Iver] Ivor's name appeared on paylist No. 12 for his work as a road labourer from August 1 to October 20, 1832. He was a very hardworking man and, as he tried different projects to earn money or goods for barter to provide for his family, his frustration with all levels of government becomes clear from his actions and in his correspondence with officials.

The 1842 Adelaide Township census locates George [Iver] Ivor as a "proprietor" in Adelaide Village on Lot 11 NER, after 10 years of living in Ontario. He has 101 acres, of which 14 acres are improved. That year he produced 30 bushels of oats, 20 bushels of peas and 200 bushels of potatoes; he has three cattle, two horses and one hog. On the property is a tavern and a store where spirits are sold. He operated a distillery in Adelaide Village. In his household are three "natives of Ireland": George, Mrs. Ivor and son, David, and five "natives of Canada," of which four are school-age children.

A series of letters from George B. Ivor to the Crown Lands office in Montreal dating from March 4, 1835, show that he had purchased village Lot 11, front range, from Joseph W. Nielsen, who had a store there in 1832. Two other village lots are recorded as sold to George Ivor. On February 18, 1846, Ivor asked for permission to put up a house on Lot 10, Egremont Street, Adelaide Village. In the reply he is informed that a valuation of that lot was approved by the Executive Council and that he would have the opportunity to purchase the lot, but the Department of Crown Lands refused permission to build until he acquired a title of purchase.

On May 30, J.B. Askin wrote from London to the Associate Commissioner of Crown Lands in Montreal complaining about Ivor's actions: *"On the map of the village you will observe an enclosure of about 20 acres made by one George B. Ivor under the pretence of purchasing it from the Crown and converting it into a small farm. He has also thrown a dam across one of the main streets leading from the Egremont Road interiorly and built a distillery where the fence is shown in red ink. I have heard a remark that Mr. Ivor has an application to the Government already for the purchase of Lot 12 north on the main or Egremont Road which he has not yet paid for."* Askin then suggested that since Lots 1 and 2 on the north side of the Second Street were vacant, they might be given to the Methodist Church, and thus the other lots in the village would be enhanced.

On May 5, 1849, the Council of the District of London had given an acre, Lots 13 and 14, on the north side of King Street, for a school in Adelaide Village. The February 25, 1850, Adelaide Township Council Minutes record that on the application of John Hoare, Anthony Preston and William Bray, trustees of S.S.#10, *"such streets as necessary, to approach the school site in the Village of Adelaide and which are now closed, be order to be opened and that the clerk now write to Mr. Ivor to request him to open them forthwith. It seems that George Ivor has enclosed this land and is using it for his own purposes."*

At the January 21, 1850, council meeting, a motion was passed recommending George Ivor be licensed as a tavern keeper, but this was not seconded. At the next council meeting, a motion was passed that no tavern, except as already licensed, should be allowed in the township during the present year.

The 1852 census lists George Ivor as a grocer and innkeeper, located on part of Lot 11, Con. 1 and 2 NER, and also the east part of Lot 19, Con. 1 NER. Very little has been learned of George Bestwick Ivor's later life or that of his children. He died in Detroit. Through his experiences in Adelaide that have been documented, we realize that he entered into many ventures to support his family: farming, storekeeping, and operating a distillery. The wheels of government apparently rolled too slowly for George Ivor, a man of action.

JOHN JAMIESON

John Jamieson, one of the early settlers in Adelaide Township, kept a diary between April 1852 and June 1854. This document, a copy of which is in the library at the University of Western Ontario, has been very valuable to our understanding of life in the County of Middlesex in the 1850s.

Jamieson had been a teacher in the town of Largs in his native Scotland before he immigrated to Canada with his sister and his daughter. It seems that they had very fond memories of their old home. John notes in his diary that his sister received annual flower seeds from Scotland, while he received the occasional newspaper with a letter.

Pioneer life was quite hard in some ways, and the Jamiesons were very much at the mercy of the Canadian weather. John Jamieson records late frosts which destroyed everything he had planted, droughts which left the hay so short that it was impossible to cut, thunderstorms which brought down trees and, of course, snow. During one particularly dry period, a brush fire got out of control, burning a great deal of the Jamieson's fence line. Not only did they have to fight the fire, John also had to stay awake all night, guarding his crops from the neighbours' cattle. They came very close to losing their home to the fire, but were saved by a well-timed thunderstorm. The meticulous record Jamieson kept of the weather has been useful recently to scholars interested in climate changes in the area. One interesting seasonal reference is to "The Canadian Band" starting each spring—it seems that this was the local name for the frog song on spring nights.

From reading the diary, one obtains a sense of the sort of person John Jamieson was. He was a religious man, a Presbyterian, who attended Sunday services whenever they were held, and he was concerned over the infrequency. He seemed pleased when the Reverend William Deas was appointed to minister to the community of a permanent basis. He almost always recorded at whose home the service was held, the subject of the sermon, or the text which inspired it, and the attendance (which seems to hover around 30 people). In September 1853, the congregation held a meeting to discuss where and when they would build a church.

Just as there was no church building for the Presbyterian community, there was no school for the children. Much to Jamieson's satisfaction, a resolution was passed to levy a tax to hire a teacher and provide the young people with an education. Although Jamieson had taught in Scotland, he had to go to London to write an examination in order to receive certification to teach in Canada. This return to teaching meant that there was less time to work his land, only the mornings and evenings on school days. In the diary entries about farming, it is evident just how much neighbours depended on each other. People helped out when they were needed, not just when it was convenient for them.

John Jamieson continued to live in the community at Lot 4, Con. 1 NER, and his name appears as an elder in the session books of the West Adelaide Presbyterian Chapel in 1856. He was secretary of the Congregational Meetings from 1853-1856.

In 1855, at the December 25 meeting, John Jamieson was appointed to keep the key of the church, provide stove wood, kindle up the stove one hour before the meeting (during the winter), sweep the floor and clean the windows. For this work, he was to receive the sum of £3, 5*s*, for a year. In the Minutes of March 6, 1867, reference is made to pay *"the late John Jamieson $13 for firewood."* This is the only record of his death. The burial was probably in the West Adelaide Chapel.

It was largely due to John Jamieson's efforts that the first West Adelaide Presbyterian Chapel was constructed. He was a hardworking Christian man, dedicated to helping his community, church, school, family and neighbours.

WINNIE KINCADE, 1888-1975

Winnie "Wyn" Kincade, from a family of six children, grew up on the Second Line South of Adelaide Township on her parents' farm, the east half of Lot 3, Con. 2 SER. She attended S.S.#8 Adelaide for her early education. From these rudimentary school days evolved Winnie's varied teaching career in many parts of Ontario. Her influence affected many students and, as a lover of history, she wrote about historical figures to help young people understand their country's story.

Winnie Kincade's mother died when Winnie was 10 years old and her father moved the family to Mt. Brydges. Here, Winnie attended Mt. Brydges Continuation School. She graduated from London Normal School in 1924 and began her teaching career at Longwoods Public School, Caradoc Township. She travelled back and forth to school by motorcycle. Making her base at the family home in Mt. Brydges so she could care for her father, Winnie taught in public schools in Lobo and Caradoc, and at the Thorndale Continuation School. She took every opportunity to study at the University of Western Ontario, from which she earned her B.A. degree. Other teaching assignments were Windsor Junior High School, Bermuda Government School, Thamesville and Dutton Continuation Schools. She earned her M.A. from the University of Michigan. Other teaching experiences were in Dryden, Wellington and Midland high schools. The Kincade house in Mt. Brydges became a boarding house for area teachers. While teaching in Caradoc from 1919-1923, Jessie Grant (later Mrs. John T. Crawford) boarded there. Winnie took loving care of her father until his death in 1941.

In a 1973 article in the Mt. Brydges Womens' Institute Tweedsmuir History, Vol. 1, Helen Coulter writes about Winnie's never-ending desire to help young people attain success with their studies. Her interests were people and writing. *"Her keen sense of humour, her wit, and enthusiasm for fun drew all ages, but especially young people, to her. The Kincade home was a gathering place for young folks for both serious meetings and for frolics."*

In St. Andrew's Presbyterian Church, Mt. Brydges, Winnie was the beloved teacher of a young men's Sunday School class, and a leader in the Dramatic Club. She directed and acted in plays, which were enjoyed by the community and provided funds for a new furnace and a new organ for the church.

While gathering material for her books, Winnie travelled extensively in all the Canadian Provinces. The theme of her books is a survey of the historical monuments of Canada., including one about Ontario, entitled The Torch: Ontario Monuments to Great Names. This book can be borrowed for reading from the University of Toronto, Special Collections Library.

Winnie's tombstone is engraved with a torch, a country school and a book, and reads:

Miss Winnie Victoria Pearl Kincade
B.A., M.A.
September 1, 1888 – March 18, 1975
Daughter of William J. Kincade and
Mary Arrand Kincade
Teacher, author and lover of Canadian history
Friend of the author of life

THOMAS RADCLIFF, 1794-1841

About 1832, Thomas Radcliff bought a considerable estate in Middlesex County where, a little later, he founded Adelaide Village, named in honour of the consort of William IV, who had come to the throne two years earlier. Radcliff was a striking figure. Physically, he has been described as a veritable son of Anak, standing 6'5" and weighing 210 pounds. At the time of his arrival in Canada, Thomas Radcliff was in his late 30s, and already had a long and distinguished military career.

Born in Ireland, he was a descendant of the ancient Saxon family of Radcliffe, of Waldstein Waters, England. He could trace his family lineage back to more than a century before the Norman conquest, his ancestors having come to England 841 A.D. His father, Rev. Thomas Radcliff, held numerous lucrative positions in the church.

Young Thomas Radcliff was educated at Trinity College, Dublin, and joined the famous 27th Enniskillen Regiment at the age of 17. About 1815, Radcliff found himself a veteran with nothing to do. His family was wealthy and when, eventually, his thoughts turned to the land across the Atlantic, it was with the idea of setting himself up as a replica of the landed gentlemen of the Old Country.

Radcliff wrote home voluminous letters regarding the new land in which he settled and, in 1837, these were collected in book form and published in Ireland under the title, "Authentic Letters from Canada."

Meanwhile, MacKenzie's agitation against the Family Compact had stirred Upper Canada and the climax was reached in the Rebellion of 1837. It is doubtful if Radcliff was an extreme Family Compact man, but there was never any doubt of his loyalty. Sir John Colborne, himself a veteran of the Peninsula, appointed Radcliff to command the Middlesex Militia.

Ultimately, in the operations along the Detroit frontier, Radcliff had as many as 5,000 untrained militia under his command, who were almost entirely dependent for provisions and accommodations upon his good management. For these services, Col. Radcliff received the formal thanks of the Parliament of Upper Canada. At the close of the troubled period of 1837-1838, he was appointed a member of the Legislative Council. In 1841, he was offered the appointment of collector for the Port of Toronto.

The appointment would probably have been welcome, as Radcliff's Canadian landed estate, so ambitiously planned, had apparently failed to measure up to his expectations. His experience paralleled that of many who found it impossible to transplant to this new land the institutions they had known in the Old Country. He was devoted to the defense of Canada against the threatened rebel inroads, and these activities had interfered materially with the operation of his properties.

The hardships of pioneer life, however, and the difficult conditions in the western district, following upon years of arduous campaigning, had undermined his health. Thomas Radcliff died at the untimely age of 47, before he could accept the Toronto appointment.

WILLIAM RAPLEY, d.1897

William Rapley was a sturdy pioneer who left his mark on the countryside. He came from Sussex, England, at the age of 18. His mother died at sea and his father died soon after arriving in the wilderness of Adelaide, leaving William in charge of his younger siblings. At that time, only seven families resided in the Township of Adelaide and they befriended the orphans.

William Rapley cleared a farm and built a fine log house with a huge fireplace and all the comforts of the times. He helped clear the Egremont Road to Sarnia. William married and raised a family, to whom he gave all the advantages possible. In 1857, he sold his property to the Great Western Railroad, their line running through his section. He and his family relocated to Strathroy, where he began his mercantile livelihood.

In 1860, Strathroy became an incorporated village, with William Rapley as a member of the first council, later reeve, then mayor and the first deputy-reeve. He was interested in politics and was an active politician for many years, a pronounced Reformer, doing much to advance the cause in Middlesex. Sir George Ross, who was his leader, dubbed him "The Grand Old Man." William Rapley crossed the ocean many times on business, and was in the company of Sir G.W. Ross when they attended Queen Victoria's Jubilee.

His first marriage took place at Katesville, where the rector was Rev. D.E. Blake, father of Hon. Edward Blake. At 72, troubled by slight deafness, he retired to his beautiful home where he passed some 10 years in the happy companionship of a large circle of relatives and friends. Until his retirement, he was a leading merchant and grain buyer.

PATRICK JAMES "PAT" STAPLETON

Pat Stapleton has always enjoyed sports, especially hockey, which for 19 years was his profession. He has enjoyed sharing his love of the ice and the game, especially with young people. He believes that hockey provides an opportunity to learn life skills, and he has always encouraged young people to be the best they can be. He participates in many events to promote sportsmanship, leadership and the effects of a positive mental attitude.

Pat Stapleton was born in Sarnia, Ontario, where he played minor hockey until 1954. He played four years of Junior "B" hockey in Sarnia and two years of Junior "A" hockey with St. Catherine's Tee Pees. In 1960, Pat went professional and played professional hockey for 19 seasons. Pat spent four years playing minor professional with EPHL-Sault Ste. Marie and Kingston and with WHL-Portland. He played 10 years in the NHL with Boston and Chicago. His last five years of professional hockey were played in the WHA in Chicago, Indianapolis and Cincinnati.

In 1966, Pat had been playing professional hockey for six years when he purchased Lloyd and Vera Muxlow's farm. The property was approximately 249 acres and had land on the north and south sides of Egremont Drive. One month before the Stapletons were to move in, the barn and the outbuildings were destroyed by fire. They rebuilt the buildings in 1967 through 1969, and celebrated the completion of the barn with a neighbourhood barn dance. Originally, the farm operated as a cow/calf operation. Polled and Horned Herefords were the main type of cattle used in the operation. Since then, Pat bought additional property, and developed his farm into a substantial beef operation.

In 1972, Pat became a member of the original Team Canada. Team Canada became the first NHL team to play against the Soviet Union. Team Canada defeated the Soviet Union in the "unforgettable epic series." Pat also played the Soviet Union in 1974 as a captain of Team Canada, this time being a member of the World Hockey Association (WHA).

During his hockey career, Pat was elected to play on the All-Star Team in every league that he played, including the NHL, where he was league all-star defenseman with the Chicago Black Hawks. He has played on 10 championship teams, and was captain of the Chicago Black Hawks.

Pat is one of only four defensemen in the history of the NHL who had six assists in one game. He is the first defenseman to set the record of 50 assists in an NHL season. He still holds the defenseman record for 17 assists in a Stanley Cup Playoff, and is the only defenseman in the WHA who had six assists in one game.

Pat Stapleton is the only person to have played, coached, managed and owned a professional hockey club. This team was the Chicago Cougars of the WHA. He also built and operated ice rinks in the Chicago area.

HUBERT TACK, d.1981

After Hubert Tack was discharged from the Army in 1948, he and his wife, Amelia, bought the farm on Lot 26, Con. 1 NER, which was owned by Jennie Gunson. While Hubert was in the Army, he was an instructor in the Medical Corp from 1940-1946. Hubert and Amelia Tack have two sons, Paul and Tom. In 1962, the Tack family sold the farm and moved to Strathroy.

BLANCHE WESTLAKE, 1794-1866

The Westlake family history has a long and illustrious background, originating in Cornwall and Devon, West of the Lake Country—thus the name "Westlake." Blanche (Woolcock) Westlake was born in Devonport, England. She married in Stoke Damerel, Devon, on May 9, 1815. Her husband, Walter Westlake, was a career British navy man and retired from serving in the Plymouth Dock Yards. Blanche, Walter and her two young brothers (some thought they were sons or nephews, but we could not substantiate it) immigrated to Canada in 1832, hoping to receive a land grant for Walter's years of service. Unfortunately, Walter died at sea in 1832, and Blanche and her brothers continued to York (Toronto). She made her way to Adelaide and endured severe hardships here.

Since there were few options open for widows in those days, and not being without means, Blanche Westlake opened an inn at Adelaide Village. She was a jolly lady and, over the years, her "Royal Adelaide Inn" became a popular place for weary travellers and townsmen alike. Here, she would have the opportunity to greet her patrons graciously as she was accustomed in her home in England. She must have brought a social brightness to this bleak backwoods village. It would be expected that some men were attracted to Mrs. Westlake's charms and business acumen, but she quickly discouraged this kind of attention. Many council meetings and other important meetings were held at her inn in the early days, and later, as reported in the Adelaide Township Council Meeting Minutes beginning in 1850.

On March 16, 1837, Blanche petitioned the Land Committee of the Executive Council for Free Deeds for Lot #4 front and rear, town of Adelaide, on which she had erected a very large frame house, probably the site of her first inn. She also asked for a grant of 100 acres of Lot 3, Con. 5 NER, as occupied by her brother, William Woolcock.

In another petition, she asked that her brother be permitted to have his status changed to that of indigent settler. This might be indicative of her innate business sense, as she might be able to purchase the land cheaply if he did not fulfill his settler's duties. Blanche acquired the patent for Lot 3, Con. 5 NER, consisting of 147 acres. It is probable that she paid her brother as well as other help to work to meet the requirements of clearing the land and the road allowance, and to build a settler's shanty.

In 1839, Blanche wrote a letter to Hon. Sullivan, Commissioner of Crown Lands, Toronto, for approval to purchase the front and rear lots of Lot 1, Con. 5 NER. She had already had a forge built for a blacksmith shop on this property, for the benefit of locals and travellers passing through the village. On November 6, 1839, Thomas Radcliffe wrote this note to assist Blanche in her efforts to buy the land: *"I certify That Mrs. Blanche Westlake has cleared that Lot alluded to in her petition in the village of Adelaide and built a Blacksmith Shop thereon as stated and that the petitioner is a spirited and improving settler and deserves every encouragement. Thos. Radcliffe."*

The 1842 census shows Blanche living by herself in Adelaide Village at Lot 11, Con. 1 NER. In July 1843, Blanche Westlake, widow, and John Stroud Hoare, Master Builder, were granted permission by the Executive Council to purchase land in the Village of Adelaide, Blanche to purchase the east half of Lot 9, Con. 1 SER, and John Hoare the west half of Lot 9, Con. 1 SER. Blanche made a financial donation to the building of the West Adelaide Presbyterian Chapel in 1853. Perhaps this was a goodwill contribution, or it may have been a business strategy to appeal to the Presbyterian patrons who had a choice of inns in Adelaide Village at that time.

In 1846, Blanche received 100 acres of Crown land being the east half of Lot 2, Con. 2 SER. In 1856, she sold 50 acres of this land to Richard Randall, and in 1864, she sold the other 50 acres to Lawrence Cleverdon. The 1851 census shows that Blanche's niece, Marian, lives with her. Blanche owns Lot 1, the south half of Lot 2, the north half of Lot 5, the east half of Lot 9, the west half of Lot 11, the east half of Lot 2, and Lot 3, Con. 1 NER. In 1855, Blanche sold the 147 acres of Lot 3, Con. 5 NER, to John Root, 18 years after her brother William Woolcock had occupied it.

Blanche was buried in St. Ann's Anglican Cemetery. This feisty, industrious pioneer, a "widow in the woods," made a considerable contribution to the development of Adelaide Village.

HUGH WILEY, 1820-1906

In 1837, Hugh Wiley left County Down, Ireland, with his parents to join the other Wileys that had already established in Adelaide Township. Hugh was a teenager, with no idea of what lay ahead. On the ship, he cared for his parents as they lay suffering from cholera. His father died and was buried in a grave at Grosse Isle, the Health Inspection Station in the St. Lawrence River. By the time he and his mother reached Hamilton, she succumbed from the plague, and was buried somewhere near the port. Young Hugh made his way to Wiley's Corners, where three older siblings had settled previously. At first, he took up blacksmithing and plied his trade at the corner of the Second Line North and Sideroad 12 (Seed Road). In 1842, Hugh bought 50 acres of the west half of Lot 4, Con. 2 NER, from Alexander Johnston. In 1852, he purchased the other 50 acres. In 1881, he sold the 100 acres to John Conkey.

In many ways, Hugh Wiley was very generous, but his reputation as an eccentric curmudgeon has lasted to the present day. In 1853, he offered land for a chapel and graveyard, but his brother John's offer was accepted as a more convenient location on the Egremont Road corner. Hugh Wiley provided mortgage money for his widowed niece, Rebecca Wiley Wilson, to provide farms for her sons, and he financially aided his brother, John, on several occasions. He became a money lender for others who needed a loan as Adelaide land records show. His motives as a philanthropist may be weighed against records that show he received interest of $400 on one mortgage of $1,000. However, records show the principal of another loan was paid off in 1929, 23 years after Hugh's death.

"Uncle Hugh," as he was called by the West Adelaide connection, never married. Stories of housekeepers who did not find him an easy employer have filtered down through time. Because of his bachelor status and eccentricities, very few people knew of his family connections and the "Uncle" name became disconnected from any family line. The penuriousness of his personal life is in contrast with his display of generosity when he donated the steel church shed for the use of the West Adelaide Church congregation.

Jack Wilson used to help Uncle Hugh with his farm work. A non-believer in banks, Hugh stored his money in an iron box. One night he asked Jack to get a lantern and help him hunt for some coins he'd lost on the sideroad, as he was returning to Clelands', where he made his home in later years. As Hugh grew older and more cantankerous, Allen Cleland made him take a bath. The old man retorted that he wouldn't leave Allen a penny—and didn't!

In his will, Uncle Hugh stated his genealogical relationship with all his nieces and nephews, to whom he left $1,000 each. In the codicil to the will, he doubled his legacy, but he decreased by half the amount left to his invalid niece, Isabella Cleland. This gesture reveals some quirk in his nature. His estate amounted to $32,000, a tremendous fortune for a teenaged orphan to acquire by 1906. In accordance with a request he made to his lawyer, Hugh Wiley's red granite tombstone is the largest and grandest in West Adelaide Cemetery—ever the neighbourhood "character"!

JOSEPH "JOE" WOODLOCK, 1872-1951

Joe Woodlock attended the second S.S.#6 School on the southwest corner of Lot 5, Con. 1 SER, the Healey farm. Siblings John, Joe and Melina were unmarried, so the only stories of their lives in the community come from neighbours or the occasional item in the Strathroy newspaper.

To his neighbours in the farming community on the Main Road, Joe seemed to be a man belonging to another era. He was considered an exceptionally smart man, self-educated because of his avid reading habits and exploratory mind. He had great perseverance and patience, always interested in working out an idea for an "invention." Joe wanted to be a railway engineer, so he went to work on the Grand Trunk Railroad operating out of London.

John Woodlock, Joe's older brother, had been running the family farm for some time and when he died in 1911, Joe gave up his dream of becoming a railroad engineer and resignedly returned home to work the farm and be with his younger sister, Melina. Joe became the janitor at the schoolhouse on his property, and he always had the wood fire lit at 7:00 a.m. He read books in the school until the students came and then went home. Eventually, he reread the books in the school many times. Joe was a very capable speaker who was in demand as chairman of school concerts and neighbourhood socials. Debating clubs at the school and at Adelaide Township Hall were very popular. Joe's team often won as he was widely read, an exceptional orator; he studied everything he could on a subject and worked out a strategy to present his points effectively. He was very witty and his humour added to his presentations.

When the newspaper arrived, Joe read it before he did anything else. Joe's mind was not centred on the demands of farming. By 1938, Joe was aging, so he cut back on farm work. He quit growing grain, and hay was his principle crop.

One time, Joe went to the London Fair, where he watched a hawker making orange juice using a metal squeezer. Joe saw that this turned the squeezer green, and he thought a glass squeezer would be better. Two years later at the fair, lemon squeezers were manufactured from glass. Before they were invented, Joe made a rip saw from a regular saw by filing the teeth to point ahead. One time, he was cutting grain and he took the notion that he could fix the springs on the binder to hold the tops of the sheaves so that the bottoms would come out first. This worked out okay, except when the wind came up and the sheaves fell over. So he worked away to make the sheaves bigger and the springs stronger so they would stand up. Joe never tried to get a patent for his ideas, because he thought that if he could figure something out, anyone else could do the same.

The Woodlocks could always be counted on for their votes to support the Liberal candidate in every election. Once, Joe decided to run for Adelaide Township Council. That year, many neighbourhood men threw their hats into the political ring and he was defeated. The next year, he was asked to run again—in an impressive speech, he decisively told his supporters that he had put his name in and they didn't want him, so he was finished with local politics… "and the rest of ye can go to @#*&%!"

Joe is buried in All Saints Cemetery, Strathroy.

CHAPTER FOURTEEN

Memories

ADELAIDE TOWNSHIP TOLL ROAD

Several pioneer reminiscences make vague reference to a tollgate on the Egremont Road, at the corner of the Strathroy Road by Mahon's Inn. Proof of a toll collection is found in the 1861 census of Adelaide Township: William Oke, 33, whose occupation is given as "toll house," lived in St. John's Ward (Egremont Road), born in England, a Wesleyan Methodist, with his wife, Charlotte, 33, and Canadian-born children, Philip, 13, and Richard, 10.

In the "History of Middlesex County, Goodspeed, 1889," it is stated that Adelaide Township had six miles of toll road on the Sarnia Road, and that the toll road income in the period from January 1, 1852, to December 31, 1868, was $2,460.77. (Lobo Township's portion: eight miles on the Sarnia Road was $12,563.74 for the same period.)

In June 1851, Middlesex County Engineer, Freeman Talbot, recommended that improvements should be made to the road beginning at the Proof Line of London Township to the western boundary of Adelaide Township. He suggested that a charcoal road be built through Adelaide and a gravel road built for London and Lobo Townships. The 20-mile repair would include new culverts and one big bridge. Then, three tollgates were erected. In December 1865, Toll Gate No. 3 Sarnia Road was rented to A. McArthur. It was found that many travellers cheated the tollgate keepers by taking to the fields, or going a longer way to get to their destinations, so profits were negligible. In 1882, the gates and buildings were sold outright.

ARRAND GATHERINGS

When George, Mary Ann (Martin) and "Baby Thomas" arrived in Upper Canada in 1836, William IV was the King of England. The only holiday celebrated annually, except Christmas, was on June 4, George III's birthday. This day was a holiday from the 1760s into the 1860s, through the reign of George IV and William IV, and into the reign of his granddaughter, Victoria. Consequently, this holiday was chosen for the Arrand family gatherings.

With the completion of the new homestead and an apparent good harvest, a well-remembered gathering was held on Saturday, June 4, 1849. Later, there was a trend to celebrate the Queen's birthday on May 24, and a few Arrand gatherings were changed to that date. However, this did not suit the spacing of leisure that was allowed between spring planting and hay harvest, so the date for family gatherings was changed back to June, to be celebrated on the third Saturday of that month.

In 1922, the gatherings had become too large to be held at the farm homestead, and it was decided to meet at Springbank Park in Byron. The name was changed from "gathering" to "reunion." It was still held on the third Saturday in June, a slack period for the farmers of Ontario and Michigan. In 1990, the Arrands celebrated the 141st family gathering and the 67th reunion.

AS THOUGH THE QUEEN WERE A GUEST

Many elderly persons carry with them vivid memories of an old-fashioned Christmas. My mother and her first cousins can recall highlights of Christmas in the 1880s, 1890s and early 1900s.

Their grandmother, Mary (Cawrse) Taylor, came to Canada as a girl of 18 with her mother, father, brothers and sisters, from Cornwall, England. Great-grandmother went into service and supervised others in a captain's house. Apparently, she had worked for Queen Victoria—at what, no one knows—and in Canada, she worked for other noted people. Indeed, she had learned to prepare for Christmas as if the Queen were a guest.

Living grandchildren can recall happy, festive occasions when married sons and daughters, husbands, wives and children were present. George Taylor and Matilda (Smithrim) Taylor, Elizabeth (Taylor) Smithrim and Richard Smithrim, Grace (Taylor) Inch and Frank Inch Sr., Sarah (Taylor) Hawken and William Hawken, Clara (Taylor) Cowan and Leslie Cowan, and Charles Taylor and Katherine (McNeil) Taylor, and my grandparents, Jane Ellen (Taylor) Dinning and Robert Dinning, were present. Aunt Bedena, the unmarried daughter, assisted in the later years, doing much of the work.

In the large brick house at the west end of the Eighth Line, Lot 1, Con. 4, Metcalfe Township, now only cattle pasture, Christmas was held. The dinner was set first for adults and then children. The women helped to prepare the meal. A blizzard blew in one Christmas and families arrived by cutter, remaining all night. Another was so mild everyone played croquet on the bare lawn.

When Charles, the younger son, married and took over the farm, William and Mary Taylor moved to Strathroy. Here, they bought a frame house on Metcalfe Street near the arena from Robert Bentley, a retired Katesville merchant. At this location, Aunt Clara and Aunt Bedena prepared Christmas for all.

Before Christmas, the white frame house was thoroughly cleaned. Silverware was polished until it glistened. Although the children still received presents in stockings at home, a large Christmas tree stood in one corner, surrounded by presents and gaily decorated with paper chains of red and green, and long white strings of popcorn.

The family gathered around this tree after their arrival Christmas Day, and opened gifts, many of which were handmade. Women received embroidered table covers, cushion tops, handkerchiefs with tatted edges, fancy dishes, and colourful vases their descendants now treasure as antiques. All received knitted sweaters and scarves, and men and boys got warm socks and cozy mittens. The men often received ties, and moustache cups with colourful scenes. Perhaps a Christmas card would be received, to adorn the parlor table all year.

Toys for children were simple. Girls received dolls in dainty embroidered dresses, tea sets and doll cradles. Boys received homemade sleds, skates, tin soldiers, Noah's arks, and rocking horses. There were games, books of fairy tales and adventure stories like Robinson Crusoe and Treasure Island, some of Dickens' books, and Elsie and Pansy books for girls.

Oh, what meals the family ate at Christmas! Typically, there were a variety of English and Canadian dishes. Great-grandmother and the unmarried daughters had baked cakes, pies and cookies. Christmas dinner included turkey, goose, turnips, fresh cabbage salads, pickles, and plum pudding and Christmas cake for dessert, decorated with icing and red and green wintergreen candies.

Supper consisted of cold fowl, boiled ham and cheese brought by Uncle Frank Inch, who operated a cheese factory in Kerwood. Uncle Frank sliced the ham as neatly as cheese for great-grandfather, who had arthritis.

Besides the cake and cookies, dessert consisted of custard, fruit and apple pies, sometimes made from dried apples. Preserved thimbleberries, raspberries and blackberries were also served, as well as oranges, a delightful change from dried apples. Bowls of hickory nuts, walnuts, beechnuts and hazelnuts from the neighbouring forests filled small spots on the table. Children especially, tried to take a little of each food.

A well-remembered candy in those days was a conversation lozenge in pale pastel shades of pink, yellow, green, white and mauve, inscribed with sentimental verses such as "You are my sweetheart."

In the afternoon, games such as crokinole and parchesi were played, but no cards. An unusual game was played eating almonds. If someone found an almond with two kernels, he would give one of them to another person. When the pair met again the next day, the first to say "filopena" received a gift from the other person.

By Jane Laughton

BEFORE UNIVERSAL IMMUNIZATION

During the first two decades of this century, there was one word from a doctor's lips that could strike terror into the heart of every parent—diphtheria. In the winter of 1924, such a terror came to Mr. and Mrs. John A. Campbell of Lot 2, Con. 1 NER. Two of their daughters, Lily and Annie, were diagnosed with diphtheria. Those of us who raised our children behind the safe barrier of immunization can scarcely imagine how these parents felt. Besides their two beloved daughters, Mr. and Mrs. Campbell had five other children. Who would be next?

The Campbells suffered not only from concern about their children and the endless nursing care of those who were ill, but also were bereft of the support of their friends and neighbours. The disease was so serious that no one was even allowed to go to the door. I remember my mother preparing food to help out, and my father taking it to the line fence where Mr. Campbell would pick it up. The next day he would return our dishes when he picked up food for that day. I am sure many of the neighbours did the same. I remember standing on a chair at our east window and watching this exchange. I was too young to understand why a family that had always been so warm and welcoming had suddenly shut the door against their friends.

Eventually, the day came when Annie's body gave up the fight against the ravages of this disease. Because of the nature of the death, the funeral had to be held the next day. When the funeral sleigh and Mr. and Mrs. Campbell, in their cutter, started the lonely drive to the cemetery, my father and his brother met them at the road in their cutter. As they passed the McChesney farm, Mr. and Mrs. W.J. McChesney joined them. The sad little procession made its way along the church sideroad to West Adelaide Cemetery and, after a simple service, they started home. Years later, I heard my father say it seemed so heartless to turn away from that new grave without even shaking hands with Mr. and Mrs. Campbell. I think it always bothered him that he could not do more for them.

What would the Campbells find when they opened the door of their house? Another sick child? Lily's condition worsening? Their prayers were surely answered when, day by day, Lily began to gain strength. Years later, she married Howard Wardell and moved to Sarnia, where they raised their family.

By Evelyn (Fletcher) Clifton

CHAUTAUQUA MEMORIES

I remember Chautauquas (pronounced "shuh-tah-kuh-wah"), evening events where people sat outdoors on makeshift seats or a chair (if one was lucky). There were no halls or buildings available for these early large events. [Merriam Webster's Collegiate Dictionary, Tenth Edition, reads, "*An institution that flourished in the late 19th and early 20th centuries providing popular education combined with entertainment in the form of lectures, concerts, and plays often presented outdoors or in a tent.*" A member of the Adelaide Township Heritage Group commented that it was typically an event where one might take a date.]

Anna Jean McCoskery tells me that Chautauquas are still held in New York. I remember attending such events when I was a girl in public school. Since there was no radio in most homes, these concerts were a very enjoyable occasion!

By Margaret Wardell (Demaray)

FOOD PREPARATION OF DAYS' PAST

Before anyone could make pickles, there had to be a supply of vinegar. If you wanted to make vinegar, you started several months before the pickling season. First, the homemaker checked the "mother of vinegar" in last year's vinegar jug. This was a slimy, pale-brown substance in the bottom of the vinegar jug. If the "mother" looked fresh, it was returned to a well-washed jug with a little of the old vinegar. Then the jug was filled with fresh cider and let stand for several weeks until vinegar formed. It was a much stronger concoction than the white wine vinegar we buy in stores today. Sour pickles were usually made in crocks and covered with a mixture of vinegar, spices and a little sugar. Early settlers made and consumed vast quantities of pickles. I have read that one reason many lived to such an advanced age was due to the amount of vinegar they consumed. Today, we hear of the therapeutic value of honey, garlic, and vinegar remedies. Maybe the "ancients" knew more than we give them credit for.

Baking

First, let us remember that in the early days, there were no electric stoves that gave a constant heat to the oven. Wood-burning stoves were the best to be had. First, the cook had to choose wood that would burn steadily, and remember to keep adding wood as it burned down. Some baked goods required hotter ovens than others. Most women could tell if the temperature was right just by putting her hand in the oven for a moment.

In the early days, all bread was made at home. In big families, bread might have to be made two or three times a week. The homemaker usually had a very large bowl in which she mixed flour, salt, sugar, butter or lard, yeast and warm water. When these ingredients were thoroughly mixed, she turned the whole thing out on a floured surface to knead by hand. This involved turning the dough over and over, and punching it into a cohesive lump of dough. This would take 10-20 minutes. The dough was then returned to the bowl, covered with a clean cloth, set in a warm place and allowed to double in size. The dough was then turned out a second time on a floured surface and kneaded. This time, it was shaped into loaves and put in baking pans. It was again set in a warm place to "rise" to double in size. The loaves were then put into the oven to bake.

By reading old cookbooks, it seems that greater use was made of molasses and spices than is the case today. Often, the family went into the woods to collect nuts, which were then shelled and used in cooking. Most baking was much plainer than we do today. Every recipe started from "scratch"—no packaged mixes. Most old recipes indicate that a great many eggs were used in baking. Baking powder was not of a consistent strength, and I suspect that eggs were used as a leaven. Pies did not seem to enjoy the popularity they do today. Many and varied were the cakes that were baked. It would seem that most were layer cakes and every cook strove to produce the highest "tall cake." Many varieties of plain cookies, along with tea biscuits and johnny-cake made with cornmeal, filled the pantry shelves. The skillful cook was also proficient in stove management.

GERMAN PRISONER-OF-WAR

Hans Bednartz was a merchant marine working on a ship loaded with coconut that was on its way to Germany. The Allies stopped the ship in the Indian Ocean and, rather than surrender, the German sailors blew it up. The men were pulled from the water and kept in the dark hold of an Allied ship until they reached Halifax. Hans recognized the area as he had been there before, and he spoke and understood English, which he had picked up during his travels.

The prisoners were taken to Northern Ontario to cut wood and then sent to Fingal. At that time, Clarence Patterson was looking to hire some help and, through the employment office in London, was matched up with Hans. Apparently, earlier in the war, other families had working prisoners-of-war, so the idea was not new. Neighbours said that the family would be killed in their beds, but Hans was a good man, reliable and hard working.

Once a month, his wages were paid to the government and, at this time, officials checked to see if both parties were happy with the arrangement. The government supplied all of Hans' clothes: a blue shirt with a 12"-wide, round, red patch on the back; a cloth cap with a red patch on top, in order to be seen from the air; and blue pants with thick red stripes down each leg. Hans was Roman Catholic, but every Sunday he went to the United Church in Kerwood with the Patterson family. He usually borrowed a white shirt or sweater from Clarence, because he didn't like to go to church with that red patch showing.

The family was to give Hans $10 per month for personal spending, but he was not allowed to buy anything except consumables like candy, peanuts and gum. He wasn't allowed to make purchases himself so he gave the money to Bob Patterson, who was eight years old at the time. Bob bought items for Hans when the family went to Strathroy on Saturday nights.

Hans built ships in bottles, something he had done in his spare time while at sea. He sold the smaller bottles for $5 and the larger bottles for $10 each. The detail inside these bottles was amazing with small wooden houses, churches, lighthouses on the shore, and a sailing ship positioned on the water, sails unfurled. With the money he made from selling the bottles and with the help of the Pattersons, he sent parcels home to his mother and family, mostly non-perishable groceries, clothes, etc. His father and two brothers-in-law had died during the war, and his mother, his sisters and their children lived together in one residence.

Hans, who was 22 at the time, worked at the Patterson farm from April 1 to November 1, 1944. He had to leave the country with the other war prisoners on December 1 of that year. The family was sad to see him go, and Hans considered running away so he could stay in Canada. Clarence told him to go back to Germany voluntarily and then apply to immigrate, and he would help by being his sponsor in Canada.

Hans worked in a coal mine in Essen, Germany, for a year, during which he and the Pattersons corresponded regularly. Suddenly, the letters stopped and it was found out later that there had been an explosion in the coalmine and Hans had died. His family couldn't understand or write English, and all contact with the Pattersons stopped.

By Helen (Patterson) Thynne

GRATTAN BARS

Once upon a time in 1923, a long-legged foal was born on the horse farm of Archie Pedden. Sixteen months later, this colt, Grattan Bars, was sold by his owner in partial trade for some nondescript calves. Fred Thrower of Kerwood, a man who made no pretensions to horsemanship, paid the sum of $10, and the yearling grew into a stallion that ran like the wind. Thrower trained and drove him and, as a four-year-old, Grattan Bars started 11 times, winning every time and breaking nine Canadian track records. He broke the world's record in London for half-mile heats, winning in 59½, 1.00½, and 1.00, driven by Gord Litt. He was a cherry bay stallion with black points, standing 15.3 hands. In the summer of 1928, he campaigned at 1,020 pounds.

Grattan Bars' speed was so great, he became the talk of Canada, and his fame spread across the border to the U.S. During 1928, he won three $25,000 purses in a 13-day period.

A mere five years after Thrower purchased him, Grattan Bars retired undefeated at the height of his career, worth $100,000. In his first year of retirement, he earned $30,000 in stud fees. Then, tragedy struck. Another stallion attacked Grattan Bars in the pasture and the champion died of his injuries.

Vic Fleming, Grattan Bars' regular driver, stated on many occasions that he was one of the fastest horses he ever handled, commenting, "Grattan Bars never extended to the limit. He raced like an unleashed thunderbolt."

Grattan Bars came from a proud racing family. Grattan Royal, his sire, was World Champion for siring pacers. Polly Bars, his dam, was by Monbars 3, who was foaled in 1889 and, in his day, a sensational trotter. The progeny of Grattan Bars carried his name onto racetracks for many years, and the memory of the 1928 Ontario "wonder horse" lives on in the racing world everywhere.

GROWING UP IN ADELAIDE TOWNSHIP

The hours and hours of work helping to make maple syrup were rewarded with, first, a small motorcycle that my Dad bought for two gallons of syrup, and then a pony for which I traded a gallon of syrup and 50 bales of straw. I got the better end of the deal.

My Mom always kept ducks and geese, for as long as I can remember. She sold them in London at the Garden Market. Every Tuesday, starting in September, we killed 50, scalded them to remove the feathers, and then moved the naked, headless birds to the basement for the next step. On Wednesday, we waxed them and then picked them, a process developed to remove the very fine pinfeathers. I can remember making wax hands to scare my friends and family, and also waxing the chopped-off heads and leaving them in places for someone to find, until Mom found out! Wednesday nights usually found me cleaning these ducks—I always got this disgusting job, heaven knows why. After about the twentieth one, I started making up excuses to leave, to get a drink or something to eat, only returning to find that no one had gotten angry enough to take over and finish the job. Oh, well! If everything went okay and the gall of the bird didn't get broken, we usually finished about midnight. The whole family got involved and, if you happened to visit on Wednesday night, another chair appeared for you to sit on. My reward for all of this was a trip to London on a school day, to help transport the fowl to market and then eat lunch at the Red Barn Restaurant, which was better than anything!

Starting school was an adventure at the age of five. I started earlier because my birthday is in the early fall. I started in the one-room schoolhouse about a mile from home, and walked to and from school. My sisters had already graduated to high school. I vaguely remember that there were only three or four of us in the class. We enjoyed recess; we made grass houses from dried grass and fallen branches. The older boys found great fun in collapsing them with someone in them—and then we would start all over again!

We were moved to the new school at the beginning of the year, Adelaide Central School. I rode a bus, and it was a brand new school! My teacher was Flossie Hall, whom I adored. I remember one day while attending school in Grade 1, I discovered something missing from my attire while in the washroom. I refused to come out, even for the principal, until my Mom brought the necessary item from home. I don't know if anyone else in my class knew, but it was enough that my favourite teacher had to rescue me from my dilemma.

The principal was certainly someone to be reckoned with, the infamous Annie Courtis. Any child who didn't have fear in their hearts before knowing her, certainly did after. She ruled in a time when discipline meant hands-on. She was also a teacher who believed in interacting with her students. At recess, she would help choose soccer teams and then take up a position on one team or the other. One thing for sure, no one was brave enough to body-check Miss Courtis! I kept in touch with her through high school and when I got married, I sent her an invitation to the ceremony. She was very pleased to attend, as she really did care about her students. She even got involved in a bun-throwing episode at the reception—an entirely different side of Miss Courtis! The cracker came when I overheard her telling guests the antics of the bride in past years—talk about a blushing bride! Although I feared her throughout school, I gained respect and appreciation in the years to follow. She was a principal and teacher who was human as well.

In the 1950s, the most prized item I owned was a Timex watch, for which I pestered Mom for days, even months. The watch was offered through a company that sold plastic seat covers. If you bought the seat covers at $29.95, you received the watch as a bonus. Mom eventually gave in and I was the proud owner of a Timex watch with a real leather band. I, of course, wore it everywhere and proudly displayed it to all who would look. One Saturday, I was playing at the McPhail farm, and Mary and I had decided to play in the barn. We were jumping from the big wood beams into the grain, which my Dad was combining for Ray McPhail. It was dusty and I decided to remove the watch so it wouldn't get lost. I took if off and placed it on the beam, back against the edge where it met the roof. Mary and I spent hours playing and, when Dad finished, he and I rode home on the combine. It was Mom who noticed the watch was missing at suppertime and wanted to know what happened to it. I had no idea where or when or how I could have lost it! The air was blue and I was in serious trouble. No matter how hard I tried, I couldn't remember where it was. Eventually, the Timex watch was forgotten. Mom wouldn't get me another no matter how hard I promised not to lose it. Another year passed and harvest season rolled around again. Dad was combining again, and Mary and I were jumping from the beams as usual. While posing for a jump, I noticed something shiny on a beam on the other side of the barn. Lo and behold, I found my precious watch and it was still running! I have kept that watch to this day, but it doesn't work anymore.

By Georgina Fleming

GROWING UP IN KERWOOD

Children of our day made their own amusements. In the winter, we skated on the pond and rode on the back of bobsleds. In the spring, we went to the sugarbush at Charlie Foster's and Seymour Langford's. We drank sap straight from the trees, and poured hot syrup on the snow to form delicious toffee!

In the summer, we hiked through the woods, walked alongside railroad tracks, fished in little creeks, and played ball at the park. We blew the whistle on the steam engine that was used at the pea factory during pea harvest. We played in the empty butter boxes at the creamery until we were chased away! In the fall, we gathered beechnuts, walnuts and hickory nuts, and saved them to eat in the winter.

On my first day at school, S.S. #7 Adelaide, my sister drove me in an old Model-T touring car and asked Donald Pollock to look after me while I was playing in the schoolyard. I fell and started to cry, and the other kids consoled me. One of them asked me what I wanted to be when I grew up. I replied that I wanted to be a farmer and grow mentholatum and all-day suckers. Childhood was such a happy, carefree time of life!

By George Leacock

I REMEMBER

- Picking milkweed pods on the way to and from school to be used for lifejacket stuffing during WWII.
- Getting up at 3:00 a.m. and packing the 1928 Chrysler with turkeys to be sold at the outdoor market in London for Christmas.
- Driving a team of horses at threshing time, and

Mother preparing dinner and supper during the harvest for a gang of men with hearty appetites in the late 1930s and early 1940s.
- The installation of a hydro pole outside the farmhouse when we converted from a Delco system to Ontario Hydro in 1939.
- Having men from the Chatham area operate a "doodle bug" in search of oil, and drilling for it during the very cold winter of 1939.
- Walking a mile or more to the Adelaide Village general store for bread or to attend St. Ann's Anglican Church Sunday School; also, the minister coming to the farm for Sunday dinner.
- Walking a mile or more to S.S. #10, where Grades 1-8 were taught by one teacher, and where we used a slate for arithmetic class; also, the teacher stayed at our house.
- Having two turkey vultures (buzzards) as pets during the summer and fall of 1940, and their return in 1941.
- A funeral held at the farm when I was nine years old, and a farm sale on November 9, 1943, then moving from Adelaide to Strathroy in 1944.
- Fond memories of the neighbours up and down the Egremont Road, when it was a gravel road with very little traffic.

By Cliff Branton Jr.

INTERVIEW WITH JAMES MARSHALL

I left Glasgow, Scotland, in March, 1929, and came to Canada to be a farmer. I did not know a cow from a horse but there was no work at home, so we were willing to try anything. This work plan was organized by a church in Glasgow. Fifty of us boys came out together and I did not know anyone. My sister came ahead in January of that year on a similar scheme.

My ship was The Duchess of Bedford, which later sank from a torpedo hit. I was sick for a couple of days on the crossing. We landed at St. John, New Brunswick, and then went by train to Georgetown, Ontario, where we stayed in a United Church hostel. I stayed for about a week to become acclimatized. Then, on April 29, I was sent to a farm near Carlisle, Ontario, to work for George Gale, a farmer in his seventies. I was there for only three weeks, as I was no help to him. He wrote to Toronto to somebody in charge to find out what to do with me. I was sent to work for Jack Gunson in Adelaide Township. I was instructed to go to Ailsa Craig, then by train to the Lucan Junction, and then to Strathroy. It would have been easier to walk across country to the Gunson farm than to make that trip by rail!

At the station in Strathroy, tall Jack Gunson, a man in his sixties, was waiting. The Gunsons had come from London Township to try farming on clay. We got to the farm, Lot 23, Con. 1 NER, after we turned down a gravel road and dropped into a mud hole. That's an example of clay farms in the spring. I finally got used to farming.

Will Gunson died in 1926, and Jack died of pneumonia in 1939, leaving his wife, Jennie, to run the farm alone. Jennie asked me if I wanted to go to another farm, Lot 26, Con. 1 NER. I did, and I stayed there for a few more years. I became acquainted with the neighbours on the main road, including Herbert Tomlinson and his daughter, Thelma; George Freele, who lived on the farm beside the school, and his father, Fred Freele, who lived on a farm to the east; Jack Ward and his brother, George; Mrs. Wes Able, who married Revington Stanley, after her first husband's death; Henry Roberts, who lived on the Tom Whiting farm, and his son, Eldon Roberts, who fought in WWII.

Tom Whiting gave the land for S.S. #3 school, Lot 28, Con. 1 SER, and Dick Whiting gave the land for Bethel United Church, Lot 28, Con. 1 NER. Dick's wife, Olive Dann, ran a dress shop in Strathroy for many years. She was Mrs. Ivan Lewis' sister.

In 1943, I met Eva Mitchell of the Fourth Line South, Adelaide Township, and we were married in 1945. Eva and Jennie Gunson found it hard to get along. Eva's father was in ill health, so we went and lived with her parents on the Mitchell farm, west of Strathroy. Jennie sold the farm to Hubert Tack, now deceased. Hubert served in WWII.

Eva and I rented the farm from her mother but she wanted to sell, so we relocated to Strathroy. I trucked freight for the C.N.R. and then went into the moving business. I sold that business, worked at Franklin Electric for 11 years, and then retired. I returned to work for a while, taking a job at the Farmers' Outfitting Store, and then finally retired for good.

James and Eva Marshall are now residents of Country Terrace in Komoka, Ontario

KEYSER CENTURY FARM

Our farm, being a century farm, has always been in the Murray name. My grandfather, Patrick Murray, being the first owner in 1852, was also one of the first pioneers in this area. He cleared the land and built a log house in which he and his family lived. The house was situated in the field in front of our present house, only farther to the east side. I do not know how long they lived in the log house, but I heard my father, John Murray, say that he was seven years old when they moved into the brick house, which is now more than 100 years old (on Lot 5, Con. 4 NER).

The brick with which it is built came from Keyser's brick yard. I think they were called "slop brick," sun dried. The walls are three bricks thick, and it required 44,000 bricks at a cost of $5 per thousand. The bricklayer was a man by the name of William Franks.

The woodwork in the interior of the house is still the original, some being bird's eye maple in the natural colour. What once was the dining room became a kitchen, with cupboards and a sink installed. We now have hydro, furnace and a bathroom.

The frame structure at the back, comprised of a kitchen and woodshed, was moved and now stands not far from the house, being used as a shelter for machinery. A garage has been built in its place. The open veranda on the front of the house has been taken down and is now an enclosed veranda, which somewhat changed the appearance of the house.

By Mrs. Ev (Murray) Herrington, 1971

LIGHT BY COAL OIL AND OTHER THOUGHTS

My earliest memory is of coal oil or kerosene lamps. Every household had a special can for bringing the coal oil from the store. It had an opening in the top for pouring in the new oil and a spout on the side for pouring oil into the lamps. Because there was seldom any way of closing this spout, the usual method was to jam a potato onto the spout. These lamps didn't give very bright light, although we managed. It was considered bad luck to put three lighted lamps on a table, so we managed with two. The lamps came in many sizes and styles.

Each morning, the lamps had to be prepared for use again. First, we had to be sure there was enough oil for the night. When we filled the bowl of a lamp, we had to be very careful not to spill oil, not even a little, because when the lamp was lit, even a few drops of oil could be a fire hazard. Next, we trimmed the wicks. If they weren't cut just right, they would smoke when lit. This created an unpleasant smell and caused smoke to gather on the inside of the glass chimney. This reduced the amount of light, and no homemaker wanted to be caught with a smoky chimney.

The chimneys were miserable things to clean! The worst of the smoke could be removed with a crumpled newspaper. Then we steamed the inside, usually by holding the chimney over the spout of a teakettle and then polishing it with a cloth. I was often excused from this job, as my mother was very particular about the sparkle of her lamp chimneys and I sometimes left fingerprints on the glass. Honestly, I didn't do it just to get out of a disagreeable job!

Even the youngest child learned about the dangers of these lamps. If a lighted lamp was upset or knocked over, it usually resulted in a house fire. The flame of the lamp would instantly ignite the spilled oil. In seconds, there was a flash fire. If any of the oil splashed on clothing, almost certain death resulted as the fire spread so rapidly. To add to the constant fear of fire was the fact that no rural area had organized firefighters—even urban communities did not have adequate protection. People formed bucket lines as they passed pails of water from the water source to the fire. The most that could be hoped for was getting people out alive, and maybe some of the principal furnishings.

In 1943, I stood in one of those bucket lines and, although we worked hard and quickly, in the end we acknowledged the strength of the fire as we watched the roof of a house collapse and the walls crumble. Ray and Donelda Brock were homeless, but the good rural folks gathered to help them and in a short time, they moved into another house, where they raised their family and lived for nearly 50 years.

Put Another Stick In The Stove

When I was growing up, the only fuel we had was good hardwood from our own woodlot. Attached to the back of our house was a large woodshed. Each fall, my father made sure this shed was very full, the wood piled neatly in rows. The larger blocks were piled separately to one side, and we used these at night to try to keep the fire going. On the other side was a pile of lighter, smaller wood to be used for cooking and throughout the day. At one end was a special pile of very dry wood of types that would ignite easily. This was finely split to make kindling for starting the fires.

The main source of heat in the house was usually the kitchen stove. In most homes, it was situated so that a length of pipe ran from the stove into the chimney, then into the next room or through the ceiling to a room upstairs. These pipes gave off some heat, but it wasn't very noticeable when the snow was falling and the wind was blowing. I slept in such an upstairs room for four years when I taught in my first country school. Although I had the warmest bedroom, I often took my clothes into bed with me, so they would be warm in the morning before I put them on.

Most houses had a stove just for heating in some other room, but often these were saved for guests. Very few farm homes (and not many town homes) had furnaces. Even with a furnace, the pipes just went to registers in the floor upstairs. Sometimes there was a register in each room but often there was just a register in a central hall. These furnaces were huge wood-burning affairs or, later, coal-burning. There were no forced air fans to circulate the heat.

My Brown grandparents had a furnace, and I thought the best thing about it was the way you could put bricks near the firebox on a cold day. When the bricks were very hot, grandfather wrapped them in newspapers and tucked them around our feet, whether we were driving in a car without a heater or going home in a cutter. We'd be about halfway home before we got really cold feet. These furnaces only worked by gravity. Those wood heat-producing units had a special cozy warmth that hasn't been replaced by methods used today.

In the summertime, the homemaker had a special problem in those days getting her cooking and baking done. A fire in the stove emitted heat both winter and summer. Some women got up early in the morning to get the baking done before the strongest heat of the day. There was a real art in knowing just how hot a fire was needed for baking. An oven hot enough to turn out golden pies would make cookies burn.

In the winter, someone had to watch the fire to see if it needed wood. If the fire burned down too low, it had to be carefully built up again. Sometimes, the room would get quite chilly before the fire got going again.

The real problem was keeping the house warm all night in the middle of a freezing February! Just before bedtime, we tried to have a deep bed of coals in the firebox. That was the time to carefully put a special block in the stove and close all the drafts. Hopefully, there would be a few coals left in the morning to start the fire quickly. If not, you started with paper and kindling and gradually built up a new fire, all the while shivering in the cold room.

Later, people began to use coal. This gave a more even heat and burned all night. When the coal was brought into the house and put into the stove or furnace, a lot of black dust was created. Still later, we had oil space heaters. Wonder of wonders, these incredible square heat-producers were equipped with fans, so the heat was better circulated.

Funerals

Since the beginning of time, funeral customs have varied according to the geographic location and the religion of the local inhabitants. There are slight variations from province to province but, overall, Canadian customs are much the same.

It may surprise young people to know that, in Ontario, funerals were at one time conducted from the home of the deceased. My grandparents were all buried from home, but my grandmothers were among the very last to be buried from home in our community. They were both well advanced in years and didn't like the idea of funeral homes.

I suppose the custom of having home funerals came about because most people died at home. In the early days, there were few hospitals. Doctors made house calls in those days. Also, families were larger and very few women or girls worked outside the home, so there was always lots of help to care for people who were sick. In the country, friends and neighbours helped by taking turns with the nursing, or bringing in food to ease the workload. When it was known that the patient was only hours from death, one or two of the closest neighbours would come to stay with the family until after the person died. The undertaker came to the home and prepared the body for burial. After the advent of motorized hearses, he would remove the body to his establishment and return it to the house when he had completed his preparations.

The family of the deceased was often required to provide accommodation for relatives coming from a distance. Public transportation was slow and uncertain. In the early part of this century, very few people had cars. If they did, the cars travelled much slower than today and they were not well equipped for night travel.

It is only in the last 30-35 years that people began gathering in churches or community halls for lunch after funerals. Before that, close friends, neighbours, pallbearers and relatives from a distance, were asked back to the house for a full sit-down meal. Usually, relatives from a distance sat down to eat first. The immediate family, such as widow/widower and children, were also seated at this time. I remember in 1936, when my grandfather died, we set the dining room table four times. Someone must have been in the background, frantically washing dishes!

Some customs were strictly observed in the first 40 years of this century but are no longer in use. As soon as a person died, all the blinds in the house were closed except in the kitchen and they would remain closed until after the funeral. The undertaker had an arrangement of black or purple velvet, often in the shape of a cross, with flowers or ribbons in the centre that he hung on the front door of the house. Friends or strangers going by would see this and slow. On the way to the cemetery, even 50 years ago, any oncoming traffic would pull off to the side of the road and wait until the funeral procession had passed. In the early days, some of the horses did not welcome having to observe this custom. Until recent times, the women of the family all wore black to the funeral and the men wore black ties and black armbands. Many widows wore black the rest of their lives. One of my grandmothers was a widow for 30 years and I never saw her in anything but black.

Hawks and Chicks

Quick! Take off your aprons and wave them frantically skyward, or grab a towel and do the same, or bang a couple of metal lids together! Above all, wave your arms and shout as loudly as you can! Why all this fuss? Look at those three hawks circling above the farmyard! "Now Grandma, take it easy. We knew someday you might flip out, but for now just relax and enjoy the view of those hawks soaring and gliding."

Well, back in the olden days, let's say in the 1920s, baby chicks weren't hatched in a brooder or kept in a special facility all of their lives. In spring, some of the hens would stop laying eggs and become broody. That meant they wanted only to sit on a nest and make soft clucking sounds. Then, someone fixed a fresh nest for the hen, usually in an open box with lots of clean straw. In a couple of days, someone put 10-12 eggs under the hen and, in about 14 days, each egg hatched into tiny, fluffy chicks. The next day, the hen and her chicks were moved from the brooding nest to an outdoor coop. These coops were triangle-shaped with slats across the front for ventilation, and each held one hen and her tiny chicks. The chicks were kept warm under the hen's wings.

Now, how did we feed these little balls of fluff? For about three days, they ate boiled, mashed egg yolk, mixed with some very fine oatmeal or chick starter from the feed store. Also, the eggshells were dried in the oven, crushed fine, and given to the chicks for grit. In a few days, the front of the coop would be raised so that the chicks could run free.

Now back to the hawks! A hawk considers a baby chick a real treat. If you waved your towel and shouted, maybe the hawks would soar away to some other chicken coop or try for a mouse. If you expected to raise many laying hens or roasting fowl, you had to look skyward whenever you went outside, and be ready to "hawk scare."

Horseless Carriages

Horseless carriages (cars or automobiles) weren't always as they are now. Look at some old photographs and you will see that the roof was once made of a heavy, treated cloth, and stretched over a frame. The sides were curtains with small mica panels to let in a little light. If the weather was bad, you could dome these curtains to the roof and the top of the doors. It wasn't as bad as it sounds, because no one drove cars during the winter months anyway.

Then, someone thought of using solid doors, with the upper half made of glass. The first glass windows were actually lowered and raised by an attached strap. Those old cars had running boards that were fun to stand on, with one arm through the window to hitch a ride. The top speed of the car was probably no more than 35-40 miles per hour. In spite of that, I suspect it wasn't very safe—but it sure was fun! I found out that an uncle was more likely than a parent to let you hitch a ride on the running board.

To start a car, one took a bent piece of metal called a crank, put it in a hole in the front of the car and, when the crank was turned rapidly, it engaged with some part of the inner mechanism to start the motor. It helped if you had someone sit in the car and move two little handles near the steering wheel to adjust the gas and carburetor.

A warm coat, scarf, mitts, a hat and warm boots were typical "driving attire" because the early cars had no heaters. A blanket or robe was often needed, to put around your legs. The air conditioning system consisted of lowering the windows. It did bring in some cooler air, but also dust from the gravel roads. I remember driving all the way to London on gravel roads.

Feeding The Threshers

Threshing meals! Now that was an experience, 12-15 hard-working men to feed! Usually the farmer's wife did not have to provide breakfast, but if she did, it would only be for two or three extra men. The big meal was always served at noon, so the women of the family had to be up and working as soon as or even before the men. There was no restriction on how many slices of meat or how many pieces of pie anyone had.

Typical Dinner Menu: Roast beef, mashed potatoes, two kinds of vegetables, gravy, two or three kinds of pickles, stacks of bread, applesauce, maple syrup, tea biscuits, johnnycake, three or four varieties of pie, and gallons of tea.

Typical Supper Menu: Cold roast beef, home-fried potatoes, cabbage salad, more bread, pickles, two kinds of canned fruit, at least two kinds of layer cake, plates of cookies, and again, gallons of tea.

When I was involved in helping with the threshing meals, the farm homes did not have hot running water. All the water for dishes and cooking had to be heated in a reservoir on the stove or in kettles on top of the stove. There was no nice, comfortable sink to wash dishes in, but an old fashioned dishpan instead.

MAIL DELIVERY ON R.R. #5, STRATHROY

Before the 1920s, mail was dropped at specific residences and farmers had to walk to those residences for their mail. Mary Brown's home on the Featherson (Robotham) Sideroad was one place where mail was delivered. Another was Crathie Post Office.

Then, during the 1920s, mail was delivered to all homes except for those on sideroads—the farmers there had to walk to the corner for their mail. Postage for a letter was 1¢ at the time.

For many years, Bill Rapley delivered the mail every morning in his horse and buggy on R.R. #5. As an act of kindness, he obtained money orders and occasionally purchased and delivered bread to individuals who couldn't make it to town. During cold or stormy weather, he stopped at E. McKeen's home at Lot 17, Con. 3 NER, to get warm. He would put his horse in the stable and eat his lunch next to the cookstove before continuing to deliver to the homes on the other half of the route. By the early 1930s, he used a car for transportation. One morning, Walter Brown found Bill Rapley at the Robotham Sideroad, where he had suffered a stroke. After that, Stanley Wardell delivered the mail for several years.

MAKING MAPLE SYRUP

As we eat our pancakes drowned in maple syrup, I am sure we never think of all the cold, wet, back-breaking labour that the earliest settlers put in to procure that sweet delectable known as maple syrup. The early settlers were very glad to have this sweetener either in liquid form or boiled enough to make cakes of maple sugar. Each settler who had a grove of hard maple trees tapped them in the early spring.

I believe that in the very early days they slashed into the trunk and inserted a piece of bark to serve as a little trough, to carry the sap from the slash to a pail or other container. But since I don't know much about that method, I will tell you how my father made maple syrup. In the very early spring, he would go to his woodlot at the back of the farm. With a hand-operated auger, he would bore holes in the south side of maple trees, then drive in a metal spile with a wire hook attached, and hang a sap bucket from the hook. The spile was inserted on a slight slant to take advantage of the natural flow of the sap. The spile had a small hole in the end that went into the tree to allow the sap to escape. The ideal weather was warm in the daytime to allow the sap to flow to the branches, and frosty at night to slow the flow down and cause the rush of sap the next day. My father had a series of tracks through the bush over which he could drive a team of horses pulling a sleigh, which carried a large barrel. The pails were carried from the trees one by one through soft, slushy snow and dumped into the barrel. When the barrel was full, the sleigh was driven back to the "sugar shanty" and the sap was dumped into a large storage tank. Hopefully, the barrel would be filled two or three times in a day.

The "sugar shanty" usually was a roofed, three-sided shack. The arch and boiling area closed in the fourth side. There was a rough bunk where the person watching the fire at night might catch a little cold sleep. There was often a space where the horses could be tied at night.

The fire was built in an area where two cement or stone walls were built about 3' apart and long enough to support two syrup pans, depending on the length of the syrup pans. Wood to fire the arch was fed into the end farthest from the storage tank. The logs for the fire were 2-3' in length. Wood was cut and stored in the shanty as carefully as wood for the house. Sap was drained out of the storage tank by a tap into the back syrup pan. As the sap boiled down in the front pan and became closer to the syrup state, more warm sap was added from the back pan. Keeping just the right amount of heat under that front pan was an exact science, with only experience and judgment as a guide. If it wasn't boiled enough, it wasn't a good flavour and was thin. If it was boiled too much, the syrup might scorch in the bottom of the pan and taste bitter. When he thought the syrup was almost finished, my father took a dipper and poured the syrup slowly back into the front pan. He was judging the colour and thickness of the syrup. When the syrup was ready to "take off," the pan was quickly removed from the heat. The syrup was poured into a large can and taken to the house. Now, the women took over for the process known as "cleaning the syrup." To do this, the syrup was put in a large boiler to reheat on the stove. Then a well-beaten egg was added to the syrup. This was to cause any impurities to rise to the surface to be skimmed off. When no more could be skimmed off, the syrup (in our house, anyway) was strained through a woollen cloth. Only then was it ready for canning. For family use, it was put into sterilized sealers and well-sealed. For sale, it was put in one-gallon cans. I can remember my father selling syrup in Strathroy for $5 a gallon. During the Depression of the late 1920s and early 1930s, when farmers in Ontario were loading freight cars with apples and potatoes to send to the most depressed areas of Western Canada, my father always included some half-gallon tins of maple syrup, which could be divided among more families.

In the very early days before syrup pans, a large kettle was suspended from a tripod of poles tied together at the top, and a fire was built under the kettle.

By Evelyn (Fletcher) Clifton

MEMORIES FROM AMSTERDAM TO ADELAIDE

Gunner Ben Gamble and I met in Amsterdam when his regiment was on leave there. I was a city girl working as a seamstress in a clothing factory. During the war, we were forced to make uniforms for the German army.

Ben and I decided to wait to be married until I came to Canada. When he returned to Canada, he sent me a diamond ring, a box of clothing, and money to pay my expenses to Canada. In April 1947, I took a plane to Sweden, where I booked passage on the Crisppholm to New York. I arrived there on May 10, 1947, and sent Ben a telegram. When I reached Toronto on the train, the conductor knew I needed help and he took me around a shortcut to get on the London train, so Ben missed me and had to drive home alone! Meanwhile, Ben's sister, Quida, and her husband, Art Hammond, met me at the London station. We drove to the Gamble homestead where I met Ben's parents. At the time, I thought this gray-haired couple was old-fashioned. Here I was, speaking broken English and wearing my modern clothes. I was afraid that I wouldn't fit in.

On May 17, 1947, Ben and I were married by Rev. Pearce in the Anglican Chapel in Thorndale. We moved to Lot 3, Con. 2 NER, to the Arthur and Marjorie Conkey farm, already purchased by Ben and his brother-in-law, Art. Ben and I lived in the back part of the house where the kitchen was, and there was a veranda across the east side. Here I had a good view of West Adelaide Church, Second Line North, and the sideroad. At first, I was very lonely. I had lived in the bustling city of Amsterdam all my life and now I was in the wide, open spaces of Adelaide Township, where nothing much seemed to happen. My family and friends were far away and Ben was too busy with farm work to spend much time with me. One day, as I was sitting on the back veranda, crying and wondering why I was here, I realized that life could only get better for me, but that I would have to do something to change it. I reached out to the neighbours and made visits to Glenys Wilson, Donelda Brock, Marjorie Arrand, and Grace Conkey, who were always very jolly. I knew that I had to learn to drive, so one day I took the car out to the hayfield and taught myself. I flattened a lot of hay, but Ben didn't say anything about that. It wasn't too long before I got my driver's license in Watford—from a man who ran a grocery store and did driver testing on the side. That was a proud day for me! The first place I drove was to Topping's store at Keyser. The Toppings were always very friendly to me.

Art Conkey had left his black cattle on the farm that first summer. I went back to the field to see Ben and the cattle all came around me. I was terrified, as I didn't know what they might do to me. Remember, I was a city girl. I had never been close to cattle before. I had a garden, although I didn't know much about it, but Ben helped me.

I joined the Helen Scott Society and I enjoyed the meetings and talking with the other girls. I had learned English in school, but I still didn't speak the language well. I baked peanut butter cookies and all the girls at the meeting said they were good. I remember when Marjorie Arrand took me to the movie theatre in Watford one night to see a Lucille Ball show.

I'll never forget the shock of my first threshing. I was not used to seeing men so dirty! Ben put out pails of water so the threshers could clean up before the meal. And their appetites! I never before saw men eat so much, so fast and with such poor manners! I had made pies and one neighbour ate a whole blueberry pie—I couldn't believe my eyes! Some of the neighbours stared at me so much that I was embarrassed. I guess they weren't used to newcomers, especially a Dutch city girl trying to be a farmer's wife.

The outdoor toilet was always one of my worst experiences. You froze in the winter, and sometimes a snake would get into the outhouse. One day, I saw a snake on the two-holed seat, and I went back to the house and got an axe—then I cut that snake in two! The head went down the one hole and the tail slid down the other. I finally felt as if I was getting some control over this farm life!

At this time, Ben rented land near Adelaide Village on Highway 22 from a Mr. Brock. First, he grew 100 acres of corn. The thorn bushes were terrible and, because of the clay, we had to rotate the crops. Ben raised Barred Rock chickens and sold the eggs in Arkona. He had sows and piglets. He bought some cows and, at first, we separated the milk and sold the cream to Kerwood. Ben never wanted me to help outside as he felt a woman's work was in the house, so I knitted, sewed, and looked after the children. Elsie was born in Strathroy Hospital on our first anniversary, May 17, 1948, so I wasn't as lonely with a daughter to care for. Martha Joan was born in 1950, but she lived just three weeks as she was born with a hole in her heart. With the medical technology available today, she could have been helped. Ben (1952) and Dalyce (1955) were born while we lived in Adelaide.

When Ben sold the farm, I wanted to stay, but Ben was ready to leave. Maggie Wilson invited our family for a farewell lunch. We had sandwiches, tea and cake. We bought a new home in Byron in 1959, and Glen was born that year in Strathroy Hospital with Dr. Vine attending. None of us liked living in Byron, so we bought a farm in Usborne Township, Huron County. Earl was born in 1961 and Marlene in 1963. My husband, Ben, died in November 1981, as the result of an unfortunate car accident while he was on his way to our other farms. With the help of Glen and Earl, this city girl from Amsterdam is still farming!

By Alida "Aly" (Van Elsland) Gamble

MEMORIES OF ALMA (SWIFT) PEARSON

My first 11 years of life were spent on the Eighth Line of Metcalfe Township and then my family moved to Strathroy. I went to London Normal School and was hired for Napperton School, S.S. #5 Adelaide, where I taught in 1927-1929. At first, I boarded with the Harold Currie family. The Curries were involved in many political activities. I remember the time that Agnes McPhail, the first woman MPP, stayed there all night when she spoke at a political meeting in Strathroy. I sat beside her at the Currie's dining room table at supper, spellbound to be in the company of such an important lady! At that time, Mr. Currie was the Secretary-Treasurer for that school section.

When my Dad bought a car, a 1928 Model-A Ford, he let me drive it to the school. One day, Annie Sullivan rode with me when I went out to see Lawrence Parker, the Trustee, about a school matter. I cut the turn too short as I drove into their driveway and the wheels on one side went over the culvert. The Parker boys, my new students, helped push me out. You can imagine how embarrassed I was for them to see their new teacher in this predicament! On snowy days, our neighbour, William Sullivan, drove me to school with the horse and cutter.

Surprisingly, there was a grand piano in the Napperton School, but I could not play it. The enrolment was small, just over 20 students. Some of my students were: Verne, Grant and Marguerite Earley; Charlie and Jim Parker, whose father was a school trustee; Grant Parker, whose father was Frank Parker; Clare and Irene Parker, whose father was Russell Parker; Lewis and Bev Morgan; Harold and Marjorie Westgate; Mervin Shepherd; and Clare Crandon.

At that time, the school trustees tried to hire the least expensive teacher they could get. When I asked for a raise at Napperton, the School Board didn't exactly chase after me, so I got a job on Pelee Island for the next two years.

MEMORIES OF ANN ELLIOTT

I went to S.S. #3 Adelaide, Mary Bolton's school. I was raised in Lobo Township on the townline, but my family attended S.S. #3 and Bethel United Church on Highway 22, the Sarnia Gravel.

I was a student in the school when the tornado went through on June 23, 1944. The sky got very dark and the wind was very strong. The teacher, Edna Patterson, was afraid that the school would blow down, so she decided to evacuate us. We lined up to go out, but the air pressure on the door (which opened inward) was so great that we couldn't open it, so we were effectively locked inside. Afterward, someone explained the reason that happened. A tornado creates a vacuum as it draws all the air into the centre. When this happens, the air pressure on the inside of a closed building becomes greater than the air pressure outside, and if it becomes more than the structure can stand, the building explodes out. The centre was not near us. On that summer day, the building did not explode. The tornado, however, made great cracks in the school's brick walls, so the building was condemned. Some of the students were sent to S.S. #2 Crathie, and some to S.S. #10 Adelaide. That was the beginning of school bus rides for us.

My maiden name was Ann Stanley, and we lived on the Adelaide Lobo Townline in Lobo, where "Friendly Acres" is now, beside Con. 12. In those days, of course, we walked the three miles to school. We had a sister who had been shot accidentally when she was five years old, and was unable to walk that far. Three of us pulled her to school in a wagon or on a sleigh, and sometimes our parents (Mr. and Mrs. R.J. Stanley) drove us in a car or in a horse and buggy.

MEMORIES OF ANN (PENNINGTON) DYMOND

The first trip I remember taking with my mother and father was to New Liskeard in Northern Ontario in the summer of 1938. We made the trip in a 1930 Buick, along with Lawrence and Mae Grogan. We visited the Grogan's daughter and son-in-law, Ruby and Reg Scriven, who lived in that area. I remember stopping in Callander to see the Dionne Quintuplets as they played in their yard. We could see them, but they could not see the tourists.

Our S.S. #9 school was a lovely brick building. In the morning, we would put a potato inside the furnace door and by lunchtime, it was perfectly cooked. This, to me, was the best school in the township.

By Grade 5, there were not enough pupils to keep the school open, so the students were taken to S.S. #4. Miss Pearl Windover was hired as teacher. My father or my sister, Kay, drove our car and took S.S. #9 children to the school. We really missed our nice school because S.S. #4 didn't have a basement, library or cloakrooms. Also, the snow drifted in the windows and the stove was enclosed with metal sheets. Water had to be carried in from the Henderson's well.

For Grade 6, 7 and 8, our teacher was Flossie (Grogan) Hall. For the next several years, the pupils moved between S.S. #4 and S.S. #9. David Robotham was the driver for the S.S. #4 pupils. He regularly gave me a ride, since I was the only one attending S.S. #9 at his end of the route. Some of the winter trips were very difficult. Dad used to take the children, covered with blankets and cowhide robes, in the horse-drawn sleigh. He didn't follow

Bruce Evans' homemade plywood school bus (mid 40s) carried 25-30 pupils to Strathroy High School.

the roads, which were deeply drifted, but went through fields and over fences.

Throughout public school, Marguerite Purdy Johnson was our music teacher, and she came once a week. I also took private piano and vocal lessons from her for many years. I believe my first piano lesson cost 25¢. Each year, a music festival was held, and I was always involved in the singing competition between all the schools in the township. This was always a scary evening, when I became very nervous. Thanks to Mrs. Johnson's encouragement, music has been an enjoyable part of my life to this day.

Thinking over my years, there are many pleasant memories. I was lucky to be raised in a loving home with kind and understanding parents and sisters. We were members of West Adelaide Presbyterian Church, and my mother was a life member of the W.M.S. Although it was the end of the Depression years and wartime rations, we never lacked food or heat. I recall the aroma of fresh-baked bread, hot biscuits, freshly churned butter, pies, cakes and cookies, which were always there, thanks to Mom. Meat, eggs, milk and cream were the result of my father's long hours of work. Every spring, Dad tapped the maple trees in our woods and, after many nights spent in the sugar shanty, we had enough maple syrup to last until the following spring. It was always "Rise early!" for Dad, as he headed to the barn to milk the cows. I can still hear him singing, "Oh the birds and the bees in the sycamore trees on the big Rock Candy Mountain!" as he sat down to lace his boots for the long day ahead.

As I spent many hours playing alone (no other children lived close to us), I learned to appreciate nature. I chased butterflies and dragonflies, watched tadpoles, fished off the bridge at the Hodgson farm across the road, and enjoyed the big garden that gave us many good meals.

The next big step in my life began when I started high school at Strathroy Collegiate. At first, there was no school bus and I rode on the London-Forest bus, boarding at the corner of Kerwood Road and Egremont Road. Shortly after the beginning of 1947, school bus service was available (with Bruce Evans as the driver) all through my high school years. During my days at S.D.C.I., there were only eight classrooms, a library, home economics, shop, gymnasium and assembly hall.

Electricity was finally available on our farm in 1948, which was a source of great excitement! No more coal oil lamps, no more wood stove, and what a pleasure to have a refrigerator!

MEMORIES OF ANNIE (SULLIVAN) FIDLER

I began my teaching career in a rural school in Sombra Township for a salary of $300. At this time, my mother was in poor health and I wished to be nearer to home, so I left after two years. Dad (William Sullivan) and my brother, Harold, went to a school board meeting at Crathie to see about getting a position for me there. Frank Bolton and Bill Graham interceded on my behalf and the job was mine.

I bought a second-hand car for $150 and drove my friend, Helen Allum, out to S.S. #4 Adelaide, on the Second Line North, and I returned to Crathie School, S.S. # 2. In the winter, Helen boarded with Walter and Olive Brown. My father had a good road horse and, on blustery days, he drove me out to school in the cutter. On one stormy day, we ran into a huge snow bank and the horse, in its fluster, broke the shaft away from the cutter. Tom Elliott came along and rescued us.

The Pedden children, Alex, Charlie and Christine, would walk across the field in the dead of winter to start the fire in the long iron stove. I would stand beside them, shivering, until the school became warmer.

Christmas concerts were an important event in a rural community and we held ours in Crathie Hall with Bob McCubbin as Master of Ceremonies. Valentine's Day was always eagerly anticipated in the country school, but February 14 often brought severe storms. One year, I put all of my Valentines in a box and took them to Lindsay Wardell's, where I stayed all night so the children wouldn't be disappointed if I couldn't get to school.

There were an average of 25-28 students in the school. Donna Nettleton, Christina Graham, and Murray Oliver started with me. In my last year at Crathie, Marjorie Wardell, Marguerite McDonald, and Beatrice Oliver passed their entrance exams to Strathroy High School. I had been dating Art Fidler for some time and on one snowy winter day, Downham's Nursery almost shut down as Art and his brother, Frank, came over to help Dad get me out to the school.

At that time, Mr. James Sexton was the School Inspector. One spring day when the sap was running, I brought a dishpan from home. The kids collected sap from the trees behind the school. They brought it in and dumped it into the dishpan on the stove, where we boiled it to try to get some maple syrup. What a mess! The girls and boys spilled sap on themselves and all over the floor by the stove. I happened to look out and, to my horror, saw Mr. Sexton arrive! I was very nervous, wondering what he would think of this sticky mess. I told the students to speak clearly and say, "Good afternoon, Mr. Sexton," and they did. He listened to my weak explanation for the mess. Then he went to the front of the room and announced to us all, "This is concrete material. What a wonderful lesson—you can't beat concrete material!" I felt absolutely limp!

MEMORIES OF CAROL GROGAN

I can remember Mom picking cucumbers for the pickle factory from our cucumber patch, and picking strawberries and raspberries also. We had a peach orchard and I recall accompanying Mom and Dad on our selling excursions. How convenient it would be today to have a bushel of peaches delivered to our door!

Mom was always a great cook and is, still today, at 89 years young. I remember the aroma of her delectable homemade buns. The thought of them even now makes my mouth water! Meals always ended with two or three desserts, usually pie, cake and homemade peaches or pears. It is a wonder we did not have a weight problem back then, but I guess everyone was busy and simply worked off those extra calories.

As a child growing up, I did not spend much time in the kitchen. Mom was too proficient at canning, cooking and baking, so I had plenty of time for riding ponies and sharing Dad's love for baseball. When I was 20, he was my baseball coach with the Arkona team and we had a winning season. Shirley Hendrick and Barbara Eves (Murray) were members of this team.

The corner general store at Keyser's was more than just an establishment that stocked bread, flour, tea, coffee and candy. Many of the neighbourhood men would congregate there on a Saturday evening to catch up on the news in politics, farming and weather. As a child, I can remember my Dad coming home from Topping's store with a brick of ice cream for our family of five. What a treat! We put some maple syrup over it and savoured the moment until the next time. Frequently, on a Saturday evening, I would accompany my Dad to the store to make my purchase of 10¢ worth of candy. What a dime could buy back then!

As I travel back in time to 1959, the corner store also brings back another memory for me. Carole (Pedden) Meyers and I attempted showbiz at Keyser's store. We introduced ourselves with a record player, a record of "He's Got The Whole World In His Hands," and we proceeded to sing our little hearts out one afternoon to any fortunate (or unfortunate) person who entered the store. We even had the audacity to pass a plate around to be compensated for the entertainment we had just provided. What nerve... but what a memory.

Life growing up at Keyser's was fun. The one-room school was close enough to walk home for lunch. S.S. #1 and #2 would certainly come alive at Christmas concert time. I had many girls my age to play with, Barbara (Murray) Eves, and Joanne and Lorraine George, who are both married and live out west now. I played many games of bingo with Carole (Pedden) Meyers and her brother, Archie, in their Grandma and Grandpa Topping's house each summer. My Dad had several ponies and much enjoyment was derived from them. In the winter, one of the ponies would be hitched up to the cutter and we would take enormous delight in a ride up and down the road.

With the opening of Adelaide Central School in 1960, it created new friends, new teachers, new experiences and many wonderful memories. It helped to prepare you for the bigger world of Strathroy High School and college or university.

In 1961, our household had two family additions. Dan Coward and his sister, Linda, had lived their lives up to this point in London, but adapted well to life on the farm. Today, Dan and his family still live in Adelaide.

Mom is happy living in Strathroy, visiting with friends, going for groceries, driving to get her hair done and dropping in at the town hall to play Euchre periodically. She enjoys visits from Rev. Miles and people from the West Adelaide Presbyterian congregation. She keeps in touch with her Keyser's Corners neighbours, George and Doris George, who also live in Strathroy. She immensely enjoys the hugs, kisses and visits from her seven grandchildren and spouses, and her six great-grandchildren. Fortunately for Mom, her family lives and works in the Strathroy area.

By Carol Lynne Grogan (1949), daughter of David and Hazel (Vernon) Grogan

MEMORIES OF DON WALKER

Winter

My father had to take the horse and cutter through the fields to town to get groceries, as the snow in the roads was too deep. I could run along the tops of the snow banks and touch the telephone wires. One day, my Dad and about 10 other men were shoveling out Hickey's hill to get to town to buy groceries. As they worked, Bill Daniels came along with a snowplow and, after some more shoveling, got through. The men climbed onto the back and rode to the next big drift to shovel again. They got home about 8:00 p.m.

Another time, in the middle of the night, my Dad and some other men, including "Spike" Martin, the O.P.P. officer, walked through knee-deep snow looking for a downed army plane, which was found on Bill Nettleton's farm. You can imagine the excitement of a small boy to see his first plane—and be allowed in it as well!

S.S. #10

In winter, the only warm, comfortable seats were those in the first row surrounding the old box stove—except for the day Lorne Elliott got to school early and packed the stove absolutely full from top to bottom and end to end. All of the windows had to be opened, and the stovepipes and stove were cherry red! It never happened again.

When they were building Highway 22, we found neat places to hide on the other side of the road. When classes resumed after dinner, we were warned not to cross the road again. Nevertheless, boys being boys and girls being girls, away we went again at recess. When we came in from recess, Mrs. Harris lined up all 28 children in the anteroom and gave us the strap. I was the last. We never crossed the road again.

I remember the Monday morning when we arrived at school only to find that every door and window had been chewed nearly all the way through. The Glenns, who were janitors of the school, had locked in their dog, Laddie, when they cleaned on Saturday.

We played baseball for Adelaide and our home diamond was in Ed Brooks' pasture field.

Lloyd Robotham told me how he and a group of other young men used to go "coon" hunting. They had a big hollow tree that was full of "coons" and they made plans to cut it down on a certain night. When they got there, the tree was cut down and they never knew who did it. It's funny but it paralleled a story my Dad told me 40 years earlier, about which I'd been sworn to secrecy. They got one raccoon.

Uncle Gordon taught at S.S. #4 Adelaide when John Seed and Evan McCabe were five years his junior and going to school. One day, they shredded his strap into neat little shoelaces. They pushed their luck all day, trying to irritate Uncle Gordon enough to be given the strap. Finally they succeeded, only— to their dismay—Uncle Gordon had a second strap that was not shredded.

I remember going to card parties at Adelaide Village, put on by St. Ann's. These were followed by a dance, with Mrs. Waltham playing the piano and Walt Feasey on the fiddle.

MEMORIES OF ED HEALY

Ed was born on his father's farm on what is now Highway 22. He moved to his present home as a small boy. He remembered that his father brought some of the lumber from the barn to build a barn on the new farm. He told us his father sold 62 acres to the county to build the county home. Ed had pleasant memories of neighbours filling silos and other kinds of bees, when they needed to work together to accomplish the bigger tasks.

Ed was a farmer and cattle drover for many years. He told us of a trip to Scotland with a boatload of cattle. There was no refrigeration, so the meat had to be shipped on the hoof. He bought and sold cattle through Lambert Sales Yard.

Ed told us of driving the cattle through town to ship on the railroad. He said the stockyard in Kerwood was one of the busiest in this part of Ontario, and he described how cattle were bought for 2¢ a pound during the Depression.

Mrs. Healy told stories of grave markers being destroyed in the Catholic cemetery in Adelaide Village, and of an unmarked cemetery at Strathmere Lodge.

MEMORIES OF EVAN HARRIS

Evan Harris was born on the farm where he still resides. His great-great-grandfather, Sam, received the land by Crown deed. His family came from Wiltshire, England, and he isn't sure why they chose to immigrate to Canada. The following are some of his recollections:

I remember seeing my first airplane in Strathroy at one of the parks. My father died when I was six years old, so I don't remember much but I do recall going to town with him when he took cream to the creamery. We had mail delivery for as long as I can remember and we got our first telephone, which Elden Carrothers installed, in 1915.

I remember that a neighbour was murdered in a house on our farm in the 1800s. The murderer was never arrested.

I remember when the Farmer's Bank in Kerwood went bankrupt and a number of farmers lost money. One man sold his farm, put the money in the bank, and lost it all!

I attended school at Napperton and I remember Christmas concerts at Mt. Zion Church. The church shed was sold to a neighbour across the road for a drive shed, and it is still standing today at Wm. Parker's farm.

I had just started farming when the Depression began. I had a few cows and I remember selling three 800-pound steers for $100. I also remember when Harold Eastman was nominated for reeve.

One memory I recall very vividly is of the 1944 tornado and the ruin it caused, destroying so many barns and severely damaging most of the houses in a three-mile stretch. It was the only time I was glad I lived on the sideroad, because all I lost from the tornado was an orchard at the end of the farm.

MEMORIES OF FARMING

Butchering

Uncle Richard Brock and Grandfather George Brock Jr. talked about the sows that had farrowed in the spring running wild with their piglets in the woods and fields. They would fatten on beechnuts, mushrooms and roots. There were few fences dividing the farms along the concession, so in the fall the neighbours would round up their own pigs, identified by a splash of paint, a cut in the ear, or a brand.

Butchering day was a busy time. Water was boiled in an iron kettle over a tripod in the yard. The pig was flipped onto its back, and then stabbed with a butcher knife through the heart and the large artery so the pig bled to death, squealing and twitching. Then, the pig was laid on a board or a door to be scalded. A mixture of ashes or lye was put into a barrel (one cup to a barrel of water or in a 1:7 proportion), and strong men dunked the pig in and out quickly so as not to burn the skin before the hair set. If scalded properly, the hair came off easily when the sow's skin was scraped with a hoe. If slaughtering an old sow, weighing over 300 pounds, the men put sacks over it and poured the boiling water and lye mixture over the sacks. In the next step, the pig was hung by the hind legs with a stick through the back tendons to keep the carcass open. A handsaw was used to saw it down the back. The heart, liver and kidneys were taken out and saved for a separate use, and the entrails were taken to the bush for wild animals. The carcasses were left overnight to "cool out" and, in the morning, they were loaded into a wagon and taken to London to be sold on the market.

Food for the Family

There were different ways to preserve pork for

family use. The sides were rubbed with salt and hung up to cure in the back kitchen. A sheet was placed over the carcass to protect it from flies. In winter, the pork side was hung up to freeze. Sealing the meat and fat in glass sealers was an alternative. Stories are told of burying the salted meat in grain in the granary to keep it dark and to prevent spoilage. The pork heads, tails and hocks were boiled and the resultant "jell" and meat were scraped off to make headcheese, a delicacy in most households. Fresh pork and spareribs were always a treat, because so much meat in those days was salted.

Pork Hides

A few farmers would skin the pigs and cure the hides. In early days, the cobblers used these to make shoes, mitts and gloves. The skin was scraped repeatedly, "worked," and treated to achieve a good quality leather. Adelaide Village had several shoemakers. Clerk Anthony Preston and James Abernatky helped unskilled farmers by making boots for everyone in the household. Sometimes, cobblers came to the farms and stayed with the families while they were fitted with new footwear. Some Brock hides were sold to Hyman Tannery in London.

From an interview with Ray Brock

MEMORIES OF GEORGE D. ROBOTHAM

George D. Robotham attended S.S. #4 Adelaide, where Earl McInroy was his first teacher. The first few days at school were spent sitting at a double desk with his neighbour, Dougald Campbell. Lard pails or honey pails served as lunch containers. George walked the 1½ miles to school in spring and fall, but in the winter, his mode of transportation was a horse. He left the animal in the stable of Evan McCabe, a neighbour who lived close to the school. Before and after school, George did chores—helping to milk the cows and feeding them. When they were in the senior grades at S.S. #4, George and his brothers, Lloyd, Wilfred and Bill, were the school custodians.

Among several salesmen who travelled from farm to farm selling their wares were the tea salesman with loose tea, Watkins, Rawleighs and Fuller Brush, with spices, brushes, liniments and cleaners. Nutritious food for the family was obtained by keeping a large vegetable garden, butchering designated farm animals, and collecting eggs from the hens. Money from the sale of milk, cream and eggs provided income to buy the remainder of the groceries.

George remembers his father butchering a pig and rubbing salt on it to keep the flies off, but the animal heat was not all out of its body. The whole pig spoiled and had to be buried, an expensive, but timely reminder to young boys about waiting until an animal is completely cold before curing.

George remembers his mother storing eggs in the oats for the winter when the henhouse was too cold for hens to lay eggs. She baked bread, pies, tarts, cookies and cakes. Some of the cream was churned into butter. Summer and fall were busy times for preserving a variety of fruits, and making pickles and relish, followed by storing vegetables from their garden.

Upon completion of Grade 8, George attended Strathroy District Collegiate Institute for a short time. Money was scarce and, with no means of transportation to school, he quit. In the spring of 1934, at the age of 15, George went to work for his Aunt Laura and Uncle George Foster. He worked six days a week and every other Sunday for $60 a year, plus his room and board. He remembers one summer without rain when they harvested only a couple of loads of hay and the crops were very sparse. Several sunny, frosty winter days found him with the horses and sleigh in the bush cutting wood, which was hauled to heat the farmhouse. Frozen food was a natural occurrence as the cold weather froze the sandwiches he had taken for his lunch.

He spent eight years working for and living with Clarence and Helen Patterson. He had his first experience of tapping maple trees and boiling sap in a big kettle in the woods. He rode his bicycle from the Patterson farm near Kerwood to Strathroy to go to the movies. Admission to the theatre was 25¢. Dances and Euchre parties were regularly held at the Anglican Hall in Kerwood. Helen Patterson, Gwen and Mabel Waltham taught George how to play Euchre and how to dance. Most of the time, Reg Freer and Gwen Waltham provided the music. Later, Margaret "Cran" King played the piano. While at Pattersons, George purchased his first car, a 1927 Chevrolet. He spent some time working for Fred and May Sullivan on their farm on the Second Line South of Adelaide Township. Later, he drove a gravel truck for Gordon and Dorothy Galbraith on the

Kerwood Road. Road gravel was loaded from Gravel Hill on Sideroad #3 and the townline (now known as Townsend Road), Chambers Pit, and several surrounding area pits.

Later, George worked for Richardson Feed Mill in Kerwood. Some days he delivered feed to area farmers for their livestock and fowl, and some days he worked in the mill. At times, he was sent to Sarnia to get loads of lumber and steel roofing. Loads of coal were delivered to some of the area homes.

While working for Bob and Lottie McCubbin, George and Ken Phillips looked after the farming operation when Bob was this area's M.P. in Ottawa.

George went to work for Bill and Alma Daniels of Daniel's Garage at Hickory Corners. While there, he helped to wire the garage for electricity. He began to drive a school bus, transporting students to Strathroy District Collegiate Institute. Sometimes he arrived with the tow truck at the scene of an accident. Stock car racing was popular, with Bill Daniels driving car #203.

At this time, George became a Mason, joining Masonic Doric Lodge 289 at Lobo Village. He married Loftena Pearl Muxlow, daughter of Loftus and Viola "Langan" Muxlow, formerly of Adelaide Township. In 1958, they had a son, William George Robotham. For a short time, George worked for Jim Smith at Wards Water Supply in London.

When Adelaide Township Central School opened in 1960 with Annie Courtis as principal, George became the full-time custodian and bus driver. He serviced the buses, which were kept in the bus barn at the school. He drove a regular route to Adelaide School until his retirement in 1984. Several days throughout the years, stormy weather and heavy snow, accompanied by high winds, caused poor visibility and clogged roads, which kept the students home. The blizzard of January 1971 came rapidly after the students were in school, and the weather was too severe for buses to transport them home. All of the students from Kindergarten to Grade 8, the teachers, George, and another bus driver, Spike Smith, had to spend the night at the school. Although the hydro went out temporarily several times, it continued to stay on; consequently, the heating system kept working. The following morning, two snowplows cleared the sideroad. George and Spike drove a bus to Strathmere Lodge to get food. Everyone found the wieners on buns very tasty. Thankfully, by 5:00 pm that night, the snowplows had cleared Adelaide roads enough for the buses to get students home safely. George drove his bus from school to Hickory Corners, up the townline to Keyser's and back the Kerwood Road to Ralph Arrand's gate before he met a snowplow that cleared the road for him to return to the school.

MEMORIES OF GEORGE FOSTER

In 1934, George Foster signed a contract to deliver mail to the people of R.R. #3 Kerwood. He took over these duties from Mr. Smith, who used a horse and milk wagon to travel the route. Frances Fonger remembers Mr. Smith arriving about 3:00 p.m.; the 40-mile route would take all day. George used a Model-A Ford that, during the Christmas season, would be packed full to the roof. Apparently, it took until noon each day to sort all of the Christmas cards and packages. The mail came via the C.N.R. railway station in Kerwood. When his daughter, Gwen, was old enough, he began to take her along, probably enjoying the company.

At Keyser's Corners, an old gentleman named Mr. Parker kept the store. He was confined to a wheelchair. He had a little dog that always met George at the store and carried the mail in his mouth up to his master at the house on top of the hill.

There was a postmasters' and mail carriers' picnic at Port Stanley one year, which George Foster attended with his family.

Many farmers met George at the mailbox for their mail and to pass the time of day. Many times, George would stop to help get cattle, etc., off the road, or to help someone hang a picture or move furniture or other items. In return, many helped him in different ways, always willing with a tractor-pull if needed. Keyser's store was about halfway around the route, and George always stopped there for soda pop and to deliver the store's mail. Many ladies would call the store to order small quantities of groceries, and George would deliver them with the mail. He always enjoyed the stop at the store with Mr. and Mrs. Laverne Topping, and later, Mr. and Mrs. Frank Gare. Mail was also delivered to the East Williams Mutual Fire Insurance office, located at John McLeish's home and later at Frank Gare's.

Sometimes, the roads were very bad during the winter, but George's law was that the mail must get through. He always exhausted every effort to drive the car in bad weather, occasionally being stuck in the snow and calling on the nearest tractor to pull him out. When Gwen and her brother, Jim, were old enough, they would walk the mail through the sideroads and George would pick them up at the other end. There were times when the roads would be blocked for days. Often, farmers would drive their tractors to pick up their own as well as their neighbour's mail. One time, George Foster and George Robotham delivered the mail in a horse and cart. It took them all day.

There was a bachelor named Mr. Rawlings who lived on R.R. #3. He didn't have a car, so about once a week he would ask for a ride to Wisbeach store to get his groceries. The storekeeper would drive him back home. Mr. Rawlings was a very generous man and always gave Jim and Gwen silver or pennies if they were riding along with George. He was quite old and not very well. Eventually, Mr. Rawlings was unable to make the trip to the store, so he made a grocery list and George would pick up what he needed at Keyser's store and deliver them. Also, he couldn't get to the bank, so George would take his cheques to the bank and bring back his grocery money. As he became less able to cope, George would go in every day and get him what he needed for the day. George bought food for him that needed little preparation. Also, he made appointments with the doctor and took him to Strathroy for them. One Saturday, George and Jim found his door locked. They had to break it open and found Mr. Rawlings had died in the night. George waited for the police and doctor and, later, went to Dennings Funeral Home and made the arrangements for his funeral. A few relatives were contacted and they came to take over. The Foster family really missed Mr. Rawlings.

Things changed as the years went by and the mail was delivered by truck to the Kerwood Post Office. Evan Denning and his family trucked mail to Kerwood for many years. At the post office, the mail was sorted into canvas pockets, which were rolled up and unrolled in the car as the mail was delivered. This was a very good system, but took a lot of wall space to hang up the three Kerwood mail routes. When Mrs. Conkey retired, the office moved to Reg and Eileen Freer's home in Kerwood. The mail was sorted into slots and then packed into boxes for delivery. The mail is still sorted in this manner today.

On December 10, 1966, George delivered the mail as usual. In the afternoon, he was helping his son Jim on a recreation room project. He suffered a heart attack and did not recover. The post office lost a dedicated friend and mail courier of 32 years that day. No one had ever taken his place in all those years; he was always on the job. Only during the last few years did Gwen, Jim, or Bob Patterson take the mail so that George was able to go on a few holiday trips.

MEMORIES OF GRADE 3 SCHOOL PROJECT

While in Grade 3, we studied the topic of Farm Life. We studied in class, learning about the farms in our area, and then we went on a tour of farms.

We had an incubator in our classroom and experienced a close-up study of baby chickens. We learned how they were hatched. We were to watch the eggs to see how they progressed, and how long it took for a baby chick to be born. This was an exciting time in the classroom. At the end of the study, there was a draw where everyone in the classroom put his or her name in to see who would take a baby chick home. I was the lucky winner of a baby chick—it was the first thing I ever won! I had to tell my Mom (Evelyn Sumner) and get her permission to bring it home. Mom approved, and within a few days, we had ourselves a baby chick at home. We found out later that it was a rooster chick, and named him Tweety-Pie. Tweety-Pie began to grow up, and my Grandfather Russell Squire made an outdoor cage for him. We tied him by the leg with an old pair of nylons so he could stray to the driveway. Tweety-Pie sure did create some excitement for my family and me. Tweety-Pie stayed with my family for a few years, until I began to lose interest in him. Many people said that Tweety would probably end up on the kitchen table, but they were wrong. My Mom promised that wouldn't happen to my bird; it was up to me what we should do about him. One day, I came home from school and Mom suggested a new home for Tweety-Pie—Storybook Gardens in London. I agreed that it would be a good place for him. Mom called Storybook Gardens and they agreed to take Tweety-Pie.

A few years later, when my niece and nephew, Lisa and Steven Smith, had Mrs. McDougal for their

Grade 3 teacher, they studied farm life, too. They were surprised when they heard that their Aunt Nancy had a pet rooster, and called me up to ask about him.

By Nancy A. (Sumner) Hepburn

MEMORIES OF HANSFORD WOOD

When I was a boy, I attended the local school, S.S. #3 Adelaide. I walked to school unless the weather was stormy, and then one of my parents would take me by horse and buggy or cutter. Walking to school, I noticed some pieces of wood in low spots in the road, so I asked my father what they were. He said that, when the road was first put through, the low spots in the road were always wet, so the early settlers dropped trees into the crevices. They referred to it as a "corduroy" road.

In those days, everyone led a simple life and there was more community spirit. We never had much money. Every farm had a small herd of cows, some hens, and horses. Winters were hard, as the cows were generally dry, and hens didn't lay. In the winter, a farmer would go to the bush, cut long poles, and draw them up into a pile. In the spring, a fellow would come along with an engine and circular saw and go from farm to farm, sawing it into short lengths. Neighbour helped neighbour, and some cut wood in the bush with a crosscut saw, if he could get someone to help pull the saw.

Eggs were 10¢ a dozen and up, and butter was around 25¢. The main crops in this area were oats, corn, wheat, hay, and some peas for the cannery. When the settlers first started, they cut hay with a scythe and raked it with a wooden rake.

At threshing time, neighbours helped. There were often 15-20 men doing the threshing. This job made a lot of work for the women at mealtime. I remember one particular threshing dinner: I was at one end of a long table and the gentleman at the other end said, "There's one piece of pie left on the plate, who wants it?" and I said "I do—throw it over," and he did just that! It's a wonder, but I caught it.

What did we do for entertainment in those days? We made our own. We had our little country church, Bethel Wesleyan, built in 1870. It became United in 1925, with the last service in 1958. We had Christmas concerts with the help of the pupils of S.S. #3. We had box socials at Valentine's Day, and sometimes house parties. Strawberry socials were in June, and the Sunday School picnic was in the summer. We had a fowl supper in September when we had our anniversary. One year, we got up a play called "Miss Mollie." We had a debating team and took on other churches. The ladies had a Women's Society and Ladies Aid.

The church stood on a 1-acre lot donated by Mr. Whiting of the east half of Lot 28, Con. 1 NER (now owned by Bob McCormick). Once a year, the menfolk had a bee to cut wood for the box stove, and to clean stovepipes. For other entertainment, you could go to the theatre in town, where admission was 15¢ for children, 25¢ for adults.

Everyone had a few cattle to sell and some farmers bought extra cattle to feed. After the first war, cattle prices got up to 20¢ or so a pound. However, when the Depression started in the late 1920s and early 1930s, the cattle price plunged. Some buyers bought cattle and never took them. My father bought some cattle in the fall for $3^3/4$¢ a pound, fed them all winter, and sold them in the spring for $3^3/4$¢ a pound. We should have spent our time sitting in the house!

We bought a 1930 Model-A Ford for $715; they allowed us $100 trade-in on our Model-T Ford. Hired help was cheap in those days; we hired a young fellow for $15 a month. I helped my neighbour cut wood with a crosscut saw from 1:00 to 5:00 p.m. for 50¢, and in the fall, you could hire out to pick potatoes at $2 a day.

At one time, each farmer could do work on the road near his farm and he was credited for doing the work when his taxes were due. They called it "road work." Before trucks, all of the gravel was put onto the road by team and wagon, and the wagon was loaded by manpower. After they dumped their load, they would race the wagons back to the gravel pit.

MEMORIES OF HAROLD EASTMAN

"Without friendship, life is nothing." Harold Eastman understood this—it was one of the credos by which he lived. Perhaps he cited this quotation to you at some time—and no doubt told you that Cicero had written this over 2,000 years ago. He was a great fellow to pass on such bits of wisdom to explain his meaning... and he could remember where he had read it!

Harold was a friend to everyone. No age or generation gaps existed in his relationships. He wanted to be "Harold" to everyone—from nine to 90. He discouraged the use of the title, "Mr. Eastman." He knew everyone in Adelaide Township and seemed to know everyone in the rest of Middlesex County, too. He was always interested in the news from Adelaide. He was interested in the families, their joys, babies born, educational progress, marriages, re-marriages, new farming techniques, new farm machinery, business successes. He knew and *remembered* the family connections of present and previous generations. He knew how the children turned out when they grew up, where they lived, how their jobs were going. He could go back two or three generations and tell a story that held up a mirror to reflect what was happening right now. What a memory he had for dates and detail!

Last summer, Harold told me that the part of municipal politics that he enjoyed the most was getting to know all the people. As reeve, he had a *reason* to drive around the township and visit. Both his door and his time awaited those who needed to talk to him.

When he left Adelaide, Harold's grassroots philosophies and interest in his fellow man were still part of his fabric, even as he wore his city suits. He was a keen, caring and dedicated diplomat of his time. Like some others of that era, he was proud to fulfill his public duty. No person was too prominent or too insignificant for his attention. His humour and practical wisdom seemed to expedite problem solving. To reach a beneficial solution with a minimum of difficulty, and without causing loss of face or hard feelings, was his technique of diplomacy. Perhaps that is why he was considered an "institution."

A late 1800s New Hampshire poet, Sam Walter Toss, wrote a poem a day for a newspaper syndicate. His optimism, humour, and homespun philosophy must have caught Harold's imagination in some newspaper. Gladys says that this was one of Harold's favourite quotations and it was one whose ideas he emulated: *"Let me live in my house by the side of the road, and be a friend to Man."*

Throughout Harold's life, he cared about others. In his early days, he was surrounded by the warmth and nurturing of his extended family. People in the neighbourhood became part of this extended family: he became a younger brother to some, then an older brother, a father figure, and then a wise elder. As we hear family and community stories while collecting material for our Adelaide Township Heritage project, we begin to understand more about the early days. There seemed to be something special about the Second Line South neighbourhood because of the concerned and supportive families living there. Harold had a way of making people feel special and worthy.

Born at the beginning of a new century, Harold was a fifth-generation Canadian. He had a deep appreciation for his roots and those of his neighbours. Although it has been said, "tradition wears a snowy beard," Harold came at it differently and youthfully. He saw very clearly what was here and now, and the possibilities of both the present and the future. Isn't the very name Eastman interesting? The man of the east, the place where a new day begins: that was Harold.

It was always a delight to visit Harold and Gladys. You were made to feel very welcome; they were always gracious. "How's so and so? Did he get that job he was hoping to get? Your grandfather's brother used to keep his racehorse in the barn across the road!" And so the conversation would go, on each visit, as stories were told with accurate details and dates.

Harold, we thank you for being our friend in your "house by the side of the road."

Anna Jean McCoskery, 1995

MEMORIES OF HELEN "HON" (SULLIVAN) CLARKSON

I was born on the farm on the Second Line South, Lot 3, Con. 3 SER. For a few years, our mail was picked up at the Wonderland Post Office, on the present-day farm of Mrs. Ross Chambers, at Lot 3, Con. 2 SER. My brother, Stewart, was two years older than I was. For about seven or eight years, cousin Mabel Sullivan lived with us after her mother died. Uncle Will Sullivan arranged for the children to live with relatives and, after Herb Langford purchased the farm, the family was reunited when Uncle Will moved to town and remarried. Mabel enjoyed staying with her Uncle Ed and Aunt Clara and going to S.S. #8 with us and the other Sullivan cousins.

We walked barefoot down the dusty road to school in the warm months. I started to school with teacher Ethel Jury. We acted very rambunctious with one teacher; we even jumped out through the window when we went to use the toilet. The next teacher, Ella Acton (later Harris), was hired to make us behave and she really "cleaned our clocks," but we liked her anyway. Many of the teachers boarded just down the road at Ernie Dowding's. He was the school caretaker.

During good weather, Evelyn Carrothers and I rode with Jack Sullivan, who drove a horse and buggy to the high school in Strathroy. In the winter, we boarded with Mabel Sullivan (now McCandless). In high school, top priorities were basketball, softball, and a busy social life. Other Adelaide Township students were Ben Ball, Velma Petch, Jessie Petch, Thelma Payne, Isabelle Chittick, Annabelle Cairns (later Mrs. Bill Wright of Strathroy, who lived with her aunt, Mrs. Chittick, in Kerwood), and Alice McKeen from northern Adelaide.

The Bethesda Church activities were our social outlet, and we looked forward to the dinners and concerts. I remember several of the ministers: Rev. Moorehouse, Rev. Brooks and Rev. Stenlake. In the winter, we enjoyed the skating rink in the drive shed. Baseball was popular for a few years. Bert Petch and Jack, Allan and Ferg Dowding, along with my brother, Stewart, played ball any chance they got.

After high school, I went to Westervelt Business College and started work at the Supertest Office on Richmond Street in London. Through mutual friends, I met Art Clarkson from Toronto, and we were married in 1942. We lived in London and Art managed the Goodrich Store. Our son, Tom, was born in 1946, and Jim was born two years later.

The accidental death of my brother, Stewart, took a great toll on my parents. In 1937, there was a 50-year anniversary of Bethesda Church, and visitors stayed at our place. A plane from the London Flying Club was there to give people the thrill of their first plane ride. Stew drove us there, and said that he was going to walk over and see the plane take off. The plane went up, circled too low, and as it nosed toward the ground, it hit Fred Sullivan and Stewart. Stewart lived until the next morning; his 28-year life was over. This newfangled attraction, intended to bring pleasure to our rural event, caused lifelong heartache for our family.

The Sullivan cousins (Jack, Annie and I) are all 88 years old and very thankful for our good health.

MEMORIES OF JOHN R. BALL

When John's parents were living near Hickory Corners, they decided their (approximately) 50-acre farm was too small. They bought a 200-acre farm in Adelaide, which needed many repairs. Their sons were nine, eight, six, and the youngest, John, was two. Five years later, another son was born. They had a farewell party, with the customary presentation of a large family Bible and an address. They were moved by their neighbours and friends with horses and wagons for the 12-mile distance. The children attended S.S. #6 in Adelaide.

Although their new neighbours were Roman Catholics of Irish descent, the difference in religion didn't change the fact that they were often dependent upon each other. Local bees were held for such occasions as threshing, and building or repairing stables and barns. In times of sickness, remedies were shared and housekeeping or nursing assistance was provided as needed. When both parents had to be away for shopping trips, etc., babysitting services were exchanged.

The town hall at the east end of Adelaide Village was used for such occasions as municipal nominations, concerts and dances, but most of the social gatherings occurred in people's homes. Young people within two or three miles had regular square-dancing parties. A fiddler and a square-dance caller were invited. A caller is someone who sings, or calls, the dance pattern instructions, such as "Join hands and circle left" or the much-anticipated "Swing!"

Occasionally during the winter, there were sparrow matches, and the easterners tried to bag more sparrows than the westerners. The losers were required to provide a social evening in one of their homes, where oyster soup and crackers might be the reward.

At Christmas time, the church usually provided a Christmas concert at which many of the students performed. The teacher usually arranged a similar concert for the families of the school section. There were plays, songs, and a few speeches and gifts for the pupils, with someone dressed up as Santa Claus.

The first moving picture I ever saw was shown in the school one evening on a hand-operated projector lighted by an acetylene gas lamp.

A special event happened each year between Christmas and New Year in the school, the annual school meeting. On Wednesday morning, the men of the school section met in the school to attend to the business affairs of the school for the following year. A report was submitted to the District Inspector. First on the agenda was the status of the teacher. Did she/he keep order? Take proper care of school property? Was the salary appropriate? There was often a bit of quibbling, but the result was usually a continuation of the status quo. The next item would be the caretaking: sweeping every morning, washing of the floors during holidays, lighting the fire by 8:00 a.m. in cold weather, etc. Reverse bidding for the yearly contract was usually brisk, and ended up in favour of a nearby neighbour who had a child old enough to qualify, at a ridiculously low compensation. Then, the contract would be let to supply the necessary number of cords of split maple and beech stove wood, again awarded after open bidding. The highlight of the meeting was the election of a new trustee for a period of three years. The senior trustee acted as Secretary/Treasurer, and their duties included making purchases of chalk, ink, etc., when requested by the teacher, paying the teacher, and for other services as arranged at the meeting. The election was usually considered privately before the meeting, and went off without incident or embarrassment. Then, the gathering was over and the ratepayers went home to report the results.

Funerals were different in those days, usually held in the home of the deceased. The number of buggies following the hearse to the graveyard often determined a person's rank in the community. Appearance at the funeral by at least one member of each family in the neighbourhood was considered necessary, no matter how pressing tasks might be at home. Funeral directors provided death notices (small cards in black and white envelopes) to be mailed to friends and relatives. Usually, there were more people waiting outside the house than there were inside. Horses were tied to every tree and post available in the yard, waiting to join the lineup to go to the cemetery. Neighbours arrived with sandwiches and cakes to be eaten after the service, but I do not remember that gifts of flowers were commonplace.

Auction sales were another community event worth remembering. On occasion, public debates attracted a good deal of notice. Women got together for regular meetings of the Women's Missionary Society, especially when they were packing a bale to be sent to relieve some dire need in a foreign land.

Weddings were another special social occasion, and these were often held in the bride's home. My mother was married on October 25, 1893, on the front verandah of my grandfather's new home in Caradoc Township.

MEMORIES OF LIFE AT KEYSER'S CORNERS

S.S. #1 and #2 Adelaide and West Williams always had a large enrolment from Grades 1 to 8. Marguerite Johnson taught music once a week and Gordon Young was the School Inspector. My teachers were: Grade 1—Vivian (McKenzie) Conkey; Grade 2—Ross Gregory; Grade 3—Jessie (Petch) Bice; and Grades 4 through 8—Mary Ellen (Paterson) McKenzie.

We had a treat once or twice a year, when Dewart Hunter from the National Film Board visited our school with his projector, reels and movies. Some of the older students were school caretakers. Green wood is difficult to burn, so some of the boys carried dry kindling from home to help get the fire in the stove started. On cold winter mornings, we sat clustered around the stove with our coats and boots on to keep warm, until the fire had been going long enough to warm the room. Ink was frozen in our inkwells on those frigid mornings.

Our drinking water was pumped from the same outdoor well where we washed our hands, letting the water flow back into the well through the cracks. We all drank water from the same dipper in the pail, but there was very little illness. Little time was spent in the bathroom as we used an outdoor privy—one for the boys and one for the girls.

We had regular plays, recitations, songs and musical drills for our Christmas concerts, presented for parents and community. We did not have a stage in our school, so we used the Foresters' Hall, which was across the fields. What fun! We always had one or two rehearsals, trudging over the hills and across the creek in the cold, deep snow (we never thought of walking down the road.) This same hall was the community hall as well as the Lodge home, where progressive Euchre parties and dances were held during the winter. No babysitters were required as the whole family attended. When the young grew weary, they slept on the pile of coats on the benches. What a cruel and rude awakening at midnight, going out, half-asleep, into the freezing cold to go home.

We all learned to dance at a young age. I have wonderful memories of Ev Herrington calling the square-dances. On bright, sunny winter days at noon, we went sleigh riding and tobogganing on the hills across the road from the school. Our teacher played with us in the snow.

On Arbour Day, the first Friday in May, we raked the lawn and cleaned the schoolyard all morning. In the afternoon, we were invited to Wilbert and Annie McLeish's farm. We went for canoe rides in the creek near their house, usually with a pail along to bail out water from a slow leak. Some of us went for horseback rides. The afternoon ended with a wiener roast. One year, Ivan and Lola McLeish allowed us to go into their bush for a walk, winding along the paths, crossing streams, and identifying wildflowers.

In the spring, our school had a ball team. Doris was the pitcher. At noon, we played against Springbank School, where Jean Colgan was the teacher. Dave Grogan was the umpire.

Sunday School picnics were held in the pavilion at Ipperwash Park with dinner at noon followed by games, contests and swimming (after the allotted two hours following dinner). Then, the leftovers were eaten, completing an enjoyable day before we headed home.

Family Christmas with all the trimmings was an exciting time. Roast turkey, duck or goose, plum puddings and Christmas cakes were served, with the cooking and baking keeping the women very busy. Oranges, hard candies, jellybeans and cream candies were real Christmas treats! Practical items such as clothing, pencils, pens and books were the usual gifts.

By Doris (Murray) Robotham

MEMORIES OF LOREEN (MRS. JOHN) BROWN

My Dad taught himself to play the violin. As a young boy, he made a bow out of a stick and a horse's tail for the strings. Father saw that he could play, so he bought a $13 violin. His mother taught him to read notes and he took a few lessons from Professor Gordon in Strathroy. Dad played in Walker's orchestra; he also played banjo and many other instruments. The Bethel Baptist Church in Strathroy had a radio program in Sarnia at one time. The program included a sermon and my Dad played the violin.

I remember the tornado of 1944. The roof slates we lost from our home were replaced for 70¢ each. My mother was making strawberry jam in the back kitchen, which was left intact. She said the tornado sounded like a freight train, and she just hung onto the table and prayed. A window blew in, and glass was driven into the linoleum floor. There was a cut across the piano bench, the music cabinet was gouged and the door was torn off—there was only one hinge left on the cabinet, which I still have, minus the hinge. The barn was destroyed. Turkeys and chickens were scattered, but there were few casualties among our farm animals. Dan Campbell's hen house turned on its foundation; he never saw his 75 Barred Rocks again.

MEMORIES OF PHYLLIS PHILLIPS OF DOWN FAMILY FARM

My memory takes me back over the years during which this property, Lot 15, Con. 2, has been home to me. I have become acutely aware of just how our lifestyle has changed since those early years.

One of my first childhood memories was long before the days of snowmobiles, cars and four-wheel-drives. Travel to and from Strathroy was done by horse and buggy, cutter or bobsleighs. I do remember our first car was a Model-T Ford that caught fire on a family outing, and caused us panic-stricken children to bale out with much haste.

The tantalizing aroma of our mother's home-made bread filled our home on a weekly basis, and smelled almost heavenly to us when we burst through the door from school.

A poignant childhood memory was when our brother, Ivan, was stricken with a serious heart ailment and confined to bed for one year. It was at this time that Dr. Vine became, not only our physician, but also a dear friend who made weekly visits. In later years, when war broke out and Ivan wanted to enlist in the air force, our family was united in the hope that he wouldn't be accepted due to his heart problems. However, that was not to be and as the weeks flew by and his training was over, he was bound for overseas duty. I have tender thoughts of my mother packing food boxes that could be better described as bundles of love. Those boxes were sent on a long journey across the ocean via boat. They were well-wrapped in sugar sacks and sewn with strong thread to ensure the contents stayed intact during passage. Those years were trying for our family, as the safety of our soldier boys was utmost in our minds. Ration coupons were the order of the day. What a blessed relief when the war ended and our brother and cousins returned safe and sound.

My teen years passed quickly. I married in 1950 and moved from Adelaide to East Williams, where my husband, Ken, was working for his uncle, Bob McCubbin. We lived on one of his farms for two years and it was during this time that our daughter, Marilyn, was born. My father passed away in 1952 and we returned to my homestead to sharecrop with my mother. After four years, Ken and I purchased the farm when my mother remarried and moved to Toronto. Our son, Robert, was born and our family was now complete. In 1970, Marilyn married Burton Dolbear and moved to Strathroy. We could soon boast of our grandchildren, Laurie, Lincoln and Sarah.

MEMORIES OF RALPH AND JACOBA BOS

Our introduction to Adelaide Township goes back to 1953, when we rented a farm owned by Fred Brent. Fred lived on the neighbouring property on the northeast corner of Egremont Road and Kerwood Road. The only building on this 100-acre farm was a dilapidated brick house (without electricity or indoor plumbing) that was once occupied by two elderly women and their brother, Joe Woodlock. The house stood bleak and empty, but it was alive with the sounds of mice and squirrels that had found a warm haven in the furnished rooms.

With a few rolls of flowered wallpaper from the Eaton's catalogue, lots of elbow grease and a calendar from the implement dealer, our new home became livable and quite inviting. The fact that the path to our cozy nest was a sea of mud bothered us very little. Following our marriage in Sarnia we drove home, left the pickup truck at the road, and my new husband carried me all the way down the long lane into the house, where the coal oil lamp spread a soft glow over the new linoleum.

We soon got to know our neighbours, who invited us for supper, or just came to visit and lend a hand where needed. Ray and Donelda Brock lived kitty-corner across the road from us, and the George Ball family was just walking distance away on Kerwood Road.

For us, as newlyweds and new Canadians in the community, it was wonderful to know that neighbours were there to help just a telephone call away. We were quite proud of our telephone in those days, partly because it was the only modern invention in our humble home, and partly because it allowed us to contact the whole neighbourhood in an emergency. Turning the crank that hung from this solid wood wall telephone case produced a loud ringing, bringing all the party line neighbours to their phones to find out where their help was needed.

One windy Sunday morning when the wood stove was roaring and Ralph was at church, and our first-born child, David, was content in his playpen, I heard a crackling sound coming from the stove pipes that wound their way close to the papered kitchen ceiling. The pipes were glowing red, and I could smell fire. Grabbing a blanket, I wrapped up the baby and placed the precious bundle on the floor near the back door. Then I turned the crank on the telephone long enough to alert the neighbours, who, upon picking up the receiver, heard my anxious cry: "Fire at Ralph Bos' place!" Within minutes, cars and pickup trucks lined our laneway, where no smoke or flames were visible since the fire had thankfully burned itself out.

Autumn of 1954 brought hurricane Hazel to the Toronto area, and heavy rains to our part of the country. The untiled heavy clay soil soon became a gray sea of mud, unapproachable for man and machinery. Crops rotted in the sodden fields, dashing our hopes for a good yield from the sugar beets and soybeans still in the field.

In the beginning of December 1954, disaster struck our young family when Ralph was seriously injured. His shotgun accidentally discharged while he was on a hunting trip in the woods bordering on our farm. Many prayers were answered when, after several hours of emergency surgery in the old Strathroy hospital, Dr. Sharpe was able to say that his patient had survived. While Ralph was recuperating, the neighbours came with tractors and equipment and a team of horses, to harvest whatever they could off the fields, which were frozen solid by then.

The following year, 1956, we left Adelaide Township and moved to Strathroy. We rented an apartment close to the office of Jackson Bakeries, where Ralph had found a job driving a delivery truck. By that time, we had two sons, very few earthly possessions and a pile of debts. Little did we realize that one day we would be making a prosperous living in Adelaide Township.

During the nine years we lived in Strathroy, we were blessed with four more children, Alice, Irving, Annette and Renee. Ralph's steady income enabled us to pay off our debts and buy a small house with enough land to keep a milk cow.

In 1963, Mrs. Justina De Groot put her farm up for sale. Her place was known as the Lewis place, located on Lot 23, Con. 1 NER. The solid brick, seven-room house was built around the turn of the century, possibly by Mr. Lewis himself. We bought the 100-acre farm, complete with equipment and milk cows, which we soon had to sell. We cashcropped the land and pastured some beef cattle. The kids had ponies to ride and the fertile clay soil produced bounteous vegetables for our growing family. Two more sons, Randall and Marvin, were born to us on the farm, making our family complete with five sons and three daughters.

In the spring of 1968, we faced another challenge when Jackson Bakeries, Ralph's employer for 13 years, found it had become unprofitable to deliver bread to customers. It therefore closed its doors for good, leaving many workers unemployed.

After much deliberation, we decided to take the plunge and set up a butchering business, catering mostly to custom slaughtering for farmers in the area. Some people, including the bank manager we had asked for a loan, wondered if we had taken leave of our senses to be taking risks like that. After more prayerful consideration and support from family and friends, including the manager from another bank, we went ahead.

In October 1968, we held an official open house. We proudly showed friends and neighbours our newly built abattoir, which still smelled of paint and fresh cement.

Twenty years later, we again held an open house. This time it was to welcome the new owners of Ralph Bos Meats Ltd., our son, Peter, and his wife Mary, who live next door to the shop in a home they built in 1984. Both had worked in the slaughterhouse for many years, and their teenage children have become valuable helpers in the meat processing business.

The venture we began with much trepidation turned out to be a profitable enterprise, providing a busy but enjoyable lifestyle in which the whole family could participate.

By Jacoba Bos

MEMORIES OF SCHOOL AND MY TEACHER, FLOSSIE (GROGAN) HALL

When I was just a little girl
In my early childhood days,
I had a very special friend
Whose memory with me stays.
She was my favourite teacher,
With her kind and patient ways.
She taught me many a lesson
In those one-room schoolhouse days.
Sometimes she would reward us
With a little gift she bought,
But always in that little gift
She had placed some special thought.
My mind goes back to a picture frame,
No picture did it hold.
Instead there was a single poem
Upon a mat of gold.
The message in that printed verse
I never will forget.
I need not gaze upon the words,
I can recite it yet.
For all these years upon my wall
This picture could be seen
The memories and the message
So much to me did mean.
Wherever I moved,
My picture moved, too.
It had so much meaning
The words were so true.
Now I must share with you the words
That, to me, are so dear.
I hope they mean as much to you
I've loved them all these years.

*By Ann (Pennington) Dymond,
in memory of her favourite teacher,
Flossie (Grogan) Hall,
Teacher at S.S. #9 and #4, 1943-1946*

MEMORIES OF SCHOOL AT S.S. #9

My first memory of school life happened about the second day of school at S.S. #9. It was a very rainy day and the rain beating on the tin roof made a terrible clatter. Having been born and raised in a large home with a full-sized attic above our top floor, I guess I had never heard rain beating on a roof so loudly and I began to cry. A very concerned teacher, Mae Watson, tried to console me and assure me that everything was alright.

Another incident occurred with Miss Watson, also when I was in Grade 1, I believe. It was wartime and everyone did their part to help, so pupils knitted squares for use as washcloths, or the pieces were sewn together to make blankets. Since my grandmother, Mary Ellen (Nell) Conkey, had taught me to knit before I went to school, I enjoyed knitting when assignments were finished. I guess I did not have my own needles, so I was using a pair of Miss Watson's. Again, due to wartime, the needles were not metal but made of something like bone (I don't know if they had plastic yet). As I was knitting, one needle snapped in half. Oh! What a catastrophe for a little girl! What did I do then? Yes, you guessed it—I cried. Miss Watson came to the rescue once again. "What is the matter, Ann?" Sobbing, I said, "I broke your needle." My smiling teacher said, "Oh dear, that's nothing to cry about. We'll just find another one." One more crisis was averted, thanks to a kind and understanding teacher.

The next situation I can recall happened in Grade 3 or 4 with another teacher, Marjorie Campbell (now Wyatt). Miss Campbell boarded at our home and I was walking home with my teacher, and Ruby and Doris Topping. As we passed Alf Cuddy's farm, a ram from Cuddy's was out on the road. I guess he thought we were in his territory and he proceeded to chase us. Ruby, Doris and I ran on ahead, leaving Miss Campbell to take care of the ram. As he came close to her, she hit him over the head with her lunchbox, hard enough that, for the remainder of the year, her box had a big dent in it from the ram's hard head!

After S.S. #9 and S.S. #4 were joined in September 1942, transportation was needed for the pupils. I guess I was lucky because, being near the boundary of the school sections, I got a ride no matter which school was open. I recall that in the winter of 1944-1945 when the snow was so deep, my Dad hitched the team of horses to his sleigh and, having built a completely covered little chamber on the sleigh, began the long trek over fences and through fields to pick up the pupils. The sun barely peeking over the horizon, Dad travelled up the Second Line North as far as Bob Adams' place, then back to S.S. #4, dressed in his raccoon coat, hat and full-length mitts. With the children safely deposited at school, he started back home, only to repeat the journey at the end of the school day. Thankfully, this was not necessary for long as parents refused to send their children in these conditions, and school was closed until the roads could be cleared.

These are just a few incidents but I must say my elementary school years hold many fond memories of fellow students and very kind, understanding, dedicated teachers.

By Ann (Pennington) Dymond

MEMORIES OF ST. ANN'S ANGLICAN CHURCH IN ADELAIDE VILLAGE, AND S.S. #10

From 1930-1939, I went to church and Sunday School at St. Ann's. I played the organ for the Sunday School class. Mrs. Fred Brent played organ for the church and she was my favourite Sunday School teacher. I belonged to the Anglican Young People's Assoc., which met in Adelaide Township Hall. We were in plays and competed with other A.Y.P.A. groups, especially Kerwood. I was Secretary for a few years. We put on dances; my father played the fiddle and I chorded for him. We also played baseball against other A.Y.P.A. teams and once my sister, Myrtle, was hit with a ball and broke her glasses.

One time, the older women were having a quilting bee in a small house in the village and the men were outside cutting up wood. The flywheel from the saw flew off and sliced through the house! Fortunately, no one was injured.

For a time at S.S. #10, there were only five students and three of them were Brantons! My father was instrumental in having Grade 5 taught as his two daughters were starting to high school together and he wanted to keep them at home. Poor Miss Velma Petch had to teach all the other grades, as well as the subjects in First Year High School. She did well, though, as I passed Grade 13 (Fifth Form) with First Class Honours and received a two-year scholarship to the University of Western Ontario!

I remember the school fairs at Adelaide Township Hall. We had to march in with a banner, dressed in navy skirts or pants, and white blouses. We competed in many areas—vegetables, flowers, animals, and even darning a sock! I tried the darning but failed miserably.

We always had Christmas concerts at the hall for the church and at the school. When my little brother was two years old, I played organ for him while he sang "Away In A Manger." He still has a good voice!

By Mabel E. (Branton) Barkman

MEMORIES OF VERA MCDONALD

Vera remembered that, when she was eight or 10 years old, she went with her Dad to the pasture to repair a windmill. They saw gypsies camping at Paine's school, where there was water. It was a multicoloured caravan, and she saw people wearing bright, flamboyant clothing, and horses roped together.

Vera's father travelled from farm to farm, repairing machinery. She recalled socials and fowl suppers at Bethesda Church, and dances in Crathie on Friday nights. George Walker played in an orchestra, and girls attended with their boyfriends. The Epworth League sponsored the Strawberry Festival at Bethesda.

Mr. Billington delivered mail at R.R. #5 Strathroy, accompanied in his buggy by his dog. Vera was allowed to ride around the route with him.

Vera walked to the high school in Strathroy with Aubrey Lyons and Ben Ball, who boarded with Mrs. Douglas.

Vera received gold medals at her 1929 commencement for highest marks in entrance exams and grammar, presented by Dr. McCabe.

In 1909, Montreal Cement Company had a competition. Morley Petch designed a porch with pillars and won Third Prize. The porch is still there; its pillars were made of carved cherry logs. Morley was very creative and artistic. He invented and built his own cement mixer, powered by a gasoline motor. He helped build Grattan Bars' horse barn.

Vera recalled the Thrower-Humphrey reunions at the Petch home in Strathroy, with attendance by more than 100.

By Anna Jean McCoskery and Marguerite Cuddy

MY LOVE AFFAIR WITH ADELAIDE VILLAGE

Although I have only spent a very small portion of my life in Adelaide Village, it has always had a very special place in my heart. I believe I was only about nine months old when my parents, Russell and Ada (Bishopp) Dowding, moved to Adelaide Village. They had moved from the farm on Second Line South, Adelaide Township, due to my father's ill health. For a brief time, we lived in the house just west of the doctor's residence (later occupied by Aldersons) and it was while we lived there that Santa Claus came one Christmas Eve, before my brother and I had gone to bed. It was so exciting—I can remember the big sack he carried on his back, with a beautiful doll sitting right at the top of his pack. He said he would go to check on the Brooks family and come back later if we promised to get right to bed—you can bet no two children ever scurried to bed faster! It was many years later when I learned that Santa Claus was actually played by Dr. Jones from next door, but that experience is still a wonderful memory.

My parents bought the old hotel and operated it as a tourist home during the 1920s. It was a prosperous time and, on the main route between Sarnia and London and during the summer months, we had visitors from numerous U.S. states, as well as other places in Ontario. There is a record of the "Register" that lists names and addresses. It is quite surprising to see the distances some people travelled in those days. No one was ever turned away and I can remember waking up on the floor when mother had given my room to strangers when all of the "tourist" rooms were filled. In the 1930s, tourists had no more money for travelling because of the Depression. My parents began to sell groceries and gas, and meals were served, mainly for the councillors who met once a month.

When electricity became available on the main road, the work crew boarded with us. That was in 1930, the year my sister was born. I can remember walking the two miles to S.S. #6. I loved school and skipped some grades, taking my high school entrance exams after only five years. There were so many activities during those school days. It always seemed to me that no matter what class I was in, I was always near the front with the "little kids," for we were lined up according to height. It was a real thrill when my best friend, Marguerite Brooks, won the T. Eaton Trophy in 1933, a Silver Rose Bowl; I "keep" this well-polished, cherished treasure in my home.

In the village, St. Ann's Church was an important part of my growing-up years. I attended Sunday

School there, and I still have a New Testament and Birthday Book given from St. Ann's with the lovely inscription on the front page written by Eliza Brent. During the Depression, there were a number of houses in the village that were unoccupied. Most of these had been left unlocked, with some furniture and other items left behind. We girls (Louise Nichol, Marguerite Brooks and I) often wandered through out of curiosity, never taking anything. One house was locked, so this presented a challenge to us. One afternoon it was decided that we should attempt to try to get in by opening an upstairs window, after climbing onto the lean-to at the back of the house. Since I was the smallest, I climbed on shoulders and finally made it but horror of horrors—the owner, Mr. Gurr, drove into the yard! Everyone scurried away and left me huddling on the roof for what seemed an eternity! Mr. Gurr never glanced up to the roof. I was probably hiding behind a chimney or something, terrified, and eventually he left. By this time, I was too frightened to get down and it was necessary to get a ladder and older brothers to help. We never attempted to break in there again.

Looking back, it seems to me there were many special occasions for girls. Once a year, there was a "Little Helpers" party in connection with St. Ann's Sunday School, as well as a picnic that was usually held at Bright's Grove, if I remember correctly. "Uncle Dick" Brock had a children's party during the summer, and women in the neighbourhood helped with the food and games. We played "Go in and out the Windows," "Drop the Handkerchief," and "Farmer in the Dell," and it was a very happy time. Birthdays were another event that called for a celebration. I really felt cheated for my birthday is in March, and it always seemed to me there was a big blizzard on that day. I was told there was a very bad one at the time of my birth and it seemed to me that tradition continued throughout my growing-up years! Marguerite had her birthday in May and Louise had hers on June 14, which usually had perfect weather for an outdoor party. When Louise turned 12, her mother said that was the last year for her to have a party, and I have a photo of that last, very special party.

Velma Petch was the teacher at S.S. #10 and there were so few students to attend that school, the possibility of its closing arose. Several students were about to leave for high school, including Mable and Myrtle Branton, Anna Brock, and Agatha Carroll. I believe the Trustees obtained permission for the teacher to instruct First Year High School. Since Miss Petch drove right past our place in the village, it was arranged that she would pick me up and I would join the class. It was a good year and as I remember we all passed, ready to go into Second Year High School at the conclusion of the term. In the meantime, my brother felt he was old enough to start working on our farm, and my father shuttled back and forth between the farm and the village. My mother, sister and I were living in the village and my brother and aunt at the farm, with my father living part-time at both places. My mother was very anxious for us to be a family together all the time, so when a suitable tenant was found, we moved to the farm. I was very unhappy to leave the village and all my friends. After two years at home on the farm, I finally got back to school, leaving to board in London and attend South Collegiate there. Most weekends when I came home, my first stop was at Adelaide Village because the bus came through there, and I would stay overnight with Marguerite and have a good time visiting with friends, often returning on Sunday unless I could get a ride back to London with someone. One summer, when I was attending school in London, I came home for the holidays. My job that year was picking berries in Arkona with some other Adelaide girls. I barely made enough money to buy my textbooks for the next term! I was 17, and Winslow Hendrick (one of the boys who had attended S.S. #6) and I dated during that summer. It was 1939 and just at the beginning of the war. The romance faded when I went back to school and he went sailing on the Great Lakes. I graduated from South Collegiate, took a business course and started working. Another Adelaide Village resident, Shirley Finkbeiner, and I shared "housekeeping rooms" while she attended school. It was wartime and many soldiers were stationed in London, so it was a common practise for girls to go in groups to the many dances that were held. We presented ourselves as dancing partners for the servicemen. I met a soldier, Jack Kaler, and we were married May 30, 1942. About six months later, he was given a Medical Discharge and we moved to British Columbia, where I've lived for the last 50 years.

In 1988, Winslow Hendrick stopped in to see Donelda, as he frequently did on his return visits to Adelaide over the years, and "matchmaker" Donelda went into action. Both Winslow and I had been widowed; my husband died in 1973 and Winslow's wife in 1985. After a period of 49 years, when neither of us knew anything about the other, it took a number of telephone calls, letters and visits, but eventually a wedding date was set. Naturally, we chose that day that had been so special to each of us, May 30. In 1990, we were married in New Westminster, B.C.

By Vera (Dowding) Kaler Hendrick

REMEMBRANCES OF ALICE (MCKEEN) LUMSDEN

I remember the busy days on the farm when today's modern equipment was unknown. A pastime for women was hooking attractive rugs—some for gifts, others to scatter throughout the house. The materials used were found in old skirts, coats and other woollen garments, using dyes from onionskin and a few commercial dyes. Wool picking bees were held to pull wool apart. It was then taken to a Strathroy factory to be made into mitts and stockings.

I remember gathering chicken eggs; the hens would often hide their nests. At seeding time, grain was spread by hand and later harrowed in by a tree branch pulled by oxen. To get grass seed, ripe heads of timothy were cut with scissors, put into bags along rail fence rows, and then flailed out. Following grain threshing, the clean straw was used to fill straw ticks for the beds, to make straw hats, etc. Bees were held to pare apples and then the apples were dried and stored for winter. Apple and vegetable "pits," which stored food in winter, were not opened until after Christmas.

After a barn raising, a house party and dance would be held. I remember the long walks to church. Uncle Joe Little, a travelling minister, often stopped at homes in the East Adelaide congregation on his way to Warwick.

I remember our grandparents talking about rows of small, black, copper-toed shoes that were polished in preparation for Sunday church.

A periodic visitor would travel in a small wagon, collecting bags of rags and other articles. These would be traded for soap, shoe polish, granite cups, tin cups, stove polish, etc. Wandering native people travelled with baskets of basswood strips, and they would barter them for farm produce. Tallow candles were made of strained beef and mutton fat. These were safer to use than coal oil lamps. In my home, as in others, the bible was read and devotions were held each evening before the family went to bed.

REMEMBRANCES OF ALICE TOPPING

From my room at Strathmere Lodge, I have been asked to recall some memories of my yesteryears. As a young girl, I took a sewing course in Sarnia. Then from my home, I did dressmaking, clothing alterations, made new garments—whatever was needed. The young ladies didn't go out to work then as they do today. After my marriage, when I became the mother of three daughters, I made all of their dresses, until they reached high school and wanted to wear store-bought garments.

After my husband, Laverne, sold the farm and bought the Parker's store at Keyser, the store became our livelihood. The Keyser store was a popular spot each evening when folks dropped in, and these visits provided an opportunity to catch up on community news.

REMEMBRANCES OF EILEEN (SISSON) CAMERON

Having lived the early years of my life in Adelaide Township, I still have many happy memories. Let me begin with my remembrances of our one-room school, S.S. #11. I was in the Junior First Class when WWI began in 1914. Back then, we started school after the Easter holiday. The war became a very important part of our education, as evidenced by the songs we sang. "There's a Long, Long Trail A-Winding" was added to the usual "Twenty Froggies Went to School." We learned about places that weren't mentioned in the history or geography books. The "War Books" issued to the schools were required reading.

When the influenza epidemic struck in 1918, the Medical Officer of the Ministry of Health instructed all pupils to wear a cube of camphor around our necks, tied in a piece of cloth attached to a string. In addition, we were to keep a handkerchief daubed with eucalyptus oil in our pocket. The school took on a medicinal odour, but I can't recall that anyone got the flu. It was a new disease that some folk jokingly called "hen flew endways."

I recall the pleasure of walking along the dusty roads to and from school. Returning from school, we explored a little roadside stream east of Harvey Harris's. There, we enjoyed the Maiden's Blush apples that fell outside the fence at what has been the "Ward place" for many years, and hunted for tiny shells in the swampy stretch west of the Bellairs' place. We rarely saw a car, but sometimes we would see a fish peddler with his horse and democrat—the fish packed in ice. A chant sometimes sounded from the older pupils, "Fresh fish, all alive, six rotten out of five!" If weather was bad, our folks would come for us with horse and buggy, or in winter, a cutter or bobsleigh. We kept pretty comfortable on the mile-long walk to school, dressed in our long underwear, two pair of stockings, a wool cloth coat, knitted toboggan cap, mitts, and a wide wool scarf over the face. Sometimes, part of our outdoor wraps had to be kept on until the big box stove heated up the room. There were no storm windows then. We wasted no time getting into our outdoor gear at 15-minute recesses or the hour at noontime, to play "Fox and Goose" or skate (those without skates slid on their rubbers). "Old Witch," "May I," "Ante-I-Over," "Run Sheep Run," "Farmer in the Dell," "Nuts" and "May" were warm weather games. Or—it was off to the backyard for a ballgame! I recall playing the character Amy in "Little Women," using the woodpile for a stage to act out the story. Indoor games were "Fruit Basket Upset," "Clap In and Clap Out," and "Birds in the Bush," to name a few. I recall stilts our father made for sister Gladys, brother Clare and me. We were very popular when we took them to school.

Until 1913, the Mullifarry Post Office was at the home of Mr. and Mrs. Charlie Down, and I was big enough then to cross the road from my home to get the mail. The lady who delivered the mail to the Downs' was a very thin person, dressed all in black, riding in a black buggy, drawn by a black horse. To my childish eyes, she looked like a witch.

ROSE CRANDON RECOLLECTS

I sailed to Canada on the Queen Mary. I was a war bride and I arrived here in July 1946. I took the train from Halifax to London and it was a month before my husband, Wilfred, came home.

Wilfred and I met at a village dance in Bagshot, Surrey. Wilfred "Bill" was recovering from jaundice in hospital and he attended the dance. He took me home. Wilfred and I were married in Windlesham Church, Surrey, England, on February 23, 1946. I was afraid to be in Canada on my own, but his parents met me in London and made me very welcome. They were very good to me.

I have enjoyed living in Canada for almost 50 years. Our anniversary is on February 23 and that will be 50 years.

SCHOOL DAYS OF ANNA JEAN (WILSON) McCOSKERY

As a student:

I attended S.S. #9 Adelaide for six years under the superb tutelage of Mae (Watson) Dodge. She was a very fair, even-tempered instructress who kept us in line because we wanted to please her. While researching the Minutes of the Trustees for this Adelaide history book, I was pleased to learn that my father, Wilfrid Wilson, had presented the motions to purchase the Books of Knowledge and build a sand-table to help the students learn more about geography. How well I remember the pleasure of making islands, rivers and deltas, and attempting to clump the sand into the shape of continents, then sprinkling leftover globs to make the Rocky Mountains down North America and South America. Ours was an especially attractive schoolhouse, a brick building on a high cement block basement. Cement steps led to a covered portico and the boys' and girls' entrances, where a large window gave students the opportunity to peek into the teacher's room and the library, which was off limits for general use. There was a large wood furnace in the basement and a huge register on the main floor, which was a favourite place to stand on cold winter mornings. The cement-floored basement, with its high ceilings and large windows, was a good rainy-day playroom for such games as "Stop Light," "Cross Over" and "Kick Ball." Most of my schooldays were spent with fellow students Mac Murray, Dorothy Topping, Lee Benedict, Doris Topping and Betty McNaughton, so Miss Watson didn't have a large enrolment to frazzle her. When she left our school, I thought she had quit because of her age. I was surprised that she taught the next year in Strathroy, and I felt utter disbelief when she married Earl Dodge! To a young child, the teacher seems ancient! Mae and I had many laughs about this in later years.

Walking to S.S. #9 each day was difficult for me, being a distance of two miles "around the road" and 1½ miles "across the fields." On a normal spring or fall morning, I put on my rubber galoshes to keep my feet dry from the morning dew, and headed off through the orchard, climbed the wire fence, and skirted Arthur Conkey's woods. I angled across through his pasture field, walked my board-for-a-bridge over the creek, and came out on the #3 sideroad (now Wilson Road) by the sumac bushes. There I'd leave my galoshes, turned upside down in case of rain. Now came the easy part. I crossed the sideroad to the church and then went down the Second Line (now Cuddy Drive) to the school. Sometimes I'd see the Grogan boys' blue car—with yellow wire wheels—as they gathered their high school passengers. The return walk at 4:00 p.m. was uneventful unless there was a heavy rainfall, when I would find my board bridge shortcut had washed away. Then, I had to walk the extra distance across to our laneway and in the long driveway to the house.

During the hunting season of the fall months, many American hunters shared my homeward path. Mother dressed me in a red cap and scarf so they wouldn't confuse me with pheasants or rabbits, or whatever their license permitted them to kill. I was terrified each time I heard a gunshot, but my luck held out! Wintertime over this route was frightening. On Monday mornings, Dad would stomp a path through the Conkey woods and go over it several times to pack the snow firmly. I can still sense my fear of seeing a boogey-person of some ilk behind each shadowy tree. In those days, there were heavy snowfalls and the #3 sideroad could become treacherously deep, so I'd go to Aunt Hattie Cuddy's (next door from the school) and spend the rest of the week.

As I reflect on this walking experience, I realize that there was time to appreciate wildflowers, weeds, birdcalls, Hungry Hollow brachiopods, and corals in the gravel on the road. Near the end of Grade 8, I inherited the Cuddy boys' bicycle and that made the daily trips to school much easier!

As a Teacher:

I have fond memories of my beginning teaching career in the one-room school at S.S. #8 Adelaide. The community school enrolment was small at that time. It was supplemented by busloads of scholars from S.S. #11, which had been destroyed by the tornado of 1944. The children were Marilyn, Bev, George, Shirley and Joan Earley, Gary Chambers, Norbert, Lawrence and Renée Deschamps and later Mary, Ian and Hugh Stirton, Louis Jansen , Ruth Ann Wright, Jim Atchison, Raymond Tucker, Donald, Bob and Leroy Demaray, Whitford and Wesley Petch, Vernon, Renita, Ronnie, Cecil, Jack and Stuart Brown, Bill, Allen Del , and Judy Dowding and John Larocque. For a few years, the Hawkins and Blanchard children came. These students did not attend S.S. #8 at the same time, and I may have missed some names. I remember well that I had 39 students in eight grades one year, with three reading groups in Grade 1—that was a handful!

Many students were driven in small buses or cars with transportation paid by the Adelaide Township School Board. Now, years later, I'm not sure how some came to school, such as George Rawlinson, Glen Paine, the Hendras, the Joris children and Joe Hoefnagels. It would seem too far for them to walk. A group came by bus from the edge of Strathroy: Jack Mason, the Gordons (Donald, Sheila and Glenn), the Cuddys (Bruce, Barbara and Doug), the Thomsons (David and Ida), and Glen Hathaway. Ron Massie and Doug Zavitz came to the country school from Head Street North. Ronnie and Bobby Crandon, and Jimmy and Velma Cooper came from the Napperton area. When one considers the mix of very young students with older ones, and the fact that there was no telephone at the school, it is rather surprising that there was no serious disaster.

One winter morning, Donald Gordon was running in the schoolyard when he tripped over a frozen, snow-covered anthill, and broke off a front tooth. I don't remember how his family was contacted, but I probably sent someone to Roy Demaray's house next door to make the call, as I could not leave the other students. With blackboards only on the front wall of the class, it was hard to have enough seatwork available. I made use of wallpaper books by writing the arithmetic and reading questions with crayon, as this was in "pre-magic marker" days. Large newsprint sheets purchased at the Age Dispatch and tacked to the wall supplemented the blackboard. At home, I had three or four gelatin hectograph duplicating systems rigged up on cookie sheets. I received "The Canadian Teacher" magazine and the literature and English composition pages were an asset, as they were typed with special hectograph ink and could be printed off.

Everyone worked together to help in the learning process and in the organization of the school itself. As I look back, it seems that the others appreciated what each of us did. These students accomplished a great deal and were not "spoon-fed" as I found in later teaching situations in Strathroy and Mississauga, when I instructed only one grade per classroom. On a few occasions, we all cooperated to prepare a Christmas dinner. Each child had a task—they made Jell-O, peeled and cooked potatoes, opened cans of peas and heated them, set out the chilled tomato juice, arranged the cooked turkey (provided by the Cuddys) on platters, and made up plates of Christmas goodies provided by several mothers. We had a two-burner hot plate on which the students took turns preparing soup in the winter months. To this day, I can't face canned soup for lunch!

We tried planting a school garden but a hard clay band went right across the corner of the property, so that idea was abandoned. I was very proud of the S.S. #8 gang when we won recognition for planting the most and best-planted evergreens on Arbour Day for the Ausable Conservation Authority, on land behind the gully west of St. Ann's church. I still look for those evergreens, but they seem to have disappeared over the years! Another area of S.S. #8 expertise was in baseball. I admit we probably trained too much, but they were a "hotshot" team at one time. One of the secrets was having a strong catcher who zinged the ball to Renita Brown on second base, who then tagged the unsuspecting runners who didn't realize that "girls" could catch a ball! We even took three school trips that I remember. We went to the River Rouge Ford Plant and Greenfield Village, to the Detroit Zoo and to Niagara Falls.

We didn't win as many prizes as Crathie School at the school fair competitions. However, in the spring when the students learned I was leaving to go to Colborne School in Strathroy, they put forth extremely painstaking and creative efforts to prepare entries for the Adelaide School Fair. They entered every category for the fair, which was judged in the summer. S.S. #8 took top prizes in nearly every category from individual to group entries and really "creamed" the other schools. How we gloated—the teacher as much as the students! I felt that it was a warm good-bye gesture to me after my eight years there.

Of course, Christmas concerts were important in the community. We would go to Bethesda Church and practise on the stage. There was exceptional talent in the school community in both drama and music. Vern Brown hammed it up as he acted and sang his way through "I Never See Maggie Alone." Don Demaray's solo, "O Holy Night," brought tears to the eyes of those who recognized an exceptional voice. Everyone had a role in the concert from acting as a shepherd or one of the magi, dancing daintily in the Maypole Dance, or acting out "Alice Blue Gown." It might have seemed that the school concert was regarded as the measure of a teacher's competence in the classroom! Those were formative years for all of us at S.S. #8 as we matured together, honing our skills for the future.

SCHOOL EXPERIENCES OF GORDON GROGAN

I drove a car to Strathroy High School because there weren't any buses. I took several students with me each day. There were many difficult trips with snow, mud, flat tires, etc. One very scary event was in the fall of the year, when it began to snow as school ended and we were leaving for home. As we travelled from school, we had seven or eight students in the 30 model Ford, plus supplies for the Keyser store. The car had a hand windshield wiper, and it gradually became difficult to keep the windshield clean and observe the safe area of the road. As we crossed the "main road highway," travelling on what is now Highway 81, I drove too close to the edge of the road and we all landed in a ditch in approximately 4' of water, the car on its side. The driver's side of the car was above the water so I quickly broke the window, crawled out, and then broke the back window. Everyone got out safely before the water rose too high in the car. We were out but very cold and wet. How fortunate we were as a nearby neighbour, Mr. Elliott, took us into his home and called our parents, who came to the rescue.

I recall that this happened on a Friday and all of us were back to school on Monday, with a different car. The following students were in the car: Gordon Grogan, Ruby Grogan, Walter Grogan, Ian McKenzie, Colin McKeen, Wilson McNab, Mac Cuddy and Kenneth George.

LAUNDRY

The first thing on laundry day (usually Monday, but I have no idea why!), the woman of the house filled what was known as a wash-boiler with water. This boiler, which was 18-24" deep, just fit on the front two lids of the stove. When the water was hot, white articles such as towels and sheets were put in the water and soft soap was added. Everything was then thoroughly boiled, and stirred with a smooth stick that was kept handy nearby. The clothes were then removed to a laundry tub or manual washing machine. If the laundry had been put in a laundry tub, the woman then scrubbed them on a washboard. Stains were rubbed with a bar of soap. If there was a washing machine in the home, it was operated by hand, which was a heavy job. In our house, Mother used the washing machine some of the time, and Dad or the hired man did this job for much of the laundry. Make no mistake! These early manuals were not equipped with any kind of wringer.

Everything—even sheets, towels, men's work pants and heavy long underwear—had to have the soapy water wrung out, and receive at least two rinses by hand. Women's hands must have been strong, and also very sore, at the end of laundry day. In those days, rinse water had "bluing" added to whiten the clothes. Bluing was bought at the grocery store. It came in about 1"-cubes, which were tied into a square of old cotton and swished around in the rinse water. It dissolved very quickly, so care had to be taken not to get too much in the water. Older women with white hair often rinsed their hair in bluing water—then their white hair really gleamed!

Finally, the happy day came when people could purchase an electric washing machine. These machines, which cleaned the laundry by agitating the soapy water, were equipped with electric wringers. The wet laundry had to be lifted out of the water and put through the wringer. This had to be repeated with the rinse waters, but no one complained, because it was a tremendous improvement over the washtub and washboard!

By Evelyn (Fletcher) Clifton

THE DUTCH FARMER IMMIGRANT
A Prelude to Immigration

The liberation laid waste to many villages and wreaked havoc on the land. Hundreds of farm buildings were destroyed; livestock lay dead, scattered in the fields. Rebuilding and starting anew wasn't easy. The replacement cattle brought to market for the so-called "bereft farmers" were mostly culls, often carrying diseases such as tuberculosis or brucellosis, so it became difficult to reestablish a healthy herd. Other factors, such as the scarcity of arable land, added to the general malaise, the tiny parcels of land having been split once too often already.

At about this time, the Dutch government sent delegates to Canada on fact-finding missions in order to help solve the plight of farmers' sons wanting to farm. They painted a rosy picture of "the land of plenty" and soon, farm families were taking English lessons, putting their farms up for sale, and waiting for word from the immigration office of a confirmed Canadian sponsor.

A condition of sponsorship was that the minimum length of stay was one year at prearranged wages. In our particular case, our sponsor did not live up to the terms of the contract; we were put up in shabby, nondescript quarters and only paid if work was available.

We broke our contract and moved to Ontario, finally settling in Adelaide Township. We were to be among the first of a long list of Dutch immigrants to choose that particular area.

One may wonder why so many settlers of Dutch origin came to live in Adelaide Township. The answer is simple—they brought each other! Sponsorship was tied to land ownership. A Dutch immigrant who had purchased a farm could sponsor a relative or friend in turn. With so much farm land available, letters undoubtedly went back and forth, urging others to come.

Strangely enough, of the numerous farmer immigrants to come to Canada, many ended up in entirely different occupations. This was due, in no small measure, to the freedom to establish oneself in any type of enterprise, unhampered by restrictions. These seemingly unlimited opportunities provided a challenge grasped by many.

THE GENERAL STORE

Can anyone today imagine going into a grocery store with plain wooden counters, plain wooden floors and plain wooden shelves, which were behind the counters and inaccessible to the customer? I have not mentioned a fresh produce counter or a frozen food department, because 100 years ago these didn't exist. The general store, as it was called then, also had one side for dry goods, such as yard goods of all kinds, threads, needles, pins, buttons, hooks, hosiery, hats, gloves, ribbons and lace.

The back of the general store sold such items as hay seed, garden rakes, nails, hammers, fencing, axes and saws. By the beginning of the 20th century, stores could probably obtain sewing machines, cream separators and stoves by special order. One-stop shopping isn't a new idea, just an old one reinstated.

Most people, even those living in town, grew a couple of apple trees as well as cherry and plum trees, and bush fruit such as gooseberries and currants, so a storekeeper had very little call for fresh fruit with the possible exception of apples. The same was true of fresh vegetables. Most people had large gardens, and grew vegetables for their own use. Sometimes, the stores stocked such vegetables as potatoes, turnips and dried white beans.

Transportation of such foods as oranges, lettuce, grapes and green onions was very slow, and there were no climate-controlled freight cars, so the loss in transit was too great to make the regular importation of such foods feasible. Most merchants tried to import a few oranges for the week before Christmas.

The main food stock in such stores included salt, flour, white sugar, brown sugar, yeast, baking soda, baking powder, currants, nuts, oatmeal and cornmeal. Stores stocked such home remedies as liniments, cough mixtures and salves. As soon as processing of tinned vegetables became common, the stores stocked peas, corn and beans, but little else. As for cereal, corn flakes and puffed rice were available, but other varieties were slow in appearing. Of course, there was always oatmeal in stock!

In larger centres, there were butcher shops but the supply was very limited, because butcher shops had the same problem as the housewife, keeping meat fresh without refrigeration. Bakeries were only commonplace in towns, and the available products were limited to bread and rolls. Most housewives produced their own bread, using "elbow-grease" to knead the dough—not an electric bread maker!

THE HERRINGTONS OF KEYSER'S CORNER

Ethel and Bert Herrington were married on April 6, 1910, at West Adelaide Presbyterian Church, and took up residence at Lot 6, Con. 5 in Keyser's Corner. The property had been in the Herrington family since 1850. Up until the time of Bert's marriage, his parents had lived there, so they moved into a home already prepared for them. I remember a nice apple orchard, flowering bushes, peonies, and a wood with hickory nuts.

At one time, Keyser's Corner had been a busy social and business community, but I only remember the cheese factory and the little corner store. The cheese factory burned down about 1917. We were in school at the time—the teacher let us stand at the window and watch the excitement.

There was a small Methodist Church next to the school, which was torn down about 1913. My grandparents attended the church and Grandma (Rose Thorpe Herrington) sang in the choir. When my folks married, Grandma and Grandpa moved to Arkona and then they attended the Presbyterian Church.

My mother played the organ at West Adelaide Church until she married, so we continued to go there. One thing that stands out in my mind is the annual Christmas concerts. They had recitations, little plays, and concerts—to a youngster, these events were wonderful! Santa Claus always came and there was a present for each child under the tree. I used to wonder how he knew exactly how many presents to have in his bag.

I can remember one Sunday in particular. Grandpa Wilson had purchased a new car. The following Sunday, my Uncle Sam drove it to church. He sailed down the side road, came around the corner without slowing down, and zoomed into the church drive! He managed to stop right behind a buggy that was letting a woman out. There wasn't much room between the car and the buggy when he hit the brake!

Wilbert and Hattie Murray, and May and Lawrence Grogan were neighbours and friends of my parents. It was always exciting when they came to visit. Dad fiddled, Mother played the piano, and May and Hattie sang.

Geordie and Mag Conkey lived across from the church at that time, and one Christmas they held a square dance in their home. Toots Conkey, son of Fred Conkey, was there, and he danced with me two or three times. It was the most fun I'd ever had. I have thought many times about how kind he was to me when I was a youngster.

Mr. and Mrs. Parker had the corner store when we lived on the farm. One day, my mother sent me to the store for some reason. The Parkers were eating their lunch at a table. They had three places set with place mats and, at the third place, their pet cat sat on a high chair with his forefeet on the table, where he ate like a gentleman!

By Jean (Herrington) Dunn

THE PRESERVATION OF FOOD

A hundred years ago or more, mothers were just as interested in keeping their families well fed as they are today. Filling food may have had a higher priority than nutrition, our chief concern today.

Preservation of Meat

Meat was probably the food that was of first importance. In the winter, beef could be hung in a back kitchen, wood shed, or other unheated building to be frozen naturally. Although it seems that long-ago winters were colder, there was always the risk of a thaw.

Beef and venison were sliced very thin and then dried by placing the meat in shallow pans, which were then placed on a warming shelf of the stove. This was a slow process, and much diligence was needed to control spoilage. Dried beef had to be soaked in water to reconstitute the moisture content. The strips could then be fried, baked in the oven, or cubed for stews.

Later, when glass jars became readily available, beef roasts were cut in thick slices by hand and then cooked in the oven. When the beef was tender, it was packed in glass jars with the liquid from the roasting pan and then sealed. It was desirable that a fair amount of fat be included as it helped with the sealing process. When needed, the meat and liquid were removed from the jars and reheated in the oven. It was a lot of work, but the results were very tasty. Pork could be dealt with in several ways. The shoulders and hams were cut to the size of roasts and then "cured."

To Cure 100 Pounds of Pork:

Make a brine sufficient to cover the meat and strong enough to float an egg. Dissolve in warm water: six pounds of table syrup and four ounces of saltpeter. Just before pouring this liquid over the meat, add two ounces of baking soda. Leave hams and shoulders in the brine for three weeks, and sides of pork for two weeks. Remove from brine. Wipe dry and rub with corn meal. Paint with essence of smoke. Put in cotton bags and hang in a cool, dry place. Before cooking, meat must be soaked in water overnight.

Another Cure of 100 pounds of Pork:
 Four pounds of salt
 Two pounds of brown sugar
 Black pepper to taste
 Red pepper to taste
 2½ oz. saltpeter

Mix all ingredients and rub in all you can. Let stand for two weeks and then rub in the remainder. Store in cotton bags in a cool, dry place.

Sides of pork were often sliced by hand and fried, then packed in large crocks, a layer of meat covered with fat from frying. When the crock was full, a large plate was placed over the meat with a weight (such as a stone) on top to prevent air spaces from forming. When required, the amount needed for the family was dug out and warmed up in a frying pan.

Preservation and Storage of Fruit and Vegetables

Fruits of all kinds grew well and produced a full harvest in this part of Ontario. Every settler tried to get two or three apple trees growing as soon as possible. Apple trees usually produced a good crop of fruit and, if packed carefully in a barrel and stored in a cool place, the fruit kept well. Later, the apples might be peeled, cored, and thinly sliced in preparation for drying. When thoroughly dry, the apple slices were hung in cotton bags.

Berries such as raspberries, both wild and garden variety, could also be dried in shallow pans, and later soaked in water and cooked. Many fruits, such as pears, plums and strawberries, did not dry well. When glass jars came into use, all fruits could be preserved in a thick syrup using the canning method, and sealed with a glass lid and metal jar ring. Great care was taken in sterilizing the jars, filling them brim full, and being sure they were securely sealed.

Corn, peas and white beans could also be dried. Corn was cut from the cob before drying. When glass sealers came into common use, corn and peas were also canned.

Onions were hung in bunches and allowed to dry for use in the winter. Herbs such as sage and mint were also dried.

Vegetables such as potatoes, carrots, and turnips were kept in a cool part of the basement or stored in a root cellar. These root cellars were often small brick or stone buildings behind the house that were used only for the storage of vegetables. They were also sometimes dug into the side of a hill and the walls shored up with planks. This method provided moisture for the vegetables.

Preserving Eggs

It is possible to keep eggs for at least three months without freezing or drying them. Even in the early days, farmers and some people in small towns kept a few hens for their own use. By today's standards, the feeding, housing, and care of poultry was very primitive. Hens laid more eggs during the summer months, so egg prices were low. During the winter months, the hens produced fewer eggs, so prices were higher. The farmers wanted to have as many eggs to sell as possible during the winter, when prices were higher. During the late summer and early fall, peak production periods, the farmers filled a large crock with water and then added "water glass." This was a product purchased at the drug store which would keep the eggs fresh for two or three months. Each week during high production, the housewife would add a few eggs to the crock with the water glass mixture.

By Evelyn (Fletcher) Clifton

THE RAYMOND BROWN STORY

For those who have known him as I have, they will readily admit that Raymond Brown was quite a remarkable man, if not a genius. When I first met him, I was immediately struck by his disarming smile and warm voice. It must have been 1951 or thereabouts and we probably needed something fixed on our old 1937 Chevy.

Ray, as he was called locally, ran a garage-cum-television repair shop down the Second Line South toward the Kerwood road. He sold Admiral televisions and provided aerial installation. This was no small feat, since television was in its infancy then, and his only competition was located in London.

By the time I arrived in Canada I was 19, and I had ridden in a motorized vehicle exactly twice. Within a month of our arrival, I found myself driving the family sedan. It's true what they say about a young man's fancy turning to cars. I was fascinated by the many intriguing items in Ray's shop. Ah, the smell of oil and rubber, the fan belts and gaskets, the tools on the wall!

In my broken English, I asked Ray for a job and, sure enough, he said I could start right away. Everything was a mystery to me. Things got worse when Ray, standing in the pit under a car, asked me for the vice grips from up on the wall rack. I didn't have a clue what it was, so I pointed to a tool on the board. "No, no, not that—over a bit, down a little, to your right!" He kept gesturing, that little smile lingering on his lips. He wasn't about to come out of that pit, no sir! I must have pointed at every tool on that board until I finally pointed to the right one. Thoroughly disgusted with myself, I asked Benny Webb of Cowan's Automotive in London to deliver a Herbrand tool catalogue when he dropped by on his weekly call. One week later, I had learned the name of every tool in that book by heart!

Of all the various shops and dealerships I was to work in afterwards, none was equipped like Ray's. He had the facility to bore out cylinders, grind crankshafts in the vehicle, and hone piston and kingpins.

Ray saw to it that I became registered as an apprentice mechanic and indirectly started me on a lifelong career that is still going today, 45 years later. Incidentally, the first tool set I purchased while in his employ is still in my possession, fully intact to this day.

The upcoming television craze demanded more and more of his time. Between selling and servicing sets, we were busily engaged assembling antennas, pipes for the masts, guy wires and corner stakes. We hoisted them up with block-and-tackle from a ladder as high as 100' in order to bring in Detroit and Buffalo stations. My job was to run from post to post to loosen the snubbers a little at a time as the mast was raised high enough for a new length of pipe to be screwed onto the one above it.

One of Ray's inventions was the rotating mechanism. A steel ball resting in a dimple in a steel plate supported the mast. An arm with a counterweight attached to the mast at window height, with a rope threaded through the windowsill, allowed turning of the aerial from inside the home.

It follows that less and less time was spent on car repairs. I had vowed to become a licensed mechanic and now saw my chances of learning the trade diminished. I left and continued my training elsewhere, but still owe Ray a debt of gratitude for giving me that first opportunity at a brand new career.

By Hubert Timmerman

THROUGH THE YEARS

Adelaide Township was to be known as a unique settlement because of its type of settlers. A group from England joined the nucleus of Irish inhabitants, and among them all, town planning became a lively topic of conservation. They intended to build an opera house where the treasures of music would be available. Others felt that a club would provide cultural and social advantages. For the first few seasons, however, nothing mattered so much as to conquer the forest for the construction of homes, and to clear and till the unyielding earth.

William Thomas Murdock was born in 1835, and everything was a real adventure to him. His mother, Anne, loved music and often sang the old Erin songs. Tommy, as he was called then, soon joined her, and John Currie taught him to clog dance. He also loved to visit his grandmother Patterson, who would tell him tales of leprechauns that lived in the moors back home. "Tales or tunes are none better nowhere than in auld Ireland, my son, and don't you ever forget it," she'd say.

Tremendous effort and adventures were reaping their rewards for our pioneers. Where once their cabin stood among dark and forbidding forest trees, now it was in a sunlit clearing. There were fields of grain, a small orchard, a plot of green vegetables, and even flower beds. William Sr. was particularly interested in cattle, and he had acquired a small herd of Shorthorns, three good horses and some pigs. Anne found time to care for the chickens and a few fat geese, so that the larder had eggs and sometimes a bird for the table. Truly, as William said, the Lord had prospered all their undertakings, and they were happy.

Community life was not lacking in Adelaide, because the settlers made no pretense of living to themselves. The club and the opera house were never realized, but a school and a church were in operation. Little Tommy Murdock attended the log school for six months of the year, learning to read, spell, write and figure in a decidedly proficient manner. The school provided a meeting place for an occasional social and for worship on Sunday. Political meetings took place at this sanctum of learning, upon which occasion the eloquence and wit of these sons of Blarney came into play. Politics were keenly alive and hotly contested to the huge enjoyment of the settlers, and very definitely a benefit of the district.

Next door to the school property lived the Rapleys. David Rapley was a huge man with a remarkable tenor voice and two crippled legs, crushed by a falling tree in his first years in Canada. Anne told him, wistfully, of her love of music and lack of an instrument. A plan took shape in David's mind that music should be a worthy part of this community, even without instruments. Accordingly, it was "given out" on Sunday that anyone desiring to join a choral society should come to the Rapley home on Friday night. Nine people came. The next week the group numbered 12 and, from that time on, David Rapley's Singing School played a wonderful part in the neighbourhood. It provided a choir for Sabbath day services, and was the background of all entertainment, which meant pleasure and profit to every participant.

David Rapley died the second winter of his singing school. His illness became acute within hours, and his great voice was heard no more. The friends and neighbours gathered for David's funeral. He was put to rest in a small plot of land owned and cleared by his son, William. When the service was over, William stood forth in the group and made an announcement.

"My friends," he said, "We are here today as a tribute of respect to your friend and my beloved father. You all know how his unfortunate accident crippled his activities. Yet, he overcame his impediment to use his fine voice as a means of pleasure and instruction in this settlement, still in its infancy. I know you wish to accord him an honoured place in your memories. Therefore, I have decided to give this plot of land to the community as a resting-place for those who, like my father, have ceased from their labours. This land shall be the property of our church, and remain in our midst as a memorial to the pioneers of Adelaide Township." The area near the school and close to the Fourth Line was consecrated as the first cemetery of the township. David Rapley's grave was almost a shrine in their midst for many years, especially for those who had loved to hear his voice.

The Murdock's youngest daughter was Roseanne. She was the delight of the family, but one day she fell ill with a high fever. Despite all efforts, she died. Anne was stricken numb. Roseanne Murdock, the darling of the house, went to a quiet spot in the graveyard where David Rapley lay.

Anne never recovered from the loss of her baby. She went about her duties as usual, but never sang again. William watched her anxiously, and decided that a new interest must come quickly. A new house was to be built. Anne never showed great enthusiasm about the new home. William Thomas went to choir practise on Friday nights now, and William realized that he was growing up rapidly. William spoke to Anne, saying, "We must have more young folks about now. Tommy must learn to be nice to the 'Colleens.'" So, a Christmas dance was arranged.

With prodigal hand, Anne sacrificed her finest fowls, and for days, the spicy odour of Christmas baking filled the house. Anne's cooking had long since become a fine art. Her shortbread, mincemeat and fruitcake were delicious to the last morsel! William Thomas and his father went back with the team to the woodlot, brought back evergreens to trim the sunny rooms, and popped corn in great clusters to festoon a tree in the hall.

The party was a great success. William Thomas proved a capable host, dancing with the shy girls, joking with the saucy ones, and leading some carol singing in a strong, clear baritone that reflected credit upon Anne's training. Anne and William watched their grown son with pride.

By Jessie Murdock Gilmore, 1945

TRANSPORTATION TO STRATHROY COLLEGIATE INSTITUTE

In the 19th century, very few children attended high school. If they did, they often obtained room and board in Strathroy or Parkhill. Usually a relative or close friend provided accommodation.

Some students travelled to school each day by buggy or cutter. They put their horse in a stable, fed it, and walked to the high school. During the winter, the town boys would try to hitch a ride on the cutter. Often in the winter, one's hands were so cold upon arrival they could scarcely release the spring on the snap of the breaching. Although the student was covered with a windproof buffalo robe and had a hot brick at his or her feet, the cold was able to penetrate. On particularly frigid mornings, icicles would hang from the horse's nose—sometimes up to 8" long!

The driver had to be alert after a windy night, because a cutter runner might drop over the edge of a snow bank. Sometimes the cutter rolled over, and the students had a soft landing in the snow bank. The driver might be dragged several feet if he or she was unable to hold onto the reins.

Occasionally after a snowfall, followed by freezing rain and the formation of an ice crust, the driver would suddenly stop and refuse to proceed because of injury to the horse's legs. After tramping the snow and ice around the horse, an about-face was made and the horse would trot home.

During the 1930s, the Grogan boys, who lived near Keyser's Corner, transported many boys and girls who lived on the Second Line north of Egremont Road to Strathroy at a cost of $1 per week. Walter Grogan drove six or seven boys in his grandfather's Model-T Ford. Gordon Grogan drove an equal number of girls in a big blue Essex that had glass windows. After the Grogans, Mac Cuddy and then Keith McInroy drove to the school. Over the years, Wardell, Branton, McKeen, McKenzie, McIntyre, Muxlow, McInroy, George, Cuddy, McNabb, Ayre and Grogan children took this journey daily.

On Highway 22, most students were able to take the Arkona bus to school. East of Highway 81, Andy Matthews rode his bicycle to school when possible. The Earley and Pollock boys supplied transportation for students living in the south part of Adelaide. In the 1940s, free busing was provided for public and high school students. Previously, children walked to public school.

WHAT IS SO RARE AS A DAY IN JUNE?
(The Tornado of 1944)

Such a line might well have described a certain Friday morning in late June 1944 on the Second Line South of Adelaide Township. The warm, smooth air carried that peculiar fragrance identified with curing hay. The wagons, mostly horse-drawn, were making their way to the various fields to haul in the hay. Most of the farmers could clear their fields before milking time and then, on Saturday morning, cut the hay to lay curing in the sun while they attended the Saturday afternoon school picnic.

What a life, and what a pleasant, ideal day to clean the exterior windows of the house!

As the afternoon wore on, there was a gradual darkening of the western sky. The hay hauling became a bit hurried, but a good rain shower would do the gardens and fields a lot of good. The sky became even darker, and then the rush was on to get that last load of hay under cover before a heavy rainstorm arrived. All those clean windows of the morning were quickly closed against the coming of heavy rain.

The wide, deepening cloud became almost black, and it turned and twisted on itself like the boiling brew in a witch's cauldron. The cloud sank lower, and there was a murky, yellow glow at the edges. Tiny twigs blew around, and sturdy old maples and elms bowed to the cloud as if begging for relief. Then the whine was heard. I heard that same whine 40 years later in Haliburton County, and it is a sound unlike any other.

Suddenly, the Second Line South exploded! Tree limbs, lawn chairs, pieces of harness, tools, roofing materials, house doors and much more were all whirling before our eyes. I couldn't hold the car I was driving on the road. Then, it was over. Eyes could not take in the devastation, minds could not comprehend the extent of such destruction. Now, through the media of television, we see tornadoes from all around the world—but in 1944, we might only see the odd newspaper picture. Every square yard had a story to tell. Barns partly or entirely damaged lay like twisted piles of kindling; porches were torn off houses; harness was found under an upstairs bed; small green tomatoes had blown through broken windows; books and pictures were found miles away; and mighty trees lay in a convoluted mass, often with a farm implement beneath. One almost had to concentrate to recognize the landscape that only minutes before had been so familiar. The whole neighbourhood was torn apart in such a way that no pen will ever be able to describe the horror, the feeling of disorientation, the utter disbelief.

One man rushed to his house to stop the door from swinging so violently. At that instant, the wind reached its peak, carrying both door and man to the eaves of a 2-storey house. Then both came crashing to the ground, and the door splintered from top to bottom. The man lay nearby, his body bruised and broken, while his life ebbed away. The friends and neighbours of the grieving Payne family did what good rural people have always done. They came, leaving their own problems at home, to support the family in every way. Men arrived with tools to cut away fallen trees, repair the front porch, and replace broken windows. Women came with mops and pails to scrub away the dust, dirt and trash that had blown into the house. Later, they returned with baskets laden with baked goods. Still later, when Archie Payne's body was brought back to his house, they returned to spend time with his family. In 1944, funerals were usually held in the home. When this tragedy occurred, I spent several days in the Payne home, and I saw people turn from their own trauma and do the expected. As I think back, I often wonder if the opportunity to do things that come naturally (showing support for neighbours) helped others come to terms with their own shock and grief.

I remember standing in one farmyard with the farmer and gazing in disbelief at what had been a reasonably good barn. We didn't say much. What was there to say? That is one thing I remember about those first few days after the storm—the quietness of nature and people alike. Beside us in that farmyard was a very excited young boy. They were going to have to build a new barn. I am not sure his father was quite so excited about building a new barn. The irony of it is that 50 years later, almost to the day, that boy stood as a man in the same yard and watched the "new barn" burn to the ground.

I imagine, after the first shock passed, most people thought of sheltering their families and caring for livestock. Many homes were without electricity and telephone. First, windows were replaced and yards were cleared. Being steadfast people of the land, they took on one phase of restoration at a time, until the landscape changed again. New buildings began to appear and repairs were made to others; maybe a roofline was changed or doors and windows were relocated. Because they kept looking ahead and doing what had to be done, they pulled their lives together and discovered there is life after a tornado. I don't suppose the adults were ever quite as young again. Some of the teenagers probably grew up sooner than they might have otherwise. Very few of the families affected by the tornado left the community.

By Evelyn (Fletcher) Clifton

Dr. Jones of Adelaide Village

Cartoons "practicings" drawn by Dr. Jones of Adelaide Village

ADELAIDE TOWNSHIP HERITAGE GROUP VOUCHERS

Aarts, Tony
Adkin, Dennis
Aerts, Shirley
Aitken, Dora
Aitken, Alan & Cathy
Akins, Myrtle A.
Arrand, Brad
Arrand, David
Arrand, Irene
Arrand, Kathleen
Arrand, Marjorie
Aziz, Barbara
Baker, Ralph & Arnolda
Bakker, Debbie
Barber, Arlene
Barclay, Brad & Peggy
Barkley, Miriam
Baxter, Jackie
Bett, Mike
Bettinson, Mr. & Mrs. R.F.
Bloomfield, Betty
Bobier, Tim & Shirley
Boere, Frank & Brigette
Boersma, Ralph
Bolton, Barbara
Bolton, Richard & Louise
Bos, John
Bos, Ralph
Boshart, C.
Bowley, Mr. & Mrs. Walter
Brand, Terri
Brander, Peter
Brent, Anna
Brock, Ray & Donelda
Brooks, Karen
Brown, Cecil & Winnie
Brown, Jack M.
Brown, James & Joanne
Brown, Mr. & Mrs. Gerald
Brown, Mrs. Loein
Brown, Philip W.
Brown, Terry A.
Brown, Vernon
Bryson, Dorothy
Budden, Mr. & Mrs. Allen
Butler, Wm. & Phyllis
Butler, Noreen
Bycraft, Patti
Bycraft, Thelma
Bylsma, Rick & Jacqueline
Cadman, Marian
Cairns, Stan
Callcott, Joyce
Callon, V.
Cameron, Eileen & Archie
Campbell, Jack & Rita
Campbell, Mrs. Gladys M.
Campbell, Ellen
Campbell, Grace
Campbell, Capt. R.E.
Carrothers, Mrs. Marguerite
Carrothers, Ivan
Carruthers, Fran
Chambers, Beryl
Clarke, Barry
Clarkson, Helen
Clifton, Evelyn
Cochrill, Dick
Coneybeare, Betty
Conkey, Gordon W.
Conkey, Donald S. & Joan
Corbett, Charles

Coward, Dan & Marilyn
Crandon, Clare
Crandon, Larry & Fran
Cuddy, A. M.
Cuddy, Marguerite
Cunningham, Mrs. I.
Currie, Shirley
Currie, John
de Bruyn, Adrian
de Bruyn, Jim & Lisa
de Ruiter, Frank & Freda
DeJong, Andy & Patty
Dekker, George & Florie
Dekker, Henry
Demaray, Don
Denning, Ruth
Derks, Gerry & Mary
Devet, Gerald
Dortmans, Elizabeth
Dortmans, John Jr.
Dortmans, John & Nellie
Dortmans, John & Rita
Dortmans, Sue
Dowding, Melvin
Dowding, Jack & Mary
Dowding, Bill
Down, Roy
Down, Gerry
Downham, George & Tina
Dunlop, Wilbert
Dymond, Bob & Ann
Earley, Bev
Earley, Bob
Earley, George
Eastman, Harold & Gladys
Edwards, John
Elliott, Jack
Evans, Dale
Ewen, Alick & Donna
Faber, Christine
Feddema, John
Ferrington, Gerald & Marilyn
Fleming, Georgina
Foster, Marjorie
Freer, Eileen
Freer, Mr. & Mrs. Ron
Freitag, Marilyn
Fuller, Marion
Galsworthy, Freda
Galsworthy, Ken & Nancy
Gamble, Diana
Gare, Frank
Gare, Evelyn
Gaunt, Irene
Geerts, Anne
George, Ken & Evelyn
George, Mrs. Lyle
Giffen, Linda
Glenn, Jim
Goddard, Robert
Goertz, Pete
Goncalves, Lucia
Gordon, Bill & Donelda
Gorman, Mr. & Mrs. Robert
Gough, Steve
Grant, Denver
Green, Darlene
Grinsven, John
Grogan, Gordon, & Ruby
Grogen, Barry & Sharon
Groot, Bill

Gubbels, Martha
Guikema, Martin
Haan, Al
Haan, Louis
Hammer, Sylvia
Hammond, Margaret
Hamstra, Wick
Hanssen, A.
Harnett, Grace
Harris, Evan
Harris, Bruce & Donna
Harris, David J.
Haskett, J.
Haumann, Barbara
Hawken, LeVerne & Adeline
Hawken, Mrs. Gordon
Hayne, Rev. Bob & Barbara
Healy, Bob & Marylou
Hemsted, Anna
Hemsted, Ida Belle
Hendrick, Bruce
Hendrickx, Mary Ann
Herrington, Ivan & Marilyn
Herrington, Mac & Marion
Herrington, Wm. & Gayle
Heywood, Karen
Heywood, Ruth
Hicks, Jack & Mary Lou
Hodgins, Lorraine
Hoefnagels, Morris & Willy
Hoffner, Fred
Houben, Michael & Maria
Howard, Doreen
Hueston, Bill & Marion
Humphrey, Mack & Eileen
Hy-Way Collision Ltd.
Ireland, Wm. K.
Jadischke, Gustav & Beverley
Jansen, Peter & June
Jansen, Jim & Tracey
Jansen, Lou
Janssen, A.
Janssens, John
Johnston, Michelle
Jordan, Bill
Joris, Hubert
Joris, Rick
Joynt, Dan & Bonnie
Kaler, V.
Kane, Virginia
Kanters, Frank & Lori
Kanters, Frank & Adriana
Kemp, Anne
Kennes, Carol
Kersten, John
Kilbourne, Frances
Kincade, Karl & Linda
Kingma, Jerry
Klahsen, Abraham
Kline, Cathy
Kobes, Clarence K.
Koetsier, Jack & Liz
Lake, Ritchie
Laker, Melvin
LaLonde, Marc & Debra
Landon, Brian & Debbie
Langford, Max & Marjorie
Langs, Doug
Leech, David
Lenting, Judy
Lewis, Rita

Lightfoot, Alma E.
Linker, John & Helen
Linton, Mrs. Greta
Locke, Ruth
Looman, Pauline
Looper, Elizabeth
Lumsden, William & Marion
MacDonald, Larry
MacDonald, Vera
Mahler, Jeanette
Mann, Robert
Marshall, Robt. C.
Martin, Fred L.
Martin, Harold J. & Diane
Martin, Helen
Matthews, Bill
Matthews, Jim & Dorothy
McCormick, Bob
McCoskery, Anna J.
McDougall, Mr. & Mrs. Lloyd
McGregor, Mr. & Mrs. Alex
McIntosh, Mr. & Mrs. Pat
McIntrye, David
McKeen, C. D.
McKenzie, Lillian
McLean, Cameron
McLean, Allan
McLean, Glen & Carol
McLeish, Edward A.
McNab, Karen
McNab, Mr. & Mrs. Wilson
McPhail, Ray
Mead, Carl
Medlyn, Phillip & Linda
Miatello, Bev
Miller, Shirley
Milliken, Dave
Milliken, Earl & Ruth
Minten, Peter
Mitchell, Jean
Morgan, Mr. & Mrs. Ernest
Morgan, Richard & Sharron
Morgan, Milo
Morgan, Wm. & Judith
Muma, Joe
Muma, Sandra
Murray, Bill & Doris
Muxlow, Vera
Naus, Henry & Rosemary
Nethercott, Jack & Vivian
Newman, Margaret
Nichols, Phyllis
Noordhof, Angela
Noordhof, Tony & Tracy
Ogg, Laila
Oomen, Chris
Paas, C.
Paff, Bonnie
Parker, Grant & Phyllis
Parker, Wm. & Elizabeth
Parsons, Al
Parsons, Don
Parsons, Margaret
Patterson, Bob & Donna
Pedden, Alex
Pedden, Archie
Pedden, Brenda
Pedden, Mrs. Winnie
Peeters, Martin & Linda
Pelkman, Anne

Perry, Margaret
Petch, Elva, J.
Petch, Helen
Petch, Wesley
Petch, Whitford
Peters, Bob & Willie
Peters, Pat
Pierce, Bonnie
Pollock, Don M.
Postma, Charlotte
Powell, David
Pranger, Mrs. Henry
Pyke, Mrs. Jean
Quinn, Dorothy
Redmond, Mr. & Mrs. Gordon
Reid, John
Reitsma, Ed
Richardson, Leila
Robertson, Dave
Robertson, Wm. & Mary
Robinson, John & Marie
Robotham, George & Doris
Robotham, Lloyd
Robotham, Robert & Pearl
Robotham, William
Roder, Norman
Rogers, Annie L.
Routley, James
Routley, Ken & Marge
Rowe, John & Donna
Rowland, Jack
Ruby, Greg
Saettler, Margaret
Salomons, Charly
Salomons, K.
Sandercock, Marjorie
Saunders, Jim & Dianne
Scherba, Dave
Shirley, Donald & Jane
Shrier, Mr. & Mrs. Kenneth
Silver, Dave & Carol
Sisson, Muriel
Smith, Mrs. Leola
Smith, Everett & Betty
St. Louis, Lola
Stapleton, Pat & Jacqueline
Stead, Evan & Evelyn
Stephenson, Jack & Sharon
Stevenson, Clayton
Still, Miss Leslie
Stirton, Ian
Stokman, Gertrude
Stott, Glenn
Stradnick, Mrs. Pat
Struthers, Jean L.
Strybosch, Harry & Josephine
Strybosch, John & Sandra
Sutherland, Clare & Helen
Tadgell, Ronald
Tamminga, G.
Taylor, Wray & Elizabeth
Taylor, June
Tedball, John
Tedball, Evelyn
Thomas, Elizabeth
Thompson, Jane
Thomson, Murray & Alice
Thorn, Reg
Thynne, Mrs. Helen
Timmerman, Hugh

Timmermans, Gertrude
Timmermans, John
Timmermans, Martin
Toth, Gary & Carol
Trethewey, Larry & Patty
Unger, Shirley
Van Damme, Joe L.
Van der Deen, Ivan
Van Dinther, Nellie
Van Dongen, John & Joanne
Van Erp, Peter & Lorraine
Van Erp, John
Van Giffen, Martin & Rita
Van Gorkum, Thelma
Van Grinsven, T.
Van Sas, Louis & Dorothy
VandeKemp, Bert & Gloria
Vanden Wielen, Henry & Kathryn
VandenEynden, John & Laura
Vanderelst, Martin & Jane
Vanderhoek, Hilda & Ray
Vanderkant, Rita
VanLeishout, John & Annie
Veenstra, John
Verhoeven, Bernard
Verhoeven, Jim
Verkley, Jeff
Verkley, Tom & Cathy
Walker, Don & Anne
Wallace, Ronald & Janet
Waltham, Ken & Marilyn
Ward, Don
Ward, Cliff
Wardell, Alan D.
Wardell, Eleanor
Wardell, Kay
Wardell, Merle
Watson, Lois
Wedge, Lois
Westgate, Helen
Whiting, Marilyn
Whytock, Marjorie
Wilcox, Wayne
Wilson, Ken
Wilton, Keith & Dorothy
Winter, Dorothy
Woerz, June
Wood, Hansford
Wood, John
Wood, Keith
Woods, Joe
Woods, Vera
Wrightman, Harvey & Irene
Zavitz, Norma
Zimmerman, Gladdis

EDITOR'S NOTE

The Voucher Lists were compiled by several persons. Our apologies for any errors or omissions that may have occurred.

LIST OF DONORS

This book, which began many years ago in March 1994, is a product of labour and love. Without the kind—in fact, overwhelming—support of so many individuals and corporations over these many years, it would not have seen the light of day. We wish to acknowledge those who have made it possible for the history of our wonderful township to be published. This list includes cash donations only, not contributions "in kind":

Under $100

Lorien Brown
S. Miller
Marguerite Cuddy
P. & J. Jansen
Capt. R. Campbell
Anne Kemp
Ivan Carrothers
Clayton Stevenson
W. Bowley
Jean Struthers
Lillian McKenzie
Aletha Sweet
Eileen McKenzie
Bert Van De Kemp
Helen Clarkson
Orville Hodgson
Carol McLean
Harold Wilson
Joe Woods
Glencoe Grain/Seed
John Dortmans
Ray McPhail
June Woerz
Gladys Eastman
Leila Richardson
Lorne McDougall
Fieny McDougall
Leo Van Geffen
Jeff & Mary Maes
Grace Campbell
Marjorie Whytock

$100-499

Kerwood Oddfellows
Don McChesney
Cargill Ltd.
Jean Baker
Ed McLeish
Cliff & Margaret Wardell
Bruce Hendrick
Ray Brock
Anna Jean McCoskery
Dale Evans
Lobo Mutual Insurance Co.
Bernice Evans
Wescast Industries
St. Willibrord Community Credit Union
Cliff Holland Trucking
Andrew Wright
Archie & Dorothy Pedden
Pedden's Collector Plates
Langs Bus Lines Ltd.
Carpet Care & Sales Ltd.
Green Scheels Pidgeon
Ken Matthews Ltd.
George Earley
Bob Earley
Bev Earley
Marilyn Freitag
Donald Pollock
Mike Bett
Wilson McNab
Ken Galsworthy
Don Gare
George Robotham
Andre Aerts
John Bos
Gerry Derks
Stuart Brown
Jack Brown
Bill Murray
David Ball
George Matthews
Norm Brooks
John Veenstra
Dan Joynt
Don Stuart
Tony Strybosch
David Robertson
Jack Hicks
Carol McLean
Enbridge Pipelines Ltd.

$500-999

I O O Foresters
Spriet Associates
Richard Brock

$1,000 and over

Cuddy International

SOURCES

Resources for this book were culled from a vast number of people, historical publications and newspapers. The following sources may have been quoted within this work:

Extracts from the *London Free Press*, various dates

Extracts from the *Strathroy Age Dispatch*, various dates

The Egremont Road, by Eleanor Nielsen, Lambton Historical Society, 1993

The History of Middlesex County, Goodspeed, 1889

The Aftermath of the Rebellion, J.M.S. Careless, 1987

London 200, An Illustrated History, Orlo Miller, London Chamber of Commerce, 1992

Welcome to Flander's Field—The First Canadian Battle Of The Great War, Dancocks, McLelland and Stewart, 1988

A Military History of Canada, D. Morton, 1990

Ordeal by Fire, Ralph Allen, Popular Library, 1961

Arthur Currie: The Biography of a Great Canadian, Hugh M. Urquhart, J. McDent, 1950

Over the Top: The Canadian Infantry in the First World War, John F. Meek, 1971

Years of Conflict 1911-1921, Century of Canada series, Grolier Limited, 1983

The Last Lion, William Manchester, Little Brown, 1983

A.W. Currie, Dancocks, 1985

To Seize the Victory, J. Swettenham, Ryerson, 1965

Death So Noble, Jonathon Vance, UBC Press, 1997

A Nation Forged in Fire, J.L. Granatstein and D. Morton, 1989

Strathroy, The Garden of Canada, 1834-1934, compiled and edited by Clifford R. Cox, undated

The Founding of Strathroy, Strathroy Museum, undated

Numerous early historical documents from the Provincial Archives, the Ontario Historical Society, and the London and Middlesex Historical Society

INDEX

A

AARTS, Leonardus and Wilhelmina	31
AARTS, Tony and Gerdie	31
ABERNETHY	32
ABMA, Fred and Alice	32
ADAIR, James and Becky	33
ADAMS, Byron and Lois	33
ALDERSON, Graham and Beverley	34
ALEXANDER, Joseph and Janet	34
ANDERSON, Alexander and Mary Jane	35
ANDERSON, Henry and Maggie	36
ARCHER, William and Della	36
ARMSTRONG, John and Jane	36
ARRAND, Clifford and Frances	37
ARRAND, George and Kathleen	38
ARRAND, William and Della	38
AULD, Robert and Joyce	39
AUSTIN, Edward and Mary Ann	39
AYRE, Robert and Jane	39
AYRE, William and Mary Jane	40

B

BALL, Thomas and Emma	41
BARKER, Paul and Brenda	42
BARRETT, Richard and Louisa	42
BAXTER, Reginald and Florence	43
BELLAIRS, James Peel Stevenson and Maria	43
BENEDICT, Ellwood and Alma	45
BETT, Michael and Barbara	46
BEYNEN, Hubert and Johanna	46
BISHOPP, George and Mary Jane	47
BLOOMFIELD, Stanley and Betty	47
BOERE, Jim and Susan	47
BOERSEMA, Marten and Elly	47
BOGUE, James and Ezelia	49
BOLTON, Richard and Frances	51
BOLTON, William and Harriet	51
BOS, Ralph and Jacoba	54
BOSHART, Carl and Suzanne	55
BOWLEY, Walter and Eva	55
BRADSHAW - LOUGHEED	55
BRANAN, Richard and Anna Maria	56
BRAND, David and Terry	58
BRANDON, Alan and Michelle	437
BRANTON, Thomas and Mary Ellen	58
BRAVENER, Robert and Sarah	60
BRENT, Fred	60
BROCK, George and Isabella	61
BROCK, Ray and Donelda	66
BROOKS, Hugh and Elizabeth	66
BROOKS, Mike and Veryle	67
BROTHERS	68
BROWN, Allan and Mary Ellen	69
BROWN, Gerald and Patricia	70
BROWN, James and Jane	70
BROWN, John	71
\BROWNE, Matt and Lily	72
BUCHANAN, John Stewart and Mabel	73
BUNTING	74
BURDON, Benjamin and Wilhelmina	74
BURROWS, Henry and Mary	75
BUTLER, William and Mary	77
BUTTERY, John and Anna	79
BYCRAFT, Craig and Patti	81
BYLSMA, Rick and Jacqueline	81

C

CALLAGHAN – WALSH – O'DONNELL	437
CALLCOTT, Bill and Joyce	82
CAMPBELL, Archie J. and Annie	82
CAMPBELL, Ernest and Mary	83
CAMPBELL, John and Nettie	84
CAMPBELL, John S. and Margaret	85
CARROTHERS, John and Harriet	85
CARSON, John and Eliza	87
CATCHPOLE, Alfred and Edna	88
CAWRSE, Charles and Grace	88
CHAMBERS, Thomas and Ann	89
CHOUFFOT, Jacques and Martha	93
CLELAND, Robert and Lillie	93
CLELFORD, William and Ann	95
CLEVERDON	95
CONKEY, Arthur and Margaret	98
COOPER	101
COWAN, Tyler and Kelley	103
CRANDON, Reginald and Frances	103
CRUMMER, John and Margaret	104
CUDDY, James and Violet	105
CUDDY, John T. and Esther	107
CUNNINGHAM, Carl and Margaret	109
CURRIE/CURRY/CORRIGAN	109

D

DALE	112
de BRUYN, Adrian and Joan	113
DEKKER, Henry and Magdalena	113
DELL, Bassnett and Elizabeth	114
DEMARAY/desMarets	114
DEMARAY, Wesley and Orville	125
DEMPSTER, Robert and Elizabeth	126
DERKS, Gerry and Mary	126
DEVET, Casey and Mary	126
DOAN, Joseph and Edith	127
DODGE, Henry and Elizabeth	127
DORTMANS, Harry and Nellie	128
DORTMANS, Hein and Johanna	128
DORTMANS, John and Nellie	129
DOUGLAS, Thomas and Cicily	130
DOWDING, Thomas and Martha	131
DOWLING, Patrick and Mary	134
DOWN, George and Celia	134
DOWNER - NAPPER	135
DOWNHAM, Howard C.	140
DUGGAN, Patrick and Annabella	140

E

EARLEY, George and Jane	140
EARLEY	142
EASTMAN, Benjamin and Mahetable	145
ELLIOTT, Allan and Clara	148
ELLIOTT, Cliff and Kay	149
ELLIOTT, Thomas and Effie	149
EMERICK, Francis and Susan	150
EMMONS, George and Emma	150
EVOY, Thomas, James and Elizabeth	152

F

FEASEY, Robert and Carolyn	153
FEATHERSTONE, John and Mary	154
FEDDEMA, Gosse and Theodora	154
FEDDEMA, Rienk and Pietje	155
FINKBEINER, Samuel and Hazel	156
FLETCHER, Donald and Annie	156
FLETCHER, James and Anne	157
FONGER, Ivan and Margaret	157
FOSTER, George and Laura	158
FOSTER, George and Marjorie	159
FREELE	160
FULLER, Obadiah and Charlotte	162
FULLER, William and Mary	163
FYDELL, Rev. Fred and Sarah	164

G

GALLOWAY, James and Anna	164
GARE, George Sr. and Jane	165
GAST, Elmer and Sarah	167
GEORGE, Edwin and Florence	167
GEORGE, George and Doris	168
GEORGE, James and Mary Ann	168
GERRY, David and Jemima	170
GERRYTS, Harry and Tina	171
GIFFEN, William and Mary	171
GLENN, George and Margaret	172
GLOVER, James and Eliza	174
GOATCHER, Stephen	174
GODDARD, Robert and Carolyn	175
GOLDRICK, Edward and Elizabeth	175
GOSDEN	178
GOUGH, Steve and Betty	180
GOVERS - YOUNG	437
GRAHAM, Duncan and Mary	180
GREEN, Lee and Hazel	181
GROGAN, Lawrence and May	181
GROOT, Adrian and Katrien	183
GUIKEMA, Martin and Jane	186

H

HAAN, Al and Aafke	186
HANNA, John and Jane	187
HANSFORD, John and Mary	187
HARRIS, Samuel	188
HAWES, Alfred and Annie	193
HEALY, James and Rosanna	193
HEMSTED, Donald and Anna	195
HENDERSON	195
HENDRICK, John and Patience	197
HENDRIKX, Lyle and Mary Ann	198
HENRY, William and Francis	199
HERRINGTON, Roscoe and Mary	200
HERRINGTON, Trueman	201
HICKS, Jack and Mary Lou	201
HOARE, John and Anne	202
HODGSON, Thomas and Elizabeth	202
HOEFNAGELS, Marinus and Wilhelmina	203
HOFFNER, Joseph and Theresa	203
HOFSTEEDE, John and Nellie	204
HOLDEN, Moses and Elizabeth	204
HOUBEN, John and Maria	205
HOULTON, Henry and Eliza	206
HOWE, Russ and Jeannie	207
HULL, Robert and Anne	207
HUMPHREY, Mack and Eileen	208
HUMPHRIES, John and Maria	209

I

INCH	210
INGHAM	211
IRELAND	211
IRWIN, Joyce and Margaret	214

J

JACKSON, Jo and Vaike	216
JADISCHKE, Wilhelm and Frieda	216
JAMES, Thomas and Alice	217
JAMIESON, John	217
JANSEN, Alfons and Lucia	219
JANSEN, Lou and Mary	220
JANSEN, Peter and June	220
JOHNSTON, Alexander and Margaret	220
JOHNSTON, John	221
JOHNSTON, Steven and Michelle	222
JONES, Dr. Samuel O.H. and Agnes	222
JORIS, Harry and Maria	223
JOYNT, John and Edythe	223

K

KAISER, Harold and Lynne	224
KELLY (CALLAGHAN), William and Mary	225
KEYSER, Philip Henry and Maria	225
KINCADE, William and Eliza	227
KING, Fred and Elsie	229
KINGMA, Rimmer and Antje	230
KLAVER - HOOGSTRA - SANDERS	230
KLINKER, Bob and Jane	231
KNIGHT, James and Jane	231
KOBES, Johannes and Gayle	232

L

LAMBERT, Doug and Fran	233
LAMBIE, James and Edna	233
LANDON, Brian and Debbie	234
LANGAN, James and Ellen	234
LANGFORD, Herbert and Margaret	235
LARGE - BRAY - LANG	236
LEACOCK, William and Emma	238
LEE, John and Bertha	239
LENTING, Jacob and Jurjendina	239
LEWIS, Frank and Isabell	240
LEWIS, John Sr. and Elizabeth	240
LEWIS, Len and Marianne	241
LIGHTFOOT, Thomas and Jane	241
LINKER, John and Helen	242
LINTON, William and Elizabeth	242
LOCKE, George W. and Ruth	242

M

MacDONALD, Angus and Sarah	243
MacDONALD, Larry and Mary	244
MacDONALD, Morris and Vera	244
MacKENZIE, John and Anne	245
MAHON, William and Araminta	245
MANN	246
MANNING	247
MARSHALL, Robert and Vesta	248
MARTIN, Hiram and Hannah	249
MATTHEWS, Stephen and Hope	251
MATTHEWS	252
McADAM, Wesley and Jean	255
McCABE, Ross and Mary	256
McCARTHY, Martin and Ann	256
McCHESNEY, William and Jane	258
McDONALD, Hugh and Mary	260
McDOUGALL, Lloyd and Fieny	261
McELMURRY	262
McGREGOR, Don and Karin	262
McINROY, Alexander "Sandy" and Ann Jane	263
McINTYRE, David L. and Jean	266
McKEEN, William and Margaret	266
McKenzie, Duncan and Janet	267
McKENZIE, James and Margaret	268
McLEAN	269
McLEISH, William and Harriet	271

McNAB, John and Ellen	276
McPHAIL, Ray and Ruby	277
MEE, Patrick and Mary	278
MILLARD, Frank and Phyllis	279
MILLER, Robert and Mary	279
MILLIGAN, John and Jean	281
MILLIKEN, Earl and Ruth	282
MINER, Truman and Elizabeth	282
MINIELLY	283
MINTEN, Peter and Jacqueline	283
MINTON, Joseph and Johanna	284
MITCHELL, John and Mary Ann	284
MITCHELL, John Sr. and Barbara	284
MONTAGUE, Joseph and Rhoda	287
MOORE	288
MORGAN, George W. and Elizabeth	289
MORGAN, Richard Sr. and Jane	290
MULLAN, John and Ellen	298
Murdock, William and Ann	298
Murray, James and Catherine	301
MUXLOW, Edwin and Harriett	309
MUXLOW, John Thomas and Ethel	310

N

NAUS, Henry and Rosemary	310
NAUTA, Karst and Aley	311
NEELANDS, Rev. John and Anna	311
NETHERCOTT, William and Blanche	311
NETTLETON, William and Jane	312
NEWELL, Alexander and Lorena	313
NEWTON, William and Christina	314
NICHOL, Edward and Maria	315
NICHOLS, William and Mary	316
NOORDHOF, John and Catherine	318

O

O'CALLAGHAN, Terrance and Catherine	318
OGG, Robert and Laila	319
OLIVER	319
OLIVER, Henry and Ellen	320
OOMEN, Chris and Nancy	321

P

PAAS, Jan and Ebeltje	321
PAFF, Vern and Eileen	321
PAINE, Joseph and Elizabeth	321
PARKER, James and Amey	322
PATTERSON, Robert and Samuel	323
PATTERSON, Thomas	325
PATTERSON	325
PEARSON, Len and Anne	325
PEDDEN, Andrew and Margaret	325
PEGLEY, Robert and Mary Ann	327
PENNINGTON, Thomas and William	329
PERRIE, Rev. James and Marion	332
PERRY, Margaret	332
PERRY, Robert and Thelma	332
PETCH, Francis and Mary	333
PETERS, John B. and Hendrika	336
PHILLIPS, Ken and Phyllis	336
PLAXTON, William and Susan	337
POLLOCK, William and Minnie	337
POSTHUMUS, Ypke and Gerda	338
POSTMA, Peter and Charlotte	338
POWELL, David and Linda	338
PRESTON, Charles and Jean	339

R

RANDALL, William and Ann	340
RAPLEY, Charles and Frances	340
RAPLEY, David and Harriet	341
RAPLEY, William and Jane	342
RAWLINSON, Fred and Nora	343
REDMAN, Howard and Dora	343
REDMOND - JIGGINS	343
REDMOND, William and Elizabeth	343
REINHARDT, John and Elizabeth	344
REITSMA, Edward and Elizabeth	345
RICHARDSON, Clare and Jessie	346
RICHARDSON, James and Mary Jane	346
RIVERS	347
ROBINSON, Robert and Diana	349
RUBOTHAM (ROBOTHAM), George and Margaret	349
ROBOTHAM, George D.	352
ROMBOUTS, Adrian and Mary	353
ROUTLEY, Jim and Elizabeth	353
ROUTLEY, Ken and Marjorie	353
ROWBOTHAM, Dan and Susaan	353
ROWLAND, Jack Sr. and Ethel	353
RUBY, Glenn and Lianne	354
RUPP, Christian and Linda	355

S

SANDS, David and Margaret	355
SAUL, John	355
SCOON, John A. and Helen	357
SCOTT, Robert and Martha	358
SEED, John and Margaret	360
SHAMBLAW, John and Lily	364
SHIELDS, William and Latetia	365
SHRIER, Jacob and Mary	366
SIFTON	367
SISSON, Herbert and Charlotte	368
SLATER, Thomas and Margaret	370
SMITH, Charles and Marie	370
SMITH, Everett and Betty	370
SMITH, John and Susannah	371
SMITH, John Graham and Francis	371
SMITH, Leonard and Marta	372
SMITH	372
SNELL, William and Henrietta	373
SOETEMANS, David and Riekie	375
SPRUYT, Nicholaas and Wanda	375
STEAD, Henry and Effie	375
STEELE, John and Janet	376
STEVENS, Samuel and Ruth	376
STEVENSON, Clarence and Bessie	378
STILL, Charles and Frances	378
STIRTON, Gordon and Margaret	379
STOKMAN, Jim and Gertrude	379
STRYBOSCH, Harry and Josephine	380
SULLIVAN, John and Letitia	381
SUMNER, Don and Evelyn	382
SUTHERLAND, Clare and Helen	383

T

TAMMINGA, Gerrit and Bouwchiene	383
TAYLOR, Daniel and Elizabeth	384
TEDBALL, Milton and Eileen	385
TEDBALL, Orville and Evelyn	385
THOMAS, Gordon and Helen	386
THOMAS, Lou	386
THOMPSON - FAUNT	386
THOMPSON, George and Eliza	388
THOMPSON, Grant and Hazel	389
THOMSON - SHOTWELL	389
THOMSON, George and Irene	390
THORPE, Ransom and Hulda	391
THROWER, Charles and Sarah	392
TIMMERMANS, Cornelius and Theodora	393
TIMMERS, Johannus and Johanna	396
TOMLINSON, William and Ann	397
TOPPING, John and Ann	397
TOTH, Gary and Carol	399
TRETHEWEY, Larry and Patricia	399

U

UNGER, Floyd and Shirley	399

V

VAN AERT, Tony and Anne	400
VAN DAMME, Josephus and Emelie	400
VAN de KEMP, Bert and Gloria	401
VAN de VEN, John and Martha	401
VAN DINTHER, Peter and Nellie	402
VAN DONGEN, John and Joanne	402
VAN ERP, Gerrit (Jerry) and Patricia	403
VAN ERP, Theodore and Aleogonda	403
VAN GEFFEN, Martin and Helen	403
VAN GRINSVEN, John and Tina	404
VANDER VLOET, Tony and Mary	404
VANDERBEETEN, Anthony and Ardina	405
VANDERHOEK, Wietze and Syke	407
VEENSTRA, John and Jean	407
VERHEYEN, Brian and Lynn	407
VERHOEVEN, Cornelis and Mary	408
VERKLEY, Peter and Gezina	408
VOKES, James and Mary	409

W

WALKER, James and Margaret	409
WALKER, Robert and Margaret	410
WALLACE	410
WALSH, Patrick and Mary Ellen	412
WALTHAM, John and Elizabeth	412
WARDELL, Joseph and Letitia	414
WARDELL, Orville and Mabel	416
WARDELL, Raymond and Barbara Joan	416
WESTGATE, George and Gertrude	417
WHITING, David and Eliza	418
WILEY, David and Ann	418
WILEY, John and Eleanor	420
WILEY, John and Mary	422
WILKINS, Matthew and Sarah	423
WILKINSON, Joseph and Mary	423
WILLIAMS, Roger S. and Maria	425
WILLISTON, John and Martha	425
WILSON, Ed and Effie	426
WILSON, Francis and Jane	426
WILSON, Hugh and Jane	427
WILSON, Hugh and Mary Ann	427
WILSON, Samuel and Rebecca	427
WOOD, William and Mary	433
WOODS	434
WOOLLEY, Warren and Naomi	435
WRIGHT, Edwin and Anna Maria	436
WRIGHTMAN, Harvey and Irene	436
WYATT, Edward and Melissa	436

Acknowledgement

To everyone who spent many hours researching, writing and proofreading this book – our sincerest thanks.

*Adelaide Township
Heritage Group*

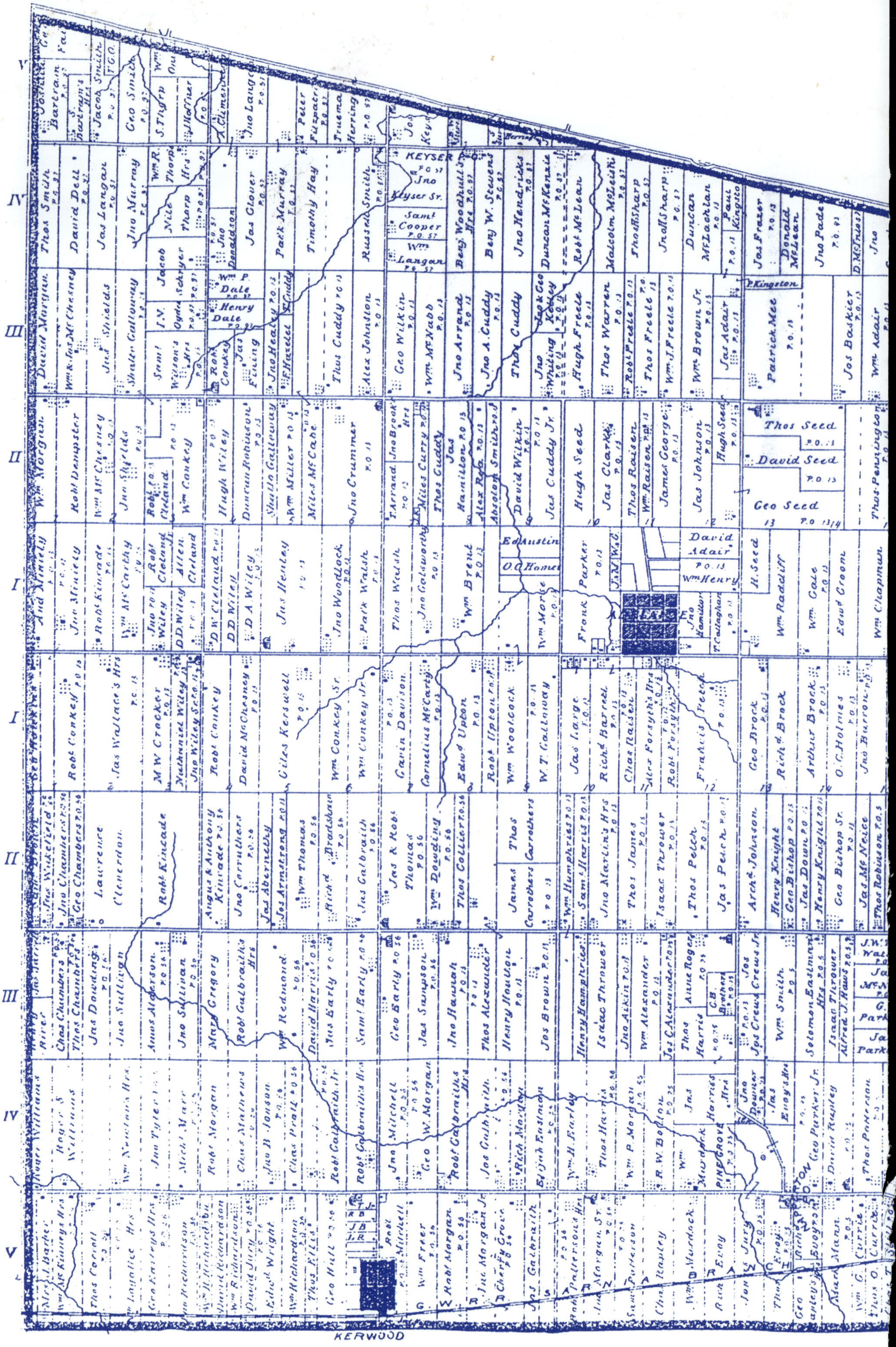